HANDBOOK OF RESEARCH AND POLICY IN ART EDUCATION

Edited by

Elliot W. Eisner
Stanford University

Michael D. Day
Brigham Young University

NAEA NATIONAL ART EDUCATION ASSOCIATION

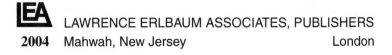
LAWRENCE ERLBAUM ASSOCIATES, PUBLISHERS
2004 Mahwah, New Jersey   London

Director, Editorial: Lane Akers
Executive Assistant: Bonita D'Amil
Cover Design: Sean Trane Sciarrone
Textbook Production Manager: Paul Smolenski
Full-Service Compositor: TechBooks
Text and Cover Printer: Hamilton Printing Company

This book was typeset in 10/12 pt. Times, Italic, Bold, Bold Italic. The heads were typeset in Helvetica Bold, and Helvetica Bold Italic.

.

Lawrence Erlbaum Associates, Inc., Publishers
10 Industrial Avenue
Mahwah, New Jersey 07430
www.erlbaum.com

Library of Congress Cataloging-in-Publication Data

Handbook of research and policy in art education / edited by Elliot W. Eisner,
    Michael D. Day.
        p.   cm.
    Includes bibliographical references and indexes.
    ISBN 0-8058-4971-8 (case : alk. paper)—ISBN 0-8058-4972-6 (paperbound : alk. paper)
    1. Art—Study and teaching—North America—History.   2. Art—Study and
    teaching—North America—Research.   I. Eisner, Elliot W.   II. Day, Michael D.

N103.H36   2004
707′.1′073—dc22   2003025839

Books published by Lawrence Erlbaum Associates are printed on
acid-free paper, and their bindings are chosen for strength and durability.

Printed in the United States of America
10   9   8   7   6   5   4   3   2   1

Contents

List of Contributors

Patricia Amburgy, Associate Professor of Art Education at The Pennsylvania State University

Terry Barrett, Professor of Art Education, The Ohio State University

H. Gene Blocker, Philosophy, Professor Emeritus, Ohio University

Paul E. Bolin, Senior Lecturer, Art Education Program, The University of Texas at Austin

Doug Boughton, Professor of Art and Education, School of Art, Northern Illinois University

Judith M. Burton, Professor and Director, Programs in Art and Art Education, Teachers College Columbia University

Graeme Chalmers, Professor of Art Education in the Department of Curriculum Studies at the University of British Columbia; Faculty of Education's David See-Chai Lam Chair in Multicultural Education

Michael D. Day, Professor, Department of Visual Arts, Brigham Young University

Stephen Mark Dobbs, Executive Vice President, The Bernard Osher Foundation, San Francisco; Executive Director, The Taube Foundation, Belmont; and, Adjunct Professor of Humanities, San Francisco State University

Arthur Efland, Professor Emeritus of Art Education, The Ohio State University

Elliot W. Eisner, Lee Jacks Professor of Education and Professor of Art, Stanford University

Mary Erickson, Professor of Art, in the School of Art, in the Herberger College of Fine Arts, Arizona State University.

Kerry Freedman, Professor of Art and Education, School of Art, Northern Illinois University

Norman Freeman, Professor of Cognitive Development, University of Bristol, UK

Lynn Galbraith, Associate Professor of Art, University of Arizona

Constance Bumgarner Gee, Associate Professor, Public Policy and Education, Vanderbilt University

Claire Golomb, Professor Emerita, Department of Psychology, University of Massachusetts at Boston

Kit Grauer, Associate Professor of Art Education, University of British Columbia

Lois Hetland, Research Associate, Project Zero at the Harvard Graduate School of Education

Samuel Hope, Executive Director, National Association of Schools of Art and Design

Anna M. Kindler, Professor and Dean School of Creative Arts Sciences and Technology The Hong Kong Institute of Education, and Professor, Department of Curriculum Studies University of British Columbia (on leave)

E. Louis Lankford, Des Lee Foundation Endowed Professor in Art Education, University of Missouri-Saint Louis and The Saint Louis Art Museum.

John Matthews, Professor, Visual & Performing Arts, National Institute of Education, Nanyang Technological University, Singapore

Carol Myford, Associate Professor, Department of Educational Psychology, Focus in Measurement, Evaluation, Statistics and Assessment, University of Illinois at Chicago

David Pariser, Professor of Art Education, Faculty of Fine Arts, Concordia University

Michael Parsons, Professor of Art Education, The Ohio State University

Hilary Persky, NAEP Program Administrator, Educational Testing Service, National Assessment of Educational Progress

F. Robert Sabol, Chair of Art Education, Purdue University, West Lafayette, Indiana

Kelly Scheffer, Director of Education and Outreach, The Contemporary Art Museum St. Louis

Alice Sims-Gunzenhauser, Assessment Specialist, Arts and Languages Group, Assessment Development Division, Educational Testing Service

Ralph A. Smith, Professor Emeritus of Cultural and Educational Policy, University of Illinois at Urbana-Champaign

Lissa Soep, Lecturer in Education, University of California, Berkeley

Mary Ann Stankiewicz, Associate Professor of Art Education, The Pennsylvania State University

Mary Stokrocki, Mary Stokrocki, Professor of Art Education, Herberber College of Fine Arts, Department of Art, Arizona State University

Patricia Stuhr, Professor and Chair The Department of Art Education, The Ohio State University

Graeme Sullivan, Associate Professor of Art Education, Department of Arts and Humanities, Teachers College, Columbia University

Frances Thurber, Edwin Clark Professor, Chair, Department of Art and Art History, University of Nebraska at Omaha

John Howell White, Chair and Professor of Art Education, Department of Art Education and Crafts, Kutztown University

Brent Wilson, Professor of Art Education, The Pennsylvania State University

Ellen Winner, Professor of Psychology, Boston College; Senior Research Associate, Project Zero, Harvard Graduate School of Education

Enid Zimmerman, Professor and Coordinator of Art Education and Gifted and Talented Education Programs, Curriculum and Instruction Department, Indiana University School of Education

Introduction to the *Handbook of Research and Policy in Art Education*

Elliot Eisner and Michael Day

The *Handbook of Research and Policy in Art Education*, which we have had the privilege of editing, marks a milestone in the field of art education. The initial forays into the teaching of art emerged in America around the middle of the 19th century. It was largely practical in orientation, a means through which girls might secure some of the skills that at that time were believed to define their gender. Art education also enabled manufacturers whose work depended on the design of their products to find able apprentices, trained in drawing, who could contribute to the success of their businesses. Even throughout the first half of the 20th century, the general orientation of the field was focused on matters of craft, on the making of the beautiful image, and on the development of creativity, especially in young children. What this hallmark handbook represents is an effort to bring together research and theory, policy and concepts that guide and give shape to what people in art education try to accomplish. It should not be said that there is a uniform chorus of opinion concerning what members of the field ought to embrace with respect to its aims and its content. There is, indeed, a healthy diversity. The section of the *Handbook* dealing with emerging visions describes some, but not all, of these competing orientations.

The *Handbook* also serves as a kind of assertion—an assertion that the field of art education has a body of scholarship to which prospective teachers of art and surely those aspiring to scholarship in the field should have access. This volume represents an effort to define some of the categories needing attention and to share with readers some of the ideas that researchers and other scholars have generated with respect to them.

Those familiar with other fields—such as the study of teaching, music education, the field of general curriculum—are aware of the fact that in these fields, research handbooks have already been published; some are in their second and third editions. In many ways, those fields have had a closer affinity to scholarship and research than has the field of art education. As we have indicated, the roots of art education are found in the practice of teaching arts and crafts, for arts and crafts served as the major models for teachers and scholars wishing to understand what might be done at the practical level. Theory and research were to come later. Research was not a term that had high currency in the field. The first research journal serving art education on a national level was *Studies in Art Education* which was initially published in 1960. In a sense, in this *Handbook* the field proclaims its affinity to scholarship and takes its place among fields that take their scholarship seriously.

For many working in the educational community, such as principals and superintendents of schools, and parents and teachers, the idea that there is a body of scholarship around the practice of teaching painting or the creation of sculpture will come as something of a surprise if not a shock. In this sense, the *Handbook* is also a testimony to others that working in the arts in school, classrooms, out-of-school settings, and higher education, is not simply a matter of emulating prior practice—Although a part of it certainly is—but that it is built on reflection and the effort to understand how complex forms of thinking can be promoted. Thus, the *Handbook* can be considered a kind of mapping of some of the territory that art educators and others interested in visual art education might consider when attempting to understand the parameters of the field. If the map is a good one, it will change over time. Useful work in the field of art education not only describes the field as it is but also provides the material through which scholars can generate new ideas and new directions in which to travel. Tautologically speaking, the process of change is marked by change. We hope that the *Handbook* contributes not only to change but also to improvement.

It is also important, we think, to say something about what the *Handbook* is not. It is not a body of fixed conclusions. It is not a recipe book for how to do things. It is not a dictionary. It is a resource for one's professional reflection. This reflection includes, of course, new ideas about any aspect of the field, ideas that have the potential to give it direction or to yield insights that deepen our understanding of what is teachable, learnable, and what can potentially be experienced in and through art.

In doing scholarship, especially in a field that embraces the idea that art is a distinctive and important form of human experience, there is a tendency in using technical language and high-level abstractions to lose sight of the concrete conditions that give professional activity in this field significance. In other words, it is possible to forget the art in the effort to understand the psychology. We assert this possibility as a caution because it would be a small victory, if victory at all, to lose the essence of the field by becoming preoccupied with ideas and policies that somehow forget that to which they are instrumental in the first place. In trying to understand art you have to keep the albatross flying while you study it. The paradox is related to the ability to survive dissection in order to understand what makes a life vital, whether that life exists in the presence of an individual or in the vitality of a field.

A word about the intended audience—like most editors, we hope this volume will be read by virtually everybody. Realistically, however, we know that is not going to happen. The main audience for this *Handbook* consists of scholars in education, particularly those interested in the social and individual factors affecting performance in the visual arts in whatever setting they happen to occupy. This population includes professors and graduate students, undergraduate students in education, and researchers in education in virtually all research fields for which the ideas examined and discussed in this volume are relevant. Increasingly, researchers in education are coming to recognize that there are many ways the world can be represented; all of the arts are among the ways people experience and know the world. Researchers are helping us understand how people use the arts to learn, experience, and see what otherwise may be obscure. Put another way, the times are receptive to an enlarged rather than to a reductive conception of the content and aims of education. In some ways, those in art education understood this before most working in other fields.

ORGANIZATION OF THE HANDBOOK: SECTIONS AND CHAPTERS

A Word About Beginnings

At a November 1999 meeting of the National Art Education Association (NAEA) Research Commission in Washington DC, Elliot Eisner suggested that a handbook for research and policy in art education would be an important contribution to the field. Professor Eisner convinced Commission members of the need for such a document and developed a proposal that was endorsed by the Commission and subsequently approved by the NAEA Board of Directors. Michael Day, a member of the Research Commission, was invited to serve as coeditor with Eisner.

Eisner and Day formulated section topics to include important issues while avoiding vagueness due to lack of specificity. This was by no means a simple task and might have been approached any number of ways. The categories for the six sections were intended not only to be broad enough to allow for creativity and innovation by the section editors but also to provide sufficient direction and a reasonable focus. During this process, the question was often asked: "What is being left out?"

It is difficult, if not impossible, to include every significant issue and topic in a publication such as this. Although the *Handbook* is broad and inclusive in its organization and intent, it is not comprehensive. Scholars will note areas of interest and import that are not addressed, research that is not reviewed, important references that are not cited, and discussions that are not included in this work. Hopefully, these shortcomings and unintended omissions (as well as 828 pages of scholarly writing) will serve to provoke discourse and motivate discussion. We invite and welcome critical response to this effort, particularly as such discourse results in improved efforts to fulfill the needs of the research and scholarly community with interests in the field of art education.

Roles of the Editors

Following formulation of categories for the six sections of the *Handbook*, our most significant contribution was to select persons to serve as section editors. Our approach was to choose experienced and respected scholars with records of research and publication within the arena of the respective section topics. Each editor accepted significant responsibility for crafting his or her section. They selected authors, suggested topics, and determined the scope of their respective sections. They were responsible for editing the works of the authors they selected, seeing that deadlines were met, and maintaining communication between the general editors and the section authors. The two general editors maintained a lighthanded relationship that allowed each section editor to proceed with few restrictions.

We mention with some pride that all who worked so hard on this endeavor contributed their efforts as academic volunteers. None received remuneration for the countless hours and painstaking research required for creating and editing each chapter. Their reward is the satisfaction gained by generous professionals in the advancement of the field of knowledge and practice to which they are dedicated.

When we invited the section editors to assume responsibility for the selection of chapter authors, we did not have, nor did we want to have, a specific format or array of criteria to be used in preparing chapters. Consistent with the arts, we value diversity, and the reader will find among the chapters a wide range of writing styles and approaches to scholarship. Some display the traditional accoutrements of scholarly social science research, whereas others display interpretive and other forms of qualitative scholarship. We find this diversity quite acceptable and consistent with the general field's interest in the cultivation of productive differences.

We indicated that the six section editors were responsible for selecting authors for their sections. We reviewed those proposed appointments and had a hand in shaping the appointments. In addition, the section editors were responsible for reviewing the chapters, at least at an initial level. We reviewed the chapters as well but left final decisions regarding the form and content of the chapters to the section editors.

It should be clear from our work that the Handbook as a whole is a collective effort of scholars committed to the importance of the work and willing to take on what is a detailed and at times arduous and complex process. We are extremely grateful to the section editors for the important contribution that they made to the Handbook.

Relationship of Research and Practice

Earlier we discussed the connections between research and practice in the field of art education, described the growing theoretical and conceptual sophistication of members in the field, and reviewed the ways in which the field has changed with respect to these issues since its birth around the middle of the 19th century. But there is another issue that should be addressed pertaining to the uses of research. It has to do with the relationship of practice, research, policy. Practice, being a practical endeavor, deals inevitably with particular situations. Theory, particularly theory in the sciences, always addresses abstractions and in large measure, idealizations of a phenomenon. As a result, theory and other conceptual apparatus needs to be appraised not by its formulaic contributions to problem solving in the practical world, but by the insight and guidance it affords practitioners in addressing what are always uniquely particular circumstances. No student, for example, is identical to any other even though they may share many similarities. The teacher needs to fine-tune teaching practices to suit specific groups or individuals. Thus, theory is a guide in human affairs, not a formula for action. For those who seek prescriptions, the Handbook will be a disappointment; it has none to provide. What it will provide are ideas that can serve as guides for serious and often difficult reflection upon local circumstances. We believe there is much in the Handbook to provide that kind of guidance and insight. Looked at metaphorically, theoretical material provides an aperture through which to peer. The contours of that aperture differ from discipline to discipline, from theoretical perspective to theoretical perspective. No single aperture tells the whole story, and all put together at the same time create an occlusion; nothing can be seen because there is no longer an opening. Thus, apertures are useful as individuals acquire the skill to see through them and the flexibility to shift apertures at will. Hence, graduate education in some sense is concerned with providing students with a variety of such apertures and developing the appetite and flexibility to look through many of them. Because these apertures are made by humans, knowledge about a state of affairs is, in the end, a construction that is influenced by the tools with which one works and the forms of representation one uses to describe, reveal, and display what one has learned.

Policy in Art Education

The first section of the Handbook is designed to illuminate core value questions regarding the purposes of art education. How a field defines its purposes, that is, the objectives it seeks to attain, is critical for virtually all that follows because the kind of research, for example, that one undertakes, the kind of preparation provided for prospective teachers, the ways in which the field interprets itself to the larger community are all shaped by policies pertaining to the fundamental functions of the field. The section on policy looks at these functions from a range of perspectives and examines research that purports to justify art education by its contributions to extra-artistic outcomes such as academic achievement. Thus, policy helps shape the direction of one's research questions and the consequences of research—what has been learned through it—help shape policy. There is an ineluctable dialectic between the two.

Learning in Art

The second section of the *Handbook* focuses on development and learning in art. Art education has a long history of efforts to describe what is often referred to as "stages" of children's art. These stages have been regarded, in the main, as genetically unfolding processes that manifest themselves in graphic form. To understand development, one needed to assume a biologically driven framework—a framework that is being problematized today. There is now a growing emphasis on the impact of culture on children's and adolescents' image-making. This emphasis on culture tends to diminish the importance of biological imperatives and emphasize matters of value, opportunity to learn, and the like. Indeed, art itself is seen as a cultural artifact. What one values aesthetically, it is claimed, is dependent on how one has been socialized. Thus, the artistic development of children is, for some, to be regarded as the product of learning rather than as the consequences of an unfolding of genetically conferred capacities. The section on development and learning in art presents an array of perspectives, some of which conflict with one another.

Assessment

Assessment in the visual arts constitutes the third section addressed in the *Handbook*. Given the implementation of educational policies that mandate the testing of students in virtually all subject areas, assessment becomes particularly critical in the field of art education. It is critical because the field embraces outcomes that are not simply routine or definable in their entirety in advance; it values outcomes that are imaginative, diverse, and interesting in any number of ways. Thus, there may not be a single criterion or even a set of criteria or rubrics as they are called that can adequately represent what students have learned. And yet there is considerable pressure on art educators to formulate standards and use them to evaluate what students have accomplished. This leaves the field in a bind. If conventional standards and assessment practices are not employed, the field might lose even the marginal position it now enjoys. If, however, conventional approaches to assessment are employed, all in the name of validity and reliability, doing so might undermine the distinctive values the field seeks to achieve. These, and other issues are particularly important in the assessment arena, and the section itself represents perspectives on assessment that extend from the interpersonal critique in the visual arts to large-scale assessment of student outcomes as represented by the National Assessment of Educational Progress. The reader should come away from this section with a broad appreciation of the varieties of assessments and the programs in which these assessments function.

Historical Currents in Art Education

Another mark of the emergence of art education within the academic discourse is increased attention paid in recent years to histories of the field. As a subject too often regarded as peripheral to the central core of general education, art education has a history of shifting rationales. The field has transformed itself through a series of justifications that promised a variety of educational benefits for students. At various periods in the history of art education, these justifications have promised to prepare students for the industrial work place, to foster creativity, to provide for a healthy integration of personality, to develop the aesthetic lens for understanding, and to assist students to more adequately negotiate the contemporary world of commercial applications in art and visual culture. These and other rationales have waxed and waned in practice and in academic discourse, and most have persisted to some extent in the art curricula and publications of art education.

This section of the *Handbook* presents two ambitious chapters: one that addresses and discusses art education in the 19th century, and one that offers a perspective on art education in the 20th century. Both chapters relate the histories of this field within the larger contexts of general education and social, political, and cultural events that influence education.

Teaching and Teacher Education

Teaching is obviously central to the field of art education, yet art teaching is relatively unstudied by researchers and scholars. If the body of research on teaching art is weak, one might ask, what guides the preparation of new teachers? Questions relevant to contemporary educational policy abound, suggesting a pressing need for competent, informative, and insightful research. In today's economic environment, what motivates college students to choose teaching as a goal? What are the potential enticements for prospective art teachers to join the profession? In the face of a general teacher shortage, how might the profession recruit prospective teachers, support new teachers, and retain experienced professionals? What are the characteristics of art teachers' professional lives in their classrooms? In what ways do values promoted within their university preparation interact with practical pressures new teachers experience from the institutions in which they serve? What are the available avenues for certification to teach? How might an art teacher's experience vary according to the state, the community, the school district, and according to the school situation they choose? What are the implications of current emphasis on assessment, newer instructional technologies, and educational standards on the working lives of art teachers? These and many other interesting and vital questions associated with teaching and teacher preparation are addressed, analyzed, and discussed in this section, and a thorough analysis of research methods and methodologies employed in their study is offered in a separate chapter. The seven authors of this section serve the field in establishing a research base about art education teaching and teacher education. The chapters range widely across topics of teaching and teacher education, from the status of current research to suggestions for future directions, all with the unique focus of art education.

Emerging Visions of Art Education

As we mentioned earlier, art education has undergone significant change over the past 2 centuries. Change in art education, perhaps more than in other areas of the curriculum, has been complete and radical far beyond the mere updating of subject content. Philosophies, theories, and rationales for art in general education have been transformed from one paradigm to another. But before significant change can occur, a vision is required that articulates, motivates, and provides direction for the desired change.

An educational paradigm is a relatively complete and stable pattern of ideas, propositions, and theories that provide guidance for practice. It is a more consistent set of ideas in comparison with an educational vision, which can be viewed as a candidate for paradigmatic status. Visions, no matter how grand, need on to be acted on to become real. Ideas, clearly, are important. Without them change has no rudder. But change also needs wind and a sail to catch it. Without them there is no movement. A vision might be more tentative and speculative than a paradigm as it offers new ideas and directions, competes for status through advocacy of change, and inspires disciples to pursue the vision.

In this section, authors are free to present their proposals for the futures of art education. They are free to speculate on possibilities for improvement, create convincing portraits of new visions, and advocate directions that compete with the discipline-based paradigm that is salient in the field today. The chapters in this provocative section are offered with an invitation for readers to speculate, critique, and contribute their own views and visions of the field of art education. In the spirit of creative scholarly discourse, this invitation serves as a fitting end-piece for the *Handbook of Research and Policy in Art Education*.

I

Historical Currents in Art Education

1

Learning from Histories of Art Education: An Overview of Research and Issues

F. Graeme Chalmers
University of British Columbia

This chapter provides an overview of historical work, mostly by art educators. As an introduction, it differs in focus and intent from the two following chapters in which the authors discuss and interpret art education histories within the light of other cultural and educational histories. It seems important to begin this chapter, and indeed this section of the Handbook, with a question: Why study (or ignore) art education's histories?

Mary Erickson (1979) has suggested that there are four reasons to study art education's histories. History initiates us into the field of art education and helps us to develop a sense of belonging. A knowledge of history helps us to clarify contested ideas, and helps us to formulate questions to be asked about the present and future of art education. In short, attention to histories of art education helps us to understand "how we came to be where we are" (Stankiewicz, 2001a). In a recent *Translations: From Theory to Practice*, Stankiewicz (2001a) uses these concepts: initiation, identity, and ancestors; clarifying concepts; asking questions; and abolishing ghosts and myths, to structure her discussion of the "why" of historical studies in art education published since 1990. Among others who provide answers to the question: "Why study (or ignore) art education's histories?" are Chalmers (1993), Erickson (1977), Efland (1992), Eisner (1992) and Soucy and Webb (1984). With only a few exceptions (such as the authors of the two following chapters), art educators have generally been slow to relate their work to either other histories of education or social, political, and cultural histories in general. (For a discussion of this issue see especially Soucy, 1991.)

Although it crops up from time to time as a conference topic, to date, few authors have addressed issues around the teaching of art education history to preservice teachers and to graduate students. Notable exceptions include Edmonston's (1985) presentation at the first Pennsylvania State University history of art education conference and Stankiewicz's (2001b) text for teacher education students—a major "history" contribution to the Davis "Art Education in Practice" series.

A BRIEF HISTORY OF ART EDUCATION HISTORIES

Don Soucy's (1990) very comprehensive analysis of literature in the history of art education has been called "the first truly historiographic essay in our field" (Stankiewicz, 2001a). Although Soucy's analysis has informed more recent reviews of art education history by other scholars (e.g., Raunft, 2001, and Stankiewicz, 2001a), there are also a number of earlier, but still useful, listings and descriptions of historical research in art education. Examples include Farnum's (1941) contribution to the *Fortieth Year Book of the National Society for the Study of Education* and Keel's (1965) chapter in the *Sixty-Fourth Year Book* and his earlier review in *Studies in Art Education* (Keel, 1963). In addition, Hamblen's (1985a, 1985b) work, addressing issues of selection and interpretation in histories of art education published up to the mid-1980s is valuable; Norris's (1979) comprehensive bibliography of primary and secondary sources in art education history is simply a listing, but is nevertheless of value to the serious scholar; and Soucy's (1985a, 1985b) earlier attempts to address the limits and potentialities of research in art education history provide seminal reviews that have influenced subsequent work in art education history.

For example, Soucy (1985a, 1985b, 1990) made us very aware that when writing their histories, too many art educators have depended on secondary sources. Many histories have been based on the pioneering but limited work of Isaac Edwards Clarke (1885, 1892). Efland and Soucy (1992) trace Clarke's influence on those who depended on his work when writing their own histories (e.g., Belshe, 1946; Chapman, 1978; Eisner, 1972; Eisner & Ecker 1966; Farnum, 1941; Gaitskell, 1948; Gaitskell, Hurwitz, & Day, 1982; Green, 1948; Hubbard, 1966; Kaufman, 1966; Saunders, 1976; W. G. Whitford, 1923). This heavy reliance on Clarke resulted in some biased and flawed, but nevertheless influential, histories. For example, two generations of art teachers-in-training learned their art education history from Logan's (1955) *Growth of Art in American Schools* and Keel and Saunders' (1966) special issue of *Art Education*. As the authors of the two following chapters show, we now embrace work with competing foci, methodologies, and interpretations.

The "growth" of art education history in doctoral dissertations, professional publications, conferences, and conference presentations has been a fairly recent phenomenon. Fifty years ago, very few doctoral dissertations focused on art education history, and, when they did, they tended to be fairly general (e.g., Belshe, 1946; Green, 1948; Hubbard, 1966; Rios, 1954). Korzenik (1995a), looking back on the next generation of historical research by graduate students, found examples of more specific and focused interest. In the mid-1960s, *Studies in Art Education* (1965) and *Art Education* (Keel & Saunders, 1966) both gave art education history a boost with the publication of special issues; and 20 years later, scholars such as Amburgy, Bolin, Efland, Soucy, Stankiewicz, and others did much to foster historical studies in art education. Beginning in 1985, the three Pennsylvania State seminars in art education history did most to revive interest in the study of art education's past and to bring together scholars interested in historical inquiry (Amburgy, Soucy, Stankiewicz, Wilson, & Wilson, 1992; Anderson & Bolin, 1997; Hoffa & Wilson, 1985) as did Soucy and Stankiewicz's (1990) edited text, *Framing the Past: Essays on Art Education.*

ART EDUCATION HISTORY AS "RESEARCH"

Within historical research in art education, styles of historical investigation, selection, and interpretation vary. In their introduction to *Remembering Others: Making Invisible Histories of Art Education Visible*, Bolin, Blandy, and Congdon (2000) remind us that "each writer and historical document offers only a limited perspective on issues which are extremely complex, both in their occurrence and in their interpretation" (p. 2). We are sensibly cautioned by these and other authors that there is no single history of anything. To identify newer approaches to historical research and writing, Bolin et al. cite Burke (P. Burke, 1991), who posits that historians are working toward enlarging what is considered to be worthy of historical study; moving beyond the study of historical documents, providing multiple responses to historical questions; and acknowledging that there is no such thing as an objective history. Art educators are increasingly realizing that, even when dealing with the same subject, many different histories can be written (Bolin, 1995a; Efland, 1995; Erickson, 1985; Hamblen, 1987, 1992; Korzenik, 1985a; Michael & Morris, 1985; Smith & LaPierre, 1995; Soucy 1985a; Stankiewicz, 1995a, etc.). Sometimes we have engaged in inspiring evangelism and have presented our research as hagiographic stories of saints, for example, Zweybruck's (1953) work on Franz Cizek as the "father" of art education.

Now art education histories are presented more as attempts to understand what really happened within wider ideological and social contexts. More art educators doing historical work are asking critical questions and using a wide range of interdisciplinary perspectives. For example, in the following chapter, Amburgy, Bolin, and Stankiewicz provide an excellent model for viewing 19th century art education within such contexts. Similarly, "invisible," "overlooked," and "obscured" histories of art education are increasingly addressed in a number of papers in Bolin et al.'s (2000) recent anthology, and by others such as Pearse (1997) and J. C. Smith (1992). Bolin et al. state that they sought to "provide a place for... 'family memory and community recollection'... to move toward recognizing and apprehending more of the frequently neglected, but extremely important experiences that should be noted within the history of art education" (p. 3). As Lemerise (2000) argues, this approach helps "diminish the propensity for hagiography that reinforces the cult of heroes" (p. 43).

The variety of research methods employed by those who "do" art education history have been effectively discussed by Marché (2000), Smith and La Pierre (1995), Stankiewicz (1995a), and others. Oral histories have been favored by, among others, Dambekains (1997), Stewart (1986), Stokrocki (1992, 1995), and Yates (1993); whereas Ashwin (1975), Korzenik (1983), and Pinto and Smith (1999) have been attracted to artifactual histories and working with ephemera. The use of archives for art education history has been a particular concern for Morris and Raunft (1995) and Stout (1985).

As in other areas of art education research, there has been a perceived schism between historical research and practice (Caldwell, 1997; Erickson, 1979). In an article in *School Arts*, Gaitskell (1953) alerted teachers to the fact that "Art education has a history," and in her recent book *Roots of Art Education Practice*, Stankiewicz (2001b) specifically focuses on art education histories for art teachers. To help us understand and reflect on our practice is a definite purpose of this section of the *Handbook*.

BROAD PERSPECTIVES ON ART EDUCATION HISTORY

There are a relatively small number of single-authored books that attempt to present comprehensive histories of art education either in schools or in higher education. Among the classics are works by Bell (1963), Carline (1968), Efland (1990), Goldstein (1996), Logan (1955), S. MacDonald (1970), Pevsner (1940), P. Smith (1996a), Sutton (1967), and Wygant (1983, 1986, 1993). "Historical" chapters appear in most of the older "art teacher education" texts (e.g., Chapman, 1978; Eisner & Ecker 1966; Gaitskell, Hurwitz, & Day, 1982; Haney, 1908; Hubbard, 1967; Kaufman, 1966; Whitford, 1929) as well as in some more recent editions. As an example of historical content in a well-used text, we can consider Laura Chapman's (1978) historical chapter "A Perspective on Art Education." Chapman labels the period 1820 to 1920

"The beginning of art education" and discusses art as skill in drawing, art for cultural refinement, and art as craft and folk tradition. The period 1920 to 1940 is labeled "The Progressive movement" and includes a discussion of art as self-expression, integrated and correlated art, and art in everyday living. In her review of the 2 decades 1940 to 1960, titled "Mid-century Developments," Chapman, discusses experimentation with materials, art education during the Second World War, art as a developmental activity, and art as creative behavior. The final section introduces the roots of some more recent practices: art as a body of knowledge and art and the social order.

THE RESEARCH INTERESTS OF ART EDUCATION HISTORIANS

The histories of ideas (sociocultural, economic, aesthetic, political, philosophical, religious ideologies and their influence on art education) have interested a number of researchers (e.g., Amburgy, 1985, 1990; Baker, 1982; Briggs, 1995; Chalmers, 1992a; M. Collins, 1997; Degenhart, 1986; Efland 1983a, 1983b; Freedman, 1986, 1992; Kern, 1985; Martin, 1991; McWhinnie, 1992; 1997; Moore, 1991, 1997; Palmer, 1978; Purdue, 1977; Sahasrabudhe, 1997; Saunders, 1961, 1990; Smalley, 1997; Stankiewicz, 1997a, 1999; Weiley, 1957; Wood & Soucy, 1990). The role of government in art education has been studied by Hoffa (1985) and Korzenik (1987a). Again, the following two chapters provide excellent examples of work with such foci.

Researchers have also given attention to changing conceptions of art curriculum content/ policy and teaching (Beittel, 1997; Bohn, 1968; Brown, 1985; Dana, 1953; Efland, 1984, 1988; Freedman, 1985, 1987a, 1987b, 1988; Freedman & Popkewitz, 1988; Korzenik, 1990; Mattil, Hoffa, Hausman, & Ecker, 1997; Mazio, 1976; Miley, 1994; Pasto, 1967a, 1967b; Stankiewicz, 1984a, 1984b, 1990, 1992a, 1992b, 1997a, 2000; Werner, 2000). Related to changing conceptions of art curriculum is an interest in technology and curriculum materials, including drawing books, plaster casts, teaching aids (see Davis, 1996; Katter, 1985; Mazio, 1976; McNutt, 1988, 1990; Sellink, 1992; Stankiewicz, 1995b; Turner, 1997, and others). Schoolroom decoration, picture study, and aesthetic education have interested Amburgy (1985), Gaughan (1990), Geahigan (1997), Jansen (1992), Jones (1974), B. L. MacDonald (1997), P. Smith (1986), Stankiewicz (1988), and others.

Regional and case studies seem to have been the particular forté of Canadian art education historians. Gaitskell (1948), Tait (1957), and Wood (1986) gave attention to the Province of Ontario. Lemerise (1992, 1995, 1997), Lemerise and Couture (1990), Lemerise and Sherman (1990), and Stirling (1997) have focused on Québec. Amburgy and Soucy (1989) and Soucy (1986a, 1986b) have focused on Nova Scotia and the Maritime Provinces, with Pearse and Soucy (e.g., 1987) giving particular attention to Halifax. Rogers (1983, 1985, 1990) has given most attention to British Columbia. As is documented in the following chapter, North American art education historians have probably focused most on Massachusetts, and especially on Boston (e.g., see Bailey, 1900; Bolin, 1985, 1987, 1990, 1995b, 1997; Efland, 1985a, 1985b; Korzenik, 1987a, and others); Pennsylvania has been the focus of work by Chalmers (1996, 1998), De Angeli Walls (1993, 1994), Marché (1995, 1997a, 1997b), and Winkelman (1990); Chicago by Amburgy (1997) and Finley (1992); Dayton, Ohio, by Loucks (1991); the Milwaukee public schools by Riley (1987); Puerto Rico by Galanes (1998); and the Southwest by P. Smith (1999) and Stokrocki (2000). Stark (1985) studied the regional influences of the Oswego Movement, and Freedman (1989) and Saunders (1985) studied the Owatonna Project.

The lives of art educators, art students, and artists have been of major interest to art education historians. However, as stated previously, some of the resulting accounts have been exercises in "saint-making" rather than critical histories. Among the biographical studies of art educators,

Possible topic [handwritten margin note]

most work has been on Walter Smith (e.g., Barbosa, 1984; Chalmers, 1985a, 2000a; Green, 1966; Rocke, 1952; Sheath, 1982; P. Smith, 1992). Work on Viktor Lowenfeld has been published by LaPorte (1997), Peter Smith (1982a, 1983, 1985a, 1989), and others. Arthur Wesley Dow has interested Hook (1985) and Mock-Morgan (1976, 1985). Zahner (1987, 1992) has completed work on Manuel Barkan, and Sherman and Efland (1997) have published work on Victor D'Amico. Kenneth Beittel has interested Okazaki (1997) and Zurmuelen (1991). Henry Schaefer-Simmern has been studied by Berta (1994); Henry Turner Bailey by Stankiewicz (1997b); and Albert Anderson (1997) focused on Charles Godfrey Leyland. Chalmers (1985b, 1994) and Rogers (1984, 1987) have studied art educators associated with the South Kensington diaspora. On her own (Sessions, 1997) and with Richard Johnston (Sessions & Johnston, 2000), Billie Sessions has studied the life and work of ceramics educator Marguerite Wildenhain. June King McFee (Congdon & Degge, 1997), Mary Dana Hicks Prang, Rila Jackson, and other women associated with art education at Syracuse (Stankiewicz, 1983, 1985a,b); Eugenia Eckford Rhoads, Marion Richardson, Natalie Robinson Cole (P. Smith, 1984, 1990, 1996b), and Charlotte Perkins Gilman (Gaudelius, 1997) are among the many women art educators that have interested contemporary historians (see additional studies cited later under Gender Issues).

Autobiographical studies of art educators are perhaps more available in art education than in other curriculum areas. Beginning in 1972, the art education program at Miami University in Oxford, Ohio, has sponsored a series of autobiographical lectures by well-known art educators. In 2001, the lectures (Raunft, 2001) were published by the National Art Education Association. In this volume, which includes contributions by 28 art educators, some accounts are more helpful to historians than others. The following art educators reflect on aspects of their lives: Rudolf Arnheim, Victor D'Amico, Ralph Beelke, Laura H. Chapman, Natalie Robinson Cole, Stanley Czurles, Elliot W. Eisner, Edmund B. Feldman, Charles D. Gaitskell, Pearl Greenberg, Eugene Grigsby, Jr., George W. Hardiman, Jerome Hausman, Albert Hurwitz, Ivan E. Johnson, Kenneth Lansing, Frederick Logan, Viktor Lowenfeld, Edward L. Mattil, June King McFee, Mary Adeline McKibbin, John A. Michael, Henry Schaefer-Simmern, Harold Schultz, Frank Wachowiak, Foster Wygant, Theodore Zernich, and Edwin Ziegfeld. Ralph Raunft (2001) introduces this volume with a strong discussion of "autobiography and issues of meaning." He states:

> Autobiographies, through their narrative emplotments and reflections of the authors, give order and meaning to life and are different than experience. A specific autobiography... has specific focus, range and limitations, yet reflects the uniqueness of each lecturer with regard to their personal and professional lives. With every autobiography, we see an author's self-awareness being structured into some order that mediates between subjective and objective reality. The question of reality forces the reader or researcher to look at an autobiography in the context of memory and the self.... (p. xii)

Although not strictly *auto*biographical, some histories utilize the insights of close family relationships. For example, Guilfoil (2000) writes about her father (Frederick George Kurz) as artist, designer, and educator, and, her niece Lemerise (2000) provides particular insights into the life and work of Canadian art educator, Irene Senecal.

Artists as educators and the education of artists, areas of growing interest among art historians, have received particular attention by D. B. Burke, (1987), Carroll (1994), Chamberlin-Hellman (1981), Davis (1996), Funk (1990), Hinterreiter (1967), Johns (1990), McRae (2000), Pearse (1986, 1992), P. Smith (1987, 1991), Toub (1997), and others. The lives of art students, too, have received some attention, for example, in Korzenik's *Drawn to Art* (1985b). Other examples of work in this genre are Glavin's (1993) careful use of archival resources to reconstruct the early art education of Maurice Prendergast. Art historians, too, have become increasingly interested in this type of work, for example, in "The Lure of Paris" Weinberg (1991) studied American painting students and their French teachers, and Klayman's (1981) dissertation reported on the art education of John Singleton Copley.

Throughout the 1980s and 1990s, gender issues have especially interested art education historians. Women art educators and art education for young women have been the foci of studies by Bermingham (1993), De Angeli Walls (1993), Dwyer (1989), Efland (1985a), Hazelwood (1999), Korzenik (1987b), McNeill (1992, 1995), Siskar (1997), P. Smith (1984, 1988a, 1996), Stankiewicz (1982a, 1982b, 1982c, 1983, 1985, 1993), Stankiewicz and Zimmerman (1984, 1985), Weisberg and Becker (1999), Zimmerman (1989, 1991), and others (see White's chapter on 20th-century art education. Within the context of gender studies, art education for young men has not received the same attention as art education for young women. Among the exceptions are studies by Chalmers (2001), Haslam (1988), and Madhok (1994).

Histories of professional associations have received some attention and John Michael (1995) has addressed particular methodological issues in writing such histories. Van Dommelen (1985) studied the history of the Pennsylvania Art Education Association; MacGregor (1979), the Canadian Society for Education through Art; Michael (1997) and Saunders (1992), the National Art Education Association; and Rhoades (1987), the International Society for Education through Art. Within the larger associations, some subgroups have usefully documented their history; a good example is Check's (2000) history of the founding of the Lesbian, Gay, and Bisexual Issues Caucus of the National Art Education Association.

Within our field, there are a number of celebratory institutional and program histories, often published as centenary projects by the institutions themselves. Among those who have studied art schools are Chalmers (2000a), Dean (1924), Hoyt and Field (1898), and others who focus on the Massachusetts Normal Art School; Marsh (1983) who focuses on the Corcoran School of Art; Dwyer (1989) focuses on the Pittsburgh School of Design for Women; Phelan (1995) on the School for American Craftsmen; Soucy (1989, 1996) and Soucy and Pearse (1993) on the Nova Scotia College of Art and Design; and Suplee (1995, 1997) on the Barnes Foundation. Chalmers (1996, 1998) and De Angeli Walls (1993, 1994) have both made detailed historical studies of the Philadelphia School of Design for Women. Chalmers (1996, 1998) and Morse (2001) also looked at its precedent, London's Female School of Design (later the Royal Female School of Art); and Weisberg and Becker (1999) studied the (American) women at Paris's the Académie Julian. In a nicely focused study on the successor to the Philadelphia School of Design for Women, "Whatever happened to the art education class of 1942," Fitzpatrick (2000) focuses on the art educational experiences of six women who graduated from the Moore College of Art in 1942. From both personal memory and library research, Phyllis Gold Gluck (2000) evokes the heady days of the art school of the Educational Alliance and its role in Jewish American life on Manhattan's Lower East Side.

Among historical studies of university art education programs and departments are work by Siegel (1981) on Adelphi University; Johnson (1985), on the University of Arkansas; Dambekains (1996), on the Pennsylvania State University; Wygant (1959), on Teachers' College, Columbia; Stankiewicz (1979), on Syracuse; Fitzpatrick (1992), on the University of Iowa and Indiana University; and McNeill (1992), on the University of Missouri.

Marché (1995, 1997a,b) studied 60 years of changes in art education in a Pennsylvania School district, and Funk (2000) has made a case study of education in the 1930s Federal Art Project.

Histories of publications have also received some attention. Together Brewer (1999), Chalmers (1999), Chapman (1999), and Collins (1999) reviewed 40 years of *Studies in Art Education*. Shumaker (1985) analyzed the content of *Art Education* from 1948 to 1984, and Stephenson (1997) used the contents of *School Arts* to examine depression-era art materials.

Possible topic

In his studies of Pedro deLemos and Native American presence in art education (e.g., White, 1997, 2001), and in his chapter in this *Handbook*, John Howell White has also made extensive use of the contents of *School Arts*.

Haynes (1993, 1997) and Henry and Nyman (1997) have studied the roots of multicultural art education practice. Chalmers (1992a) studied the origins of prejudice in our field. Although documentation of the lives and work of African American artists is increasing, less has been written about those who were also educators. Exceptions include the work of Augusta Savage (Cochran, 2000, and J. C. Smith, 1992) and studies by Claxton (1997), C. A. Hollingsworth (1988), Hubbard (1985), P. Smith (1987, 1988b), and Stanford (1984). Audrey Dear Hesson, the 1951 first black graduate in art education from the Nova Scotia College of Art and Design, is the subject of a fascinating oral history by Harold Pearse (2000). Native American art education has received some historical attention (see Chalmers, 2000b; Eldridge, 2001; P. Smith, 1999; Stokrocki, 1997; White, 1997). McCollister (2000) documents the work of a number of persons who worked with a traditional Blackfoot (Idaho) arts program between 1976 and 1981.

Forman (1968) and Stankiewicz (1984b, 1988) have addressed European precedents in general. Histories of the South Kensington Diaspora and its impact in other parts of the world, including North America, have been provided by Chalmers (1985a,b, 1994, 2000a), Denis (1995), Rogers (1983, 1984, 1985, 1987), and Sproll (1994). Germanic foundations are the topic of studies by Ashwin (1981), Morris, Raunft, and Pfeiffer (1985), Moynihan (1980), P. Smith (1982a, 1982b), Whitford (1994), and others. The influence of Swedish Sloyd is the topic of Eyestone's (1992) study, and American influences on art education in Brazil and Japan have been studied by Barbosa (1984), Foster (1992), and Okazaki (1994).

Art education for special populations has received limited historical attention (e.g., Troeger, 1992; Zimmerman, 1985). Abrahamson (1985) studied implications for art education and art therapy found in the work of Henry Schaefer-Simmern; Chalmers (1992b) reported on learning to draw in the military; and Abia-Smith (2000) writes about historical and contemporary approaches to museum education for visitors with disabilities.

Radio art education has been the topic of studies by Bolin (1992), Funk (1998), and Kelly (1992). Although aspects of children's art and early childhood education have been of research interest to many art educators, children's art seems to have been of less interest to historians. (Exceptions include Finnegan, 1997; Freedman, 1989b; Korzenik, 1981; Leeds, 1989; Pariser, 1985; Sienkiewicz, 1985; Tarr, 1989; Turner, 1992; and Wilson, 1985, 1992). An interest in industrial arts education and manual training is evident in the work of most art educators who study the 19th century. The topic has been the specific focus of work by Anderson (1992), Bennett (1926, 1937), Gerhard (1997), Maffei (2000), Saunders (1976), and Stanford (1984). Clark (1985, 1992), Joyce (1997), and others have contributed histories of testing and assessment; and histories of museum education, becoming more numerous in the field of museology, have been the focus of work by a few scholars in art education (e.g., Abia-Smith, 2000; Din, 1998; Newsom & Silver, 1978; Ott, 1985, 1992; Schroeder, 1992; Svedlow & Troxell, 1997; Zeller, 1989).

REFERENCES

Abia-Smith, L. (2000). Historical and contemporary approaches to museum education and visitors with disabilities. In P. Bolin, D. Blandy & K. G. Congdon (Eds.), *Remembering others: Making invisible histories of art education visible* (pp. 113–124). Reston, VA: National Art Education Association.

Abrahamson, R. E. (1985). Henry Schaefer-Simmern's research and theory: Implications for art education, art therapy, and art for special education. In H. Hoffa & B. Wilson (Eds.), *History of art education: Proceedings of the Penn State Conference* (pp. 247–255). College Park, PA: The Pennsylvania State University, College of Arts & Architecture School of Visual Arts.

Amburgy, P. M. (1985). Loved illusions and real beliefs: The concept of aesthetic experience. In H. Hoffa & B. Wilson (Eds.). *History of art education: Proceedings of the Penn State Conference* (pp. 35–39). College Park, PA: The Pennsylvania State University, College of Arts & Architecture School of Visual Arts.

Amburgy, P. M. (1990). Culture for the masses: Art education and progressive reforms, 1880–1917. In D. Soucy & M. A. Stankiewicz (Eds.), *Framing the past: Essays on art education* (pp. 103–116). Reston, VA: National Art Education Association.

Amburgy, P. M. (1997). Arts and crafts education in Chicago, 1890–1920. In A. Anderson & P. Bolin (Eds.). *History of art education: Proceedings of the Third Penn State International Symposium, October 12–15, 1995* (pp. 384–388). College Park, PA: The Pennsylvania State University Art Education Program, School of Visual Arts.

Amburgy, P., & Soucy, D. (1989). Art education, romantic idealism, and work: Comparing Ruskin's ideas to those found in 19th century Nova Scotia. *Studies in Art Education, 30*(3), 157–163.

Amburgy, P. M., Soucy, D., Stankiewicz, M., Wilson, B., & Wilson, M. (Eds.). (1992). *History of art education: Proceedings of the Second Penn State Conference, 1989.* Reston, VA: The National Art Education Association.

Anderson, A. (1997). Charles Godfrey Leland: Pioneer craft educator. In A. Anderson & P. Bolin (Eds.), *History of art education: Proceedings of the Third Penn State International Symposium, October 12–15, 1995* (pp. 367–374). College Park, PA: The Pennsylvania State University Art Education Program, School of Visual Arts.

Anderson, A., & Bolin, P. (Eds.). (1997). *History of art education: Proceedings of the Third Penn State International Symposium, October 12–15, 1995.* College Park, PA: The Pennsylvania State University Art Education Program, School of Visual Arts.

Anderson. J. D. (1992). Art and the problem of vocationalism in American education. In P. M. Amburgy, D. Soucy, M. A. Stankiewicz, B. Wilson, & M. Wilson (Eds.), *History of art education: Proceedings of the Second Penn State Conference, 1989* (pp. 12–15). Reston, VA: The National Art Education Association.

Ashwin, C. (1975). *Art education documents and policies 1768–1975.* London: Society for Research into Higher Education.

Ashwin, C. (1981). *Drawing and education in German speaking Europe: 1800–1900.* Ann Arbor: UMI Research Press.

Bailey, H. T. (1900). *A sketch of the history of public art instruction in Massachusetts.* Boston: Wright & Porter.

Baker, D. W. (1982). *Rousseau's children: An historical analysis of the romantic paradigm in art education.* Doctoral dissertation, Pennsylvania State University, State College.

Barbosa, A. M. (1984). Walter Smith's influence in Brazil and the efforts of Brazilian liberals to overcome the concept of art as an elitist activity. *Journal of Art and Design Education, 3*(2), 233–246.

Beittel, K. R. (1997). Fateful fork in the road: The 1965 *Red Book.* In A. Anderson & P. Bolin (Eds.), *History of art education: Proceedings of the Third Penn State International Symposium, October 12–15, 1995* (pp. 533–539). College Park, PA: The Pennsylvania State University Art Education Program, School of Visual Arts.

Bell, Q. (1963). *The schools of design.* London: Routledge & Kegan Paul.

Belshe, F. B. (1946). *A history of art education in the public schools of the United States.* Doctoral dissertation, Yale University, New Haven, CT.

Bennett, C. A. (1926). *History of manual and industrial education up to 1870.* Peoria, IL: The Manual Arts Press.

Bennett, C. A. (1937). *History of manual and industrial education 1870–1917.* Peoria, IL: The Manual Arts Press.

Bermingham, A. (1993). The aesthetics of ignorance: The accomplished woman in the culture of connoisseurship. *Oxford Art Journal, 16*(2), 3–20.

Berta, R. (1994). *His figure and his ground: An art educational biography of Henry Schaefer-Simmern.* Doctoral dissertation, Stanford University, Stanford, CA.

Bohn, D. (1968). "Artustry" or the immaculate misconception of the 70's. *History of Education Quarterly, 8*(1), 107–110.

Bolin, P. (1985). The influence of industrial policy on enactment of the 1870 Massachusetts Free Instruction in Drawing Act. In H. Hoffa & B. Wilson (Eds.), *History of art education: Proceedings of the Penn State Conference* (pp. 102–107). College Park, PA: The Pennsylvania State University College of Arts & Architecture School of Visual Arts.

Bolin, P. (1987). *Drawing interpretation: An examination of the 1870 Massachusetts "Act Relating to Free Instruction in Drawing."* Doctoral dissertation, University of Oregon, Eugene.

Bolin, P. (1990). The Massachusetts Drawing Act of 1870: Industrial mandate or democratic manoeuvre? In D. Soucy & M. A. Stankiewicz (Eds.), *Framing the past: Essays on art education* (pp. 59–68). Reston, VA: National Art Education Association.

Bolin, P. (1992). Art over the airwaves: A brief examination of radio art education in the United States, 1929–1951. In P. M. Amburgy, D. Soucy, M. A. Stankiewicz, B. Wilson, and M. Wilson (Eds.), *History of art education: Proceedings of the Second Penn State Conference, 1989* (pp. 274–278). Reston, VA: The National Art Education Association.

Bolin, P. (1995a). Matters of choice: Historical inquiry in art education. In P. Smith & S. D. La Pierre (Eds.), *Art education historical methodology: An insider's guide to doing and using* (pp. 44–52). Pasadena, CA: Open Door Publishers for the Seminar for Research in Art Education.

Bolin, P. (1995b). Overlooked and obscured through history: The 1875 legislative bill proposed to ammend the Massachusetts Drawing Act of 1870. *Studies in Art Education, 37*(1), 55–64.

Bolin, P. (1997). The "National Peace Jubilee and Musical Festival," June 1869: Historical context for the petitioners of drawing education. In A. Anderson & P. Bolin (Eds.), *History of art education: Proceedings of the Third Penn State International Symposium, October 12–15, 1995* (pp. 347–354). College Park, PA: The Pennsylvania State University Art Education Program, School of Visual Arts.

Bolin, P., Blandy, D., & Congdon, K. (Eds.). (2000). *Remembering others: Making invisible histories of art education visible*. Reston, VA: The National Art Education Association.

Brewer, T. (1999). *Studies in Art Education*: 1979–1989. *Visual Arts Research, 25*(1), 14–18.

Briggs, P.S. (1995). *The influence of Unitarianism on the inclusion of art education in the common schools of Massachusetts, 1825–1870*. Doctoral dissertation, Pennsylvania State University, College Park.

Brown, H. (1985, February). Academic art education and studio practices. *American Artist, 49*, 42–53.

Burke, D. B. (1987). Louis Comfort Tiffany and his early training at Eagleswood 1862–1865. *The American Art Journal, 19*(3), 29–39.

Burke, P. (1991). *New perspectives on historical writing*. University Park, PA: Pennsylvania State University Press.

Caldwell, C. (1997). A gestalt for art education: Integrating the history of art education in preservice art education. In A. Anderson & P. Bolin (Eds.), *History of art education: Proceedings of the Third Penn State International Symposium, October 12–15, 1995* (pp. 37–40). College Park, PA: The Pennsylvania State University Art Education Program, School of Visual Arts.

Carline, R. (1968). *Draw they must: A history of the teaching and examining of art*. London: Edward Arnold Ltd.

Carroll, K. L. (1994). Artistic beginnings: The work of young Edvard Munch. *Studies in Art Education, 36*(1), 7–17.

Chalmers, F. G. (1985a). South Kensington and the colonies II: The influence of Walter Smith in Canada. In H. Hoffa & B. Wilson (Eds.), *History of art education: Proceedings of the Penn State Conference* (pp. 108–112). Reston, VA: National Art Education Association.

Chalmers, F. G. (1985b). South Kensington and the colonies: David Blair of New Zealand and Canada. *Studies in Art Education 26*(2), 69–74.

Chalmers, F. G. (1992a). The origins of racism in the public school art curriculum. *Studies in Art Education, 33*(3), 134–143.

Chalmers, F. G. (1992b). An officer and a gentleman: Teaching drawing in the military. In P. M. Amburgy, D. Soucy, M. A. Stankiewicz, B. Wilson, & M. Wilson (Eds.). *History of art education: Proceedings of the Second Penn State Conference, 1989* (pp. 259–263). Reston, VA: The National Art Education Association.

Chalmers, F. G. (1993). Commentary "doing" histories of art education. *Studies in Art Education, 34*(4), 254–256.

Chalmers, F. G. (1994). Narrow and sectarian pretensions: George Gustavus Zerffi and the teaching of art history. *Canadian Review of Art Education, 21*(1), 15–26.

Chalmers, F. G. (1996). The early history of Philadelphia School of Design for Women. *Journal of Design History, 9*(4), 237–252.

Chalmers. F. G. (1998). *Women in the nineteenth-century art world. Schools of art and design for women in London and Philadelphia*. Westport, CT: Greenwood Press.

Chalmers, F. G. (1999). *Studies in Art Education*: The first 10 of 40 years, *Visual Arts Research, 25*(1), 2–6.

Chalmers, F. G. (2000a). *A 19th century government drawing master: The Walter Smith reader*. Reston, VA: National Art Education Association.

Chalmers, F. G. (2000b). Art education in "Indian" residential schools in British Columbia. *Canadian Review of Art Education, 27*(1), 21–35.

Chalmers, F. G. (2001). Art education in a manly environment: Educating the sons of the Establishment in a 19th century boys' school. *Studies in Art Education, 42*(2), 113–130.

Chamberlin-Hellman, M. J. (1981). *Thomas Eakins as a teacher*. Doctoral dissertation, Columbia University, New York.

Chapman, L. (1978). *Approaches to art in education*. New York: Harcourt Brace Jovanovich.

Chapman, L. (1999). *Studies in Art Education*: Decade two. *Visual Arts Research, 25*(1), 7–13.

Check, E. (2000). To be seen is to be: The founding of the Lesbian, Gay, and Bisexual Issues Caucus of the National Art Education Association. In P. Bolin, D. Blandy, & K. G. Congdon (Eds.), *Remembering others: making invisible histories of art education visible* (pp. 137–146). Reston, VA: National Art Education Association.

Clark, G. A. (1985). Early inquiry, research, and testing of children's art ability. In H. Hoffa & B. Wilson (Eds.), *History of art education: Proceedings of the Penn State Conference* (pp. 276–285). College Park, PA: The Pennsylvania State University, College of Arts & Architecture School of Visual Arts.

Clark, G. A. (1992). Using history to design current research: The background of Clark's drawing abilities test. In P. M. Amburgy, D. Soucy, M. A. Stankiewicz, B. Wilson, & M. Wilson (Eds.), *History of art education: Proceedings of the Second Penn State Conference, 1989* (pp. 191–199). Reston, VA: The National Art Education Association.

Clarke, I. E. (1885). *Art and industry. Drawing in the public schools.* U.S. Senate Report, 46th Congress, 2nd Session, Vol. 1. Washington, DC: Government Printing Office.

Clarke, I. E. (1892). *Art and industry.* Part 2. *Industrial and manual training in public schools.* U.S. Senate Report, 46th Congress, 2nd Session, Vol. 7. Washington, DC: Government Printing Office.

Claxton, R. W. (1997). *The infusion of African-American art from 1880 to the early 1990s for middle and high school art education.* Doctoral dissertation, The Ohio State University, Columbus.

Cochran, M. T. (2000). Let us march on 'til victory is won: The life and work of Augusta Savage. In P. Bolin, D. Blandy, & K. G. Congdon (Eds.), *Remembering others: Making invisible histories of art education visible.* (pp. 98–107). Reston, VA: National Art Education Association.

Collins, M. (1997). Tactility, habit and experience: The influence of William James and John Dewey on Kimon Nicolaides' *The natural way to draw.* In A. Anderson & P. Bolin (Eds.), *History of art education: Proceedings of the Third Penn State International Symposium, October 12–15, 1995* (pp. 175–184). College Park, PA: The Pennsylvania State University Art Education Program, School of Visual Arts.

Collins, G. (1999). *Studies in Art Education* 1989–1999. *Visual Arts Research, 25*(1), 19–26.

Congdon, K. G., & Degge, R. M. (1997). June King McFee's life and work: Constructing a feminist approach to biography for art education. In A. Anderson & P. Bolin (Eds.), *History of art education: Proceedings of the Third Penn State International Symposium, October 12–15, 1995* (pp. 138–146). College Park, PA: The Pennsylvania State University Art Education Program, School of Visual Arts.

Dambekains, L. (1996). *Curriculum and the collective mind: Changing paradigms in the Pennsylvania State University's Department of Art Education, 1960–1970.* Doctoral dissertation, College Park: Pennsylvania State University.

Dambekains, L. (1997). Oral history in the search for curriculum and the collective mind. In A. Anderson & P. Bolin (Eds.), *History of art education: Proceedings of the Third Penn State International Symposium, October 12–15, 1995* (pp. 540–548). College Park, PA: The Pennsylvania State University Art Education Program, School of Visual Arts.

Dana, L. P. (1953). Where is the new approach better? *School Arts, 53*(2), 15–17.

Davis, E. B. (1996). American drawing books and their impact on Winslow Homer. *Winterthur Portfolio, 31*(2/3), 141–163.

De Angeli Walls, N. (1993). Art and industry in Philadelphia: Origins of the Philadelphia School of Design for Women, 1848–1876. *The Pennsylvania Magazine of History and Biography, 117*(3), 177–199.

De Angeli Walls, N. (1994). Educating women for art and commerce. *History of Education Quarterly, 34*(3), 329–355.

Dean, M. (1924). *History of the Massachusetts Normal Art School 1873–1924.* (Reprinted from issues of *Massachusetts Normal Art School Alumni Association Bulletin* with slight changes and additions). Boston: Massachusetts Normal Art School.

Denis, R. C. (1995). The Brompton Barracks: War, peace, and the rise of Victorian art and design education. *Journal of Design History, 8*(1), 11–25.

Din, H. W. (1998). *A history of children's museums in the United States, 1899–1997: Implications for art education and museum education in art museums.* Doctoral dissertation, The Ohio State University, Columbus.

Dwyer, B. C. (1989). *Nineteenth century regional women artists: The Pittsburgh School of Design for Women 1865–1904.* Doctoral dissertation, University of Pittsburgh, Pittsburgh, PA.

Edmonston, P. (1985). Teaching the history of art education: Methodological issues and topics. In H. Hoffa & B. Wilson (Eds.), *History of art education: Proceedings of the Penn State Conference* (pp. 359–374). College Park, PA: The Pennsylvania State University, College of Arts & Architecture School of Visual Arts.

Efland, A. (1983a). School art and its social origins. *Studies in Art Education, 24*(3), 149–157.

Efland, A. (1983b). Art and music in the Pestalozzian tradition. *Journal of Research in Music Education, 31*(Fall), 165–178.

Efland, A. (1984). Curriculum concepts of the Penn State Seminar: An evaluation in retrospect. *Studies in Art Education, 25*(4), 205–211.

Efland, A. (1985a). Art and education for women in nineteenth century Boston. *Studies in Art Education, 26*(3), 133–140.

Efland, A. (1985b). The introduction of music and drawing in the Boston schools: Two studies of educational reform. In H. Hoffa & B. Wilson (Eds.), *History of art education: Proceedings of the Penn State Conference* (pp. 113–124). College Park, PA: The Pennsylvania State University, College of Arts & Architecture School of Visual Arts.

Efland, A. (1988). *Studies in Art Education*: Fourth invited lecture. How art became a discipline: Looking at our recent history. *Studies in Art Education, 29*(3), 262–274.

Efland, A. (1990). *A history of art education: Intellectual and social currents in teaching the visual arts.* New York: Teachers College Press.

Efland, A. (1992). History of art education as criticism: On the use of the past. In P. M. Amburgy, D. Soucy, M. A. Stankiewicz, B. Wilson, & M. Wilson (Eds.), *History of art education: Proceedings of the Second Penn State Conference, 1989* (pp. 1–11). Reston, VA: The National Art Education Association.

Efland, A. (1995). Historical research methods for art educators. In P. Smith & S. D. La Pierre (Eds.), *Art education historical methodology: An insider's guide to doing and using* (pp. 62–69). Pasadena, CA: Open Door Publishers for the Seminar for Research in Art Education.

Efland, A., & Soucy, D. (1992). Who was Isaac Edwards Clarke, why did he do what he did, and why should we care? In P. M. Amburgy, D. Soucy, M. A. Stankiewicz, B. Wilson, & M. Wilson (Eds.), *History of art education: Proceedings of the Second Penn State Conference, 1989* (pp. 138–149). Reston, VA: The National Art Education Association.

Eisner, E. W. (1972). The roots of art in schools: An historical view from a contemporary perspective. *Educating Artistic Vision* (pp. 29–63). New York: Macmillan.

Eisner, E. W. (1992). The efflorescence of the history of art education: Advance into the past or retreat from the present? In P. M. Amburgy, D. Soucy, M. A. Stankiewicz, B. Wilson, & M. Wilson (Eds.), *History of art education: Proceedings of the Second Penn State Conference, 1989* (pp. 37–41). Reston, VA: The National Art Education Association.

Eisner, E. W., & Ecker, D. (1966). What is art education? Some historical developments in art education. In E. W. Eisner & D. Ecker (Eds.), *Readings in art education* (pp. 1–13). Waltham, MA: Blaisdell Publishing Company.

Eldridge, L. (2000). Dorothy Dunn and the art education of Native Americans. *Studies in Art Education, 42*(4), 318–332.

Erickson, M. (1977). Uses of history in art education. *Studies in Art Education,18*(3), 22–29.

Erickson, M. (1979). An historical explanation of the schism between research and practice in art education. *Studies in Art Education, 20*(2), 5–13.

Erickson, M. (1985). Styles of historical investigation. *Studies in Art Education, 26*(2), 121–124.

Eyestone, J. E. (1992). The influence of Swedish Sloyd and its interpreters on American art education. *Studies in Art Education, 34*(1), 28–38.

Farnum, R. B. (1941). The early history of art education. In G. Whipple (Ed.), *Fortieth Yearbook of the National Society for the Study of Education*. Chicago: University of Chicago Press.

Finley, K. D. (1992). Cultural monitors: Clubwomen and public art instruction in Chicago, 1890–1920. In P. M. Amburgy, D. Soucy, M. A. Stankiewicz, B. Wilson, & M. Wilson (Eds.), *History of art education: Proceedings of the Second Penn State Conference, 1989* (pp. 252–258). Reston, VA: The National Art Education Association.

Finnegan, J. E. (1997). Elizabeth Harrison and the kindergarten: Art education as social reform. In A. Anderson & P. Bolin (Eds.), *History of art education: Proceedings of the Third Penn State International Symposium, October 12–15, 1995* (pp. 113–119). College Park, PA: The Pennsylvania State University Art Education Program, School of Visual Arts.

Fitzpatrick, V. L. (1992). Curriculum changes in fine arts education at the University of Iowa and Indiana University. In P. M. Amburgy, D. Soucy, M. A. Stankiewicz, B. Wilson, & M. Wilson (Eds.), *History of art education: Proceedings of the Second Penn State Conference, 1989* (pp. 159–163). Reston, VA: The National Art Education Association.

Fitzpatrick, V. L. (2000). Whatever happened to the art education class of 1942? In P. Bolin, D. Blandy, & K. G. Congdon (Eds.), *Remembering others: Making invisible histories of art education visible* (pp. 44–57). Reston, VA: National Art Education Association.

Forman, B. I. (1968). Early antecedents of American art education: A critical evaluation of Pioneer Influences. *Studies in Art Education, 9*(2), 38–51.

Foster, M. S. (1992). Exchanges between American and Japanese art educators: What did they learn from each other? In P. M. Amburgy, D. Soucy, M. A. Stankiewicz, B. Wilson, & M. Wilson (Eds.), *History of art education: Proceedings of the Second Penn State Conference, 1989* (pp. 104–108). Reston, VA: The National Art Education Association.

Freedman, K. (1985). Art education and the development of the academy: The ideological origins of curriculum theory. In H. Hoffa & B. Wilson (Eds.), *History of art education: Proceedings of the Penn State Conference* (pp. 19–27). College Park, PA: The Pennsylvania State University, College of Arts & Architecture School of Visual Arts.

Freedman, K. (1986). A public mandate for personal expression: Art education and American democracy in the 1940s and 1950s. *Arts and Learning Research, 4,* 1–10.

Freedman, K. (1987a). Art education and changing political agendas: An analysis of curriculum concerns of the 1940s and 1950s. *Studies in Art Education, 29*(1), 17–29.

Freedman, K. (1987b). Art education as social production: Culture, society and politics in the formation of curriculum. In T. S. Popkewitz (Ed.), *The formation of school subjects* (pp. 63–84). New York: The Falmer Press.

Freedman, K. (1988). Abstract expressionism and art education: Formalism and self-expression as curriculum ideology. *The Bulletin of the Caucus on Social Theory and Art Education, 8,* 17–25.

Freedman, K. (1989a). The philanthropic vision: The Owatonna art education project as an example of 'private' interests in public schooling. *Studies in Art Education, 31*(1), 15–26.

Freedman, K. (1989b). Narcissism and normalcy: Historical foundations of art education for young children. *Canadian Review of Art Education, 16*(1), 21–33.

Freedman, K. (1992). Educational discourse as cultural representation: Modernism in school and the media. In P. M. Amburgy, D. Soucy, M. A. Stankiewicz, B. Wilson, & M. Wilson (Eds.), *History of art education: Proceedings of the Second Penn State Conference, 1989* (pp. 220–225). Reston, VA: The National Art Education Association.

Freedman, K., & Popkewitz, T. S. (1988). Art education and social interests in the development of schooling: Ideological origins of curriculum theory. *Journal of Curriculum Studies, 20*(5), 387–405.

Funk, C. (1998). The *Art in America* radio programs, 1934–1935. *Studies in Art Education, 40*(1), 31–45.

Funk, C. (1990) *The development of the professional studio art training in American higher education 1860–1960.* Doctoral dissertation, Columbia University Teachers' College, New York.

Funk, C. (2000). Education in the Federal Art Project. In P. Bolin, D. Blandy, & K. G. Congdon (Eds.), *Remembering others: Making invisible histories of art education visible* (pp. 85–97). Reston, VA: National Art Education Association.

Gaitskell, C. D. (1948). *Art education in the Province of Ontario.* Doctoral dissertation, University of Toronto, Toronto.

Gaitskell, C. D. (1953). Art education has a history. *School Arts, 53*(2), 6–7.

Gaitskell, C. D., Hurwitz, A., & Day, M. (1982). *Children and their art. Methods for the elementary school.* New York: Harcourt, Brace & World.

Galanes, C. (1998). *An historical analysis of elementary level art education supported by the Puerto Rican Department of Public Instruction from 1898–1990.* Doctoral dissertation, Louisiana State University, Baton Rouge.

Gaudelius, Y. (1997). Optimist reformer: Charlotte Perkins Gilman and the revision of architectural education. In A. Anderson & P. Bolin (Eds.), *History of art education: Proceedings of the Third Penn State International Symposium, October 12–15, 1995* (pp. 120–128). College Park, PA: The Pennsylvania State University Art Education Program, School of Visual Arts.

Gaughan, J. M. (1990). *One hundred years of art appreciation education: A cross comparison of the picture study movement with the discipline-based movement.* Doctoral dissertation, University of Massachusetts.

Geahigan, G. (1997). Reflections on a model of art criticism in the picture study literature. In A. Anderson & P. Bolin (Eds.), *History of art education: Proceedings of the Third Penn State International Symposium, October 12–15, 1995* (pp. 434–442). College Park, PA: The Pennsylvania State University Art Education Program, School of Visual Arts.

Gerhard, C. (1997). The influence of Gustaf Larsson on manual training in the United States. In A. Anderson & P. Bolin (Eds.), *History of art education: Proceedings of the Third Penn State International Symposium, October 12–15, 1995* (pp. 421–426). College Park, PA: The Pennsylvania State University Art Education Program, School of Visual Arts.

Glavin, E. (1993). The early art education of Maurice Prendergast. *Archives of American Art Journal, 33*(1), 2–12.

Gold Gluck, P. (2000). The Educational Alliance art school. In P. Bolin, D. Blandy, & K. G. Congdon (Eds.), *Remembering others: Making invisible histories of art education visible* (pp. 58–70). Reston, VA: National Art Education Association.

Goldstein, C. (1996). *Teaching art: Academies and schools from Vasari to Albers.* New York: Cambridge University Press.

Green, H. (1948). *The introduction of art as a general subject in American schools.* Unpublished doctoral dissertation, Stanford University, Stanford.

Green, H. (1966). Walter Smith: The forgotten man. *Art Education, 19*(1), 3–9.

Green, H. B. (1966). Walter Smith: The forgotten man. *Art Education 19*(1), 3–9.

Grigor, A. (1985). *The one and the many: Concepts of the individual and the collective in art education during the progressive era in education 1920–1960.* Doctoral dissertation, Concordia University, Montreal.

Guilfoil, J. (2000). Frederick George Kurz an artist, designer, and educator. In P. Bolin, D. Blandy, & K. G. Congdon (Eds.), *Remembering others: Making invisible histories of art education visible* (pp. 198–200). Reston, VA: National Art Education Association.

Hamblen, K. A. (1985a). Historical research in education: A process selection and interpretation. In H. Hoffa & B. Wilson (Eds.), *History of art education: Proceedings of the Penn State Conference.* (pp. 1–10). College Park, PA: The Pennsylvania State University, College of Arts & Architecture School of Visual Arts.

Hamblen, K. (1985b). An art education history chronology: A process of selection and interpretation. *Studies in Art Education, 26*(2), 111–120.

Hamblen, K. (1987). Using written history to understand levels of professional maturity. *Arts and Learning Research, 5*(1), 120–131.

Hamblen, K. A. (1992). Shifting historical interpretations. In P. M. Amburgy, D. Soucy, M. A. Stankiewicz, B. Wilson, & M. Wilson (Eds.), *History of art education: Proceedings of the Second Penn State Conference, 1989* (pp. 200–208). Reston, VA: The National Art Education Association.

Haney, J. P. (1908). The development of arts education in the public schools. In J. P. Haney (Ed.), *Art education in the public schools of the United States* (pp. 21–77). New York: American Art Annual.

Haslam, R. (1988). Looking, drawing and learning with John Ruskin and the Working Men's College. *Journal of Art and Design Education, 7*(1), 65–79.

Haynes, J. S. (1997). The roots of multicultural art education practice: Social and cultural factors of the 1950s and 1960s that influenced a secondary urban art program. In A. Anderson & P. Bolin (Eds.), *History of art education: Proceedings of the Third Penn State International Symposium, October 12–15, 1995* (pp. 81–87). College Park, PA: The Pennsylvania State University Art Education Program, School of Visual Arts.

Haynes, J. S. (1993). Historical perspectives and antecedent theory of multicultural art education: 1954–1980. *Visual Arts Research, 19*(2), 24–34.

Henry, C., & Nyman, A. (1997). Images for multicultural art education: An historical examination. In A. Anderson & P. Bolin (Eds.), *History of art education: Proceedings of the Third Penn State International Symposium, October 12–15, 1995* (pp. 88–94). College Park, PA: The Pennsylvania State University Art Education Program, School of Visual Arts.

Hinterreiter, H. G. (1967). Arthur Lismer: Artist and art educator. A reflection on his life, work and philosophy. *School Arts, 66*(5), 21–28.

Hoffa, H. (1985). From the New Deal to the new frontier: The role of government in arts. In H. Hoffa & B. Wilson (Eds.), *History of art education: Proceedings of the Penn State Conference* (pp. 338–345). College Park, PA: The Pennsylvania State University, College of Arts & Architecture School of Visual Arts Education.

Hoffa, H., & Wilson, B. (Eds.). (1985). *History of art education: Proceedings of the Penn State Conference.* College Park, PA: The Pennsylvania State University, College of Arts and Architecture School of Visual Arts.

Hollingsworth, C. H. Jr. (1988). *Viktor Lowenfeld and the racial landscape of Hampton Institute during his tenure from 1934–1946.* Doctoral dissertation, The Pennsylvania State University, College Park, PA.

Hook, D. (1985). The Fellonosa and Dow relationship and its value in art education. In H. Hoffa & B. Wilson (Eds.), *History of art education: Proceedings of the Penn State Conference* (pp. 238–242). College Park, PA: The Pennsylvania State University, College of Arts and Architecture School of Visual Arts.

Hoyt, D., & Field, M. L. (1898). *Historical sketches of the Massachusetts Normal Art School Alumni Association and the Massachusetts Normal Art School.* Boston: Privately Printed.

Hubbard, C. A. (1985). Black art education from slavery to the 1940s: The pioneering years. In H. Hoffa & B. Wilson (Eds.), *History of art education: Proceedings of the Penn State Conference* (pp. 163–165). College Park, PA: The Pennsylvania State University, College of Arts & Architecture School of Visual Arts.

Hubbard, G. (1966). Art in general education: An historical review with contemporary implications. *Art Education, 19*(1), 11–13.

Hubbard, G. (1967). *Art in the high school.* Belmont, CA: Wadsworth.

Jansen, C. R. (1992). Historical development in art appreciation studies. In P. M. Amburgy, D. Soucy, M. A. Stankiewicz, B. Wilson, & M. Wilson (Eds.), *History of art education: Proceedings of the Second Penn State Conference, 1989* (pp. 215–219). Reston, VA: The National Art Education Association.

Johns, E. (1990). Thomas Eakins and pure art education. *Archives of American Art Journal, 30*(1–4), 71–76.

Johnson, T. D. (1985). *History of art education at the University of Arkansas at Pine Bluff, 1873–1973.* Doctoral dissertation, University of Oklahoma.

Jones, R. L. (1974). Aesthetic education: Its historical precedents. *Art Education, 27*(9), 12–16.

Joyce, A. I. (1997). The historical evolution of evaluation and assessment in art education: From anomaly to paragon of educational efficacy. In A. Anderson & P. Bolin (Eds.), *History of art education: Proceedings of the Third Penn State International Symposium, October 12–15, 1995* (pp. 320–328). College Park, PA: The Pennsylvania State University Art Education Program, School of Visual Arts.

Katter, E. (1985). Hands-on instructional resources for the teaching of art: A historical perspective. In H. Hoffa & B. Wilson (Eds.), *History of art education: Proceedings of the Penn State Conference* (pp. 295–314). College Park, PA: The Pennsylvania State University, College of Arts & Architecture School of Visual Arts.

Kaufman, I. (1966). *Art education in contemporary culture.* New York: Macmillan.

Keel, J. S. (1963). Research review: The history of art education. *Studies in Art Education, 4*(2), 45–51.

Keel, J. S. (1965). Art education, 1940–64. In Hastie, W. Ried (Ed.), *The sixty-fourth yearbook of the National Society for the Study of Education* (pp. 35–50). Chicago: The National Society for the Study of Education.

Keel, J. S., & Saunders, R. J. (Eds.). (1966). *Art Education, 19*(1) (special history issue).

Kelly, M. F. (1992). "Let's draw," 1936–1970: Elementary art education by radio. In P. M. Amburgy, D. Soucy, M. A. Stankiewicz, B. Wilson, & M. Wilson (Eds.), *History of art education: Proceedings of the Second Penn State Conference, 1989* (pp. 279–286). Reston, VA: The National Art Education Association.

Kern, E. J. (1985). The purposes of art education in the United States from 1870 to 1980. In H. Hoffa & B. Wilson (Eds.), *History of art education: Proceedings of the Penn State Conference* (pp. 40–52). College Park, PA: The Pennsylvania State University, College of Arts & Architecture School of Visual Arts.

Klayman, R. (1981) *The education of an artist: The American years of John Singleton Copley, 1738–1774*. Doctoral dissertation, University of New Hampshire, Durham.

Korzenik, D. (1981). Is children's work ART? Some historical views. *Art Education, 34*(5), 20–24.

Korzenik, D. (1983). Art education ephemera. *Art Education, 36*(5), 18–21.

Korzenik, D. (1985a). Doing historical research. *Studies in Art Education, 26*(2), 125–128.

Korzenik, D. (1985b). *Drawn to art: A nineteenth-century American dream*. Hanover, NH: University Press of New England.

Korzenik, D. (1987a). Why government cared. In *Art education here* (pp. 59–74). Boston: Art Education Department, Massachusetts College of Art.

Korzenik, D. (1987b). The art education of working women. In D. Faxon & S. Moore (Eds.), *Pilgrims and pioneers: New England women in the arts*. New York: Midmarch Arts Press.

Korzenik, D. (1990). A developmental history of art education. In D. Soucy & M. A. Stankiewicz (Eds.), *Framing the past: Essays on art education* (pp. 201–212). Reston, VA: National Art Education Association.

Korzenik, D. (1995). Looking back on twenty years of graduate student's historical research. In P. Smith & S. D. La Pierre (Eds.), *Art education historical methodology: An insider's guide to doing and using* (pp. 35–43). Pasadena, CA: Open Door Publishers for the Seminar for Research in Art Education.

La Porte, A. M. (1997). Drawing the line: Lowenfeld and coloring books. In A. Anderson & P. Bolin (Eds.), *History of art education: Proceedings of the Third Penn State International Symposium, October 12–15, 1995*. College Park, PA: The Pennsylvania State University Art Education Program, School of Visual Arts.

Leeds, J. A. (1989). The history of attitudes towards children's art. *Studies in Art Education, 30*(2), 93–103.

Lemerise, S. (1992). Study of the relationship of the art field and the social context to art education, applied to Québec in the 1960s. In P. M. Amburgy, D. Soucy, M. A. Stankiewicz, B. Wilson, & M. Wilson (Eds.), *History of art education: Proceedings of the Second Penn State Conference, 1989* (pp. 79–84). Reston, VA: The National Art Education Association.

Lemerise, S. (1995). Contextes historiques et actuels des rapports entre l'art et l'education au Quebec. *Canadian Review of Art Education, 22*(2), 155–166.

Lemerise, S. (1997). Drawing in the pedagogical press of French Québec. In A. Anderson & P. Bolin (Eds.), *History of art education: Proceedings of the Third Penn State International Symposium, October 12–15, 1995* (pp. 302–310). College Park, PA: The Pennsylvania State University Art Education Program, School of Visual Arts.

Lemerise, S. (2000). When a short narrative fits into a larger historical context: Irène Senécal, 1901–1978. In P. Bolin, D. Blandy, & K. G. Congdon (Eds.), *Remembering others: Making invisible histories of art education visible* (pp. 41–43). Reston, VA: National Art Education Association.

Lemerise, S., & Couture, F. (1990). A social history of art and public art education in Quebec: The 1960s. *Studies in Art Education, 31*(4), 226–233.

Lemerise, S., & Sherman, L. (1990). Cultural factors in art education history: A study of English and French Quebec, 1940–1980. In D. Soucy & M. A. Stankiewicz (Eds.), *Framing the past: Essays on art education* (pp. 183–200). Reston, VA: National Art Education Association.

Logan, F. M. (1955). *Growth of art in American schools*. New York: Harper & Brothers.

Loucks, R. S. (1991). *From art education to industrial arts: Public schools in Dayton Ohio, late 19th through early 20th century*. Doctoral dissertation, University of Cincinnati, Cincinnati, OH.

MacDonald, B. L. (1997). *The Perry Magazine for School and Home (1898–1906): An analysis of its historical location within the schoolroom decoration and picture study movements*. In A. Anderson & P. Bolin (Eds.), *History of art education: Proceedings of the Third Penn State International Symposium, October 12–15, 1995* (pp. 404–421). College Park, PA: The Pennsylvania State University Art Education Program, School of Visual Arts.

MacDonald, S. (1970). *The history and philosophy of art education*. New York: American Elsevier Press.

MacGregor, R. N. (1979). *A history of the Canadian Society for Education Through Art*. Lexington, MA: Ginn Custom Publishing.

Madhok, P. (1994). *The drawing books of Henry Peacham and Jan de Bisschop and the place of drawing in the education of a Renaissance gentleman*. Doctoral dissertation. Urbana-Champaign: University of Illinois.

Maffei, N. (2000). John Cotton Dana and the politics of exhibiting industrial art in the U.S., 1909–1929. *Journal of Design History, 13*(4), 301–318.

Marché, T. (1995). *A history of change in the art program of a suburban Pennsylvania school district (educational reform)*. Doctoral dissertation, Indiana University, Bloomington.

Marché, T. (1997a). Sixty years of art at Penn Manor: A continuum of change. In A. Anderson & P. Bolin (Eds.), *History of art education: Proceedings of the Third Penn State International Symposium, October 12–15, 1995* (pp. 225–231). College Park, PA: The Pennsylvania State University Art Education Program, School of Visual Arts.

Marché, T. (1997b). Examination of factors affecting change in a Pennsylvania school district's art program from 1924 to 1992. *Studies in Art Education, 39*(1), 24–36.

Marché, T. (2000). Toward a community model of art education history. *Studies in Art Education, 42*(1), 51–66.

Marsh, A. T. (1983). *Washington's first art academy, the Corcoran School of Art, 1875–1935*. Doctoral dissertation, University of Maryland, College Park.

Martin, J. (1991). Why teach art? Herbert Read's early essays on the revolutionary significance of an education through art. *Canadian Review of Art Education, 18*(2) 136–150.

Marzio, P. (1976). *The art crusade. An analysis of American drawing manuals, 1820–1860*. Washington, DC: Smithsonian.

Mattil, E., Hoffa, H., Hausman, J., & Ecker, D. W. (1997). 1965 Penn State Seminar and subsequent events. In A. Anderson & P. Bolin (Eds.), *History of art education: Proceedings of the Third Penn State International Symposium, October 12–15, 1995* (pp. 505–516). College Park, PA: The Pennsylvania State University Art Education Program, School of Visual Arts.

McCollister, S. (2000). Gloria Dillard and the traditional Indian arts program in Blackfoot, Idaho 1976–1981. In P. Bolin, D. Blandy, & K. G. Congdon (Eds.), *Remembering others: Making invisible histories of art education visible* (pp. 149–163). Reston, VA: National Art Education Association.

McNeill, P. L. (1992). Ella Victoria Dobbs and Verna M. Wulfekammer: Teaching art in the university elementary school. University of Missouri, 1912–1936. In P. M. Amburgy, D. Soucy, M. A. Stankiewicz, B. Wilson, & M. Wilson (Eds.), *History of art education: Proceedings of the Second Penn State Conference, 1989* (pp. 150–153). Reston, VA: The National Art Education Association.

McNeill, P. L. (1995). *Verna Mary Wulfekammer at the University of Missouri: Factors affecting her career development in art education, 1928–1968*. Doctoral dissertation, University of Missouri, Columbia.

McNutt, J. K. (1988). *The introduction of plaster casts into the public schools of the United States: 1870–1900*. Doctoral dissertation, Florida State University, Tallahassee.

McNutt, J. K. (1990). Plaster casts after antique sculpture: Their role in the elevation of public taste in an American art institution. *Studies in Art Education, 31*(3), 158–167.

McRae, R. O. (2000). *Toward an understanding of the Beaux Arts curriculum: A survey of six United States sculptors educated in Beaux Arts academies in the first half of the twentieth century*. Doctoral dissertation, Texas Tech University, Lubbock.

McWhinnie, H. J. (1992). A consideration of the roots of the formalistic aesthetic in art education history. In P. M. Amburgy, D. Soucy, M. A. Stankiewicz, B. Wilson, & M. Wilson (Eds.), *History of art education: Proceedings of the Second Penn State Conference, 1989* (pp. 157–158). Reston, VA: The National Art Education Association.

McWhinnie, H. J. (1997). Manuel Barkan's models of inquiry paper: Some reflections on the Penn State Seminar. In A. Anderson & P. Bolin (Eds.), *History of art education: Proceedings of the Third Penn State International Symposium, October 12–15, 1995* (pp. 549–555). College Park, PA: The Pennsylvania State University Art Education Program, School of Visual Arts.

Michael, J. (1995). History of art education associations. In P. Smith & S. D. La Pierre (Eds.), *Art education historical methodology: An insider's guide to doing and using* (pp. 26–34). Pasadena, CA: Open Door Publishers for the Seminar for Research in Art Education.

Michael, J. (Ed.). (1997). *National Art Education Association: Our history, celebrating 50 years 1947–1997*. Reston, VA: National Art Education Association.

Michael, J. A., & Morris, J. W. (1985). The difficulty of studying the history of art education research and publication. In H. Hoffa & B. Wilson (Eds.), *History of art education: Proceedings of the Penn State Conference* (pp. 354–358). College Park, PA: The Pennsylvania State University, College of Arts & Architecture School of Visual Arts.

Miley, R. B. (1994). *A critical examination of Henry Turner Bailey's method of pedagogical art criticism in context*. Doctoral dissertation, Florida State University, Tallahassee.

Mock-Morgan, M. E. (1976). *A historical study of the theories and methodologies of Arthur Wesley Dow and their contribution to teacher training in art education*. Doctoral dissertation, University of Maryland, College Park.

Mock-Morgan, M. E. (1985). The influence of Arthur Wesley Dow on art education. In H. Hoffa & B. Wilson (Eds.), *History of art education: Proceedings of the Penn State Conference* (pp. 234–237). Reston, VA: National Art Education Association.

Moore, J. J. (1991). *William James and art: Perspectives for art educators*. Doctoral dissertation, Harvard University, Cambridge.

Moore. J. J. (1997). William James and art education: Links between the pragmatists and the progressives. In A. Anderson & P. Bolin (Eds.), *History of art education: Proceedings of the Third Penn State International Symposium, October 12–15, 1995* (pp. 167–174). College Park, PA: The Pennsylvania State University Art Education Program, School of Visual Arts.

Morris, J. W., Raunft, R., & Pfeiffer, J. (1985). Ideoplastiche Kunst: The ideas of influence of Max Verworn. In H. Hoffa & B. Wilson (Eds.), *History of art education: Proceedings of the Penn State Conference* (pp. 225–233). College Park, PA: The Pennsylvania State University, College of Arts & Architecture School of Visual Arts.

Morris, J. W. & Raunft, R. (1995). Archives and their role in art education research. In P. Smith & S. D. La Pierre (Eds.), *Art education historical methodology: An insider's guide to doing and using* (pp. 1–15). Pasadena, CA: Open Door Publishers for the Seminar for Research in Art Education.

Morse, B. (2001). *A woman of design, a man of passion: The pioneering McIans*. Lewes, UK: The Book Guild.

Moynihan, J. P. (1980). *The influence of the Bauhaus on art and art education in the United States*. Doctoral dissertation, Northwestern University, Chicago, IL.

Newsom, B. Y., & Silver, A. Z. (Eds.) Issues in art museum education: A brief history. In *The art museum as educator* (pp. 13–20). Berkeley, CA: University of California Press.

Norris, R. A. (1979). *History of art education: A bibliography: Secondary and primary sources*. Columbus, OH: Published by Author.

Okazaki, A. (1994). Japanese art education: The contribution of western modernism and American art programs during the 1920's. *Journal of Multicultural and Cross-Cultural Research in Art Education, 12*, 50–65.

Okazaki, A. (1997). Understanding the "other" in art education: A biographical interpretation of Beittel's writing. In A. Anderson & P. Bolin (Eds.), *History of art education: Proceedings of the Third Penn State International Symposium, October 12–15, 1995* (pp. 41–51). College Park, PA: The Pennsylvania State University Art Education Program, School of Visual Arts.

Ott, R. W. (1985). Art education in museums: Art teachers as pioneers in museum education. In H. Hoffa & B. Wilson (Eds.), *History of art education: Proceedings of the Penn State Conference* (pp. 286–294). College Park, PA: The Pennsylvania State University, College of Arts & Architecture School of Visual Arts.

Ott, R. W. (1992). Euphoria to glory: Early exhibitions and art education. In P. M. Amburgy, D. Soucy, M. A. Stankiewicz, B. Wilson, & M. Wilson (Eds.), *History of art education: Proceedings of the Second Penn State Conference, 1989* (pp. 287–291). Reston, VA: The National Art Education Association.

Palmer, R. D. (1978). *A history of the concept of imitation in American art education*. Doctoral dissertation, Pennsylvania State University, College Park.

Pariser, D. (1985). The juvenalia of Klee, Toulouse-Lautrec and Picasso: A report on the initial stages of research into the development of exceptional graphic artistry. In H. Hoffa & B. Wilson (Eds.), *History of art education: Proceedings of the Penn State Conference* (pp. 192–202). College Park, PA: The Pennsylvania State University, College of Arts & Architecture School of Visual Arts.

Pasto, T. (1967a). A critical review of the history of drawing methods in the public schools of the United States 1. *Art Education, 20*(8), 2–7.

Pasto, T. (1967b). A critical review of the history of drawing methods in the public schools of the United States 2. *Art Education, 20*(9), 18–22.

Pearse, H., & Soucy, D. (1987). Nineteenth century origins of Saturday morning art classes for children in Halifax, Nova Scotia. *Studies in Art Education, 28*(3), 141–148.

Pearse, H. (1992). Arthur Lismer: Art educator with a social conscience. In P. M. Amburgy, D. Soucy, M. A. Stankiewicz, B. Wilson, M. Wilson (Eds.), *History of art education: Proceedings of the Second Penn State Conference, 1989* (pp. 85–88). Reston, VA: The National Art Education Association.

Pearse, H. (1997). Imagining a history of Canadian art education. In A. Anderson & P. Bolin (Eds.), *History of art education: Proceedings of the Third Penn State International Symposium, October 12–15, 1995* (pp. 3–24). College Park, PA: The Pennsylvania State University Art Education Program, School of Visual Arts.

Pearse, H. (1986). Arthur Lismer and the roots of Canadian art education. *ATA Journal, 8*(1), 18–26.

Pearse, H. (2000). Discovering the first black graduate and rediscovering the first art education program of the Nova Scotia College of Art and Design. In P. Bolin, D. Blandy, & K. G. Congdon (Eds.), *Remembering others: Making invisible histories of art education visible* (pp. 26–36). Reston, VA: National Art Education Association.

Pevsner, N. (1940). *Academies of art past and present*. New York: DaCapo.

Phelan, A. (1995). 50 years at the School for American Craftsmen. *Ceramics Monthly, 43*(Feb), 51–56.

Pinto, W., & Smith, P. (1999). An artifact as history in art education. The Chautauqua Industrial Art Desk. *Art Education, 52*(1), 19–24.

Purdue, P. (1977). *Ideology and art education the influence of socialist thought on art education in America between the years 1890–1960*. Doctoral dissertation, University of Oregon, Eugene.

Raunft, R. (Ed.). (2001). *The autobiographical lectures of some prominent art educators*. Reston, VA: National Art Education Association.

Rhoades, J. E. (1987). *A history of the origin and development of the International Society for Education through Art: the Edwin Ziegfeld legacy*. Doctoral dissertation, The Ohio State University, Columbus.

Riley, M. C. (1987). A history of the development and determinants of Milwaukee public school arts policy from 1870–1930: Critique of a dissertation by A. B. Troiana. *Bulletin of the Council for Research in Music Education, 94*(Fall), 72–75.

Rios, J. F. (1954). *History of art education in the secondary schools of the United States from 1900 to 1950*. Doctoral dissertation, University of Texas, Austin.

Rocke, J. (1952). Walter Smith—A pioneer of art education 1836–1886. *Yorkshire Illustrated*, 15.

Rogers, A. W. (1983). *The beautiful in form and colour: Art education in British Columbia between the wars*. Masters thesis. University of British Columbia, Vancouver.

Rogers, A. W. (1984). William P. Weston, artist and educator. *Art Education, 26*(5), 27–29.

Rogers, T. (1985). British art education in the schools, 1895–1910 and its influence on the schools of British Columbia. In H. Hoffa & B. Wilson (Eds.), *History of art education: Proceedings of the Penn State Conference* (pp. 87–93). College Park, PA: The Pennsylvania State University, College of Arts & Architecture School of Visual Arts.

Rogers, A. W. (1987). *W. P. Weston, educator and artist: The development of British ideas in the art curriculum of B.C. public schools*. Doctoral dissertation, University of British Columbia, Vancouver.

Rogers, A. W. (1990). Art education curriculum in British Columbia between the wars: Official prescription—unofficial interpretation. In D. Soucy & M. A. Stankiewicz (Eds.), *Framing the Past: Essays on Art Education* (pp. 153–166). Reston, VA: National Art Education Association.

Sahasrabudhe, P. (1997). The expressionist era in education: The grounding for a Victor D'Amico pedagogy. In A. Anderson & P. Bolin (Eds.), *History of art education: Proceedings of the Third Penn State International Symposium, October 12–15, 1995* (pp. 495–502). College Park, PA: The Pennsylvania State University Art Education Program, School of Visual Arts.

Saunders, R. J. (1961). *The contribution of Horace Mann, Mary Peabody Mann, and Elizabeth Peabody to art education in the United States*. Doctoral dissertation, The Pennsylvania State University, College Park, PA.

Saunders, R. J. (1976). Art, industrial art and the 200 years war. *Art Education, 29*(1), 5–8.

Saunders, R. J. (1985). Owatonna: Art education in Camelot. In H. Hoffa & B. Wilson (Eds.), *History of art education: Proceedings of the Penn State Conference* (pp. 152–157). College Park, PA: The Pennsylvania State University, College of Arts & Architecture School of Visual Arts.

Saunders, R. J. (1990). Elizabeth P. Peabody's quest for art in moral education. In D. Soucy & M. A. Stankiewicz (Eds.), *Framing the past: Essays on art education* (pp. 35–46). Reston, VA: National Art Education Association.

Saunders, R. J. (1992). The making of the National Art Education Association: Names, initials, and group identity crises. In P. M. Amburgy, D. Soucy, M. A. Stankiewicz, B. Wilson, & M. Wilson (Eds.), *History of art education: Proceedings of the Second Penn State Conference, 1989* (pp. 164–169). Reston, VA: The National Art Education Association.

Schroeder, C. (1992). A history of education in American museums. In P. M. Amburgy, D. Soucy, M. A. Stankiewicz, B. Wilson, & M. Wilson (Eds.), *History of art education: Proceedings of the Second Penn State Conference, 1989* (pp. 292–295). Reston, VA: The National Art Education Association.

Sellink, M. (1992). As a guide to the highest learning, an Antwerp drawing book dated 1589. *Simiolus, 21*(1/2), 40–55.

Sessions, B. (1997). Marguerite Wildenhain: A woman of choice substance. In A. Anderson & P. Bolin (Eds.), *History of art education: Proceedings of the Third Penn State International Symposium, October 12–15, 1995* (pp. 129–137). College Park, PA: The Pennsylvania State University Art Education Program, School of Visual Arts.

Sessions, B., & Johnston, R. (2000). Marguerite Wildenhain: the visible core. In P. Bolin, D. Blandy, & K. G. Congdon (Eds.), *Remembering others: Making invisible histories of art education visible* (pp. 11–25). Reston, VA: National Art Education Association.

Sheath, N. (1982). *Some events in the life of Walter Smith*. Chesham, UK: Chesham Church Printing.

Sherman, L., & Efland, A. (1997). Educational discourse and the visual documentation of practice: Victor D'Amico, Modernism and Child Art. In A. Anderson & P. Bolin (Eds.), *History of art education: Proceedings of the Third Penn State International Symposium, October 12–15, 1995* (pp. 486–494). College Park, PA: The Pennsylvania State University Art Education Program, School of Visual Arts.

Shumaker, E. A. (1985). A content analysis of the journal *Art Education* from 1948 through 1984. In H. Hoffa & B. Wilson (Eds.), *History of art education: Proceedings of the Penn State Conference* (pp. 315–328). College Park, PA: The Pennsylvania State University, College of Arts & Architecture School of Visual Arts.

Siegel, G. B. (1981) *Adelphi University's Children's Center for Creative Arts and its relationship to arts education practices in the United States 1937–1977*. Doctoral dissertation, New York University, New York.

Sienkiewicz, C. (1985). The Froebelian kindergarten as an art academy. In H. Hoffa & B. Wilson (Eds.), *History of art education: Proceedings of the Penn State Conference* (pp. 125–137). College Park, PA: The Pennsylvania State University, College of Arts & Architecture School of Visual Arts.

Siskar, J. F. (1997). Laura Hill Chapman: A biography of a woman art educator. In A. Anderson & P. Bolin (Eds.), *History of art education: Proceedings of the Third Penn State International Symposium, October 12–15, 1995* (pp. 147–165). College Park, PA: The Pennsylvania State University Art Education Program, School of Visual Arts.

Smalley, S. F. (1997). From Allan Kaprow's happenings in the mid-1960s to what has happened since: A review of the expansive contemporary art world (1965–1995) and its challenges for the art educator. In A. Anderson & P. Bolin (Eds.), *History of art education: Proceedings of the Third Penn State International Symposium, October 12–15, 1995* (pp. 565–569). College Park, PA: The Pennsylvania State University Art Education Program, School of Visual Arts.

Smith, J. C. (1992). Augusta Savage, sculptor/educator. In J. C. Smith (Ed.), *Notable black American women* (pp. 979–983). Nashville, TN: Gale Research Press.

Smith, P. (1982a). Lowenfeld in a Germanic perspective. *Art Education, 35*(2), 25–27.

Smith, P. (1982b). Germanic Foundations: A look at what we are standing on. *Studies in Art Education, 23*(3), 23–30.

Smith, P. (1983). *An analysis of the writings and teachings of Viktor Lowenfeld: Art educator in America.* Doctoral dissertation, Arizona State University.

Smith, P. (1984). Natalie Robinson Cole: The American Cizek? *Art Education, 37*(1), 36–39.

Smith, P. (1985). The Lowenfeld motivation revisited. *Canadian Review of Art Education Research, 12,* 11–17.

Smith, P. (1986). The ecology of picture study. *Art Education, 39*(Sept.), 48–54.

Smith, P. (1987). Lowefeld teaching art: A European theory and American experience at Hampton Institute. *Studies in Art Education, 29*(1), 30–36.

Smith, P. (1988a). The role of gender in the history of art education: Questioning some explanations. *Studies in Art Education, 29*(4), 232–240.

Smith, P. (1988b). The Hampton years: Lowenfeld's forgotten legacy. *Art Education, 41*(6), 38–42.

Smith, P. (1989). Lowenfeld in a Viennese perspective: Formative influences for American Art Education. *Studies in Art Education, 30*(2), 104–114.

Smith, P. (1990). An art educator for all seasons: The many roles of Eugenia Eckford Rhoads. *Studies in Art Education, 31*(3), 178–183.

Smith, P. (1991). The case of the artist-in-the-classroom with special reference to the teaching career of Oskar Kokoschka. *Studies in Art Education, 32*(4), 239–247.

Smith, P. (1992). A troublesome comedy: The causes of Walter Smith's dismissal. In P. M. Amburgy, D. Soucy, M. A. Stankiewicz, B. Wilson, & M. Wilson (Eds.), *History of art education: Proceedings of the Second Penn State Conference, 1989* (pp. 269–273). Reston, VA: The National Art Education Association.

Smith, P. (1996a). *The history of American art education. Learning about art in American Schools.* Westport, CT: Greenwood Press.

Smith, P. (1996b). Another vision of progressivism: Marion Richardson's triumph and tragedy. *Studies in Art Education, 37*(3), 170–183.

Smith, P. (1999). The unexplored: Art education historians' failure to consider the Southwest. *Studies in Art Education, 40*(2), 114–127.

Smith, P., & La Pierre, S. D. (Eds.). (1995). *Art education historical methodology: An insider's guide to doing and using.* Pasadena, CA: Open Door Publishers for the Seminar for Research in Art Education.

Soucy, D. (1985a). Approaches to historical writing in art education: Their limits and potentialities. In H. Hoffa & B. Wilson (Eds.), *History of art education: Proceedings of the Penn State Conference* (pp. 11–18). College Park, PA: The Pennsylvania State University, College of Arts & Architecture School of Visual Arts.

Soucy, D. (1985b). Approaches to historical writing in art education: Their limits and potentialities. In H. Hoffa & B. Wilson (Eds.), *History of art education: Proceedings of the Penn State Conference* (pp. 11–18). Reston, VA: National Art Education Association.

Soucy, D. (1985). Present views of the past: Bases for the future of art education Historiography. *Canadian Review of Art Education Research, 12,* 3–10.

Soucy, D. (1986). (Ed.). A history of Maritime art education. *ATA Journal, 8*(1).

Soucy, D. (1986). Religion and development of art education in 19th century Nova Scotia. *Arts and Learning Research, 4,* 36–43.

Soucy, D. (1987). Social factors in nineteenth century art education: A comparison between Nova Scotia's public and private schools. *The Bulletin of the Caucus on Social Theory and Art Education, 7,* 49–54.

Soucy, D. (1989). More than a polite pursuit: Art college education for women in Nova Scotia, 1887–1930s. *Art Education, 42*(2), 23–24, 37–40.

Soucy, D. (1990). A history of art education histories. In D. Soucy & M. A. Stankiewicz (Eds.), *Framing the Past: Essays on Art Education* (pp. 3–34). Reston, VA: National Art Education Association.

Soucy, D. (1991). Art education history and Canadian educational history: Their potential to inform each other. *Canadian Review of Art Education, 18*(1), 13–31.

Soucy, D. (1996). *Training for art-related employment: Community support for Halifax's art school. 1887–1943.* Vancouver: Doctoral dissertation, University of British Columbia.

Soucy, D., & Pearse, H. (1993). *The first hundred years: A history of the Nova Scotia College of Art and Design.* Fredericton, N.B.: University of New Brunswick.

Soucy, D., & Stankiewicz, M.A. (Eds.). (1990). *Framing the past: Essays on art education.* Reston, VA: National Art Education Association.

Soucy, D., & Webb, N. (1984). History—Who cares? *Art Education, 36*(5), 37–38.

Sproll, P. A. C. (1994). Matters of taste and matters of commerce: British government intervention in art education in 1835. *Studies in Art Education, 35*(2), 105–113.

Stanford, W. W. (1984). *Black Americans and vocational and practical art education—an historical development: 1750–1954*. Doctoral dissertation, University of Wyoming.

Stankiewicz, M. A. (1979). *Art teacher preparation at Syracuse University, the first century*. Doctoral dissertation, Ohio State University, Columbus.

Stankiewicz, M. A. (1982a). Searching for women art educators of the past." In E. Zimmerman & M. A. Stankiewicz (Eds.), *Women art educators*. Bloomington, IN: Mary Rouse Memorial Fund & Women's Caucus of the National Art Education Association.

Stankiewicz, M. A. (1982b). The creative sister: An historical look at women. The arts, and higher education. *Studies in Art Education, 24*(1), 48–56.

Stankiewicz, M. A. (1982c). Woman, artist, art educator: Professional image among women art educators. In E. Sommerman & M. A. Stankiewicz (Eds.), *Women art educators*. Bloomington, IN: Indiana University.

Stankiewicz, M. A. (1983). Rila Jackson, pioneer at Syracuse. *Art Education, 36*(1), 13–15.

Stankiewicz, M. A. (1984a). Self-expression or teacher influence: The Shaw system of finger painting. *Art Education, 37*(2), 20–24.

Stankiewicz, M. A. (1984b). "The eye is a nobler organ": Ruskin and American art education. *Journal of Aesthetic Education, 18*(2), 51–64.

Stankiewicz, M. A. (1985a). A Generation of Art Educators. In H. Hoffa & B. Wilson (Eds.), *History of art education: Proceedings of the Penn State Conference* (pp. 205–212). College Park, PA: The Pennsylvania State University, College of Arts & Architecture School of Visual Arts.

Stankiewicz, M. A. (1985b). Mary Dana Hicks Prang: A pioneer in art education. In E. Sommerman & M. A. Stankiewicz (Eds.), *Women art educators II* (pp. 22–38). Bloomington, IN: Indiana University.

Stankiewicz, M. A. (1988). Form, truth, and emotion: Transatlantic influences on formalist aesthetics. *Journal of Art and Design Education, 7*(1), 81–95.

Stankiewicz, M. A. (1990). Rules and invention: From ornament to design in art education. In D. Soucy & M. A. Stankiewicz (Eds.), *Framing the past: Essays on Art Education* (pp. 89–102). Reston, VA: National Art Education Association.

Stankiewicz, M. A. (1992a). From the aesthetic movement to the arts and crafts movement. *Studies in Art Education, 33*(3), 165–173.

Stankiewicz, M. A. (1992b). Time, antimodernism, and holiday art. In P. M. Amburgy, D. Soucy, M. A. Stankiewicz, B. Wilson, & M. Wilson (Eds.), *History of art education: Proceedings of the Second Penn State Conference, 1989* (pp. 209–214). Reston, VA: The National Art Education Association.

Stankiewicz, M. A. (1993). Women's clubs, art and society. *Arts and Learning Research, 10*(1), 48–57.

Stankiewicz, M. A. (1995a). So what: Interpretation in art education history. In P. Smith & S. D. La Pierre (Eds.), *Art education historical methodology: An insider's guide to doing and using* (pp. 53–61). Pasadena, CA: Open Door Publishers for the Seminar for Research in Art Education.

Stankiewicz, M. A. (1995b). Drawing book wars. *Visual Arts Research, 12*(2), 59–72.

Stankiewicz, M. A. (1997a). Perennial promises and pitfalls in arts education reform. *Arts Education Policy Review, 99*(2), 8–14.

Stankiewicz, M. A. (1997b). The celestial city of culture: Henry Turner Bailey's "City of Refuge." In A. Anderson & P. Bolin (Eds.), *History of art education: Proceedings of the Third Penn State International Symposium, October 12–15, 1995* (pp. 427–433). College Park, PA: The Pennsylvania State University Art Education Program, School of Visual Arts.

Stankiewicz, M. A. (1999). Chromo-civilization and the genteel tradition (an essay on the social value of art education). *Studies in Art Education, 40*(2), 101–113.

Stankiewicz, M. A. (2000). Discipline and the future of art education. *Studies in Art Education, 41*(4), 301–313.

Stankiewicz, M. A. (2001a). Recent research in history of art education. *Translations, 10*(2), 1–6.

Stankiewicz, M. A. (2001b). *Roots of art education practice*. Worcester, MA: Davis.

Stankiewicz, M. A., & Zimmerman, E. (1984). Women's achievements in art education. In G. Collins & R. Sandell (Eds.), *Women, art, and education* (pp. 113–140). Reston, VA: National Art Education Association.

Stankiewicz, M. A., & Zimmerman, E. (Eds.). (1985). *Women art educators II*. Bloomington, IN: Indiana University.

Stark, G. K. (1985). The Oswego Movement 1861–1903 (Education in Art). In H. Hoffa & B. Wilson (Eds.), *History of art education: Proceedings of the Penn State Conference* (pp. 138–151). College Park, PA: The Pennsylvania State University, College of Arts & Architecture School of Visual Arts.

Stephenson, W. (1997). Coping with a lack of art materials in the depression era as reflected in *School Arts Magazine*. In A. Anderson & P. Bolin (Eds.), *History of art education: Proceedings of the Third Penn State International Symposium, October 12–15, 1995* (pp. 232–237). College Park, PA: The Pennsylvania State University Art Education Program, School of Visual Arts.

Stewart, J. N. (1986). *The Penn State Seminar in art education: An oral history*. Doctoral dissertation, Florida State University, Tallahassee.

Stirling, J. C. (1997). The politics of drawing: theory into practice: Walter Smith's influence in post-secondary Québec industrial arts schools, 1876–91. In A. Anderson & P. Bolin (Eds.), *History of art education: Proceedings of the Third Penn State International Symposium, October 12–15, 1995* (pp. 355–366). College Park, PA: The Pennsylvania State University Art Education Program, School of Visual Arts.

Stokrocki, M. (1992). Interviews with students: Thomas Munro as teacher of aesthetics and art criticism. In P. M. Amburgy, D. Soucy, M. A. Stankiewicz, B. Wilson, & M. Wilson (Eds.), *History of art education: Proceedings of the Second Penn State Conference, 1989* (pp. 296–300). Reston, VA: The National Art Education Association.

Stokrocki, M. (1995). Oral history: Recording teaching folklore and folkways. In P. Smith & S. D. La Pierre (Eds.), *Art education historical methodology: An insider's guide to doing and using* (pp. 16–25). Pasadena, CA: Open Door Publishers for the Seminar for Research in Art Education.

Stokrocki, M. (1997). Towards an ethnohistory of Amerindian art education: Navajo cultural preservation vs. assimilation. In A. Anderson & P. Bolin (Eds.), *History of art education: Proceedings of the Third Penn State International Symposium, October 12–15, 1995* (pp. 71–80). College Park, PA: The Pennsylvania State University Art Education Program, School of Visual Arts.

Stokrocki, M. (2000). Commentary: Historical research in the southwest: Ignored and undervalued. *Studies in Art Education, 42*(1), 83–86.

Stout, L. J. (1985). Children's art in archives. In H. Hoffa & B. Wilson (Eds.), *History of art education: Proceedings of the Penn State Conference* (pp. 203–204). College Park, PA: The Pennsylvania State University, College of Arts & Architecture School of Visual Arts.

Studies in Art Education. (1965). Historical research in art education; symposium. *Studies in Art Education, 26*(2), 67–128.

Suplee, B. P. (1995). *Reflections on the Barnes Foundation's aesthetic theory, philosophical antecendents, and 'method' for appreciation*. Doctoral dissertation, Pennsylvania State University, College Park.

Suplee, B. P. (1997). Art education at the Barnes Foundation: Seven decades of "learning to see." In A. Anderson & P. Bolin (Eds.), *History of art education: Proceedings of the Third Penn State International Symposium, October 12–15, 1995* (pp. 271–278). College Park, PA: The Pennsylvania State University Art Education Program, School of Visual Arts.

Sutton, G. (1967). *Artisan or artist? A history of the teaching of arts and crafts in English schools*. Oxford: Pergamon Press.

Svedlow, A. J., & Troxell, R T. (1997). Building on traditions: Reflections on American art museum education. In A. Anderson & P. Bolin (Eds.), *History of art education: Proceedings of the Third Penn State International Symposium, October 12–15, 1995* (pp. 255–263). College Park, PA: The Pennsylvania State University Art Education Program, School of Visual Arts.

Tait, G. E. (1957). *The history of art education in the elementary schools of Ontario*. Doctoral dissertation, University of Toronto, Toronto.

Tarr, P. (1989). Pestalozzian and Froebellian influences on contemporary elementary school art. *Studies in Art Education, 30*(22), 115–21.

Toub, J. (1997). The legacy of Oskar Kokoschka's International School of Seeing. In A. Anderson & P. Bolin (Eds.), *History of art education: Proceedings of the Third Penn State International Symposium, October 12–15, 1995* (pp. 211–217). College Park, PA: The Pennsylvania State University Art Education Program, School of Visual Arts.

Troeger, B. J. (1992). You past is our future: The development of art programs for special populations. In P. M. Amburgy, D. Soucy, M. A. Stankiewicz, B. Wilson, & M. Wilson (Eds.), *History of art education: Proceedings of the Second Penn State Conference, 1989* (pp. 181–185). Reston, VA: The National Art Education Association.

Turner, D. (1992). A history of exhibitions of children's art: Practices, motives and outcomes. In P. M. Amburgy, D. Soucy, M. A. Stankiewicz, B. Wilson, & M. Wilson (Eds.), *History of art education: Proceedings of the Second Penn State Conference, 1989* (pp. 175–180). Reston, VA: The National Art Education Association.

Turner, D. (1997). The real world: The history of technology in art education. In A. Anderson & P. Bolin (Eds.), *History of art education: Proceedings of the Third Penn State International Symposium, October 12–15, 1995* (pp. 238–245). College Park, PA: The Pennsylvania State University Art Education Program, School of Visual Arts.

Van Dommelen, D. B. (1985). A history of the Pennsylvania Art Education Association. In H. Hoffa & B. Wilson (Eds.), *History of art education: Proceedings of the Penn State Conference* (pp. 346–353). College Park, PA: The Pennsylvania State University, College of Arts & Architecture School of Visual Arts.

Weiley, E. A. (1957). *Socio-economic influences in the development of American Art education in the nineteenth century*. Doctoral dissertation, University of Michigan, Ann Arbor.

Weinberg, H. B. (1991). *The lure of Paris: Nineteenth-century American painters and their French teachers*. New York: Abbeville.

Weisberg, G. P., & Becker, J.R. (1999). *Overcoming all obstacles: The women of the Académie Julian*. New York: Dahesh Museum & Rutgers University Press.

Werner, R. J. (2000). Arts education policy in the twentieth century. *Arts Education Policy Review, 101*(3), 15–16.

White, J. H. (1997). Native American presence in *School Arts*: The deLemos legacy, 1919–1949. In A. Anderson & P. Bolin (Eds.), *History of art education: Proceedings of the Third Penn State International Symposium, October 12–15, 1995* (pp. 95–104). College Park, PA: The Pennsylvania State University Art Education Program, School of Visual Arts.

White, J. H. (2001). Imaging (native) America: Pedro de Lemos and the expansion of art education (1919–1950). *Studies in Art Education, 42*(4), 298–317.

Whitford, F. (1994). *The Bauhaus: Masters and students by themselves*. New York: Overlook.

Whitford, W. G. (1923). A brief history of art education in the United States. *Elementary School Journal, 29*, 109–115.

Whitford, W. G. (1929). Introduction: Brief history of art education in the United States. *An introduction to art education* (pp. 7–18). New York: D. Appleton & Co.,

Wilson, B. (1985). Towards an iconography of children's motifs, signs and symbols: The messages of a 75–year-old diary. In H. Hoffa & B. Wilson (Eds.), *History of art education: Proceedings of the Penn State Conference* (pp. 185–191). College Park, PA: The Pennsylvania State University, College of Arts & Architecture School of Visual Arts.

Wilson, B. (1992). Children's schooled and unschooled images from the nineteenth and early twentieth centuries: Art education, cultural hegemony, and the 'intentions' surrounding three sets of visual artefacts. In P. M. Amburgy, D. Soucy, M. A. Stankiewicz, B. Wilson, & M. Wilson (Eds.), *History of art education: Proceedings of the Second Penn State Conference, 1989* (pp. 226–233). Reston, VA: The National Art Education Association.

Winkelman, R. J. (1990). *Art education in the non-public schools of Pennsylvania, 1720–1870*. Doctoral dissertation, Pennsylvania State University, College Park.

Wolf-Ragatz, M. P. (1988). *Tactile education: Its history and potential for art education*. Doctoral dissertation, University of Georgia, Athens.

Wood, A. B. (1986). The hidden curriculum of Ontario school art 1904–1940. *Ontario History, 78*(4), 351–369.

Wood, A. B., & Soucy, D. (1990). From Old to New Scotland: Nineteenth century links between morality and art education. In D. Soucy & M. A. Stankiewicz (Eds.), *Framing the past: Essays on Art Education* (pp. 47–58). Reston, VA: National Art Education Association.

Wygrant, F. (1959). *A History of art education at Teacher's College, Viewed as response to social change*. Doctoral dissertation, Teachers College, Columbia University, New York.

Wygrant, F. (1983). *Art in American schools in the nineteenth century*. Cincinnati: Interwood Press.

Wygant, F. (1986). *Art in American schools: 1900–1970*. Cincinnati: copyright held by author.

Wygant, F. (1988). Dewey and Naumburg: An unresolved debate. *Canadian Review of Art Education, 15*(20), 29–39.

Wygant, F. (1993). *School art in American culture 1820–1970*. Cincinnati: Interwood Press.

Yates, F. E. (1993). *Remembering artist and educator Maude I. Kerns: An historical study using oral history techniques and a contextual approach*. Doctoral dissertation, University of Oregon, Eugene.

Zahner, M. (1987). *Manuel Barkan: Twentieth century art educator*. Doctoral dissertation, The Ohio State University, Columbus.

Zahner, M. (1992). Manuel Barkan: Twentieth-century art educator. In P. M. Amburgy, D. Soucy, M. A. Stankiewicz, B. Wilson, & M. Wilson (Eds.), *History of art education: Proceedings of the Second Penn State Conference, 1989* (pp. 170–174). Reston, VA: The National Art Education Association.

Zeller, T. (1989). The historical and philosophical foundations of art museum education in America. In N. Berry & S. Mayer (Eds.), *Museum education history, theory, and practice* (pp. 10–89). Reston, VA: National Art Education Association.

Zimmerman, E. (1985). Art talent and research in the 1920s and 1930s: Norman Charles Meier and Leta Stetter Hollingworth's theories about special abilities. In H. Hoffa & B. Wilson (Eds.), *History of art education: Proceedings of the Penn State Conference* (pp. 269–275). College Park, PA: The Pennsylvania State University, College of Arts & Architecture School of Visual Arts.

Zimmerman, E. (1989). The mirror of Marie Bashkirtseff: Reflections about the education of women and art students in the 19th century. *Studies in Art Education, 30*(3), 164–175.

Zimmerman, E. (1991). Art education for women in England from 1890–1910 as reflected in the Victorian periodical press and current feminist histories of art education. *Studies in Art Education, 32*(2), 105–116.

Zurmuehlen, M. (1991). Kenneth Beittel: A re-interpreting presence in art education. *Visual Arts Research, 17*(1), 1–11.

Zweybruck, N. (1953). Cizek as father of art education. *School Arts, 53*(2), 11–14.

2

Questioning the Past: Contexts, Functions, and Stakeholders in 19th-Century Art Education

Mary Ann Stankiewicz
Patricia M. Amburgy
The Pennsylvania State University

Paul E. Bolin
The University of Texas at Austin

To this day the older teachers tell of the halcyon days when Walter Smith lectured on drawing and design, and the greatness of great men.
—Bailey, 1893, p. 6, Bailey Papers, Box 13

North American histories of 19th-century art education have most often been written for art educators by other art educators who have been, perhaps unduly, influenced by Isaac Edward's Clarke's political and economic interpretation (Soucy, 1990). Not only did Clarke valorize Walter Smith as the great man in American art education, but he focused on public school drawing instruction for children and technical training for industrial workers with Massachusetts, his home state, as the wellspring.[1] In Clarke's version of the halcyon days, and in the stories of those imbued with his interpretation, the primary context for art education was northeastern industrial cities, the dominant function the preparation of human capital for economic success, and the chief stakeholders the capitalists of Massachusetts. These themes continued to color art education history through the end of the 20th century and are reflected in this essay, a review and synthesis of major secondary sources on the history of North American art education during the 19th century.

As in other forms of research, historians tend to find what they seek; that is, historical research is governed by our assumptions, working definitions, and preferred metaphors. For example, both Henry Turner Bailey (1865–1931) and Arthur Efland used a fluid metaphor to characterize underlying structures of art education. Writing at the end of the 19th century, Bailey quoted Ralph Waldo Emerson, describing the idea of art education falling like rain on the mountain tops of the best minds then running down, "'from class to class, until it reaches the masses and works revolutions'" (p. 1). These rivers of thought had united, from Bailey's perspective, to form a millrace, an energetic stream that powered New England manufacturing. For Efland (1990), streams of ideas also come together, but in harmonious confluence where the

---

[1] The parallel in Canadian art education histories seems to be a tendency to privilege Ontario as the model, obscuring the diversity of Canadian experiences (Pearse, 1997).

effects of historical movements linger even after the movement has ceased. Bailey's metaphor reflects the tendency, which continued into the 20th century, for history to be plotted top-down with a focus on the work of "great" minds, underlying beliefs in a predestined class structure and in progress through political revolutions which should, nonetheless, affirm the rightness of great men.

Efland's streams, on the other hand, evoke the multiple voices and hopeful eclecticism emerging, along with recognition of the power that ideas of race and citizenship have had on schooling, in late 20th-century art education (Spring, 2001). As paradigms for art education have changed, histories of art teaching and learning have taken different forms. Some historical research in the last three decades has questioned received wisdom, probing more deeply into the social contexts where art education has occurred, examining the functions it has been asked to serve, and questioning the varied stakeholders who have advocated art education for themselves or others. Rather than simply describing how the streams of thought have fallen from mountaintops to masses, recent writers have begun to probe the landscape, the social structures and functions of visual art education, the greatness of great men.

WHAT SOCIAL FUNCTIONS DID ART EDUCATION SERVE
CIRCA 1800–1912?

In colonial and 19th-century North America, art education served the needs of practical education, spiritual education, liberal education, moral education, and polite or ornamental education. Prior to colonization, indigenous peoples in North America had not conceived of an ideal art apart from society. Both practical and ritual objects were carefully shaped, prestige denoted and enhanced by decoration. The family was the first teacher, elders transmitting eye and hand skills along with beliefs and rituals. Even before British and French colonists began to leave their marks on the northeast, Catholic explorers and missionaries brought Spanish traditions and Baroque styles to the southwest. Emigrant artists taught native apprentices to paint and sculpt religious images that, in turn, could be used for spiritual instruction through art. Traditional hierarchies maintained the artisan status of the Spanish artist and prevented native artisans from gaining master status until colonial domination was reduced. The Academy of San Carlos, founded in 1781, brought neoclassical influences and European models of instruction to Mexico City, while use of indigenous materials changed styles and methods of working taught to apprentices in what is now New Mexico (Fane, 1996; Hail, 1987; Metropolitan, 1990; Smith, 1996).

In southwestern cities, as in the northeast, local artists offered lessons to those with time and inclination to learn and cash to pay. Functions and definitions of art derived from European notions of drawing as a genteel pastime and "the heroic ideals of high art" (Harris, 1982, p. 9). These functions were often combined, so that Benjamin Franklin, for example, recommended that youths in Pennsylvania academies receive a practical education that included everything useful and ornamental as a means for upward mobility. Thomas Jefferson's unrealized plan for the University of Virginia included the fine arts with the liberal expectation that higher education would develop innate reason, improve individual virtue and social worth, thus contributing to the creation of a natural aristocracy. After seeing Parisian architecture and sculpture, John Adams wrote his wife Abigail that a young country most needed the useful, mechanic arts and should postpone study of the polite arts until his grandchildren's generation. Polite education, as the term was used in the early Republic, was preparation for participation in genteel society, for displaying one's good taste and artistic accomplishments at formal entertainments in the gracious homes of refined ladies and gentlemen (Bermingham, 2000; Bushman, 1992; Cremin, 1980; Efland, 1990; Spring, 2001; Strazdes, 1979; Winkelman, 1990; Wygant, 1983).

Theoretical and Rhetorical Foundations

Arguments for the value of art education varied depending on who was speaking and for whom art instruction was intended. Political leaders, like Franklin, Jefferson, and Adams, tended to focus on art's value to the state and citizens. During most of the 19th century, only white male property owners enjoyed full citizenship in the United States. Thus, it is not surprising that much of the early rhetoric advocating art education addressed the interests of the dominant class of "enlightened gentlemen" (Miller, 1966, p. 16). This rhetoric was rooted in the world of the courtesy book, instructional literature originally written for Renaissance courtiers for whom drawing was both a refined amusement and a means to develop appreciation of art (Bushman, 1992; Strazdes, 1979).

European, British and Scottish influences contributed to the aesthetic theories of the early Republic. A North American gentleman most likely would have agreed with the empiricist philosopher John Locke that drawing was more useful than writing for communicating ideas, favored the neoclassical style of Sir Joshua Reynolds, believed in Lord Kames' theory of aesthetic universals as standards of taste for the privileged few, and accepted the associationist psychology of the Scotsman Archibald Alison (1757–1839). Alison argued that taste was an emotion that connected sensations to memories, experience and environment, leading to the exercise of imagination. These associations led one to appreciate beauty or the sublime. Thus, exposure to great works of art was expected to improve intellect, behavior, and taste among the better classes, lifting the elite mind from materialism to higher pursuits (Efland, 1990; Miller, 1966; Storr, 1992; Winkelman, 1990).

Between about 1790 and 1840, arguments by college presidents and student orators, speakers at literary societies and mechanics' institutes, dialogs among artists and patrons broadened these arguments to create a discourse of aesthetic didacticism, a generalized rhetoric that proposed a special connection between art and republican social order. This discourse ameliorated American distrust of the visual arts as sensuous pleasures. Grounded in Renaissance humanism, aesthetic didacticism began from the belief that art making was an intellectual project with techniques related to the highest forms of creativity. Works of art could embody and communicate ideals. Principles of criticism could be formulated and taught to people who would understand and judge works of architecture, painting and sculpture, but also be able to apply their improved critical faculties to social life. Rules governing the intellectual and technical aspects of art making could be taught to aspiring artists with natural talent. Education, as the primary means for individual improvement, should, therefore, include the arts as a benign influence on the general public in a democratic society (Harris, 1982; Storr, 1992).

By the 1840s, visual art had begun to enter the discourse of educational reform. Beautification of school buildings through painting, remodeling, and landscaping was recommended in the northeast as a way to cultivate taste and improve behavior. The sentimental novelist, Lydia Sigourney (1791–1865), recommended that classrooms aim for the elegance of a parlor. Few proper parlors, however, housed blackboards or encouraged children to draw on individual slates with powdery white chalk, schoolroom innovations that laid the practical foundation for drawing in common school education. Drawing served a range of school subjects: infant geographers were expected to develop clearer concepts of place and location by drawing maps; future surveyors learned spatial relations through studying perspective and proportion; geometry and beginning drawing were coterminous, as were penmanship and drawing. Object drawing based on ideas from Pestalozzi entered the curriculum during the same period as a means to help children observe objects accurately and acquire clearer ideas (Davis, 1992; Dobbs, 1972; Efland, 1990; Stankiewicz, 2000, 2001; Stevens, 1995; Winkelman, 1990).

As art education was democratized, it shifted from being chiefly a concern of elite male leaders to occupying the attentions of women and men who sought to ape their betters or find work in growing art industries. At the same time that the emerging middle classes began to seek art education for themselves, the upper classes perceived art education as means to maintain their cultural authority. Genteel art education for refinement, manners and morals was advocated by upper-middle-class women and men for their own children and for the deserving poor, for example, single or widowed middle-class women who had fallen on hard times. Art and design schools specifically for women were established as philanthropic enterprises in Boston, New York, and notably Philadelphia (Chalmers, 1998a, 1998b; Korzenik, 1985; Waller, 1992; De Angeli Walls, 1993, 1994).

Art education came to be perceived as having special benefits for young women. Ornamental education for social display through subjects such as embroidery was most popular prior to 1815, though lists of types of fancywork and ornamental subjects could be found in catalogs of private schools well into the century. Some writers cautioned that such accomplishments failed to help a woman meet her responsibilities as wife and mother. Other authors, including some ministers and women who wrote didactic novels, advice books, and treatises on female education, positioned art as a positive moral influence. Art, they argued, naturally appealed to woman's sensitive nature and the study of art would better prepare her for her destiny as wife, mother, and teacher (Cott, 1977; Douglas, 1977; Flynt, 1988; Harris, 1982; Parker, 1984; Ring, 1983; Stankiewicz, 1982; Winkelman, 1990).

WHAT FORMS OF ART EDUCATION WERE AVAILABLE IN NORTH AMERICA DURING THE EARLY-19TH-CENTURY ERA OF INDUSTRIALIZATION, URBANIZATION, AND MIDDLE-CLASS FORMATION?

Colonial North America lacked both an organized art world and systematic schooling, but as the beginnings of industrialization and urbanization challenged Jefferson's vision of a rural Republic, art education could be found in formal and informal education, through apprenticeships, in art and design schools, and in nonpublic schools. Against the elitism of political theories of art, the humanist rhetoric of aesthetic didacticism, the practical introduction of drawing in service to technical literacy, and the amateurism of art in woman's sphere, artists struggled to secure a professional identity. Inspired by the academic ideals of Sir Joshua Reynolds (1723–1792), painters and sculptors sought to move beyond the imitative labor of portraiture and conventions of craftsmanship, to establish a unified community with a national market, its own critics and journals, specialized studio spaces and educational institutions. Although ambitious North American artists throughout the 19th century regarded European study as a necessary finish to their art education, art academies were established in the late 18th century. With other Philadelphia artists, Charles Willson Peale (1741–1827) founded the Columbianum in 1794. Its program of lectures and classes in drawing from casts and life was modeled on the British Academy, but the organization faltered within its first year. Art academies were founded in New York in 1802 and again in Philadelphia in 1805. As the artist's status rose, belief in the noble soul of the artistic genius contributed to conceptions of the artist as teacher and minister. Families like the Peales, Sartains, and Weirs were recognized not only as gifted artists but also as educators and tastemakers (Bolger, 1976; Burns, 1996; Efland, 1990; Fahlman, 1997; Harris, 1982; Martinez & Talbott, 2000; Marzio, 1976).

Drawing Books

As American artists struggled to create their own professional communities with formal schools for artist training and galleries and museums to display their work, an emerging middle class sought the kinds of art education formerly available only to upper-class amateurs. This art education was provided through new institutions such as venture schools, chartered academies and seminaries that provided secondary education for practical life, and publicly funded school systems. The introduction of drawing into Massachusetts' common schools will be the focus of a separate section below. The growth of printers and publishers created an important supporting context for art education, providing reproductions and drawing books.

From about 1820 to 1860, more than 145 drawing books were published in the United States. These books, written for the most part by working artists who shared a common vision of the meaning of art and the best methods for art making, were available to almost everyone. Prices ranged from as little as a quarter to more than twenty dollars for oversize tomes in multiple volumes. Engraved illustrations and expensive bindings increased costs; pocket-sized, lithographed booklets could fit almost any budget. Drawing cards also provided examples that could be copied, usually without instructions or rules (Marzio, 1976).

Drawing books and cards were intended as practical guides to drawing with the goals of teaching Americans how to perceive meaning in great art and beauty in nature. The goals of the books tended to be utilitarian rather than ornamental. Although some were intended specifically for women, the books appealed to both sexes as sources for disciplined knowledge of drawing, as means to educate the taste of workers and consumers and thus to encourage economic prosperity. These drawing manuals promulgated the belief that drawing was a universal language that anyone could learn. At the same time, they sought to develop a distinctly American art with examples of northeastern landscapes, combining a universal aesthetic with nationalism in subject matter and style (Andrus, 1977; Davis, 1992; Korzenik, 1985, 1999; Marzio, 1976).

One of the first drawing books was John Rubens Smith's *Juvenile Drawing Book*, published in 1822. Smith (1775–1849), who would publish five different drawing manuals, immigrated to Boston from England about 1806. Just as writing masters used examples printed on copperplate for their classes as the basis for early penmanship books, so Smith used examples prepared for his classes as the basis for his books. As artist–teachers, Smith, Rembrandt Peale (1778–1860), John Gadsby Chapman (1808–1889), and other art crusaders brought authority to their arguments for the importance of drawing. Their books addressed multiple audiences: individuals seeking self-education, families, and schools. Artists like Winslow Homer (1836–1910) and Thomas Eakins (1849–1916), whose high school art classes followed a curriculum developed by Peale, initially developed drawing skills from copybooks. On-the-job instruction in lithographic workshops helped Homer and other artists refine these rough skills. Would-be artists, especially those in rural areas or who lacked later opportunities for advanced study or apprenticeship, used drawing books as primary means of learning, remaining on the threshold of professional competence (Barnhill, Korzenik, & Sloat, 1997; Davis, 1992, 1996; Johns, 1980; Korzenik, 1985, 1999; Thornton, 1996; Vlach, 1988).

Collegiate Art Education

Aesthetics and criticism entered the American college early in the 19th century through courses in moral philosophy taught to seniors by college presidents and through courses in classic language and culture. Bowdoin College established the first collegiate gallery in 1811, setting a precedent for colleges to collect and display works of fine art and curiosities. Yale purchased Colonel John Trumbull's art collection in 1831, building a gallery the following year and constructing a building for a professional art school in 1864 to 1867. Syracuse University claimed the distinction of establishing the first degree-granting College of Fine Arts in 1873, just a year before Charles Eliot Norton (1827–1908) was appointed Professor of Fine Arts at Harvard. Women's colleges introduced art history about the same time: Vassar in 1874 and

Wellesley in 1875. By the end of the 1870s, art history had become a popular fad in women's colleges, as well as a component of professional and liberal education for men (Efland, 1990; Harris, 1976; Smyth & Lukehart, 1993; Stankiewicz, 2001).

Art Museums

Artists in 18th-century Boston and Philadelphia established the earliest North American picture galleries. Exhibiting copies of European paintings along with portraits they had painted, artists like John Smibert and Robert Edge Pine provided exemplars for aspiring artists and aesthetes. Charles Willson Peale's museum, opened to the public in 1782, included natural history and fine arts with the intention of providing rational amusement to Philadelphians. After the Civil War, wealthy citizens of New York and Boston led other cities in establishing public museums to encourage study of the fine arts, provide examples for artisans and designers, and instruct the public. Philadelphia's museum was a legacy of the 1876 Centennial Exhibition in that city. Other American museums traced the impetus for their founding to London's 1851 Crystal Palace exhibition and the establishment of the South Kensington Museum, today the Victoria and Albert. The collection of casts that furnished Edgerton Ryerson's (1803–1882) educational museum for Upper Canada, now Ontario, in 1856 was based on this English precedent. Civic and cultural leaders who imported European reproductions and artworks for public display thus continued the colonialization of North America, displacing approaches to art education trans-planted earlier with a newer British model (Alexander, 1983, 1987; Harris, 1962; Tompkins, 1973; Zeller, 1989).

WHERE AND WHEN DID ART EDUCATION ENTER PUBLIC SCHOOLS IN NORTH AMERICA?

Cities and towns in various regions of the northern United States were, by the 1850s, formally introducing the study of drawing into public schools. Throughout the years just prior to the eruption of the Civil War, many forms of drawing appeared within a growing number of public school classrooms. This swelling interest in drawing education helped to initiate the first statewide legislation of drawing as a subject of study within the public school curriculum. Updating statutes to take effect in the new decade, Massachusetts lawmakers ratified legislation in December 1859 declaring that drawing, along with algebra, vocal music, physiology, and hygiene, should be taught in public schools. With passage of this legislative act the subject of drawing was listed specifically among permitted academic subjects that might be taught in any public school (Belshe, 1946; Bennett, 1926; Clarke, 1885; Green, 1948; McVitty, 1934; Stankiewicz, 2001; Wygant, 1983, 1993).

Massachusetts' Petition for Drawing Instruction

Nearly a decade later, in June 1869, a select group of 12 individuals and 2 businesses delivered a formal petition to Massachusetts lawmakers requesting, in part, that this legislative body appeal to the Board of Education to report some definite plan for introducing free instruction in drawing in all towns with more than 5,000 inhabitants. The 14 signers of this petition had firm ties to business and textile manufacturing in Boston and the surrounding region, but they had other ties as well. Some were linked through strong vocal and written advocacy for substantial governmental tariffs placed on manufactured goods imported from Europe. A number regarded commercial trade protection and teaching Americans skills in mechanical and industrial drawing as kindred avenues for advancing the economic climate in America, particularly in the northeast, a region that depended heavily on industrial manufacturing. Many of the drawing education petitioners had graduated from Harvard College during the early 19th century, and throughout their lives maintained close ties with this educational institution. In the 1860s, eight of the 12 individuals who signed the drawing petition acted as members of overseer committees for Harvard, helping to set policy and direction for this prominent establishment. These petitioners were also connected by religious affiliation; many were vocal and active Unitarians within and around Boston. Reverend Edward E. Hale (1822–1909), a spokesman for the petitioning group, was one of Boston's most prominent Unitarian ministers. Overlapping business, political, educational, and religious beliefs and activities appear to have motivated these petitioners to spearhead the industrial drawing movement in Massachusetts (Bolin, 1985, 1986; Efland, 1983, 1985b, 1990; Saunders, 1976).

Massachusetts lawmakers quickly heeded the petitioners' request for an investigation into the promotion of publicly supported drawing education within the state. In June 1869, legislators endorsed a Resolve that the State Board of Education explore the feasibility of legislating instruction in mechanical drawing within public schools of larger cities. At the conclusion of the legislative session, the Board of Education undertook efforts to carry out the lawmakers' request. A Special Committee on Drawing, consisting of three members of the Massachusetts Board of Education and Board Secretary Joseph White, worked throughout the fall and winter of 1869 and into the spring of 1870 gathering information and insight on drawing education offered from interested citizens throughout the state of Massachusetts. The Special Committee on Drawing received a wide range of responses from concerned individuals about the purposes and practices of drawing in public schools and the suitability of enacting drawing education legislation. In the spring of 1870, the Massachusetts Board of Education unanimously forwarded to the legislature a formal recommendation to require the teaching of elementary and free hand drawing in all public schools of the commonwealth (Bolin, 1986, 1990).

Institutionalizing Drawing Instruction

With passage of the Act Relating to Free Instruction in Drawing, signed into law on May 16, 1870, Massachusetts became the first state to mandate drawing education as part of the public school curriculum. The next step was to find a director for drawing as recommended by the educational and drawing experts consulted earlier. The Committee investigated individuals within the United States who could possibly administer the drawing program for Boston, but made a decision to hire an art master from across the Atlantic. Charles Callahan Perkins (1823–1886), a wealthy Bostonian knowledgeable in the arts, who had traveled extensively in Europe, was asked to recommend a person to fill this position. Perkins suggested the School Committee contact Sir Henry Cole, director of the South Kensington School in London, and ask him to nominate graduates of his National Art Training School. Cole recommended Walter Smith (1836–1886) who was then directing the Art School at Leeds (Billings, 1987; Bolin, 1990, 1995; Chalmers, 2000a; Efland & Soucy, 1991; Korzenik, 1985; Stankiewicz, 2001).

In October 1871, Walter Smith arrived in Boston, with his family, and commenced his professional work in Massachusetts as both the State Director of Art Education and the Director of Drawing for the Public Schools of Boston. In his dual positions, Smith showed himself to be an individual of tremendous dedication and energy, who throughout his tenure spoke and wrote zealously on behalf of drawing education. Smith was both explicit and adamant regarding the type of drawing that should be taught, and for what purpose this subject ought to make its way into public school classrooms. Industrial drawing was distinguished from ornamental and professional branches by its importance as a factor in trades and manufactures. Furthermore, Smith believed that all children of normal intelligence could learn to draw and that, in the lower grades, drawing should be taught by regular instructors, not specialists. One of Smith's challenges was providing clear and precise lessons that teachers without art training could present successfully (Belshe, 1946; Chalmers, 2000a; Clarke, 1885; Dean, 1923/24; Efland, 1990; Eisner, 1972; Green, 1948, 1966; Haney, 1908; Marzio, 1976; Sheath, 1982; Wygant, 1983).

Massachusetts Normal Art School

Smith worked unwaveringly throughout his tenure in Massachusetts to achieve his goals, soon realizing that a teacher education facility with a focus on drawing instruction needed to be established. Serious discussions with the legislature regarding the founding of a school for the preparation of art teachers were initiated in the spring of 1872. The Massachusetts Normal Art School (MNAS) began operations on November 6, 1873, in Boston, with Smith taking the reins as school principal in addition to his responsibilities as state agent and city supervisor for industrial drawing. During Smith's nine years as director of the MNAS, hundreds of students passed through its doors. Many graduates and certificate holders supervised drawing in neighboring states, disseminating Smith's methods throughout the northeast and into eastern Canada. In addition, Smith traveled throughout the northeastern United States and eastern Canadian Provinces talking to multitudes of educators, citizen groups, and lawmakers about his purposes and practices of drawing education, inscribing his mark on many of these locations (Chalmers, 1985a, 1985b, 1990, 2000a; Efland, 1990; Stirling, 1997; Wood & Soucy, 1990).

Walter Smith's Departure

Throughout Walter Smith's time in Massachusetts, there was open tension and confrontation between Smith and various others. These disputes reached a climax in the early 1880s. In a vote taken by the Boston School Committee on April 26, 1881, Henry Hitchings (d. 1902), art teacher at the English High School in Boston, was elected to replace Walter Smith as Director of Drawing for the Boston Public Schools. Little more than a year later, in early July 1882, the Board of Education voted to dismiss Walter Smith from his dual positions as State Director of Art Education and Principal of the Massachusetts Normal Art School. Much speculation has occurred regarding reasons for Walter Smith's dismissal from his three professional positions in Massachusetts, but the precise motivations for his removal are not known. Were the key factors Smith's bitter and open controversies with competing authors and publishers of drawing textbooks, Smith's "old fashioned" and demanding teaching methods, personality conflicts that took place between Smith and those around him, nationality and denominational conflicts, or a squabble that occurred over the cost of the building rented to house the Massachusetts Normal Art School? No conclusive explanations have been given (Chalmers, 2000a; Dean, 1923/24; Efland, 1990; Green, 1948, 1966; Korzenik, 1985; Smith, 1992).

Industrial Drawing Textbooks and Controversies

The production and dissemination of printed materials to teach drawing expanded tremendously in the second half of the 19th century. Fueled by technological printing developments, including the invention of chromolithography, and by a burgeoning education market within and outside of school, authors and publishers of drawing textbooks, drawing cards and other instructional drawing materials vied for sales. By the outbreak of the Civil War, 35 book companies had published drawing manuals, and were attempting to sell their books to public schools throughout the eastern United States (Marzio, 1976, 1979; Stankiewicz, 1985).

Woolworth, Ainsworth, and Company began publishing William Bartholomew's drawing books in 1868, although Bartholomew had been producing drawing books and cards for publication since the 1850s. Bartholomew (1822–1898) was born in Boston, but spent time as a cabinetmaker at Post Mills, Vermont. He returned to Boston to study art, and soon began a nearly 20-year career as a teacher of drawing in Boston's English High School and the Girls High and Normal School, beginning his efforts there in the early 1850s. Bartholomew, now a painter whose major interest was in representational drawing, adapted his books to the industrial drawing movement, helping them maintain an influence beyond New England. Battles between Woolworth, Ainsworth, and Company and J. R. Osgood, who had begun publishing Walter Smith's drawing books, testify to the importance of the potential market for school drawing books. For a number of months accusations flew between the two parties. However, as Smith gained a firmer foothold in Massachusetts by way of his professional positions, disputes between his publisher and the publisher of Bartholomew's drawing books diminished. For a short period Smith's confrontations over textbooks subsided, but then turned volatile in another direction (Bennett, 1926; Efland, 1985a; Korzenik, 1985; Wygant, 1983).

Walter Smith's editor, John S. Clark, severed ties with J. R. Osgood and Company in 1874, to join the publishing firm of L. Prang and Company. The Prang Company purchased the publication rights to Smith's popular *American Textbooks for Art Education*, which were published in a range of formats by Prang and Company beginning in 1875. In the next half-decade, the publication partnership of Louis Prang and Walter Smith solidified their hold on the very profitable art education market. Korzenik (1985) has described it in these terms: "Fortunes were to be made on the orders coming in from all the states for Walter Smith's books, drawing cards, and drawing models, and up to 1882, Smith had a virtual monopoly, shared only by his publisher" (p. 240) (Korzenik, 1985; Marzio, 1976; Wygant, 1983).

With great sums of money to be secured and power to be grasped, Prang and Smith's relationship was at loggerheads, even as early as 1876. The disputes between author and publisher grew more vehement and vocal through the late 1870s, as each attempted to establish a more secure financial foundation, at the other's expense. In the days just prior to Smith's dismissal from his position as Director of Drawing for the Public Schools of Boston in the spring of 1881, confrontations between Smith and Prang were featured in Boston newspapers, supporting interpretations that Prang may have helped force Smith out of Massachusetts. The Massachusetts Drawing Act of 1870 helped to cultivate an environment wherein drawing education was viewed as a lucrative commodity. The open competition demonstrated between differing ideologies and practices of drawing instruction is evidence of the great value authors and publishing companies placed on this educational market that was expanding throughout the United States and Canada (Chalmers, 2000a; Korzenik, 1985; Stankiewicz, 1986; Wygant, 1983).

Drawing Education in Other States

Passage of "An Act Relating to Free Instruction in Drawing" provided the motivation and model for other state legislatures. The states of Maine, in February 1871, and New York, in May 1875, established laws requiring that drawing be instituted as a curricular subject in the public schools of these states. In the year following passage of drawing education legislation in New York, lawmakers in Vermont enacted legislation establishing free-hand drawing as a required subject of study in public schools. Drawing instruction continued to gain attention in the public schools of other New England and eastern states throughout the final quarter of the 19th century, even though many states did not enact legislation either permitting or requiring drawing as a subject of study for students in their public schools. Between 1870 and 1907, however, lawmakers in 12 states established drawing as a required subject of study in public school. Through this same period, drawing was approved as a public school subject by cities or towns in 31 other states (Commissioner of Education, 1882; Clarke, 1885; Cubberley, 1934; Saunders, 1976).

WHY WAS ART EDUCATION IMPORTANT IN THE INDUSTRIALIZED, URBAN SOCIETY OF LATE 19TH CENTURY NORTH AMERICA?

As the 19th century drew to a close, there were significant changes in North American communities. Patterns of social life were altered by rapid industrialization, the growth of cities, the arrival of new immigrants, and increasing numbers of women who joined new immigrants and others in the industrial workforce. The forms of art education that emerged at the end of the century reflected and, to some degree, shaped the changes that occurred in social life. Manual training, arts and crafts, design and composition, picture study, the kindergarten movement, and early experiments in progressive education were both protests and accommodations to the conditions of industrialized, urban society.

Manual Training

Like industrial drawing, manual training was introduced into schools in response to calls for more "practical" forms of education. From the perspective of businessmen who supported it, manual training was a form of vocational education that would prepare students for work in mills and factories. From the perspective of educators, however, manual training was conceived as a form of general education. In the 1880s, educators who supported manual training argued that it was not "trade training," or preparation for particular forms of work. They argued that students would develop hand and eye coordination by learning to use tools for working with wood and metal. The skills gained through manual training would be beneficial for all students, whatever their vocational destination in life (Cremin, 1961; Fisher, 1967; Kliebard, 1999; Stamp, 1970).

In principle, manual training was beneficial for all students, but in practice it was most often provided for the children of First People nations, African American children, the children of new immigrants, and working-class children. Some children were deemed more in need of manual training than others to develop character and prepare them for work. Typically, both moral and economic reasons were given for establishing manual training programs in public and private schools; however, in the boarding schools that were established for African American and Native students, an expectation that the institutions should be self-supporting sometimes took precedence over students' education. In such cases, manual training consisted of little more than the manual labor needed to sustain the institutions. In boarding schools organized on the "half-and-half" plan, students attended classes in the mornings and spent afternoons performing the same manual chores, again and again, in the schools' shops, fields, and laundries. Boarding schools stripped away students' Native cultures, including their art forms. Native art forms were not included in the curricula of boarding schools until after the turn of the 20th century (Adams, 1995; Anderson, 1988; Chalmers, 2000b; Coleman, 1993; Kliebard, 1999; Lazerson, 1971; Miller, 1996; Spring, 2001; Titley, 1986).

In practice, manual training was also shaped by assumptions about gender roles, along with assumptions about race and class. As many public schools began to offer classes in woodworking and metal work for boys, girls began to receive instruction in cooking and sewing. Over time, as educators began to see vocational training as a central goal of schooling, many public schools established programs for girls in home economics, called "domestic science" or "household arts." Such programs were based on an assumption that all girls, whatever else they might do temporarily, were destined by nature to be homemakers. The establishment of home economics programs at the turn of the 20th century was especially significant in the context of urban industrial society, because increasing numbers of women were leaving home to enter the industrial workforce. As a form of vocational preparation, home economics programs had more to do with preserving nostalgic ideals of home and family than with preparing women for the contemporary world of work (Kessler-Harris, 1982; Powers, 1992; Rury, 1991; Tyack & Hansot, 1990).

When manual training was first introduced into North American schools in the 1880s, most educators were resistant to the idea of vocational education. By the turn of the century, however, many of them came to see not only manual training but also all of public schooling as preparation for work. At the same time that views about the purpose of education were changing, the nature of work in industrial society was changing as well. With the development of new technology and assembly line methods of production, workers no longer needed the kinds of knowledge and skills that might be developed through manual training programs. Instead of hand and eye coordination and qualities such as self-direction, the kinds of "skills" industrial workers needed were an ability to follow orders and to perform simple, repetitive tasks. Increasingly, educators joined businessmen in criticizing manual training at the turn of the century, not because it was vocational preparation, but because it was an anachronistic, outmoded form of vocational training in an industrial age (Cremin, 1961; Kliebard, 1999; Lazerson, 1971).

Arts and Crafts

As manual training seemed increasingly outmoded to educators who supported vocational training, educators who still supported general education and manual training began to join forces with arts and crafts enthusiasts. In the United States, a successful precedent for joining manual training with art instruction had already been established by Charles Godfrey Leland (1824–1903). In 1881, Leland had opened the experimental Industrial Art School in Philadelphia to give grammar school students experience with what he called the "minor arts." The school's curriculum included classes in design, modeling, painting, pottery, embroidery, repoussé, woodcarving, and carpentry. Leland viewed instruction in crafts as a form of general vocational preparation. Rather than giving students specific skills that would prepare them for a particular trade, he held that crafts education taught students how to work.[2] Leland's assistant J. Liberty Tadd (1854–1917) took over as director of the school in 1884, and the school continued to be acclaimed a success under Tadd's guidance. The school served as a model for similar programs in other North American communities, as well as being recognized abroad (Anderson, 1997; Baker, 1984; Stankiewicz, 2001).

Before establishing the Industrial Art School in Philadelphia, Leland had lived for 10 years in Britain where he became acquainted with the ideas of John Ruskin (1819–1900) and William Morris (1834–1896), two of the leading figures in the British Arts and Crafts movement. A romantic idealist, Ruskin held that a society's moral character was reflected in the quality of its art, both fine and applied. Morris adapted Ruskin's moral aesthetic to a craft ideal, holding there should be joy and dignity in labor, rather than the fractured, demeaning character of toil in modern capitalist society.[3] Along with a philosophical basis for the British Arts and Crafts movement, Morris provided examples of the craft ideal in practice with his firm Morris and Co., organized in 1875, and the Kelmscott Press, founded in 1890 (Boris, 1986; Kaplan, 1987).

---

[2]Leland published *The Minor Arts* in 1880. His book served as an early reference work on many "lost" crafts for arts and crafts enthusiasts in Britain and the United States.

[3]Ruskin was a prolific writer, publishing dozens of books and pamphlets over the course of his lifetime. His works were compiled and indexed by E. T. Cook and Alexander Wedderburn in *The Works of John Ruskin*, published in 39 volumes from 1903 to 1912. Among Ruskin's most influential works were "The Nature of Gothic," the sixth chapter of the second volume of *The Stones of Venice*, published in 1853; the five volumes of *Modern Painters*, published from 1843 to 1860; and *The Elements of Drawing*, published in 1857. Morris's works were complied by his daughter May Morris in *The Collected Works of William Morris*, published in 24 volumes from 1910 to 1915.

The Arts and Crafts movement in the United States flourished between 1890 and 1910. Arts and crafts ideals were spread through arts and crafts societies, periodicals, and classes. Instruction was offered in a variety of settings, including summer schools, design schools, and settlement houses, as well as public schools. Working people were part of the Arts and Crafts movement in Britain, but in the United States, the movement was predominately a middle- and upper-class phenomenon. This blunted the movement's social criticism and altered many of its central ideals. In the United States, advocates of arts and crafts included social reformers, tastemakers who focused on the appearance of objects, and those who saw arts and crafts as a hobby or leisure activity. Guiding ideals in the American Arts and Crafts movement included work, taste, and therapy (Amburgy, 1997; Boris, 1986; Lears, 1981).

Jane Addams (1860–1935) and Ellen Gates Starr (1860–1940) were among the social reformers concerned with work in American society. Addams and Starr were cofounders of Hull House, a widely acclaimed social settlement in Chicago. Whereas Starr believed it was important to change the nature of industrial work in order to restore what Morris called "joy in labor," Addams focused on changing workers' perceptions.[4] In the Labor Museum at Hull House, workers could see demonstrations of traditional skills and displays of hand-crafted objects, and come away with a new understanding of the history of labor that imparted significance to their own positions in the modern workforce. In seeking to change the way workers viewed their work rather than the work itself, Addams' position was one of accommodation to modern conditions of labor (Amburgy, 1990; Lears, 1981; Stankiewicz, 1989).

Many of the arts and crafts societies focused on taste. The Society of Arts and Crafts, Boston, founded in 1897, was an example. Although there were conflicts between social reformers and tastemakers in the early years of the organization, the conflicts were resolved when a change in leadership established a firm commitment to exhibition and sales. Other arts and crafts societies similarly focused on educating consumers' taste by mounting exhibitions of handcrafted items and maintaining salesrooms that offered handcrafted items for sale (Boris, 1986; Cooke, 1997; Kaplan, 1987).

One of the most compelling ideas within the Arts and Crafts movement was a belief that crafts were primitive, natural activities. As middle-class Americans achieved more wealth and leisure at the end of the 19th century, they increasingly began to fear they were becoming overcivilized, out of touch with "real life." Plagued by doubts about the reality of modern life, many came to see arts and crafts as a source of primal, authentic experience. In this context, handwork came to be viewed as a means of therapeutic rejuvenation (Lears, 1981).

In other contexts, crafts were associated with primitive cultural experience and children's development. According to the "culture epoch theory" then popular, children's development replicated the stages of development through which the whole human race had passed. According to the theory, early stages of children's development corresponded to early stages of racial development. Since decorative arts and traditional crafts were associated with supposedly primitive stages of human history (which included both past cultures and contemporary cultures, such as those of Native Americans), children were believed to have a natural affinity for arts and crafts. Charles Godfrey Leland and Arthur Wesley Dow were among those who applied the culture epoch theory to teaching art (Boris, 1986; Kaplan, 1987; Moffatt, 1977; Stankiewicz, 2001).

---

[4]Starr's views on contemporary work are set out in "Art and Labor," an article published in the collection *Hull-House Maps and Papers* in 1895. Addams' views appear in "The Art-Work Done by Hull-House, Chicago," an article published in the July 1895 issue of *Forum*. Addams also discusses the significance of art for working people in her books *Democracy and Social Ethics*, published in 1902, and *Twenty Years at Hull-House*, published in 1910.

Design and Composition

Arthur Wesley Dow (1857–1922) was a key figure in the Arts and Crafts movement at the turn of the century. Through his work as an artist, a theorist, and a teacher of teachers, Dow made important contributions to art education that would shape the field for decades to come. The contributions of Denman Waldo Ross (1853–1935) were equally important, although not as often recognized in histories of art education. Ross and Dow were similar in emphasizing formal aspects of art over narrative content, but they differed in the elements and principles of design they stressed in their theories and their approaches to teaching. Ross's theory of design was based on three central principles: balance, rhythm, and harmony. The important elements in his theory were tones (value and color), measures (size or area), and shapes. For Dow, the central elements of art were line, color, and notan (light and dark). These elements were arranged according to five principles of composition: opposition, transition, subordination, repetition, and symmetry. A general overarching principle was proportion, or good spacing.[5] Whereas Ross emphasized studying the past and a thorough preparation of students before they created original compositions, Dow emphasized originality in students' work, even the work of beginners (Green, 1999; Moffatt, 1977; Stankiewicz, 1988, 1990, 2001).

Dow's own development as an artist had been deeply influenced by the *ukiyo-e* woodcuts of Katsushika Hokusai. In his books and teaching, Dow included examples of art from both eastern and western cultures. He was not alone in his admiration for the art of nonwestern cultures. By the 1890s, many artists, along with much of the general public, had become familiar with decorative arts from around the world as a result of the Aesthetic movement.

The Aesthetic Movement

The Aesthetic movement flourished in the United States in the 1870s and 1880s. Like the Arts and Crafts movement, the Aesthetic movement had originated in Britain as a reaction to social changes that came with industrialization; however, instead of challenging the structure of capitalist work relationships, the Aesthetic movement offered a way of believing in the power of art without the kind of social critiques mounted by Ruskin, Morris, and others. The Aesthetic movement placed artistic values above ethical ones. Its central ideal was art for art's sake, a celebration of universal form and style apart from the historical, social, and moral contexts in which works of art were created or used. Although the Aesthetic movement was centered in the decorative arts, it was also apparent in arts such as painting and architecture. The Aesthetic movement reflected and helped reshape Americans' ideas about nature, religion, political economy, and gender in ways that were in keeping with an urban, industrial way of life (Stein, 1986).

In art education, Aesthetic beliefs had initially been disseminated by the South Kensington system of teaching drawing and design, brought to North America by Walter Smith. Over time, elements of both Aestheticism and the Arts and Crafts movement were combined in textbooks published by the Prang Educational Company in the late 19th and early 20th century (Stankiewicz, 1992a).

Schoolroom Decoration and Picture Study. In the 1880s and 1890s, Ruskin's belief that people's social environment shaped their taste and character became a rationale for placing reproductions of art in schoolrooms. In 1883, the Art for Schools Association was founded

---

[5]Ross's major work on design was his book *Theory of Pure Design*, published in 1907. Dow's major work was *Composition*, first published in 1899. *Composition* was one of the most influential books of all time in the field of art education. It went through twenty editions, with the last one appearing in 1941.

in Britain with Ruskin as president of the association. In the United States, the Boston Public School Art League was established in 1892. Similar organizations were soon founded in other American cities. One of the most influential was the Chicago Public School Art Society, established in 1894 with Ellen Gates Starr as its first president. In addition to developing students' character, goals of schoolroom decoration included Americanization of new immigrants, providing a more home-like atmosphere in schools, and subduing "rough boys" (Boris, 1986; Dobbs, 1972; Efland, 1990; Finley, 1992; Stankiewicz, 1992a, 2001).

The movement to decorate schools, which became a popular cause in the United States in the 1890s, soon expanded to include a systematic study of pictures as part of the art education program in schools. The picture study movement, which lasted from the mid-1890s until the 1920s, focused on appreciation of masterpieces to develop students' character and taste. Moral lessons were based on the subject matter or stories represented in images, and students were given information about the lives of the artists. In upper grades, students might also analyze formal qualities. The images used for picture study were typically black and white or sepia reproductions, created through the halftone process that had recently been perfected. Reproductions were available from the Prang Educational Company, Perry Prints, and other suppliers. Books and articles on picture study also supported the picture study movement (Stankiewicz, 1984).

Professionalization in Art Education

Textbooks, journals, and professional organizations played important roles in strengthening art education as a profession at the end of the 19th century. In the 1870s, when drawing was first introduced into many schools, most teachers were not trained to teach art; in fact, teacher preparation of any sort was still minimal, especially for teachers in the primary and grammar grades. For this reason, most teachers relied on textbooks to teach various subjects in school (Cuban, 1993).

As drawing became an established part of school curricula, textbooks for school-based instruction became available to teachers. Textbooks for schools offered progressive instruction over 12 grades, a feature that distinguished school series from the drawing books that had been popular earlier in the century. Walter Smith's books were one of the first series of textbooks developed specifically for schools. By the end of the century, however, Smith's books were eclipsed by other series published by Prang that combined a pedagogy based on students' interests with comprehensive content in constructive, representational, and decorative art. As teachers and art supervisors departed from textbook-driven methods of teaching and began to create their own art curricula, there were conflicts with textbook publishers such as Prang (Marzio, 1976; Stankiewicz, 1986, 2001).

Periodicals also played an important role in supporting new movements and keeping teachers and art supervisors informed about developments in art education. *The Perry Magazine*, published from 1898 to 1906, helped promote schoolroom decoration and picture study. J. C. Witter's journal *Art Education*, published from 1894 to 1901, covered a range of professional topics. The *School Arts Book*, first published in 1901 as the *Applied Arts Book*, is still being published today. Then as now, it was an important source of professional information for art educators. Henry Turner Bailey (1865–1931), one of the founders of the journal, served as editor of *School Arts* from 1903 to 1917. Bailey influenced the course of art education at the turn of the century and beyond through his work as editor, as well as his many books and articles on art education (Efland, 1990; MacDonald, 1997; Stankiewicz, 2001).

Professional organizations were another means by which leaders in art education helped shape the direction of the field in the 19th and early 20th centuries. In 1883 the National Educational Association established its Department of Art Education. Members of the department presented many reports on the status of American art education, including the influential report of the Committee of Ten on Elementary Art Education, completed in 1902. In 1893 two other important organizations were established: the Manual Training Teachers Association of America and the Western Drawing Teachers Association. After several evolutions in name and membership, the Manual Training Teachers Association joined forces with art teachers in eastern states and eventually became the Eastern Arts Association. Similarly, the Western Drawing Teachers Association combined with manual training teachers in the Midwest and evolved into the Western Arts Association (Efland, 1990; Jacobs & Francis, 1985; Wygant, 1997).

The Kindergarten Movement and Progressive Education

The kindergarten movement originated in the work of the German philosopher and educator Frederich Froebel (1782–1852). Seeking to reform current educational practices that were based on memorization, punishment, and discipline, Froebel designed a curriculum based on play. Educational activities in his kindergarten were structured around a series of progressive "gifts and occupations" that taught young children concepts of universal form and number (Brosterman, 1997; Efland, 1990).

Elizabeth Peabody (1804–1894) opened the first English-speaking kindergarten in the United States in 1860. The first training school for kindergarten teachers was established in St. Louis in 1873. One of the most influential centers for promoting the kindergarten and Froebelian principles was the Chicago Kindergarten Club, established in 1884 by Alice Harvey Putnam (1841–1919), one of Peabody's students, and Putnam's student Elizabeth Harrison (1849–1927). For the most part, economically privileged women were leaders of the kindergarten movement. They established privately supported kindergartens that, over time, came to be absorbed into public school systems in many cities. The role of privileged women in promoting kindergartens was similar to the role played by privileged men who established privately funded centers for manual training that eventually became part of the public school system in cities such as Chicago. Some advocates of kindergarten education claimed that young children's working with Froebelian gifts and occupations was a foundation for the kind of practical education offered by manual training in the grammar grades (Efland, 1990; Finnegan, 1997; Lazerson, 1971; Saunders, 1990; Snyder, 1972).

An emphasis on active learning and practical education was also apparent in the early stages of the progressive movement in education. Francis Wayland Parker (1837–1902) and John Dewey (1859–1952) were two of the prominent figures in progressive education in Chicago at the end of the 19th century. Instruction in art was an important part of the curriculum in the practice school affiliated with Parker's Cook County Normal School, as it was in Dewey's Laboratory School.[6] By psychologizing the value of art in students' lives, Parker and Dewey were forerunners of modernist conceptions of art education (Amburgy, 1990; Korzenik, 1992; Sidelnick, 1995).

Women's Contributions to Art Education.   Women were not only the leaders of the kindergarten movement. Through their work in other kinds of voluntary organizations, including settlement houses, arts and crafts societies, and women's clubs, they made significant contributions to many aspects of art and education in the late 19th and early 20th century.

---

[6]Parker's views on education were published in his *Talks on Pedagogics* in 1894. Dewey's major works on education at the turn of the century include *The School and Society*, published in 1899, and *The Child and the Curriculum*, published in 1902. *Schools of Tomorrow*, written with his daughter Evelyn Dewey, was published in 1915. Dewey's major philosophical treatise on education, *Democracy and Education*, was published in 1916.

Although much of the written history of 19th-century art education has focused on the ideas and accomplishments of men, feminine accomplishments in the form of ornamental education helped lay a foundation for art in public schools. Beliefs that women are naturally suited to teach the young led to the reality that most K-12 art teachers have been women, contributing to a lower status for art in society. The role of women in art education remains a site for critical historical research (Blair, 1994; Boris, 1986; Finley, 1992; Stankiewicz, 1989, 2001; Stein, 1986).

HOW DID ART EDUCATION IN THE EARLY 20TH CENTURY DIFFER FROM ART EDUCATION A CENTURY EARLIER?

By the beginning of the 20th century, art educators had developed a professional self-consciousness that set them apart from classroom teachers and from artists. The early histories of art education written by Clarke (1885) and Bailey (1893, 1900) located art education in formal, often publicly funded, institutions for education, ignoring the varied mixture of informal and formal delivery systems found at the beginning of the century. Art education was located in the political context of northeastern industrial expansion and the cultural context of European academic art traditions. Art educators themselves, civic leaders and capitalists, philanthropists and politicians, were drawn as the chief stakeholders, though women were active in the background actually delivering art instruction. Walter Smith was the great man centering the composition, while systematic art education for schoolchildren, industrial workers, and teachers radiated outward from his position as expert. Stacks of sequential drawing books in the corners of the canvas bore the imprint of publishers rather than artist–authors and were designated for schools rather than individuals, families, and schools.

By the end of the 19th century, art education had become both a reflection of cultural hierarchy and a means of reproducing that hierarchy (Levine, 1988). The rhetoric focused on social control of the masses through art, with little more than lip service to Franklin's belief in upward mobility through art education. The aesthetic didacticism that had argued for beneficial connections between art and life was being displaced by aesthetic distance, formal design, and the isolation of art from life. The rich, if sometimes overwhelming, range of motives found at the beginning of the century was replaced by advocacy for art as a tasteful retreat from pressures of modern life (Stankiewicz, 1997). On the other hand, art educators were committed to bridging the gap between art and life. Growing recognition that children's drawings served different functions than adult art-making resonated with earlier beliefs that art contributed to intellectual as well as emotional growth. In kindergartens, museums, and settlement houses, as well as in many schools, young people were introduced to visual art as one element for improving life.

WHAT ARE SOME CRUCIAL QUESTIONS AND TOPICS FOR FUTURE HISTORICAL RESEARCH?

In spite of the number of publications relevant to the history of 19th century art education produced during the past 3 decades, more research can be done. A number of the strongest dissertations in this area have not been followed by more accessible articles or books. Many of the most provocative sources have been researched and written by non-art educators. More than other research methods, historical research benefits from interdisciplinarity. The references for this chapter include sources from art history; history of education; social, cultural, and economic history; gender and ethnic studies, as well as American studies. These secondary sources can fund more comprehensive interpretations of primary source material or be mined for suggestive topics.

What kinds of art education existed in venture schools, seminaries, and academies early in the 19th century? Who sought this kind of art instruction and why? How were drawing books actually used and what did one learn from them? How did systematic art education develop in cities other than Boston? What were the relationships among art museums, schools of art and design, and public school art programs? How have publishers of textbooks and reproductions supported or constrained art teaching? What forms of art education were available to First People nations, African Americans, and immigrants? What roles have institutions for adult education, such as Chautauquas and correspondence schools, played in general art education? What impacts did world's fairs and similar cultural expositions have on dissemination of ideas in art education? How was 19th century art education affected by technological and cultural changes that contributed to the emergence of popular and visual culture?

More detailed, personalized studies based on archival research are needed to address these and other questions. At the same time, art education history is entering a state where larger syntheses and cross-cultural comparisons can begin to be done. We are just beginning to move beyond the halcyon days of Walter Smith and into the scarcely charted waters, both calm and crashing, which will help us better understand how art educators and art education have come to be as they are.

REFERENCES

Adams, D. W. (1995). *Education for extinction: American Indians and the boarding school experience, 1875–1928.* Lawrence: University Press of Kansas.

Alexander, E. P. (1983). *Museum masters: Their museums and their influence.* Nashville, TN: The American Association for State and Local History.

Alexander, E. P. (1987). Early American museums from collections of curiosities to popular education. *The International Journal of Museum Management and Curatorship, 6,* 337–351.

Amburgy, P. M. (1990). Culture for the masses: Art education and progressive reforms, 1880–1917. In D. Soucy & M. A. Stankiewicz (Eds.), *Framing the past: Essays on art education* (pp. 103–114). Reston, VA: National Art Education Association.

Amburgy, P. M. (1997). Arts and crafts education in Chicago, 1890–1920. In A. A. Anderson, Jr., & P. E. Bolin (Eds.), *History of art education: Proceedings of the Third Penn State International Symposium* (pp. 384–388). University Park, PA: Pennsylvania State University.

Anderson, A. A., Jr. (1997). Charles Godfrey Leland: Pioneer crafts educator. In A. A. Anderson, Jr., & P. E. Bolin (Eds.), *History of art education: Proceedings of the Third Penn State International Symposium* (pp. 367–373). University Park, PA: Pennsylvania State University.

Anderson, J. D. (1988). *The education of Blacks in the south, 1860–1935.* Chapel Hill, NC, and London: University of North Carolina Press.

Andrus, L. F. (1977). *Measure and design in American painting, 1760–1860.* New York: Garland.

Axelrod, P. (1997). *The promise of schooling: Education in Canada, 1800–1914.* Toronto: University of Toronto Press.

Bailey, H. T. (1893). *Industrial drawing in the public schools of Massachusetts: A sketch of its history.* Henry Turner Bailey Papers, Box 13. Special Collections, University of Oregon Libraries, Eugene, Oregon.

Bailey, H. T. (1900). *A sketch of the history of public art instruction in Massachusetts.* Boston: Wright & Potter.

Baker, D. W. (1985). J. Liberty Tadd, who are you? *Studies in Art Education, 26,* 75–85.

Barnhill, G. B., Korzenik, D., & Sloat, C. F. (Eds.). (1997). *The cultivation of artists in 19th-century America.* Worcester, MA: American Antiquarian Society.

Belshe, F. B. (1946). *A history of art education in the public schools of the United States.* Unpublished doctoral dissertation, Yale University.

Bennett, C. A. (1926). *History of manual and industrial education up to 1870.* Peoria, IL: Author.

Bermingham, A. (2000). *Learning to draw: Studies in the cultural history of a polite and useful art.* New Haven: Yale University Press, published for the Paul Mellon Centre for Studies in British Art.

Billings, K. L. (1987). *Sophisticated proselytizing: Charles Callahan Perkins and the Boston School Committee.* Unpublished master's thesis. Massachusetts College of Art, Boston.

Blair, K. J. (1994). *The torchbearers: Women and their amateur arts associations in America, 1890–1930*. Bloomington: Indiana University Press.

Bolger, D. (1976). The education of the American artist. In *In this academy: The Pennsylvania Academy of the Fine Arts, 1805–1876: A special bicentennial exhibition organized by the Pennsylvania Academy of the Fine Arts.* (pp. 51–74). Philadelphia: Pennsylvania Academy of the Fine Arts.

Bolin, P. E. (1985). The influence of industrial policy on enactment of the 1870 Massachusetts Free Instruction in Drawing Act. In B. Wilson & H. Hoffa (Eds.), *History of art education: Proceedings of the Penn State Conference* (pp. 102–107). Reston, VA: National Art Education Association.

Bolin, P. E. (1986). Drawing interpretation: An examination of the 1870 Massachusetts, "Act Relating to Free Instruction in Drawing." *Dissertation Abstracts International, 47,* 2425A.

Bolin, P. E. (1990). The Massachusetts Drawing Act of 1870: Industrial mandate or democratic maneuver? In D. Soucy & M. A. Stankiewicz (Eds.), *Framing the past: Essays on art education* (pp. 59–68). Reston, VA: National Art Education Association.

Bolin, P. E. (1995). Overlooked and obscured through history: The legislative bill proposed to amend the Massachusetts Drawing Act of 1870. *Studies in Art Education, 37*(1), 55–64.

Bolin, P. E. (1997). The "National Peace Jubilee and Musical Festival," June 1869: Historical context for the petitioners of drawing education. In A. A. Anderson, Jr., & P. E. Bolin (Eds.), *History of art education: Proceedings of the Third Penn State International Symposium* (pp. 347–354). University Park, PA: Art Education Program, School of Visual Arts.

Boris, E. (1986). *Art and labor: Ruskin, Morris, and the craftsman ideal in America.* Philadelphia: Temple University Press.

Briggs, P. S. (1995). *The influence of Unitarianism on the inclusion of art education in the common schools of Massachusetts, 1825–1870.* Unpublished doctoral dissertation, The Pennsylvania State University, University Park.

Brosterman, N. (1997). *Inventing kindergarten.* New York: Harry N. Abrams.

Burns, S. (1996). *Inventing the modern artist.* New Haven: Yale University Press.

Bushman, R. L. (1992). *The refinement of America: Persons, houses, cities.* New York: Vintage Books.

Chalmers, F. G. (1985a). South Kensington and the colonies: David Blair of New Zealand and Canada. *Studies in Art Education, 26*(2), 69–74.

Chalmers, F. G. (1985b). South Kensington and the colonies II: The influence of Walter Smith in Canada. In B. Wilson & H. Hoffa (Eds.), *History of art education: Proceedings of the Penn State Conference* (pp. 108–112). Reston, VA: National Art Education Association.

Chalmers, F. G. (1990). South Kensington in the farthest colony. In D. Soucy & M. A. Stankiewicz (Eds.), *Framing the past: Essays on art education* (pp. 71–85). Reston, VA: National Art Education Association.

Chalmers, F. G. (1998a). Teaching drawing in 19th-century Canada—Why? In K. Freedman & F. Hernández (Eds.), *Curriculum, culture, and art education: Comparative perspectives* (pp. 47–58). Albany: State University of New York Press.

Chalmers, F. G. (1998b). *Women in the 19th-century art world: Schools of art and design for women in London and Philadelphia.* Westport, CT: Greenwood Press.

Chalmers, F. G. (2000a). *A 19th century government drawing master: The Walter Smith reader.* Reston, VA: National Art Education Association.

Chalmers, F. G. (2000b). Art education in "Indian" residential schools in British Columbia. *Canadian Review of Art Education, 27,* 21–35.

Clarke, I. E. (1885). *Art and industry* (Vol. 1) (Senate Ex. Doc. No. 209). Washington, DC: Government Printing Office.

Coleman, M. C. (1993). *American Indian children at school, 1850–1930.* Jackson: University Press of Mississippi.

Commissioner of Education. (1882). *Report of the Commissioner of Education for the year 1880.* Washington, DC: Government Printing Office.

Cooke, E. S., Jr. (1997). Talking or working: The conundrum of moral aesthetics in Boston's arts and crafts movement. In *Inspiring reform: Boston's arts and crafts movement* (pp. 17–31). Wellesley, MA: Davis Museum and Cultural Center, Wellesley College; New York: distributed by Harry N. Abrams.

Cott. N. F. (1977). *The bonds of womanhood: Woman's sphere in New England, 1780–1835.* New Haven: Yale University Press.

Cremin, L. (1961). *The transformation of the school: Progressivism in American education, 1876–1957.* New York: Alfred A. Knopf.

Cremin, L. A. (1980). *American education: The national experience, 1783–1876.* New York: Harper & Row.

Cuban, L. (1993). *How teachers taught: Constancy and change in American classrooms 1880–1990* (2nd ed.). New York: Teachers College Press.

Cubberley, E. P. (1934). *Public education in the United States: A study and interpretation of American educational history.* Boston: Houghton Mifflin.

Davis, E. B. (1992). Training the eye and the hand: Drawing books in 19th-century America (Doctoral Dissertation, Columbia University). *Dissertation Abstracts International* (Order Number 9313576).

Davis, E. B. (1996). American drawing books and their impact on Winslow Homer. *Winterthur Portfolio, 31*(2/3), 141–163.

Dean, M. S. (1923/1924). *A brief history of the Massachusetts Normal Art School 1873 to 1923–'24*. Boston: Massachusetts Normal Art School.

de Angeli Walls, N. (1993). *Art, industry, and women's education: The Philadelphia School of Design for Women, 1848–1932*. Unpublished doctoral dissertation, University of Delaware.

de Angeli Walls, N. (1994). Educating women for art and commerce: The Philadelphia School of Art and Design, 1848-1932. *History of Education Quarterly, 34*(3), 329–355.

Dobbs, S. M. (1972). Attic temples and beauty nooks: The schoolroom decoration movement. *Intellect, 101*, 43–45.

Douglas, A. (1977). *The feminization of American culture*. New York: Avon Books.

Efland, A. D. (1983). School art and its social origins. *Studies in Art Education, 24*(3), 149–157.

Efland, A. D. (1985a). Art and education for women in 19th century Boston. *Studies in Art Education, 26*(3), 133–40.

Efland, A. D. (1985b). The introduction of music and drawing in the Boston schools: Two studies of educational reform. In B. Wilson & H. Hoffa (Eds.), *History of art education: Proceedings of the Penn State Conference* (pp. 113–124). Reston, VA: National Art Education Association.

Efland, A. D. (1990). *A history of art education: Intellectual and social currents in teaching the visual arts*. New York: Teachers College Press.

Efland, A. D., & Soucy, D. (1991). A persistent interpretation: Education historiography and the legacy of Isaac Edwards Clarke. *History of Education Quarterly, 31*(4), 489–511.

Eisner, E. W. (1972). *Educating artistic vision*. New York: Macmillan.

Eisner, E. W., & Ecker, D. W. (1966). *Readings in art education*. Waltham, MA: Blaisdell Publishing Company.

Fahlman, B. (1997). *John Ferguson Weir: The labor of art*. Newark: University of Delaware Press.

Fane, D. (Ed.). (1996). *Converging cultures: Art & identity in Spanish America*. New York: The Brooklyn Museum in association with Harry N. Abrams, Inc.

Finley, K. D. (1992). Cultural monitors: Clubwomen and public art instruction in Chicago, 1890–1920. In P. M. Amburgy, D. Soucy, M. A. Stankiewicz, B. Wilson, & M. Wilson (Eds.), *History of art education: Proceedings of the Second Penn State Conference, 1989* (pp. 252–258). Reston, VA: National Art Education Association.

Finnegan, J. E. (1997). Elizabeth Harrison and the kindergarten: Art education as social reform. In A. A. Anderson, Jr., & P. E. Bolin (Eds.), *History of art education: Proceedings of the Third Penn State International Symposium* (pp. 113–119). University Park, PA: Pennsylvania State University.

Fisher, B. (1967). *Industrial education: American ideals and institutions*. Madison: University of Wisconsin Press.

Flynt, S. L. (1988). *Ornamental and useful accomplishments: Schoolgirl education and Deerfield Academy 1800–1830*. Deerfield, MA: Pocumtuck Valley Memorial Association and Deerfield Academy.

Green, H. B. (1948). *The introduction of art as a general education subject in American Schools*. Unpublished doctoral dissertation, Stanford University.

Green, H. B. (1966). Walter Smith: The forgotten man. *Art Education, 19*(1), 3–9.

Green, N. E. (1999). Arthur Wesley Dow: American arts & crafts. *American Art Review, 11*, 214–221.

Hail, B. A. (1987). Traditional Native American art of the plains and northern woodlands. In G. C. Schwartz, *Patterns of life, patterns of art* (pp. 9–22). Hanover, NH: University Press of New England.

Haney, J. P. (Ed.). (1908). *Art education in the public schools of the United States*. New York: American Art Annual.

Harris, J. C. (1976). *Collegiate collections 1776–1876*. South Hadley, MA: Mount Holyoke College.

Harris, N. (1962). The gilded age revisited: Boston and the museum movement. *American Quarterly, 14*, 545–566.

Harris, N. (1982). *The artist in American society*. Chicago: University of Chicago Press.

Jacobs, R., & Francis, B. D. (1985). Ninety years of the Western Arts Association. *Art Education, 38*(4), 32–35, 37.

Johns, E. (1980). Drawing instruction at Central High School and its impact on Thomas Eakins. *Winterthur Portfolio, 15*(Summer), 139–147.

Kaplan, W. (1987). *"The art that is life": The arts and crafts movement in America, 1875–1920*. Boston: Little, Brown.

Kessler-Harris, A. (1982). *Out to work: A history of wage-earning women in the United States* (especially pp. 171–179). New York: Oxford University Press.

Kliebard, H. M. (1999). *Schooled to work: Vocationalism and the American curriculum, 1876–1946*. New York: Teachers College Press.

Korzenik, D. (1985). *Drawn to art: A 19th-century American dream*. Hanover, NH: University Press of New England.

Korzenik, D. (1992). Foreign ideas for American originals: Francis Wayland Parker. In D. Thistlewood (Ed.), *Histories of art and design: Cole to Coldstream* (pp. 38–54). Harlow, Essex, England: Longman, National Society for Education in Art and Design.

Korzenik, D. (1999, March). Becoming an art teacher c. 1800. *Art Education, 52*(2), 6–13.

Lazerson, M. (1971). *Origins of the urban school: Public education in Massachusetts, 1870–1915.* Cambridge, MA: Harvard University Press.

Lears, T. J. J. (1981). *No place of grace: Antimodernism and the transformation of American culture, 1880–1920.* New York: Pantheon Books.

Levine, L. W. (1988). *Highbrow/lowbrow: The emergence of cultural hierarchy in America.* Cambridge, MA: Harvard University Press.

MacDonald, B. L. (1997). *The Perry Magazine for School and Home* (1898–1906): An analysis of its historical location within the schoolroom decoration and picture study movement. In A. A. Anderson, Jr., & P. E. Bolin (Eds.), *History of art education: Proceedings of the Third Penn State International Symposium* (pp. 404–420). University Park, PA: Pennsylvania State University.

Martinez, K., & Talbott, P. (Eds.). (2000). *Philadelphia's cultural landscape: The Sartain family legacy.* Philadelphia: Temple University Press.

Marzio, P. C. (1976). *The art crusade: An analysis of American drawing manuals, 1820–1860.* Washington: Smithsonian Institution Press.

Marzio, P. C. (1979). *The democratic art.* Boston: David R. Godine, Published in association with the Amon Carter Museum of Western Art, Fort Worth.

McVitty, L. F. (1934). *The rise of art education in the United States.* Unpublished master's thesis, University of Pittsburgh, Pennsylvania.

Metropolitan Museum of Art. (1990). *Mexico: Splendors of thirty centuries.* New York Author.

Miller, J. R. (1996). *Shingwauk's vision: A history of Native residential schools.* Toronto: University of Toronto Press.

Miller, L. B. (1966). *Patrons and patriotism: The encouragement of the fine arts in the United States, 1790–1860.* Chicago: University of Chicago Press.

Moffatt, F. C. (1977). *Arthur Wesley Dow (1857–1922).* Washington: Smithsonian Institution Press.

Parker, Rozsika. (1984). *The subversive stitch: Embroidery and the making of the feminine.* New York: Routledge.

Powers, J. B. (1992). *The "girl question" in education: Vocational education for young women in the progressive era.* London/Washington, DC: Falmer Press.

Ring, B. (1983). *Let virtue be a guide to thee: Needlework in the education of Rhode Island women, 1730–1830.* Providence: Rhode Island Historical Society.

Rury, J. L. (1991). *Education and women's work: Female schooling and the division of labor in urban America, 1870–1930.* Albany: State University of New York Press.

Saunders, R. J. (1976). Art, industrial art, and the 200 years war. *Art Education, 29*(1), 5–8.

Saunders, R. J. (1990). Elizabeth P. Peabody's quest for art in moral education. In D. Soucy & M. A. Stankiewicz (Eds.), *Framing the past: Essays on art education* (pp. 35–45). Reston, VA: National Art Education Association.

Secretary of the Commonwealth. (1870). *Acts and resolves passed by the General Court of Massachusetts, in the year 1870.* Boston: Wright & Potter, State Printer.

Sheath, N. C. C. (1982). *Some events in the life of Walter Smith.* No location: Author.

Sidelnick, M. (1995). Colonel Francis Wayland Parker: Legacy of an artist-teacher. *Art Education, 48*(6), 18–22.

Smith, P. (1992). A troublesome comedy: The causes of Walter Smith's dismissal. In P. M. Amburgy, D. Soucy, M. A. Stankiewicz, B. Wilson, & M. Wilson (Eds.), *History of art education: Proceedings of the Second Penn State Conference, 1989* (pp. 269–273). Reston, VA: National Art Education Association.

Smith, P. (1996). *The history of American art education: Learning about art in American schools.* Westport, CT: Greenwood Press.

Smyth, C. H., & Lukehart, P. N. (Eds.). (1993). *The early years of art history in the United States.* Princeton, NJ: Department of Art History and Archaeology, Princeton University.

Snyder, A. (1972). *Dauntless women in childhood education 1856–1931.* Washington, DC: Association for Childhood Education International.

Spring, J. (2001). *The American school 1642–2000* (5th ed.). Boston: McGraw-Hill.

Soucy, D. (1990). A history of art education histories. In D. Soucy & M. A. Stankiewicz (Eds.), *Framing the past: Essays on art education* (pp. 3–31). Reston, VA: National Art Education Association.

Stamp, R. M. (1970). Evolving patterns of education: English-Canada from the 1870s to 1914. In J. D. Wilson, R. M. Stamp, & L.-P. Audet (Eds.), *Canadian education: A history* (pp. 314–336). Scarborough, ON: Prentice-Hall.

Stankiewicz, M. A. (1984). "The eye is a nobler organ": Ruskin and American art education. *Journal of Aesthetic Education, 18*(2), 51–64.

Stankiewicz, M. A. (1985). A picture age: Reproductions in picture study. *Studies in Art Education, 26,* 86–92.

Stankiewicz, M. A. (1986). Drawing book wars. *Visual Arts Research, 12*(2), 59–72.

Stankiewicz, M. A. (1988). Form, truth, and emotion: Transatlantic influences on formalist aesthetics. *Journal of Art and Design Education, 7,* 81–95.

Stankiewicz, M. A. (1989). Art at Hull House, 1889–1901: Jane Addams and Ellen Gates Starr. *Woman's Art Journal, 10,* 35–39.

Stankiewicz, M. A. (1990). Rules and invention: From ornament to design in art education. In D. Soucy & M. A. Stankiewicz (Eds.), *Framing the past: Essays on art education* (pp. 89–101). Reston, VA: National Art Education Association.

Stankiewicz, M. A. (1992a). Barbarian or civilised: Ellen Gates Starr, T. C. Horsfall and the Chicago Public School Art Society. In D. Thistlewood (Ed.), *Histories of art and design: Cole to Coldstream* (pp. 55–68). Harlow, Essex, England: Longman, National Society for Education in Art and Design.

Stankiewicz, M. A. (1992b). From the aesthetic movement to the arts and crafts movement. *Studies in Art Education, 33*, 165–173.

Stankiewicz, M. A. (1997). The celestial city of culture: Henry Turner Bailey's "City of Refuge." In A. A. Anderson, Jr., & P. E. Bolin (Eds.), *History of art education: Proceedings of the Third Penn State International Symposium* (pp.427–433). University Park, PA: Pennsylvania State University.

Stankiewicz, M. A. (1999). Chromo-civilization and the genteel tradition (An essay on the social value of art education). *Studies in Art Education, 40*(2), 101–113.

Stankiewicz, M. A. (2000). Embodied conceptions and refined taste: Drawing enters the Lowell schools. *Visual Arts Research, 26*(2), 1–14.

Stankiewicz, Mary Ann (2001). *Roots of art education practice*. Worcester, MA: Davis Publications.

Stein, R. B. (1986). Artifact as ideology: The aesthetic movement in its American cultural context. In D. B. Burke, *In pursuit of beauty* (pp. 23–51). New York: Metropolitan Museum of Art.

Stevens, E. W., Jr. (1995). *The grammar of the machine: Technical literacy and early industrial expansion in the United States*. New Haven: Yale University Press.

Stirling, J. C. (1997). The politics of drawing: Theory into practice: Walter Smith's influence in post-secondary Quebec industrial art schools, 1876–91. In A. A. Anderson, Jr., & P. E. Bolin (Eds.), *History of art education: Proceedings of the Third Penn State International Symposium* (pp. 355–366). University Park, PA: Art Education Program, School of Visual Arts.

Storr, A. V. F. (1992). *Ut pictura rhetorica: The oratory of the visual arts in the early republic and the formation of American cultural values, 1790–1840*. Unpublished doctoral dissertation, University of Delaware.

Strazdes, D. (1979). The amateur aesthetic and the draughtsman in early America. *Archives of American Art Journal, 19*(1), 15–23.

Thirty-fourth annual report of the Massachusetts Board of Education. (1871). Boston: Wright & Potter, State Printers.

Thornton, T. P. (1996). *Handwriting in America: A cultural history*. New Haven: Yale.

Titley, E. B. (1986). Indian industrial schools in western Canada. In N. M. Sheehan, J. D. Wilson, & D. C. Jones (Eds.), *Schools in the west: Essays in Canadian educational history* (pp. 133–153). Calgary: Detselig Enterprises Limited.

Tompkins, C. (1973). *Merchants and masterpieces*. New York: E. P. Dutton & Co.

Tyack, D., & Hansot, E. (1990). *Learning together: A history of coeducation in American schools*. New Haven: Yale University Press.

Vlach, J. M. (1988). *Plain painters: Making sense of American folk art*. Washington, DC: Smithsonian Institution Press.

Waller, B. (1992). Aping their betters: Art appreciation and social class. In P. M. Amburgy, D. Soucy, M. A. Stankiewicz, B. Wilson, & M. Wilson (Eds.), *History of art education: Proceedings of the Second Penn State Conference, 1989* (pp. 16–27). Reston, VA: National Art Education Association.

Winkelman, R. J. (1990). *Art education in the non-public schools of Pennsylvania, 1720–1870*. Unpublished doctoral dissertation, The Pennsylvania State University.

Wood, B. A., & Soucy, D. (1990). From old to new Scotland: 19th century links between morality and art education. In D. Soucy & M. A. Stankiewicz (Eds.), *Framing the past: Essays on art education* (pp. 47–56). Reston, VA: National Art Education Association.

Woolworth, Ainsworth, and Company. (1873). *Drawing in the public schools. A brief history of its origin and progress*. New York: Author.

Wygant, F. (1983). *Art in American schools in the 19th century*. Cincinnati: Interwood Press.

Wygant, F. (1993). *School art in American culture 1820–1970*. Cincinnati: Interwood Press.

Wygant, F. (1997). The N.E.A. Committee of 10: The good, the true, and the beautiful. In A. A. Anderson, Jr., & P. E. Bolin (Eds.), *History of art education: Proceedings of the Third Penn State International Symposium* (pp. 389–396). University Park, PA: Pennsylvania State University.

Zeller, T. (1989). The historical and philosophical foundations of art museum education in America. In S. Mayer & N. Berry (Eds.), *Museum education: History, theory, and practice* (pp. 10–89). Reston, VA: National Art Education Association.

3

20th-Century Art Education: A Historical Perspective

John Howell White
Kutztown University

IMAGING THE MODERN HOMELAND

In the previous chapter, Bolin, Amburgy, and Stankiewicz show that by the end of the second decade of the 20th century the central conditions for today's art education had been established. This feat included the framing of the field under the general term "Art Education" in 1914 by Royal Bailey Farnum (Plummer, 1985). By the end of the First World War, North American culture and U.S. art educators were on parallel courses, establishing mature cultural identities while healing wounds caused by war, technology, and social change. Citizens were conflicted over allegiances to European cultural roots and their independent aspirations, which were grounded in multiple experiences of life in North America (Committee on the Function of Art in General Education, 1940; White, 2001). The influx of immigrants, which had precipitated education's earlier Americanization emphasis, had been severely restricted as a result of postwar isolationism. European Modernism had a tenuous grasp on North American aesthetics. Despite the opening of Alfred Stieglitz's Gallery 291 and the International Exhibition of Modern Art (Armory Show, 1913), it would take until after the Second World War to fully immerse American culture in Modernist ideals. Along the way, Albert Barnes' Foundation began in 1922, the periodical, *Creative Art,* was published in 1927, the Mexican Muralists entered the New York scene in the late 1920s, and the Museum of Modern Art opened in 1929. It should not be surprising then that Modern Art, as an object of study, was slow to reach North American classrooms. Still, Modernism in the larger sense, as a way to envision change based on action, universal principles, and individual experience, was perfectly aligned with American Pragmatic philosophy (Moore, 1997; White, 1998). That philosophy, which associates inquiry with embodied responses to a changing world, provides a framework through which art education found a place in schooling (Freedman & Popkewitz, 1985).

Healing Hands

At the end of the 19th and beginning of the 20th centuries, educators and anthropologists alike were interested in the role of the human hand in both individual and cultural development.

Handwork and crafts were considered developmentally important in that (a) the hand was the earliest tool through which thinking was organized and by extension (b) that technologies and tools, as the extension of hands, were seen to influence and structure people and cultures.

A belief in craft as a healing agent was applied to people, homes, communities, and industry. Handicrafts, pressed into the service of social work, were used as occupational, emotional, and social therapies to promote the well-being of children who were disabled, orphaned, or wayward (Koch, 1924, 1927a, 1927b; Levitas, 1920; McMahon, 1928; Pasto, 1967). For soldiers returned from World War I, with a significant sense of physical, mental, and social displacement, handicrafts provided therapeutic benefits. In locations throughout the country, handicrafts were pressed into service to rehabilitate soldiers injured and traumatized by both world wars (Duveneck, 1921; Green, 1948; Kilgore, 1922; Koch, 1921, 1923; Morris, 1920).

The war also highlighted the role of industrial arts and design in healing the economy. The effects of the submarine blockades of shipping from Europe had focused North American attention on its industrial products. The Art Alliance of America held an exhibition at this time of machine made textiles, perhaps the first example of machine-made products being displayed as art (Bement, 1941). Returning soldiers in turn highlighted the needs of late adolescents and adults to obtain skills needed in industry. A growing interest in Industrial Arts, thanks in part to the federal Smith–Hughes Act of 1917 and an increased awareness of the education needs of both industry and adults, influenced art educators to develop programs that were directly related to the common objects of everyday life.

A civic agenda for art, which had roots in the City Beautiful Movement promoted by women's clubs and other civic organizations, was accelerated by war, technology, industry, the depression, and a widening awareness of rural conditions. Crafting artworks provided community and civic awareness. In the 1920s, community organizations like the American Legion initiated Art Weeks, first in Philadelphia and elsewhere in Pennsylvania, which spread across the country (Grattan, 1925; Ludwick, 1930; Mechlin, 1925). In classrooms, lessons pertaining to Holiday Art, pageantry, and celebration and festivals provided links to community values and everyday life. Teachers attended a growing cottage industry of summer schools in New England, California, Chicago, and New York or joined sketch clubs, like Philadelphia's Fleischer Memorial, where people gathered to develop their drawing skills. Crafting artworks provided a sense of community and a civic infrastructure (Gluck, 2000).

Crafts were incorporated into public school drawing through Manual Training, Industrial Arts, and Applied Arts programs. Their inclusion was influenced by concerns related to industry, social management, and theories of child and race (Amburgy, 1990; Efland, 1990a, 1990b; Stankiewicz, 2001; Wygant, 1993). Hammock and Hammock's (1906) textbook reflects the common practice including craft with drawing and design as a significant domain for art educators. *School Arts Magazine* (originally, 1901, The *Applied Arts Book*) editors, Fred Daniels, Henry Turner Bailey, Anna Lorette Cobb, and Pedro deLemos focused on Drawing and Painting, Design, and Handcrafts. Monthly thematic issues were related to each of these areas. Lemos' work, which clearly stressed crafts traditions, was disseminated nationally through textbooks, *Applied Art: Drawing, Painting, Design, and Handicraft* (1920), *The Art Teacher* (1934), and a wide range of instructional portfolios.

University educators Frederick Bonser of Teachers College and Charles Bennett of Bradley University in Peoria, Illinois were instrumental in the promotion of Manual and Industrial Arts through program development and publications (Bennett, 1917, 1934, 1937; Welling, 1935). The first PhD (1914) granted from Teachers College in a field of study associated with art education was in Industrial Arts (Burton, 2001a). At the University of Missouri, Ella Victoria Dobbs established an Applied Arts Department, which included education methods courses in art and handwork. Verna Wulfekammer carried Dobbs' work forward and developed a vibrant weaving program (McNeill, 1992, 2001). In *Illustrative Handwork for Elementary School*

Teachers, Dobbs (1920) provides explicit directions for grade school teachers to use drawing and physical activity, such as work at the sand table, bookmaking, illustration, and mapmaking, to integrate knowledge through physical activity (McNeill, 1992). Dobbs' book relates handwork to a more general cultural interest of progressive educators in the organization of curricula around themes, which were understood through the grouping of associated activities. This approach parallels work by the Activity Movement at Teachers College, which emphasized action-in-the-world and handwork as a cross-disciplinary method of inquiry (Whipple, 1934).

The shift from Manual Arts to Industrial Arts marks a shift from the handmade to the designed environment. Designers from Europe were attracted by American wages in the late 1920s; and in the depression, the significance of the "everyday," including everyday objects, became important. The Metropolitan Museum of Art (MET) began mounting exhibitions of Industrial Art in 1918 (Bach, 1927). In 1929, The Association of Art and Industries held the first Exhibition of Modern American Decorative Art in Chicago. Industrial arts programs, initially associated with training for specific industries, came to be more broadly associated with design, aesthetics, and consumerism (Cheney & Cheney, 1941; Stankiewicz, 1990; Freedman, 1989).

Industrial Arts, which was primarily for young boys, dealing as it did with work outside of the home, in the world, and with machines, formalized a gender split already operational in Manual Arts programs (Stankiewicz, 2001). The Household Art Movement, an integrated program that drew from science, sociology, and art, was targeted for girls (Goldstein & Goldstein, 1926). It specialized in home products such as handmade clothing, interior design, and handicrafts. Anna Cooley headed the Department of Household Arts at Teachers College (Smith, 1996a). The Art Institute of Chicago utilized the Better Homes Institute of its Extension Department to provide programming to create an awareness of aesthetics in everyday life (Zeller, 1989). In-school art programs, Household Arts, were connected with Everyday Art. The American Crayon Company, working with Bonnie Snow and Hugo Froehlich, published *Everyday Art* (1922–1974). Snow and Froehlich had developed a substantial following through their summer school work with Louis Prang and the publication of their 8-volume series, *Industrial Arts Textbooks* (Everyday Art, 1925; Katter, 1985; Snow & Froehlich, 1916, 1919) These two movements, although not formalized as strongly in academic settings, exerted an enormous influence on art teachers, who sought ways to connect with progressive ideas.

Household Arts and Everyday Art were seen by many educators as a means to reestablish the integrity of the American home. During the depression, art teachers commonly used everyday materials associated with these movements (Efland, 1983b; Stephenson, 1997). They also were seen as a way to reconnect Americans with their cultures of origin. In Baltimore, the "Homelands Exhibition" provided a display of the household arts of local immigrants (Karr, Winslow & Kirby, 1933). In *School Arts Magazine* volumes in the 1920s and 1930s were devoted to Americana themes like "Home," "Sunny South," "Pennsylvania," "Rural," "Our Country," "Home & Garden," "City and Town," "Farm," "Community Life," and folk traditions from other places like "Other Lands," "Orient," "Art Abroad," "Spain," "Czechoslovakia," and "Mexico." Lemos connected folk arts with an emerging interest in home, community, and daily life. The paradigmatic example of this was the reverence, perhaps misplaced, in which art educators, Modern artists, and American culture held Southwestern Native American art. Their art was romantically seen as a pure example of a successful integration of art with community life (Bernstein & Rushing, 1995; Brody, 1971, 1997; Eldridge, 2000; Hyer, 1990; Smith, 1999; Stokrocki, 2000; White, 1997, 2001a, 2001b; Zastrow, 1982, 1985).

The opportunity presented by these developments was not wasted on the entrepreneurial initiatives of American business. Commercial ventures were eager to capitalize on and to promote art education. *School Arts Magazine's* first advertisement (1905) was for Binney and Smith's Crayola Crayons. Although advertisements in 1907 were balanced among materials, art reproductions, and art services such as summer schools, by 1920, consumable art supplies dominated the advertising sections. Commercial interests were not only promoted through advertisements but also through rich networks of commercial people and teachers. At a Western Arts Association meeting in 1923, William H. Milliken of Binney and Smith and other "commercial men" formed "the Ship" (1923), an organization for suppliers of art materials to communicated with and influenced art education associations (Farnum, 1960). Art educators and commercial men often formed comfortable working relationships (Gregory, 1982). By the end of World War I, art education's use of prepared instructional materials and supplies associated with handicrafts had been clearly established.

Designing an Image

Accompanying the democratic emphasis on learning by doing, scientists, artists, and educators alike searched for underlying principles that could guide all people to frame the moral, aesthetic, and instrumental aspects of their inquiry. Structural approaches to art making were prefigured in the work of postimpressionists and color theorists. In art education, Arthur Wesley Dow, Denman Ross, and Jay Hambridge in the United States, Aldolfo Best-Maugard in Mexico, and William Weston in Canada influenced a shift in studio instruction from imitating historic ornament to establishing principles of design (Brenner, 1929; McWhinnie, 1985; Rogers, 1984, 1990; Stankiewicz, 1990; Wygant, 1985). Design promised the democratization of beauty, even though it was accomplished through the abstraction of visual experience into intellectual categories though language.

At Teacher's College, Belle Boas carried Dow's work into the schools through her own teaching of preservice students, her influential textbook, *Art in the Schools* (1924), and her editorial oversight of *Art Education Today* (1935–1952). Boas used design foundations in the first two chapters of her text, after which she moved toward a more progressive methodology emphasizing the child's interests and imagination (Boas, 1924, Smith, 1996a; Wygant, 1993; Zimmerman, 1982). A move away from Dow's ideas can be seen in Cleveland, Ohio, art supervisor Margaret Mathias' *The Beginnings of Art in the Public Schools* (1924). Mathias shifts the emphasis by relegating design principles to the end of the text, following a chapter on classroom arrangement. Her primary focus is first on the child's world and second on different materials (Mathias, 1929; Wygant, 1993).

A search for underlying patterns also contributed to the child study movement's interest in the ways images are constructed and perceived. Initial studies of children's drawings conducted in Germany, by Kerschensteiner (1903), Lambrecht (1904), and Stern (1905), and in America, by Arthur Clark (1897), surveyed material that had been produced by children. At Teachers College, Edward Thorndike devised Standardized tests to study children's visual development. His *A Scale of Merit of Drawings by Pupils 8 to 15 Years Old* (1913) and *Test of Esthetic Appreciation* (1916) were designed to identify a normal range of child behaviors for making and responding to art (Clark, 1985, 1987; Korzenik, 1995a).

In the city of Philadelphia, an oddly construed center of art education activity, funded by the philanthropic impulses of Albert Barnes, was being established. The primacy of education in the Barnes Foundation's mission highlighted another aspect of the healing that was taking place in America, the reintegration of art and life. Barnes invited John Dewey to develop an education program to promote the analysis, appreciation, and enjoyment of artworks. For Barnes and Dewey, the fine arts and the decorative and folk arts had been artificially separated from one another, in a kind of class warfare. The Foundation's art collection consisted of works by Cezanne, Renoir, Matisse, Van Gogh, Seurat, Picasso, Modigliani, and Pippin; but it also contained a variety of artworks from different times and places including African sculpture, Native American art, folk arts, and crafts works.

Barnes, Dewey, and Thomas Munro sought to develop a sequential structure for guiding the viewer's appreciation of artworks. Although this structure stressed expressive and formal aspects of art experiences, it also historicized art within traditions of reference. The education program thus contributed a structure and a history for talking about art that went beyond the moral lessons of picture study and the pure formalism of Dow, Ross, and Hambridge. Experience with the arts could focus on commonalities that could in turn unite rather than separate people. In order for this to occur, they proposed that a larger organizing principle, aesthetic experience, was available to understanding connections among the arts (Hollingsworth, 1994; McWhinnie, 1994, 1992; Stokrocki, 1992; Supplee, 1994, 1997; Wygant, 1985, 1988a, 1988b).

Design, as a solution to disorder, was also applied to the structuring of curricula and the organization of the professional status of art educators around a common language. James Haney (1908) and William Whitford (1933) articulated definable features of the field and their histories (Efland, 1990b). Art supervisors for states and cities, like Pennsylvania's Valentine Kirby, Baltimore's Leon Winslow, and New England's Royal B. Farnum, designed curriculum through organizational structures such as units, lessons, and articulated goals. At Teachers College, James Kilpatrick's Project Method brought together diverse knowledge and skills through units developed around organized themes. The design of curriculum allowed for the "correlation" of subjects through the identification of relationships among subject areas (Efland, 1990a; Guay, 1997; Katter, 1985; Wygant, 1993).

As these programs matured, design and consumerism provided a means to extend Industrial Arts beyond trade education and the industrial was embraced within the everyday. For example, Leon L. Winslow, Director of art education for the city of Baltimore, repositioned Industrial Arts within art education though units "correlated" with other subjects. Winslow advocated units of study such as for first grade, "What I saw at the circus," or for sixth grade "The origin and development of athletes." Lessons were then developed in relation to the following criteria: art information (knowing technical information about art), creative expression (applying studio skills), art appreciation (revealing beauty), industrial information (relating to organizational topics), and related information (referencing contextual information) (Klar, Winslow, & Kirby, 1933). Winslow's ideas were extended in *The Integrated School Art Program* (1939). There he recommended texts like *Art and the Machine* (Cheney & Cheney, 1936, 1941) and *Enriched Community Living* (Burnett & Hopkins, 1936).

Creating a World

The failures of science and technology, experienced by people alienated by work and the experience of World War I, produced a different sort of hope for art educators: that art education could heal, revive, and integrate people's emotional disconnection with the world. In a move perhaps unfathomable from a tradition-based perspective, hopes for this rejuvenation were placed in and on children. The Progressive Education Association, founded in 1919, developed Seven Cardinal Principles to guide the development of curriculum (Wygant, 1993). On the island of Manhattan, contact with the art of European Modernism, the psychology of Sigmund Freud and Carl Jung, the pedagogy of Franz Cizek from Vienna, and the political art of Mexico exerted a palpable influence. These educators saw that the primary site of healing would take place in the healthy development of the self (Freedman, 1989b, 1992, 1998; Hacking, 1995).

Margaret Naumberg, founder and director of the Walden School, was instrumental in the development of the field of art therapy (Agell, 1980; Hagaman, 1985; Packard, 1980; Troeger, 1992). Florence Cane, Naumberg's sister and the school's art teacher, broke with the emphasis John Dewey had placed on the role of social habits in education (Agell, 1980; MacIver, 1989; Packard, 1980, Smith, 1996; Wygant 1988, 1993). In this rarified atmosphere of private school attention and New York art world allure, Naumberg and Cane formed the prototype for the

— Lowinfield

Modernist artist–teacher. Cane developed what she saw as a culturally neutral classroom, freed of artworks and other associations with the past. Cane's methods promoted the free use of the student's body so that marks could be made in an uninhibited manner. The role of the art educator was to unfold the layers of culture that inhibited this inner artist. For this to occur, the foundations of art education shifted from the crafting of drawings and objects to an expression of feelings developed "through" the inhibition of restrictive responses (Cane, 1926, 1929, 1951; Freedman, 1987, 1989, 1998; MacIver, 1988; Thistlewood, 1990; Smith, 1996a; Wygant, 1988a, 1988b). The use of the metaphor "through" characterizes a focus on the child as emerging into a different sort of ideal person: a freely expressed human being.

The teaching of creative expression was lubricated through the use of soft and wet artist materials such as crayons, pastels, and tempera paints, as opposed to the hard dry pencils of the 19th century. By the late 1920s, North Carolina art educator Ruth Shaw had invented the ideal vehicle for unrestrained creativity, finger paint, marketed in the mid-1930 by Binney and Smith (Stankiewicz, 1984, 2001). Not surprisingly, Shaw moved from North Carolina to New York via Europe (1932) to teach at the Dalton School. Children produced art works at Progressive Education schools throughout the country that bore a remarkable likeness to the work of Georgia O'Keefe and Arthur Dove, American Modernists in the Stieglitz Circle associated with Cane and Naumberg (Cane, 1929). While self-expression paralleled free speech as identifying symptoms of the construction of American democratic values, viewed differently, it seems that above all else children, free or not, mimic adult values (Korzenik, 1995; Wilson & Wilson, 1977).

DISTRIBUTING CULTURE

From the 1920s to the 1940s, the movement of ideas and peoples, shaken by wars, displaced by shifting economic conditions, and uncertain as to the form that self-government might take, created new opportunities and perspectives. The federal government played a limited role in art education's development, although depression-era programs (WPA) provided the groundwork for later federal initiatives (Funk, 2000). The vibrancy of Modernism, however, influenced conservative and radical changes that were distributed through the dissemination of people, ideas, and artifacts.

Philanthropy

The most influential supporters of research in art education were philanthropic foundations, of which the Carnegie Corporation of New York (CCNY) was the dominant force. Since the end of World War I, the CCNY had been interested in funding adult and community education. Its funding of art education proved to be less successful than its support of scientific research (Freedman, 1989a; Funk, 1990, 1998; Lagemann, 1989). However, the CCNY was the primary supporter of the American Federation of the Arts (AFA) founded in 1909 (Funk, 1998; Levy, 1914; Mechlin, 1925).

The AFA was an arts advocacy group composed of a collection of business and art professionals, artists, and educators. The AFA published the *American Magazine of Art* (*Art and Progress* until 1909; *Magazine of Art*, 1937–1953), which provided regular information about art education, including the AFA convention notes and annual reports. From 1912 it published the *American Art Annual*, founded by Florence Levy in 1898, which listed national art organizations. It also published Mrs. Everett Pattison's (1923) *Art in Our Country*, a survey of notable monuments, architecture, and art works throughout the United States (Levy, 1914; Mechlin, 1925; Pattison, 1923).

The AFA was an arbiter and promoter of taste and culture including the merits of out-door advertising, community art projects, art museums, art in the schools, and war memo-rials. It took as one of its missions an advocacy for the creation of the National Gallery of Art. Its other activities included a "portfolio service," which circulated prints to schools, clubs, and individuals. As an extension of this program, the first art education through ra-dio, *Art in Everyday Life*, was broadcast out of New York on WEAF in 1925 (Mechlin, 1925).

The CCNY had been apprehensive about funding art education, citing the Barnes Foundation as one of the few successful initiatives (CCNY, 1924, 1930). In 1924, Richard F. Bach, Director of the Metropolitan Museum of Art, and Frederick Keppel produced *The Place for Art in American Life*, a report for the CCNY that commented on the sad state of art education, which was perceived as a "fad or a thrill" (CCNY, 1925, 1930; Everyday Art, 1925; Funk, 1998; Keppel & Duffus, 1933; Tannahill, 1932). Keppel's work spurred the CCNY to fund its second community arts center, after Santa Barbara, California, in Cedar Rapids, Iowa, from 1926 to1934. Still, CCNY was hesitant to support programs when the administrative structure in the art education was undeveloped. By 1930, with the election of a strong AFA president, Frederic A. Whiting, from the Cleveland Museum of Art, and the country in the midst of a depression, the CCNY was ready to intensify its support by funding several community arts projects (CCNY, 1938).

The most successful of these was the Owatonna project (Owatonna, MN, 1932–1939). Robert Hilbert at the University of Minnesota was one of a number of educators concerned with the promotion of art in rural education (Hibert, 1924, 1925). Melvin Haggerty of The University of Minnesota and Henry Suzzalo of CCNY envisioned the structure of the project; afterward Edwin Ziegfeld, Barbara Smith, and Hilbert became influential members of the team. Owatonna focused on "Art as a way of life" using aesthetics and design for the understanding of the role of industrial products in everyday life (Freedman, 1989; Kern, 1985). As a research project, it was designed to (a) develop a method of community analysis, (b) develop a course for the study of art, and (c) develop the community's interest in the arts by involving the community in adult education, classroom curricula, and teacher education (Saunders, 1985). As an alternative to socialist reactions to capitalism, Owatonna embraced the education of the citizen-as-consumer, whose lives were filled with imported images and things (Belshe, 1946; Burton, 2001b; Efland, 1965, 1990; Freedman, 1987, 1989a; Haggerty, 1935; Jones, 1974; Logan, 1955; Saunders, 1985; Smith, 1996a; Stankiewicz, 2001; Wygant, 1995; Ziegfeld, 2001; Ziegfeld & Smith, 1944).

Cultural Capital

American art museum educators sometimes emphasize the aesthetic properties of art works; other times, they stress historical relatedness, interdisciplinary relationships, and opportunities for social advocacy (Cherry, 1992; Ott, 1985; Svedlow & Troxell, 1997; Wittmann, 1966; Zeller, 1989). At the beginning of the century, the Boston Museum of Fine Arts' Benjamin Ives Gilman saw art objects as ideals that model excellence. Art museums, unlike science museums, were seen as places to experience and be impressed rather than taught (Zeller, 1989). Progressive Education contributed several versions of museum education wary of too many cultural influences and historical connections. In 1928, Margaret Lee of the Carnegie Institute in Pittsburgh instituted two Saturday art classes for children, the Tam O'Shanters and the Palettes. Reflecting the influence of Franz Cizek, students learned first to imitate a studio process, which was in turn related to artworks in the galleries (Judson, 1989). Similarly, Francis Taylor at the Worcester Art Museum in the early 1930s believed that use of media and processes could provide opportunities for empathetic relationships with art works (Zeller, 1989).

The use of studio experiences found their greatest resonance in the museum work of Arthur Lismer and Victor D'Amico. At the Art Gallery of Toronto, Lismer founded the Children's Art Centre in 1932. The Centre was later replicated in 17 other locations throughout Canada. Lismer saw both the child artist and the artist-as-child sharing in a universal act of creative expression, which represented the wonder of life (Korzenik, 1995). Exhibitions of children's work from these centers traveled abroad in 1934 and throughout Canada in 1937 (Hinterreiter, 1967; Pearse, 1988, 1992, 1997; Saunders, 1954; Turner, 1992).

In New York, Victor D'Amico also advocated a form of creative expression that assumed a universal creative impulse, which could be awakened through the use of materials. D'Amico's work as the head of the art department at the progressive Fieldston School (1926–1948) prepared him to develop programs for the Museum of Modern Art (MOMA) such as The Young People's Gallery, a space to exhibit high school art (1938). While there, he organized The Children's Art Carnival (1942–1969) funded by the Rockefeller Foundation. The Carnival included a motivational workspace and a creative workspace, both of which could be viewed by adults from a separate viewing area. D'Amico's work also traveled. He sent the Children's Carnival to Trade Fairs in Milan, the World's Fair in Brussels, and to New Deli (D'Amico, 1960, 2001; Efland, 1990; Kim, 2001; Newson & Silvers, 1978; Sahasrabudhe, P., 1997, 2001; Sherman & Efland, 1997).

Thomas Munro advocated a different form of relationship with the arts. As curator of education at the Cleveland Museum of Art, Munro developed programs that closely tied the art museum with certified art educators. Munro based his teaching on aesthetics and art criticism, with an emphasis on logic and clarity of language. Although his emphasis was not ahistorical, neither was it contextual. As with the program at the Barnes Foundation, where he worked for 4 years, works were related to one another as the function of different aesthetic values with the provision that unity was a common characteristic of outstanding work (Logan, 1965; Ott, 1985; Stockrocki, 1992; Zeller, 1989).

Henry Kent at Metropolitan Museum of Art developed programs to correlate art works with other subjects. One of his teachers, Anna Curtis Chandler (1917–1934), dramatized art works through stories related to the narrative of the image and its historical period. Chandler dressed in period attire, formed groups of children into tableau vivants, produced plays, turned these into books, and eventually (1932) developed two programs for CBS's *American School for the Air* (Zeller, 1989; Zucker, 2001).

Kenneth Chapman, then working for the Museum of New Mexico, used motifs from pottery chards to teach university students and Indian School children about historical traditions in Native American pottery. To formalize this study, he established the Indian Art Fund to develop an extensive collection of Native American pottery and other crafts. This initiative motivated John D. Rockefeller Jr. to support the establishment of The School for American Research (White, 2001).

In the 1930s, museum educators like Francis Henry Taylor of the Worcester Museum, Philip Youtz of the Pennsylvania (later Philadelphia) Museum of Art and the Brooklyn Museum, and Theodore Low of the Walters Art Gallery resisted the notion that artworks speak for themselves, and that art appreciation and studio production could adequately address the meaning of artworks. These educators saw art objects as rich resources that functioned in relation to language, other objects, and social customs. For Theodore Low, the most radical of the group, museum visitors need be provided with multiple methods of interpretation and points of entry to understand the artworks as cultural history (Zeller, 1989).

Mass Media and the Technologies of Delivery

Newly emerging technologies in image reproduction and transmission allowed people to see and hear about art, in their own homes and schools (McNeill, 1997; Wygant, 1993).

Photography and magazines such as *School Arts* (1901–present), *Everyday Art, The Masses, Creative Art, Keramic Studio, Ladies Home Journal*, and so forth, provided images and commentary to their subscribers. In 1925, the AFA introduced adults to art education through the radio series, *Art in Everyday Life*. The first program in the series, *Its Importance to You and Me*, by Robert W. De Forest emphasized the availability of aesthetic perception to all who saw beauty in everyday objects. Florence Levy's *The Museum of Art: How To Use and Enjoy It* emphasized adult education, the integration of art and life, and an orientation toward a consumer society (American Magazine of Art, 1925; Forest, 1926; Levy, 1925; Mechlin, 1925).

In 1929, two radio initiatives, *The Ohio School of the Air*, conducted by William H. Vogel, and *The American School of the Air* (ASA), the more widely distributed NBC broadcast, focused on the use of radio for curriculum development (Bolin, 1992). These broadcasts were intended for teachers who, equipped with a set of corresponding art reproductions and instructional materials, would facilitate connections among the announcer, the images in the sets, and their students (Bolin, 1992; Zucker, 2001). Articles in art education periodicals such as "Children's Radio Broadcasting in the USSR" (School Arts, 1934) suggest art educators' widespread interest in the use of technology in their field.

The early integration of mass media was also used for the education of adults in rural areas. Early programs out of Buffalo, New York, in 1930, Kentucky in 1932, Kansas in 1942, and Pittsburgh featured radio talks supplemented with photographs of the art works published in local newspapers (Bolin, 1992; Salkind, 1985). The most successful of these programs, the weekly (1934) *Art in America* broadcast by WJZ in New York, was subsequently carried by 37 affiliates (Bolin, 1992; Cahill & Barr, 1934; Funk, 1998, 1990).

The radio was also used to broadcast programs that taught people how to make art. Of these, James Schwalbach's *Lets Draw* (1936–70) produced over the *Wisconsin School of the Air* was highly successful (Bolin, 1992; Kelly, 1992). For 34 years, Schwalbach developed programming that emphasized art making, not as a step-by-step process but as a creative act that stressed symbolism over formalism or expressionism (Kelly, 1992). As the show developed, audience participation was encouraged through various techniques such as guest artists, art groups, manuals, teachers' guidelines, and prizes.

The use of radio for art education gave way to film and television. The first broadcast about art on television occurred in conjunction with the inauguration of the new MOMA building in 1939. The program, a Belgian movie about Van Eyck's *Adoration of the Lamb*, included commentary by MOMA's Alfred Barr accompanied by musicians playing 15th-century instruments. This was followed by art critic Emily Genauer's survey of the masterpieces at the New York Worlds Fair. Television, because it provided images, became a model medium for providing adult art education (Kastner, 1940).

Art educators also used television for instructional purposes. Ed Mattil, Gil Albert, Joe Servillo, and Alice Schwartz put together *Key to the Cupboard* in the 1950s. The program consisted of short segments of appreciation, application, and history presented by Schwartz, a friendly mouse puppet, and an art historian. Mattil and Schwartz produced *Meaning in Art*, a 60-program, 6-year series funded and used by the Pennsylvania State Department of Public Instruction. Swartz also produced *Images and Things* for Indiana University (Mattil, 2001).

Migrations

Although isolationist impulses following World War I limited immigration, Western European immigrants, existent minority populations, and crafts from around the world increasingly influenced art education. Some of these influences came from within the country. While Pedro deLemos was editor (1919–1950), Native American crafts played a prominent role in *School Arts Magazine*. Native American crafts from the pueblos of the American Southwest were seen as the ideal Household Art in which art and life were integrated. Classroom teachers responded to these articles with articles of their own, describing how they incorporated Native American crafts and designs into their classrooms. In mainstream culture, traditional Native American work was being elevated from relic to art as evidenced by a 1919 exhibition in New York organized by Mabel Dodge Luhan and John Sloan (Cahill, 1922; Smith, 1999; White, 2001a, 2001b, 2001c).

It was common practice for art education periodicals like *School Arts* and *Everyday Art* to feature crafts from folk traditions around the world. A 1933 *School Arts* issue devoted to the art of the Soviet Union demonstrates the scope this practice, which lasted through the Second World War. Probably the most radical influence from outside of mainstream art education culture came in the form of murals from Mexico. The political and educational works of Mexican artists, like Diego Rivera, Jose Orozco, and Frida Kahlo; and art educators, like Adolf Best Maugard; were popular with both progressive and conservative art educators (Barbosa, 2001; Brenner, 1929; Clark, 1926; Pepper, 1935; Taylor, 1935). Although socialist political messages of the muralists may not have been embraced over time, appropriation of public spaces by art teachers through mural projects continued to gain legitimacy. Jose Orozco's work as Visiting Lecturer at Dartmouth College (1932), where he painted a mural on the Baker Library, pioneered the implementation of artist-in-residence programs (Green, 1948).

Immigrants, many Jewish, fleeing unstable conditions in Western Europe in the 1930s and 1940s, brought with them sophisticated ideas developed in Europe's urban centers. The closing of the Bauhaus by the Nazi regime in 1932 resulted in the immigration of some of its central figures to North American colleges and universities: Annie and Joseph Albers to Black Mountain, then Yale; Walter Gropius to Harvard; Lazlo Maholy-Nagy to Illinois Institute of Design; Gorgy Kepes to MIT, and so forth. The Bauhaus curriculum, which placed a priority on materials and design, became so pervasive that art educators came to see the Bauhaus as the origin of a design-based curriculum (Edwards, 1982; Efland, 1990; Wygant, 1993). The effects of this influence could be seen in art education periodicals from the mid 1930s through the 1970s. Their unsentimental embrace of the machine age meshed with pragmatic Americans looking for a fresh place to start after the strain of WWII. Bauhaus-trained and independent-minded Marguerite Wildenhain was an influential figure in the American Studio Potter Movement of the 1940s and 1950s whose Pond Farm in California contributed to a new tradition of summer studio workshops (Sessions, 1997, 2000).

Events in Europe affected not only artists but also researchers including Henry Schaeffer-Simmern (1896–1978), Viktor Lowenfeld (1903–1960), and Rudolf Arnheim (1904–). Schaeffer-Simmern was influenced by the research of Gustaf Britsch, Franz Cizek, and Gestalt psychology. He theorized the universal availability of artistic cognition and the teacher's role as a guide toward increasingly more complex forms of visual thinking. In *The Unfolding of Artistic Activity* (1948), Schaefer-Simmern's research became available to American art educators (Abrahamson, 1980a, 1980b, 1985, 1992, 2001; Smith, 1982b, 1996a).

Viktor Lowenfeld's immigration to the United States in 1939 had an enormous influence. From Austria he brought an interest in haptic perception derived through his work with the blind, stages of development identified by Kerschensteiner, a visual-haptic theory of art initiated by Alois Riegel, and the creative expression of Cizek (Arnheim, 1983; Lowenfeld, 2001; Saunders, 2001; Smith, 1982a, 1987, 1989, 1996a). While teaching at the Hampton Institute (1939–1946), he refined his visual-haptic theory, wrote *Creative and Mental Growth* (1947), and developed a respect for his African American students. It was his work at The Pennsylvania State University (1946–1960), where he established the program in art education (1946), that confirmed his influence on art education. Lowenfeld was a charismatic colleague, mentor, and teacher (Beittel, 1982; Edwards, 1982; Hausman, 1982b; Madenforte, 1982; Saunders, 1982; Youngblood, 1982). His image of art education as a process through which a child's maturation is enhanced and developed sequentially came to dominate the field (Efland, 1976a).

His psychology-based theories legitimized and privileged handwork. They also integrated the value of craft brought forward from manual arts and creative expression ideas from progressive education (Efland, 1990; Kauppinen, 1985; King, 1991; LaPorte, 1997; Lowenfeld, 2001; Michael, 1981, 1982a, 1982b; Michael & Morris, 1984; Saunders, 1960, 1961, 2001; Smith, 1982b, 1983, 1987, 1996a).

By the time of Rudolf Arnheim's arrival in 1940, the passage to America of Jewish intellectuals dismissed from German universities was well established. Arnheim was a Gestalt psychologist whose early work involved the study of the illusion of movement in film. Psychology grounded his argument for the primacy of perception in cognition, as opposed to language. These ideas were articulated primarily through *Art and Visual Perception* (1954) and *Visual Thinking* (1969). Arnheim's research paralleled the influence of Bauhaus pedagogy and prepared the way for aesthetic education and art-as-language metaphors of the 1970s (Behrens, 2001; Corwin, 2001; Korzenik, 1993; Pariser, 1984).

ORGANIZING THE PROFESSION

The CCNY noted, in 1930, that its interest in developing a systematic means of initiating and administrating national arts research projects was difficult given the lack of a coherent organizational structure associated with art education. It took until after the end of World War II for a professional organization of art educators and research programs at the doctoral level to develop to the point where they could take on a systematic study of the profession.

Building Consensus

The development of the National Art Education Association (NAEA) is a study of the interplay among national, regional, and individual visions and needs. Since 1883, there had been a Department of Art affiliated with the National Education Association (NEA), but by 1913 it had become fully appropriated by a Manual Training and Industrial Arts affiliate group, which in turn was dropped by NEA in 1919. The strength of the field rested within regional organizations (Clark, 1926; Michael, 1997, 2001; Saunders, 1992).

Keppel and Bach's 1924 report, which characterized attitudes toward art education as a fad or a frill, generated a lot of talk (CCNY, 1932; Knouff, 1924; Smith, 1996a; Tannahill, 1932). It also contributed to the founding in 1924 of the Federated Council on Art Education (FCAE) to facilitate communication among arts organizations on issues concerning education in public schools, museums, and colleges and universities (Whiting, 1926). The FCAE made little headway, but it did reinforce Royal Bailey Farnum's commitment to a national organization.

Throughout the 1930s and 1940s there continued to be competing visions for the appropriate way to structure a national organization. One strain developed out of the NEA, which in 1933 reestablished a department of art. The problem with this solution was its inability to integrate with the powerful the regional organizations. By 1947, with a membership of only 127, it was apparent that this organizational structure must change. Through this period, the NEA served as a placeholder for what would become the NAEA (Saunders, 1966, 1978, 1992).

Along the way, the needs for a national organization had been recognized from within the regional organizations themselves. In 1935 Farnum, through his office at the FCAE, polled the profession and found that there was an interest within the regional associations to develop a national coalition. At the end of 1935, Farnum disbanded the FCAE and started the National Association for Art Education (NAAE). Although the regional associations endorsed this project, within 2½ years it became apparent the NAAE could not address national needs (Saunders, 1978, 1992).

A more selective initiative developed in 1942 at the MOMA, where Victor D'Amico organized of The Committee on Art Education (COAE). Unlike the political agenda of the NAAE, the COAE was a forum where art educators, often associated with museums and universities, could gather and learn from influential artists and artworld personalities. This committee was guided by D'Amico's advocacy for an artist–teacher model. The COAE developed into a national organization, holding meetings at university locations throughout the country and providing a forum for researchers, artists, and educators. It was, however, a product of D'Amico and MOMA. His retirement and the fading of progressive education precipitated its end in 1969 (D'Amico, 2001; Freundlich, 1985; Sahasrabudhe, 2001).

The final stages of the founding of the NAEA took place in 1947. Marion Quin Dix of the EAA was instrumental in developing relationships with the NEA. Dix, together with Italo deFrancesco and Adella Church of the Art Department of the NEA, strategized a plan for the Council of Affiliated Art Associations. Their plan was presented to the Art Department at the NEA and regional representatives at the NEA national conference in Atlantic City. The political problems of representation were solved first by Dix's appointment of Edwin Ziegfeld as temporary chair and through a summer meeting in Cincinnati, where the relations between the national and the regional associations were formalized (Burton, 2001; Saunders, 1992; Ziegfeld, 2001). The NAEA was housed at Kutztown University until Ralph Beelke, in 1958, moved it to Washington (Beelke, 2001; Gregory, 1982, 1983, 1985a, 1985b; Michael, 1997).

The arts continued to be a useful means for healing, in this case to unite a world community still recovering from World War II. The founding of UNESCO by the United Nations was based on this vision. In 1951, Charles Gaitskell, Thomas Munro, and Edwin Ziegfeld met with Herbert Read and Trevor Thomas for a seminar in Bristol, England, to discuss the formation of the International Society for Education through Art (INSEA). Edwin Ziegfeld was again elected president of a newly formed art education organization. After the Bristol conference, Gaitskell, who had also attended the first NAEA conference in New York (1951), returned to Canada determined to create The Canadian Society for Education through Art (CSEA), which was formed in 1955 (Gaitskell, 2001; Lemerise & Sherman, 1997; Qualley, 1997; Rhodes, 1985; Saunders, 1954; Shoaff-Ballanger & Davis, 1997).

Developing a Research Agenda

Art education's professional organizations resulted from social and political needs that transcended both local and regional interests. The theoretical basis for these shared interests needed to be defined through research (Keel, 1963, 1965). Prior to World War II, art education had neither an established research identity nor a systematic approach to funding projects. The research that had been conducted was done by psychologists or educators, often funded by philanthropic, as opposed to by federal, sources (Hoffa, 1994).

Higher education programs for the training of art teachers, beginning with the Massachusetts State Normal School (Mass College of Art) in 1873, were widespread in the United States and Canada. Teachers College had a sustained history in education research, but its first PhD in art education was not granted until the late 1930s (Burton, 2001). This situation changed with the GI Bill of Rights (1944). Universities now needed a supply of qualified professors with advanced degrees whose perspective could inform the field (Eisner, 1965b; Stankiewicz, 2001). The period after World War II also precipitated a shift in the gender of the heads of university art education departments. Prior to 1950, it was common for women to head art education programs. As programs shifted to include both the training of teachers and the education of research professionals, the gender of the heads of art education programs shifted from women to men (Edwards 1982; Hutchens, 2001; Logan, 2001; Smith, 1996).

Loosely constructed, art education has a history of research through the work of people like Florence Cane, Marion Quin, Ruth Faison Shaw, Natalie Robinson Cole, and Sallie Tannahill, whose qualitative methods informed their ideas about teaching (Cole, 2001; Gregory, 1982; Hausman, 1982a; Smith, 1985a, 1985b; Stankiewicz & Zimmerman, 1984). But it was primarily psychologists and educators who developed empirical studies related to the field. At the University of Minnesota, psychologist Florence Goodenough (1924, 1926) conducted the *Draw-a-Man Test* and Measurement *of Intelligence by Drawings*. At the University of Iowa, psychologist Norman C. Meier designed the *Meier-Seashore Art Judgment Test* (1929) and *Meier Art Tests* (1942) (Clark, 1985, 1987, 1992; Clark, Zimmerman, & Zurmuehlen, 1987; Weider, 1977; Whitford, 1926; Zimmerman, 1985a, 1985b; Zurmuehlen, 1985).

In addition to these tests for intelligence, curriculum research, like the Owatonna Project, was conducted to assess educational programs and surveys, and reports such as *Art in American Life and Education* (Whipple, 1941) provided an overview of the field. The most significant longitudinal research was the Eight-Year Study (1932–1940) by the Progressive Education Association with funding from the Carnegie Fund for the Advancement of Teaching. The purpose of the study was to examine the relationship between high school courses and college success rates. Although not specifically an art education project, it did show that high school students would select art courses if free to do so. It also showed that those same students had equal or improved results in college compared to students whose courses were prescribed (Logan, 1955; Plummer, 1969, 1985; Wygant, 1993).

The research developed in these early years was influenced by psychology and creative expression. The publication of this research was also important to identify the field. In 1948, *Art Education*, the journal of the NAEA, was first published (Michael, 1997; Schumaker, 1997). In 1949, the Eastern Arts Association created the *Research Bulletin*. As the regional associations became absorbed into NAEA, the bulletin was transformed in 1958 into *Studies in Art Education* (Brewer, 1999; Chalmers, 1999; Chapman, 1999; Collins, 1999). In 1970, NAEA's Kenneth Beittel and June McFee worked to establish the Seminar for Research in Art Education (SRAE) to develop new knowledge about the field (Qualley, 1997).

New research funds were available after the United States government's passage of the Cooperative Research Act (1954), the Elementary and Secondary Education Act (1965), and the National Arts and Humanities Act (1965), which created the National Endowment for the Arts. In place now were three levels of organization: a national professional organization, a system to educate researchers in the field, and a system for disseminating emerging ideas. Such initiatives marked the maturation of art education. The influence of researcher and project administrators, as opposed to the classroom teachers, initiated questions about the relationship between the tacit knowledge of the practitioner and the theoretical and empirical knowledge of the researcher/administrator. Fundamental questions arose regarding the authority upon which art education was based and the goals that its practitioners might set for themselves (Eisner, 1965a; Stankiewicz & Zimmerman, 1984; Strommen, 1988).

QUESTIONS OF IDENTITY

As the national identities of Art Educators were established, people holding divergent perspectives could engage in informed critical discussion. The later part of the 20th century chronicles how the field responded to these differences. Despite the ascent of New York City to the status of the cultural capital of Modernism, the descendants of that project, artists and art educators alike, became increasingly dissatisfied with enterprises like creative expression that viewed inquiry as culturally and historically detached.

Establishing Prototypes

Until the beginning of the cold war, the federal government had shown little interest in either education or the arts, let alone art education. New Deal initiatives (1933–1939), like the Works Progress Authority (WPA), were the first government programs designed to assist the arts (Funk, 1990). But these were not research, education, or even welfare programs but work relief programs designed to help artists suffering during the depression. Following World War II, the Soviet Union's development of nuclear capabilities (1949) and their launch of Sputnik into orbit (1957) provoked a rethinking of the federal neglect of education (Efland, 1990a, 1990b, 2001). Like the conditions that influenced the state of Massachusetts to legislate its Drawing Act in 1870 (see previous chapter), the federal government now looked to education to improve its competitive position in the world (Bolin, 1990; Farnum, 1925).

Educators began to frame their language around what was basic. Schools were seen to promote learning as opposed to social development. The Council for Basic Education, a nonprofit organized to promote this mission for education, was formed in 1958 (Down, 1979; Smith, 1966). Following the passage of the National Defense Education Act (1958), mathematics and science representatives from CCNY, the National Science Foundation, the National Academy of Sciences, and the American Association for the Advancement of Science gathered to discuss curriculum development at the Woods Hole Conference. Jerome Bruner's (1960) account of the conference in *The Process of Education* proposed that the work of scientists, mathematicians, and so forth, was structured, disciplined, and based on a history of prior practitioners. Bruner's scheme valued the uniqueness of the relationships between knowledge and skills that constituted disciplined inquiry. It also looked to experts in the disciplines to reveal what their work entailed. Educators needed to identify what subjects could be said to be disciplines, identify the ways that inquiries in those disciplines are structured, and translate those structures into a developmentally appropriate sequence of instruction for students (Efland, 1988, 1990). Art educators now had to make the case that the arts were disciplined and basic. This self-questioning is evidenced by a series of articles for *Studies in Art Education* that addressed the fundamental identity of art education as a discipline (Dobbs, 1979; Erickson, 1979).

Oddly enough, it was scientists Jerrold Zacharias and Joseph Turner, members of the President's Science and Advisory Committee's Panel on Educational Research and Development, who saw the need for a balance between science and the arts (Efland, 1984). Their Yale Seminar on Music Education (1963) was the first of 17 projects in the arts funded by the Arts and Humanities Department of the USOE (Efland, 1990a, 1990b; Hoffa, 1977). Kathryn Bloom, the newly appointed director (1963–1969) of the USOE–A&H, understood that there was a need to fund research initiatives in the arts. Her first project, *The Seminar on Elementary and Secondary Education* in 1964 held at NYU, picked up on the tradition of Victor D'Amico at MOMA, which favored the expertise of art professionals over art educators. This initiative foreshadowed the Arts-in-Schools program of the National Endowment for the Arts (NEA) and the Arts in Education Program of the John D. Rockefeller III Fund (Ecker & Hausman, 2001; Fowler, 1980; Hoffa, 1997). At The Ohio State University, the USOE funded David Ecker's *The Research and Development Team for the Improvement of Teaching Art Appreciation*, which marked an intensification of the role of aesthetics in art education. The most far-reaching project was *A Seminar in Art Education for Research and Curriculum Development* (1965) held at Penn State. The Seminar was organized by Ed Mattil, Ken Beittel, Elliott Eisner, David Ecker, Jerome Hausman, and Manuel Barkan (Efland, 1984; Mattil, 1997). The conference included philosophers, artists, art critics, psychologists, and art educators. It was informed by Manuel Barkan's (1962) conception of art education as being structured around art production, art criticism, and art history, June King McFee's concerns for the social dimensions of art, and

Ecker's ideas that art was involved with the qualitative aspects of experience (Beittel, 1997; Ecker, 1963, 1997; Efland, 1984; Hamblen, 1997; Hausman, 1997; Hoffa, 1997; Lanier, 1963; Mattil, 1966, 1997; McWhinnie, 1997; Smith, 1997; Zahner, 1997). Following the Penn State Conference and Kathryn Bloom's stay at the USOE, art education developed in two directions: one dominated by art educators and the other by arts administrators.

The Penn State Seminar contributed to a series of aesthetic education initiatives, involving responding to art in structured ways that provided guidelines for developing curriculum. Ralph Smith's (1966a) book, *Aesthetics and Criticism in Art Education,* and journal (1966b), *The Journal of Aesthetic Education,* informed this discussion. Manuel Barkan, Laura Chapman, David Ecker, and Jerome Hausman submitted a successful proposal to the USOE for the development of an Aesthetic Education Program, to be administered by Barkan, Chapman, and Evan Kern followed by Stanley Madeja at the Central Mid western Regional Educational Laboratory (CEMREL) (Chapman, 1982, 2001; Efland, 1987; Jones, 1974; Kern, 1997; Madeja, 1977a, 1977b, 2001). Initiatives included the development of CEMREL kits and instructional packages for classroom use. Aesthetic education kits were also developed for Eisner's Kettering Project (1967–1969) at Stanford University. Kettering boxes, intended for the use by nonspecialists in elementary classrooms to teach art, delivered a sequenced curriculum structured around art production, history, and criticism (Clark, 1975; Copeland, 1983; Eisner, 1968, 1970, 1972, 2001b; Dobbs, 1992; Wygant, 2001). And in at the Southwest Regional Education Laboratory (SWRL), Duane Greer, working through ideas developed by Harry Brody and Rudolf Arnheim, used the disciplines of art criticism, aesthetics, art history, and studio production to provide models for structuring lessons (Dobbs, 1992; Efland, 1990). These initiatives provided the basis from out of which the Getty Center for Education in the Arts (later Getty Education Institute for the Arts) developed its art education project under the direction of LeiLani Lattin-Duke (Wilson, 1997). Greer coined the term Discipline-Based Art Education (DBAE) for the approach the Getty would take in providing curriculum development institutes for elementary classroom teachers in art instruction (Clark, Day, & Greer, 1987; Greer, 1984; Greer & Rush, 1985; Wilson, 1997).

These initiatives envisioned a public education that could instruct all students in ways to approach art and that would provide meaningful experiences throughout their lives (Chapman, 1982). The discipline-based initiatives shared a reasonable premise: Start with what society wants children to become, determine its attributes, and then figure out how to teach it. However, it was on this point the Social Reconstructionists took issue with what they perceived as DBAE's limited perspective. For example, they claimed that the academy's record on social equity was spotty and that the kinds of knowledge academics hold is a small portion of what informs visual culture (Jagodzinski, 1997). Criticism also came from art educators associated with creative expression and child development (Burton, Lederman, & London, 1988; Greenberg, 2001).

The other strain of art education, following the legacy of the USOE and a perspective that looks toward discipline experts, held that qualitative experiences through direct exposure to the arts, through artist-in-residence and event programming supported by adequate staffing, was the best means of ensuring an authentic arts experience for students. This was the possibility that motivated the work of Kathryn Bloom, who left the USOE to direct the Arts in Education Program (AIE) (1968–1979) at the John D. Rockefeller III Fund. The AIE developed programs throughout the country (Bloom, 1980). These programs provided a foundation for future community-based initiatives (Eddy, 1980). The remaining USOE connection to art education was through its funding of the Alliance for Arts in Education and the National Committee for Arts for the Handicapped in 1975 (Killen, 1999a, 1999b). Both projects were directed through the Kennedy Center. These programs depended on state arts councils and community art centers, rather than on public schools, to administer and deliver programming.

These differing directions in programming reveal long-standing differences in focus. Art educators by and large look for ways to structure learning. Arts professionals look for ways to promote art-related experiences for students. In the 1990s, the legacy of federal support declined and there was less emphasis on experiential opportunities like the Artist-in-the-Schools Program or academic research. The central directive of federal policy, since the Goals 2000 initiative in 1994, has been the promotion of assessment and National Standards (Beittel, 1997; Clark, 1992; Dambekalns, 1997; Ecker, 1997; Eisner, 2001; Hamblen, 1997; Hausman, 1997, 2001; Hoffa, 1985, 1994, 1997; Joyce, 1997; Marche, 1997; Mattil, 1997; McWhinnie, 1997; Payne, 1985; Pittard, 1985; Smith, 1997; Zahner, 1992, 1997).

Establishing Inquiry

Throughout the century, inquiry was an issue in art education. Florence Levy (1910) wanted art to "guide his spirit of inquiry"(p. 121). From the 1950s art educators suggested that both making and perceiving art engage us in problem-solving and posing activities (Efland, 1987; Eisner & Ecker, 1966; Jansen, 1992; Kern, 1987; Smith, 1987). Most influential in its revelation of the limited ways that this is incorporated into teaching was Arthur Efland's (1976, also 1983a) "The School Art Style: A Functional Analysis."

Many art educators have stressed the making of art as a form of critical engagement. David Ecker (1963) revisited the ideas of John Dewey stressing the artistic process as a series of problems that are qualitative as opposed too theoretical. The artist both poses and solves these problems. Eisner (1962) and Paul Torrance and Paul Hendrickson (1961) studied creativity as a form of inquiry. Edmund Feldman (1962) placed the artist in a greater social context (Feldman, 2001). Artists engage in existential problems, the solutions for which model solutions for all of us (Chalmers, 1999).

Closely related to the idea of art making as a form of inquiry, requiring a self-reflexive consciousness is the concept of art as a language/symbol system. As early as 1925 *School Arts Magazine* had an issue titled *Visual Education*. George Kepes' (1944) *Language of Vision* and Rudolf Arnheim's (1969) *Visual Thinking* presented highly influential conceptions of what it means to think visually. Nelson Goodman (1976) contributed his theory that visual art is not a language per se but rather a symbol system, dense in its semantic features but lacking a rule-governed syntax. Goodman's ideas grounded Howard Gardner and David Perkins' work on Project Zero at Harvard University. Gardner's Multiple Intelligence Theory and Project Zero's ARTS PROPEL research project provided a model for considering reflection as consciously developed component of studio activity. The ARTS PROPEL model also incorporated the use of process portfolios as part of its curriculum (Gardner, 1989).

One of the lasting achievements of the discipline-based initiatives was the incorporation of language as a critical component of art education. Although there had been a tradition in art education for appreciating and discussing art works, art educators became interested in the ways language facilitates the development of conceptual structures for understanding art. For this to have been accepted, language and images needed to be seen not only as symbolic systems but also as interdependent systems (Mitchell, 1994; Parsons, 1998; Wilson, 1966). Texts that emerged from the aesthetic education movement, like Hubbard's and Rouse's (1973) *Art: Meaning, Method, and Materials* and Chapman's (1978) *Approaches to Art in Education* and (1985) *Discover Art*, directed the field's attention to a careful use of language (Hubbard, 1982; Neil, 1985; Siskar, 1997). Eliot Eisner's (1972) *Educating Artistic Vision* stressed the need for structuring thought. Edmund Feldman's (1970) *Becoming Human through Art* and June King McFee's (1967) *Preparation for Art* applied the importance of language to the social function of art. Mary Erickson developed strategies for using language to frame historical relationships. Feldman's work on art criticism was extended through the writings of Terry Barrett (1994), whose *Criticizing Art* not only amplified methodologies for critically approaching art works but also enriched the field by promoting the use of contemporary art. Barrett's model suggested that the choice of artworks may also provoke inquiry. Marilyn Stewart's (1997) *Thinking through Aesthetics* emphasized the importance of a careful use of language to develop conceptual relationships.

Establishing Community

Art education has a long history of being connected to community work. Dewey's spiral curriculum operated out of the assumption that a child first knows his or her own world and subsequently applies this knowledge to other places, times, and cultures (Efland, 1995b). Initiatives like the city beautiful movement, art weeks, pageantry, rural education, community centers, Progressive Education, WPA, Mexican Muralists, Industrial Arts, Household Arts, Owatonna, and correlated art have all been closely linked to community development. The goal of these efforts, however, was to Americanize, uplift, or train students as they came to assume mainstream values (Amburgy, 1990; Freedman, 1989, 1998; Funk, 1990, 2000; Stankiewicz, 2001).

The conception of art education as being connected to possibilities for critical inquiry required a recognition of critique as being "for," "through," and "based on" the perspectives of different communities of interest. Community-based initiatives sought ways to acknowledge those divergent community voices and to use community resources. Civil Rights initiatives, accelerated by World War II, Brown v. Topeka in 1954, the Civil Rights Act of 1964, and philosophical issues, related to the social construction of meaning, called into question essentialist notions of exemplary artworks and academic models of inquiry (Haynes, 1993). If art was a deeply social human activity, then differing communities of experience might bring different values to the field (Haynes, 1993, 1997).

Mainstream art educators, for the most part, were very slow to acknowledge their complicity in the underrepresentation of minority concerns either as content or as method (Henry & Nyman, 1997). *School Arts Magazine* before World War II had few works by African or African American artists. One exception was the Barnes Foundation, which consistently supported African American artists and educators (Jubilee, 1982). During the 1920s and the early years of the depression, the Harmon Foundation developed eight art centers throughout the country to promote African American artists. Artists who developed and showed at the New York center, like Aaron Douglas, Hale Woodruff, and Palmer Hayden, went on to establish influential careers (Grigsby, 1977; Hubbard, 1985, 1992). Also in New York, Augusta Savage developed the Savage Studio of Arts and Crafts in 1931 (Cochran, 2000). Lowenfeld's work at the Hampton Institute informed the efforts he made to support African American art educators at The Pennsylvania State University. Under his advisement, John Biggers (1955) produced an unorthodox dissertation, *The Negro Woman in American Life and Education: A Mural Presentation.* Lowenfeld's encouragement and Biggers dissertation exhibit an understanding of a need in the field to find alternative ways of articulating concerns of different communities of thought (Grigsby, 1977; Smith, 1982a, 1996).

Art educators Edmund Feldman (1962, 1970), June King McFee (1961, 1966, 2001a, 2001b), Vincent Lanier (1963), and F. Graeme Chalmers (1973, 1974, 1978, 1984, 2000) provided important leadership in developing systematic ways to understand the arts as a form of social practice (Baxter, 1989). At the University of Oregon, McFee developed the Institute for Community Art Studies and established a graduate program that focused on social and anthropological issues (McFee & Ettinger, 2001). At the Penn State conference, McFee's (1966) "Society, Art, and Education" was the clearest statement of a need for socially responsive art education. Her textbooks, *Preparation for Art* (1961) followed by *Art, Culture, and Environment*

(1977) with Rogena Degge were important texts (Congdon & Degge, 1987; McFee, 2001). The NAEA in 1971 recognized the importance of diverse voice through the establishment of the Committee on Multiethnic concerns (Grigsby, 1997; Qualley, 1997). Vincent Lanier's (1969) "The Teaching of Art as Social Revolution" presses issues related to the social theory and Chalmers' (1996) *Celebrating Pluralism* presents a social reconstructionist agenda in some contrast to the more conservative impulses of earlier discipline-based initiatives.

Feminist art educators developed a more radical critique of the depth to which art education theories and practices were grounded in perspectives based on privilege and power. They questioned why art education, which has always had a high percentage of women practitioners, has framed its history in relation to male leadership, instructed students through the use of artists, artworks, and artforms that replicate male privilege, and promoted male-biased conceptions of curriculum and instruction. Georgia Collins (1977) and Sandra Packard (1977) took a critical look at the status of women and women's perspectives in art education. Collins maintained that not only were women in art education systematically excluded from leadership positions, but also curriculum models were being developed out of aesthetic principles that reflected male sensibilities, which assume hierarchies and dominance, as opposed to female sensibilities, which value integration and connectedness (Collins, 1977; Collins & Sandell, 1984; Sacca, 1989, 2001).

These efforts never produced coherent overarching curriculum initiatives backed by the financial power of the USOE or the Getty but they have had a tremendous influence on the development of curricula that reflect feminist sensibilities (Congdon & Zimmerman, 1993; Patterson, 1997; Sacca & Zimmerman, 1998; Speirs, 1998; Stankiewicz & Zimmerman, 1984, 1985; Zimmerman & Stankiewicz, 1982). Issues of equity also led to the founding of the NAEA's Women's Caucus in 1975, the Caucus on Social Theory in 1982, and the Lesbian/Gay/Bisexual Issues Caucus in 1996 (Check, 2000; Qualley, 1997). Minority rights were explored on several fronts. The emphasis on exemplars in art education, reflected in the Back-to-Basics and Excellence movements, was radically critiqued as a false conception of the value art education holds for students. Kristin Congdon and Doug Blandy's (1987) *Art in a Democracy* stretched the traditional methodologies associated with the field. They also brought art education's attention to issues related to folk artists and people with disabilities (Abia-Smith, 2000; Bolin, Blandy, & Congdon, 2000; Congdon, 1985; Congdon, Blandy, & Bolin, 2001; Traeger, 1992). Textbooks, too, responded to the broader conception of community. Eldon Katter and Marilyn Stewart (2001) in their series *Art and the Human Experience* emphasized community through thematic units developed around broadly shared human processes. Researchers like Christine Ballangee Morris (2000) and Mary Stokrocki (1997, 2001) applied ethnographic and community-based research methods toward understanding the visual cultures of various peoples. Recently, art educators have sought to redefine the field through the study of visual culture, material culture, and mass arts (Bolin & Blandy, 2003; Chapman, 2003; Duncum, 2001; Freedman, 2000). These initiatives stress the importance of the intersection of community and critically as the foundations of the field. They advocate for a critical pedagogy that connects students with their lives through an examination of the roles images, artifacts, and performances play in the construction of identity (Chapman, 2003).

CONCLUSION

Art educators continue to wonder about the relation between art education's role as a tool for critical self-examination and/or a tool for uniting people around shared beliefs. Art educators also continue a vital dialog between social reconstructionist perspectives based on multi-centered, situated approaches to learning and conservative perspectives, promoted through initiatives such as *A Nation at Risk* and *Goals 2000*, which embrace definable standards based on exemplary models. Between these two stances, however, there is much agreement on the value of an embodied understanding of critical theory as a means to develop relations between art and life. This emphasis on criticality differs significantly from earlier approaches that used aesthetic distance as a means to bridge that same gap.

One senses from viewing the past, when North American people looked to craft, design, and authentic self-expression as a means to heal and reintegrate their lives, that emerging technologies and their social repercussions influenced art's role in education. As was true then, technologies frame our perceptions, provide images to study, the means to study them, tools to manipulate them, and lifestyles to be embraced and resisted (Garoian & Gaudelius, 2001). In this mediated world of visual culture, both cognition—embodied in forms such as art, art classrooms, and mass culture—and technologies—embodied within us—effect cultural practices in dynamic and unforeseen ways. These interactions present art educators with tremendous opportunities to reconfigure their field in relation to a wider range of cultural practices. Art educators ask not only how an image made in London might be transported to, understood, critiqued, emulated, and resisted in rural Mississippi, but also how an image made in Mississippi might transform the lives of its makers and the lives of others.

The history of art education is informed by the dynamics of these movements. As an area of research within the field, it contributes to the stories that we tell about who we are and why we do what we do. As the relationships among images, words, social institutions, and folk and progressive practices and beliefs intermingle, art education's history becomes a more complex tale of shared and unshared interests, of odd alliances and understandable disagreements, which will become increasingly reliant on research by others and critical self-examination to develop its stories in useful ways.

REFERENCES

Abia-Smith, L. (2000). Historical and contemporary approaches to museum education and visitors with disabilities. In P. Bolin, D. Blandy, & K. G. Congdon (Eds.), *Remembering others: Making invisible histories visible* (pp. 113–124). Reston, VA: NAEA.

Abrahamson, R. (1980a). Henry Schaeffer-Simmern: His life and work. *Art Education, 33*(8), 12–16.

Abrahamson, R. (1980b). The teaching approach of Henry Schaeffer-Simmern. *Studies in Art Education, 22*(1), 42.

Abrahamson, R. (1985). Henry Schaeffer-Simmern's research and theory: Implications for art education, art therapy, and art for special education. In B. Wilson & H. Hoffa (Eds.), *History of art education: Proceedings of the Penn State Conference* (pp. 247–255). University Park, PA: The Pennsylvania State University College of Art and Architecture, School of Visual Arts.

Abrahamson, R. (1992). Gustaf Britsch: His theory, life, and implications of his theory for tomorrow's art education. In P. Amburgy, D. Soucy, M. A. Stankiewicz, B. Wilson, & M. Wilson (Eds.), *History of art education: Proceedings of the Second Penn State Conference, 1989* (pp. 133–137). Reston, VA: NAEA.

Abrahamson, R. (2001). Henry Schaeffer-Simmern: A biographical study. In R. Raunft (Ed.), *The autobiographical lectures of some prominent art educators* (pp. 349–356). Reston, VA: NAEA.

Agell, G. (1980, April). The history of art therapy. *Art Education*, 8–9.

Amburgy, P. (1990). Culture for the masses: Art education and Progressive Education, 1880–1917. In D. Soucy & M. A. Stankiewicz (Eds.), *Framing the past: Essays on art education* (pp. 103–116). Reston, VA: NAEA.

Amburgy, P., Soucy, D., Stankiewicz, M. A., Wilson, B., & Wilson, M. (1992). *History of art education: Proceedings of the Second Penn State Conference, 1989*. Reston, VA: NAEA.

American Magazine of Art. (1925). Other Federation activities, *American Magazine of Art, 16*(3), 144–148.

Anderson, A., & Bolin, P. (1997). *History of art education: Proceedings of the Third Penn State International Symposium, Oct 12–15, 1995*. University Park, PA: The Pennsylvania State University.

Arnheim, R. (1954). *Art and visual perception: A psychology of the creative eye*. Berkeley, CA: University of Los Angeles Press.

Arnheim, R. (1969). *Visual thinking*. Berkeley, CA: University of California Press.

Arnheim, R. (1983). Viktor Lowenfeld and tactility. *Journal of Aesthetic Education, 17*(2), 19–29.

Art Education Today (1935–1952). New York: Teachers College Press.

Bach, R. (1924). The place of art in American life. *Office Memorandum, 1*(9), CCNY.

Bach, R. (1927). American Industrial Art. *American Magazine of Art, 18*(1), 27–29.

Barbosa, A. M. (2001). The Studies in Art Education Invited Lecture, 2001: The Escuelas de Pintura al Aire Libre in Mexico: Freedom, Form, and Culture. *Studies in Art Education, 42*(4), 285–297.

Barkan, M. (1962). Transition in art education: Changing conceptions of curriculum content and teaching. *Art Education, 15*(7), 27–28.

Baxter, L. R. (1989). Interview with Vincent Lanier. *Canadian Review of Art Education, 16*(2), 87–100.

Beelke, R. (2001). In R. Raunft (Ed.), *The autobiographical lectures of some prominent art educators* (pp. 77–94). Reston, VA: NAEA. (Originally presented 1977)

Behrens, R. R. (2001). Rudolf Arnheim: A biographical study. In R. Raunft (Ed.), *The autobiographical lectures of some prominent art educators* (pp. 357–362). Reston, VA: NAEA.

Beittel, K. (1982). Lowenfeld and art for a new age. *Art Education, 33*(6), 18–21.

Beittel, K. (1997). Fateful fork in the road: The 1965 Red Book. In A. Anderson & P. Bolin (Eds.), *History of art education: Proceedings of the Third Penn State International Symposium, Oct 12–15, 1995* (pp. 533–538). University Park: The Pennsylvania State University.

Belshe, F. (1946). *A history of art education in public schools of the United States.* Ann Arbor: UMI.

Bement, A. (1941). The development of industrial design in America. In G. M. Whipple (Ed.), *The fortieth yearbook of the National Society for the Study of Education: Art in American life and education* (pp. 93–99). Bloomington, IL: Public School Publishing Co.

Bennett, C. (1917). *The manual arts.* Peoria, IL: The Manual Arts Press.

Bennett, C. (1934). *Industrial arts in modern education.* Peoria, IL: The Manual Arts Press.

Bennett, C. (1937). *History of Manual and Industrial Arts education, 1870–1917.* Peoria, IL: The Manual Arts Press.

Bernstein, B., & Rushing, W. J. (1995). *Modern by tradition.* Albuquerque, NM: Museum of New Mexico.

Blandy, D., & Congdon, K. (1987). *Art in a democracy.* New York: Teachers College Press.

Boas, B. (1924). *Art in the schools.* New York: Doubleday, Doran & Co.

Bolin, P. (1990). The Massachusetts Drawing Act of 1870: Industrial Mandate or democratic maneuver? In D. Soucy & M. A. Stankiewicz (Eds.), *Framing the past: Essays on Art Education* (pp. 59–68). Reston, VA: NAEA.

Bolin, P., & Blandy, D. (2003). Beyond visual culture: Seven statements of support for material culture studies in art education. *Studies in Art Education, 44*(3), 246–263.

Bolin, P., Blandy, D., & Congdon, K. G. (2000). *Remembering others: Making invisible histories visible.* Reston, VA: NAEA.

Bolin, P. E. (1992). Art over the airwaves: A brief examination of radio art education in the United States, 1929–1951. In P. Amburgy, D. Soucy, M. A. Stankiewicz, B. Wilson, & M. Wilson (Eds.), *History of art education: Proceedings of the Second Penn State Conference, 1989* (pp. 274–278). Reston, VA: NAEA.

Brenner, A. (1929). Children of revolution.*Creative Art, 4*(2), 36–40.

Brewer, T. M. (1999). Forty years of *Studies in Art Education:* 1979–1989. *Visual Arts Research, 25*(1), 15–27.

Brody, J. (1971) *Indian painters & White patrons.* Albuquerque, NM: University of New Mexico Press.

Brody, J. (1997). *Pueblo Indian painting: Tradition and Modernism in New Mexico, 1900–1930.* Santa Fe, NM: School of American Research Press.

Burnett, M. H., & Hopkins, L. T. (1936). *Enriched community living.* Wilmington, DE: State Department of public Instruction.

Burton, J. (2001a). Doctoral programs at Teachers College. In J. Hutchens (Ed.), *In their own words: The development of doctoral study in art education* (pp. 10–27). Reston, VA: NAEA.

Burton, J. (2001b). Edwin Ziegfeld. In R. Corwin (Ed.), *Exploring the legends: Guideposts to the future* (pp. 75–99). Reston, VA: NAEA.

Burton, J., Lederman, A., & London, P. (1988). *Beyond DBAE: The case for multiple visions of art education.* New York: University Council for Art Education.

Cahill, E. (1922). America has its "primitives." *El Palacio, 12*(9), 126–131.

Cahill, H., & Barr, A. H. (1934). *Art in America in Modern Times.* New York: Reynal & Hitchcock.

Cane, F. (1926). Art in the life of the child. In G. Hartman (Ed.), *Creative expression through art* (pp. 155–162). Washington: Progressive Education Association.

Cane, F. (1929). Art and the child's essential nature. *Creative Art, 4*(2), 29–33.

Cane. F. (1951). *The artist in each of us.* New York: Pantheon Books.

Carnegie Corporation of New York. (1925). *Report of the President and the Treasurer.* New York: CCNY.

Carnegie Corporation of New York. (1930). *Report of the President and the Treasurer.* New York: CCNY.

Carnegie Corporation of New York. (1938). *Report of the President and the Treasurer.* New York: CCNY.

Chalmers, F. G. (1973). The study of art in a cultural context. *Journal of Aesthetics and Art Criticism, 32*(2), 249–256.

Chalmers, F. G. (1974). A cultural foundation for education in the arts. *Art Education, 27*(1), 21–25.

Chalmers, F. G. (1978). Teaching and studying art history: Some anthropological and sociological considerations. *Studies in Art Education, 20*(1), 18–25.

Chalmers, G. (1984). Cultural pluralism and art education in British Columbia. *Art Education, 36*(5), 22–26.

Chalmers, G. (1999). The first 10 of 40 years of *Studies in Art Education. Visual Arts Research, 25*(1), 2–6.

Chapman, L. (1982). *Instant art, instant culture: The unspoken policy for American schools.* New York: Teachers College Press.

Chapman, L. (1999). Studies in Art Education: Decade two. *Visual Arts Research, 25*(1), 7–13.

Chapman, L. (2001). In R. Raunft (Ed.), *The autobiographical lectures of some prominent art educators* (241–254). Reston,VA: NAEA. (Originally presented 1994)

Chapman, L. (2003). Studies in the mass arts. *Studies in Art Education, 44*(3), 230–245.

Check, E. (2000). To be seen is to be: The founding of the Lesbian, Gay, and Bisexual Issues Caucus of the National Art Education Association. In P. Bolin, D. Blandy, & K. G. Congdon (Eds.), *Remembering others: Making invisible histories visible* (pp. 137–146). Reston, VA: NAEA.

Cheney, S., & Cheney, M. (1941). *Art and the machine.* New York: McGraw-Hill.

Cheney, S., & Cheney, M. (1941). Art and the machine. In G. M. Whipple (Ed.), *The fortieth yearbook of the National Society for the Study of Education: Art in American life and education* (pp. 93–99). Bloomington, IL: Public School Publishing Co.

Cherry, S. (1992). A history of education in American Museums. In P. Amburgy, D. Soucy, M. A. Stankiewicz, B. Wilson, & M. Wilson (Eds.), *History of art education: Proceedings of the Second Penn State Conference, 1989* (pp. 292–295). Reston, VA: NAEA.

Clark, A. (1926). The Pacific Arts Organization. *School Arts Magazine, 25*(7), 388–391.

Clark, G. (1975). Art kits and caboodles: Alternative learning materials for education in the arts. *Art Education, 28*(5), 27–30.

Clark, G. (1985). Early Inquiry, research, and testing of children's art abilities. In B. Wilson & H. Hoffa (Eds.), *History of art education: Proceedings of the Penn State Conference* (pp. 276–285). University Park: The Pennsylvania State University College of Art and Architecture, School of Visual Arts.

Clark, G. (1987). Early inquiry, research, and testing of children's art abilities. In G. Clark, E. Zimmerman, & M. Zurmuehlen (Eds.), *Understanding art testing: Past influences, Norman C. Meier's contributions, present concerns, and future possibilities* (pp. 1–26). Reston, VA: NAEA.

Clark, G. (1992). Using history to design current research: The background of *Clark's Drawing Ability Test.* In P. Amburgy, D. Soucy, M. A. Stankiewicz, B. Wilson, & M. Wilson (Eds.), *History of art education: Proceedings of the Second Penn State Conference, 1989* (pp. 191–199). Reston, VA: NAEA.

Clark, G., Day, M., & Greer, D. (1987). Discipline-based art education: Becoming students of art. *Journal of Aesthetic Education, 21*(2), 129–196.

Clark, G., Zimmerman, E. & Zurmuehlen, M. (1987). *Understanding art testing: Past influences, Norman C. Meier's contributions, present concerns, and future possibilities.* Reston, VA: NAEA.

Cochran, M. T. (2000). Let us work on 'til victory is won: The life and work of Augusta Savage. In P. Bolin, D. Blandy, & K. G. Congdon (Eds.), *Remembering others: Making invisible histories visible* (pp. 98–108). Reston, VA: NAEA.

Cole, N. R. (2001). In R. Raunft (Ed.) *The autobiographical lectures of some prominent art educators* (pp. 67–76). Reston, VA: NAEA. (Originally presented 1976)

Collins, G. (1977). Considering an androgynous model for Art Education. *Studies in Art Education, 18*(2), 54–62.

Collins, G. (1999). Studies in Art Education, 1989–1999. *Visual Arts Research, 25*(1), 19–26.

Collins, G., & Sandell, R. (1984). *Women, art, and education.* Reston, VA: NAEA.

Collins, M. (1997). Tactility, habit, and experience: The influence of William James and John Dewey on Kimon Nicolaides' *The Natural Way to Draw.* In A. Anderson & P. Bolin (Eds.), *History of art education* (pp. 175–184). University Park: The Pennsylvania State University.

Committee on the Function of Art in General Education (1939). *The visual arts in general education.* New York: D. Appleton-Century Inc.

Congdon, K. G. (1985). Women folk artists as educators. In M. A. Stankiewicz & E. Zimmerman (Eds.), *Women art educators II* (pp. 192–209). Bloomington, IN: Indiana University.

Congdon, K. G., Blandy, D., & Bolin, P. E. (2001). *Histories of community-based art education.* Reston, VA: NAEA.

Congdon, K. G., & Degge, R. M. (1997). June King McFee's life and work: Constructing a feminist approach to biography for art education. In A. Anderson & P. Bolin (Eds.), *History of art education* (pp. 138–146). University Park: The Pennsylvania State University.

Connell, W. (1980). *A history of education in the twentieth century.* New York: Teacher's College Press.

Copeland, B. (1983). Art and Aesthetic Education learning packages. *Art Education, 36*(3), 32–35.

Corwin, R. (2001). *Exploring the legends: Guideposts to the future.* Reston, VA: NAEA.

Corwin, S. K. (2001). Rudolf Arnheim. In R. Corwin (Ed.), *Exploring the legends: Guideposts to the future.* Reston, VA: NAEA.

D'Amico, V. (1960). *Experiments in creative art teaching: A progress report on the Department of Education, 1937–1960.* The Museum of Modern Art. Garden City, NY: Doubleday & Co.

D'Amico, V. (2001). In R. Raunft (Ed.), *The autobiographical lectures of some prominent art educators* (pp. 47–58). Reston, VA: NAEA. (Originally presented 1973)

Dambekalns, L. (1997). Oral history in the search for curriculum and the collective mind. In A. Anderson & P. Bolin (Eds.), *History of art education* (pp. 540–548). University Park: The Pennsylvania State University.

Dobbs, E. V. (1920). *Illustrative handwork for elementary school subjects: A desk manual for teachers.* New York: The MacMillan Co.

Dobbs, S. (1979). *Art education and back to basics.* Reston, VA: NAEA.

Dobbs, S. (1992). The Kettering Project: Memoir of a paradigm. In P. Amburgy, D. Soucy, M. A. Stankiewicz, B. Wilson, & M. Wilson (Eds.), *History of art education: Proceedings of the Second Penn State Conference, 1989* (pp. 186–190). Reston, VA: NAEA.

Down, A. G. (1979). Art, education, and the Back to Basics Movement. In S. Dobbs, (Ed.), *Art education and back to basics* (pp. 28–38). Reston: NAEA.

Duncum, P. (2001). Visual culture: Developments, definitions, and directions for art education. *Studies in Art Education, 44*(2), 101–112.

Duveneck, J. (1921). The community house. *School Arts Magazine, 20*(5), 253–258.

Ebken, R. (1960). *Prospect and retrospect: The Eastern Arts Association, 1910–1960.* Kutztown, PA: Kutztown Publishing Co.

Ecker, D. (1963). The artistic process as creative problem solving. *The Journal of Aesthetics and Art Criticism, 21*(3), 283–290.

Ecker, D. (1997). Some thoughts on the Penn State Seminar. In A. Anderson & P. Bolin (Eds.), *History of art education* (pp. 515–516). University Park: The Pennsylvania. State University.

Ecker, D., & Hausman, J. (2001). From artist-teacher to artist-researcher: First person accounts of the growth of doctoral study in art education at New York University. In J. Hutchens (Ed.), *In their own words: The development of doctoral study in art education* (pp. 152–159). Reston, VA: NAEA.

Eddy, J. (1980). Beyond "enrichment": Developing a comprehensive community-school arts program. In J. Hausman (Ed.), *Arts and the schools* (pp.157–204). New York: McGraw-Hill.

Edwards, D. (1982). Lowenfeld as mentor. *Art Education, 33*(6), 38–40.

Efland, A. (1976a). Changing views of children's artistic development: Their impact on curriculum and instruction. In E. Eisner (Ed.), *The arts, human development, and education* (pp. 65–86). Berkley, CA: McCutcheon Publishing Company.

Efland, A. (1976b). The school art style: A functional analysis. *Studies in Art Education, 17*(2), 37–44.

Efland, A. (1983a). Art education during the great depression. *Art Education, 36*(6), 38–42.

Efland, A. (1983b). School art and its social origins. *Studies in Art Education, 24*(3), 149–157.

Efland, A. (1984). Curriculum concepts of the Penn State Seminar: An evaluation in retrospect. *Studies in Art Education 25*(4), 205–211.

Efland, A. (1987). Curriculum antecedents of Discipline-Based Art Education. *Journal of Aesthetic Education, 21*(2), 57–94.

Efland, A. (1988). Studies in Art Education: Fourth invited lecture. How art became a discipline: Looking at our recent history. *Studies in Art Education, 29*(3), 262–274.

Efland, A. (1990a). *A History of art education: Intellectual and social currents in teaching the visual arts.* New York: Teachers College Press.

Efland, A. (1990b). Art education in the 20th century: A history of ideas. In D. Soucy & M. A. Stankiewicz (Eds.), *Framing the past: Essays on art education* (pp. 117–138). Reston, VA: NAEA.

Efland, A. (1995). The Spiral and the lattice: Changes in cognitive learning theory with implications for art education. *Studies in Art education, 36*(3), 134–153.

Efland, A. (2001). Overview of the 20th century. In R. Corwin (Ed.), *Exploring the legends: Guideposts to the future.* Reston, VA: NAEA.

Eisner, E. (1965a). American education and the future of art education. In W. R. Hastie (Ed.), *The sixty-fourth yearbook of the National Society for the Study of Education, Part II-Art Education.* Chicago: University of Chicago Press.

Eisner, E. (1965b). Graduate study and the preparation of scholars in art education. In W. R. Hastie (Ed.), *The sixty-fourth yearbook of the National Society for the Study of Education, Part II-Art Education.* Chicago: University of Chicago Press.

Eisner, E. (1968). Curriculum making for the wee folk: Stanford University's Kettering project. *Studies in Art Education, 9*(3), 45–56.

Eisner, E. (1970). Stanford's Kettering Project: Appraisal of two year's work. *Art Education, 23*(8), 4–7.

Eisner, E. (1972). *Educating artistic vision.* New York: The Macmillan Company.

Eisner, E. (2001b). In R. Raunft (Ed.), *The autobiographical lectures of some prominent art educators* (pp. 281–290). Reston, VA: NAEA. (Originally presented 1996)

Eisner, E., & Ecker, D. (1966). What is art education? Some historical developments in art education. In E. Eisner & D. Ecker (Eds.), *Readings in Art Education* (pp. 1–13). Waltham MA: Blaisdell Publishing Co.

Eldridge, L. (2001). Dorothy Dunn and the art education of Native Americans: Continuing the dialogue. *Studies in Art Education, 42*(4), 318–332.

Erickson, M. (1979). An historical explanation of the schism between research and practice in art education. *Studies in Art Education 20*(2), 5–13.

Everyday Art (1925). How may art come into its own. *Everyday Art, 4*(1), 3–5, 14.

Everyday Art (1922–1974). Sandusky, OH: The American Crayon Co.

Farnum, R. B. (1925). The Massachussettes Normal School and her leaders. *School Arts Magazine, 24*(5), 266–277.

Farnum, R. B. (1960). The story of The Eastern Arts Association. In R. Ebken (Ed.). *Prospect and retrospect: The Eastern Arts Association, 1910–1960* (pp. 11–25). Kutztown, PA: Kutztown Publishing Co.

Fast, L. (1999). Fine and practical arts in Ontario elementary school policies (1840–1940): Lessons to be learned. *Canadian review of art education, 26*(3), 114–133.

Feldman, E. (1962). Dilemma of the artist. *Studies in Art Education, 4*(1), 4–10.

Feldman, E. (1970). *Becoming human through art*. Englewood Cliffs, NJ: Prentice-Hall.

Feldman. E. B. (2001). In R. Raunft (Ed.), *The autobiographical lectures of some prominent art educators* (pp. 193–210). Reston, VA: NAEA. (Originally presented 1989)

Forest, R. (1925). Art for the schoolroom. *American Magazine of Art, 16*(3), 142–1944.

Forest, R. (1926). Art in everyday life: A radio talk. *American Magazine of Art, 17*(3), 127–129.

Fowler, C. (1980). *An arts in education source book: A view from the JDR 3rd Fund*. New York: The JDR 3rd Fund.

Freedman, K. (1987). Art education and changing political agendas: An analysis of curriculum concerns of the 1940's and 1950s. *Studies in Art Education, 29*(1), 17–29.

Freedman, K. (1989a). The philanthropic vision: The Owatonna Art Education Project as an example of "private" interests in public schooling. *Studies in Art Education, 31*(1), 15–26.

Freedman, K. (1989b). Nacissism and normalcy: Historical foundations of art education for young children. *Canadian Review of Art Education, 16*(1), 21–33.

Freedman, K. (1992). Educational discourse as cultural representation: Modernism in school and the media. In P. Amburgy, D. Soucy, M. A. Stankiewicz, B. Wilson, & M. Wilson (Eds.), *History of art education: Proceedings of the Second Penn State Conference, 1989* (pp. 220–225). Reston, VA: NAEA.

Freedman, K. (1998). The importance of Modern Art and Art Education in the creation of a national culture. In K. Freedman & F. Hernandez (Eds.), *Curriculum, culture, and art education*. New York: SUNY Press.

Freedman, K. (2000). Social perspectives on art education in the U.S.: Teaching visual culture in a democracy. *Studies in Art Educations, 41*(4), 314–329.

Freedman, K., & Hernandez, F. (1998). *Curriculum, culture, and art education*. New York: SUNY Press.

Freedman, K., & Popkewitz, T. (1985). Art education and the development of the academy: The ideological origins of Curriculum theory. In B. Wilson & H. Hoffa (Eds.), *History of Art Education: Proceedings of the Penn State Conference* (pp. 19–27). University Park, PA: The Pennsylvania State University College of Art and Architecture, School of Visual Arts.

Freundlich, A. L. (1985). The Committee on Art Education. In B. Wilson & H. Hoffa (Eds.), *History of art education: Proceedings of the Penn State Conference* (pp. 329–333). University Park, PA: The Pennsylvania State University College of Art and Architecture, School of Visual Arts.

Funk, C. (1990). *The development of professional studio training in American higher education, 1860–1960*. Unpublished doctoral dissertation, Teachers College, Columbia University.

Funk, C. (1998). The Art in America Radio Programs, 1934–1935. *Studies in Art Education, 40*(1), 31–45.

Funk, C. (2000). Education in the Federal Art Project. In P. Bolin, D. Blandy, & K. G. Congdon (Eds.), *Remembering others: Making invisible histories visible* (pp. 85–97). Reston, VA: NAEA.

Gaitskell, C. D. (2001). In R. Raunft (Ed.), *The autobiographical lectures of some prominent art educators* (pp. 119–130). Reston, VA: NAEA. (Originally presented 1979)

Gardner, H. (1989). Zero-Based arts education: An introduction to ARTS PROPEL. *Studies in Art Education, 30*(2), 71–83.

Garoian, C., & Gaudelius, Y. (2001). Cyborg Pedagogy: Performing resistance in the digital age. *Studies in Art Education, 42*(4), 333–347.

Gluck, G. (2000). The Educational Alliance School. In P. Bolin, D. Blandy, & K. G. Congdon (Eds.), *Remembering others: Making invisible histories visible* (pp. 58–70). Reston, VA: NAEA.

Goldstein, H., & Goldstein, V. (1926). *Art in everyday life*. NY: MacMillan & Co.

Goodenough. F (1926). *Measurement of intelligence by drawing*. Yonkers-on-Hudson, NY: World Book.

Goodman, N. (1976). *Languages of art*. Indianapolis, IN: Hackett.

Green, H. (1948). *The introduction of art as a general subject in American Schools.* Ph.D. Dissertation. Palo Alto, CA: Stanford University.

Greenberg, P. (2001). In R. Raunft (Ed.), *The autobiographical lectures of some prominent art educators* (pp. 331–348). Reston, VA: NAEA. (Originally presented 2000)

Greer, D. (1984). A discipline-based view of art education. *Studies in Art Education, 25*(4), 212–218.

Greer, D., & Rush, J. (1985). A grand experiment: The Getty Institutes for Educators on the Visual Arts. *Art Education, 37*(1), 24–35.

Gregory, A. (1982). Marion Quin Dix: A people picker and an innovator in American education. In E. Zimmerman & M. A. Stankiewicz (Eds.), *Women art educators* (pp. 59–71). Bloomington, IN: Indiana University Press.

Gregory, A. (1983, July). Origins of the NAEA: An interview with Ralph Beelke. *Art Education*, 14–17.

Gregory, A. (1985a). Ruth Elise Halvorsen: An advocate of art for all. In M. A. Stankiewicz & E. Zimmerman (Eds.), *Women art educators II* (pp. 131–147). Bloomington, IN: Indiana University.

Gregory, A. (1985b). Ruth M. Ebken: A concerned art educator. In M. A. Stankiewicz & E. Zimmerman (Eds.), *Women art educators II* (pp. 148–159). Bloomington, IN: Indiana University.

Grigsby, E. (1977). *Art & ethnics: Background for teaching youth in a pluralistic society.* Dubuque, IA: William C. Brown & Co.

Grigsby, E. (1997). People of color: Their changing role in the NAEA. In Michael, J. (Ed.), *The National Art Education Association: Our history—Celebrating 50 years 1947–1997* (pp. 167–180). Reston, VA: NAEA.

Guay, D. (1997). Integrated, correlated, and cross-disciplinary art education in public schools: Some roots and a questionable harvest. In A. Anderson & P. Bolin (Eds.), *History of art education* (pp. 203–210). University Park: The Pennsylvania State University.

Hacking, I. (1995). *Rewriting the soul: Multiple personality and the science of memory.* Princeton, NJ: Princeton University Press.

Hagaman, S. (1985). Mary Hunttoon: Artist, teacher, and therapist. In M. A. Stankiewicz & E. Zimmerman (Eds.), *Women art educators II* (pp. 82–99). Bloomington: Indiana University.

Haggerty, M. (1935). *Art a way of life.* Minneapolis: University of Minnesota Press.

Hamblen, K. (1985). An art education chronology: A process of selection and interpretation. *Studies in Art Education, 26*(2), 111–120.

Hamblen, K. (1997). Developing a theory of historical self-criticality based on the 1965 Penn State Conference and subsequent events. In A. Anderson & P. Bolin (Eds.), *History of art education* (pp. 525–532). University Park: The Pennsylvania State University.

Hammock, C., & Hammock, A. (1906). *The manual arts for elementary schools: Drawing, design, construction.* Boston, MA: Heath & Co.

Haney, J. P. (1908). *Art education in the public schools of the United States.* New York: American Art Annual.

Hardiman, G. W., & Zernich, T. (2001). In R. Raunft (Ed.), *The autobiographical lectures of some prominent art educators* (pp. 301–310). Reston, VA: NAEA. (Originally presented 1998)

Hastie, W. R. (1965). *The sixty-fourth yearbook of the National Society for the Study of Education, Part II-Art Education.* Chicago: University of Chicago Press.

Hausman, J. (1982a). Marion Quin Dix: Facilitator, helper, colleague, and friend. In E. Zimmerman & M. A. Stankiewicz (Eds.), *Women art educators* (pp. 72–73). Bloomington, IN: Indiana University Press.

Hausman, J. (1982b). Viktor Lowenfeld—Remembrances of a friend and colleague. *Art Education, 33*(6), 15–17.

Hausman, J. (1997). Some remarks on the 1965 Penn State Seminar. In A. Anderson & P. Bolin (Eds.), *History of art education* (pp. 512–514). University Park: The Pennsylvania State University.

Hausman, J. (2001). In R. Raunft (Ed.), *The autobiographical lectures of some prominent art educators* (pp. 291–300). Reston, VA: NAEA. (Originally presented 1997)

Haynes, J. S. (1993). Historical perspectives and antecedent theory of multicultural art education: 1954–1980. *Visual Arts Research, 19*(2), 24–34.

Haynes, J. S. (1997). The roots of multicultural art education practie: Social and cultural factors in the 1950s and 1960s that influenced a secondary urban art program. In A. Anderson & P. Bolin (Eds.), *History of art education* (pp. 81–87). University Park: The Pennsylvania State University.

Henry, C., & Nyman, A. (1997). Images for multicultural art education: An historical examination. In A. Anderson & P. Bolin (Eds.), *History of art education* (pp. 88–94). University Park, PA: The Pennsylvania State University.

Hilbert, R. (1924). Art in relation to the rural community. *Everyday Art, 3*(2), 14.

Hilbert, R. (1925). Art in relation to the rural community. *Everyday Art, 3*(7), 11–14.

Hinterreiter, H. G. (1967). Arthur Lismer/Artist and art educator: A reflection on his life and work. *School Arts, 66*(5), 21–28.

Hodik, B. (1992). The art education of the designer: A case study of Alvin Lustig (1915–1955) and his contributions to art education. In P. Amburgy, D. Soucy, M. A. Stankiewicz, B. Wilson, & M. Wilson (Eds.), *History of art education: Proceedings of the Second Penn State Conference, 1989* (pp. 154–156). Reston, VA: NAEA.

Hoffa, H. (1977). History of an idea. In S. Madeja (Ed.). *Arts and aesthetics: An agenda for a future* (pp. 61–80). St. Louis: CEMREL.

Hoffa, H. (1985). From the New Deal to the New Frontier. In B. Wilson & H. Hoffa (Eds.), *History of art education: Proceedings of the Penn State Conference* (pp. 338–346). University Park: The Pennsylvania State University College of Art and Architecture, School of Visual Arts.

Hoffa, H. (1994). *Revisitations: Ten little pieces on art education.* Reston, VA: NAEA.

Hoffa, H. (1997). Penn State '65: Context and consequences. In A. Anderson & P. Bolin (Eds.), *History of art education* (pp. 509–511). University Park: The Pennsylvania State University.

Hollingsworth, C. H. (1994). Port of sanctuary: The aesthetic of the African/African American and the Barnes Foundation. *Art Education, 47*(6), 41–43.

Hubbard, C. (1985). Black art education from slavery to the 1940s. The pioneering years. In B. Wilson & H. Hoffa (Eds.), *History of art education: Proceedings of the Penn State Conference* (pp. 163–165). University Park: The Pennsylvania State University College of Art and Architecture, School of Visual Arts.

Hubbard, C. A. (1992). The African-American artist and patronage: A comparison of private and public contributions. In P. Amburgy, D. Soucy, M. A. Stankiewicz, B. Wilson, & M. Wilson (Eds.), *History of art education: Proceedings of the Second Penn State Conference, 1989* (pp. 241–243). Reston, VA: NAEA.

Hubbard, G. (1982). Mary Rouse: A remembrance. In E. Zimmerman & M. A. Stankiewicz (Eds.), *Women art educators* (pp. 7–17). Bloomington, IN: Indiana University Press.

Hutchens, J. (2001). *In their own words: The development of doctoral study in art education.* Reston, VA: NAEA.

Hyer, S. (1990). *One house, one voice, one heart: Native American education at the Sante Fe Indian School.* Sante Fe, NM: The Museum of New Mexico Press.

Jagodzinski, J. (1997). *The nostalgia of Art Education. Reinscribing the master's narrative, 38*(2), 80–94.

Jones, R. L. (1974). Aesthetic education: Its historical presidents. *Art Education, 27*(9), 12–16.

Joyce, A. I. (1997). The historical evolution of evaluation and assessment in art education: From anomaly to paragon of educational efficacy. In A. Anderson & P. Bolin (Eds.), *History of art education* (pp. 320–328). University Park: The Pennsylvania State University.

Jubilee, V. (1982). The Barnes Foundation: Pioneer patron of black artists. *Journal of Negro Education, 51*(1), 40–49.

Judson, B. H. (1989). Master teachers at the Carnegie. *Art Education, 42*(2), 41–47.

Karr, W., Winslow, L., & Kirby, V. (1933). *Art Education in principle and practice.* Milton Bradley Company.

Kastner, A. (1940). Television, artist, and public. *Magazine of Art, 33*(10), 581, 599–600.

Katter, E. (1985). Hands-on instructional resources for the teaching of art: A historical perspective. In B. Wilson & H. Hoffa (Eds.), *History of art education: Proceedings of the Penn State Conference* (pp. 295–314). University Park, PA: The Pennsylvania State University College of Art and Architecture, School of Visual Arts.

Katter, E., & Stewart, M. (2001). *Art and the Human Experience.* Worcester, MA: Davis Publications.

Keel, J. S. (1963). Research review: The history of art education. *Studies in Art Education, 4*(2), 45–51.

Keel, J. S. (1965). Art education, 1940–1964. In W. R. Hastie (Ed.), *The sixty-fourth yearbook of the National Society for the Study of Education, Part II-Art Education* (pp. 35–50). Chicago: University of Chicago Press.

Kelly, M. F. (1992). "Let's Draw," 1936–1970: Elementary art education by radio. In P. Amburgy, D. Soucy, M. A. Stankiewicz, B. Wilson, & M. Wilson (Eds.), *History of art education: Proceedings of the Second Penn State Conference, 1989* (pp. 279–286). Reston, VA: NAEA.

Keppel, F. P., & Duffus, R. (1933). *The arts in American life.* New York: McGraw Hill.

Kern, E. (1985). The purposes of art education in the United States from 1870–1980. In B. Wilson & H. Hoffa (Eds.), *History of art education: Proceedings of the Penn State Conference* (pp. 40–52). University Park: The Pennsylvania State University College of Art and Architecture, School of Visual Arts.

Kern, E. (1987). Antecedents of Discipline-Based Art Education: State Departments of Education curriculum documents. *Journal of Aesthetic Education, 21*(2), 35–56.

Kilgore, A. (1922). Our soldier boys and modeling. *School Arts Magazine, 21*(6), 357–359.

Killeen, D. (1999a). Can we learn from the past? A history of the Kennedy Center Alliance for Arts Education: Part 1: Defining the agenda. *Arts Education Policy Review, 101*(1), 14–22.

Killeen, D. (1999b). Can we learn from the past? A history of the Kennedy Center Alliance for Arts Education: Part 2: Controlling the agenda. *Arts Education Policy Review, 101*(2), 7–19.

Kim, H. (2001). Art education in the Museum of Modern Art (1930s–1950s). In K. G. Congdon, D. Blandy & P. Bolin (Eds.), *Histories of community-based art education* (pp. 19–28). Reston, VA: NAEA.

Klar, W., Winslow, L. L., & Kirby, C. V. (1933). *Art education in principle and practice.* Springfield, MA: Milton Bradley Co.

Koch, F. (1921). Teaching the disabled veteran to draw. *School Arts Magazine, 20*(6), 315–321.

Koch, F. (1923). Making artists of veterans at Bayley's Harbor Way. *School Arts Magazine, 22*(6), 323–330.

Koch, F. (1924). Teaching art to kiddies who can't hear teacher. *School Arts Magazine, 24*(2), 67–71.

Koch, F. (1927a). Teaching school arts to a big city's wee cripple. *School Arts Magazine, 27*(1), 8–11.

Koch, F. (1927b). Teaching the cannons of practical arts to the sightless. *School Arts Magazine, 27*(4), 203–209.

Koos, M. (2000). Helen Merritt: An original art educator. In P. Bolin, D. Blandy, & K. G. Congdon (Eds.), *Remembering others: Making invisible histories visible* (pp. 37–40). Reston, VA: NAEA.

Korzenik, D. (1993). Arnheim and the diversity of American art. *Journal of Aesthetic Education, 27*(4), 143–153.

Korzenik, D. (1995). The changing concept of artistic giftedness. In C. Golomb (Ed.), *The development of artistically gifted children: Selected case studies* (pp. 1–29). Hillsdale, NJ: Lawrence Erlbaum Associates.

Lagerman, E. C. (1983). *Private power for the public good: A history of the Carnegie Foundation for the Advancement of Teaching.* Middletown, CT: Wesleyan University Press.

Lanier, V. (1963). Schismogenisis in contemporary art education. *Studies in Art Education, 5*(1), 10–19.

Lanier, V. (1969). The teaching of art as social revolution. *Phi Delta Kappan, 50*(6), 314–319.

Lanier, V. (1990). The future is behind us. *Canadian Review of Art Education, 17*(1), 51–62.

Lemerise, S., & Sherman, L. (1990). Cultural factors in art education history: A study of English and French Quebec, 1940–1980. In D. Soucy & M. A. Stankiewicz (Eds.), *Framing the past: Essays on art education* (pp. 183–200). Reston, VA: NAEA.

Lemos, P. (1920). *Applied Art: Drawing, painting, design, and handicraft.* Mountain View, CA: Pacific Press Publishing Ass.

Lemos, P. (1931). *The Art Teacher.* Worcester, MA: The Davis Press.

Levitas, A. (1920). Handicrafts for wayward boys. *School Arts magazine, 19*(6), 335–339.

Levy, F. (1910). Art Education in the public schools of New York. *Art & Progress, 1*(5), 119–123.

Levy, F. (1925). Radio talk: The museum of art, how to use and enjoy it. *American Magazine of Art,* 425–428.

Logan, F. (1955). *Growth of art in American schools.* New York: Harper & Brothers.

Logan, F. (1965). Developments of art education in the twentieth century. In J. Hausman, J. (Ed.), *Report of the Commission on Art Education* (pp. 49–68). Reston, VA: NAEA.

Logan, F. (2001). Doctoral study in art education. In J. Hutchens (Ed.), *In their own words: The development of doctoral study in art education* (pp. 1–9). Reston, VA: NAEA.

Lowenfeld, V. (2001). In R. Raunft (Ed.) *The autobiographical lectures of some prominent art educators* (pp. 1–16). Reston, VA: NAEA. (Originally presented 1958)

Madeja, S. (1977a). Arts and aesthetics: An agenda for the future. St. Louis, MO: CEMREL Inc.

Madeja, S. (1977b). *The arts, cognition, and basic skills.* St. Louis, MO: CEMREL Inc.

Madeja, S. (2001). Remembering the aesthetic education program: 1966–1976. In K. G. Congdon, D. Blandy, & P. Bolin (Eds.), *Histories of community-based art education* (pp. 117–126). Reston, VA: NAEA.

Madenfort, D. (1982). Lowenfeld, myself, and the tragic dream. *Art Education, 33*(6), 22–24.

Majewski, M. (1985). Lowenfeld's first graduate student: Ruth Freyberger. In M. A. Stankiewicz & E. Zimmerman (Eds.), *Women art educators II* (pp. 160–180). Bloomington, IN: Indiana University.

Mathias, M. (1924). *The Beginnings of Art in the Public Schools.* New York: Charles Scribner's & Sons.

Mattil, E. (1966). *A seminar in art education for research and curriculum development. Cooperative research project V-002.* University Park: The Pennsylvania State University.

Mattil, E. (1997). Opening remarks. In A. Anderson & P. Bolin (Eds.), *History of art education* (pp. 505–508). University Park, The Pennsylvania State University.

Mattil, E. (2001). In R. Raunft (Ed.), *The autobiographical lectures of some prominent art educators* (pp. 155–172). Reston, VA: NAEA. (Originally presented 1984)

McFee, J. K. (1961). *Preparation for art.* Belmont, CA: Wadsworth Publishing.

McFee, J. K. (1966). Society, art, and education. In E. Mattil, (Ed.), *A seminar in art education for research and curriculum development. Cooperative research project V-002* (pp. 122–140). University Park: The Pennsylvania State University.

McFee, J. K. (2001a). In R. Raunft (Ed.), *The autobiographical lectures of some prominent art educators* (pp. 131–142). Reston, VA: NAEA. (Originally presented 1981)

McFee, J. K. (2001b). The School of Eduation and The Department of Art and Architecture doctoral program in art education at Stanford University, 1957–1962. In J. Hutchens (Ed.), *In their own words: The development of doctoral study in art education* (pp. 59–66). Reston, VA: NAEA.

McFee, J. & Ettinger, L. (2001). The doctoral program in art education at The University of Oregon 1965–1993. In J. Hutchens (Ed.), *In their own words: The development of doctoral study in art education* (pp. 80–102). Reston, VA: NAEA.

McKibbin, M. (1960). Fifty years of theory and practice. In R. Ebken (Ed.). *Prospect and retrospect: The Eastern Arts Association, 1910–1960* (pp. 62–79). Kutztown, PA: Kutztown University.

McMahon, F. (1928). Orphan art. *School Arts Magazine, 27*(6), 369–371.

McNeill, P. (1992). Ella Victoria Dobbs and Verna M. Wulfekammer: Teaching art in the University Elementary School, University of Missouri, 1912–1936. In P. Amburgy, D. Soucy, M. A. Stankiewicz, B. Wilson, & M. Wilson

(Eds.), *History of art education: Proceedings of the Second Penn State Conference, 1989* (pp. 150–152). Reston, VA: NAEA.

McNeill, P. (1997). The school and the camera. In A. Anderson & P. Bolin (Eds.), *History of art education* (pp. 246–252). University Park: The Pennsylvania State University.

McNeill, P. (2001). Verna Wulfekammer's story. In K. G. Congdon, D. Blandy, & P. Bolin (Eds.), *Histories of community-based art education* (pp. 92–102). Reston, VA: NAEA.

McWhinnie, H. J. (1985). Jay Hambridge and art education. In B. Wilson & H. Hoffa (Eds.), *History of art education: Proceedings of the Penn State Conference* (pp. 243–246). University Park, PA: The Pennsylvania State University College of Art and Architecture, School of Visual Arts.

McWhinnie, H. (1994). Some reflections on the Barnes Collection. *Art Education, 47*(6), 22–34.

McWhinnie, H. (1997). Manuel Barkan's models of inquiry paper: Some reflections on *The Penn State Seminar*. In A. Anderson & P. Bolin (Eds.), *History of art education* (pp. 549–555). University Park, PA: The Pennsylvania State University.

Mechlin, L. (1925). The Cleveland convention. *American Magazine of Art, 16*(7), 348–375.

Michael, J. (1982a). *The Lowenfeld Lectures: Viktor Lowenfeld on art education and art therapy.* University Park, PA: The Pennsylvania State University.

Michael, J. (1982b). Viktor Lowenfeld. *Art Education, 33*(6), 13–14.

Michael, J. (1997). *The National Art Education Association: Our history—Celebrating 50 years 1947–1997.* Reston, VA: NAEA.

Michale, J. (2001). John A. Michael. In J. Raunft (Ed.), The autobiographical lectures. (pp. 211–230). Reston, VA: NAEA.

Mitchell, W. J. T. (1994). *Picture theory.* Chicago: University of Chicago Press.

Moore, J. (1997). William James and Art Education: Links between pragmatists and progressives. In A. Anderson & P. Bolin (Eds.), *History of art education* (pp. 167–174). University Park, PA: The Pennsylvania State University.

Morris, C. (2000). A sense of place: The Allegheny Echoes Project. In P. Bolin, D. Blandy, & K. G. Congdon (Eds.), *Remembering others: Making invisible histories visible* (pp. 176–187). Reston, VA: NAEA.

Morris, E. (1920). Hospital handicraft. *School Arts Magazine, 19*(6), 319–322.

Newsom, B. Y., & Silvers, A. Z. (1978). *The art museum as educator.* Berkley, CA: University of California Press.

Packard, S. (1977). An analysis of current ststistics and trends as they influence the status and future of women in the art academe. *Studies in Art Education, 18*(2), 38–48.

Packard, S. (1980, April). The history of art therapy education. *Art Education,* 10–13.

Parsier, D. (1984). A conversation with Rudolf Arnheim. *Studies in Art Education, 25*(3), 176–184.

Parsons, M. (1998). Integrated curriculum and our paradigm of cognition in the arts. *Studies in Art Education, 39*(2), 103–116.

Pasto, T. (1967). A critical review of the history of drawing methods in public schools of the United States II. *Art Education, 20*(9), 18–22.

Pattison, E. (1923). *Art in our country.* Washington, DC: American Federation of Art.

Payne, J. A. (1985). Manuel Barkan's *Foundations of Art Education*: The past is prologue In B. Wilson & H. Hoffa (Eds.), *History of art education: Proceedings of the Penn State Conference* (pp. 259–264). University Park, PA: The Pennsylvania State University College of Art and Architecture, School of Visual Arts.

Pearse, H. (1992). Arthur Lismer: Art educator with a social conscience. In P. Amburgy, D. Soucy, M. A. Stankiewicz, B. Wilson, & M. Wilson (Eds.), *History of art education: Proceedings of the Second Penn State Conference, 1989* (pp. 85–88). Reston, VA: NAEA.

Pearse, H. (1997). Imagining a history of Canadian Art Education. In A. Anderson & P. Bolin (Eds.), *History of art education* (pp. 16–25). University Park: The Pennsylvania State University.

Pepper, A. (1935). A Mexican school of sculpture. *Art Education Today.* New York: Teachers College.

Pittard, N. (1985). Preliminary considerations concerning aesthetic education. In B. Wilson & H. Hoffa (Eds.), *History of art education: Proceedings of the Penn State Conference* (pp. 166–176). University Park, PA: The Pennsylvania State University College of Art and Architecture, School of Visual Arts.

Plummer, G. (1969). Unclaimed Legacy: The eight year study. *Art Education, 22*(5), 4–6.

Plummer, G. (1985). Collage: People, places and problems in our historical continuum. In B. Wilson & H. Hoffa (Eds.), *History of art education: Proceedings of the Penn State Conference* (pp. 213–218). University Park, PA: The Pennsylvania State University College of Art and Architecture, School of Visual Arts.

Qualley, C. (1997). Memberships and affiliate groups. In Michael, J. (Ed.), *The National Art Education Association: Our history—Celebrating 50 years 1947–1997* (pp. 101–132). Reston, VA: NAEA.

Rhodes, J. (1985). Initial findings on the origins of the International Society for Education Through Art. In B. Wilson & H. Hoffa (Eds.), *History of art education: Proceedings of the Penn State Conference* (pp. 334–337). University Park, PA: The Pennsylvania State University College of Art and Architecture, School of Visual Arts.

Rogers, A. (1990). Art education curriculum in British Columbia between the wars: Official prescription—Unofficial interpretation. In D. Soucy & M. A. Stankiewicz (Eds.), *Framing the past: Essays on art education* (pp. 153–166). Reston, VA: NAEA.

Rogers, T. (1984). In our past: William P. Weston, artist and educator. *Art Education, 36*(5), 27–29.

Sacca, E. (1989). Invisible women: Questioning recognition and status in art education. *Studies in Art Education, 30*(2), 122–127.

Sacca, E. (2001). Epilogue. In R. Corwin (Ed.), *Exploring the legends: Guideposts to the furture.* Reston, VA: NAEA.

Sahasrabudhe, P. (1997). The expressionist era in education: The grounding for a Victor D'Amico pedagogy. In A. Anderson & P. Bolin (Eds.), *History of art education* (pp. 495–502). University Park, PA: The Pennsylvania State University.

Sahasrabudhe, P. (2001). Victor D'Amico. In R. Corwin (Ed.), *Exploring the legends: Guideposts to the future.* Reston, VA: NAEA.

Solkind, L. (1985). Maud Ellsworth: Art educator and master teacher. In M. A. Stankiewicz and E. Zimmerman (Eds.), Women art educations II (pp. 114–130), Bloomington, IN: Indiana University.

Saunders, R. J. (1954). *The parallel development of art education in Canada and the United States, with emphasis on the history of art education in Canada.* Unpublished master's thesis, The Pennsylvania State University, University Park.

Saunders, R. (1960). The contributions of Viktor Lowenfeld to art education: Part I: Early influence on his thought. *Studies in Art Education, 2*(1), 6–15.

Saunders, R. (1961). The contributions of Viktor Lowenfeld to art education: Part II: *Creative and Mental Growth. Studies in Art Education, 2*(1), 6–15.

Saunders, R. (1978). First Steps: The FCAE & the NAAE: A brief history.*Art Education, 31*(7), 18–22.

Saunders, R. (1982). The Lowenfeld motivation. *Art Education, 33*(6), 26–31.

Saunders, R. (1985). Owatonna: Art education's Camelot. In B. Wilson & H. Hoffa (Eds.), *History of art education: Proceedings of the Penn State Conference* (pp. 152–158). University Park, PA: The Pennsylvania State University College of Art and Architecture, School of Visual Arts.

Saunders, R. (1992). The making of the National Art Education Association: Names, initials, and group identity crisis. In P. Amburgy, D. Soucy, M. A. Stankiewicz, B. Wilson, & M. Wilson (Eds.), *History of art education: Proceedings of the Second Penn State Conference, 1989* (pp. 164–169). Reston, VA: NAEA.

Saunders, R. (2001). Viktor Lowenfeld. In R. Corwin (Ed.), *Exploring the legends: Guideposts to the future.* Reston, VA: NAEA.

School Arts Magazine (1901–present). Worchester, MA: Davis Publications.

School Arts Magazine (1934). *Children's Radio Broadcasting in the USSR.* Worchester, MA: Davis Publications.

Schultz, H. (2001). In R. Raunft (Ed.), *The autobiographical lectures of some prominent art educators* (pp. 95–108). Reston, VA: NAEA. (Originally presented 1978)

Sessions, B. (1997). Marguerite Wildenhain: A woman of choice substance. In A. Anderson & P. Bolin (Eds.), *History of art education* (pp. 129–137). University Park: The Pennsylvania State University.

Sessions, B. (2000). Marguerite Wildenhain: the visible core. In P. Bolin, D. Blandy & K. G. Congdon (Eds.), *Remembering others: Making invisible histories visible* (pp. 11–25). Reston, VA: NAEA.

Sherman, L., & Efland, A. (1997). Educational discourse and the visual documentation of practice. In A. Anderson & P. Bolin (Eds.), *History of art education* (pp. 486–494). University Park: The Pennsylvania State University.

Shoaff-Ballanger, S., & Davis, D. J. (1997). Professional conferences for art educators: A pilgrimage to excellence. In Michael, J. (Ed.), *The National Art Education Association: Our history—Celebrating 50 years 1947–1997* (pp. 133–144). Reston, VA: NAEA.

Smith, M. (1966). *A decade of comment on education 1956–1966.* Washington: Council on Basic Education.

Smith, P. (1982a). Lowenfeld in a Germanic perspective. *Art Education, 33*(6), 25–27.

Smith, P. (1982b). Germanic foundations: A look at what we are standinson. *Studies in Art Education, 23*(3), 23–30.

Smith, P. (1985a). Natalie Robinson Cole: The American Cizek? *Art Education, 37*(1), 36–39.

Smith, P. (1985b). Natalie Robinson Cole: The American Cizek? In M. A. Stankiewicz & E. Zimmerman (Eds.), *Women art educators II* (pp. 100–113). Bloomington, IN: Indiana University.

Smith, P. (1987). Lowenfeld teaching art: A European theory and American experience at Hampton Institute. *Studies in Art Education, 29*(1), 30–36.

Smith, P. (1996). *The history of American art education: Learning about art in American schools.* Westport, CT: Greenwood Press.

Smith, P. (1997). Allan Kaprow and the artist-in-the-classroom. In A. Anderson & P. Bolin (Eds.), *History of art education* (pp. 556–564). University Park: The Pennsylvania State University.

Smith, P. (1999). The unexplored: Art education historians' failure to consider the Southwest. *Studies in Art Education, 40*(2), 114–127.

Smith, R. (1966a). *Aesthetic and criticism in art education*. Chicago: Rand McNally.

Smith, R. (1966). (Ed.), The Journal of Aesthetic Education.

Smith, R. (1987). The changing image of Art Education: Theoretical antecedents of Discipline-Based Art Education. *Journal of Aesthetic Education, 21*(2), 3–34.

Snow, B., & Froehlich, H. (1916, 1919) *Industrial arts textbooks. Books 1–8*. Chicago: Laidlaw Brothers.

Speirs, P. (1998). *Collapsing distinctions: Feminist art education as research, art, and pedagogy*. Unpublished doctoral dissertation: The Pennsylvania State University.

Stankiewicz, M. A. (1982). Woman, artist, art educator: Professional image among women art educators. In E. Zimmerman & M. A. Stankiewicz (Eds.), *Women art educators* (pp. 30–48). Bloomington, IN: Indiana University Press.

Stankiewicz, M. A. (1984). Self expression or teacher influence: The Shaw system of finger painting. *Art Education, 37*(3), 20–24.

Stankiewicz, M. A. (1990). Rules of Invention: From ornament to design in Art Education. In D. Soucy & M. A. Stankiewicz (Eds.), *Framing the past: Essays on art education*. Reston, VA: NAEA.

Stankiewicz, M. A. (2001). *Roots of art education practice*. Worcester, MA: Davis Publications Inc.

Stankiewicz, M. A., & Zimmerman, E. (1984). Women's achievements in art education. In G. Collins & R. Sandell (Eds.), *Women, art, and education*. Reston, VA: NAEA.

Stankiewicz, M. A., & Zimmerman, E. (1985). *Women art educators II*. Bloomington, IN: Indiana University.

Stephenson, W. (1997). Coping with a lack of art materials in the depression era as reflected in *School Arts Magazine*. In A. Anderson & P. Bolin (Eds.), *History of art education* (pp. 232–237). University Park, PA: The Pennsylvania State University.

Stokrocki, M. (1992). Interviews with students: Thomas Munro as a teacher of aesthetics. In P. Amburgy, D. Soucy, M.A. Stankiewicz, B. Wilson, & M. Wilson (Eds.), *History of art education: Proceedings of the Second Penn State Conference, 1989* (pp. 296–300). Reston, VA: NAEA.

Stokrocki, M. (1997). Toward an ethnohistory of Amerindian art education: Navajo cultural preservation vs. assimilation. In A. Anderson & P. Bolin (Eds.), *History of art education* (pp. 71–80). University Park: The Pennsylvania State University.

Stokrocki, M. (2000). Commentary: Historical research in the Southwest: Ignored and undervalued. *Studies in Art Education, 42*(1), 83–86.

Strommen, E. (1988). A century of children drawing: The evolution of theory and research concerning the drawings of children. *Visual Arts Research, 14*(2), 13–24.

Suplee, B. (1994). The eccentric hanging of the Barnes Foundation. *Art Education, 47*(6), 35–40.

Suplee, B. (1997). Art education at the Barnes Foundation: Seven decades of "learning to see." In A. Anderson & P. Bolin (Eds.), *History of art education* (pp. 271–278). University Park: The Pennsylvania State University.

Swift, J. (1990). Memory drawing and visualization in the teaching of Robert Catterson-Smith and Marion Richardson. In D. Soucy & M. A. Stankiewicz (Eds.), *Framing the past: Essays on art education* (pp. 139–152). Reston, VA: NAEA.

Tannahill, S. (1932). *Fine arts for public school administrators*. New York: Teachers College Press.

Taylor, F. (1935). Observations on art education among school children of Worcester. In B. Boas (Ed.), *Art Education Today* (pp. 40–42). New York: Teachers College Press.

The American Magazine of Art. (1925). Other federation activities. *The American Magazine of Art, 16*(3), 144–148.

The American Magazine of Art. (1925). Mr. De Forest's radio talk. *The American Magazine of Art, 16*(3), 1948–1949.

Thistlewood, D. J. (1990). Educating in contemporary art: the first decade of the London Institute of Contemporary Arts. In D. Soucy & M. A. Stankiewicz (Eds.), *Framing the past: Essays on art education* (pp. 167–182). Reston, VA: NAEA.

Troeger, B. J. (1992). Your past is our future: The development of art programs for special populations. In P. Amburgy, D. Soucy, M. A. Stankiewicz, B. Wilson, & M. Wilson (Eds.), *History of art education: Proceedings of the Second Penn State Conference, 1989* (pp. 181–185). Reston, VA: NAEA.

Welling, J. B. (1935). Art education as a social study. In B. Boas (Ed.), *Art Education Today* (pp. 55–60). New York: Teachers College Press.

Whipple, G. M. (1934). *The thirty-third yearbook of the Society for the Study of Education, Part II—The Activity Movement*. Bloomington, IL: Public School Publishing Co.

Whipple, G. M. (1941). *The fortieth yearbook of the National Society for the Study of Education: Art in American life and education*. Bloomington, IL: Public School Publishing Co.

Whitford, W. (1926). Research in art education. *School Arts Magazine, 25*(5), 269.

Whitford, W. (1933). Analysis of the art curriculum. *School Arts Magazine, 32*(10), 582–587.

White, J. (1997). Native American presence in *School Arts*: the deLemos legacy, 1919–1949. In A. Anderson & P. Bolin (Eds.), *History of art education* (pp. 95–104). University Park: The Pennsylvania State University.

White, J. (1998). Pragmatism and art: Tools for change. *Studies in Art Education, 39*(3), 215–229.

White, J. (2001a). Imaging (Native) America: Pedro deLemos and the expansion of art education (1919–1940). *Studies in Art Education, 42*(4), 298–317.

White, J. (2001b). The ethnic aesthetics of Pedro deLemos: Editor, *The School Arts Magazine* (1919–1950). In D. Blandy, P. Bolin, & K. Congdon (Eds.), *Histories of Community-based Art Education* (pp. 182–197). Reston, VA: NAEA Publications.

White, J. (2001c). Pedro J. deLemos: Progress and restraint. *School Arts Magazine, 101*(3), 12–14.

Whittmann, O. (1966). The museum and its role in art education. *Art Education, 19*(2), 3–6.

Wieder, C. (1977, February). Three decades of research on child art: A survey and critique. *Art Education, 30*(2), 5–10.

Wilson, B. (1997). *The quiet revolution: Changing the face of arts education.* Los Angeles: The Getty Education Institute for the Arts.

Wilson, B., & Hoffa, H. (1985). *History of art education: Proceedings of the Penn State Conference.* University Park, PA: The Pennsylvania State University College of Art and Architecture, School of Visual Arts.

Wilson, B., & Wilson, M. (1977). An iconoclastic view of the imagery sources in the drawings of young children. *Art Education, 30*, 4–13.

Winslow, L. (1939). *The integrated school art program.* New York: McGraw–Hill.

Wygant, F. (1985). Art structure: Fundamentals of design before the Bauhaus. In B. Wilson & H. Hoffa (Eds.), *History of art education: Proceedings of the Penn State Conference* (pp. 158–162). University Park, PA: The Pennsylvania State University College of Art and Architecture, School of Visual Arts.

Wygant, F. (1988a). Dewey and Naumberg: An unresolved debate. *Canadian Review of Art Education, 15*(2), 29–39.

Wygant, F. (1988b). A response to professor MacIver. *Canadian Review of Art Education, 16*(1), 59–60.

Wygant, F. (1991). Efland's long view of art education. *Journal of Aesthetic Education, 25*(2), 40–46.

Wygant, F. (1993). *School art in American culture.* Cincinnati, OH: Interwood Press.

Wygant, F. (2001). In R. Raunft (Ed.), *The autobiographical lectures of some prominent art educators* (pp. 311–331). Reston, VA: NAEA. (Originally presented 1999)

Youngbood, M. (1982). Lowenfeld's unremitting legacy. *Art Education 33*(6), 32–36.

Zahner, M. (1992). Manuel Barkan: Twentieth-century art educator. In P. Amburgy, D. Soucy, M. A. Stankiewicz, B. Wilson, & M. Wilson (Eds.), *History of art education: Proceedings of the Second Penn State Conference, 1989* (pp. 170–174). Reston, VA: NAEA.

Zahner, M. A. (1997). A seminar in art education for research and curriculum development: Analysis of private ideologies and public policy. In A. Anderson & P. Bolin (Eds.), *History of art education* (pp. 517–524). University Park: The Pennsylvania State University.

Zastrow, L. (1982). American Indian women as art educators. In E. Zimmerman & M. A. Stankiewicz (Eds.), *Women art educators* (pp. 88–95). Bloomington, IN: Indiana University Press.

Zastrow, L. M. (1985). The changing role of Native American women as teachers of art. In M. A. Stankiewicz & E. Zimmerman (Eds.), *Women art educators II* (210–218). Bloomington, IN: Indiana University.

Zeller, Neil (1989). The historical and philosophical foundations for art museum practice in America. In N. Berry & S. Mayer (Eds.). *Museum Education: History, theory, and practice.* Reston, VA: NAEA Press.

Zimmerman, E. (1982). Belle Boas: Her kindly spirit touched all. In E. Zimmerman & M. A. Stankiewicz (Eds.), *Women art educators* (pp. 49–58). Bloomington, IN: Indiana University Press.

Zimmerman, E. (1985a). Art talent and research in the 1920s and 1930s: Norman Charles Meier's and Leta Stetter Hollingworth's theories about special abilities In B. Wilson & H. Hoffa (Eds.), *History of art education: Proceedings of the Penn State Conference* (pp. 269–275).University Park, PA: The Pennsylvania State University College of Art and Architecture, School of Visual Arts.

Zimmerman, E. (1985b). To test all things: The life and work of Leta Steller Hollingsworth. In M. A. Stankiewicz & E. Zimmerman (Eds.), *Women art educators II* (64–81). Bloomington, IN: Indiana University.

Zimmerman, E., & Stankiewicz, M. A. (1982). *Women art educators.* Bloomington, IN: Indiana University Press.

Zucker, B. (2001). Anna Curtis Chandler: Art educator nonpareil at the Metropolitan Museum of Art. In K. G. Congdon, D. Blandy, & P. Bolin (Eds.), *Histories of community-based art education* (pp. 8–18). Reston, VA: NAEA.

Zurmuehlen, M. (1985). Norman C. Meier: His relationships with artists and students. In B. Wilson & H. Hoffa (Eds.), *History of art education: Proceedings of the Penn State Conference* (pp. 265–268). University Park, PA: The Pennsylvania State University College of Art and Architecture, School of Visual Arts.

Zurmuehlen, M. (1991). Kenneth Beittel: A re-interpreting presence in art and education. *Visual Arts Research, 17*(1), 1–11.

II

Policy Perspectives Impacting
the Teaching of Art

4

Policy and Arts Education

Ralph A. Smith
University of Illinois, Urbana-Champaign

INTRODUCTION

As this *Handbook* indicates, policy questions and issues surface when decisions are made about the purposes and objectives of arts education, curriculum design, teaching and learning strategies, the selection of content, teacher preparation, administration, and types of advocacy and research. A judicious and coherent policy is one that is ethically acceptable, descriptive of the state of affairs it is intended to realize, implementable, and amenable to assessment. There are also questions about the sources of policy and the forces driving it.

What then is the state of affairs that policy for visual art education intends to bring about? Who should decide such policy, and how is policy enacted and implemented? How is it to be assessed and who should be the assessors? What are the conditions and forces influencing changes in policy? Policymaking is often a function of collaboration among federal agencies, states, and communities, professional arts organization, institutions of higher education, cultural organizations, and a variety of special-interest groups. States, school districts, and local school boards, moreover, usually provide some leeway in the selection of content, methods of implementation, and instruments of evaluation, as evidenced, for example, in the implementation of the national standards for arts education. The tendency of professional arts associations has been to emphasize the distinctive educational values of arts education and how they might be realized in the young. Federal and private organizations, often in tandem, tend to concentrate on national priorities. Special-interest groups further complicate matters. Because a serious tension exists between professional arts education associations and a complex of federal and cultural organizations with potent lobbying powers, a major issue for the field of art education has become the preservation of the core values of art education. Such tension raises issues about the sources of policy, the credibility of policymakers, and the dynamics and politics of collaboration.

All policymaking ultimately derives from more or less explicit assumptions about the inherent values of art and how they figure in justifications of art education. What, for example, are the more immediate values of artistic and appreciative activities in art education and their effects on other human values considered to be important? Contributors to this section have much to say about this issue as well as several others: the dilemma of policymakers in a period of cross-purposes (Hope), the uses and abuses of advocacy (Gee), the credibility of research claims (Hetland and Winner), the state and fate of aesthetic literacy (Smith), the mixed consequences of multiculturalism (Blocker), and the problems of understanding new and controversial art in both classrooms and museum education programs (Lankford and Scheffer).

The most informed writer about policy for arts education is Samuel Hope. He has written extensively about the subject and has been a leader in formulating and enacting policies, having played a major role in the creation and publication of the national standards for arts education. Moreover, as an executive editor of *Arts Education Policy Review*, he helps maintain an important forum for debates concerning policy relating to K-12 arts education. He thus brings a valuable background to a discussion of visual art education.

What stands out in Hope's views on policy is not only his treatment of a series of policy issues, each one of which he illuminates by asking a number of key questions, but also his making a case for policy-based research. His articulation of issues and questions, which range from discussions of purposes, techniques, youth cultures, technology, and teacher preparation to philosophy, curriculum, support sources, and standards, constitutes a primer for thinking about policymaking. Making distinctions between the survival and the health of the field and between activism and wisdom-seeking, he highlights the basic values of the field, the degree of control the field has over maintaining and attaining such values, and the forces that impede their realization. Most important, he emphasizes putting policy analysis and enactment in the service of a substantive art education that emphasizes the creation and experience of works of visual works of art for their intrinsic values in contrast to views that place art education in the service of extraneous goals.

Whereas Hope provides a general framework for thinking about policy, Constance Baumgarner Gee examines a number of specific examples of policymaking that could have potentially adverse consequences for what Hope calls the security and health of the field. Having written extensively about the subject, she is principally concerned with the abuses of advocacy and the emergence of a complex of federal, cultural, and university collaborations that have less to do with the young realizing art's distinctive values than with connections between art education and nonarts outcomes. Accordingly, she stresses the importance of asking key questions and making important distinctions. For example, what can school-based programming do that arts organizations cannot? To what extent do the objectives, overt and covert, of arts organization contribute to the erosion of school-based learning? Should it be assumed that any kind of art activity is educational and that anyone associated with art is an educator? If so, what are the consequences for the support of school programs of art education and professional teacher-preparation programs? Is there empirical support for those claiming significant nonarts benefits of art education? Gee's stance is critical and skeptical and questions whether the field of arts education associations can effectively compete with a powerful arts organization complex whose priorities are often at odds with those of the field. Gee sees an encouraging sign, however, in the successful effort of the arts education associations to counter legislation that would give arts organizations considerable influence over policymaking. Her own convictions about the values of art education are grounded in reasonable assumptions about the contributions of art education to spirit, mind, and body, and in her belief that engagement with works of art is one of the greatest satisfactions of human experience.

One would think that anyone taking a serious interest in the arts would concentrate on their manifold aesthetic properties and meanings, which is to say their intrinsic values. The same should be true of the objectives of research programs that study the dynamics of teaching art. Yet a considerable amount of research is being devoted not to discovering the ways the young develop knowledge about art's intrinsic value but to attempts to detect the effects of arts education on such cognitive non-arts outcomes as reading, mathematical, and spatial reasoning skills, not to mention a variety of social behaviors. In short, research is centered more on art's instrumental than on its core values. This priority seems to have two motivations. One motivation addresses the national concern about the eroding of basic skills in the population and a number of social problems that the schools are believed capable of ameliorating. The other motivation stems from curiosity about the ways the brain functions when undergoing certain kinds of acts. In her chapter, Gee enumerates a surfeit of instrumental values that advocates say are realizable through the study of the arts. What does a systematic and comprehensive assessment of such research conclude?

This was this question Lois Hetland and Ellen Winner set out to answer in REAP (Reviewing Education and the Arts Project). Using the method of meta-analysis, they synthesized clusters of individual studies that tested the effects of arts education on learning in non-arts domains. The results of the research were first published in the *Journal of Aesthetic Education* (Summer/Fall, 2000), copies of which provided reading material for participants in a conference sponsored by the Getty Center that further addressed the problem of transfer. The proceedings of the conference were published by the Getty in *Beyond the Soundbite: Arts Education and Academic Outcomes* (Los Angeles, 2001). The results of the REAP study were also the subject of a symposium in *Arts Education Policy Review* (May/June, 2001), and an executive summary of the study was distributed by the National Art Education Association as part of its series that translates theory into practice.

Stating that REAP offers the most trustworthy knowledge currently available about the relations of arts education and cognitive transfer, Hetland and Winner concluded that overall there is as yet no compelling evidence that the study of art forms leads to improved academic performance. There were some exceptions. The use of dramatic techniques in the general classroom not surprisingly improved verbal skills. Musical instruction was shown to have had some effect on types of spatial reasoning, but Hetland and Winner nonetheless say that these studies provide no basis for thinking that policies should mandate listening to classical music for its extra-aesthetic benefits, whatever the audience. The Mozart effect, moreover, remains problematical so long as the mechanism responsible for it has not been found. With regard to the effects of visual art education, of most interest to readers of this *Handbook*, Hetland and Winner likewise found no compelling evidence to support claims for cognitive transfer. Different kinds of arts-rich education revealed no enhancement of either reading or math skills; the finding was the same for the effects of music instruction. Examinations of dance fared no better, although the paucity of dance studies was noted. It is not, say Hetland and Winner, that the studies they assessed have no value; the better-designed ones may provide insight into how the brain functions when undergoing certain kinds of activities. It is rather that cogent relevance to policy has not been established. Accordingly, the authors advise muting positive claims about the mechanisms of causative transfer.

Not only that. The authors question investing so much effort in studying arts education's instrumental effects and ask whether there are important noncognitive outcomes of art education that are motivational and dispositional in character. Another approach might investigate whether the methods of teaching art suggest useful ideas for teaching other subjects. In short, the writers call for the right kinds of arguments for art education and the right kinds of evidence to support them. "The best hope for the arts in our schools," they write, "is to justify them by what the arts can do other subjects cannot do as well or cannot do at all."

The conviction that art education should do what it alone can do best also pervades contemporary writings about aesthetic education. Such writings conclude that education in the arts serves learning well by developing aesthetic literacy in the young, which is best attained by refining creative, perceptual, and reflective capacities. After indicating different senses of aesthetic education and its close ties to the branch of philosophy known as aesthetics, Ralph

Smith distinguishes between domain and nondomain interpretations; the former centers on the study of the arts and the latter on a variety of contexts in which aesthetic sensibility can find expression

Before addressing contemporary literature and issues, Smith recalls the ideas of three generative writers on aesthetic education, Friedrich Schiller, Herbert Read, and John Dewey, whose expansive notions of aesthetic education inspired other theorists of arts education to argue the case for a more humane and aesthetic life. Consonant, however, with the prevalent temper of the second half of the twentieth century, expansive notions of aesthetic education gave way to more restrictive domain interpretations. Accordingly, Smith devotes less attention to nondomain interpretations that encompass, for example, the aesthetics of the natural environment and efforts to examine various aspects of education from aesthetic perspectives.

Questions and issues that arise in discussions of domain interpretations of aesthetic education center on the viability of such key concepts as aesthetic experience, aesthetic value, and aesthetic judgment. After a period when critical analysis (from both Anglo-American and Continental perspectives) questioned the tenability of certain aesthetic concepts, there has been a revival of interest in the aesthetic. Motivating this sentiment was the realization that too much was being lost in efforts to deaestheticize the experience of art. Moreover, the restoration of the aesthetic brought with it arguments for a closer relationship between aesthetic and ethical values.

Among the challenges facing policy for art education is a cluster of issues associated with multiculturalism. H. Gene Blocker, who has written extensively about the topic and spent considerable time living in different cultures, sorts out the basic problems and makes recommendations for policy. Blocker first mentions practical, theoretical, private, and cultural reasons for having art education: that is, self-expression, informed knowledge and appreciation of the art world, enrichment of life, and assimilation of the young into their culture. He then emphasizes that we are concerned with multiculturalism because North America itself constitutes an ongoing evolution of the integration and assimilation of different groups. While the roots of American culture have been primarily, but not exclusively, European, he says that the evolutionary process must now continue with the integration and assimilation of non-European groups. But so far as art education is concerned, how to do this has generated a wide-ranging discussion that extends from radical ideological interpretations of multiculturalism to more accommodating and conciliatory viewpoints. Although Blocker strongly favors the idea of cultural diversity and the assimilation of the young into their cultures, he devotes a large part of his chapter to exposing a number of myths and misconceptions that have influenced questionable policy decisions. Blocker's work and disposition prompt him to recommend complementing Western conceptions of values, art, and aesthetics but without being anti-Western or anti-modern; and he cautions against the possibility of instilling in students a hatred of their culture that is the result of ignorance. Calling for sober reflection and consideration, he sides with those who say that all multicultural studies need not be about victimized minorities or express anti-Western sentiment. Nor is multiculturalism necessarily divisive.

Among the salient points Blocker makes is a recognition that multiculturalism is grounded in Western ideals of democracy and its ideals of equality, diversity, and freedom. Moreover, the charge that Western art and aesthetic theory have been preoccupied primarily with "art for art's sake" proceeds from ignorance of Western aesthetics. Nor is the relatively detached appreciation of art uniquely Western. It is also stressed in some non-Western aesthetic traditions, for example, those of China and India. Knowledge about non-Western forms of art, moreover, is usefully conveyed by museum education programs, that is, in venues often condemned by anti-Western critics for their alleged role in defining and advancing Western art. Last, in the place of a multiculturalism that insists on introducing the young chiefly into the arts of their own ethnic backgrounds—African art for African Americans, etc.—there should be an intercultural education that stresses a balance between assimilation into one's own culture and transcendence of it in order to build a more catholic sense of self. Blocker's recommendations call for greater depth and breadth in the definition of multiculturalism, better understanding of both Western and non-Western art and aesthetics, and more emphasis on the non-Western and native roots of American culture.

In his discussion of multiculturalism Blocker referred to postmodern critics of art museums who faulted them for what they took to be elitist policies typical of Western cultural institutions. Blocker countered by saying that such criticism notwithstanding, museums can play important roles in providing authentic knowledge about non-Western and native cultures. Louis Lankford and Kelly Scheffer address a different kind of problem museums have in fulfilling their educational obligations. They stress the need for policies and procedures regarding exhibitions of controversial art. Their discussion ranges from a description of the response of art museums to ever-changing concepts of art, the meaning of controversial art, types of controversies museums must contend with (e.g., internal organizational problems and external relations with the public and the media), to the character of the works themselves. For example, what should attitudes be toward works that are not only fragile, impermanent, confrontational, morally offensive, and of questionable origin and ownership, but also toward works that are more statements about art than aesthetically interesting objects. Consequently, the staffs of museums must be well versed in the history of Western art, cultural differences, and the changes that have occurred in the modern era, not to mention in philosophical aesthetics that provides insight into the problems of defining, interpreting, and evaluating art. Aesthetic education in the schools has similar responsibilities in preparing teachers of art for schools charged with inducting the young into the world of art, including the world of art museums. Many of the issues associated with controversial art are brought out in the authors' extended discussion of Alma Lopez's *Our Lady*.

5

Art Education in a World of Cross-Purposes

Samuel Hope
National Association of Schools of Art and Design

This chapter considers a number of policy challenges for the field of art education. It suggests basic orientation to policy considerations and proposes several sets of research questions that need perpetual attention. Distinctions are drawn between the survival and the health of the field. Purposes, techniques, youth cultures, technology, teacher preparation, philosophy, curricula, support resources, and standards are considered as major areas of policy analysis. The conclusion recommends the development of a more extensive research-based policy capability for the field of art education.

ART EDUCATION AND QUESTIONS OF POLICY

To study art education is to discover and engage a field rich with achievement and promise. On one hand, this comes as no surprise because art education encompasses and embraces great artistic and intellectual traditions of work in and about visual form, each of which with its own habits of mind, approaches to achievement, and history. On the other hand, the accomplishments of art educators in the United States represent something special. Many contextual factors work against serious instruction in things visual. Gains in art education have been purchased through the extraordinary dedication of individual teachers working alone and in groups. In one sense, art education in the United States is defined by the unremitting struggle to sustain a reasonable purpose: developing basic visual knowledge and skills in individual students.

Like all other fields, art education works in a context created by forces over which it has little control. It also has areas of responsibility where it can exercise significant control. A third reality is not discussed as much as it should be. This reality can be demarcated by asking several illustrative questions: What choices does the field make about dealing with conditions that appear to be beyond its control? How well does the field delineate and then protect those things that are essential to its survival? How does the field manage the relationship between decisions in areas it cannot control and decisions in areas it can control? How much and what kind of thinking is being done about the short- and long-term ramifications of real or prospective changes? What are the forces influencing areas over which the field has little or no control? How are distinctions made between dysfunction and obsolescence? What lies immediately ahead that represents a challenge, an opportunity, or a significant danger? How does the field and its organizations determine the nature and conditions of its interaction with others?

In-depth answers to these kinds of questions are normally sought through policy studies. The field of art education has been fortunate to have a number of outstanding thinkers who, from time to time, have devoted themselves to such questions.[1] The field has made significant advances in policy sophistication over the last 30 years. Time and experience have shattered a number of naïve illusions. The formulation of national standards for student learning has provided a critical reference point for policy development (Consortium of National Arts Education Associations [Consortium], 1994). Still it remains questionable whether the field of art education has sufficient policy analysis capabilities given the scope and magnitude of its efforts and responsibilities. Because art education is primarily funded by local government, and because local school governance is connected in various ways to state and federal governments, and because governments at all levels support arts and humanities councils, most of the field's external policy attention is focused on government or government-influenced issues as they arise. Such efforts continue to be important. No amount of sophistication can be too great when dealing with the political, legislative, and organizational issues of governmental education and arts policies. But there is more, much more. Governmental policies are not developed in a vacuum. All policies are based on ideas, and ideas are conceived, developed, promoted, and funded. Ideas grow from basic points of view. Basic points of view or core beliefs are the foundations for policy frameworks that compete with each other (Gerzon, 1996; Hope, 2002). Understanding these frameworks and their interaction is critical.

It is important to remember that, in the United States, individuals working in the most powerful governmental positions convince a majority of the people to vote for them. This means that governments both reflect and direct. Many nongovernmental forces create values and influence decisions at all levels in all sectors. In the policy realm, to focus on government and government-sponsored organizations without attending to other contextual forces is dangerous and potentially destructive. For example, marketing techniques used to inveigle children and youth create the social and aesthetic environment for formal art education in the schools. Decisions about the nature and content of messages and items that create youth cultures are far more influential than anything said or done about art education by the federal government, and have at least as much influence on student learning as the decisions of local school boards.

This juxtaposition of education and marketing illustrates a truth about present conditions. Considered comprehensively, the pressures and issues in the context for art education reveal a world of cross-purposes. Not only are there direct and obvious oppositions, but also there are situations where what seems positive in the short term turns out to be negative in the long term. Cross-purposes work not only against the visual arts and art education but also within them. For example, freedom of expression and public support are important conditions for the visual arts. Regularly, one is achieved at the expense of the other.

This chapter provides an overview of many policy issues that influence the present and future of school-based education in things visual. In the text, the terms *art* and *visual art*

---

[1]From time to time, writers such as Laura H. Chapman (1982, pp. 113–130), Charles Dorn (2001), Elliot Eisner (2001), Constance Bumgarner Gee (1999a, 199b), and Ralph Smith (1987, 1993, 1995) issue warnings and recommendations based on policy analysis. Tom Hatfield, the executive director of the National Art Education Association (NAEA), has nurtured policy orientations in the work of that association. Such efforts can be the foundation for building enhanced capabilities.

and *things visual* are used to encompass and address all of the many specializations in art, design, crafts, architecture, and film/video; art and design history; criticism; philosophy of art; and so forth that constitute work in the visual world. Although each of these fields and their specializations have their own policy concerns, this chapter is devoted to considerations of policy matters affecting the whole as the basis for general education in things visual—art education—from early childhood through the high school years.

The chapter begins with several points about policy, continues with a discussion about the survival and health of art education, and concludes with an annotated list of policy areas and questions. It looks toward the possible future of policy research in art education. Its purpose is to construct and connect possibilities that would place policy analysis and action in the service of substantive art education as a counter to forces that would place art education in service to policy goals external to matters of instruction and individual enlightenment and competence in things visual.

POLICY AND ITS POWERS

Essentially, policy means some sort of engagement with simple or complex efforts to make successful decisions or to influence the decisions of others. Obviously, decisions can be made with or without research, the application of significant intellectual technique, or any thought at all. Policy may also refer to larger, established frameworks that govern specific decisions. For example, in the United States many endeavors are supported by maintaining a tax system that provides incentives for individual giving. This overall policy produces a framework for millions of individual and group decisions about philanthropy and fundraising. This framework— embedded in the American way of doing things—is both generated and reflected by many federal and state policies.

Beyond these generalities about policy lie many critical issues. Each decision has consequences. Some decisions are better than others. Some approaches to decision making obscure rather than clarify and produce illusions rather than illuminations of reality, thus leading to danger, dysfunction, or loss. These considerations are particularly important when considering issues of policy research. Research is a critical part of sophisticated policymaking. But often, there is no time for in-depth research before decisions must be taken. This means that chances for success usually improve to the extent that research-based thinking and projecting have been done in advance. Such thinking and projecting are primary purposes of intelligence operations in government, commerce, and the military; and of market research in advertising.

When research and policymaking are connected, what makes the result valuable? What predicts a good decision? A way to begin answering is by drawing a distinction between policy as activism and policy as wisdom seeking. All entities and efforts have a purpose. Some have given more thought to their purposes or stated them with greater precision than others, but purpose is present, either by design or by default. Activism can take any purpose and disconnect it from the greater reality. Activism tends to narrow perspective so that everything is evaluated and projected on the basis of what happens with respect to a single issue. Single-reference activism has significant powers to destroy the healthy connections between research and policy. Normally, such activism has no interest in what has been learned before; no willingness to consider, understand, or support the interlocking elements of larger systems; no patience; no sense of humor; and a highly selective acceptance of the facts. Activists already have all the answers. There is no question that activism can influence decisions. American society at present is replete with individuals and groups with a single objective, a deep understanding of activist techniques, and not much else. Opposition and obstruction are high arts. The activist approach is not very careful about what it does except in its own narrow sphere of interest. Thus, activism has tremendous corrosive powers. More hidden are the abilities of master politicians in all fields to manipulate activists unmercifully, thus adding cynicism to myopia. Few readers of this chapter can be unaware of the significant problems art education has experienced for decades due to efforts of activists in education and in the arts to reduce attention to sequential curricula, qualified specialist teachers, time and resources within the school day, and so forth, in pursuit of goals they consider having higher priority.

In a policy arena pervaded with activisms where activist techniques appear to win regularly, there is great temptation to put all of a field's policy chips on the activists' square. But devoting everything to the games of activism can obscure and obstruct the steady pursuit of reasonable purposes, for such a pursuit is multidimensional. It requires making all sorts of connections, including connections with activisms and activists. Pursuing purposes steadily over time calls for policy development based on wisdom seeking, on understanding, on seeing the relationships of parts and wholes, and on synthesis. Research plays a critical role here, for research brings information, data, and various analytical techniques to decision making oriented to showing things as they are. To activists, the only research that matters is that which supports the current focal point of their activism; to them research is a branch of propaganda.

Policy analysis devoted to wisdom seeking is different: It tells the known truth as comprehensively as possible at the time of telling. It develops a sense of where the make-or-break variables for a field and its practitioners really are and how they are evolving. Wisdom-seeking policy analysis also tells the truth about what is not known. It separates what is fact from speculation. Wisdom-seeking policy analysis does not minimize the presence of opposition to the pursuit of basic purpose. For example, it recognizes that forces opposing serious art education in the schools are far greater than one or two press-pilloried individuals, a political party, or any particular organization or group. Wisdom-seeking policy analysis does not demonize or join community swoons; rather, it explains. Policy informed by research and connected to the steady pursuit of reasonable purpose does not advance, promote, or reinforce illusions. It does not imply that supporting this person or cause will solve everything, or make everything appreciably better than that person or cause can make it. At the national level, this kind of policy development focuses on functions to be served more than the methods to be employed. For example, it is more concerned about what students are learning than about drawing polarized distinctions between artists and arts teachers.

The comprehensive, thoughtfully engaged approach of wisdom-seeking policy analysis is thus able to consider ramifications and deliver warnings. It can identify and illuminate conflicting agendas. It is comfortable with asking the question, "What can go wrong with this apparently good idea?" It can help to avoid long-term losses at the cost of short-term gains. It can ask hard questions about projects, language, jargon, and scope of thought contained in ideas and operations as they relate to the steady pursuit of reasonable purpose. It can lay out strategic and tactical options and present the strengths and weaknesses of each.

Policy analysis and development based on wisdom seeking have produced spectacular advances in all kinds of situations and enterprises. But history—ancient, modern, and recent—is full of examples where wise policy advice was ignored. In the activist environment of early 21st century America, ignoring wisdom-seeking policy analysis is a natural consequence of struggles to gain power *over* things. Such struggles regularly obscure the primary purpose of education to develop individual powers *in* things. Onrushing events and funded activisms devalue efforts to bring policy analysis and development into the slower rhythm of the research-based decision making that supports teaching the substance of visual content in ways that produce individual competence and understanding.

A field's decision about focused activism versus steady pursuit of reasonable purpose partially reveals its concept of leadership. Today, within the broad field of arts education, there is so much activism on the part of professional arts advocates and education reformers that sets of images and cultures reinforce each other to produce an illusion that the evolving interplays and progressions of activisms lead the field. To the extent that this view dominates, the steady pursuit of reasonable purpose based on content is obscured. Expertise, images thereof, and references thereto are transferred from the profession to the activist group with the biggest megaphone available at any particular time. By continuously acquiescing to such conditions, a field can lose control of its internal purpose, thus diminishing the areas over which it has control and expanding the number of areas where it is controlled by other forces. The wrong weighting between activism and steady pursuit of purpose produces serious strategic conse-quences. The steady pursuit of reasonable purpose through wise policy decisions increases the field's identity and security. Activisms supporting sets of projects, purposes, or educational fads damage and eventually destroy field identity and security.[2]

Clearly, policy is a serious and complex arena containing tools that must be used carefully. To be effective over the long term, the wisdom-seeking approach must dominate. Art education would not be where it is today without significant wisdom-finding capabilities. The National Art Education Association has worked especially hard to keep attention focused on disciplinary content, vigorous teaching, and field identity and security. All these achievements provide a strong foundation for building policy capabilities of greater sophistication and scope. This means an expansion in the kinds of research associated with art education. It means more connections with contextual issues in ways that analyze and synthesize these issues into a relationship with the reasonable purposes of art education. It means that policy analyses for art education must be generated by individuals centered in things visual, or, at least, things artistic. Let us look further at why all these are important.

SURVIVAL AND HEALTH

For the human body, the distinction between survival and health is fundamentally clear. There is a strong relationship; but one is not the same as the other. When the terms are used beyond biology, confusion and conflation are common. It is natural for a field and the professionals within it to seek improvement. Searches for improvement often produce criticism about the present, as though the present is the enemy of the future. If care is not taken, messages associated with efforts to improve health can be transformed into inaccurate messages about survival. There are many dangers here, and avoiding them begins with making clear distinctions among issues of survival, issues of health, and the degree to which issues of health have an impact on survival. Thoughtful policy analysis is critical because it can produce reasonable valuations for losses and gains. Activists tend to treat every setback as a survival issue and present it in those terms. The cumulative effect is a pernicious image of failure and decline irrespective of the facts.

What *are* the survival issues for the field of art education? What are the true make-or-break variables? These may be formulated in various ways, but here are several things that the field must have in order to exist.

1. There must be a definition of content and purpose sufficient to distinguish art education from other fields. The field must answer the question, "What is unique about what we do and the content for which we are responsible?"

---

[2]Security here refers to the continuing ability of the field of art education, or of any field, to continue fulfilling its primary—and to some extent unique—responsibilities. Security means far more than job security.

2. A sufficient number of policymakers and/or the public must believe in the work of the field. For these people, the field must answer the question, "Why are the unique things we do worthwhile?"
3. There must be a group of professionals capable of practicing effectively in the field and advancing it. These individuals must be able to answer questions 1 and 2 as a preface to the question, "What should I/we be doing in this field?"
4. There must be a body of people who prepare new professionals. In addition to answering the first three questions, they must answer the questions, "What do future professionals in this field need to know and be able to do?" and "What of this is most important to teach in the time available?"
5. There must be students able and willing to learn.
6. There must be basic resources: curriculum, time, materials, and facilities, for example.

Take any one of these things away for an appreciable period of time, and art education's survival is threatened. This is true at every level: from the single school to the nation as a whole.

By itself, the list reveals little that is not already understood; it should be used regularly in policy analysis to consider statements, ideas, decisions, and projections about the arts and art education. For example, the loss of any one entity, whether it be an arts council, a university teacher preparation program, a particular philanthropic effort, programs in a school district, and so forth, tragic as it may be, is not a survival issue for art education in general. This truth is not cruel; rather, it is enabling.

Thoughtful policy analysis puts gains and losses in perspective and thereby enables more appropriate decisions about next steps. A loss of distinction between tactical setbacks and strategic necessities can produce conditions where one of the strategic survival factors is threatened in subtle ways while attention is focused too exclusively on real or potential tactical losses. For example, in recent years there have been continuing attempts to deny the field of art education its uniqueness by asserting that it is important only to the extent that it achieves objectives beyond teaching and learning in and about things visual, for example, that its primary purpose is to illuminate or teach other subjects. From a survival perspective, tactical losses such as specific entities or programs are minimal in comparison with any potential strategic loss of the field's identity with unique purposes and content. To the extent that such a strategic loss is sustained, the ground is cut from under all the other make-or-break variables. Indeed, the field's identification with a unique and reasonable purpose is the most important survival element of all.

Over the years, art teachers and their organizations have seen local, statewide, and even national policies evolve that strike at one or more of the six survival variables identified earlier. Yet, although there have been and remain many local tragedies and disappointments, overall, the field has survived and shows every indication of continuing to do so. In policy terms, survival elements are those that cannot be lost or traded away in any circumstances. This is why analyses of ramifications are so essential as ideas are put forward about art education and its future. Proposals to improve the field that attack or weaken these strategic necessities are not worth following. Partnerships that do not protect the survival points are questionable and perhaps dangerous. When internal yearnings for improvement are reflected in actions and rhetoric that corrode the strategic base, they need shunting into more productive channels.

Of course, the health of the field is linked to its survival. But for purposes of seeking time-specific situation analyses as the basis for developing plans and projections, the health of the field deals with quality, quantity, and choices about such issues as curriculum balances and methodology. Questions about any one of these issues can be posed in terms of health or in terms of survival. For example, efforts to improve quality can be presented either as an opportunity to build on gains already achieved through the hard work of professionals, or as an attempt to correct failures caused by professionals. The first strengthens the conditions for survival; the second weakens them, particularly to the extent that the second support arguments that the visual arts can be taught by those unprepared or barely prepared in the content of the field. Another example: Issues of quantity can be discussed either in terms of a larger rationale or as the primary rationale. An illustration is (a) using low enrollment numbers in art education to justify policies that provide more opportunities for students to gain knowledge and skills in this unique of field of study, or (b) using low enrollment statistics as an indication of popularity and market share, thus, justifying the reduction or the termination of programs.

These two examples demonstrate how critically important it is to deal with health issues in a way that analyzes their potential effect on policies related to survival. Vigorous debates over content balances in curricula and specific teaching methodologies are important to the advancement of the profession. But there is no reason to conduct these debates in ways that weaken the basic strategic survival positions of the field as a whole. Such self-discipline and self-regulation within a field are facilitated when each professional has a fundamental understanding of what is at stake.

Issues of survival and health are not and cannot be influenced or decided by art educators alone. Clearly, art education interacts with other fields and their interests, both within and beyond the arts and education. The intensity and complexity of these interactions, unfolding primarily in a climate of activism, make it even more important to understand and act in recognition of the fundamental survival issues. Such an approach is essential for establishing a reasonable basis for cooperation, even though establishing and articulating this basis will bring charges of setting up barriers or failing to cooperate. But attention to survival and health means entering into all relationships and considering all ideas by asking several strategic policy questions:

1. Will the action we are contemplating cause us to diminish or deny the uniqueness of our field; that is, what can the visual arts do that no other field can do?
2. Will it harm understanding of what we do and its importance among those who make fundamental decisions about our survival, including parents and students?
3. Will it diminish understanding of the need for professionals to conduct the work of our field?
4. Will it damage our ability to recruit, develop, and support future professionals?
5. Will it decrease the number of students we are able to serve with substantive, sequential art education?
6. Will it diminish the fundamental resources we must have in order to teach?

These questions have been posed in negative terms, because the purpose of asking them is to prevent decisions that have negative effects. If, in reviewing a past or potential decision, the answer is "no" to the questions, or "no, just the opposite," then the decision is not touching a survival issue.

Another way to obtain a quick policy sense about issues of survival and health is to play a game of *take away*. What happens to the field of art education in terms of survival and health if a certain thing is taken away? By doing this exercise, one learns that the field is stronger than the rhetoric about it often implies. For example, the field has had the tragic experience of losing art education programs in many cities and even in the whole state of California. In those locales, survival criteria were not maintained; but, nationally the field as a whole survived and continued building its capabilities. Now, some of these terrible losses are starting to be reversed. Another example: For quite a few years now, many have been concerned about the possible loss or severe diminution of the National Endowment for the Arts. Although such a loss seems unlikely, the survival of the Endowment is not a make-or-break variable for the field of art education. There is no apparent direct link between the survival of any governmental arts or education entity in Washington and the survival of art education as a field. The strategic survival issues are placed elsewhere and are not linked to federal agencies and quangos (quasi-autonomous governmental organizations, e.g., the President's Committee on the Arts and Humanities, The Arts Education Partnership) as much as to ideas, professional practice, students, and local resource streams. Looking at prospects and issues this way may appear to be cold and calculating; but in reality, it produces the kind of understanding and sensibility that enable a field to protect what is necessary for survival and work for improvement in its health while maintaining productive relationships based on realistic assessments of associated efforts and activities.

The preceding paragraph must not be interpreted as expressing a lack of concern for specific local conditions or for the well-being of agencies and organizations that individuals or groups consider important. On the contrary, it argues that these concerns can be addressed more effectively by keeping them in perspective. Normally, for the field as a whole, this means treating them as health issues rather than as survival issues. Keeping the national distinction avoids the problem of extrapolating local or specific situations beyond their real scope and thus producing or contributing to a negative overall image for the field of art education. When survival really *is* at stake, nationally or locally, there will be no history of overstatements and false alarms to dilute attention.

Such an approach is critical in addressing the issue of justification. Confusions about survival and health can lead to serious misjudgments about how to justify. Constantly portraying issues of health as issues of survival produces a climate of crisis that borders on continuing panic. In turn, this atmosphere produces the tendency to justify art education in fashionable terms, moment to moment. Such an approach is extremely dangerous, implying that the field has no unique mission that serves as a basic foundation for its work, it attacks a strategic necessity. To the extent that the mission is always defined in terms of "the cause of the moment," to that same extent art education loses its identity. This is a perfect example of how short-term gains can contribute to long-term losses. If art education has every purpose, then it has no purpose of its own. Of course, art education is always under pressure—a fate shared with all fields. Allowing those external to the field, or the field itself, to deal with every problem in survival terms produces too many external and internal negatives and multiple cross-purposes. Research-based, wisdom-seeking policy analysis has a significant role to play in reviewing events and ideas, conditions, and prospects and sorting them in terms of their effect on health, survival, or the relation between the two. Produced and presented on a broad scale, such analyses will no doubt show that the survival probability for art education is quite high if the fundamental strategic conditions can be maintained. What are some of the issues that need watching if the future is to be secured?

POLICY ISSUES AND QUESTIONS

Purposes

Previously, the case has been made for the importance of a unique, reasonable purpose, for answering the question, "What does the field of art education do that nothing else can do?" This question is predicated on a more fundamental question in terms of student learning, "What does study of the visual arts accomplish that nothing else can accomplish?" On the surface, these questions seem rhetorical. However, the questions are important because the answers provide a foundation for almost all else. The answers are not always easy to give because the world of the visual is multifaceted; many-splendored; and rich with specializations, points of view, and connections to other fields. The visual arts have many uses and thus are used in many ways. In addition to their roots in artistic action, they have connections with history, the therapeutic, social and political action, marketing, and personal response and fulfillment on all sorts of levels. But such multiple connections are not unique to the visual arts. Neither are multiple uses, and so, a primary policy question is the extent to which educational purposes are centered primarily on the visual arts themselves or on their connections and uses. In a comprehensive curriculum, there is not an either/or answer, but rather a spectrum upon which different answers are appropriate at different times and places.

This inclusive approach is in contrast to a more activist position that chooses one point on the spectrum and defends it against all others. In one critique of the single-answer approach, Eisner (2001) writes

> However, the study of visual culture, influenced by critical theory, pays less attention to culture's aesthetics than to its politics. Students study the art of popular culture to understand the sociology or politics of the image. In this view, what we sometimes refer to as the fine arts are seen not so much as dazzling or even high human achievements, but as products representing what those in power choose to praise. (p. 8)

To delve into this matter further as an educational policy issue, it is instructive to conduct another take-away exercise. When this is done, one finds that a focus on making or understanding something visual creates the uniqueness around which art education centers its work. Going further, one finds that in human terms, the visual arts and its specializations evaporate or transform into something else unless there is or has been creation of a work. It is the creation of or attention to the presence of a work of art or design or craft or architecture or film or any other visual manifestation that identifies the field uniquely.

This condition comes as no surprise. All disciplines and fields of endeavor involve the ability to do something or the results of having done something in that field. Medicine is about the practice of medicine, fundamentally. Mathematics is about the ability to think and work mathematically. Scholarship in the humanities is centered on the production of scholarly work. The connections of medicine, mathematics, and humanistic scholarship to history, therapeutics, social and political action, and so forth are all real and important, but they are not a substitute for the central core activity of the field. The core activity enables the connections. Connections, honestly made, reveal the centrality of the core activity.

This point is important because the adverse justification climate, discussed earlier, can foster rhetoric implying that producing work in a visual medium is secondary to the connections of visual arts with other purposes, worthy as they are. It is not unusual to see articles indicating that the first purpose of the visual arts now is to support political action and social change. Certainly, the visual arts can do this to some extent, but they are not unique in having this ability. They may be able to bring a unique dimension and poignant force to political and social change, but political and social change and the visual arts either separately or in the aggregate are not the same thing. Each is at least as big as the other. Conflating them diminishes both, and in the present climate, visual content loses. A larger vision for art education has already been articulated. The national voluntary K-12 standards for the visual arts recognize the critical importance of learning to do work and communicate in things visual. They support visual history and analysis and connections with other disciplines. The standards acknowledge how rich purposes can be without abandoning the essence, the prime mover of effort in the visual realm (Consortium, 1994).

The thing that art can do uniquely is art itself. At a most basic level, the history of a thing does not make the thing; making the thing produces the basis for its history. Aesthetic response, if the words retain their standard meanings, indicates reaction to a thing that already exists. These are not advertising points for studio-based learning, but rather basic realities that help place all the elements of art education into perspective: first, to deliver the best possible education to students; and second, to protect a strategic necessity of the field, that is, a clear and honest articulation of reasonable and unique purpose—what it does that nothing else does. From a policy perspective, the question of purpose is extremely important because a field insecure about or divided over purposes, or appearing to be insecure or divided enables individuals or groups with other agendas to work one set of purposes against another and vitiate the field's security, both in image and in fact.

From time to time, various visual specializations and professions fall into the trap of denying a home base in fundamental visual content. Professional aspirations coupled with yearnings to produce effective public relations can lead to pronouncements that an individual or a field *centered in visual content* is really centered in psychology, assessment, politics, therapy, sociology, media, communications, and so forth. At times, this can produce conditions where connections are called for and denied in the same set of rhetorical or organizational gestures. The problem is denying visual content roots rather than being proud of or advancing the cause of a field that uses or produces multidisciplinary work.

Policy-oriented research about purposes would focus on such questions as:[3]

1. How unified and clear is the field's message about its unique purpose, both in general and to specific audiences?
2. If there is a lack of basic clarity or unity, what forces, issues, or prospects are producing disagreement or confusion at a fundamental level?
3. To what extent are healthy arguments over secondary purposes, connections with other things and disciplines, methodologies, and weightings of curricular elements producing either the image or the fact of a loss of a central unique purpose?
4. How can decisions in the present and in the immediate future be crafted to promote creativity, debate, and advancement in the field while maintaining a clear internal and external focus on central disciplinary purposes.
5. What are the indicators that the field is gaining or losing understanding about the fundamental purpose of art education among specific groups?

Technique: Visual

All theories notwithstanding, every field considered basic has a body of factual information, terminology, and techniques for doing work in that field. A student in a 12th grade calculus class has far more mathematical technique than the 1st-grader struggling to write and understand numbers; study has produced a progression of technical ability that supports creative applications. In some fields, the technique is the content, but in most others technique is a means for creating or working with content. This is just as true with regard to the techniques of scholarship as it is with the techniques of making works in visual form—design, fine arts, craft, architecture, film, and so forth. In every field technique enables more: Those who have it can understand more and do more than those who do not.

Reading through much of the art education literature, especially that of the last few decades, one senses a real ambivalence about and sometimes antipathy to technical studio skill. This fear may be more present in writing about art education than in art education itself, but whatever the case, the field's overall position on the acquisition of studio technique is critical. Where does

---

[3]Throughout the chapter, sample policy questions are posed in terms of "the field." However, questions work equally well for smaller units, such as a state, school district, school, or collegiate program that prepares art teachers. It cannot be emphasized too strongly that these are only *some* of the questions that could be asked about each topic and that the topics are only *some* of the topics to be addressed by comprehensive policy effort.

it lead policy for art educators themselves to suggest that writing is intellectual but drawing is not (Best, 2000).

This chapter is not the place to debate the issue; it is more productive to point out that art education is working under significant pressures antipathetic to the fundamental generative techniques for producing work in visual form due to a number of forces that are not correlated in the same way for any other field. These include combinations and collisions of desires to nurture creative expression in a psychological sense; to move art education beyond creative expression defined as play time with art materials; to join contemporary movements in the visual arts that substitute verbal conceptualization for visual sophistication; and to produce or introduce shocking spectacles. Attempts to divorce visual art from technique and craft are not evident across the whole range of visual action. But the forces of opposition are formidable, and without strategic understanding, it is possible that those who seek a rich, comprehensive art education that includes but goes beyond studio technique may be presenting their goals in ways that deny their own field its most basic technical foundation.

Of course, it is possible to focus on the acquisition of specific studio techniques to a point that limits contact with important matters of history and analysis or applications in and connections to fields of specialization within the visual world. But it is equally possible to deny technique its importance in a way that undercuts the role of technique in delineating the uniqueness of the visual arts in all their manifestations as a school discipline that is basic to general education. For just as the acquisition of technique in languages, mathematics, the sciences, and historical and social analyses is a major part of what each of those disciplines teach uniquely, so is the acquisition of artistic and intellectually based visual technique a major part of what art education teaches uniquely.

Several continuing policy and research questions are:

1. How is studio technique understood and valued internally and externally as a component of art education? What are the ramifications of the answer to this question that impinge on strategic necessities for the survival or health of the field?
2. What are the distinctions and relationships among creative expression, studio technique, historical knowledge, and analytical technique?
3. How is the field dealing with distinctions and relationships between (a) studio technique and technology (Healy, 1998) and (b) studio technique and artistic freedom?
4. What are the policy ramifications of presenting studio technique as being either confining or liberating? How can policy analysis help clarify indications of the difference in specific situations?

Youth Cultures

The visual arts are being taught to students heavily influenced by mass-produced youth cultures. Targeted marketing to children and youth has reached such intensity, sophistication, and coverage that such traditional cultural formation powers as the home, school, and religion have lost overall influence (Hymowitz, 2000, 2001; Ruggerio, 2000). Specific reaction is manifested in home schooling, school vouchers, and charter schools, all to some extent attempts to swing the pendulum back to local adult control. But irrespective of how these particular struggles turn out, youth cultures will always be a critical policy issue for art education.

Analytical questions can begin with the values promoted by a particular youth culture concerning the nature of work, patient application to the development of knowledge and skills, willingness to tackle difficulty, and the relationship between individual and community. A youth culture that sends the usual current messages—everything must be fun; everything must be sensational; everything must be simple; everything must be new; everything must change constantly; everything must be fast; everything must be easy; everything is essentially about "me," what's "cool" is what adults don't like—is not supportive of serious education in any discipline, much less the visual arts.

It is not unusual to hear admonitions that educators should meet students where they are. This sounds reasonable, even logical. However, accepting this view means that both policy and educational challenges are defined by how far students are from the nature of the discipline to be studied. Particularly powerful questions arise here if one believes that education is to lead people to knowledge and skills they do not currently have.

Several perennial policy questions in this area are:

1. What are the forces creating youth cultures at various levels, pre-K−12? To what extent can the values promoted by these youth cultures be generalized?
2. To what extent are the values and messages being promoted by these cultures consistent with the acquisition of knowledge and skills in the visual arts?
3. If there are consistencies, how can they be reinforced? If there are inconsistencies, how can these be addressed in ways that promote student learning?
4. What is the role of art teachers and the field of art education in addressing issues of youth culture at individual, classroom, school, district, local, state, and national levels?
5. What is the field's responsibility to students regarding their ability to understand visual manipulation in the messages they receive?

Technique: General

We are constantly being bombarded with information and analysis about technology—practical applications of scientific discoveries in machinery, drugs, and electronic systems. In general, very little is said about technique—applications of technological habits of mind in all dimensions of life. Readers of this *Handbook* are familiar with problems that occur when everything is considered a science, whether it is or is not. The 20th century was replete with disasters caused by misplaced faith in scientific and technical approaches. Policymaking can be severely and dangerously skewed by reliance on technical means alone. Yet, technique is widely favored as the initiator of action, is pervasive, and is the mode of choice for major forces influencing education policy. It is critical to remember that the technical imperative when applied to policy is intended to produce a single decision for everyone. Thus, purely technical thinking is in severe contrast to artistic thinking, where there is no standard solution, but rather a continuing development of individual solutions.

As stated previously, technique and technical thinking play powerful roles in making art, studying it, and presenting it. But technique alone is never enough in any of the arts. Most arts professionals understand this, but many outside the arts who have heavy influence on the conduct of art education do not. Clear evidence is seen in means proposed to attain higher levels of accountability in elementary and secondary education. The proliferation of techniques, systems, standards, measurements, evaluations, assessments, and standardized tests all indicate how powerful technical thinking is in our society as a whole and in education. The wonderful and continuing successes in machine technology only reinforce the idea that the same mode of thought can be applied to every problem, irrespective of its nature. The result is loss of faith in and respect for professional judgment and individual professional action (Ellul, 1964; Hope, 1990; Ortega y Gasset, 1961).

Art education policy development will proceed for some time under conditions that overweigh the importance of technical thinking. Policy analysis is critical to understanding how this problem is unfolding and in what areas at specific times and over time.

The following policy research questions have continuing importance:

1. How is technical thinking—one-size-fits-all ideas, systems, and evaluations—manifested in the present context for art education? How are technique-based ideas evolving in areas that impact the strategic fundamentals of the field? What opportunities and problems exist or are possibilities or probabilities?
2. What messages can the field best present about the issue of technique and technical thinking? How can the field of art education inform students and the public at large about positive and negative relationships between creativity and technical thinking?
3. In terms of the health of the field, what are the potential impacts of technological thinking on concepts of evaluation, accountability, and funding. To the extent that the answer is negative, what can be done to counter trends or to ameliorate their effects?
4. How can the field prepare its future professionals to work with the challenge of technological thinking as it evolves? What are the potential impacts of this issue on teacher preparation curricula?

Technique: Applied

The field of art education is deeply concerned with art content, but it is equally concerned with technique and methodology. The field includes attention to studio technique, scholarly technique, research technique, educational technique, evaluation technique, and so forth. Such sets of technique and their relationships are typical in all fields of endeavor. Specializations arise within fields concerned with specific techniques or from methodologies associated with specific bodies of work—restoration in the visual arts, for example. But the work of art education and particularly its policy context are regularly impacted by applications of other bodies of technique. Political and advertising techniques are two of the most powerful. In the visual arts, it is clear that there is a vast difference between imitating how an artist or designer acts and being successful at what an artist or designer does. Imitation can only go so far. The same is true of politics and promotion. For art educators interacting with professional politicians or promoters, imitation is not enough. Both of these sets of techniques are powerful producers of illusions.[4] Because politics and promotion have deep relationships with policy and policymaking, any policy effort intending to support art education must attend to political and promotional techniques per se, to the illusions they can create, and to their applications, both separately and together, in specific circumstances.

This means far more than the fundamental tasks of watching and reacting to specific legislation, regulation, or messages. It means developing the capability to understand what each game is and how it is being played, especially because the games never end. For example, it is extremely critical to know when consultation is sought on a real or symbolic basis, when the field is being involved or bypassed regarding matters affecting its health or survival, when incidents are being extrapolated into norms in order to advance a particular rearrangement of powers, and so forth (Gee, 1999a, 1999b).

---

[4]For example, the results of polls are of little use when developing policy when those polled have little understanding or knowledge of a subject. Public opinion derived from the most super of super majorities regarding questions of neurosurgery is worthless. This is why there is significant concern among experts in any field about ratings or decisions based on polling technique. Another example is evaluation technique that assumes all achievement can be expressed in mathematical terms. Another is promotional technique applied to education when celebrity presence is substituted for student learning.

Several continuing research-based policy analysis questions in this area are:

1. What sets of technique—promotional, political, fundraising, accountability related, and so forth—beyond the field of art education have the most impact on policy development either in or affecting the field?
2. What are the features of these sets of techniques? How have they been applied in ways that affect art education? How are they being applied now? What applications seem most probable in the immediate future? What among these is supportive, benign, or dangerous?
3. What external sets of techniques, or specific generic techniques within them, are most supportive of art education by their very nature? Which are most destructive by their very nature? What are the indicators that techniques or their applications are becoming dangerous to the health or survival of the field?
4. How can the field best position itself to address issues of technique as well as content in policy debates? What kinds of specific research are needed to gain these capabilities? What is the content of this research in general, or for specific circumstances?

Technology

Magnificent achievements in technology are among the glories of civilization. Advances in computing, with their direct applications to communication and their heavy reliance on things visual, represent a new level of opportunity and continuing promise for art education. They have lifted a number of design fields into new levels of career prestige and raise issues of design content in K-12 art education (Davis, 1998). Technology has enlarged the meaning of technique development in the visual arts. Beyond these and many other technological facts and issues lie a number of serious policy matters associated with content and the development of visual thinking.

The computer enables many things, including illusions: Access becomes confused with capability; mouse and keyboard technique becomes confused with intellectual skill; compilation becomes confused with knowledge; and so forth. Policy analysis can look at the whole field of technology, its relationships to education in general, and its specific relationships to visual learning of all kinds. For example, a major policy question is how to keep technology from narrowing possibilities rather than expanding them. If visual experience beyond the natural daily context is primarily confined to what can be seen on a computer screen, experience narrows and the full promises of technology are not being realized. Technology issues are not easy (Gelernter, 2001), and approaches to them that favor a comprehensive and substantive art education require deep understanding of numerous issues and their relationships, including the massive funding of political and promotional operations to promote the sale of technological equipment.

A number of standing policy questions in this area are:

1. What technological capabilities do we have now, and what capabilities are projected in the immediate future?
2. How do these specific technologies and the composite effect of their continuing development relate to the field's specific goals for student learning in various areas of the visual arts?
3. What is involved in establishing policy positions that enable the field to both support and critique technology as appropriate? What kinds of alliances to support or critique are created, and what are the ramifications of these alliances?
4. What are the economic issues associated with technology? Examples include the replacement of teachers by technical means, distance learning, constant provision of current equipment, efficiencies of delivering instruction, and so forth.

Teacher Preparation

Like other school disciplines, the field of art education has done a lot of deep thinking about teacher preparation. Standards, constant professional discussions about methodology, curriculum and methodological philosophies, and from time to time an overabundance or shortage of teachers are all standard subjects. Much past and continuing work in this area is policy oriented; thus, an expansion of the field's policy analysis effort would involve connecting specific issues of teacher preparation policy with the other kinds of policy issues that we have been discussing.

A major factor here is that knowledge is expanding at a rapid rate. Skill requirements are expanding also. But the time available is not expanding. Indeed, financial and other pressures are causing many states and institutions to reduce the number of hours required for an undergraduate degree to at or near 120 semester hours. Increasingly, contextual forces are influencing professional decisions about content, sequence, and method. In response to political pressures generated by the education reform movement, teacher preparation is being freighted with all sorts of accountability mechanisms. Pursued and established through vigorous, sophisticated applications of political and advertising techniques, these accountability mandates carry significant dangers along with their intended, purported benefits for student learning. For example, at the same time that there is a vast intensification of accountability mechanisms in teacher preparation, and indeed in teaching as a lifelong career, teacher shortages are producing alternative certification plans that simply bypass current and prospective accountability systems.

Clearly, policy analysis in this arena is a continuing responsibility because the field is unlikely to have the will, patience, or resources to turn on a dime every time there is a call for change. Constant changes and self-enlarging systems are ingredients in recipes for dysfunctions, which in turn usually produce more changes and new or bigger systems. If such a cycle is now apparent, or becomes part of the field's contextual future, a policy-oriented analytical approach continually focused on student learning in the visual arts has the best chance of keeping the field out of danger and, indeed, of helping it to advance as changes and systems proliferate and confusion mounts.

Sample research-based policy questions for this area are:

1. How does the field best keep teacher preparation focused on the knowledge and skills necessary to develop competencies in the visual arts in individual students?
2. What external pressures seem most influential on teacher preparation policies? What are the sources of these pressures?
3. How can the field best respond to that which appears problematic or destructive? To what extent can policy research and analysis enable the field (a) to predict difficulties and be somewhat ready to meet them and (b) be proactive in ways that maintain control or preempt activism by forces that attack or erode conditions for effective teacher preparation?
4. What kinds of orientations to policy issues should be part of the content of teacher preparation?

Intellectual and Curriculum Issues

The proliferation of theory in every field is, in part, an offshoot of the scientism that pervades our age. Theorizing coupled with overspecialization can develop a self-vitiating power within a field, a power that sustains itself toward ultimate irrelevance (Elkins, 2001; Ruddick, 2001). A careful policy effort can critique both theorizing and specialization without showing disrespect to the productive powers of each. It can also analyze the ramifications of specific theories and the findings of specific specializations with regard to their potential impacts on the survival and health of the field. It can make useful distinctions between theory as explanation and theory as ideology. Thoughtful policy analysis cuts through jargon to meaning for decision making. It refuses to accept buzz words such as interdisciplinary, elitism, multiculturalism, diversity, self-esteem, and so forth, as indicators of automatic positives (Smith 1989, 1995). Almost all these concepts are double-edged in some way. For example, interdisciplinarity is an important goal for education. An individual's ability to integrate the knowledge, skills, modes of thoughts, points of view, and content of two or more disciplines is a tremendous achievement. But too often, interdisciplinarity is used to obscure or obviate the need for knowledge or skill development in specific disciplines sufficient to enable their combination in an interdisciplinary effort or project. Likewise, multiculturalism can indicate an expansion of knowledge to include information, languages, and approaches used by those beyond one's home culture. But multiculturalism can be used propagandistically to deny or denigrate the achievements of Western cultures, thus advocating, and at times, producing a new narrowness (Windschuttle, 2002).

The purpose of policy analysis in such matters is not to stop or start intellectual efforts, theories, discussions, promotions, or debates, but rather to understand their potential impacts on primary goals for student learning in the K-12 years and the work of the field to support such learning.

A number of important policy questions in this area are:

1. What ideas in all applicable fields are providing the most influence on the present evolution of art education as a field? To what extent is there a distinction in levels of influence between ideas generated within and those generated beyond the field?
2. What are the ramifications of these ideas for the security and health of the field? How easily can apparently good or beneficial ideas be turned against the fundamental purposes or strategic necessities of the field? How likely are such turnings?
3. What are the indicators that concepts, ideas, and modes of thought external to the visual arts are beginning to overshadow, obscure, or obviate visual content? For example, how do art educators know when to become concerned that they are teaching toward a single idea more than teaching the visual arts specifically and/or comprehensively?
4. Given the fact that ideas come and go, and given what is known now, what bodies of ideas are likely to constitute the next few waves of fads and trends? What positives and negatives are evident in these potentials?

Funding and Rhetorical Support

Surveying the whole field of art education pre-K-12, two things are obvious. First, billions of dollars are being spent on art education each year, mostly from local tax revenues. Second, these funds, as large in the aggregate as they are, are insufficient to the need. Clearly, funding is so critical that it regularly overrides almost all other policy considerations. The pressures to operate in this way push any field away from comprehensive policy considerations. In other words, constant funding pressures can reduce the possibility of doing the kind of work that would reduce these pressures over time in many cases. At the very least, these pressures diminish prospects for the kind of advancements that a broader policy analysis would surely bring. Although there is a great deal of understanding about funding patterns and the relationships of policy to funding at local, state, and federal levels, at base, art educators and those who represent them must know how to work the system as it evolves (Hooker, 1987). How fast and in what directions are funding mechanisms changing?

Rhetorical support is important not only in and of itself but also for its relationship to funding. Rhetorical support comes in word-based testimonies but also symbolically through grant programs, publication of achievements, recognitions and prizes, and all forms of speaking and writing, including policy analyses themselves. Both funding and rhetorical support announce the presence of a field to those outside it. Normally, each comes at a price. The role of policy analysis in this area is to consider the real and total cost of the price required or exacted. This real and total cost needs to be calculated in terms of not only student learning but also the survival and health of the field, because the survival and health of the field are essential for student learning in things visual. How many grants have been entered into without calculating the cost of what will happen when the grant stops, an almost certain inevitability?

Clearly, major policy efforts must be devoted to obtaining necessary funding and gaining the most positive rhetorical support possible. But research-based, wisdom-seeking policy analysis can place this continuing effort in a larger context that connects it to such things as the operations of political and advertising technique; issues arising from one or more youth cultures and reactions to them; movements in the worlds of ideas, realities, and potentials for technical means, and so forth.

A number of important policy questions in this area are:

1. What does a composite picture of primary funding sources and patterns for art education reveal about priorities for maintaining and increasing financial report? Where should the most concern about funding be focused?
2. What is the relative weight of secondary funding; what are the various types of rhetorical support; and what do the answers tell the field about concentrations of promotion and development energies?
3. How well is the field doing in connecting issues of financial and rhetorical support to goals and objectives for student learning. What forces in the context are supporting or disrupting such connections?
4. What kinds of projective research and analysis are needed to deal with future funding and future issues of rhetorical support? For example, what is the role of the individual teacher?

Standards and Resources

The field of art education is naturally concerned about standards and resources. It is both true and fun to say that we have standards because we have the visual arts, not the visual arts because we have standards. Standards based on great achievements in the fine arts, design, crafts, architecture, film, and so forth, exist and continue to evolve. In 1994, the art education field joined other arts disciplines in publishing a consensus-based set of national voluntary standards for K-12 students (Consortium, 1994). Such results always represent a compromise; thus, no one person can be entirely satisfied with the result. But after a long developmental struggle, the standards hit the target sufficiently to gather broad support as a baseline document for use in state and local circumstances. The policy impact of this standards effort is extremely positive for the most part; for example, approximately 47 states have either endorsed the standards or developed their own standards based on the National Standards. Effects from the standards effort are still being felt and will be felt for many years to come. For one thing, the standards text provides one formulation of the fundamental uniqueness of the content that is the responsibility of the art education field. Therefore, because the text protects that uniqueness, it or another text that serves the same purpose is a matter of basic security in the policy arena. For example, the standards cannot be achieved by students without teachers who have expertise in subject matters based in or centered on the visual arts. Meeting the standards requires resources and the development of student learning year after year throughout elementary and secondary schooling. By the nature of the context they delineate, the standards indicate that regular study, not casual experience, is necessary to develop competence. Indeed, the articulation of the unique content of art education in the standards is an anchoring reference point for almost all other decisions, thus, for policy analysis, research, and development.

Standards written in ways to ensure that they can serve as an anchoring reference point are a critical necessity tied to basic security in ways that are not always readily apparent. Anchoring policy to student learning is essential, but such anchoring works only if student learning is defined in terms of specific knowledge and skills centered on the discipline in question. Thus, not only is the presence of standards a critical policy issue, but also the nature of standards and the purposes they reflect are equally critical. Not just any standards will do. This is why standards revisions are among the most critical decisions, particularly in fields like art education that are not broadly understood to be fundamental or basic. Policy efforts regarding standards must draw upon an understanding of both (a) all the forces directly opposing or subtly countering substantive learning and (b) the danger of substituting formulations or methodologies for basic content. They must foster an acute sensibility to positive and negative relationships between that which is foundational and that which is faddish or trendy. They must be based on a clear understanding about distinctions between what is essential for the survival for the field and what is good for the health of the field.

A number of perennial policy questions in this area are:

1. How are standards affecting policies at various levels and locations, and how are policies affecting the fulfillment and application of standards?
2. How secure are specific sets of standards, and what are the potential meanings of any insecurities for student learning?
3. Are there ideas or policy initiatives that essentially undermine capabilities to achieve standards while purporting to support standards? For example, to what extent are there instances of specific parts of the standards being abstracted and overemphasized in preemptory ways?
4. What are the prospects that the field can control any effort or attempt to change the national standards of 1994? What are the policy ramifications and research needs if it appears that the field either can retain or may lose control?
5. What rhetorical relationships between resources and standards are most effective in gaining additional opportunities and resources for student learning?

Other Policy Areas

The previous list of topics is only a beginning and is intended to show, by example, the kinds of work research-based policy analysis should do. Other areas such as demographics, economics, relationships with organizations and groups in the arts, culture, and education, media, and general education policy are also extremely important and need attention.

FUTURE ISSUES

Famed business consultant Peter Drucker (1970) is often credited with the thought that research, policy analysis, and projection are not so much about predicting the future, but rather for studying the futurity of present decisions (p. 131). The kinds of questions posed previously can be asked constantly over time. No matter how much policy-oriented work is done, no matter how much research and thinking are accomplished, there are always unpredictable events that alter everything. September 11, 2001, is a case in point. In a few minutes, cultural conditions changed radically (Brooks, 2001; Knight, 2001). In situations like the present, and indeed all the time, a wisdom-seeking analytical effort can reveal what is happening and what might happen in a way that relates to what might or should be done in the field's area of responsibility. Even if we do not know what is next, we can know what is now and create out of our knowledge, research, and sensibilities optional scenarios of what might be next, and how we might lead or respond. After all, this is what intelligence analysts are doing in all the areas that affect our basic security as a nation.

Present and future policy analysis cannot ignore the presence of values, inclinations, and interests that produce different views and interpretations of situations, and thus about what should be done next. In all fields where there is active policy analysis, there are serious disagreements. In the main, these disagreements sharpen understanding, except when activism or yearnings for a certain result obscure the truth or the potential opportunities and dangers inherent in possible conditions, decisions, and ramifications. Overall, much writing labeled arts policy is really advocacy. Advocacy never finds any danger in its own recommendations. Advocacy is a critical piece of the arts and arts education effort. But it is based on promotional technique—not on policy analysis—and thus is not a sufficient base for solid decision making. In arguing that advocacy is not enough to accomplish the purposes of a recent report published by RAND and The Pew Charitable Trusts, McCarthy, Brooks, Lowell, and Zakaras (2001) write that,

> In undertaking this research, we made no initial assumptions about the proper role of government in the arts, or about the value of one kind of artistic expression or experience over another. We have tried to avoid any type of advocacy for the arts in order to try to conduct the kind of impartial, empirical analysis that forms the basis of sound policy. (p. 3)

The dangers of building the kind of policy analysis capability necessary to address the complexities outlined previously are several and serious. Among them are backlashes to findings that counter or express concern about long-advocated positions, decisions, or directions; roiling public disagreements over interpretations of facts; the development of evidence that contradicts or confirms beliefs held as myths; critiques of positions and actions taken by powerful groups and forces in the arts, education, and culture generally; vulnerability to the charge that the field is being selfish in focusing everything on its own goals for student learning, its fundamental security, or its health; charges of failure to cooperate, to be good partners, and so forth. Let it be noted that these possibilities exist in every field where sophisticated research-based policy analysis and synthesis are well established.

What alternatives does the field of art education have? Policy is always with us, created either by design or by default. The art education field is where it is today, because a number of leaders in various sectors of the field have been courageous in addressing policy issues associated with basic survival and continuing health. Most of these efforts have grown from a highly developed personal sensibility coupled with great expertise, a bloodhound's nose for the scent of danger, the will to speak out, and in many cases, a position from which to be heard. The aggregate result of these efforts over the years has provided more security for the field than many realize. Without a continuation and intensification of these efforts, a vacuum will be created as complexities mount. Essentially, the field has two choices: a) to develop and intensify its capability to understand and influence policy on its own behalf or (b) to accept and react to the policy decisions of others. It is virtually certain that the art education field risks grave peril if it allows those external to the field free reign to shape its policies and policy context.

A policy effort of greater capability is needed to ensure that the field has capabilities for warning itself about potential problems ahead. Reacting forcefully is important, but it is not enough. Danger is not always obvious immediately. The same is true of golden opportunities.

The capability development advocated here cannot be acquired quickly. It is needed, not just for art education but also for all the disciplines in the general field of arts education. Policy analytical capabilities in all these fields have grown over the past 2 decades. Experience has been a great teacher. Associations such as NAEA are working with a far greater policy sophistication than ever before. There is an urgent need for more data and information about current conditions. The facts themselves are valuable, but when used as the basis for strategic analysis, their value increases many times over. Indeed, the policy capability needed is the ability to analyze in specific areas *and* to synthesize these analyses into composites that give the overall picture of status and prospect that in turn leads to wise decisions.

Developing these capabilities means creating a relatively small group of professionals steeped in research and analysis, content and technique, who are able to draw information from a wide variety of sources, make connections, and develop integrated evaluations of import that are reasonably accurate most of the time. These professionals are not dictators, but thought provokers serving the field by watching and attending to its basic security and fundamental health more than to its temporary image. They pay particular attention to ideas and movements that narrow vision and to coercive illusions that lead art educators to deny, diminish, or denigrate the basics of their own field.

The tremendous needs for increases in student learning that require the field to advance call for the development of a research-based policy capability, tied first to continuous pursuit of the reasonable and unique purposes of the field. It is indeed immaterial or unnecessary for such an effort to be closely associated organizationally with advocacy, partnerships, or the larger connections among art, politics, and philanthropy that occupy the attentions of what is usually called arts policy or cultural policy on the national scene. It seems in this point in its development, the field of art education would benefit most from an overt intelligence operation based in a few universities, connected to applicable policy issues, and devoted to supporting the field's powerful and critical interests in increasing and advancing student learning. Moving forward in this direction can certainly improve prospects for advancing the health of the field, and may even be critical to its long-term survival in a world of cross-purposes.

AUTHOR NOTE

Samuel Hope is Executive Director of the National Association of Schools of Art and Design and an Executive Editor of *Arts Education Policy Review* magazine.

Correspondence concerning this article should be addressed to Samuel Hope, Executive Director of the National Association of Schools of Art and Design, 11250 Roger Bacon Drive, Suite 21, Reston, Virginia 20190. E-mail: shope@arts-accredit.org.

REFERENCES

Best, H. M. (2000). Art, words, intellect, emotion. *Arts Education Policy Review, 101*(6), 3–11; 102(1), 3–10.

Brooks, D. (2001, November 5). The age of conflict. *The Weekly Standard,* 19–23.

Chapman, L. (1982). *Instant art, instant culture: The unspoken policy for American schools.* New York: Teachers College Press.

Consortium of National Arts Education Associations. (1994). *National Standards for Arts Education.* Reston, VA: Music Educators National Conference. Author.

Davis, M. (1998). Making a case for design-based learning. *Arts Education Policy Review, 100*(2), 7–15.

Dorn, C. M. (2001). Art education and the iron triangle's new plan. *Arts Education Policy Review, 103*(1), 3–11.

Drucker, P. L. (1970). Long range planning. In *Technology, management, and society* (pp. 129–148). New York: Harper & Row.

Eisner, E. W. (2001). Should we create new aims for art education? *Art Education, 54*(5), 6–10.

Elkins, J. (2001). The ivory tower of tearlessness. *The Chronicle of Higher Education*, November 9, B, 7.

Ellul, J. (1964). *The technological society*. New York: Alfred A. Knopf.

Gee, C. B. (1999a). "For you dear—anything!" Omnipotence, omnipresence, and servitude "through the arts," Part I. *Arts Education Policy Review, 100*(4), 3–18.

Gee, C. B. (1999b). "For you dear—anything!" Omnipotence, omnipresence, and servitude "through the arts," Part II. *Arts Education Policy Review, 100*(5), 3–22.

Gelernter, D. (2001, January). Computers and the pursuit of happiness. *Commentary*, 31–35.

Gerzon, M. (1996). *A house divided: Six-belief systems struggling for America's soul*. New York: Most/Tarcher, Putnam Publishing Group.

Healy, J. M. (1998). *Failure to connect: How computers affect our children's minds for better and worse*. New York: Simon & Schuster.

Hooker, M. (1987). Moral values and private philanthropy. *Grantmakers in the Arts Reader, 12*(1), 1–38.

Hope, S. (1990). Technique and arts education. *Design for Arts in Education, 91*(6), 2–14.

Hope, S. (2002). Policy frameworks, research, and k-12 schooling. In R. Colwell & C. Richardson (Eds.), *The new handbook of research on music teaching and learning handbook for research in music education* (pp. 5–16). New York: Oxford University Press.

Hymowitz, K. S. (Spring, 2000). The teening of childhood. *American Educator*, 20–47.

Hymowitz, K. S. (Spring, 2001). Parenting: The lost art. *American Educator*, 4–9.

Knight, C. (2001, November 4). What exactly can art heal? *Los Angeles Times*, 8.

McCarthy, K. F., Brooks, A., Lowell, J., & Zakaras, L. (2001). *The performing arts in a new era*. Phiiladelphia: RAND and the Pew Charitable Trusts.

Ortega y Gasset, J. (1961). *The modern theme*. New York: Harper & Row.

Ruddick, L. (2001, November 23). The near enemy of the humanities is professionalism. *The Chronicle of Higher Education*, B, 7–9.

Ruggiero, V. R. (Summer, 2000). Bad attitude: Confronting the views that hinder students' learning. *American Educator*, 10–48.

Smith, R. A. (1989). *The sense of art: A study in aesthetic education*. New York: Routledge.

Smith, R. A. (1993). The question of multiculturalism. *Arts Education Policy Review, 94*(4), 2–18.

Smith, R. A. (1995). Elitism and populism. In *Excellence II: The continuing quest in education* (pp. 97–114). Reston, VA: National Art Education.

Windschuttle, K. (2002). The cultural war on western civilization. *The New Criterion, 20*(5), 4–16.

6

Spirit, Mind, and Body: Arts Education the Redeemer

Constance Bumgarner Gee
Peabody College, Vanderbilt University

A large number of public agencies, nonprofit organizations, and private sector companies are engaged in arts and arts education advocacy campaigns. A broad range of assertions about the capacity of the arts to assist in spiritual and moral development, improve academic performance, and induce psychological and even physiological well-being are used to promote support for all types of arts and arts education programming. Federal arts groups characterize the services of artists and arts organizations as being indispensable to successful school-based arts instruction. This chapter analyzes the interests of various arts groups in arts education, the motivations behind various advocacy claims, and the likely repercussions of hard-driving marketing on K-12 arts education. The author concludes that state and municipal commitment to K-12 arts education will further erode as a direct result of failure to distinguish between the purposes and capabilities of schools and those of arts organizations with regard to student learning in the arts. The responsibilities and jurisdiction of schools must be delineated clearly and firmly, the outcome of which must be assured support for programs and research designed specifically for the advancement of school-based arts study. Arts educators are urged to proclaim those distinctions in the public arena just as they also must differentiate between more and less credible arts education advocacy claims.

In the spring of 2001, I was asked to contribute a chapter addressing the relationship of advocacy and K-12 art education to this *Handbook*. I had recently completed a chapter on the impact of various types of advocacy on music education for a research compendium similar to this one but organized by MENC, The National Association for Music Education (Gee, 2002). After having spent many months examining a broad range of arts education advocacy materials and reflecting on the intended and unintended consequences of various advocacy campaign promises and priorities for K-12 music education, I resisted emerging myself in a visual arts view of the same subject. I had read and reread every variation of the proof and promise that arts education raises SAT scores; improves reading, math, and spatial skills; increases overall academic performance; and builds self-esteem, self-discipline, creativity, community cohesion, and greater tolerance for difference. I had read that those qualities and achievements bolstered "workforce readiness" among America's young people and that a strong and ready workforce ensured our global competitiveness, a condition critical to our national security. Like others who have analyzed the proliferation of such justifications for arts education (Chapman, 2001; Eisner, 1998; Hope, 1985, 2002; Smith, 2002), I had come to believe that those claims and the techniques used to market them were seriously eroding the field's identity, credibility, and purpose (Gee, 1999b). But unlike others of greater faith and longer memory, I had accepted the inevitability of the destruction. I had arrived at the sad conclusion that, try as we might to brake its forward motion, the momentum of the marketing machine was so powerful as to be unstoppable and, that ultimately it would flatten every dissenter or counter any idea that stood in its path.

It is terribly difficult to write in defense of a belief or idea once faith in one's ability to make a difference has been lost. But although faith may be absent, hope lingers wistfully. Thus, I set about this task much like the Peanuts character, "Repeat" (the younger brother of Lucy and Linus), approached a drawing assignment in his first-grade art class. Seated at his side, Repeat's pig-tailed classmate turns to inform him, "We're suppose to draw each other's face." "Well, turn your head... I can only draw a side view face," he replies. Striking a pensive pose, she says, "I'm trying to have an expression of someone looking to the future with hope." "That's all right," replies Repeat, "I'm just drawing your ear."

And so I began to draw an ear, just an ear.

UNDERSTANDING THE WWW OF ARTS EDUCATION ADVOCACY

There is—to paraphrase Jerry Lee Lewis—a whole lotta arts education advocacy going on. Typing "arts education advocacy" into Google Search in August 2001 linked you to 234,000 Web sites; entering the same command in August 2002 links you to 309,000. Represented among those sites are state and local arts agencies; state alliances for arts education, artist alliances, arts centers, museums, performing arts organizations, national and state arts education associations, school districts, arts lobbyist groups; and private individuals advertising their capacities in arts advocacy, marketing, and conference speaking. There are 501(c)(3) performing, visual, and media art organizations that combine advocacy activities with the provision of "arts and education" or "arts in education" or just plain arts education programs and workshops. There are 501(c)(4) tax-exempt groups that lobby city council members and state and federal legislators on behalf of the arts education advocacy and programming efforts of 501(c)(3) tax-exempt organizations; of school districts; and of local, state, and federal public arts and cultural agencies. Public grant-making agencies such as the National Endowment for the Arts (NEA) and state and local arts councils advocate for arts education and for recognition and support of their own role and of the roles of arts organizations and artists in ensuring the success of arts education programming. Private philanthropic organizations and community foundations advocate for broad support of arts education. Along with public arts agencies, they seek to influence arts education policy, funding, programming, and practice through grant making for arts education-related projects and research, through the sponsorship of symposia, and through the publication and promotion of symposia proceedings and sponsored research. This information can be downloaded at the blink of an eye.

Chief among Washington-based publishers and distributors of arts education advocacy materials are Americans for the Arts, the NEA, the National Assembly of State Arts Agencies, the Kennedy Center Alliance for Arts Education, the Arts Education Partnership, and the President's Committee on the Arts and the Humanities. These federal arts agencies and federalized arts organizations, virtually one and the same with shared administrative staff, board membership, and advisory panels (and, therefore, philosophy and missions), are largely inter-changeable.[1] Self-promotion is the primary interest of these organizations and arts education serves them well in this respect. They seek to convince politicians, policymakers, and community leaders that they (and their state and local sister arts agencies and organizations and artist dependents) are essential to the work of arts education in all venues and at all phases and levels. Through their own in-house publications and through publication of research that they themselves sponsored, they assert their collective importance as the primary factor in successful arts education programming and as the main change agent in effective reform.[2]

Critical Links: Learning in the Arts and Student Academic and Social Development (Arts Education Partnership, 2002) is the federal arts cooperative's latest attempt to influence public policy by way of channeling arts education funding and research toward math, reading, and social service agenda. Financed by the NEA and the U.S. Department of Education, *Critical Links* was published in answer to the Arts Education Partnership's charge by its own research task force to create such a compendium. Weighted heavily with educational psychologists, *Critical Links* research reviewers and project advisors decided that the compendium would include "studies of the academic and social effects of arts learning experiences" rather than studies focused on learning in the arts (p. ii). The stated purpose of the compendium is to "recommend to researchers and funders of research promising lines of inquiry and study suggested by recent, strong studies of the academic and social effects of learning in the arts." A "parallel purpose" was to influence designers of arts education curriculum and instruction to attend more specifically to "the arts learning experiences that are required to achieve those effects" (p. iii).

Critical Links also serves as a vehicle for another more clandestine purpose, that is, the advancement of federal arts' decades-old practice of using arts education as a means to sustain political support and public funding. Whereas public arts subsidies are always in question and may be viewed as a political liability, no politician has been heard to say that education in the

---

[1]See Gee (2002, pp. 944–945) for a description of the intimate interconnectedness of the NEA and other Washington-based arts organizations and advocacy groups and the U.S. Department of Education.

[2]*Gaining the Arts Advantage* (President's Committee on the Arts & the Humanities and the Arts Education Partnership, 1999) provides a ready-made example of the arts bureaucracy's aggrandizement of various elements of the arts community as being front and center in K-12 arts education. The report's "central finding" asserts: "The single most critical factor in sustaining arts education in... schools is the active involvement of influential segments of the community in shaping and implementing the policies and programs of the district." *Influential segments of the community* is translated to mean "... individuals and groups from the broader community actively engage[d] with one another in arts and arts education activities inside and outside of the schools" (p. 9). The number one "critical success factor" is reported as being: "The Community—broadly defined as parents and families, artists, arts organizations, businesses, local civic and cultural leaders and institutions" (p. 11). *Champions of Change* (President's Committee on the Arts and the Humanities & the Arts Education Partnership, 1996) promotes seven arts intervention projects as replicable "models of excellence" for improved student achievement and education reform. The in-school and "nonschool" projects focused entirely on the work and contributions of "outside providers" of arts education—that is, local artists and arts groups that provide services within or outside of the school setting, during or after school hours. An Americans for the Arts advocacy pamphlet (2001a) queries: "Who works to ensure that arts education enriches the life of every child in America? Answer: Americans for the Arts" (p. 3). The pamphlet explains that Americans for the Arts ensures every American child an arts education through the distribution of its YouthARTS Tool Kit ($75) "to hundreds of local organizations to provide ideas and strategies for creating successful ['afterschool'] youth arts programs in their communities" (p. 3).

One might rightly wonder about the invisibility of the professional arts educator in these celebratory reports of arts education victories. It is clear these organizations are very much about the business of making it appear that they (and their sister organizations at the state and local levels) drive all steps forward in arts education. It is not difficult to understand their political motivations. Although the arts bureaucracy has used arts education as a public relations tool for decades, the practice intensified dramatically in the mid-1990s when Congressional intimidation of the NEA was at its most severe. See Gee (2002) for a more detailed description and analysis of the promotional activities of these organizations.

arts for young people is unworthy of support. Thus, high-profile association with "bringing the arts to America's children," while attaching the purpose of such programming to whatever social or educational cause is currently revving up the media, is a smart and effective means to generate political goodwill. Advocacy publications such as *Critical Links* are useful in legitimizing such maneuvering and posturing.

The publication, however, is really a transparent and unabashed attempt to portray methodologically weak studies as "strong" research. In other cases, the intent is to transform tenuous correlations into highly significant ones that might, if no one pays much attention, slither toward causation. Most of the studies were recycled from previous federal arts advocacy publications including *Champions of Change* (President's Committee on the Arts and the Humanities and the Arts Education Partnership, 1996) and *Eloquent Evidence* (Murfee, 1995).[3] No part of any of the 62 studies included in *Critical Links* is reprinted; instead, each of the studies is summarized by 1 of 14 research reviewers. A second reviewer joins the primary reviewer in commentary on the study's "contribution to the field of arts education and its implications for future research and/or practice" (p. ii). Yet, another hand is evident in what was selected from each of these commentaries for excerpt. This relay of summarizing and editing makes it difficult to determine the merit and tenor of the original study. The careful reader notices the almost total disconnection between reported noneffects and cautionary language found in the summaries and the cocksure tone of the excerpts. The busy political aid or school board member would be greeted with the dazzling good news that arts students "earned better grades and scores, were less likely to drop out of school, watched fewer hours of television, were less likely to report boredom in school, had a more positive self-concept, and were more involved in community service" (p. 69). *Critical Links* concludes with an inventory of 53 "core relationships" between arts learning and academic and social outcomes, all of which are said to "show evidence of transfer in the sense that learning activities in the arts have various effects beyond the initial conditions of learning" (Catterall, 2002, p. 154). Using this criterion for evidence of transfer, one might wonder if it is possible to identify any type or smidgen of learning that cannot be linked to improved academic and behavioral outcomes.[4]

Other organizations prominent in the arts education advocacy business include the American Symphony Orchestra League, the American Association of Museums, the American Arts Alliance (comprised of the Association of Art Museum Directors, Association of Performing Arts Presenters, Dance/USA, OPERA America, and the Theatre Communications Group), and the National Coalition for Music Education (comprised of MENC, The National Association for Music Education, National Academy of Recording Arts & Sciences, and National Association of Music Merchants [NAMM]). The National Coalition for Music Education and VH-1 Save the Music Foundation produced *The Music Education Advocacy Kit* (1999) complete with a video, a CD-ROM, an advocacy guidebook, posters, and several packets of pamphlets for distribution. A drawing of Albert Einstein playing a violin covers the front of the kit and all the accompanying materials. The co-opted Dr. Einstein makes the point that "Music makes you smarter!"

The Walt Disney Company appears to have persuaded an infantile Dr. Einstein to join corporate America in enlisting other deceased geniuses in the arts education enterprise. Having already produced Baby Mozart, Baby Beethoven, and Baby Bach, The Baby Einstein Company recently released Baby Vivaldi (Entertainment Wire, 2002). Baby Van Gogh and Baby Shakespeare attest as well to Baby Einstein's interest in the visual and literary arts. Information on the benefits of music on brain development is packaged with each CD courtesy of the

---

[3] In "Does Experience in the Arts Boost Academic Achievement?" Elliot Eisner (1998) offers an edifying critique of *Eloquent Evidence*.

[4] For a more extended discussion of *Critical Links*, see the symposium in *Arts Education Policy Review* (2003).

American Music Conference, the public relations arm of NAMM and a consultant for *The Music Education Advocacy Kit*.[5]

Upstaging Albert Einstein as a caring and glamorous proponent of arts education is Barbie Queen of the Prom, reincarnated most recently as Art Teacher Barbie. Trying to make a living in Los Angeles as an elementary art teacher, Barbie is truly concerned about arts education.[6] Her Barbie Cares Supporting Children in the Arts Web site states that "kids engaged in the arts score better on standardized tests. . . [and] perform better in core subjects like reading and math" (Mattel, Inc., 2002). Supermodel Cindy Crawford seconds Barbie, adding that "the arts build self-confidence and encourage kids to be more active in community affairs and promote creative expression and individuality" (Entertainment Industry Foundation, 2002). Both are spokespersons for the Entertainment Industry Foundation's National Arts Education Initiative of which the Arts Education Partnership was an initial beneficiary.

The National Governors Association (NGA) Center for Best Practices in cooperation with the NEA and with "significant research assistance" from the National Assembly of State Arts Agencies published an issue brief encouraging the use of arts-based education "as a money- and time-saving option for states looking to build skills, increase academic success, heighten standardized test scores, and lower the incidence of crime among general and at-risk populations" (NGA, 2002, p. 1). Reported successes of "arts-based" educational programs among at-risk and incarcerated youth appear to be of particular interest to the NGA. According to the report, arts involvement provides an avenue "by which at-risk youth can acquire the various competencies necessary to become economically self-sufficient over the long term, rather than becoming a financial strain on their states and communities" (p. 1).

Americans for the Arts and the Advertising Council have mounted a multiyear *National Arts Education Public Awareness Campaign* (Americans for the Arts & the Advertising Council, 2002) that promises to "secure approximately $28 million annually in donated television, radio, print, and online advertising time and space" (p. 2) for sponsors, most of which are state and local arts agencies.[7] The official campaign theme is: *The Less Art Kids Get, The More It Shows. Are Yours Getting Enough? Art. Ask for More.* The convoluted justification for the campaign hinges on the response to a question included in the *National Arts Education Public Awareness Campaign Survey* commissioned by Americans for the Arts (2001b). When parents were asked whether they were "satisfied with the amount of arts education that their children receive at both their local school and through community arts organizations" (p. 8), schools received a 68% approval rating and community arts organizations received a 70% approval rating. Thus, the campaign organizers' "creative strategy" is to convince parents "that there is a problem with the small amount of art their children are getting. . . [and] to move parents and concerned citizens from being complacent with what they have to demanding even more art for

---

[5]See Gee (2002, pp. 945–947) for a more detailed description of the content and character of the music education advocacy conducted by various music associations.

[6]Art Teacher Barbie is lucky to have a job, as there are only 29 full-time elementary visual arts teachers in the Los Angeles Unified School District (LAUSD) for the 2002–2003 school year. There are 476 elementary schools in the LAUSD. Each teacher serves 5 to 7 schools on a rotating basis. This means that 154 or 32% of LAUSD's elementary schools have a few weeks access to a visual arts teacher. However, things are looking up for Barbie and her art teacher colleagues; there were no LAUSD elementary art teachers in the 1999–2000 school year. Music Teacher Barbie is more fortunate; she has 146 colleagues and is only required to serve in 5 schools each year. (Richard Burrows, Director of Arts Education, LAUSD, telephone interview, August 21, 2002).

[7]Sponsors or "official partners" are allowed to join the campaign at one of three levels: "basic" with access to print ads, "intermediate" with access to print and radio ads, or "premiere" with access to print, radio, and television ads. The sponsoring organization is provided ready-made ads and public service announcements to which it can attach its logo or dub in its name in affiliation with Americans for the Arts and the Ad Council. It is the responsibility of the sponsor to seek out and secure local marketing spots. State arts education organizations can participate in the print and radio portions of the campaign but not in the televised portion.

children" (Americans for the Arts & the Advertising Council, 2002, p. 2). The "main idea" to be conveyed to parents is "that some art is not enough" and that "their children are missing out because [they are not getting enough] of it" (p. 2). The six-page Official Partnership Fact Sheet does not mention what type of art is important for kids to "get" or what desirable knowledge or experience is to be had by getting more art. "Reasons to Join as an Official Partner" focus *exclusively* on opportunities for press coverage and media exposure. Again, no explanation is offered of the value or purpose of getting more art for kids other than to "gain local media attention for your organization" (p. 3). Media attention will (according to the fact sheet) lead to "more support and funding for the arts and arts education in your community" (p. 3).

The Congressional Recognition for Excellence in Arts Education Act (Senate Bill 2789, United States Congress, 2000) stands as a recent example of legislated arts advocacy. As reported in *Adviso* by the American Association of Museums (2001, January), which assisted the Arts Education Partnership in developing the legislation, S.2789, it "creates a congressional board and a citizens advisory board to establish an award for schools that demonstrate excellence in arts education curriculum" (p. 2). The advisory board is to be appointed by the congressional board based on recommendations from the Arts Education Partnership steering committee and from the arts and cultural organizations with which schools partner (S.2789, sec. 206). The first-listed awards criterion is that "the community serving the school [e.g., artists, arts organizations, businesses, and cultural leaders] is actively involved in shaping and implementing the arts policies and programs of the school" (sec. 205). The Arts Education Partnership is cited in the bill as "an excellent example of one organization that has demonstrated its. . . capacity and credibility to administer arts education programs of national significance" (sec. 202). As of November 2002, S.2789 (now Public Law No: 106-533) awaited a budget appropriation of $1 million.

Two fundamental premises drive arts education advocacy as it is currently coined and circulated. The first premise is that all arts programming is educational. The second is that most everyone involved in arts programming is considered to be an educator in the arts. Arts participation, arts learning, arts experience, arts encounters, and arts involvement—all considered to be arts education—can be obtained at community recreation centers, museums, performing arts venues, summer camps, day care centers, fairgrounds, schools, churches, prisons, hospitals, and via the Internet. Arts education services are provided by artists and artisans, K-12 arts specialists, elementary classroom teachers, state and local arts agency staff, and visual and performing arts institution personnel. Professionally credited arts educators hold no special purview within the World Wide Web of arts education advocacy. K-12 arts education holds no superior claim to fiscal or political support. As one ponders the political presence and interests of all of the various players engaged in arts education advocacy, it is important to be mindful that the purpose of the types of advocacy cited previously is to influence policy, attain position, define programs, and redirect funding.

3 FOR 3: AN ARTS EDUCATION ADVOCACY CONTENT PRIMER

Reasons given to support arts education and those who provide it fall under three broad categories of societal interest and purpose. Arts education is justified and marketed as a means to improve (a) the individual as a person, (b) the individual as a contributing member of society, and (c) the human community. Three interlacing advocacy themes further define arts education's contributions to these basic concerns of civil society. Arts education's earliest and broadest realm of proclaimed influence was and continues to be on human spirituality and morality. Closely related to spiritual and moral development is emotional maturation, another area of personal improvement that arts education is said to assist. Arts education's ability to contribute to brain and skill development has become a second and ever more popular advocacy theme in our intensely competitive, market-centered society. The notion of arts education/experience qua arts therapy as a means to improve one's emotional and physical well-being is a third overarching advocacy theme that is fast gaining momentum. Over the years, I have come to regard the trinity, Spirit, Mind, and Body, as the "YMCA Approach" to arts education.[8]

Building Better Moral Values

There are abundant variations on the commonly voiced claim that arts education contributes to the spiritual and moral development of the individual, an outcome that in turn makes for a more virtuous citizenry and principled society.[9] A virtuous person is self-aware and self-disciplined, kind to others and respectful of their beliefs and ideas, and dutiful and cheerful in tasks undertaken. The following advocacy statements proffer that view of the value of arts education:

- Arts learning experiences help students to better know themselves and to better relate to those around them.
- Arts education fosters tolerance of and appreciation for cultural and ethnic diversity.
- Arts education improves children's attitudes toward school.
- In-school and "nonschool" arts programming improves self-esteem, curbs delinquent behavior, teaches discipline, and helps students to better perform academically.
- Arts education teaches children to communicate more effectively with adults and peers.

At-risk students from low-income families—a type and class of individuals most threatening to a moral and ordered society—are said to benefit most from arts participation. Another fervent and frequent claim is that K-12 education can be "transformed through the arts." Arts programs are said to improve the school culture as a whole by breaking down barriers between subject areas, energizing teachers, motivating students, and improving the physical appearance of school buildings. Broad-scale transformation of our nation's schools into more humane, open, and uplifting places of learning is perceived as being the moral duty of a good society.

Building Better Minds and Workplace Skills

The capacity of arts education to more fully develop the human mind and improve dispositions toward learning is another essential arts advocacy theme. Frequently made claims proffering that vision of the value of arts education include:

- Students with high levels of arts participation outperform "arts-poor" students on virtually every academic performance measure.

---

[8]"Spirit, Mind, Body" is the motto of the Young Men's Christian Association (YMCA).

[9]See Jacques Barzun (1974) for an enlightened perspective on our age-old predilection to associate knowledge and support of the arts with heightened spiritual sensibilities and superior moral character. In *From Dawn to Decadence* (2000), Barzun recounts a popular argument for greater support of and participation in the arts in Renaissance Italy— "that art was conducive to order and harmony in private life and the state" (p. 156). Although renowned for its advances in the arts, the temperament of Renaissance Italy was anything but peaceful. "The melancholic and the moralists," Barzun writes, "as well as the devout, read the times as wicked and bound for perdition. Endless wars, recurrent plague, the new curse syphilis, and the readiness to murder for gain or revenge—all these frequently depicted in the Dance of Death—justified gloom. In any period it is hard to believe in the maxim *Emollit musica mores*—music makes behavior gentler" (p. 161).

- Students who study or participate in the arts score higher on standardized tests.
- Music study improves math scores and spatial skills; reading skills are enhanced by arts learning, particularly through theater and the visual arts.
- Arts education stimulates creativity, builds communications skills, promotes teamwork, and engenders "love of learning" in all subject areas.
- Arts education teaches critical thinking and higher order thinking skills, providing a competitive edge for getting a job in the future.

The frequently heard claim that "arts education improves overall academic performance" capitalizes on the collective, hazy angst that our public schools are somehow failing us. The complex concept of *academic performance* is most commonly understood as the ability to cipher and read at grade level, attainments valued first and foremost as prerequisites for gainful employment. The popularized notion of *workforce readiness* calls forth a gamut of knowledge, skills, and dispositions necessary for a smooth and efficient transition from student to worker. Of course the value assigned to various workforce attributes depends largely on which workforce one is expected to enter. As one moves up the socioeconomic chain—from employee to employer, from job to career, from laborer to professional—emphases placed on basic math and reading skills and on working well within a group shift toward the need for independent and critical thinking, creative problem solving, and individualism. Arts education is said to contribute in a significant and effective manner to all of those learning and socialization goals.

Building Better Psyches and Physiques

"Musick has Charms to sooth a savage Breast." "[M]oods and attitudes that come from the realm of the mind transform themselves into the physical realm through the emotions." "[T]here is overwhelming evidence that hormones and neurotransmitters can influence the activities of the immune system, and that products of the immune system can influence the brain." "Attending and enjoying the arts, specifically live arts experiences, is good for your health." "Making music makes you smarter and healthier and happier and helps you live longer." The first statement was written by William Congreve in 1697; it is the first line in his play, *The Mourning Bride.* The second and third statements were made, respectively, by neuroscientist Candace Pert and neurobiologist David Felten during Bill Moyer's public television series *Healing and the Mind* (Moyer, 1993, pp. 189, 215). The fourth statement was the thesis of a Hospital Audiences, Inc. (HAI) monograph funded by the U.S. Department of Health and Human Services (Spencer, 1996). The fifth statement currently headlines the one-page "research" section of the NAMM Web site (2002) and has been circulated widely since the 1999 production of "The Einstein Kit" (i.e., *The Music Education Advocacy Kit*) by the National Coalition for Music Education and VH-1 Save the Music Foundation.

Philosophers, healers, spiritual leaders, and artists across cultures and centuries have expressed their conviction in art's power to refresh the spirit and calm the mind. The power of art to stimulate as well as soothe is also well extolled. As John Dryden (1687), Congreve's friend and mentor, penned: "What Passion cannot Musick raise and quell!" (p. 2). Art, it is believed fervently, speaks to and cultivates our sensibilities; it helps us to "get in touch" with and express our "inner feelings."

According to adherents of mind/body medicine, it is our feelings or emotions that bridge the mental and physical, the physical and mental. Repression of emotion is not only believed to be detrimental psychologically but also thought to contribute to or even cause physical disease. Release of emotion, especially within the safe confines of a support group, is believed to have a positive impact on the immune system. According to Pert, "A common ingredient in the healing practices of native cultures is catharsis, complete release of emotion" (Moyer, 1993,

p. 191). In this context and for these purposes, emotions are not something to be controlled or disciplined, but acknowledged, legitimized, and nurtured. This is precisely the role of arts education when used to provide "creative outlets" for self-expression. Arts education advocates posit further that being able to creatively and effectively express oneself leads to a sense of empowerment, a decidedly positive feeling that in turn leads to a more positive overall mental state. NAMM, whose member organizations sell musical instruments, asserts that *making music makes you healthier and increases your longevity* (2002). HAI director Michael Jon Spencer, whose organization sells programs and performances, insists that simply attending an arts event is beneficial to health and wellness. Effortlessly bridging art with physical health and good medicine he asserts: "The gateway to good health starts with a healthy immune system. Positive mental and emotional states are pivotal to maintaining and strengthening this immune system. The enjoyment of the arts usually starts with the experience of pleasure, relaxation, and relief from tension and stress" (1996, p. 1).

The rationale for arts education qua arts therapy snowballs along from a first principle about the nature of art into a seemingly self-evident truth about human mind/body functions into a reasonable enough statement about a basic purpose of and justification for arts education into a broadly generalized assumption about the impact of art on health that a lot of people want and need to believe. Thus:

- Art speaks directly to our emotions; it excites, soothes, and helps us to connect with our feelings.
- Acknowledgement and release of emotion are good for our mental and physical health.
- Art education is important because it provides a creative (and safe) outlet for self-expression (i.e., the release and communication of emotion and ideas) resulting in greater self-awareness and self-worth.
- Making and experiencing art has a positive effect on our physiological well-being. As a consequence we feel better about ourselves and more empathetic toward others, dispositions which make us happier and help us to live not only fuller but also longer lives.

The logic of the sequence is far from flawless, but the conclusions are highly appealing to a broad audience; and appeal is the most important attribute of any rationale in the world of marketing, public relations, and advocacy. No advocacy group, to my knowledge, is campaigning (yet) under the banner, "Arts education is good for your immune system!"[10] However, the close

---

[10]Self-proclaimed "world-renowned artists" Vitaly Komar and Alexander Melamid (1999) gleefully encouraged aspiring art doctors to make that leap in *The New York Times Magazine* Endpaper. Announcing their book and audiotape series, *The Healing Power of Art*, they explained:

Stories of Art's curative powers fill our history books, from the Greek royal whose cracked hip was cured by a fresco to the noted American President whose lower-back pain disappeared while viewing Velázquez's beautiful and inspiring "Water Seller of Seville." While we all know that Art can deliver us from illness, its powers have always seemed random and hidden in mystery. Too often we want to benefit from Art, but we simply do not know where to begin. . . . Customized for the great museums of the world, each Healing Power of Art™ book features a detailed, annotated floor plan, indicating the best periods, artists and paintings for a wide spectrum of afflictions. The accompanying cassette tapes guide you through the museum, making your visit (and recuperation!) speedier.

Exposure to Seurat banishes pimples, Pollack assists with blood disorders, Rubens is good for the liver, and Macedonian handicrafts stop nosebleeds. (Readers who, at this point, are experiencing nausea may want to proceed to the Asian wing of Metropolitan Museum of Art for a dose of Korin.)

The ironic sting of Komar and Melamid's art caper is its "gotcha" quality. Chances are that many of the most art worldly and wary of *The New York Times* subscribers, paused, if only for a moment, thinking: Is this for real? Undoubtedly, tens of thousands of less suspicious souls glanced at the tongue-in-cheek advertisement with bland acceptance.

association of health and human service rationales for support of arts programming coupled with arts education's touted success as a self-esteem builder and therapeutic vent for self-expression offers grand incentive for protuberance of advocacy theme number 3.

PERSONAL TRUTHS AND PULP FICTION

Arts education is good for the spirit, the mind, and the body. Arts education is good for the individual, the citizenry, and the world. Variations and spin-offs of these grand themes and public purposes are the stuff of arts education advocacy efforts big and small. Whether one is a true believer in the religion of art with only the betterment of humankind in mind or an opportunist seeking to align oneself with the current doctrine of political and fiscal survival, or somewhere in between, a combination of these rewards is likely to be proffered to potential arts education proselytes (particularly proselytes with purses).

Certainly there are basic truths about the nature of art and needs of human beings and societies embedded in some of the arts education advocacy slogans. For example, the frequently heard statement that arts learning experiences help students to better know themselves and better relate to those around them speaks directly to our fundamental psychological need to connect with others and feel part of a greater whole. Attainment of a deeper knowledge of oneself and greater empathy for one's fellow classmates and citizens would seem to be important and sensible rationales for support of arts education, if in truth those are the effects of arts experience and learning. Unfortunately, proof of this assumption is not readily evident in the day-to-day business of the artworld. Robert Hughes (1993) writes, "We know, in our heart of hearts, that the idea that people are morally ennobled by contact with works of art is a pious fiction.... There is just no generalizing about the moral effects of art, because it just doesn't seem to have any. If it did, people who are constantly exposed to it, including all curators and critics, would be saints, and we are not" (p. 178).

Further afield from the centuries-old spiritual and moral development homilies about the value of arts study and exposure to the individual and society stand more recent claims of heightened academic performance, improved test scores, and healthier minds and bodies. It is by now common knowledge that most of the assertions about the effects of arts study/experience/exposure on math, reading, and test taking are much more assumption than fact.[11] A second fact is that nobody much seems to care. The marketing potential in equating correlation with causation is just too tempting; the short-term rewards are too tasty.

When the World Trade Towers fell, America's hyped-up recovery movement ricocheted off the rubble. Suddenly the entire country was in need of solace and therapy. Art the Healer, hustled along by arts agency handlers, rose up to meet those needs. Arts and Living sections of newspapers were filled with stories of art events and projects that were uniting the nation and healing individuals and communities. Americans for the Arts responded immediately creating an *Arts Healing America* section on its Web site, where hundreds of stories about the healing power of art were posted. A special preconference, *Art Heals*, was planned for Americans for the Arts' annual arts advocacy convention. As Americans for the Arts president

---

[11]There has been ongoing debate over the extent to which arts study affects achievement in core academic subjects such as math, reading, and science since the Sputnik-inspired 1950s push to improve K-12 math and science education. The findings of the Reviewing Education and the Arts Project (REAP), published first in a special issue of the *Journal of Aesthetic Education*, greatly intensified the debate (Winner & Hetland, 2000). Also see Winner and Hetland (2001) and *Arts Education Policy Review* (2001).

and CEO Robert Lynch (2001, p. 1) put it, art was no longer for art's sake; it was now "Art for the Nation's Sake." An elite group of university visual arts educators dedicated their annual meeting to discussion of "post-cataclysmic art education" and to the development of policy statements that addressed "September 11th and the need for more practical, immediate, and humane work related to the global crisis and art education's role in promoting healing and survival through policy designed to improve global social ecology for peace [*sic*]" (Council on Policy Studies in Art Education, 2002).

Exhibiting remarkable courage amidst this feverish, nationwide art therapy epidemic, *Los Angeles Times* art critic Christopher Knight asked the question: "What Exactly Can Art Heal?" (November, 2001). The idea that art is "useful for the treatment of social, spiritual or emotional disorders," Knight wrote, is "a secular version of venerating the healing power of religious paintings and statues" (p. 1). While Grunewald's *Isenheim Altarpiece* is "one heck of a painting," it did not cure those afflicted with gangrene as was its purpose. Knight cites the Arts Recovery Program, launched by the Los Angeles Cultural Affairs Department in the wake of the 1992 riots, as a latter-day version of this same idea. "Nearly a half-million dollars in scarce civic arts money was spent—and mostly wasted—on funding for nearly 150 projects that ostensibly would help to heal the battered city. That few today can quite remember what those projects were is just one measure of the program's inadequacy" (p. 2). According to Knight, public arts therapy is often more beneficial for the therapist than the patient:

> [I]t's instructive that politicians and the political class are the ones who so often champion this old-timey conception of art's purpose and value. Extolling "the healing power of art" in the face of massive social trauma handily fudges the failure of politics, and the failure of politics is at the root of things like the '92 riots and the current terrorist nightmare. . . . There's also an economic dimension to the [arts] institutional urge. Back in 1992, for example, the Arts Recovery Program was the leading edge of a larger effort on the part of the Cultural Affairs Department to transform art into a social service. With the arts under ferocious attack from conservative anti-government forces in the culture war, and with a simultaneous recession in the California economy creating fierce competition for public and philanthropic money, [arts institution] survival was at stake. . . . An alignment of the arts with social welfare projects would make the arts appear to be an indispensable humanitarian service. (p. 2)

Art the Psychotherapist specializes in self-esteem building, and of course Arts Education hangs up a shingle right next door. It is a profitable business. "The self is now the sacred cow of American culture," wrote Hughes (1993), "self-esteem is sacrosanct, and so we labor to turn arts education into a system in which no-one can fail" (p. 7). Mental health professionals (as well as cantankerous cultural critics) are (finally) questioning such ingrained assumptions. In a recent *New York Times Magazine* article psychologist Lauren Slater (2002) discussed America's "quasi-religion" of self-esteem. She summed up the shared central conclusions of three "withering" studies released in 2001: "[P]eople with high self-esteem pose a greater threat to those around them than people with low self-esteem and feeling bad about yourself is not the cause of our country's biggest, most expensive social problems" (p. 46). "The psychotherapy industry. . . would take a huge hit were self-esteem to be re-examined," she added.

> After all, psychology and psychiatry are predicated upon the notion of the self, and its enhancement is the primary purpose of treatment. . . . There is a profound tension here between psychotherapy as a business that needs to retain its customers and psychotherapy as a practice that has the health of its patients at heart. . . If you look at psychotherapy in other cultures, you get a glimpse into the obsessions of our own. You also see what a marketing fiasco we would have on our hands were

we to dial down our self-esteem beliefs. In Japan, there is a popular form of psychotherapeutic treatment that does not focus on the self, and its worth [but instead] holds as its central premise that neurotic suffering comes, quite literally, from extreme self-awareness. (p. 47)

Arts education as self-esteem therapy is riddled with the same tensions and failings. And in our heart of hearts, we know it. Knight (2001) concluded, "Art can be put to all kinds of uses but intrinsically it's amoral. The unctuous presumption of art's essential 'goodness' is a political fiction. Just about the last thing we need at a time of national emergency is yet one more political fiction" (p. 2). We also do not need any more educational fiction.

THE SIGNIFICANCE OF ARTS EDUCATION ADVOCACY FOR K-12 VISUAL ARTS EDUCATION

So what does this kaleidoscope of more and less credible claims mean for K-12 visual arts education? Beyond engendering confusion in some and cynicism in others, it does not mean much of anything for the fundamentals of teaching and learning. All the marketing slogans in the world cannot change our basic relationship with art. Art is a part of our lives because it brings us *pleasure*, not simply casual pleasure but the pleasure of engagement. Art makes us *feel*; it makes us feel alive sensuously, emotionally, and intellectually. Such pleasures are for the most part intensely personal, especially with regards to visual and literary art forms. The made-for-public-consumption rewards of arts education that headline arts advocacy campaigns are quite beside the point of why art teachers teach and why students take their courses. Nevertheless, the energy spent jumping from one bandwagon to another in the arts education advocacy parade is an unfortunate waste of resources; the dust clouds of confusion kicked up by this unceasing procession take their toll on our intellectual environment. It would be foolish to disregard the wasting effects of cynicism and disorientation on spirit and intellect.

Misspent energies and professional folly are as evident within the art education professorate as they are within the arts bureaucracy. That is where lies the field's greatest danger for disorientation and dissolution. Eagerly we wrench art education inside out to make it about healing and survival. We squander our energies making up imaginary policies for art education "to improve global social ecology for peace." If the field's best and brightest indulge in such histrionics how can we expect arts lobbyists and marketeers to show greater restraint and good sense?

So much for the anguish and hyperbole about why arts education should be supported. What is the significance of the less overt but insistent message that arts programming per se is educational and that as a consequence most everyone involved in arts programming is an arts educator? It probably means that funding for school arts programs will continue to erode as legislators, community leaders, and parents become increasingly uncertain of the value and need of school-based arts instruction. Ultimately it may mean that "arts education" will cease to stand for much of anything.

Almost 2 decades ago an editorial in *Design for Arts In Education* (1985a) stated:

[S]o much talk about the arts now seems focused on funding and the politics of funding, so much activity about art now seems based on what every possible group is doing to support it that the central importance of the individual activities of making art, teaching it, and learning about it seems increasingly lost in an orgy of advocacy and self-congratulations. (p. 2)

Since the late 1960s, the arts education community has watched a proliferating arts bureaucracy make increasingly aggressive claims on and on behalf of arts education. Comprised of public arts agencies and associations, arts service organizations, and arts lobbyist groups, this coterie portrays itself as the primary force behind arts education improvement and reform. This stance is evident in *Coming Up Taller* (President's Committee on the Arts and the Humanities & the National Assembly of Local Arts Agencies, 1996), where the perception is promoted that genuine arts learning is had through "frequent, direct contact with the artists and scholars themselves" (p. 35). The presence of "adults who are experts", in contrast to art teachers, is touted as a primary differentiating characteristic between out-of-school and in-school arts programs. Featured prominently in *Coming Up Taller*, Robert Capanna, executive director of the Settlement Music School in Philadelphia, offers an all too ready example: "Artists process their environment differently. When you put an artist in a teaching environment, they stay an artist. When you put a teacher in that environment and give them some art skills, they are a teacher with some art skills [*sic*]. And the kids know the difference" (p. 35).[12] This is but one of many such examples found throughout decades of NEA publications and echoed by the National Assembly of State Arts Agencies, Americans for the Arts, the Arts Education Partnership, and the President's Committee on the Arts and the Humanities. Such claims are made at the expense of tens of thousands of K-12 arts educators whose daily efforts in the classroom (and personal artistic qualifications) are often ignored completely or contrasted unfavorably with the youth-oriented outreach programming of arts organizations and services of visiting artists.

The National Art Education Association (NAEA) has spent considerable resources trying to lessen the impact of these claims and attacks on arts education and arts educators. In 1997, the Consortium of National Arts Education Associations (of which the NAEA is a member) with assistance from the National Association of Music Merchants organized a resistance movement. The impetus for this defiance was a barrage of intentionally misleading assertions about arts education that were being circulated by the NEA and its lobbyists in preparation for the 1997 Congressional reauthorization and budget hearings. Desperately trying to change the unhappy direction of the NEA's political fortunes, federal arts lobbyists sought to tie the wounded agency closer to arts education by way of equating the merits of high-quality K-12 arts education programming with NEA-sponsored arts exposure activities. Their goal was to capture for the Endowment any political goodwill that arts education might garner and to portray the NEA's marginal involvement with arts education as being the driving force behind any positive outcomes (real or imagined) associated with K-12 arts instruction. The vehicle for this plan to generate support for the NEA was Senate Bill 1020. Its passage would have awarded the NEA and its constituent organizations significant power over arts education funding, policymaking, and programming primarily through adoption of a federally legislated definition of arts education that made no distinction between the most inconsequential of arts-exposure activities and sequential, comprehensive school-based arts instruction. Ultimately the Consortium won the protracted and energy-consuming battle over S.1020. A subsequent telephone and fax campaign convinced the Interiors Appropriations Committee not to use the term *arts education* in conjunction with NEA appropriation language and conditions.[13]

In 1998, the NAEA broadened its efforts to alert its membership and key school administrators to the dangers inherent in the federal arts bureaucracy's claims on arts education and to curtail the escalating ballyhoo about the positive effects of arts study/experience on math,

---

[12]For a history of the denigration of K-12 arts teachers by the arts bureaucracy see Gee (1999b).

[13]See Gee (1999a, pp. 10–15) for an account of the battle over S.1020 between the Consortium of National Arts Education Associations and its supporters and the NEA and its supporters.

reading, and SAT scores. E-mail and fax missives called attention to the intent of federal arts groups to influence important areas within K-12 arts education such as teacher preparation and certification and the focus and funding of instructional programs.[14] This cadre of federal arts groups sought one goal over all others—that is, more control and cash for itself and its supporting constituency of artists and arts organizations. Gary Larson (1997), author of the NEA publication *American Canvas*, summed it up matter of factly in identifying K-12 arts education as a "revenue stream" and fiscal and political "escape route" for a persecuted nonprofit arts community. Involvement with arts education would provide "immediate payoffs, in the form of work for artists and arts organizations." Larson also proposed generating additional revenue for arts organizations through increased involvement in youth programs and crime prevention (p. 49).

More recently, the NAEA has shifted from a defensive to an offensive advocacy strategy. Recognizing the seriousness of the arts bureaucracy's challenge in the arts education policy arena, the NAEA is actively seeking to educate its members about the importance of their attentiveness to and engagement in policy formulation and implementation. At the same time, the NAEA works to maintain the field's focus on the areas and issues that it sees as being most critical to the continuing progress of visual arts teaching and learning. Through its "Where's the Art?" campaign, it hammers home the need to focus on the "nation's arts education policy and program deficiencies" (NAEA, 15 August 2002, p. 1).[15] This message is sent to every member of Congress and to every governor; and to tens of thousands of local and state school officials, state legislators, school principals, and Parent–Teacher Association leaders across the country. A "Where's the Art?" poster features an "arts education policy fact sheet" and provides directives as to ways for art teachers, parents, legislators, state officials, and arts councils to correct policies adversely affecting K-12 arts education. The fact sheet provides information on the poor standing of the arts in terms of high school graduation and university admissions requirements, its exclusion from a large majority of college and university admissions' grade point average computations, and its omission from most state learning assessment and teacher licensure programs. Instructions for art education activism make the point repeatedly that the focus must be kept on policies and strategies that lead to student learning in art—not math or reading or science. Teacher preparation; learning standards; curriculum design and development; time within the school day; graduation requirements; teaching materials, equipment, and facilities; professional development; student assessment; and teacher evaluation are the subjects of the "Where's the Art" campaign and of its charge to "Support Improving Art Education Policies." Steady streams of leaflets, posters, postcards, e-mails, and faxes attempt to keep these pivotal

---

[14] A series of self-mailers and faxes (NAEA, 1998a) made the point:

In arts education many lay-artists, amateurs, and philanthropists want to decide who should teach art, what curriculum content should be taught. . . Too often, their arts education isn't necessarily your arts education. Chances are it will turn out to be a visiting artist, a performance, a visit to a gallery or exhibit, or perhaps just pure entertainment. . . In fact, the mission of some arts groups and organizations is simple exposure to the arts.

Another leaflet (NAEA, 1998b) read:

Although millions enjoy riding in airplanes without understanding airfoil dynamics no one would seriously suggest that 'plane rides' should be substituted for school-based study of math and physics. Unfortunately, such substitutions are explicitly and implicitly made all the time with respect to arts activities that provide entertainment, exposure, and enrichment, but not education. . . . Advocacy is important, but it is not the reason for or the content of arts education. Advocacy works to convince and encourage belief. Education works to teach and encourages individual learning and competence.

[15] Fifteen different "Where's the Art?" flyers can be downloaded from the NAEA's Web site at http://www.naea-reston.org/news.html.

arts education policy issues in the sightline of local and state education and legislative decision makers nationwide.

NAEA leadership is also angling to wedge in a chair at the federal arts education policy table with a determination heretofore unseen. Meeting with Susan Sclafini, chief counselor to U.S. Secretary of Education Rod Paige, NAEA President MacArthur Goodwin tried to ensure that the NAEA's voice would be heard in future policy discussions about "improving student learning in general and visual arts education in particular" (NAEA, August 14, 2002). If past is prescient, the sharp elbows of the federal arts players will keep the NAEA pressed into the back of its seat even if it does manage somehow to push a chair up to the club table.

A large percentage of the professional art education field's advocacy efforts are conceived and conducted as a countercheck to the advocacy messages and aims of the federal arts bureaucracy. As advocacy reports such as *Critical Links* and *Gaining the Arts Advantage* make all too clear, federal arts groups are intent on directing arts education policymaking, research, and funding toward support of the types of programs and ends that best serve the needs and interests of arts agencies and organizations. These are not the same types of programs and ends that keep art educators, school officials, and political leaders focused on what it takes to best encourage student learning in art.

THE COST OF NOT MAKING DISTINCTIONS

Many arts and arts education advocates will disagree vehemently with my characterization of the arts education-related activities of entities such as the NEA, Americans for the Arts, the Arts Education Partnership, the National Assembly of State Arts Agencies, and the President's Committee on the Arts and the Humanities. Many will argue that arts education is not being diffused but *infused* into and throughout communities. They will say that the advocacy campaigns of the organizations mentioned previously support K-12 arts education by encouraging the involvement of the community (arts organization administration and staff, artists, parents, local arts patrons, and business and civic leaders) in school policymaking and instructional programs. They will counter that although K-12 arts teachers make important contributions to the education of children, so do local artists and arts organizations; and that although K-12 arts programming is important and desirable, so are after-school, weekend, and summer arts learning opportunities. After all, school is in session only 7 hours a day, 5 days a week, 9 months out of the year. Life and art are always in session (both with a distinct preference for non-school hours and environs).

Perhaps it is possible to assent to four basic convictions. First, a strong public school system is fundamental to a democratic society. Second, knowledge of an art form contributes greatly to the cultivation and pleasures of life. Third, a substantive arts education curriculum contributes significantly to the quality of the school curriculum as a whole. Moreover, as long as it is generally mandated that children attend school up to 16 years of age, American's public schools provide the most effective and democratic means by which to ensure that the greatest number of students have the opportunity to attain in-depth knowledge of an art form.

I do not doubt that most arts education advocates honor convictions about both the importance of a strong public education system in a democratic society and the role the arts can and ought to play in the education and life of the individual. There is unanimity among arts and arts education advocates of all persuasions on these points. It is the fourth conviction or, perhaps more accurately, the intensity of commitment and focus it demands, that brings disillusion and divisiveness. *The belief that the best chance to cultivate a citizenry broadly educated in the arts resides within the school curriculum and the school day requires that the improvement of school-based arts instruction be the clear and primary focus of arts education funding and research.* This fourth conviction is disillusioning because the institutionalization of regularly offered, sequentially instructed arts programming in our nation's schools has proven to be unattainable after almost a century of effort by arts educators, artists, and concerned parents. It is divisive because it demands an unadulterated focus on K-12 arts education, a perspective that in practice narrows significantly the meaning of the term *arts education* to school-based programming.

In the World Wide Web of arts advocacy, a truly incredible assortment of spirit–mind–body benefits spill forth from a cornucopia of "working partnerships" among arts agencies and institutions, arts and social service organizations, corporations, local businesses, school districts, and individual schools. This grand vision stakes out the moral high ground with its inclusiveness while standing tall as a golden example of the American entrepreneurial spirit and can-do attitude. In contrast, skepticism about the sense and truth of the promised rewards or the credibility of the promise makers seems small-minded, mean spirited, and shortsighted. Yet many questions concerning the content and consequences of full-throttle arts and arts education advocacy ought to be posed, just as questions should be raised about the specific costs, benefits, and possible unintended consequences of all grand-scale policymaking. Two questions seem central:

- Wherein lies the impetus for state and local governments to allocate the budget and expend the effort that is required to improve the quality of school arts instruction and to make the study of an art form part of the regular K-12 curricula if arts education is portrayed as being available in venues throughout the community and in after-school, weekend, and summer programs; and if artists and arts organization staff are portrayed as being ready and willing to provide arts experiences, arts exposure, arts involvement, arts learning, and arts education?
- If arts education is or can be made available so well and readily throughout the community, then why should people of social and political influence—people whose own children already have various opportunities for arts study and experience—concern themselves over the establishment, maintenance, and steady improvement of regularly offered elementary, middle, and high school arts programs?

A realistic assessment of the numerous and competing program and funding demands on state and local governments and of the unceasing requests for time and money from civic leaders provides the answers to these questions. The harsh truth is that arts education when compared to other societal needs and political interests is not and will not ever be an educational or social welfare priority for state or local governments or for most people of influence. There are simply too many more pressing claims on public and private resources. Arts education advocates promise a fantastic and unattainable assortment of returns in exchange for a fantastic and unavailable span of investment. Consequently, civic leaders and politicians shrink further away as the stated needs of the arts education enterprise become increasingly consuming and complex and as workable solutions appear to stretch further over the horizon. Diffusion of focus and scattering of energies make it less likely that arts programming of educational substance will be broadly institutionalized. By refusing to make distinctions among the programming responsibilities, parameters, and capabilities of schools and those of arts organizations, the greater decline the field will suffer and the more ineffectual and invisible it will become.

Granted, our unrelenting push to be or appear to be all things to all people is only one factor in the breaking apart and further diminishment of K-12 art education. Our university art education community has failed to establish and sustain a critical mass of high-quality preservice and in-service teacher education programs. One frequently hears academicians who are paid to teach within departments of art education proclaim that art education is no longer relevant to student learning. They argue that the study of "visual culture" or "visual culture art education" should supplant the now-stale (and worse) hierarchical concept of art education. Fervent disagreement about why, what, and how to teach and how to define art education as a professional field—or perhaps even more fundamentally if an attempt at definition should be made—mirrors the artworld infighting among cutting-edgers, traditionalists, modernists, and postmodernists. Mimicking the trends and adopting the values of the artworld do make for a perplexing if not (oxy)moronic coupling of the word *art* with the word *education*.

The promotion of visual culture studies over the study of something called "art" has emerged from an acknowledgment of the inevitable technological saturation of our society with infinite varieties of popular culture and electronic and print images. Ironically, it is that same profuse availability of coded visual stimuli and multimedia sensory experience that makes its inclusion as a school subject seem unnecessarily redundant. The overt sociopolitical agendas of many of its proponents call to question the legitimacy and sustainability of visual cultural studies within the K-12 curriculum. Art education also becomes increasingly difficult to justify as part of formal schooling as it becomes more associated with popular culture and visual culture studies. Of course at this point the school classroom would seem to offer the least conducive environment for learning to occur of this nature and scope.

Spiritless Redemption

Arts education, as characterized by arts activists, promises not only the salvation of individuals but also the path to redemption for art itself. Thirty years ago, Jacques Barzun (1974) identified in characteristic manner the growing momentum of the idea of art as redeemer. "The final paradox is that after 150 years of despising society and giving signs of despising itself, art now more than ever wants to be a social force, revolutionary, therapeutic, or simply popular. Its handicaps for this ambition are as great as those that made it fail as a religion" (p. 96). He argued that "to be valid, the idea of redemption by art would have to be popular and democratic. Secular salvation, like religious, must be open to all who seek it" (p. 89). That is, widespread secular salvation via art is not possible because of (a) the demanding and difficult (and hence exclusionary) nature of some art, particularly high art, in terms of technical mastery and deep understanding; and (b) the diversity and plurality of art which precludes the development of a unifying theology—the foundation of any religion.

The primary purpose of including art in the public school curriculum has always been to make whatever skills and benefits art is believed to provide more accessible to more people. One of the main goals of most school arts programming has been to enable students to take their first steps toward the communion table of high art. The purpose has not been the democratization of art but rather the democratization of the opportunity to get what art offers. As long as arts educators kept their gaze on the face of high art, the enterprise of arts education was able to offer the unifying theology that art could not. Arts education was able to be selective, culling from art only what it deemed most worthy of attention (or adoration), study, interpretation, and imitation. Of course the catch-22 for arts education has been the inherently elite nature of art that is brilliantly conceived and masterfully executed. Thus, arts education that has kept the study of demanding works of art at its center and rigorous expectations for teacher and student performance as its standard becomes almost as exclusionary as the art around which teaching and learning is organized. The salvation offered—that is, deliverance from ignorance about that specific art form in particular and from a mundane world view more abstractly—is neither widely attractive nor easily attained.

Will a less defined, more inclusive arts education be able to provide the widespread secular salvation that has eluded its more uptight sister? It is difficult to conceive of a more appealing and accessible theology than one that proffers deliverance of spirit, mind, and body through the arts. Interconnectivity and inclusiveness provide the anti-doctrine doctrine through which grace is given and salvation attained; content parameters and performance standards are worldly limitations to be transcended. All are invited to take communion and all will be uplifted, not only to a higher plane of art awareness but also to a higher reading, writing, and math consciousness (resulting in higher SAT score percentiles); enlightened and enlarged multicultural understandings; and elevated interpersonal skills, problem solving abilities, graduation rates, and self-esteem. Barzun's intellectual notions about what art can and cannot deliver because of its inherently undemocratic, pluralist nature are of no consequence when one believes in the benign omnipotence and omnipresence of arts education. Prodigal Art, chastened and domesticated, is brought safely into the fold (its sheep's clothing surgically fastened). Equally important, perhaps more so, is the political shelter (however unstable) provided arts agencies and organizations that have proven their allegiance to the common cause and convinced detractors of their indispensability in the delivery of a more popularly grounded, self-helping arts education. This is the broad, bland path to secular, soulless salvation.

TRYING TO HAVE AN EXPRESSION OF LOOKING TO THE FUTURE WITH HOPE

It will require an enormous amount of resolve by individual visual arts educators to keep the field intact and, to succeed, they will have to make unpopular distinctions between programs of study that have more or less or no real worth to art learning and, therefore, for art teaching. They will need to distinguish between what art education is marketed as being able to accomplish and what it actually can accomplish. And they will need to make those distinctions of merit and truth in the public arena. This does not mean the dismissal of ideas or suppression of debate; those are the tactics of overzealous advocates, not of educators. It means working conscientiously to achieve what Monroe Beardsley described "that most difficult intellectual stance which keeps us open to everything that may have worth or seeds of worth, yet without relinquishing all distinctions that give order to our thought" (1982, p. 91). The path and purposes of the contemporary artworld and of arts advocates need not be the path and purposes of art educators. The path and purposes of art and those of art education are not one and the same.

Hughes wrote, "Democracy's task in the field of art is to make the world safe for elitism. Not an elitism based on race or money or social position, but on skill and imagination. The embodiment of high ability and intense vision is the only thing that makes art popular" (1993, p. 202). Quality arts education does not seek to democratize art. It seeks to democratize the opportunity to experience the personal pleasures and special understandings gained only through knowledge of art by *teaching us about art*. Such teaching may not produce better, more tolerant, mentally and physically in-tune people who do well on standardized tests; but if the education is sound, people will end up knowing more about art. In all truth, that is the most that can be promised and *delivered*. Public life is more about promising than delivering, but art education ought not to be.

Present conditions present serious strategic choices to the art education field. If care is not taken, the field will talk itself out of a place in many schools either by promoting theories that deny the value of art on its own terms or by embracing the ever-changing advocacy agenda that promotes the kind of art in schools that requires no special professional competence in art itself and, at base, is not about student art learning at all. It will be interesting to see if the field can overcome various social and political pressures and massive psychological manipulations and maintain its integrity both philosophically and operationally. If it cannot, one of the greatest opportunities for mass art education in the history of the world will have been philosophized and propagandized away.

"Reminds me of Sputnik," an art education elder scribbled across an arts advocacy publication. There is solace and (yes!) hope to be found in her cynical observation because art education does not look anymore like science education today than it did half a century ago. Art education is still with us, and most of it is still about art. Good art teachers still strive to share with their students that which they love most about art—the masterful articulation of form, the far-reaching view, the heart-quickening vista.

I find that at the close of this chapter I have indeed sketched "just an ear." There is much more body and much more soul to be rendered if you have the will; rendered well if you have the expertise; rendered beautifully if you have the sensibility.

REFERENCES

American Association of Museums. (2001, January). Congress establishes arts education award. *Adviso*. Washington, DC: Author.

Americans for the Arts. (2001a). Who connects every American with the arts? Washington, DC: Author.

Americans for the Arts. (2001b, July). National Arts Education Public Awareness Campaign Survey. *Monograph*. Washington, DC: Author.

Americans for the Arts & the Advertising Council. (2002). A national arts education public awareness campaign (p. 2). Washington, DC: Authors. Retrieved Oct. 14, 2001 from http://www.artsusa.org/pa-campaign/factsheet.html

Arts Education Partnership. (2002). In R. J. Deasy (Ed.), *Critical links: Learning in the arts and student academic and social development*. Washington, DC: Author.

Arts Education Policy Review. (2001). [Symposium] REAP: How good a harvest? *Reviewing Education and the Arts Project, 102*(5).

Arts Education Policy Review. (n.d.) [Symposium] Critical Links: Learning in the arts and student academic and social development. Forthcoming.

Barzun, J. (1974). Art the redeemer. *The use and abuse of art*. New Jersey: Princeton University Press.

Barzun, J. (2000). *From dawn to decadence*. New York: HarperCollins.

Beardsley, M. (1982). Aesthetic experience regained. In M. J. Wreen & D. M. Callen (Eds.), *The aesthetic point of view: Selected essays* (pp. 77–92). Ithaca, NY: Cornell University Press.

Catterall, J. S. (2002). The arts and the transfer of learning. In R. J. Deasy (Ed.), *Critical links: Learning in the arts and student academic and social development*. (pp. 151–157). Washington, DC: Arts Education Partnership.

Chapman, L. H. (2001). Can the arts win hearts and minds? *Arts Education Policy Review, 102*(5), 21–23.

Council on Policy Studies in Art Education. (2002). Same time next year? Reflections on visual culture and post-cataclysmic art education. Unpublished program summary, January 25, 2002.

Design for Arts in Education. (1985a). A positive attitude, a cautionary approach, and question after question. [Editorial] *86*(3), 2–4. (*Design for Arts in Education* was renamed *Arts Education Policy Review* in 1992)

Design for Arts in Education. (1985b). *Less than substance, more than fluff*. [Editorial] *87*(2), 2–6.

Dryden, John (1687). A song for St. Cecilia's Day, 1687 (stanza 2, line 16). Retrieved Nov. 15, 2001, from http://www.library.utoronto.ca/utel/rp/poems/dryden

Eisner, E. W. (1998). Does experience in the arts boost academic achievement? *Art Education, 51*(1), 7–15.

Entertainment Industry Foundation. (2002). Barbie Cares Supporting Children in the Arts joins the entertainment industry foundation to launch EIF's national arts education initiative. Retrieved on August 10, 2002, from http://www.eifoundation.org/2002/naei.html

Entertainment Wire. (2002, May 7). "Baby Vivaldi." Newest addition to the award-winning line of audio CDs.

Gee, C. B. (1999a). For you dear Anything! Omnipotence, omnipresence, and servitude "through the arts"—Part 1. *Arts Education Policy Review, 100*(4), 3–17.

Gee, C. B. (1999b). For you dear Anything! Remembering and returning to first principles—Part 2. *Arts Education Policy Review, 100*(5), 3–22.

Gee, C. B. (2002). The "use and abuse" of arts advocacy and its consequences for music education. In R. Colwell & C. Richardson (Eds.), *The new handbook of research on music teaching and learning* (pp. 941–961). New York: Oxford University Press. (Reprinted in *Arts Education Policy Review, 103*(4), 3–21)

Hope, S. (1985). Promotion: Past failures, present urgencies. *Design for Arts in Education, 87*(2), 14–22.

Hope, S. (2002). Policy frameworks, research, and K-12 schooling. In R. Colwell & C. Richardson (Eds.), *The new handbook of research on music teaching and learning* (pp. 5–16), New York: Oxford University Press.

Hughes, R. (1993). *Culture of complaint: A passionate look into the ailing heart of America.* New York: Warner Books.

Knight, C. (2001, November 4). *What exactly can art heal?* Retrieved on November 8, 2001, from http://www.calendarlive.com

Komar, V., & Melamid, A. (1999, September 9). The healing power of art. *The New York Times Magazine,* Endpage. New York: *The New York Times.*

Larson, G. O. (1997). *American Canvas.* Washington, DC: National Endowment for the Arts.

Lynch, R. L. (2001, December). Art for the nation's sake. *ArtsLink.* Washington, DC: Americans for the Arts.

Mattel, Inc. (2002). Arts teacher of the year search. Retrieved on August 10, 2002, from http://www.barbie.com—parents section.

Moyer, B. (1993). *Healing and the mind.* New York: Bantam Doubleday Dell Publishing Group, Inc.

Murfee, E. (1995). *Eloquent evidence: Arts at the core of learning.* Washington, DC: President's Committee on the Arts and Humanities.

National Art Education Association. (1998a). *Should arts teachers teach the arts?* Reston, VA: Author.

National Art Education Association. (1998b). *Art is not made basic through advocacy.* Reston, VA: Author.

National Art Education Association. (2002). *Where's the Art?* Poster. Reston, VA: Author.

National Art Education Association. (2002, August 14). NAEA president meets with chief counselor to U.S. secretary. NAEA policy update memorandum. Reston, VA: Author.

National Art Education Association. (2002, August 15). NAEA releases "Where's the Art?" campaign flyers. NAEA media release.

National Coalition for Music Education and VH-1 Save the Music Foundation. (1999). *The Music Education Advocacy Kit.* New York: Authors.

National Association of Music Merchants. (2002). *Making music makes you smarter.* Retrieved March 3, 2002, from http://www.namm.com/education/research/frame_research.html

National Governors Association. (2002). The impact of arts education on workforce preparation. Retrieved on May 15, 2002, from http://www.nga.org/center

President's Committee on the Arts and the Humanities and the Arts Education Partnership. (1996). *Champions of change.* Washington, DC: Author.

President's Committee on the Arts and the Humanities & the National Assembly of Local Arts Agencies. (1996). *Coming up taller: Arts and humanities programs for children and youth at risk.* Washington, DC: Author. (NALAA merged with the American Council for the Arts in January 1997 to form Americans for the Arts)

President's Committee on the Arts and the Humanities & the National Assembly of Local Arts Agencies. (1999). *Gaining the arts advantage: Lessons from school districts that value arts education.* Washington, DC: Author.

Slater, L. (2002, February 3). The trouble with self-esteem. *The New York Times Magazine.* New York: *The New York Times.*

Smith, R. A. (2002). Recent trends and issues in policy making. In R. Colwell & C. Richardson (Eds.), *The new handbook of research on music teaching and learning* (pp. 23–32). New York: Oxford University Press.

Spencer, M. J. (1996). *Live arts experiences: Their impact on health and wellness* [Monograph]. New York: Hospital Audiences, Inc.

United States Congress. (2000, November). Congressional recognition for excellence in arts education act. Retrieved on August 20, 2002, from http://thomas.loc.gov/cgi-bin/query/D

Winner, E., & Hetland, L. (Guest Eds.). (2000). The arts and academic achievement: What the evidence shows [Special Issue]. *The Journal of Aesthetic Education, 34*(3–4).

Winner, E., & Hetland, L. (Eds.). (2001). *Beyond the soundbite: Arts education and academic outcomes.* Los Angeles: J. Paul Getty Trust.

7

Cognitive Transfer From Arts Education to Nonarts Outcomes: Research Evidence and Policy Implications

Lois Hetland
Project Zero, Harvard Graduate School of Education

Ellen Winner
Department of Psychology, Boston College and Project Zero, Harvard Graduate School of Education

This chapter reports methods, findings, and implications for research and policy from 10 meta-analytic reviews of the effects on nonarts cognition from instruction in various art forms. Three analyses demonstrate generalizable, causal relationships: classroom drama and verbal achievement, music listening and spatial reasoning, and music learning and spatial reasoning. Five do not allow causal conclusions: multiarts and academic achievement, arts-rich instruction and creativity, visual arts and reading, dance and reading, music and reading. Findings for two analyses are equivocal: dance and spatial reasoning and music and mathematics. The authors urge arts education researchers to keep research syntheses in mind when conducting studies and advise policymakers to support arts programs that demonstrate learning in the arts.

Both researchers and policymakers in arts education seek understanding, yet they differ in what satisfies that quest. Researchers pursue enduring puzzles—puzzles that expand to require new insights from the next study, or even from studies conducted by later generations of researchers. Following the trail of evidence wherever it leads, research advances incrementally, often over the course of decades. Scholars develop patience with this glacial pace, with one study leading to another as they probe another nuance, a further connection. Policy, on the other hand, cannot afford patience. Policymakers need to act, and they need to act now. Children grow up, money is allocated, and programs are implemented, always today. The urgency of policy contrasts starkly with the slowly accruing clarity developed through the enterprise of research.

Despite these fundamentally different drives, both researchers and policymakers can benefit from the research produced by REAP (Reviewing Education and the Arts Project, Winner & Hetland, 2000): quantitative syntheses of individual studies that test the effects of arts education on learning in nonarts domains. Although the latest study may seem like the answer for awhile, its allure and veracity fade as the next new study rises on the horizon. No matter how well designed, single studies offer only partial answers, particular to the settings, persons, and procedures of their design. In contrast, the lens provided by looking at the evidence amassed from a body of studies on a given question can clarify apparently contradictory evidence and allow clear patterns to emerge that can guide further research as well as practical applications in policy. By combining and comparing findings from all available studies that address similar questions, syntheses help researchers understand variation, develop better methods, and identify new questions. The same summaries offer policymakers what they need most—the best evidence available at a given time upon which to base decisions (Light & Pillemer, 1984).

In today's educational climate, academic skills seem to be valued exclusively, and all too often the arts are seen as expendable frills. In such an environment, arts advocates need to convince decision makers of the rightful place of the arts in the schools. But as they look to research to build their case, they find scattered evidence, and much of it is not about the inherent value of the arts for children, but rather about the instrumental value of the arts—their effects on basic academic skills whose importance is undisputed.

Arts educators and advocates have argued with increasing fervor over the past 2 decades that the arts are a means to improved basic academic skills. For example, according to a 1995 report by the President's Committee on the Arts and Humanities, "teaching the arts has a significant effect on overall success in school" (Murfee, 1995, p. 3). The report justifies this claim by noting that both verbal and quantitative SAT scores are higher for high school students who take arts courses than for those who take none. And former Secretary of Education Richard Riley stated that "The arts teach young people how to learn by giving them the first step: the desire to learn" (Fiske, 1999, p. vi).

But what is the research base on which such claims are made? These claims were not based on summaries of the research evidence for transfer of learning from the arts to academic subjects, because no summary had been conducted to assess the strength of the case or to understand the mechanisms of transfer, who benefited, and under what conditions. We therefore set out to identify and synthesize all studies on this question since 1950. In this chapter we describe our methodology and present the results of 10 quantitative syntheses. Three of our syntheses revealed a clear case for transfer. In two syntheses, the claims are equivocal. In five, we had to conclude that there is (at least as yet) no compelling evidence that study in an art form leads to improved academic functioning. At the conclusion to this chapter we answer critics who have misinterpreted us as arguing that the arts therefore do not help children. We argue instead that the arts have great value in a child's education but that this value is due first and foremost to the importance of learning in the arts. Although arts study may in some cases instill skills that strengthen learning in other disciplines, arts programs should never be justified primarily on what the arts can do for other subjects.

SYNTHESIZING EVIDENCE THROUGH META-ANALYSIS

The REAP reviews were conducted using a technique called meta-analysis, a quantitative synthesis in which the unit of analysis is the study rather than the person. Although meta-analysis is only now becoming commonplace in educational research, it is the standard for synthesis in public health, medicine, epidemiology, psychology, and agriculture (where it was first used). Meta-analyses bring coherence to research domains, and consequently they are among the most cited forms of research (Cooper & Hedges, 1994). Policymakers, especially, should benefit from understanding how meta-analyses are conducted so that they can weigh the quality of two research syntheses that review the same information.

A meta-analysis can do several things that a traditional narrative review of the literature cannot. First, a meta-analysis can tell us the average strength of the relationship between arts and academic outcomes derived from many studies. That information is preferable to generalization from a single study (which by its nature is particular to the settings, procedures, and subjects it assesses). It is also preferable to merely counting the number of studies achieving significance at a level of, say $p < .05$ (which is misleading because the same effect could be statistically significant or not depending only on how many subjects were included in an analysis; studies with larger sample sizes generate more effects judged as "significant"). Second, a meta-analysis tells us how reliable (i.e., how likely to be reproduced in next studies) this average effect size is. Meta-analyses also allow us to test hypotheses: By coding studies for important variables (e.g., length of arts study, or whether arts were taught separately or integrated into the curriculum) and then comparing average effects for the different groups, we can see the influence of particular variables. Thus, a meta-analysis is far more than a summary—it makes it possible to generate and explore new hypotheses that cannot be explored in single studies (such as whether particular research designs demonstrate larger effects than others, or whether published studies show larger effects than unpublished ones).

Although the fundamental goal of meta-analytic procedures is to cumulate evidence that aids understanding of past research and guides future inquiry, meta-analytic methods are similar to other types of quantitative research. Methodological standards for meta-analytic reviews are summarized in *The Handbook for Research Synthesis* (Cooper & Hedges, 1994). Along with texts by meta-analytic specialists such as Rosenthal (1991, 1995), Light and Pillemer (1984), and Mosteller and Colditz (1996), the *Handbook* served as the methodological foundation for REAP.

Meta-analysts first define a research question and a sampling frame for a population of studies (i.e., they set principles about the kind of studies to be included in the analysis). Then the search for studies (the "subjects" of a meta-analysis) begins with the aim of finding an unbiased sample of studies that fairly represents all the studies conducted on the relevant research question. Next, studies are coded objectively for potential moderator variables that may influence the effect size resulting from different "treatments" (in this case, different forms of arts education). These might include, for example, length of time of arts study, quality of arts class, level of teacher expertise, genre of art studied, study design, or outcome measure employed.

When studies do not routinely report effect sizes (as is all too often the case), analysts must first compute effect sizes from reported data such as means, sample sizes, and significance levels. Each study contributes one average effect and one significance level to the group average, computed through standard statistical procedures. In further analysis, effect sizes for sub-groups of studies can be compared to test whether moderator variables influence the sizes of average effects.

In the work described in this chapter, we first searched for all studies, published and un-published, carried out since 1950, which examined the relationship between arts study and academic achievement. In our search, we used seven computer databases, reviewed reference lists of acquired articles, contacted over 200 scholars in the field, and hand-searched 41 journals from the previous 50 years. Such an exhaustive, systematic search with redundant channels is the best way to identify the "fugitive" literature, which helps to minimize a common threat to validity of meta-analytic findings from sampling bias. This kind of search also reduces the likelihood of bias caused by combining only published studies. Published studies are gen-erally "significant," since researchers often do not submit studies for publication when they have not demonstrated significance at $p < .05$ (i.e., the level of likelihood at which, were the study conducted 100 times, the reported effect would be achieved in 95 of the trials). Includ-ing a disproportionately high number of published articles in meta-analyses may artificially raise average effects and/or combined significance levels, leading to inflated, inaccurate results (Rosenthal, 1994).

From those articles identified in the REAP search we included only studies that actually quantified (a) some kind of nonarts, cognitive outcome; (b) results from subjects who received some type of arts instruction or exposure; (c) results that compared subjects who received arts to subjects in a control group who received either no treatment or, better, an alternate treatment. Because of the volume of studies, the REAP analyses could not examine the evidence for the claimed social outcomes of the arts such as improved academic motivation or increased school attendance—Studies addressing these questions remain to be synthesized. Nor did we include studies in which teachers expressed their belief that students' cognitive skills were boosted by the arts (because this was not a direct measure of cognitive improvement), nor studies that showed improvement from arts study without comparison to a control group who received no arts study over the same period of time. We found almost 200 studies that met our criteria for inclusion. We then defined criteria for inclusion for the 10 separate meta-analyses and sorted the studies accordingly.

Since meta-analyses combine only quantitative findings, it is worth a brief digression at this point in the description of our methods to discuss whether our results represent an unbiased sample of the research conducted on questions of arts transfer. To be included in a meta-analysis, qualitative results must include numerical values (e.g., as they did in Heath's [1998] qualitative study, which was included in the Winner & Cooper [2000] analysis summarized in the following section). Without numerical values, studies cannot contribute directly to a meta-analytic average effect size. However, that fact reduces neither the contribution of qualitative studies to meta-analyses nor the value of meta-analyses as unbiased summaries. Qualitative data contribute to meta-analytic reviews in their discussion sections, not in the quantified results. That is because in the ongoing investigation of psychological and behavioral phenomena qualitative research contributes different kinds of evidence than do its quantitative cousins. Qualitative research does not attempt to calculate the size of a relationship, but rather seeks to inform by triangulating examples of phenomena observed in lived contexts, by "thick" description and by categorical analysis of the nature and dimensions of relationships. Ideally, qualitative and quantitative approaches to a given question build upon one another, focusing on the problem first in one way, then in another way, as befits particular puzzles. In review and summary of a field, qualitative data contribute observations that inform interpretations of numerical results and contribute hypotheses that can be tested quantitatively—either within the qualitative study itself or in related quantitative study later on.[1] Thus, qualitative studies located by REAP's exhaustive search, as well as those studies rejected because they did not meet study inclusion criteria, should not be expected to contribute to the quantitative cumulation of effects. But they do help to explain why the numerical findings turned out as they did. They suggest avenues and techniques for future investigation.

After locating studies through our search procedures, REAP researchers classified them by both art form and nonarts outcome (e.g., visual arts and reading, music and mathematics). For each set of comparable studies, we developed codes for potential moderator variables and conducted descriptive, inferential, and interpretive analyses. Descriptive analysis yields a description of the characteristics of the studies in the sample, with the most important of these being an average effect size from combining the studies. Along with the average effect, we reported the range of effects (largest and smallest), the quartiles (25th, 50th—also called the median, and 75th percentiles), and the percentage of effects greater than zero.

Inferential analysis shows how likely results of the synthesis are to generalize to next studies. When reading the summaries, note the 95% confidence intervals around the average effect size. When these intervals span zero, confidence that a positive effect actually exists is

---

[1]Quantitative methods such as contrasts, which were employed extensively in the REAP reviews, explore similar questions through data-analytic procedures, but these methods are possible only in later developmental stages of research when specific directional hypotheses can be advanced based on previous qualitative and quantitative work.

typically reduced. Another inferential statistic is also very useful to policymakers—the "t test of the mean Zr." This test makes it possible to determine how generalizable the results are to future studies on the same research questions—higher confidence is indexed by lower p levels associated with tests of the mean Zr.

Interpretive analyses help us to assess to whom the results apply and under what conditions. Our interpretive analyses consisted of contrast tests to assess which features of programs and research design influence the size of the reported effects.

The heart of a meta-analysis rests on the calculation of an "effect size" for each study, because these individual effect sizes allow us to calculate the size of effects when combined and compared across studies. Effect sizes show the strength of the relationship between two variables, in this case, between some type of arts study and some cognitive or academic outcome. Two of the most common statistics used to show effect size are d and r. Because simple algebra can readily transform one index to another (e.g., an r at low values such as those found in the REAP analyses can often be doubled to get a rough estimate of an equivalent d), the choice of effect size statistic is mainly based on ease of interpretation for a particular audience and on the ability to compute the chosen statistic for the body of primary studies being reviewed.

In the analyses reported here, we used r, as recommended by Rosenthal (1991, 1994, Rosenthal & Rosnow, 1991). This statistic can be used even when a study has more than two conditions, as did many of the studies analyzed by REAP. In contrast, d, which is the standardized difference between two means, is meaningless for experiments employing three or more conditions, because differences cannot be computed for more than two groups. The effect size r is also readily interpreted by readers unfamiliar with statistics, because it can be translated into percentages of subjects helped or not helped by a treatment. Rosenthal (1991) demonstrates this translation using a binomial effect size display (BESD) (Rosenthal & Rubin, 1982, Rosenthal, Rosnow, & Rubin, 2000).[2]

Effect size rs range from -1.0 (a perfectly correlated negative effect) to $+1.0$ (a perfectly correlated positive effect). In general, meta-analysts interpret rs of .10 as small, of around .24 as medium, and above .37 as large effects (Cohen, 1988). However, these are rules of thumb defined statistically, not by influence on the field, so these quantities should not rigidly direct interpretations about the importance of any given effect. Small effects sometimes matter a lot (e.g., if they index a small number of students who stay in school as a result of a treatment) and sometimes very little (e.g., if they index a rise of a few points on a standardized test). A classical example of an important effect that might be considered small comes from Smith, Glass, and Miller (1980), in which psychotherapy yielded $r = .32$, and consequential effects from biomedical research are often much smaller—even as low as $r = .034$ (Steering Committee of the Physicians Health Study Research Group, 1988).

As stated by Rosenthal and Rosnow (1991), the relationship between level of statistical significance and effect size can be understood as follows:

$$\text{Significance Test} = \text{Effect Size} \times \text{Study Size}.$$

Simply put, the larger a study's sample size, the more significant the results will be.[3] The same small, moderate, or large effect size could be significant or not *depending only on the size*

---

[2]To make this simple calculation, divide the reported effect size r by 2 and add it to .50 (e.g., for $r = .20$, $1/2r = .10$; $.10 + .50 = .60$ or 60%). That quantity is the percentage of people who are helped by the treatment; so for .60, 60 of every 100, or 600,000 of every million are helped). Subtract that number from 100 for the number not helped (i.e., for this example, 40%, or 400 per 1000, or 400,000 per million not helped).

[3]This is true unless the size of the effect is truly zero, in which case a larger study will not produce a result that is any more significant than a smaller study. Effect sizes of exactly zero, however, are rarely encountered.

of the sample, and this is frequently forgotten in the interpretation of research results. Thus, complete reporting of the results of any study requires reporting both effect size and level of significance. All too often, studies report only half the necessary information—how likely an effect would be to occur again (the *p* value). But without knowing how large the effect is, we cannot judge the importance of its likelihood of re-occurrence. Reporting effect sizes is becoming standard practice in other fields (see the APA task force on statistical significance, Wilkerson, 1999), and arts education research publishers should require it.

In summary, we sought to employ standardized methods to ensure reliability (i.e., would replication of our analysis result in similar answers?) and validity (i.e., did we analyze what we intended to?). We do not claim that REAP is the final word on the effects of arts on cognitive transfer to nonarts areas. As more research accrues, the evidence may well require different conclusions. But we venture to assert that our findings represent the most trustworthy knowledge currently available about the question of cognitive transfer.

WHAT THE META-ANALYSES REVEALED

Support for Three Instrumental Claims

As noted earlier, our findings revealed three areas in which a causal relationship between arts and some nonarts cognitive outcome was demonstrated: classroom drama and verbal achievement; music listening and spatial reasoning; and music instruction and spatial reasoning.

Classroom Drama and Verbal Skills. Perhaps the most well-researched arts to academics transfer literature focuses on the effects of "classroom drama." Classroom drama refers to using acting techniques within the regular classroom curriculum. This stands in contrast to theater, or the production of plays. In an earlier synthesis of this area, Kardash and Wright (1986) meta-analyzed 16 studies of classroom drama and found positive relationships between drama and reading, oral language development, self-esteem, moral reasoning and various drama skills (with an average effect size of $r = .32$, equivalent to $d = .67$). A second meta-analysis was conducted by Conard (1992) on the effect of classroom drama on verbal achievement, self-concept, and creativity. This analysis combined 20 studies, 6 of which were included in Kardash and Wright's analysis. Again a positive effect was found, with an average effect size of $r = .23$ (equivalent to $d = .48$). Neither of the two previous meta-analyses teased apart specific components of classroom drama that might influence academic achievement. Nor did these previous studies separate the different kinds of outcomes that were affected and so were not able to determine which area or areas of academic achievement were more strongly related to classroom drama.

Podlozny (2000) found almost 200 experimental studies probing the effect of classroom drama on academic achievement. Over 40% of these studies tested verbal achievement outcomes, and it is this body of literature that Podlozny examined meta-analytically as part of REAP. Eighty studies were included in her meta-analysis. The studies tested and compared the effect of classroom drama on seven distinct verbal outcomes. To test which instructional qualities might influence the size of effect, Podlozny identified and assessed three components of classroom drama—*enactment, plot* (level of structure), and *leader* (teacher's level of involvement).

By definition, dramatic instruction entails enactment of some pretend, imaginary situation. But the form of enactment can range widely. Stories can be enacted by creating dialog, for example, while sitting in a circle on the floor (called *verbal enactment* by Podlozny), or through pantomime (*physical enactment*). Further, enactment may be performed by the child *(self enactment)* or through puppets, toys, or other objects *(distanced from self)*. Enactment often involves combinations of these four features (verbal/action/self/distanced from self). Because 75 of the 80 studies engaged children in verbal, physical, self-drama, Podlozny was unable to test the effect of type of enactment, but such an examination merits future attention.

Plot may be *structured*, as when children are given a story or script, relatively *unstructured*, as when children are simply given themes to act out, or combine structured and unstructured plots.

The *leader* (i.e., teacher) can take the part of a character *(in-role)*, work as a coach outside of the dramatic frame *(facilitator)*, or work at a distance from the action *(removed)*, answering questions, but not serving as a driving force for the activity.

Podlozny (2000) classified studies in terms of whether they directly tested material students had actually enacted in their drama sessions *(direct)* or whether tests were of entirely new material *(transfer)*. This distinction was made to determine whether enacting a story simply helped children better read, understand, and recall a particular story that they had acted out, or whether the experience of acting out a story helped children's verbal skills more generally.

Podlozny examined seven verbal outcomes:

In 17 studies with oral recall outcomes, the drama group heard and enacted the stories and the control group heard but did not act out the stories. Students were then tested on oral recall.

In 14 studies with written recall outcomes, the drama group read and then enacted the stories while the control group read, then discussed, and were drilled on vocabulary from the stories. Children were tested only on stories that had been taught.

In 20 studies with reading achievement outcomes, the drama group typically read a story or play and enacted it while the control group simply continued with their regular reading classes. Both groups were then given a standardized reading comprehension test. Thus, in this body of studies children were always tested on new material. Hence, any effect demonstrates transfer of reading comprehension skills to new material.

In 18 studies with reading readiness outcomes, the drama group heard a story and acted it out, while the control group either heard the same story and discussed but did not enact it, reenacted themes from field trips or from other experiences (and hence did not hear the story), or engaged in cut and paste and categorizing activities (here they neither heard the story nor engaged in any enactment). This body of studies again only tested children on new material.

In 20 studies with oral language development outcomes, students in the drama group typically engaged in creative dramatics (storytelling, role-playing, puppetry) as well as discussion while the control group watched filmstrips and engaged in arts other than drama. Later, the oral language of all children was assessed, sometimes when talking about new material, other times when talking about the stories that they had enacted.

In 10 vocabulary studies, children in the drama group engaged in creative drama activities, including role-play, pantomime, movement, and improvised dialog, while the control group had no special treatment. Later all children were given a vocabulary test, sometimes with words from the stories that had been taught and other times with new words.

In eight studies with writing skills outcomes, writing samples were assessed for skills such as audience awareness, story structure (beginning, middle, and end), organization, and elaboration. Typically children in the drama group first participated in a discussion about writing and then engaged in improvisation, pantomime, and movement; developed story ideas, improvised story scenes, and drafted stories. The control group also participated in a discussion about writing, but then they simply continued with their regular language arts program before drafting their stories. Stories were analyzed according to a narrative writing scale. In some of the studies, children wrote stories related to themes they had enacted. In others, they wrote stories on new material.

Classroom drama was found to have a strong positive effect on six of the seven verbal outcomes examined. The largest effect size was for written story recall, where an average effect size of $r = .50$ was found (equivalent to $d = 1.15$; 95% confidence interval was $r = .37$ to $r = .73$; t test of the mean $Zr = 3.91$, $p < .0025$). This is an extremely large effect. Studies assessing the effect of drama on oral language were also moderate to large ($r = .30$, equivalent $d = .63$), followed by story understanding as measured orally, reading readiness, writing, and reading achievement ($r = .27, .25, .24, .20$, respectively, equivalent to $d = .56, .52, .49, .41$). All of these effects were robust: t tests of their mean Zrs indicate that the results generalize to future studies, and none of the confidence intervals spanned zero. Vocabulary was also enhanced ($r = .06$, equivalent $d = .12$), but unlike the other six effect sizes, this one was not statistically significant (the 95% confidence interval $r = -.07$ to $r = .19$ spanned zero, and the t test of the mean $Zr = 1.01$, $p < .24$).

The type of plot used in the drama instruction influenced the effectiveness of the instruction. Working with structured plots resulted in larger average effects when story comprehension and structure were the outcomes. When oral language development was the outcome, working with unstructured plots in improvised role-play (or combinations of structured and unstructured plots) resulted in larger average effects. Podlozny (2000) explained that because oral language development is not directly related to story structure and comprehension, this variation can be readily explained. Emphasis on extemporaneous and improvised speech is more facilitative of oral language development than working with scripted plots, which emphasize acting within the confines of the particular story or script. Interestingly, structured and unstructured plots were equally effective for oral measures of story understanding and vocabulary.

Level of teacher involvement could only be investigated as a factor in studies assessing story understanding, as none of the other studies described the role of the teacher. This factor proved to be related to the effectiveness of drama instruction for studies measuring story understanding. Following Dansky's (1980) "multistage" model of effects, Podlozny (2000) had hypothesized that leader "in-role" might increase the occurrence and/or quality of dramatic play, which, in turn, might increase academic achievement.

For the question of whether drama helps students with new texts, Podlozny's (2000) seven analyses demonstrate higher effect sizes for material studied directly. However, to a lesser but still impressive degree, the analyses also show that drama helps learners understand new texts. As Podlozny says, "What is remarkable is not that drama's strongest effects are direct ones, but rather that drama does have the power to foster skills that then transfer to new material" (p. 266).

With respect to the age at which drama is most likely to result in enhanced verbal skills, the evidence was inconsistent. Although the meta-analyses by Kardash and Wright (1986) and by Conard (1992) both found that classroom drama was more effective for younger children, five of the seven meta-analyses performed by Podlozny (2000) showed no relationship between age and effect size. Of the remaining two, one showed that the effect was stronger for younger children (writing achievement), whereas the other found that the effect was stronger for older children (oral language).

Also contrary to both of the previous meta-analyses, five of Podlozny's (2000) seven meta-analyses found that drama was equally effective for average, low SES, and learning disabled students. The remaining two analyses (those assessing written story understanding and reading achievement) found that drama was actually more effective in promoting verbal skills when the children involved were from low SES populations. This finding is consistent with Smilansky (1968), who reports that exposure to drama increases the achievement levels of poor students. One explanation is that children from disadvantaged backgrounds may not have engaged in as much creative, dramatic play nor experienced success through participating in engaging instruction. Classroom drama instruction may provide a "boost" to these students, helping them to acquire a deeper level of story understanding.

The most important finding of these meta-analyses on classroom drama is the demonstration that drama not only helps children to master the texts they enact but also often helps them to master new material not enacted. The transfer of skills from one domain to another is generally not thought to be automatic: It needs to be taught (Salomon & Perkins, 1989). In the field of classroom drama, however, transfer appears to be naturally designed into the curriculum, even if teachers are not labeling it as such. If teachers of classroom drama did more to teach explicitly for transfer, these effects might be even stronger.

Music Listening and Spatial Reasoning. Since the prestigious journal, *Nature,* published the report by Rauscher, Shaw, and Ky (1993) that described a temporary increase in spatial reasoning by college students after listening briefly to certain kinds of music, the public has been beset by innuendoes from that now famous letter. Did the results support then Georgia Governor Zell Miller's decision to give all Georgia newborns a CD of classical music? Or Florida's mandate that day care centers should play 30 min of classical music daily? Or that Mozart CDs marketed to children could improve mathematics scores later in life if listened to carefully? They did not. The leap from this single laboratory experiment to policies for children's learning and to marketing strategies for prenatal courses and CDs was unwarranted and never supported by the researchers. But does that make the study or the numerous replication attempts of no interest? Indeed not—They are of great scientific interest, because they suggest that the mind may work in ways we had not previously thought.

Hetland (2000a) identified 36 relevant experiments (2,469 subjects) that could be synthesized through meta-analysis. The analysis included experiments conducted in laboratory settings with adults (i.e., college students) who listened briefly to a musical stimulus that was predicted to enhance spatial reasoning compared to at least one control condition predicted not to enhance spatial reasoning. Replication studies also employed some measure of spatial reasoning and made enough data available to compute an effect size (i.e., the degree of relationship between the musical condition and the score on the outcome measure).

None of the replications reproduced the original experiment exactly. Many used the same music as that used in the 1993 experiment (i.e., the *Allegro con spirito* from Mozart's Sonata for Two Pianos in D major, K. 448), but some researchers predicted that enhanced spatial reasoning would result from listening to other movements or pieces by Mozart, other classical music (e.g., Schubert, Mendelssohn), a piece by the contemporary composer, Yanni, and musical stimuli comprised only of pure rhythm or pure melody.

Replications also varied by the measures used to index spatial reasoning. "Spatial reasoning" is a term that encompasses a range of intellectual processes, much as the term "heart attack" refers to a variety of medical traumas. The Paper Folding and Cutting subtest of the Stanford–Binet: Fourth Edition, a task used in the original experiment and in many of the replications, is a good example of the type of task Rauscher and Shaw (1998) call "spatial–temporal" and which they predicted would be enhanced by listening to certain types of music. The Paper Folding and Cutting subtest requires subjects to imagine folding and cutting paper in ways similar to actually folding and cutting paper snowflakes.

Researchers attempting to replicate the original experiment used a variety of other tests as well, some of which do not meet Rauscher and Shaw's (1998) criteria for spatial–temporal tasks. For example, Matrices tasks do not qualify as spatial–temporal. In matrice-type tasks, one figure is missing from a gridded pattern of figures, usually 3 by 3, ordered vertically and horizontally according to rules of logic (add the figures, subtract the figures, enlarge the figures in specific ways). Such tasks do not require flipping and turning objects mentally, nor doing so in sequential steps. The Pattern Analysis subtest of the Stanford–Binet also does not qualify as spatial-temporal, because, although it requires mentally flipping and turning objects, it provides subjects a model to match and compare while solving the task.

Another important variation in replications is the different types of control conditions employed (note that experiments often used more than one). These included silence (used in about three quarters of the experiments), audiotapes of verbal instructions designed to lower blood pressure (used in about half of the experiments), natural and man-made sounds (5 of 36 experiments), texts read aloud (3 of 36 experiments), and music that researchers thought was not complex enough or sufficiently like Mozart to enhance spatial–temporal skills (used in about one fourth of the experiments). For example, 5 of 36 experiments used a piece by Philip Glass called "Music with Changing Parts," which is almost hypnotically repetitious, and others used various "relaxing" music (one was described as "angelic female voices"). Still others used disco and rock music, presumably thought to be distracting.

Six preliminary analyses determined whether experiments with such diverse controls could be combined responsibly into a single analysis. The first two preliminary analyses replicated and compared analyses to a previous meta-analysis (Chabris, 1999). The other four preliminary analyses included studies that employed more than one control to directly compare scores on spatial–temporal tasks following different control conditions (Silence vs. Relaxation tapes, Silence vs. Noise, Silence vs. Nonenhancing music, Relaxation vs. Nonenhancing music).

The Music versus Silence analysis yielded a moderately sized average effect of $r = .24$ (equivalent $d = .48$), compared to the small average effect Chabris (1999) found, which was equivalent to $r = .07$ ($d = .14$). The Music versus Relaxation analysis yielded a moderate to large average effect of $r = .33$ (equivalent $d = .70$), compared to Chabris's similarly sized average effect equivalent to $r = .29$ ($d = .57$). Because Hetland's (2000a) sample is more representative of all the studies conducted on this research question (due to the exhaustive nature of the search and to including both published and unpublished studies), these results are more likely to represent the true effect size for the theoretical "universe" of studies on this research question.

Note that the relative size of the effects for the first two preliminary analyses is similar to Chabris's analysis (i.e., Music vs. Silence has a smaller effect than Music vs. Relaxation). At face value, this finding lends support to the arousal theory, according to which music enhances spatial performance because it arouses. Unless overstimulated, an aroused person performs better on tests; relaxation is likely to produce lower arousal than merely sitting in silence. However, the third preliminary analysis suggests that arousal does not account for the difference in effect sizes, because when scores following silence and scores following relaxation were compared directly, they were essentially the same ($r = -.02$, with the minus sign indicating that scores following relaxation were trivially higher on average, not lower). The remaining preliminary analyses suggest that differences in scores following various control conditions when directly compared were not consequential or systematic (Silence vs. Noise, $r = .02$; Silence vs. Nonenhancing music $r = -.05$; Relaxation vs. Nonenhancing music, $r = -.02$). As a result of these analyses, the various control conditions used in the experiments appeared to produce essentially similar results and, thus, could be combined legitimately into a single analysis. Including all the identified experiments lends Hetland's (2000a) analysis considerable statistical power and summarizes all the laboratory data with adults identified as relevant to the question about music's temporary enhancing effect on spatial task performance.

The first main analysis (36 experiments, 2,469 subjects) compared tasks that qualified as spatial–temporal (31/36) to other types of spatial measures (5/36). Contrast analysis showed that the moderately sized and highly generalizable mean effect ($r = .22$, $d = .46$, 95% confidence interval $r = .14$ to $r = .31$; t test of the mean $Zr = 5.34$, $p < .0001$) results from higher effect sizes in experiments using spatial–temporal measures. The average of the experiments employing spatial–temporal measures alone is $r = .20$. Experiments employing only nonspatial–temporal measures yielded an average effect of $r = .04$, and experiments that used a combination of spatial–temporal and nonspatial–temporal measures showed an intermediate effect size ($r = .15$). Thus, this analysis supports the conclusion that music's influence is specific to spatial–temporal measures, rather than to all types of spatial measures. Such specificity is evidence against the general arousal hypothesis.

The second main analysis included only those 31 experiments (2,089 subjects) that employed spatial–temporal measures. Again, the analysis showed a moderately sized relationship between listening briefly to music and enhanced performance on spatial–temporal measures ($r = .25, d = .50$), which is highly generalizable (95% confidence interval: $r = .14$ to $r = .35$; t test of the mean $Zr = 4.84$, $p < .0001$). However, two problems limit the strength of the conclusions that can be drawn from the analysis.

First, the effect sizes of the individual studies varied too much to be considered as sampled from a single population of studies (Range: $r = -.20$ to $r = .67$, $SD = .25$, heterogeneity test, $\chi^2 (30) = 101.90$, $p < .0001$), and only some of the variation could be accounted for by moderator variables. Of the seven potential moderator variables identified, four did not influence the size of effect significantly (type of enhancing music used, subject gender, carryover from previous spatial activation, and publication status). The remaining three did explain some of the variation. Experiments that employed a relaxation tape control did have larger than average effect sizes ($r = .34$). However, because the third preliminary analysis showed no difference in scores following Silence and Relaxation when compared directly, it is likely that unidentified procedures of the laboratories that used relaxation as a control account for the systematic differences in effect sizes, rather than the control condition itself. This conclusion is affirmed by the results of a sensitivity analysis that temporarily removed studies from labs that contributed five or more experiments with relaxation controls. Both the Rauscher studies (average $r = .40$; Rauscher, Bowers, & Kohlbeck, 1999; Rauscher & Hayes 1999; Rauscher & Ribar, 1999; Rauscher, Shaw, & Ky, 1993; 1995) and the Rideout studies ($r = .42$; Rideout, Dougherty, & Wernert, 1998 [experiments 1 and 2]; Rideout, Fairchild, & Urban, 1998; Rideout & Laubach, 1996; Rideout & Taylor,1997) had higher than average effects.

Such an observation leads to speculation about the procedures used by various labs. An analysis of study quality showed that experiments with stronger designs (i.e., designs that were less vulnerable to threats of internal validity) had higher average effects, and both the Rauscher and Rideout experiments ranked average or above on these criteria. Thus, the variation in effects is unexplained by study quality and cannot be attributed to errors by the researchers. The most likely explanation for the effect is that these two laboratories emphasized to subjects the importance of attending closely to the music. It is possible that doing so allowed the music to have an effect, whereas other experimental procedures allowed subjects' attention to wander. Colwell (2001) references a literature in music education that supports a conclusion that focused attention produces a different cognitive response than does casual listening. Such an explanation should be addressed in the design of future studies.

The second limitation is that a mechanism could not be unequivocally identified as causing the effect. Experiments did not provide enough data to explore plausible alternate hypotheses to the "trion" priming model proposed by Leng and Shaw (1991); alternatives such as arousal, preference, or mood as causal mechanisms; or the theory that the element of rhythm links musical and spatial processes (Parsons, Martinez, Delosh, Halpern, & Thaut, 1999), or the possibility that musical sophistication and training result in listening analytically and increasing the effect.

In summary, the synthesis of the Mozart Effect studies is of scientific interest, because the highly significant, moderately sized effect indicates that a relationship does exist between musical and spatial reasoning, as far as can be assessed from the studies conducted to date. It appears that spatial and musical processing areas of the human mind/brain are not entirely independent, but it is uncertain whether they influence each other because they are nearby, such that activation of one "primes" activation of the other; or because they overlap, such that development of certain musical processing areas would simultaneously develop the particular type of spatial reasoning defined as spatial–temporal.

Further research must disentangle the cognitive mechanism that causes the effect. For example, neither priming model—either Shaw's "trion" or Parson's "rhythm" models—is conclusively affirmed or refuted, although both remain promising. In addition, future research must distinguish the effect conclusively from potential artifacts of procedures (e.g., subjects' attention to musical stimuli, or subject or experimenter effects that align results with unconscious expectations of subjects or researchers) or research design variations (e.g., control stimuli that are equally preferred by subjects or that can be measured as equally arousing or mood altering). The analysis does not have direct implications for education, because the experiments were not about learning, but rather about how the human mind processes two types of information: musical and spatial. However, the result does suggest that studies in which subjects are taught music could plausibly result in spatial learning. A group of such studies was synthesized by Hetland (2000b), and is described in the following section.

The lack of mechanism for the Mozart Effect finding means that the effect is still questionable, and future research may yet demonstrate that the effect is an artifact of research design. Although the best evidence to date is that the effect appears to hold up, that does not imply that policy should mandate listening to classical music for any audience. Future research needs to test specific hypotheses about the mechanism underlying this effect, but this laboratory finding with college students implies nothing for the education of children, much less infants *in utero*. If parents or teachers wish to play classical music for themselves or their children, they should by all means do so for any number of reasons. However, based on what we know at present, no one should expect that listening to music alone will aid children's future scores on standardized tests of academic achievement.

Music Instruction and Spatial Reasoning.   A second body of studies has often been confused with the Mozart Effect studies, but it deserves consideration in its own right. Hetland (2000b) identified 19 studies in which children ages 3 to 12 engaged in programs of active music instruction for up to two years.[4] The studies included in the music instruction analysis were conducted in schools or other instructional settings and used a variety of musical pedagogies and measures of spatial reasoning. To be included in the analysis, studies had to have one or more control conditions, with or without an alternate treatment. About one third had an alternate treatment for controls consisting of instruction in language, instruction in reading or mathematics on the computer, or passive instruction in music. Almost all had a nontreatment control (17/19), either in addition to a treated control group or as the only comparison group.

In studies included in the analysis, music instruction involved combinations of the following: singing, playing musical games, learning notations, improvising or composing music, moving responsively to music, including clapping, and playing instruments. The instruments used in the programs were combinations of voice, piano, xylophones, snare drum, and classroom rhythm instruments (triangles, tambourines, rhythm sticks, finger cymbals, hand-chimes, and bells).

Measures used in the studies varied widely, and because the results of the Mozart Effect analysis indicated that only spatial tasks defined as spatial–temporal were enhanced by music, type of task was the distinguishing feature for three groups of studies analyzed in separate meta-analyses. The first analysis included studies that employed spatial–temporal tasks, the second

---

[4]Costa-Giomi's study (1999) lasted for 3 years, but only the first 2 years of data could be analyzed.

included studies employing nonspatial–temporal tasks, and the third included studies that employed a variety of spatial tasks that could not be clearly distinguished by the criteria for spatial–temporal tasks.

The first instructional analysis included 15 studies (701 subjects) employing such spatial–temporal tasks as the Object Assembly subtest from the WPPSI-R or WISC-III, in which children assemble a puzzle of a familiar object without seeing a model of the completed image. Studies using other tasks were also included: A program designed by Matthew Peterson in Gordon Shaw's lab used a measure called the Spatial–Temporal Animation Reasoning or STAR, and other studies used spatial subtests of other standardized tests for children (i.e., Developing Cognitive Abilities Test, the Wide Range Assessment of Visual Motor Abilities, and the Kaufman, Woodcock-Johnson, and McCarthy batteries).

The average effect size was large by meta-analytic standards ($r = .37$, $d = .79$), and the results were highly generalizable (t test of the mean Zr was 7.50, $p < .0001$). Most interestingly, despite great variation in the music programs and spatial–temporal measures employed, there was relatively little variation in effect size among the studies included. All had effects greater than zero, the 95% confidence interval was $r = .26$ to $r = .48$, the SD was less than half the size of the effect at .16, and studies were decidedly drawn from a single population (χ^2 (14) = 20.37, $p = .12$). We can conclude from these results that the analysis is highly robust.

Contrast analysis of 17 potential moderator variables explored potential reasons for the effect found in this analysis. The most interesting finding is that 13 of these moderators did not influence the size of the effect systematically, even though many of them are factors that often have been found to influence learning. These potential moderators include socioeconomic status, duration of instruction, parental involvement, test reliability, teacher and experimenter expectancy effects (unconscious expectations of subjects or experimenters that bias results), the Hawthorne effect (a tendency of any new program to have a positive impact), methods of group assignment, and study quality. In addition, and of particular interest to music educators, keyboard instruction proved no more influential than the other forms of active music instruction tested, despite a reasonable assumption that the spatial layout of the keyboard might be an important contributor in enhancing spatial outcomes. In addition, effect sizes did not vary for those studies that used different keyboard instruments (pianos and xylophones), nor for studies that either did or did not use responsive movement in the music program, nor for studies that either did or did not ask students to create or improvise musically. In other words, the large effect found for the analysis is very stable in relation to a host of variables that might have affected it one way or the other. The effect is not an artifact.

There were, however, two moderator variables that did impact the size of effect. Effect sizes were somewhat larger in studies with individual rather than group lessons, and in studies in which children learned standard notation (rather than either no notation or preparatory types of notation such as Kodaly hand signs). However, the more relevant finding from a policy perspective is that large effects were obtained in both group and individual formats (group lessons $r = .32$, individual lessons $r = .484$) and with and without standard notation (no notation: $r = .36$, standard notation: $r = .39$).

There were also two moderator variables that were nearly significant. The first is the publication status of the article (published articles $r = .29$, unpublished articles $r = .47$). Publication status is often used as a proxy to index study quality; however, a direct analysis of quality showed no difference between studies with higher and lower ratings on threats to internal validity, so the publication result has not been adequately explained. The other variable of interest was subject age (comparing 3- to 5-year-olds to children 6 years of age or older). Because the comparative effect sizes of the two groups were fairly large (3 – 5 year, $r = .44$, ≥ 6 years $r = .27$), the effect is noteworthy. Future research should test whether enhancing effects from music programs are greater for younger children, as was the case here.

The second instructional analysis (5 studies, 694 subjects) included studies with Raven's Matrices as the outcome measure. Based on the results of the contrast on measures in the Mozart Effect analysis, which found a lower average effect ($r = .04$) for nonspatial–temporal measures compared to spatial–temporal measures ($r = .20$), a lower effect size could be anticipated for this analysis. That proved to be the case. The average effect for the nonspatial–temporal measures analysis in the instruction studies ($r = .08, d = .16$) was much lower than the average effect of the spatial–temporal measures analysis ($r = .37, d = .79$). The average weighted r was even lower ($r = .03, d = .07$), which may be the more informative statistic, because four of the studies were similar in size (ranging from 147 to 179 subjects) and only one differed (40 subjects). The effect was not generalizable (the 95% confidence interval spans zero at $r = -.10$ to $r = .27$, t test of the mean $Zr = 1.23$, $p = .29$), and the studies were from a single population ($\chi^2 (4) = 5.72, p = .22$). This result provides support for the claim that the effect of music instruction is specific to spatial–temporal and not nonverbal tasks generally, such as Raven's, that rely more on general logic.

The third instructional analysis included nine studies (655 subjects) that employed a range of spatial measures not readily classifiable as either spatial–temporal or nonspatial–temporal. Thus, this analysis tested whether the enhancing effects of music instruction extend beyond spatial–temporal measures to other, less clearly defined, types of spatial reasoning. Some studies used both spatial–temporal and nonspatial–temporal measures (i.e., several used more than one spatial subtest from the WPPSI-R and only reported a global score), some used tests that may be spatial–temporal but that are difficult to classify (e.g., Children's Embedded Figures Test, or "drawings and words presented in lacunary and ambiguous form" Zulauf, 1993/1994, p. 114). One study used a task that relies mainly on spatial memory (Bead Memory task from the Stanford–Binet: Fourth Edition).

The average effect found in this analysis ($r = .26, d = .55$) is lower than the effect in the spatial–temporal analysis, but it is still of moderate size. In addition, it is generalizable (95% confidence interval $r = .16$ to $r = .36$; t test of mean $Zr = 6.11$, $p = .0003$) and represents a single population of studies ($\chi^2 (4) = 8.87, p = .35$). From this we can conclude that music instruction may not be limited to enhancing spatial–temporal tasks but may enhance spatial reasoning more broadly. Further research is needed to affirm this finding, however, because the measures are quite diverse.

For the instructional analysis, there is a solid, generalizable finding that, for children aged 3 to 12, active instruction in music—not listening alone, although listening is a component of such instruction—enhances performance on a specific type of spatial task classified as "spatial–temporal." Further, the third instructional analysis for mixed spatial measures suggests that this enhancement may extend more broadly to some nonspatial–temporal forms of reasoning, although not to matrices tasks (as shown in the second analysis).

However, before policymakers mandate music instruction as a means to enhance children's spatial abilities, important questions about the value to education of such an effect need to be raised. Remember that not all types of music programs have been tested, and that, in fact, the musical treatments combined may be different from each other in important and as yet unspecified ways. More research describing the components of music instruction is needed to clarify just what teachers and students do in music instruction that aids skill in spatial reasoning. Further, the music studies analyzed were only for students between ages 3 and 12, so we cannot generalize to infants, toddlers, or adolescents. Further, because the spatial tests were conducted within a few weeks of the end of the music instruction, we do not know how long any enhancing effect lasts. And because only one longitudinal study extending beyond two years currently exists, and that showed students without music instruction catching up to those with piano instruction during the third year of instruction (Costa-Giomi, 1999), we do not know if music instruction is effective in fostering spatial reasoning after the first two years of instruction.

Perhaps even more important is the question of whether the effects of music instruction on spatial tests translate to better success in school. They might, or they might not. First, "real-world" spatial problems, whether found in mathematics or the block corner or the ball field, may or may not be predicted by success on paper-and-pencil or table-task tests such as those used in these studies. Second, a corollary to this problem is that many classrooms do not give students a chance to use spatial skills, because instruction may not offer opportunities to apply spatial reasoning to school subjects. In such cases, unfortunately, enhanced spatial ability would not necessarily lead to improved success in school. To reap the benefits of any enhancement of spatial reasoning resulting from music instruction, therefore, schools would also need to ensure that instruction emphasize spatial approaches to learning. Third, because spatial reasoning is multidimensional (e.g., consider the differences in designing a bridge, packing a car trunk, or finding your way around a new city) it is not clear where the effects of the specifically spatial–temporal tasks would show up. Thus, although this is a solid finding, its implications for educational policy are not self-evident.

No Support for Five Instrumental Claims

Arts-Rich Education and Verbal and Mathematical Achievement.   Perhaps the most commonly heard instrumental claim for the arts is that they lead to enhanced standardized test scores, higher grades, and lowered high school drop out rates. Just what is the evidence for such claims?

Winner and Cooper (2000) synthesized studies that examined the relationship between studying the arts (type of art course was not specified) and verbal and mathematical achievement. These studies do not allow us to determine which form or forms of arts students studied. Thus, all we can say about this body of data is that it examines the effects of studying the arts (which could mean intensive study of some combination of visual arts, music, drama, and dance) on academic achievement. Because our meta-analyses combine studies that examine the effects of a variety of art forms, we refer to these as "multiarts" meta-analyses.

In the studies synthesized, students were either exposed to the arts as separate disciplines, or they received such exposure but were also given an arts-integrated academic curriculum. Unfortunately, few of the studies explained in much detail anything about the nature and quality of the arts instruction, or about what it really meant to study an academic subject with arts integration. Academic achievement in these studies was measured primarily in the form of test scores (composite verbal and quantitative scores, or verbal and quantitative scores separated) but also sometimes in the form of academic grade point averages or receipt of academic awards.

We first examined the correlational studies—studies that compared the academic profile of students who do and do not study the arts either in school or in after school programs. For example, we included in the analysis James Catterall's study in which he demonstrated that students who are highly involved in the arts in middle school and high school outperform those who are not involved in the arts on a multitude of academic indicators, and this relationship holds even for students in the lowest SES quartile of the United States (Catterall, 1998; Catterall, Chapleau, & Iwanaga, 1999). These students earned higher grades and test scores than those that were not involved in the arts. The high arts students were also less likely to drop out of high school, and they watched fewer hours of television than did the low arts students. We included Shirley Brice Heath's (1998) study showing that at-risk students who participate in after-school arts organizations for at least 9 hr a week over the course of at least a year are ahead of a random national sample of students on a wide range of academic indicators: Their school attendance is higher, they read more, and they win more academic awards. And we included data from the college board revealing that the average SAT scores of students with 4 years of high school arts was higher than the scores of those who took no arts courses at all in high school (College Board, 1987–1997).

Three meta-analyses synthesizing the correlational studies were performed, each on a different academic outcome (composite verbal and quantitative outcomes summed; verbal outcomes; quantitative outcomes). All three correlational analyses showed a clear relationship between academic achievement and studying the arts. All three effect sizes were significantly different from zero, as shown by a t test. When we examined the five studies that used composite outcomes (verbal and mathematics achievement indicators summed), we found a small but highly significant relationship ($r = .05$, equivalent to $d = .10$, 95% confidence interval $r = .03$ to $r = .08$, t test of the mean $Zr = 5.97$, $p = .004$). When we examined the 11 studies that used verbal outcomes (and this included 10 years of the College Board data), we found a small to medium relationship ($r = .19$, equivalent to $d = .39$), which was also highly significant (95% confidence interval $r = .17$ to $r = .22$, t test of the mean $Zr = 16.52$, $p < .0001$). And when we examined the 11 studies that used mathematics outcomes (and this included 10 years of the College Board data), we again found a small to medium relationship ($r = .10$, equivalent to $d = .20$) that was highly significant (95% confidence interval $r = .07$ to $r = .14$, t test of the mean $Zr = 6.36$, $p < .0001$).

These three meta-analyses show that students in the United States who choose to study the arts are students who are also high academic achievers. But because the studies on which these meta-analyses were based were correlational in design, they allow no causal inferences. Does art study cause higher scores? Or do those with higher scores take more art? Or, is there a third variable, such as parental involvement, that causes both greater arts study and higher test scores? We cannot tell. Unfortunately, however, studies such as these have often been used erroneously to support the claim that studying the arts *causes* test scores to rise.

One plausible noncausal interpretation of the findings is that high academic achievers (no matter what their SES) may be more likely to choose to study the arts than low academic achievers. This could occur for several reasons. High academic achievers may attend schools strong in both academics and the arts; they may come from families that value both academics and the arts; or they may have high energy and thus have time for and interest in both academics and the arts.

One piece of evidence for the high-energy hypothesis comes from the study by Heath (1998). Heath's study included not only students involved in after-school arts organizations but also those in two other kinds of after-school organizations: those focusing on sports and those focusing on community service. All three groups were intensively involved in their choice of organization. Heath allowed us access to her unpublished data, and we compared the likelihood of winning an academic award for the arts versus the sports students. Although both groups were significantly more likely to win an academic award than a random national sample of students, we found no difference between these two groups. Eighty-three percent of the group of 143 arts-involved students and 81% of the sports-involved students won an academic award, compared to 64% of the national sample. The finding that both intensively involved sports and arts students did well academically is consistent with (though does not prove) the possibility that these are highly motivated students to begin with. Perhaps the drive factor is what impels these students both to involve themselves in an after-school activity in a serious way and to do well in school. It is also possible that these students get "hooked," whether on sports or arts, and when they are thus engaged their energy is productively channeled.

Some support for the drive hypothesis comes from a comparison pointed out by Eisner (2001). He compared the SAT advantage of students taking 4 years versus 1 year of arts to that of students taking 4 years versus 1 year of either an elective academic subject such as science or a foreign language. Students who specialized in any subject, whether in arts or in an academic elective, all had higher SATs than those who had only 1 year in that subject (with academic specialization yielding a far greater advantage than arts specialization). For example, in 1998, although students with 4 years of arts had verbal SAT scores that were 40 points higher than those with only 1 year of arts, those with 4 years of a foreign language had verbal SAT scores that were 121 points higher than those with only 1 year of foreign language. Similarly, although students with 4 years of arts had mathematics SAT scores that were 23 points higher than those with only 1 year of arts, those with 4 years of science had mathematics SAT scores that were 57 points higher than those with only 1 year of science. Students who specialize or focus might have higher energy than those who do not, and this higher drive could account for their higher academic achievement. It is also possible, however, that the very process of sticking to something (whether art or an academic subject) leads to better academic performance in other areas.

Another reason for the strong correlation found between arts study and SAT scores could be that our highest achievers study the arts in order to enhance their chances of admission to selective colleges. It should be noted, in this regard, that the academic profile of students choosing to take the arts has risen consistently over the last decade. When Vaughn and Winner (2000) plotted the relationship between SAT scores and taking 4 years of arts in high school (compared to taking no arts), we found that this relationship grew stronger each year beginning with the first year in which the data are available (1988) and continuing through 1999 (the last year of data we examined). Rising effect sizes for the arts–SAT relationship are shown in Figure 7.1. Thus, the comparative SAT advantage for students with 4 years of arts grew greater each year. As our most selective colleges become more competitive each year, students may feel they need to build resumes showing strength in a nonacademic area such as an art form.

An examination of the relationship between arts study and academic achievement in other countries proves extremely instructive. In the Netherlands, Haanstra (2000) found that students who take the arts in high school to prepare for a national exam that includes the arts attain the same educational level as those with no arts electives. This study, which controlled for students' SES, shows that in the Netherlands, taking the arts in high school does not predict the ultimate educational level attained. In the UK, Harland and colleagues (Harland, Kinder, Lord, Stott, Schagen, & Haynes, 1998) found that the greater the percentage of arts courses taken in high school, the poorer the performance on national exams at the end of secondary school. Harland explained this finding by noting that in the UK, the only students who are permitted to prepare for more than one arts subject for their secondary school exams are those who are academically weak. This contrasts sharply with educational policy in the United States. Academically weak

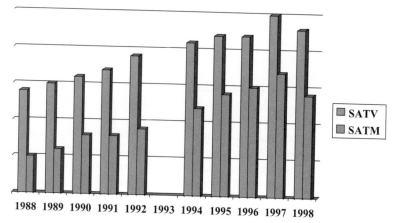

FIG. 7.1.   Rising effect size rs for the relationship between SAT scores and 4 years of arts courses compared to no years, 1988–1998 (1993 missing).

students in the United States are steered into remedial academic courses, not into the arts. The comparison between the findings in the United States and those in the Netherlands and the UK suggest that the relationship between arts study and academic achievement is not a causal one but instead reflects different cultural values about who should study the arts.

We reasoned that even if self-selection (high achievers choosing to study arts) explains the correlation in the United States, there might still be some causal force at work. Might it not be that once high achievers self-select into the arts, the arts then foster cognitive skills which translate into even higher academic performance? We were able to test this hypothesis by examining the data in James Catterall's study mentioned earlier (Catterall, 1998; Catterall, et al., 1999). Catterall reported longitudinal data on students who self-selected into the arts in 8th grade and remained highly involved in the arts through the 12th grade. If both factors were at work, we would expect the effect sizes showing the strength of the relationship between arts involvement and academic performance to rise over the years. But we found no change. The effect size showing the relationship between studying the arts and academic achievement was $r = .18$ (equivalent to $d = .37$) for students in the 8th grade, and this effect size remained unchanged in 10th and 12th grades. Although these data come from only one study, they come from a very large-scale study: There were 3,720 students who were highly involved in the arts from the 8th through the 12th grades, and the same number who were not particularly involved in the arts over that time period. The data fail to support the view that the arts are what is causing the academic achievement of these students to be higher than that of students relatively uninvolved in the arts.

Although the correlational studies, and the meta-analyses synthesizing them, do not permit causal inferences, studies with an experimental design do allow such inferences. We examined two bodies of experimental studies testing the causal claim that when students study the arts, their academic achievement rises. These studies compared academic performance before and after studying the arts. Typically, these studies examined students at the elementary school level who had studied the arts for a year and who studied the arts both as separate disciplines and as integrated into the academic curriculum. The academic growth of these students was then compared to the growth of similar students not exposed to any special arts program.

We found 24 studies testing the hypothesis that verbal skills improve as a consequence of studying the arts and 15 studies testing the hypothesis that mathematics skills improve. The meta-analysis performed on the verbal outcomes yielded a mean effect size r of .07 (equivalent to $d = .14$). This effect size was not statistically significant. The 95% confidence interval was $r = .01$ to $r = .14$. In addition, a t test of the mean Zr showed that the mean effect size found was not significantly different from zero. Moreover, the 19 studies in which the arts were integrated into the curriculum yielded a mean effect size identical to that of the five studies in which the arts were only studied separately. Thus, we had to conclude that we had found no evidence that studying the arts, including the arts integrated with academic subjects, resulted in enhanced verbal skills.

The meta-analysis performed on the mathematics outcomes yielded a mean effect size of $r = .06$ (equivalent to $d = .12$). Again the 95% confidence interval included zero, and the t test of the mean Zr showed that the mean effect size was not significantly different from zero. In this case we could not statistically compare the studies with and without arts integration, because all but two were based on an arts-integrated curriculum. Again, then, we had to conclude that we found no evidence that studying the arts, including the arts integrated with academic subjects, resulted in enhanced mathematics achievement.

Thus, we can see that there is (yet) no evidence that studying the arts, or studying an academic curriculum in which the arts are somehow integrated, results in higher verbal and mathematics achievement, at least as measured by test scores, grades, or winning academic awards.

Arts-Rich Education and Creativity.   Does studying the arts lead to enhanced critical and creative thinking outside of the arts? This claim seems more plausible than the claim that the arts lead to higher verbal and mathematical test scores, and we felt optimistic about this section of our research. Unfortunately, we found no studies testing this claim by assessing any kinds of thinking skills besides those measured by standard paper-and-pencil creativity tests (Moga, Burger, Hetland, & Winner, 2000). We found four studies comparing the creativity test scores of students who took arts courses versus those who did not. When we entered the verbal creativity scores into a meta-analysis, we found $r = .05$, equivalent to $d = .10$. This relationship was not statistically significant at $p = .64$ (95% confidence interval $r = -.21$ to $r = -.31$, t test of the mean $Zr = .81$, $p = .50$). We did find a small- to medium-sized relationship ($r = .19$, equivalent to $d = .39$) between studying arts and figural creativity tests (which themselves are visual tests), but even this relationship did not withstand the most important significance test because it was not significantly different from zero (95% confidence interval $r = -.05$ to $r = .44$, t test of the mean $Zr = 3.19$, $p = .09$). It seems reasonable to suggest that paper-and-pencil creativity tests are not the right kinds of outcomes to be using, as these tests primarily assess fluency and cleverness. Future research should examine more qualitative creative thinking outcomes, such as the ability to find new problems (Getzels & Csikszentmihalyi, 1976).

Visual Arts and Reading.   Can studying the visual arts help remedial readers improve their reading? This is the assumption guiding several programs set up in New York City, such as the Guggenheim Museum's Learning To Read Through the Arts, Reading Improvement Through the Arts, and Children's Art Carnival. In these programs, children with reading difficulties are given experience in the visual arts, which is integrated with reading and writing. For example, children drew and then wrote and read in connection with what they drew. These programs generally find that remedial readers improve their reading scores quite considerably. They then conclude that this improvement is due to the arts experience students received. Unfortunately, these programs failed to compare the effects of an arts-reading-integrated program with the effects of an arts-alone program. Therefore, we cannot know whether the reading improvement that undoubtedly did occur was a function of art experience, art experience integrated with reading, or simply from the extra reading experience and instruction.

We examined two groups of studies: those that compared an arts-only instruction to a control group receiving no special arts instruction (nine studies); and those that compared an art-reading-integration treatment to a control group receiving reading only (four studies). The first group allowed us to see whether instruction in visual art by itself teaches skills that transfer to reading skills; the second group allowed us to test whether reading integrated with art is more effective than reading instruction alone.

A meta-analysis of the studies testing the effects on reading of art instruction alone yielded a small effect ($r = .05$, equivalent to $d = .10$) which could not be generalized to new studies (95% confidence interval $r = -.30$ to $r = .54$, t test of the mean $Zr = .53$, $p = .61$). A meta-analysis of the studies testing the effects of art-reading-integrated instruction yielded a mean effect size of $r = .23$ (equivalent to $d = .47$), and again this result could not be generalized to new studies (95% confidence interval $r = .03$ to $r = .45$, t test of the mean $Zr = 2.003$, $p = .14$). Moreover, this effect was entirely due to reading readiness outcomes, and these are visual outcomes. There was no effect for reading achievement outcomes.

Thus, we had to conclude that there is no support for the claim that the visual arts enhance reading skills. Programs that help remedial readers improve their reading through a reading-arts-integrated program are likely to work well because of the extra, intensive reading training that the children receive, independently of the fact that this training is fused with drawing.

Dance and Reading. It is difficult to imagine how dance could enhance reading at the level of decoding, though one could hypothesize that by enacting stories through dance, comprehension of these stories might deepen. In Chicago, a program called Whirlwind had sought to improve basic reading skills in young children through dance (Rose, 1999). One of the activities that children in this program engage in is "dancing" their bodies into the shapes of letters. By virtue of this activity, these children in fact improved their beginning reading skills significantly more than did a control group which did not get the same kind of "dance" instruction. Unfortunately, however, we cannot conclude that the dance activity is what led to the reading improvement, because the control group did not get an equivalent kind of letter training. It must be added, as well, that the activity of putting one's body into the shape of letters is not authentic dance, though in fact it may prove to be an excellent way of helping children remember letters.

We searched for studies that examined the effect of dance on reading which also had appropriate control groups (Keinanen, Hetland, & Winner, 2000). A meta-analysis on the four identified studies showed a small effect size between dance and reading ($r = .10$, equivalent to $d = .20$), but this effect size was not significantly different from zero (95% confidence interval $r = -.21$ to $r = .42$, t test of the mean $Zr = 1.03$, $p = .38$). Thus, we concluded that there is no evidence that dance is a tool to enhance reading. However, the main finding of this analysis is the paucity of studies that test the relationship between dance and nonarts learning of any kind. Until more studies are conducted, the case cannot be made convincingly one way or the other.

Music and Reading. Music has also been claimed to be a way to improve reading skills, possibly because of the effect of learning to read music notation. In reading of both text and music notation, the written code maps onto a specific sound; hence, perhaps practice in reading music notation paves the way for learning to read linguistic notation. In addition, perhaps listening to music trains the kind of auditory discrimination skills needed to make phonological distinctions. It is also possible that music enhances reading skills only when students learn to read the lyrics of songs.

As part of the REAP project, Butzlaff (2000) located six experimental studies testing music's effect on reading and performed a meta-analysis on these studies. He found a mean effect size of $r = .18$ (equivalent to $d = .37$). This average was based on quite varied effect sizes, and the effect size was not significantly different from zero (95% confidence interval $r = -.21$ to $r = +.52$, t test of the mean $Zr = 1.06$, $p = .34$). So, we have to conclude that there is no evidence thus far that learning music aids the development of reading.

Equivocal Support for Two Instrumental Claims

Dance and Spatial Reasoning. Keinanen et al. (2000) were able to find four studies assessing the effect of dance instruction on nonverbal performance IQ scales and on nonverbal paper-and-pencil spatial reasoning tests. The average effect size yielded by a meta-analysis on these studies was $r = .17$ (equivalent to $d = .35$), and this was statistically significant (95% confidence interval $r = .06$ to $r = .29$, t test of the mean $Zr = 3.46$, $p = .04$). We can conclude that dance does enhance nonverbal skills. This finding constitutes a case of near transfer and is not surprising because dance itself is a visual–spatial form of activity. In addition, although it is a positive relationship, it is based on very few studies. The bigger story in dance remains that very little research has been conducted to test rigorously the relationship between dance and nonarts learning.

Music and Mathematics.   In 1999, a study published in *Neurological Research* received a lot of publicity (Graziano, Peterson, & Shaw, 1999). This study reported that piano-keyboard training along with computer-based spatial training led to greater improvements in mathematics than when spatial training was combined with computer-based English-language training. Vaughn (2000) searched for other studies examining the power of music to stimulate mathematical thinking and found six studies. Meta-analysis of these studies found an average effect size of $r = .13$ (equivalent to $d = .26$), the confidence interval did not span zero (95% confidence interval $r = .03$ to $r = .23$), and the t test of the mean $Zr = 2.49$, which was nearly significant (considering the .05 level as a cutoff) at $p = .06$. These findings suggest that there may indeed be a causal link between some forms of music instruction and some forms of mathematics outcomes. But no firm conclusions can be drawn at this point, because the finding was based on only six experiments. Moreover, of these six results, only two yielded medium-sized effects ($r = .31, .20$, equivalent to $d = .65, .41$), one yielded a small to medium-sized effect ($r = .17$, equivalent to $d = .35$), and the remaining three were below .10, the level considered to be small (one of which was actually negative.) Thus, more research on this question is needed before we can be sure about the result.

RESEARCH IMPLICATIONS OF REAP

Although the findings are not entirely negative, and although the limits of the analysis are carefully articulated by the authors, it is important to stand back from their findings and ask whether the game is essentially over.... Some would say that it had never really begun. (Perkins, 2001, p. 117)

Meta-analytic syntheses such as those conducted during REAP are not the final word on a research area. Instead they clarify what the research has thus far shown and guide attention to questions that remain to be asked. The REAP research summarized here assesses what we know to date about cognitive transfer from arts education to nonarts learning. In addition to informing policymakers about what research has to tell us about transfer from arts to nonarts learning at this point in time, the results of the REAP analyses can be used to guide future studies on this complex question. And, as David Perkins suggests in the previous quotation, one of the implications of REAP is that, as arts education researchers, we need to play a better game about transfer from arts to nonarts learning.

A better game, in our view, means that we need to (a) shift the areas of research focus and (b) refine the research methods.

Shifting the Focus

First, we believe that the field needs a renewed focus on teaching and learning *in* the arts. To continue building strong practice and to provide support for doing so, both policymakers and practitioners need descriptions and evidence for what arts instruction achieves at its core. It is the responsibility of researchers to provide that evidence.

Second, we need research that examines possible noncognitive transfer outcomes of arts education: the social, motivational, or dispositional effects of arts instruction. For example, when schools take the arts seriously, do they become more inclusive environments, more tolerant of differences, more focused on social justice? Do students in such schools attend more regularly, stay in school longer, work in a more disciplined manner in nonarts subjects, and/or show a willingness to reflect on and revise their work in nonarts subjects?

Third, we need to investigate how other subject areas can learn about good teaching and deep learning by looking at arts classes. For example, we might test the effects of arts-as-entry-points in a variety of subjects: Do students with certain kinds of profiles engage more deeply in subject matter when arts are used as entry points? Which students? How? And when? Would students in mathematics or English classes benefit from greater proportions of class time being devoted to working on projects while teachers offer individual consultations on ongoing work, similar to the way studio art courses are run? Or would science, history, or language classes benefit from the kind of regular, midproject critiques that are common in studio arts courses?

Fourth, we need to search for reasonable "bridges" between specific arts and specific subject matters. It may be more reasonable to expect transfer from the arts to higher order cognition (reflection, critical thinking, creative thinking, ability to tolerate ambiguity and resist premature closure when solving a "messy problem" with no clear right answer) than to more basic-level skills such as spelling or vocabulary (Eisner, 2001; Perkins, 2001; Tishman, MacGillivray, & Palmer, 1999).

Fifth, we need to examine the effects of *explicit* teaching for transfer in the arts. Perhaps it is only when teachers make clear that the skills being taught in arts classes can be used in other subject areas, can help students see how they might do so, and/or can work with students to reflect on and practice making such connections that students become able to transfer skills learned in the arts.

Improved Research Methodology

Research in arts education also needs to be improved methodologically. Our reviews of the literature revealed that many researchers in the arts have not applied standard social science methodology for the rigorous conduct and reporting of research. This may be due to the fact that much arts education research has been conducted in schools, rather than in the laboratory, and field-based research is always more complex than laboratory research. In addition, arts education research has been hampered by not having been routinely well funded; hence, arts researchers have not had as many opportunities to learn from mistakes as have researchers in mathematics or science or reading. But we should face the need for improved methodology, rather than feel defensive. Doing so is what will help advance understanding of the complex issues surrounding teaching and learning in the arts.

Perhaps the first and most important research implication from REAP is that the field needs to embrace the value of synthesis: More arts education scholars need to develop skill in meta-analysis (cf. Rosenthal & Hetland, 2001). Because meta-analytic procedures and methods are codified and described explicitly, meta-analytic reviews are more replicable than traditional reviews and allow reviewer bias to be revealed over time through the scientific process. In this way, the weaknesses of meta-analysis, which in our view is the best (though imperfect) way to summarize research, will improve. With improved synthesis, our findings become more trustworthy.

A corollary to the need to embrace synthesis is the need for clearer reporting of empirical research. Arts journals should require that studies report effect sizes; exact quantities for all significance tests performed (i.e., t, F, or χ^2); their associated degrees of freedom and exact p levels (even for "nonsignificant" findings[5]); confidence intervals, tables of Ns, means, and standard deviations for all groups; and ANOVA or regression tables where appropriate. All of these quantities are necessary for accurate synthesis, and accurate synthesis is necessary

---

[5]The Task Force on Statistical Inference, American Psychological Association, recommends reporting exact ps so that distinctions can be assessed along a continuum, rather than at an arbitrarily defined cutoff between "true" and "false." When researchers report only whether $p \leq .05$ rather than reporting exact ps, "likelihood" is assessed as a cliff. Such reporting of results equates as equally likely probabilities of, for example, $p = .06$ and $p = .50$ (one-tailed), when they are not equivalent. A $p = .06$, one-tailed, indicates that if the null hypothesis were true we would find a t of this size in the predicted direction only 6% of the time. A $p = .50$, one-tailed, however, indicates that if the null hypothesis were true we would find a t of this size in the predicted direction 50% of the time (Wilkinson, 1999).

if practice and policy are to rely on research. In addition to such reporting, researchers need to identify threats to validity and alternative explanations of results. These always exist and always require explanation. And finally, any study of arts learning, whether learning in the arts or learning transferred from the arts, should report clear descriptions of teaching methods, because the characteristics and quality of teaching certainly affect how well students can use what they learn flexibly and appropriately.

A second research implication from REAP is that we need to end the pointless debate about whether qualitative or quantitative paradigms are most appropriate in the arts. Both methodologies aid our understanding of the complex and subtle phenomena involved in artistic learning and practice. Skill with one paradigm supports skill in the other. Quantitative research is not inherently reductive; qualitative research is not inherently fuzzy. Researchers in the arts need to be trained in both qualitative and quantitative paradigms and then employ the methods that best suit the questions they wish to answer.

A corollary to the appropriate use of paradigms is that arts education researchers should learn from innovative methods developed in other disciplines. Many areas of education (e.g., mathematics, reading, writing, science), and other social, behavioral, and biomedical areas of research, including social and clinical psychology, anthropology, sociology, medicine, and public health, have had more resources devoted to research over time than have the arts. The arts would be wise to use the good fortune of these domains as sources of information about how sophisticated methodologies can help us answer questions of interest in our own field.

A third implication is that we need to design studies more rigorously. "You can't fix by analysis what you bungle by design" (Light, Singer, & Willett, 1990). Such rigor includes conducting two kinds of studies: those that develop theories and those driven by theory, with both kinds focused on defining the mechanisms that link treatments and outcomes. Longitudinal designs need to be conducted more commonly, and contrasts need to be employed more routinely. Assignment to experimental groups should be randomized at the level of the individual whenever possible and, when not feasible, matched at least for IQ, SES, parental education, and parental arts background. And studies must employ control groups with alternative treatments (besides arts) so that specific hypotheses can be tested and potential confounds disentangled.

A fourth research implication from REAP is that we need to turn our attention to the development of measures. If we value students learning, for example, to perceive, think, and understand in addition to acquiring technique and memorizing information, then we need to develop tests that allow students to demonstrate, and teachers, states, and researchers to assess, those qualities. An underutilized technique in arts assessment is rating by expert judges. It is central in the arts (e.g., in the assessment of portfolios for admission to arts schools, in qualifying processes for juried exhibitions) and in other disciplines in which nuance separates levels of quality (e.g., judging of figure skating and gymnastics at the Olympic level). And, when cognitive transfer from the arts to other subjects is of interest, researchers need to include measures of learning in the art form itself and compare that to learning in the other subject(s). Higher levels of transfer outside of the arts should reflect greater learning in the parent domain (Bransford & Schwartz, 1999).

With attention to these topics and methods, arts education research will be able to advance quickly from the benchmark defined by REAP in 2000.

POLICY IMPLICATIONS OF REAP: HOW SHOULD WE JUSTIFY ARTS EDUCATION?

Perhaps the most important policy implication of the research reported here is that arts education policy should not be based on instrumental outcomes for the arts, whether or not these outcomes can be demonstrated. If they cannot be demonstrated, the case is clear: We must make honest arguments for the importance of the arts. But even in cases where they can be demonstrated, we should not use instrumental outcomes as justifications. We need to distinguish between core justifications for teaching the arts and instrumental ones. Core justifications are the central reasons: They are about learning in the disciplines of the arts themselves. Instrumental reasons are the side effects—enhanced learning in nonarts disciplines, which may or may not occur. It is self-destructive to justify the arts on the basis of instrumental effects. If the arts are given a role in our schools because people believe the arts cause academic improvement, then the arts will quickly lose their position if academic improvement does not result, or if the arts are shown to be less effective than direct instruction in literacy and numeracy. Instrumental claims for the arts are a double-edged sword. It is implausible to suppose that the arts can be as effective a means of teaching an academic subject as is direct teaching of that subject.

When instrumental reasons become the chief justification for arts education, arts teachers may feel compelled to teach the arts in a way that will enhance academic (rather than artistic) understanding. They may turn strings of music notations into multiplication problems and bill this as music education, the kind likely to improve mathematics scores. Or they may teach the physics of sound in music class rather than the aesthetics of sound, or have students build musical instruments (because that may improve their spatial abilities) rather than learn to play these instruments.

It is time to state the right arguments for the arts in our schools and to begin to gather the right kind of evidence for these arguments. The best hope for the arts in our schools is to justify them by what the arts can do that other subjects cannot do as well, or cannot do at all.

The two most important reasons for studying the arts are to enable our children to be able to appreciate some of the greatest feats humans have ever achieved (e.g., a Rembrandt painting, a Shakespeare play, a dance choreographed by Martha Graham, a Charlie Parker jazz improvisation), and to give our children sufficient skill in an art form so that they can express themselves in this art form. The arts are the only arenas in which deep personal meanings can be recognized and expressed, often in nonverbal form.

In reaction to our work, arts advocates have said that we are just returning to "arts for arts sake" arguments, and that these old arguments just won't wash. But this is an admission of defeat. If we realize that the arts are as important as the sciences, and that the purpose of education is to teach our children to appreciate the greatest of human creations, then the arts will have a stronghold in our schools. But if we become swayed by today's testing mentality and come to believe that the arts are important only (or even primarily) because they buttress abilities considered more basic than the arts, we will unwittingly be writing the arts right out of the curriculum.

AUTHOR NOTE

The research reported in this chapter was supported by the Bauman Foundation, and we thank John Landrum Bryant for his support and guidance. Full reports on the meta-analyses summarized here are published in an invited special double issue of the *Journal of Aesthetic Education,* Fall/Winter 2000, Volume 32, Nos. 3–4. We thank Ralph Smith for his editorial guidance. Hetland's music analyses are reported in her dissertation, Harvard Graduate School of Education, 2000. A conference devoted to presentation and critique of the meta-analyses reported here was held at the Getty Center, August 24–25, 2000, and the proceedings of the conference have been published by the J. Paul Getty Trust as *Beyond the soundbite: Arts education and academic outcomes,* 2001. We thank the president and chief executive officer of the J. Paul Getty Trust, Barry Munitz; deputy director of the Getty Grant Program, Jack Meyers; and the Getty staff for their support in these endeavors. An Executive Summary of these analyses is published in the *Arts Education Policy Review,* May/June 2001. We thank Sam Hope for his editorial guidance.

We wish to acknowledge the researchers from our project team, whose papers are summarized in this chapter: Kristin Burger, Ron Butzlaff, Monica Cooper, Mia Keinanen, Erik Moga, Ann Podlozny, and Kathryn Vaughn. Additionally, we thank Ron Butzlaff, Robert Rosenthal, and Richard Light, for statistical advice throughout the project; and Howard Gardner, David N. Perkins, and Judith Singer, for generous review and counsel. We also wish to thank the research assistants who helped us at various times throughout the project: Kristin Burger, Lisa French, Kimberlee Garris, Nandita Ghosh, Maxwell Gomez-Trochez, Jessica Gordon, Joanna Holtzman, Jenny Martin, Elisabeth Moriarty-Ambrozaitis, Brian Moss, Melissa Mueller, Leah Okimoto, Nina Salzman, and Daniel Schneider. Finally, for their generosity and cooperation in answering questions about their work, we thank the researchers whose work we reviewed.

Correspondence concerning this article should be addressed to Lois Hetland, Project Zero, Harvard Graduate School of Education, 124 Mt. Auburn Street, Suite 500, University Place, Cambridge, MA 02138. E-mail: Lois@pz.harvard.edu

REFERENCES

Bransford, J., & Schwartz, D. L. (1999). Rethinking transfer: A simple proposal with multiple implications. *Review of Research in Education, 24,* 61–100.

Butzlaff, R. (2000). Can music be used to teach reading? *Journal of Aesthetic Education, 34*(3–4), 167–178.

Catterall, J. (1998). Involvement in the arts and success in the secondary school. *Americans for the Arts Monographs, 1*(9).

Catterall, J., Chapleau, R., & Iwanaga, J. (1999). Involvement in the arts and human development: General involvement and intensive involvement in music and theater arts. In E. Fiske (Ed.), *Champions of change: The impact of the arts on learning* (pp. 1–18). The Arts Education Partnership and The President's Committee on the Arts and the Humanities.

Chabris, C. (1999). Prelude or requiem for the 'Mozart Effect?' *Nature 402,* 826–827.

Cohen, J. (1988). *Statistical power analysis for the behavioral sciences* (2nd ed.). Hillsdale, NJ: Lawrence Erlbaum Associates.

Colwell, R. (2001). The effects of early music experiences. In E. Winner & L. Hetland (Eds.), *Beyond the soundbite: Arts education and academic outcomes* (pp. 89–98). Los Angeles: J. Paul Getty Trust.

College bound seniors: A profile of SAT and achievement test takers. The College Board, Princeton, NJ: 1987–1992; 1994–1997.

Conard, F. (1992). *The arts in education and a meta-analysis.* Unpublished doctoral dissertation, Purdue University, West Lafayette, IN.

Cooper, H., & Hedges, L. V. (Eds.). (1994). *The handbook of research synthesis.* New York: Russell Sage.

Costa-Giomi, E. (1999). The effects of three years of piano instruction on children's cognitive development. *Journal of Research in Music Education, 47*(5), 198–212.

Dansky, J. L. (1980). Cognitive consequences of sociodramatic play and exploration training for economically disadvantaged preschoolers. *Journal of Child Psychology and Psychiatry and Allied Disciplines, 21,* 47–58.

Eisner, E. (2001). What justifies arts education: What research does *not* say. In M. McCarthy (Ed.), *Enlightened advocacy: Implications of research for arts education policy practice* (pp. 19–29). The 1999 Charles Fowler Colloquium on Innovation in Arts Education. College Park: University of Maryland.

Fiske, E. (Ed.). (1999). *Champions of change: The impact of the arts on learning.* Washington, DC: Arts Education Partnership and President's Committee on the Arts and Humanities.

Getzels, J., & Csikszentmihalyi, M. (1976). *The creative vision: A longitudinal study of problem finding in art.* New York: Wiley.

Graziano, A., Peterson, M., & Shaw, G. (1999). Enhanced learning of proportional math through music training and spatial-temporal training. *Neurologoical Research, 21*(2), 139–152.

Gregory, R. J. (1996). *Psychological testing: History, principles, and applications* (2nd ed.). Boston: Allyn & Bacon.

Haanstra, F. (2000). Dutch studies of the effects of arts education on school success. *Studies in Art Education 41*(3), 19–33.

Harland, J., Kinder, K., Lord, P., Stott, A., Schagen, I., Haynes, J. (2000). *Arts education in secondary schools: Effects and effectiveness.* York, UK: National Foundation for Educational Research.

Heath, S. (1998). Living the arts through language and learning: A report on community based youth organizations. *Americans for the Arts Monographs, 2*(7).

Hetland, L. (2000a). Listening to music enhances spatial-temporal reasoning: Evidence for the "Mozart effect." *Journal of Aesthetic Education, 34*(3/4), 105–148.

Hetland, L. (2000b). Learning to make music enhances spatial reasoning. *Journal of Aesthetic Education, 34*(3/4), 179–238.

Kardash, C. A. M., & Wright, L. (1986). Does creative drama benefit elementary school students? A meta-analysis. *Youth Theatre Journal, 1*(3), 11–18.

Keinanen, M., Hetland, L., & Winner, E. (2000). Teaching cognitive skill through dance: Evidence for near but not far transfer. *Journal of Aesthetic Education, 34*(3–4), 295–306.

Leng, X., & Shaw, G. L. (1991). Toward a neural theory of higher brain function using music as a window. *Concepts in Neuroscience, 2*(2), 229–258.

Light, R. J., & Pillemer, D. B. (1984). *Summing up: The science of reviewing research.* Cambridge, MA: Harvard University Press.

Light, R. J., Singer, J. D., & Willett, J. B. (1990). *By design: Planning research on higher education.* Cambridge: Harvard University Press.

Moga, E., Burger, K., Hetland, L., & Winner, E. (2000). Does studying the arts engender creative thinking? Evidence for near but not far transfer. *Journal of Aesthetic Education, 34*(3–4), 91–104.

Mosteller, F., & Colditz, G. A. (1996). Understanding research synthesis (Meta-Analysis). *Annual Review of Public Health, 12*(1), 1–23.

Murfee, E. (1995). *Eloquent evidence: Arts at the core of learning.* Report by the President's Committee on the Arts and the Humanities.

Parsons, L. M., Martinez, M. J., Delosh, E. L, Halpern, A., & Thaut, M. H. (1999). *Musical and visual priming of visualization and mental rotation tasks: Experiment 1.* Manuscript in preparation, San Antonio: University of Texas.

Perkins, D. (2001). Embracing Babel: The prospects of instrumental uses of the arts for education. In E. Winner & L. Hetland (Eds.), *Beyond the soundbite: Arts education and academic outcomes* (pp. 117–124). Los Angeles: J. Paul Getty Trust.

Podlozny, A. (2000). Strengthening verbal skills through the use of classroom drama: A clear link. *Journal of Aesthetic Education, 34*(3–4), 91–104.

Rauscher, F. H., Bowers, M. K. & Kohlbeck, K. (1999). [Mozart effect and laterality.] Unpublished raw data, University of Wisconsin at Oshkosh.

Rauscher, F. H., & Hayes, L. J. (1999). *The effects of music on spatial-temporal task performance: Exploring task validity.* Manuscript submitted for publication.

Rauscher, F. H., & Ribar, R. J. (1999). Music and spatial-temporal task performance: Effects of arousal and preference. Manuscript in preparation. University of Wisconsin at Oshkosh.

Rauscher, F. H., & Shaw, G. L. (1998). Key components of the Mozart effect. *Perceptual and Motor Skills, 86,* 835–841.

Rauscher, F. H., Shaw, G. L., & Ky, K. N. (1993). Music and spatial task performance. *Nature, 365*(6447), 611.

Rauscher, F. H., Shaw, G. L., & Ky, K. N. (1995, February). Listening to Mozart enhances spatial-temporal reasoning: Towards a neurophysiological basis. *Neuroscience Letters, 185,* 44–47.

Rideout, B. E., Dougherty, S., & Wernert, L. (1998). Effect of music on spatial performance: A test of generality. *Perceptual and Motor Skills, 86,* 512–514 [experiments 1 and 2].

Rideout, F. H., Fairchild, R. A., & Urban, G. E. (1998). *The "Mozart Effect" and skin conductance.* Paper presented at Eastern Psychological Association, Boston, MA.

Rideout, B. E., & Laubach, C. M. (1996). EEG correlates of enhanced spatial performance following exposure to music. *Perceptual and Motor Skills, 82,* 427–432.

Rideout, B. E., & Taylor, J. (1997). Enhanced spatial performance following ten minutes exposure to music: A replication. *Perceptual and Motor Skills, 85*(1), 112–114.

Rose, D. (1999). *The impact of Whirlwind Basic Reading through Dance Program on first grade students' basic reading skills: Study II.* Chicago: 3-D Group.

Rosenthal, R. (1991). *Meta-analytic procedures for social research.* Newbury Park, CA: Sage.

Rosenthal, R. (1994). Parametric measures of effect size. In H. Cooper & L. Hedges (Eds.), *The Handbook of Research Synthesis.* New York: Russell Sage Foundation.

Rosenthal, R. (1995). Writing meta-analytic reviews. *Psychological Bulletin, 118*(2), 183–192.

Rosenthal, R., & Hetland, L. (2001). Meta-analysis: Its use and value in arts education research. In E. Winner & L. Hetland (Eds.), *Beyond the soundbite: Arts education and academic outcomes* (pp. 1–16). Los Angeles: J. Paul Getty Trust.

Rosenthal, R., & Rosnow, R. L. (1991). *Essentials of behavioral research: Methods and data analysis.* New York: McGraw-Hill.

Rosenthal, R., Rosnow, R.. L., & Rubin, D. B. (2000). *Contrasts and effect sizes in behavioral research: A correlational approach*. Cambridge, UK: Cambridge University Press.

Rosenthal, R., & Rubin, D. (1982). A simple, general purpose display of magnitude of experimental effect. *Journal of Educational Psychology, 74*, 166–169.

Salomon, G., & Perkins, D. N. (1989). Rocky roads to transfer: Rethinking mechanisms of a neglected phenomenon. *Educational Psychologist, 24*(2), 113–142.

Smilansky, S. (1968). *The effects of sociodramatic play on disadvantaged preschool children* New York: Wiley.

Smith, M. L., Glass, G., & Miller, T. I. (1980). *The benefits of psychotherapy*. Baltimore: Johns Hopkins University Press.

Steering Committee of the Physicians Health Study Research Group. (1988). Preliminary report: Findings from the aspirin component of the ongoing physicians' health study. *New England Journal of Medicine, 318*, 262–264.

Thorndike, R. L., Hagen, E. P., Sattler, J. M. (1986). *The Stanford-Binet scale of intelligence*. Riverside, IL: Chicago.

Tishman, S., MacGillivray, D., & Palmer, P. (1999) *Investigating the educational impact and potential of the Museum of Modern Art's Visual Thinking Curriculum: Final report*. Unpublished manuscript.

Vaughn, K. (2000). Music and mathematics: Modest support for the oft-claimed relationship. *Journal of Aesthetic Education, 34*(3–4), 149–166.

Vaughn, K., & Winner, E. (2000). SAT scores of students who study the arts: What we can and cannot conclude about the association. *Journal of Aesthetic Education, 34*(3–4), 77–90.

Wechsler, D. (1967). *Manual for the Wechsler Preschool and Primary Scale of Intelligence*. New York: The Psychological Corporation.

Wilkinson, L. (1999, August). Statistical methods in psychology journals: Guidelines and explanations. *American Psychologist, 54*(8), 594–604.

Winner, E., & Cooper, M. (2000). Mute those claims: No evidence (yet) for a causal link between arts study and academic achievement. *Journal of Aesthetic Education, 34*(3/4), 11–75.

Winner, E., & Hetland, L. (Eds.). (2000). The arts and academic achievement: What the evidence shows. *Journal of Aesthetic Education, 34*(3/4).

Zulauf, M. (1993/1994). Three-year experiment in extended music teaching in Switzerland: The different effects observed in a group of French-speaking pupils. *Bulletin of the Council of Research in Music Education, 119*, 111–121.

8

Aesthetic Education: Questions and Issues

Ralph A. Smith
University of Illinois, Urbana-Champaign

This chapter examines questions and issues that arise in formulating policies that bear on the philosophy and practice of aesthetic education. After mentioning different meanings of the term aesthetic education, *subsequent discussion centers on three generative thinkers and the ideas of a number of contemporary theorists. A final section identifies issues that present challenges to policymakers.*

THE MEANINGS OF AESTHETIC EDUCATION

An aesthetically educated person may be understood to subscribe to values and possess dispositions that in important respects are distinctive. The respects in which such values and dispositions are unique, and the methods by which they might be developed are, however, subject to interpretation. *Aesthetic education* may imply arts education programs that develop aesthetic literacy in matters of creating and appreciating art, the fostering of a distinctive sensibility irrespective of the subject or context of teaching, or combined arts programs unified by aesthetic concepts and principles. Although an aesthetic point of view can be taken toward practically anything, aesthetic education may also concern itself with interest in natural and humanly constructed environments and in objects and activities of everyday life, not to mention the art of living itself. Curriculum theorists have also examined various aspects of schooling—teaching, learning, evaluation, administration, and school atmosphere—from aesthetic perspectives. Several theorists (discussed under Contemporary Theorists) have interpreted aesthetic education as sustaining a close relationship with the branch of philosophy known as aesthetics because of the educational relevance of the latter's analysis of aesthetic concepts and methods of inquiry. In short, just as the reach of the aesthetic is extensive (Hepburn, 2001), so is that of aesthetic education. There are restrictive and more expansive senses of the terms. In this chapter, interpretations covering discrete school subjects such as art or aesthetic education will be designated domain interpretations in contrast to nondomain interpretations that are more expansive. Domain interpretations of aesthetic education may be regarded as programmatic definitions that highlight benefits associated with particular viewpoints. They thus are similar to definitions of art that, as Morris Weitz (1956) has indicated, are in effect invitations to entertain varieties of artistic excellence. Scheffler (1960, pp. 31) has also likened the logic of definitions of education to definitions of art. Consistent with this handbook's emphasis on art education as a subject and on interpretations of aesthetic education in the literature, this chapter devotes more space to domain interpretations of aesthetic education.

THREE GENERATIVE THINKERS: SCHILLER, READ, DEWEY

Friedrich Schiller (1759–1805)

Schiller was an 18-century German dramatic poet, philosopher, and man of letters whose career unfolded during the turbulent modern era when the power of the state and the privileged classes was coming under attack in the name of Enlightenment principles of reason, freedom, and democracy. Many thinkers of the time believed that history was steadily evolving in a direction that would grant individuals greater freedom and control over their lives. Although Schiller admired the ideals and promise of the French Revolution, he was dismayed by its cruelty and concluded that Man was not yet ready for freedom. He held that before the State could become properly constituted, its citizens had to harmonize their own conflicting impulses. Schiller drew ideas not only from the discipline of aesthetics—newly established by Alexander Baumgarten (1954) and systematized by Immanuel Kant (1952)—but also from his close association with the poet Johann Wolfgang von Goethe. He also relied on his own considerable strengths as a dramatic playwright.

In his *Letters on the Aesthetic Education of Man* (1954),[1] Schiller attempted to provide an account of the conditions that could release in Man what he called the living springs of human life, by which he meant those qualities of life that are realized in experiences of Beauty. Such springs of life would be set free in a fusion of sensuous and formal impulses, a reconciliation made possible through an integrating impulse that Schiller termed *play*. The experience of Beauty, in other words, was a necessary condition for the emergence of a full humanity. Schiller found the play impulse ideally exemplified in the integrations of form and content evident in the great works of the cultural heritage. That is, the instrument of aesthetic education "is the Fine Arts, and their well-springs are opened up in their immortal examples" (p. 51). Although he prescribed no particular curriculum or pedagogy, Schiller was persuaded that the fostering of aesthetic culture was the next phase in the evolution of civilization. The aesthetic path must be taken "because it is through Beauty that man makes his way to Freedom" (p. 9).

Modern philosophic analysis has questioned Schiller's metaphysics and psychology and wondered at his extraordinary faith in aesthetic education's ability to advance the cause of morality and human freedom (Beardsley, 1966a, pp. 225–230). The inspirational force of his message, however, was not lost on writers who continued to emphasize the civilizing powers of the arts and the role of art in integrating various human impulses. Above all, by recognizing the potential it held for achieving political and social stability—what he called the promotion of aesthetic culture—Schiller presented a strong justification for aesthetic education.

---

[1] Of the two standard translations of Schiller's *Letters*, the Snell (1954) version is referenced in the text because it was translated with the general reader in mind (cf. the translation by Wilkinson & Willoughby, 1967, which contains a lengthy introduction, German and English texts, and an extensive bibliography).

Herbert Read (1893–1968)

Read was a poet, critic, art historian, editor, philosopher, pacifist, anarchist, and educational theorist. But he is perhaps best characterized as a humanist in a world of politics who was at odds with received cultural, intellectual, and educational traditions that he thought were inhibiting the full realization of individuals' potentialities. He was appalled by the living and working conditions in the burgeoning factory towns of the industrial revolution, and he had come to believe that specialization, division of labor, and technical rationality were fracturing the sense of community he had experienced during his rural upbringing. His exposure to the horrors of World War I as well as his early literary training helped shape a poetic sensibility reminiscent of Schiller's. It is thus not surprising that Read evokes Schiller in his description of the kind of education that could ameliorate the effects of dehumanization or in his prescription for a fitting instrument for accomplishing it—the method of aesthetic education (Read, 1964, 1966). But there are differences as well.

As Read's educational writings (1956, 1960, 1961a, 1961b, 1966) reveal, he drew his inspiration not solely from Schiller but, like Schiller, also from Plato's theory that the pattern of moral virtue could found in the structure of the physical universe. The path to moral goodness therefore lay in individuals' repeating this pattern in their own lives. Plato had perceived certain laws of the physical universe—for example, the laws of harmony, proportion, balance, and rhythm. Because he had found these laws exemplified not only in the phenomena of nature and in all living things, but also in fine examples of music, dancing, gymnastics, poetry, sculpture, and painting, Plato recommended making the rhythmic arts basic in teaching the young.

Read combined Plato's and Schiller's ideas with those of writers prominent in his own time, for example, the social thought of Marx, Morris, and Ruskin and the psychological theories of Freud and Jung (Thistlewood, 1984).[2] The former group of thinkers sensitized Read to the dehumanization of society that was being wrought by an industrial machine culture, one of the consequences of which was a decline in the quantity and quality of humanly crafted objects. From the latter group he adopted certain aspects of psychoanalytical theory. For example, notions about the structure and dynamics of the unconscious played significant parts in his thinking about the artistic process and aesthetic education. The operations of the unconscious being essentially sensuous and sexual in nature—Read characterized his philosophy of education as a salutation to Eros (Wasson, 1969)—they stood in opposition to the constraints placed on human behavior by traditional moral codes. Read believed that dipping into the unconscious, especially into its potent image-making powers, opened up paths to greater self-realization. Thus, the crucible of the unconscious, which may be thought of as a cauldron of memory images, feelings, and inherited attributes called archetypes, was to supply source material for the creative imagination. Whatever impeded access to unconscious processes was therefore to be discouraged, for it was only by utilizing such processes as resource material that individuals could express their creative powers. Because Read thought that modern artists were particularly adept at plumbing the unconscious, he devoted a major portion of his career to championing their efforts.

Read's thought and career contain several complexities and contradictions that cannot be dealt with here. Suffice it to say that from his aesthetics, social philosophy, conception of psychological processes, and interpretation of modern art, it was but a natural step to an educational aesthetics aimed at freeing human experience from the repressive tendencies of contemporary life and schooling. In contrast to Schiller's emphasis on the value of studying the great works of the tradition, Read's pedagogy tended to demote the art object. He believed conventional modes of awareness encouraged passive responses and perpetuated a conception of inert knowledge.

---

[2] See Thistlewood (1984) for the evolution of Read's social and psychological ideas.

Wanted instead was what Dewey called learning by doing. Read consequently favored pedagogy grounded in processes that emphasized creative self-expression. Given the idiosyncrasies of learners and the individual dispositions of teachers, Read's preferred method of aesthetic education was less a set of specific procedures than a selection from a collection of practices; in other words, whatever worked for a particular student.

The impact of Read's writing was literally global. It is especially evident in his influence on the International Society for Education through Art, which periodically confers an award in his name. As was the case with Schiller, the spirit of Read's message counted for more than his theoretical formulations. Few teachers had the patience or background to digest the theoretical intricacies of *Education through Art* (1956). And by the time Read published *The Redemption of the Robot* (1966), a summary for the general reader of his encounters with education through art, contemporary art education theory was beginning to move in a different direction.

John Dewey (1859–1952)

Dewey's roots and preoccupations resemble Read's. He had experienced early childhood in a rural environment, expressed concerns about dislocations caused by social change, and criticized educational traditions and institutions he believed were hostile to reform. He also held pedagogical ideas compatible with Read's, for example, the notion that art should be experienced for both its consummatory value and its potential for the transformation and reconstruction of experience.

Dewey's distaste for dualisms and his deep feeling for the unity of experience reflect the strong influence of Hegel. However, in the course of evolving a naturalistic empiricism, Dewey abandoned Hegel's metaphysics. Instead, he favored a Darwinian biosocial conception of human development that conceived experience as interaction between an organism and its environment or, in Deweyan terminology, doings and undergoings. Among the numerous dichotomies that troubled Dewey, there was one of particular relevance to this chapter, namely, what Dewey considered an unfortunate bifurcation between art and everyday life. This separation was epitomized by the pedestal conception of museum art discussed in *Art as Experience* (1934, pp. 7–9). His countervailing strategy called, first of all, for striving to reintegrate art into common experience. That effort in turn proceeded through two steps. The first was defining everyday experiences in a way that revealed their inherently dramatic character. The second was claiming that whenever experience exhibits a certain organization and possesses certain qualities it may be regarded as art. This meant that all forms of experience—intellectual, social, political, and practical—could under certain conditions be so regarded. Presumably the world of modern work with its typical disjunctions between means and ends could be reconfigured to provide experiences that qualified under Dewey's definition.

Not unlike Read who wrote eloquently about works of fine art while at the same time dethroning the art object for pedagogical purposes, Dewey alternated between two views of art. And according to some writers (e.g., Gotshalk, 1964, pp. 131–38), Dewey did so at the price of creating some confusion. He seemed to favor the view of the work of art as constituted by certain qualities of experience regardless of the context of that experience. But Dewey also discussed art in the conventional sense, namely, as humanly constructed material objects, as works of fine art. Much of what Dewey knew about fine art was learned from Albert Barnes, the director of the Barnes Foundation that is renowned for its collections of art and educational programs. Dewey's dedicating *Art as Experience* to Barnes reflects the extent of Barnes's influence on his aesthetics (Glass, 1997). Consistent with Dewey's view of experience, his pedagogical recommendations placed emphasis on the designing of problem-solving situations. Implemented in the University of Chicago laboratory school, they aimed at establishing continuity between the activities of school and society (Jackson, 1998; Tanner, 1997).

As these brief summaries of three generative thinkers indicate, a line of argument can be traced from the writings of Plato in antiquity to Schiller's ideas in the 18th century to those of Herbert Read and John Dewey in the 20th century. The unifying thread consists in these thinkers' conviction that aesthetic education should be integral to the upbringing of the young. Concentrating on the modern period, serious discussion of aesthetic education begins with the writings of Schiller, many of whose main concerns were taken up in different ways by Read and Dewey. All three writers were preoccupied with such problems as the dehumanizing consequences of political and social dislocation, the alienation inherent in modern productive processes and institutional arrangements, the reductionism in values, and the disruption of the continuity of nature and human experience. For Schiller, the violence of the Reign of Terror during the French Revolution provided the impetus for his analysis of aesthetic education that set forth conditions for a more a humane and democratic society. For Read, it was the advent of industrialization and the alienation of the proletariat that prompted his recommending a pedagogy capable of reuniting in human experience what modern life and production methods had sundered. In his broadly defined view of art as a certain kind of worthwhile experience, Dewey's concerns were similar to Schiller's and Read's.

RECENT DEVELOPMENTS

In an article on the history of aesthetic education, Ronald Moore (1998) organizes his remarks around two sets of questions that he thinks are representative of contemporary discussions of aesthetic education: questions about the role of the arts and aesthetic experience in the education of the young, and questions about the role of aesthetics (mainly philosophical aesthetics) in aesthetic education. Moore reviews writings from antiquity to the present in order to discover how philosophical theorizing about aesthetic education has interpreted the roles of the arts and aesthetic experience in both private and public life and what such roles suggest for the education of young persons. He concluded that this legacy of philosophical thought testifies to the seriousness with which writers have typically regarded the functions of the arts and the aesthetic in human experience. These functions, moreover, have been understood in connection with basic principles that unite the life of the individual with that of the state, principles that were to be comprehended within a context of theory embracing the exercise of both mind and sensibility. Growth in aesthetic literacy was believed to progress through a series of stages from simpler to more complex tasks and achievements, a notion that has become almost axiomatic in contemporary research on aesthetic development. Moore draws the conclusion that the reason the arts have occupied an important place in philosophies is that "they, more than any other topics of study, transcend limitations of time, place, and personality to reveal what human beings and their societies are and may be" (p. 91).

CONTEMPORARY MOVEMENTS TOWARD AESTHETIC EDUCATION

References to aesthetic education began to appear more frequently in discussions of arts education around mid-20th century. Read was still expounding his notion of aesthetic education as the method for education, and Dewey's ideas about schooling and pedagogy enjoyed favor with educators of a progressive bent, notwithstanding Dewey's dislike of the term progressive education. But with the death of Dewey in 1952 and Read's in 1968, theorists had begun to favor a less expansive and encompassing conception of aesthetic education, one that saw it as a substantive subject in its own right and thus deserving of a place in a program of general education.

Although the lines of influence were not always direct, a number of writings anticipated later developments in the 1960s and beyond. For example, a year before Dewey's passing, Harry S. Broudy (1951), whose theory of aesthetic education was to have substantial influence on subsequent developments in art and aesthetic education, outlined the problems any educational aesthetics must address. Among these were the problems of explaining the peripheral status of arts education in the schools and the low level of taste prevailing in the society. Broudy also recognized the need not only for understanding the nature of aesthetic experience but also for identifying the criteria of aesthetic value and, most important, justifying aesthetic education. Further, in the 1950s, Thomas Munro (1956, pp. 3–24), who had a long association with the educational activities of the Cleveland Museum of Art and the American Society of Aesthetics, urged the establishment of close relationships between aesthetics and school learning. School arts activities were to provide data for aestheticians to interpret that could then be used to make recommendations for teaching art. Munro understood the aims of aesthetic education to be the furtherance of the artistic and aesthetic strains of human experience and the transmission of the cultural heritage in ways designed to help students develop a sense of vocation and a commitment to citizenship. Similarly, the writing team of David Ecker and E. F. Kaelin (1958) pointed out the relevance of aesthetics to the task of clarifying the purposes of art education programs, whereas Edmund Feldman (1959) went so far as to assert that all research in art education should take its lead from aesthetics in order to detect the philosophical assumptions underlying teaching and learning about art.

The writings referred to previously, and others in a similar vein, in effect set the agenda for the 1960s. Thus, Manuel Barkan (1962) conjectured that the future of reform in art education would lie in the effort to make the aesthetic life a reality for theorists, teachers, and students alike. Sensing what was in the air, Elliot Eisner (1965) wrote that the emerging interest in the aesthetic constituted a new era in art education. Eisner regarded aesthetic education as humane education in and through the arts. To achieve the aims of this kind of education, he thought it would be necessary to generate ideas by exploring not just the behavioral sciences but also the history and the philosophy of art. In the introduction to a book of readings on aesthetics and criticism in art education, Smith (1966) acknowledged the change in thinking about the scope of art education. Recognizing a need, he also established in the same year the *Journal of Aesthetic Education* (1966–) which provided a forum for serious discussions about the nature and problems of aesthetic education.[3] Portions of Eisner and Ecker's (1966) book of readings likewise emphasized the relevance of aesthetic theory. A year later, *Art Education*, the journal of the National Art Education Association, devoted a special issue (Smith, 1967) to aesthetic education. These developments in aesthetic education were symptoms of a watershed in American cultural life and education. In the 1950s and 1960s, New York City became the center of the international art world; the national endowments for the arts and the humanities came into being; and unprecedented support became available for a rash of seminars, symposia, and conferences on arts education.

Interest in aesthetic education carried over into the 1970s, which well may be regarded as the decade of aesthetic education. Indicative is Brent Wilson's (1971) statement in a handbook devoted to examining the nature of educational evaluation. He said that "the central purpose of art instruction is to assist students in achieving reasonably full aesthetic experiences with works of art and other visual phenomena which are capable of eliciting such experience" (p. 510). Continuing their collaboration, Ecker and Kaelin (1972) identified a peculiarly aesthetic domain of educational research, the principal focus of which was on aesthetic experiences of works of art. In the 1970s, Smith edited two more anthologies that had a bearing on the nature

---

[3] In his history of art education, Efland (1990, p. 240) takes 1966 as a critical year for aesthetic education.

of aesthetic education. One (Smith, 1970) examined the relations of a number of aesthetic concepts to arts education and education generally, whereas the other (Smith, 1971) subsumed art-educational writings under the topics of aims, curriculum, design and validation, and teaching and learning. While in the 1950s Broudy had outlined mandatory questions to be addressed by any theory of educational aesthetics, he in effect answered them in his *Enlightened Cherishing* (1972). The reprinting of this book in the 1990s was a sign of its continuing importance.

The shift in orientation that was occurring in the field of art education also produced a number of textbooks that either stressed the idea of aesthetic education or were compatible with it. Feldman's *Becoming Human through Art: Aesthetic Experience in the Schools* (1970) was significant for its subtitle alone. The text, Feldman said, "can be regarded as either an art education text with a strong aesthetic bias, or an aesthetic education text with a strong art education bias " (p. v). Certain parts of Eisner's *Educating Artistic Vision* (1972) were also consonant with the idea of aesthetic education. But standing out as the most ambitious effort to reform art education in the 1970s—prior, that is, to the Getty venture of the 1980s and 1990s—was the aesthetic education program of the Central Midwestern Regional Educational Laboratory (CEMREL).

In *Through the Arts to the Aesthetic: The CEMREL Aesthetic Education Curriculum*, Stanley S. Madeja (the program's director) with Sheila Onuska (1977) set out the scope and accomplishments of CEMREL's program and reviewed some of the problems it had faced. "Aesthetic education in its simplest sense," wrote the authors, "is learning how to perceive, judge, and value aesthetically what we come to know through the 'senses'" (p. 3). The St. Louis laboratory generated and supported an array of activities ranging from developing curriculum materials and sponsoring research to convening symposia and conferences. The laboratory's publishing program produced yearbooks on different topics (e.g., Madeja, 1977, 1978; Engel & Hausman, 1981). The program concentrated on developing curriculum units for the elementary years that were organized around the notions of integration, unity, and organicity. Although these notions reflect the influence of Read and Dewey, they were complemented by the findings of modern cognitive studies.[4]

If the 1950s can be regarded as having set an agenda for aesthetic education, the 1960s as having produced a literature that began to communicate the significance of its points of view, and the 1970s as having actualized some of the possibilities of implementation, the 1980s and 1990s were marked by initiatives to build further on established foundations. In a number of places, Vincent Lanier (e.g., 1982) designated aesthetic literacy as the end of art education, and Madeja and D. N. Perkins (1982) edited a series of discussions on the phenomenology of aesthetic response. Most noteworthy, however, was the extensive involvement in art education by the Getty Center for Education in the Arts (renamed the Getty Education Institute for the Arts; in the 1990s, it was ultimately dissolved), which was one of several operating entities of the J. Paul Getty Trust.[5]

Directed by Leilani Lattin Duke for 17 years, the Getty venture took its lead from theorists of art education who were convinced of the importance of integrating several interrelated fields of study for purposes of art instruction. The Center advanced an approach to art education termed disciplined-based art education. This approach stressed that the teaching of art should be grounded in the content and methods of art making, art history, art criticism, and aesthetics (Getty, 1985). Publications by Smith (1989), Brent Wilson (1997), and Stephen Mark Dobbs

---

[4]For additional discussions of CEMREL's aesthetic education program, see Barkan, Chapman, and Kern (1970), and a special issue of the *Journal of Aesthetic Education, 4*(2), 1970, Madeja, guest Ed.

[5]Following a change of leadership at the Getty Trust in the late 1990s, the Education Institute for the Arts was discontinued.

(1998) provide accounts of the origins and evolution of the Getty's efforts. A book of readings edited by Smith (2000), which contains selections from an extensive annotated bibliography of the literature of DBAE, supports the conclusion that the selection of the discipline of aesthetics was felicitous. This branch of philosophy received the greatest attention from scholars and theorists of art education because of its usefulness for justifying art education and providing content and suggestions for teaching. Also noteworthy was the Getty's adoption of Broudy's philosophy of general education that advanced ideas about aesthetic education distributed throughout many of his writings. Broudy (1987) further contributed a monograph to the Getty publication program and participated as a faculty member in a number of its summer institutes.[6] Additional Getty involvements in aesthetic education in the 1990s included support for Michael Parsons and H. Gene Blocker's *Aesthetics and Art Education* (1993), a volume in the Getty series Disciplines in Art: Contexts of Understanding, and the reprinting of Broudy's *Enlightened Cherishing* (1994). The chapter in this handbook by Stephen Mark Dobbs presents a more comprehensive description of the Getty's activities in art education.

Smith's *The Sense of Art: A Study in Aesthetic Education* (1989b) also appeared in the period under discussion, as did *Aesthetics and Arts Education,* an Anglo-American anthology edited by Smith and Alan Simpson (1991), and yet another anthology, *Aesthetics for Young People,* edited by Moore (1995). Textbooks, for example, E. Louis Lankford's (1992) *Aesthetics: Issues and Inquiry* and Marilyn Stewart's (1992) *Thinking through Aesthetics,* also deserve mention. Furthermore, the 1992 NSSE yearbook, *The Arts, Education and Aesthetic Knowing,* edited by Bennett Reimer and Smith, contains chapters with discussions of aesthetic experience and learning. Finally, the publication of encyclopedia articles on aesthetic education by Eisner (1992),[7] Moore (1998), and Smith (1998, 2002a) attests to the existence of a substantive literature on aesthetic education.

CONTEMPORARY THEORISTS

For the greater part of the second half of the 20th century the foremost American philosopher of aesthetic education was Harry S. Broudy. Throughout his long career he consistently assigned an important place to aesthetic education in both his philosophical and his educational writings (e.g., 1961, 1964a, 1964b). In his major statement on the subject, *Enlightened Cherishing* (1972), he defined aesthetic education as an important kind of value education that addressed the perennial educational problem of teaching virtue, that is, the problem of developing norms and standards for individuals' pursuit of a good life. Part of such a life is what Broudy called *enlightened cherishing,* which he understood as a love of objects and acts that is justified by knowledge. Because Broudy considered human choices and judgments to be pervaded by aesthetic judgments and stereotypes, he recommended a perceptual approach to aesthetic education that was aimed at cultivating students' capacities to derive satisfaction and insight from works of art that express the meaning of the more complex and subtle forms of human experience. In short, aesthetic education as general education was to provide the context for students' acquiring both creative and appreciative skills, what Broudy termed the *arts of expression and impression.*

According to Broudy (1987), the fundamental importance of aesthetic education was further secured by the assumption that the imaginative perception of works of art develops a rich store of images that energizes and directs not only the experience of works of art but also the

---

[6]See Greer (1997) for Broudy's participation in the Getty's efforts to reform the teaching of art.

[7]Eisner's (1992) article on aesthetic education is identical to the one in the fifth edition of the *Encyclopedia of Educational Research* (1983).

perception and interpretation of other phenomena. The magnitude of Broudy's influence is evident in the philosophical guidance he provided for over 3 decades to numerous agencies, institutions, and programs concerned with art and aesthetic education. A special issue of the *Journal of Aesthetic Education* (Vandenberg, 1992) contains discussions of his contributions to aesthetic education as well as a bibliography of his writings.

In a number of places, Maxine Greene (e.g., 1978, 1981) discusses the unique pleasure people seek to derive from works of art but are often unable to realize due to their lack of adequate knowledge and skill. Greene (1981) takes the goal of aesthetic education to be the development of aesthetic literacy, which she defines simply as the capacity to unlock the inherent values of works of art. She takes such values to consist in a greater perceptual awareness of the qualities and meanings of works of art, an expanded imagination and enhanced appreciation of ordinary life and natural phenomena, and an enlarged sense of personal freedom. Aesthetic education may also ameliorate the stringent technological imperatives of modern life and help individuals avoid stereotyped ways of thinking and feeling. She stresses that because aesthetic literacy implies knowledge of art and mastery of requisite interpretive skills, it is also necessary to foster a general grasp of aesthetics and a degree of critical acumen, both of which enable young persons to engage works of art more effectively. Above all, teachers must be sensitive to the subjectivity of individual experience. Generally speaking, gaining competency and sensitivity in the aesthetic domain allows persons to live more vivid, intense, and satisfying lives. The influence of Greene's thinking can be seen in her numerous writings about arts education and in her impact on the aesthetic education programs of Lincoln Center for the Performing Arts (Greene, 2001).

Smith's (1989b, 1991, 1992, 1995) interpretation of aesthetic education differs from most others in its explicit advocacy of a humanities point of view. He holds that because any well-developed sense of art presupposes not only some familiarity with artistic creation and performance but also acquaintance with aesthetic concepts, art history, and principles of criticism, teachers of the arts should strive for general knowledge in each of these areas. Smith considers works of art to be artistic statements that are distinctive for their dramatic forms of expression, their place in the history of artistic accomplishment, and their exemplification of the human impulse to impose significant form on unshaped material. He believes that works of art are prized particularly for their constitutive and revelatory values. By this he understands their capacity to infuse experience with aesthetic energy and to provide insight into a range of human and natural phenomena. He takes *reflective percipience* to designate the general goal of aesthetic education; it is a disposition that enables the young to traverse the world of art with a degree of intelligence, sensitivity, and autonomy. Discussions of Smith's contributions to aesthetic education theory, as well as a bibliography of his writings, can be found in a special issue of the *Journal of Aesthetic Education* (Hausman & Reimer, 2000).

David Swanger (1990), a philosopher of education and a poet, approaches his conception of aesthetic education through an examination of the relations of art, ideology, and society in a democratic culture. Ideology, understood as a set of beliefs that stubbornly resist change and the need to engage it are animating notions in Swanger's thought. Art's inherently radical and destabilizing power enables it effectively to exert pressure on the status quo, which it does by virtue of its freshness and creativity. By involving students in artistic activities under the guidance of a practicing teacher–artist, aesthetic education can encourage the young to seek and appreciate aesthetic values in other areas of life. As a secondary goal, Swanger suggests aesthetic education can help move a materialistic consumption-minded society toward a more conservation-conscious way of living that he terms *prosumption*.

In *Aesthetics and Education*, Michael J. Parsons and H. Gene Blocker (1993) combine educational and philosophical interests in explaining how aesthetics can contribute to the attainment of art education objectives. Aesthetics helps students understand the nature of aesthetic concepts as well as a number of conundrums that will enable them to develop their own views about the character, meaning, and value of art—in short, a rudimentary theory of art. In their discussion of multiculturalism, modernism, and postmodernism, the authors reject extreme positions in favor of more temperate and balanced stances. They defend the aesthetic as both a separate category and criterion of excellence and emphasize the importance of the arts for understanding the life of the emotions. The authors also stress the need for teachers to take into account stages of aesthetic development, a topic on which Parsons (1987) has done extensive research. The collaboration between a philosopher and an educational theorist that produced *Aesthetics and Education* was a distinguishing feature of volumes in a Getty publication venture. By bringing together scholars in the disciplines and specialists in art education, the series aimed to demonstrate the possibility of relating theory to practice.

H. B. Redfern (1986), a British philosopher who is familiar with the American literature on aesthetic education, assumes that aesthetic education has as its purpose the cultivation of aesthetic discrimination and judgment in the arts. Accordingly, the concepts of aesthetic experience, feeling, imagination, and critical evaluation figure importantly in her attempts to clarify a number of aesthetic issues. Redfern characterizes aesthetic experience as a special kind of imaginative attention that, owing to the nature of perception and the percipient's indispensable personal involvement, has both affective and cognitive dimensions. The refining of perception and judgment is in fact what makes aesthetic education possible. The basic pedagogic question then for any theory of aesthetic education is how to develop in students the disposition to regard things from an aesthetic point of view. More concerned to point out problems than to recommend practical curriculum suggestions, Redfern nonetheless questions whether young people should be allowed to leave school without having become acquainted with the great works of the cultural heritage or without having been instructed in the nature and application of critical standards.

By and large, contemporary American philosophers have not expressed interest in aesthetic education. Three notable exceptions are E. F. Kaelin, Monroe C. Beardsley, and Marcia M. Eaton.

Kaelin (1989) argues that art is important by virtue of the potential benefits that accrue when persons accept the imperatives of an aesthetic situation. Such a situation requires openness to the expressive surfaces of artworks and a willingness to permit their various aspects to control imagination and perception. In addition to reaping the rewards of intensified and clarified experiences, individuals also are helped in choosing their futures. They can do this by creating new forms of aesthetic value and by vicariously participating in the imaginative works of others. Kaelin further thinks that aesthetic experiences have potential for contributing to desirable social outcomes. For example, once persons, through the influence of aesthetic education, are disposed to enjoy aesthetic experiences, they may act to strengthen the institutions of the artworld, whose principal function he takes to be the preservation and replenishment of aesthetic value. Because individuals enter into aesthetic situations freely and solely for the sake of the unique advantages they derive from their interactions with artworks, art can lead them to a better appreciation of the value experiences available in an open society. They may also be made aware of the contrast in which their situation stands to the policies of totalitarian societies that closely monitor the creation and experience of art. Kaelin's thought is echoed in the aesthetic writings of Louis Lankford (1998) as well as in the guiding philosophy of the Getty-supported Southeast Institute for Education in the Visual Arts (see, e.g., Lindsey, 1998). Further discussions of Kaelin's contributions to aesthetic education theory as well as a bibliography of his writings can be found in a special issue of the *Journal of Aesthetic Education* (Spring, 1998).

In his discussion of the uses of aesthetic theory in the formulation of national and educational policy objectives, Beardsley (1982a) sets forth a concept of aesthetic welfare that subsumes a number of related ideas. The aesthetic welfare consists of the sum of all aesthetic experiences being undergone in a society at a given moment. The degree to which such welfare is being realized depends largely on the existence of aesthetic wealth within a society, which wealth is constituted by the totality of all aesthetically worthwhile objects as potential sources of aesthetic welfare. A democratic society should also be notable for aesthetic justice, which makes it necessary to provide through schooling and easy access to art opportunities for all individuals to participate in the life of culture. The existence of a condition of aesthetic welfare also presupposes individuals' trained aesthetic capacities to benefit from aesthetic experiences. To round out the picture there should be what Beardsley calls aesthetic auxiliaries, namely, teachers, cultural service workers, and others responsible for providing access to aesthetic value. Although teachers may find this account by itself useful in justifying and sketching the functions of aesthetic education, they may also find helpful Beardsley's discussion of the inherent values of art and his classification of types of critical statements and reasons. (1981, pp. 454–489).

In a later essay that discusses the relations of art and culture, Beardsley (1982) acknowledges a different kind of criticism, called cultural criticism, that typically takes interest in the nonaesthetic aspects of works of art. But he states that cultural criticism cannot avoid taking account of the judgments of aesthetic criticism. In order to do justice to each of a variety of cultural strands, cultural critics must be sensitive to the differences and divergences among them as identified and characterized by aesthetic criticism. Therefore, rather than eliminating or replacing aesthetic criticism, cultural criticism must embrace it and build upon it in order to "make room for, and preserve the distinctively aesthetic point of view (p. 372)."[8] Beardsley's influence is reflected in the writings of Smith (1989) and of those who found his analysis of aesthetic experience appropriate for conducting museum studies (e.g., Csikszentmihalyi & Robinson, 1990). Lankford's (2002) discussion of museum education compares Beardsley's, Csikszentmihalyi's, and Smith's understanding of aesthetic experience.

Yet another aesthetician interested in the theoretical and practical problems of aesthetic education is Marcia M. Eaton. In a number of books, articles, addresses, and workshops, she preserves what she thinks is worthwhile in the concept of aesthetic experience and demonstrates the practical uses of aesthetics. Essentially a contextualist, Eaton (1989) makes traditions, which she calls forms of life, central to her definitions of art, aesthetic experience, and aesthetic value. Traditions are an important part of what we think with during aesthetic experience because they not only provide the language for talking about art but also, in some instances, determine the manner in which we treat it. Hence, something is a work of art if it is a humanly made artifact that is experienced in such a way as to direct the attention of respondents to features considered worthwhile in aesthetic traditions. In other words, aesthetic experience involves taking delight in those intrinsic properties of artworks that traditionally have been considered worth perceiving and reflecting upon. A work's aesthetic value, it follows, resides in those of its qualities that traditions have stamped capable of rewarding interest and contemplation and of inducing delight. Eaton takes the aesthetic seriously and believes that having aesthetic experiences enriches life "not only by providing pleasure but by sensitizing, vitalizing, and inspiring human beings" (p. 9). In a work that refines and synthesizes earlier writings, Eaton (2001) discusses the close relationships between aesthetic and ethical merit and the significance of such relations for policies that would sustain a sound arts education, a healthier environment and community life, and aesthetic life generally. "A person leads an aesthetic life," she writes, "if he or she, through perception and reflection, tries to organize

---

[8]For other examples of his educational writings, see Beardsley (1966b, 1970a). See also Smith (1984) for the evolution of Beardsley's thinking about the nature of aesthetic experience.

life in terms of patterns of intrinsic properties similar to those displayed by works of art, and delights in this reflection for its own sake (p. 113)."[9]

This *Handbook* is devoted primarily to matters of research and policy in education in the visual arts, but is worth pointing out that the field of music education has also produced a substantive literature on aesthetic education (e.g., Leonhard & House, 1959; Mark, 1999; MENC, 1971; Schwadron, 1967), and it finds its most systematic treatment in the writings of Bennett Reimer (1989, 1992). In a chapter in an NSSE yearbook, Reimer (1992) states that the purpose of aesthetic education is the development of the capacity for aesthetic knowing in its creating, performing, and responding aspects. Aesthetic cognition, a type of knowing that is sui generis, deserves a place among the important ways of knowing because it provides access to works of art that are exemplary expressions of subjective reality. Believing that the structures and forms of artworks capture the internal dynamics of feeling in a manner not available to other modes of knowing, Reimer describes four kinds of knowing that have pedagogical relevance. Two of these types constitute the essence of aesthetic knowing ("knowing of or within" and "knowing how") while the other two are auxiliary kinds ("knowing that" and "knowing why"). Music education is effective, claims Reimer, when it encourages, improves, and enhances not only musical reaction but also musical creativity and a serious understanding of music; and is most effective when it disposes the young to value the qualities and import of music. Further discussions of Reimer's contributions to aesthetic education and a bibliography of his writings can be found in a special issue of the *Journal of Aesthetic Education* (Richmond & Webster, 1999). The field of music education has also produced two handbooks of research comparable to this one (see, e.g., Colwell, 1992; Colwell & Richardson, 2002).

BEYOND AESTHETIC EDUCATION AS ART EDUCATION

The foregoing review of contemporary writings about aesthetic education centered primarily on domain interpretations of aesthetic education that, while paying some attention to the appreciation of nature and the environment, tended to concentrate on the teaching of the arts. Another literature takes a broader view of aesthetic education. Beyond respect for the continuing influence of traditional ideas, it reveals a keen interest in nature, the environment, and the arts of everyday living, as well as an eagerness to understand a spectrum of educational phenomena from artistic and aesthetic perspectives.

Environmental and Natural Aesthetics and Aesthetic Education

Arnold Berleant and Allen Carlson (1998) indicate the spectrum of theoretical and practical issues that, depending on how they are resolved, can affect the direction of theoretical inquiry and, it may be assumed, policymaking for aesthetic education. Key questions revolve around the tenability of a distinction between environmental aesthetics and natural aesthetics and whether environmental aesthetics is the more encompassing notion. Moreover, if there are fundamental differences between experiences of the environment and those of nature, do they support an argument for two separate theoretical orientations? Also, what role should aesthetic appreciation play? Are concepts applicable to the appreciation of works of art also applicable to the appreciation of the environment and nature? Still further, what is the relationship between aesthetic and ethical values in policy decisions about such matters? Might aesthetic considerations contribute toward moral ends? There is evidence, the authors say, that an environment rich in positive aesthetic value can augment a sense of well-being in individuals

---

[9]For further examples of aesthetics applied to educational situations, see Eaton (1992, 1994a, 1994b).

and reduce physical and social ills—an important consideration, if credible, for policymakers to take into account. Finally, can the various areas of nature—woodlands, bodies of water, geological formations—be said to constitute genres, in the way we speak of genres in art? Contributors to the special issue coedited by Berleant and Carlson (1998) discuss the aesthetics of scenic and nonscenic nature, the character of appreciation and the role of imagination in the experience of the environment and nature, fact and fiction in talk about the environment and nature, and special topics such as forests and gardens.[10]

In introducing a symposium on natural aesthetics in the *Journal of Aesthetic Education,* Stanley Godlovitch (1999) distinguishes between cultural and natural aesthetics; the former takes humanly fashioned artworks as the primary objects of inquiry and the latter an array of qualities that compose the phenomena of nature. Given the diminishing reserves of unmodified nature, the need is ever more urgent to preserve and replenish nature's qualities. Godlovitch (1999) assigns natural aesthetics the task of exploring issues involved in defining aesthetic contact with nature. Godlovitch thinks that the significance of such inquiry to aesthetic education is clear: "Insofar as aesthetic education aims further to enlarge our appreciation of the value of the world we inhabit, natural aesthetics reminds us of the irreplaceable riches outside our urban centers" (p. 2). Contributors to the symposium addressed such topics as the expressive powers of gardens, creativity in nature, natural sounds, and the appreciation of natural beauty.

Godlovitch's belief that there still remains much to be done in the area of natural aesthetics does not diminishe the value of work that has already been done and that may be said to have laid the foundations for general, natural, and environmental aesthetics. For example, Yrjö Sepänmaa (1986) constructed a model for environmental aesthetics and indicated at some length its practical applications. The model shows how the environment may be depicted and understood as an aesthetic object and points out the need for ethical as well as aesthetic judgments in the framing of environmental and educational policy. In a section on applied environmental aesthetics, Sepänmaa takes aesthetic education to be an umbrella concept that covers both art and environmental education, the common objective of which is the development of taste (p. 139). Having adopted Beardsley's (1981) scheme of critical statements, he thinks this goal can be approached via proper descriptions, interpretations, and evaluations of the environment. Marcia Eaton (1989, 2001) also discusses the uses of aesthetic theory in studies of the environment. She bases her argument on the sort of delight believed to be a major attribute of aesthetic experience. She then extends her definitions of art and aesthetic experience to the natural environment and highlights the distinctive qualities and pleasures inherent in experiencing it aesthetically. Also of interest are Eaton's comments about flaws found in environmental studies that rely primarily on legal, psychological, and quantitative methods in formulating policy recommendations. These shortcomings can be corrected only by complementing such methods with the aesthetic and ethical values distinctive of humanistic perspectives.

Aesthetic Dimensions of Education

Readers scanning the literature of education from the last decades of the 20th century will perhaps be struck by the intensity of efforts to articulate the qualitative aspects of practically all facets of schooling. One explanation interprets these efforts as a corrective to behavioral learning theory and its misapplication of quantitative criteria to features of teaching and learning that are resistant to such forms of measurement. Another suggests that a proclivity for the qualitative is a manifestation of a culture that, for better or worse, increasingly relies on aesthetic

---

[10]See Carlson (2000) for the appreciation of nature, art, and architecture; and Carlson (2001), for curriculum recommendations for teaching an appreciation of landscape.

criteria for making judgments in a variety of contexts, aesthetic and otherwise (Barzun, 1974). Whatever the reasons, interest in the qualitative dimensions of learning is evident in Eisner's (1992) encyclopedia article on aesthetic education. After alluding to the history of aesthetics and defining aesthetics as philosophical inquiry into the nature of the arts and natural phenomena, Eisner discusses the influence of Herbert Read, John Dewey, Susanne Langer, Rudolf Arnheim, and Nelson Goodman on theories of aesthetic education. He discusses Langer's belief in the potential of artworks for presenting meaningful forms of feeling and notes Arnheim and Goodman for their views on the capacity of works of art to generate insight and understanding. In discussing Read and Dewey, Eisner draws attention to their broad conceptions of the aesthetic. Examples are Read's notion that artistic making is not confined to the arts but occurs whenever there is a satisfactory exercise of skill, sensibility, and imagination; and Dewey's insistence that experience may be regarded as art whenever its components have a dramatic organization. Although Eisner has contributed significantly to domain interpretations of art education, a sizable portion of his writing as an educational theorist has been devoted to illuminating facets of education from artistic and aesthetic viewpoints (see, e.g., Eisner, 1991). Endeavors like these, in contrast to domain interpretations that are more restrictive, may be regarded as reflections on the aesthetic foundations of education generally. Other chapters in this handbook deal with the qualitative aspects of education in greater detail.

Vernon Howard (1992), a philosopher and performing artist, borrows from both classical and modern philosophy in his variations on the theme of cultivating the sensibilities, an educational objective that he thinks has been neglected in learning theory. Such fostering of sensibilities, he believes, is possible in any domain of human development and constitutes "a kind of continuing 'aesthetic education'" (p. 152) that operates through a variety of perceptual and symbolic activities characteristic of the distinctively human. Howard organizes his argument around such concepts as imagination (the most important), practice, example, and reflection. Although indebted to Schiller and Dewey, Howard gives a special twist to his discussion with extrapolations from modern philosophical and psychological studies of the mind.[11]

Donald Arnstine (1967, 1970, 1995) sees a fundamental similarity between aesthetic experiences and learning that he thinks is particularly important in developing new dispositions. Learning that approximates aesthetic experience is distinguished from rote learning and is educationally significant because it requires reconciling discrepancies and overcoming obstacles put in the path of the learner. Arnstine acknowledges that Dewey's method of intelligence is one fruitful way to develop dispositions, but he thinks having aesthetic experiences is another. He understands aesthetic experience in terms of the perception of form (essentially unified aspects of design and composition) and the intrinsic satisfaction such perception can afford. Because the experience of form not only is highly gratifying but also leads to the recognition of discrepancies between it and one's own ordinary experience, Arnstine speculates about the use of an aesthetic-experience model for learning in numerous educational contexts. Such a model, for example, permits seeing teaching as an art and teachers as dramatists and dramatic actors (cf. Travers, 1974, 1979). Although urging more frequent recourse to the arts throughout the curriculum, Arnstine clearly believes that a domain interpretation of art education is less important than accentuating the various aesthetic aspects of schooling. *Aesthetic Concepts and Education* (Smith, 1970) contains several essays along comparable lines, including Arnstine's. Authors indicate ways in which aesthetic concepts such as aesthetic experience, aesthetic argument and judgment, performance, play, medium, creativity, metaphor, and intention can illuminate various aspects of teaching and learning. A number of writers, however

---

[11] Also see Howard's (1986) imaginatively composed letter by Schiller to a later age (cf. Grossman, 1968, and Kimball, 2001, on Schiller's educational thinking). Kimball's article is representative of contemporary reevaluations of traditional aesthetic ideas.

(e.g., Beardsley, 1970, pp. 19–20; Gotshalk, 1968, p. 49; and Smith, 1970, p. 62), caution that the application of aesthetics to teaching and learning should not be pushed to the points at which analogies, metaphors, and parallels begin to break down. But the problem here, and ultimately a question for policymaking, is how much weight policymakers should give to nondomain, in contrast to domain, interpretations of aesthetic education.

QUESTIONS, ISSUES, AND RECONCILIATIONS

The questions and issues that bear on policymaking for aesthetic education are not necessarily unique to that subject area. Yet aesthetic education, as was pointed out earlier, requires special consideration because it has two major literatures—one that advocates domain and one that advocates nondomain interpretations. The following discussion will confine itself to domain interpretations of aesthetic education. They are more representative of contemporary writings about the field and also lend themselves more readily to effective policymaking. It is simpler, moeover, to make recommendations for a subject area than for something that is diffused throughout the curriculum. Although this restriction makes matters more manageable, there are still theoretical and practical issues that, depending on how they are resolved, will affect the substance of policy thinking. Thoughtful and responsible statements of aims, for example, are systematically tied to questions about curriculum design, teaching and learning, evaluation, research, and teacher education.

One issue has to do with the viability of the very idea of aesthetic education itself. Some of its key concepts—for example, aesthetic experience—have been subjected to critical scrutiny by philosophical analysis, social science, and cultural criticism. Applying the principle of Occam's Razor—a principle that asserts concepts should not be unnecessarily multiplied—some writers have produced a body of criticism that concludes that the aesthetic attitude is a phantom (Dickie, 1965) and continued reference to it an impediment to clear thinking. The innate complexity of human experience and the difficulty of isolating its separate strands suggest that it is better simply to speak of the experience of art instead of a distinct kind of experience. What is more, the finding of anthropological studies that the languages of many cultures contain no concepts for art and aesthetic experience has led to the rejection of the proposition that one of the principal functions of artworks is to induce aesthetic experience. Nor does the concept play a major role in postmodern theory (more on which later), which tends to understand works of arts less as occasions for aesthetic experience than as opportunities for cultural criticism and deconstructivist analysis. Clearly, if it is the case that aesthetic concepts have little or no philosophical validity or are socially and politically irrelevant, then any theory of aesthetic education that makes them central will be suspect and pose problems for policymaking. Indeed, the label *aesthetic education* may have to be abandoned.

Critiques of the aesthetic, however, are not the whole story. A serious body of argument opposes the elimination of traditional aesthetic concepts. The feeling is that something important is lost when theory overemphasizes social and political considerations at the expense of aesthetic values. This realization has generated a revival of interest in the idea of aesthetic experience and its continuing relevance to aesthetic education (Eaton & Moore, 2002). Eaton's writings on the importance of the aesthetic have been mentioned. Noël Carroll (1999, 2000, 2001) is another writer who believes that aesthetic experience is neither myth nor phantom. On the contrary, he claims it satisfies a basic human need and has evolutionary significance.[12] And in a variant of postmodern thought that departs from typical interpretations, George Shusterman (1992, 1997) advances a pragmatist aesthetics that recalls the ideas of Schiller and

---

[12] See Dissanayake (1988) for anthropological evidence of art's necessity.

Dewey. He recommends giving serious attention to the kinds of aesthetic experiences provided not only by works of high culture (by which he sets some store) but also by works of popular culture and the arts of living.

T. J. Diffey (1986) likewise holds that the idea of aesthetic experience deserves systematic clarification and should not be summarily dismissed as something empty and nonsensical. Michael H. Mitias (1986, 1988) has further written extensively about the importance of the concept. In short, after a period during which traditional aesthetic ideas had come under a cloud, efforts are being made to salvage what is worthwhile in them—with, to be sure, some refinements in analysis and its areas of application. Policymakers and educational theorists therefore need not fear endorsing interpretations of arts education that feature aesthetic experience.

Even if, as a substantive literature suggests, the master concepts of aesthetic education are viable, there are still policy issues regarding aesthetic education's basic purposes. Nor can reflection on the objectives of aesthetic education ignore the functions of cultural institutions, the state and health of the art world, popular standards of taste, and so forth. In short, it is still necessary to answer the sorts of questions Broudy asked at mid-20th century.

Most important is that attempts to clarify the purposes of aesthetic education—that is, the benefits expected to accrue from such education—should be based on some understanding of the inherent values of art. Any such understanding has implications not only for methods of art instruction but also for research and teacher preparation. If, for example, it is proposed that the arts should be taught primarily for nonarts outcomes—say, the development of basic reading and mathematical skills, the amelioration of social problems, or the promotion of a political agenda—then assessment and research will have to discover the relationships between instruction in the arts and the realization of such extrinsic objectives. On the other hand, if it is believed that the arts should be taught for their inherent values, for the distinctive advantages that derive from studying and experiencing works of art, then policy for aesthetic education will reflect a clear conception of such values. Revealing in this connection is Ellen Winner and Lois Hetland's discussion in this *Handbook* of the distinction between core (aesthetic) and nonart values and the authors' report on what research shows on cognitive transfer—and, more significantly, what it fails to show—about the often-claimed efficacy of arts education for the development of a range of basic skills.

But if the core values of art are its inherent values, what are inherent values? In his answer to this question, Beardsley (1981, pp. 571–577) distinguishes between the more immediate and the more distant effects of art, that is, two kinds of inherent value. The more immediate values of art may be understood as the refinement of perception and discrimination and the development of imagination. More distant values may be said to consist of certain desirable psychological outcomes as well as the fostering of mutual sympathy and a readiness to shape human life on the model of art and aesthetic experience. The actualization of such values, however, if they are to qualify as the inherent values of *art*, must derive from the experience of the distinctive aesthetic features, qualities, and import of artworks. At a time when theorists of art education increasingly try to justify art education programs in terms of nonaesthetic and nonarts values (see, e.g., Clark, 1996; Efland, Stuhr, & Freedman; 1996; and Hutchens & Suggs, 1997), policymakers must ask themselves whether too high a cost is being paid in sacrificing art's inherent values. The question of the purpose of art and aesthetic education may thus come down to supporting aesthetic literacy versus promoting cultural criticism.

Exponents of art education who favor introducing students to cultural criticism or, alternatively, immersing students in cultural studies, believe themselves to be in the vanguard of a postmodern era. Because their position conflicts in major respects with the view holding that aesthetic education should strive to realize the inherent values of art as discussed earlier, some steps toward understanding what is meant by postmodernism would seem to be in order. Attaining such understanding is not easy. In his discussion of postmodern art, Christopher

Jencks (1987, p. 7) states that postmodernists themselves often do not know what the term means, and Irving Sandler's (1996) survey of postmodern art reveals a striking diversity of styles. Likewise, Linda Hutcheon (1993) says about postmodernism "that there is little agreement on the reasons for its existence or on evaluation of its effects" (p. 612). Interpretations of postmodernism, for example, tend to vary according to the national and cultural backgrounds of writers—say, French, German, or American.

In an effort to discern some common denominators, Hutcheon notes that the term *postmodernism* seems to refer to a period of artistic, cultural, and scholarly activity since the 1960s that represents either a continuation of late modernism or a rupture with modernist assumptions about such basic notions as knowledge, reality, meaning, truth, objectivity, communication, and value. The term postmodernism may refer variously to eclecticism in artistic creation and performance, the cultural logic of late capitalism, the condition of knowledge in an information age, a shift in emphasis in the kinds of philosophical problems studied, and the literature of an inflated economy. Characteristic of postmodern analysis is its use of standard linguistic conventions and traditional forms in order to subvert them. This strategy, says Hutcheon, combines both complicity and subversion with a liberal dose of irony and parody that often thwarts comprehension. With the objective of dissolving traditional hierarchies of value, she also points out that postmodernism further aims to undermine an array of conventional distinctions, for example, between genres, art forms, theory and art, and high and popular culture.

One strand of postmodernist thought, deconstructionism, is worth mentioning for its pronounced hostility to questions of value. One consequence is that discussions of the excellence and substance of works of art cannot even arise. Indeed, a judgment of something's being "great" is often considered risible. In commenting on deconstruction, S. J. Wilsmore (1987) goes so far as to say that "deconstructionist skepticism, taken to its logical conclusion, would deny the existence of art altogether. It ceases to express itself within the artistic forms of humanism, and ends in nihilism" (p. 338).

Despite all this, the posture of postmodernism has been enthusiastically endorsed by a number of art educators. David Carrier (1998), however, who reviewed several of their books sympathetically, was nonetheless prompted to say that "the problem with almost all discussions of postmodernism is that they are singularly ill-adapted to popularization" (p. 101). The premises of postmodernism, he writes, erects formidable obstacles to educational adaptations not only by virtue of its variety of its meanings and modes of expression but also through its denial of the possibility of objective judgment and the pursuit of truth. Carrier further notes that postmodernist art educators cast teachers in the role of agents of social change, but this is a burden many of them may be unwilling and unable to assume under the conditions of contemporary schooling. In short, postmodern interpretations of art education are prone to serious oversimplification. Such an assessment, along with those by Jencks and Hutcheon, helps to explain why Smith (1989b, pp. 89–103) agrees with critics of postmodernist theory who claim that it is excessively given to questionable hypotheses, often impenetrable prose, inherent contradictions, nihilism, and in some cases sheer dogmatism. In summary, postmodernist thinking has the potential for confounding, even for dissolving, domain interpretations of aesthetic education that are predicated on the retention of important distinctions and hierarchies of value.

Discussions of the relationships between policies for domain interpretations of aesthetic education and some of the most prevalent forms of contemporary thought are typically adversarial. Yet, more relaxed reactions to postmodernism can be found in the literature. Joseph Margolis (1986), for example, suggests that deconstruction is merely a cautionary tale that underlines the complex relations between language and reality but does not do much of anything else; it leaves the lives of individuals unaffected. We must, he says, keep doing what we have always done and must keep doing. Contra postmodernism, George Steiner (1985) continues to believe "that there are interpretations of works and meanings that can be perceived, analyzed and chosen over others," and that masterworks of the cultural heritage "exist in a hierarchy of recognition which extends from the classical summits to the trivial and mendacious" (p. 1275). Annette Barnes (1988) also thinks that it is possible to justify interpretations of artworks, albeit within a given culture that shares certain forms of life, customs, and traditions. Thus, we can "assume that we have better or worse understandings of texts—correct and incorrect understandings, not merely more or less ingenious or creative or workable ones—including texts of authors, critics, and metacritics" (pp. 104–105).[13] Similarly, it is still thought possible to disagree about the quality and value of experiences. Martin Schralli (2002), moreover, while recognizing an anticipation of postmodernist stances in Dewey's abstention from a quest for certainty, nonetheless finds the seeds of a constructive postmodernism in Dewey's description of what is involved in having a special kind of experience. Such experiences are "vital experiences in the ongoing experience of human beings that stand out" and "rise to such a level of felt integrity and completeness that they become remarkable and durably memorable" (p. 62). In other words and contrary to deconstructionist thinking, judgments of value remain tenable.

What is more, it may be the case that certain divergences between conventional and postmodernist views are bridgeable. Parsons and Blocker (1993, pp. 62–65) have perhaps pointed the way. Having clarified the relationships between facts and interpretations, reality and appearance, and objectivity and subjectivity—distinctions blurred or denied in postmodernist theory—they take the following view. Differences between truth and falsity and between reality and appearance are discernible relative to particular situations, and such discernment forms a basis for meaningful communication. Skepticism about the ultimate validity of such distinctions is therefore no excuse for avoiding the effort to recognize artistic traditions and their usefulness for gaining insight into the present. "Teaching," say the authors, "has always been the attempt to pass on our best understanding of the present so that our students will make sense of the future" (p. 65).

Resistance to the idea of aesthetic education comes from other quarters as well. Defenders of the status quo persuaded of the value of their own outlooks understandably feel no need to change their views. Others have criticized aesthetic education on the grounds that one of its key concepts, aesthetic experience, is too subjective for quantitative measurement (Efland, 1992). Yet, it is still the case that inferences about internal states of mind are commonly made and accepted as defensible. Eaton (1989) and Csikzentmihalyi (1990, 1997) are two writers who believe it is possible to assess whether a person has taken an aesthetic point of view toward something.

What then can policymaking for aesthetic education do in a period in which, as Samuel Hope puts it in his chapter in this section, writers about aims are at cross-purposes or, as Barzun (2000, p. xvii) has suggested, when culture is stalled? Considering the extremism and acrimony that often attend discourse about divergent viewpoints, the prospects for working out reasonable compromises might not appear to be good. Although the characterization is perhaps slightly overstated, the dispositions of traditionalists and progressivists seem irreconcilable; postmodernists and modernists often are not on speaking terms; proponents of high culture seldom have anything in common with those of popular culture; and defenders of the artistic accomplishments of Western civilization are assailed by its detractors. That there should be

---

[13]In deconstructivist writings, the term *text* initially implied the texts of literature. Eventually, however, other works of art were also so regarded, with similar assumptions being applicable to them.

disagreement about purposes is understandable in a democratic society that assigns the control of schools to states and local communities. But unchecked proliferation of options and ill will produce deadlock.[14]

The picture, however, is not totally bleak. Intimations of a possible rapprochement, or at least a workable approximation of it, may be detected in the literature of aesthetic education reviewed in this chapter. One prospect is offered by Parson and Blocker's effort to bridge differences between modernists and postmodernists and by Schiralli's propositions for a constructive postmodernism. Another is found in Kaelin's emphasis on the values of aesthetic communication and on the potential of aesthetic experience to ensure the proper functioning of cultural institutions. Also suggestive is Beardsley's concept of aesthetic welfare and his attempt to reconcile cultural criticism and aesthetic criticism, as are, some limitations notwithstanding, the national standards for arts education (MENC, 1994). All offer pathways and thus contribute substance to policy deliberations. Extreme postmodernist criticism of the deconstructivist type, however, is a cul-de-sac, as are social-science and cultural-studies conceptions of art education. If carried to their logical conclusion, the latter could result in the transformation of aesthetic education into sociology—an outcome about which, among others, Anita Silvers (1999) and John A. Stinespring (2001) have registered serious reservations.

In conclusion, although the preceding discussion of questions and issues in aesthetic education may have contained some judgments and alluded to some preferences, the primary concern of this chapter has been indicate the viability of the idea of aesthetic education and to present the questions and issues it poses for policymaking. What is promising at the beginning of a new century is the presence of features in the contemporary theoretical landscape that suggest continuing discussion about the meaning and nature of aesthetic education. Among these are the increasing volume of substantive writings on the subject of aesthetic education, the continued publication of the *Journal of Aesthetic Education* that serves as a serious forum for writers, and the creation of a committee on aesthetic education within the American Society for Aesthetics.

AUTHOR NOTE

Ralph A. Smith is Professor Emeritus of Cultural and Educational Policy at the University of Illinois at Urbana-Champaign. He was the founder of the *Journal of Aesthetic Education* and was its continuous editor from 1966–2000.

Appreciation is extended to publishers for permission to draw from two previously published materials: Ralph A. Smith (1988). Contemporary Aesthetic Education (Vol 2, esp. pp. 93–95). *Encyclopedia of aesthetics–four volume set*, edited by Michael Kelly, copyright 1998, New York: Oxford University Press; and Ralph A. Smith (2001). (Vol 1, esp. pp. 207–208). New York: Elsevier Science.

Correspondence concerning this chapter should be addressed to Ralph A. Smith, 360 Education, 1310 S. Sixth Street, University of Illinois at Urbana-Champaign, IL 61820. E-mail: ras@uiuc.edu

---

[14]The notion of stalemate or a stalled culture, writes Barzun (2000), helps to explain "a floating hostility to things as they are," that in turn "inspires the repeated use of the dismissive prefixes *anti-* and *post* (anti-art, post-modernism) and the pressure to *reinvent* this or that institution"(p. xvii). Also see Smith's (2001) Culture in a Bind. *Arts Education Policy Review 102*(3), 37–39, review of Barzun's (2000) *From Dawn to Decadence.*

REFERENCES

Arnstine, D. (1967). *Philosophy of education: Learning and schooling.* New York: Harper & Row.

Arnstine, D. (1970). Aesthetic qualities in experience and learning. In R. A. Smith (Ed.), *Aesthetic concepts and education* (pp. 21–44). Urbana: University of Illinois Press.

Arnstine, D. (1995). *Democracy and the arts of schooling.* Albany: State University of New York Press.

Barkan, M. (1962). Transition in art education: Changing conceptions of curriculum and theory. *Art Education, 15*(7), 12–18.

Barkan, M., Chapman, L., & Kern, E. J. (1970). *Curriculum development for aesthetic education.* St. Louis: CEMREL.

Barnes, A. (1988). *On interpretation.* New York: Basic Blackwell.

Barzun, J. (1974). *The use and abuse of art.* Princeton: Princeton University Press.

Barzun, J. (2000). *From dawn to decadence: 500 years of Western cultural life.* New York: HarperCollins.

Battin, M. P., Fisher, J., Moore, R., & Silvers, A. (1989). *Puzzles about art: An aesthetics casebook.* New York: St. Martin's Press.

Baumgarten, A. G. (1954). *Reflections on poetry* (K. Aschenbrenner & W. B. Holther, Trans.). Berkeley: University of California Press. (Original work published 1735)

Beardsley, M. C. (1966a). *Aesthetics from classical Greece to the present: A short history.* New York: Macmillan.

Beardsley, M. C. (1966b). The aesthetic problem of justification. *Journal of Aesthetic Education, 1*(2), 29–39.

Beardsley, M. C. (1970a). The classification of critical reasons. *Art Education, 20*(3), 17–20.

Beardsley, M. C. (1970b). Aesthetic theory and educational theory. In R. A. Smith (Ed.), *Aesthetic concepts and education* (pp. 3–20). Urbana: University of Illinois Press.

Beardsley, M. C. (1973). Aesthetic welfare, aesthetic justice, and educational policy. *Journal of Aesthetic Education, 7*(4), 49–61. Also in R. A. Smith and R. Berman (Eds.), *Public policy and the aesthetic interest* (pp. 40–51). Urbana: University of Illinois Press.

Beardsley, M. C. (1981). *Aesthetics: Problems in the philosophy of criticism* (2nd ed.). Indianapolis: Hacker.

Beardsley, M. C. (1982). Art and its cultural context. In M. J. Wreen & D. M. Callen (Eds.), *The aesthetic point of view: Selected essays* (pp. 352–370). Ithaca, NY: Cornell University Press.

Berleant, A., & Carlson, A. (Eds.). (1998). Introduction: Environmental aesthetics [Special issue]. *Journal of Aesthetics and Art Criticism, 56*(2).

Broudy, H. S. (1951). Some duties of a theory of educational aesthetics. *Educational Theory, 1,* 190–198.

Broudy, H. S. (1961). *Building a philosophy of education* (2nd ed.). Englewood Cliffs, NJ: Prentice-Hall.

Broudy, H. S. (1964). The structure of knowledge in the arts. In Stanley Elam (Ed.), *Education and the structure of knowledge* (pp. 75–106). Chicago: Rand McNally.

Broudy, H. S. (1994). *Enlightened cherishing: An essay in aesthetic education.* Urbana: University of Illinois Press. (Originally published 1972)

Broudy, H. S. (1987). *The role of imagery in learning.* Los Angeles: Getty Center for Education in the Arts.

Broudy, H. S., Smith, B. O., & Burnett, J. (1964). *Democracy and excellence in American secondary education.* Chicago: Rand McNally.

Carlson, A. (2000). *Aesthetics and the environment: The appreciation of nature, art, and architecture.* New York: Routledge.

Carlson, A. (2002). Education for appreciation: What is the correct curriculum for landscape? *Journal of Aesthetic Education, 35*(4), 97–112.

Carrier, D. (1998) [Review of the books *Postmodern art education: An approach to curriculum & Art education issues in postmodern pedagogy*] *Journal of Aesthetic Education, 32*(1), 99–101.

Carroll, N. (1999). *Philosophy of art.* New York: Routledge.

Carroll, N. (2000). Art and the domain of the aesthetic. *British Journal of Aesthetics, 40,* 191–208.

Carroll, N. (2001). *Beyond aesthetics.* New York: Cambidge University Press.

Clark, R. (1996). *Art education: Issues in postmodernist thought.* Reston, VA: National Art Education Association.

Colwell, R. (Ed.). (1992). *Handbook of research on music teaching and learning.* New York: Schirmer Books.

Colwell, R., & Richardson, C. (Eds.). (2002). *The new handbook of research on music teaching and learning.* New York: Oxford University Press.

Csikszentmihalyi, M. (1997). Assessing aesthetic education: Measuring the ability to "ward off chaos." *Arts Education Policy Review, 99*(1), 33–38.

Csikszentmihalyi, M., & Robinson, R. E. (1990). *The art of seeing.* Malibu CA: J. Paul Getty Museum & Getty Center for Education in the Arts.

Dewey, J. (1934). *Art as experience.* New York: Minton, Balch.

Dickie, G. (1965). Beardsley's phantom aesthetic experience. *Journal of Philosophy, 62,* 129–136.

Diffey, T. J. (1986). The idea of aesthetic experience. In M. H. Mitias (Ed.). *Possibility of aesthetic experience* (pp. 3–12). Dodrecht: Martinus Nijhof.

Dissanayake, E. (1988). *What is art for?* Seattle: Washington University Press.

Dobbs, S. M. (1998). *Learning in and through art: A guide to discipline-based art education*. Los Angles: Getty Education Institute for the Arts.

Eaton, M. M. (1989). *Aesthetics and the good life*. Cranberry, NJ: Associated University Presses.

Eaton, M. M. (1992). Teaching through puzzles in the arts. In B. Reimer & R. A. Smith (Eds.), *The arts education, and aesthetic knowing* (pp. 151–168). 91st Yearbook of the National Society for the Study of Education, Pt. 2. Chicago: University of Chicago Press.

Eaton, M. M. (1994a). Philosophical aesthetics: A way of knowing and its limits. In R. Moore (Ed.), *Aesthetics for young people* (pp. 19–31). Reston, VA: National Art Education Association.

Eaton, M. M. (1994b). Context, criticism, and art education: Putting meaning into the life of Sisyphus. *Journal of Aesthetic Education, 23*(1), 95–110.

Eaton, M. M. (2001). *Merit, aesthetic and ethical*. New York: Oxford University Press.

Eaton, M. M., & Moore, R. (2002). Aesthetic experience: Its revival and its relevance. *Journal of Aesthetic Education, 36*(2),17–36.

Ecker, D., & Kaelin, E. F. (1958). Aesthetics in public school teaching. *College Art Journal, 17*, 382–391.

Ecker, D., & Kaelin, E. F. (1972). The limits of aesthetic inquiry: A guide to educational research. In L. G. Thomas (Ed.), *Philosophical redirection of educational research* (pp. 258–286). 71st Yearbook of the National Society for the Study of Education, Pt. 1. Chicago: University of Chicago Press.

Efland, A. (1990). *A history of art education*. New York: Teachers College Press.

Efland, A. (1992). Ralph Smith's concept of aesthetic experience and its curriculum implications. *Studies in Art Education, 33*, 195–209.

Efland, A., Stuhr, P., & Freedman, K. (1996). *Postmodern art education: An approach to curriculum*. Reston, VA: National Art Education Association.

Eisner, E. W. (1965). Toward a new era in art education. *Studies in Art Education, 6*(20), 54–62.

Eisner, E. W. (1991). *The enlightened eye: Qualitative inquiry and the enhancement of educational practice*. New York: Macmillan.

Eisner, E. W. (1992). Aesthetic education. In *Encyclopedia of educational research* (6th ed., Vol. 1, pp. 39–42). New York: Macmillan.

Eisner, E. W. (1997). *Educating artistic vision*. New York: Macmillan. (First published 1972. Reprinted by the National Art Education Association)

Eisner, E. W., & Ecker, D. (Eds.). (1966). *Readings in art education*. Waltham, MA: Blaisdell.

Engel, M., & Hausman, J. (Eds.). (1981). *Curriculum and instruction in arts and aesthetic education*. St. Louis: CEMREL.

Feldman, E. B. (1959). Research as the verification of aesthetics. *Studies in Art Education, 1*(1), 19–25.

Feldman, E. B. (1970). *Becoming human through art: Aesthetic experience in the schools*. Englewood Cliffs, NJ: Prentice-Hall.

Getty Center for Education in the Arts. (1984). *Beyond creating: The place of art in American schools*. Los Angeles: J. Paul Getty Trust. Author.

Glass, N. R. (1997). Theory and practice in the experience of art: John Dewey and the Barnes Foundation. *Journal of Aesthetic Education, 31*(3), 91–105.

Godlovitch, S. (1999). Introduction: Natural aesthetics [Symposium]. *Journal of Aesthetic Education, 33*(3), 1–4.

Gotshalk, D. W. (1964). On Dewey's aesthetics. *Journal of Aesthetics and Art Criticism, 23*, 131–138.

Gotshalk. D. W. (1968). Aesthetic education as a domain. *Journal of Aesthetic Education, 2*(1), 43–50.

Greene, M. (1978). *Landscapes of learning*. New York: Teachers College Press.

Greene, M. (1981). Aesthetic literacy and general education. In J. F. Soltis (Ed.), *Philosophy and education* (pp. 115–141). 80th Yearbook of the National Society for the Study of Education, Pt. 1. Chicago: University of Chicago Press.

Greene, M. (2001). *Variations on a blue guitar*. New York: Teachers College Press.

Greer, D. W. (1997). *Art as a basic: The reformation of art education*. Bloomington, IN: Phi Delta Kappa Foundation.

Grossman, W. (1968). Schiller's aesthetic education. *Journal of Aesthetic Education, 22*(1), 31–41.

Hausman, J., & Reimer, B. (Guest Eds.). (2002). In pursuit of excellence: Essays in honor of Ralph A. Smith [Special Issue] *Journal of Aesthetic Education, 36*(2).

Hepburn, R. W. (2001). *The reach of the aesthetic*. Ashgate: Burlington, VT.

Howard, V. A. (1982). *Artistry: The work of artists*. Indianapolis: Hackett.

Howard, V. A. (1986). Schiller: A letter on aesthetic education to a later age. *Journal of Aesthetic Education, 20*(3), 8–11.

Howard, V. A. (1992). *Learning by all means: Lessons from the arts*. New York: Peter Lang.

Hutchens, J., & Suggs, M. (Eds.). (1997). *Art education: Content and practice in a postmodern era*. Reston, VA: National Art Education Association.

Hutcheon, L. (1993). Postmodernism. In *Encyclopedia of contemporary literary theory* (pp. 612–613). New York: Oxford University Press.

Jackson, P. W. (1998). *John Dewey and the lessons of art*. New Haven: Yale University Press.

Jencks, C. (1987). *Post-Modernism: The new classicism in art and architecture*. New York: Rizzoli.

Journal of Aesthetic Education. (1966–). Urbana: University of Illinois Press.

Journal of Aesthetic Education. (Spring 1998). *32*(1). [Special Issue] Essays in honor of Eugene F. Kaelin.

Kaelin, E. F. (1989). *An aesthetics for educators*. New York: Teachers College Press.

Kant, I. (1952). *Critique of judgment* (J. C. Meredith, Trans.). Oxford: Clarendon Press. (Original work published 1790)

Kimball. R. (2001). Schiller's "aesthetic education." *The New Criterion, 19*(7), 12–19.

Lanier, V. (1982). Aesthetic literacy as the product of art education. In J. Condous et al. (Eds.), *The product of a process* (pp. 115–121). The Netherlands: De Trommel.

Lankford, E. L. (1992). *Aesthetics: Issues and inquiry*. Reston, VA: National Art Education Association.

Lankford, E. L. (1998). Aesthetic experience in a postmodern age: Recovering the aesthetics of E. F. Kaelin. *Journal of Aesthetic Education, 32*(1), 23–30.

Lankford, E. L. (2002). Aesthetic experience in consructivist museums. *Journal of Aesthetic Education, 36*(2), 140–153.

Leonhard, C., & House, R. W. (1959). *Foundations and principles of music education* (2nd ed.). New York: McGraw Hill.

Lindsey, A. (1998). Before our very eyes. *Journal of Aesthetic Education, 32*(1), 17–22.

Madeja, S. (Guest Ed.). (1970). Curriculum and aesthetic education [Special issue] *Journal of Aesthetic Education, 4*(2).

Madeja, S. (Ed.). (1977). *The arts and aesthetics: An agenda for the future*. St. Louis: CEMREL.

Madeja, S. (Ed.) (1978). *The arts, cognition, and basic skills*. St. Louis: CEMREL.

Madeja, S., & Onuska, S. (1977). *Through the arts to the aesthetic: The CEMREL aesthetic education program*. St. Louis: CEMREL.

Madeja, S., & Perkins, D. N. (Eds.). (1982). *A model for aesthetic response*. St Louis: CEMREL.

Margolis, J. (1986). Deconstruction: A cautionary tale. *Journal of Aesthetic Education, 20*(4), 91–94.

Mark, L. (1999). A historical interpretation of aesthetic education. *Journal of Aesthetic Education, 33*(1), 9–15.

Mitias, M. H. (Ed.). (1986). *Possibility of the aesthetic experience*. Dordrecht: Martinus Nijhof.

Mitias, M. H. (1988). *What makes an experience aesthetic?* Amsterdam: Rodopi.

Moore, R. (Ed.). (1995). *Aesthetics for young people*. Reston, VA: National Art Education Association.

Moore, R. (1998). History of aesthetic education. In *Encyclopedia of aesthetics* (Vol. 2, pp. 89–93). New York: Oxford University Press.

Munro, T. (1956). *Art education: Its philosophy and psychology*. New York: Liberal Arts Press.

Music Educators National Conference. (1971). *Toward an aesthetic education*. Washington, DC: Author.

Music Educators National Conference. (1994). *National standards for arts education*. Reston, VA: Author.

Neperud, R. W. (Ed). *Context, content, and community: Beyond postmodernism*. New York: Teachers College Press.

Parsons, M. J. (1987). *How we understand art: A cognitive developmental account of aesthetic experience*. New York: Cambridge University Press.

Parsons, M. J., & Blocker, H. G. (1993). *Aesthetics and education*. Urbana: University of Illinois Press.

Read, H. (1956). *Education through art* (3rd ed.). New York: Pantheon.

Read, H. (1960). The third realm of education. In *The creative arts in education* (pp. 36–65). Cambridge: Harvard University Press.

Read, H. (1961a). *The grass roots of art*. Cleveland: World.

Read, H. (1961b). *Art and industry*. Bloomington: Indiana University Press.

Read, H. (1966). *The redemption of the robot: My encounters with education through art*. New York: Strident Press.

Redfern, H. B. (1986). *Questions in aesthetic education*. Boston: Allen Unwin.

Reimer, B. (1992). What knowledge is of most worth? In B. Reimer & R. A. Smith (Eds.). *The arts, education, and aesthetic knowing* (pp. 20–50). 91st Yearbook of the National Society for the Study of Education, Pt. 2. Chicago: University of Chicago Press.

Reimer, B. (2003). *Philosophy of music education; Advancing the vision* (3rd ed.). Upper Saddle River, NJ: Pearson Education, Prentice Hall. (First edition published 1970)

Richmond, J. W., & Webster, P. R. (Guest Eds). (1999). Musings: Essays in honor of Bennett Reimer [Special issue] *Journal of Aesthetic Education, 33*(4).

Sandler, I. (1996). *Art of the post-modern era: From the late 1960s to the early 1990s*. New York: HarperCollins.

Scheffler, I. (1960). *The language of education*. Springfield, IL: Charles C. Thomas.

Schiller, C. F. (1954). *On the aesthetic education of man in a series of letters* (R. Snell, trans.). New York: Frederick Unger. (Original work published 1795)

Schiller, J. C. F. (1967). *On the aesthetic education of man* (E. M. Wilkinson & L. A. Willoughby, Eds. & Trans.). Oxford: Clarendon Press. (Original work published 1795)

Schiralli, M. (2002). Anxiety and uncertainty in aesthetic education. *Journal of Aesthetic Education, 36*(2) 52–66.

Schwadron, A. A. (1967). *Aesthetics: Dimensions for music education*. Washington, DC: Music Educators National Conference.

Sepänmaa, Y. (1986). *The beauty of environment: A general model for environmental aesthetics*. Helsinki: Suomalainen Tiedeakatemia.

Shusterman, R. (1992) *Pragmatist aesthetics: Living beauty, rethinking art*. Cambridge, MA: Blackwell.

Shusterman, R. (1997). The end of aesthetic experience. *Journal of Aesthetics and Art Criticism, 55*, 29–41.

Silvers, A. (1999). Multiculturalism and the aesthetics of recognition: Reflections on *Celebrating Pluralism* (Review of the book *Celebrating pluralism: Art education and cultural diversity*). *Journal of Aesthetic Education, 33*(1), 95–103.

Smith, R. A. (Ed.). (1966). *Aesthetics and criticism in art education: Problems in defining, explaining, and evaluating art*. Chicago: Rand McNally. (Reprinted 2001 with a new introduction and bibliographic note by the National Art Education Association, Reston, VA)

Smith, R. A. (Guest Ed.). (1967). Aesthetic education [Special issue] *Art Education, 20*(3).

Smith, R. A. (Ed.). (1970). *Aesthetic concepts and education*. Urbana: University of Illinois Press.

Smith, R. A. (Ed.). (1971). *Aesthetics and problems of education*. Urbana: University of Illinois Press.

Smith, R. A. (1979). Is teaching really a performing art? *Contemporary Education 51*(1), 31–35.

Smith, R. A. (1984). The aesthetics of Monroe C. Beardsley: Recent work. *Studies in Art Education, 25*(3), 141–150.

Smith, R. A. (Ed.). (1989a). *Discipline-based art education: Origins, meaning, and development*. Urbana: University of Illinois Press.

Smith, R. A. (1989b). *The sense of art: A study in aesthetic education*. New York: Routledge.

Smith, R. A. (1992). Toward percipience: A humanities interpretation for arts education. In B. Reimer & R. A. Smith (Eds.), *The arts, education, and aesthetic knowing* (pp. 51–69). 91st Yearbook of the National Society for the Study of Education, Pt. 2. Chicago: University of Chicago Press.

Smith, R. A. (1995). *Excellence II: The continuing quest in art education*. Reston, VA: National Art Education Association.

Smith, R. A. (1998). Contemporary aesthetic education. In *Encyclopedia of aesthetics* (Vol. 4, pp. 93–96). New York: Oxford University Press.

Smith, R. A. (Ed.). (2000). *Readings in discipline-based art education: A literature of educational reform*. Reston, VA: National Art Education Association.

Smith, R. A. (2001). Aesthetic education. *International encyclopedia of the social and behavioral sciences*. (Vol. 1, pp. 206–210). New York: Elsevier Science.

Smith, R. A. (2001). Culture in a bind. *Arts Education Policy Review 102*(3), 37–39.

Smith, R. A., & Levi, A. W. (1991) *Art education: A critical necessity*. Urbana: University of Illinois Press.

Smith, R. A., & Simpson, A. (Eds.). (1991). *Aesthetics and arts education*. Urbana: University of Illinois Press.

Steiner, G. (1985, November 8). Viewpoint: A new meaning of meaning. *Times Literary Supplement*, p. 1262.

Stewart, M. (1997). *Thinking through aesthetics*. Worcester, MA: Davis Publications.

Stinespring, J. A. (2001). Preventing art education from becoming "a handmaiden to the social sciences." *Arts Education Policy Review, 102*(4), 11–18.

Swanger, D. (1990). *Essays in aesthetic education*. San Francisco: Mellon Research University Press.

Tanner, L. N. (1997). *Dewey's laboratory school: Lessons for today*. New York: Teachers College Press.

Thistlewood, D. (1984). *Herbert Read: Formlessness and form: An introduction to his aesthetics*: Boston: Routledge & Kegan Paul.

Travers, R. M. W. (1974). *Empirically based teacher education*. Occasional Paper 1. Society of Professors of Education. Minneapolis: College of Education, University of Minnesota.

Travers, R. M. W. (1979). Training the teacher as a performing artist. *Contemporary Education, 51*(1), 14–18.

Vandenberg, D. (Guest Ed.). (1992). Essays in honor of Harry S. Broudy [Special Issue] *Journal of Aesthetic Education, 26*(4).

Wasson. R. (1969). Herbert Read now: A salutation to eros. *Journal of Aesthetic Education, 3*(4), 11–25.

Wilsmore, S. J. (1987). The new attack on humanism in the arts. *British Journal of Aesthetics, 27*(4), 335–344.

Wilson, B. (1971). Evaluation of learning in art education. In B. Bloom, J. T. Hastings, & G. F. Madaus (Eds.), *Handbook of formative and summative evaluation of student learning* (pp. 499–558). New York: McGraw-Hill.

Wilson, B. (1997). *The quiet evolution: Changing the face of art education*. Los Angeles: Getty Education Institute for the Arts.

Winner, E., & Hetland, L. (Guest Eds.). (2000). The arts and academic achievement: What the evidence shows. [Special Issue] *Journal of Aesthetic Education, 34*(3–4).

9

Varieties of Multicultural Art Education: Some Policy Issues

H. Gene Blocker
Ohio University

This paper reviews the wide-ranging debate concerning multicultural art education since its inception just over a decade ago. Various senses of multicultural art education are reviewed, along with different measures of the extent to which minority art and culture need to be integrated into and separated from the dominant culture; and, finally, competing conceptions of the emphasis needed in multicultural art education of political engagement and aesthetic detachment. In the process, some suggestions are offered for future policy decisions.

INTRODUCTION

In order to see multicultural art education in its proper perspective, we need to step back for a moment and consider why we offer art education in the first place. First of all, we should have to admit that in all education there is an inevitable measure of tradition and inertia; we do it like this because this is how we have always done it (or as far back as we can collectively remember), not because we have good reasons for doing so. This is not necessarily or entirely wrong; what has worked in the past surely contains some value. Nonetheless, it is always useful, from time to time, to take a long, hard, critical look at what precisely we are trying to accomplish (and whether we are succeeding).

Art education practice is partly an effort to give children a chance to express themselves, to explore their talents in drawing, painting, and so forth. This is what we might call the "practical" side of art education. But we are also trying to help youngsters become more informed and appreciative of the artworld, and that involves knowledge of artists, styles of art, history of art, and so on. This represents the more "theoretical" side of art education—the sort of thing encouraged by advocates of discipline-based art education (DBAE).

But why engage in the latter? What are we trying to accomplish on the more theoretical side of art education? We do this partly out of a sense of promoting the "liberal arts"—the idea that this sort of informed appreciation and taste "liberates" an individual, hopefully enabling individuals to better enjoy paintings, music, theater, and so forth, and thereby enrich their lives. This is an old but still very good reason, and one we might see as the more "private" side of art appreciation.

But we also want to help young people assimilate into their own culture, and this is the more "public" side of art education. This is why students in Korea will learn more of the history of Korean art than that of, say, North Africa. In China today there is a considerable effort to introduce Chinese aesthetic education as a means of developing a sense of national solidarity.

And this brings us to the question, why then *multi*cultural art education? Because our (North American) culture *is* multicultural, meaning that it cannot be narrowly specified religiously or ethnically or racially (in the sense in which the virtually monolithic cultures of Japan or Kuwait, e.g., very nearly can). And this is for two reasons: The first is that our culture is the product of many different ethnic groups settling in North America over several centuries, and the second is due to the amazing "shrinking world" phenomenon. Every child needs to have some sense of Arabic, Japanese, Chinese, and African contemporary cultures as part of the world with which they, as Americans, must interact. Even if we did not have millions of Islamic students in our classes in America, the events of September 11 make clear our need to learn more about and to teach our students more about Islam. Of course, this involves more than art education, but it certainly includes art, and art is a good place to begin with young children.

We sometimes lose sight of the fact that we have already constructed two enormous multicultural integrations. First were the many European ethnic groups into one "Western" or "European," albeit English-speaking, culture; and second were the many perceived racial groups of the late 19th and early 20th centuries into one "white," mainly "European" group.

In the early years of American settlement, our culture was predominantly British, of course; but long before independence American culture had become heavily influenced by Dutch, German, French, and other European nationalities; and through territorial conquest, what we now call "Hispanic" (itself a cultural mix of Spanish and Native American); and still later, Russian Jews, Mediterranean, and Slavic peoples. Imagine if Ben Franklin (who in the 18th century worried about Germanic influence) were alive today, he would see a broadly "Europeanized" American culture vastly transcending British culture.

We need to reflect on this long and remarkable process of assimilation that has been racially as well as culturally integrative. At one point in the nation's history, Anglo-Saxon was regarded as a superior "race," in competition, not with Asian or African races, but with Celtic (Irish), Italian, Slavic, Jewish peoples. As late as the early 20th century, these were considered separate races. One obvious sign of assimilation is that all these are now seen as one white race, embodying, more or less, one European culture. Before Hispanic became an accepted term for classifying Americans, Spanish-speaking citizens of that part of the United States which had formerly been part of Mexico, successfully petitioned American census authorities to classify them as white—similarly for people from the Indian subcontinent (on the grounds that they are, after all, of "Aryan" descent). In other words, there has already been an enormous assimilative construction. After the Second World War, many American young people felt the need to see Europe and not just Scotland or Poland from whence their ancestors hailed, but Europe. In short, the primary cultural roots of white Americans are European.

And that cultural construction (from British to European) remains the biggest part of America's cultural roots—not only in terms of population but also in terms of contribution to American culture. It would be a serious mistake to discount that. But because that is not the whole story of American cultural history, the process of assimilation and integration must continue. Specifically, the study of European art and culture must now be complimented with that of non-European art and culture which has significantly contributed to North American culture—Native American, African, Hispanic, Chinese, Indian, Jewish, and Arabic. The contribution of Africa to American culture is obvious and overwhelming. Less pronounced has been the integration into American culture of various Native American roots, early Chinese immigrants; and later, Vietnamese, Japanese, Korean, and Indian, not to mention millions of immigrants from various Islamic countries. There are now more Muslims in the United States than there are Jews, and if this should strike us as surprising, it is only because Muslims have not yet become as well assimilated into mainstream American culture as have the Jews. Most non-Jewish school children will know a little something about Chanukah, for example; but most will either know nothing about Ramadan or think of it as something practiced in countries outside the United States.

Today, although many Americans find a comforting sense of identity in their supposed racial origins, race continues to decline as a concept of any serious scientific import at the same time as more and more Americans choose to identify their racial designation as "Mixed." The task of constructing a still greater cultural integration beyond the broadly white European American culture must therefore continue. The question is, how to accomplish this?

MULTICULTURALISM AS DIVERSITY, EQUALITY, AND A RELATIVISED AESTHETICS

Now after more than a decade of multicultural art education, it is time to take a careful look at what multicultural art education has become. The first thing to note is that it is still far from clear what "multicultural art education" means; a review of the recent literature reveals many quite different objectives under this one umbrella. As Elizabeth Manley Delacruz writes (1996), "Multiculturalism, by definition, refuses to be just one thing" (p. 92).

Of course, it means primarily increasing diversity instead of concentrating exclusively or almost exclusively on European "high art" since the Renaissance (and art before and after which influenced and was influenced by that). The objective is to consider non-European art—the art of Asians, Africans, Arabic/Islamic, and Native Americans. But this goal of increased diversity can itself lead to at least two quite different goals, as Anita Silvers notes (1999, p. 95), either to *exclude* supposedly racist or sexist Western artworks (e.g., *Huckleberry Finn*, *Venus de Milo*) or to *include* more non-European artworks (and, of course, with a limited curricular timetable, to do the latter inevitably involves the former). This is especially important, as Silvers points out, in countries such as the United States and Canada whose population is increasingly diverse and which therefore requires a pedagogy that is "responsive to the growing diversity of the population" (p. 95). As Peter Smith (1994) puts it, "Sooner or later, practices of the schools must reflect the will of a changing population" (p. 13). And as Bob Milgrom said in an informal discussion, "American culture *is* Multicultural."

But that apparently innocuous first move immediately introduces vexed theoretical considerations as to why European art has been privileged all these centuries, involving as it does the presumed status of the art critical standards by which European art is considered superior (and why high European art is considered better than European folk art). Otherwise it is not easy to explain why we would want to expand our art curriculum to include art that was inferior. If we have a good standard, which has been used to establish a canon of the best art in the world, why would we possibly want to change that?

The need for this shift in attention is clearly shown in John A. Stinespring's (1996) "Moving from First-stage to Second-stage Multiculturalism in the Art Classroom." The first stage is simply including many non-European artworks and art traditions previously excluded (and excluding some from the European canon to make room for the new additions). But as Stinespring notes, "those admitted must endure comparison in terms of criteria upon which the previously admitted had been recognized. . . . As a result, they may seem to be second-rate. . . As a result, negative stereotypes might be reinforced rather than dispelled" (p. 50). In the second stage, we have to reexamine (and alter) our criteria, "examining our own unacknowledged assumptions and biases," as Joanna Frueh (1991) writes of feminist art criticism, "developing ways to write about art that will serve as new models for art critical discourse" (p. 50).

Thus, we come to the second common objective of most multiculturalists, which is that of introducing a diversity of non-European art as *equal in value* to European art. As Silvers (1999) puts it, "doing so means embracing the idea that the beliefs, values, and practices of all cultures are equally important" (p. 95). But if so, then we cannot avoid the vexing theoretical question of whether there are multicultural art critical standards for distinguishing good from mediocre art as opposed to a single universal set of standards which privilege European art. If we are committed to the objective of presenting diverse art of diverse cultures as having equal aesthetic worth, then we may have to embrace a relativized notion of artistic excellence—different art from different cultures being equally valuable for different cultural reasons.

DOES MULTICULTURAL ART REQUIRE A MULTICULTURAL AESTHETICS?

Clearly, if we are to encourage both diversity and the notion of relative equality, then we have to be more open to diverse standards of artistic excellence. As Delacruz (1995) argues, this does not mean aesthetic anarchy or nihilism, but a new more expansive aesthetics: "What multicultural art education teaches is that there is no single universal aesthetic" (p. 58). K. A. Hamblen (1991) makes a similar point. Paulette Spruill-Flemming (1990, 1991) and Graeme Sullivan (1993) also emphasize the need to get away from the Eurocentric notion of judging the value of artworks by autonomous aesthetic standards (art for art's sake, aesthetically detached or distanced from other, nonaesthetic everyday considerations—the romantic idea of the lonely artist struggling outside of and often contrary to the larger society). Instead, they argue, we must begin to look at art in its larger sociopolitical–economic context, not just by adding a few non-European artworks but by looking at *all* art in this broader social context in terms of which art, including non-European art, will be judged by its role in the larger social context. As Delacruz (1995) says, "Multicultural art education is a reconceptualization of the nature of art itself and our manner of interacting with it" (p. 59) (also see Ambush, 1993; Collins & Sandell, 1992; Hart, 1991; Sullivan, 1993).

Doug Blandy and Kristin Congdon (1987) also argue that art criticism must "recognize the cultural, political, sociological, ecological and economic aspects of art" (p. 15). Adrienne Hoard (1990) stresses the culturally relative development of different standards of appreciation and assessment. Christine Ballengee-Morris and Patricia L. Stuhr (2001) argue that art education must be based on a politically engaged social reconstructionist multicultural approach. Deborah Ambush (1993) thinks the emphasis should be on the student's development of a sense of self. Mary-Michael Billings (1995) proposes a twofold approach to multicultural art education, including both a more politically motivated "issues" orientation and a "thematic" approach that seeks to relate art to individual student's own life experiences. But in either case the move is away from an exclusive or predominant formalist focus on the art object, whether toward the social context or toward the inner self of the viewer (i.e., the student's sense of self).

On the other hand, some commentators have argued that multicultural art education does *not* necessitate a new aesthetic theory, but can be reconciled within a revised Western aesthetics. In particular, F. Graeme Chalmer's (1987) *Celebrating Pluralism: Art, Education, and Cultural Diversity* argues for the compatibility of the political standpoint of multicultural art education with the more traditional aesthetic detachment of DBAE. Silvers (1999) finds Chalmer's approach ultimately "futile," though she agrees with him that "multiculturalism's quintessential enabling ideas are central to, and therefore available within, the practice of the disciplines of aesthetics, art criticism and art history" (p. 102). The problem she finds with Chalmers is that he finds it necessary to achieve the desired integration of multicultural art education with traditional aesthetics (especially DBAE) by reducing aesthetics to sociology (thereby denying to aesthetics the relative autonomy which it traditionally enjoyed), which Silvers claims is neither necessary nor advisable. Nonetheless, both Silvers and Chalmers agree that traditional Western aesthetics, in one or more of its various forms, is adequate to deal with multicultural art.

My own sympathies lie with this last group of writers. As I have argued for many years (Blocker, 1993, 2000, 2001), there is no qualitative evolution (or "progress") of art and no major international kind of art that can in general be said to be intrinsically better than any other. As an enthusiastic admirer of traditional African, pre-Columbian meso-American, and ancient Chinese tomb art, I have argued and would maintain that, although we need to examine non-Western systems of aesthetics (for precisely the same reasons we need to be open to non-Western art and systems of thought generally), there is no reason to think that evaluating non-Western art by Western aesthetics standards will systematically show the inferiority of all non-Western art. The best of traditional African, Chinese, Indian, Native American art (especially that of Middle America) can hold its own against the best of Western art, even when judged by Western standards.

On the other hand, I have been criticized over the years for embracing the idea of a *general cultural* evolution. I do see an evolution from Old Stone Age hunting and gathering to New Stone Age agricultural to Bronze and Iron Age large-scale literate to industrialized and modern cultures. But I do *not* see modern culture as exclusively Western, though much of it originated there (witness Japan), any more than I can see Bronze and Iron Age culture be exclusively tied to the Middle East where it originated. Wherever they begin, world cultural movements sooner or later become multicultural and international.

Admittedly a delicate balancing act perhaps, nonetheless I think it is a mistake first to identify all Modernism with European culture; and second, either to denigrate European culture as the origin of the worst aspects of Modernism or to praise the superiority of European culture for the more positive aspects of Modernism.

It is also a mistake to think of all Western aesthetics as the formalist, New Criticism, art for art's sake sort which postmodern critics attack for its lack of social contextual relevance. Western aesthetics has been concerned with the issues of social and political engagement for at least a hundred years. We need to remind ourselves that Marxist and neo-Marxist aesthetics is not, after all, non-Western or anti-Western, but is itself a part of Western aesthetics. The precise degree of aesthetic autonomy and social relevance is a debate *within* Western aesthetics. When we introduce our students to *any* art, we should try to place it within its social and historical context, but this is no less true of Greek temple art than it is of Mayan ceremonial art. Nor should we think that any art that serves a nonaesthetic, utilitarian function cannot also serve an aesthetic function. This has also been long debated *within* Western aesthetics. Otherwise, insisting on the most narrow, purist formalist (New Criticism, art for art's sake) notion of "fine art" would exclude Greek, Roman, medieval Christian art, and indeed all Western art prior to the modern period (beginning roughly in the 16th century). And by the same token it is only through ignorance of non-Western aesthetics traditions that we assume there is no aesthetic tradition (of a relatively detached appreciation of art for art's sake) in certain periods of China and India.

Some investigators attempt to fill in the information gap that exists in our knowledge (or lack of knowledge) of non-European art. But this knowledge of roots must be accurate. All Americans, including African Americans, need to learn more about Africa (and so for Chinese, Jewish, Indian Americans). But we must never assume we know the essentials of European art and culture just because we are white; African art and culture, just because we are black; and so on; this realization must be carefully understood and our schools can and should help. Fortunately some art educators are working to improve this situation: Norman DePillars (1990), by showing how Native Americans and Africans have been misunderstood, and Jacqueline Chanda (1992, 1993), by admirably filling a large hole in our knowledge of African art and society. As both DePillars and Chanda argue, part of our misunderstanding is based on simplistic and inadequate stereotypes which reduce a wide variety of cultures and art styles within Native American groups and among various African tribal groups to one monolithic—and largely mistaken—cliché.

On the other hand, Dipti Desai (2000) argues that so-called attempts to achieve "accurate" and "authentic" representations of culture, of the sort we see in Chanda, and those of DePillars, may be just as Western-biased as those more obviously stereotyped and marginalized accounts they are meant to correct, especially where these more "accurate and authentic" accounts are associated with the display of non-Western art in metropolitan art museums. This position is strongly resisted by Renee Sandell and Cherry Schroeder (1994) and by Karen Branen and Kristin Congdon (1994), who support the role of the museum in promoting multiculturalism as a positive hopeful move. Because of my own experience in the Cleveland area, I would have to agree with this last group of writers. Surely one of the best ways to awaken the interests of Cleveland inner-city minority students in their cultural heritage is to show them in the most accurate way possible the arts and crafts of their African, Chinese, Indian, Native American, Arabic, and so forth, ancestors through various outreach programs of the Cleveland Museum of Art (including both visits to the museum and classroom visits by museum personnel). To complain that this approach presents the art of minority cultures through the European slant of the "art museum," however true, overlooks the larger point that this is surely the best, and in many cases the only, way to bring actual art works and trained experts to explain them to minority students. It is also a hopeful way to interest minority students (who will one day become adults) in the support of the museum that they can now see as a source of non-Western as well as Western art.

MULTICULTURALISM AS ANTI-WESTERN

If what was stated in the previous section is so, then several questions arise. First, why hasn't this been done before; and second, why is it being so vigorously resisted in some circles today? This leads many commentators to adopt a radical political and ideological stance that claims ignoring non-European art or treating it as inferior is part of the larger neocolonial agenda of Europeans to dominate non-Europeans. This is the neo-Marxist (or neo–neo-Marxist) view that the agenda of international economic interests is to exploit and oppress not only developing countries but also the poor and underprivileged in their own countries. This is the anti-Western side of multicultural education. Sometimes multiculturalism appears as a kind of self-hatred focused on European culture, including art, as though all the violence, greed, and selfishness in the world springs from that source and should now be overcome or at least ignored. Despite the fact that this geopolitical position is often assumed and taken for granted in discussions of multicultural art education, it should be seriously questioned. Insofar as Western culture tends to be identified with modern world culture, it is surely a mistake to encourage in our children a blanket hatred and rejection of Modernism in all its forms (from human rights and democracy to individualism and freedom), an ideal toward which the rest of the world aspires. Our approach must be more balanced and emphasize both positive (democratic) values and negative aspects (the legacy of slavery, colonialism, and other forms of economic exploitation).

Apart from its one-sidedness, the contrast usually drawn between European culture and other cultures is really an ancient contrast *within* a schizophrenic European culture, between the more rationalist, analytic aspect and the more romantic, holistic, intuitive, and poetic side of Western culture going back at least as far as Plato's reference to the ancient quarrel between poetry and philosophy. Whenever we (Westerners) become tired or disgusted with the more rationalist, analytic side of our own collective culture, we turn to other cultures for a confirmation of the romantic side of our own culture. It is questionable why, in our quest for diversity, we need to deny the contribution of Europeans in art, literature, philosophy, music, architecture, and so forth, to world culture.

Nonetheless this radical geopolitical agenda leads other writers to emphasize the need of art educators to demonstrate the role of art in combating contemporary social injustice in their own societies. Elizabeth Sacca (1993) urges art teachers to develop their students' understanding of the political role of the artist that often opposes and is opposed by society. Vincent Lanier (1987) and Jan Jagodzinski (1982) stress the role of art as promoting a program of radical social change. For example, Jagodzinski (1996) argued on Lacanian grounds that the multicultural program of the Getty Center for Education in the Arts (which has supported DBAE) was essentially racist. Arthur Efland (1997) points out, however, that Jagodzinski's comments were based on a single Getty advertisement and seemed more designed to capitalize quixotically on the stereotypical differences between big business (i.e., Getty, and therefore right-wing fascist) and himself as a left-wing liberal espousing radical ideas. Elliot W. Eisner (1998) also defends the Getty program, especially in its response to critics through the work of outgoing director Lielani Lattin Duke. We do need to stress the social and political character of art and artists (as Western aestheticians have been doing for at least 100 years), but we should acknowledge that much of this social-protest art is directed *against* antimodernist cultures (e.g., against restrictions on both women's rights and child slavery).

Without incorporating some sociological, anthropological, and political theories, as suggested earlier, with aesthetic theory, the presentation of a smorgasbord of bits and pieces of art objects from around the world—especially where this is an add-on to the main course of European art since the Renaissance—will only succeed in producing what Ralph Smith (1983) calls "ethnic tourism." Considered interesting but strange, exotic other art will inevitably take its place in student's minds as inferior to European art (which is after all the main thing). This is the distinction Keith Swanwick (1994) and others draw between "multicultural" and "intercultural." Multicultural often becomes, according to Swanwick, in reference to musical multiculturalism, a sort of "musical tribalism" in which those in one musical tradition observe from the outside bits and pieces of other musical traditions as interesting and exotic oddities without absorbing or entering into those other musical traditions. This, according to Swanwick, is very different from what some call "intercultural," which involves transcending one's own musical tradition in order to absorb elements of other musical traditions, making them, or at least parts of them, one's own, a view defended by Wayne Bowman (1994).

The problem here is the old problem of how to simultaneously achieve sufficient depth and breadth? How can art educators be expected to learn enough and spend enough class time teaching non-Western art forms without spreading themselves and their content too thin? For this reason Estelle R. Jorgensen (1988) urges Stanwick to "retreat to a less radical position and go along with the framers of the *National Standards for Arts Education* in suggesting that a few contrasting musical traditions be studied" (p. 81). Clearly, whatever approach one adopts, the project of multicultural art education is going to be much more involved and difficult than many have imagined. As Grant and Sleeter (1998) point out, "Many of those who embrace the concept [of multicultural art education] tend to oversimplify or understate the degree of change called for and are content with merely injecting a few folk customs and ethnic heroes into the curriculum" (p. 9). This is made even worse when these artworks are taken out of cultural context and reproduced in class projects, using empty milk cartons, for example; or students making Halloween-style African-like masks out of construction paper.

MULTICULTURALISM AS WESTERN HEGEMONY

This raises yet another sensitive issue. Many minorities do not want to assimilate into the majority culture which is their right which we should all respect. Many come to North America to earn some money or escape persecution and then return home; and while here, they maintain as high a degree of ethnic purity as possible. Although this is their right, it is not the bigger picture, not the longer, mainstream history of America, which is the story of assimilation. Generally, as soon as their children are born in America, they become part of the assimilative process. The new talk about multicultural diversity should not blind us to the historical fact that it took generations for other groups of Americans to assimilate, for example, the Greek, Polish, and Italian ethnic groups. The idea that ethnic groups used to assimilate quickly but now demand more cultural separation is historically questionable. German communities in Texas continued to speak German for over a hundred years. At various points in America's history there were factories in which Italian or Croatian was exclusively spoken. However, eventually these groups did assimilate and it is no less true today. More likely, the "melting pot" has never melted quickly, but melt it did and continues to do so today. Perhaps the main difference is that ethnic groups today may seek a different balance between integration and cultural separation. They seek to teach their children the languages and customs from their countries of origin, for example, and thereby enrich American culture.

For this reason many minority cultures do not perceive and do not want to perceive their own art as a relativised segment of international diversity to be taken up by art students in a playful Disneyland-type construction program. Sometimes on pain of death or dismemberment, African masks were not to be seen by anyone, even of the same tribal society, who was not a member of that secret society. They were sacred objects whose power needed to be respected. Is it fair, some writers ask, to require these societies to "give up" their objects for the casual, playful, entertaining role of diversity education?

Ironically, or paradoxically, as Taylor, Gutmann, Rockefeller, Walzer, and Wolf (1992) point out in *Multiculturalism and "The Politics of Recognition,"* the whole conception and ideal of diversity and equality (with the relativistic notions these ideas imply) are European, liberal, democratic ideals. James Banks (1993) has also argued that multicultural education is based on and is a logical extension of modern Western ideals of democracy and equality. Delacruz (1995) discusses "the democratic principles upon which multiculturalism is based: equity, diversity, and social justice" (p. 57). As Peter Smith (1994) puts it:

> The United States was founded during the so-called Age of Enlightenment, and white Americans in general have internalized certain enlightenment notions. Among these is the idea that persons can somehow stand outside their own life experiences. Is this in itself a Western imperialist notion? If it is, then certain strands in multiculturalistic thinking are a priori tainted. (p.140)

This is the positive side of Modernism discussed earlier.

Another irony is that in order to avoid Eurocentric hegemony, we are forcing a European ideal on non-European cultures fighting for their collective lives, that is, aborigines of Australia, Maoris of New Zealand, African traditionalists, and Native Americans in North, Central, and South America. As Ronald N. MacGregor (1994) writes:

> At what point does talk about we, the family, or we, the tribe, become talk about we, the people? How does one reconcile the egalitarian tradition of liberal democracy implied in "we the people" with the arguments of interest groups who insist that their survival as a group depends on their being accorded special status? (pp. 4–5)

The same problem affects the multicultural treatment of Islamic art and culture whose adherents may be opposed to the modern liberal, enlightenment idea that all religions and cultures are equal. Indeed, Stuart Richmond (1995) argues that the democratic Western liberal perspective of American public schools is probably not a good way to present multicultural art education, especially as it tends to emphasize sociopolitical concerns at the expense of artistic and aesthetic concerns. This liberal tradition is but one of many world traditions, and because non-Western art arises within these other world traditions, it should be interpreted according to these other world traditions and not be biased from a Western point of view.

Nonetheless, despite the need to be sensitive to perceptions of various minority communities, we cannot and should not abandon, but embrace, the Modernist foundations of multiculturalism, for the entire agenda of multicultural art education is based on the liberal, democratic ideal of the integration of diverse cultures treated as equals.

MULTICULTURALISM AS CULTURAL SEPARATION OR INTEGRATION

In schools of mainly minority students, multiculturalism has come to mean an emphasis on Black or Hispanic art and culture as a way to restore the damaged self-esteem of these students outside the dominant culture. Here African American students learn about African culture; Native American students study Native American art; and so on. As Sandra C. Dilger (1994) points out:

> For the child with non-Western parents, the impact of a Western curriculum on that student's self-concept, sense of pride, and cultural knowledge can be adverse.... Unfortunately, instead of combining to form a new people in a new land, most of the immigrant and ethnic groups that have come to America 'stick to the bottom' of the proverbial melting pot. (p. 50)

Although, as Anna M. Kindler (1994) points out, such an approach actually "limits the ability of a child exposed to cultural variety from birth, to select, define, and construct a personal cultural heritage from all that is available in a culturally diversified environment" (p. 54). She mentions her personal experience with her son who became very involved with Haida images when the family moved to Canada.

One sense of multiculturalism is therefore to let children and their families select the art and culture of their own supposed heritage. If they are African American they will concentrate on African art; if they are Jewish Americans, Jewish art and culture; and so on. I would join those authors who challenge this conception, arguing that children need to learn and assimilate the art and culture of their respective countries (and art and culture of the United States contains more than African and Jewish elements, though it includes these ingredients), and also because in most cases students have a mixed heritage. How many African Americans have no non-African ancestors? How many Jewish Americans have zero non-Semitic ancestors? I am not referring only to blood lines, for many African American and Jewish American families lived for centuries in North America and Europe. Not all pride in one's heritage is bad, of course, and Jewish Americans and African Americans and Chinese Americans have a right to know about and feel some pride in the artistic culture of their ancestors. But this should not be limited to their remote pre-American ancestors but should also include the contributions to American culture of their American-born ancestors, including, for example, 100 years of Chinese opera in San Francisco; a wealth of Jewish American comedy, entertainment, and literature; and African American jazz, blues, and gospel music.

As Aristotle said of becoming virtuous, it is a matter of striking the right balance—it takes practice and continuous readjustment. Currently many Jewish Americans are turning more to their Jewish roots, whereas many African Americans are turning away from a narrow Afrocentrism. How much written and spoken Chinese language should Chinese Americans learn? The main point is that there is room for both the attempt to cling to cultural roots and the attempt to contribute to an enlarging American culture. This can be done by bringing new meaning to these newer designations: "Jewish American," "African American," and "Chinese American." Hernandez (1993), Marantz (1993), and Feinstein (1989) also object that an exclusivist notion of cultural pluralism is divisive and will balkanize the nation. As Peter Smith (1994) points out, one problem with this approach to multicultural art education is that it is not only divisive, pitting minority against dominant culture, but also frustrating for African Americans who have little real knowledge or sense of African culture and thus find it difficult if not impossible to identify with Africa beyond simplistic stereotypes. Surely better, as Smith suggests, would be a study of the contributions of African Americans to mainstream American culture. "In the case of African American heritage, accessible identification might be more feasible through the study of great musicians and visual artists who grew up in American culture" (p. 17). This would have the added benefit of integrating African American students into the larger American culture where they must, after all, sink or swim in their individual struggles for success in life.

These writers urge an alternative (to which I would add my voice): Give all American students a sense of the diversity of their American cultural roots. The emphasis here should be not only to give each student a sense of the cultural contributions of all ethnic groups which have made a significant contribution to American art and culture but also to show how these different ethnic groups made that contribution through assimilation within the broader American culture. Jazz and blues are good examples, and although they have African roots, they are also played on European, not African, instruments (e.g., cornet, clarinet, banjo, guitar, and piano) and incorporate European musical scales and harmonies. Consider the example of American gospel music. At first it might seem that this is a distinctively African contribution to American religion, but we must also consider the evangelical movement in 17th-century Britain as various Protestant groups broke with the Church of England, encouraging "enthusiasm," speaking in tongues of the Quakers, Shakers, and others, emphasizing the Holy Spirit entering the heart of the individual believer, producing spontaneous emotional expressions of religiosity, traditions which are still alive and well in America today, not only in Black churches but also in Southern and Appalachian white churches.

CONCLUSION

As many art educators have thus recognized, there are many quite different goals grouped together under the general heading of multiculturalism. Collins and Sandell (1992) mention four such goals that provide us with a good summary of what we have been saying. These are the goals of "attack multiculturalism" in which the dominant culture is criticized for its neocolonial hegemony; "escape multiculturalism" in which the malevolent dominant culture is simply ignored in favor of more friendly cultures; "transformative multiculralism," which selects the best parts of different cultures and tries to blend them together into a kinder and more gentle culture; and "repair multiculturalism," which seeks to improve the self-image of minority students damaged by the dominant culture.

No wonder, then, says Delacruz (1995), that so many "myths, misconceptions, misdirections" surround multicultural art education. In Banks's (1993) discussion, four such myths stand out: that multicultural education is only for victimized minorities, that all multicultural education is opposed to Western culture, that all multicultural education is divisive, and that in any event multicultural education is a fad that will pass. After a decade of intense debate and experimental educational practice, we can see that this is certainly not a fad that will soon pass. Rather we have entered a time of sober reflection and consolidation, and above all a time to seek consensus, balance, and good sense.

In my review of the work of many contributors to multicultural art education over the past decade, I have tried to articulate what I see as the "logic," or "argument," which seems to lead from the need for diversity to an anti-Western ideology. In my view, for reasons I have stressed here, the need for diversity is undeniable; and this need does indeed lead "logically" to the respecting of diverse artistic cultures as being of equal value. But I have argued that this does *not* reasonably lead, as many have supposed, to a rejection of Western aesthetics, Western art, or Western values. Above all, I have argued, this should not lead us to interpret multicultural art education as an attempt to segregate students by their supposed minority cultural roots, that is, African art for African-American students, Hispanic art for Hispanic students, and so on. Instead, we should continue to move in the direction of exploring the diverse cultural roots of American culture, especially of American art, for example the African roots of American music which are of vital interest for *all* our students to know. I have also stressed the need for genuine, "authentic" knowledge of non-Western art and culture and the important role that metropolitan museums can play in providing that knowledge base. In the process, I would hope that we would recover a better understanding not only of non-Western aesthetics standards but also of the breadth and diversity *within* Western aesthetics.

AUTHOR NOTE

As a philosopher specializing in aesthetics, two things have brought me into the thick of the debate surrounding multicultural and cross-cultural art and art education. The first was Ralph Smith's invitation to join with Michael Parsons in writing the aesthetics "discipline" book, *Aesthetics and Education* (University of Illinois Press, 1993) for the Discipline-Based Art Education series. The second was my long-standing interest in non-Western art, especially that of West Africa and Pre-Columbian Central America, and the ancient art of China (*The Aesthetics of Primitive Art*, University Press of America, 1994), which, in turn, led to my interest in non-Western aesthetics (*Contemporary Chinese Aesthetics*, coedited with Zhu Liyuan, Peter Lang, 1995), and the symposium which I organized and to which I contributed, "Non-Western Aesthetics" *The Journal of Aesthetic Education, 35*(4), 2001 (which included African, Chinese, and Native American aesthetics). As a result of all this I am often asked to teach a required course in philosophy of art for art education majors. In all these ways I have been very happily drawn into the contentious fray of multicultural and cross-cultural art education.

REFERENCES

Ambush, D. (1993). Points of intersection: The convergence of aesthetics and race as phenomenon of experience in the lives of African American children. *Visual Arts Research, 19*(2), 13–23.

Ballengee-Morris, C., & Stuhr, P. L. (2001). Multicultural art and visual culturaleducation in a changing world. *Art Education, 54*(4), 6–13.

Banks, J. A. (1993). Multicultural education: Development, dimensions, and challenges. *Phi Delta Kappan, 75*(1), 22–28.

Billings, M. (1995). Issues vs. themes: Two approaches to a multicultural art curriculum. *Art Education, 48*(1), 21–24.

Blandy, D., & Congdon, K. G. (1987). *Art in a democracy.* New York: Teachers College Press.

Blocker, H. G. (1993). Aesthetic value in cross-cultural, multicultural art study. *Art Education Policy Review, 95*(3), 26–29.

Blocker, H. G. (2000). "Art Education and Postmodernism." In R. A. Smith (Ed.), *Readings in discipline-based art education: A literature of educational reform* (pp. 370–373). Reston, VA: National Art Education Association.

Blocker, H. G. (2001). Non-Western Aesthetics. [Symposium]. *The Journal of Aesthetic Education, 35*(4).

Bowman, W. (1994). *Music without universals: Relativism reconsidered.* Paper presented to the Philosophy of Music Education: International Symposium II, University of Toronto.

Branen, K., & Congden, K. (1994). An elementary school museum celebrates community diversity. *Art Education, 47*(4), 8–12.

Chalmers, F. G. (1987). *Celebrating Pluralism: Art, Education, and Cultural Diversity.* Occaisional paper 5. The Getty Education Institute for the Arts.

Chalmers, F. G. (1987). Culturally based versus universally based understanding of art. In D. Blandy & K. G. Congdon (Eds.), *Art in a democracy* (pp. 4–12). New York: Teachers College Press.

Chanda, J. E. (1992). Alternative concepts and terminologies for teaching African art. *Art Education, 45*(1), 56–61.

Chanda, J. E. (1993). *African arts and cultures.* Worcester, MA: Davis.

Collins, G., & Sandell, R. (1992). The politics of multicultural education. *Art Education, 45*(6), 8–13.

Delacruz, E. M. (1995). Multiculturalism and art education: Myths, misconceptions, misdirect ions. *Art Education, 48*(3), 57–61.

Delacruz, E. M. (1996). Approaches to multiculturalism in art education curriculum products: Business as usual. *The Journal of Aesthetic Education, 30*(1), 85–97.

DePillars, N. (1990). Multiculturalism in visual arts education: Are America's educational institutions ready for multiculturalism? In B. Young (Ed.), *Art, culture and ethnicity* (pp. 115–134). Reston, VA: National Art Education Association.

Desai, D. (2000). Imaging difference: The politics of representation in multiculturalart education. *Studies in Art Education, 41*(2), 114–129.

Dilger, S. C. (1994). Developing policy and programs for multicultural art education: Curriculum and instruction responsive to cultural diversity. *Art Education, 47*(7), 49–53.

Efland, A. (1997). The demonization of the Getty Education Institute for the Arts: A commentary. *Studies in Art Education, 39*(1), 89–91.

Eisner, E. W. (1998). The Getty Education Institute for the Arts. *Studies in Art Education, 40*(1), 4–7.

Feinstein, H. (1989). Beware the chant of pluralistic pluralism. *Art Education, 42*(6), 6–7.

Frueh, J. (1991). Towards a feminist theory of art criticism. In H. Smagula (Ed.), *Revisions: New perspectives of art criticism* (pp. 50–64). Englewood Cliffs, NJ: Prentice-Hall.

Grant, C., & Sleeter, C. E. (1998). *Turning on learning: Five approaches for multicultural teaching plans for race, class, gender, and disability* (2nd ed.). Upper Saddle River, NJ: Prentice-Hall.

Hamblen, K. A. (1991). Beyond universalism in art criticism. In D. Blandy & K. G. Congdon (Eds.), *Pluralistic approaches to art criticism* (pp. 7–14). Bowling Green, OH: Bowling Green State University Popular Press.

Hart, L. M. (1991). Aesthetic pluralism and multicultural art education. *Studies in Art Education, 32*(3), 145–159.

Hernandez, F. (1993). From multiculturalism to *Mestizaje* in world culture. *VisualArts Research, 19*(2), 1–12.

Hoard, A. W. (1990). The black aesthetic: An empirical feeling. In B. Young (Ed.), *Art, culture and ethnicity* (pp. 155–168). Reston, VA: National Art Education Association.

Jagodzinski, J. (1982). Art education as ethnology: Deceptive democracy or a new panacea? *Studies in Art Education, 23*(3), 5–9.

Jagodzinski, J. (1997). The nostalgia of art education: Reinscribing the master's narrative. *Studies in Art Education, 38*(2), 80–95.

Jorgensen, E. R. (1998). Musical multiculturalism revisited. *The Journal of Aesthetic Education, 32*(2), 77–88.

Kindler, A. M. (1994). Children and the culture of a multicultural society. *Art Education, 47*(7), 54–60.

Lanier, V. (1987). Misdirect ions and realignments. In D. Blandy & K. G. Congdon (Eds.), *Art in a democracy* (pp. 4–12). New York: Teachers College Press.

MacGregor, R. N. (1994). Diversity and divisiveness. *Art Education, 47*(7), 4–5.

Marantz, K. A. (1993). *Multicultural myths in a politically correct era.* Paper presented at the 1993 International Society for Education through Art World Congress, August, Montreal, Canada.

Richmond, S. (1995). Liberalism, multiculturalism, and art education. *The Journal of Aesthetic Education, 29*(3), 15–25.

Sacca, E. J. (1993). Art, native voice, and political crisis: Reflections on art education and the survival of culture at Kanehsatake. *Visual Arts Research, 19*(2), 35–43.

Sandell, R., & Schroeder, C. (1994). Talking about art: From past to present, here to there: Preservice art teachers' collaborations with a museum. *Art Education, 47*(4), 18–24.

Silvers, A. (1999). Multiculturalism and the aesthetics of recognition: Reflections on *Celebrating Pluralism, The Journal of Aesthetic Education, 33*(1), 95–103.

Smith, P. (1994). Multicultural Issues: Dilemmas and hopes. *Art Education, 47*(7), 13–17.

Smith, R. A. (1983). Forms of multi-cultural education in the arts. *Journal of Multicultural and Cross-Cultural Research in Art, 1*(1), 23–32.

Spruill-Flemming, P. (1990). Linking the legacy: Approaches to the teaching of African and American art. In B. Young (Ed.), *Art, culture and ethnicity* (pp. 135–154). Reston, VA: National Art Education Association.

Spruill-Flemming, P. (1991). Pluralism in African American aesthetics and art criticism. In D. Blandy & K. G. Congdon (Eds.), *Pluralistic approaches to art criticism* (pp. 60–65). Bowling Green, OH: Bowling Green State University Popular Press.

Stinespring, J. A. (1996). Moving from first-stage to second-stage multiculturalism in the art classroom. *Art Education, 49*(7), 48–53.

Sullivan, G. (1993). Art-based art education: Learning that is meaningful, authentic, critical, and pluralist. *Studies in Art Education, 35*(1), 5–21.

Swanwick, K. (1994). *Musical knowledge: Intuition, analysis and musical education.* London: Routledge.

Taylor, C., Gutmann, A., Rockefeller, S., Walzer, M., & Wolf, S. (1992*). Multiculturalism and "the politics of recognition."* Princeton, NJ: Princeton University Press.

10

Museum Education and Controversial Art: Living on a Fault Line

E. Louis Lankford
University of Missouri-St. Louis

Kelly Scheffer
*University of Missouri-St. Louis,
and St. Charles Community College*

No art museum is immune from the risk of controversy associated with works of art, regardless of the nature of the museum's collections or exhibitions. Controversy usually arises when individuals who are unaffiliated with a museum judge an exhibited work of art to be egregiously offensive and take action to undermine the museum's authority to determine the content of its galleries. An artwork is most commonly judged to be offensive if it violates dominant beliefs, values, tastes, and mores of society, especially those pertaining to sex or religion. It is argued that art controversies are partially by-products of audience development aimed at building a larger and more diverse visitor base and a willingness by museums to accept more risks with exhibitions of contemporary art. To illustrate their points, the authors describe circumstances of a controversy that flared when the Museum of International Folk Art exhibited Our Lady, an artwork by Alma López that triggered strong reactions from the Hispanic Catholic community of Santa Fe, New Mexico. Throughout the paper, reference is made to special challenges that museum educators, both staff and volunteer docents, face during a controversy. In the final sections, the authors provide a number of concrete proposals for how museums, and museum educators in particular, can effectively prepare for and respond to controversy.

Let us begin with a fundamental assertion: *Any work of art may be controversial.* As any veteran art museum educator can verify, the reality is that however much people may agree with each other, they still collectively hold an infinite variety of opinions, values, and perceptions. Nowhere is this more evident than in responses to works of art. No artwork is so mundane or so innocuous as to be exempt from stirring the fires of indignation; no artwork is so laudable as to be immune from critical scrutiny and condemnation. Most of the time people can tolerate differences of opinion concerning art, but from time to time those differences can become almost unbearable. When works of art for one reason or another perturb people in the extreme, such that lines are drawn and defensive and offensive actions are taken by opposing sides, it is a case of controversial art. Fortunately extreme cases are relatively rare, but when they do occur they can rock artistic careers, shake up entire museums, and cause the artworld to quake.

For museum educators it is like living on a fault line; when an earthquake hits they are near the epicenter because it is their responsibility to address questions of interpretation and value raised by the public concerning artworks exhibited in their museums. Like anyone living on a fault line, it is advisable to prepare for the possibility of earthquakes and to have a plan of response if one occurs.

Controversial art is not altogether a bad thing. Impassioned dialog fuels the exploration and examination of ideas that make a difference in the way people think about, value, and live with art. Thoughtful and challenging dialogs are vital for sustaining meaningful relationships within the artworld and between the artworld and other segments of society. Unfortunately, when art becomes controversial, the dialog can cease to be constructive. People on either side of an issue can react fervidly or contemptuously and, as often as not, unpredictably.

For museum administrators, trustees, curators, and educators the stress does not end when the controversy does. This eyewitness account by curatorial administrator Lonnie Bunch (1995), who was referring to the spate of museum controversies that occurred in the late 1980s and early 1990s, applies as much today as when it was written: "The recent controversy over museum exhibits has left many in the profession uncertain, angry, and fearful. They wonder whether this criticism is a momentary storm or the dawning of an Ice Age of conservative change and control" (p. 34). Bunch asserted that museums would be making a mistake if they attempted to tip-toe around the continuing threat of controversy instead of facing it head on: "Much of the current controversy and debate revolves around profound issues and central questions that will shape and inform the direction, role, and importance of museums for many years to come" (p. 34). In art museums, those issues and questions revolve around what may or may not be exhibited, conditions under which art may be exhibited, and the scope of educational products and programs associated with exhibitions.

American museums are in many ways dependent on public opinion, and this dependence applies to more than funding. The people who step through a museum's doors provide the opportunity for the museum to realize its mission of education and service. Museums are trusted institutions of society, to whom the public looks for answers and enlightenment. Controversial art represents a perceived breach in that trust by those who feel offended, and it is in the museum's best interest to vigorously pursue a resolution of the dispute. Everyone who works at the museum is a stakeholder, and in a sense, every member of society is too, for when a museum is under fire its abilities to represent the artworld and fully and effectively serve the community are at risk.

On the following pages the nature of controversial art will be examined, particularly as it affects museum educators. It is argued that art controversy is in part a by-product of art museums' reaching out for larger and more diverse audiences, as well as an inclination by curators to take more risks with exhibitions. Art is most commonly judged to be controversial by an audience if it violates accepted beliefs, values, and mores of society, especially those pertaining to sex or religion. Each of these elements contributed to a controversy that flared up when the Museum of International Folk Art (MOIFA) exhibited *Our Lady,* a digital photo-collage print by Alma López. How this artwork became the center of controversy, and the museum's response to the crisis, makes for an interesting and enlightening story. In the final sections of this paper, strategies are proposed that address ways museums can prepare for and respond to controversy.

DIVERSITY AND EXHIBITION RISK FACTORS FOR CONTROVERSY

It seems clear that museums are more at risk than ever before of inadvertently stirring up troubles for themselves. As one museum executive pointed out when talking about controversy, "It's not a matter of *if* it's going to happen to you; it's a matter of *when*" (cited in Platt, 1990, p. 40). Ironically, good intentions can net both positive and negative consequences. Good intentions have motivated audience development at museums, as well as the willingness to exhibit cutting-edge and nonmainstream art. But has there been a price to pay?

"Paying" for Audience Development

For quite some time, art museums have been earnestly working to open their doors to a broader audience, to count among their visitors a more diverse mix of citizens that are truly representative of the communities they serve. As outlined in a policy statement adopted by the American Association of Museums (AAM, 1992):

> Museums have the potential to be enriched and enlivened by the nation's diversity. As public institutions in a democratic society, museums must achieve greater inclusiveness. Trustees, staff, and volunteers must acknowledge and respect our nation's diversity in race, ethnic origin, age, gender, economic status, and education, and they should attempt to reflect that pluralism in every aspect of museums' operations and programs. (p. 8)

It takes a long time and a lot of effort to shed a reputation of elitism and attract new audiences while not disenfranchising established patrons. Extensive advertising, blockbuster exhibitions, and an expansion of family and target-audience programming have successfully lured visitors through the unfamiliar portals of their regional art museums. Opportunities abound for museum educators to enrich the lives of individuals of all ages and walks of life, and museums have set about to build audiences that will sustain them into the future. Yet larger and more diverse audiences multiply the possibility of controversy. Although reaching wider audiences is a worthwhile goal, acceptance of an increased risk of controversy is a price museums must pay. This is not to suggest that museums should cease trying to reach broader audiences, but rather that museums should concurrently plan and initiate measures to address controversy.

In its *Strategic Plan 1998–2000* for preparing to enter the 21st century, the American Association of Museums (AAM) identified increased audience diversity as one of the key "challenges and opportunities" facing museums:

> Continuing demographic change and the growth of a borderless global environment is changing the context in which museums work. Museums will need to become more responsive to the resulting diversity in every aspect of their governance, staffing, and program and audience development. (www.aam-us.org/news.cfm?mode=LIST&id=4, 1997)

New audiences carry with them new perceptions, biases, and predispositions. Newer visitors lack the advantage of having followed the evolutionary history of exhibitions at a museum, whereas frequent visitors are less likely to be unduly shocked by contemporary artworks if they have followed trends through years of exhibitions. Novice visitors for whom "art" means a print reproduction of the Mona Lisa are far more likely to be stricken by the variety of modern and contemporary art, or any form of art unfamiliar to them. Although many will certainly respond timidly with a simple "I just don't get it," and chalk it up to either their own lack of knowledge or the crazy state of the world today, others are inclined to take offence and lay the blame for their incensement on the artist, the artwork, and the museum (or more precisely the museum staff) that had the audacity to exhibit such things. *If* art museums *are* being brazen with their exhibitions, they are flaunting their audaciousness before an ever larger and more diverse audience. The good news is that although there is an increased risk of controversy, larger and more diverse numbers also create a bigger pool of museum supporters, which is crucial for museums to be able to continue exhibiting potentially controversial work. As the AAM asserted in its report, *Excellence and Equity: Education and the Public Dimension of Museums* (1992), "Museums serve as appropriate places to confirm and validate accepted ideas and can be forums for presenting and testing alternative ideas and addressing controversy" (p. 12).

For museum educators the challenge is twofold: to interpret controversies for a curious and sometimes hostile public, and to be effective teachers for an audience as diverse as the population itself. Seonaid McArthur, while Chairing the Committee on Education (EdCom) of the American Association of Museums, noted "the complexity of engaging a diverse audience in vital and meaningful learning experiences" and stressed interdepartmental teamwork; the application of new technologies; active public advocacy; and rigorous planning, implementation, and assessment of museum education to meet these challenges (2002).

Proliferation of Edgy Exhibitions

Art museums do seem more willing than ever before to accept risks in their exhibition planning, opening their galleries to boundary-breaking artwork and revisionist and postmodern notions of art. Folk art, outsider art, performance art artifacts, popular art, functional art, ecoartists' environmental projects, electronic media arts, kitsch—the sky's the limit on what might constitute valid content for art museum exhibitions today. The number of perplexed museum visitors has grown exponentially as a result.

The fact is that there are more museum venues exhibiting more edgy artworks than at any time in history. The artworld once depended primarily on private galleries to exhibit the work of emerging artists and nonconformist extremes in art, and galleries continue to provide such venues. Yet today's art audiences are just as likely to encounter alternative art on a visit to their local art museum. Traditional and encyclopedic art museums have joined with much newer contemporary art centers, such as the Contemporary Arts Center (CAC) of Cincinnati; the Museum of Contemporary Art (MOCA) in Los Angeles; the Wexner Center for the Arts in Columbus, Ohio; the Museum of Contemporary Art (MCA) in Chicago; and the New Museum of Contemporary Art in New York City, in offering visitors access to recent, thought-provoking, and emotion-evoking works by experimental artists. Yet more established art museums are taking a risk that visitors may be turned off. "A museum that seemed to be a bastion of tradition, a safe haven, a protector and preserver of the past, suddenly becomes a proponent of the new and the radical," observed museum director Franklin Robinson (1995), adding that museums should not shy away from exhibiting current art: "If we say that such art should not be seen in museums, we are saying that the museum is not a place to debate the central issues of our time, that these institutions are not relevant to society today" (p. 43).

Risks associated with exhibiting "edgy art" became all too evident when in the fall of 1999 the Brooklyn Museum of Art (BMA), a museum with an encyclopedic collection, prepared to open its exhibition, *Sensation: Young British Artists from the Saatchi Collection.* Risks associated with this exhibition could not have escaped the notice of the BMA's director and staff, for a similar version of *Sensation* had earlier generated controversy when exhibited at the Royal Academy of London (Becker, 2001). In fact, the BMA's marketing seemed determined to capitalize on the show's reputation in order to attract larger, younger, and more diverse audiences (Becker, pp. 16–17).

> Did [BMA Director] Lehman go too far? Did he compromise his institution and overly sensationalize Sensation? The preshow publicity and the signage at the show warned that the exhibition "may cause shock, vomiting, confusion, panic, euphoria, and anxiety." The show was presented as if it were some drug with possible side effects or an amusement park ride to be entered at one's own risk. But the only one who suffered all these symptoms was probably Lehman himself. (Becker, p. 17)

Even before the exhibition opened in Brooklyn, the mayor of New York publicly denounced the exhibition, attempted to cut off public funding to the BMA, and sought to revoke its lease because the "*Sensation* exhibition included paintings that the mayor thought were 'sick' and 'disgusting' and offensive to people with deeply held religious views" (Strauss, 2001, p. 44). Legal battles and public debates raged for months before the controversy faded, the BMA's funding and lease intact (Rothfield, 2001). There were a host of correlative circumstances that acted to ignite and fuel the fires of controversy at the BMA, not least being political and economic motivations, and media frenzy.

But for each BMA *Sensation* there are many other instances of museums exhibiting potentially controversial art without suffering such consequences. For example, the encyclopedic Saint Louis Art Museum hosted a major contemporary art exhibition titled *Wonderland* during the summer of 2000. Curated by Rochelle Steiner, *Wonderland* featured large indoor and outdoor installations and site-specific works by international artists. Among the several highlights were an urban survivalist farm with live chickens and a vegetable crop prepared by Atelier van Lieshout, Pipillotti Rist's twin video projections of a lovely young woman gleefully smashing out windows of automobiles parked along an urban street juxtaposed with breezy images of wildflower fields, and an audio-tour by Janet Cardiff that led visitors outside and along an earthen path through woods adjoining the museum. Nearby museum galleries exhibited pieces from the museum's permanent collection, including Impressionist paintings; Egyptian mummies; Early Renaissance altarpieces; landscapes by artists of the Hudson River School; Asian bronzes; Pre-Columbian ceramics; and other artworks representing various styles, cultures, and time periods. Many visitors who came to see the mummies and Monet also had a startling introduction via *Wonderland* to some of the most progressive artwork on the world scene at the time. Visitors were challenged to expand their concept of art and confront a variety of global issues. In this case, although there was some concern expressed by adult visitors about Rist's video setting a poor example of behavior for impressionable younger visitors, overall *Wonderland* was well attended and well received.

The success of *Wonderland* is an indication that a significant market is ready for and interested in a wide variety of sometimes challenging works of contemporary art. Indeed, there are signs of growth nationwide among institutions exhibiting contemporary art. The Walker Art Center in Minneapolis can boast that it is 1 of the 10 most visited art museums in the United States (www.walker.art.org, 2002). The Corcoran Gallery of Art in Washington, DC, with its long history of collecting and exhibiting the work of living artists, is poised to construct a major new wing. The new wing itself announces to the world the risk-taking character of the institution. Designed by innovative architect Frank Gehry, the polished surfaces and multilayered facade of the new wing will create a startling and thought-provoking stylistic counterpoint to the Corcoran's existing Beaux Arts building (www.corcoran.org, 2002). The Walker is also planning a major building addition, and both the CAC in Cincinnati and the Contemporary Art Museum of Saint Louis are in the process of constructing larger new museum buildings.

Because so many museums with more traditional collections are enthusiastically embracing the diverse media and messages of contemporary art, it is important for those (and all) art institutions to be aware of the variety of situations that can spark controversy. Familiarity with recent cases of controversy, and an understanding of some of the reasons why visitors have difficulty comprehending art works, can help museums anticipate and effectively manage controversy should it arise. Museum staff and members of the public who are entrenched in the artworld may not be aware of the difficulty most visitors experience when trying to decipher the dizzying array of materials and messages of contemporary art. Nor, for that matter, do they always recognize or fully appreciate the immense challenge this presents for museum educators. In the best circumstances, museums can use controversy as an opportunity to expand and deepen visitor learning in the museum.

WHAT MAKES ART CONTROVERSIAL?

Controversy is certainly nothing new to the artworld—It has been commonplace throughout its history. Many of the works we herald as artistic masterpieces were considered by contemporary audiences to be controversial: Some of the figures in Michelangelo's *Last Judgment* were painted over after his death because they were perceived as touching one another in perverse ways; Manet's *Olympia* required around-the-clock guards at the 1865 Salon des Refusés; Rodin's sculpture *The Kiss* was considered too graphic for public display at the 1886 World's Fair and placed behind a curtain; Dada exhibitions in Germany in the 1920s were forcibly shut down by police. Many museum visitors today would not bat an eye at a painting like *Olympia* and would agree that nudity, violence, sexuality, and political themes have a legitimate place within the world of art. Nevertheless, novices and even seasoned museum visitors sometimes "draw the line when such themes could be construed as pornographic, tasteless, or blasphemous" (Tapley, 2002, p. 51). Just where the public may draw that line is difficult to predict.

So what constitutes controversial art today? The Oxford Dictionary describes controversy as a "prolonged argument or dispute." By its very definition, "controversy" spells trouble, but it is a fuzzy term—A "prolonged argument or dispute" can take many forms and can be sparked by a variety of situations. Art controversies can occur within the context of a museum, commercial galleries, community art centers, university galleries, school art exhibitions, and public art projects. Within the realm of the art museum, controversy can ignite among staff and departments, or can be initiated by the public. No matter what its source, controversy can tax museum resources and staff, place reputations at risk, and threaten future funding.

Controversies on the Inside

Controversies that arise within the museum can create rifts between staff or departments and can undermine the smooth operation of the institution. Issues of authenticity and quality, and how well acquisitions fit into the museum's collection, can be the focus of controversy, especially when acquisition funds are limited. Arguments over expenditures and budgets can create tension within or between departments, impeding the ability of the museum to operate as a cohesive whole.

Among the most recent sources of controversy within museums are conservation issues. Some media employed by contemporary artists are difficult if not impossible to conserve, which creates questions regarding the validity of spending large portions of already limited acquisition funds on works that may not stand the test of time. Video and other digital media present a particular problem, as the technology on which their presentation depends may one day become obsolete. Works that require special accommodations that may tax strapped budgets may also create controversy within the museum. Marc Quinn's *Self* (1991, private collection), for example, is a cast of the artist's head created from Quinn's own frozen blood. The work is housed in a refrigerated unit that must be in constant operation, and one power failure could compromise the artwork and the investment. Works like Quinn's are often displayed in temporary exhibitions or relegated to private collections due to the additional costs of preserving such pieces. Whether to conserve a work of art that was intended by the artist to decay over time is another cause for debate within the museum—Should the museum honor the intentions of the artist or preserve their investment?

One of the most pressing problems facing museums today concerns the acquisition of works with questionable origins. Works that were confiscated from private collectors and museums by the Nazis, art that was removed from its country of origin (such as work from Ancient Greece and Egypt), and works tied to particular cultures and religious groups (such as American Indian artifacts) are at the center of hot debates concerning issues of rightful ownership and repatriation. These are particularly sensitive issues for museums to consider: Who is the "rightful owner" of such works and how is ownership determined? Once brought to the attention of the general public, such debates can quickly become front-page news and affect the public's perception of the integrity of the museum.

This Is Art?

Although internal controversies can have a profound impact on the efficiency of museum operations, it is public controversy sparked by a specific work of art or exhibition that museums dread. Artworks can be perceived by museum visitors as controversial for many reasons, ranging from the content or message the works convey to the media, styles, or forms in which they were created.

Contemporary art is particularly difficult for some viewers to understand because its content and appearance often differ from what many museum visitors are familiar with. Many contemporary works look different from traditional works of art, and some viewers may question the meaning and artistic validity of works that are created from nontraditional materials. Contemporary artists have created works from a wide range of materials, from blood to trash to ordinary objects from everyday life, and it is often difficult for viewers to understand why these works are considered "art." Installation pieces and works that are displayed in unusual ways (other than on the wall or a pedestal), performance pieces, and works that blur the boundaries between "art" and "reality" (such as Ann Hamilton's *Seed Bed,* an installation at the inaugural exhibition of the Wexner Center that literally presented the life cycle of moths) can be fodder for controversy because they break from our society's traditional concepts of art.

Works of art that are not deemed aesthetically pleasing by visitors are also ripe for controversy. Art has long been equated with beauty, but many of today's artists are addressing "ugly" issues and are often more concerned with conveying a message than with creating beautiful aesthetic objects. Works created collaboratively or appropriated from other artists or the mass media can also spark controversy. Works such as these challenge conceptions of artistic genius based on creativity and originality and may be dismissed by some viewers as invalid. Although these issues do not often spark large-scale controversy with potentially serious consequences, they are the types of issues often faced by museum educators in the galleries.

Confrontational Art

There is no paucity of "hot-button" issues in contemporary society, including those pertaining to sexism, racism, ageism, social class divisions, the environment, foreign policy, and more. Many issues attract keen interest from a broad cross-section of society. But controversy is often sparked by artworks that are perceived by a particular segment of the population as derogatory to their beliefs. The BMA's *Sensation* exhibition featured several works that were perceived as controversial, most notably Chris Ofili's mixed-media artwork, *The Holy Virgin Mary,* that was composed in part of cutouts from pornographic magazines and lumps of elephant dung. Ofili's work was attacked by various Christian groups who viewed the painting as blasphemous (see Rothfield, 2001). The *Sensation* incident illustrates the potential for serious consequences resulting from controversial art. Publicly funded museums are at special risk because they draw on taxpayer dollars, so they must be particularly aware of the possible repercussions of displaying works that have a high potential to offend. But art museums have to carefully balance the fear of potential consequences with the drive to fulfill their mission statements and provide the public with the opportunity to view, and learn from, art that may be controversial.

Works that are viewed as ethically or morally offensive or as promoting cruelty also come under fire by the viewing public. Some of the work of British artist Damien Hirst, for example, features animals suspended in glass cases of formaldehyde. Hirst creates works that are purposely provocative, but many viewers have difficulty overcoming the confrontational and often gruesome aspects of the work. Gunther von Hagens's plasticized human corpses have also come under fire recently. Although Von Hagens claims that his work is not any different from the cadavers used in medical schools or from the displays in natural history museums, and that the pieces give viewers new respect for the human body, some people see his work as macabre and believe that he has crossed a line by treating the human body as if it were "something as pliable as sculptors' clay" (Andrews, 2001, p. 1). Despite many objections from religious and activist groups, people have waited up to 3 hours to see Von Hagens's work throughout Europe and Japan. This illustrates a positive aspect of controversy—It often gets people through the door and gets them thinking about not only the ideas presented by the artist but also the larger role of art and museums in society.

Sexually Charged Artworks

Sexually explicit works or works that present forms of sexuality on the fringes of the mainstream often elicit controversy from viewers, even those who are otherwise strong supporters of the artworld and of freedom of expression. Few in the art museum world need to be reminded of the heated debate surrounding Robert Mapplethorpe's *X-Portfolio* or the enormous impact it had on federal funding of the arts (see Lankford, 1992b). Museums faced with the choice of whether or not to display works with graphic sexual content invariably flash back to the Mapplethorpe storm, especially if the museum operates using public funds, no matter how small the percentage of the museum's total budget. Past controversies and their ramifications can affect the decisions of museum staff and boards for many years after the initial flames have been extinguished, and can ultimately result in a kind of self-censorship.

Some museums, however, have faced the potential for controversy head on and exhibited graphic works, albeit with some protective measures in place. The William Benton Museum at the University of Connecticut, for example, exhibited several pieces that had the potential to be construed as pornographic in a 2000 exhibition entitled *Genealogies, Miscegenations, Missed Generations*. This small university museum was able to carry out a successful, well-received exhibition without controversy by issuing preemptive warnings and carefully working out the mission of the Benton (Starger, 2000, p. 16). Erin Valentino, the exhibition's curator, and Sal Scalora, the Benton's new director, separated two works from the main exhibition space, including Nadine Robinson's *322 Ways to Breed Mulattos for BET Music Videos, Miss America Beauty Pageants, Army Generals, and NBA Player's Girlfriends*, which featured explicit sex acts between mixed-race couples. The museum posted warning signs and a guard at the entrance to Robinson's installation and did not allow anyone under the age of 18 to enter the space. Although the artist believed that having her work segregated from the rest of the show undermined the exhibition's focus on difference (Starger, 2000, p. 18), the museum was able to avoid controversy by warning viewers of the work's potential to offend and essentially giving them the choice to look or not to look.

A well-informed public is less likely to create a ruckus over art with questionable subject matter when they feel as if the institution is sensitive to their needs and perspectives. The Benton's success is testament to the possibility of balancing sensitivity toward the viewing public with support for freedom of expression and acknowledgment of differences in perception. As Scalora asserted, "A museum is a special place...I believe that a museum's function is to try to come up with the best solution so that many kinds of statements can be heard" (cited in Starger, 2000, p. 18).

Whether a statement made by an artist becomes a source of controversy depends on a multitude of factors distinct from the work of art itself. The content of the exhibition or collection in which the work is displayed, the reputation of the museum, and the physical setting that houses the work can all serve as mitigating or exacerbating forces in the unfolding of controversy. In addition, the social and ethnic makeup of a museum's audience can play a large role in the formation and resolution of controversy. As the saga of *Our Lady* at the Museum of International Folk art illustrates, larger societal issues influence the nature of controversy and the way that it plays out.

OUR LADY

One of the most interesting cases of controversial art in recent history began with the February 2001 opening of "Cyber-Arte: Where Tradition Meets Technology" at the Museum of International Folk Art (MOIFA) in Santa Fe, New Mexico, one of four museums operated by the Museum of New Mexico. The work at the center of the controversy was *Our Lady*, a digital photo-collage print created by Alma López, an artist based in Los Angeles. *Our Lady* is reminiscent of widespread imagery of the Virgin of Guadalupe, an icon strongly linked to Hispanic Catholicism. The image features a muscular contemporary Hispanic woman "with attitude" in the role of the Virgin (Keller, 2001, p. 30). She stands in contrapposto, one knee cocked and her hands on her hips. Unlike traditional images of the Virgin of Guadalupe, her head is not covered and she engages the viewer—she is self-assured and her gaze is somewhat confrontational. Only a grouping of flowers pasted over her breasts and pelvis covers her body, and her open cloak is covered with images from an Aztec relief sculpture of the moon goddess/warrior Coyolxauhqui. The putti that holds with outstretched arms the crescent on which the Virgin stands is a bust of a contemporary woman—with short hair, bare breasts, and pierced nipples—who hovers in front of the wings of a butterfly. The figures are surrounded by garlands of roses reminiscent of sentimental antique lithographs and superimposed patterns suggestive of tacky wallpaper and faded red velvet. Taken as a whole, the image makes reference not only to notions of Hispanic Catholicism but also to social stereotypes regarding Hispanic women and culture.

Over 11,000 brochures featuring *Our Lady* were mailed by MOIFA as exhibition announcements in September of 2000, and the museum received six complaints based on the image in the brochure before mid-March, 2001. Although they were able to successfully address these complaints, the museum correctly interpreted their arrival as a sign of possible controversy to come (A. Gomez, personal communication, November 22, 2002). Thomas H. Wilson, director of the New Mexico Museum, had been aware of the potential for controversy presented by this work but was confident that the exhibit had been developed according to existing museum policies and procedures. Nevertheless, curator Tey Marianna Nunn carefully prepared MOIFA's 60-some docents to discuss *Our Lady* in the context of art history, images of the Virgin of Guadalupe, and the depiction of women and nudity in art; the intention was not just to prepare the docents to educate the public but also to prepare them to respond to issues that might arise in the gallery (A.Gomez, personal communication). The opening of the exhibition and panel discussion on February 25 featuring López, Nunn, and the three other artists featured in the exhibit attracted over 400 attendees, but was without incident. Wilson and MOIFA employees were taken by surprise when the Our Lady of Guadalupe Parish presented him and MOIFA Director Joyce Ice with a four-page letter. State Cultural Affairs Officer J. Edson Way (through whom Wilson reports to the governor of New Mexico) and Linda Hutchison, Way's deputy, also received copies of the Parish's complaints. The letter, which contained several citations referring to canon law, asked Way to "remove the sacrilege art" and "all Catholic sacred images and icons from the museum" and "return" them to the Archdiocese of Santa Fe. It also demanded the return of "tainted" money earned by the museum through public admissions. Further, the letter requested the resignation of Wilson and Ice due to actions perceived by the parish to be culturally insensitive (cited in Keller, 2001, p. 31). In addition to the letter, the church had issued a news release, and reporters and protesters were already outside the front doors of the museum.

The letter from Our Lady of Guadalupe Parish and initial demonstrations were just the beginning of a slew of protests, letters (including over 24,000 preprinted postcards mailed from locations across the country), e-mails, phone calls, and media-hyped public meetings that would consume Wilson and MOIFA's staff for the next several weeks. An interactive component of the exhibition set up by the museum, consisting of an "altar" with a computer monitor displaying a screen saver and space around the computer to leave "offerings," had been erected to the reflect the overarching themes of the exhibition as a whole. This had to be dismantled and replaced with a notebook for comments when local artists opposing the exhibition of *Our Lady* began bringing large objects such as tires, bags of trash, and dead fish into the gallery space (A. Gomez, personal communication). The media was present when a group of 125 protesters gathered at the museum a week later, and reporters soon made the conflict front-page news. Word spread very quickly due to local television coverage as well as coverage by CNN, the BBC, the Associated Press, international art publications, the Mexican media, and many major newspapers around the country. Web sites appeared on the Internet expressing contrasting opinions of the artwork, the artist, and the controversy. The issue soon caught the attention of the New Mexico government. Although the Republican governor supported the right of MOIFA to exhibit the work, seven Democratic members of the state House signed a petition to persuade the museum—with vague threats to decline pending funding requests—to remove the work.[1] Suits were filed against Nunn, Ice, and Wilson for not having public hearings before the opening of the exhibition.[2] The Archbishop of Santa Fe, the Catholic League of Religious and Civil Rights, the American Association of Museums, the American Civil Liberties Union of New Mexico, and the National Coalition Against Censorship joined local organizations and individuals in what was quickly becoming a battle of epic proportions, spurred on primarily by people who had never set foot into the exhibition space (A. Gomez, personal communication).

In an effort to resolve the conflict and allow the expression of public opinion, the museum's board of regents invited comment and participation at its next meeting, scheduled for April 4. On April 3, Wilson released to the public a statement addressed to the board that reflected the museum's belief that the work should remain on view and provide an impetus for the review and possible revision of museum policy:

> In creating this exhibition and selecting this particular image, the Museum of International Folk Art followed standard procedures and guidelines. . . In view of the present situation, current procedures, albeit evolved over ninety years, may not be enough. We are currently developing policy and guidelines in regard to sensitive materials in our collection and exhibitions. Such review of sensitive materials might well involve the participation of interested communities. (Cited in Keller, 2001, pp. 32–33)

Sparked by Wilson's public statement and media announcements regarding the opportunity for public involvement in the decision-making process, over 600 people showed up for the regent's meeting. Only 300 or so were admitted into the building because of space limitations

---

[1] According to Gomez, there was no indication of funding cuts as of mid-November 2002.

[2] A state district court judge ruled that Nunn was not at fault for not requesting public input before the opening of the exhibition.

and safety concerns, leaving an angry crowd of between 300 and 400 people to wait outside. Aurelia Gomez, MOIFA's Education Director, characterized this first public hearing as the most stressful part of the controversy because the museum staff felt physically threatened by the opposition, resulting in the premature adjournment of the meeting (A. Gomez, personal communication). López flew to Santa Fe from Los Angeles to read a prepared statement, but was unable to do so before the meeting was abruptly ended. While waiting for security escorts, López and curator Tey Marianna Nunn were accosted by several men. As Nunn recalls, "We were suddenly surrounded by eight or ten men saying 'crucify her' and calling us *fea* [ugly] as we left. I was very shocked and upset that what I consider my culture would do this to me." López was also traumatized by the encounter, as she had already received e-mailed threats to her safety. Nunn viewed the situation as a defeat: "We were effectively silenced since they ended the meeting before we could present our statements" (cited in Keller, 2001, p. 33).

In order to appease the throngs of people who wished to make comments and participate in the regent's decision, an open forum (lasting eight hours) was held at the 1,200-seat convention center in Santa Fe. Over 600 people attended over the course of the day, including four genera-tions of Guadalupana/os, members of Our Lady of Guadalupe Parish, MOIFA staff and trustees from the Museum of New Mexico system and other museums, artists and art professionals, activists, and representatives of many other segments of the population. Many of MOIFA's do-cents, who had been on the front lines since the beginning of the controversy, also attended the open forum and paid for a local advertisement in support of the museum (A. Gomez, personal communication). Members of the New Mexico state government were also present, including the first lady, the secretary of state, and the speaker of the house. The professionally managed meeting was more peaceful than the previous, but many attendees were upset that the cultural affairs director of Santa Fe, who acted as the meeting's facilitator, allowed the deacon of Our Lady of Guadalupe Parish to make an opening statement lasting 11 minutes, whereas museum supporters were not given comparable time to speak. Many supporters felt that the proceedings were unbalanced in favor of the fundamentalist groups, who had, as Gomez observed, "packed the house" (A. Gomez, personal communication).

Although *Our Lady* remained on exhibit until October 2001, when the exhibition was closed early in what MOIFA director Joyce Ice called "a spirit of reconciliation" (cited in Keller, 2001, p. 35). The conflict that arose in Santa Fe is demonstrative of the all-consuming, media-saturated controversies that can arise from a single work of art. As Ice explained, "This focus on one piece of art in one small exhibit takes on its own energy, almost like a whirlwind that pulls things into it. It's become a metaphor for issues of difference and diversity; the economic divide in Santa Fe, the sense of art being for the elite and not the common people" (cited in Keller, 2001, p. 35). Poet, photographer, and former New Mexico State Arts Council director Bernie López keenly described the nature of the controversy:

> What's really going on has nothing to do with art. This region encompasses predominately Catholic areas still associated with their Spanish colonial antecedents. A great deal of land is gone, customs are gone, and the remaining spiritual realm is seen as threatened. Everything else is gone. With all this passionate emotional feeling about a changing way of life, a changing world, art becomes the catalytic factor, the pressure point at which these feelings emerge. (cited in Keller, 2001, p. 33)

Although most cases of controversial art are not based as strongly on a particular culture as is the *Our Lady* controversy, the series of events surrounding the MOIFA exhibition illustrate the complexities that underlay such incidents. Although MOIFA holds the largest collection of folk art in the world, and contemporary Hispanic art, often with religious themes, is exhibited regularly in the Hispanic Heritage Wing, the museum was in this case seen as the enemy: It exhibited to the public an image that was perceived as an affront to Hispanic Catholic tradition and beliefs. Such a fierce attack by a segment of the population that was well represented in the museum's collection was completely unexpected.

Despite the discouraging and stressful series of events that MOIFA endured, from an educational standpoint the experience proved to be what Gomez characterized as "one of the greatest things to have ever happened" at the museum (personal communication). Although this comment may initially be surprising, Gomez was in fact expressing a larger view of the impact this incident had on the community: As a result of extensive publicity about the controversy, people all over town engaged in thoughtful dialogs about art, artists, the nature of artistic expression, the value of images, and the role of art museums in culture and society. Several local schoolteachers used the controversy as an opportunity to discuss the Bill of Rights and freedom of expression with their students (A. Gomez, personal communication).

For a time, art was the hot topic in Santa Fe and beyond—but the museum staff also learned important lessons that will help them handle controversy in the future. The museum staff involved in the saga of *Our Lady* became aware of the value of careful assessment at each stage of exhibition planning. The support of the museum board is of paramount importance when museum staff and volunteers are under fire. The value of thorough preparation of docents for addressing visitors' questions was underscored. Perhaps most importantly, the MOIFA staff learned the importance of providing visitors with opportunities to voice their opinions. As Barbara Hagood, Director of Marketing and Public Relations, explained, "we have taken the approach of allowing the person to vent or explain without trying to justify our position concerning the museum's mission and free expression. People want to be heard, and by listening, we let them know that we welcome a spirited discussion about our differences" (cited in Keller, 2001, p. 35). It is important to allow the public to express their opinions without fear of feeling disregarded or patronized by an "elitist" museum staff.

Although the MOIFA controversy provided many opportunities for discourse and learning for both the public and the museum staff, it was a unique case, as are all cases of controversy. Each case plays out differently, and although lessons learned from one controversy may be applied to the next, it is important for museums to develop broad and flexible policies and procedures that will accommodate a wide variety of situations and aid in the management of unexpected flare-ups. As Wilson discussed the *Our Lady* controversy with fellow museum professionals around the country, he discovered that anticipating what artworks might ignite controversy is difficult for most museum staff. As Wilson explained:

> We are still in the process of learning lessons. It would be irresponsible not to take seriously the sensitivities of people who have objections, so we're working internally to see how we can meet those sensitivities... One lesson that was underscored is the extreme importance of having well thought out and written polices and procedures that will set guidelines and standards, so you're relying on time-tested polices. (cited in Keller, 2001, p. 33)

POLICIES AND PROCEDURES
FOR ADDRESSING CONTROVERSY

Although the problems that arise from controversial art are unique to each case and institution, generalizations can be made that allow for the creation of broadly based policies that can serve as a framework to assist museum personnel in preparing for and coping with controversy. The creation of policies is especially important considering that, as often as not, controversy arises unexpectedly. Exhibitions and works of art that are considered fairly benign by curators, museum educators, board members, and others closely associated with the museum may be considered malignant by some members of the viewing public. Fortunately, policies and procedures that are carefully crafted might be applied to placate the offended when controversies arise and ensure that some controversies be avoided altogether.

In the most general terms, a museum policy is a governing or operating principle. These principles should reflect the museum's mission. Policies are often philosophically grounded, although there may be economic, political, educational, or other foundations for a policy. Because each case of controversy has unique characteristics and is context specific, museum policies should be broad enough to encompass a range of possibilities and flexible enough to adapt to individual circumstances. Because social and cultural mores evolve as time passes, every museum's strategic plan should include periodic review and revision of policies pertaining to controversy management. As Cathryn Keller, the former chief communications officer of the Museum of New Mexico sagely noted in her reflections on the *Our Lady* controversy, "it is unlikely that any institution would be accused of being over-prepared if it addressed, in its strategic and crisis planning, the possibility of dealing with strong public sentiment and organized opposition to an exhibition or program" (2001, p. 35).

A procedure is an articulated plan of action that is designed to fulfill the intent of a policy. Such procedures may include the who, what, when, where, and how of carrying out a policy. For example, it may be (and probably should be) a museum's policy to record and respond to serious visitor complaints. If a docent receives a complaint about a work of art from a visitor during a tour, a procedure can be followed for reporting the incident that includes providing the docent supervisor with an accurate written description of the nature of the complaint, the immediate response of the docent to the visitor (which may itself have been framed by a policy), and if possible the name and contact information of the person expressing the concern. The docent coordinator may then follow procedures for formally responding to the visitor, record keeping, and reporting the incident to other administrators at the museum.

It is usually a good idea for museum staff and volunteers to be trained in procedures. Training should include not just the mechanics of carrying out a procedure but also education about its purpose. Understanding the purpose of the procedure used in the previous example would assist docents in being able to distinguish between serious complaints that should be reported and everyday, nonthreatening complaints that are unnecessary to report. It is serious business if a visitor claims that a work of art is a profound sacrilege and aggressively demands that it be removed from an exhibition. But a visitor scowling at an Abstract Expressionist painting, claiming that his 6-year-old niece could do as well and voicing the opinion that it is not art and should not be in the museum's collection is much less significant. Museum educators hear such remarks every day.

In practice, museum policies and procedures act in concert to maintain consistency of purpose and performance across the museum. Policies and procedures should be in place that are applicable to all levels and in every department of the museum, and all staff and volunteers should be well informed about them. Museum educators should collaborate with others across the museum as well as with one another in their education departments to frame policies and procedures that will provide guidance and security for docents and staff educators when working with the public.

What follows are generalized proposals for addressing controversial art. Any of these may be suggestive of policies, procedures, or both. To be useful, educators and other museum personnel must adapt these proposals to their particular institutional and community contexts. The proposals are divided into two sections: Preparing for Controversy and Responding to Controversy, although in practice these categories are not exclusive but mutually informative; that is, preparations reveal their optimum usefulness only when the museum is forced to respond to controversy, and responses reveal strengths and shortcomings of the preparations.

Preparing for Controversy

Museums that have conscientiously prepared for controversy are less likely to experience the need to respond to a controversy that has gotten out of hand. The actions required for preparation help to build positive museum–community relationships that are vital for staving off local discord. Preparations also serve the purpose of raising the awareness of museum staff to common causes and potentials for controversy, thereby increasing the likelihood that these are taken into consideration when plans and decisions are made.

Meet the Mission

One of the most effective defenses against controversy is the ability to demonstrate that exhibitions and programs are consistent with the stated mission of the museum. Reference to the centrality of a museum's mission is made in the AAM's *Code of Ethics for Museums:* "[The governing authority of a museum shall ensure that] the museum's collections and programs and its physical, human, and financial resources are protected, maintained, and developed in support of the museum's mission" (AAM, 2000).

Although museum staff may be cognizant of these relationships, visitors and the general public may be unaware. Due to the tumultuous and complex nature of recent art controversies, it has become advisable for museums to more clearly and openly articulate the essential connection between a museum's mission and its exhibitions and programs. Statements to that effect could be included in introductory text panels, docent tours, audio-tours, brochures and catalogs, and so forth. In essence, this task becomes part of the educational responsibility of the museum, which is stressed in the AAM's policy document *Excellence and Equity* (1992): "The educational role of museums is at the core of their service to the public. This assertion must be clearly stated in every museum's mission and central to every museum's activities" (p. 8). Keeping the mission visible is more than an exercise—It serves to inform and remind the public of the purpose of the museum, and it helps to keep the museum's mission foremost in the minds of curators and educators.

Prepare the Docents

Before *Our Lady* was available for public viewing, docents at MOIFA were given an intense, comprehensive education about the context and significance of the artwork. This no doubt contributed significantly to their determination and ability to carry on in the face of controversy. Only one docent took a leave of absence during the exhibition, and there were other extenuating circumstances affecting that docent's decision (A. Gomez, personal communication). Effective docent training builds knowledge that fosters confidence in the galleries. Informed and confident docents and tour guides are more likely to retain their composure when visitors act shocked or offended and are better equipped to respond to visitors' misinformed interpretations or damning judgments of works of art.

Instilling knowledge about works of art and exhibitions is only part of a docent's preparation for controversy. Docents should be familiarized with the museum's policies and procedures that pertain to controversy and be permitted and encouraged to collaborate with museum staff in developing complementary guidelines that are specific to docents' responsibilities and circumstances. This can help provide docents with an added sense of ownership and empowerment regarding the museum's preparation for and response to controversies.

It might be a good idea to activate an Internet listserv to encourage docents to describe incidents that have occurred in the galleries and share strategies they used or observed in use that addressed difficult or challenging situations. This would be a form of peer teaching as well as a way for docents to keep abreast of developments should a controversy arise. This could also be used as a tool for education staff to provide information, reassurance, feedback, and suggestions to volunteer docents.

Apply Inquiry-Oriented Education

All museum educators, both staff and volunteers, should possess a repertoire of instructional strategies designed to engage visitors in meaningful learning encounters with works of art. In today's "meaning-making" museums visitors are not passive learners to which knowledge is transmitted, but active learners engaged in questioning, analyzing, comparing, examining, interpreting, evaluating, and synthesizing (Hein, 1998). The current trend toward participatory learning and interactive exhibits and programs is grounded in constructivist learning theory, which posits that learners construct knowledge in personal ways but are greatly influenced by social environments, and that new ideas and information must be integrated with prior learning in order to be comprehensible and applicable (Hein & Alexander, 1998). This helps to explain why visitors often have difficulty understanding or appreciating innovative works of contemporary art: An artwork can be so different from visitors' art historical frame of reference and so removed from their concept of art that they literally do not know what to make of it. For some visitors, the result is a feeling of hopeless puzzlement; for others, it is hostile rejection of an artwork perceived as an affront.

Fortunately, the fields of art and aesthetic education provide models for teaching and learning that are capable of guiding visitors from states of puzzlement to comprehension, and sometimes from hostility to acceptance or at least tolerance. In particular, art criticism can be useful as an approach to grasping the qualities and meanings of a work of art. Relevant aesthetic concepts may be explored to enlarge visitors' frames of reference, and associated works in art history may be examined to enrich the breadth and depth of visitors' perceptions. Studying a work of art critically can help visitors sort out their thoughts and feelings regarding a controversial work of art and then form justifiable judgments. As Ralph Smith (2000) stated, "Art criticism. . . is the refinement of perception and the rendering of qualitative judgments and is born of the human need to perceive clearly and to separate the meritorious from the meretricious" (p. 50).

One of the most effective ways of engaging in criticism with visitors is through dialog. When visitors to a museum encounter a work of art that startles, puzzles, delights, or offends them, it is common for them to want to talk about their experiences of the work. Educators skilled in dialog and inquiry will invite comments and questions from visitors and use these as the basis for engaging them in a participatory analysis and interpretation of the work of art. If the work is at the center of a highly publicized controversy, visitors will probably also want to discuss larger social, institutional, or aesthetic issues related to the controversy. In such cases, aesthetic inquiry delving into the art world and the role and significance of art in society can be meaningful. Dialog is an effective approach to these topics as well (Lankford, 1992a).

In a constructivist museum, visitors should come to expect educators to pose probing questions designed to get visitors to analyze their own opinions and values. For example, "What is it about this work of art that makes you uneasy?" Follow-up questions are usually essential to encourage visitors to peer beneath their initial reactions: "Do you think the artist is trying to make a statement with this artwork, or perhaps get us to think about an issue? Can a work of art that you think is ugly or offensive still be powerful and constructive in its impact and teach us something valuable?" By getting visitors to engage in self-examination of their concepts and biases, and by having several visitors engage in dialog with one another, alternative perspectives may emerge. In fact, the museum educator—who must listen carefully and present varied perspectives in a balanced way—is often the first to perceive things differently!

One great advantage of applying a dialog-and-inquiry approach to education in the galleries is that it invites alternative interpretations and reveals differing perspectives on the significance of works of art. As David Carr (2001) asserts,

> Every museum owes its users an opportunity to think beyond the museum, to make judgments of their own. Toward this, every museum should pose and illuminate questions that are inherently difficult to address. Such questions may be taken back to the galleries to provoke new observations or as easily carried into the everyday spaces that follow the museum experience. (pp. 77, 79)

Carr is an advocate for museums that "nourish differences of perception and response," and he calls for programs that "involve controversy, alternative interpretations, [and] emerging points of view" (2001, p. 29). This can be especially valuable advice in the case of controversial art. Someone may express outrage about a particular work of art, and that opinion may be countered by one or more alternative and perhaps more positive and meaningful interpretations and assessments. Of course, if dialog deteriorates into diatribe and contentious debate, it escalates the controversy and encourages people to dig in to save face, and ultimately no one wins and nothing is gained. It is important for the educator to be the mediator, attempting to be at least tolerant if not accepting of every idea and maintaining a constructive and respectful climate wherein all feel comfortable expressing their views and all are encouraged to consider alternatives (Lankford, 1992a). Referring to all types of museums, Lonnie Bunch (1995) summarized the value of considering multiple perspectives:

> Museums must not look to educate visitors to a singular point of view. Rather, the goal is to create an informed public that can analyze, criticize, understand, and manipulate history, culture, art, and science so that it informs their lives and aids them in addressing the issues, problems, and normal dilemmas of life. (p. 59)

Provide Educational Outreach

Perhaps the best guarantee of artistic freedom for current and future generations of artists and museum visitors is a well-educated citizenry, specifically citizens who have had the benefit of comprehensive, sequenced art and aesthetic education throughout their years of schooling. Two outcomes of this would be a decrease in the threat of vehement controversy and a significant increase in thoughtful and constructive dialogs and decisions. It is not usually those who frequent art museums who ignite and fan the flames of controversy; protest and derision often come from those who have never viewed the contested exhibition but are acting on word of mouth. If citizens were educated to be informed and critical thinkers about art they would be far less likely to jump to conclusions, particularly conclusions based on the judgments of others who have a prejudicial agenda.

But to be genuinely prepared to make mature and responsible decisions about art, particularly controversial art, people need to understand and learn to assess the social contexts in which artworks are produced and exhibited. Unlike in the early days of Impressionism when shocked audiences seemed gripped with apoplexy, or decades later when Abstract Expressionism became the brunt of jokes, one seldom hears great and widespread consternation regarding works of art because they are judged to be poorly composed, stylistically bizarre, technically crude, or just plain ugly. These are ultimately concerns tied to individual assessments of visual qualities. Because controversy today is almost invariably borne in a context of social issues, it is useful to learn about the social dynamics by which art is nurtured and sustained, or left vulnerable and besieged.

Museum education outreach is one way to provide such lessons to a broader public. Programs may be offered in schools, community centers, libraries, or other places where people commonly gather to learn. A good starting point is to consider with students the sorts of social roles that exist in the artworld. Artists, art dealers, art critics, gallery operators, art teachers, art historians, museum curators, art patrons, museum educators, museum visitors, and a host of others interact with each other to achieve goals that have both personal and collective values. Sometimes different segments of society mesh with the artworld, but sometimes they collide; and when that happens controversy can be the result (Lankford, 1992b, p. 249).

For students of high school age and older, the concepts of "freedom of expression" and "artistic freedom" should be examined. The United States Constitution extends rights of freedom of speech to American citizens, and over time this has come to be interpreted as being applicable to a much broader range of expression, including literature and the visual and performing arts. Freedom of expression has been a key defense for those accused of producing or exhibiting exploitative, incendiary, pornographic, sacrilegious, or otherwise offensive art. It is impossible to underestimate the importance of freedom of expression to the artworld and to the status and security of art's place in society. In order to protect worthwhile artworks that some may find offensive, there must be tolerance for even the trite and sensational, lest art become subject to condemnation and removal at the whim of any social group that may complain. Students, especially those who hope to play significant roles in the world of art, should recognize that freedom of expression is a privilege that must be protected and should not be abused. Decisions that affect art today can have far-reaching and long-lasting effects on culture (Lankford, 1992b, p. 250). If the artworld loses one battle for freedom of expression, society as a whole—not just the artworld—has lost ground. Once a right or privilege is lost, it can be difficult to regain.

To further prepare students who are middle-school-aged and older to reasonably and intelligently address contentious works of art, familiarize them with some of the reasons works of art can be controversial. As has been pointed out, works of art can become controversial because viewers are offended by political, sexual, religious, or other content that varies significantly from the values and mores of members of the community. Understanding the basis of people's objections can help art advocates better prepare for and respond to controversies.

Museum education outreach programs should aim to prepare present and future audiences to be more accepting of artwork that is unfamiliar. To begin, it is useful to challenge students with work that is, for them, new and different. Although some visitors are eager to encounter something challenging and new, many are uncomfortable because they feel either inadequate in their abilities to interpret the art or assaulted by art forms or themes that are radically different from what they know and prefer. By encouraging students, perhaps through carefully calculated incremental steps, to fairly attend to unfamiliar work and consider the diverse meanings and values of a wide range of art forms, museum educators are providing students with more opportunities for enjoying and appreciating art throughout their lives.

It is useful for students to understand that one work of art may suggest alternative interpretations, and that ultimately there is no absolute interpretation. Liberated from the pressure of coming up with "the correct" interpretation, visitors will probably find themselves less frustrated and intimidated by difficult works of art. Similarly, timid visitors should be reassured that there is no one way that a person is "supposed" to feel or respond when experiencing a work of art.

Be Vigilant About the Risk of Controversy

Museums are busy places, and it is easy to forget about preparing for the risk of issues that have not even arisen. Yet, there is ample evidence in the museum world to indicate the wisdom of being prepared. Because controversy affects an entire museum, the most appropriate way to prepare for it is to draw on perspectives from a cross-section of the museum's organizational units. A plan to address controversy need not be a stand-alone document but can be incorporated into an existing policy and procedures handbook. Before a plan is approved, all personnel should have an opportunity to review and comment on it. Regular assessment and possible revision should be built into the museum's long-range strategic plan, and museum staff and volunteers should receive periodic refresher training.

Because education is, or should be, central to a museum's mission, it is imperative that museum educators play leadership roles in formulating and implementing any plan. All staff should remain vigilant for signs of controversy in the museum or community. Docents and staff educators spend so much time with the general public that they may be able to notice a controversy simmering *before* it boils over.

As museums set about the process of preparing for possible controversies, it can be useful to learn about policies and procedures that are in place at similar institutions, particularly those museums that have already been confronted with the need to address a controversy. Sharing ideas and information along these lines should be considered a responsibility among museum professionals. Museum controversy has been the subject of AAM conference sessions and should continue to be a regular part of professional development.

Undertake Visitor Research

Museums may undertake visitor research and evaluation for any number of reasons: public relations, marketing, programming, and strategic planning, among others. Demographic data about visitors and the community can be helpful when seeking to target new audiences or sustain audience loyalty. When an exhibition or program is still in development, front-end evaluation may be used to gauge audience reception and the effectiveness of the learning encounter before it is installed or utilized in the museum (Diamond, 1999).

A combination of quantitative and qualitative research might yield useful insights into the interests and motivations of visitors to the museum. If those involved in planning exhibitions and programs are well informed about their audience and the community they serve, they can more accurately predict and avoid controversy. Informed museum educators and curators are more sensitive to issues within the community

Develop Community Support Networks

One of the most important steps that a museum can make in preparing for controversy is to build bridges to the local community. Local government officials, administrators of community organizations, and other community leaders should be made to feel that the museum cares about ideas and issues that are of concern to the community. A museum should go out of its way to keep the community informed about its current and upcoming projects, programs, and exhibitions. Input from members of the community should be actively sought before, during, and after staging special exhibitions or programs, and the museum should make it known that the community's input was carefully considered when making decisions. Most community leaders are quick to discern when their input is a form of tokenism—openly sought but seldom heeded—and this can ultimately work against the museum.

The AAM emphasizes building community relationships in its policy documents and initiatives. For instance, the AAM Board of Directors established a major nationwide task force in 1998 to realize its *Museums and Community Initiative* (2002), whose purpose was "to explore the potential for renewed, dynamic engagement between museums and communities" and to help ensure that museums have the resources they need to enhance and attend to their "civic missions." The AAM's *Strategic Agenda* (1997) stresses that "museums are both community institutions and institutions that can build community. They can be places where ideas and civic values can be discussed and shared." In the same document, the AAM also promotes community collaborations:

> Partnership and collaboration are increasingly important means through which organizations of every kind accomplish their purposes. Museums will need to develop greater facility in forging innovative and mutually advantageous partnerships and collaborative arrangements with other not-for-profit institutions, with business enterprises, and with government at every level.

If controversy strikes, having a positive relationship with community leaders can be invaluable in buttressing the museum's position. As Geoffrey Platt, Jr., the AAM's director of government affairs, asserted:

> Your museum, if it hasn't already, will one day come under the public microscope in an unprecedented way. Some exhibition, policy, or event will trigger your museum being called to account, and likely not in an arena of your choice....your greatest allies in coping with an accountability crisis [are] public officials, but only if those persons are "on board" well before they might be needed. (1990, p. 40)

Museum educators should be integral to the processes of building and sustaining positive community ties. Education is almost always a central issue in any community, so a high-profile education program will build good will as well as increase the museum's audience and improve visitors' gallery experiences. Museum educators are, after all, in the business of making artworks in the museum as accessible as possible to the public. But aside from building good will and support, museum educators can benefit by connecting with the community. For example, community networks can be very useful in establishing venues for outreach programs and advising how best to develop interests and address the concerns of local citizens. An education advisory board comprised of K-12 and higher education art educators could provide ideas and feedback to help assess and improve museum programs. The AAM Committee on Education endorsed community engagement in its policy document, *Excellence in Practice: Museum Education Standards and Principles* (2002):

> (a) Develop and maintain sound relationships with community organizations, schools, cultural institutions, universities, other museums, and the general public, (b) reflect the needs and complexities of a changing society, (c) shape content and interpretation toward relevant issues and create a broad dialogue. (www.edcom.org/about/standards)

Responding to Controversy

Despite efforts to avoid controversy, museums will always face the possibility that some artwork or exhibition will offend a segment of the population. Every day of the year except Mondays and holidays a wide variety of artworks are considered by museum visitors to be offensive. Most of the time, nothing serious comes of it, but then there are instances when controversy erupts. If the museum has thoroughly prepared, it should be able to meet the challenge. Most of the following *response* proposals consist of an extension and application of previous *preparation* proposals.

Respond Promptly and Directly

There is ample evidence that an art controversy will snowball once it appears before the public eye. A quick response directed to the person or group lodging the complaint may satisfy the offended and contain the scope of the controversy. Unfortunately, word of mouth is swift in some communities; and to make matters worse, sometimes those offended seem more eager to gain media attention for their cause than to attempt to resolve an issue directly and discreetly with the museum.

Nevertheless, as MOIFA administrators learned, it is important that people who are offended by a work of art be reassured that the museum cares about their perceptions and feelings. A prompt response accompanied by careful listening demonstrates that the museum is sensitive to serving the community and preserving public trust.

Museum educators may be thrust by circumstance to attend to offended visitors in the galleries, say, in the course of a tour or other program. It is probably best to politely acknowledge visitors' concerns, indicate that you appreciate their perceptions, and promise that personal attention will be promptly paid to the matter if they are willing to provide contact information. Avoid assuming a defensive attitude or debating issues with offended visitors in the galleries.

It is advisable that all museum staff and volunteers be consulted when forming the museums' official position with regard to a controversy, and that all museum personnel be thoroughly familiarized with the position before it is made public. Anyone associated with the museum might be approached and questioned by a curious or concerned citizen, particularly when a controversy is widely reported in the media. Presenting a unified and consistent position regarding the controversy will help to build and sustain the museum's image and reputation as an institution grounded in convictions, integrity, and a commitment to reliability in fulfilling its public service responsibilities.

Associate the Mission of the Museum With Larger Social Good

At a time when museums are striving to better attract and serve their communities, it is distressing to say the least when controversy assumes an "us versus them" character. It is important to remind both museum personnel and the public that more is at stake than the reputation of the institution. Also at stake are the museum's ability to serve a diverse public and the museum world's collective responsibility to preserve freedom of expression for all.

In order to serve its community well, a museum must attempt to represent the range of perceptions, opinions, and values held by members of the local community *and* by others representing larger contexts of culture and society. Attitudes and beliefs that may be uncommon within the museum's immediate community may be expressed in some form by the museum's exhibits in order to further educate the public about the diversity of human experience. This means that conflicts occurring in society from local to global levels might be reflected in a museum's exhibitions. Although this may result in controversy, it may be considered a necessary risk for museums to bear. In his defense of MOIFA during the *Our Lady* controversy, AAM President and CEO Edward H. Able, Jr., referred to such risks:

> Museums have a responsibility to preserve and enlighten, and often advance new and challenging interpretations of art, history, and science. . . .As publicly accountable institutions, museums owe their communities a high level of transparency about their actions. But the governing authority of the museum must also be the final point of authority for decisions about what the museum will exhibit and, in doing so, it must be willing on occasion to risk disapproval so that the ultimate goal of the museum, the dissemination of knowledge, is fulfilled. (AAM, 2001, p. 4)

Able's comments also apply to upholding an important democratic principle. When controversy at a museum includes an external demand that one or more works of art on exhibit be removed, freedom of expression is put on the line (Lankford, 1992b). In order to continue to explore new ideas and present unique observations and thought-provoking perspectives on issues, artists must be able to express themselves freely within a social context that allows and ideally even encourages such expression. Museums that seek to present alternative perspectives and stimulate public dialog about important topics and issues must be able to mount exhibitions that may not conform to values and opinions commonly held in the community. Adult audiences should be able to choose which exhibits to view and study (or avoid) without coercion from museums or external agencies. Visitors and critics must be able to independently determine what they judge to be worthwhile within an exhibit. All of these elements are linked under the conceptual and protective umbrella of freedom of expression.

Attempts by special interest groups to condemn artists and artworks, to coerce museums to limit or censor what they choose to exhibit, or to prescribe what visitors may or may not see are contrary to the spirit of freedom of expression. In efforts to preserve and defend its reputation, exhibitions, and programs from attack, a museum would do well to fold into its rationales and arguments references to serving the larger public good. This would situate a museum more securely within the context of a broad family of museums and link individual mission statements with widely held collective purposes. Further, to reiterate an assertion presented in the *preparation for controversy* section: Education is key to preserving freedom of expression, and education is a common purpose of most museums today.

Call on Community and Museum Allies for Support

Community leaders, museum advisory boards, and other museums and institutions can provide valuable support to a museum under fire: for example, by utilizing influence or authority to help protect the museum's resources, assisting with community education programs and public forums, and offering legal or managerial advice. Community leaders might be able to provide insights into the root causes or issues motivating complaints by members of their constituency, and advisory boards may be able to facilitate constructive communications or otherwise intervene between the offended parties and the museum. Supportive statements issued to the public and press by respected citizens and community leaders can significantly improve the museum's position in the public eye as well as bolster the museum's internal morale. Similarly, when other museums in the community and across the nation publicly advocate the museum's position, it affirms the principles that have guided the museum's decisions.

Utilize the Controversy as an Opportunity to Expand and Enrich Education

Many people, including some who may never have visited the museum, will want to learn more about the controversy, hear various sides of the issues, and see for themselves the work in question. Community interest, visitor numbers, and the diversity of visitors may significantly increase during a controversy. Requests to add or modify tours and programs may be expected. For museum educators it will be the best of times and the worst of times. Workloads may increase, but so will demand, respect, and appreciation for high-quality education. Educators might consider adding a symposium to other scheduled programs and invite outside scholars to discuss the artworks and issues at hand. Adding additional educational material to brochures, text panels, and tours might be possible. Believe it or not, this might also be a good time to recruit new docents. Not everyone in the community is against the museum during a controversy; many will side with the museum and feel motivated to demonstrate their support through volunteer service. Although earnest and eager in their wish to serve, new volunteers should still receive complete and thorough training prior to instructing the public. For those unwilling or unable to undergo docent training, there are usually other ways that volunteers could be of service to a museum education department. Increased volunteerism has obvious long-term benefits that will outlive the controversy.

Document the Controversy

Once the controversy has died down, museum personnel might understandably be inclined to put the whole matter behind them. But far more beneficial to the museum would be a careful review of the sequence of events, an analysis of community motivations and of the impact of actions taken, and an assessment of how the museum handled the incident. Taking the time to reflect on and document the controversy can pay off should similar issues arise again. Lessons learned from a controversy can be applied to revision of museum policies and procedures and can inform and strengthen a museum's ability to avoid, prepare for, and respond to controversy in the future.

CONCLUSION

Controversial art is a blessing and a curse. On one hand, it spurs society to think seriously about the meaning and value of art; on the other hand, it causes rifts between social factions and the art world. When controversy rears its head at any museum, art museums everywhere shudder in consternation. Yet by conscientiously developing policies, procedures, and educational programs and strategies to prepare for and respond to controversy, art museums may be able to avoid controversy altogether or minimize its negative impact.

One could rightly argue that many of the proposals presented in this paper are descriptive of good museum education practice regardless of whether or not controversial art is in the picture. Except there are two significant differences: First, when museum educators are aware of and sensitive to the causes, risks, and impact of controversy, they can add relevant nuances to the content and delivery of their public programs, and as any seasoned educator can tell you, details matter. Second, if museum educators are cognizant of ideas, issues, policies, and procedures associated with controversy, then should controversy arise they will know what to do.

Avoiding controversy should not be taken to the extreme of functioning as a sort of institutional in-house censorship. Art has always been and continues to be a powerful means of expression, and ideas and values expressed are not always pretty and untroubled. No matter what steps are taken, some people will find certain works of art objectionable. A major strength and purpose of any art museum is its commitment to presenting diverse points of view and not shy away from issue-laden and thought-provoking art. In fulfilling this mission, art museums contribute to the great dialog that is the exercise of freedom of expression.

REFERENCES

American Association of Museums. (1992). *Excellence and equity: Education and the public dimension of museums*. Washington, DC: Author.

American Association of Museums. (1997). *Strategic Agenda FY 1998–2000*. Retrieved January 29, 2003, from http://www.aam-us.org/news.cfm?mode=LIST&id=4

American Association of Museums. (2000). *Museum ethics*. Retrieved January 29, 2003, from http://www.aam-us.org/aamcoe.cfm

American Association of Museums. May (2001). Virgin Mary controversy continues. *Aviso,* 4.

American Association of Museums. (2002). *Museums and community initiative*. Retrieved January 29, 2003, from http://www.aaus.org/initiatives/m & c/history.cfm

Andrews, E. L. (2001). Plasticized corpse: Is it art? Retrieved April 3, 2001, from www.shul.org

Becker, C. (2001). The Brooklyn controversy: A view from the bridge. In L. Rothfield (Ed.), *Unsettling "sensation": Arts-policy lessons from the Brooklyn Museum of Art controversy* (pp. 15–21). New Brunswick, NJ: Rutgers University Press.

Blair, L. (1996). Strategies for dealing with censorship. *Art Education 49*(5), 57–61.

Bunch, L. G. (1995). Fighting the good fight: Museums in an age of uncertainty. *Museum News 74*(2), 32–35, 58–62.

Carr, D. (2001). Balancing act: Ethics, mission, and the public trust. *Museum News 80*(5), 28–32, 71–81.

The Corcoran Gallery of Art. (2002). *The Gehry wing.* Retrieved January 29, 2003, from http://www.corcoran.org/general/support_fs.html

Diamond, J. (1999). *Practical evaluation guide: Tools for museums and other informal educational settings.* Walnut Creek, CA: Alta Mira Press.

EdCom. (2002). *Exellence in Practice: Museum Education Standards and Principles.* Retrieved January 29, 2003, from http://edcom.org/about/standards.shtml

EdCom. (2002). *Standards and Best Practice in Museum Education.* Retrieved January 29, 2003, from http://edcom.org/about/standards

Hein, G. D. (1998). *Learning in the museum.* London: Routledge.

Hein, G. D., & M. Alexander. (1998). *Museums: Places of learning.* Washington DC: American Association of Museums.

Keller, C. (2001). Faith and the first amendment Santa Fe Style. *Museum News 80*(4), 30–35.

Lankford, E. L. (1992a). *Aesthetics: Issues and inquiry.* Reston, VA: National Art Education Association.

Lankford, E. L. (1992b). Artistic freedom: An art world paradox. In R. A. Smith & R. Berman (Eds.), *Public policy and the aesthetic interest* (pp. 236–253). Urbana: University of Illinois Press.

McArthur, S. (2002). *Standards & best practice in museum education: Introduction.* Retrieved January 29, 2003, from http://www.edcom.org/about/standards

Platt, G., Jr. (1990). Controversy: No longer a question of *if*, but *when. Museum News 69*(2), 40.

Robinson, F. W. (1995). The moral dilemma of American art museums. *Museum News 74*(2), 42–43.

Rothfield, L. (Ed.). (2001). *Unsettling "sensation": Arts-policy lessons from the Brooklyn Museum of Art controversy.* New Brunswick, NJ: Rutgers University Press.

Smith, R. (2000). DBAE: A humanities interpretation. In R. Smith (Ed.), *Readings in discipline-based art education: A literature of educational reform* (pp. 46–51). Reston, Virginia: National Art Education Association.

Starger, S. (2000). Dealing with controversial art at the William Benton Museum. *Art New England 21*(4), 16–18.

Stauss, D. A. (2001). The false promise of the first amendment. In L. Rothfield (Ed.), *Unsettling "sensation": Arts-policy lessons from the Brooklyn Museum of Art controversy* (pp. 44–51). New Brunswick, NJ: Rutgers University Press.

Tapley, E. (2002). Scrutinized art: The many faces of visual art censorship. *Art Education 55*(6), 48–52.

The Walker Art Center. (2002). *Visiting The Walker.* Retrieved January 29, 2003 from http://www.walker.art.org

III

Learning in the Visual Arts

11

Introduction: Development and Learning in Art

Anna M. Kindler

University of British Columbia/Hong Kong Institute of Education

INTRODUCTION

A baby moves her finger across a spilled milk and looks with an interest at a mark that her gesture leaves behind. A toddler holding a felt pen with a firm grip hits a sheet of paper covering it with a rain of dots. A preschooler attentively adds lines to an oval explaining that his dog has just run away. A third-grader completes a collage made of tiny pieces of orange paper to celebrate Halloween. Her companion adds another Little Kitty drawing to the margins of the notebook. A teenager, with his hands and face splashed with mud adds finishing touches to a vase swirling on a potters wheel while his classmate carefully sketches a still life compiled in the back of the art room. A college student frustrated with the low speed of his computer transforms a scanned photograph he took with the help of Photoshop. An artist leans over a large canvas in a spacious studio. Her friend stands in a doorway of a gallery contemplating her latest work. What accounts for changes in pictorial behavior that may lead from a play with spilled milk to an art exhibition?

Questions about the origins and nature of pictorial behavior and attempts to describe a developmental journey that may lead from first acts of representation to artistic accomplishment recognized by and acclaimed within the artworld have long been of interest to art education. What motivates the infant's interest in her early graphic marks? How do these early discoveries transform into pursuit of imagery that carries with the desired level of accuracy and precision the meaning intended by its creator? What cognitive processes propel change; and what psychobiological and/or cultural factors bear influence on the invention, learning, or mastery of pictorial systems that effectively function within the boundaries of relevant cultural expectations? How do manifestations of representational intent materialized within the pictorial domain enter the sphere of visual arts?

From the time when art has abandoned its academic definition in the modernist era and ventured into the territory of visual imagery that in the present day and age knows no limits or rules of category membership, the possibility to answer some of these questions has become increasingly problematic. Yet, these questions remain significant to art education as the field continues its struggle to design curricula and implement pedagogy that would allow children and adolescents to meet their artistic potential.

This section of the *Handbook* focuses on the relationship between the learner and the domain of art. It inquires about the developmental factors that underlie acquisition of artistic knowledge, skills, and competencies and explores origins and developmental pathways of human ability to manipulate symbol systems that shape the world of art. How do people construct artistic knowledge? What processes guide development of art-related abilities? How do biological and sociocultural influences impact on development in pictorial representation? What founds aesthetic judgment and reasoning? A team composed of leading art educators, cognitive scientists, and psychologists was invited to address these and other related issues that are of significance to curriculum development and implementation in art education.

The section on "Development and Learning" in art is organized into six chapters, each focusing on a specific aspect of the developmental debate. It opens with a discussion of theories and models of artistic development that suggests a need for a significantly revised approach to the developmental question. The subsequent chapters address specifically the origins of development in pictorial representation and expression; the "nature vs. nurture" dilemma, with special emphasis on the role of culture as a determinant or mediator of artistic behavior; development in three-dimensional representation; the origins and developmental pathways of aesthetic judgment and reasoning; and finally, consideration of talent and exceptionality in the visual arts. Each chapter offers a comprehensive overview of research conducted in the area of its focus, points to its relevance to the teaching of art and identifies issues that merit further inquiry.

The opening chapter by Anna Kindler asks provocative questions regarding the "impossibility" of artistic growth and questions the link between specific psychobiological and/or cultural phenomena with a comprehensive notion of development in art. It raises doubts about the epistemological appropriateness of defining "artistic development" as a distinct phenomenon and reframes studies in artistic development as segments of knowledge relevant to the domain rather than defining a universal set of processes necessary and sufficient for artistic progression. These doubts and questions are raised in the context of a comprehensive review of research in art, education, psychology, cognitive sciences, and neuroscience, which has attempted to shed light on processes engaged in manipulation of artistic media resulting in outcomes that may fit diverse definitions of art.

The chapter includes a presentation of different theoretical models and offers a critique of their conceptual strengths as well as weaknesses often linked to assumptions that do not stand the test of cultural or historical relevancy. Much attention is given to models that consider multiple trajectories of growth in the development of pictorial representation as they effectively address some of the shortcomings of the single-endpoint, linear conceptions of development in art. Yet, Kindler points to the fact that even these more open and broad conceptions are bound by limitations which prevent them from accurately accounting for the vast universe of processes responsible for all possible dimensions and venues of what could be considered as improvement in artistic performance.

The author's doubts about "artistic development" echo Wilson's observation about "child art" being a cultural construction and extend it to the broader realm of development in art. Kindler makes a reference to Csikszentmihalyi's (1988, 1999) systems approach to creativity that highlights the interaction among an individual, a "domain," and a "field" and suggests that confluence theories of creativity may signal a possible way to restructure discourse about artistic development in the future. She notes, however, that flexibility and elasticity of the concept that such theories afford come at the expense of precision and consistency of meaning that may reduce pragmatic, practical value of these accounts.

John Matthews, whose long-standing research interests have focused on beginnings of expressive and representational thought in infancy, addresses in his chapter "the art of infancy." Drawing on the results of his and other scholars' work, Matthews argues that even the earliest pictorial behavior is not limited to a simple sensorimotor exploration. He presents evidence suggesting that both as process and as product, early drawings carry a profound meaning and represent significant outcomes of cognitive activity. Matthews' account of development in early childhood, while largely limited to consideration of two-dimensional imagery, explores significance of different pictorial media, including what he refers to as "electronic paint" providing insights into very young children's attempts to employ computer technology for expressive and representational purposes.

Matthews draws attention to the importance of social and interpersonal contexts in early pictorial representation and brings his extensive teaching experience in early childhood environments to complement formal research findings in his analysis of their significance. His British upbringing and education combined with years of working in Singapore provide him with a good platform to address issues of culture and its impact on artistic development and learning. This chapter benefits from Matthews' firsthand experience with cross-cultural inquiry and expertise in early childhood art education practices in selected settings in North America and Asia. A unique aspect of Matthews' contribution is consideration of gender issues in early childhood classrooms. The author claims that, given the demographics of the early education workforce, learning environments are typically "designed *by* females, *run* by females, for females." His discussion of "sexism in the nursery" considers negative impact of gender-biased practice on both girls' and boys' development in expression and representation.

Matthews is careful to point out that artistic development in early childhood is not a process of unilinear unfolding limited to the domain of graphic representation. He describes the process as a much more complex endeavor that benefits from adult intervention rather than from interference. He supports "scaffolded" or "mediated learning" in early childhood art education where adults and young children become "companions as intellectual adventurers" in the context of play.

The following chapter is contributed by Brent Wilson who, together with Marjory Wilson, pioneered the notion of development in art as a form of cultural learning. In their groundbreaking 1977 article "An Iconoclastic View of the Imagery Sources of Young People," the Wilson's contradicted long-standing models of development that attributed changes in pictorial production to internal, psychobiological mechanisms and proposed instead a conception that pointed to the fundamental role of culture in development of pictorial representation. Brent Wilson has remained faithful to this idea through decades of his research, and this chapter is a logical extension of his earlier work. In "Child Art After Modernism: Visual Culture and New Narratives" Wilson argues that "child art" is in itself a cultural construction and that conceptions of development as a natural unfolding of representational abilities resulted from a confusion brought upon the modernist set of values and resulted in a "grand narrative of art education" that has greatly constrained art education practice. Wilson claims that there is nothing natural about artistic development and that assumption that children are more creative than adults is nothing but a cultural artifact. His views, which some art educators may consider controversial, are carefully supported with cross-cultural research evidence and with engaging anecdotes and narrative that describe children's engagement with visual culture. Wilson advocates the need for a comprehensive theory of art/visual culture that would allow rewriting a philosophy of child art and art education relevant to and reflective of the reality of children of the present day.

Discussion of artistic development has traditionally been focused on development in two-dimensional pictorial representation, and the number of studies addressing processes that found performance in three-dimensional media has been very limited. One of the few researchers who has devoted significant time exploring development in three-dimensional representation is Claire Golomb, a psychologist with a long standing interest in visual arts. In her contribution to the *Handbook*, Golomb describes and analyzes research that traces the origins of children's engagement with clay from their first prerepresentational actions to sculptures with clear representational intent and outcomes marked by technical and expressive success. She frames her presentation with a backdrop of history of art making in three-dimensional media on the one hand and accounts of developmental progression in drawing, on the other.

The author argues that although there are some similarities in which development across two- and three-dimensional media progresses, such as the initial use of global, minimally differentiated forms, she notes significant medium-specific differences. For example, she argues that while increased differentiation has long been considered as one of the hallmarks of progress in drawing, the process of differentiation in clay sculpture tends to level off in middle childhood. She attributes this to the tension between the desire for uprightness and detail that need to be mediated in the context of the physical properties of the medium and the technical difficulties in coping with its demands.

Golomb points out that studies of development in clay clearly document that even very young children exhibit basic three-dimensional understanding and that their representational concepts are three-dimensional in nature. This offers further support to theories that reject intellectual immaturity thesis as accounting for the outcomes of young children's engagement with artistic media. It is rather a limited experience with the medium, lack of practice and technical skill, as well as lack of knowledge of traditions and practices that prevail in the medium that account for the "primitive" appearance of young children's early sculptures.

Golomb recognizes limitation of a clinical approach that marks much of research referred to in her chapter and suggests the need for more inquiry conducted in "studio-like environments where professional assistance is made available, where work is sustained over several sessions and the young artist's conceptions can evolve (and be systematically studied) over time." This places art educators in a very good position to contribute to the generation of knowledge in this area that could help guide improvement in classroom practice.

Discussion about development and learning in art would not be complete without consideration of artistic reasoning and aesthetic judgment. Norman Freeman's chapter focuses on aesthetic thinking and explores ways in which people acquire assumptions about pictorial functions, decide about what is important in pictures, and formulate opinions about their artistic worth. Freeman notes that the concepts of expressivity, attractiveness, and recognizability are at the core of aesthetic reasoning about pictorial images and presents an overview of research that examined how these concepts function in human reactions to artifacts.

Referring to his theory of pictorial reasoning (Freeman, 1995), the author devotes much of the chapter to the exploration of pictorial communication. He argues that a broad analysis of pictorial reasoning requires attention to four entities: artist, viewer, picture, and referent. From a developmental perspective, Freeman notes that although children as young as 3 years of age understand that viewer–picture relations can vary and that people differ in their pictorial preferences, this "is a long way from understanding viewers as representational agents whose culturally relative pictorial judgments will vary depending on what they bring to the viewing situation."

Freeman's theoretical position interacts with Parsons' (1987) notion, attributing great significance to "pictorial assumptions" that viewers bring to an aesthetic experience. He is careful to note that these assumptions remain closely related to the core four terms that he identified in pictorial communication and demonstrates how the salience and weighting of these components may vary and how they affect an aesthetic reaction. The author highlights the fact that communication through images involves a variety of "cultural devices" that eventually "bridge the gap between minds and between physical and mental reality." He articulates the role that education can play in helping people challenge and reshape their pictorial assumptions in order to make them better equipped to respond to changes and innovations in art.

Finally, David Pariser and Enid Zimmerman provide a thorough account of research on development, identification, and nurturing of artistic talent. The chapter begins with an introduction of the complex nature of the concepts of gifted and talented and the tendency to associate giftedness with superior academic abilities and talent with exceptional abilities in the arts. The authors contradict this distinction by referring to Winner's (1996) description of giftedness that identifies generic cognitive characteristics that mark exceptionality across academic and artistic fields. This definition points to the talented children's early and rapid development of skills within a symbolic domain in ways that exceed standard expectations for individuals of the same age. It also notes talented children's "urge to master" that domain and an exceptional ability to find unique solutions to problems that they encounter along their learning journey and relative independence in their learning pursuits. Drawing on Jellen and Verduin's work (1986), Pariser and Zimmerman highlight the need to consider the concept of artistic talent in ways that account for not only specific cognative abilities but also affective (empathy and sensitivity) and cognative (interest and motivation) dispositions. They refer to a body of research concerned with personalities and backgrounds of artistically gifted individuals to demonstrate that a broad spectrum of factors contributes or interacts with artistic exceptionality.

Recognizing the complex nature of the concept of artistic giftedness and the difficulty that it poses in attempts to generalize and apply it in practical tasks of identification and nurturing of such gifts, the authors refer to a collection of case studies of individuals who, within their local cultural contexts, have been identified as artistically gifted as well as to those whose artistic talent has been recognized and acclaimed in global contexts. Studies of children selected for participation in art enrichment programs designed for individuals demonstrating artistic giftedness, prodigies, and world-famous artists whose juvenile work became a subject of study allow for deeper levels of understanding of how the concept of artistic giftedness functions within societies.

Among important dimensions of this chapter are its cross-cultural focus and attention given to the consideration of gender and socioeconomic factors in the discussion of artistic exceptionality. These become particularly relevant when the issues of identification of talent are raised and when solutions are proposed relative to the actions needed to sustain and support artistic gifts. Although the authors, drawing on their comprehensive review of related research, identify a generic set of strategies for development of curricula that support creativity and talent development, they are also careful to note the need to account for contextual factors in seeking most relevant and appropriate solutions. Pariser and Zimmerman make it clear that the notion that artistically gifted children should be "left to their own devices" is nothing but a myth. They point to the evidence suggesting a strong impact of educational opportunities and the role of teachers in nurturing and development of artistic talent and call for more research documenting this need and identifying successful practice.

In summary, the chapters compiled in this section compose together a broad landscape of inquiry into the nature of artistic development and learning and suggest how it can be further shaped to inform and support insightful practice in art education.

REFERENCES

Csikszentmihalyi, M. (1988). Society, culture and person: A system view of creativity. In R. J. Sternberg (Ed.), *The nature of creativity*. New York: Cambridge University Press.

Csikszentmihalyi, M. (1999). Implications of a systems perspective for the study of creativity. In R. J. Sternberg (Ed.), *Handbook of creativity*. Cambridge: Cambridge University Press.

Freeman, N. H. (1995). The emergence of a framework theory of pictorial reasoning. In C. Lange-Kutter & G. V. Thomas (Eds), *Drawing and looking*. Hemel Hempstead, UK: Harvester Wheatsheaf.

Jellen, H. G., & Verduin, J. R. (1986). *Handbook of differentiated education of the gifted: A taxonomy of 32 key concepts*. Carbondale, IL: Southern Illinois University Press.

Parsons, M. J. (1987). *How we understand art*. Cambridge: Cambridge University Press.

Wilson, B., & Wilson, M. (1977). An iconoclastic view of the imagery sources of young people. *Art Education, 30*(1), 5–15.

Winner, E. (1996). *Gifted children: Myths and realities*. New York: Basic Books.

12

Researching Impossible? Models of Artistic Development Reconsidered

Anna M. Kindler

University of British Columbia/Hong Kong Institute of Education

INTRODUCTION

The term *child development in art* has become a part of the core vocabulary in the field of art education. It has graced book titles, become a name for university courses, and established itself as a focus of a well-defined area of scholarly inquiry that has attracted contributions from the fields of psychology, art, and education. Intuitively, most people have a notion of what this term entails. Images of scribbling children mastering their drawing skills over a long period of time to eventually be able to produce images that clearly communicate the artist's intent readily come to mind. People who are not experts in art often see artistic development in rather simplistic and unilinear ways—as an ability to progress from pictorial production that "looks like nothing" to creation of images that "look like something." Psychologists interested in cognitive underpinnings of pictorial behavior tend to focus on changes in denotation systems, figure differentiation, segmentation and contouring, volumetric and surface representation, and the use of other pictorial devices indicative of advancement in the utilization of graphic symbol systems. Depending on their cultural origins, artists and art educators may point to the improvements in technique and ability to control and manipulate the medium or to an increase in complexity, detail, and expressiveness of images. However, even this apparent diversity of possible indicators or measures of growth seems dramatically limited and seriously insufficient in relation to the vast universe of art, in the world "after the end of art" (Danto, 1997) where the definition and potential for "art" remain open-ended.

The concept of "artistic development" becomes highly problematic in the absence of systematic and consistent criteria, requirements, or values against which it could be assessed. The ability to achieve mastery in pictorial realism is neither a necessary nor a sufficient condition for artistic success. Technical proficiency has proven redundant in some manifestations of art. Complexity and elaboration have been dethroned to embrace synthetic simplicity, and absence of form gained artistic credibility matching that of a tangible artifact. Interest in cultural pluralism has incorporated into the domain of "art" (at least in the Western understanding of the term) objects and actions that require understandings, abilities, and skills increasingly diverse and hard to trace along a developmental continuum. Information technology, multimedia applications, and proliferation of images within the scope of visual culture have further extended the already ungraspable universe. In this context, can we still contemplate a possibility of "artistic development" as a discrete, universally shared phenomenon of a sequence that associates psychobiological and sociocultural factors with an increase in "artistic" performance?

The "ill-defined" nature of the category "art" represents only one aspect of the problem. The other comes from uncertainty, highlighted by lack of credible evidence, that artistic performance in visual arts involves separate and distinct cognitive processes that may be a subject to their own pattern of development. Even within a very narrow definition of art there is little evidence to suggest that growth or progression within the domain can be attributed to a set of developmental processes and their sequence characteristic and unique to this area of experience. A close examination of theories concerned with development in art suggests that they have been based on a principle of "the closest match" between development of selected general cognitive abilities and practical competencies with what has been deemed as key attributes or characteristics of art.

For example, in his book *Art and Representation* Willats (1997) proposes a developmental theory based on changes in the use of denotation systems: from ones where regions stand for volumes to ones where lines are used to denote contours and edges and in gradual emergence of what he regards as "higher" modes of representation of space in drawings: from topology and extendedness through orthogonal, horizontal, vertical, and oblique projections to the use of linear perspective. Although no-one in their right mind would argue that ability to use linear perspective in drawings precedes attempts to represent special relationships through topological representations in early spontaneous pictorial work of youngest children, it remains that application of linear perspective is hardly indicative of artistic success and within certain cultural contexts has historically remained irrelevant. Evidence of reaching a more advanced developmental stage according to Willat's theory is relevant only to a limited artistic tradition and is hardly a predictor of artistic success. Furthermore, having had taught orthographic, isometric, and perspective drawing for several years, I have failed to observe any developmental facility in terms of my students' ability to apply the three systems. In fact, orthographic projections of displayed models were at times more difficult for some students to produce than were perspective renditions, especially if students employed simple grids facilitating applications of the technique. At least for some students it seemed more difficult to correctly decompose the model into surface representations than to create an image that could be judged and corrected in relation to the three-dimensional appearance of the referent. In any case, learning of perspective drawing was clearly a process of acquisition of a skill that could be reduced to a series of step-by-step instructions and their careful execution—hardly a hallmark of "development." It is true that Western culture has attributed a high value in art to linear perspective, but there is no strong evidence suggesting that its superiority is anything but a judgment call that reflects preference toward visual realism over retaining actual angles, dimensions, or proportions within the represented objects.

It is important to note that my reservations regarding the concept of "artistic development" are framed differently from arguments presented by Hagen (1985) as she declared that "there is no development in art" (p. 59). Hagen, who conducted a systematic analysis of projection systems focusing on the use of primary geometry and light in a drawing (1985, 1986) concluded that in these respects there was no evidence of existence of any clear developmental patterns. From my perspective, however, such a conclusion is, again, far removed from the context of art and what does and does not matter within its universe. I would consider Hagen's "no development" stance as problematic as Willat's insistence on development—in that what they have suggested applies only to a very limited subset of what art and artistic engagement may possibly build on, even within the domain of drawing. Hagen (1985) correctly notes that acquisition of drawing skills geared toward visual realism relies heavily on "mastery of specifically taught canons" and the gradual acquisition of motor skills rather than being a prerogative or evidence of the existence of "a developmental progression with ordered stages that differ qualitatively from each other" (p. 76). Still, her conceptualization of developmental question remains framed within the great Western narrative of academic art and could easily be contested based on the narrowness of the criteria of development in art that she selected.

One point on which I strongly converge with Hagen is the notion that hierarchy in pictorial systems (whether restricted to consideration of geometry, as has been in Hagen's case, or not) can be highly misguided or culturally biased and that an alternative model of a parallel growth in a range of systems that are of equal status provides a more appropriate model for describing changes in human pictorial attempts. In fact, understanding of "development" as an increase in pictorial repertoires rather than as a cumulative linear growth within a system that has a single endpoint has underlined the work of Wolf and Perry (Wolf, 1994; Wolf & Perry, 1988) and the model of development in pictorial representation that Bernard Darras and I have proposed (Darras & Kindler, 1993; Kindler & Darras, 1994, 1997, 1998) . Within the context of my present claim questioning the concept of "development in art," it is important to note that our model has been presented on earlier occasions within the "development in art " discourse because of its relevance and usefulness to the field of art education rather than due to our commitment to the concept of "artistic development." This stance has been particularly well articulated by my research partner whose interest in imagery has consistently been less related to art education than my own focus (Darras, 1996, private communication, 1998–2001). Our model addressed the development of pictorial representation largely within a two-dimensional space, and from its onset our claim has been to incorporate or account for a vast universe of pictorial imagery that may or may not be classified as art. In other words, we have attempted to describe some principles underlying differentiation or change relative to the use of pictorial systems that may be used in the contexts of diverse applications, some of them falling within the vast territory of art and others situated outside its boundaries.

I have already eluded to a fundamental difficulty related to the concept of development in art—namely, the vastness and ill-defined nature of the artistic domain. There are some specific aspects to this complexity that pose serious obstacles to articulation of a coherent and comprehensive developmental theory in this area of human experience that I will try to highlight in this section. In this chapter, as I address selected obstacles to articulation of a coherent, comprehensive theory of development in art, I will try to present perspectives that exemplify both theoretical limitations and contributions that constitute attempts to transcend them.

PROBLEMATIC NATURE OF OPERATIONAL DEFINITIONS OF "ART"

In order to cope with the vastness of the concept of art, contributors to the debate about the nature of development have resorted, explicitly or implicitly, to the use of operational definitions or limiting assumptions corresponding to the focus of their inquiry. A good example of an explicit attempt to frame the concept of art for the purpose of a developmental theory is Hagen's explanation that limits art to "two-dimensional creations of skilled people, whether painted, drawn, etched, engraved and photographed, or even programmed," production that "is always skilled labor, the end product of developed technique." Hagen discounts "intention, function, and aesthetic appeal" of an image and excludes "sculpture, crafts and artifacts," "startlingly beautiful patterns of nature or the happy accidents of chance construction, or the uncontrolled expressions of children," or "snapshots of summer camp and family picnics" from the category of art (Hagen, 1986, p. 3). Although such operational definition may be satisfying to a perceptual psychologist, it clearly would raise serious issues with art historians, artists, and art educators.

Implicit exclusions have been embedded in a majority of developmental theories that focused on development in pictorial representation in a two-dimensional plane, or more specifically, drawing. Some of the most influential, longstanding theories (e.g., Arnheim, 1974; Lowenfeld, 1943; Luquet, 1927) as well as recent models (e.g., Cox, 1992; Kindler & Darras, 1997, 1998; Matthews, 1999; Milbrath, 1998; Willats, 1997) exemplify this focus on two-dimensional work. Notwithstanding the important place of drawing within the world of art to say that a model of artistic development could be complete without consideration of sculpture, installation, or other forms of art that make use of three-dimensional space would be inconceivable. The issue of neglect of three-dimensional imagery and other forms of representation including those that involve cooperation of multiple modalities of expression will be further discussed in a separate section later in this chapter.

IMPORTANCE ATTRIBUTED TO VISUAL REALISM

Some of the most prevalent and influential developmental theories have rested on the assumption that experimentation with pictorial devices is directed toward finding and adopting solutions that lead to the creation of "simile" (Darras, 1996)—images that display a high degree of visual resemblance to their referents. Luquet (1927) argued that children's learning in drawing is concerned with and motivated by an interest in producing recognizable representations. The criterion for measuring growth has been a progression from "fortuitous realism" through "failed realism" and "intellectual realism" to finally arriving at the "visual realism" stage. Victor Lowenfeld's work (1943) has further asserted this general conception of artistic growth in his own stage theory that consists of early scribbling and preschematic stages, followed by the schematic stage and the stage of "dawning realism." Although Lowenfeld contended that the final "stage of reasoning" characterized by naturalism (visual realism) refers especially to the developmental progression of "visuallyminded children," and that "haptic individuals" may instead focus on expressive qualities in their work as a result of their heightened awareness of muscular, kinesthetic sensations and experiences, the general direction of his developmental account has clearly favored specific cultural models, namely, visual realism and expressiveness characteristic of modernist art. Lowenfeld also closely linked artistic and mental growth that favored, from a developmental perspective, a great amount of detail in a drawing over a more synthetic image. Linking an increase in drawing differentiation to a greater level of a child's awareness of his or her environment placed more complex drawings higher on a developmental scale—with no consideration of the drawing's intent of purpose, which could have well accounted for a selective elimination of detail.

More recent studies of development have also largely focused on drawing development with visual realism as its endpoint (e.g., Chen, 1985; Cox, 1992; Milbrath, 1998; Willats, 1997). This is well exemplified in the work of Milbrath, who asserted that "drawing of less talented children reflects categorical properties rather than visual properties" (1998, p. 41) and considered "remarkable visual realism" (p. 369) in drawings as an indicator of artistic talent. As I have signaled earlier, concern over visual realism also underlined the developmental account formulated by Willats, who argued that changes in children's drawings are prompted by "a series of interactions between picture production and picture perception" (p. 318). According to Willats, children progress from drawings that offer, in their estimation, acceptable solutions to pictorial problems (drawing that seem "right") to drawings that also "look right."

It is interesting to note that the criterion of visual realism has underlied developmental accounts by scholars otherwise representing differing perspectives on the specific causes or mechanisms accounting for appearance of drawings. For example, Piaget closely linked cognitive development with development in drawing and regarded early pictorial work of children as evidence of their cognitive deficit (e.g., Piaget & Inhelder, 1956). Freeman (1980, 1995), who disagreed with the cognitive deficit theory and suggested that it is not the lack of knowledge about the world but rather the lack of ability to translate it in a drawing is responsible for an "immature-looking" pictorial production of children, nonetheless characterized development as a move from object-centered to view-centered description, pointing to the developmental superiority of realism-based representation. Optical realism also remained the endpoint of development in work of many neo-Piagetian researchers concerned with artistic development (e.g., Porath, 1997; Reith, 1995).

Although it certainly is true that some of the pictorial work of children, adolescents, and adults tends to gravitate toward visual realism, there is also a range of imagery that emerges in spontaneous pictorial production that is not concerned at all with the appearance of things. It is very common, for example, for young children to produce drawings that focus on actions rather than on objects and where iconicity is restricted to the kinetic dimension (e.g., Kindler, 1999; Kindler & Darras, 1994, 1997, 1998; Matthews, 1999; this volume; Wolf & Perry, 1988). This highlights another problem embedded in classical theories of development: a general lack of consideration of the relationship between the purpose and the intention behind a pictorial attempt and the choice of expressive media, which will be discussed in the next section of this chapter. Furthermore, there is no evidence to suggest that an ability to produce realistically looking replicas of the world is regulated by a developmental mechanism. On the contrary, most adults never reach this "endpoint" in their pictorial production, and those who attain such ability typically acquire it through extensive training situated within culturally based forms of apprenticeship.

The problem with relying on visual realism as a benchmark for artistic growth has been exposed by Arnheim (e.g., 1966, 1974), whose work challenged the assumption that the concept of development should be tied to the notion of art as a copy of reality. Arnheim noted that children and artists alike do not necessarily strive to "copy" a scene but rather concern themselves with the creation of equivalences guided by their own internal graphic logic and which only structurally or dynamically correspond to the objects to be represented. Like a hobby horse, in Gombrich's (1985) essay, that does not need to visually resemble a horse but "becomes a horse" because a child can ride on it, in pictorial representation there is a range of graphic solutions that allow the creation of well-functioning pictorial substitutes. Arnheim's theory has greatly influenced the developmental work of Golomb (e.g., 1992, 2002), who concluded that "based on empirical findings reported by different investigators, one has to reject a unilinear view of developmental progression toward realism in artistic development" (2002, p. 48) The ecosystemic approach recently advocated by Darras (2002) further highlights the fact that visual culture is composed of systems of imagery that do not necessarily consistently favor a visual/mimetic or a schematic/pictographic orientation but that also include systems that select, integrate, and mix different aspects of these two traditions.

ISSUES OF PICTORIAL INTENT AND PURPOSE

One of the greatest problems with traditional developmental theory has been the focus on the issue of "translation" of a three-dimensional reality into a two-dimensional plane with little or no attention given to the nature of decision making and to the intentions behind the pictorial act. In her recent critique of accounts of "drawing development as a unidirectional progression towards optical realism," Golomb (2002) noted that such theory "ignores the diversity of cultural models and the effectiveness of alternative modes of representation that depend on the intention of the artist" (p. 18). One of the earliest studies that systematically explored young children's capability to use multiple drawing systems within a timeframe of a single "stage" in relation to diverse drawing tasks was conducted by Bremmer and Moore (1984). These researchers demonstrated that even very young children have and exercise choices in selecting such systems depending on the context and purpose of their drawings.

Their findings complemented Project Zero researchers' work concerned with early symbolization that lead to the broadening of the definition of representation and to the identification of distinguishable drawing systems in production by children as young as 12 to 15 months of age (Shotwell, Wolf, & Gardner, 1980). In their critique of traditional stage theories, Wolf and Perry (1988) referred to the work of sociolinguist Dell Hymes who argued that language acquisition by children was not limited to learning of a language but rather "languages—ways of using words in face-to-face conversations and long-distance communications, in arguments and songs, in writing and in speech, in poems and recipes" (p. 17). By analogy, Wolf and Perry suggested that the use of pictorial language is not restricted to a developmental acquisition of one system of visual representation and have argued that depending on the context different drawing systems may be utilized. Atkinson (1991) further provided examples to substantiate the claim that children have an ability to access multiple pictorial systems.

"FROM ENDPOINTS TO REPERTOIRES"

The notion of possible multiple endpoints of artistic development has underlined theoretical contributions that reconceptualized development in drawing as a growth in pictorial repertoires (e.g., Golomb, 2002; Kindler, 1999; Kindler & Darras, 1994, 1998; Matthews, this volume; Pariser, 1995, 1997; Wolf, 1994; Wolf and Perry, 1988). Unlike classical developmental theories that regarded visual realism as an ultimate destination of artistic growth, these more recent accounts consider the strive toward realistic representation as only one of the possible avenues of development in the pictorial domain.

Wolf and Perry (1988) defined a "drawing system" as a "set of rules designating how the full-size, three-dimensional, moving, colored world of ongoing visual experience can be translated into a set of marks on a plane surface" (p. 19). They noted that these rules referred to at least two categories of issues: consideration of kinds of information crucial to the representational success and aspects of pictorial behavior of the individual engaged in the drawing task that may also carry meaning. In Wolf and Perry's account, the earliest drawing systems are not graphic in nature and involve object-based representations where very young children may use paper or felt pens in a course of symbolic play. In other words, in these types of representations, drawing materials themselves become substitutes for referents. They also identify gestural representations that are concerned with motions rather than with objects that eventually lead to point-plot representations at approximately 20 months of age. Wolf and Perry argue that "existence, number and position" (p. 21) take precedence here over shape, color, or volume. As they describe other drawing systems; those that involve consideration of shape and relative size, as well as systems that situate objects in a larger space or that call for application of rules of projective geometry, Wolf and Perry assert that development in drawing consists of a growth in pictorial repertoires as well as of an evolution and improvement within each of the drawing systems. They claim that the ability to use the most recent, newly acquired system is less relevant to the concept of progress in the pictorial domain than the ability to select from among the attained choices a system that best matches a specific pictorial task.

The notion of pictorial repertoires has also been central to the model of development proposed by Kindler and Darras (1997, 1997b, 1998). This model attempted to chart some possible avenues of acquisition and roads toward mastery of pictorial systems that collectively add to pictorial repertoires from which cultures and individuals prioritize and select depending on their purpose and values. Relying on Peirce's semiotic theory, we have argued that development in graphic representation can be explored through examination of the use of icons, indexes, and symbols that constitute components of signs (1997). We suggested that the range of graphic production of children, adolescents, and adults can be treated and interpreted as systems of dynamic signs that are subject to change, mutation, and evolution as a function of diverse teleologies or purposes and to shifts in salience of different attributes of a concept that becomes selected or prioritized in the act of representation. This process leads to development of pictorial repertoires that are cumulative rather than substitutive in nature, that rely on single or multiple modalities of expression in representation attempt, and that can be purposefully selected from depending on contexts and specific pictorial tasks.

Our account of development pointed to the close and circular relationship among changing teleologies of representational behavior, shifting semiotic saliences, and growing pictorial repertoires. We have argued that change in pictorial imagery results from this dynamic system where a shift in one of the elements affects changes in other components. A new teleological orientation or purpose can influence selection of different conceptual and/or visual attributes of objects to be represented, but it can also emerge as a result in shift in importance given to specific aspects of the object/concept. Similarly, a new pictorial repertoire may emerge as a result in changing purposes or teleologies, but it may also open the door to new pictorial teleologies and endpoints.

In explaining the origins of pictorial behavior, we benefited from work of Varela (1989), who proposed that cognitive activity emerges at the crossroads of activities of the sensorimotor type, on the one hand, and the activities of the central nervous system, on the other. We have argued that an interaction of sensorimotor activities, which are subject to environmental influences and activities of the central nervous system, allows for emergence of the teleology of representation. This teleology develops from the ability to recognize similarities and differences in movements opening the door to the creation of first iconic signs. An ability to re-create kinetic acts with an awareness of their identity or similarity to an earlier movement is at the foundation of representation, as it allows for both production of icons of gestures and experimentation that would lead to the development of new, different signs. We consider gestures as iconic signs of movement and regard icons of gestures as first observable behaviors within the domain of representation. Our approach here is congruent with Wolf and Perry's (1988) assertion that pictorial development must be traced further back in its origin than to the first tangible marks left on a surface.

I have also argued that iconic gestures are at the heart of an important pictorial repertoire that children spontaneously use well beyond infancy (Kindler, 1999). The "I am the picture" repertoire (p. 336) relies on the interplay of gestural, visual, vocal, and verbal cues and is manifested in "action pictures" that gain in elaboration, complexity, intentionality of specific purpose, and ability to carry explicit meanings. However, these "action pictures" are grounded in the same teleology of representation and general iconic principles as the earliest iconic manifestations, testifying to the fact that the first, initial iconic behaviors neither atrophy nor become replaced with more sophisticated pictorial systems. Instead, they function in parallel to other repertoires that can emerge later in life and have found ways to claim a place within the realm of professional art through the performance-based artists such as Allan Kaprow or Rebecca Horn (e.g., Henri, 1974).

In Darras and Kindler's model, the shift of salience from the kinetic aspects of movement to the marks or traces that they can leave on a surface leads to the emergence of teleology of figuration. Now figurative aspects of a gesture trajectory that have acquired a static dimension can be further explored, interpreted, and modified. As has been the case earlier, a pictorial repertoire of icons of traces has a potential to be sustained and developed beyond early childhood years and boundaries of a dilettante production. The notion of indexality in image making and creation of imprints not only is common to many pictorial efforts of toddlers and older children but also surfaces in works of mature artists such as Matisse and in artistic techniques such as printmaking.

The existence of icons of traces in early phases of pictorial experimentation also allows for consideration of another teleology where repetition of icons creates a sufficient increase in the number of graphic elements to create structures of special organization. This teleology of organization is still closely tied to the kinetic dimension and in its earliest manifestations results in "icons of rhythms" that capture trajectories of multiple movements with a varied degree of kinetic diversity. Such icons of rhythms create the possibility for two new qualitatively different teleologies and resulting pictorial repertoires: one, drawn out of an analysis and interpretation of forms; and the other, concerned with the dynamic dimension and potential for representation that unfolds in time. In the Darras and Kindler model, the former is referred to as a teleology of autonomy where interest in regularity of marks, closure, and coherence contributes to development of "icons of forms." Closed shapes separating segments of space create intrinsically semantic forms that communicate roundness, harmony, and coherence (Arnheim, 1974) and lend themselves to reinterpretation as a result of child's interactions with his or her environment. An increase in realization of the potential to create graphic marks that can "stand for" objects and people in the environment leads to the emergence of teleology of description with icons of objects that satisfy the need to communicate by achieving a desirable level of basic correspondence between the intention and the interpretation of the image. We have argued, however, that icons of objects as they emerge in early pictorial production are seldom created in isolation from vocal, verbal, or gestural commentary. In other words, the semiotic process in which they play a role is not restricted to graphic communication and relies on a much more extensive range of modalities of expression.

A parallel development of the "teleology of narration" highlighted, in our model, the fact that representation of static aspects of experience calls for a different pictorial system than representation concerned with dynamic events. "Icons of actions" documented in a toddler's drawings by lines or dots, generated through a process of play imitating a driving car or a jumping rabbit, leave cars and rabbits outside of the picture. The existence of a car in these drawings is required only for the action to take place, and it can be sufficiently asserted through verbal or vocal clues. Again, it has been documented that in pictorial production of older children, in drawings where "the bare essence of the story" matters (Kindler, 1999, p. 336), children readily refer to this early acquired pictorial repertoire.

We have also pointed to the early emergence of two additional teleologies of pictorial behavior that combine interest with narration and description, with an emphasis on either the story-telling aspects or the descriptive mandate of representation. We noted that depending on the salience attributed to each of these dimensions children select different pictorial repertoires. It is only within the realm of imagery concerned with "how things look" that visual realism may become of relevance.

We have never suggested that our model represents the universe of possibilities within a pictorial domain but have noted that the emergence of pictorial teleologies that we have described is sufficient for the system of "initial imagery" (Darras, 1985, 1986; Darras & Kindler, 1993) to emerge. This pictorial system that characterizes production of preadolescent children, "nonartistic" adolescents, and adult art novices, in addition to being present in exemplars of prehistoric art, comprises simple but stable schema that satisfy the basic needs of representation. We highlighted the fact that although this system is often degraded as "primitive" or immature, its schematic and "generic" qualities and ability to capture the essence rather than the particular make it exceptionally strong and effective in its universality, economy of means, and effectiveness in communication as it exemplifies Arnheim's (1974) notion of an internal strive toward simplicity. We also noted that initial imagery is often employed in the context of representation that incorporates gestural or verbal elements and as such is not deficient in lack of detail or elaboration.

A recent study by Kailin (2002) offers additional support to the repertoire-based models by demonstrating that elementary-school-aged children have a very good understanding of different pictorial systems and different strategies that can support learning of each of them. For example, participants in Kailin's study made it clear that copying is the most effective strategy in becoming good at cartoon drawings, whereas looking closely at an object and being coached step by step may most effectively lead to success in "life-drawing" tasks that are concerned with visual realism. They further indicated that drawing emotions may best be learned through a study of the work of artists or even that of peers or drawing alongside someone else.

Although the repertoire-based accounts of development have addressed some limitations of classical-stage theories, they still fall short of describing "development in art." First, they have been focused primarily on development in two-dimensional representation; and second, they have not attempted to delineate developmental mechanisms specifically responsible for production of art as opposed to other kinds of pictorial imagery. In fact, the category of "art" has hardly been central to these theoretical positions and has entered the picture only to the extent to which some of the production that they attempted to explain could be classified as art according to selected cultural and historical criteria. Kindler and Darras (1997) made it explicit that although certain categories of imagery tend to be classified as art and others may more readily belong to the category of "visual communication," there are certainly no clear demarcation lines that could be consistently applied for the purpose of this differentiation and that the boundaries between these categories are subject to fluctuation depending on historical and cultural perspectives and values.

DEVELOPMENTAL MODELS AND CULTURAL AESTHETIC BIAS

Wilson (1997, this volume) has convincingly argued that "child art" is a concept of the modernist era and that cultural biases and assumptions have long muddled the developmental discourse. A similar observation was made by Hamblen (1993), who claimed that models of development in art "tend to be prescriptive of art learning that conforms to the values of modernity, to the characteristics of a hierarchical society, to the institutional needs of education" (p. 45).

An excellent example of a theory heavily dependent on a specific cultural perspective is the U-curve model of artistic development proposed by researchers associated with Harvard's Project Zero (Davis, 1991, 1997a, 1997b; Gardner & Winner, 1982). The essence of the U-curve theory is that an initial outburst of artistic creativity in early childhood years is followed by a demise in the quality of children's artistic production in middle childhood, and that only in late adolescence or adulthood there is a rebirth of artistic ability, at least in the case of artistically inclined individuals.

Observations leading to this conclusion initially made by Gardner and Winner (1982) were later empirically confirmed by Davis (1991, 1997a, 1997b) in an experiment involving 5-, 8-, and 11-year-old children as well as "artistic" and "nonartistic" adolescents and adults in the United States. Participants in Davis's study were asked to make drawings representing themes of "happy," "sad," and "angry." Completed drawings were then presented to expert judges (artists), who were asked to evaluate them using a protocol based on the analysis of the "symptoms of the aesthetic" (Goodman, 1976). The judges were specifically asked to pay attention to the following criteria: overall expression, balance, and the use of line and composition, as appropriate to the target emotion being expressed. These assessments confirmed that the work of the youngest children was superior in its artistry to production to that of all other children and nonartistic adolescents and adults.

However, subsequent studies conducted in diverse cultural settings that replicated Davis's experiment (Pariser & van den Berg, 1997), including those that freed the judges from the obligation to follow strict criteria predetermined by the experimenter and allowed for application of standards that the judges themselves deemed relevant to the task, consistently failed to yield the U-curve developmental patterns (Kindler, 2001; Kindler, Liu, Pariser, & van den Berg, 2003; Kindler, Pariser, van den Berg, & Liu, 2001; Liu et al., 2002; Pariser & van den Berg, 2001). The explanation proposed by those who have expressed doubts about the U-curve theory points to the bias embedded in a Western, modernist perspective of Davis's judges. In other words, it has been argued that this developmental theory has been constructed here in relation to a very specific set of aesthetic values that are not universally shared (Kindler, Pariser, van den Berg, Liu, & Dias, 2002, 2002a). Given the fascination that modernist artists have with young children's imagery; both as collectors and as borrowers of stylistic characteristics of young children's art in their own work, it is not difficult to see that an assessment of artistic development using a scale conforming to the modernist taste would put young children's production in a very positive light. Fineberg's *The Innocent Eye* (1997) systematically documents the intimate relationship between children's art and the creative output of modernist artists. The author highlights Picasso's admiration of the "visual inventiveness of children" and pointed to its connection with the artist's "own extraordinary access to the memories and urges of childhood that most of us have buried beyond the reach of our adult consciousness" (p. 137). Similarly, Franciscono claimed that Dubuffet "turned in the 1940s to children's drawings as a means of cutting to the truth of the ordinary experience" (1998, p. 116). If artists such as Picasso, Duchamp, Klee, or Miro modeled some of their work on young children's imagery, it is only natural that the work of young children would, conversely, carry elements characteristic of the modernist artists.

The thesis of dependency of the U-curve theory on a particular aesthetic tradition associated with a specific period in history of art is further substantiated by the fact that in selected North American (Canada) as well as South American (Brazil) and Asian (Taiwan) cultural contexts nonartist adult judges and children and adolescent judges alike consistently failed to evaluate young children's drawings as superior to images produced by other age groups (Kindler, Pariser, van den Berg & Liu, 2002; Kindler, Pariser, van den Berg, Liu, & Dias, 2002, 2002a). Developmental patterns found among different age and art-expertise groups resembled, in a majority of cases, either a rising line or "dragon-like" curves with a general upward direction. Only selected expert judges who have been heavily exposed to the modernist tradition in their own artistic training produced patterns reminiscent of the U-curve.

This is not to say that the U-curve model does not describe some aspects of a phenomenon that fits the "development in art" discourse. Within the modernist ethos of elevation of child art to serve as an exemplar of excellence in the domain, it is certainly possible to argue that artistic development indeed takes a dip and that, paraphrasing the famous Picasso's statement, it takes a lifetime before an artist can attain the quality of a child's imagery in his or her mature artistic production. However, it is necessary to remember the qualifying conditions of this assertion; and given the limitations that they impose, it is difficult to argue that the U-curve model defines universal patterns of artistic development.

NATURAL DEVELOPMENT OR CULTURAL LEARNING?

Although much consideration has been given to the concept of artistic development as a natural unfolding of cognitive abilities, some researchers have argued that there is nothing "natural" or "developmental" about acquisition of drawing skills and that it all is confined to cultural learning. This theory receives significant attention in a separate chapter (Wilson, this volume) and consequently will not be given much elaboration here. It is important, however, to highlight Wilson and Wilson's theoretical contribution to the debate about development in art (Wilson & Wilson, 1977, 1982, 1985; Wilson, 1997).

Unlike Arnheim (1974) or Golomb (1992), who posited that artistic development involves children inventing graphic language, Wilson and Wilson (1977, 1982, 1985) argued that such language is strictly culturally acquired. They suggested that with the exception of the earliest years of life that are marked by development of general cognitive abilities relevant to consideration of artistic process, all images created by children or adolescents can be traced back to preexisting schemata that are socioculturally shared. They claimed that such schemata become naturally shared among peers and are adopted from imagery that permeates visual worlds in which children grow up.

In essence, their argument reverses Lowenfeld's (1943) claim that if not for the interference of the external world, every child would grow up to be an artist. According to the Wilsons, it is precisely this interference that lays foundations for artistic accomplishment. Research in art education and psychology offers numerous examples demonstrating powerful influences of sociocultural contexts on the development of pictorial imagery of children (e.g., Burton, 1980; Golomb, 1974; Hamblen, 1999; Kindler, 1992, 1994, 1995; Kindler & Darras, 1994; Kindler & Thompson, 1994; Thompson & Bales, 1991)—many of them clearly very productive in encouragement of children's artistic activity.

Leaving expert theories aside for a moment, it may be of interest to consider children's views regarding the nature/nurture influence on their artistic progression. Kindler and Darras (1995) conducted a study of 3- and 5-year-old children in France and Canada concerned with young children's conceptions of the nature and modes of the acquisition of drawing skills. They found that although most of their interviewees contended that people get better at drawing with age, they have not attributed this improvement simply to maturation. This was especially the case with the 5-year-old children, who overwhelmingly discounted the natural improvement hypothesis and claimed that they and others learn how to draw from others by being taught, through copying and through practice. A recent study by Kailin (2002) further demonstrated that forms of interaction with the environment such as "learning to draw the object step-by-step," "looking at other children's drawings," or "copying" rather than natural maturation are consistently identified by children as possible means of improvement in their artistry.

One of the most significant implications of the Wilsons' position is realization of the power and influence of visual culture. This impact of exposure to and engagement with visual worlds has been signaled by the "Flynn effect" (Darras, 2002) in terms of its impact on cognition. Flynn (1987) conducted a study comparing, across 14 cultural settings, IQ scores obtained within several decades and noted a consistent, significant increase over time. Progressive elimination of alternative hypothesis of the cause of this increase (such as improvement in nutrition, increase in quality of education, etc.) led to the observation that the improvement was almost exclusively noted on nonverbal tasks that relied on visual–spatial competencies. It was eventually stipulated that the change in visual environment and the resulting growing expertise in visual analysis account for the new patterns of the IQ test results. This is consistent with the notion forwarded by Fish and Scrivener (1990), who observed that:

> Despite scholarly arguments for a greater emphasis on visual modes of thought (. . .), Western culture and education are still dominated by verbal/propositional reasoning and information storage. New evidence of the importance of mental imagery in memory, reasoning and invention, and research that reveals the awesome proportion of the brain that is dedicated to vision, emphasize the need to redress the imbalance. (p. 125)

SELF-CONTAINED GRAPHIC LANGUAGE OR COLLABORATION OF MULTIPLE MODALITIES OF EXPRESSION?

The majority of accounts of artistic development regarded development in graphic representation as restricted to a single-symbol system. This view has been especially well articulated by Arnheim, whose notion of visual thinking involved thinking within a medium and stipulated development of ability in creation of pictorial equivalences in negotiation within the medium properties. This notion has been also strongly entrenched in the thinking of neo-Piagetian psychologists concerned with development in the pictorial realm. I recall a roundtable session on graphic development at a Jean Piaget Society International conference in Geneva several years ago, where a suggestion of a possible existence of a more integrated cognitive system—in which gestures, vocal/verbal and graphic forms are inseparably bound and create a plurimodal language of early childhood that subsequently becomes broken down into culturally accepted categories of movement, language, and graphic worlds (Kindler & Darras, 1996)—was quickly dismissed because the notion of the need to study simultaneously phenomena that have traditionally been fragmented without breaking them into the component parts seemed impossible to conceive.

Yet, in recent years there has been a growing interest in more integrated conceptions of early cognition involving pictorial behavior. The work of Matthews (1994, 1999, this book) well documented the interplay of different modalities of expression in visual representation in early childhood. Evidence from cognitive sciences contributed further evidence that "the mind uses imagery and verbal processes for complementary and interdependent purposes" and that "it may be an error" to separate them (Fish & Scrivener, 1990, p. 125). Parsons expresses similar sentiment arguing that "systems approach to cognition identifies the different arts as each being a different symbol system" and "requires thought to stay within boundaries of a single medium it is dealing with on the assumption that, if it moves from one system to another, it loses its coherence" (Parsons, 1998, p. 106). He expresses concern that such an understanding of cognition in the arts "transforms a dimension of difference into a principle of separation" not compatible with his view of artistic learning. Efland's (2002) recent book *Art and Cognition* offers additional support to the more complex and integrated notion of artistic learning.

MEANING VERSUS FORM: WHAT ABOUT DEVELOPMENT IN "ARTISTIC THINKING?"

Another question relevant to the concept of development in art addresses the salience of the production aspect, which has traditionally been at the heart of the developmental debate in art education, in relation to the nature of artistic thought. In other words, to what extent performance within a medium can be considered as a sole or even as a key determinant of "artistic development?" One does not need to resort to examples of conceptual art to argue that the quality of thinking and ability to identify, pose, and solve problems within the realm of artistic creativity are fundamental to art. If the meaning and message in art can be regarded as equally or, at times, even more important than the form, then a question regarding developmental pathways guiding growth in "artistic thinking" becomes central to the concept of "development in art." It also becomes of interest to explore how "artistic thinking" intersects with cognitive processes that account for abilities to translate artistic ideas into tangible artifacts within a selected medium along a developmental continuum.

One area of research that attempted to provide some answers to the first question has been the inquiry concerned with the nature and development of artistic creativity. Although the relationship between art and creativity can certainly be problematized, especially from a cross-cultural perspective, and the definition of creativity poses no fewer problems than does the definition of art, it may be worthwhile to examine accounts of development in creativity in the context of developmental discourse in art, given the strong common association of the two concepts. The ability to generate original ideas, find new associations, and build innovative, unconventional connections among concepts that characterize creative behavior tends also to be associated with artistic accomplishment.

Sobel and Rothenberg (1980) argued that artistic creativity is related to the development of homospatial thinking—"a particular type of cognitive operation involving highly complex mental imagery" where "images and representations derived from any sensory modality" (including visual) are consciously brought into the same special location" (p. 994). The resulting mental conception allows for the production of new forms and structures, and their integration, which characterizes creative endeavors, as documented in research on distinguished artists, musicians, and creative individuals in other fields (Rothenberg, 1979). However, this research has left many questions unanswered regarding the specific links between the homospatial processes and their creative function, nor has it given any indication that development in homospatial thinking would be characteristic of artistic development as opposed to creative activity in other areas.

Tucker, Rothwell, Armstrong, and McConaghy (1982) presented some evidence linking allusive (loose) thinking and the type of creativity exhibited by acknowledged artists. They differentiated between a low-level creativity associated with divergent thinking that involves an ability to "generate or produce, within some criterion of relevance, many cognitive associates, and many that are unique" (Wallach & Kagan, 1965, in Tucker et al., 1982, p. 840) and allusive thought demonstrated by successful visual artists. The researchers have acknowledged, however, that "with changes in accepted art forms, allusive thinking could become more or less valuable to artists" (p. 840) and contented that creation of nonrepresentational art, for example, particularly benefits from this kind of thinking. In other words, they acknowledged that development in allusive thinking would not necessarily effectively support development in all domains or styles of art.

An interesting account of development in artistic creativity was also proposed by Smolucha and Smolucha (1980), who posited that such creativity emerges at the intersection of analogical thinking (thinking that characterizes children's symbolic play) and logical thinking. They argued that visual artists have an ability to perceive and manipulate perceptual resemblances (which they called isomorphisms) between different things to create multiple levels of meaning by consciously controlling their analogical thinking and oscillating between the analogical and logical modes of thought. Considering perception of isomorphisms as a function of sensorimotor thought, Smolucha and Smolucha suggested that, in the visual arts, isomorphisms function as means of implying relationships between seemingly unrelated parts and allow a work of art to acquire multiple levels of interpretation. They argued that "imagination has its origins in the sensorimotor domain in the form of mental images which are reconstructions of external reality" and that "these mental representations can be used to represent more abstract ideas by semiotic extension" (p. 97). When Smolucha and Smolucha put their theory to an empirical test by constructing a series of tasks that allowed the measurement of manipulations of isomorphisms and the collection of scores of fluency and flexibility of divergent behavior of subjects ranging in age from 2 to 57, they discovered a J-shaped developmental pattern indicating that "artistic creativity is at its highest in adulthood" (p. 98). They noted that this contradicted the U-curve model and suggested possible further qualitative change in artistic cognition that could be attributed to the improved collaboration between the two forms of thinking and a desired state of equilibrium between the analogical thinking based on sensorimotor thought, on the one hand, and the verbal–logical thought, on the other.

An interesting insight into the consideration of the nature of artistic growth and its socio-cultural determinants comes from studies by Petrov (1996, 1998), who explored the creativity of artists in relation to relative brain asymmetry. Using expert ratings categorizing stylistic orientations of over 200 European artists from the mid-15th century to the mid-19th century and plotting these judgments against bipolar scales on indicators of the two opposing types of information processing that characterize left- and right-hemispheric functions, he concluded that these two types of processes "are periodically dominant during the evolution of the socio-psychological life of a society" with a mean duration of each cycle of approximately 20 to 25 years. He predicted "a new half-cycle of L-brain prevalence in the next several years, with such features as rationality and predominant role for verbal elements, theoretical concepts, reflexive processes, etc." to dominate in the visual arts (1998, p. 229). According to Petrov's theory of evolution in art in relation to shifts in value that favor or deemphasize selected types of information processing, it could be stipulated that developmental models such as the U-curve proposition generated within a particular cycle would likely carry a respective bias.

None of the aforementioned approaches have, however, unconditionally linked artistic development to specific forms of thinking exclusive to the domain; nor have they suggested that these account for the entire realm of artistic production. Although these approaches suggested possible connections between certain characteristics or modes of thought and creative activity, no claims were made of a comprehensive theory of artistic development.

ARTISTIC DEVELOPMENT AND THE BRAIN

Although research in neuroscience has not led, as of yet, to any attempts to formulate comprehensive accounts of development in art, several studies conducted especially over the past decade have contributed important insights into the nature of human artistry. Relevance of such research to art education has recently been explored by Dake (2000), who outlined a number of studies concerned with neurological foundations of visual perception, cognition, and selected art-related behaviors, such as thumbnail sketching.

A body of work in neuroscience has been concerned with identification of brain areas involved in artistic activity. For example, Miller and Tippet (1996) identified right frontal lobe as the area particularly involved in visual problem solving. Elliot (1986) demonstrated that integration and synchronization of functions of the right and left hemispheres relate to creative visual thinking. Changeaux (1994) argued that artistic creativity involves not only cortical areas of the visual system located in the posterior (occipital) part of the brain that are responsible for analysis and synthesis of forms, colors, spatial locations, and movement pertaining to the objects and figures in the external world that fund creation of a mental image, an inner representation of the external world, but also cortical areas located in front of the visual areas in temporal and parietal regions that are responsible for recognition and spatial localization. He further claimed that there is a strong evidence of involvement of "a number of complex and heterogeneous areas in the brain cortex located in the front most part of the brain, on the frontal lobe" (p. 192), where "transitory assemblies of active neurons, or pre-representations, are formed and remain in the conscious short-term memory (. . .) in order to compose a "fundamental thought," a mental stimulation of the picture" (p. 194). Changeaux also noted the significance of cells found in sensorimotor areas of the cortex—which through the spinal cord "send their orders to the muscles (of the hand) that carry them out" (p. 195)—and the role of cerebellum in guiding visual movement. He argued that whereas invention of art is a cultural phenomenon and is not linked to any particular predisposition of human brain, he also contended that humans possess an ability to "unlock the pre-frontal cortex" (Leroi-Gourhan,

1965, in Changeaux, 1994, p. 200) in ways that allow for evolution of mental and cultural representations that make use of "neural structures of reasons" (p. 200).

Neuroscientists Zeki and Lamb (1994) asserted in their "Credo (manifesto of physiological facts)" that "all visual art must obey the laws of the visual system" (p. 607) and that "no theory of aesthetics" (and by extension, possibly also a theory of development in art) that is not substantially based on the activity of the brain is ever likely to be complete, let alone profound (Zeki, 1999). In this context, it could be argued that development in art could perhaps be described in relation to the development of visual brain. Zeki and Lamb's work clearly suggests a possibility to study and articulate "relationships between the organization of the brain and its manifestations in art" (p. 633).

The concept of visual brain (Zeki, 1999) challenged a longstanding tradition of regarding vision as consisting of two separate cortical processes located in separate areas. According to the traditional conception of the "seeing eye" and the "understanding brain," the process of seeing originated with an impression of an image of the visual world on the retina that was transferred and decoded by the visuosensory cortex (the primary visual cortex also referred to as area V1). It was posited that interpretation, or making sense of the image, happened in a different part of the brain, the "association cortex," in the context of present and past impressions. According to this theory, seeing was regarded as a passive process that engaged active cognitive involvement only at later stages of processing.

In contrast, Zeki's (1999) visual brain theory stipulates that vision "is an active process in which brain, in its quest for knowledge about the visual world, discards, selects and, by comparing the selected information to its stored record, generates the visual image" (p. 21). Zeki noted that visual brain functions in ways that can be paralleled to the tasks undertaken by artists when they create images. One of the important dimensions of such common tasks is a search for essentials and "seeking of knowledge in ever-changing world" (p. 12) while overcoming the fundamental problem of vision, the fact that "the image at the eye (retinal image) has countless possible interpretations" (Hoffman, 1998, p. 13). Hoffman argues that an ability to interpret retinal images that are in constant flux in consistent and coherent ways is fundamental to "visual intelligence."

According to Hoffman, visual intelligence is a universal gift acquired rapidly in early childhood years with "each normal child, without being taught, reinvent(ing) the visual world, (. . .) much the same way" (p. 13). Hoffman parallels development of visual intelligence to the processes of language acquisition by suggesting that children learn "the rules of universal vision" (p. 14) in a way similar to that in which they gain linguistic ability. He refers to Steven Pinker's quote: "The crux of the argument is that complex language is universal because children actually reinvent it, generation after generation—not because they are taught, not because they are generally smart, not because it is useful to them, but because they just can't help it" (Pinker in Hoffman, 1998, p. 15).

Zeki (1999) notes, however, that engagement in artistic tasks has the potential to influence visual brain processes and documents how some artists trained in their craft have an ability to "override" some of the prewired mechanisms. Using the example of Monet, he claims that artists who deliberately paint something differently from the ways in which they see it have two subdivisions of the frontal cortex of their brain that naturally become activated in different sets of circumstances to communicate with each other. This could suggest that engagement with visual imagery can allow for forms of neural interactions and dynamics that otherwise may not be achieved.

Zeki also proposes the notion of "modularity of visual aesthetics" that relates to the earlier described conceptions of artistic development as a growth in pictorial repertoires. Through research involving mapping of neural activation zones in relation to different pictorial tasks, Zeki concluded that "different modes of painting make use of different cerebral systems"

(p. 215) and suggested that it may be possible to speak of distinct neurologies of nonobjective, representational, and narrative art.

ARTISTIC DEVELOPMENT REVISITED

In this chapter, I have questioned the concept of artistic development on several grounds. I have argued that its definition may not be possible because of the ill-defined nature and vastness of the domain which it attempts to describe. In this context, I have identified a number of limitations of single-endpoint models of development, pointing to their insufficiency and embedded cultural bias. I have suggested that even the repertoire conceptions of artistic growth that address many of these limitations are not free from constraints of preoccupation with a predominantly two-dimensional medium of expression. I also highlighted the fact that the processes described in these and other theoretical attempts to define artistic development, regardless of their specific situation within a given field of scholarly inquiry, identify, analyze, and interpret behaviors and phenomena that are not necessarily restricted to artistic endeavor. My suspicion regarding the appropriateness of asserting that artistic development is a self-contained category encompassing a unique set of cognitive processes that develop in a systematic, organized manner along one or even more dimensions has further been reinforced by the lack of any credible evidence pointing in this direction.

It may be worthwhile to refer here to Gardner's theory of multiple intelligences (Gardner, 1983, 1993a). Although this theory is often invoked in art education to substantiate claims about the uniqueness of cognitive processes relative to artistic learning, it is important to note that "artistic intelligence" does not figure among the seven distinct intelligences identified by Gardner. The spatial intelligence especially associated with artistic creativity characterizes not only painters or sculptors but also sailors, engineers, and surgeons. Perhaps even more importantly, Gardner cautions that it is a combination of different types of intelligence rather than a single intelligence that possibly accounts for one's success within a domain. So even if development in different aspects of cognition may benefit development of a particular intelligence, it is the interaction of such developmental processes and their selective combination that would account for achievement in artistry.

The 10th anniversary edition of *Frames of Mind* (Gardner, 1993b) includes reference to Csikszentmihalyi (1988) and Feldman's (1980) work from whom Gardner borrows the concepts of "domain" and "field." These concepts may also be of help in the discussion of difficulties in defining artistic development. Csikszentmihalyi's "systems approach" to creativity "highlights the interaction of the individual, domain, and field. An individual draws upon information in a domain and transforms or extends it via cognitive processes, personality traits, and motivation. The field, consisting of people who control or influence a domain (e.g., art critics and gallery owners), evaluates and selects new ideas. The domain, a culturally defined symbol system, preserves and transmits creative products to other individuals and future generations" (Sternberg & Lubart, 1999, p. 10). In essence, in Csikszentmihalyi's model creativity is neither biologically determined nor socially constructed but instead builds on certain psychobiological predispositions that are realized within a specific area of human endeavor and are further subjected to recognition by designated experts. The systems view of creativity implicates a triadic relationship among individual society, and culture as collaborators in the creative process. Reciprocal interaction between the individual and the culture allows for transmission of information that is necessary to distinguish "new" from "old," original from trivial. In Csikszentmihalyi's (1999) model, the interaction between the individual and the field stimulates novelty, whereas the interaction between the field and the domain allows one to select it.

This confluence theory of creativity signals perhaps a new way in which artistic development discourse could be structured. Although many existing accounts have pointed to the simultaneous role of the "nature and nurture" factors in development in art, no theoretical model has combined the biological, social, and cultural elements in ways that are quite as explicitly stated and systematically connected. The advantage of this approach is that it introduces a sense of relativity to the concept that makes it elastic enough to fit the changing landscape of art and different sets of cultural values. The problem, just as with Csikszentmihalyi's theory of creativity, is, however, that this elasticity also introduces a great deal of imprecision to the concept and makes it a subject to interpretations and understandings that can possibly become divergent to the point of rendering the discourse meaningless.

Having invested years of work researching what well may be nonexisting as a unique, well-defined, domain-specific phenomenon, or at least nondescribable in ways that can maintain a high degree of consistency over time, I am firm in my belief that this time has not been wasted. For even if "development in art" may only be an illusion created out of our need to precisely define and grasp phenomena that account for achievement of human artistry, research concerned with changes in graphic representation in early childhood years—strategies that people of different ages and cultural experiences employ in solving pictorial problems and ways in which they approach, classify, and make sense of the visual world—is of great value to the field of art education. It informs us about the universe of factors and interactions between psychobiological and cultural processes that selectively support or distract us from art-oriented pursuits. It highlights the complexity of artistic performance and asserts the value and uniqueness of this complexity. It offers a collection of cases and examples that collectively build a significant body of knowledge. It directs us to shift attention from waiting for a developmental unfolding toward accepting responsibility for guiding our students through a multidimensional and multifaceted journey of learning. But perhaps, most of all, it makes us realize how little we still know about the nature of the artistic process, about the ways in which it engages different facets of human cognition, and about how it relates to the functions of the "emotive" and "visual brain." Exploration of these phenomena in their own right without the mandate to formulate theories of "development in art" will in no way diminish the relevance of the outcomes of this research on art education—as long as art education will continue to be concerned with the visual world and our students' ability to fully experience and contribute to it.

REFERENCES

Arnheim, R. (1966). *Towards a psychology of art.* Berkeley: University of California Press.

Arnheim, R. (1974). *Art and visual perception.* Berkeley: University of California Press.

Atkinson, D. (1991). How children use drawing. *Journal of Art and Design Education, 10*(1), 57–72.

Bremmer, J., & Moore, S. (1984). Prior visual inspection and object naming: Two factors that enhance hidden feature inclusion in young children's drawings. *British Journal of Developmental Psychology.* 2. 371–376.

Burton, J. M. (1980). Developing minds: Beginnings of artistic language. *School Arts,* 6–12.

Changeaux, J. P. (1994). Art and neuroscience. *Leonardo, 27*(3), 189–201.

Chen, M. J. (1985). Young children's representational drawings of solid objects: A comparison of drawing and copying. In N. Freeman and M. V. Cox (Eds.), *Visual order: The nature of development of pictorial representation.* Cambridge, England: Cambridge University Press.

Cox, M. (1992). *Children's drawings.* London: Penguin Books.

Csikszentmihalyi, M. (1988). Society, culture and person: A system view of creativity. In R. J. Sternberg (Ed.), *The nature of creativity.* New York: Cambridge University Press.

Csikszentmihalyi, M. (1999). Implications of a systems perspective for the study of creativity. In R. J. Sternberg (Ed.), *Handbook of creativity.* Cambridge: Cambridge University Press.

Dake, D. M. (2000). Brain compatible visual education. *Translations, 9*(3), 1–6.

Danto, A. (1997). *After the end of art: Contemporary art and the pale of history.* Princeton, NJ: Princeton University Press.

Darras, B. (1996). *Au commencement etait l'image: Du dessin de l'enfant a la communication de l'adulte.* Paris: ESF.

Darras, B. (2002). Les formes du savoir et l'education aux images. *Recherches en communication, 18,* 1–14.

Darras, B., & Kindler, A. M. (1993). Emergence de l'imagerie: Entre l'essence at l'accident. *Mediascope, 6,* 82–95.

Darras, B., & Kindler, A. M. (1997). L'entrée dans la graphosphere: Les icons de gestes et de traces. Approche semiotique et cognitive. *MEI: Revue Internationale de Communication, 6,* 99–113.

Davis, J. (1991). *Artistry lost: U-shaped development in graphic symbolization,* Doctoral dissertation. Harvard Graduate School of Education, Cambridge, MA.

Davis, J. (1997a). The "U" and the wheel of "C:" Development and devaluation of graphic symbolization and the cognitive approach at Harvard Project Zero. In A. M. Kindler (Ed.), *Child development in art,* (pp. 46–58). Reston, VA: National Art Education Association.

Davis, J. (1997b). Drawing demise: U-shaped development in graphic symbolization. *Studies in Art Education, 38*(3), 132–157.

Efland, A. (2002). *Art and cognition. Integrating the visual arts in the curriculum.* Reston, VA: National Art Education Association.

Elliot, P. (1986). Right or left brain cognition, wrong metaphor or creative behavior. It is prefrontal lobe volition that makes the human difference in release of creative potential. *Journal of Creative Behavior, 20*(3), 203–214.

Feldman, D. (1980). *Beyond universals in cognitive development.* Norwood, NJ: Ablex.

Fineberg, J. (1997). *The innocent eye. Children's art and the modern artist.* Princeton, NJ: Princeton University Press.

Fish, J., & Scrivener, S. (1990). Amplifying the mind's eye: Sketching and visual cognition. *Leonardo, 21*(1), 117–126.

Flynn, J. R. (1987). Massive IQ gains in 14 nations: What IQ tests really measure. *Psychological Bulletin, 101,* 171–191.

Franciscono, M. (1998). Paul Klee and children's art. In J. Fineberg (Ed.), *Discovering child art* (pp. 95–121). Princeton, NJ: Princeton University Press.

Freeman, N. H. (1980). *Strategies of representation in young children: analysis of spatial skills and drawing processes.* London: Academic Press.

Freeman, N. H. (1995). The emergence of a framework theory of pictorial reasoning. In C. Lange-Kutter & G. V. Thomas (Eds.), *Drawing and looking.* Hemel Hempstead, UK: Harvester Wheatsheaf.

Gardner, H. (1983). *Frames of mind. The theory of multiple intelligences.* New York: Basic Books.

Gardner, H. (1993a). *Frames of mind. The theory of multiple intelligences* (10th anniversary ed.). New York: Basic Books.

Gardner, H. (1993b). *Multiple intelligences. The theory in practice.* New York: Basic Books.

Gardner, H., & Winner, E. (1982). First intimations of artistry. In S. Strauss (Ed.), *U-shaped behavioral growth.* New York: Academic Press.

Golomb, C. (1992). *The child's creation of a pictorial world.* Berkeley, CA: University of California Press.

Golomb, C. (2002). *Child art in context: A cultural and comparative perspective.* Washington, DC: American Psychological Association.

Gombrich, E. H. (1985). *Meditations of a hobby horse and other essays on the theory of art.* Chicago: University of Chicago Press.

Goodman, N. (1976). *The Languages of art.* Indianpolis: Hackett Publishing Co.

Hagen, M. A. (1985). There is no development in art. In N. H. Freeman and M. V. Cox (Eds.), *Visual order: The nature and development of pictorial representation.* Cambridge: Cambridge University Press.

Hagen, M. A. (1986). *Varieties of realism: Geometries of representational art.* Cambridge: Cambridge University Press.

Hamblen, K. (1993). Developmental models of artistic expression and aesthetic response: The reproduction of formal schooling and modernity. *Journal of Social Theory in Art Education, 13,* 37–56.

Hamblen, K. (1999). Local knowledge: Within children's art work and outside school culture. *Visual Arts Research, 25,* 14–24.

Henri, A. (1974). *Total art. Environments, happenings, performance.* New York: Praeger.

Hoffman, D. D. (1998). *Visual intelligence.* New York: Norton.

Kailin, N. (2002). *Children's views on teaching and learning in drawing.* Unpublished master's thesis. University of British Columbia, Vancouver.

Kindler, A. M. (1992). Worship of creativity and artistic development of young children. *Canadian Society for Education through Art Journal, 23*(2), 12–17.

Kindler, A. M. (1994). Artistic learning in early childhood: A study of social interactions. *Canadian Review of Art Education, 21*(2), 91–106.

Kindler, A. M. (1995). Significance of adult input in early childhood artistic development. In C. M. Thompson (Ed.), *The visual arts and early childhood learning.* Reston, VA: National Art Education Association.

Kindler, A. M. (1998). Artistic development and art education. *Translations, 7*(2), 1–6.

Kindler, A. M. (1999). "From endpoints to repertoires:" A Challenge to art education. *Studies in Art Education, 40*(4), 330–349.

Kindler, A. M. (2001). From the U-curve to dragons: Culture and understanding of artistic development. *Visual Arts Research*, *26*(2), 15–29.

Kindler, A. M. (2001). *Visual culture and the visual brain: Exploring possibilities of visual education*. Paper presented at the International Symposium in Art Education. Taipei, Taiwan, R.O.C.

Kindler, A. M., & Darras, B. (1994). Artistic development in context: Emergence and development of pictorial imagery in early childhood years. *Visual Arts Research*, *20*(2), 1–13.

Kindler, A. M., & Darras, B. (1995). Young children's understanding of the nature and acquisition of drawing skills: A cross-Cultural study. *Journal of Multicultural and Cross-Cultural Research in Art Education*, *13*, 85–100.

Kindler, A. M., & Darras, B. (1997a). Map of artistic development. In A. M. Kindler (Ed.), *Child development in art*. Reston, VA: NAEA.

Kindler, A. M., & Darras, B. (1997b). Development of pictorial representation: A teleology-based model. *Journal of Art and Design Education*, *16*(3), 217–222.

Kindler, A. M., & Darras, B. (1998). Culture and development of pictorial repertoires. *Studies in Art Education*, *39*(2), 147–167.

Kindler, A. M., Liu, W. C., Pariser, D., & van den Berg, A. (2003). A cultural perspective on graphic development: Aesthetic assessment of local and foreign drawings in Taiwan. *Research in Arts Education*, May (5), 23–47.

Kindler, A. M., Pariser, D., van den Berg, A., & Liu, W. C. (2001). Visions of Eden: The differential effects of skill on adult judgments of children's drawings: Two cross-cultural studies. *Canadian Review of Art Education*, *28*(2), 35–63.

Kindler, A. M., Pariser, D., van den Berg, A., Liu, W. C., & Dias, B. (2002). *Navigating cultures in graphic development: Testing the cultural socialization thesis*. Paper presented at the 9th International Literacy and Education Research Network Conference on Learning, Beijing. China.

Kindler, A. M., Pariser, D., van den Berg, A., Liu, W. C., & Dias, B. (2002a). Aesthetic modernism, the first among equals? A look at aesthetic value systems in cross-cultural, age and visual arts educated and non-visual arts educated judging cohorts. *International Journal of Cultural Policy*, *8*(2). 135–152.

Kindler, A. M., & Thompson, C. (1994). *Social interactions and young children's artistic learning*. Paper presented at the National Art Education Association conference, Baltimore, MD.

Lange-Kuttner, C., & Reith, E. (1995). The transformation of figurative thought: Implications of Piaget and Inhelder's developmental theory for children's drawings. In C. Lange-Kuttner & E. Reith (Eds.), *Drawing and looking* (pp. 75–92). London: Harvester Wheatsheaf.

Liu, W. C., Kindler, A. M., Pariser, D., & van den Berg, A. (2002). *Taiwanese children and adolescents' judgments of developmental patterns in aesthetic growth*. Proceedings of the 17th Congress of the International Association of Empirical Aesthetics Takarazuka, Japan, 4–8 August. 277–282.

Lowenfeld, V. (1943). *Creative and mental growth*. New York: Macmillan.

Luquet, G. H. (1927). *Le dessin enfantin*. Paris: Alcan.

Matthews, J. (1994). *Helping children to draw and paint in early childhood: Children and visual representation*. (0-8 Series, Series Ed. Tina Bruce). London: Hodder & Stoughton.

Matthews, J. (1999). *The art of childhood and adolescence*. London: Falmer Press.

Milbrath, C. (1998). *Patterns of artistic development in children*. Cambridge: Cambridge University Press.

Miller, L., & Tippet, L. (1996). *Effects of focal brain lesions on visual problem-solving*. Neuropsychologia, *34*(5), 387–398.

Pariser, D. (1995). Looking for the muse in some of the right places. *American Journal of Education*, *107*, 155–169.

Pariser, D., (1997). Graphic development in artistically exceptional children. In A. M. Kindler (Ed.), *Child development in art* (pp. 183–192). Reston, VA: National Art Education Association.

Pariser, D., & van den Berg, A. (1997). The mind of the beholder: Some provisional doubts about the U-curve aesthetic development thesis. *Studies in Art Education*, *38*(3), 158–178.

Pariser, D., & van den Berg, A. (2001). Teaching art versus teaching taste: What art teachers can learn from looking at a cross-cultural evaluation of children's art. *Poetics: Journal of Empirical Research on Literature, the Media and the Arts*, *29*, 331–350.

Parsons, M. J. (1998). Integrated curriculum and our paradigm of cognition in the arts. *Studies in Art Education*, *39*(2), 103–116.

Peirce, C. (1931–35). *Collected papers*. Cambridge, MA: Harvard University Press.

Pemberton, E. F., & Nelson, K. E. (1987). Using interactive graphic challenges to foster young children's drawing ability. *Visual Arts Research*, *13*(2), 29–41.

Petrov, V. (1996). Quantitative estimates of left- and right-hemispherical dominance in art. *Leonardo*, *29*(3), 201–205.

Petrov, V. (1998). The evolution of art: An investigation of cycles of left- and right-hemispherical creativity in art. Leonardo, *31*(3), 219–230.

Piaget, J. (1929). *The child's conception of the world*. New York: Harcourt, Brace & World.

Piaget J., & Inhelder, B. (1956). *The child's conception of space*. London: Routledge & Kegan Paul.

Piaget, J., & Inhelder, B. (1969). *The psychology of the child*. London: Rutledge & Kegan Paul.

Porath, M. (1997). A developmental model of artistic giftedness in middle childhood. *Journal for the Education of the Gifted, 20*, 201–223.

Rothenberg, A. (1979). *The emerging goddess: The creative process in art, science and other fields*. Chicago, IL: University of Chicago Press.

Shotwell, J. , Wolf, D., & Gardner, H. (1980). Styles of achievement in early symbolization. In M. Foster & S. Brandes (Eds.), *Symbol as sense: New approaches to the analysis of meaning* (pp. 115–199). New York: Academic Press.

Smolucha, L. W., & Smolucha, F. C. (1980). A Fifth Piagetian stage: The collaboration between analogical and logical thinking in artistic creativity. *Visual Arts Research, 11*(2), 90–99.

Sobel, R. S., & Rothenberg, A. (1980). Artistic creation as stimulated by superimposed versus separated visual images. *Journal of Personality and Social Psychology, 39*(5), 953–961.

Sternberg, R. J., & Lubart, T. I. (1999). The concept of creativity: Prospects and paradigms. In R. J. Sternberg (Ed.), *Handbook of creativity*. Cambridge: Cambridge University Press.

Thompson, C., & Bales, S. (1991). "Michael doesn't like my dinosaurs." Conversations in a preschool classroom. *Studies in Art Education, 33*(1), 43–55.

Tucker, P. K. , Rothwell, S. J. , Armstrong, M. S., & McConaghy, N. (1982). Creativity, divergent and allusive thinking in students and visual artists. *Psychological Medicine, 12*, 835–841.

Varela, F. (1989). Autonomie et connaissance. Paris: Seuil.

Willats, J. (1997). *Art and representation*. Princeton: Princeton University Press.

Wilson, B. (1997). Child art, multiple interpretations and conflicts of interest. In A. M. Kindler (Ed.), *Child development in art*. Reston, VA: National Art Education Association.

Wilson, B., & Wilson, M. (1977). An iconoclastic view of the imagery sources in the drawings of young people. *Art Education, 30*(1), 5–15.

Wilson, B., & Wilson, M. (1982). The case of a disappearing two-eyed profile: Or how little children influence the drawing of little children. *Review of Research in Visual Arts Education, 15*, 19–32.

Wilson, B., & Wilson, M. (1985). The artistic tower of Babel: Inextricable links between cultural and graphic development. *Visual Arts Research, 11*(1), 90–104.

Wolf, D. (1994). *Development as the growth of repertoires*. In M. B. Franklin & B. Kaplan (Eds.), *Development and the arts* (pp. 59–78). Hillsdale, NJ: Laurence Erlbaum Associates.

Wolf, D., & Perry, M. (1988). From endpoints to repertoires: Some new conclusions about drawing development. *Journal of Aesthetic Education, 22*(1), 17–34.

Zeki, S., & Lamb, B. (1994). The neurology of kinetic art. *Brain, 117*, 607–636.

Zeki, S. (1999). *Inner vision: An exploration of art and the brain*. Oxford: Oxford University Press.

13

The Art of Infancy[1]

John Matthews
National Institute of Education, Singapore

PENCIL AND PAPER AND ELECTRONIC PAINT: OBSERVATIONS OF VERY YOUNG CHILDREN DRAWING

Robert, a 3-year-old, is seated at a table in a nursery class in London, England, facing a computer. He is starting to draw with electronic paint, using a mouse-driven, computer paintbox program. With this medium, marks do not appear on the surface against which he presses and moves the drawing instrument, the mouse, but on a separate monitor, vertically orientated in front of him. A few illuminated spots and dashes are already glowing on the screen, the product of his prior investigations. He is now trying to work out how he managed to achieve these visual effects. He is trying to coordinate the different actions necessary to produce a trace on the screen. Sometimes he presses the mouse button but forgets to move the mouse; sometimes he moves the mouse but forgets to press the button. He allows the mouse to come to rest, fingering it and looking up at the screen between times. He appears to thoughtfully study the device and ponder the problem. He does not utter a word, although he may be listening to the gentle advice of the investigator sitting next to him. Finally, using three very distinctive drawing actions, he manages to make colored traces appear on the screen. First of all he uses a vigorous arcing motion, the movement mainly issuing from his shoulder, the mouse moving repeatedly left and right. Then he makes several pushing and pulling movements, away from and toward his own body. Finally, he makes a continuous rotational movement, describing big ellipses on the table and causing segments of colored ellipses to whirl across the screen. While continuously moving the mouse in circles on the table, he looks intently at the colored lines as they furiously orbit the screen (Figure 13.1).

Here is another observation from another part of the world. Chinese children, between the ages of 2 ½ and 3 ½ years, sitting around a table in a childcare center in Singapore, are about to draw, using 2B pencils on A4 size, white cartridge paper. The children have been told that

---

[1] Note: In this chapter I have used the pronouns "she," "her," and "hers" throughout, except when I refer to the child's caregiver, at which times I use the pronouns, "he," "him," and "his."

FIG. 13.1.   Robert, 3 years old, uses electronic paint.

they can draw anything they like. Some of them have not drawn before and a few of them hesitate, looking with slight bewilderment at the paper and pencils, and then up at the teacher. One such child apparently misconstrues the task to be one of writing. Her friend sitting next to her "explains," not using speech, but only mimetic, elliptical, hand movements made in the air over the paper, suggestive of drawing rather than of writing.

The majority of the children, however, set off drawing immediately and with great enthusiasm. Many of them appear to investigate the properties of the medium, testing the pencil point against the paper surface and setting the pencil into motion, creating trails of graphite. Some the children stab the pencil repeatedly against the paper, making clusters of dots. Some markings are made with great speed, whereas at other times the children decelerate the pencil's movement, studying closely the lines that appear. It is not long before carefully controlled shapes appear, not always made slowly, but that nevertheless appear to be the product of purposeful construction rather than of accident (Figures 13.2–13.6).

As the children draw, some of them call out in Chinese Mandarin. One child says her drawing is a "Mo gui"—a "ghost." Another child cries, "Wo de fei ji fei le!" ("My aeroplane is flying!") (Figure 13.3). Others join in, adding new ideas; for example, "Wo de fei ji zhao huo le!" ("My aeroplane is on fire!") (Figure 13.5), or make vocalizations that sound like the sirens of an ambulance or a fire engine. Sometimes, a child will lift her drawing paper into the air and move it gracefully through space (Figure 13.4) (Matthews, 2003) (Figures 13.7–13.9).

TRIVIAL ACTIONS OR THE BEGINNINGS OF VISUAL EXPRESSION AND REPRESENTATION?

I begin with these two descriptions of very young children's activities in order to initiate a discussion about the role of art in development and learning. I refer to all the visual and performing arts, but I am going to focus on the example of drawing. It is possible that, in a few years, PCs will become "boring" (Gurterl, 2001) and "useless doorstops" (*The Economist*, 2001, p. 12), but I think it is always going to be the case that making marks on two-dimensional surfaces, of one kind or another, is going to remain central to the way human beings think and live. I believe that analysis of early drawing episodes, like those described earlier, takes

FIG. 13.2. *Horizontal arcs* and *push-pulls*, plus dots or points made by a *vertical arc*, or stab of the pencil, constitute *First-Generation Structure*. Shortly afterwards, in this drawing, the child also makes closed shapes into which points or dots are located. The topological relationship of inside and outside is encoded into 2D.

us straight to the heart of fundamental issues in art, education, representation, and human development.

In psychology, there is much controversy about the way in which very young children's activities, like those described previously, should be interpreted. Should this be of concern to people interested in art education? Yes, because such trivial-seeming actions are in fact the beginnings of visual expression and representation. These actions signal the child's discovery of semiotic systems, which will form the basis of later symbol use, without which thinking

FIG. 13.3.   When horizontal arcs or push pulls are "opened-up," as it were, a *continuous rotation* is formed.

is impossible. How we interpret the beginnings of children's art also tells us a great deal about how we conceptually construe the development of artistic and aesthetic thought through later childhood and into adolescence. Conceptualisations about development and education are often tacit, unconscious, and unarticulated. Yet, these unquestioned assumptions have profound effects on the way we provide for what is crudely termed *art education* and how we understand its role in the development of mind as a whole.

IS THIS JUST SENSORIMOTOR EXPLORATION?

In considering the two previous observations, some people will allow that the children are learning to coordinate motor actions and use tools. This is probably as far as agreement will go. From here, there will be a dramatic divergence of opinions about the ways in which learning takes place and how this learning should be supported. For example, some people will argue that children learn to use tools (be they computers, pencils and paper, or anything else) only by imitation and instruction from adults around them, whereas other people might take the opposite stance, arguing that, although children may need some help (perhaps with complicated devices like computers), children more or less find out how to use tools, "naturally," by themselves (for a new approach to children's use of electronic and lens media, see Ma Ying & Leong, 2002, and Chan & Matthews, 2002, forthcoming).

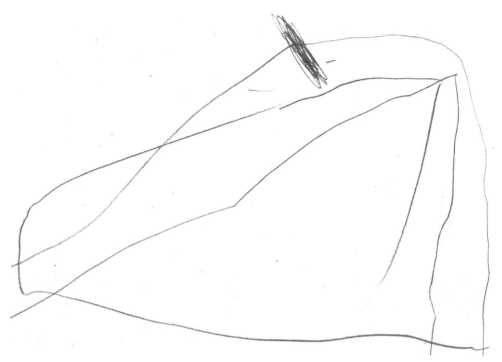

FIGS. 13.4–13.8. These drawings represent the dynamic and configurative aspects of an airplane's flight and subsequent crash. (It is important to note that, with the exception of Fig. 13.7, similar action representations, which record trajectory and moment of impact—including airplane crashes—occur prior to the September 11, 2001, tragedy.)

FIG. 13.4. This 3-year-old discovers the important structural principles of *crossing lines, attaching lines to a baseline* (especially at approximate right angles), *attaching lines to the beginnings and endings of lines* and making *direction changes in continuous contact lines*. He uses these dynamic structures to describe an airplane's flight. "Wo de fei ji fei le," he cries, in Chinese Mandarin ("My airplane flies."). This then is an *action representation*; it encodes the movement of an object.

As for further levels of meaning, *at least in terms of expression and representation*, according to many theories both old and new, there simply are none. The vast majority of traditional and current studies on the development of children's art, although acknowledging that such episodes signal the beginnings of tool mastery, claim that otherwise they mean nothing. Such theories profoundly and destructively influence education.

At this point it is important to note that there are a few writers who do not subscribe to the view that these episodes mean nothing. The work of Wolf and Fucigna (1983), Chris Athey (1990), Costall (1993, 1995, 2001), and Kindler and Darras (1997, 1997a, 1997b), for example, makes the point quite explicitly (in their different ways) that the beginnings of drawing are important. But these are the notable exceptions. Although many people might concede that the previously cited behaviors are expressive in a reflexive, hystrionic sense, most people would not consider the actions as the intelligent expression of emotion or the mindful representation of events and objects.

Yet, a deeper analysis of the drawings, both as process and artifact, reveals that they are elegantly orchestrated and have profound meaning. Some of the children make markings that appear to be the product of exploration of the materials in themselves. Other children produce shapes that might possibly be intended to represent something—though the representational

FIG. 13.5. In contrast, his friend sitting next to him draws a *configurative representation* of an airplane. He makes an elongated closure to represent the closed volume of the airplane. He captures the shape and structure of an object. He encodes inside and outside relationships. Perhaps the internal closures represent windows, or people, or both. Additionally, the child is able to elongate the closure to describe the salient length of the fuselage. After producing this drawing, he physically picks up the drawing paper and moves it gracefully through the air, as if "flying" his drawn airplane. This behavior forms another kind of *action representation*. He is trying to link configurative and dynamic aspects of the object.

intention is far from clear in terms of likeness to the shape of any physical object. One might also notice that in this single session, some of the children move from the former type of drawing to the latter.

For some people, it is tempting to account for this change in terms of an "age-stage" relationship, with children moving from "primitive" to "advanced" modes of drawing as they grow older. This notion derives from theories initiated over a century ago, including that of Sully (1895), reformulated during the 20th century by Buhler (1930), Piaget and Inhelder (1956), and Lowenfeld and Brittain (1970) and which continue to exert influence in more recent years (Cox, 1993; Selfe, 1983; Snyder, 2000; Snyder & Thomas, 1997; Thomas & Silk, 1990).

This is indeed the conventional wisdom, yet it turns out that there is a great deal wrong with this conceptualization, as we will see later. What is meant by the terms "primitive" and "advanced" (and other similar terminology) typically used to describe this staged development? What gauge of measurement is being employed? If, for example, the gauge implies developmental increments from supposedly inferior, chaotic-looking, haphazard "scribbles" to shapes more clearly defined in terms of line (and, therefore, supposedly "superior"), the theory straightaway runs into difficulties. In fine-grained analaysis of children's spontaneous drawing actions, like the episodes described previously, it is sometimes the younger children who form clearly delineated shapes, whereas some of the older children seem to make haphazard looking

FIG. 13.6.   A 3-year-old Chinese girl makes this closed shape and then, underneath it, some intense push-pull marks, while she cries out, "Wo de fei ji zhao huo le." ("My airplane bursts into flame.") In drawings like this, a contrast is made between the initial coherence and the integrity of a closed volume and its subsequent destruction, often represented as explosive marking.

configurations. Moreover, some other children, who commenced by producing clearly delineated shapes, seem to "regress" to make apparently haphazard drawings. Are such cases merely the "exception which proves the rule"; merely little dips in a developmental graph which, overall, steadily climbs toward the peak of "correct" representation? Or do they signal more serious flaws in a classical "stage theory" of development?

At a larger scale of analysis, it is often argued that there exists, in general, an overall stage-by-stage progression toward the goal of the "visually realistic" image. But what does this mean? In other studies I made, children between 2 and 4 years of age were presented with opaque and transparent cubes to draw (Matthews, 2001a). Although it might be said that, generally speaking, as the children grow older, they try to capture more *view-specific* information in their drawings—that is, information about the shapes of the objects as observable from their own stationpoint—the ways in which this is achieved are not predicted by stage theory (Matthews, 2001a & b) (see Figures 13.10–13.13).

FIG. 13.7.   This 2-year-old uses both dynamic and configurative modes to represent a terrorist sui-cide plane about to impact against the side of a building. Again, she captures inside and outside relationships. The interiorized marks may represent a combination of windows and people. The ex-plosive marking registers moment of impact. She also encodes the salient extension of the shapes of both objects, the tower building and airplane, along a longitudinal axis and a lateral axis, respectively.

Moreover, in contrast to the popular assumption, these and other observations often show that children seem to observe and encode the visible aspects of the objects in their earliest drawings. The representational approaches or systems children employ remain invisible to most observers because they are not described by conventional theory—*nor can they be*. Most developmental theories describe a progression from meaningless mark-making through a symbolic, rather than a representational, stage and finally to a visually realistic stage. This journey is usually described with important landmarks in representation reached at roughly similar ages.

In contrast, new theoretical approaches reveal that children capture representational in-formation about movement, structure, and vision in their earliest drawings, in a purposeful experiment with visual and dynamic structure. Moreover, the individual's route through her developmental landscape is unique; dependent on a bewildering variety of factors that can never be described in advance by a simplistic, linear, stage theory. On the other hand, nor is it correct to think that development is totally idiosyncratic. It is equally mistaken to conclude that development is totally without "biases" or "values" (Edelman, 1987; Thelen & Smith, 1994; Thelen, Schoner, Scheier, & Smith, 2000, p. 184).

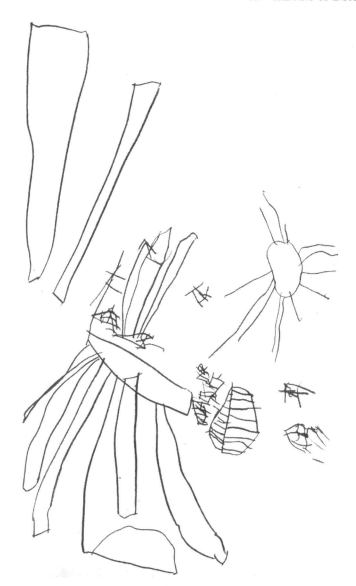

FIG. 13.8.   The differentiation, permutation, and combination of structural principles, closure, and right-angular attachment allows this Chinese Singaporean 3-year-old to make this complex configuration. Developments of right-angular attachment, include *core and radial* (closed shape with radial lines attached at perimeter, to the right), and *U shape on a baseline*. These latter closures are elongated (perhaps representing "wings") attached at approximate right angles to a single, elongated closure (perhaps representing airplane "fuselage").

So is there a way to reconcile what appears to be, on the one hand, an orderly "stage like" development with these contrasting and contradictory variations? What determines the change the child makes from one moment to the next? Are the children moving from one drawing procedure to another with the passage of time; and if so, does this imply a sort of "developmental time," implicit in most developmental theories, involving a mysterious, unseen process vaguely termed "*maturation*"? Or is it a moment-to-moment time, involving here-and-now practice within a social and cultural environment, with physical materials, which (in these

FIG. 13.9.   A complex configuration that combines, closure, core, and radial right-angular attachment, and a development of crossing lines, its *grids*. This drawing also describes a complex narrative
about the journey of an airplane.

examples) are themselves the product of human culture? We might suggest that these different
time scales are one and the same. Yet, given that children clearly do not develop with a uniform,
clockwork predictability, it is difficult to see how such a confluence can be possible. Here, as
elsewhere, we will encounter curious paradoxes in accounts of development.

MEDIA DIFFERENCES

Further argument will pivot around the differences in the drawing materials used by the children: traditional versus electronic media. Are these to be considered completely distinct activities, each with its own unique characteristics and task demands? Do media differences cause
substantially different patterns of development in visual expression and representation? The
rhetoric of IT entrepreneurs would often have it so, yet there is no research evidence to justify
this claim. For example, Robert, in the previous observation, in addition to using e-paint, uses
traditional materials, including pencil on paper. There are, of course, obvious differences between his electronic painting and his pencil and paper drawings (Matthews & Jessel, 1993a,
1993b). Some of these media differences are rather startling and demolish certain cherished notions of staged development. For example, John Jessel and I found that, in contrast to children's
use of physical pigments, when practical and other constraints put a limit on the selection and
number of colors children can use, when using a computer paintbox program, 3-year-olds may
be capable of managing a palette of hundreds of colors. At least some abilities, once thought

FIGS. 13.10–13.13.   These drawings represent very young children's representation of a cube set placed before them. Although some of the very youngest children's drawings are unrecognizable as views of the objects, they are descriptions in which topological and dynamical features of the cube are represented in a process that captures the children's changing attention to the object in relation to the drawing process. Such drawing processes are not satisfactorily explained by simple classification into either intellectually realistic or visual realistic categories.

FIG. 13.10.   Lee Mei Hong (2 years, 11 months) uses a line which bisects points along a route. This is an example of the use of the attractor, *collinearity*. She may use it to represent a surface which has significant landmarks along its route—corners or edges.

tied to a "developmental stage," have more to do with the possibilities of the specific medium (Golomb, 1974, 1992, 1993).

Yet, despite significant differences among media, it is equally true to say that, in other respects there are some remarkable resemblances between Robert's e-paintings and his pencil and paper drawings, for example, in terms of certain shapes and the actions used to produce them. For instance, he deploys a *horizontal arcing*, *push-pulling* action and a *continuous rotation* to trail colored lines around the screen. These are first-and second-generation structures we observe in the Chinese children's use of pencil and paper. These seem to be deep structures found in children's earliest drawings thoughout the world (Matthews, 1999, 2003).

SOCIAL AND INTERPERSONAL CONTEXTS

What about the adult supervision of these activities? Do children need any? Some famous pioneers of children's art make the claim that children need little adult supervision, and some go so far as to shun any adult help at all, insisting that this will "corrupt" a "natural" development (Cizek, in Derham, 1947, 1961; Kellogg, 1969; Viola, 1942). At the other end of the spectrum of

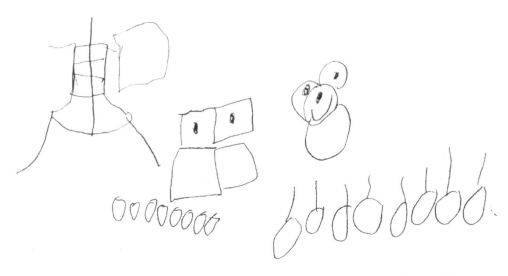

FIG. 13.11. Oh Kai Lun (4 years, 5 months) tries a variety of ways to represent the cube. He may be combining information about multiple faces of the object which join at vertices. This is achieved in two main ways: members of a new family or a set of structural principles. One way is to make a grid, which suggests joined multiple faces; the other way is drawing separate, discrete shapes and abutting them together.

FIG. 13.12. Chua Wei Li (3 years, 4 months). After drawing a front face of the cube as an approximate rectangle, Wei Li draws a separate, discrete, second face which she abutts to the first face. She manages to distort this second shape out of the rectangular, skewing it to the right. She may be trying to show the top face receding from the viewer.

FIG. 13.13.   Ang Yee Fong (4 years, 10 months) moves through a series of experiments, starting with undifferentiated closure, to the addition of faces, one to another, the shapes of which she carefully transforms in order to arrive at possible views of a cube. In this case, the denotational function of the line is changing to represent interior edges, in which faces are conceived as sharing boundaries rather than as individual, discrete shapes (Willats, 1997).

child-art pedagogy are people who maintain that children's learning is dependent on imitation or instruction from adults (van Sommers, 1984; Cox, Cooke, & Griffin 1995) .

During the drawing session with the Singaporean Chinese children, a kindly smiling teacher crouches down close to the children in turn and talks to them about their drawings. During Robert's investigation of the computer, he receives advice from the adult sitting next to him. How, if at all, does adult intervention affect the childrens' actions? Is there an optimal type of interaction that will assist development; and if so, of what does it consist?

Cultural exemplars that surround the child do indeed play a part in development (Martlew & Connelly, 1996; Wilson, 1985, 1997, 2000, and this volume; Kindler, Darras, & Kuo 2000; Kindler, this volume). This and other research show that the process through which development interacts with culture is subtle and complex and is by no means a straightforward copying or following of instructions. Robert finds ways of operating the mouse which have not been suggested by, or copied from, the adult companion (for example, a *swivelling* action of the mouse upon its own axis—Matthews & Jessel, 1993a, 1993b).

Similarly, the Chinese children find ways of using the pencil and paper medium that are neither advised nor even dreamed of by their teachers. In a later observation, these same children (between 3 and 4 years of age) produce images, the likes of which they could never have encountered in their visual and pictorial environment. Consider Figures 13.10, 13.11, 13.12, and 13.13, which represent cubes placed before the children, with the request that they draw these from observation (Matthews, 2001b). These drawings capture the structure of the object in relationship to the drawing surface and in relation to the child's changing attention over time. Piaget might have termed these drawings "intellectually realist," but a careful reading of his later theory shows that he did not intend a rigid dichotomy between "intellectual realism" and "visual realism" (Beilin & Pufall, 1992) as today's conventional wisdom has reduced his theory. The children use dynamic systems that capture the structure of the object irrespective of viewpoint and in relationship to the drawing surface and to their own changing perceptions and understandings of the objects. Note that many of the children are quite capable of drawing simple rectangles, and indeed this is the first solution to present itself to them. Significantly, although their teachers are delighted with this solution, the children clearly are not and persist in making drawings that are not like any known image of the object they could have seen before. The point I am making here is that, whereas drawings like this are habitually regarded as the consequence of some failing on the part of the children, to either perceive or produce the visual shapes of an object, on the contrary, the children are shown to be quite capable of producing rectangular shapes that may serve as analog for the visual array, which are found satisfactory by adults. However, the children themselves are clearly dissatisfied with this as the key to the solution of representing the object. They are clearly trying to do something else (Arnheim, 1954, 1974; Matthews, 2002). This "something" warrants their complete attention to the drawing task, from which they are almost completely indistractible.

CULTURE AND RACE

It is hard to conceive of a child's encounter with visual media outside of a social context of some kind, and research does indeed show that children's art is influenced by the images they see around them (Wilson, 1985, 1997, 2000, this volume). Nevertheless, it is crucial to grasp that a simple imitation model is insufficient to account for the process of development. The interaction between the social group development and the individual development involves systems we understand very little.

If we were to link these questions with other vexing ones about the differences between the races and cultures to which the children belong, the result would seem to be a complicated puzzle! Will there be a significant difference in the way you learn to use tools depending on whether you are a Chinese child living in Singapore or a young Caucasian living in London, or whether you belong to some other ethnic group from another place? If so, what are these differences? Are these differences of *content* (or "subject matter"); or are they differences in *structure* (by this term I mean the combination and permutation of lines, shapes, forms, colors, and actions as entities in themselves), or both? The effects of acculturation in children's art, as revealed by research, demolishes any simplistic "universalistic" model of development (see Kindler, 1996a, 1996b, 1997, this volume; Kindler et al., 2000; Wilson, 1985, 1997, 2000, this volume). On the other hand, there is ample evidence to show (contrariwise) that, especially in infancy, some aspects of children's drawing throughout the world are essentially the same, certainly in terms of structure and often in content too. How can both these apparently contradictory data be simultaneously true?

There is a striking resemblance between Robert's drawings (both in electronic paint and in pencil) and those of some of his Chinese Singaporean peers, both in terms of shape and in terms of the actions that produced them. If some aspects of development seem universal, and other aspects seem to vary; what is it that develops, and what is it that varies? Does it make sense even to ask this question? That is, can we separate nature and nurture? How do we describe development in such a way as to resolve what appear to be irreconcilable conflicts among different interpretations?

At this point, some readers might be asking: Why make such a fuss about such trivial actions? What have they to do with either art or education? What difference will it make to their education if children do not do these activities at all? The answer to these questions is that actions such as those described previously play a fundamental role in development and learning. These apparently trivial behaviors are emergent representation and expression. To suppress early modes of representation (*representation* here meaning the way we give form to objects and events) and expression (*expression* here meaning the way we give form to emotion) is to limit the extent and depth to which the child can make an infrastructural investigation of semiotic systems essential to her survival.

How you understand (or misunderstand) the development of art in childhood will set up a train of consequences in terms of how you plan learning experiences for children. Some designs for learning will stimulate and promote development. Some will not. This chapter argues for the need for a *developmental* explanation of that which we term *children's art*; a theory that describes the changes which occur in children's representation and expression, not in terms of a gradual adjustment to the requirements of the supposed content of the "subject-area" "art," or in terms of the gradual "correction" of children's of representational models, either external or internal, but in terms of a process spontaneously generated from within the child in relation to the physical and psychological environment; and in response to the properties of the medium; a process driven by the child's own intentions, motivations, and priorities (Light, 1985).

THE IMPORTANCE OF CHILDREN'S SPONTANEOUS ART

I stress the need to understand and support the *spontaneous* art of children. The children described previously have not been given a set task. It is especially important at the present time to reaffirm the significance and meaning of children's spontaneous drawing, painting, and other forms of representation and expression. Children's spontaneous use and organization of visual and other media plays a central role in the development of intelligence; yet, tragically, there appears at present to be a general devaluing and downplaying of young children's spontaneous art (Costall, 2001). The truth of this is easy to see if one considers any number of "national" curricular initiatives that, even though they might span occidental and oriental cultures, are curiously similar (Berliner & Biddle, 1995; Kelly, 1990; NIE Corporate Seminar, 2001; Simon, 1988).

A SCRIBBLING STAGE, OR THE BEGINNINGS OF EXPRESSION AND REPRESENTATION?

The observations with which this chapter started are of the phase of drawing which a classical model of development terms the *scribbling stage*. According to this traditional approach, these markings are not really drawings at all. They are usually considered meaningless. This, as we will see, turns out to be catastrophic misconception. This mistake undermines our understanding and support of the beginnings of representational thought and has serious repercussions on the way we understand and provide for later visual expression and representation in the arts.

As I noted earlier, a few people do appreciate the very beginnings of representational and expressive thought (including Athey, 1990; Costall, 1993, 1995, 2001; Darras & Kindler, 1997; Kindler & Darras, 1997a, 1997b; Wolf & Fucigna, 1983). However, these new theoretical approaches are exceptions to the general denigration and incomprehension of spontaneous early representation.

As Wolf and Fucigna (1983) point out, given discoveries made about other aspects of infant cognition, the misconceptualization about the beginnings of visual art is anomalous. Ingenious studies now reveal hitherto unexpected precocial competence of newborns in their perception of objects and events, and in their preverbal communication skills. Yet, no analogous level of infant cognition is considered applicable to very young children's use of visual media. In some respects, a recent theory of the modular structure of the brain, which posits specialized areas designated to particular functions rather mitigates against the idea of transference of skills from one domain to another. For example, Steven Pinker, arguing for the theory of neurological modularity and against the idea of the brain as a sort of all-purpose, symbol-making device, writes of the "grammatical genius" of very young children while simultaneously claiming that "... a three year old... is quite incompetent at the visual arts..." (Pinker, 1994, p. 1994).

This view is shared by many; yet, it is both sad and ironic. As we will shortly see, children have visual systems of expression and representation long before speech but early painting and drawing episodes also share a similar structure with that of conversational language (Chafe, 1994; Matthews, 1999). These expressive and representational modes are emergent at the outset of development, and their structural possibilities are, like those of language, infinite. Although it seems to be the case that the brain is composed of systems dedicated to particular forms of processing, this turns out to be only half the story. It is not the separateness of these sensory and cognitive domains which is their most significant feature, but rather their cooperative interconnectedness (Thelen & Smith, 1994; Thelen et al., 2000).

At present, and albeit with a few notable exceptions (references as above), it remains true that early drawing or paintings are, at best, considered sensorimotor practice and preliminary investigation of materials, and random and meaningless in terms of expression and representation. Whether the materials derive from electronic media or from paper and pencil technologies, such exercises are usually considered motoric rather than mindful, physical rather than mental. This attitude stems from traditional developmental theories which assume the "intellectual" to be distinct from (and superior to) the physical, the dynamic, and the visual. According to any number of theories, increases in "cognitive maturation" gradually coupled with the "physical" mastery of objects will eventually allow "proper" drawing to take place (Lowenfeld, 1939, 1967; Peter, 1996; Piaget, 1956).

According to a classical model of development and its variants, the drawing episodes described earlier are the first faltering steps in a long march toward "accurate" representation. The earliest "mark-making" does not even win the uncritical and sentimental approval with which later childhood drawings are sometimes greeted, drawings which, albeit strange-looking to some adults, are at least recognizable as attempts to represent the shapes of things. This traditional model conceives of development in the visual arts as a progression from supposedly inferior, primitive forms of representation, through a sequence of successive "stages" to supposedly increasingly superior forms, until the final endpoint of "correct" representation is reached.

THE PARADIGM OF VISUAL REALISM

The presumed destination of this developmental journey varies from time to time and from culture to culture, but the reader should know about one influential terminus and the sequence of famous landmarks en route. This is the supposed journey toward "visual realism." To readers acquainted with modern and contemporary art, it may seem anachronistic to measure children's drawings in terms of how "visually realistic" they look. Many will argue that no sophisticated art educator nowadays expects educational outcomes in terms of photographic or linear perspective verisimilitude to external, physical reality. Some may claim that conceptual skills now replace the emphasis on the "retinal" and on the motor skills required to produce it.

Yet, the paradigm of visual realism, in various guises, remains persistent and pervasive. Despite recent research, curriculum guides based on the century-old premise that development moves from inferior to superior modes of representation and culminates in a visually realistic endstate, continue to be published today (e.g., Bates, 2000; Peter, 1996).

By describing this paradigm and the influence it continues to exert on the interpretation of "children's art" sets the stage for a discussion about alternate approaches to development in the visual arts. Some of these approaches are radically different from the traditional model and its variants and resituate that which is termed *art education*, at the center, rather than at the periphery of the curriculum.

THE STAGE THEORY OF DEVELOPMENT IN THE VISUAL ARTS

One classical stage theory of development in the visual arts derives from a hybrid of the work of Jean Piaget (Piaget & Inhelder, 1956) and George Luquet (1927, 2001). It runs something like this: A preliminary "scribbling" stage is replaced by a stage of "fortuitous realism" in which the child chances upon and then consciously tries to repeat what is initially the product of accident. This in itself an astonishing idea, because, in contrast to what we know about other aspects of development, the move to representation from no representation at all is, according to this theory, the result of accident.

There are a number of variations of the "happy accident" theory of children's development. For example, in Rhoda Kellogg's influential version, "scribbling" is significant only in terms of the accidental assemblage of a vocabulary of shapes which will at some later date (at around 3 years of age) serve a useful purpose of making controlled "designs," "aggregates," and pictures (Kellogg, 1969). In view of what we know about other aspects of the infant's development, it would seem to be a bizarre situation for children to persist in an activity that has no purpose or meaning for them. Kellogg's case also typifies another common error: that of the adult researcher herself projecting her own ideas into the child's drawings. For example, her classification system has influenced several generations of scholars and educators; yet, careful inspection of the drawings of the very young reveals that the "twenty basic scribbles," as categorized by Kellogg, do not, in fact, exist.

Maureen Cox notes that, in contrast to the folklore about children's drawing, there is no evidence to support the idea that the beginnings of visual representation and expression are based on what are initially the products of accident (Cox, 1993, 1997). Unintended events do indeed play a vital role in all aspects of development, but this role is not explained in the terms of the traditional theory. It is ironic that the traditional approach, although mistaking "accident" to be the main mechanism of development, at the same time fails to see the true significance of the "accidental."

INTELLECTUAL REALISM AND VISUAL REALISM

Following the stage of "fortuitous realism," so the story continues, children start to produce drawings that most adults still find strange but in which they think they recognize representations of objects. One characteristic of these drawings, and the main reason why adults find them difficult to understand, is that they do not show any possible view of an object (Willats, 1997). These drawings are often termed *intellectually realistic* drawings, the basic idea being that they capture what the child intellectually "understands" about the object, rather than the optical shape of the object projected to the eye held still at a fixed position. The idea here derives from an even older fallacy, which has no evidence to support it, that the basis of the human vision is a form of perspectival "retinal image," somehow "corrupted" by conceptualization and perhaps involving language (Costall, 1993, 1995, 2001).

In its simplest form, intellectually realistic drawings are supposed to show what the child *knows* rather than what the child *sees*. Advocates of this theory might classify some of the

FIGS. 13.14–13.19. Although such drawings are crudely categorized as either intellectually realistic (object centered) or visually realistic (viewer centered), each drawing is extremely complex, combining many systems which capture visual, dynamic, kinesthetic, and haptic forms of information as well as logical, mathematic, and linguistic analogs of the object. Such systems are emergent at the outset of representational development, for example, in the drawings of cubes (Figures 13.10–13.13). Figures 13.14–13.19 are probably designed and organized with respect to imagined potential human actions, imagined lines of sight, and interrelationships between persons and objects. Each drawing uses different combinations of systems which capture different sorts of information about objects and events. The ways in which these systems are combined depends on the child's priorities.

FIG. 13.14. An Australian child, Campbell (4 years, 7 months), draws people sitting around a table on which rest objects. In this drawing, the child preserves the rectangular shape of the tabletop and the relationship of the people sitting around it. Campbell also uses a *proto-occlusion* and *hidden-line elimination* to show the salient boundary at which people's waists or bodies meet the table edge. Drawings like this are sometimes misleadingly termed *intellectually realistic* or *object-centered* drawings.

drawings of cubes produced by the Chinese Singaporean preschoolers (discussed previously—e.g., Figure 13.11) as "intellectually realistic." According to this theory, the stage of intellectual realism is supposed to be finally replaced by the next stage, in which the situation is reversed, and the child now draws what he or she *sees* rather than what he or she *knows*. Drawings of the cube like that in Figure 13.13 might be enlisted to support this idea of development from the former "stage" to the latter stage. This idea, as we will see, is spurious. Development remains unexplained by the notion of a simple shift from knowledge-based drawings to drawings based on optical information. Rather, an entirely new approach is called for, which describes a series of intertwined dynamic systems deployed by the child and which are present, in embryo, as it were, from the outset of drawing (Figures 13.14–13.16).

The notion of two distinct types of drawing, one intellectually realistic, the other visually realistic, dates back over 100 years but was perhaps most fully articulated by Piaget (Piaget & Inhelder, 1956), who appropriated the ideas from George Luquet's brilliant (1927, 2001) study of children's drawing (first English translation, Costall, 2001). Luquet established a methodology of immense value to us today. Instead of merely studying finished drawings collected from school teachers (the favored method of other researchers at that time), and in preference to contriving experimental drawing tasks, Luquet made sensitive observations of children's *spontaneous* drawing processes. He discovered that the child uses a range of different *modes of representation*, to which *the child, not the adult*, gives the sense and meaning. Such meanings are not always to be discerned within the finished drawing but can be detected by

FIG. 13.15.   A 6-year-old Londoner's drawing of people standing near a table on which rest objects. Again, the child has captured information about some objects irrespective of viewpoint, including the table and some of the objects on it, for example, the cake with six candles on it (toward the right side of the table). Other configurations also capture major axes of the object represented but are more *canonical* in their organization, in that they also capture an exemplar view of the object. Consider, for example, the sticky-tape dispenser near the bottom edge of the table at the middle. Unlike the human figures in the Campbell's drawing, however, the figures here are all coordinated along an overall vertical axis. Also unlike him, she does not use occlusion and hidden-line elimination but superimposes configurations of people over configuration for table.

unobtrusive, supportive observations of the drawings as processes in time. The importance of this approach cannot be overemphasized.

Although Piaget, like other writers, arranged Luquet's modes of representation into a tiered-stage hierarchy, with the supposedly most primitive at the bottom leading, step by step, to the supposedly most superior at the top, Luquet never intended this. On the contrary, he considered all modes equally valid and powerful approaches to representation (Costall, 1993, 1995, 2001). Piaget himself also appears to have changed his mind about the stage model, and in his later work, development involves change of emphasis within a dialectical relationship among perception, cognition, and representation.

Made in the same era and in the same country in which Picasso and Braque were inventing Cubism (apparently Luquet was not aware of this), Luquet's discoveries are of equal importance to their pictorial revolution. The significance of Luquet's work has yet to be grasped by the vast majority of contemporary psychologists, early childhood professionals; and art educators (Costall, 2001).

Although the terminology has been updated, so that, deriving from the work of David Marr (1982), "intellectual realism" becomes "object-centered," whereas "visual realism" becomes "viewer-centered," the theory remains essentially unchanged. There persists today the false dichotomy between a supposedly forerunning, inferior mode of object-centered intellectual realism, thought to capture the child's "cognitive" understanding of the object, in terms of concepts and language (what the child "knows" about the object), followed by a supposedly

FIG. 13.16.   A 7-year-old Chinese Singaporean child's drawing of people sitting at a table on which rest objects. In this case, the child sacrifices the true shape of the tabletop by using a drawing system in which oblique lines can mean horizontal edges which recede from a notional viewer of the picture. She can also use occlusion and hidden-line elimination to show different views of the people, their relationship to the table, and their relationship to each other. This use of occlusion and hidden-line elimination is more complex than that of Campbell. This kind of drawing is sometimes termed *viewer-centered*—or even (misleadingly) "visually realistic."

superior mode of "viewer-centered" visual realism, thought to convey "perceptual" information (what the child "sees"). Although rarely defined by its proponents, the basic idea is that the child finally manages to overcome her intellectualist tendencies and show the 'true' optical shape of the object in terms of the projection of the image, in light, from the object to the retina of the eye of a viewer observing the scene from a fixed position. This model, or one of its variants, underpins many recent experimental studies of children's drawing and most descriptions of development in drawing. It continues to exert a powerful influence on the ways in which we evaluate and provide for children's learning in the arts. So deep-seated is this concept, that some psychologists go to extraordinary lengths to support it, even enlisting as evidence the works of a handful of artistically gifted, autistic children (Eames & Cox, 1994; Freeman, 1987; Marr, 1982; Pariser, 1981; Selfe, 1977; Snyder, 2000; Snyder & Thomas, 1997; Winner, 1982). For an alternative approach, see Seow (2000).

Costall (1995, 1997, 2001) notes that the theory of a dichotomy between two modes of representation has a further dichotomy within it, for there exists an alternate version that, in direct contrast to the one described previously, regards the intellectually realistic mode as the authentic, child art; while perspective now becomes the corrupting influence. Several great pioneers of children's art seem to have thought like this, for example, Cizek (in Viola, 1942), Derham (1947, 1961), Richardson (1948), and Lowenfeld (1939, 1967). This approach claims a more or less wholly natural, unfolding creativity isolated from cultural context. Generally speaking, this approach, which had its heyday in the earlier part of the 20th century, is now in decline, and art educators have more recently striven to reconceptualize art as a teachable subject. The reason for this turnaround is due to the implausible developmental and pedagogical implications of a model that assumes development to be universal yet simultaneously individualistic and which fails to acknowledge the effects of social cultural context (Kindler, 1996a, 1996b, this volume; Kindler et al., 2000; Piscitelli, 2001; Wilson, 1985, 1987, 2000, this volume). It gives no clear role to the teacher, other than as a provider of materials. Indeed, in its most extreme form, this approach shuns any teaching of art to children, considering this a pollutant of a wholly natural, unfolding creativity (Wilson, 1985, this volume).

However, I feel it important to point out that nowadays it is often overlooked that early proponents of the natural, unfolding creativity of the child were not entirely wrong. They had good reason to oppose the repressive approaches to art education practiced in Europe and in the West in the late 19th and early 20th centuries. In recent years, a typical replacement of the "childhood innocence" model is equally ill-conceived and destructive. There now dominates an approach, which is ignorant and disdainful of children's spontaneous art, and indeed, distrustful of all unsupervised learning (Matthews, 1996, 2003). Many contemporary curricula reflect paranoia about human freedom and plan its control right from the outset, even from preuterine life! (Bruce, 2002, personal communication). Sometimes, these interventions are well intentioned, and again range in their degree of sophistication. However, at their crudest, they overtly prohibit any actions of the child not prescribed beforehand by the teacher or the curriculum writers. At its extreme end, children are "sent to Coventry" for not obeying explicit representational rules (usually of the most trite nature), or even have their work torn up in front of the class (Neo, 2001). Other, more recent approaches take control of children's activities in more subtle ways, appropriating, while at the same time distorting, key Vygtoskyian ideas about "scaffolding" or "structuring" the child's tasks, or else use terms like *mediational intervention*, or *focusing the children's attention*. Such approaches, hijack key concepts of developmental education but, because they fail to understand them, distort them and misuse them. Whether subtle or crude, both have the same result. They take the intellectual and emotional actions out of the child's hands, both literally and metaphorically. They both rob children of their own development. The former approach is merely semiliterate and cruel, whereas the latter one uses a more expanded vocabulary; that is all. They are both obsessed with the social control of knowledge. For those of you who still doubt me, take a look at the walls of early childcare centers and primary schools—See how much genuinely spontaneous children's art is displayed. If it exists at all, it is done outside the cage of contemporary curricula.

It might, of course, be argued that "art" is not recognized as important enough to adopt *any* pedagogical approach that would require any systematic and purposeful action, and certainly this state of affairs exists and is equally destructive. However, just because a "subject"-led and "subject"-defined conceptualization of education allows what we crudely understand as children's art to escape, by default, as it were, curricula guidelines, does not, in itself result in any freedom of expression or representation. Far from it. The vacuum created by this other form of ignorance simply allows the unquestioned prejudices and assumptions free reign—They come in by the back door, as it were.

Whether mild or heavy-handed, overt or covert, with some important and notable exceptions, an art training is adopted, based on adult conceptualizations about the "subject-area," "art." In the current (and sometimes ill-conceived) fervor for early years' "intervention," it is invariably overlooked that the early pioneers of children's art, including Lowenfeld, Richardson, Derham, Kellogg, and Cizek, did have a point. There *are* important aspects of development that *you should leave alone.*

Both conceptualizations, the one based on a mythical innocence of children's art, and the other, teacher-centered, task-orientated, subject- and examination-driven, are really flip sides of the same counterfeit coin. Both are based on the paucity of developmental theory and on the same fallacious dichotomy between visual perception and cognition. This confusion has been readily exploited for reasons of social control, by wilfully confusing a laissez-faire approach with genuine learner-cenetred education (Blenkin & Kelly, 1998, 1996, 2001).

In most interpretations of normal children's drawing development, the "visually realistic" image is supposed to be finally recovered through a series of developmental "stages." Again, there are two versions of this approach. In one story, one stage leads to the next stage, with visual realism growing out of intellectual realism. In the alternate version, visual realism is thought to be present all along, but repressed by intellectual realism, the product of the child's developing cognition (Costall, 1993, 1995, 2001). Alan Costall notes that both versions of the story can be turned to use if you wish to denigrate the art of a range of cultures. Depending on which version you go for, both nonperspectival art and realistic cave painting can be insulted as "primitive." When the early appearance in human history of visually realistic art threatens to disrupt a Western ethnocentric view of art history, it can be accounted for as the automatic product of an "innocent," or even "autistic" vision; on the other hand, when intellectually realistic art is encountered, one can do an about-face and claim that, this too is the result, not of intelligent human effort and aesthetic decision making but is likewise the product of "child-like" (i.e., "unintelligent") minds.

Variants of both stage or repression versions of this theory have had far-reaching effects on the interpretation of children's development in visual representation. For example, much influential recent experimental work is based on this traditional notion of a dichotomy between these two modes: intellectual and visual realism. Often, it is the repression version that is assumed. The idea behind these experiments is that very young children in fact possess, all along, abilities to show views, unpredicted by the traditional stage theory of development, but that these abilities are repressed by an intellectually realistic tendency (Costall, 1995, 1997).

EXPERIMENTAL STUDIES OF CHILDREN'S DRAWING

From about the 1980s on, ingenious experiments about children's drawing have been designed with the intention of teasing out children's abilities to show *view-specific* information assumed repressed by the intellectually realistic mode (see Freeman & Cox, 1985). Typically, the child is asked to draw something set before her, and asked to show, in her drawing, a view of the object obtainable only from her position. Sometimes one object will be placed behind another, with respect to the child's line of sight. In other experiments, a familiar object will be placed before the child, but with a characteristic feature concealed from the child's point of view. For example, the experimenter might position a teacup in such a way that the cup's handle is hidden from the child's position (Davis, 1985). The criteria on which the child is judged to have achieved representation of view-specific information include the presence of *occlusion*, a view-dependent overlap of the further object by the nearer one, a relationship that can be shown in a drawing by omitting lines representing the hidden-edges of the further object (*hidden-line elimination*), or when the child succeeds in omitting a feature of the object that cannot be seen from her position.

Typically, very young children (those approximately 3 to 5 years of age) even when viewing one object in front of another, so that the farther object is partially occluded by the nearer, will avoid the use of occlusion and hidden-line elimination in their drawings, and draw both objects in their entirety. They preserve the continuous outline of the object, even at the expense of distorting this outline (Piaget & Inhelder, 1956; Willats, 1997; Matthews, 1997, 1999, 2001a). Or, if a salient feature of an object (e.g., the handle on the teacup) is hidden from the child's line of sight, the younger child will persist in including this feature in her drawings.

Arguments abound about how this should be interpreted. It cannot be explained as a motor problem—Many children of 2 to 3 years of age possess the abilities to form the necessary shapes and line junctions (Phillips, Hobbs, & Pratt, 1978; Willats, 1981, 1985, 1997).

Intelligent decision making must surely be involved. One reason children avoid the use of occlusion and hidden-line elimination is because this violates their understanding of the object as a coherent solid with an uninterrupted surface (Piaget & Inhelder, 1956; Willats, 1985, 1997; Reith & Kuttner, 1995; Matthews, 1984, 1994, 1999a, 2002, forthcoming). However, this cannot be a sufficient explanation in itself, because there are instances in which even a three or four year-old will sacrifice the coherence of a boundary line in order to show a view (Matthews, 1999a). This occurs when occlusion and hidden-line elimination are even more salient to the child than the coherence of the object. For example, consider how Campbell draws people sitting around a table, 'cutting off' their configurations at their chests, in order to show the salient meeting of the table's edge with the body (Figure 13.14).

Some writers have suggested that children are reluctant to omit characteristic features of objects (e.g., the handle of the teacup), even if these are occluded from their station point, because the children feel that doing so would make instant identification of the object by a viewer other than themselves too difficult. Psychologists of this persuasion argue that the child wants to show the best exemplar or *canonical* description of the object (Davis, 1985).

This idea has similarities with the intellectually realistic (object-centered) theory, but there is a subtle difference in emphasis between these approaches, which raises awkward questions. The object-centered description is supposedly based on the structure of the object irrespective of any viewpoint, including that of the young artist herself. The canonical description, on the other hand, suggests that the child is aware of the communication requirements of a notional viewer other than themselves. This "other" could be either a real person, present or not present, or a hypothetical person. Together with other data (which I will discuss later), and in contrast to popular opinion and traditional Piagetian theory, producing a canonical description suggests children have some understanding of the requirements of a viewer of the drawing.

Other internal conflicts in the model of intellectual and visual realism also tend to explode the theory from within. The object-centered (or intellectually realistic) drawing, strictly speaking, captures the true shapes and axes of the object irrespective of any particular viewpoint. Now, in many such intellectually realistic drawings, the represented object is easily identified. However, other drawings, also categorized as intellectually realistic or object-centered, are decidedly unrecognizable (see Figure 13.19). According to the theory of intellectual realism, this should not happen because, by definition, children are supposed to produce object-centered drawings precisely in order to capture the most recognizable axes and characteristics of objects. In contrast to the original Marrian definition of object-centered description (Marr, 1982), certain of these drawings assuredly do not capture the main axes of the object; yet neither do they capture a view of the object. Nor did Marr originally intend his theory of object-centered descriptions, which he described in terms of interiorized algorithms and rules, to form any kind of "image" or "picture" that could be set down on paper with a pencil. The classic theory is insufficient explanation for many different types of drawings all crudely lumped together under the category of intellectual realism. A totally new explanation is needed (Figures 13.17–13.19).

Left to their own devices, very young children tend not to draw objects from observation—at least not in the way in which adults typically define observational drawing, as a species of "still-life" drawing. However, as Alan Costall (1993, 1995, 2001) notes, it is not just the artificiality of the experimental situation that is in question. As with the experiments on neonate "cognition," such experimental work succeeds in undermining the "age-stage" relationship postulated by Piaget and others but leaves no theory to replace it.

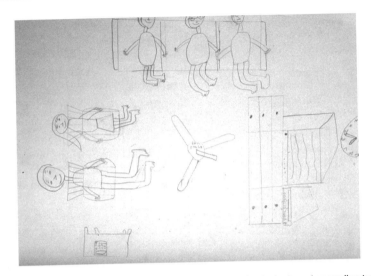

FIG. 13.17.   A drawing by a Singaporean 7-year-old. This drawing is designed according to imagined human lines of sight and actions plus hypothetical views of the scene (it is as if we were looking down through the ceiling, beyond the ceiling fan, into the room).

THE KNOWLEDGE INDUSTRY

Although contemporary curricula may offer variants of this stage theory, what they have in common is that they all seek to control how people represent reality. Even though many enlightened educators have fought a lifetime for a more expanded version of what it means to be "visually literate" (Eisner, 1985, 1997, 1998, this volume), many teachers are often hampered by tight controls on how they conceptualize and provide learning experiences for their pupils. Many teachers are forced to comply to agendas fixed by people who know very little about development and education, and who talk in terms of the "skills and understandings" assumed the prerequisite for whatever kind of "objectives," "attainment targets" are demanded to be reached in this "value-added," "knowledge industry." I have here used the terminology of England's and Singapore's National Curricular, but equivalent terms, extrapolated from consumerism, echo drearily in educational circles around the world. Although contemporary curricula may include approaches to art making derived from the contemporary art scene, and although the terms *process* and *development* are sprinkled like confetti throughout recent curriculum documents, in many, if not most contemporary curricula, "process" is not intended to mean transformational growth of intelligence, but merely the step-by-step assembly of an end product already preenvisaged in the mind of the teacher—or more accurately, in the mind of curriculum planners working under directives of a government. Hence, most purportedly "developmental curricula" are developmental only in the most trivial sense of the term. This applies to the teaching of many other subject areas, but in art, such "skills and understandings" derive from an approach to art making which retains a notion of "correct" representation at its center. Although, these days, this endpoint might not be visual realism in the strict sense of a linear perspectival, optical image; there invariably exists, buried in the heart of contemporary curricular, the supposition that development is a process in which the child gradually corrects severe deficits and shortcomings in her drawing until she achieves perfect adjustment to a representational norm. This may be disguised with a greater or lesser degree of sophistication. However, it makes little difference whether the curriculum is couched in premodern, modern, or postmodern terms, or in the third-rate science fiction rhetoric about the educational liberation

FIG. 13.18. A 6-year-old Londoner's drawing of horses in a field. Initially, the child tries to draw the structure of the object irrespective of viewpoint. A good example is the configurations for horse with the legs extended from the body (middle top and the bottom right). It is akin to Figure 13.15 in which the legs of the table are extended from each corner. In subsequent attempts, the child increasingly moves toward configurations designed to combine both the structure of the object and the notional views of the object (for example, the configuration for horse at middle left, which partially occludes legs that are farther from a notional viewer).

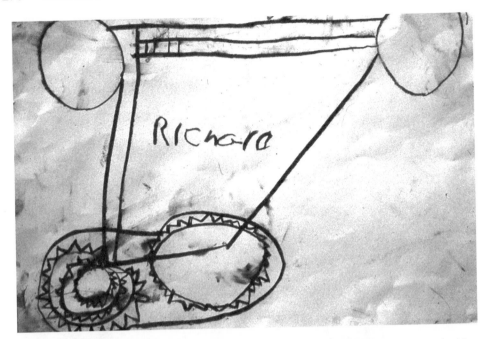

FIG. 13.19.   This is a 6-year-old Londoner's drawing of a bicycle. The bicycle was present beside the child. He interprets the object according to attractor systems which direct him to certain aspects, features, and characteristics of the object rather than to others. Although such a drawing is often classified under the heading "object-centered' or "intellectually realistic," it is different the from Figures 13.14, 13.15, 13.17, and 13.18, in that it cannot really be claimed that it captures the main axes of the object but rather the axes of psychological interest to the child. These structures are held together in a drawing process which unfolds in time and space, recording the child's attention to axes of the object in relation to the drawing as an event.

promised by Information Technology (IT). Whichever variant is adopted, the ghost of this old theory continues to haunt much of present-day pedagogy. This is because contemporary plans for art form a small part of a political agenda for education overall. Most of the rhetoric of IT entrepreneurs push the use of electronic media toward simulation of a reality that is desirable only to them and to their highly lucrative businessess. Thus, what passes for "progress" in IT likewise reflects an obsolete paradigm of simulation and replication; all that has changed is that the desired endpoint is the "virtually real." Rarely are children allowed to investigate electronic media freely, for their own purposes (for an exception to this, see Matthews & Chan, 2003, forthcoming; Matthews & Jessel, 1993a, 1993b).

Although visionary educators like Seymour Papert (2000) and Mitchell Resnick (2002), in their use of electronic media with children, advocate truly child- and learner-centered education based on principles first introduced by Froebel (Papert, 2000; Resnick, 2002), use of electronic media in schools is sometimes decidedly uncreative. The electronic blackboard has merely replaced the physical one. Children merely become slaves of a new, electronic sweatshop.

THE NEED FOR A DEVELOPMENTAL ACCOUNT
OF CHILDREN'S ART

As Alan Costall (1993, 1995, 2001) points out, we still require a *developmental* explanation of children's art. If traditional staged models have proved inadequate, then, so too have accounts which merely invoke "cultural influence" while failing to offer any explanation of the mechanisms through which the child might select from society's images. Clearly, children do change as they get older! One week the infant cannot walk; the next week she can. How has the child achieved this? One day, the child produces a particular type of drawing; the next day, a rather different one. How—and why—does the child move from one mode of representation to another?

New approaches to development begin to address these questions. Early drawing processes described in the observations made earlier involve the children generating complex ideas about representation and expression. These ideas are neither preformed in the brain, nor are they stumbled on or learned after abandoning (perhaps with some coercion from adults) a series of false trails until the "correct" solution is reached. Rather, right from the beginning of life, the infant discerns and exploits the expressive and representational possibilities of her body actions, which are then amplified and extended with various media (Bruner, 1964, 1972). These media may include drawing, painting, and other "art" materials, but they essentially consist of anything she can get her hands on (Kress, 1997), even spilt milk or regurgitated food (Matthews, 1984, 1994, 1999, 2002, forthcoming). This is a self-generated, seamless continuum of expressive and representational modes in which children work out how symbols, signs, and representations encode ideas, thoughts, feelings, objects, and events.

Before discussing new approaches to children's art, it is important to consider more closely some important theories of intellectual and emotional development.

TRADITIONAL STAGED THEORIES OF HUMAN DEVELOPMENT

Although aspects Piaget's theory are misleading, some of its central ideas and tenets remain powerful and germane. In his early work, he developed a powerful, naturalistic methodology in which he carefully observed and interpreted the actions of his own children. As with Luquet's naturalistic methods, the importance of this approach cannot be overstated. Piaget revealed that children were not miniature adults but had their own characteristic ways of knowing the world which were different from those of adults. Piaget's theory offers a powerful description of the child's intellectual and emotional development. He conceived of development in terms of successive revolutions in cognition in which the child radically revised her ways of knowing.

THE IMPORTANCE OF SELF-LOCOMOTION

Especially important is the central place in cognitive development Piaget accorded the infant's self-initiated, self-directed, and self-controlled movement. That development emerges from actions of the body remains a crucial insight. Piaget's theory established children's learning as a dynamic, rather than as a passive process. The child learned and developed through a continuous, self-initiated interaction with the environment. This idea radically changed approaches to education, especially for the early years and at primary school level. It is also at the core of certain new understandings of children's art. The essential point here is that action is *self*-initiated, *self*-directed, and *self*-controlled. Research shows that passive movement does not stimulate cognition. For example, classic experiments involving the passive movement of cats, when they are wheeled on trolleys around environments instead of being allowed to explore the environment by themselves, show that passive movement fails to initiate development in visual systems in the cats' brains (Held & Hein, 1963). More recently, studies show that infants with independent crawling and walking experience develop spatial understandings quicker than those without (Bertenthal et al., 1984; Bushnell & Boudreau, 1993; Thelen,

Schoner, Scheier, & Smith, 2000; Thelen & Smith, 1994). Self-driven by curiosity, they move around the environment and find out about surfaces, contours, edges, and textures of things. They discover what the backs of things look like, what lies hidden behind or inside other things, and how one can use things. Following on from the importance of self-locomotion, Piaget has another extremely cogent hypothesis that action is gradually *interiorized* in the brain to become *thinking*.

It is true that some aspects of his theory have been seriously challenged. Piaget thought of the brain as an all-purpose, symbol-making, and problem-solving device; whereas contemporary neuroscience provides evidence that it is composed of modular structures, each one designated a particular function. However, as I mentioned earlier, there are shortcomings with the modular approach too, in that it vastly underemphasizes the interconnected cooperation of perceptual modes. We will return to this issue, for it has an important bearing on development and learning.

As we will shortly see, recent experiments in neonate perception, sensorimotor actions, and interpersonal skills reveal that newborns have hitherto unsuspected abilities, which seem to confound Piaget's age-stage relationship. Even if we modify this relationship, trying to account for individual differences, questions remain about how the child moves from one stage to another. Piaget himself came to acknowledge this problem in his later work, when he reconceptualized development as a spiraling, rather than as a steplike process (Beilin & Pufall, 1992). Other basic problems remain, however. Does the theory really mean that development is universal, despite differences in social and cultural contexts? So many data contradict this notion. For example, unlike Piaget's account of the development of spatial representation, it is certainly not the case that people generally end up producing linear-perspective drawing! Even if we take any truly basic skill, achieved at a roughly predictable time in development, we find stunning variation in onset, manner, and timing. For example, studies show that the developmental trajectory of learning to walk is unique to each individual infant. From a distance, as it were, development might seem stagelike, orderly, and linear; when looked at in close-up and in greater detail, we discover astonishing and complex variations among individuals within the same culture, before we even get on to consider "cultural variation" (Thelen et al., 2000; Thelen & Smith, 1994).

As was mentioned near the beginning of this chapter, neither can development be explained as totally idiosyncratic, completely context related, or utterly reliant on imitation from culture. Nor does the compromise position, so often trotted out, of "interaction between nature and nurture," resolve these problems (Thelen et al., 2000; Thelen & Smith, 1994), because it perpetuates a false dichotomy between what are presumed to be two separate processes, supposedly joined together (in a bewildering variety of combinations), in ways as yet unknown.

VYGOTSKY AND THE INTERPERSONAL DIMENSION OF LEARNING AND DEVELOPMENT

Piaget was interested in the development of interiorized schemata within individuals, and many writers have criticized him for underestimating the impact of the cultural and social contexts on development and learning. In fact, a close reading of Piaget shows that he considered the interaction between unfolding schemata and the social and interpersonal environment essential. He thought that in this open system, any novel experience opened up a set of possible futures.

This would, of course, include social and interpersonal experiences. It is this interpersonal, social, and cultural dimension of development and learning that is stressed by the great Russian psychologist, Lev Vygotsky (1966). Vygotsky's theory postulates a "zone of proximal development," in which the direction the child's development is moving becomes the key issue. Vygotsky showed that what the child achieved with some help was more significant than what she achieved unaided. The role of the adult caregiver thus becomes crucial because he is required to understand, anticipate, and support the child's development toward a potential future developmental state. Bruner, and his colleagues too, significantly added to our understanding of the importance of adult support for early learning and how culture and its various technologies "amplify" naturally unfolding abilities of infants (Bruner, 1964, 1972). That mediated involvement with tasks of representation causes sustained gains in cognition is convincingly evidenced by position emission tomographic and magnetic resonance imaging of the development of cortical and subcortical structures in the brain (Klein, 2001).

However, not all Vygotsky's predictions are borne out by close observation of children's actions. It can be shown that children form structural and representational understandings, not by induction into adult models but through a process they generate by themselves, which is, technically speaking, "creative" (Chomsky, 1980, pp. 222–223). Currently, there is a danger that the role of the adult, in terms of his guidance of the child, has been overemphasized and in ways that Vygotsky never intended (Bruce, 2001, personal communication). The current stress on the supposed necessity of "focusing the child's attention" toward educational endpoints in the mind of the adult is a serious misunderstanding of the role of the adult companion (Klein, 2001). This distortion of the interpersonal dimension of children's development ignores crucial aspects of Vygotsky's theory that show the creative and self-generative character of children's *play* and its centrality in the development of symbolic thought (Vygotsky, 1966). Play will be discussed later in this chapter.

THE INTERPERSONAL DIMENSION OF DEVELOPMENT

Recent studies of mother and baby diads have offered further insights into the interpersonal dimension of development (Klein, 2001; Trevarthen, 1995). These new studies reveal that the neonate is able to participate in acts of communication with the caregiver. Such studies have important implications for our understanding of children's cognitive development. It may be that these "protoconversations" are the precursors of expressive and representational thought (Trevarthen, 1975, 1988, 1995). Infants assign representational and expressive values to objects and events within a psychological envelope formed between infant and caregiver. When parents play with their babies, they tend to naturally exploit the multimodal linkages among different sensory information (Thelen et al., 2000; Thelen & Smith, 1994). This not only assists the infant's conceptualization of events and objects by helping the infant coordinate, sight, sound, touch, and movement, it also simultaneously reenforces the analogic or metaphoric aspects among different perceptual domains which are to play a crucial part in visual representation (Matthews, 1999, 2000).

This has important implications for the growth of children's art and its interpersonal support. Far from being passive recipients of culture, blank pages on which culture is to be written, studies show that babies take part in the "creation of culture" (Trevarthen, 1995; Trevarthen & Grant, 1979, p. 566). What is more, most parents behave as if their baby's actions had meaning. We will return to this later, for this offers insights about the origin and growth of creative thought, and how it might best be supported in the interpersonal and social environment.

INFANTS' UNDERSTANDING OF EVENTS AND OBJECTS

Recent experiments on neonate perception suggest that babies are not born as "tabular rasa," or blank slates. They seem to respond intelligently and with purpose toward objects and events that they have never experienced before. Elizabeth Spelke (1976, 1990) and others, who made these ingenious experiments, originally interpreted these precocial abilities as evidence that the neonate comes into the world equipped with rudimentary concepts of volumetric solids and their movements in space and time. However, more recently, some investigators have questioned this idea. Theories about innate ideas are problematic, for they entail internal representations which preprogram development (Thelen et al., 2000; Thelen & Smith, 1994). It may be that, in contrast, to nativist theory, repeated experiences form attractor systems in the baby's brain causing developmental pathways to be carved. Each new encounter either slides into and deepens a preexisting attractor (if the experience is similar) or changes it (if it is dissimilar). As each attractor system is triggered into action, so it offers opportunities for further structural and representational possibilities, and so on, until, eventually, the developmental landscape is etched with paths, some of which overlap, forming what we call concepts. I believe that this is what Piaget intended by his theory of *schemas*. According to this approach, nothing is preshaped in the brain, nor is knowledge a static thing, but is the result of continuous interaction within a context, a "dynamic assembly" made in real time and space (Thelen & Smith, 1994, pp. 90, 166) .

On the other hand, it should be understood that development cannot just go anywhere. The infant's actions are driven by biases or *values* (Edelman, 1987) and as the systems evolve so they create a history and a set of potential futures that unfold in certain directions rather than in others. Given a generalized human situation, the child is likely to encounter new experiences in a certain sequence, and that is why development may assume a stagelike regularity. If so, why, in experimental situations, does the infant appear to display "knowledge" or capabilities not normally seen? Some investigators now think that this is not the result of the liberation of preformed ideas normally repressed in the brain. Rather, these unanticipated capabilities may be the consequence of a seamless and continuous interaction of cooperative systems that have encountered atypical, carefully tailored situations. This theory helps resolve the apparent contradictions between universal development and its variations. What we call "children's art" is a stunning example of this process.

Whichever way neonate perception is interpreted, it has great significance for people interested in the development of children's art. The neonate's interests in movement, position, and shape are the emergent concepts on which children's early forms of representation will be based (Athey, 1990; Matthews, 1994, 1999, 2003).

Although these studies of neonate cognition have altered our understandings of the abilities of infants and young children, the mysteries about development are deepened rather than explained. The evidence of precocial abilities in infants may challenge traditional stage theories, but they nevertheless remain part of, and share a bias with, a research tradition initiated by Piaget, Vygotsky, and Bruner. This bias has, to some extent, distorted our understanding, not only of children's art but also of cognitive development overall.

What these theories, old and new, have in common is that they assume that development is essentially a moving away from "here and now" actions in a sensorially rich, perceptual world, toward an evermore disembodied, abstract, formal, *and therefore superior* mode of thinking (Thelen & Smith et al., 2001; Thelen & Smith, 1994). This notion has had enormous consequences, not only for the way in which we interpret children's development in art but also for the way in which intellectual and emotional development, as a whole, is conceptually construed. In an important sense, the confusion about, and devaluing of children's art merely mirrors a misconception about learning and development overall.

RECENT DEVELOPMENTS IN EARLY CHILDHOOD EDUCATION

It is within early years' education that the theory of a learner-centered and developmental curriculum is most fully articulated. In the subject-orientated curriculum, the transmission of the "knowledge" within the discipline or subject domain is assumed to automatically confer intelligence to the student. It will surprise many readers to learn that there is no scientific evidence to support this conventional wisdom (Blenkin & Kelly, 1988, 1996). In contrast, there is overwhelming evidence that developmental curricula defined by Athey (1990), Bruce (1987, 1991), Blenkin and Kelly (1988, 1996), and Katz (1992) and early mediation between caregiver and infant (Klein, 2001) produces sustained gains in intelligence, caring, sharing and happiness.

The developmental curriculum is planned with reference to processes of human development. Early childhood education is, at best, an approach to learning not tied to the transmission of any particular culture or body of knowledge. In such a curriculum, what is available within the subject area is significant only insofar as it contains process, instruments, and experiences, which might stimulate and promote human development (Blenkin & Kelly, 1996). Researchers including Chris Athey, Tina Bruce, Lilian Katz, Geva Blenkin, Vic Kelly, Lisl Steiner, and Victoria Hurst reevaluate the ecological and developmental niche of early childhood and prepare learning experiences designed to map onto and nourish an unfolding development spontaneously generated from the child. Although recent studies reveal capabilities of babies and infants, unpredicted by earlier psychological theory, Lilian Katz (1992) enquires about what young children *should* be learning rather than merely what they are *capable* of learning in contrived situations.

There are important recent developments in the pedagogy of early years. There is a concern about the child's personal individual development and the social and interpersonal aspects of learning, including a renewed interest in the work of Vygotsky (Abbot, 2001). A multiprofessional approach stresses the caring and emotional side of education (Bruce, 1987, 1991, 2001). Regimes in the best nursery and childcare centers are no longer based on regulatory aspects of behavior or controlling conflict but on promoting human development (Abbot, 2001).

In Britain, after about 20 years of suppression of the developmental dimension of children's learning, in favor of the transmission of information, and after years of what really amounts to systematic persecution by successive governments of early years' theorists and practitioners, the penny is finally starting to drop that the curriculum for the very young cannot, and must not, be a watered-down version of endstate-orientated, subject-driven teaching, but has to acknowledge processes of human development (Blenkin & Kelly, 1996, 2001; Bruce, 1991, personal communication, 2001; Simon, 1988).

It will take some time for this idea to really sink in. Governments tend to flip developmental theories around so as to turn them, from *descriptions,* into stage-by-stage *requirements* of children. This strategy echoes a tendency in developmental theory itself that, by a sleight-of-hand, often turns descriptions of development into explanations for it (Thelen & Smith, 1994). Hence, education is often misconceptualized in terms of the construction of the "ideal" adult. Typically, a curriculum, originally designed for the older child and adolescent, is diluted down to a simplified form, in the forlorn hope of making subject-driven, exam-orientated teaching palatable to ever-younger children. This simply has the effect of "damaging the disposition to learn" in early childhood (Katz, 1992). Likewise, many parents are persuaded— by entrepreneurs of the simplistic, "quick-fix" method—to think of early years' education as a premature "hot-housing" of shallow cognitive skills, word recognition, and recitation. Pushed to its extreme, the transmission model of teaching causes suicidal stress in very young children.

THE SUPPRESSION OF THEORY ABOUT THE ART OF THE VERY YOUNG

There persists a pervasive ignorance about the meaning and significance of children's spontaneous drawing, painting, and of children's expressive and representational uses of other media.

Children's spontaneous drawings are often devalued in favor of either prescriptive, "cottage industries" in which children are prematurely trained in diluted versions of still-life practice or else are led, step by step, toward a banal, stereotyped end product preenvisaged in the mind of the teacher (or more precisely, in the mind of a government-controlled curriculum designer). It hardly matters if this endpoint is a Christmas angel made from yoghurt cups and cotton wool, or a pastiche of Monet's water lily pond, the destruction to development is identical. Many governments' crude conceptions of development and learning (most of which have proved ineffective, if not disastrous) have exacerbated tendencies to teach toward inappropriate paradigms of visual expression and representation which only succeed in undermining development. However, there are signs that the tide is beginning to turn. We have increasing evidence about development in infancy that confirms the need for a developmental, learnercentered education, supported by adult companions. Hopefully, this is beginning to ameliorate the worst effects of the "aims and objectives" model. There is a long way to go, however.

PLAY

Ironically, although contemporary (and traditional) education has been told repeatedly by its controllers that it must prepare pupils for the future, this is precisely what it fails to do. As Partington and Grant (1984) point out, these plans invariably involve children being prepared for contemporary goals that are obsolete before the children leave school. Only by supporting the hypothetical realities children construct in play and representation will children be able to cope with whatever "probabilistic future" unfolds (Partington & Grant, 1984, p. 76).

It is within early years' education that the significance and meaning of play in human development and learning is most fully realized. There is an important relationship between play and children's use of art media, because it is within play that the child discovers and exercises skills in symbolization, representation, and expression; skills that are carried over— or "transported"—to use Dennie Wolf's terms (Wolf & Fucigna, 1983, p. 1), to visual and other media.

Play is crucial for the child's understandings and use of symbols, signs, and representations. Yet, with some important exceptions, notably in Scandinavian and some North American early childhood education, where the concept of play is central to development and education, in many parts of the world, play is not generally well supported by education systems. When, if at all, play is mentioned, it often turns out that the term *play* is misused to mean adult-supervised and adult-dominated tasks designed to extrapolate those aspects of learning the adult deems important. The child needs opportunities for complete freeplay, in order to temporally uncouple means from ends in tasks, allowing her to investigate processes as entities of interest in themselves and worthy of repeated investigation, replication, and combinatorial variation. In Vygotskian terms, play allows the child to separate words from objects, and actions from meanings (Vygotsky, 1966). This has some important consequences for learning. By releasing objects and actions from their usual functions and meanings, the child is able to detect characteristics not otherwise revealed when these objects, and the actions performed on them, are tied to adaptation to object-mastery.

When objects and action are set free from their constraints in adaptation to reality, this allows the child to form the combinatorial flexibility noted by Bruner (1964) so necessary if a deep reading and use of semiotic systems are to occur. Children's use and organization of art media are a part of this process. Ludic activities allow hybrid families of thoughts and ideas to be formed within hypothetical or analog realities in which they can be tested. It allows the far-reaching connections to be made among different seeming phenomena, which allow creative, autonomous thought to develop.

Sexism in the Nursery

By far the most serious mistake made in early years' education is the systematic repression, by the dominant female workforce, and as a matter of policy, of many important aspects of symbolization and representation—almost invariably singling out these in the play of boys. Boys' play is catastrophically misinterpreted as indicative of male hegemony and violence. A review of how the play of boys and girls in early years is studied and interpreted reveals breathtaking assumptions about the supposed "gendering" and "sex-typing" of play simply accepted as obvious truths, or "givens," neither requiring—nor allowing—any challenge or query as to their veracity. These unquestioned assumptions are damaging to both boys and girls (Matthews, 2003, forthcoming). This problem is exacerbated by the paucity of men involved in early childhood education. In Australia, for example, early childhood teachers number 98% women, a figure echoed roughly throughout the world (Sumsion, 1999). As Sumsion points out, men have only "visitors' rights" in the early childhood setting. Yet, although gender equality is discussed constantly in early years education, the major, and usually *only*, topic on the agenda, is how to stop boys from "dominating" play space, time, and equipment! For example, Pat Gura talks of boys play with blocks in terms of "...a self-perpetuating cycle...inextricably bound up with territory and dominance" (quoted in Cubey, 1999, p. 14). Such bleak and negative terms have been accepted without question for a decade or more. Boys' play is almost invariably interpreted as nothing more or less than male domination of play materials and the beginning of male domination of females. Pat Cubey, writing about how, in the name of gender equality, "this problem was addressed" has this to say: "...there was a change.... *Differences between structures boys and girls built could no longer be detected*" (my italics) (Cubey, 1999, p. 15). This statement is staggering, not only in its implicit sexism but also (ironically) in its assumption that, either, there is no difference between boys' and girls' play, or that this induced homogeneity is in fact desirable. No recognition seems to be made of the overall setting in which this mythological male domination is supposed to take place. A learned blindness seems to prevent the researcher (usually female) seeing the overall context, which is that of a workplace, designed *by* females, *run* by females, *for* females.

Yet, girls also suffer badly because of this misreading. The kind of play in question is typically multilayered in terms of meaning and function. The first level of play deals with structural relationships within objects and scenes and causal relationships in events. At this level, geometries of lines of sight are organized within hypothetical worlds in which space, depth, mass, trajectory, and velocity are organized as components of imaginary, overarching, spatiotemporal realities. In this freeplay, temporal and spatial events may be arranged and rearranged at will. At a superficial level, many of these plays seem to involve warlike or aggressive themes. However, every time a pretend missile is launched, the child works out the characteristics of its trajectory within a gravity field, its point of arrival, or moment of impact in an allocentric world. Sometimes, this play emulates the behavior of objects within a 1G field, like the one in which human beings usually live. At other times, it is a hypothetical reality. Whichever is the case, the child's questions about where things come from, where things go, and what eventually happens to them remain part of a powerful substrate for the child's theory about reality. The subject matter of such games may be imaginary events: Spider Man, for example, swinging from building to building; or they may be representations of the possibly real, anything from a car crash to a sneeze. Or, they may represent the actually real, for example, terrorist suicide planes exploding against the side of a building (see Figure 13.6) (Matthews & Chan, 2002; forthcoming; Ma Ying & Leong, 2002).

A second level of play involves the understanding of psychological states which, to a great extent, hold together the structure of events and objects. This is an imaginary world peopled by imaginary agents, who have their own intentions and motivations. The child has to learn, not only about what makes objects "go," but also about what makes people "go." Sometimes the former is dependent on, or linked in complex ways, to the latter. This play reality analogs the real world and helps the child know how it is glued together by forces that are both physical and psychological.

This level is linked with the symbolization of internal energy and power, some of which may be sexual, but which is also concerned with issues about viewpoint, lines of sight, the characteristics of trajectory, and moment of impact or point of arrival (Athey, 1990; Matthews, 1999, 2003). Supposed "gunplay" is part of a family of representational modes concerned with the causal relationships within events.

At a further level, the meanings of play will have to do with the affirmation of personal power, of being an agent who can affect the world as well as control her own feelings toward it. These levels will be connected to expression and organization of sexual energy (of both boys and girls). These will be levels concerned with the the interiorization and resolution of internal emotional conflict. They will feel their own aggression and need to do something about it, but they will also have to understand the aggression (both overt and covert) of others around them. The child has to deal with her own anger and the anger of others. The internal struggle between forces of good and evil is a way of working out themes of justice. These themes are rarely recognized by those who think in terms of "war" or "gun play" and how to stamp them out.

Play may also reflect actual physical and mental violence the child witnesses or endures within the family or the social setting. This violence may be that which the child receives from her parents, but may also be the beatings and batterings her parents inflict on each other. Or, again, the violence may be of the more discreet, veiled variety, where, for example, parents disguise their own perpetual state of war with social niceties. It is impossible to say which kind is worse for the child to deal with.

However, these are extreme cases. The ordinary, "well-balanced" child only finds her balance through using the kind of play most often banned in nursery and early years. The prohibition of ("gun play" so-called), and superhero–superheroine play is destructive to both girls and boys. It is absolutely crucial for early years' education that this play should not be confused with gender issues or manipulated for dubious purposes of social engineering.

Nor is this play simply an imitation of adult exemplars. The notion that children merely copy what they see on television or film is an illusion created by poor theories about development and learning. Such blinkered vision effectively conceals the true meaning and purpose of children's play. Children take from available imagery only those aspects that fit into their own unfolding agenda of representational concerns.

The use of superhero and superheroine play is part of a continuum of representation and metaphor that commences in babyhood. These imaginary beings are really "Fantasy Guardian Angels" (Partington & Grant, 1984, p. 76) essential for children's development. They range from the "Teletubbies' and the 'Powerpuff Girls' of infancy, to "CatDog" and "Harry Potter" of later childhood, and, in adolescence, to "Superman," "Coldplay," "Britney Spears," and "Kylie." In adulthood, they may take the form of great scientists, artists and politicians, religious leaders, and so on. For example, it must be apparent that I admire Piaget and Vygotsky. I do not say no to watching Kylie, either!

At a deep level of description, children's play is about control and understanding of personal power, and superheroes or heroines play an essential role. Imaginary superheros and superheroines are psychological devices for coping with imaginary problems and crises in hypothetical realities. These mythological beings are transformed and interiorized through development to become part of the makeup of adult mental life necessary to cope with real-life situations.

Aside from the extraordinary situation of very young boys being required to pay the price of (supposed) adult male violence, any approach that seeks to suppress forms of "gun" or "fighting" play is fundamentally and dangerously flawed. It is true that some kinds of play are disruptive, repetitive, noisy, and even boring to some adults.

The reason for this is that "fighting" play does not usually receive proper support and so remains at an impoverished level. Far from receiving the support that would deepen and enrich the level of play, players encounter active discouragement and disapproval. This dislike communicates itself to children and tends to distort, limit, and impoverish their play. When one participates in and supports this type of play, communicating to the children an understanding of it, they are delighted. Men are often good at this kind of interaction.

At this point, it is vital to note that the adult participation in play I intend is not be confused with the kind used to subvert its real meaning toward sanitized, socially sanctioned aspects. The intention should be not of changing the representational values of the forms used, but of developing play in its own terms. The fundamental principle for interaction and provision is to identify the mode of representation taking place, beyond descriptions of its surface content.

Children know perfectly well that they are pretending. In essence, they understand that they are symbolizing—long before they would ever use this word. It is a tragic irony that adult teachers apparently fail to understand what the 3-year-olds in their care understand perfectly. Girls also play these games of violence, yet it remains invisible to the largely female workforce. The term "gender equality" in early-years' education is, at present, just a joke. A nonpartisan study of play is vital. There is really no point in young children—boys or girls—attending nurseries or under-fives centers unless this real violence to children's representational plays stops. Grownups might confuse reality with representation, but children, as a rule, do not.

NEW APPROACHES TO CHILDREN'S DEVELOPMENT IN THE VISUAL ARTS

Play is linked to the ability to form expressive and representational thought in art materials, and it is to children's use and organization of visual media in infancy and childhood we now turn. In contrast to traditional approaches, recent studies suggest a far different model of development in expression and representation (Athey, 1990; Duncum, 1993, 1999; Kindler & Darras, 1997; Matthews, 1994, 1999, 2003; Smith, 1983; Wolf & Fucigna, 1983; Wolf & Perry, 1988).

We are also indebted to Norman Freeman and Maureen Cox's (1985) experimental work, which has spurred other writers (sometimes by disagreement) along promising avenues of research (Freeman & Cox, 1985).

This chapter has focused especially on the visual arts, but there exists new research into the beginnings of dance and musical understandings (e.g., Young, 2000). Some of these new approaches no longer measure children's development against an unquestioned adult paradigm of what is assumed to constitute a "correct" or "accurate" representation. Rather, they attempt, in their different ways, to identify the modes of representation employed by children as consequences of children's own intentions, motivations, and priorities (Kindler & Darras, 1997; Light, 1985). In some of these recent accounts, the development, use, and organization of visual media are seen as a dialectical relationship among the thinking child, the representational or expressive intention, the unfolding possibilities afforded by the medium, and the interpersonal environment (Matthews, 1994, 1999; Wolf, 1984). The pedagogical implications are enormous. It is only by identifying and supporting children's emergent modes of expression and representation that their creative thinking will be nurtured and encouraged.

CHILDREN DRAWING ATTENTION: DEVELOPMENT OF VISUAL REPRESENTATION AND EXPRESSION AS A DYNAMIC PROCESS

The traditional staged theory has it that, as children grow older, the changes that occur in their drawings reflect changes in their interiorized mental models, as these are successively adapted to match an external reality. Although, as mentioned previously, many would deny adopting "visual realism" as a learning end state, we are justified in claiming that the old-fashioned model remains behind the scenes, because, however updated the curriculum is from the original, "retinal" model, the notion that there is one reality to which everyone must conform, one developmental endpoint toward which all must be coerced, remains central to contemporary pedagogy as directed by controlling power groups.

The evidence from recent research suggests that the developmental route children take in visual representation and expression is complex and involves a progression through a series of dynamical systems. These systems involve an interaction between an infrastructural inquiry of visual and dynamic structure for its own sake plus its expressive and representational uses. The visual structures children generate may follow one of a number of pathways through an epigenetic landscape which allows representational experiments in which children recover the structure of objects and events. That many children resolve the indeterminacies in their drawings through an increased coordination of view-specific information is just one of an infinite series of possible developmental pathways.

The first generation of structure is shaped by the natural oscillations of the skeletal and muscular frame (Smith, 1983) and consists of three basic marking actions: *horizontal arc, vertical arc*, and the *push-pull* (Matthews, 1984, 1994, 1999, 2002, forthcoming). This first generation of structure is clearly seen in the previous observations of the Chinese children and of the English boy, Robert, using e-paint. Depending on the convergence of a variety of developmental trajectories and on the number of ways these might interact, further generations of structure emerge. *Right-angular structure, parallelism, colinearity, connectivity*, and *closure* are among the first. *Beginnings and ending, rising and falling, higher and lower, inside* and *outside, hollowness, boundary*, and *connectivity* are forms and relationships that quickly follow. As these structures are simultaneously differentiated, combined, varied, and reiterated, extremely complex forms are created. As children develop, they realize a further level of representation and metaphor, along with mathematical and linguistic analogs. For example, in the Singapore nursery, connectivity among forms manifests itself in the drawing of right-angular attachment of wing to aircraft. In other drawings, topological characteristics of the airplane as a closed volume with a continuous surface, plus inside and outside relationships are recovered in terms of closures with nuclei. In addition to the importance of recovering the location and shape of an object, very young children are concerned with its movement. Some of the Chinese children represent going around, going up, going down, going into from outside, getting outside from inside, and the journey from "a" to "b", in terms of either discrete displacements or continuous line.

An example of the latter *action representation* is when one child, while synchronizing rising and falling musical vocalizations, waves his drawing paper into the air and moves it gracefully through three dimensions of space and the dimension of time, as if representing the airplane's flight. These dynamic understandings are also encoded on the drawing surface. The beginnings and endings of journeys are demarcated by marking the beginnings and endings of lines. The interest in trajectory and point of arrival are combined with other emergent understandings, including those of ascent and descent, which may be mapped onto the two-dimensional surface in rising and falling arcs. In the previous observation of the Chinese children, the interest in the trajectory and destiny of objects sometimes manifests itself in terms of descriptions of air disasters which encode an airplane's trajectory in space–time and its moment of impact (Chan & Matthews, 2002; Matthews, 1984, 1994, 1999). As shown in the observations of the young Chinese Singaporeans, such dynamic representations are often accompanied by spoken narrative and onomatopoeic vocalizations which underscore and analog the visual sequence.

These understandings are carried across media domains and combined together. The permutations are, literally, endless. From the beginning, the child realizes the multilayered possibilities in semiotic chains of meaning (Atkinson, 2003). This is where children's visual and dynamic representation links with other aspects of cognition.

EMERGENT WRITING

Writing also develops on the drawing surface. Children set themselves the task, often with little adult assistance, of differentiating between a range of semiotic systems; those that specify immediately to the visual system three-dimensional relationships and those that are encoded in a different ways, for example, letters, words, and numbers.

It is as if the child is asking, how is it that the shape of objects and events can be represented, with a pencil, on the flat surface, side by side with shapes representing the sounds that come out of people's mouths? How is it that the groups and sequences of marks can stand for words and ideas? How can things in the world be assigned values or "numbers," in yet another system? How is it that these very different phenomena can be encoded equally well in two dimensions?

To gain this understanding involves the child's differentiation and organization of family of semiotic systems. The child has the task of working out internal relationships within selfcontained systems and how these different systems interrelate with each other as well as representing things, events, actions in the world, plus ideas, thoughts, and feelings inside people's brains. We can see this process happening continuously in the drawings of the very young. Sometimes children receive help from their peers—an important but little discussed aspect of mediated learning. For example, in the Singaporean observation cited previously, one child, using mimetic hand movements, explains to her friend that their task is one of drawing rather than writing!

That making these differentiations is a profound undertaking is borne out by the ongoing controversy among "grownup" semioticians and linguists. Language, for instance, has traditionally been assumed to be arbitrary and conventional. Whereas pictorial images specify directly to the visual systems the form of things in the world, this does not appear to be the case with language. But the distinction between the written and drawn may not be clear-cut. We see this in the children's early experiments with the representation of both writing and speech. In two dimensions, plus the dimension of time, they capture the oscillating, rhythmical structure of both sound waves and handwriting or, as a queue of discrete configurations, in terms of print.

On a macro scale too, languages seem to coordinate a range of different devices. One example is Chinese, which combines both pictorializations and abstractions which themselves can be further subdivided into different classes of sign. Additionally, some writers suggest that the time-honored distinction between the arbitrary or conventional and the pictorial is a false one. Fascinating new work suggests that language may also have natural origins and be rooted in action and perception (Allott, 2001). The topological, geometrical, and dynamic understandings formed in the drawings of the Singaporean Chinese children referred to previously, are among the dynamic metaphors in which language is first embedded (Johnson, 1987; Matthews, 2001; Thelen & Smith, 1994).

LOGICOMATHEMATICAL THOUGHT, MUSIC, AND DANCE

While coordinating, in a two-dimensional world, the causal relationships within events, mathematical understandings are formed. Emergent counting occurs when one-to-one correspondences are made between action and sound and image. The child might, for example, make empathic vocalizations to coincide with and underscore impacts of brush or pencil. This synchrony also forms rhythmical, musical, and dance understandings. Later on they may call out number names, albeit not always in the correct sequence ("..one, two, fourteen," says Hannah as she carefully counts three marks—Matthews, 1999) but nevertheless grasping that an arbitrary "numeron" may be tagged to an action (Gelman & Gallistel, 1983).

The child makes the discovery that everything is countable, from pencil marks to steps and hops. Children may also start grouping objects in little heaps at designated locales: a pile of toys on a chair or a heap of orange peelings in granddad's shoe. This is really an aspect of spatial and temporal ordering (Athey, 1990). The children are essentially *classifying*. Later on, this classification will be encoded into drawing systems; for example, when Joel, at around $2\frac{1}{2}$ years, groups marks according to type inside a closed shape, and when, later on, he physically partitions the closed shape with lines forming gridded subdivisions. As children group marks and shapes according to their characteristics, so we see the beginning of mathematical set theory.

AESTHETICS

None of these emergent understandings can be separated from the child's senses of *composition*, *design*, and *aesthetics* (see Freeman, 1995, and this volume). However, in many studies of children's development in representation, these are often considered as separate, complicating issues which may be safely neglected. Of course, for purposes of analysis, it is sometimes necessary to separate different aspects of representation. Ultimately, however, the way children design the object with reference to the picture surface involves aesthetic sensibilities (Costall, 1991, personal communication). Some children appear to have an aesthetic response to the effects and qualities of the movements, marks, color, and space in their own work. This drives what they do next.

Piecemeal identification of particular devices and structures children use in their work is not in itself sufficient; one has to try to ascertain what holds together these interrelated devices and strategies. As Claire Golomb (1992) has noted, this aesthetic dimension is not an optional "extra" to research. It is an integral driving force of children's art, deriving from bursts of attention to events and objects of extreme emotional significance (Trevarthen, 1995). This is in stark contrast to the traditional notion that children only become aesthetically aware at around middle childhood. Dennie Wolf (1984, 1989) and Claire Golomb (1974, 1992) have noted that infants are perfectly aware that, though drawing may correspond with reality, it is simultaneously a lawful, self-sufficient structure, in no way reliant on physical laws of the "real" world or the "linear deriviatives of objects" (Rawson, 1982).

EXPRESSION OF EMOTION

Additionally, children use media to express, and to come to terms with, their own desires and fears; the joy and pain of being alive. These are not separate items but part of a seamless and continually interacting dialectical relationship, set in motion as soon as the baby starts to exploit the expressive possibilities of her own body actions. These expressive actions are formed within an interpersonal "bubble" of space formed between the infant and her caregiver (Stern, 1977, p. 29). Eventually, this bubble extends into both the physical and the psychological environment as well as becomes interiorized, forming an analog space, in which hypothetical realities are constructed, built on axes based on understandings of human motivations and intentions originally constructed within the psychological interpersonal envelope.

Far from "scribbling," the flight of the pencil across the two-dimensional surface forms a representational attractor into whose orbit many other aspects of the child's actions, thoughts, and feelings are swept. My studies show that young children's attention immediately alights on the structural opportunities that emerge on the drawing surface, detecting those that best allow representational inquiry into the nature of unfolding events, the structure of objects, and the motivations of people.

Many drawings crudely classified intellectually realistic are based on the imagined intentions of imagined human agents in imagined worlds. A thinking, feeling, and human pilot, constructed in the child's mind, controls the airplane drawn in the Singaporean nursery. Perhaps the airplane contains passengers. If it crashes, the imaginary rescuers of the injured will also be motivated by imagined human emotions. The drawing event becomes a spatiotemporal theater, complete with vocalized ambulance sirens and related narrative. All of this signifies a powerful empathic identification on the part of the child with events unfolding on the drawing surface. Some of these children are drawing for the very first time, yet in their ephemeral tracings, a hypothetical world is built, in which events, objects are organized with respect to the child's understanding of physical and causal relations and human psychology.

These understandings form the basis for symbolization and representation, without which entry into the expanded world of semiotic systems children will encounter in school and in society will be impossible. The concept of children's art is a fairly recent one. It is a useful concept in the sense that it has put children's emergent representation on the map, but it has also created definitional problems (Fucigna, 1983). What I term *children's art* includes the representational and expressive aspects of all the actions of children. It is not simply a question of whether art makes you "smart"; in the sense of improving your child's literacy and numeracy, rather, without that which is crudely termed children's art, no thinking at all is possible.

ADULT AND CHILD COMPANIONS AS INTELLECTUAL ADVENTURERS

Although, like language acquisition, the beginnings of representational thought are self-initiated in early infancy, representation will never fully develop unless certain optimal interpersonal conditions prevail. This is true of all semiotic systems. For example, lacking adequate support from the interpersonal environment, language ability is severely curtailed and remains at a primitive level (Pinker, 1994). The interpersonal and social conditions are the crucial factors in determining whether creativity is fostered or stunted.

Earlier on, I remarked that, in contrast to the general demeaning of children's early representation, there exists a group of people who do appreciate it and offer support. Among this number are parents. They do not give marks out of 10 for walking, talking, and drawing (though in repressive societies, there is a concerted effort to make parents think like this).

FIELDS OF WONDER AND HAPPINESS

The interesting question is, why, exactly, do some parents delight in the first signs of representation, for example, marks made on a scrap of paper which may not remotely resemble the shape of anything in the world, which are despised by so many, and which count for nothing in education? Why do many parents praise their child for stabbing a piece of paper with a pencil, and excitedly saying "ducks," or "people," or 'bees', or any number of other imaginary object or creature, not to mention events like the wind blowing or a balloon bursting?

The answer is, the value that "good-enough" parents (Bettelheim, 1987; Winnicott, 1971) place on their children's actions. The importance of this answer is that it helps us understand the beginnings of representation within an interpersonal context and offers a clue about how this development might best be fostered. Parents generally interact with their babies with the certainty that their babies' actions have meaning.

This interplay is held together by a field of emotion between the partners, in which each is sensitive to a universal, biological rhythm in which any variation in tempo, cadence, and stress becomes significant in terms of affect (Trevarthen, 1995). Each partner tunes into the rhythm of the other's actions, timing his or her own contributions to fit into the other's momentary pauses, in an elaborate dance of face, eyes, arms, and hands. It is within this interpersonal envelope of space, that actions, shapes, and objects are given representational and expressive value.

It is crucial to note, however, the subtle distinction between intervention and interference. Parents do not teach their children to speak; rather, they try to understand what their babies are trying to tell them (Pinker, 1994). The same is true of many parents' relationship with other forms of their children's emergent representation. They look, listen, and learn. "Scaffolded" or "mediated learning" may not involve a great deal of words on the part of the parent. Nor does it mean that the adult physically takes over the child's tasks of construction. Although the adult might minimally help the child with physical mastery, his or her real support is the way he or she helps the child hold the task together psychologically. I have seen brilliant teachers, apparently doing nothing, sitting, quite still, like Buddha, next to a child. Yet their apparently minimal involvement, as "light as a butterfly" (Hart, 1968), has been crucial to the development of child's autonomous and creative thought.

The process is a seamless flow in which all manner of random disturbance is incorporated into the dialog among adult, child, and the construction medium, whether this be pencil and paper, electronic paint, the use of a videocamera, or the transient movements of the body in time and space alone. The patterning and structure of these interactions offer hope and suggestions for how the beginnings of expressive and representational thought might be developed. Early interaction between parent and child, in which they embark side by side on an intellectual adventure, forms the basis of education.

CONCLUSION: THE SIGNIFICANCE OF CHILDREN'S ART

In contrast to traditional, classic accounts, development in visual representation is not best described as primarily an adaptation to a visual reality presumed to exist in some absolute sense independently of any forms of representation. Rather, the child seems to generate possible realities on the drawing surface in a manner akin to the way hypothetical realities are constructed in pretend play. In the case of drawing, the structures generated in this medium act as attractors that guide the child's attention to certain forms, relationships, and features within the environment. In contrast to the theory that the basis of human vision is a retinal, perspective image, recent theories, including those of computer vision, suggest it more likely that it consists of the structures we encounter in very young children's drawings (Biederman, 1987; Gibson, 1975).

The developmental sequence is very variable and flexible, suggesting a process not driven by preformed, internal representations or program but set into motion by the generation of "attractor" systems (Lorenz, 1963), which, with repeated experiences (supported by adult companions), converge in real time and space and in doing so create opportunities for further structural discoveries (Thelen & Smith, 1994). The ways in which initially independent developmental trajectories might intertwine are infinitely complex (Matthews, 2001).

There are no "stages" of "scribbling," "intellectual," or "visual realism." The "dynamic assemblies" launched in infancy are the beginnings of a seamless trail which incorporates a range of sensorial information and emergent language right from the outset (Thelen & Smith, 1994, pp. 90, 166). Similar modes of representation and expression are applied to a range of media, from regurgitated milk to electronic media. Each unique situation not only offers up different and immediate effects but also presents further crossroads of potential developmental routes. In a recent study, Rebecca Chan and I distributed videocameras to 2- and 3-year-olds. The ways in which these new media will impact on development cannot, as yet, be known— There is no history of how children develop in their use of moviemaking. Yet we are already witnessing another example of how available media interact with an unfolding process of development.

We found that these very young children explore these new media with emergent concepts they are forming with other media. For example, the emergent concept of "going through" a bound volume or tube is applied to the "virtual" tube of the camera's viewfinder. Understandings forming in other situations about lines of sight and point of view are further stimulated by the use of the videocamera. The child finds out about her individual viewpoint, and how it is determined by her movement and position. She makes the paradoxical discovery, which forms the basis of all understanding, that her own individual viewpoint is, at one and the same time, unprivileged yet unique.

These concerns are similar to those that are represented in drawing. Many psychologists start from the unquestioned assumption that drawing, by definition, is the recording of what James Gibson terms a "frozen" visual array (Gibson, 1979, p. 71). Such psychologists behave as if this paradigm were transparently obvious to the child. Nothing could be further from the truth. In the beginning, the child has not yet conceptualized the drawing surface as representing a window opening out onto a momentary glimpse of the object as if seen from one fixed position at one moment in time. Similar to the movie making described previously, though in an entirely different form, the process of drawing records the child's own process of attention to objects and events, imaginary or real, in relation to the medium over time.

Nor does this dynamic relationship disappear as the child grows older; rather, it undergoes transformation, so that, by about roughly age 4 or 5, she starts to realize not only the possibilities of the drawing surface for showing views of the object from a notional viewpoint but also the use of the objects as "pivots" (Vygotsky, 1966, p. 546) around which chains of metaphoric and structural analogy may be formed in emergent drawing rules (Willats, 1997).

Although some drawings may show object-centered and/or viewer-centered information, this is best understood as a consequence of an empathic identification the child makes with the unfolding representational opportunities emerging on the drawing surface, a process that began in infancy when dynamic systems of representation were set in motion.

Although, as they grow older, many children do produce drawings that increasingly specify three-dimensional relationships, this is an imaginative construction formed along a continuum which started with the first markings. The child's resolution of three-dimensional space into the two-dimensional surface is one of an infinite number of solutions to the problem of resolving internal conflicts and ambiguities that arise on the drawing surface. This sorting out of structural indeterminacies on the surface of the paper may, in turn, at a deeper level, reflect both the resolution of internal conflict and the wonder of being alive.

The conclusion of this chapter consolidates the main ideas about the significance and meaning of children's art and its role in human development. It reaffirms children's representational and expressive actions as members of a unitary cluster of modes that interact together in a dialectical relationship and drive development.

There is a vital need to reevaluate the role of childhood, the ecological niche it occupies, and how best the beginnings of intellectual and emotional life might be supported. An important part of these beginnings is the emergence of representation and expression. For, within deceptively trivial-seeming actions performed by very young children on a range of objects and materials are located the beginnings of representational thought. The child will use anything that comes to hand to launch a project about the representation of events and objects and the expression of feeling. Intertwined with this, an infrastructural inquiry is set in motion which will form the basis of the child's later encounter with symbols and signs. Children's ability to deep-read the various ways in which their worlds are written may, to a great extent, be dependent on the formation of early representation in infancy and how well this has been supported and nurtured.

REFERENCES

Abbot, L. (February 9, 2001). *Two talks on early childhood education.* Specialised Education Group, National Institute of Education, Nanyang Technological University, Singapore.

Allott, R. (2001). *The natural origin of language: Vision, action, language.* Great Britain: Able Publishing.

Atkinson, D. (2003). *Art education: Identity and practice.* Dordrecht/Norwell, MA: Kluwer Academic Publishers.

Arnheim, R. (1954, 1974). *Art and visual perception: The psychology of the creative eye.* Berkeley, CA: University of California Press.

Athey, C. (1990). *Extending thought in young children: A parent-teacher partnership.* London: Paul Chapman.

Bates, J. K. (2000). *Becoming an art teacher.* Belmont, CA: Wadsworth.

Beilin, H., & Pufall, P. B. (1992). *Piaget's theory: Prospects and possibilities.* Hillsdale, NJ: Lawrence Erlbaum Associates.

Berliner, D. C. (1995). *The manufactured crisis:myths, fraud, and the attack on the American public schools.* Reading, MA: Addison Wesley.

Bertenthal, B., Campos, J., & Barrett, K. (1984). Self-produced locomotion: An organizer of emotional, cognitive, and social development in infancy. In R. Emde & R. Harmon (Eds.), *Continuities and Discontinuities* (pp. 175–210). New York: Plenum Press.

Bettelheim, B. (1987). *A good enough parent.* London: Thames & Hudson.

Biederman, J. (1987). Recognition by components: A theory of human image understanding. *Psychological Review, 94,* 115–147.

Blenkin, G. M., & Kelly, A.V. (Eds.) (1988, 1996). *Early childhood education: A developmental curriculum* (2nd ed.). London: Paul Chapman.

Blenkin, G., & Kelly, A.V. (October, 2001). *Talks about early childhood education,* Ministry of Education, Singapore.

Bruce, T. (1987). *Early childhood education.* London: Hodder & Stoughton.

Bruce, T. (1991). *Time to play in early childhood education.* London: Hodder & Stoughton.

Bruner, J. S. (1964). The course of cognitive growth. In *American Psychologist* (vol. 19, pp. 1–15).

Bruner, J. S. (1976). The nature and the uses of immaturity. In J. S. Bruner, A. Jolly, and K. Silva (Eds.), *Play—Its role in development and evolution.* Harmondsworth, England: Penguin.

Buhler, K. (1930). *The mental development of the child.* London: Kegan Paul.

Bushnell, E. M., & Boudreau, J. P. (1993). Motor development in the mind: The potential role of motor abilities as a determinant of aspects of perception development. *Child Development, 64,* 1005–1021.

Chafe, W. (1994). *Discourse, consciousness and time: The flow and displacement of conscious experience in speaking and writing.* Chicago: University of Chicago Press.

Chan, R., & Matthews, J. (2002). *Trajectory and impact: The representation of the terrorist suicide plane crashes in the U.S.A, in the drawings of 2 to 3 year olds in Singapore.* Unpublished research study.

Chomsky, N. (1980). *Rules and representation.* Woodbridge Lectures Number Eleven, Columbia University Press.

Costall, A. (July/August, 1993). Beyond linear perspective: A Cubist manifesto for visual science. *Image and Image Computing, 11*(6), 334–341.

Costall, A. (1995). The myth of the sensory core: The traditional versus the ecological approach to children's drawings. In C. Lange-Kuttner & G. V. Thomas (Eds.). *Drawing and looking: Theoretical approaches to pictorial representation in children* (pp. 16–26). Hemel Hempstead: Harvester.

Costall, A. (1997). Innocence and corruption: Conflicting images of child art. *Human development: Artistic development* (Vol. 40, No. 3, pp. 133–144). Basel: Karger.

Costall, A. (2001). Introduction and notes to Luquet, G. H. (1927). In *Children's Drawings ('Le Dessin enfantin').* (Alan Costall, Trans. and Commentary). London/New York: Free Association Books.

Cox, M. V. (1993). *Children's drawings of the human figure.* Hillsdale, NJ: Lawrence Erlbaum Associates.

Cox, M. V., Cooke, G., & Griffin, D. (1995). Teaching children to draw in the infants school. *Journal of Art & Design Education, 14,* 153–163.

Cox, M. V. (1997). *Drawing of people by the under 5s.* London: Falmer Press.

Cubey, P. (1999). Exploring blockplay. *Early Chidhood Practice: The Journal for Multi-Professional Partnerships, 1*(1).

Darras, B., & Kindler, A. M. (1997). L'entrée dans la graphosphere: les icons de gestes et de traces. Approche semiotique et cognitive. *MEI: Revue Internationale de Communication, 6,* 99–113.

Davis, M. D. (1985). The canonical bias: Young children's drawings of familiar objects. In N. H. Freeman, & M. V. Cox (Eds.), *Visual order: The nature and development of pictorial representation* (pp. 202–230). Cambridge: Cambridge University Press.

Derham, F. (1961, 1973). *Art for the child under seven* (5th ed.). Canberra: Australian Pre-school Association.

Duncum, P. (1993). Ten types of narrative drawing amongst children's spontaneous picture-making, *Visual Arts Research, 19*(1), 20–29.

Duncum, P. (1999). A multiple pathways/multiple endpoints model of graphic development. *Visual Arts Research, 25*(2, issue 5).

Eames, K., & Cox, M. V. (1994). Visual realism in the drawings of autistic, Down's syndrome, and normal children's drawing. In G. Butterworth (Ed.), *British Journal of Developmental Psychology, 12,* 234–239.

Economist, The (September 8–14, 2001). "Over the hill at twenty" (p. 12).

Edelman, G. M. (1987). *Neural Darwinism.* New York: Basic Books.

Eisner, E. (1985). *The art of educational evaluation: A personal view.* London: Falmer Press.

Eisner, E. (1997). *Keynote paper on visual arts education.* Presented at the *International Conference on "The Arts and Education in Hong Kong": An International Symposium,* Hong Kong Convention Centre, Lyric Theatre, Academy for Performing Arts, March 20–22, 1997. Hong Kong.

Eisner, E. (1998) *The enlightened eye: Qualitative inquiry and the enhancement of educational practice.* Upper Saddle River, NJ: Merrill/Prentice Hall.

Fineberg, J. (1997). *The innocent eye: Children's art and the modern artist.* Princeton, NJ: Princeton University Press.

Freeman, N. H. (1987). Current problems in the development of representational picture production. *Archives de Psychologie, 55,* 127–152.

Freeman, N. H., & Cox, M. V. (Eds.) (1985). *Visual order: The nature and development of pictorial representation.* Cambridge: Cambridge University Press.

Fucigna, C. (1983). Research proposal: MA thesis. Tufts University, MA.

Gelman, R., & Gallistel, C. R. (1983). The child's understanding of number. In M. Donaldson, R. Grieve, & C. Pratt (Eds.), *Early Childhood Development and Education* (pp. 185–203). Oxford: Blackwell.

Gibson, J. (1979). *The Ecological Approach to Visual Perception.* Boston: Houghton Mifflin.

Golomb, C. (1974) *Young children's sculpture and drawing: A study in representational development.* Cambridge: Harvard University Press.

Golomb, C. (1992). *The child's creation of a pictorial world.* Berkeley, CA: University of California Press.

Golomb, C. (1993). Art and the young child: Another look at the developmental question, *Visual Arts Research, 19*(1), 1–16.

Guterl, F. (September 17, 2001). The boringness of computers, *Newsweek,* p. 35.

Hart, J. (1967). Lecture at Goldsmiths School of Art, London: University of London.

Held, R., & Hein, A. (1963). Movement produced stimulation in the development of visually guided behavior. *Journal of Comparative and Physiological Psychology, 56,* 872–876.

Jackendoff, R. (1994). *Patterns in the mind: Language and human nature.* New York: Basic Books.

Johnson, M. (1987). *The body in the mind: The bodily basis of meaning, imagination, and reason.* Chicago: Chicago University Press.

Katz, L. (1992). *The Ruth Wong Memorial Lecture on early childhood education.* Nanyang Technological University, Singapore.

Kellogg, R. (1969). *Analyzing children's art.* Palo Alto, CA: National Press Books.

Kelly, A. V. (1990). *The national curriculum: A critical review.* London: Paul Chapman.

Kindler, A. M. (1996a). Myths, habits, research and policy: The four pillars of early childhood art education. *Arts Education Review, 97*(4), 24–30.

Kindler, A. M. (1996b). Artistic learning in early childhood: A study of social interactions. *Canadian Review of Arts Education, 21*(2), 91–106.

Kindler, A. (Ed.) (1997). *Child development in art.* Reston, VA: National Art Education Association.

Kindler, A. M., & Darras, B. (1994). Artistic development in context: Emergence and development of pictorial imagery in early childhood years. *Visual Arts Research, 20*(2), 1–13.

Kindler, A. M., & Darras, B. (1997a). Development of pictorial representation: A teleology-based model. *Journal of Art and Design Education, 16*(3), 217–222.

Kindler, A. M., & Darras, B. (1997b). Map of artistic development. In A. M. Kindler (Ed.), *Child development in art.* Reston, VA: NAEA.

Kindler, A. M., Darras, B., & Kuo, A. (2000). When a culture takes a trip: Evidence of heritage and enculturation in early conceptions of art. *International Journal of Art & Design Education, 19*(1), 44–53.

Klein, P. (2001). Promoting flexibility of mind in the 21st century: A mediational approach. Keynote paper, *The thinking child: Nurturing a generation of learners, International Conference,* organized by NTUC Childcare and RTRC Asia, supported by Ministry of Community Development and Sports, Suntech City Auditorium, Singapore.

Kress, G. (1997). *Before writing: Rethinking the paths to literacy.* London: Routledge.

Lange-Kuettner, C., & Reith, E. (1995). The transformation of figurative thought: implications of Piaget and In-helder's developmental theory of children's drawings. In C. Lange-Kuttner, & G. V. Thomas (Eds.), *Drawing and looking: Theoretical approaches to pictorial representation in children* (pp. 75–92). Hemel Hempstead: Harvester, Wheatsheaf.

Light, P. (1985). The development of view-specific representation considered from a socio-cognitive standpoint. In N. H. Freeman & M. V. Cox (Eds.), *Visual order: The nature and development of pictorial representation* (pp. 214–229). Cambridge: Cambridge University Press.

Lorenz, E. (1963). Deterministic non-periodic flow. *Journal of Atmospheric Sciences, 20,* 130–141.

Lowenfeld, V. (1939). *The Nature of Creative Activity.* New York: Macmillan.

Lowenfeld, V. (1967) *Creative and Mental Growth.* 3rd edition. New York: Macmillan.

Lowenfeld, V., & Brittain, W. L. (1970). *Creative and mental growth.* New York: Macmillan.

Luquet, G. H. (1927). *Le dessin enfantin.* Paris: Alcon. English translation with introduction by Alan Costall, *Children's drawings.* London/New York: Free Association Press.

Luquet, G. H. (2001). *Children's drawings. (Le dessin enfantin,* Translated and with an introduction by Alan costal). London/New York: Free Association Press.

Marr, D. (1982). *Vision: A computational investigation into human representation and processing of visual information.* San Francisco: Freeman.

Martlew, M., & Connolly, K. J. (1996). Human figure drawings by schooled and unschooled children in Papua New Guinea. *Child Development, 67,* 2743–2762.

Matthews, J. (1996). Art education as a form of child abuse. In W. C. Lee, L. Perera, & J. Yap (Eds.) *Looking at culture* (pp. 55–60). Artres Design & Communications (First published in 1992 in *Commentaries: Journal of National University of Singapore.* Banned in Singapore until 1996).

Matthews, J. (1997). Liang ge dong xi bu yi yang (Mandarin for "Two objects not the same"): A study of how Singaporean children between ages 2 and 5 years differentiate, in drawing, between a sphere and an elongated, straight-sided ovoid. *Visual Arts Research, 23*(1, Issue 45, pp. 73–96). Chicago: University of Illinois.

Matthews, J. (1999a). *The art of childhood and adolescence: The construction of meaning.* London: Falmer Press.

Matthews, J. (1999b). *The conversational structure of very young children's use of visual media.* Paper presented at the 4th Conference of English in Southeast Asia, National Institute of Education, Nanyang Technological University, Singapore, November 22–24, 1999.

Matthews, J. (2001a). *Within the picture: Reconsidering intellectual and visual realism in children's drawing.* A paper prepared for *"II International Congress in Children's Art,"* September 27–29, 2000, University of Madrid, Spain.

Matthews, J. (2001b). Children drawing attention: Studies from Singapore. In *Visual arts research.* Chicago: University of Illinois.

Matthews, J. (2001c). *Taking the toys from the boys: The suppression of male symbolisation in early years' education.* Unpublished paper.

Matthews, J. (2003). *Drawing and painting: Children and visual representation* (2nd ed.). (0–8 Series, Series Ed. Tina Bruce). London: Paul Chapman.

Matthews, J. & Chan, R. (2002). *How two year olds in Singapore use electronic lens media to make movies.* Unpublished research study.

Matthews, J. & Chan, R. (2003). *Representation and epresentation: Very young children use digital video cameras and digital still cameras.* Unpublished research study.

Matthews, J., & Jessel, J. (1993a). Very young children and electronic paint: The beginnings of drawing with traditional media and computer paintbox (shortened version). *Early Years, 13*(2), 15–22. London.

Matthews, J., & Jessel, J. (Spring, 1993b). Very young children use electronic paint: A study of the beginnings of drawing with traditional media and computer paintbox (original version). *Visual Arts Research, 19*(1, Issue 37), 47–62.

Ma Ying, J., & Leong, W. Y. J. (2002). *The art of childhood and adolescence: The construction of meaning: Exhibition catalogue.* Visual and Performing Arts, National Institute of Education, Nanyang University, Singapore.

NIE Corporate Seminar (February 10, 2001). National Institute of Education, Nanyang Technological University, Singapore.

Neo, J. (2001). *I Not Stupid.* Movie: Raintree Pictures.

Papert, S. (September 6, 2000). Dialogue session with Seymour Papert: *How technologies can provide new ways to learn.* Singapore Science Centre: Singapore.

Pariser, D. (1981). Nadia's drawings: Theorizing about an autistic child's phenomenal ability. *Journal of Studies in Art Education, 22,* 20–29.

Partington, J. T., & Grant, C. (1984). Imaginary playmates and other useful fantasies. In P. K. Smith (Ed.), *Play in animals and humans* (pp. 66–76). Oxford: Basil Blackwell.

Peter, M. (1996). *Art for all–II: The practice.* London: David Fulton Publishers.

Phillips, W. A., Hobbs, S. B., & Pratt, F. R. (1978). Intellectual realism in children's drawings of cubes, *Cognition, 6,* 15–33.

Piaget, J., & Inhelder, B. (1956). *The child's conception of space.* London: Routledge/Kegan Paul.

Pinker, S. (1994). *The Language Instinct.* London: Penguin.

Piscitelli, B. (2001). *Re-reading art for the child under seven.* Seminar paper, School of Early Childhood, Centre for Applied Studies in Early Childhood, Queensland University Research, Brisbane, Australia.

Power, C. (May 13, 2002). Speaking up for themselves. *Newsweek,* pp. 40–41.

Pufall, P. (1997). Framing a developmental psychology of art. In B. Rogoff (Ed.), *Human Development* (Vol. 40, No. 3, pp. 169–180). Karger: Basel.

Rawson, P. (1982). Lecture at Goldsmiths School of Art, University of London, London, England.

Resnick, M. (July 27, 2002). Learning through playful invention and exploration. National Institute of Education, Nanyang Technological University, Singapore.

Selfe, L. (1977). *Nadia: A case of extraordinary drawing ability in an autistic child.* London: Academic Press.

Selfe, L. (2000). *Normal and anomalous representational drawing ability in children.* London: Academic Press.

Seow, A. W. (2000). *Daniel: A case of an autistic child's drawing—what can the drawings of an autistic teach us about development and representation?* Academic exercise, (Hons degree), Visual and performing Arts, National Institute of Education, Nanyang University, Singapore.

Simon, B. (1988). *Bending the rules: The Baker "reform" of education.* London: Lawrence & Wishart.

Smith, N. R. (1983). *Experience and art: Teaching children to paint.* New York: Teachers College Press, Columbia University.

Snyder, A. (February 4, 2000). The genius within. *Science at Nine: Frontiers.* BBC Radio

Snyder, A., & Thomas, M. (1997). Autistic artists give clues to cognition. *Perception, 26,* 93–96.

Spelke, E. S. (1976). Infant's intermodal perception of events. *Cognitive Psychology, 8,* 533–560.

Spelke, E. S. (1990). The origins of visual knowledge. In D. N. Osherton, S. M. Kosslyn, & J. M. Hollerbach (Eds.), *An invitation to cognitive science: Visual cognition and action* (pp. 99–128). Cambridge, MA: MIT Press.

Stern, D. (1977). *The first relationship: Infant and mother.* Glasgow: Fontana.

Sully, J. (1895). *Studies of childhood.* London: Longmans, Green.

Sumsion, J. (1999). James' story: A decade in the life of a male early professional. *Early Childhood Development and Care, 159,* 5–16.

Thelen, E., Schoner, G., Scheier, C., & Smith, L. B. (2000). The dynamics of embodiment: A field theory of infant perseverative reaching. *Behavioural and Brain Sciences, 24*(1). Preprinted on internet: http//www. cogsci.soton.ac.uk/bbs/Archive/bbs.thelen.html

Thelen, E., & Smith, L. B. (1994). *A dynamic systems approach to the development of cognition and action.* A Bradford Book, Cambridge, MA/London, England: MIT Press.

Thomas, G. V., & Silk, A. M. J. (1990). *An introduction to the psychology of children's drawings.* London/New York: Harvester Wheatsheaf.

Trevarthen, C. (1975). Early attempts at speech. In R. Lewin (Ed.), *Child alive* (pp. 62–80). London: Temple Smith.

Trevarthen, C. (June 23, 1988). *Human communication is emotional as well as cognitive—from the start.* A talk given at the Medical Research Council's Cognitive Development Unit, Euston, London.

Trevarthen C. (1995). Mother and baby—seeing artfully eye to eye. In R. Gregory, J. Harris, P. Heard, & D. Rose (Eds.), *The artful eye* (pp. 157–200). Oxford: Oxford University Press.

Trevarthen, C., & Grant, F. (February, 1779). Infant play and the creation of culture. *New Scientist,* pp. 566–569.

van Sommers, P. (1984). *Drawing and cognition: Descriptive and experimental studies in graphic production.* Cambridge: Cambridge University Press.

van Sommers, P. (1995). Observational, experimental and neuropsychological studies of drawing. In C. Lange-Kuttner, & G. V. Thomas (Eds.), *Drawing and looking: Theoretical approaches to pictorial representation in children* (pp. 44–61). London/New York: Harvester Wheatsheaf.

Viola, W. (1942). *Child art.* London: University of London Press.

Willats, J. (1981). What do the marks in the picture stand for? The child's acquisition of systems of transformation and denotation. *Review of Research in Visual Arts Education, 13*, 78–83.

Willats, J. (1985). Drawing systems revisited: The role of denotation systems in children's figure drawings. In N. H. Freeman & M. V. Cox (Eds.), *Visual order: The nature of development of pictorial representation.* Cambridge, UK: Cambridge University Press.

Willats, J. (1997). *Art and representation: New principles in the analyses of pictures.* Princeton, NJ: Princeton University Press.

Wilson, B. (1985). The artistic tower of Babel: Inextricable links between culture and graphic development. *Visual Arts Research, 11*, 90–104.

Wilson, B. (1997). Types of child art and alternative developmental accounts: Interpreting the interpreters. In B. Rogoff (Ed.), *Human Development* (Vol. 40, No. 3, pp. 155–168). Basel: Karger.

Wilson, B. (December 28–31, 2000). Paper, *2000 Asia-Pacific Art Education Conference, Regional Experiences and Prospects in the New Century, Hong Kong Institute of Education,* Hong Kong.

Winner, E. (1982). *Invented worlds: The psychology of the arts.* Cambridge, MA: Harvard University Press.

Winnicott, D. (1971). *Playing and reality.* Tavistock.: London.

Wolf, D. (1984). Repertoire, style, and format: Notions worth borrowing from children's play. In P. K. Smith (Ed.), *Play in animals and humans.* Oxford: Basil Blackwell.

Wolf, D. (1989). Artistic learning as a conversation. In D. Hargreaves (Ed.), *Children and the arts.* Milton Keyes: Open University Press.

Wolf, D., & Fucigna, C. (1983). *Representation before picturing.* Paper presented at the Symposium on Drawing Development, British Psychological Society International Conference on Psychology and the Arts, University of Cardiff.

Wolf, D., & Perry, M. D. (1988). From endpoint to repertoire: Some new conclusions about drawing development. *Journal of Aesthetic Education, 2*(1), 17–34.

14

Child Art After Modernism: Visual Culture and New Narratives

Brent Wilson
Penn State University

INTRODUCTION: CHILDHOOD AND THE DISCOVERY OF CHILD ART

This chapter is built on an ironic assumption that child art, which is generally assumed to be a natural artifact of childhood which is essentially unaffected by culture, is itself a cultural construction. For more than a century, the practices of art education have been based on the notion that child art is something that children make by themselves and that children are creative in ways different from those of adults. Like the French philosopher Lyotard's (1984) claims about modernism, this belief was the "grand narrative" of art education. It unified our values and guided our practices. Now, in the postmodern era, that unifying narrative has fragmented into a surprisingly varied surfeit of little stories. I wish to examine the evolution of our grand narrative and to employ the very evidence that the proponents of child art have used to make the case for its naturalness and its creativeness to argue that child art is not natural, that its special character is the result of adult intervention, and that children are no more, and perhaps less, likely to be creative than are adults. Then I will have the task of characterizing some of the new stories that are beginning to be told about children's visual cultural activities—and, of course, I will need to point to the ideologies and theories underlying then.

The child art master narrative existed in two separate versions that will take some time to untangle. Beginning in the mid-19th century, one was told by modern artists and their ideological co-conspirators, the critics. The other was recounted by pedagogues and art educators who were sometimes joined by psychologists—who were not so much concerned with art as they were with the contents of children's minds revealed by their drawings. Interestingly, the groups, whose stories were so ideologically similar, hardly took note of the other. Nevertheless, both versions of the child art/modernist master narrative revealed a rebellion against the rule-governed ways that art was taught and learned in the premodernist era. They championed the "natural," freedom from rules, creativity, and individual expression. The best place to begin my tale is with the era before these beloved modernist traits mattered.

HISTORICAL EVIDENCE OF THE ART-LIKE PRODUCTS
OF CHILDREN: MANIFESTATIONS OF CULTURAL STYLES

The story of the cultural influences on child art began in the West long before adults conceived of child art. Nevertheless, modernist blinders led us to see only the similarities in children's drawings from different times and places, not the differences.

In an interview with Ernst Gombrich, Jonathan Miller (1983) commented:

> Now you say in *Art and Illusion* that we can learn a lot about the use of schemata by looking at the way in which the child draws. This has changed very little in 500 years, even 2000 years, and I'm sure that the pictures by Egyptian children were exactly the same [as today].

To which Gombrich replied:

> Yes, I think that's roughly true. Though our children are influenced nowadays by picture books they see or the shows they watch they are pretty much impermeable to these influences.

Gombrich's response is surprising because more than any other art historian he has shown that even when an artist makes a careful observational drawing, say of a person's head, the artist relies on culturally acquired schemata for how to draw noses, eyes, lips, faces, heads, and hair. The artist, as Gombrich has shown so convincingly in his *Art and Illusion*, adjusts or customizes the acquired general schemata in order to reproduce the model's individual features (1965, pp. 146–178). It is fascinating that at the beginning of his chapter, Formula and Experience, he quotes from Ayer's 1916 pedagogically oriented writing,

> The trained drawer acquires a mass of schemata by which he can produce a schema of an animal, a flower or a house quickly upon paper. This serves as support for the representation of his memory images and he gradually modifies the schema until it corresponds with that which he would express. (pp. 146–147)

Gombrich's thesis is that for more than 500 years artists in both the East and the West have used "how to draw" books as their source for general schemata.

In responding to Miller, perhaps Gombrich wished not to appear to disagree with his interviewer. In a later piece of writing about child art, Gombrich notes that it is a mistake to believe that the child draws without rules (1998). I think, however, that Gombrich, who did not direct much attention to the study of children's drawings, underestimated the extent to which schemata and rules are casually acquired. Children acquire all sorts of schemata from other children. And, of course, drawing schemata and rules are constructed within cultures. Gombrich's thesis can be applied more generally than he may have realized.

A very long time ago I learned that whatever influences affect adults' behaviors, also affect the behaviors of children. This is why, when I examined the images of children drawn from, say, 100 to 700 years ago, I saw in them characteristics not found in children's images today. I had no difficulty detecting stylistic differences. Those differences, manifestations of various forms of cultural influence, may come in the form of either specific adult direction willingly accepted by children or more general cultural schemata that children acquire from a variety of visual cultural sources, often other children, and which they in turn use and pass on to other children. Let's look at the evidence.

From Graphic Play to Art: Apprenticeships in a Time When There Was No Child Art

Surely for as long as adults have carved and modeled sculpture, painted designs and narratives on walls, and made and decorated the ritual objects that we in Western civilization have come to call art, we can be certain that children have watched their elders shape things and then made their own naive versions of adult art. But to claim that these early manifestations of children's graphic and plastic play was child art would be wrong. The concept, 'child art,' had not yet been invented. There is scant evidence that adults paid attention to the visual artifacts that resulted from children's play. If we want to gain an historical perspective on the graphic products of young people we must go to two sources. The first is art history and the second is the few self-initiated images that, through quirks of fate, have survived.

In recounting the *Lives of the Artists*, Vasari describes how gifted artists-to-be attracted the attention of adults. His story of the image of a sheep scratched on a smooth rock by the young shepherd boy, Giotto, is the perfect example. The drawing so astounded Cimabue that the artist immediately asked for permission to have the boy as his apprentice (Vasari, 1894, p. 94). The story may be apocryphal, but it tells an essential truth. Adults paid attention to the artlike things children produced only when they showed evidence of precocity—when the child, at a very early age, could imitate the art of adults.

We are still fascinated by artistic prodigies today. Take, for example, the case of Wang, Yani (Ho, 1989), whose astonishing images captivated the world. At the age of 3, after using her father's paints without his permission, Yani, who possessed a passion for artmaking, began to paint monkeys that resembled the *xieyi hua*, or a freer more naive-appearing style of Chinese ink and brush painting. At age 4, Yani traveled around China giving painting demonstrations, and by the time she was a teenager she had a traveling retrospective exhibition that began at the Smithsonian's Sackler Gallery in Washington, DC. Yani's precocity and her output provide a fascinating view of the interaction of early interest, talent, and tutoring, however informal, by her father and her use of the modes and models she found in traditional Chinese painting. Indeed, it was her early mastery of elements of the traditional *xieyi hua* style that led to Yani's notoriety and our fascination with her artworks. Yani's story both reaffirms our beliefs in the innocence of children and their innate creativity, while, ironically, at the same time it reinforces our belief that everyone who achieves mastery in any disciplined undertaking must master rule-governed skills—which Yani mastered precociously.

For more than 500 years, young boys (seldom girls—Artemisia Gentileschi, Vigée LeBrun, and Rosa Bonheuer are among the notable exceptions—as are the young girls shown receiving instruction in Jan Steen's *The Drawing Lesson* [Walsh, 1996]) perceived to have artistic talent were apprenticed to a master. We have a sizable collection of prints, drawings, and paintings that reveal the history of how young artists were educated in the Western world. Many of these prints and drawings were shown together for the first time in a remarkable exhibition, *The Children of Mercury: The Education of Artists in the Sixteenth and Seventeenth Centuries* (Muller, 1984). For example, an anonymous Florentine engraving, ca. 1460 shows "Children of Mercury" applying their skills to painting, modeling, and carving—sureness of hand counted most because the young, like their masters, were artisans (Rubin, 1984, p. 12.) Fialetti's etching, *Artist's Studio*, Venice, 1608, shows a group of five apprentices, the youngest of whom appears to be no more than 5, drawing from plaster casts (Amornpichetkul, 1984, p. 108). Another fascinating print of an artist's studio, *The Invention of Oil Painting* (Fig 14.1), made during the second half of the 16th century by Theodor Galle (after Johannes Stradanus), shows a young 7- or 8-year-old apprentice drawing images probably taken from a copy book; a slightly older 9- or 10-year-old apprentice drawing from a plaster cast; and an apprentice in his late teens or early 20s painting a portrait from a sitter; while at the center of his studio, the master

COLOR OLIVI.

Colorem oliŭ commodum piĉToribus,   Inuenit insignis magisṭer Eyckius.

14.

FIG. 14.1.   Theodor Galle after Johannes Stradanus, *The invention of Oil Painting*, second half of the 16th century, engraving. The Fine Arts Museum of San Francisco, Achenbach Foundation for the Graphic Arts, purchase, 1966.

paints the allegorical St. George and the Dragon (Bleeke-Byrne, 1984, p. 31). Artists-to-be were treated as much more than mere artisans. They learned the theory and philosophy of art along with skills. No drawing shows this better than Lomazzo's *Art Academy* (ca. 1565–1570) where the aspiring artist is encouraged by Mercury, who symbolizes skill, and by Minerva who symbolizes wisdom and learning in the liberal arts. Art making was seen as an activity of the hand and the brain.

These prints reveal one thing: Becoming an artist meant acquiring skills and following rules—the rules established by adults to which Gombrich points in his "Formula and Experience" (1965, pp. 146–147). The art of young people counted, only when, after a long apprenticeship, their drawing, painting, and sculpture had acquired the look and styles of adult artists. But surely, children who were selected, usually because they were perceived as having talent, had to do something to attract the attention of adults. In the West we have a small body of evidence that reveals the self-initiated graphic works of children and young people.

Historical Evidence of Self-Initiated Drawing and Cultural Style: A Sampling of Cases

From medieval to modern times, the results of graphic play provided adults with evidence that some children should be apprenticed to a master. The few remnants of their graphic play also provide little glimpses into the influence of visual culture on children's drawings—the kind

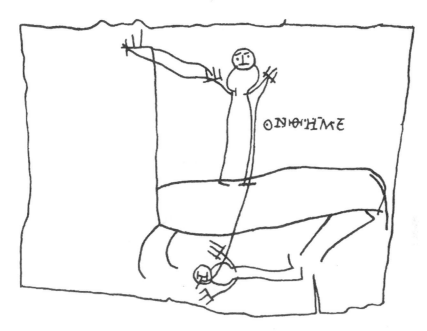

FIG. 14.2. *Onfim striking his enemy*, ca. 1224–1238. The inscription in the top right corner reads, "Onfim" (APN reproduction of an archeological copy of a birch bark drawing, 1984).

of visual culture to which Gombrich and other art historians (and art educators) have paid little attention. For example, the frozen tundra of Russia has provided the drawings of young Onfim who, at some time between the years 1224 and 1238, drew pictures of battles on birch bark tablets that had been prepared for his school lessons (Yanin, 1985). Interestingly young Onfim's figures (Figure 14.2) contain hands that look like rakes—the same configuration found in the drawings that Sully collected in Britain 750 years later—and seldom found elsewhere. It is as if the configuration used by Onfim spread throughout Europe and was one of the preferred ways of making hands for more than half a millennium. The rakehands seen pervasively in late-19th-century European children's drawings and seldom in children's drawings in other parts of the world point to the most common form of influence on children's drawings: schemata acquired from other children. Indeed, as I studied Egyptian children's drawings and observed numerous instances of bodies made with an X-form, because contemporary Egyptian children have little access to images from ancient Egypt, I became convinced that they had acquired the X-body from other children who had passed the form down from Pharaonic times (Wilson & Wilson, 1984).

Jean Héoard, the tutor to Louis XIII, saved the drawings of the young prince, from the time when he was 4 years of age, and they are now in the Bibliotheque Nationale in Paris (Rubin, 1984, p. 14). After examining the human figure drawn by the future king at age 6, one is led to wonder if, in 1607 at the age of 6, the young prince might have copied from an artist's portrait when he drew a detailed and realistic face on a crude head and body. In a single drawing it is possible to see how, when a child observes the work of an adult, the child's drawing reveals the direct influence of the style of the adult graphic model.

In the drawings of older children and adolescents it is possible to see the influence of what might be thought of as a general era style. For example, Johannes, a young Dutch boy, drew figures (Figure 14.3) in his school text book in the early 16th century (Rubin, 1984, pp. 16–17). At nearly the same time, in about 1520, the Italian artist Gian Francesco Coroto painted the portrait of a young boy shown holding a drawing of a human figure—perhaps his self-portrait

FIG. 14.3.   "Johannes," *Ensign with Two Dogs*, ca. 1520–1525, pen and ink, in Horatius, *Epistole*, Paris 1503? The Hague, Koninklijke Bibliotheek.

(Gardner, 1980, p. 9). It is fascinating that both the drawings by Johannes and the drawing held by the young boy painted by Coroto exhibit a similar style—a small circular body and very long legs. It is as if the two boys had mastered an era style, perhaps influenced by the costumes of their day as well as by the work of adult artists. These drawings were not based on schemata learned by apprentices; they are what young people learn merely by looking at the drawings of their peers.

Young people's drawings also reveal the influence of their visual culture—and even a longing for the culture from which they have been removed. In the 1870s, youth from Native American tribes were sent to the Carlisle Indian School in Pennsylvania. For a short period of time, before their teachers began to see their drawing as subversive, young boys drew pictures of battles and buffalo hunts. Interestingly, their horses have the characteristics of a common Plains Indian style as well as the distinct stylistic differences of the Sioux and the Comanche adults found in the ledger books (Wilson, 1997a).

From the scant bits of evidence to which I have pointed we can be fairly certain that children have probably made artlike things for as long as adults have made what we now call art. Moreover, the self-initiated artlike things children made were products of their time—Children's drawings, just as those of adult artists, possess the style and character of a time and place. They provide evidence for my claim that even when young people do not receive formal instruction they borrow graphic schemata from the surrounding visual culture. These drawings also provide evidence to support and to broaden Gombrich's "Formula and Experience" thesis. Nevertheless, these remnants should not be considered child art; they should merely be considered the residue of graphic play.

However, before I complicate the notion of child art even further, I must provide a brief account of how child art was "discovered." At what point did adults begin to think of the drawings of children as art? When did children's drawing cease to be merely the byproducts of children's graphic play or the precursor of an apprenticeship in an artist's studio? When and why did children's graphic play become art?

CHILDHOOD CREATIVITY AND THE MODERN ARTIST

In the mid-19th century, something quite extraordinary occurred. It was a Swiss pedagogue and graphic narrator Rudolph Topffer who, so far as we know, first wrote about child art as a special category. In 1848, Topffer's posthumously published book, *Reflections et Menus Propos d'un Peintre Genevois*, contained two chapters devoted to child art (Schapiro, 1979, p. 61). Topffer was a teacher, caricaturist, and illustrator of children's stories and perhaps with his education as an artist, with his own work as a graphic narrator—now we would call him a cartoonist—and with his schoolteacher's insights into the drawings of children, he could raise questions about the little *mannekin* or rudimentary figures drawn by children.

One of the most fascinating aspects of his writing is his speculation about childhood creativity. He wondered if the apprentice painter was less an artist than the young child who has received no formal instruction in art! Indeed, Topffer makes the astonishing statement that there is less difference between Michelangelo-the-untutored-child artist and Michelangelo-the-immortal than between Michelangelo-the-immortal and Michelangelo-the-apprentice (Shapiro, 1979, p. 61). To Topffer, the child's spontaneous graphic inventions were seen as closer to the creative expressions of great artists than were the works of artists whose drawings displayed mere conventional skill.

Gautier in his *L'art Moderne* was, according to Schapiro, "enchanted by Topffer's assertion of the superiority of children's art" (1979, p. 62). In the opinion of Schapiro (1979, p. 63) Topffer's ideas also influenced Champfleury. It is through Champfleury that child art came to be linked with modernism. And it is modernism that holds the key to the idea that the child could create art.

In writing about the work of Courbet in 1855, Champfleury echoed Topffer and said of the painter, "between Courbet as a child and Courbet as a master, there was no Courbet 'apprenti'" (Schapiro, 1979, p. 82). Now we have the opportunity to see the full extent of the relationship between child art and the embryonic notion of modern art. Each in his own way, Champfleury and his colleague Courbet, championed popular and naive images. Let me try to illustrate how important this idea is to the development of the idea of child art.

In his enormous 1854–1855 painting, *L'Atelier* (the long title is *The Painter's Studio, Real Allegory, Resolving a Phase of Seven Years in My Artistic Life*) Courbet presents himself at work on a painting while a model and a little boy observe. On the right, Courbet paints friends and colleagues from the artistic and literary world, Baudelaire and Champfleury notably among them. Courbet has painted what Werner Hofmann has called a "*Tableau clef.*" One of its many interpretations is as an allegory of the ages of man (Hofmann, 1977). The artistic journey begins with an infant being nourished by its mother. Next one of the two young boys representing childhood stands watching, seemingly transfixed by the painter's power to creat visions of reality from mere paint. The second boy is show drawing at the feet of Champfleury, the critic who first drew Courbet's attention to the supposed freshness of folk art. Is it possible that Courbet presents little boy drawing at Champfleury's feet as a sign of a creative power which flows directly from childhood spontaneity to adult boundary breaking?

In this monumental painting in which Alan Bowness (1972) claims Courbet invented modern art, we glimpse (through the triangle formed by Courbet, Champfleury, and the child) the first chronicle in paint of childhood creativity. It is auspicious, to say the least, that, in this first major dramatic production of modernism, the child has been cast in the role of the artist, placed among artists, and given nearly equal billing. In this painting, a radical view of creativity and the supposed inventive force of children's drawing entered if not the consciousness at least the subconscious of the artistic avant-garde—but not of the pedagogues.

It was not long before the seemingly spontaneous images of children that appeared so devoid of conventional artistic rules were woven into the ideology of modernism. Artists were adamant in their beliefs about the creativity and originality of child art. In an article he contributed to the *Blaue Reiter* almanac (probably the first journal to publish children's art for artistic reasons (Miesel, 1970, p. 44), Macke praised the art of children and aborigines "who have their own form, strong as the form of thunder." And in a letter to his fellow artist Macke, Marc proclaimed,

> We must be brave and turn our backs on almost everything that until now good Europeans like ourselves have thought precious and indispensable. Our ideas and ideals must be clad in hairshirts, they must be fed on locusts and wild honey, not on history, if we are ever to escape the exhaustion of our European bad taste. (Wiedmann, 1979, p. 223)

Kandinsky wrote of the cosmic and spiritual forces that could be sensed and expressed when free of convention. And children who had not had the time to be enslaved by convention were, along with primitive peoples, the possessors of clear channels to the primal forces of creativity. In Kandinsky's own words:

> We shall appreciate that the inner sound is intensified when it is separated from conventional practical meanings. That is why children's drawings have such a powerful effect upon independent-thinking, unprejudiced observers. Children are not worried about conventional and practical meanings, since they look at the world with unspoiled eyes and are able to experience things as they are, effortlessly.... Thus, without exception, every child's drawing reveals the inner sound of objects.

Kandinsky goes on to decry adult efforts to instruct children in their artistic endeavors and concludes with, "Now the gifted child not only ignores externals but has the power to express the internal so directly that it is revealed with exceptional force (as they say, 'so that it speaks!')." (Miesel, 1970, p. 59).

In effect, if this unconventional, untrammeled, unfiltered creative expression, which children possessed, was regained by artists, it would be, they reasoned, the means by which they could capture the essence of objects rather than their external appearances. The simplicity, directness, and apparent abstractness of children's images reinforced the idea that children saw and expressed reality with a universal wholeness that any modern artist would hope to emulate.

In the postmodern era it is somewhat surprising that the notion that children's art is uninfluenced by culture persists both in art education and, interestingly, in art history. Jonathan Fineberg (1997) has written an entire book, *The Innocent Eye: Children's Art and the Modernist Artist*, chronicling the influence of child art on artists. Fineberg provides a chronicle of the beliefs that the artist possesses a childlike spirit, that the child is closer to nature than is the adult, and that the child is an unknowing seer (1997, pp. 2–3). These are his beliefs, too. He writes:

> It is, by now, commonplace to recognize the freshness of vision that children possess and how often it "innocently" reveals profound insights. Moreover, we admire child art for its expressive directness and its ability to communicate an emotion to a wide range of viewers. But aren't these characterizing traits of child art also qualities for which we praise the great paintings in museums? (Fineberg, 1997, p. 21)

Fineberg never questions the modernist assumption that children's art is creative or that it originates entirely with the child. Of course his interest is the influence of child art on modern artists, not child art per se.

It is difficult to deny that artists saw in the images of children the expressive qualities that they had already begun to achieve in their own work. Nevertheless, it is misguided to believe that in appropriating the images of children, artists freed themselves from cultural influences. Hofmann, for example, writes, "In the case of Klee and Penck, of Miró and Dubuffet. . . the 'natural' is the result of a learned, artistic skill. . . . Has someone used naiveté here in order to disguise himself? This potential ambivalence is overlooked by most supporters of modern "primitivism" (Hofmann, 1977, p. 13). In short, the adoption of images from child art may have resulted from artists' desire, in the spirit of Rousseau, to free themselves from societal norms and academic rules, but in so doing they merely adopted another set of "rules" or conventional schemata found in the images of children.

It is also notable that in his writing about the discovery of child art Fineberg makes virtually no mention of the art educators and pedagogues who have studied children's art whose views are contrary to his own, and whose views lead to very different conclusions about the character of childhood innocence and creativity. It's time to look at the second discovery of the "art" of children.

PEDAGOGUES AND POETS DISCOVER CHILD ART

Pedagogues discovered child art on walls. In Milan in the winter of 1883/1884, Corrado Ricci, the Italian poet and philosopher, took refuge under a portico to escape a sudden shower. While waiting for the rain to subside he observed the drawings that children had scrawled spontaneously on the walls. The drawings by older children which were high on the wall he thought crude; those lowest, and presumably by the youngest, were, Ricci (1887) wrote, "least technical and logical; they were nevertheless, characterized by a greater decency." The experience was sufficiently moving that they "reconciled me to the art of the little ones and suggested to me the present study" (translated by Maitland, 1894) which became *L'arte dei Bambini* published in 1887 which was the first entire book devoted to child art. Interestingly, it came a full generation after Topffer's two chapters on the art of the child and Courbet's *The*

Studio. It is just as interesting that the setting in which Ricci discovered the art of little children was a social one in which they could borrow graphic schemata from one another.

Ricci was not alone in his discovery of child art. At nearly the same time the Austrian art student, Franz Cizek, observed children drawing on a wall opposite his room in Vienna (Viola, 1936). Fascinated by children's strong desire to draw, Cizek provided children with art materials. On his return to his native Bohemia, Cizek was surprised to discover that children there made drawings that were virtually the same as those made by the children he had encouraged in Vienna. He concluded that children's drawings developed according to natural laws, showed the drawings to his expressionist artist friends (one of the few documented points of contact between modern artists and a pedagogue), and eventually, after several tries, received permission to establish a juvenile art class for children where the educational philosophy was "let the child create." For his pioneering efforts he became known as the "father of child art."

Of course there were many other fathers and mothers of child art in the United States and in Europe. In 1893, the American, Earl Barnes (1893), unaware of the work of Ricci, published his own study of children's drawings, and when he learned of Ricci's book, he had a portion of it translated and published in the United States (Maitland, 1894), so that differences between his research and that of Ricci could be noted, and so that he would escape the charge of plagiarism that he feared someone might level at him. But Barnes should not have been concerned with plagiarism; he and a sizable number of his colleagues, frequently unbeknownst to one another, were affected by the spirit of their time as they all enthusiastically discovered child art. In the space of the dozen years before the turn of the century, psychologists, philosophers, educators, and art educators had published an enormous number of important studies on child art. In 1904 in Britain, Partridge published what was the first visual account of developmental stages in the art of the child. In Munich in 1905, Kerschensteiner, who had just been appointed as our equivalent of art supervisor for the city, collected many thousands of children's drawings and data on the children and published them in one of the most impressive books on child art that has ever been written. In France in 1913, Luquet published a marvelous book on the story drawings of his daughter; and in 1927, another, relating to the art of children in general (translated in English, Costall, 2001). Cizek's disciple Viola gave a detailed account of a year of Cizek's teaching—a topic to which I shall return shortly. Lowenfeld, who was acquainted with Cizek's juvenile art classes in Vienna considered Cizek an intuitive teacher whose pedagogy had no theoretical underpinning. Lowenfeld filled the theoretical void by writing of the haptic and visual types of creation in his *The Nature of Creative Activity* (1939), and then his *Creative and Mental Growth* (1947). With *Spontaneous and Deliberate Ways of Learning* (1962), Burkhart and a host of researchers at Penn State and around the world followed Lowenfeld's lead in providing a framework of empirical data to support the ideology that children's art was creative.

Although the artists and their informants and the pedagogues and psychologists took their separate courses through the world of child art, they arrived at a nearly identical set of beliefs about that world. The literature reveals the nearly universal collective unquestioned set of assumptions: (a) The child is a natural artist who needs only encouragement, not formal instruction Indeed adult influence will disrupt the natural flowering of artistic creative expression. (b) Children's art comes from "deep down inside" (Cole, 1966)—from individual and innate sources. (c) Art provides a way for children to express feelings about themselves and their worlds. Children have no need to depict the exterior appearance of things. (d) Form and abstraction are intrinsic to child art, and the artist and the child see the world as light, color, and mass. (e) The art of children and of tribal peoples are a model of primal and unfettered creativity for modern artists to emulate. (f) All former artistic conventions (at least of the Western variety) were to be avoided. Every artist and every child had the obligation to invent an individual style of art, and through the harnessing of individual creative energies art could then remain in a perpetual state of renewal, modernism could last forever, and there would be a perennial avant-garde. (g) In this ideal modernist state, artistic growth came not through formal instruction but through nature and the organic unfolding of intrinsic creative energy. Indeed, Cizek spoke wistfully of an island in the sea where the world's children could be sent to unfold naturally, free from the influence of adult visual culture. It is amazing to me that many art educators still believe these assumptions to be true and continue to construct their pedagogical practices in light of them. I wish to argue that it is art educators, not children, who created what we call child art.

SCHOOL ART AND CREATIVE EXPRESSION: THE MOST CULTURALLY CONTROLLED IMAGERY

Perhaps the best place to begin is with Arthur Efland's "The School Art Style: A Functional Analysis" (1977). Efland claims, as I do, that art pedagogues created child art—a form of art that "doesn't exist anywhere else except in schools, and it exists in schools around the world" (p. 38). Efland characterizes its principal products, media, and topics, and writes of two primary functions of school art. One is that "the school art style is to provide behaviors and products that have the look of humanistic learning"—the appearance of creativity. The second function is that because school art is fun and easy, it has a morale-boosting function—It leads children to enjoy school (p. 41).

I wish to extend Efland's argument by showing how teachers create *child art* (the term that I wish to substitute for Efland's "school art"). For my illustration, I'll go to the pedagogy of "the father of child art." By the 1920s, Franz Cizek's juvenile art classes in Vienna (Figure 14.4) had become the Mecca to which art teachers from Europe, Britain, and America traveled to learn from the Father of Child Art how to stimulate and motivate children's creative expression. In 1942, Cizek's disciple, Wilhelm Viola, wrote of a year of Cizek's teaching. A close examination of the transcript of one of Cizek's lessons is revealing.

On the 30th of November, 30, 1935, Cizek asks his young students:

What nice things would you like to do to-day? Think about it and tell me! *Child*: I shall make a doll's pram. I shall make a "Krampus" [1] *Child*: I should like to make a window where Santa Claus has put something. *Cizek*: We shall take a block [a sheet of paper] with the long side at the bottom. Or would you prefer it the other way round. Children: No! *Cizek*: Who wants it in this way? (shows the block with the long side at the bottom. All the children want it this way.) *Cizek*: We shall draw a line down the center. This is a wall. At one side of the wall Santa Claus will stand, and on the other side—who will stand there? The "Krampus." At the side of the paper near the window[2] we have Santa Claus, and at the side of the paper near the door we have the "Krampus." How does Santa Claus look? *Child*: He wears a mitre. *Child*: And a long coat. *Cizek*: Yes, a long coat. But you should begin with the head. How does his head look? *Child*: It's like a man's head. *Cizek*: What kind of head has he? *Child*: A very funny head. *Cizek*: He has a long beard and beautiful white hair. *Child*: No I don't believe it. *Cizek*: What has he on his head? *Child*: A mitre. *Cizek*: Do you know hat a mitre looks like? But you can draw it better than describe it. Who can describe the mitre? *Child*: I. *Child*: I. *Child*: I. *Child*: Like a bishop. *Child*: There is an arch and it closes down and at the top is a cross, and that is all. *Cizek*: I shan't bother you to describe it—draw it. Begin with the head, then the mitre, and then the rest. Start! But don't make the head too small!

---

[1] "Krampus" and Santa Claus come to the children on the evening of December 5th. "Krampus" is the devil and Santa Claus is the good bishop. It is a kind of forerunner of Christmas and a great event in children's lives in Roman Catholic countries. Santa Claus brings fruits and sweets to the good children, and "Krampus" is supposed to thrash the naughty ones.

[2] Undoubtedly some of the very young children would not know left and right.

FIG. 14.4. "A child explaining her work to others," Photo by R. J. Bohl, Vienna, reproduced in W. Viola (1936), *Child art and Franz Cizek* (p. 23). Vienna: Austrian Junior Red Cross.

Cizek (later): You all must begin with the mitre near the top of the paper—as Trude did. Not in the middle! Otherwise it would be a wee Santa Claus. *Cizek* (to one child): You have done the head and mitre, but don't forget his eyes and eyebrows. (Viola, 1942, pp. 112–113)

Through his careful use of language, Cizek has instructed the children to paint a particular subject, to orient their paper horizontally, to divide the page in half, to paint large, to use specific colors. Before the session is over, Viola has recorded Cizek saying "You should draw each hair separately." "You must make your decorations thicker. "Don't make a few quick strokes, but cover your paper carefully." "You can't paint a single line. You can only paint what is between two lines. You must have double lines." "When I say, Now do the eyes, you should not make blots, but eyes with lids, pupils, and all the parts of the eyes" (Viola, 1942, pp. 114–115).

What I wish to claim is that the teachers of child art, the Cizeks, the Lowenfelds, the Frank Wachowiaks, the Blanche Jeffersons, the Natalie Robinson Coles, and all the other gifted art teachers—the teachers whose students created such luscious examples of child art, *themselves*, through their language, their motivations, and their instructions, their guiding techniques and processes—created child art! Ironically, the art of children, which we art educators have assumed to be the most spontaneous, the freest, the most creative, the least influenced, is actually the foremost example of cultural influence. This influence was noted as early as 1925, when, after his visit to Professor Cizek's classes in Vienna, Thomas Munro (1956) concluded:

In short, it was obvious that in spite of the attempt at preserving spontaneity, several different types of influence had affected the work of both groups (the younger and older children). The teacher himself, first of all, was doing more than he realized; in no other way could the marked likeness between the pictures, which stamped them at once as Cizek products, be explained. (pp. 237–241)

In addition to Cizek's directions to his students, Munro lists children copying from one another, and especially the children's seeing, in the works displayed in the school, the kinds of works that they themselves should create. Munro (1956) concludes his critique of Cizek's teaching with two astonishing statements:

> The idea of keeping a child's imagination in a state of absolute purity and freedom is from the start impossible. The very attempt at such an end is evidence of the false psychology which has affected much writing on art education: of the old belief that some 'self' within the child is bursting for expression and release, and that all outside forces tend to repress and enslave it. (p. 239)

Munro concludes his critique with:

> The old academic methods tends to be restrictive; not, as the free expressionists suppose, because it imparts traditions, but because it imparts too few traditions.... The Cizek plan, far from achieving its end of freedom, robs and restricts the student when it shuts out all but a few influences, and these few none of the best. (pp. 240–241)

The Cult of Childhood (George Boas, 1990) has had a very long run. In some parts of the world—I could cite Japan where Lowenfeld in the 1980s and 1990s was still the most quoted art educator—beliefs about the natural art of the child show few signs of diminishing. It is difficult to believe that "cultural primitivism"—the nearly 150-year-old belief that earlier states are better and purer because they are more innocent—continues to shape art educational practices.

If we art educational researchers were interested in the complete spectrum of cultural influences on children's images, we would direct our studies to the products of art classrooms present and past. We could become historians of child art conducting analyses of the styles of art produced by the students of the gifted practitioners of child art. Our studies of children's artworks would reveal the remarkable differences in the visual culture of, say, Cizek's and Natalie Robinson Cole's classrooms. Our studies could be directed to the striking differences in the school art within China, Taiwan, and Japan and the even greater differences when "child art" of the East is compared to products from Western art classrooms. Yes, our studies would surely show that art teachers and their pedagogical practices have created distinct styles of child art.

MODERNIST NOTIONS OF CREATIVITY: THE MISGUIDED AVOIDANCE OF CONVENTION

Modernist ideologists, whether the artists or the pedagogues such as Cizek, prized child art because of its apparent creativity and freedom from conventional imagery. They viewed the spontaneous and unrestrained images as evidence that the child had not yet succumbed to the confining affects of artistic rules. Indeed, it was their goal to keep the child artist and the adult that the child would become forever free from such restrictions. They believed that, through the positive outcomes of art education, adults—perhaps even entire societies—might be transformed from a state of unimaginative slavery to rules to a condition of never-ending creative well-being. The goal was admirable, but the understanding of creativity and the means through which it is achieved was hopelessly flawed. Of course "insidious" society and its conventions always prevailed. As children grew older, their painting and drawings appeared to become less spontaneous, more deliberate, and they were filled with images that seemed to have been copied from a great variety of conventional sources.

The child art ideologues had missed one important point—that there is a crucial distinction between (a) avoiding artistic rules altogether; and on the other hand, (b) acquiring artistic rules, conventions, and skills and then playing with those rules and images—stretching them and inventively recombining them to in one way or another to create something new. The story of 20th-century art is filled with examples of artists such as Duchamp, Picasso, and Calder, who rejected conventional rules and replaced them with new images, new functions, and new definitions that actually redirected the history of art into new channels. But is it possible to extend, combine, and go beyond rules and conventions—if they haven't been acquired? It is this aspect of artistic creativity that the proponents of child art and creative expression had not understood—perhaps have still not understood.

There is a simple way to think about the child and artistic creativity. It has to do with states that I refer to as preconventionality, conventionality, and postconventionality. The young child, at the very beginning of his or her mark-making, exploratory modeling, and assembling/constructing phase, exists in a state where he or she knows very little of artistic conventions. Almost immediately, however, the child begins to notice and use the configurations, marking patterns, and various kinds of art-making activities of other children and adults. For example, some Egyptian children make tadpole figures with square heads—a convention that they learn from other children. What I have termed the *preconventional stage* is actually a very short-lived period characterized by the acquisition of conventional images that pervade child subcultures within larger cultures. Most of the images and configurations used by children are not invented by them; they are borrowed from other children. In other words, the preconventional is actually characterized by considerable borrowing. And as I have already indicated, this preconventional period was capitalized on by child art pedagogues such as Cizek who unknowingly encouraged children to emulate the art of other children.

I think of the conventional phase as the time when, in one way or another, young people begin to acquire the rudiments of such things as perspective, conventional ways to draw human figures, facial features, landscapes, and the like—the sorts of things acquired from how-to-draw books and from some art teachers. It is fascinating to note that Gombrich (1998), in his essay of Violett-le-Duc's *Histoire d'n dessinateur* (1879), provides an insightful account of how young people acquire rules. The young apprentices about which I have already written provide the paradigm example of the conventional phase. In the West very few art programs currently exist, either in schools or in special art classes, that provide comprehensive instruction in the rules and conventions of traditional artistic production—a fact for which we should, perhaps, be grateful. In Taiwan, for example, where entrance to some schools requires young applicants to demonstrate mastery of conventional artistic skills, I have examined children's portfolios filled with ordinary carefully rendered Western-style still-life drawings and paintings produced in special outside-school art classes. Nevertheless, where instruction does not exist formally, some young people often informally acquire conventions of drawing. Most notably, the conventional phase is a time when children emulate images from the popular media (Wilson & Wilson, 1977). My studies show that most Japanese children learn to draw in the manga style—and many master the style to a remarkably high degree (Figure 14.5) (Wilson, 1997b, 2000a, 2002).

The postconventional phase, in my view, is reached by only a few individuals who have sufficiently mastered conventional art styles and ideologies to the point that they have become dissatisfied by their limitations. The dissatisfaction leads to such things as rejection, significant extension, reapplication of images of one mode of art to another mode of art, or on rare occasions, to the creation of an entirely new form of art. The extensions, reapplications, new combinations, and especially the new forms, I think, must result in the creation of something of cultural and historical significance to qualify as postconventional. In short, I have set the bar high—so high that no child, and few if any youth, is capable of reaching it. After all, only a few adults do.

FIG. 14.5.   When Japanese Children were asked to draw stories, over half the kindergarten children drew characters derived from manga; two thirds of the characters drawn by sixth-grade children were based on manga. The large-eyed female figures at the upper left were made by kindergarten children; those in the middle were drawn by second- and fourth-grade children; and those at the lower part of the page were drawn by sixth-grade children.

The child art pedagogues did not distinguish between child "art" that was preconventional and the postconventional and creative work of rule-breaking artists (who sometimes appropriated children's images). Art teachers mistakenly believed that they could hold children in a permanent preconventional state and that their young charges, thus free of convention, could be forever creative. This feat was both practically and logically impossible.

Of course what I have not taken into account is idiosyncratic longings, gifts, quirks, handicaps, whatever, that lead nearly every individual to produce artlike things that are, to a lesser—a very lesser—or a greater degree, unique. This uniqueness may occur at the preconventional and the conventional phases as well as at the postconventional phase. Indeed, in my view, art educators should encourage idiosyncratic behavior, the minor breaking of artistic rules and conventions, inventive and imaginative combining of images, and a stretching from the known to the unknown at any phase of a young person's development. This is precisely what Wilson, Hurwitz, and Wilson (1987) tried to encourage in *Teaching Drawing from Art*. It is probably time for art educators to rethink the meaning of the term *creativity*, especially when creativity is defined as working without constraints. It is through conventional constraints first acquired, then subsequently rejected and subverted that creativity arises.

POSTMODERNISM ENTERS ART EDUCATION: QUESTIONING THE MODERNIST NARRATIVE

Through much of the 20th century, art educators felt the pangs of defeat whenever they saw evidence that children's drawing and painting had become corrupted by adult imagery—often imagery of the "worst" sort, stolen from popular visual culture. In the 21st century, as we now know, children are always "corrupted" by cultural conventions. This, however, was not a popular position to take in the 1970s. In 1977, Wilson and Wilson published "An Iconoclastic View of the Imagery Sources of Young People." In it we claimed that virtually every image drawn by teenagers could be traced to sources such as popular visual culture, how-to-draw books, and by the schemata used by other young people. The article was greeted by some art educators as an affirmation of how they themselves had learned to draw; and by others, as an outrageous attack on the basic principles of modern art education. Rudolph Arnheim (1978) was the most eloquent critic. He wrote, "Iconoclasm, I thought was the smashing of traditional icons. Instead what Brent and Marjorie Wilson attempted to do with their 'Iconoclastic View' was the opposite, namely the exhumation of the mummies of nineteenth century art drill." Of course we had not made any claims about pedagogy—just that young people usually borrowed their images rather than invent them. Arnheim's and others' criticism notwithstanding, we knew that our eyes were not deceiving us; we could see that children's imagery was highly influenced by culture. Consequently we set out to take the very evidence that was used to support the claim that children's images unfolded naturally and show that those same drawings contained powerful evidence of cultural influence.

The Disappearing Two-Eyed Profile

In his *L'arte Dei Bambini*, Ricci (1887) noted that 70% of the profiles drawn by Italian children showed the two eyes of the full face. Sully (1896) presented scores of children's drawings, of which 54% are two-eyed profiles. Partridge, in 1902, wrote that the mixed profile, which included the two-eyed profile, was one of the developmental characteristics of children's drawings—that they began by showing figures from a frontal view, then drew profiles with two eyes, and finally profiles with only one eye showing. In the hundreds of figure drawings collected by Kerschensteiner (1905) in Munich prior to 1905, approximately 30% were two-eyed profiles, and Levinstein (1905) in Germany also reported that 34% of children's figure drawings were two-eyed profiles. In her book on the Draw-a-Man test, Goodenough (1926) shows two eyed-profiles, but does not analyze them. About 5% of Goodenough's sample from American children's drawings made between the years 1917 and 1923 are two-eyed profiles (Figure 14.6). In Lowenfeld's books, *The Nature of Creative Activity* (1939) and *Creative and Mental Growth* (1947, 1957), the partially sighted boy, D. H. who searches for his lost pencil, is a two-eyed profile. However, in the figure drawings collected for the 1960s standardization of the Draw-a-Man test (Harris, 1963) there are no two-eyed profiles. This once common

FIG. 14.6. Three two-eyed profile figures, reproduced in J. Sully (1896), *Studies of childhood* (p. 341). London: Longmans, Green, and Co. Fifty-four percent of the human figures reproduced in Sully's chapter on "The Young Draftsman" are two-eyed profiles. The figure on the left has a rake hand, the same schema used by Onfim in the 13th century, and seldom used by American children today.

feature of children's drawings declined and disappeared in Europe and America. Why? Wilson and Wilson (1981) speculate that perhaps more than 200 years ago, somewhere in Europe, a young child drawing on a wall looked higher up and seeing the profile of face drawn by an older child thought to himself or herself, I should draw like that. After completing a profile, the child might have puzzled, thought to herself, don't people have two eyes (explained by Luquet, 1927, as intellectual realism)? A second eye was added, and the two-eyed profile was born. Other children in the town copied it on other walls; one child from the village visited another town, drew it on another wall, and soon other children were carrying the schema from town to town; and in time the image spread throughout Europe, to Britain, and with schemata carrying children it emigrated to America.

But why was the two-eyed-profile so common, and why did it disappear? When it was present in high numbers, children (and adults who drew much like children) were nearly the sole source of imagery (usually found on walls) from which children could acquire their graphic schemata. Around the beginning of the 20th century with the increased availability of paper for drawing and the invention of rapid printing, children were presented with a myriad of graphic sources in comics and illustrated books from which to borrow schemata. When the two-eyed profile was only one schemata among many, its potency was first diminished and then lost entirely—except that Picasso began painting the two-eyed profile in 1927. Actually, Picasso may have drawn it as a child, and if not, he probably saw it in the drawings of Spanish and French children.

It is also worth noting that the two-eyed profile is still being drawn by some children. In the early 1980s in Egyptian villages where there were virtually no magazine or book illustrations, I found a sizable number of children who drew the two-eyed profile (Wilson & Wilson, 1984). Egyptian children draw a profile face with their numeral 4—which looks like a 3 drawn in reverse. The presence of the profile was an invitation for some children, who as Luquet has theorized sometimes draw what they know, not what they see (Luquet, 1927), to draw the two-eyed profile—and its presence was an invitation for many other Egyptian village children to draw what they had seen other children draw.

An Overview of Studies of Cultural Influences on Children's Drawings

Since the 1970s, researchers have been studying manifestations of cultural influence in the drawings of children and youth. I wish to note some of the major contributions to this growing body of literature—a literature that reveals the tension between modernist and postmodernist views of the images of children, the sources of those images, and how students should be educated in art.

The anthropologist Alexander Alland, Jr. in his book *Playing with Form: Children Draw in Six Cultures* (1983), filmed children, ages 2 to 8 in Japan, Bali, Taiwan, Ponape, France, and the United States in order to analyze their step-by-step drawing process. He used his insights to challenge modernist beliefs about the universality of developmental stages and to argue that the differences he observed reflect rules that are specific to cultures. His attention to rules rather than to style and his inattention to the drawings of older children resulted in his ignoring many of the most obvious manifestations of visual cultural differences.

The National Society for Education in Art and Design 1989 Conference held at the British Museum in London resulted in the publication of *Drawing Research and Development* (Thistlewood, 1992). The book reveals the growing separation between those who believe that children's imagery is from internal and personal sources and those who explain development in terms of the acquisition of cultural schemata. John Matthews (1992) and Nancy Smith (1992) attended to the internal sources, while Elsbeth Court (1992) analyzed universal features and social influences in the drawings of rural Kenyan children. Taha Elatta (1992) documented the distinct patterns of design used by children and youth in different parts of the Sudan. Wilson and Ligtvoet (1992) had Dutch, American, and Italian children (in 1986) complete art assignments originally given to Dutch children in 1937 by a follower of Cizek. Focusing on schemata children used for drawing trees, we found that there were significant cultural differences among the groups of contemporary children and especially between the contemporary children and the 1937 Dutch children. One of our most important conclusions was that, ironically, the Dutch follower of Cizek had managed to entice children to produce drawings that were far more elaborate, detailed, and exquisite than those of today's children who were used to working with less teacher supervision and considerably less discipline. After completing the study, I was reminded of a statement attributed to Lowenfeld as he registered his disappointment at the rather dismal results achieved by some of the student teachers in Penn State's Saturday morning art classes: "It may be child art, but it isn't good child art!" Cizek, Lowenfeld, and their followers everywhere know how to create the visual cultural conditions that encourage—or direct—children to produce gorgeous things.

This apparent decline in the quality of child art has attracted a variety of speculations regarding the underlying causes. For example, in *Child Development in Art* an anthology published by the National Art Education Association (Kindler, 1997), Rudolf Arnheim praises the "overall quality, variety, and originality of works chosen by teachers and a Japanese jury" for an international exhibition of children's art. He then speculates that perhaps it is the mass media such as television that detract children's attention from art making. He goes on to claim that "We see children losing their spontaneous creativity when they copy comic strips and similar commercial imagery, and there have been art educators who neglected their mission by asking their pupils to faithfully imitate inferior models" (Arnheim, 1997, pp. 14–15). Arnheim has not examined teaching practices. Nevertheless, the decline in "spontaneous creativity," he notes, probably results because many American art teachers do not acquire the skills and techniques employed by Cizek, Lowenfeld, and their followers to make child art appear spontaneous and expressive. In the time after modernism, should they? In *Child Development in Art*, Duncum

(1997) examines the sex, power, and violence, and the many other subjects and themes of children's unsolicited drawings. Together they present a striking contrast to the topics typically assigned by teachers. In my own chapter in the same book (Wilson, 1997a), I claim that child art is an open concept, subject to debate, redefinition, and multiple interpretations. In a tremendously important chapter mapping artistic development, Kindler and Darras (1997) provide a theory that specifies the complex sets of factors, cultural and natural, and their relationships needed to account for the many different strands of artistic development.

Two recent anthologies, *The Cultural Context: Comparative Studies of Art Education and Children's Drawings* (Lindström, 2000) and *The Arts in Children's Lives: Context, Culture, and Curriculum* (Bresler & Thompson, 2002), deal specifically with the relationships among children, the arts, and culture. Just at its title applies, *The Arts in Children's Lives*, sensitively examines the complex intertextual relationships among the arts, both high and popular; development; cultural contexts; and curriculum. In both anthologies, the selection of papers and their content show a lessening of the tension between modernist/naturalist accounts of artistic development and postmodernist/cultural accounts of artistic achievement. Cultural accounts of children's lives in and out of school are beginning to feel natural.

Studies of Cultural Influence That Might Be Conducted

Every textbook in art education, every art education magazine, and every exhibition and catalog of exhibition of children's art contain the raw material for studies of cultural influences on the art of children. They call for the question: Why do these images look as they do? How does the visual culture of school-based art education programs interact with students' and teachers' interests in popular visual culture and other aspects of visual culture to shape the images made in school?

For example, I open a catalog of children's art: *Shen Zhen Shi Er Hui Hua Zuo Pin Xuan Ji printed in China* (Zhang, 1997). On pages 14 and 15, six works are reproduced. The first image on page 14 shows a woodcut or linoleum cut by a 13-year-old whose teacher and her print, it appears, were influenced by Russian art educational media and practices in a time when Russian and Chinese relations were closer than they are today. The image is reminiscent of European 20th-century woodcuts, and, especially, it has the character of the prints of the Swiss-French artist Felix Vallotton (1865–1925), whose woodcuts were influential in reviving interest in the medium. Many school images have a similar complex visual cultural lineage. Below the print on the left is a charming ink and brush painting of a cat and basket of flowers by a 7-year-old (Figure 14.7A and 14.7B). It is painted in a style similar, very similar, to that of Yani whom I mentioned earlier. And, of course, Yani's work is related to that of Xi Bi-shi (1863–1957), who is sometimes called the Chinese Picasso; and that of Shi Lu (1919–1982), whose paintings of cats could have been the model for the child's painting. The 86-page catalog has a dozen other works that show the influence of Yani or of Xi Bi-shi or of Shi Lu. My hunch is that it is the child prodigy Yani, more than artists Xi Bi-shi and Shi Lu, who has inspired innumerable Chinese children and their teachers to emulate her images and bask in the glow of her fame. Next to the Yani-like painting is another ink and brush painting of lotus blossoms and a bird by a 9-year-old. It is rendered in a precise and elegant linear style of brush painting. Page 15, at the top and at the bottom, shows two typical child art images done in what appears to be combinations of marker and water-based paint. One painting, by a 10-year-old, is of a family festival with children dancing while parents look on. The second work, at the bottom, shows 14 children around a building. The animals fill the building—We know this because we have a characteristic child art x-ray view of its contents. The eye-shaped clouds, however, each have spiral-formed interiors—typical Chinese cloud designs. The middle work on page 15 is by a 9-year-old. It shows an aspiring young master of ceremonies holding a microphone as he entertains animals—the most prominent of which is a King Kong-like guerilla looking over

FIG. 14.7A & B.   Children's art from a Chinese catalog. Zhang, H. (1997). *Shen Zhen shi shao er hua zuo pin xuan ji* (Shen Zhen city children's drawing and painting portfolio) pp. 14–15. Shen Zhen Municipal Art Education Committee.

the boy's right shoulder. The boy and the animals are done in the "cute" style of comics and cartoons. These six works reveal the school art educational world of Chinese children and their teachers. It is a world where myriad bits of visual culture swirl around the globe and around China before they settle in fascinating ways in children's school art. For every image produced in school, we need to ask: What are the sources of the images that have settled within the students' works? What did the teacher ask the students to do, and why? What conditions did the teacher impose? How many degrees of freedom were the children allowed? What do the images mean to the teacher, to the children who produced them, and to the children's parents? Do these images matter, and if so, then why?

FIG. 14.7. *Continued*

Colleagues in the Netherlands, Sweden, Germany, and Finland are way ahead of art educators in the United States in analyzing and charting the influences that underlie the visual cultural artifacts children produce under the direction of teachers. Pirkko Pohjakallio (1998) has asked: "What can we learn from children's pictures?" She has collected Finish school art products and uses them to answer questions about the role of art education in shaping things such as national identity and gender roles. *Kind und Kunst: Zur Geschichte des Zeichen— und Kunstunterrichts* (1977) (Child and Art: On the History of Drawing and Art Education) produced by the Society of German Art Educators provides a marvelous critical overview of German art education and its practices. The visual images by themselves reveal the social, cultural, political, and ideological forces that have shaped German art education since the 1870s. Like their German colleagues, Dutch scholars Ben Koevoets and Herbert van Rheeden wrote *Geen dag sonder lijn: Honderd jaar tekenonderwijs in Nederland 1880–1980* (1980). Their

100-year history reveals international currents that have washed over Dutch art education. It is fascinating to note the political concerns that underlie the German view of art education that are largely absent from the Dutch history. These two books tell us about art in two European countries' education, and they tell us something about the interests and ideologies of their authors. The visual cultural histories of art education in the United States await their writers.

CHILDREN, ART, AND VISUAL CULTURE IN THE 21st CENTURY

From our contemporary perspective, it is possible to look on the era which saw the "discovery of child art" and see it differently. Child art and beliefs about innocence and creativity are the products of modernism's grand narrative (Lyotard, 1984). At the beginning of the 21st century, we art educators have the task of creating our own narratives, and it is not and will not be a single postmodern narrative. Rather, I think that we will critically construct and reconstruct many small narratives that account for children's and for the art educators' use of visual culture—and perhaps these narratives will include the creation of minor aspects of postmodern visual culture. We art educators must base our narratives on new sets of beliefs about children, art, visual culture, and education in art and visual culture. We must begin to contemplate how our practices will continue to change as we relinquish many of our cherished modernist beliefs about child art, creative expression, and about the desirability rather than about the undesirability of cultural influences.

We must ask ourselves the following: questions: (a) How would art education change if we no longer believed that every child is an artist? (b) Would we teach differently if we believed that artistic conventions must necessarily be acquired before creativity is possible? (c) Would we treat our students differently if we understood that there are no developmental stages and no natural unfolding in art—if we assumed that artistic development depends on various forms of cultural influence and instruction, that artistic development is the acquisition of a variety of different cultural schemata and forms? (d) How would art education change if we were to assume that child art is a product of adult art educators? Would we art educators still wish to continue creating child art if we were to realize that it is our creation more than the children's creations? (e) What would art education be like if we assumed that there were many forms of visual culture produced by children and youth—and that these visual cultural forms have many different functions and purposes for the child, for education, and for society? (f) What challenges would art education face if we were to assume that the benefits children derive from art-making activities flowed from the popular as well as from the high arts? These are only a few of the challenges we face as we construct art and visual cultural curricula and instructional practices for the new century.

A New Paradigm: The Visual Culture of Children and Youth

In his *Structure of Scientific Revolutions* (1970), Thomas Kuhn characterized "normal science" as periods of time when a theory or a set of theories dominate. These theories provide the hypotheses that are tested. The assumptions underlying the theories are so strong and so pervasive that when empirical data emerge that would disprove the theories, the evidence is overlooked for surprisingly long periods of time. It is only when the evidence becomes so pervasive and so obvious that it cannot be ignored that new theories are constructed to account for the evidence. Modern art educators, like scientists, overlooked most of the evidence that they themselves created "natural" child art. Observations such as those made by Thomas Munro: that Cizek controlled the "art" created by his students and that children in his classes were merely copying one another, were ignored for most of the 20th century, because we wanted to believe that children were naturally creative artists. In art education, we have come to a time where we must construct a new paradigm that replaces our assumptions about child art and creative expression. I wish to offer a series of propositions that might be useful in constructing the next theories—not a grand narrative, but lots of little stories—pertaining to the visual cultural education of children and youth.

Child Art Is a Construct: The Visual Culture of Children and Youth Is Also a Construct

There is nothing natural about the artlike activities of children. Art is one aspect of the vast global visual phenomenon constructed within various human cultures. It is important to note that art teachers, pedagogues, theoreticians, psychologists, art historian; oh, and children have collaboratively constructed child art—which has become a minor aspect of visual culture. Readers will detect that here I am echoing, Barthes's (1977) claim that it is folly to believe that a text—an artwork or a visual cultural artifact—is authored by a single individual. Barthes's "death of the author" applies to the visual culture produced by young people every bit as much (perhaps more) as it pertains to the images produced by adults. Every artifact of visual culture is in actuality a tapestry of interwoven texts.

Every visual artifact produced by a young person is a product pervaded by culture. The very possibility that children might engage in artlike behavior is a cultural construct, and children's early mark-making, modeling, and constructing activities are frequently initiated by adults and then viewed by and classified by them through cultural lenses. Every example of child art—and even the paradigm collections of the art of the child become candidates for reinterpretation as visual culture shaped primarily by adults. As such, when interpreted as cultural products, these collections of child art will probably reveal more about, say, adult pedagogical intentions than about children and their motives and desires (Wilson, 1997a, 1997b, 1997c).

The Term Child Art Is Ideological

Every visual artifact produced by a young person may and should be considered from ideological perspectives. That is to say from political perspectives, colonial and postcolonial perspectives, from philosophical perspectives, from modern and postmodern perspectives. The most revealing, and perhaps the most important ideologies surrounding the visual products of young people are also those that are most hidden. It is much easier for me to recognize the ideologies that motivate others than it is to recognize my own. I assume that this is frequently the case for others as well. One of the most important tasks for those of us who teach art and who inquire into the visual cultural products of young people is to uncover hidden ideological positions held by ourselves and other pedagogues who have initiated students' art-making activities and to recognize our own biases.

This point is so important that I think an illustration is in order. Adults have used child art for blatant propaganda purposes—and they have gotten away with it because children are assumed to be innocent and unbiased observers or victims of the events that surround them. Japanese children's drawings were sent to the United States just prior to World War II to extol Japan's peaceful intentions. Collections of children's drawings from Spain showing the bombing of towns were circulated in Britain and in the United States during the Spanish Civil War to promote the Spanish Republican cause. German art textbooks contain children's images that denigrate the Allied forces. In my "Innocent Graphic Accounts or Adult Propaganda: A Critical History of Children's War Art" (Wilson, 1997c), I provide an overview of a variety of additional cases where adults either wittingly or unwittingly use children's art to promote adult causes.

Every exhibition of children and youth art must be viewed as an ideological statement—if nothing more than to promote the cause of art education in the schools. Frequently, however, the intentions are less benign. The "Kids Guernica" project initiated in the 1900s, motivated by adults' desires for world peace, as worthy as its goal may be, is just another example of how adults shape the images of children to promote adult purposes.

The Emergence of Visual Culture: Multiple Forms of Child and Youth Culture

The discipline of visual culture reflects a growing tendency to reject conventional classifications of art and replace them with critical studies of image making within and among different groups and strata of human cultures. Young peoples' self-initiated images and performances either relate to or reflect advertisements, television, photography, and video and cinema in their various guises, various forms of digital imagery, the internet, comic strips, material culture, crafts, folk images, world art, the images of amateur and professional artists, new and emerging art forms such as performance and installation, and intermedia forms of art. Moreover each of these aspects of visual culture has the potential to become the content of art programs for children and youth. The various established and emerging forms of visual culture and the ways in which children and educators use them should also become the content of research in art education. In our postmodern time, distinctions among high art, low art, popular art, and mass culture have disintegrated, and the political and ideological are as important in the visual culture of young people as aesthetic and expressive qualities once were in child art.

Visual culture presents challenges to the way in which we art educators have traditionally thought about our field. It also presents opportunities to reconceive and broaden our thinking about the images that children and youth make and use.

Child art has become a problematic term—Perhaps it was from the beginning. I have concluded, ironically, that the term should probably be reserved for those images children produce under the direct control of adults who engage in the kinds of preliminary motivating activities employed by Cizek, Lowenfeld, and other proponents of "creative expression." (Cizek's lesson presented earlier in this chapter is a paradigm example.)

Kindler and Darras have theorized about the vast terrain of children's imagery development and to its "pluri-media" character (1997). As we begin to broaden our study of the image-making capacities of young people, the discipline of visual culture reminds us that the "map" will show how children and youth emerge as photographers, makers of films and video art, the producers of a multitude of forms of digital imagery, how they become quasi-performance artists, installation artists, comic book artists (Wilson, 2000b).

To state the obvious conclusion from my observations, stage-based developmental accounts based on a natural unfolding fail to stand up to scrutiny. Feldman (1980) has offered a brilliant theoretical and empirical critique of developmental stage theory in which he demonstrates that even with Piaget's cognitively grounded levels of map drawing—levels that are far more rigorously constructed, say than Lowenfeld's or any other stage formulation in art education—children perform in several levels simultaneously. In short, the levels do not exist; nor do stages of artistic development. Moreover, young peoples' development in the realm of visual culture is nonlinear, nonhierarchical, multidimensional, and multipurposeful (Kindler & Darras, 1997). Young people produce visual artifacts with pencils, markers, pens, brushes, and with cameras, computers, found objects, and their bodies; and in the future, they will produce visual culture in ways that we cannot now imagine. The mastery of skills and concepts relating to new media, new art forms, digital imaging, and other emerging forms of visual culture have hardly been addressed in art education. This brings me to my next point.

*The Visual Cultural Artifacts of Children and Youth Must Always Be
Viewed in Relationship to Adult Visual Culture*

Any visual artifact produced by a young person has cultural antecedents. These forms that exist prior to their emulation by young people provide the models and the technologies. These visual cultural forms are also surrounded by theories that define their characteristics, functions, and values. As new forms of visual cultural texts emerge and attract theory and criticism—and this is especially the case with the visual arts which, continually redefine themselves through subversion and rejection of previous forms, conceptions, and styles—we must be prepared to redefine our conceptions of child and youth visual culture—including our conceptions of the kinds of artlike things that young people make, might make, and might be encouraged to make in and around schools.

As art and visual cultural theorists explore issues such as gender, colonialism, and postcolonialism, politics, the environment, various form of globalism, class, race, economics, technology, the body, and cyborgs, we art educators should probably assume that each new area of exploration provides an opportunity to understand young peoples' visual culture in new ways.

Multiple Interpretations Based on Interests and Conflicts of Interest

In our postmodern era we no longer assume that there is a single privileged "true" interpretation of an artwork, visual cultural artifact, or other text. We have entered a time when multiple interpretations are not just desirable, they are necessary. The interests and conflicts of interest, differing experiences and viewpoints, values, and assumptions of interpreters add meaning to visual cultural texts. When it comes to the visual culture and artlike products of children and youth, we have hardly begun to consider the implications of images interpreted from different perspectives—from the vantage point of the child, the teacher, the empirical researcher, the semiotician, the postmodern philosopher (Wilson, 1997a, 1997b, 2000b).

At present, we have a growing number of theoretical constructs that may be applied to the visual cultural products of young people. Duncum's article (2001) is especially useful. Even what has been called child art is a collection of narratives, and these narratives are continually being written by a variety of groups—psychologists, art historians, teachers, researchers, advocates, anthropologists, artists, and politicians. Preschool children, elementary school age children, teenagers, I should note, have seldom been invited to create their own narratives about the visual culture they create. Nevertheless, each group creating these narratives have varying and often conflicting interests. And as I have already noted, the authors of these narratives are often unknown to one another. Psychologists and pedagogues often do not read the research conducted by individuals in other fields, and the interpretations and narratives of young people are seldom documented.

School Art Education Must Be Viewed in Terms of Power and Control

Since the late 19th century when art pedagogues began to promote and produce the "natural" art of children, they were dismayed by children's attraction to images from the popular visual culture and took various steps to discourage their production. To the child art pedagogues, these images were evidence of an insidious infiltrating of undesirable cultural images that would corrupt and impede the naturally flowering childhood creativity. As the pedagogues went about their task of thwarting popular visual culture, as I have already argued, they engaged in practices that quite utterly shaped children's within-school visual output in order to conform to expectations of what child art should look like in subject matter, theme, style, and expression. This exercise of power in the control of children's images was, of course, conducted with the best of intentions and genuine concern for the well-being of children.

We art pedagogues have no choice; although thoughts of power and control over the images of children may make us feel uncomfortable, still we will shape the visual products of our students. The questions that we must continually ask ourselves are: How am I controlling my students? What are the consequences of encouraging some forms of children's and youths' visual culture and discouraging other forms? I think that we must engage in the continual interpretation of the products of art schooling. The visual products of young people should be interpreted in light of who benefits and even who gains advantage over whom and for what purposes. There are motives for making, for controlling making, and for interpreting the visual cultural products made by young people. Each motive serves different interests. Art teachers' interests are different from young peoples' interests. Young peoples' interests are different from researchers' interests. Arts education advocates' interests may differ from both young peoples' and art teachers' interests.

Is it possible to develop pedagogical practices that no longer pit school art against out-of-school visual cultural products; that no longer pit the interests of children against those of their teachers; that no longer pit high art against popular visual culture; that pit political, ideological, and narrative art against art that glorifies sumptuous aesthetic qualities, expressiveness, design, and pleasing form? Perhaps the resolution of these dialectics is impossible. Nevertheless, surely the sensitive examination of the ideologies underlying the opposing interests would benefit art education.

School Art and Children's Out-of-School Visual Culture: A Continuing Dialectic

School art and children's art are marginal classifications within the larger world of art and the enormous realm of visual culture. Child art is shaped by conventional classifications of art. If we say that children make art, and for me this is still an open question, it is because the category "art" exists within a culture. The forms of art such as painting, sculpture, printmaking, crafts—and, for child art, the more problematic classifications such as photography, digital art forms, video, installation, and performance affect the way children's visual cultural productions are classified and interpreted. As forms of visual culture evolve to include things such as MTV and video games, children and young people will make visual cultural forms based on them. Because children create visual culture that is nothing like school art, will we art educators take note and incorporate these forms into schooling?

The media with which children are permitted to work in schools comprise cultural influences that shape child art. The differences between children's school art and their out-of-school visual cultural artifacts can often be detected by media alone. School art is produced on standard sheets of paper and made with soft media such as colorful tempera and acrylic paint, whereas out-of-school visual culture is enormously varied—from fine-tipped gel pens on lined paper to huge constructions of cardboard boxes, board, and other found objects. Regardless of how open school art practices might become, it is likely that the rhizomatic (Wilson, 2002) character of the visual culture children produce outside the school will always be more varied and unpredictable than school art.

The themes, topics, and subject matter around which children are encouraged to create school art reflect educators' cultural beliefs about the innocence of children. School art is concerned primarily with topics from everyday life, holidays, festivals, and illustrations of fairy and folktales. Children's out-of-school visual cultural artifacts, again, have an enormous range which includes diagrams, narratives, exercises that reveal struggles to master cultural conventions—often borrowed from popular culture, themes of war, love, hate, sexual relationships, death, struggle, and other topics from which many teachers believe children should be protected. Do art educators have something to learn from children and young people?

The within-school/outside-school dialectic has many more dimensions than I can point to at this time. Nevertheless, I should note that while teaching in Taiwan, I observed that elementary school art teachers and classroom teachers give students art homework assignments. The products of these assignments have characteristics of both in-school and out-of-school visual culture. In them, children have more degrees of freedom to experiment with the themes, subjects, and styles of popular visual culture. In some ways they bring to resolution a dialectic that I had assumed would never be resolved.

The Philosophy of Child and Youth Visual Cultural Education

Much of what I have written in this chapter would have been strengthened if it had been written from a cohesive philosophy of art or a comprehensive theory of visual culture. I have claimed (Wilson, 2000b) that a philosophy of art is the singlemost underdeveloped area pertaining to the visual artifacts produced by children and youth. If an art object becomes a work of art by virtue of the interpretations that it attracts, as Danto claims (1986, p. 4), then we art educators have lots of interpreting to do before we transform the things children make (and that we compel them to make) into artworks. The interpretative task becomes all the more complicated when visual appearance and aesthetic qualities no longer count and when art is anything that is interpreted as art (Danto, 1997, p. 13). About the possibility of a philosophy of child art I have written:

> I end my plea for a philosophy of art pertaining to young people with this thought: If art has entered its post-historical phase where artworks can be anything and where they can have any conceivable look, and since teachers exert considerable control—and in many instances nearly complete control—over the images created by children in their classroom, then in this time after the end of art, should teachers consciously assign children to create all sorts of art? Should art teachers use children's acquiescence and malleability to get them, for example, to create artworks that question the assumed nature of child art, to produce child-artworks that look like adult-artworks, to make artworks in which there is a conscious effort to mix child-like and artist-like images, to make artworks that mimic and mix styles, to make artworks that are consciously anti-visual or anti-aesthetic, to make works for the purpose of attempting to transform them into artworks through multiple acts of interpretation?
>
> If teachers were deliberately to persuade young people to work ironically—for that is what I have just suggested, then would the purpose of children's image-making be in effect to raise philosophical questions about the nature of child art? Does this kind of activity have a desirable educational payoff? (Wilson, 2000b, p. 244)

CONCLUSION

The Japanese artist Takashi Murakami (2000) has written the Super Flat Manifesto in which he claims:

> The world of the future might be like Japan today—super flat.
>
> Society, customs, art, culture: all extremely two-dimensional. It is particularly apparent in the arts that this sensibility has been flowing steadily beneath the surface of Japanese history. Today, the sensibility is most present in Japanese games and anime, which have become powerful parts of world culture. One way to imagine super flatness is to think of the moment when, in creating a desktop graphic for your computer, you merge a number of distinct layers into one. (p. 5)

Murakami writes that although this "is not a terribly clear example," the feeling he gets from this flattening is "a sense of reality that is very nearly a physical sensation." He continues, "the reason I have lined up both the high and low of Japanese art...is to convey this feeling. I would like you, the reader, to experience the moment when the layers of Japanese culture, such as pop, erotic pop, otaku, and H.I.S.-ism, fuse into one"(Murakami, 2000, p. 20)

I wonder if, perhaps, there is a theory of art and visual cultural education embedded within Murakami's manifesto. I must confess, however, that I am as intrigued with the layers that are flattened as with the flattening—which I am not sure I understand. If art education were to celebrate visual culture, what might an instructional unit look like. Surely it would consist of layers—lots of layers. I believe that artworks and visual cultural artifacts that are designated for inclusion in art curricula should be drawn simultaneously from global/universal sources, from East and West, from national sources, and from local sources. They call out for interconnecting and contesting. This is the basis for the new visual cultural *narratives* that underlie art education. I have tried to approach the topic from multiethnic and multiarts positions. I have rejected the notion that there is a common language for dealing with young peoples' visual cultural products. Pedagogues and researchers must subject their own practices and inquiry to ongoing critique. I have claimed that opposing views are useful, that local knowledge should compete with the notion of a world system, and that in the 21st century the study of children's images will most likely consist of many intersecting intertextual stories rather than one master modernist narrative.

REFERENCES

Alland, Jr., A. (1983). *Playing with form: Children draw in six cultures*. New York: Columbia University Press.

Amornpichetkul, C. (1984). Seventeenth-century Italian drawing books: Their origin and development. In Jeffery M. Muller (Ed.), *The Children of Mercury: The education of artists in the sixteenth and seventeenth centuries* (pp. 108–118). Providence, RI: Department of art, Brown University.

Aronsson, K., & Junge, B. (2000). Intellectual realism and social scaling in Ethiopian children's drawings. In L. Lindström (Ed.), *The cultural context: Comparative studies of art education and children's drawings* (pp. 135–159). Stockholm: Stockholm Institute of Education Press.

Arnheim, R. (1978). Expressions. *Art Education, 31*(3), 37–38.

Arnheim, R. (1997). A look at a century of growth. In A. M. Kindler (Ed.), *Child development in art* (pp. 9–16), Reston, VA: The National Art Education Association.

Ayer, F. C. (1916). *The psychology of drawing with special reference to laboratory teaching*. In E. H. Gombrich (Ed.). (1965). *Art and illusion*. New York: Bollingen Foundation.

Barnes, E. (1893). A study of children's drawings. *Pedagogical Seminary, 2,* 451–463.

Barthes, R. (1977). The death of the author. *Image, Music, Text* (S. Heath Ed. & Trans.). New York: Hill.

Barzun, J. Quoted in A. K. Wiedmann. (1979). *Romantic roots in modern art*. Surrey, England: Gresham Books.

Belting, H. (1987). *The end of the history of art?* Chicago and London: University of Chicago Press.

Bleeke-Byrne, G. (1984). The education of the painter in the workshop. In Jeffery M. Muller (Ed.), *The Children of Mercury: The education of artists in the sixteenth and seventeenth centuries* (pp. 28–39). Providence, RI: Department of art, Brown University.

Boas, G. (1990). *The cult of childhood*. Dallas: Spring Publications, Inc.

Bresler, L., & Thompson C. M. (2002). *The arts in children's lives: Context, culture, and curriculum*. Dordrecht, The Netherlands: Kluwer Academic Publishers.

Bowness, A. (1972). *Courbet's 'Atelier du Peintre* (50th Charlton Lecture on Art). Newcastle upon Tyne: University of Newcastle upon Tyne.

Burkhart, R. C. (1962). *Spontaneous and deliberate ways of learning*. Scranton, PA: International Textbook Company.

Cole, N. R. (1966). *Children's arts from deep down inside*. New York: The John Day Company.

Court, E. (1992). Researching social influences in the drawings of rural Kenyan children. In D. T. Thistlewood (1992). *Drawing research and development* (pp. 51–67). Harlow, Essex: Longman.

Cox, M. V. (2000). Children's drawings of the human figure in different cultures. In L. Lindström (Ed.), *The cultural context: Comparative studies of art education and children's drawings* (pp. 119–134). Stockholm: Stockholm Institute of Education Press.

Danto, A. C. (1986). *The philosophical disenfranchisement of art*. New York: Columbia University Press.

Duncum, P. (1997). Subjects and themes in children's unsolicited drawings and gender socialization. In A. M. Kindler (Ed.), *Child development in art* (pp. 107–116). Reston, VA: The National Art Education Association.

Duncum. P. (2001). Theoretical foundations of an art education of global culture and principle for classroom practice. *International Journal of Education and the Arts 2*(3).

Efland, A. (1976). The school art style: A functional analysis. *Studies in Art Education 7*(2), 37–44.

Elatta, T. (1992). Sudanese graphic imagery: A survey for art education. In D. T. Thistlewood (Eds.), *Drawing research and development* (pp. 68–74). Harlow, Essex: Longman.

Feldmen, D. B. (1980). *Beyond universals in cognitive development.* Norwood, NJ: Ablex.

Fineberg, J. (1997). *The innocent eye: Children's art and the modern artists.* Princeton: Princeton University Press.

Gardner, H. (1980). *Artful scribbles: The significance of children's drawings.* New York: Basic Books.

Gombrich, E. H. (1965). *Art and illusion.* New York: Bollingen Foundation.

Gombrich, E. H. (1998). Viollet-le-Duc's *Historie d'un dessinateur.* In J. Fineberg (Ed.), *Discovering child art* (pp. 27–39). Princeton: Princeton University Press.

Goodenough, F. L. (1926). *Measurement of intelligence by drawings.* New York and Burlingame: Harcourt, Brace & World, Inc.

Harris, D. B. (1963). Children's drawings as measures of intellectual maturity: A revision of the Goodenough Draw-a-Man Test. New York: Harcourt, Brace & World, Inc.

Ho, C. W. (1989). *Yani: The brush of innocence.* New York: Hudson Hill Press.

Hofmann, W. (1977). The painter's studio: Its place in nineteenth-century art. In Petra ten-Doesschate Chu (Ed.), *Courbet in Perspective* (pp. 110–120). Englewood Cliffs, NJ: Prentice-Hall.

Kind und Kunst: Zur Geschichte des Zeichen—und Kunstunterrichts. (Child and Art: On the History of Drawing and Art Education). (1977). Berlin: Society of German Art Educators.

Kerschensteiner, D. G. (1905). *Die entwickelung der zeichnerischen begabung.* (The development of drawing talent). Munich: Gerber.

Kindler, A. M. (Ed.) (1977). Child development in art. Reston, VA: National Art Education Association.

Kindler, A., & Darras, B. (1997). Map of artistic development. In A. M. Kindler (Ed.), *Child development in art* (pp. 17–44). Reston, VA: The National Art Education Association.

Koevoets, B., & van Rheeden, H. (1980). *Geen dag zonder lijn: Honderd jarr tekenonderwijs in Nederland 1880–1980.* Haarlem: Fibula-Van Dishoeck.

Kuhn, T. S. (1970). *The structure of scientific revolutions.* Chicago: The University of Chicago Press.

Levinstein, S. (1905). *Kinderzeichnunger bis zum 14 Lebensjahre. Mit Parallelen aus der Urgeschichte, Kulturgeschichte, und Völkerkunde.* Leipzig: Voigtländer.

Lindström, L. (Ed.). (2000a). *The cultural context: Comparative studies of art education and children's drawings.* Stockholm: Stockholm Institute of Education Press.

Lindström, L. (2000b). Family vs. peers: Themes in Mongolian and Cuban children's visual narratives. In L. Lindström (Ed.), *The cultural context: Comparative studies of art education and children's drawings* (pp. 179–206). Stockholm: Stockholm Institute of Education Press.

Lowenfeld, V. (1939). *The nature of creative activity.* New York: Harcourt, Brace & World.

Lowenfeld, V. (1947). *Creative and mental growth: A textbook on art education.* New York: The Macmillan Company.

Lowenfeld, V. (1957). *Creative and mental growth* (3rd ed.). New York: Macmillian.

Luquet, G. H. (1913). *Les dessins d'un enfant.* Paris: F. Alcan.

Luquet, G. H. (1927). *Le dessin enfantin.* Paris: Alcan (5th ed. published in 1991 by Delachaux and Niestle [Lausanne and Paris]; and the English edition, A. Costal [Tr.] (2001). *Children's drawings.* London/New York: Free Association Books)

Lyotard, J. F. (1984). *The postmodern condition: A report on knowledge.* G. Bennington, et al. (Trans.). Minneapolis: University of Minnesota Press.

Matthews, J. (1992). The genesis of aesthetic sensibility. In D. T. Thistlewood (Ed.), *Drawing research and development* (pp. 26–39). Harlow, Essex: Longman.

Miesel, V. H. (1970). *Voices of German Expressionism.* Englewood Cliffs, NJ: Prentice-Hall.

Miller, J. (1983). *States of mind.* New York: Pantheon Books.

Maitland, L. (1894). The art of little children. A translation of portions of C. Ricci's *L'Arte Die Bambini.* In *Pedagogical Seminary,* 1894, *3,* 302–307.

Muller, J. T. (1984). *The Children of Mercury: The education of artists in the sixteenth and seventeenth centuries.* Providence, RI: Department of Art, Brown University.

Munro, T. (1956). *Art education: Its philosophy and psychology: Selected essays.* Indianapolis: Bobbs-Merrill Company, Inc.

Murakami, T. (2000). *Superflat.* Tokyo: MADRA.

Partridge, L. (1902). Children's drawings of men and women. *Studies in Education, 3*(7), 163–179.

Pohjakallio, P. (1998). Reflections on the art education history. In L. Lindström, (Ed.). *Nordic visual arts research: A theoretical and methodological review* (pp. 63–67). Stockholm: Stockholm Institute of Education Press.

Ricci, C. (1887). *L'Arte Dei Bambini.* Bologna: Nicola Zanichelli. In L. Maitland (Trans.), in *Pedagogical Seminary,* 1894, *3,* 302–307.

Rubin, L. (1984). First draft artistry: Children's drawings in the sixteenth and seventeenth centuries. In Jeffery M. Muller (Ed.), *The Children of Mercury: The education of artists in the sixteenth and seventeenth centuries* (pp. 20–27). Providence, RI: Department of art, Brown University.

Schapiro, M. (1979). Courbet and popular imagery: An essay on realism and naivete. In *Modern art: 19th and 20th centuries* (pp. 47–85). New York: George Braziller.

Smith, N. R. (1992). Development of the aestheic in children's drawings. In D. T. Thistlewood (1992). *Drawing research and development* (pp. 130–140). Harlow, Essex: Longman.

Sully, J. (1896). *Studies of childhood*. London: Longmans, Green, and Co.

Thistlewood, D. T. (1992). *Drawing research and development*. Harlow, Essex: Longman.

Vasari, G. (1894). In Mrs. Jonathan Foster (Trans.), *Vasari's lives of the most eminent painters, sculptors, and architects*. London: George Bell and Sons.

Viola, W. (1936). *Child art and Franz Cizek*. Vienna: Austrian Junior Red Cross.

Viola, W. (1942). *Child art*. London: University of London Press.

Wachowiak, F. (1985). *Emphasis art* (4th ed.). New York: Harper & Row.

Wiedmann, A. (1979). *Romantic roots in modern art*. Surrey, England: Gresham Books.

Walsh, J. (1996). *Jan Steen: The drawing lesson*. Los Angeles: J. Paul Getty Museum.

Wilson, B. (1974). The superheroes of J. C. Holtz plus an outline of a theory of child art. *Art Education, 16*(1), 2–9.

Wilson, B. (1976). Little Julian's impure drawings. *Studies in Art Education, 17*(2), 45–62.

Wilson, B. (1987). Histories of children's styles of art: Possibilities and prospects. In B. Wilson & H. Hoffa (Eds.), *History of art education: Proceedings of the Penn State Conference* (pp. 177–184). Reston, VA: The National Art Education Association.

Wilson, B. (1992). Primitivism, the avant garde, and the art of little children. In D. Thistlewood (Ed.), *Drawing: Research and development* (pp. 14–25), Harlow, Essex, England: Longman.

Wilson, B. (1997a). Child art, multiple interpretations, and conflicts of interest. In A. M. Kindler (Ed.), *Child development in art* (pp. 81–94), Reston, VA: The National Art Education Association.

Wilson, B. (1997b). Types of child art and alternative developmental accounts: Interpreting the interpreters. *Human development, 40*, 155–168.

Wilson, B. (1997c). Innocent graphic accounts or adult propaganda? A critical history of children's war art. In A. Anderson & P. Bolin (Eds.), *History of art education: Proceedings of the Third Penn State International Symposium* (pp. 311–319). University Park, PA: The Art Education Program.

Wilson, B. (2000a). Empire of signs revisited: Children's *manga* and the changing face of Japan. In L. Lindström (Ed.), *The cultural context: Comparative studies of art education and children's drawings* (pp. 160–178). Stockholm: Stockholm Institute of Education Press.

Wilson, B. (2000b). Epilogue: The Vilnius Conference and the future of child art: A philosophical agenda. In L. Lindström (Ed.), *The cultural context: Comparative studies of art education and children's drawings* (pp. 237–246). Stockholm: Stockholm Institute of Education Press.

Wilson, B. (2002). Becoming Japanese: *Manga*, children's drawings, and the construction of national character. In L. Bresler & C. M. Thompson (Eds.), *The arts in children's lives: Context, culture, and curriculum* (pp. 43–55). Dordrecht, The Netherlands: Kluwer Academic Publishers.

Wilson, B., Hurwitz, A., & Wilson, M. (1987). *Teaching drawing from art*. Worcester, MA: Davis.

Wilson, B., & Ligtvoet, J. (1992). Across time and cultures: Stylistic changes in the drawings of Dutch children. In D. T. Thistlewood (1992). *Drawing research and development* (pp. 75–88). Harlow, Essex: Longman.

Wilson, B., & Wilson, M. (1977). An iconoclastic view of the imagery sources in the drawings of young people. *Art Education, 30*(1), 4–12.

Wilson, B., & Wilson, M. (1984). Children's drawings in Egypt: Cultural style acquisition as graphic development. *Visual Arts Research, 10*(1), 13–26.

Wilson, B., & Wilson, M. (1987). Pictorial composition and narrative structure: Themes and the creation of meaning in the drawings of Egyptian and Japanese children. *Visual Arts Research, 13*(2), 10–21.

Wilson, M., & Wilson, B. (1982). The case of the disappearing two-eyed profile: Or how little children influence the drawings of little children. *Review of Research in Visual Arts Education*, (Issue 15), 1–18.

Yanin, V. (1985). The drawings of Onfin. *School Arts, 84*(7), 6–8.

Zhang, H. (1997). *Shen Zhen shi shao er hua zuo pin xuan ji* (Shen Zhen city children's drawing and painting portfolio) (pp. 14–15). Shen Zhen: Shen Zhen Municipal Art Education Committee.

15

Sculpture: Representational Development in a Three-Dimensional Medium

Claire Golomb
University of Massachusetts at Boston

INTRODUCTION

Representational development in the visual arts is a uniquely human endeavor that emerges relatively early and quite spontaneously in ontogenetic development. It is a symbolic activity that sets humans apart from their closest non-human relatives, the great apes; and to date, there is no convincing evidence that symbol (language) trained apes create representational drawings and sculptures (Boysen, Berntson, & Prentice, 1987; Miles, 1990; Miles, Mitchell, & Harper, 1996; Smith, 1973). Great apes can recognize photographs and drawings of people and objects; however, findings regarding their ability to produce representational drawings are ambiguous at best.

Reports on apes' modeling with clay have not yet been published, but some research has been undertaken with capuchin monkeys who are noted for their skillful tool use. When provided with clay, stones, sticks, paints, and leaves, the monkeys modified the array of items and with their hands and stones reshaped the clay (Westergaard & Suomi, 1997). Their actions included squeezing, tearing, and rolling the mass, striking it against the cage, and incorporating leaves into the clay mass. When provided with sticks, stones, and a slab of clay fastened to the floor, the capuchins used their hands as well as the sticks and stones as marking tools and produced at least one set of lines across the surface of each form, a nonfigurative pattern which, according to the authors, is indicative of the monkeys' nonrepresentational behavior that lacks any symbolic significance (see Figures 15.1A and 15.1B).

The prolonged exposure of some symbol trained apes to drawing and painting implements, and the generally negative findings regarding their capacity for symbolic representation in this medium, highlights the amazing achievements of young children who, without training or great effort, evolve their first basic representational shapes, name them, and expect others to recognize them.

A chapter devoted to representational development needs to define what is meant by this term, and what the boundaries of this concept are. The concept of *representation* in its broad meaning refers to thought that is based on a system of differentiated symbols and their referents,

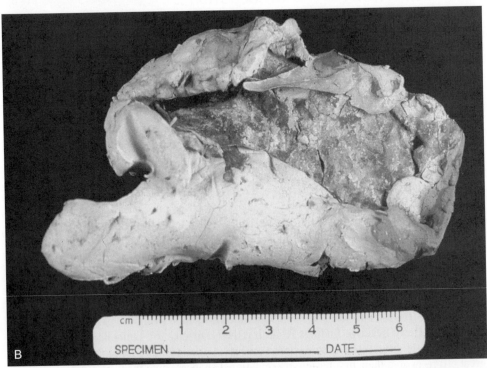

FIG. 15.1.   A & B Clay productions of Capucin monkeys. Reproduced with the permission of Gregory Charles Westergaard.

that is, signifiers and their meaning (signified) that can be evoked in thought and in the absence of the real object (Piaget, 1951). In the more restricted sense of the visual arts, representation refers to the invention of pictorial or plastic forms that can stand for the intended object without confusing the symbol with its referent (Golomb, 2002, 2003). In the development of child art we need to differentiate between mere sensorimotor actions on a medium such as pounding the clay and intentional actions designed to create a specific object that can stand for an aspect of the world. The concept of representation implies an understanding that a mental action such as a thought can lead to the intention to create specific shapes that bear some likeness to the object and thus can stand for it. Above all, representation involves a mental activity that goes beyond the perception of objects and events and transforms them with the means available in the chosen medium.

The systematic study of the development of modeling or sculpting in clay,[1] plasticene, or playdough has so far received only scant attention in marked contrast to the intensive scrutiny of drawing development that dates its beginnings to the end of the 19th century. Since this time, children's drawings have continued to engage investigators for over 100 years, and their interest in this subject has led to large collections of child art, to numerous exhibitions, often in conjunction with the work of adult artists, and to an extensive list of publications. The paucity of published studies on three-dimensional art most likely reflects the technical difficulties of working with clay which is a messy medium, difficult to handle, and requires special care transporting, preserving, and storing the fragile sculptures. In contrast, drawings are relatively easy to elicit, collect, evaluate, and preserve.

Despite those difficulties, the first decades of the 20th century saw a series of publications on the clay sculptures of children and, in some cases, of the models created by blind children (Bergemann-Könitzer, 1928, 1930; Löwenfeld, 1939; Märtin, 1932; Matz, 1912, 1915; Münz & Lowenfeld, 1934; Potpeschnigg, 1912; Wulff, 1927). These pioneering studies reflect the interest of artists, psychologists, and art educators in the role the plastic medium plays in the mental life of normal and handicapped children. Löwenfeld's interest in different modeling styles, which he derived from his early studies with the blind, led to his formulation of a contrasting typology of "haptic" and "visual" types, which he somewhat later extended to all artistic expression in drawing as well as in modeling (Löwenfeld, 1939, 1947). These early studies broadened the scope of inquiry beyond drawing development as a measure of conceptual development, but the absence of adequate experimental controls and statistical analyses limits the conclusions that can be drawn from these reports. Surprisingly, to this day, basic research in this domain has been very sparse; the published reports are few in number and their focus is primarily pedagogical, that is, to facilitate the use of the medium in creative and expressive ways and to provide art teachers with instructions on how to teach children to work with clay (Burton, 1981; Edwards, Gandini, & Forman, 1993; Grossman, 1980; Haas, 1998; Haas & Gavitch, 2000; Hagen, Lewis, & Smilansky, 1988; Ley, 1980; Löwenfeld, 1939; Sherman, Landau, & Pechter, 1977; Topal, 1986), with some authors listing the number and type of body parts that are modeled at different ages (Brown, 1975, 1984). A different focus can be found in writings that explore the therapeutic and/or diagnostic benefits of clay, drawing, puppets, and stories in the treatment of emotionally disturbed children (Case & Dalley, 1990; Kramer, 2000; Rubin, 1984). With few exceptions (Golomb, 1972, 1973, 1974, 2002; Golomb & McCormick, 1995) studies devoted to modeling have not been concerned with the three-dimensional conceptions that underlie children's work with clay, conceptions which are at the core of children's approach to sculpture.

---

[1] In the past, some authors have drawn a distinction between the methods employed by sculptors, the artists who work in stone, and modelers, artists who work with clay, wax, or plaster. This distinction has not been sustained over time, and I shall not distinguish between these terms and use both to describe children's work in clay or playdough.

Sculpture is an ancient art that dates back to prehistoric times, to 32,000 bce (before the common era), and the earliest figures document *Homo sapiens'* ability to create images in the tangible form of ivory, clay, and stone (Bahn & Vertut, 1997; Leroi-Gourhan, 1982; Sanders, 1985). Although we do not know with any degree of certainty what role these early sculptures may have played in the life of our distant ancestors, the care with which they were sculpted and the diverse locations in which they were found indicate that they fulfilled a significant function in the communal life of Cro Magnon man, a hunter's society establishing itself in Europe during the Ice Age of the Upper Paleolithic period. The first known sculptures of humans and animals are statuettes modeled in the round in ivory and stone, indicating a fully formed three-dimensional representational conception of the figure, with a carbon dating of 32,000 bce. Even during the Upper Paleolithic, the early period of modern man in Europe, anthropologists and archeologists have documented diverse stylistic models in the representation of the human figure (Delporte, 1993). Diversity of models is also the case in the sculptures from the Neolithic period in the Balkans (4500–3000 bce), witness the coexistence of diverse styles which ranged from expressive and naturalistic portraits to highly stylized versions (Sanders, 1985). Throughout this period and throughout the Balkans, Sanders notes the continued significance of clay modeling and firing of pots and figures in kilns, a technically accomplished art form which extended over 1,500 years. Although Sanders records stylistic changes over time in the direction of greater simplification of the human figure, she does not support the notion of a general developmental progression either from abstract forms to naturalistic ones or, in a reverse direction, from realism to abstract representation. Reviewing different historical periods, Sanders points to discontinuities in artistic forms that indicate changing sociocultural conceptions and lifestyle. Throughout art history she identifies a recurrent tension between an inclination toward naturalism and one toward schematization or simplification.

Given this brief historical perspective on the earliest known forms of art making in a three-dimensional medium, and the finding that sculpture played a significant role in the cultural life of Cro Magnon man in Europe, we want to know how such an interest in modeling might find expression in childhood. Do we find evidence for a rule-governed developmental course; and, if so, are its defining characteristics best conceived in analogy to drawing development, or are they subject to the unique constraints and possibilities of the three-dimensional medium? In drawing, the artist is faced with a flat, two-dimensional surface, and the representation of depth requires special techniques to create the illusion of the third dimension. This condition does not apply to clay, plaster, or plasticene, and questions regarding the evolution of representational concepts in these media are of considerable interest for an understanding of artistic development and related competencies.

To the extent that drawing development has served as a model for the analysis of representation in a three-dimensional medium, its progression is said to begin with an undifferentiated global circle, then to proceed from one-dimensional lines to two-dimensional geometric shapes or regions, and to culminate with three-dimensional lines that represent the sides of objects receding into depth, strategies that yield a more differentiated portrayal of an object or scene. In the absence of developmental data, on the basis of his analysis of prehistoric sculpture and in a partial analogy to drawing development, Arnheim (1974) hypothesized that the development of sculpture might begin with an undifferentiated blob or sphere of clay. From this simple beginning, development will proceed to the use of one-dimensional sticks and slabs arranged within one plane and culminate in patterns that represent the cubic object in the third dimension, thus enabling the sculptor to model figures in the round. If one were to transpose this view of the historical antecedents of sculpture to the developmental domain, one might conceive of the sticks and/or snakelike shapes children roll with playdough or clay as equivalents for one-dimensional lines, the pounding or flattening of the clay which yields a thin flat layer as an equivalent for a two-dimensional region on a page, whereas modeling all sides of the cubic object would indicate a three-dimensional approach to sculpture.

Underlying this analysis of historical and ontogenetic development is the assumption that similar principles of differentiation apply to both media, a position that seemed to find some support in the limited data on children's modeling with clay, especially, in the finding of the frontally modeled and horizontally placed human figures (Brown, 1975, 1984). This view appeared to be quite compatible with the widely accepted notion that children's persistent use of two-dimensional strategies in drawing and their considerable difficulty with representing a scene in perspective was a mark of their conceptual immaturity to be overcome with the acquisition of concrete operational and formal operational reasoning (Case, 1992; Dennis, 1992; Piaget & Inhelder, 1956; Milbrath, 1998; Porath, 1997).

However, the concept of differentiation in artistic development may find different forms of expression in different media, and a literal and premature application of what we may have learned from drawing development, a medium that lacks the third dimension, may be misleading. Perhaps, children have a basic understanding of the three-dimensional nature of the clay medium and what it can afford them and develop, early on, simple but three-dimensional representational concepts of the modeling task. The reasons children model the canonical frontal view of a human and place this figure in a horizontal orientation need to be explored, and it is premature to interpret such findings in terms of children's limited three-dimensional concepts. Of course, it would be futile to expect children's sculpture to meet the stringent requirement of modeling in the round, to conceive of the emerging figure from all its sides, which is a highly sophisticated approach developed in Greece in their large-scale sculptures around 400 bce . Modeling in the round requires the sculptor to consider all potential views as he or she works on a particular aspect or side. We might, however, consider more elementary aspects of three-dimensional representation, for example, the upright standing posture of a figure, and the child's intention to model more than a single frontal side. Such a conception of three-dimensional representation in sculpture provides a new perspective on its development in children.

I now turn to a review of two studies that were designed to explore children's representational concepts in the three-dimensional medium of playdough and clay, and to findings that provide some insight into the role of significant variables that affect the modeling of diverse objects. These studies were conducted at two different times, and both address the development of three-dimensional conceptions in children's sculpture (Golomb, 1972, 1973, 1974, 2002; Golomb & McCormick, 1995).

The first study focused on the emergence of representational conceptions and the transition from a nonrepresentational attitude to the evolution of effective "models" of the human figure. The participants in this study were 300 American and Israeli children enrolled in preschool, kindergarten, and first grade (Golomb, 1972, 1974). Their ages ranged from 2 to 7 years. Children were seen individually and given a standard portion of playdough with the request to make a doll, a mommy, and a daddy. Following the modeling tasks, each child was also asked to make a drawing of a mommy and a daddy. These data and the extensive protocols that record each child's behavior during the session provide us with a fairly clear picture of the early representational concepts that find expression in this medium.

The second study provides a more comprehensive account of children's models of inanimate and animate objects and records the developmental changes that occur in the conceptions and executive skills of children throughout the childhood years. The participants were 109 children ranging in age from 4 to 13 years (Golomb, 2002; Golomb & McCormick, 1995). They were enrolled in preschool centers, kindergarten, and elementary-junior high schools through seventh grade. We also included an adult sample of 18 liberal arts students who were enrolled at an urban university. Approximately one half majored in the visual arts or took art courses; the others were students of psychology. Each participant was seen individually over one to two sessions, and for each task was provided with a ball of clay 4 in. in diameter. A detailed record was made on all facets of the construction process with careful attention to the modeler's actions and comments which were also tape recorded. The sculptures were preserved for examination, analysis, and scoring. This study aimed for a more detailed examination of the variables that affect the three-dimensional treatment of inanimate and animate objects, namely, complexity, symmetry, balance, and familiarity. Of these variables, *complexity* refers to the number and arrangement of differentiated elements that comprise an object and vary from a few simple to many diverse elements. *Symmetry* refers to the number of sides of the volumetric object that have the same or similar characteristics; these can vary from complete symmetry of the six sides of a cube to the partial symmetry of a four-footed animal whose two long sides are near symmetrical, to the bilateral symmetry of the human figure whose front and back sides are distinctly different. *Balance* a variable that is quite specific to the clay medium, refers to the construction of a freestanding sculpture, which requires some understanding of its mechanical properties and the technical difficulty of balancing an upright figure. *Familiarity* refers to knowledge of the object and the availability of practiced representational models. Thus, for example, familiarity with drawing might predispose a child who has not yet worked with clay to rely on a well-practiced graphic model (or schema) and transpose it to the clay medium.

We selected these variables to study their impact on modeling of diverse objects and to distinguish among the effects of the medium, instruction, and the child's concept of the object. We were especially interested in delineating the developmental progression, whether it follows the dimensional pattern established for drawing, from one- to two- to three-dimensional use of lines most commonly assumed (Lark-Horowitz, Lewis, & Luca, 1967) or whether dimensionality plays a different role in this medium.

In order to provide an integrated review of the findings, the results from the two studies are combined into a single and unified report.

FROM PREREPRESENTATIONAL ACTIONS TO THE FIRST MODEL OF A HUMAN

When presented with clay or playdough, the youngest children in our sample (2.0–2.8) tend to hold the material passively in their hands, turn it aimlessly, or use it in conjunction with other toys, for example, sticking it on blocks or vehicles. Somewhat later (2.8–3.2) they tend to handle the matter more actively, squeezing, folding, poking, pinching, and flattening the playdough. Children seem to enjoy handling the soft and pliable material, but in the beginning their actions do not show a representational intention. Eventually, children discover the rolling motion, rolling the dough back and forth on the table top which yields the first visually coherent and pleasing unit in playdough (plasticene or clay). Without apparent planning, the child has created his first articulate shape in this medium, a stick or snakelike shape, and somewhat later he or she discovers how to make the more difficult rounded shape of a ball or irregularly shaped sphere. With the creation of these basic elements we note, in short succession, a sequence of prerepresentational interpretations that are characteristic of a transition from mere action on the medium to a first inkling of representational possibilities: Romancing, Imitative Actions, Reading Off, and Verbal Designation.

Romancing, the first of these representational devices, is the child's attempt to respond to the request of an adult or an older child to explain what he or she has made. Lacking any real concept of what "making or modeling" might involve, Romancing is a kind of forced interpretation of an accidentally produced formation, and the ensuing fantasy narrative develops quite independently of form quality and is not yet tied to a perceptual likeness.

A somewhat more advanced form of prerepresentational interpretation can be seen in *Imitative Actions,* in which a piece of rounded playdough or clay is bounced in imitation of a ball, a blob is moved across a table in imitation of a car or an animal walking, and a flattened lump of clay is equated with making meat patties. Although these actions imply the object by imitating one of its functions, they do not aim to create a perceptual likeness. Romancing and imitative actions serve as short-lived substitutes for representation proper; they mark a transitional phase of development when functional representational concepts and models are as yet lacking.

Reading Off and *Verbal Designation* are somewhat more advanced forms of prerepresentational devices. Reading off is based on an incidental discovery of perceptual similarity between the blob of clay and a real object. It relates to the "looks" of the product and thus is less arbitrary and fanciful than Romancing. Verbal Designation is the most advanced of the prerepresentational devices invented by the child and serves as a useful aid to representation in that the parts, though not yet modeled, are verbally identified. In this case, the verbal identification of parts no longer depends on the matter's chance appearance, and the figure, though still crude and minimally differentiated, is made to conform to the child's original intention. Parts are now interpreted according to some principle such as location on a vertical axis: Top is head, center is tummy, and bottom is legs. Designation requires the notion of correspondence, and the discovery that the top of the bulky structure can stand for the upper part of a person is a significant step and further representational development depends on it.

EARLY MODELS OF THE HUMAN FIGURE

Following the earlier exploration of the medium and discovering what can be done with it, children develop three basic models of a human, and we can follow their evolution from a minimally differentiated figure to a more detailed model that bears some resemblance to the object it is meant to represent. These models include the *upright standing column*, a lengthened blob of dough, crudely shaped, held up in the air, or placed erect on the table; *a ball with facial features* poked out or separately formed; and the *layout model* which consists of an arrangement of separately formed parts that represent the facial features but can also include arms and legs (Figures 15.2A–15.2C). In relatively short time, depending on practice with the medium, these early models undergo differentiation: The upright standing one-unit column figure undergoes internal subdivision of its parts; the ball with facial features develops into a tadpole figure, consisting of a sphere and legs; and the layout model becomes a *graphic model* (Figures 15.3A–15.3D). The latter is a linear model which derives its concepts and procedures from drawing, in that it outlines the major body parts with thin strips of dough (clay), or creates the stick figure which is a variant of the graphic model.

From these early sculpting models we can infer the representational concepts that gave rise to them. As in drawing, they are characterized by generality, such that a global form can stand for another global entity, in this case a person. Verticality, uprightness, and facial features serve as defining attributes of the human figure. Considering the technical difficulty of working with playdough or clay, the determination to create a specific object and the ability to sustain this intention while shaping the mass is a significant achievement. It reveals the capacity to subordinate the modeling action and the child's verbal designation of parts to a central, dominant representational intention. Indeed a profound distance exists between the prerepresentational child who merely acts on the medium and the child who makes a crude column with designated parts.

Progress in modeling can be seen in the differentiation of the parts of the human figure that are now distinctly modeled. We see continued developments in the three early models with

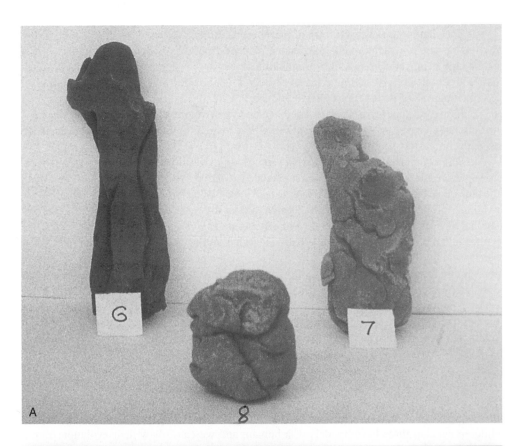

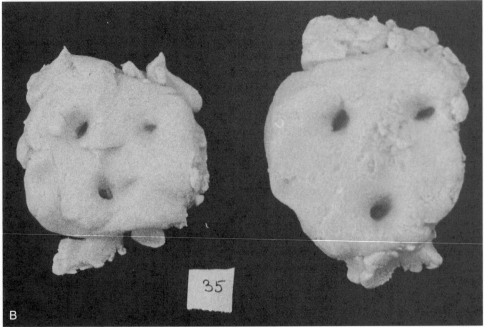

FIG. 15.2. Early models of the human figure. A. Upright standing column. Boys, ages 3.6–4.0. B. Ball with facial features. Boy, age 4.6. C. Lay-out model composed of eyes, nose, mouth, body, and legs. Girl, age 5.4.

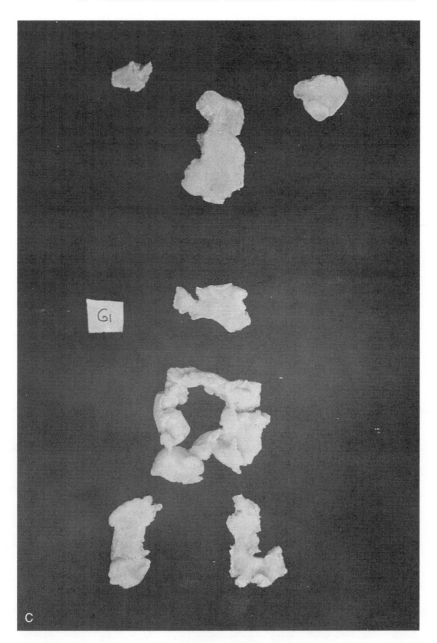

FIG. 15.2. *Continued*

the *upright standing* figure composed of several solid parts, the *horizontal* figure constructed of solid rounded or flattened parts, and the more detailed *graphic outline* figures (Figures 15.4A–15.4C).

The primitive one-unit figure splits apart and now includes, at the very least, a separately formed head, body, and legs, though it is often armless and faceless. The horizontal figure represents a compromise formation between the three-dimensional upright standing figure and the flat two-dimensional model of graphic origin. Once it develops a differentiated trunk and legs, its appearance varies from the crude and slightly lumpy construction of younger children

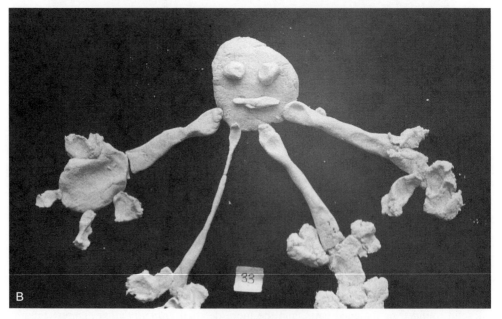

FIG. 15.3. Beginning differentiation in the early models of the human figure. A. Upright standing columns composed of two parts: head and body. Boy, age 4.0, girl, age 3.8. B. Tadpole figure composed of head and limbs. Girl, age 4.4. C. Graphic model. The major parts are outlined with thin strips of playdough or clay. Girl, age 5.9. D. Stick figure, a variant of the graphic model. Figure comprises a head with prominent facial features, body, arms, and fingers. Girl, age 4.9.

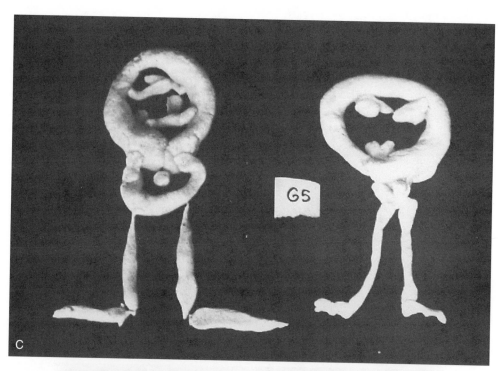

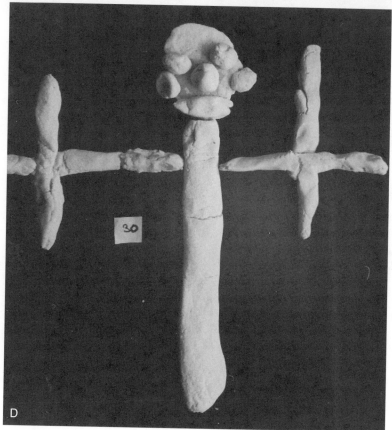

FIG. 15.3. *Continued*

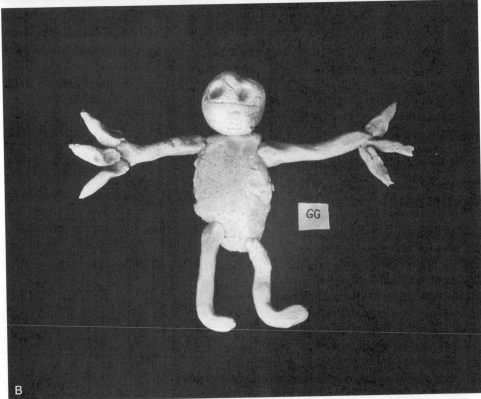

FIG. 15.4. Differentiated models of the human figure. A. Upright standing Man, Woman, and Figure Bending. Boy, age 7.6. B. Horizontally placed figure composed of head, eyes, body, arms, and fingers, legs, and feet. Boy, age 5.9. C. Graphic models of the human figure composed of a solid head, outlined body, arms, legs, and fingers. Girl, age 5.9.

FIG. 15.4.   *Continued*

to the skillfully and symmetrical production of the more experienced children. The graphic model in playdough, the descendant of the earlier layout model and of the graphic tadpole figure, persists and is perfected. The figure, outlined with strips of dough, closely follows the characteristics of the drawn line. These figures demonstrate careful planning and measuring the length of sides. Overall, the tendency is toward greater differentiation of the parts, modeling arms and hands, legs and feet, and distinguishing between the upper and the lower torso.

In each of the three sculpting models the figure passed through a process of orderly differentiation determined by the properties of the medium and the specific model employed. The main emphasis is on the differentiation of forms and the creation of balanced and symmetrical structures. Once this has been achieved, the overall proportions of the figure improve gradually and attention extends beyond the frontal view. Here it is important to note that frontality carries special weight in the representation of the human figure. In the case of the human body, the frontal aspects are the most important and informative ones; they define the character of the person, gender, affect and intentionality, direction of movement, and social communication. In sculpture, as in real life, humans relate most directly through their senses, which favor the representation of the canonical frontal view, and this view receives the most attention from our young sculptors. In modeling, unlike drawing, the human figure is often faceless and armless, whereas the trunk is more often included, even in the models of young children. Overall, in sculpture we find less attention to detail and little ornamentation.

Models are temporary solutions, and the adoption of a model does not imply its continued use. On the contrary, the child who spends a great deal of time with this medium tends to discard the less suitable model and invents other means of representation. This is especially evident in the graphic model which is unstable, cannot be lifted without serious dislocation of its parts, and requires patience and fine motor coordination. For these reasons the graphic model tends to be exchanged for more solidly modeled forms that are more suited to the task at hand. We also note significant individual differences, with some 3-year-olds creating advanced sculptures, whereas some 4- and 5-year-olds produce undifferentiated tadpoles. Above all, models should be considered as tentative solutions, temporary and flexible formulae for representation and not printouts of an underlying conceptual schema, a finding which is well documented in the next study that examines children's models on diverse tasks.

CHILDREN'S REPRESENTATION OF INANIMATE, HUMAN, AND ANIMAL FIGURES IN CLAY

So far we have focused on modeling the human figure in young children. We now turn our attention to the modeling conceptions and skills of older children engaged in a range of different tasks. The aim of this expanded study is twofold: (a) to determine the order in which representational concepts emerge in the medium of clay and (b) to clarify the impact of selected task variables on the child's ability to represent objects in a three-dimensional manner.[2]

The order of stages or phases in the development of three-dimensional representation is primarily addressed in terms of the *posture* of the figure (upright standing or placed horizontally on the table), the child's attention to *multiple sides* of the modeled object, and the *manner* in which the *medium* is used, for example, by hollowing out and creating protrusions, thus suggesting the inside as well as the outside of the figure. We wished to examine the hypothesis that three-dimensional development in sculpture follows the same progression conventionally established for drawing or, alternatively, that children exhibit from the beginning a basic three-dimensional representational conception of the object that undergoes differentiation with development.

In the study of task variables, we payed special attention to the difficulty associated with modeling specific objects, notably the human figure. Previous studies had noted similarities in the drawing and modeling of a person, which seemed to suggest the dominance of children's two-dimensional strategies of representation in both media. This interpretation ignored the uniquely difficult problem of representing the human figure in an upright fashion without recourse to an armature (a kind of wire scaffold). A contrasting hypothesis that considered the horizontal posture of the modeled human figure a function of this particular task and its medium was not considered, and this issue is raised in our second study where we consider the previously mentioned variables of complexity, symmetry, balance, and familiarity.

We chose eight tasks that varied along these selected dimensions. The tasks were modeling a Cup, Table, Man, Woman, Person Bending to Pick Up a Ball, Dog, Cow, and Turtle. According to our analysis of potential task effects, objects that are familiar to the child, simple in construction, easily balanced, and have symmetry of sides, are the most likely candidates for successful three-dimensional modeling. These conditions apply most fully to the Cup and the Table. Animals are more complex in structure and comprise a larger number of differentiated parts that require skillful planning. They are, however, relatively stable (balanced) in structure with bodies resting on four legs placed perpendicular to the horizontal axis of the body, which facilitates an upright posture. Animals are also quite symmetrical, with two major sides, the long sides, near-duplicates of each other. Instead of a dominant canonical view that favors a single side, which is the case for the human, in four-footed animals there is competition between frontal and side views (Golomb & Farmer, 1983; Ives & Rovet, 1979) which calls

---

[2]It is important to keep in mind the distinction between working with mass and a three-dimensional conception of a figure that is to be modeled on all sides and placed standing upright. The fact of working in a three-dimensional medium does not by itself guarantee a three-dimensional conception and/or production.

attention to more than a single side or view. In terms of familiarity, most children are familiar with the animals we selected, either from direct experience or from picture books, with dogs and turtles somewhat more familiar to urban children than cows that are mostly known from picture books.

Finally, the human figure, though the most familiar object, is also the most complex one in this series of tasks. Its structure is organized along the vertical axis, and its relatively disproportionate parts which include head, neck, body, arms and hands, legs and feet make it difficult to balance. In contrast to animals, the dominant sides of the human figure are quite distinct with marked differences between its front and its back sides. The human body calls for the vertical alignment of a large torso with two spindly legs which creates problems of balance for a standing figure, thus favoring the horizontal position. However, specification of a theme that makes posture more salient as in the Person Bending task may facilitate uprightness and attention to multiple sides.

The results of our findings highlight the importance of the variables we had identified and reveal that even young preschoolers, the 4-year-olds, entertain an implicitly three-dimensional conception of the objects they modeled.

UPRIGHTNESS

On the first two tasks, that were symmetrical in structure, familiar, balanced, and relatively simple in the construction of its parts, all the 4-year-olds, almost without exception, modeled the cup and the table in a three-dimensional upright standing fashion. Although the younger children modeled their objects more crudely than the older children, the three-dimensional attributes of uprightness and a hollowed-out center for the cup was clearly in evidence (Figure 15.5).

The great majority of animal figures were also modeled standing upright and exceeded the number of erect standing human figures. Among the human figures, the Person Bending to

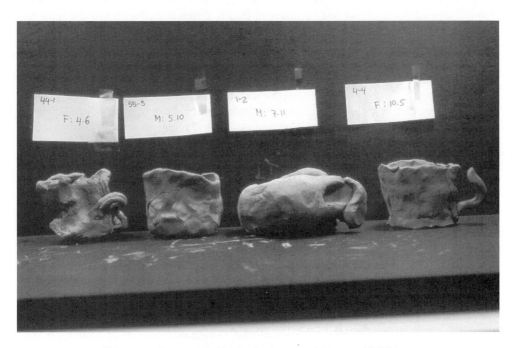

FIG. 15.5.   Cup modeled in clay by 4, 5, 7 and 10-year-old children.

Pick up the Ball was modeled more frequently in an upright posture than the Man or Woman, revealing sensitivity to the nature of the topic or theme. Findings for the total sample of children indicate that 57% attempted to model the Man and Woman figures standing which is comparable to the 50% of upright humans modeled by the adult sample. For the children this figure increased to 76% for the Person Bending (adults 100%), and peaked at 83% for the animal tasks (adults 100%).

An interesting age-related factor emerged on further analysis of the human figure task. Upright intention *decreased* with age and with the complexity of the figure, with preschoolers having the highest upright intention (71%), followed by the kindergarteners (68%), with all others trailing far behind. We found a significant relationship between the posture of the human figures and the degree of their differentiation (complexity). As the figure increases in detail, children find it harder to make it standing, thus resorting to a horizontal posture. These finding suggest that at an early stage in the modeling of young children, 4- and 5-year-olds employ a primitive three-dimensional strategy which yields crudely modeled upright standing humans. Once the figure becomes more differentiated in the number and proportions of its parts, the spindly legs cannot support the head, neck, and torso, at which point horizontality provides a reasonable solution to the task the child has set herself. The adults in our sample face the same technical problem and they adopt a similar solution in regard to posture.

In contrast to the human figures, animal figures, their horizontally placed body resting on four legs that provide a stable base, were mostly modeled in an upright fashion.

MODELING OF SIDES AND DIMENSIONALITY SCORES

In addition to upright posture, modeling of sides comprised another aspect of our dimensionality assessment. The findings from the human and animal tasks indicate that even our youngest children in this study, the 4-year-olds, were inclined to model more than a single side of an object, especially in the case of the animals. Overall, the tendency was to create an upright standing animal, its head and body orientation clearly differentiated such that the head was modeled frontally and the body in side view. Attention was also payed to the underside of the body and the shaping of the legs. Children worked attentively on up to six sides of an animal, and in the process of modeling they turned the figure upside down and to the side to create the different parts.

Dimensionality is a composite measure that includes number of sides modeled, uprightness, and procedures such as hollowing out, creating protrusions, indicating parts located inside the body (open mouth, tongue, teeth, earlobes) or underneath clothing. In general, dimensionality scores increased with age, with Animal figures gaining higher scores than the humans and the Person Bending gaining higher scores than the Man and Woman figures. This age-related increase in children's scores tends to level off at ages 8 or 9, but scores again increase for the adult sample. It is worth noting that despite the leveling off in dimensionality scores, and the somewhat crude appearance of the majority of the sculptures, the *attitude* of the older children differed from that of the younger ones. This was noticeable in their persistence with the task, in the repeated attempts to revise their model often three or four times, and in their efforts to smoothen the appearance of the clay figure.

FIGURAL DIFFERENTIATION AND REPRESENTATIONAL MODELS

As with the findings from our earlier reported study on the evolution of the modeled human figure, figural differentiation was mostly age related. The majority of our participants created three-dimensional models that were held upright, free standing, or standing with some support.

Variability in style and degree of differentiation was common in each age group and characterizes children's performance across all tasks. Thus, for example, children who employed a graphic model on the human sculpture switched to solidly shaped upright standing animals. Different strategies might be employed on the three animal tasks which suggests the exploratory and experimental nature of children's approach to modeling rather than the print-out of an underlying conceptual model (Figures 15.6A and 15.6B; Figures 15.7A and 15.7B).

Differentiation is the hallmark of development and with experience children create more detailed figures, introduce measurement, guide their own progress, make corrections, and gain greater satisfaction from the end product. In the case of the human figure we note a more differentiated torso; shoulders; the inclusion of a neck; and clothing such as shirts with sleeves, flaring skirt or pants, an occasional tie, hat, belt, earrings, mustache, beard, zipper, shoelaces, and heels (Figures 15.8A and 15.8B).

As the human figures gains in detail it is mostly placed horizontally. Although the sculptures continue to be modeled quite crudely, older children attempt to introduce motion and gesture, attend to proportions, and convey more information. The technique of the older children is often not better than that of younger ones; but their attitude toward the task, the serious reflection, and the concentrated time devoted to their efforts distinguish between them. One of the main differences in the work of our children and adults concerns the sexual differentiation of the human figure. In the case of children, it was rare to find sexually distinctly modeled humans; but in the adult sample those differences became very marked by the inclusion of breasts, penis, buttocks, broader shoulders for the male, thinner waists and broader hips for the female (Figures 15.10 and 15.11B).

Differentiation of the animal models can be seen in collars on the dog, bells, horns, and udders on the cow, and spots on the turtle. There is also more attention to size differences, with the dog smaller than the cow, and attempts to introduce actions (Figures 15.9A–15.9C). Along with planning, reflection and increased skill comes a more critical awareness and a negative evaluation of the final product.

Construction style, that is, the manner in which children compose their figures, involves two strategies: internal subdivision of the lump of clay by pinching, pulling, and subtracting clay from a single unit or addition of separately modeled parts. In our sample, the additive method was more frequently employed than internal subdivision, and it was unrelated to age and differentiation of the figure and also independent of the sequence of construction. Regarding the sequence of ordering the parts during construction, the majority of humans were composed in a top-to-bottom sequence. Next came the inverse order of bottom to top that in many cases facilitated the figure's upright stance, followed by a sequence that modeled the body first. In the case of animal figures, the body was always the first part modeled, indicating that ordering of the body parts was generally flexible and adapted to the nature of the task. Overall, figures in clay were constructed with utmost simplicity, devoid of detail and adornment, often faceless, but most commonly including the trunk.

Modeling a figure in clay seems to make its own demands, and although facial features are rarely omitted in the drawn human figure where they seem to constitute the figure's defining characteristic, the prevalence of faceless figures in clay was high, with approximately one third of the humans lacking facial features. In animal figures these omissions reached 40%.

SUMMING UP

Our major questions concerned the development of three-dimensional concepts in modeling with clay and the order in which dimensional strategies evolve. Our findings indicate that when children become representational in this medium, approximately during their fourth or fifth year, they exhibit some basic three-dimensional understanding as indicated by their attention

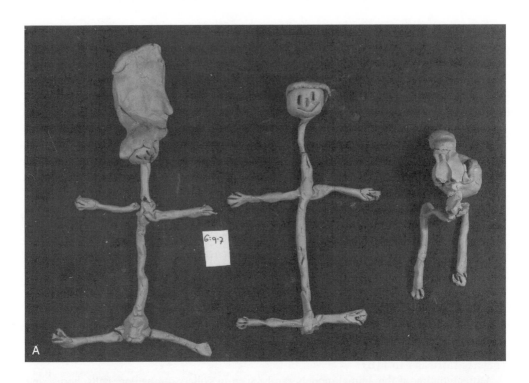

FIG. 15.6.   Distinctive modeling of humans and animals. Girl, age 9.7. A. Humans are modeled as stick figures: the Woman with a prominent hairdo, the man with short hair, and the Person Bending with a bent back and shoulders. B. Animals are modeled on all sides and standing.

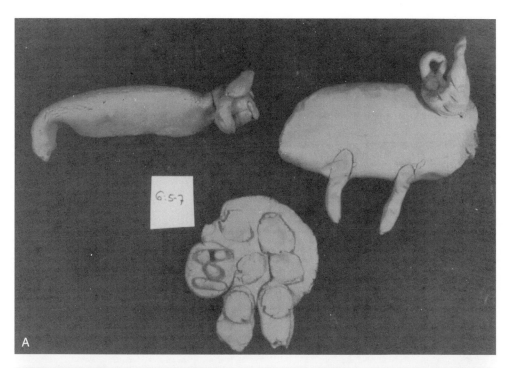

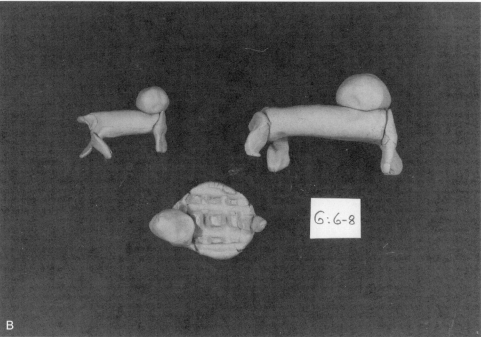

FIG. 15.7.   Exploration of different animal models. A. The Dog, standing upright, is modeled from all sides, with differentiated front and side views; the Cow, placed horizontally, is constructed quite solidly, equipped with two legs, its head, horns, and facial features aligned with the side view; the two-legged Turtle is flattened, its head turned frontally and aligned with its body. Girl, age 5.7. B. Dog and Cow, differentiated by their size, are modeled upright and are quite similar in their construction of head, body, and legs. The Turtle is modeled with a top-view in mind that emphasizes head, body-shell with prominent markings, and a tail; legs are invisible. Girl, age 6.8.

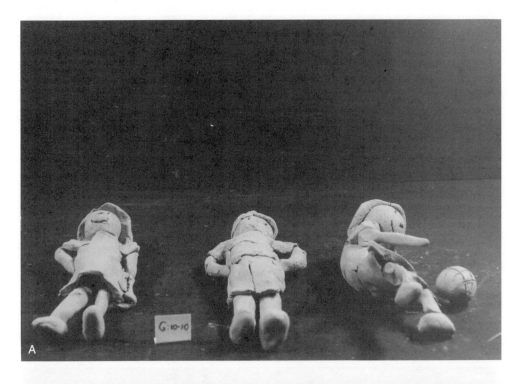

FIG. 15.8A & B. Human figures with differentiated torso and clothing that suggest the underlying body. Girls, ages 10.9 and 10.10.

FIG. 15.9. Differentiated animal figures. A. Cow with udders. Boy, age 7.4. B. Dog with collar, Cow with bell, Turtle with markings on the shell that covers a separately formed body. Girl, 10.10. C. Dog and Cow modeled with attention to their respective size differences. Boy, age 10.2.

(Continued)

FIG. 15.9. *Continued*

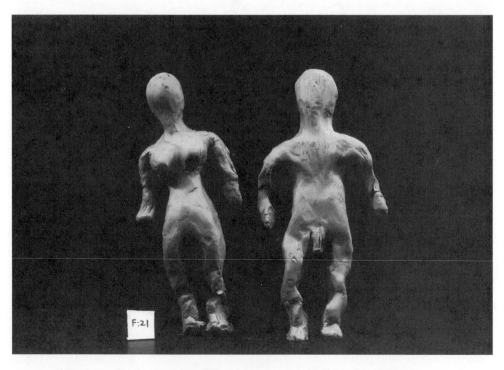

FIG. 15.10. The human figure of the adult artists shows greater sexual differentiation.

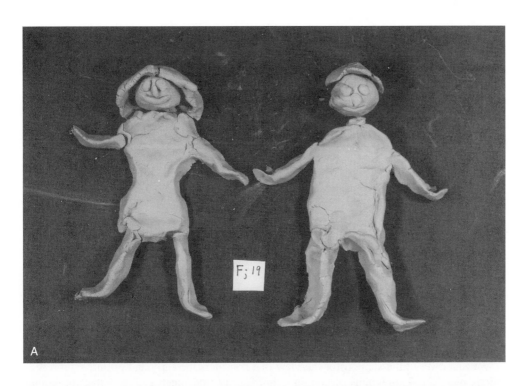

FIG. 15.11. Diverse models of the human figure created by young adults. A. Man and Woman modeled frontally and placed horizontally on the table. Female, age 19. B. Man, Woman, and Person Bending in a sitting position that circumvents the difficulty of modeling a standing figure. Male, age 25.

to multiple sides, to the volume of a figure and its upright stance. The flattened and horizontally placed human figures appear to be a somewhat later development, a function of familiarity with this difficult medium and the ambition to create a more complex and differentiated figure. Even then the tendency to work horizontally on the figure's frontal side is counteracted on the Person Bending and Animal tasks and override it. It is most striking to observe the differential treatment which the same child applies to our different tasks (Figures 15.6A and 15.6B; Figure 15.7A). Thus, the previously held notion that the singular attention to frontal aspects represents the child's conceptual limitations regarding dimensionality no longer seems tenable. From the very beginning of their work with clay children develop representational concepts that are incipiently three-dimensional in nature, and then refine them with continued practice. When their ambition to create a better likeness to the object, which requires the inclusion of a larger number of body parts, militates against the use of an upright posture, they resort to what appear to be two-dimensional strategies: flattening some of the forms in order to better attach them and placing the figure horizontally on the table.

It is perhaps surprising that the process of differentiation tends to level off during the middle childhood years. Even the sculptures of our educated adult sample shows this leveling off effect, with 50% of the humans placed horizontally and attention focused on the frontal region of the sculpture (Figures 15.10 and 15.11A). This leveling off effect is similar to what we find in drawing, and only in cases of continued practice and the motivation to acquire new representational skills do the drawings of adolescents and adults progress beyond the typical childhood drawings. Similar factors may underlie the arrest of modeling skills.

We found very little support for the view that considers the early and primitive representations merely as expressions of cognitive immaturity, and much evidence that the young artist struggles with problems older children must also confront: how to create a satisfying representation in a medium that puts a premium on balance, uprightness, and the modeling of multiple sides, all of which require great skill and practice. Given children's limited experience with modeling in clay and their lack of knowledge of the cultural traditions and practices that prevail in this medium, their early somewhat primitive constructions are to be expected. Early beginnings tend toward simplicity and economy of forms that result in global representations.

In addition to mapping representational development in clay, our findings document some of the limitations that are inherent in the transposition of interpretive models derived from the domain of drawing and applied to sculpture. This statement receives additional support from cross-cultural studies that explore the drawings and sculptures of preliterate youngsters.

CROSS-CULTURAL STUDIES

In order to establish the generality of findings from research conducted in Western industrialized societies, investigators look for additional data that will support their interpretation or call for a modification of their theory. Thus, the search is for cross-cultural research with "naive" subjects drawn from a preliterate society, not known for its artistic traditions. The search for untrained, spontaneous beginnings of art making has led many investigators to collect drawings from children and adults who live in non-Western, unschooled communities. Studies that include modeling are extremely rare and, with but few exceptions, incidental to the quest for drawing. One often quoted study, conducted during the years 1934 to 1937 in Northern Ghana by the anthropologist Meyer Fortes who, in collaboration with his wife, collected drawings from unschooled Tallensi children and adults (Fortes, 1940, 1981). Modeling was not the focus of this research, but Fortes commented on the three-dimensional nature of clay figures which played a significant role in the life of the children. He noted that children's favorite pastime was modeling small clay figures of people, horses, cattle, and other animals, 3 to 6 in. in height. Boys and girls played extensively with their clay figures which varied in quality, but the best among them were realistic representations, endowed with facial features but lacking ears. The human figures clearly indicated sex differences, modeling the females with breasts, an occasionally enlarged belly signifying pregnancy, and a slit between the legs to indicate the vulva which was decorated with a tuft of hair snipped from the artist's head. The figures of men were not given genitals; however, an enlarged scrotum was occasionally represented. Figures of chiefs mounted on horses were always dressed in bits of cloth and equipped with a hat modeled from clay. Cattle were modeled with horns; and bulls and stallions with scrota (Fortes, 1981).

In a recent study designed to collect drawings as well as sculptures from a preliterate community, Sven and Ingrid Andersson (1997) requested drawings and sculptures from children and adolescents living in a remote area of Northern Namibia, near Ruacana and the Epupa Falls at the Kunene River. The youngsters, members of the Himba tribe, did not attend school and had no previous access to paper and pencils. In a video made by the Anderssons, we meet the participants of their study and observe their approach to drawing and modeling. We note that the adolescent girls and young women wear their hair in an elaborate and highly ornamental style, adorn their neck and bare-breasted chests with decorative pendants and necklaces, and their wrists with bracelets, evidence of a developed aesthetic sense. The adolescent boys shave their hair on both sides of the skull and wear their hair plaited and hanging down the back. They also wear some necklaces and straps around the ankles and wrists, but compared to the girls, the males use fewer ornamental devices.

Provided with paper and holding the pencil gingerly, the youngsters take turns drawing small circles, lines, and figures in an inverted orientation to the drawer. The figures resemble stick figures, tadpoles, open trunk figures, and two-dimensional people with or without arms; the drawings also include circular enclosures that are identified as house and animal shed. With the help of an assistant who serves as translator, all the drawn objects are identified. Most participants draw with intense concentration, taking their time as they create the simple variants of the basic human and animal figures.

The second set of data were collected from members of the Himba tribe living at the Epupa Falls. In this study, the Anderssons first supply their subjects with clay and ask them to model a person or an animal. All the participants hold the clay in their hands as they model and shape their sculpture in the round, turning, pulling, pushing, and pinching the material to create an upright standing, quite naturalistic looking three-dimensional figure. Some create an animal quickly and very competently, modeling head, body, four legs, ears, and a curled up tail. The object is modeled by internal subdivision of its parts, and the animal is standing. The girls in this group tend to model their humans with a long neck and breasts, emphasizing hairdo and buttocks, and upright posture. The ease and confidence with which they model their figures suggest that the artist has some familiarity with clay modeling. Talent and individual differences also play a role that can be seen when we compare the work of highly adept modelers with that of others who are less skillful and create more crudely shaped figures. Following modeling with clay, the participants are provided with paper and pencils and asked to draw. The forms, figures, and configurations that emerge are very similar to the ones drawn by the first group of subjects. By comparison with their ease of modeling clay figures, the youngsters appear to be deeply immersed in the drawing efforts, seem less relaxed, and experience more difficulty. The differences between the drawn and the sculpted models of humans and animals highlight the significance of the medium of representation, which yields the abstract linear quality of the pencil drawing and the three-dimensional more naturalistic representation of clay figures, radically different constructions on the same theme. The different strategies are ingenious problem-solving approaches to the problem of representation.

NOTES ON DRAWN AND SCULPTED FIGURES

In this chapter I focused on the development of sculpture and my references to drawing and its developmental trajectories have been brief. In order to apprehend the impact of the medium on the form representations may take, one also needs to take account of some of the dominant theoretical conceptions regarding the nature of children's drawings.

Dating back to Piaget's account of drawing development (1928, 1929; Piaget & Inhelder, 1956, 1971) and under the influence of Luquet's taxonomy of child art (Luquet, 1913, 1927), Piaget viewed drawing developmental in close parallel to logicospatial reasoning. Thus, drawings provided an index of the child's conceptual development captured in the often-heard phrase "a child draws what he knows not sees." According to Piaget, prior to the emergence of concrete operational thought this knowledge is incomplete, deficient, and centered on some of the most prominent characteristics of the object. Unable to consider all essential aspects of the object, and failing to organize the elements into a coherent representation, the preoperational child omits and misplaces body parts and creates distorted and ill-proportionate figures. With the acquisition of Euclidean and projective concepts of measurement and the ability to consider the viewpoint of the observer, the concrete and formal operational child overcomes the earlier conceptual limitations and handicaps, and consequently the drawings are supposed to exhibit greater fidelity to the true appearance of objects and scenes.

Although Piaget was not interested in children's artistic development and viewed the data on drawing within the context of cognitive development and as support for his genetic epistemological theory, his writings have had a significant influence on researchers studying child art. Of course, his position has not gone unchallenged, and new data and their interpretation have contested his proposition that conceptual deficits account for the typical childhood drawings (Cox, 1992; Freeman, 1980; Freeman & Cox, 1985; Golomb, 1973, 2002, 2003; Pariser, 1995; Willats, 1997; Winner, 1996). There is now considerable evidence that the nature of the task, the medium, theme, and instruction have a considerable effect on the child's representation; and the notion of a central, unified mental image that underpins drawing is seriously questioned. Thus, for example, omission of the trunk in drawing but its inclusion in modeling cannot indicate conceptual confusion on one hand and competence on the other. Furthermore, studies that document drawing development during the late childhood and adolescent years clearly indicate that the hypothesized progression from intellectual realism to visual realism, from a knowledge-based drawing that is subjective and somewhat distorted to one that approaches optical realism, has not been supported. Without explicit training, neither children nor adults reach this level of proficiency in the projective rendering of space, suggesting that art is a domain where visual thinking and problem solving follows its own rule system which does not simply mirror the domain of logical reasoning. However, the elegance of a more unified conception of intellectual and artistic development continues to inspire students of child art, and Piaget's overarching conception of drawing development as a progression toward realism in art continues to find adherents (Case, 1992; Case & Okamoto, 1996; Dennis, 1992; Milbrath, 1998; Morra, 1995; Morra, Moizo, & Scopesi, 1988; Porath, 1997).

The data on drawing and modeling point to the existence of significant differences in the models that evolve in both media, in the construction of inanimate and animate objects, and further indicate that realism in art is not a spontaneously achieved competence but subject to cultural norms, training, talent, and motivation. Differentiation of form is a fundamental principle that underlies development in the arts, but the specific forms its expression takes is influenced by the nature of the medium and its specific tools and affordances.

In both two- and three-dimensional media, development begins with global undifferentiated forms that represent their object in a minimal and highly economical fashion, a model consisting of a basic unit which represents the *whole person*. As the figure undergoes further differentiation of its parts, frontality dominates in drawing with its emphasis on linear elements that provide clear contours and significant detail useful for indicating a subject's age, gender, activity, and relationships. In modeling, other aspects become dominant such as uprightness, the order of construction, dimensional treatment, and an earlier attention to multiple sides. In contrast to drawing, clay is a revisable medium such that the figure can be taken apart, matter can be added or subtracted, and the construction process can be reversed. In modeling we note an emphasis on the overall structure of the figure and its major components at the expense of facial features, detail, and ornamentation, a style that is reminiscent of certain historical antecedents, the prehistoric Venus statuettes, the differently modeled beautiful Cycladic figures of 2700–2000 bce, and more recently the modern sculptures of Arp, Brancusi, Moore, and others.

Finally, our study of children's modeling militates against a notion of a single underlying mental image or schema and provides evidence for considerable flexibility in the child's creation of two- and three-dimensional figures. Two-dimensional drawings, mixed models that combine the side view of an animal with its frontally depicted head, omission of features and body parts, emphasis on frontality and many other so-called faults in children's drawings need not indicate conceptual confusion or memory constraints on one hand and competence on the other. The answer is to be found in the evolution of artistic thinking, sensitivity to the possibilities and constraints of each medium, and a spontaneous awareness that a representation is not a literal imitation of an object.

CONCLUDING COMMENTS

The studies reported in this chapter provide us with a first systematic account of developmental trends in modeling and the evolution of children's three-dimensional conceptions in playdough and clay. We payed special attention to the nature of the medium, its affordances and constraints, and the effects of such task variables as complexity, symmetry, balance, and familiarity in the construction of a sculpture.

Contrary to the widespread assumption that the development in sculpture would mirror the progression in drawing from one- to two-dimensional representation and, eventually, culminates with a three-dimensional portrayal, our data indicate that basic three-dimensional conceptions emerge early on as seen in the child's intention to model an upright standing figure and his or her inclination to work, in addition to the frontal part, on multiple sides. With increasing practice in modeling, the differentiated human figure comprised of separately modeled parts tends toward horizontal placement in contrast to the upright standing animal figures. These different procedures highlight the effects of the nature of the tasks and the facilitating role of symmetry and balance in the construction of an object. The vertically aligned human figure composed of such major parts as head, neck, body, and limbs poses the problem of how to stabilize a top-heavy upper part on slender legs, whereas the symmetry of the horizontally aligned animal body and its four legs facilitates the modeling of a balanced and upright standing structure.

The significant differences between the competence of our youngsters modeling multiple sides and the skills of the prehistoric artists who sculpted their ivory statuettes in the round should not mask the similarity in their three-dimensional representational conceptions which emerges early in our young participants, suggestive of a basic competence in this domain. The findings from the cross-cultural studies we reviewed and our comparison of the diverse styles children evolve in drawing and modeling suggest that we are dealing with representational models that are characteristic of the different affordances of the two- and three-dimensional media and do not, by themselves and taken in isolation, reflect the conceptual limitations of the artist. Altogether, children's use of different models on diverse tasks indicates a considerable flexibility of representational schemas in both drawing and modeling, a finding that also calls for a reevaluation of stage conceptions in drawing as a progression toward a single endpoint, namely, optical realism in art.

Of course, the early and primitive efforts of young children's modeling are only the beginnings of a long route toward the accomplishments of the skilled artist, and our study documents only limited phases of this potential development. Our current findings call for a more extensive sets of studies on modeling that consider major aspects not addressed so far: the role of talent, motivation, practice, training, and individual differences. The usual short-term interventions that comprise most of our research are inadequate for a genuine understanding of children's representational conceptions, skill level, motivation, and ability to learn from their experience and from instructions. The work of children and adolescents ought to be studied in a more studio-like environment where professional assistance is made available, where work is sustained over several sessions and the young artist's conceptions can evolve over time. Of course, art educators are familiar with such an approach, and under facilitating conditions it ought to be possible to conduct research that meets the requirements of systematic observations and the necessary experimental and statistical controls of scientific inquiry.

REFERENCES

Andersson, I., & Andersson, S. B. (1997). *Aesthetic representations among Himba people in Namibia* (unpublished manuscript). Linköping University, Sweden.

Arnheim, R. (1974). *Art and visual perception.* Berkeley, CA: University of California Press.

Bahn, P. G., & Vertut, J. (1988). *Images of Ice Age.* Leicester, Winward, New York: Facts on File.

Bahn, P. G., & Vertut, J. (1997). *Journey through the ice age.* Berkeley: University of California Press.

Bergemann-Könitzer, M. (1928). Das plastische Gestalten des Kleinkindes. *Zeitschrift für angewandte Psychologie, 31*(2–4), 1–58.

Bergemann-Könitzer, M. (1930). *Das plastische Gestalten des Kleinkindes.* Weimar: H. Boehlaus Nachfolger.

Boysen, S. T., Berntson, G. G., & Prentice (1987). Simian scribbles: A reappraisal of drawing in the chimpanzee (*Pan troglodytes*). *Journal of Comparative Psychology, 101,* 82–89.

Brown, E. V. (1975). Developmental characteristics of clay figures made by children ages three through the age of eleven. *Studies in Art Education, 16*(3), 45–53.

Brown, E. V. (1984). Developmental characteristics of clay figures made by children: 1970–1981. *Studies in Art Education, 26*(1) 56–60.

Burton, J. M. (1981). Developing minds: With three dimensions in view. *School Arts,* February, 76–80.

Case, R. (1992). *The mind's staircase.* Hillsdale, NJ: Lawrence Erlbaum Associates.

Case, C., & Dalley, T. (Eds.) (1990). *Working with children in art therapy.* London: Tavistock/Routledge.

Case, R., & Okamoto, Y. (Eds.) (1996). *The role of central conceptual structures in the development of children's thought.* Chicago: University of Chicago Press.

Cox, M. (1992). *Children's drawings.* London: Penguin Books.

Delporte, H. (1993). Gravettian female figurines: A regional survey. In H. Knecht, A. Pike-Tay, & R. White (Eds.), *Before Lascaux: The complex record of the early Paleolithic* (pp. 243–276). Boca Raton, FL: CRC Press.

Dennis, S. (1992). Stage and structure in children's spatial representations. In R. Case (Ed.), *The mind's staircase* (pp. 229–245). Hillsdale, NJ: Lawrence Erlbaum Associates.

Edwards, C., Gandini, L., & Forman, G. (1993). *The hundred languages of children: The Reggio Emilia approach to early childhood education.* Norwood, NJ: Ablex.

Fortes, M. (1940). Children's drawings among the Tallensi. *Africa, 13,* 293–295.

Fortes, M. (1981). Tallensi children's drawings. In B. Loyd & J. Gay (Eds.), *Universals of human thought* (pp. 46–70). Cambridge, UK: Cambridge University Press.

Freeman, N. H. (1980). *Strategies of representation in young children.* London: Academic Press.

Freeman, N. H., & Cox, M. (1985). *Visual order.* London: Academic Press.

Golomb, C. (1972). Evolution of the human figure in a three-dimensional medium. *Developmental Psychology, 6*(3), 385–391.

Golomb, C. (1973). Children's representation of the human figure: The effects of models, media, and instructions. *Genetic Psychology Monographs, 87*, 197–251.

Golomb, C. (1974). *Young children's sculpture and drawing*. Cambridge, MA: Harvard University Press.

Golomb, C. (2002). *Child art in context: A cultural and comparative perspective*. Washington, DC: American Psychological Association Press.

Golomb, C. (2003). *The child's creation of a pictorial world*, 2nd. ed. Mahwah NJ: Lawrence Erlbaum Associates.

Golomb, C., & Farmer, D. (1983). Children's graphic planning strategies and early principles of spatial organization in drawing. *Studies in Art Education, 24*(2), 87–100.

Golomb, C., & McCormick, M. (1995). Sculpture: The development of three-dimensional representation in clay. *Visual Arts Research, 21*(1), 35–50.

Grossman, E. (1980). Effects of instructional experience in clay modeling skills on modeled human figure representation in preschool children. *Studies in Art Education, 22*(1), 51–59.

Haas, M. (1998). *Preschool children's exploration and expression with art materials*. Haifa: Ach Publisher.

Haas, M., & Gavich, Z. (2000). *Toddlers experience art materials*. Haifa: Ach Publisher.

Hagen, K., Lewis, M., & Smilansky, S. (1988). *Clay in the classroom: Helping children develop cognitive and affective skills for learning*. New York: Peter Lang.

Ives, W., & Rovet, J. (1979). The role of graphic orientations in children's drawings of familiar and novel objects at rest and in motion. *Merrill Palmer Quarterly, 25*(4), 281–292.

Kramer, E. (2000). *Art as therapy*. London & Philadelphia: Jessica Kingsley Publishers.

Lark-Horowitz, B., Lewis, H. P., & Luca, M. (1967). *Understanding children's art for better teaching*. Columbus, OH: Charles E. Merrill.

Leroi-Gourhan, A. (1982). *The dawn of European art*. Cambridge, UK: Cambridge University Press.

Ley, E. (1980). *Children make sculpture*. New York: van Nostrand Reinhold.

Löwenfeld, V. (1939). *The nature of creative activity*. New York: Harcourt, Brace & Co.

Löwenfeld, V. (1947). *Creative and mental growth*. New York: Macmillan.

Luquet, G. (1913). *Les dessins d'un enfant*. Paris: F. Alcan.

Luquet, G. (1927). *Le dessin enfantin*. Paris: F. Alcan.

Märtin, H. (1932). Die plastische Darstellung der Menschengestalt beim jüngeren Schulkinde. *Zeitschrift für pedagogische Psychologie, 33*, 257–273.

Matz, W. (1912). Eine Untersuchung über das Modellieren sehender Kinder, Taubstummen und Blinden. *Zeitschrift für angewandte Psychologie, 6*, 1–20.

Matz, W. (1915). Zeichen und Modellier Versuch an Volkschülern, Hilfschülern, Taubstummen und Blinden. *Zeitschrift für angewandte Psychologie, 10*, 62–135.

Miles, H. L. (1990). The cognitive foundations for reference in a signing orangutan. In S. T. Parker & K. R. Gibson (Eds.), *"Language" and intelligence in monkeys and apes* (pp. 511–539). New York: Cambridge University Press.

Miles, H. L., Mitchell, R., & Harper, S. (1996). Simon says: The development of imitation in an enculturated orangutang. In A. Russon, K. Bard, & S. T. Parker (Eds.) *Reaching into thought: The mind of great apes*. New York: Cambridge University Press.

Milbrath, C. (1998). *Patterns of artistic development*. New York: Cambridge University Press.

Morra, S. (1995). A neo-Piagetian approach to children's drawings. In C. Lange-Küttner & G. V. Thomas (Eds.), *Drawing and looking* (pp. 93–106). London: Harvester-Wheatsheaf.

Morra, S., Moizo, C., & Scopesi, A. (1988). Working memory (or the M Operator) and the planning of children's drawings. *Journal of Experimental Child Psychology, 46*, 41–73.

Münz , L., & Löwenfeld, V. (1934). *Plastische Arbeiten Blinder*. Brünn CSR: Rudolf M. Rohrer Verlag.

Pariser, D. (1995). Not under the lamppost: Piagetian and neo-Piagetian research in the arts. A review and critique. *Journal of Aesthetic Education, 29*(3), 94–108.

Piaget, J. (1928). *Judgment and reasoning in the child*. London: Routledge & Kegan Paul.

Piaget, J. (1929). *The child's conception of the world*. London: Routledge & Kegan Paul.

Piaget, J. (1951). *Play, dreams and imitation*. New York: Norton.

Piaget, J., & Inhelder, B. (1956). *The child's conception of space*. London: Routledge & Kegan Paul.

Piaget, J., & Inhelder, B. (1971). *Mental imagery in the child*. London: Routledge & Kegan Paul.

Porath, M. (1997). A developmental model of artistic giftedness in middle childhood. *Journal for the Education of the Gifted, 20*(3), 201–223.

Potpeschnigg, L. (1912). *Aus der Kindheit der bildenden Kunst. Schriften für Erziehung und Unterricht*. No 2. Leipzig: Seeman.

Rubin, J. (1984). *Child art as therapy*. New York: van Nostrand Reinhold.

Sanders, N. K. (1985). *Prehistoric art in Europe*. Harmondsworth, NY: Viking Penguin.

Sherman, L., Landau, S., & Pechter, L. (1977). A study of the young child's development in the use of clay and styrofoam as art media. *Canadian Review, 4*(1), 68–78.

Smith, D. A. (1973). Systematic study of chimpanzee drawing. *Journal of Comparative and Physiological Psychology, 82*(3), 406–414.

Topal, C. W. (1986). *Children, clay and sculpture*. Worcester, MA: Davis Publications.

Westergaard, G. C., & Suomi, S. J. (1997). Modification of clay forms by tufted capuchins (Cebus apella). *International Journal of Primatology, 18*(3), 445–467.

Willats, J. (1997). *Art and representation*. Princeton: Princeton University Press.

Winner, E. (1996). *Gifted children: Myths and realities*. New York: Basic Books.

Wulff, O. (1927). *Die Kunst des Kindes*. Stuttgart: Ferdinand Enke.

16

Aesthetic Judgment and Reasoning

Norman H. Freeman
University of Bristol

BACKGROUND BRIEFING: WHAT AESTHETIC
THINKING IS USUALLY ABOUT

Lay people and experts of all ages often find themselves making many types of decisions about what a picture shows, how it shows it, and how well it shows it. The decisions are made on many types of pictures, photographs, road signs, artworks on a wall, quick sketches, text illustrations, and more. An account has to encompass diverse types of pictures in relation to how viewers and depictors cope with difficult pictorial decisions. When people diverge about such matters as whether a picture is a "true likeness," or the conditions under which a picture "will turn out well," there is a chance of discerning their aesthetic assumptions. When the divergence is because the people concerned are of different ages, there is a chance of discerning how the demands of the pictorial domain shape development. Children grow into becoming art critics (Freeman, 1993; Golomb, 2003).

Let us take one example where viewers' opinions did not altogether tally with an artist's assumption about his work. Bernd Salfner's late-1990s hospital murals seemed to him, as producer, to associate with color, distraction, cheering up. Some of the viewers interviewed did indeed assert that. But more viewers asserted that they associated the pictures with silence and calming down. Is that a straightforward conflict of registrations? Not necessarily. It is quite possible that " the answer reflects the hope of patients to calm down by watching distracting paintings" (Salfner & Voigtmann, 1999, p. 89). The immediate point is that the artist here appealed to what he thought the viewers brought to the situation, their hopes for what a picture could do for them in that context. The artist was wondering whether viewers had indeed perceived the mural as he did, as a lively distracting piece, and then filtered their perception through their initial hopes. In summary, this brief illustration draws to our attention the sorts of issue that arise when trying to characterize aesthetic judgment. The two biggest issues are what a picture can do for a viewer (e.g., provide distraction) and what a viewer can do with a picture (e.g., extract calm). We shall look at the issues shortly, but before doing so, we have to note that those two issues are crosscut by two angles, which specify what is involved in mastery of the pictorial domain.

One angle, propounded by Freeman (1995), concentrated on the breadth of the domain to be learned, encompassing how pictures can relate to scenes, how artists can determine whether a picture turns out beautiful or not, how viewers look at pictures, and so forth. Basically, children grow an increasingly broad framework theory of art. They take this framework to different contexts, evaluating the artworks they find in places such as hospitals (Freeman, 1999). The other angle, propounded by Parsons (1987), concentrated on the increasingly reflective nature of interpretative activity. Basically, children tend to concentrate on subject matter first, then come to include ideas on the artist's expressive powers, and last may become aware of their own interpretative activities as viewers. The two angles need each other (Freeman & Parsons, 2001).

Consider one example of pictorial judgment made by people poised between childhood and adulthood. Turner (1983) took a group of 14-year-olds to the Tate Gallery. They were unanimous in disliking Derain's *Pool of London* (1906). In its time daring and savage (Fauvist), nowadays the picture does not look shocking in its liberal use of nonnaturalistic colors. The adolescents judged that Derain had not paid attention to accuracy in choice of colors. In their eyes, the picture did not respect visual facts about the scene, and they blamed the artist. Any pattern of reasoning can be characterized by what it can achieve and what it misses. What the reasoning achieved was to encompass the entities "scene" and "artist" in relation to "picture." That is surely a creditable bit of breadth. What was saliently missing was any awareness of where Derain fit in with other artists of the time. Understanding how picture production always occurs in cultural context is a deep matter. It is a shallow judgment that the artist had been undiscerning or careless in coloring.

Now let us move from a case of viewers' negative verdict to a case of positive praise. In June 2002, the great retrospective of 156 works spanning the entire career of Lucien Freud opened at the Tate Modern. A critic who reported on the preview ended with a single sentence that made three points. Those points encapsulate what many a painter would want to achieve: "I can't praise this beautifully installed show more highly than to say that after I'd seen it once, I came back for a second look, and in every gallery—every picture, even—found new things to delight the eye and engage the mind" (Dorment, 2002, p. 9). Without falling into the trap of concluding that each and every picture should please a critic in those ways, it can surely be agreed that a picture is indeed a great success if it repays repeated viewing, delights the eye, and engages the mind. In a study of a range of pictures, Belver (1989) found extremely high correlations between ratings of attractiveness and ratings of interestingness.

A functional approach to aesthetics asks how pictures do those things for a viewer. It is certainly fruitful to inquire into what determines whether particular pictures will repay repeated viewing, why those pictures should delight the eye and engage the mind for a variety of viewers. Of course, not all viewers engage with pictures from the same stance; viewers' tastes may differ, often as a function of age and experience, and their minds may be engaged in different ways. But although fully accepting that it is interesting to inquire into how pictures do things for a variety of viewers, the fact is that there is another way to approach the same set of pictorial functions.

If the aforementioned approach rightfully puts pictures at the center of any analysis, a second approach dethrones the picture from a central position in favor of the mind. The reason for that move is that the expression "how pictures do things" is metaphorical. A picture does not literally do something, because a picture is not an agent. An artist is the agent behind the production of the picture, and a functional approach thus asks what another agent, a viewer, does with a picture so as to register something of what an artist has done. Any functional account has to put the mind rather than the pictures at the center of an analysis, because "The pictorial properties of pictures can have no causal effects upon the world except via agents who register those properties" (Schier, 1986, p. 81). Analysis of viewers' interpretative decisions is appropriate to the "central fact about pictures," that they are "an intentional manifestation of mind" (Wollheim, 1993, p. 134). Interpretation will be taken to be understanding or specifying the meaning of something (see Hopkins, 1992). Viewers make assumptions about how the appearances of things relate (a) to the appearances of pictures of those things and (b) to the ways in which picture producers generate the artifacts.

The psychology of aesthetics has developed from being a fairly sedate matter of assessing preferences for picture properties to attempting to grapple with the convolutions of critical judgment that people may make. The development applies to both (a) empirical aesthetics as met in art education and in experimental psychology and to (b) philosophical aesthetics as it has influenced art education. The entry on aesthetics on page 12 of *The Oxford Companion to Art* (1970) succinctly sums up how an influential tradition of writers came to the position that the study of aesthetics should center on the study of taste and on the perception of beauty in nature and in art. Briefly, the change that has occurred in the past 50 years has been away from focusing on viewers as being driven by taste and tastes. The handbook entry ends up by noting that aesthetics extends as far as encompassing beauty that is not directly perceptible, beauty that pertains to moral and intellectual formulations and representations. It is commonplace now to focus on viewers as spontaneously using a great deal of intellect to formulate what they reckon is interesting and engaging about art. An economical way to clarify how much matters have changed in the generation since the 1970 Oxford companion is to consult a subsequent Oxford book: Kelly's (1998) *Encyclopedia of Aesthetics*.

The editorial preface of Kelly (1998) stakes out a claim that aesthetics is made up of "critical reflection on art, culture, and nature" (p. ix). Why should that characterization be so broad? A broad characterization is necessary to encompass the fact that art objects make up only one of the classes of things, which afford aesthetic experiences and thoughts, and art objects certainly relate to nature and to culture. So we can do well by taking up Kelly's gloss that aesthetics comprises the "analysis of the beliefs, concepts, and theories implicit in the creation, experience, interpretation, or critique of art" (xi). That gloss directs us to consider whether we can unearth the cognitive activity underlying the organization of a stunning variety of processes of aesthetic thought and judgment in people of all ages. Although indeed an interest in aesthetics may inexorably lead into critical reflection on art, culture, and nature, critical reflection does not have to be an austere affair, indifferent to the sensual aspects of art. Indeed, an aesthetics devoid of sensibility about feeling and expression would be a tedious, humorless affair.

A consequence of the new concentration on critical reflection, and on its constituent concepts, beliefs, theories, is to bypass the classical problem of what makes an artwork beautiful. As Kelly (1998) correctly remarks of contemporary aestheticians: "It would be unusual for them to include beauty as one of their major research topics; they talk more often about the problem of meaning or representation in connection with works of art" (p. xi). But an account of research on aesthetics that drew up its agenda so that it could not deal with developing ideas on beauty would be oddly detached from something that makers and viewers of artworks know is important to them. Again, a handy formulation is in Kelly; "Modern philosophers argued that "beauty is not a property of objects...experienced or judged as beautiful; rather it is a relational property between subjects and objects" (p. xi). Surely that is correct. We do not want to treat beauty as though it were an objective and universal property of the art object, like an object's size or texture may be. A relational stance on beauty is needed to encompass how people think about beauty, beautification, and decoration. It is most interesting that research reviewed later in this chapter shows how young children do indeed think of beauty as though it were a transparently objective property of an object; and the children then slowly develop a relational stance. Equally important, though, we must not get trapped into regarding beauty as though it were all in the eye of the beholder and entirely a matter of individual taste.

EVERYDAY AESTHETIC THINKING ABOUT PICTURES

People do not view pictures with a blank mind. How do people acquire commonsense assumptions about pictorial functions? It has been said that a picture can communicatively be worth a thousand words. The platitude is difficult to theorize, because the pictorial domain is vast. Could a single communicative metric cover road signs, rock art, and Rembrandts? How many words a picture is worth depends on what you want your words to say. If you want to say "Sam is ambivalent about appearing at the conference," you are better off with just those eight words. But if you want someone to check whether Sam has put in an appearance at a meeting you might do better to hand over a picture. Pictures can be characterized as "visual prostheses—they extend the informational system by gathering, storing, and transmitting visual information about their subjects in ways that depend upon and also augment our ability to identify things by their appearance" (Lopes, 1997, p. 144). An eclipse of the sun can be depicted so that one can view something that would blind one in reality: The picture here is a device for taking the sting out of nature. A family portrait is an aide-memoire to long-vanished events. And so forth. In none of the prosthetic instances can there ever be a truly precise match between scene and picture, a true reinstatement of a previous visual experience. Viewers acquire sophisticated beliefs about the complex relations between the appearance of things and the appearance of pictures. Global assumptions about the peculiarity of depiction animate viewers' armchair reflections. Thus, "The changing relationship with the visible world is what genuinely characterizes the 'history' of painting" and evaluation of viewers' interpretations should be organized around the question of why people "relate in a number of different ways to the visible world and its reproduction" (Vajda, 1986, p. 137).

When do children's concepts become organized to represent what is communicatively important about pictures? A study of Greek children by Maridaki-Kassotaki and Freeman (2000) proved revealing. The Greek term *kadro* literally means "frame," but also means "that which has been framed as a display piece" to embellish the home. On two trials, 1 week apart, 120 informants explained what a *kadro* is. In the explanations of 4- and 8-year-old children, these important artifacts were held to be furnishings, useful for hanging on walls. Adults and adolescents showed conceptual flexibility and referred to the use of display to commemorate artists' achievements. Further, these participants saw the displays as display of householders' judgment. You can tell someone's artistic tastes and judgments from the pictures they put on exhibition. A communicative theory of art and a critical stance are certainly in operation after middle childhood.

One can expect children gradually to develop assumptions about what pictures are good for. Pictures excel in the display of appearances that can be "emotionally engaging, eye-catching, and memorable" (Willats, 1997, p. 25). Those three aspects of pictorial vividness are usually discussed under the broad headings of *expressivity, attractiveness*, and *recognizability*. Any account of what people think about pictures has to find a way of formulating the three in a common framework.

Let us briefly survey the diversity of commonsense assumptions that a theory has to encompass. Any driver who thinks that the Canadian road authorities place pictures of moose at some roadsides as an aesthetic gesture might not survive collision with the reality. It is necessary but not sufficient to recognize the contents of the picture. Viewers have to learn to categorize such moose pictures in context for their symbolic significance. The general category under which such pictures fall is that *of advertisement* of a state of affairs that can be truth tested. Either moose are liable to be around or they are not; if they are around, either they are liable to stand in the road or they are not. However, there are other ways of categorizing roadside pictures. Some pictures might be placed to enable the authority to *express* something, as when a picture of a maple leaf in part of a province is used to assert an agency's pride in ownership. It would be an error to assume that the maple leaf advertises the danger of leaves drifting across the road, making it slippery. That is, the *communication* conveys something about the relation of the agent to the scene. Yet other roadside pictures might well be placed for *embellishment*, in an arts-support program, and advertise nothing. On the other hand, a politically aware viewer might reasonably take the artworks to advertise an expression of the financial and political support that makes such things possible. Viewers might reasonably debate whether current moose pictures are beautiful enough to (a) encourage a conservationist attitude toward the creatures, or (b) caricature the animals to look stupid and demonize them as road hazards. Even simple depictions can offer rich interpretative possibilities for viewers to exercise their reasoning on.

For the moment, the important point is that those three functions, of truth-testable representation, expressivity, and embellishment, dominate learners' thinking in semistructured interviews about pictures (Parsons, 1987). Assumptions about the three topics are not reserved for situations of deep reflection. Anyone who attests that a passport photograph is a "true likeness" of the sitter is deploying a commonsense theory of pictures. Anyone who picks up anything of Picasso's political stance from *Guernica* has some notion of an artist expressing something through an act of production. The folksy catchphrase that something "is as pretty as a picture" can coexist with the catchphrase that "beauty is in the eye of the beholder"; both have to be accounted for in identifying constraints on learners' assumptions. Such topics have a venerable philosophical ancestry. In Book 10 of Plato's *Republic*, the general principle was put forward that there are three areas of expertise that have to be considered with all artworks: expertise in representation, in manufacture, and in usage. Pictures are open to truth testing, can conserve something of the producer's expressivity, and can be appreciated as vividly attractive. Some pictures do indeed delight the eye and engage the mind.

EXPRESSIVITY

As noted in the opening section, one great theme of art theory is a shift of emphasis away from asking what qualities are "in" a picture to asking what interpretative inferences a picture invites. An artist's choice of contents can express something about that artist, and viewers might learn to make inferences about artists. That is, part of learners' commonsense theory of depiction would concern inferences about production. Artists have beliefs, desires, and feelings, and they attempt to realize some of those to communicate them to viewers. Ziller (1990) asked students to display local photographs that best described what the United States meant to them. U.S. students largely went in for "patriotism," "development," and "freedom," and the foreign students largely went in for "sports," "food," and "security." That seems to be a clear case where it is safe to interpret from the contents of the pictures to the mentalities of the artists, and where knowing something about the artists helps in viewing the pictures. But not all cases are so clear. In particular, expressivity can somehow be manifest not just in choice of contents but in both style and the "mood" of a picture.

Can viewers agree on moods expressed in pictures, irrespective of facts about the artists? Callaghan (1997) asked 15 artists to assess 64 museum pictures (none of which contained a human figure) for conveying happiness, sadness, calm, or excitement. Sixteen of the pictures for which there was over 72% agreement (they included Picasso's The *Pigeons*, Van Gogh's *A Pair of Shoes*, Monet's *Palazzo Dario*, Matisse's *The Nightmare of the White Elephant*) were then shown to untrained adults and to adult artists for them to categorize for mood. Both groups came up with a mean of 75% agreement with the assessors. A second group of untrained adults was also asked to justify their categorizations. About half the justifications focused on the quality of marks (color, line) and about a third focused on the contents as depicted. There were only 2% explicit references to either the artist ("The person who painted that must have been really blue.") or the viewer ("It makes me happy to see those trees."). Probing interviews may be needed to expose viewers' assumptions about agents (Parsons, 1987).

There is a traditional problem in explaining expressivity. One aspect of the problem lies in identifying signals of expressivity. In one study in which children were given a free choice of colors to use in portraying different emotions, light blue was commonly used to denote happiness (Caloni & Morra, 1990). There is no theory in the literature that could have predicted that particular color as expressive in that way. Gombrich (1972, pp. 28–30) discussed evidence that, in *Francoise Gilot, Femme Fleur*, Picasso painted her face a light blue in an effort to signal "an equivalent to the impression of slimness." Even worse, even if there were clear agreement on how to interpret a signal, such as a sad face, there is nothing that entails that the artist actually feels sad. In that sense, an actor can portray emotions without expressing them. It may be the case that research on expressivity will be a swift route to exposing learners' *reasoning* using commonsense beliefs about what pictures may communicate; but the gateway to the research route has not yet been found.

BEAUTY

The polemical opening paragraph of Neisser (1967) is worth rereading:

> It has been said that beauty is in the eye of the beholder. As a hypothesis about localization of function, the statement is not quite right—the brain and not the eye is surely the most important organ involved. Nevertheless it points clearly enough towards the central problem of cognition. Whether beautiful or ugly or just conveniently at hand, the world of experience is produced by the man (sic) who experiences it. (p. 3)

The person may well be the producer of experience, but the production is subject to constraints. McManus, Kumar, and Stoker (1989) synthesized 25 austere Mondrian abstracts on a computer screen and displayed each abstract accompanied by variants that had been altered by small random amounts. Inexpert viewers reliably preferred the genuine articles. Other research has substantiated and extended the findings. Solso (1994, pp. 264–269) speculated on the neural basis for the impact of Mondrians. But no-one has yet defined precisely what Mondrian was up to in the course of producing such attraction. Perhaps it is proving easier to pin down the orderliness underlying the efforts of Jackson Pollock. The canvasses appear chaotic, but the dripped paint conforms to the patterns unearthed by chaos theory in the hands of physicists and mathematicians. The statistics of chaotic systems seem to map onto Pollock canvasses which thereby "in other words, display the fingerprints of nature" (Taylor, Micolich, & Jonas, 1999, p. 25). There is not one law for nature and another law for art; the same eye that responds to natural patterns responds to artworks.

It is possible to study recognition of particular abstracts and to compare preference with preference for novel abstracts. Freeman and Parker (1973) serially projected 84 abstract shapes (from Vanderplas & Garvin, 1959), in runs of 14, followed by immediate serial presentation of each run randomly mixed with 14 shapes that had not been viewed. Participants were asked say whether they recognized each shape, and to give a preference rating for how attractive it was. Recognition accuracy was about 67%, with a preference for correctly recognized shapes over shapes correctly categorized as novel. The useful finding was that the same preference disparity appeared for shapes that were mis-recognized as familiar (false alarms) compared with preexposed shapes that were not recognized (misses). The variable that controlled attractiveness was thus not the history of viewing a particular abstract but whether the viewer categorized the abstract as triggering a recognition.

There is a class of pictures where there is something to recognize, but the artists make it difficult for untrained viewers to accomplish the recognition. One such style is cubism. Cubist pictures make it impossible to decide whether the particular human figures depicted are beautiful as people. Hekkert (1995) showed nonexpert adults 40 cubist human figure pictures of varying degrees of abstraction. Some of the pictures were rather easy to decipher as being human-figure portrayals; other pictures more obscured the portrayal. For fast-recognizable portrayals like Picasso's *Clovis Sagot*, ratings of how beautiful the pictures were was a positive function of human-figure recognizability and was unrelated to ratings of pictorial complexity. For slow-recognizable portrayals like Braque's *Man Smoking a Pipe*, there was an inverted-U function of beauty against the complexity of lines in the picture itself. In light of the aim of cubism to force viewers' attention onto the picture plane itself, it is interesting that slow recognizability did lead untrained viewers to concentrate on the complexity of the markings on the picture plane. Hekkert found a criterion shift in vocationally expert viewers: (a) With fast recognizability, ratings of beauty were a small negative function of recognizability; and (b) for slow-recognizable pictures, the inverted U of beauty against complexity vanished in favor of a null relation. Reanalysis showed that, for the experts, rated beauty was a positive function of how typical a picture was judged to be as an exemplar of cubism.

In summary, with different types of pictures, determinants of beauty can be attributed to different variables. Recognizability is often important, so let us now consider the pictorial functions of recognition.

RECOGNIZABILITY

Kose (1985) questioned 7- and 11-year-olds about photographs. Replies focused on the scenes recorded and on the medium, with virtually no mention of photographers' intents. Later, with maturity, some viewers come to distrust photography, because agents manipulate cameras to obtain various effects (see Beloff, 1985). Indeed, Lynch and Edgerton (1988) found that digital-image processors introduce much "crafting of resemblances," to make the products acceptable and comprehensible to potential viewers. Yet some viewers come to regard photography as a touchstone of communicative truth, treating the photograph–referent relation as transparent. Presumably a search for some "true likeness" is why, as Gombrich (1960) pointed out, mature viewers reject most snapshots as uncharacteristic of their referents.

A commonsense opinion about the display of appearance in photographs was crucial in a Court of Appeal landmark decision (London, October 10, 1997) reviewing a conviction for possession of indecent video photographs. The defence submitted that the prosecution had not called an expert to attest the age of children in the photographs. A substantive issue was seen to be involved; the appeal would not otherwise have been considered at Court. Lord Justice Judge and colleagues rejected the appeal on the grounds that photographs were referentially self-evident; "A brief look at the material would show whether it did or might depict a person under 16," and, in that respect, the "jury was just as able as an expert" in assessing the evidence (*R. v.* Land, 1997, p. 446). The assumption was that viewers are equal as pictorial interpreters for the task, and it was explicitly recorded that the presumption of equality applied to the defendant (O'Hanlon, 1997). It is irrelevant whether or not the photographs had been faked; that is, the causal history of production is irrelevant. The offence was held to concern representations that trigger instant recognition in all viewers.

The judge's ruling was in line with Schier's (1986) philosophical characterization of pictorial competence as a disposition to recognize a picture of a referent by using the skill involved in being able to recognize the referent itself (see also Hopkins, 1998; Lopes, 1997, p. 178). The judge's ruling seems reasonable for his purpose. Would it be reasonable to extend the ruling to cases of line drawings stylized as caricatures? Research on caricatures has become very interesting nowadays. Caricatures themselves clearly preserve the imprint of agency: Some artists have gone to great lengths to interpose themselves between reality and image. The issue here is that line caricatures are not entirely *naturalistic* (surfaces of the referent may only be implied by white spaces between the lines, and proportions can be so distorted that a real referent would be unviable). But the crucial fact about instant recognition is that some caricatures can serve as "superportraits" triggering faster and more accurate recognitions than undistorted images (see Rhodes, 1996). Pictorial *realism* can be specified as "the quality of a picture that allows us quickly and easily to recognise what it is a picture of" (Sartwell, 1994, p. 354). Realism lies "'not in quantity of information but in how easily it issues" (Goodman, 1976, p. 36). It is theoretically most interesting that caricatures, which are clearly fictional transformations of referent appearances, can be categorized by philosophers as more realistic than photographs that one signs for as "true likenesses" on identity documents.

Recognizability is not a function of how confusible a picture is with its referent. Nobody confuses a caricature with a real face, yet a caricature can indeed be as recognizable as an undistorted image (Perkins & Hagen, 1980). Something is known of the basis in the visual brain for how caricatures work. Think of a line drawing as having tonal contrasts in it that would be appropriate either to valleys cut into the surface or to ridges standing proud of the surface. Pearson, Hanna, and Martinez (1990) demonstrated that black-on-white line drawings mapped onto luminance valleys from gray-scale images. Recognition accuracy of black-on-white caricatures was thereby superior to that of white-on-black caricature; one would predict superiority in speed of recognition too, not just in accuracy of recognition (contrary to a suggestion by Biederman & Kalocsai, 1997, on comparing drawings with photographs).

Given a picture that triggers a recognition of its contents, under what conditions will a viewer be willing to "affirm a likeness"? Rhodes and McLean (1990) reported that untrained viewers recognized caricatured birds as accurately as undistorted images. Bird experts even found caricatures more recognizable than undistorted images. The important point is that the expert bird watchers had not been specially trained with caricatures. Therefore, it must have been the bird watchers' expertise in discriminating between real birds and between bird pictures that gave positive transfer to caricatures. Only some people are expert bird watchers, but all people can be regarded as expert face watchers; and a caricature advantage can indeed appear with face recognition. Caricatures may serve as better likenesses than undistorted images (see Rhodes, 1996, pp. 98–102, for conditions under which a caricature advantage holds). The advantage is a function of the degree to which a particular caricature exaggerates distinctive aspects of the particular referent face it is caricaturing. It is also possible to generate anticaricatures that deemphasize referent distinctiveness (Brennan, 1985). Rhodes, Brennan, and Carey (1987) reported that viewers' speed in recognizing caricatures of their colleagues was twice the speed of undistorted images, which was, in turn, twice the speed of anticaricatures (see Benson & Perrett, 1994; Stevenage, 1995, for cognate data).

Caricatures can also facilitate learning names for faces (Stevenage, 1995), so caricatures support the consolidation of associative memory traces. It has proved possible to model some of the caricature effects in computational research. Tanaka and Simon (1996) found higher activation for caricatures than undistorted input by back-propagation in a neural net modeling (see also Calder, Young, Benson, & Perrett, 1996, on modelling a caricature advantage in priming).

Given that caricatures are pictorially powerful in their effects on perception and memory, the next question is whether recognizability results carry through to viewers' beliefs about caricatures. We know how viewers react to caricatures in various ways that show that viewers' visual systems are registering a likeness, but are viewers likely consciously to affirm a caricature to be a likeness? Rhodes and Tremewen (1996) studied face caricatures varying in distortion and found that 30% to 50% distortions facilitated recognition, yet 10% caricatures were judged to be best likenesses (Rhodes, 1996, p. 102). However, Benson and Perrett (1994) allowed viewers also to act as artists by giving them a slider that controlled caricature distortion on the screen; and some 40% distortion was produced in a best likeness task. The stimuli were then checked for recognizability, and a satisfactory fit was obtained in the data. It seems that when participants are put in the artist's role, they tend to adopt a realist stance on ensuring that visual information "issues easily" from the drawing; and when participants are put in the viewers' role, they use more naturalistic criteria for judging likeness. Consonant with that, viewers generally rated photographs as truer likenesses than professional caricatures of famous faces in most of the conditions used by Tversky and Baratz (1985). Finally, note that photographs can be put into a caricature program and thus produce photographic caricatures. Such pictures trigger a strong naturalistic preference for undistorted images as best likeness (Benson & Perrett, 1991; Ellis, 1992). It is essential to see whether there would be a tilt toward realism when participants themselves produce photographic caricatures. It is essential to find out whether the previous empirical effects extend to recognition and judgment of aspects, such as mood.

PICTORIAL COMMUNICATION

Communication systems all involve one small set of relations between a communicator and a receiver. Constraints on those relations allow agents to agree on what information is transmitted from one mind to another. Thus, with language, "When noises have meaning they do not only have distinctive relations with human beings who use them or respond to them but also distinctive connections with some . . . states of affairs . . . in the world" (Heal, 1978, p. 367). That is, communication *of* something is from an agent *to* an agent *via* an utterance. Those four entities are the irreducible minimum needed for defining linguistic communication. Cognate terms for pictorial communication are *artist*, *viewer*, *picture*, and *referent*. They may become empirically very close-knit, as when an artist makes a self-portrait and is the first viewer of the finished product. But no matter how close-knit the relations become, those four entities are analytically distinct. A theory of pictures, whether in the mind of the scientist or in the mind of the lay viewing public, must encompass relations between the four entities. That is the main thrust of a broad analysis of pictorial reasoning (Freeman, 1995). The problem for children is that pictorial reasoning has to be spread broadly over all four entities. That is why pictorial reasoning is a lifelong endeavor (Freeman, 2000). For each of the topics of expressivity, beauty, and recognizability, it is straightforward to lay out how people can vary in their thinking. Here is an example for beauty.

1. Beauty might be assumed to be an objective *property of a picture*, much like the complexity of its lines is an objective property (as studied by Hekkert, 1995, for cubism).
2. Another assumption would be that beauty is a function of whatever *referent* is recognizable. Parsons (1987) suggested that learners in such a phase would deny that one could get a beautiful picture of an old and rusting automobile. Young children assume that if a referent were ugly, then a picture of it would necessarily be ugly in the same way as the referent itself. That rigid concept of resemblance neglects the agency of the artist.

3. A third assumption would be that the *artist* was the responsible agent, beautifying a picture regardless of the referent, analogous to the power of a decorator to do up a decrepit house. Hekkert's (1995) series of experiments revealed a component of inexpert viewers' preference as being a requirement that artists' agency be apparent in their mastery in production.

4. Finally, beauty might be assumed to be a function of the *viewer*, "beauty is in the eye of the beholder." That conception operates as though the viewer held all the power of agency in the situation and direction of fit were from picture to mind in the viewer, irrespective of what the picture might display and how powerful the artist's expressivity might be.

Is it likely that people develop very firm assumptions about pictorial beauty? It is certainly common to regard being beautiful as a prime attribute of pictorial success. Kindler and Darras (1998) interviewed 7- to 14-year-olds in British Columbia, Quebec, and France, in the absence of pictures. The question of interest here is "what is a good drawing?" The most common attribute across the cultures was that the drawing be "beautiful." Thereafter, there was interesting cultural diversity, with consideration of expressive quality being second for Quebec participants, but low for others. What we can take from that study is that in order to be the most common attribute emerging over and above a degree of cultural diversity, a conception of beauty must be rooted in some very firm assumption or other. In a probe for assumptions about pictorial beauty, Freeman and Sanger (1995) interviewed Anguillan children who had no art training beyond the chance to paint at Sunday school. Most 11-year-olds maintained that an ugly thing would make a worse picture than a pretty thing. The children's reasoning was mainly "if something is ugly, you would have to draw an ugly picture, and an ugly picture is a bad picture." That is, (a) beauty or ugliness exists in the referent, (b) it becomes transferred onto a picture surface, and (c) the terms "pretty" and "ugly" map onto "good" and "bad," so (d) if something is ugly then it must be bad. The children were in accord with the formulation of classical naturalism, where "The work of art is conceived as the mirror for natural beauty" And "... naturalism ... may be inconsistent with some of the senses of 'realism'" (Osborne, 1970, p. 767). Most 14-year-olds maintained that it did not follow that if something were ugly a picture of it would be bad and largely explained that the outcome depends on the artist's skills and enthusiasm. Those children were spontaneously shifting from focusing on the picture–referent relation to invoking the artist–picture relation that the interviewer had not explicitly mentioned. That is a shift toward regarding pictures as communications of the artist's competence (see Gross, 1973). The prediction is that the shift would be even further delayed in a systematic replication with questioning about photographs. Freeman and Sanger (1993) noted that the shift occurred in English city children some 3 years younger. The suggestion is that the same conceptual shift occurs in urban English children and Caribbean island rural children, just on a different timescale. Evidence for that suggestion came from asking children questions that explicitly mentioned other relations in the intentional net. Younger children largely applied the same resemblance argument for expressivity as for beauty, whereby an artist feeling happy or sad produces a happy or sad picture. Maybe the children were using some notion of emotional projection; but another finding does not entirely support that idea, whereby the younger children largely held that a viewer's mood could not affect viewing. For them what the picture is, is what you see. As hypothesized, the viewer was the last entity to be integrated into thinking, with a conception of viewer autonomy emerging in the older children. It is worth noting that even 3-year-olds understand that viewers differ in their liking for drawings (Hart & Goldin-Meadow, 1984); they understand that the viewer–picture relation can vary. But that is a long way from understanding viewers as representational agents whose culturally relative pictorial judgment will vary depending on what they bring to the viewing situation (see Parsons, 1987).

STUDIES OF THE EARLIEST SIGNS OF PICTORIAL REASONING

General debate over intention in production can be traced back to Luquet (1927). He argued that preschool children are accustomed to start off with an intention to draw some particular referent, and if the emerging drawing seems to resemble something else, they may switch to a new interpretation (see Freeman, 1972, for a critique). Even children as old as 4 years of age may only recently have emerged from the phase where they pretend to act as artists by stipulating what their scribbles show, suspending the truth condition of recognizability of referents. A child's scribble of mother falls short of depicting her because it "simply does not represent her as having any visual properties—properties she may be seen to have" (Lopes, 1997, p. 98). For a century, researchers have been offered the stark alternatives that early scribbles (a) reveal as-yet unmodelable connections between representational intent and product (see Smith, 1979; also Stephan, 1990, pp. 94–99), or (b) "show the utter lack of any apparent connection between a mental picture in consciousness and the movements made by the hands and fingers in attempting to draw it" (Lukens, 1986, pp. 79–80). The latter has been decisively disconfirmed, and the former has been made more precise.

A longstanding empirical problem has been that many 2–year-olds stay silent when asked what their scribbles show. It transpires that it is possible to elicit a high level of replies if the experimenter points to segments of the scribble. Adi-Japha, Levin, and Solomon (1997) identified a regularity specifying (a) what segment will elicit a representational reply and (b) under what conditions. Let us take those two in turn. Inflected lines were stronger stimuli than smooth curves. The authors showed that the distinction could be formulated in terms of a psychophysical function governing the speed of the pen. Inflections involve slowing the pen. The suggestion is that making an inflection involves an effort of production that primes focal attention to the mark. The conditions under which the inflection advantage held were illuminating. The advantage was disrupted by even moderate delay, suggesting that a memory of the act of production was important. That rules out the possibility that the advantage was solely a product of associative visual memory in which, for some reason, a greater number of inflected forms than smooth forms were stored. Congruent with that, the advantage vanished when the segments were in another child's scribble or in the experimenter's copy of the child's own scribble. Long before children's own productions can trigger content recognition in a viewer, a basis is laid for some conception of an active relation of production. There is no evidence that any of the 2-year-olds' interpretations were other than post hoc as opposed to preplanned representational intent. Some evidence for a connection between representation and fulfilled prior intention can be found by asking children to draw a segment of an otherwise finished picture. Freeman (1980, pp. 5–6) gave a 2-year-old scribbler incomplete drawings to scribble over on condition that he stated what he was going to draw before he started. The resulting scribbles were uninterpretable; but for each segment, the pen hit at the start precisely where it should to complete the drawing (for sample data on multicue control see Freeman, 1980, pp. 198–201). For viewers only of the finished product, the representational intent visible during the process of scribble production had been hidden in noise.

Systematic evidence for a connection between representation and fulfilled intention comes from 3-year-olds. Gelman and Ebeling (1997) used pictures that appeared poorly done but could be seen as representational (e.g., a bear). Children were told that the markings either (a) had arisen by accident (e.g., someone knocking over a paint pot) or (b) had been intentionally produced by someone. The children were then asked to describe each picture. The intentional group had had the artist–picture relation primed; they named the contents much more than did the unintentional group. One possibility is that the intentional group noticed the contents of the pictures more than the unintentional group did. It is feasible to do a systematic replication varying pictorial realism to counterpose intention against a successfulness of a product as it looks to a viewer. It is important to discover whether the intention effect (a) applies across the board to different levels of realism or (b) leads to a lower criterion for a recognizable picture, to encompass less realistic pictures. A more powerful study was reported by Bloom and Markson (1998). In one circumstance, preschool children were asked to draw a balloon on a string. The drawing was put away. On a separate occasion the children were asked to draw a lollipop. A balloon on a string can be visually parsed as a volume on an extended thin object and thence pictorially mapped onto a circle on a line. But so can a lollipop. If a preschool child produces virtually identical drawings of balloon and lollipop, how can anyone decide which picture is which? Bloom and Markson (1998) reported that the children who had produced the circle-line drawings used recall of own prior intention to label their own drawings; and sometimes protested if the experimenter deliberately transposed labels. Let us put the finding in formal terms: When the shape on the page did not serve its usual role in deciding what shape in the outside world was the referent, preschool children relied on a memory of the causal history of production to label what each drawing referentially communicated. The authors' general conclusion was that "Children might call a picture that looks like a bird 'a bird' not merely because it looks like a bird, but because its appearance makes it likely that it was created with the intent to represent a bird. In general, appearance—and shape in particular—is seen as an excellent cue to intention" (Bloom & Markson, 1998, p. 203).

It would be unsafe to credit the preschool children with a deep grasp of representational principles, but their pictorial decision accorded with an insistence in the literature that knowledge of causal history may legitimate an interpretation. Thus, a picture of you represents you and not your identical twin (see Schier, 1986; also Perner, 1991). It could even be true that your twin has never been drawn or photographed by anyone. The representing relation is here analogous to a written marriage contract; someone who marries you does not thereby marry your twin, not even if your parents had absentmindedly given both of you the same name which is thus written on the marriage contract. A picture of a lollipop is not a picture of a balloon even if the two can be depicted identically. An analogy can also be taken from intentional communication terms: The word "bank" denoting a riverside does not denote a financial institution even though the pronunciation is identical. The resemblance is not a relevant resemblance. From a variety of theoretical perspectives, analyses of representation and of communicative relevance crucially intersect (see Freeman, 2000; Harrison, 1997; Hobson, 1993; Schier, 1986; Searle, 1982; Sinha, 1988; Wollheim, 1987). A working definition of representational depiction should include the notion of "someone's attempt to communicate preserve, or express" something (DeLoache, Pierroutsakos, & Troseth, 1997, p. 3). Pictures not only allow a viewer "to see things but also allow one person to communicate with another. This means they are almost invariably subordinate to intention" (Kennedy, Gabias, & Pierantoni, 1990, p. 43). In Bloom and Markson's (1998) experiment, the causal history included the artist's representational intent. Bloom and Markson argued that viewers categorize pictures as functional artifacts that realize intentions. Viewers assume that if a drawing is seen to have a similar shape to something else such as a clothespin, it would be extremely unlikely that the two appearances would have been made to match by accident.

It is feasible to ask how viewers' interpretation of what they see in a picture weighs evidence from a producer's state of mind against the appearance of the finished product. Thus, in a set of studies on adult drawing where "Both skilled and unskilled artists overestimated the accuracy of rendering regardless of who created the rendering ... the artists may have recognized what the critics may have missed: the intent behind the marks ... an understanding of the intent behind a mark may translate into a higher estimation of the accuracy of the rendering" (Cohen & Bennett, 1997, p. 620).

An account of viewers' assumptions must incorporate an idea of a picture as an artifact, made by one agent (artist) and available for use by another agent (viewer) who, in the Bloom–Markson (1998) and Cohen–Bennett (1997) studies, had commissioned the artist to depict named things. Note how Bloom and Markson's formulation reflects the shift in aesthetic argument that was noted in the opening section of the present chapter: A mental analysis, rather than a picture being central, takes center stage. What is central is not the shape on the page exerting its effects on a viewer but the communicative intentions of the picture producer. Bloom (2000) argued that the intentional analysis is not peculiar to the pictorial domain. Sensitivity to communicators' intentions is central to children's learning in general. Of course, children might misread intentions, and the communicator might well be animated by intentions below the level of conscious awareness. But that is a different matter: Any learning-approach makes mistakes.

There are data showing that some preschool children confuse the properties of a referent with the properties of a picture. In general, it seems that discrimination between picture properties and referent properties is established by some 19 months of age (DeLoache, Pierroutsakos, Uttal, Rosengren, & Gottlieb, 1998) but takes time to become effective under test conditions. Preschool children may predict that a picture of an ice-cream will feel cold and be edible. Maybe some of the children have yet to learn that the medium does not transparently allow the transfer of those particular properties from the referent. However, such errors often vanish with counter-suggestion or an invitation to eat the picture (Beilin & Pearlman, 1991). More persistent failure, even in 4-year-olds, to separate picture from referent comes from studies in which a photograph is taken, then the referent is changed, and the child is asked what the photograph depicts. Updating the picture occurs, as though the depiction were tied to reality instead of being a representation of its aspect at the time of depiction (Leekam & Perner, 1991; Leslie & Thaiss, 1992; Peterson & Siegal, 1998; Slaughter, 1998; Zaitchik, 1990). However, a crucial constraint on the error was noted by Robinson, Nye, and Thomas (1994), in systematic replication involving the experimenter making line drawings. The design included a converse test in which the line drawing was changed and the child was asked to predict whether the referent would change. Updating errors were clearly asymmetrical, running from referent to picture rather than the reverse. That is, the child may regard a picture as tied to reality, but is less likely to regard reality as tied to a picture. That is at least in the right direction: A picture might become uninterpretable when its referent gets destroyed, but reality does not vanish if a picture gets destroyed. It is a plausible guess that the average 3-year-old would not be terror stricken if a drawing of her were torn up (Freeman, 1991).

Robinson, Riggs, and Samuel (1996) ran a deceptive box task in which 3- and 4-year-olds were asked what they thought was in a smartie tube, and to draw the contents, then were shown that the contents were marbles and were asked to recall what they had first thought and drawn as (mis)representations of the contents. Recall of the caption of the drawing was 70% accurate, compared with 45% accurate recall of the prior belief. In another study in which the child watched someone else doing the test, recall was 85% for drawing and 63% for belief. Let us first consider children's successes. It was easier for children to categorize a drawing as a representation that can mismatch reality than to categorize a prior belief as a misrepresentation. Children who have only a rudimentary theory of mind as indexed by the standard deceptive box test are likely to have precociously acquired a concept of depiction, and the two can readily be empirically dissociated (Slaughter, 1998).

Finally, what is the role of the viewer in young children's assumptions? Taylor (1988) showed children, between 3 and 8 years of age, pictures of animals (e.g., a giraffe), drawing attention to the aspect that was depicted (e.g., sitting). Viewers were then allowed restricted views of the picture, ranging from a tiny edge to a small part that would only just reveal what species was depicted. Half the children up to 5 years of age reported on at least one trial that even a tiny edge was sufficient for the viewer to recognize the species. Above the age of 3 years, there was less tendency also to claim that the viewer would recognize the aspect under which the referent was depicted. Pillow (1994) showed children a segment of a picture, say a triangle, and asked them what they thought it was before revealing the rest of the picture in which the triangle turned out to be the roof of a house. The procedure was repeated. On the third presentation the triangle turned out to be a shark fin. The whole procedure was repeated with a fresh viewer while the child watched. The child was asked to predict how the viewer would interpret the triangle on the third trial before seeing the whole card. The correct answer "roof" and not "shark" was only at some 50% level even in 6-year-olds. Chandler and Lalonde (1994) confirmed that one cannot rely on children under some 7 years of age to take into account in their pictorial inferences other viewers' epistemic states. The overall indication is that the viewer is the last entity to be incorporated into pictorial reasoning. It may even be the case that a slogan like "beauty is in the eye of the beholder" is actually a rather advanced formulation. The formulation appears to be a trite comment on people's tastes differing, and so it might be in the minds of many. But it is also conceivable that the formulation reflects a discovery of the agency of the viewer. If that be so, it is rather a creditable discovery that can be built on, instead of being used to foreclose discussion in line with the well-worn notion that there is nothing to argue about where differences in taste arise.

EDUCATIONAL CHALLENGES

Innovations in art put a strain on the everyday aesthetic reasoning of the viewing public. That is, artists invent a new method of production, and viewers deploy commonsense assumptions to test claims about the products. Any account of aesthetic judgment has to explain the nature of challenging encounters with artworks that might lead viewers to reflect on their pictorial assumptions (Parsons, 1987) or to reject the artwork. Many viewers exhibit resistance when entering a collection of assemblages of junk (see Matravers, 1994) or canvasses in varying shades of gray. Viewers may well reject an innovation, expressing concern and dismay at any gallery paying good money for whatever artwork it is that is taken to be an affront. And yet it would be a big mistake to let one's attention be captured by the fact of expressed rejection. That distracts one's attention from an analysis of what pictorial reasoning underlies the rejection. Often enough, expressed rejection seems to be generated by an attempt to articulate that the artist has failed to communicate. In this section we examine that possibility and ask what the educational implications are.

In the earlier section on pictorial communication, it was noted that the irreducible minimum is to consider the four terms: *artist, viewer, picture,* and *referent.* Given four terms, it follows that people might give weight to one term more than to other terms in any particular situation of a pictorial puzzle. We went through the possibility of children progressing from thinking that the beauty of a picture came directly from the referent, or scene, depicted, so that a picture acted rather like a mirror held up to nature. Another possibility was of a development to grasping the role of an artist who uses the power of agency as a beautifier, much as a decorator beautifies a blank room that is just waiting for something to be done. And two other possibilities were considered. The assumption we use in this section is that mature people become accustomed to thinking about artworks in terms of the four entities in the communication network. It follows that if a particular artwork appears to obscure the role of any one of the four entities, people will react by trying to repair the damage; so the viewers will thereby attempt to reinstate their ideas of communication.

Consider for the moment the "case of the vanishing artist." The lesson will be that it is absolutely fine to foster innovation and experimentation in art education, as long as it be accompanied by an awareness of exactly how the innovation challenges the viewing public. The fostering of such awareness in art students is in itself educational; it helps them become aware of how a diversity of other people may react to their work.

First, there has been a history of artists attempting to focus viewers' attention onto the picture by removing recognizable referents in favor of abstract patterns. Sometimes that can have unifying effects on viewers, as in responding to Mondrian abstracts, as was noted earlier. Sometimes it can misfire, as in the heyday of Abstract Expressionism where the artist might even walk over the canvas. Learners give weight to a commonsense notion that a pictorial artwork ought to be seen to be well crafted (Hekkert, 1995). Ironically, an attempt by expressionist artists physically to unite with the artwork had rendered both artist and artistry invisible, so viewers had nowhere for their concept of interpretation to grip—"anyone could do that." Art critics justified the abstracts as historically necessary, arguing from traditions of picture-to-picture fit (see Wolfe, 1975, for polemical opposition). Viewers who reasonably rely on being able to think in terms of an intact communication model, which includes an artist's relation to a picture, often resist critics' deployment of art history. Gross (1973) argued that viewers are right to expect evidence on why the artist chose as she did, and what the organization is that would allow the viewer to admire the art by admiration of artistry.

Second, consider a case where the artist seems to vanish in favor of some other agency. It is, in principle, possible for an ant to leave a pattern on the sand that looks like Winston Churchill (see Putnam, 1981). The pattern is not an artifact but a natural kind which has migrated to take the artist's position. The artist's vanishing can be repaired by anyone willing to claim the role of artist. Someone could take a cast of the sand pattern and put it on display. Production is shared between that artist and the ant as unwitting accomplice. Such is the logic behind the display of *objets trouvés* in galleries. The products rely for their effect on the ambiguity between attributing responsibility to the natural producer, to the vision of the viewer who discerned initial possibilities, and to her subsequent action as an artist. It is no accident that Damien Hirst's animal corpses framed in tanks challenge the hard-won reasoning of a vast section of the viewing public. So did Carl Andre's unframed bricks *Equivalent VIII* (see Eaton, 1988, for discussion). Recently, a movement has arisen to reinstate artists proactively—"with biological art, the artist doesn't finish his own creation. He begins the work and lets the silkworm finish it off by laying silk over the original design" (Magan, 1997, p. 3). It is safe to predict that a movement will arise to let the animal start the production and the artist intervene before or at the end. It seems equally safe to predict that the artists will have to give viewers explicit briefing about what is going on.

Third, consider cases where the artists exert their authority by removing anything that viewers would consider to be a picture. At the opening of the 2001 Turner Prize exhibition at Tate Britain, the curator announced that the prize-winning artwork was particularly significant in being a critical moment in the trend of the dematerialization of art since the 1960s. The artwork by Martin Creed was an empty room with lights spasmodically flickering. The work "has had people spluttering and complaining that anyone could have done it" (Searle, 2001, p. 3). The role of the artist had been cut out of viewers' model of thinking, and they wanted something to fill the place. To fill the place with "anyone" is not remotely satisfying. It is no remedy to tell viewers that even if they could have done it, it so happens that they had not done it. That does not answer the viewers' point. The point is to know what made the installation worth doing. And that is not easy to discern. It is even harder with the March 2002 exhibition at the Birmingham Custard Factory. Ana Benloch and Stuart Tait left the exhibition room bare. So if viewers wanted to imagine artworks, they could, but that was all the art experience that was on offer. So here, both artist agency and artwork had decisively been removed from being on offer. It is hard to think of what information to offer viewers in such a case to make up for their minds not necessarily being engaged. It would not help to tell them that a visit to the exhibition would be a bit like a visit to a restaurant that told you that you were free to imagine any food you like, and that was all you were going to get. It is hard in such a case to distinguish between artistic wit and artistic dereliction of duty. And if that was the purpose of the exhibition, it needs meticulous spelling out and assimilably offering to visitors. It might be supposed that nothing can come of nothing. But that is not entirely true. Important presentation of empty space can be done. At the opening in 1999 of Daniel Libeskind's Jewish museum in Berlin, all exhibits were kept out, by public demand. The public wanted to see and feel the empty space. The attraction grew; and by the end of the year, some half a million people had come. Libeskind had made it possible for people to come to terms with vital emotions through moving through an important space. Nothing more was necessary. But then it usually is not if you get things right. And that, ultimately, was why the Tate Britain and the Birmingham Custard Factory exhibitions were failures to engage and educate the viewing public: Nothing assured them that everything or anything had been done to get things right.

With artworks nowadays, things can be gotten right. Communication can be achieved. The concerns of the viewing public can be addressed. But to address people's minds, it is necessary to understand the assumptions they bring to the viewing situation (Parsons, 1987). It is not necessary to use information about people's assumptions to pander to their biases. But it is such a waste of an educational possibility not to be respectful of people's intuitive tendency to think in terms of communication.

In summary, communication is not confined to exchanging utterances or gestures; instead there is a variety of cultural devices whereby we try to bridge the gap between minds and between physical and mental realities. For example, photographs can make the look of things portable, communicating to a viewer how the agent felt about a scene, or what he or she remembers about it, maybe even inviting the viewer to compare her memory of the scene with that of the agent. Pictures are important prostheses, enabling protagonists to stage-manage a meeting of minds. Innovations in art may challenge viewers' habitual way of seeking meaning in art. Some innovations can readily be classified so as to make salient exactly what challenge is involved. Education may well involve explaining the challenge, respectfully. With respect, that is, toward the hard-won assumptions people develop and the pattern of reasoning they undertake when they judge artworks.

REFERENCES

Adi-Japha, E., Levin, I., & Solomon, S. (1997). Emergence of representation in drawing: The relation between kinematic and referential aspects. *Cognitive Development, 13*, 23–49.

Beilin, H., & Pearlman, E. G. (1991). Children's iconic realism: Object versus property realism. In H. W. Reese (Ed.), *Advances in child development and behavior* (Vol. 23, pp. 73–112). San Diego, CA: Academic Press.

Beloff, H. (1985). *Camera culture*. Oxford, UK: Blackwell.

Belver, M. H. (1989). *Psicologia del arte y criterio estetico*. Salamanca, Spain: Amaru.

Benson, P. J., & Perrett, P. I. (1991). Perception and recognition of photographic facial quality caricatures: Implications for the recognition of natural images. *European Journal of Cognitive Psychology, 3*, 105–135.

Benson, P. J., & Perrett, P. I. (1994). Visual processing of facial distinctiveness. *Perception, 23*, 75–93.

Biederman, I., & Kalocsai, P. (1997). Neurocomputational bases of object and face recognition. *Philosophical Transactions of the Royal Society of London (Series B) 352*, 1203–1219.

Bloom, P. (2000). *How children learn the meanings of words*. Cambridge, MA: MIT Press.

Bloom, P., & Markson, L. (1998). Intention and analogy in children's naming of pictorial representations. *Psychological Science, 9*, 200–204.

Brennan, S. E. (1985). The caricature generator. *Leonardo, 18*, 170–178.

Calder, A. J., Young, A. W., Benson, P. J., & Perrett, D. I. (1996). Self priming from distinctive and caricatured faces. *British Journal of Psychology, 87*, 141–162.

Caloni, B., & Morra, S. (1990). *Exploring the intentional depiction of emotions*. Poster at the Fourth European Developmental Psychology Conference, Stirling August, 28–31.

Callaghan, T. C. (1997). Children's judgements of emotions portrayed in museum art. *British Journal of Developmental Psychology, 15*, 515–529.

Chandler, M., & Lalonde, C. (1994). Shifting to an interpretative theory of mind. In A. Sameroff & M. Haith (Eds.), *Reasons and responsibility*. Chicago, IL: University of Chicago Press.

Cohen, D. J., & Bennett, S. (1997). Why can't most people draw what they see? *Journal of Experimental Psychology: Human Perception and Performance, 23*, 609–621.

DeLoache, J. S., Pierroutsakos, S. L., & Troseth, G. L. (1997). The Three 'R's of pictorial competence. In R. Vasta (Ed.), *Annals of child development* (Vol. 12, pp. 1–48). Bristol, UK: Jessica Kingsley Publishers.

DeLoache, J. S., Pierroutsakos, S. L., Uttal, D. H., Rosengren, K. S., & Gottlieb, A. (1998). Grasping the nature of pictures. *Psychological Science, 9*, 205–210.

Dorment, R. (2002). Intense master creates show of the summer: Review of Lucien Freud retrospective, *The Daily Telegraph*, June 19, 8–9.

Eaton, M. (1988). *Basic issues in aesthetics*. Belmont, CA: Wadsworth.

Ellis, H. (1992). The development of face processing skills. *Philosophical Transactions of the Royal Society, Series B, 335*, 105–111.

Freeman, N. H. (1972). Process and product in children's drawing. *Perception, 1*, 123–140.

Freeman, N. H. (1980). *Strategies of representation in young children: Analysis of spatial skills and drawing processes*. London: Academic Press.

Freeman, N. H. (1991). The theory of art that underpins children's naïve realism. *Visual Arts Research, 17*, 65–75.

Freeman, N. H. (1993). Drawing: public instruments of representation. In C. Pratt & A. F. Garton (Eds.), *Systems of representation in children* (pp. 113–132). Chichester, UK: Wiley.

Freeman, N. H. (1995). The emergence of a framework theory of pictorial reasoning. In C. Lange-Kuttner & G. V. Thomas (Eds.), *Drawing and looking* (pp. 135–146). Hemel Hempstead, UK: Harvester Wheatsheaf.

Freeman, N. H. (2000). Communication and representation: Why mentalistic reasoning is a lifelong endeavour. In P. Mitchell & K. Riggs (Eds.), *Children's reasoning and the mind* (pp. 349–366). Hove, UK: Psychology Press.

Freeman, N. H., & Parker, D. M. (1973). Affective preference and misclassification in a novel/familiar identification task. *British Journal of Psychology, 64*, 77–81.

Freeman, N. H., & Parsons, M. J. (2001). Children's intuitive understanding of pictures. In B. Torff & R. J. Sternberg (Eds.), *Understanding and teaching the intuitive mind* (pp. 73–92). Hove, UK: Erlbaum.

Freeman, N. H., & Sanger, D. (1993). Language and belief in critical thinking: Emerging explanations of pictures. *Exceptionality Education Canada, 3*, 43–58.

Freeman, N. H., & Sanger, D. (1995). The commonsense aesthetics of rural children. *Visual Arts Research, 21*, 1–10.

Gelman, S. A., & Ebeling, K. S. (1997, April). *The influence of shape and representational status on children's naming*. Poster presented at the biennial meeting of the Society for Research in Child Development. Washington, DC.

Golomb, C. (2003). *The child's creation of a pictorial world*. Berkeley, CA: University of California Press.

Gombrich, E. H. (1960). *Art and illusion: A study in the psychology of pictorial representation*. Oxford, UK: Phaidon.

Gombrich, E. H. (1972). The mask and the face: The perception of physiognomic likeness in life and in art. In E. H. Gombrich, J. Hochberg & M. Black (Eds.), *Art, perception and reality* (pp. 24–37). Baltimore MD: Johns Hopkins University Press.

Goodman, N. (1976). *Languages of art* (2nd ed.). Indianapolis, IN: Hackett.

Gross, L. (1973). Art as the communication of competence. *Social Science Information, 12*, 115–141.

Harrison, A. (1997). *Philosophy and the arts: Seeing and believing*. Bristol, UK: Thoemmes Press.

Hart, L. M., & Goldin-Meadow, S. (1984). The child as a nonegocentric art critic. *Child Development, 55*, 2122–2129.

Heal, J. (1978). On the phrase "theory of meaning." *Mind, 87*, 359–375.

Hekkert, P. P. M. (1995). *Artful judgements: A psychological inquiry into aesthetic preference for visual patterns*. The Hague, Netherlands: Cip-Gegevens Koninklijke Bibliotheek.

Hobson, R. P. (1993). *Autism and the development of mind*. Hove, UK: Lawrence Erlbaum Associates.

Hopkins, J. (1992). Psychoanalysis, interpretation, and science. In J. Hopkins & A. Savile (Eds.), *Psychoanalysis, mind and art: Perspectives on Richard Wollheim*. Oxford, UK: Blackwell.

Hopkins, R. (1998). *Picture, image and experience*. Cambridge, UK: Cambridge university Press.

Kelly, M. (1998). *Encyclopedia of aesthetics*. Oxford: Oxford University Press.

Kennedy, J. M., Gabias, P., & Pierantoni, R. (1990). Meaning, presence and absence in pictures. In K. Landwehr (Ed.), *Ecological perception research, visual communication, and aesthetics* (pp. 43–56). London: Springer-Verlag.

Kindler, A. M., & Darras, B. (1998). Culture and development of pictorial repertoires. *Studies in Art Education, 39*, 147–163.

Kose, G. (1985). Children's knowledge of photography: A study of developing awareness of a representational medium. *British Journal of Developmental Psychology, 3*, 373–384.

Leekam, S. R., & Perner, J. (1991). Does the autistic child have a metarepresentational deficit? *Cognition, 40*, 203–218.

Leslie, A. M., & Thaiss, L. (1992). Domain specificity in conceptual development: Neuropsychological evidence from autism. *Cognition, 43*, 225–251.

Lopes, D. (1997). *Understanding pictures*. Oxford, UK: Clarendon Press.

Lukens, H. T. (1986). A study of children's drawings in the early years. *Pedagogical Seminary, 4,* 79–110.

Luquet, G. H. (1927). *Le dessin enfantin.* Paris: Alcan.

Lynch, M., & Edgerton, S. (1988). Aesthetics and digital image processing: Representational craft in contemporary astronomy. In G. Fyfe & J. Law (Eds.), *Picturing power: Visual depiction and social relations.* London: Routledge.

Magan, C. (1997). *Arte biologico.* Toledo, Spain: Museo de Santa Cruz.

Maridaki-Kassotaki, K., & Freeman, N. H. (2000). Concepts of pictures on display. *Empirical Studies of the Arts, 18,* 151–158.

Matravers, D. (1994). Why some modern art is junk. *Cogito, 8,* 19–25.

McManus, I. C., Kumar, B., & Stoker, J. (1993). The aesthetics of composition: A study of Mondrian. *Empirical Studies of the Arts, 11,* 83–94.

Neisser, U. (1967). *Cognitive psychology.* New York: Appleton-Century-Crofts.

O' Hanlon, K. (1997, October 16). Independent law report: Jury can decide age of child in indecent photograph. *The Independent,* p. 19.

Osborne, H. (1970). *The Oxford companion to art.* Oxford, UK: Clarendon Press.

Parsons, M. J. (1987). *How we understand art.* Cambridge, UK: Cambridge University Press.

Pearson, D., Hanna, E., & Martinez, K. (1990). Computer generated cartoons. In H. Barlow, C. Blakemore, & M. Weston-Smith (Eds.), *Images and understanding* (pp. 46–60). Cambridge, UK: Cambridge University Press.

Perkins, D. N., & Hagen, M. A. (1980). Convention, context, and caricature. In M. A. Hagen (Ed.), *The perception of pictures* (Vol. 1). Alberti's window. New York: Academic Press.

Perner, J. (1991). *Understanding the representational mind.* Cambridge, MA: The MIT Press.

Peterson, C. C., & Siegal, M. (1998). Changing focus on the representational mind: Deaf, autistic and normal children's concepts of false photos, false drawings and false beliefs. *British Journal of Developmental Psychology, 16,* 301–320.

Pillow B. (1994). *Do 4-year-olds understand biased interpretation?* Poster presented at the biennial meeting of the Society for Research in Child Development, New Orleans.

Plato (1994). *The Republic* (Trans. R. Waterfield). Oxford, UK: Oxford University Press.

Putnam, H. (1981). *Reason, truth and history.* Cambridge, UK: Cambridge University Press.

R. v. Land (Michael). (1997). *Current law year handbook,* Vol. 1, 1282, No. 1160, 446. London: Sweet and Maxwell.

Rhodes, G. (1996). *Superportraits: Caricatures and recognition.* Hove, UK: Psychology Press.

Rhodes, G., Brennan, S., & Carey, S. (1987). Identification and rating of caricatures: Implications for mental representation of faces. *Cognitive Psychology, 19,* 473–497.

Rhodes, G., & McLean, I. G. (1990). Distinctiveness and expertise effects with homogeneous stimuli: Towards a model of configural coding. *Perception, 19,* 773–794.

Rhodes, G., & Tremewen, T. (1996). Averageness, exaggeration and facial attractiveness. *Psychological Science, 7,* 105–110.

Robinson, E. J., Nye, R., & Thomas, G. V. (1994). Children's conception of the relationships between pictures and their referents. *Cognitive Development, 9,* 165–191.

Robinson, E. J., Riggs, K. J., & Samuel, J. (1996). Children's memory for drawings based on a false belief. *Developmental Psychology, 32,* 1056–1064.

Salfner, B., & Voigtmann, R. (1999). The oncological pavilion in Bochum University Hospital. In M. Roselli (Ed.), *Visual art in hospitals* (pp. 73–90). Florence: Gli Ori, Maschietto e Musolino.

Sartwell, C. (1994). Realism. In D. E. Cooper (Ed.), *A companion to aesthetics* (pp. 354–357). Oxford, UK: Blackwell.

Schier, F. (1986). *Deeper into pictures.* Cambridge, UK: Cambridge University Press.

Searle, J. R. (1982). What is an intentional state? In H. L. Dreyfus (Ed.), *Husserl, intentionality and cognitive science* (pp. 259–276). Cambridge, MA: MIT Press.

Searle, A. (2001). Judges switched on as Turner prize goes to Creed of nothingness. *The Guardian,* December 10, 3.

Sinha, C. (1988). *Language and representation.* Hemel Hempstead, UK: Harvester Wheatsheaf.

Slaughter, V. (1998). Children's understanding of pictorial and mental representations. *Child Development, 69,* 321–332.

Smith, N. R. (1979). How a picture means. *New Directions for Child Development, 3,* 59–72.

Solso, R. L. (1994). *Cognition and the visual arts.* Cambridge, MA: The MIT Press.

Stephan, M. (1990). *A transformational theory of aesthetics.* London: Routledge.

Stevenage, S. S. V. (1995). Can caricatures really produce distinctiveness effects? *British Journal of Psychology, 86,* 127–146.

Tanaka, J. W., & Simon, V. B. (1996). Caricature recognition in a neural network. *Visual Cognition, 3,* 305–324.

Taylor, M. (1988). Development of children's understanding of the seeing-knowing distinction. In J. W. Astington, P. L. Harris, & D. R. Olson (Eds.), *Developing theories of mind* (pp. 207–225). Cambridge, UK: Cambridge University Press.

Taylor, R., Micolich, A., & Jonas, D. (1999). Fractal expressionism. *Physics World, 12,* 25–28.

Turner, P. (1983). Children's responses to art: Interpretation and criticism. *Journal of Art and Design Education, 2,* 185–198.

Tversky, B. T., & Baratz, D. (1985). Memory for faces: Are caricatures better than photographs? *Memory and Cognition, 13,* 45–49.

Vajda, M. (1986). Aesthetic judgement and the world view in painting. In A. Heller & F. Feher (Eds.), *Reconstructing aesthetics* (pp. 119–149). Oxford, UK: Blackwell.

Vanderplas, J. M., & Garvin, E. A. (1959). The association value of random shapes. *Journal of Experimental Psychology, 57,* 147–154.

Willats, J. (1997). *Art and representation: New principles in the analysis of pictures.* Princeton, NJ: Princeton University Press.

Wolfe, T. (1975). *The painted word.* New York: Farrar, Straus & Giroux.

Wollheim, R. (1987). *Painting as an art.* London: Thames & Hudson.

Wollheim, R. (1993). *The mind and its depths.* Cambridge, MA: Harvard University Press.

Zaitchik, D. (1990). When representations conflict with reality: The preschooler's problem with false beliefs and "false" photographs. *Cognition, 35,* 41–68.

Ziller, R. C. (1990). *Photographing the self.* London: Sage.

17

Learning in the Visual Arts: Characteristics of Gifted and Talented Individuals

David Pariser[1]
Concordia University

Enid Zimmerman
Indiana University

In this research review about art learning and talented individuals, we first introduce theoretical concepts and then discuss the educational implications of these concepts. Definitions of giftedness, talent, and creativity are discussed early in the chapter, followed by a review of research on juvenile work of great artists, cross-cultural aspects of visual giftedness, and case studies of people talented in the arts. Next, is a review of research related to art talent development and identification and educational programming for artistically gifted children including these topics: potential and process versus performance and product; educational contexts; student abilities, personalities, values, backgrounds, and gender; the impact of educational opportunities; standardized testing; and teacher characteristics. The chapter concludes with recommendations for future research on art talent development and the education of artistically talented students.

DEFINITIONS OF GIFTEDNESS, TALENT, AND CREATIVITY

There are no agreed-upon definitions for the terms *gifted*, *talent*, and *creativity*. In popular usage, the term gifted often refers to students who have superior academic abilities, and the term talented usually refers to students with superior abilities in the visual and performing arts or sports. Teachers often describe their outstanding academic students as "gifted," whereas outstanding art students are "talented." Obviously there is a hierarchy of importance with talent as a term indicating a lesser endowment. The term gifted has retained that meaning, but talented also has been defined as possessing superior abilities in a single school subject, such as mathematics, language arts, science, or the fine arts. The term *gifted and talented*, in many contexts, has been replaced by talent development. So the emphasis has shifted from identifying predetermined gifts to nurturing talents (Feldhusen, 1992; Feldhusen & Hoover, 1986).

---

[1] Authors are listed alphabetically; both contributed equally to this chapter.

Winner (1996) offered a useful discussion of giftedness and distinguishes it from "talent." She insists that the term *gifted* should apply equally to individuals with abilities in academic *and* artistic fields. Winner identifies gifted children by three traits: (a) precocity that is demonstrated by early and surprisingly great skill and ability in the mastery of a given symbolic domain. Gifted children master basics at a young age and show rapid growth in acquiring content and skills. (b) The urge to master. Gifted children value total immersion in the domain of their choice. They have an insatiable urge to absorb and learn as much and as quickly as possible. (c) Gifted children often find their own way. They do not march in lockstep with most of their peers, and very often find unique solutions to problems and sometimes do not need the "scaffolding" provided to less able learners. This is not to say that gifted children do not require any instruction, rather that their instruction needs to be qualitatively different from that offered to less gifted individuals. In our discussion we will use the term *talented* but will keep in mind the constellation of traits previously described by Winner.

There is no clear relationship among the terms *talent*, *giftedness*, and *creativity*. Sternberg and Lubart's (1999) definition of creativity as "the ability to produce work that is both novel . . . and appropriate" (p. 3) is one that has been widely accepted. According to Csikszentmihalyi (1996), talent differs from creativity in that talent focuses on the ability to do something well, and most people in the case studies about creative adults that he and his colleagues researched achieved creative success without exceptional talent being evident. Gardner (1996) categorized seven individuals as creative according to each of his seven intelligence types (Picasso was included in the spatial intelligence category). Gardner explained that talented individuals function within a well-defined domain of knowledge within a culture. On the other hand, creative individuals often "lack fit" within a domain of knowledge and only after much time and effort do they establish a body of work that comes to be valued in a culture.

Certain personality traits may play a role in determining which gifted and talented children achieve their adult potentials in areas of art and science. As a result of his case studies of adults who achieved success in the arts and sciences, Feist (1999) concluded that giftedness as measured by high IQ scores might be a poor indicator of adult creative achievement and success. He conjectured that "lack of predictive validity of aptitude tests can be explained by the small relationship between intelligence and creativity" (p. 286).

THEORETICAL ASPECTS OF ART LEARNING AMONG GIFTED AND TALENTED INDIVIDUALS

In this discussion, we stress that special abilities and gifts found in the domain of the arts are just as "intellectual" and "cognitive" as gifts associated with high performance in domains such as math and science. Let there be no mistake, the visual arts do require intelligent thought and require problem-finding and problem-solving behaviors. Gardner's (1983, 1999) research on multiple intelligences and the foundational work of Arnheim (1969) on visual thinking in the arts both firmly establish the claim for artistry as flowing out of intelligent behavior and not just simply as the expression of feelings. Thus, we assume that children gifted in the arts are every bit as intellectually endowed as those with academic gifts.

The relationships among giftedness, talent development, and creativity are challenging areas of research. Because researchers lack consensus about what constitutes creativity itself, progress in developing operational definitions of "creativity" has been slow (Clark & Zimmerman, 1992; Csikzentmihalyi, 1996; Hunsaker & Callahan, 1995; Sternberg, 1988). Although some scholars agree that creative achievement is reflected in the production of useful, new ideas or products that result from defining a problem and solving it in a novel way (Hunsaker & Callahan, 1995; McPherson, 1997; Mumford, Connely, Baughnan, & Marks, 1994; Wakefield, 1992), others distinguish between expert creative acts and those of novices. Csikszentmihalyi

(1988, 1996), Feldman (1982), and Winner and Martino (1993) referred to creativity as inventiveness within a domain of knowledge, where a creative individual's work is recognized as a significant addition to that domain, by the social institutions (or field) that monitor the domain. No talented children, they claim, have "effected reorganization of a domain of knowledge" (p. 253). If we apply these criteria to student art, it would be rare that a student would create a work of art that is original, appropriate, and recognized by members of a disciplinary field. Fineberg (1997) has shown that numerous modernist artists appropriated motifs, images, and spatial organization from drawings and paintings of young children that these artists themselves collected. This appropriation does not, however, confer on the works of the children the title of "creative innovators" any more than the artisans who created the urinal used in Duchamp's "Fountain" were path-breaking creative sculptors.

In the educational literature, problem finding, problem solving, divergent and convergent thinking, self-expression, and adaptability to new situations are all traits commonly associated with creativity (Csikszentmihalyi 1988, 1996; Mumford et al., 1994; Runco, 1993; Runco & Nemiro, 1993; Starko, 2001; Sternberg 1988, 1997, 1999). Some research demonstrates that problem-finding and problem-solving skills can be taught and students can be helped to master productive thinking and creative problem solving (Treffinger, Sortore, & Cross, 1993). Talent development can be enhanced in a "supportive, flexible, but intellectually-demanding academic environment" (Mumford et al., 1994, p. 245) by encouraging students to work consistently and responsibly when confronted by frustration. According to Feldhusen (1992), students can be taught to find problems, clarify problems, and use certain skills when attempting to solve problems. They also can be taught to monitor their own learning activities and seek and test alternative solutions.

Creativity also can be developed by adapting teaching strategies that balance students' generation of new ideas, critical thinking abilities, and their ability to translate theory into practice (Sternberg & Williams, 1996). Feldman and Goldsmith (1986a) studied six children who were prodigies in many different areas, including the arts. These researchers were convinced that all progress in learning is the result of intensive and prolonged instruction. Rostan, Pariser, and Gruber (2000), in their examination of visual artists, supported the same conclusion. Successful teachers of highly able students are knowledgeable about their subject matter, and able to communicate instructions effectively. They select important learning experiences that challenge their students to attain advanced levels of achievement.

Educators have suggested a number of strategies for developing curricula in different subjects that support creativity and talent development. Some of these suggestions include having students: (a) practice problem-finding as well as problem-solving techniques; (b) use unfamiliar materials that elicit more novel thinking and lead to new ideas, (c) experience convergent (structured) and divergent (unstructured) tasks because they need knowledge and information for skill building and open-ended tasks for self-expression; (d) rely on both visual and verbal materials; (e) be exposed to curricula with open-ended outcomes that allow for unforeseen results; (f) follow their own interests and work in groups, as well as independently; (g) choose environments that support their talents and creativity; and (h) encounter a wide range of tasks intended to encourage, reinforce, and enhance emerging talents (Feldhusen, 1995; Mumford et al., 1994; Runco, 1993; Runco & Nemiro, 1993; Sternberg & Williams, 1996).

REVIEW OF RESEARCH ON SIGNIFICANT INDIVIDUALS IN THE VISUAL ARTS

It is surprising that over the centuries art historians have not given much thought to the records of juvenile art by great artists. Even though collections of juvenilia exist for a number of world-class artists (Dortu, 1971; Duff, 1987; Glaesemer, 1973; Zervos, 1950) these collections have only recently attracted the sort of study that they deserve. It has been the task of art educators and psychologists to examine these records to see what connections exist between artwork made in childhood and that made as adults (Carroll, 1994; Dennis, 1987; Duncum, 1984; Feldman & Goldsmith, 1986a; Golomb, 1995; Murray, 1991; Paine, 1987; Pariser, 1987, 1991, 1995; Rostan et al., 2001; Porath, 1988; Winner, 1996; Zimmerman, 1995). Such records are important for at least two reasons: First, they may help answer the mystery surrounding the growth of highly successful individuals, such as Klee, Picasso, and Munch, who have contributed hugely to the visual arts. These people are, in Winner's terms, "creative with a big 'C'." Second, it is also a matter of some interest to see in what ways the graphic developmental paths of these fated individuals are similar to and/or different from the graphic development of individuals not destined for greatness.

What can be learned from looking at the juvenile work of acknowledged artists? First, these children were prolific, producing large numbers of drawings. Such productivity is the result of what has been described as the gifted child's "rage to master" (Winner, 1996); that is, an intense involvement with a given domain in the service of imaginative play.

Second, we also learn that without exception, these children experimented with spatial rendering, naturalistic likeness, and more stylized approaches to representation; and there is clear evidence of a learning process. At an exhibit of children's art Picasso said, "When I was their age, I could draw like Raphael, but it has taken me a whole lifetime to learn to draw like them" (Gardner, 1993, p. 145.) But there is little evidence to support his claim. In Picasso's case, there is ample proof that although he was a very quick study and he learned drawing techniques of all sorts with frightening speed, he most certainly did not spring forth from the head of Athena, a fully formed child/artist. Yet, that myth persists (Staaller, 1986) and colors the degree to which instruction is accepted as a bona-fide basis for artistic growth. In short, any and all artists who left a record of their struggles clearly attained graphic mastery through effort, repetition, and the assistance of good teachers.

Porath (1988) suggested that if any anomalies exist in the development of gifted children, they will be found within the various stages of development rather than across such stages. She maintains that giftedness in childhood is a matter of quick learning in a domain, within a given stage, rather than a rapid development from one intellectual stage to the next. Porath examined Paul Klee's juvenilia in the Bern museum and made the claim that gifted children are not conceptually much in advance of their chronological age peers—at least as manifested in their representation of pictorial space. Using the Harris Draw A Man Test (1963) as a measuring instrument, she found that Klee at age 6, drew people at an adult level. Yet, his organization of pictorial space was not much different from that of other 6-year-olds. She also examined a few of Lautrec's childhood drawings and the same pattern emerged—Figures were handled with sophistication, but space and perspective were still rendered at only one substage above the one expected for the child's chronological age. Pariser (1987) examined some of the same drawings and noted that although Lautrec drew horses and human figures with surprising sophistication, his birds and railroad trains were less well rendered. He, like many other children deeply involved in drawing, was a "specialist."

Porath (1988) found that well-practiced drawings were mixed in with Klee's less accomplished performances and that there was no "uniform level" to his drawing performance. Research on Klee's and Lautrec's juvenalia (Pariser, 1987, 1991) supports the observation that these two children did not show any outstanding capacity for spatial rendering at an early age; what they did show was a phenomenal inventiveness and capacity for rendering their subjects with flavor and life.

All the artists who left traces of their childhood works were clearly able to master graphic conventions favored by their cultural millieux. What is evident is that Western children destined for artistic greatness demonstrated a phenomenal ability to draw "realistically." It would be a mistake, however, to think that mastery of realistic drawing techniques is always an indicator of adult greatness. Although we lack juvenalia of world-class Asian or African artists, we do have work from a highly gifted Chinese child, Wang Yani (Tan, 1993). What she demonstrates is a gift for mastering the highly conventionalized, nonnaturalistic, visual idiom used in traditional brush painting. Yani, at age 4 was able to function fluently, creating scenes and narratives that were much out of the ordinary (Andrews, 1989; Ho, 1989) (however, we have no knowledge of Yani's present accomplishments). Yani's childhood work illustrates Winner and Martino's (1993) observation that: " What unites all children with artistic gifts is . . . the ability to master one or more of the culture's norms of artistry at a very early age" (p. 10).

There is a hypothesis that talented children explore graphic representation along several stylistic and conventional tracks. It may be that the difference between these great artists and lesser mortals lies not in their progression through basic developmental steps, but perhaps in their experimentation with a multiplicity of genres and conventions, an eclecticism that Milbrath (1998) also observed in her own study of visually talented children. Three artists, Picasso, Klee, and Lautrec, who Pariser (1987) chose to study, all experimented with a variety of representational styles and genres simultaneously and occasionally in the same image. For example, Picasso at age 12 was both mastering classical drawing techniques and copying Spanish caricatures and newspaper broadsides.

Milbrath (1998) analyzed and compared the work of what she referred to as artistically talented and less talented children. Her several hundred drawings came principally from two sources: a 10-year longitudinal study of eight highly talented children and a cross-sectional study of spontaneous drawings from children between the ages of 4 and 14. Milbrath found that the most telling difference between talented and less talented children were matters of quality and kind. The more talented children performed differently in the following three ways: (a) the variability of their drawing output was above the modal level, unlike the less talented whose variability was below the modal level; (b) they used line to indicate edges of forms rather than simply an enclosure, discovering very early that lines can function effectively as the edges of solids and planes; and (c) their drawings were more realistic, incorporating visual distortions suggesting their position vis-à-vis the object rather than "canonical" views more typical of the comparison group. Milbrath suggested that artistically talented children begin drawing representationally a full 1 to 2 years earlier than other children, have a higher degree of originality or creativity, and have strong motivation or commitment to a domain.

Milbrath (1998) proposed two hypotheses to explain the qualities of graphic work by artistically talented children. One she calls the "farther faster" hypothesis. This explains the root difference between artistically talented and less talented children as just an outgrowth of their conceptual precocity—particularly in the area of spatial reasoning. The second set of hypotheses propose that especially able children develop as they do because of their heightened figurative abilities. That is, they see (perceive), remember (have excellent visual memories), and do (draw) earlier, in qualitatively different ways from their peers. Because some gifted children such as Eytan (Golomb, 1992) share some traits with exceptionally able autistic artist-children (Selfe, 1983, 1995; Wiltshire, 1983) it is suggested that these two populations do in fact share some of the neurological components that make such phenomenal drawing performances possible.

In proposing this second set of hypotheses, Milbrath (1998) deftly incorporates several different sorts of research on child art. Researchers have identified at least three discrete elements that constitute drawing behavior: (a) the perceptual aspect that includes the mechanics of looking and analyzing what one sees; (b) the aspect of mental imagery found in mental representations and schemata used by the person making a drawing (Winner, 1996); (c) the mastery of the mechanics of the drawing process itself, planning, ordering, controlling, and monitoring the image as it appears on the page (Freeman, 1972). Milbrath claimed that the data she has collected and analyzed suggest the hypothesis that, "talented children develop as they do not because they are conceptually advanced over their less talented peers but because they possess heightened figural capacities; simply stated . . . talent in the visual arts arises out of differences in children's ability in figurative thought rather than differences in conceptual ability" (p. 355). In other words, artistically talented children see the world differently from their peers.

Milbrath's work (1995, 1998) and that of Winner (1996), Golomb (1992), and others propose the notion that there is nothing developmentally anomalous about the emergence of noteworthy graphic performance—at least not as far as issues of cognitive and technical achievement are concerned. The three artists that Pariser (1987, 1991, 1995) studied also grappled with representing space and objects in space, in the same sequence of stages as their less gifted peers. All three artists left behind a collection of childhood drawings that indicates that, as Milbrath observed, there was no underlying cognitive difference between them and other less artistically able children.

The drawings of autistic child artists (Pariser, 1981; Selfe, 1977, 1983, 1995) should be of interest to all students of children's drawing for some autistic children appear blessed with remarkable drafting skills, making images that can only be called uncanny. In particular, two children, Nadia Chomyn and Steven Wiltshire (both discussed in Selfe, 1995), made drawings that are phenomenally realistic. Nadia made her realistic drawings between the ages of 4 and 7 years—then reverted to unremarkable, age-appropriate imagery. Steven Wiltshire (now an adult) continues to draw architecture with meticulous skill. Nadia, and to a lesser degree, Stephen Wiltshire are asocial and autistic. They have received no drawing instruction, yet have mastered a style that is associated with a sophisticated understanding of the visual scene—in Steven's case, two-point perspective. The question raised by their work, is simple: How can children who are intellectually impaired, be able to render the world with such accuracy? The examples of these two children suggest that there is a neural module that makes possible such drawing skills and that this module is capable of working independently of the "cognitive" modules that classify, abstract, and so forth. In fact, abstract thought and linguistic classification seem to inhibit rather than enhance accurate drawing. It is known that the absence of conceptual information about the subject of a drawing tends to make the drawing more realistic (Bremner & Moore, 1984). In effect, the work of these two autistic children makes the point that there is no necessary connection between intellectual understanding and realistic rendering—In fact, such understanding may be a liability. The sudden efflorescence of Nadia's work also makes the point that so-called developmental sequences in graphic development are routes followed by "ordinary" children but not by exceptional children. Could one call either Stephen or Nadia "gifted," "talented," or "creative"? Both children clearly have an unusual facility in an area of art—a talent—But in neither case do they show signs of self-conscious experimentation and boundary pushing that mark significant creativity—as defined by Csikszentmihalyi (1988).

There is some preliminary research that addresses the question of how the juvenile work of great artists differs from that of children who are merely talented. In a pilot study, Rostan, Pariser, and Gruber (1998) asked: Would judges who were "blind" to the identity of the great artists find their juvenile work exceptional if it were mixed in anonymously among the work of contemporary art students? Seventy-one art students (6- through 11-year-olds) participated in the study. Although limitations of the 1998 study prevent any generalizations about the findings, it was found that the young artists' works distinguished themselves by the degree of variability manifest across the whole corpus. Such variability would suggest that they, more than the other children, experimented with different technical approaches.

Subsequent work by Rostan, Pariser, and Gruber (2001) focused on the same questions. This research involved a much larger number of great artists' juvenile drawings. There were approximately 80 juvenile drawings by great artists, and a comparison pool of 200 drawings were taken from artistically educated and naive children from European and Chinese communities in North America. The researchers found that the juvenile works of the great artists were generally ranked among the better drawings but did not stand out in any dramatic way.

CASE STUDIES OF THE LIVES OF PEOPLE TALENTED IN ART

The case study method has long been considered a productive avenue for considering the work of significantly creative adults and children alike. Luquet (1927) and Fein (1976), to name a few researchers who focus on children's drawing abilities, offer longitudinal descriptive studies of children who loved to draw. Franklin (1994), who offered a qualitative description of the working histories of two women artists, acknowledged the utility of employing Wallace and Gruber's (1989) approach to creative lives. These two psychologists produced a volume of work consisting of case studies of scientists and artists. In Gruber's "evolving systems approach," he tries to do justice to the complexity of the lives of significantly creative people. Gruber's path- breaking work was first illustrated in his book on Darwin's evolving conceptions of evolution (Gruber, 1982). In this study, Gruber presented his key notion that creative individuals, especially those of Darwin's caliber, are people with "multiple networks of enterprise"; that is, people with a number of related but parallel interests. Gruber's research is informed by five principles. Such studies should be: (a) developmental and systemic; (b) pluralistic and encompassing the multiplicity of goals that a creative person pursues; (c) culturally and socially interactive, (d) situated socially, historically, and institutionally; (e) constructionist in the sense that creative individuals select and alter their environments; and (f) reflective of the affective and experiential dimensions of an individual's work.

Studies of artistically gifted children conducted by Rostan et al., (1998, 2000, 2001) are influenced by Gruber's approach. To date, this research has generated statistical and descriptive data about the emergence of artistically gifted children. Results from the research suggest that even in childhood individuals deeply involved with a medium or an artistic practice already share certain features with adults similarly engrossed in artistic activity. Among these are high productivity, multiple interests, and a strong affinity for the discipline.

In her 1995 work, Golomb presented six case studies of unusually able children. These case studies provide researchers with profiles of children ranging from nascent world-class artists (Toulouse-Lautrec) to an autistic child with highly unusual drawing abilities (Nadia).

Sosniak (1985) interviewed a number of professionally successful pianists and identified three common phases in musical apprenticeship: (a) romance with the subject, (b) acquisition of discipline and technique, and (c) development of individuality and personal insight in musical practice. Sosniak found that each phase required a teacher with different traits. First teachers were generally characterized by their pupils as warm and empathetic, much like family members. In the second phase, teachers were less caring, but had excellent technical skills and were strongly connected to the discipline and field. Teachers for the third phase were demanding taskmasters who prepared their students for initiation into the field of musical performance. Teachers at the third level emphasized the need for students to develop their own "signature" or "voice." It would appear that Sosniak's model might provide a pattern for apprenticeship in the visual arts as well as in music. Although Bloom did not find a similar path for the sculptors he studied, it is easy to recognize the same three-step process in music talent development applies to the apprenticeships of Picasso, Lautrec, and Klee (Pariser, 1987).

These same patterns derived from Sosniak can be traced in the life histories of the two gifted children whose work and development Rostan et al. (2000) described in the initial phases of their research on artistic giftedness. Two gifted children were chosen with very different backgrounds. One (Eric) comes from a comfortable New England background, whereas the other (Bin) is a Chinese immigrant, recently arrived in the United States. Both were devoted to the visual arts, and both were strongly supported by their families.

Eric's work emerged from a stable familial and political climate. A colorist rather than a draughtsperson, he is clearly entering the second stage of Sosniak's three-stage model; he is beginning to learn about the technical aspects of art—with less dependence on a supportive emotional climate. He sees himself as an artist, is prolific in terms of output, and demonstrates the special trait identified by Winner (1996) in gifted children, namely, the "rage to master."

Bin is older than Eric is and his work is technically and conceptually far in advance of Eric's. It is distinguished by its clearly political message. One of his recent paintings is a parody of images that were prevalent during the Cultural Revolution. Bin's ability to work at a very high level in a number of different styles is one characteristic that can be observed in the work of other artists at the start of their careers. For example, Picasso, when he came to Paris in 1900 worked in the styles of Lautrec and Bonnard (Pariser, 1987). So, Bin certainly possesses at least one of the key feature of giftedness, a capacity to quickly acquire cultural conventions.

Like other adolescent artists, such as a young man described by Gardner (1980), Bin is unafraid of crossing the lines of decorum. Shocking the adult world and violating political expectations would seem to be second nature for Bin. It is evident that Bin and Eric share the same intensity of purpose. Art making is as natural and vital to them as breathing. But, the two settings in which the impulse is played out are markedly different. Family expectations are distinct. Bin is expected to carry forward his father's dreams; Eric is simply expected to articulate his own dreams and find some way of accommodating his own father's ambivalence about the artistic profession as a career.

Recently, psychologists have used multiple, individual case studies to compare and contrast the influence of personality and patterns of development on adults who have achieved success in particular domains of knowledge including the visual arts (Feist, 1999; Gardner, 1996). Csikszentmihalyi (1996), after 30 years of research and in nearly 100 interviews with creative people in many different fields including the arts, determined that even the most talented individual needs the support of a society and culture. The potentially creative person will not be able to achieve anything of importance without a constellation of conditions consisting of training, expectations, resources, recognition, hope, opportunity, and both extrinsic and intrinsic rewards.

CROSS-CULTURAL ASPECTS OF VISUAL GIFTEDNESS

Golomb (1992) reviewed the results of graphic-developmental studies in Egyptian, Lebanese, Ghanain, and North American aboriginal cultures and commented on cross-cultural comparisons of drawing development in general: "In my view, development seems to evolve across cultures in much the same way, with structurally simpler forms and figures always preceding the most complex ones. The rules for representing the world appear to be the same" (p. 337). Certain underlying features of children's graphic development thus appear to be common across all societies and cultures. Children the world over are attracted to and actively explore the problem of representing objects and experiences in a given medium. This is not to suggest that there is a universal developmental "push toward optical realism"—realism is a parochial Western concern. As Winner stated:

> The evidence from art produced by children in China, and by American children, outside of the culture of school, points to the clear conclusion that there is nothing natural about the goal of realism. What is natural and inevitable I believe, is the drive to master the pictorial conventions that are valued in one's culture or sub-culture. (p. 15)

A body of cross-cultural research comparing Chinese and Western children's performance on drawing tasks supports Golomb's (1992) and Winner's (1986) observations that many features of children's drawing development are much the same the world over. We present the results of this cross-cultural research as an example of pan-human similarities and differences in drawing development. Note that Western art as such is no stranger to China. Sixteenth century art was known in middle kingdom and ever since the turn of the century; Western academic drawing and painting approaches have been known and widely practiced in Chinese schools and art academies. As early as 1912, schools of Western-style painting existed, and the drill of European academic drawing was a common feature of Chinese art education (Kao, 1998)—and remains so to this day. The fine Arts Academy of Beijing has an intensive course in plaster-cast drawing. It may be that Western academic art has taken such a hold in China precisely because this European import, like traditional Chinese painting, is rooted in mastery of a medium and requires mastery of graphic skills. The fact that there has been at least a century of Western cross-pollination in China should be kept in mind when considering the East-West comparisons that follow.

Chinese and American children aged 4 to 6 years master rendering of topological space before rendering Euclidean space (Hoffman & Trepannier, 1982). Chinese and Canadian children of these ages do not differ in the rate of shift from topological to Euclidean rendering (Harvey, Manshu, Biao, & Jue, 1986). Chinese and British children between the ages of 7 and 12 do not differ in developmental sequences in representing space (Case, Tu, & Berg, 1992) and appear to be at the same place in a standard graphic developmental trajectory (Stratford & Au, 1988). Hong Kong Chinese children, ages 3 to 5, draw human figures in conformity with figure drawing by children from around the world (Chan & Lobo, 1992). In addition to parallels in development, there are also some noted differences. For example, Jolley, Richard, Thomas, Gly, and Zhi (1996) suggested that differences that they observed in Chinese and North American children's aesthetic responses may be due to greater emphasis in Chinese schools on mastery of detail and technical skill, as well as to early imposition of technical discipline. The Chinese children tended to be more sensitive to aesthetic dimensions when it came to responding to images. Certainly, emphasis in China on skill training and discipline fits well with an emphasis on compliance which is reported to be a key component of the Chinese socialization process (e.g., Reed, 1992).

There is evidence that even today, in the teaching of the arts in China, technical skill is viewed as the indispensable basis for development of true artistic ability and expression. When Gardner (1989a) went to China to study art programs and teaching methods, he found that most Chinese teachers "resisted the notion that one can be creative, or even begin to explore, before one has developed considerable skill. From their point of view we [Westerners] were simply and stubbornly attempting to put the cart before the horse" (p. 252). In a recent research article on drawing instruction in China, the following observation can be found: "In the Chinese weekend art schools a high level of drawing skill is considered essential: teachers argue that we cannot be creative without first becoming technically skilled, otherwise we have no way of expressing that creativity" (Cox, Perara, & Xu, 1998, p. 181).

In the case of artistically talented children from China, an example is the work of Wang Yani (Tan, 1993), a girl with precocious painting abilities. There is a record of her painting development from simple to more complex uses of value, line, brush control, and composition. The story of Yani demonstrates that the same three factors that contribute to the emergence of Western children deeply committed to the arts also contribute to the emergence of similar children in the East. These factors include support from the family, a strong (innate) affinity for the medium and the domain, and an insatiable hunger for mastery of cultural forms.

Feldman and Goldsmith (1986a), writing case studies of six child prodigies who excelled in five domains (music, chess, mathematics, foreign languages, and creative writing) stressed that "cultures vary in the importance they attach to mastery of different domains at different times" (pp. 13–14). Therefore, what is considered *a valued ability* in one culture, such as being able to copy artworks well, may not be valued in another. Artistically talented students therefore are dependent on instruction about artforms that can be communicated effectively within their cultures. Feldman and Goldsmith (1986b) claimed that potential talent cannot be developed without access to a symbol system, as well as to a domain of knowledge valued by the culture. Only those areas of artistic expression valued by a culture, or subculture, are developed sufficiently to offer organized symbol systems and domains that can be made available to artistically talented students. A student, therefore, can only be identified as talented in areas that a culture values (Feldman & Goldsmith, 1986b; Gallagher, 1985; Greenlaw & McIntosh, 1988; Zimmerman, 1992b).

Ghengis Blues is a touching and remarkable 1995 film that illustrates the socially contextualized theory of creativity proposed by Feldman and Goldsmith (1986a, 1986b) and by others. Ghengis Blues tells the story of Paul Penja, a blind San Francisco street musician from Cape Verde, whose talents for overtone singing were only recognized in Tuva, an Eastern province of Russia. Depressed and lonely after the death of his beloved wife, Penja began to listen to overtone singing on shortwave radio. Overtone singing involves voicing the notes in such a way that the overtones to a given note are plainly audible and can be played with to generate a second musical line. Penja taught himself the technique and added this style to his street-busking repertoire.

There were few overtone-singing fans in San Francisco, but one day a visiting Tuvan singer happened to hear Penja and was blown away by his abilities. He urged Penja to come to Tuva and to appear in the annual singing competition. The film documents Penja's triumph in Tuva. Penja never achieved much recognition in the United States with his traditional folk and Blues repertoire, but his special vocal talents were immediately acclaimed in Tuva where he was known as "Earthquake" for the resonance and power of his voice—and for the excellence with which he had mastered Tuvan lyrics and overtone-singing forms. Paul Penja's story illustrates the need to consider all necessary conditions for nurturance of special abilities in the arts including individual abilities, the existence of a valued symbolic domain, and the actions of the social world through a specific field. Until Penja happened across Tuvan singing, his special abilities were hidden. It still required the attention of expert judges and other members of the Tuvan culture to assess and recognize the special quality of his performance.

ART TALENT DEVELOPMENT IN EDUCATIONAL CONTEXTS

The role of the art teacher and his or her impact on an artistically talented student is great. Talented and sensitive teachers challenge their artistically talented students to have transformational experiences while making art. The students view themselves as possessing abilities to respond to and produce artwork at a very high level. In some cases, when involved with students with high interest and abilities in the visual arts, teachers can be a neutral factor or in more isolated cases can have a detrimental influence on a student's art talent development. Factors such as student behaviors, personalities, gender, cognitive abilities, age, class, and ethnicity also play important roles in the impact of educational experiences on artistically talented students.

PROGRAMMING OPPORTUNITIES

The major purpose of visual arts programs for artistically talented students is to bring together students with high interests and abilities, or potential abilities, in ways that broaden and deepen their knowledge about the world of art, sharpen their art skills, and offer them new learning opportunities rarely found in a regular classroom setting. Based on a review of literature about educating artistically talented students (Clark & Zimmerman, 1994a), a number of programming arrangements were best suited to teaching artistically talented students: (a) mixed-ability grouping including in-class enrichment, cooperative learning, and individualized instruction (e.g., self-study units and mentoring); (b) ability grouping including specialized schools (e.g., magnet schools), special classes in regular school for the entire school day (students recruited from one school or several schools), special grouping for part of the school day (e.g., pull-out programs, special courses, released time, clubs, artists-in-residence), and grouping for school-related activities (e.g., field trips, school/museum visits); and (c) acceleration, including grade skipping, early admission, and rapid progress (e.g., accelerated programs, advanced placement, credit by examination). Clark and Zimmerman (1994a) described examples of many of these programs for artistically talented students in a publication for the Research-Based Decision-Making Series supported by the National Research Center on the Gifted and Talented. They concluded that gifted and talented visual arts, secondary students need access to space and facilities that resemble those used by artists. Students also need access to professional-level books, slides, computer programs, slides, art reproductions, and periodicals, as well as to appropriate spaces that support advanced or accelerated study and problem-finding and problem-solving project work about nonstudio aspects of the visual arts.

Clark and Zimmerman (1994a) also determined that there is not a foundation of research on which to conduct meta-analysis research about programming opportunities for artistically talented students. Based on their research they suggested administrators of school-based programs for highly able secondary art students create climates in which flexibility and alternatives in program planning are encouraged. Students offerings might include (a) remaining in their school for part of the day and attending a nearby college or university for advanced courses, (b) taking part in advanced placement art courses offered in high school that earn college credits, (c) enrolling in correspondence courses with college-level art content, (d) attending fast-paced art courses in which curriculum compacting allows 2 years of a course to be covered in 1 year, (e) bypassing course prerequisites by examination, (f) earning full credit for courses by examination, and (g) entering college early.

IMPACT OF EDUCATIONAL OPPORTUNITIES ON TALENTED ART STUDENTS

There have been a number of case studies about the work of talented young artists who showed precocious abilities in the visual arts (Gardner, 1980; Goldsmith, 1992; Golomb, 1995a, 1995b; Wilson & Wilson, 1980; Zimmerman, 1995). All of these studies emphasized spontaneous artwork done by precocious youngsters, from early childhood through their adolescence, or emphasized separate time periods during the development of these young artists. Only a few case studies have focused on schooling and on the effects of differential programming opportunities and options on the development of art talent (Clark & Zimmerman, 1987b; Nelson & Janzen, 1990).

Gardner (1980) presented a case study of spontaneous drawings of a 16-year-old artistically talented adolescent and did not find that formal art instruction had much impact on Garbriel's development. Robertson (1987) reported a case study in which she intimated that formal art instruction, rather than supporting art talent development, might have been an inhibiting factor.

In case studies reported by and Golomb (1995a), formal art lessons or directed art experiences were viewed as inhibiting the visual art development of artistically gifted and talented students. Bloom (1985) and his associates reported case studies of talented individuals who, before the age of 35, had reached extremely high levels of accomplishment in their respective fields. One of the case studies (Sloan & Sosniak, 1985) focused on 20 sculptors, and the researchers concluded that the absence of formal art education before college did not appear to have a negative effect on sculptors' art development and eventual success as practicing artists.

Few researchers have studied the positive effects of accelerated or enriched learning in art on a student with high visual arts abilities, although a number of studies have shown that teaching can have a very positive impact. Wilson and Wilson (1980) studied the graphic work of a talented 15-year-old and credited the art teacher with encouraging the students' talents by stressing the value of popular, narrative models, rather than by emphasizing fine arts instruction alone. In several of Golomb's (1992) case studies, art teachers are credited with encouraging students' talents.

Zimmerman (1992b, 1995) presented a case study of Eric, a talented art student. He spoke positively of the benefits of accelerated and enriched art programs. Similarly positive comments on enriched art programs have been expressed by other talented students (Stanley, 1977; Van Tassel-Baska, 1986, 1987). To produce and be supported in maintaining his body of work, Eric spoke about the development of both the perceptual and the conceptual qualities of his artwork through expression and skill with a variety of media. The positive characteristics of the teachers Eric identified included knowledge of art skills, general knowledge about art, empathy with students, ability to make classes challenging, and the encouragement of students to be reflective about art making.

Eric was fortunate in his elementary and junior high school years to study with teachers who were flexible and taught enriched, theme-oriented classes in which students could complete assignments according to their interests, abilities, and a variety of modes, including both visual and verbal problem solving. These kinds of curriculum adaptations allowed Eric to express his skills, abilities, values, and understandings in a variety of discursive and nondiscursive contexts. He described a number of transformational experiences that allowed him to view himself as a young artist achieving his own goals, chosen in the company of other like-minded art students. The accelerated and enriched art program options in which he participated in his precollege experiences gave him the impetus to continue to study art, and his skills were later applied as an adult when he became a successful designer of interactive games. Zimmerman (1992a, 1995) concluded that artistic development is not an automatic consequence of maturation. It is instead a learned set of complex abilities that, to a great extent, are influenced by culture and the educational opportunities available within that culture.

Feldman (1980) and Feldman and Goldmith (1986a) studied children who were precocious in many different areas and were convinced that all progress in learning is the result of intensive and prolonged instruction. Talent, Feldman and Goldsmith contended, does not develop without an enormous amount of work, practice, and study, coupled with a great deal of direct assistance, guidance, and encouragement. Their conclusion that an individual's talent within a culture involves the interplay of many forces, including education, has great relevance to the education of talented visual arts students.

POTENTIAL AND PROCESS VERSUS PERFORMANCE AND PRODUCT

Although notions of talent in the arts often emphasize a superior final product, a number of psychologists and educators have also emphasized attention to the processes that lead to such products. These researchers claimed that the processes students select and pursue are more important in defining a gifted or talented performance in the arts than the products that students create. They concluded that the ability to depict the world realistically is just one indicator of talent in the visual arts; other indicators may be deep emotional involvement as, for example, in "flow" experiences described Csikszentmihalyi (1990, 1996); importance of cultural norms (Feldman, 1980, 1982); and use of paradoxes, puns, and metaphors (Tannenbaum, 1983; Zimmerman, 1992b). Researchers such as Brown (2001), Gardner (1989b), and Wolf (1989) stress the importance of using process portfolios at elementary and secondary levels in order to meaningfully assess learning over time in the arts. Getzels and Csikszentmihalyi (1976) studied young college art students and the relationship between their problem-finding behaviors and the originality of their artworks. They concluded that students' methods of discovery, visualization techniques, and the ways that they sought productive questions were often far better indicators of high ability than just their solutions to artistic problems.

Psychologists since the time of Binet and Simon (1916) have viewed intelligence traditionally as a single, measurable trait. Then in the 1980s researchers such as Gardner and Sternberg challenged the construct of a single intelligence. Gardner (1983), posited the existence of multiple intelligences: linguistic, logico-mathematical, musical, spatial, bodily kinesthetic, interpersonal, and intrapersonal. Recently, Gardner (1999) added three other kinds of intelligences to his list of seven: naturalist, spiritual and existential. One should note that Gardner does not posit a so-called "artistic intelligence" as a separate module. Artists use any and all of the intelligences available. Sternberg (1985) also posited specialized abilities, but his are related to general intelligence, whereas Gardner's intelligences are tied to separate abilities (Feldhusen & Hoover, 1986). Sternberg described aspects of intelligence that include abilities to think at high levels, to process information effectively, to achieve insights and solve problems, and to use efficient metacognitive processing systems.

Within various arts areas, many vastly different behaviors and abilities often are required for success. Students with superior drawing or painting abilities, for example, may have different sets of developed sensibilities than those talented at creating three-dimensional objects. Even within two-dimensional visual arts, different abilities and sensitivities are clearly needed in order to succeed in diverse fields such as photography, printmaking, painting, or political cartooning. Csikszentmihalyi and Getzels (1973) studied the personalities of young, college-level, visual arts students and concluded that their personalities and abilities differed substantially from those of advertising and industrial arts majors. Barron (1972) drew similar conclusions based on studies of students and professionals in acting, dance, writing, and the visual arts. Each domain required different abilities. Professionals in fields related to the arts, such as aestheticians, critics, and historians, demonstrate skills and abilities that differ greatly from those required for success by visual artists. Intelligence needed for success in the visual arts clearly cannot be defined as a "single characteristic, but as a phenomenon that contains multiple ways of dealing with knowledge" (Hurwitz & Day, 1991, p. 118).

IQ, CREATIVITY, AND ACHIEVEMENT TESTS

A contentious issue is determining the relationships among intelligence tests, creativity tests, and achievement tests, and how these relate to the identification of talent in the visual arts. One contested claim is that above average intelligence is a requirement for superior performance in the arts. Winner (1996) finds little evidence that visually gifted children consistently have high IQs in academic areas. However, the arbitrary separation of intelligence and art performance has been questioned for many years (Arnheim, 1969; Clark & Zimmerman, 1984a). During the 1970s, a number of researchers demonstrated that many highly intelligent students also were highly able in the arts, and that most highly able arts students are also highly intelligent in a traditional sense, although not all highly intelligent students possess art talent (Luca & Allen, 1974; Schubert, 1973; Vernon, Adamson, & Vernon, 1977). A high degree of intelligence has been described as necessary for acquiring the kinds of advanced techniques and skills required for superior arts performance (Luca & Allen, 1974; Schubert, 1973).

Relationships between general intelligence and art talent have not been pursued in recent research, because IQ tests have been challenged by many educators and researchers (Gardner, 1983; Gagne, 1985; Feldhusen & Hoover, 1986; Sternberg, 1984, 1985, 1986; Treffinger & Renzulli, 1986). Despite such challenges, during the 1980s, some educators and researchers continued to advocate the use of IQ tests for identification of gifted and talented students, although always in conjunction with other measures (Borland, 1986; Kaufman & Harrison, 1986; Shore, 1987).

During the 1940s, Torrance (1962, 1972) and others developed what became known as creativity tests, and creativity became a by-word in gifted and talented education (Renzulli, Reis, & Smith, 1981). When originally designed, creativity tests were used to measure general problem-solving skills and divergent thinking abilities applicable to various situations. Kulp and Tarter (1986) developed instruments to measure creativity in order to identify highly able visual arts students, and a number of authors endorsed using creativity tests to identify talented students for visual arts programs (Greenlaw & McIntosh, 1988; Hurwitz, 1983; Khatena, 1982; Parker, 1989). However, Torrance (1962) reported that creative achievements in writing, science, medicine, and leadership were more easily predicted than creative achievements in music, the visual arts, business, or industry. With a population of elementary students, Clark and Zimmerman (2001b) have demonstrated a correlation between scores on the Torrance Test of Creativity and Clark's Drawing Abilities Test.

STUDENT CHARACTERISTICS

In a review of research, based on 25 studies of identification procedures and instruments for talented art education programs, Boston (1987) concluded that "the criteria on which to identify students as being exceptional, intelligent, or talented in this subject area have yet to be agreed upon" (p. 1). This is especially true for students from economically disadvantaged families or minority groups (Richert, 1987).

As was indicated earlier in this chapter, art teachers use the term *talent* to refer to students of high ability in a specific visual arts area. There is little agreement among practitioners and researchers on how to define what constitutes high abilities in the visual or performing arts. One result of this lack of agreement is that identification recommendations for specific programs for talented art students are idiosyncratic (Bachtel, 1988; Zettel, 1979). Another is that current writers have moved away from a single criterion or definition and have endorsed multiple criteria identification practices (Clark & Zimmerman, 1984a, 1987, 2001b; Gallagher, 1985; Renzulli & Reis, 1985; Renzulli, Reis, & Smith, 1977). A third has been to avoid a generalized definition by specifying program content and goals and selecting only those students whose abilities would be served by the specific character of a program (Gallagher, 1985; Greenlaw & McIntosh, 1988; Parker, 1989).

Claims about the characteristics of artistically talented students therefore are varied and contradictory (Clark & Zimmerman, 1984a). There are many reasons for these inconsistencies: Researchers working in different cultures, times, and places have used different sets of criteria and artistically talented students have not been categorized systematically. Although examining art products for evidence of talent in the visual arts is common, it also is possible to observe behaviors that may indicate a predisposition to create art products or that manifest themselves while students actually engage in art making. Using content analysis and comparative analysis Clark and Zimmerman analyzed and grouped over 75 years of research about the characteristics of artistically talented students. The two largest categories that emerged were the observable characteristics of students' art products and observable student behavior (Clark & Zimmerman,

1984a, 1984b). Hurwitz and Day (1991) referred to task commitment and cognitive, artistic, and creative characteristics of art students as ways of defining what they termed "artistic intelligence." Other characteristics, cited by Pariser (1997), include intensity of application and early mastery of cultural forms, production of a large volume of works over a sustained period of time, nurturance from family and teachers, and thematically specialized work.

Although other examples could be offered; it is clear that there are many ways to describe and categorize the characteristics of students with talents in the visual arts, and no single set of characteristics will ever comprehensively describe all covert or overt manifestations of such talents. This would be neither possible nor desirable.

STUDENT SKILLS AND COGNITIVE AND AFFECTIVE ABILITIES

At this point, a germane question is, do skills and affective and cognitive abilities need to be accounted for in a definition of talent in the arts, or would any of these be sufficient alone as an indicator of talent? Stalker (1981), for example, included cognitive complexity (manifesting many solutions to problems), executive drawing abilities (superior skills in drawing), and affective intensity (strength of emotional responses and judgments) as parts of her definition of visual arts talent. Jellen and Verduin (1986) did not address problems of identification, but rather concepts that define gifted and talented students. They included three inclusive domains: cognitive (intelligence and imagination), affective (empathy and sensitivity), and conative (interest and motivation). These seem somewhat parallel to Renzulli et al.'s (1981) more familiar factors of intelligence, creativity, and task commitment. According to Gardner (1989), development in any skill area or talent area proceeds separately during a student's years of greatest development; they may or may not be present at the same levels at the same time, although potential for talented performances may be latent in one or all of them.

STUDENT BACKGROUNDS

Clark and Zimmerman (1992, 1994a), in reviews of research about artistically talented students, found little that dealt with the personalities of talented visual arts students or their values and backgrounds. Only a small body of research dealt with educational opportunities for such students. Researchers in psychology and art education have conducted interviews with young art students or artists, in their formative years, to gain access to their early reminiscences. Getzels and Csikszentmihalyi (1976) interviewed young artists when they were college art students and after they left school. Bloom and his associates (1985) interviewed individuals who reached high levels of accomplishment in the their fields before the age of 35. Among the people interviewed were concert pianists and sculptors as well as high achievers in science, mathematics, and sports. Siblings and the parents of these individuals also were interviewed. A few researchers have interviewed young, artistically talented students to gain information about their perceptions and understanding of life situations (Rostan et al., 1998). Chetelat (1982) interviewed six artistically talented students, aged 11 to 14, to discern differences and similarities of specific characteristics and their living and learning environments. He also studied the early childhood experiences of six eminent artists as recorded in autobiographical accounts. Using interviews and open-ended questionnaires, Guskin, Zimmerman, Okola, and Peng (1986) studied artistically talented and academically gifted students, aged 9 to 15, in order to understand how high-ability students view themselves and how they interpret their abilities. Taylor (1986), drawing extensively upon Hargreaves's (1982) work with adults, interviewed artistically talented students, aged 14 to 18, to determine how they developed a commitment to one or more art forms, and how they identified or empathized with artworks. Clark and

Zimmerman (1988) interviewed artistically talented students, aged 12 to 16, in a summer arts program on a university campus.

Some of the results of these studies are in agreement; others are not. Clark and Zimmerman (1988) found that a majority of students in their program felt good about themselves and their abilities and could accept criticism in order to improve their work. Nearly half the students mentioned the importance of winning awards as a factor in maintaining their interest in art and contributing to support from their families. The majority of students expressed pleasure at being grouped with others with similar interests and abilities. In this study, most students were aware of their art talent, were interested in improving their abilities, and were introspective about the role of the arts in their lives. A majority of students knew that they possessed unusual interest and abilities in the arts, a finding similar to those reported by Bloom (1985) and Chetelat (1982). Students had favorable views of themselves and of talented students in general, as did students in the Guskin et al. study (1986). Bloom (1985) and Chetelat (1982) also found, as did Clark and Zimmerman, that young people with talent in the arts find art-making experiences rewarding. Although Getzels and Csikszentmihalyi (1976) reported that emotional crises were stimulants to creating art, the majority of subjects in the Clark and Zimmerman study made no reference to an emotional crisis as a basis for their art making. Most of the students in the Clark and Zimmerman study reported that their families encouraged them to maintain their interest in art, although family members did not have art backgrounds. Bloom and Chetelat reported strong support from both parents and encouragement for their children. Subjects in this study reported similar support in most cases. This finding contradicts findings by Getzels and Csikszentmihalyi that young art students frequently received support only from their mothers and had harsh memories of their fathers.

Bloom (1985) reported that parents of talented students varied greatly in the level of education they had completed, the type of work they engaged in, their economic levels, and their avocational interests and activities. In the Clark and Zimmerman study, students' responses and other information verified similar findings about parents. Bloom reported, however, that the students he studied came from homes that emphasized music and the arts; few subjects in the Clark and Zimmerman study were offered such opportunities either at home or in any other aspect of their lives. Recollections of their art teachers varied widely among subjects in this study, although many recalled specific teachers who rewarded and encouraged them. Unlike Chetelat's (1982) subjects, not all recalled their art teachers positively. In this study, as well as in studies by Bloom and Chetelat, researchers found that positive motivation for art was generated among students when their artworks were selected for exhibit, when they participated in an art club, or when they were otherwise singled out for praise.

The issue of identifying and providing appropriate programs for students with superior talent in the visual arts in diverse populations is of current concern to many researchers and educators. Students from diverse backgrounds, including minority students and students from low socioeconomic groups, usually are underrepresented in one or more phases of identification programs for special educational opportunities (Richert, 1987). In Clark and Zimmerman's (2001b) study of elementary students with interest and abilities in the visual arts, they found that students from "minority" groups, who were economically challenged, could be identified as talented through sensitive measures developed locally by teachers, students, parents, community members, and artists.

DIVERSE EDUCATIONAL CONTEXTS

A number of studies point to the impact of community involvement in successful programs for rural students with high interest and abilities in the visual arts (Cleveland, 1980; Lally, 1986). Of particular interest is research that has been done in Israel on the involvement of local community members in educational programs for gifted and talented students. In a "Discovery Program," selected rural and other underserved students are identified and prepared to be accepted into the Israel Arts and Sciences Academy, a national, residential high school for very highly gifted and talented students (Amran, 1991). Several procedures were found to be helpful in ensuring the success of rural and underserved gifted and talented students, including meeting with an official from each community to solicit and guarantee his or her prolonged support; holding a series of meetings with school principals, local teachers, and parents of highly able students to ensure understanding of the program's goals and activities; and employing local people who understand community needs and values as program administrators and teachers. Such program personnel are more successful in promoting positive educational outcomes than are outsiders.

Clark and Zimmerman (1988) interviewed a random sample of 12- to 16-year-old artistically talented students. As a result of interviews with these students, it was clear that rural students with high abilities in the visual arts had fewer opportunities than students from urban areas to experience music or art, either at home or in their local communities. Students from rural areas viewed school as a social environment, and did not have many friends with similar art interests; whereas students from urban areas described a variety of places where they socialized with friends who had similar art interests. It also was suggested that a variety of authentic measures be used to collect information from students, teachers, parents, and others so that identification procedures, differentiated curricula and program options could be designed to both meet the needs of artistically talented students and at the same time provide enrichment opportunities for entire school populations. Finally, community involvement should be a high priority in rural art programs for high-ability art students. In such programs, parents, local artists, and other concerned citizens should be actively involved in all aspects of programs designed for rural, artistically talented students. Such community involvement often leads to positive communication among local school administrators, teachers, and parents who understand community values and mores.

ABILITY GROUPING IN DIVERSE CULTURES

A comparative analysis of ability grouping around the world, conducted by Arnove and Zimmerman (1999), focused on whether or not to emphasize individual differences or group commonalties, and whether excellence or equity should be foremost in policy decisions governing education. They concentrated on a few comparative cases in the United States, Japan, South Korea, France, Germany, Canada, and China. Although there are many differences in the educational and political systems in these countries, all have policies and practices that lead to sorting students and exposing them to differentiated curricula. Arnove and Zimmerman found that there were differences in the point at which differentiation occurs, how subtle the process is and the form it takes, and the extent to which selection is based not only on some criteria of merit but also on nonachievement factors. Although this study did not focus on art talent development exclusively, a number of the cases included input from art educators. The researchers concluded that "despite historical and societal differences, there is a tendency for education systems to converge on a middle point between the extremes of highly centralized educational systems with little attention to individual differences and highly decentralized systems giving little attention to group similarities" (p. 126). They noted a parallel continuum that exists between polar opposites of excellence and equity. In the countries studied, a tension between excellence and equity is manifest in policies for identifying and cultivating unique talents of gifted and talented students while simultaneously downplaying individual differences and providing access to high-quality programs for all students (Zimmerman, 1997). Arnove and Zimmerman concluded that "all countries need balanced policies that uphold this dynamic tension . . . but, at the same time, meet specific needs of students studying in a variety of contexts, connected to a particular society's political, social, and economic values" (p. 126).

GENDER ISSUES AND ARTISTICALLY TALENTED STUDENTS

Although there is a paucity of research about artistically talented girls, there is a considerable amount of research about academically gifted girls (Kerr, 1987; Reis, 1987, 1991; Silverman, 1986). There have been a few studies about artistically talented girls (Goldsmith, 1992; Golomb, 1992; Nelson & Janzen, 1990); however, there are many more longitudinal case studies about artistically talented boys and these included study of their artworks, art education, and perceptions and life situations (Duncum, 1984; Gardner, 1980; Wilson & Wilson, 1980; Zimmerman, 1995). Zimmerman (1995–1996) interviewed artistically talented teenagers and found some similarities and differences with studies about academically talented girls. She found that cultural stereotyping (Reis, 1987, 1991) was apparent in the choices of subject matter and media that girls and boys remembered using at an early age. Although all boys realized at an early age that they possessed special talents, only half the girls were aware of their capabilities in art. As did academically talented boys (Kerr, 1987), artistically talented boys developed a stronger sense of identity through their artwork than did girls. Artistically talented girls generally lacked self-esteem. Such poor self-esteem contributes to females' lower levels of achievement (Reis, 1987, 1991). Zimmerman found almost all the girls had unrealistic notions about what artists must do to achieve success. Lack of realistic and practical planning for future careers was more apparent in girls' responses than in boys'; these outcomes mirrored Kelly and Cobb's (1991) findings for academically talented girls. Silverman (1986) stressed the importance of parents and others who encouraged their daughters; she also emphasized the importance of support and assistance of males. In Zimmerman's study, most mothers encouraged their daughter's artwork; however, only 25% of the fathers were interested or supported their daughters' artwork.

Most girls in the Zimmerman study were model students, interested in getting good grades and gaining admiration from their teachers and peers; they demonstrated what Loeb and Jay (1987) described as a need for achievement through conformity. Boys were less interested in being well behaved or conscientious about their school work and were more independent and self-reliant than were girls. For artistically talented girls, the most preferred class was math, this same subject disliked by most of the artistically talented boys. This finding differs from most studies about academically talented students (Reis, 1987, 1991) and does not fit the stereotype of girls having a high incidence of math anxiety.

DISTRIBUTION AND STANDARDIZED TESTING

No discussion of issues about defining talents in the visual arts would be complete without acknowledging how talent is distributed in the world's population. A number of arts education researchers, across the years, have speculated—or displayed—that talent in the arts is normally distributed among all students in schools and the adult population, with those considered superior at the upper end and those below average at the lower end (Clark & Zimmerman, 1995, 2000; Lark-Horovitz, Lewis, & Luca, 1967; Lark-Horovitz & Norton, 1959; Munro, 1956; Sarason, 1990). If talent is taken to be normally distributed, then the possibility of standard testing in the visual arts is a viable concept. In the visual arts, however, there are few nationally standardized tests that have been used to measure preferences for design, drawing abilities, or aesthetic judgment, such as those developed by Graves (1978), Horn (1953), or Meier (1963). These tests have been evaluated by numbers of reviewers, and questions have been raised about their usefulness in respect to outmoded items and illustrations, inadequate samples, weak validities, inconsistent scoring, and lack of completeness as measures of art abilities (Buros, 1972; Clark & Zimmerman, 1984a; Eisner, 1972). A few nationally available rating scales or checklists exist and have been used with some success (Khatena, 1982; Renzulli, Smith, White, Callahan, & Hartman, 1976). At the state level, in 1990, about 23 locally designed visual arts achievement tests were in use (Sabol, 1994). Most attempts to develop standardized tests for use within a state have resulted in emphases on basic abilities that have been used as measures in other content areas (Hamblen, 1988).

An exception is Clark's Drawing Abilities Test (CDAT) that has been shown to be reliable and valid in a variety of educational contexts (Clark, 1993; Clark & Wilson, 1991; Clark & Zimmerman, 2001b). The CDAT was used as a research instrument in a federally funded project that was designed to identify high ability, artistically talented, elementary students from four different ethnic backgrounds, in seven rural schools, and to implement differentiated arts programs for them (Clark & Zimmerman, 2001b). In research about identification of students in this project, scores on the Torrance Tests of Creativity, Clark's Drawing Abilities Test, and state achievement tests were found to be correlated. Except at one site, gender was not found to be a significant variable on these tests. In the same project, locally designed identification measures, developed by teachers and community members, were found to be appropriate by teachers and staff if several, different measures were used. As a result of this study, it was recommended that local measures, the CDAT, and achievement tests be used to identify artistically talented students in rural communities with populations similar to those in this project.

Many scholars have suggested multiple criteria systems should be used for art talent development identification and assessment (Boston, 1987; Clark & Zimmerman, 1994, 2001b; Chetelat, 1982; Cox & Daniel, 1983; Hurwitz & Day, 1991; Khatena, 1989; Saunders, 1982; Stalker, 1981; Wenner, 1985, 1990). These systems include using a number of procedures such as self-nominations; peer nominations; parent nominations; teacher nominations; observations; interviews; grades in art; selected, standardized art and creativity tests; portfolios; and work samples done on site.

TEACHER CHARACTERISTICS AND STRATEGIES RELATED TO TALENTED STUDENTS' ART LEARNING

Descriptions of ideal teachers for gifted and talented students has been generated by a number of authors on the basis of armchair speculation (e.g., Gold, 1965; Khatena, 1982; Torrance, 1962). These descriptions generally are impractical because they are either idealistically unattainable or they fail to differentiate between good teachers for all students and good teachers for certain students with high abilities (Clark & Zimmerman, 1984a; Gallagher, 1975). There are a few studies about teachers of academically gifted students and still fewer about teachers of artistically talented students.

Story (1985) reported that traits most often cited in literature about successful teaching of academically gifted students were not directly identified from observed behavior patterns; rather, these traits were identified through interviews and qualitative analyses. Lundsteen (1987) advocated using qualitative methods to better understand processes of teaching academically gifted students. Although there are a few qualitative studies about teachers of academically talented students, there is a paucity of such studies about teachers of artistically talented students.

Bloom (1985) and his colleagues described characteristics of teachers of individuals who had attained world-class accomplishments before age 35. The group of individuals studied were sculptors who noted that the most important part of their professional art education was studying with teachers who were professional artists (see also, Albertson, 2001). As they progressed in their education, these sculptors related that they were taught less about skills and techniques and more about "art issues" (p. 127) that included becoming intensely involved in the study of art history and art criticism. Through projects, classes, interactions with teachers, and "copying" the work of artists, these individuals slowly learned "the language, the history, the rituals, and the techniques of making art" (p. 128).

Zimmerman (1991, 1992a) studied the teaching methods and strategies of two teachers who taught 2-week painting courses for 13- to 16-year-old artistically talented students. These two case studies of painting teachers yielded two models of teaching highly able young adolescents who were identified as talented in the visual arts. One teacher met the students' needs for developing skills and techniques; the other teacher, in addition to teaching skills and techniques, encouraged students to become engaged in art issues and to think reflectively about the context in which they were creating art. The latter teacher mirrored more qualities associated with teachers who were identified in the Bloom (1985) study as successful art teachers for talented students. It was concluded from this comparative study that if artists teach talented students they should be aware that their students may have needs for knowledge and understandings that include becoming aware of the contexts in which they make art, examining their reasons for creating art, and becoming intensely involved in art issues that go beyond the acquisition of art skills and techniques.

RECOMMENDATIONS FOR FUTURE RESEARCH

We offer these suggestions for further research in this area.

- Collaborative work by researchers in the fields of both psychology and education should explore the ill-defined terms, *talent, giftedness, and creativity.*
- Future research into the development of artistically gifted children and adults needs to incorporate two key notions in artistic development: (a) that graphic development has several end points, not just one; (b) graphic development cannot be understood as a single-minded quest for "realism."
- Future researchers should look much more closely at the development of certain features of graphic development that have up to now been overlooked such as development of expression, use of color, and the acquisition of culturally approved graphic models and conventions and the myriad of graphic properties that do not depend on the acquisition of mimetic skills.
- Future researchers should examine the relationship between those aspects of graphic development that are universally given as a function of the laws of perception and representation and those aspects that are culturally imposed norms.
- The myth that artistically talented students learn best if left to their own devices is still alive and well. We have presented a number of studies that challenge this notion. There is clearly a need for more research about the impact of educational opportunities, educational settings, and the role of art teachers on the development of artistically talented students.
- So that equitable art learning experiences can be provided for all students in a variety of educational contexts, more research about visual art talent development must be conducted. This should focus on students' backgrounds, personalities, gender orientations, skill development, and cognitive and affective abilities.

- There also is a need for researchers to focus on art talent development in cross-cultural contexts and on the impact of global and popular culture on the education of artistically talented students.
- The relationship of standards and the testing movement with processes of nuturing art learnings for artistically talented students should be clarified. In an age of performance-based outcomes, we also need to ask if the educational environments we provide are best suited to educate our talented visual arts students.
- Students' backgrounds, personalities, values, gender, and age need to be studied further as factors in the identification of art talent. Multiple criteria that are sensitive to the communities in which students learn need to be developed and studied in terms of their effectiveness in a variety of settings.
- Large-scale studies and longitudinal case studies should be conducted about the nature of programming opportunities for high-ability art students from a variety of diverse backgrounds. When program evaluations are reported, they should include discussion of both strengths and weaknesses of standardized and authentic assessment measures.

REFERENCES

Albertson, C. (2001). *Because clay has a memory. Conversations about dyslexia, ceramics and success*. Doctoral dissertation in Art Education. Concordia University, Montreal.

Amram, R. (1991). Things in action: The Discovery Program Exploration Camps. *Roeper Review, 13*(2), 82.

Andrews, J. (1989). Wang Yani and contemporary Chinese painting. In H. W. Ching (Ed), *Yani the brush of innocence* (pp. 39–50). New York: Hudson Hills Press.

Arnheim, R. (1969). *Visual thinking*. Berkeley: University of California Press.

Arnove, R. F., & Zimmerman, E. (1999). Dynamic tensions in ability grouping: A comparative perspective and critical analysis. *Educational Horizons, 77*(3), 120–127.

Atkinson, D. (1991). How children use drawing. *Journal of Art and Design Education, 10*(1), 57–72.

Bachtel, A. E. (1988). A study of current selection and identification processes and schooling for K–12 artistically gifted and talented students (Doctoral dissertation, University of Southern California). *Dissertation Abstracts International*, 49, 12A–3597.

Barron, F. (1972). *Artists in the making*. New York: Seminar Press.

Binet, A., & Simon T. (1916). *The development of intelligence in children*. Reprint: New York: Arno Press 1973.

Bloom, B. (1985). *Developing talent in young people*. New York: Ballantine Books.

Borland, J. H. (1986). IQ tests: Throwing out the bathwater, saving the baby. *Roeper Review, 8*, 163–167.

Boston, N. E. (1987). *Determining giftedness in elementary visual arts students*. South Bend, IN: Indiana University (ERIC Document Reproduction Service ED 301025).

Bremner, J., & Moore S. (1984). Prior visual inspection and object naming: Two factors enhance hidden feature inclusion in young children's drawings. *British Journal of Developmental Psychology, 2*, 371–376.

Brown, K. E. (1982). *Development and evaluation of a program for culturally diverse talented children. Dissertation Abstracts International*, 44/01A. (Publication No. AAC8311042)

Brown, N. C. M. (2001). The imputation of authenticity in the assessments of student performances in art. *Educational Philosophy and Theory, 33*(3–4), 293–305.

Buros, O. (Ed.). (1972). *The seventh mental measurements yearbook*. Highland Park, NJ: Gryphon Press.

Carroll, K. (1994). Artistic beginnings: The work of young Edvard Munch. *Studies in Art Education, 36*(1) 7–17.

Case, R., Tu, M., & Berg, R., (1992). A Cross-National Comparison of Children's Skill in Perspective Drawing. Unpublished Ms.

Chan, L., & Lobo, L. (1992). Developmental trends of Chinese preschool children in drawing and writing. *Journal of Research in Childhood Education, 6*, 93–99.

Chetelat, F. J. (1982). *A preliminary investigation into the life situations and environments which nurture the artistically gifted and talented child*. Unpublished doctoral dissertation. Pennsylvania State University, College Park.

Clark, G. (1993). Judging children's drawings as measures of art abilities. *Studies in Art Education, 34*(2), 72–81.

Clark, G., & Wilson, T. (1991). Screening and identifying gifted/talented students in the visual arts with Clark's Drawing Abilities Test. *Roeper Review, 13*(2), 92–97.

Clark, G., & Zimmerman, E. (1984a). *Educating artistically talented students*. Syracuse, NY: Syracuse University Press.

Clark, G., & Zimmerman, E. (1984b). What do we know about artistically talented students and their teachers? *Journal of Art and Design Education, 27*, 275–286.

Clark, G., & Zimmerman, E. (1987). *Understanding art testing: Past influences, Norman C. Meier's contributions, present concerns, and future possibilities.* Syracuse, NY: Syracuse University Press.

Clark, G., & Zimmerman, E. (1988). Views of self, family back-ground, and school: Interviews with artistically talented students. *Gifted Child Quarterly, 32*(4), 340–346.

Clark, G., & Zimmerman, E. (1992). *Issues and practices related to identification of gifted and talented students in the visual arts.* Storrs, CT: The National Research Center on the Gifted and Talented.

Clark, G., & Zimmerman, E. (1994). *Programming opportunities for students talented in the visual arts.* Storrs, CT: The National Research Center on the Gifted and Talented.

Clark, G., & Zimmerman, E. (1995). "You can't just scribble:" Art talent development. *The Educational Forum, 59*(4), 400–407.

Clark, G., & Zimmerman, E. (2000). Greater understanding of the local community: A community-based art education program for rural schools. *Art Education, 53*(2), 33–39.

Clark, G., & Zimmerman, E. (2001a). Art talent development, creativity, and enrichment in programs for artistically talented students in grades K-8. In M. D. Lynch & C. R. Harris (Eds.), *Fostering creativity in children, K-8: Theory and practice* (pp. 211–226). Boston: Allyn & Bacon.

Clark, G., & Zimmerman, E. (2001b). Identifying artistically talented students in four rural communities in the United States. *Gifted Child Quarterly, 45*(2), 104–144.

Cleveland, L. C. (1980). The use of community volunteers in a rural secondary school gifted and talented program. (Doctoral dissertation, Florida State University). *Dissertation Abstracts International, 41*, 10A.

Cox, J., & Daniel, N. (1983). Specialized schools for high ability students. *Gifted Child Today, 28*, 2–9.

Cox, M. V., Perara, J., & Xu, F. (1998). Children's drawing ability in the UK and China. *Psychologia, 41*, 171–182.

Crockenberg, S. B. (1972). Creativity tests: A boondoggle for education? *Review of Educational Research, 42*, 27–45.

Cronbach, L. J. (1960). *Essentials of psychological testing* (2nd ed.). New York: Harper & Row.

Cronin, V. (1966). *The romantic way.* New York: Houghton Mifflin.

Crow, L. D. (1963). Educating the academically able. In L. D. Crow. & A. Crow (Eds.), *Educating the academically able* (pp. 272–276). New York: McKay.

Csikszentmihalyi, M. (1988). Society, culture and person: A systems view of creativity. In R. J., Sternberg, (Ed.), *The nature of creativity: Contemporary psychological perspectives.* New York: Cambridge University Press.

Csikszentmihalyi, M. (1990). *Flow: The psychology of optimal experience.* New York: Harper & Row.

Csikszentmihalyi, M. (1996). *Creativity: Flow and the psychology of discovery and invention.* New York: Harper-Collins.

Csikszentmihalyi, M., & Getzels, J.W. (1973). The personality of young artists: An empirical and theoretical exploration. *British Journal of Psychology, 64*(1), 91–104.

Dennis, S., (1986). *The Development of Children's Art: A Neo-Piagetian Interpretation.* Doctoral Dissertation, Ontario Institute for Studies in Education, Toronto.

Dortu, M. (1971). *Toulouse-Lautrec et son oeuvre* (Vol. 6). New York: Collectors Editions.

Duncum, P. (1984). How 35 children, born between 1724 and 1900 learned to draw. *Studies in Art Education, 26*(1), 93–102.

Duff, J. (1987). *Wyeth: An American vision.* Singapore: Bullfinch Press.

Eisner, E.W. (1972). *Educating artistic vision.* New York: Macmillan.

Eisner, E. (1974). Examining some myths in art education. *Studies in Art Education, 15*(3), 7–16.

Eisner, E. W. (1994). *Cognition and curriculum reconsidered.* New York: Teachers College Press.

Fein, S., (1976). *Heidi's horse.* Pleasant Hill, CA: Exelrod Press.

Feist, J. (1999). The influence of personality on artistic and scientific creativity. In R. J. Sternberg (Ed.), *Handbook of creativity* (pp. 273–296). Cambridge: Cambridge University Press.

Feldhusen, J. F. (1992). *Talent identification and development in Education (TIDE).* Sarasota, FL: Center for Creative Learning.

Feldhusen, J. F., & Hoover, S. M. (1986). A conception of giftedness: Intelligence, self-concept, and motivation. *Roeper Review, 8*(3), 140–143.

Feldman, D. H. (1980). *Beyond universals in cognitive development.* Norwood, NJ: Ablex.

Feldman, D. H. (1982). *Developmental approaches to giftedness and creativity.* San Francisco: Jossey-Bass.

Feldman, D. H. (1999). The development of creativity. In R. J. Sternberg (Ed.), *Handbook of creativity* (pp. 169–186). Cambridge: Cambridge University Press.

Feldman, D. H., & Goldsmith, L. (1986a). *Nature's gambit: Child prodigies and the development of human potential.* New York: Basic Books.

Feldman, D. H., & Goldsmith, L. (1986b). Transgenerational influences on the development of early prodigious behavior: A case study approach. In W. Fowler (Ed.), *Early experience and the development of competencies*. San Francisco, CA: Jossey-Bass.

Fineberg, J. (1997). *The innocent eye: Children's art and the modern artist*. Princeton, NJ: Princeton University Press.

Franklin, M. (1994). Narratives of change and continuity: Women artists reflect on their work. In M. Franklin & B. Kaplan (Eds.), *Development in the arts. Critical perspectives* (pp. 165–192. Hillsdale, NJ: Lawrence Erlbaum Associates.

Freeman N. (1972). Process and product in children's drawings. *Perception, 1*, 123–140.

Gagne, F. (1985). Giftedness and talent: Reexamining a reexamination of definitions. *Gifted Child Quarterly, 29*(3), 103–112.

Gallagher, J. J. (1985). *Teaching the gifted child* (2nd & 3rd eds.). Boston, MA: Allyn & Bacon.

Gardner, H. (1980). *Artful scribbles. The significance of children's drawings*. New York: Basic Books .

Gardner, H. (1983). *Frames of mind: The theory of multiple intelligences*. New York: Basic Books.

Gardner, H. (1989a). *To open minds. Chinese clues to the dilemma of contemporary education*. New York: Basic Books.

Gardner, H. (1989b). Zero-based arts education: An introduction to Arts Propel *Studies in Art Education, 30*(2), 71–83.

Gardner, H. (1993). *Creating minds: An anatomy of creativity seen through the lives of Freud, Picasso, Stravinsky, Eliot,Graham and Ghandi*. New York: Basic Books.

Gardner, H. (1996). The creators' patterns. In M. A. Boden (Ed.), *Dimensions of creativity* (pp. 143–158). Cambridge, MA: MIT Press.

Gardner, H. (1999). *Intelligences reframed: Mulitple intelligences for the 21st. century*. New York: Basic Books.

Getzels, J. W., & Csikszentmihalyi, M. (1976). *The creative vision: A longitudinal study of problem finding in art*. New York: Wiley.

Glaesemer, J. (Ed.). (1973). *Paul Klee Handzeichnungen L. Kinderheit*. Bern: Kunstmuseum.

Gold, M. J. (1965). *Education of the intellectually gifted*. Columbus, OH: Charles E. Merrill.

Goldsmith, L. T. (1992). Wang Yani: Stylistic development of a Chinese painting prodigy. *Creativity Research Journal, 5*(3), 281–293.

Goldsmith, L., & Feldman D. (1989). Wang Yani: Gifts well given. In H. W. Ching (Ed.), *Yani: The brush of innocence* (pp. 51–65). New York: Hudson-Hills Press in association with the Nelson-Atkins Museum of Art, Kansas City, MO.

Golomb, C. (1992). *The child's creation of a pictorial world*. Berkeley: University of California Press.

Golomb, C. (1995a). Eitan: The artistic development of a child prodigy. In C. Golomb (Ed.), *The development of artistically gifted children: Selected case studies* (pp. 171–196). Hillsdale, NJ: Lawrence Erlbaum Associates.

Golomb, C. (Ed.). (1995b). *The development of artistically gifted children: Selected case studies*. Hillsdale, NJ: Lawrence Erlbaum Associates.

Gombrich, E. (1970). Meditations on a hobby horse or the roots of artistic form. In G. Pappas (Ed.), *Concepts in art education. An anthology of current issues*. New York: Macmillan.

Gombrich, E. (1988). *Art and illusion: A study in the psychology of pictorial representation*. Oxford: Phaidon Press. (Originally published in 1960)

Greenlaw, M. J., & McIntosh, M. E. (1988). *Educating the gifted: A sourcebook*. Chicago: American Library Association.

Gruber, H. (1982). *Darwin on man* (2nd ed.). Chicago. University of Chicago Press.

Guskin, S., Zimmerman, E., Okola, C., & Peng, J. (1986). Being labeled gifted or talented: Meanings and effects perceived by students in special programs. *Gifted Child Quarterly, 30*(2), 61–65.

Hamblen, K. (1988). If it will be tested, it will be taught. A rationale worthy of examination. *Art Education, 41*(5), 59–62.

Hargreaves, D. (1982). *The challenge for the comprehensive school*. London: Routledge & Kegan Paul.

Harris, D. (1963). *Children's drawings as measures of intellectual maturity*. New York: Harcourt Brace, and World.

Harvey, B., Manshu, Z., Biao, K., & Jue, Z. (1986). Spatial conceptions in Chinese and Canadian children. *The Journal of Genetic Psychology, 147*, 457–464.

Hoffman, R., & Trepannier, M. (1982). A cross-cultural influence on some basic graphic representations of young Chinese and American children. *The Journal of Genetic Psychology*, No. 141, 167–175.

Ho, W. C. (Ed.) (1989). *Yani: The brush of innocence*. New York: Hudson-Hills Press, in association with the Nelson-Atkins Museum of Art, Kansas City, MO.

Horn, C. C. (1953). *Horn art aptitude inventory*. Chicago: Stoelting.

Hunsaker, S. L., & Callahan, C. (1995). Creativity and giftedness: Instrument uses and *abuses*. *Gifted Child Quarterly, 39*(2), 110–114.

Hurwitz, A. (1983). *The gifted and talented in art: A guide to program planning*. Worcester, MA: Davis.

Hurwitz, A., & Day, M. (1991). *Children and their art: Methods for the elementary school* (5th ed.). San Diego, CA: Harcourt, Brace, Jovanovich.

Janson, H., & Janson D. (1952). *The story of painting for young people from cave painting to modern times.* New York: Harry Abrams.

Jellen, H. G., & Verduin, J. R. (1986*). Handbook of differentiated education of the gifted: A taxonomy of 32 key concepts.* Carbondale, IL: Southern Illinois University Press.

Jolley, R., & Thomas, G. (1995). Children's sensitivity to metaphorical expression of mood in line drawings. *British Journal of Developmental Psychology, 13,* 335–346.

Jolley, R., Thomas, G., & Zhi, Z. (1996). *The development of understanding moods metaphorically expressed in pictures: A crosscultural comparison in Britain and China.* Paper presented at The Growing Mind, Centennial of Jean Piaget's Birth Conference, University of Geneva.

Kao, M. (1998). Reforms in education and the beginning of the western style painting movement in China. In J. Andrews, & S. Kuiyi (Eds.), *A century in crisis. Modernity and tradition in the art of 20th century China* (pp. 146–172). New York: Harry N. Abrams.

Kaufman, A. S., & Harrison, P. L. (1986). Intelligence tests and gifted assessment: What are the positives? *Roeper Review, 8*(3), 154–159.

Kelly, K. R., & Cobb, S. J. (1991). A profile of the career development characteristics of young gifted adolescents: Examining gender and multicultural differences. *Roeper Review, 13*(4), 202–206.

Kerr, B. A. (1987). *Smart girls, gifted women.* Columbus, OH: Ohio Psychology.

Khatena, J. (1982). *Educational psychology of the gifted.* New York: Wiley.

Khatena, J. (1989). Intelligence and creativity to multitalent. *Journal of Creative Behavior, 23*(2), 93–97.

Kindler, A., Darras, B., & Kuo, A. (1998). Children and the world of art: Conversations with preschoolers and kindergartners about art, artists, and creativity in three cultures. *Canadian Review of Art Education,* 25(1), 67–82.

Kinney, A. (Ed.). (1995). *Introduction to Chinese views of childhood.* Honolulu University of Hawaii Press.

Kulp, M., & Tarter, B. J. (1986). The Creative Process Rating Scale. *The Creative Child and Adult Quarterly, 11*(3), 166–176.

Lally, E. M. (1986). A survey of gifted program administration in rural Alaska. (Doctoral Dissertation, University of the Pacific). *Dissertation Abstracts International, 47,* 10A.

Lark-Horovitz, B., Lewis, H., & Luca, M. (1967). *Understanding children's art for better teaching.* Columbus, OH: Merrill.

Lark-Horovitz, B., & Norton, J. A. (1959, 1960). Childrens' art abilities: The interrelations and factorial structure of ten characteristics. *Child Development, 30*(4), 433–452; *31*(1), 453–462.

Loeb, R. C., & Jay, G. (1987). Self-concept in gifted children: Differential impact in boys and girls. *Gifted Child Quarterly, 31*(1), 9–14.

Luca, M., & Allen, B. (1974). *Teaching gifted children art in grades one through three.* Sacramento, CA: California State Department of Education.

Lundsteen, S. W. C. (1987). Qualitative assessment of gifted education. *Gifted Child Quarterly, 31*(1), 25–29.

Luquet, G. (1927). *Le dessin enfantin,* Paris: Alcan.

Lutz, F., & Lutz, S. B. (1980). *Gifted pupils in the elementary school setting: An ethnographic study.* Paper presented at AERA in Boston.

McPherson, G. E. (1997). Giftedness and talent in music. *Journal of Aesthetic Education, 31*(4), 65–77.

McPherson, G. E. (1997). Giftedness and talent in music. *Journal of Aesthetic Education, 31*(4), 65–77.

Meier, N. C. (1963). *Meier Art Tests: Aesthetic Perception.* Iowa City, IA: State University of Iowa, Bureau of Educational Research and Service.

Milbrath, C. (1995). Germinal motifs in the work of a gifted child artist. In C. Golomb (Ed.), *The development of gifted child artists: Selected case studies* (pp. 101–135). Hillsdale, NJ: Lawrence Erlbaum Associates.

Milbrath, C. (1998). *Patterns of artistic development: Comparative studies of talent.* Cambridge: Cambridge University Press.

Motherwell, R. (1970). The universal language of children's art, and modernism. An address opening the plenary session of the International Exchange in the Arts (April 29). *The Scholar,* 24–27.

Mumford, M. D., Connely, M. S., Baughman, W. A., & Marks, M. A. (1994). Creativity and problem solving: Cognition, adaptability, and wisdom. *Roeper Review, 16*(4), 241–246.

Munro, T. (1956). *Art education: Its philosophy and psychology.* New York: Liberal Arts.

Munro, T., Lark-Horovitz, B., & Barnhardt, E. N. (1942). Children's art abilities: Studies at the Cleveland Museum of Art. *Journal of Experimental Education, 11*(2), 97–184.

Murray, G. (1991). *Toulouse-Lautrec: The formative years 1878–1891.* New York: Oxford University Press.

Nelson, K. C., & Janzen, P. (1990). Diane: Dilemma of the artistically talented in rural America. *Gifted Child Quarterly, 31*(1), 12–15.

Paine, S. (1987). The childhood and adolescent drawings of Henri-de Toulouse-Lautrec (1864–1901) drawings from 6 to 18 years. *Journal of Art and Design Education, 6*(3), 297–312.

Pariser, D. (1981). Nadia's drawings: Theorizing about an autistic child's phenomenal ability. *Journal of Studies in Art Education, 22*(2), 20–31.

Pariser, D. (1984). Two methods of teaching drawing skills. In R. MacGregor (Ed.), *Readings in Canadian Art Education* (pp. 143–158). Vancouver, BC: Wedge.

Pariser, D. (1987). The juvenile drawings of Klee, Toulouse-Lautrec and Picasso. *Visual Arts Research, 13*(2), 53–67.

Pariser, D. (1991). Normal and unusual aspects of juvenile artistic development in Klee, Lautrec and Picasso: A review of findings and direction for future research. *Creativity Research Journal, 4*(1), 51–67.

Pariser, D. (1995). Lautrec: Gifted child-artist and artistic monument: Connections between juvenile and mature work. In C. Golomb (Ed.), *The development of gifted child artists: Selected case studies* (pp. 31–71). Hillsdale, NJ: Lawrence Erlbaum Associates.

Pariser, D. (1997). Conceptions of children's artistic giftedness from modern and portmodern perspectives. *The Journal of Aesthetic Education, 31*(4), 35–47.

Pariser, D. (1999). The children of Kronos: What two artists and two cultures did with their childhood art. *Journal of Aesthetic Education, 33*(1), 62–72.

Pariser, D., & van den Berg, A. (2001). Teaching art versus teaching taste: What art teachers can learn from looking at a cross-cultural evaluation of children's art. Poetics. *Journal of Empirical Research on Literature, the Media and the Arts, 29*, 331–350.

Pariser, D., & Zimmerman, E. (1990) (Eds.). Special issue. Gender issues in art education. *Studies in Art Education, 32*(1).

Parker, J. P. (1989). *Instructional strategies for teaching the gifted.* Boston: Allyn & Bacon.

Passow, A. H. (Ed.). (1979). *The gifted the talented: Their education and development.* Chicago: University of Chicago Press (78th Yearbook of NSSE).

Porath, M. (1988). *The intellectual development of gifted children: A neo-Piagetian approach.* Doctoral dissertation. OISE, University of Toronto.

Reed, G. (1992). Modeling as pedagogical technique in the art and life of China. *Journal of Aesthetic Education, 26,* 75–83.

Reis, S. M. (1987). We can't change what we don't recognize: Understanding the special needs of gifted females. *Gifted Child Quarterly, 31*(2), 83–89.

Reis, S. M. (1991). The need for clarification in research designed to examine gender differences in achievement and accomplishment. *Roeper Review, 13*(4), 193–202.

Renzulli, J. S., & Reis, S. M. (1985). *The schoolwide enrichment model: A comprehensive plan for educational excellence.* Mansfield Center, CT: Creative Learning.

Renzulli, J. S., & Reis, S. M. (1994). Research related to the school-wide enrichment triad model. *Gifted Child Quarterly, 38*(1), 7–20.

Renzulli, J. S., Reis, S. M., & Smith, L. H. (1977). Two approaches to the identification of gifted students. *Exceptional Children, 43,* 512–518.

Renzulli, J. S., Reis, S. M., & Smith, L. H. (1981). *The revolving door identification model (RDIM).* Mansfield Center, CT: Creative Learning.

Renzulli, J. S., Smith, L. H., White, A. J., Callahan, C. M., & Hartman, R. K. (1976). *Scales for rating the behavioral characteristics of students.* Mansfield Center, CT: Creative Learning.

Richert, E. S. (1987). Rampant problems and promising practices on the identification of disadvantaged gifted students. *Gifted Child Quarterly, 31*(4), 149–154.

Robertson, A. (1987). Borrowing and artistic behavior: A case study of Bruce's spontaneous drawings from six to sixteen. *Studies in Art Education, 29*(1), 37–51.

Rostan, S. (1997). A study of young artists. The development of talent and creativity. *Creativity Research Journal, 10,* 175–192.

Rostan, S. M., Pariser, D., & Gruber, H. E. (1998, April). *What if Picasso, Lautrec, and Klee were in my art class? A study of the early signs of artistic talent.* Paper presented at the Annual Meeting of the American Educational Research Association, San Diego.

Rostan, S., Pariser, D., & Gruber, H. (2000). *Across time and place: A cross-cultural study of early artistic development: Two young artists.* Paper presented at the Jean Piaget Society Meeting, Montreal, Canada.

Rostan, S., Pariser, D., & Gruber H. (2001). *Cross-cultural study of artistic talent and creativity.* American Psychological Association. Paper presented at Division 10, San Francisco.

Runco, M. (1993). *Creativity as an educational objective for disadvantaged students.* Storrs, CT: The National Center on the Gifted and Talented.

Runco, M., & Nemiro, J. (1993). Problem finding and problem solving. *Roeper Review, 16*(4), 235–241.

Sabol, R. (1999). *A critical examination of visual arts achievement tests from state departments of education in the United States.* Unpublished doctoral dissertation, Indiana University, Bloomington, Indiana.

Sarason, S. (1990). *The challenge of art to psychology.* New Haven, CT: Yale University Press.

Saunders, R. J. (1982). Screening and identifying the talented in art. *Roeper Review, 4*(3), 7–10.

Schubert, D. S. P. (1973). Intelligence as necessary but not sufficient for creativity. *Journal of Genetic Psychology, 122,* 45–47.

Selfe, L. (1977). *Nadia: A case of extraordinary drawing ability in an autistic child.* London: Academic Press.

Selfe, L. (1983). *Normal and anomalous representational drawing ability in children.* London: Academic Press.

Selfe, L. (1995). Nadia reconsidered. In C. Golomb (Ed.), *The development of artistically gifted children* (pp. 197–237). Hillsdale, NJ: Lawrence Erlbaum Associates.

Shore, B. (1987). *Recommended practices in the education and upbringing: A progress report on an assessment of the knowledge base.* Indianapolos, IN: Department of Education.

Silverman, L. K. (1986). What happens to the gifted girl? In C. J. Maker (Ed.), *Critical issues in gifted education: Defensible programs for the gifted* (pp. 43–89). Austin, TX: Pro-Ed.

Sloan, K. D., & Sosniak, L. A. (1985). The development of accomplished sculptors. In B. Bloom (Ed.), *Developing talent in young people* (pp. 90–138). New York: Ballantine.

Smith, N. (1998). *Observation drawing with children. A framework for teaching.* New York: Teacher's College Press.

Sosniak, L. A. (1985). In B. Bloom (Ed.), *Developing talent in young people.* New York: Ballentine Books.

Staaller, N. (1986, September 1). Early Picasso and the origins of Cubism. *Arts Magazine, 61,* 80–90

Stalker, M. Z. (1981). Identification of the gifted in art. *Studies in Art Education, 22,* 49–56.

Stanley, J. C. (1977). Rationale of the study of mathematically precocious youth (SYMPY) during the first five years of promoting educational acceleration. In J. C. Stanley, W. C. George, & C. H. Solano (Eds.), *The gifted and creative: A fifty-year perspective* (pp. 75–112). Baltimore, MD: The Johns Hopkins University Press.

Starko, A. J. (2001). *Creativity in the classroom: Schools of curious delight* (2nd ed.). Mahwah, NJ: Lawrence Earlbaum Associates.

Sternberg, R. J. (1984). How can we teach intelligence? *Educational Leadership, 42,* 38–48.

Sternberg, R. (1985). *Beyond IQ.* New York: Cambridge University Press.

Sternberg, R. J. (1985). *Beyond IQ: A triarchic theory of human intelligence.* Cambridge: Cambridge University Press.

Sternberg, R. J. (1986). Identifying the gifted through IQ: Why a little bit of knowledge is a dangerous thing. *Roeper Review, 8*(3), 143–150.

Sternberg, R. J. (Ed). (1988). *The nature of creativity. Contemporary psychological perspectives.* New York: Cambridge University Press.

Sternberg, R. J. (1997). *Successful intelligence: How practical and creative intelligence determine success in life.* New York: PLUME.

Sternberg, R. J. (Ed.). (1999). *Handbook of creativity.* Cambridge: Cambridge University Press.

Sternberg, R. J., & Lubart, T. I. (1999). Concept of creativity: Prospects and paradigms. In R. J., Sternberg (Ed.), *Handbook of creativity* (pp. 3–15). Cambridge: Cambridge University Press.

Sternberg, R. J., & Williams, W. M. (1996). *How to develop student creativity.* Alexandria, VA: Association for Supervision and Curriculum Development.

Story, C. (1985). Facilitator of learning: A micro-ethnographic study of the teacher of the gifted. *Gifted Child Quarterly, 29*(4), 155–158.

Stratford, B., & Au, M. (1988). The development of drawing in Chinese and English children. *Early Child Development and Care, 30,*141–165.

Tannenbaum, A. (1983). *Gifted children: Psychological and educational perspectives.* New York: MacMillan.

Tannenbaum, A. (1986). Giftedness: A psychological approach. In R. J. Sternberg & J. E. Davidson (Eds.), *Conceptions of giftedness* (pp. 21–52). Cambridge: Cambridge University Press.

Tan, L. (1993). A case study of an artistically gifted Chineses girl: Wang Yani. Master's. Art Education thesis, Concordia University, Montreal.

Taylor, R. (1986). *Educating for art.* London: Longman

Torrance, E. P. (1962). *Education and the creative potential.* Minneapolis, MN: University of Minnesota Press.

Torrance, E. P. (1972). Career patterns and peak creative achievements of creative high school students twelve years later. *Gifted Child Quarterly, 26*(2), 75–88.

Treffinger, D. J., & Renzulli, J. (1986). Giftedness as potential for creative productivity: Transcending IQ issues. *Roeper Review, 8*(3), 150–163.

Treffinger, D. J., Sortore, M. R., & Cross, J. A. (1993). Programs and strategies for nurturing creativity. In K.A. Heller, F.J. Monk, & A.H. Passow (Eds.), *International handbook of research and development of giftedness and talent* (pp. 555–567). New York: Permagon.

van den Berg, A., Pariser, D., Kindler, A. M., Belidson D., & Wan, C. L. (2001). *De Gustibus non est Disputandum? Some preliminary cross-cultural tests of some transcultural theories.* A paper presented at the 5th Conference of the European Sociological Association, Helsinki.

Van Tassel-Baska, J. (1986). Acceleration. In C. June Maker (Ed.), *Critical issues in gifted education: Defensible programs for the gifted* (pp. 179–196). Rockville, MD: Aspen.

Van Tassel-Baska, J. (1987). The ineffectiveness of the pull-out program model in gifted education: A minority perspective. *Journal of Education of the Gifted, 10*(4), 255–264.

Vernon, P. E., Adamson, G., & Vernon, D. (1977). *The psychology and education of gifted children.* Boulder, CO: Viewpoint.

Wakefield, J. F. (1992). *Creative thinking: Problem solving skills and the arts orientation.* Norwood, NJ: Ablex.

Wallace, D., & Gruber, H. (Eds.) (1989). *Creative people at work: 12 Cognitive case studies.* New York: Oxford University Press.

Warner, J. (1981). John Everett Millais: Drawings from 7–18 years. In S. Paine (Ed.), *Six children draw* (pp. 9–22). London: Academic Press.

Wenner, G. C. (1985). Discovery and recognition of the artistically talented. *Journal for the Education of the Gifted, 8*(3), 221–238.

Wenner, G. C. (1990). A school for the fine(est) artists. *School Arts, 89*(9), 30–33.

Wilson, B., & Wilson, M. (1980). Beyond marvelous: Conventions and inventions in John Scott's Gemini. *School Arts, 80*(2), 19–26.

Wilson, B., & Wilson M. (1981). Review of artful scribbles: The significance of children's drawings. In H. Gardner (Ed.), *Studies in Visual Communication, 7*(1), 86–99.

Wiltshire, S. (1993). *Floating cities: Venice, Amsterdam, Moscow, Leningrad.* London: Michael Joseph.

Winner, E., & Martino, G. (1993). Giftedness in the visual arts and music. In K. A. Keller, F. J. Monk, & A. H. Passow (Eds.), *International handbook of research and development of giftedness and talent* (pp. 253–281). New York: Permagon.

Winner, E. (1989a). How can Chinese children draw so well? *Journal of Aesthetic Education, 23*, 41–65.

Winner, E. (1989b). Development in the visual arts: How universal? In N. Damon (Ed.), *Child development today and tomorrow,* San Francisco: Jossey-Bass.

Winner, E. (1996). *Gifted children: Myths and realities.* New York: Basic Books.

Winner E., & Martino G. (1993). Giftedness in the visual arts and music. In K. A. Heller, E. J. Monks, & A. H. Passow (Eds.), *International handbook of research and development of giftedness and talent* (pp. 253–281). New York: Pergamon Press.

Winner, E., & Pariser, D. (1985). Giftedness in the visual arts. *Items* (Social Science Research Council) *39*(4), 65–69.

Wolf, D. P. (1989). Portfolio assessment: Sampling student work. *Educational Leadership, 46*(7), 35—40.

Zervos, C. (1950). Oeuvres et images inedites de la jeunesse de Picasso. *Cahiers D'Art, 25*(2),

Zettel, J. (1979). State provisions for educating the gifted. In A. H. Passow (Ed.), *The gifted the talented: Their education and development.* Chicago: University of Chicago Press (78th Yearbook of NSSE).

Zimmerman, E. (1991). Rembrandt to Rembrandt: A case study of a memorable painting teacher of artistically talented 13 to 16 year-old students. *Roeper Review, 13*(2), 76–81.

Zimmerman, E. (1992a). A comparative study of two painting teachers of talented adolescents. *Studies in Art Education, 33*(2), 174–185.

Zimmerman, E. (1992b). Factors influencing the graphic development of a talented young artist. *Creativity Research Journal, 5*(3), 295–311.

Zimmerman, E. (1994–1995). Factors influencing the art education of artistically talented girls. *The Journal of Secondary Gifted Education, 6*(2), 103–112.

Zimmerman, E. (1995). It was an incredible experience: The impact of educational opportunities on a talented student's art development. In C. Golomb (Ed.), *The development of artistically gifted children: Selected case studies* (pp. 135–170). Hillsdale, NJ: Lawrence Erlbaum Associates.

Zimmerman, E. (1997). Excellence and equity issues in art education? Can we be excellent and equal too? *Art Education Policy Review, 98*(4), 20–26.

IV

Teaching and Teacher Education

18

Introduction to Teaching and Teacher Education

Enid Zimmerman
Indiana University

I have been teaching for 35 years, first as a K-12 art teacher and then as a university professor at the higher education level. Serving as a mentor to my students, and the rewarding results of those mentor–student relationships, is of great significance to me. I attempt to embody reflective teaching by focusing on the theme of mentoring as caring, that is, pedagogical nurturance of both the intellect and the spirit, because I think instruction does not terminate at the classroom door.

Collaboration with others, both in teaching and in writing scholarly articles about teaching, also is of great significance to me. Another important aspect of my teaching philosophy is viewing education from an intercultural point of view that combines aspects of multicultural, community-based, and global education perspectives. I believe in constructing an interconnected web of understanding that includes the belief that a community of knowledge can be created, both inside and outside classrooms and beyond our familiar settings. When I teach students from different backgrounds in diverse contexts, we all learn from each other.

Empowerment is a key issue for my students, who are preparing to be, or are, reflective practitioners. To this end, I have encourged these students to develop their personal, collaborative, and public voices through knowledge of and belief in one's self, through knowledge of content and pedagogy, through creating caring communities of leaders and learners, and through creation of shared success and autonomy. The end goals for these future teachers are to mentor others, to assume leadership roles, to be advocates for change, and to develop and present their work in public arenas. When I agreed to be both editor of this section on teaching and teacher education for the *Handbook on Research and Policy in Art Education,* I was influenced by what I thought was valuable, worthwhile, and meaningful for the field, as filtered through my own personal experiences and values.

While putting this section of the *Handbook* together and meandering through my files, I attempted to construct meaning from the vast array of materials I had sequestered away during my many years of teaching and of preparing future teachers. This research and my own background provided me with an opportunity to determine what I thought were the most important categories to discuss regarding teaching and teacher education. I also perused handbooks about teaching and teacher education in both general and specific subject matter areas. I asked myself what information was needed by practitioners and by those responsible for teacher education at preservice, inservice, and doctoral levels that would be beneficial in critical analyses and interpretations of current research in art education.

In 1992, I was one of a small group of arts educators who met in Annapolis, Maryland, to discuss setting a research agenda for arts in American schools in the 1990s. I prepared a paper for this conference, "Current Research and Practice about Pre-Service Visual Art Specialist Teacher Education," that was published in 1994. At that time, I concluded that how much knowledge preservice art teachers have about subject matter content, how they put that subject matter content into practice, and what impact outside influences would have on preservice programs needed to be explored through a carefully constructed research agenda. From 1993 to 1994, I served as the first National Art Education Research Commission Chair. One of the initiatives of this commission was to establish seven Research Task Forces, which met from 1994 to 1998, and produce a number of publications and initiate several research programs. Two of these Task Forces were Instruction and Teacher Education, and members were in agreement that the field of art education was in need of discovering what research was being conducted in these two areas and what research still needed to be studied and reconceptualized. In 1995, a symposium convened by Michael Day on the topic of art teacher preparation was funded by the Getty Education Institute for the Arts. His book *Preparing Teachers of Art,* published in 1997, dealt with a number of issues discussed at the meeting and also provided us with a number of useful conceptions for organizing the content of this section of the *Handbook.* I wrote a chapter in this book focusing on a demographic analysis of art teacher preparation programs in the United States and concluded that new technologies were emerging that could aid in the quest to collect demographic information about art teacher preparation programs. Once accurate information was available and easily accessible, then research efforts and practical applications for art education research studies could be enhanced. In the current research environment in art education research, much has been initiated and accomplished since I wrote the article and book chapter and organized Task Forces that coalesced around the issues and concerns about art teaching and teacher education.

In this section of the *Handbook*, I have been privileged to work with a group of seven art educators, who are pioneers in establishing a research base about art education teaching and teacher education. They have provided the most recent and expert critical analyses on this topic and have devoted much time and effort to not only reporting the current state of research but also providing conceptual frameworks from which informed perspectives about issues facing art teaching and teacher preparation can be formed and informed. This section was a collaborative process among the contributors to this chapter and myself. As a result of a meeting that took place in the year 2000 at Stanford University with all section editors and editors of the *Handbook*, Michael Day, Elliot Eisner, and I finalized the topics in this section: (a) demographics and art teacher education; (b) recruitment, certification, and retention of art teachers; (c) the practice of teaching in K-12 schools; (d) interaction of teaching and curriculum; (e) contexts for teaching art; and (f) teacher education as a field of study in art education. Each author submitted an outline that all the other authors and I read. Feedback from all involved was invaluable, prevented overlapping of information, and provided insights from a wide variety of perspectives. Then outlines were sent out again for final feedback. Authors then wrote and rewrote their chapters several times, the result being a comprehensive and well-articulated section on the status of research in art education related to teaching and teacher education. In addition, the recommendations for future art education research will be invaluable resources for seasoned as well as novice researchers and teachers who wish to to be better informed about their own practices.

This section of the *Handbook* has the potential to provide research which helps teachers and teacher educators recognize the positive aspects of accomplishments of programs and initiatives that are making differences in art education and also to uncover those places that are in need of more attention. With a well-conceived and well-documented research background, social action and positive change can be outcomes that impact how we teach, what we teach, and how we prepare teachers and researchers in art education.

Lynn Galbraith and Kit Grauer, in the chapter "State of the Field: Demographics and Art Teacher Education," explore demographic research methods, sources, and issues; develop themes and questions; develop, and describe and discuss representative examples of teacher education programs in both the United States and Canada with respect to size, location, enrollments, degrees, curriculum, and course work. Demographic research about preservice elementary classroom generalists teachers, art teachers, and teacher educators is presented next. Certification and licensure, standards and quality, and teacher quantity and quality are presented as important issues for both present and future research. Galbraith and Grauer call attention to the need for research to paint a more complete picture about the demographics of teacher education programs and faculty who prepare future art teachers as well as what is taught in these programs so as to establish a well-defined research baseline data for art education.

Mary Stokrocki, in her chapter, "Contexts for Teaching Art," presents complex contextual considerations such as physical environment, sociocultural factors, and economic and political challenges that all contribute to form, content, meaning, and value of art teaching. Her focus is research on schooling, community, intercultural, and electronic contexts for instruction in art education. Schooling contexts include studies about school culture; faculty working conditions; urban, suburban, and rural settings with respect to negotiation of learning agendas; community ethics; and inclusion of all students. Research about museum outreach programs, folk art as a source for art teaching, ethnic art in community centers, neighborhood sites, and correctional institutions are included in community contexts. Interculturalism, which blends multicultural, community-based, and global education, is presented as an area of inquiry that combines a number of past agendas and holds promise for contributory future research. In her review of studies devoted to electronic contexts for teaching, Srokrocki indicates that new models are emerging that are changing from single-site instruction to collaborative and multicontextual operations employing new media. She concludes that contexts are complex areas of research that often contain contradictory theories, practices, and outcomes; and a healthy debate about educational contexts for art teaching should be encouraged around issues such as politics of identity, multiple perspectives, and methodological concerns, making research outcomes appropriate and useful for a variety of constituents.

Mary Erickson, in her chapter, "Interaction of Teachers and Curriculum," examines how art curriculum relates to teaching through a complex of factors from three perspectives: art curriculum theories, available research, and conditions that affect individual teacher's decisions about selecting an appropriate curriculum. A review of past curriculum theories reveals that there are many proposals for curriculum reform, but few sustained efforts and bases in critical dialog. The literature in art education research reveals few studies that report on the effectiveness of large-scale curriculum efforts, although some studies can be found in areas of art-making instruction, effects of art understanding in a variety of educational contexts, and learning across the curriculum. Teachers' interactions with art curricula are influenced, according to Erickson's review, by educational traditions; preservice experiences, beliefs, and practices; and practical realities of classroom life. She recommends that researchers design studies around key variables important to art education as evidenced by past endeavors. Art teachers, she proposes, are in a position, due to their autonomy in choosing curriculum, to be a unique population for further inquiry. Last, Erickson recommends that researchers plan their studies in a manner by which they can be conducted in consortium with teachers and easily accessed by them.

Frances Thurber, in another contribution to this section, "Teacher Education as a Field of Study in Art Education: A Comprehensive Overview of Methodology and Methods Used in Research About Art Teacher Education," emphasizes the importance of finding questions of concern for art teaching and teacher education and then investigating them through appropriate methodologies. Her focus on methodologies and methods provides a conceptual framework for grounding research outcomes and informing practices encountered in the other chapters in this section. Her overview of methodological trends in art education and her diagraming of these trends presents a conceptual map that should be most helpful in charting present and future trends. Thurber has taken my original conceptual model for art education research designed more than 2 decades ago and reconceptualized its components to accommodate contemporary methodologies and methods that have proliferated since my model was originally conceived. I was teaching a graduate course about art education research when Thurber was writing this section, and my students and I had an opportunity to provide Thurber with a critique of a few earlier versions of her conceptual framework that appear in the *Handbook*. This experience provided a model for my students to experience how a community of scholars can work collaboratively to inform the field of art education. Thurber, in her chapter, first presents an historical context for research methodology in art education and then presents a number of inquiries employing contemporary methodologies in categories suggested by a review of the literature. These categories include phenomenology, hermeneutics, constructivist analyses, ethnography, ethnology, ethnomethodology, narrative and visual sociology, case studies, connoisseurship and educational criticism, critical theory, feminist approaches, paradigm research, philosophical and theoretical research, content analysis, and action and collaborative research. She then highlights specific researchers and their bodies of work based on findings from her exhaustive study of the field. Her recommendations for the field of art education call for attending to emerging trends in educational research, connecting research to past efforts, increasing collaboration among researchers from a variety of settings, developing methodologies that interface with emerging research in other areas, promoting action research by teachers, exploring the use of new media in research, and publishing results of research not only in art education but also in other fields. She encourages art education researchers to use their "colorful and creative minds" by continuing to ask intriguing questions and yet at the same time by honoring the past.

Robert Sabol, author of the chapter "Recruitment, Certification, and Retention of Art Teachers" examines how three waves of educational reform have affected the field of art education. He sets the stage for discussion of recruitment, certification, and retention in the arena of general education research and then relates these findings to preservice and inservice art teachers. In the future, Sabol predicts that recruitment, certification, and retention of art teachers will be affected by three forces: the standards movement, assessment, and technology. Research, he believes, plays a critical role and encourages others to join the ranks of those who already are conducting studies in these areas. He raises numerous questions that could be the basis of a number of needed research studies and emphasizes the need to provide support and incentives for those who are entering the field of art teaching.

In the final contribution to this section, Judith M. Burton, in "The Practice of Teaching in K-12 Schools: Devises and Desires," provides personal and professional perspectives about the practice of teaching, teachers' instructional work, their experiences in the classrooms, and what they are expected to know and be able to do. "Teachers' work," she explains, "has come to be more and more the object of public scrutiny." However, there is not much consensus about good practice and what ingredients are required for success. Burton sets forth three trends that she sees emerging from research literature about art teaching: speculative–theoretical, inferential–empirical, and the descriptive case study. Those whose research can be categorized as emanating from a speculative–theoretical perspective offer new possibilities for teaching practice; however, means of reaching innovative practices often are not addressed. Researchers who employ an empirical–inferential position often use quantitative methods for determining teachers' practices, often surveys, that meet the demands of school administrators and policymakers and add to the research base in art education. Burton calls attention, however, to the danger of making causal links between quantitative findings and classroom instruction. The complexity of classroom life, she maintains, cannot be easily captured by such studies. Taken from a descriptive case study point of view, the focus is on narrative accounts of classroom practice that often cannot be generalized beyond the contexts in which their study resides. From such narratives, Burton contends these studies hold promise for gaining insights into fundamental elements for improving classroom art practice and ensuring professional excellence.

As this section of the *Handbook* began to take form, I became aware, more than I had ever in the past, of the multifaceted and rich avenues and contexts that are available for conducting research on art teaching and teacher education. In all these chapters, there is a dynamic tension between what general education research offers the field and what art education as a specific domain within education has to offer to which no other area of education can make claim. As I reflect back on the beginning of this introduction and revisit the beliefs and values that undergird my many years of practice in art education, I question whether these are relative only to my experiences or if they are universal and, through research, can be shown to be held by others in a variety of art education settings. In art education we have an opportunity to celebrate what is unique to our field as we capitalize on our backgrounds as creative and innovative researchers and as we construct future avenues for research in art education. In order to accomplish this, we need to create bodies of work that are sustained over long periods of time, which extend from the past through the present and to the future. This section about art teaching and art teacher education provides a basis for critically examining theory and its relation to practice. It also offers a research agenda in art education for the succeeding generations of all those who have a stake in building a future where art education is valued for all those qualities that we believe are important to everyone's education. These agendas can come to fruition, with some surprises as well, if they are backed by research that demonstrates what many may already know intuitively.

REFERENCES

Zimmerman, E. (1994). Current research and practice about pre-service visual art generalist teacher education. *Studies in Art Education, 35*(2), 78–89.

Zimmerman, E. (1997). Whence come we? What are we? Wither go we? Demographic analysis of art education teacher preparation programs. In M. Day (Ed.), *Preparing teachers of art* (pp. 27–44). Reston, VA: National Art Education Association.

19

State of the Field: Demographics and Art Teacher Education

Lynn Galbraith
University of Arizona

Kit Grauer
University of British Columbia

In this chapter, existing art education data and related literature are examined in order to provide a demographic portrait of art teacher education today. Our goal is directed toward contributing to the knowledge and understanding of art teacher education in the broader community of art education scholars and educators.

We first describe research methods and databases employed in this chapter and provide an overview of how demographic research is defined in relation to art teacher education. Second, we look at issues that surround development of a demographic picture within art teacher education. Third, our inquiry focuses on questions related to three major themes: teacher education programs, preservice and practicing teachers, and teacher educators. We then follow with a discussion about other demographic issues that affect how art teachers are prepared today. We conclude with a few reflective comments about the future of demographic research within art teacher education.

DEMOGRAPHICS: RESEARCH FRAMEWORK

In this section of the chapter, our purpose is to outline what it means to conduct demographic research within art education and explore the relationship of this research to art teacher education. We also provide a rationale for the issues, themes, and questions that have shaped this inquiry.

Demographic Research: Methods and Sources

Zimmerman (1997a), citing Burton (1996), identified demographic research as the identification of specific populations using "geographic, economic, social, educational, and other parameters" (p. 29). In this chapter we pay particular attention to identifying and asking questions about teacher education programs (e.g., program size, location, and context) and specific populations (e.g., preservice teachers, practicing teachers, postsecondary art education faculty) that encompass art teacher education today.

Zimmerman (1994a) outlined certain types of research that can be employed in collecting demographic data. These methods include basic research, previous demographic research, foundational research, rationales, broad-based research, comparative research, single-group research, and trend analysis. Zimmerman (1997b) elaborated further by stating that demographic researchers often collect data through the use of surveys and by regrouping and analyzing data that have been previously collected in data banks. Richardson (1996) noted that descriptive studies of teacher education programs and systems often comprise large- or small-scale surveys or multiple case studies. These studies are designed to provide "verbal pictures of systems" (Richardson, 1996, p. 716) as they describe the characteristics of populations, programs, and the contexts of these programs. Additionally, as Sevigny (1987) noted, determining changing demographic patterns and trends within teacher education requires some understanding of traditions prior to such changes.

We began our inquiry with an extensive literature review of demographic research within art education and specifically targeted research that related specifically to art teacher education. We identified relevant sources and studies by conducting database searches such as ERIC, FirstSearch, *Dissertation Abstracts*, and Arts & Humanities Citation Index. We also examined existing syntheses of art education research (see, for example, Colbert & Taunton, 2001; Galbraith, 2002; Jones & McPhee, 1986), as well as key writings on art teacher education (see, for example, Davis, 1990; Day, 1997; Zimmerman, 1994b) and selected National Art Education Association (NAEA) publications on teaching and learning and on teacher education quality (see, for example, the *Standards for Art Teacher Preparation*, NAEA, 1979, 1999). We also consulted publications of the NAEA Research Commission (see, for example, NAEA, 1994a, 1998; Zimmerman, 1994a), along with reports and documentation from the various NAEA Research Task Forces (specifically the task forces on Demographics and Teacher Education). The NAEA executive director, Dr. Thomas Hatfield, forwarded a number of teacher-education-based reports to the authors. An examination of recent annual NAEA Convention catalogs also was conducted in a search for relevant information.

This search was extended to include applicable research located in handbooks on general education research and teacher education (see, for example, Murray, 1996; Wittrock, 1986) and other arts disciplines (see, for example, Colwell & Richardson, 2002). We also examined standards for teacher education programs outlined by the National Board for Professional Teaching Standards (National Board for Professional Teaching Standards, 1994), by the National Council for Accreditation of Teacher Education (National Council for Accreditation of Teacher Education, 2001), and by recent reports written by proponents of educational reform for teacher preparation within the United States (see, for example, National Commission on Teaching and America's Future, 1996).

In addition, the National Center for Educational Statistics (www.nces.org) and the Educational Testing Service (www.ets.org) served as useful Web site databases. Other helpful electronic databases were the report on the quality of teacher preparation issued by the U.S. Department of Education (www.title2.org/statereports/index.html) and Web sites from the departments of education within various U.S. states. These sources provided information on various licensure and certification procedures and standards.

DEMOGRAPHICS: DEVELOPING A PICTURE

Developing a Picture: Issues and Considerations

Wilson, Floden, and Fernini-Mundy (2001) argued not only that development of a research base that closely examines teacher education programs only began in the 1960s and gained momentum in the 1980s but also that research in this area is lacking. Clark (2001) maintained that the chronic discrepancy between institutional regard for the role of educator and institutional regard for the role of scholar was a constant impediment to development of teacher education as a field of study. Ducharme (1993) has posited that those faculty members who work closely with K–12 schools are regarded less highly on college and university campuses than faculty who are viewed as working in more theoretical and less practical subject disciplines. The past decade, however, has seen the rise of unprecedented new scholarship in the area of teacher education. As yet, this focus in teacher education does not appear to have the same impact on art education as it does on other fields of education.

Galbraith (1990, 1995) and Zimmerman (1994b) also noted that there is a body of research on general preservice teacher education and that research that is specifically linked to art teacher education practices is sorely lacking. Zimmerman (1997b) reaffirmed the paucity of art teacher education research and data in her demographic analysis of art teacher preparation programs in the United States. For example, after extensive research, Zimmerman found few studies related to art teacher education demographic research, and very little evidence related specifically to art teacher education practices nationwide. Burton (1998) concurred that few articles on demographic research have appeared in the published literature over the years. In his synthesis of art teacher education practices and development of discipline-based art education, Sevigny (1987) concluded that there is minimal historical documentation on teacher preparation in the visual arts. These concerns are echoed in Davis's (1990) important and historical analysis of teacher education in the visual arts: Little is known about the practice of teaching art at the various levels of schooling.

A number of reasons are possible for why the art teacher education research base is still limited in the early 21st century, specifically in terms of demographic research. Moreover, it is important to lay out these reasons in order to provide an accurate assessment of demographic research within art teacher education, for in many respects, such a discussion is central to both understanding the state of the field today and examining the possibilities for the future. First, since the early 1970s, a decrease in federal or state sources for large-scale research projects in art education sharply curbed possibilities for conducting large-scale studies or replicating previous inquiries within the United States (Chapman, 1982; MacGregor, 1998). Some researchers have sought funding from philanthropic and private organizations, such as the Spencer Foundation and the Jacob Javits Gifted and Talented Discretionary Grant Program (see, for example, Clark & Zimmerman, 1997). The former Getty Institute for Education in the Arts (previously known as the Getty Center for Education in the Arts) also sponsored research projects related to discipline-based art teacher education. This sponsorship was primarily aimed at inservice teacher education (see, for example, Wilson, 1998), although some initiatives were directed at examining preservice teacher education (see, for example, Day, 1997; Getty Center for Education in the Arts, 1988). Some of the Getty Institute's funding was supplemented by funds from the U.S. Department of Education, the National Education Association, and national foundations such as the Annenberg Institute for School Reform. Researchers have also relied on funds from higher education institutions, state organizations, or on the grants programs sponsored by the NAEA Research Commission and the National Art Education Foundation. Nonetheless, it is fair to say that research funding is generally limited and that large-scale demographic research requires some form of financial support.

Second, many researchers have embraced theoretical or qualitative methodologies (Hamblen, 1989; MacGregor, 1998) as alternatives to empirical and descriptive studies; the latter of which are often more suitable for conducting demographic research. There have been a large number of descriptive and quantitative studies over the years within art education as a whole (see, for example, Brewer, 1999a; Chalmers, 1999; Jones & McPhee, 1986), yet as Wilson (1994) reflected, experimental research has fallen into disfavor recently. Many doctoral-granting programs and students in the United States and Canada favor more humanistic arts-based research methods (Anderson, Eisner, & McRorie, 1998; Hutchens, 2001). Given this assessment, the future of art teacher education research may reveal an increasing commitment to qualitative concerns and methodologies.

Our literature review established that research on art teacher education problems can be categorized as either singular case studies or small-scale research projects reliant on observational, survey, and interview data or on summaries and interpretations of existing data. As we sorted through and read these studies, we found that some share certain demographic characteristics. For instance, as disclosed in this chapter, a few research studies focus on the beliefs and concerns of preservice teachers (see, for example, Ellingson, 1991; Grauer, 1998; Kowalchuk, 1999; Short, 1995; Thurber, 1989), and so when reexamined and analyzed together, this cluster of studies provides the beginnings of a verbal picture (Richardson, 1996) of this population. Obviously, we are unable to generalize from these groups of studies, yet they may serve as a springboard for further large-scale research or for the eventual development of a body of case study knowledge. Howey and Zimpher (1989), for example, developed a series of in-depth case studies of six teacher education programs within the United States. This work serves as a model for further data collection on teacher education programs and faculty (see, for example, Ducharme, 1993). Furthermore, the shift toward qualitative research provides researchers with opportunities for exploring the demographics of preservice and practicing teachers in terms of examining the contexts in which they learn and teach. As other chapters in this handbook section on teacher education show, researchers are conducting case study research in a variety of K-12 classroom contexts (see, for example, Anderson, 2000; Bresler, 1994; Degge, 1987; Wolfe, 1997; Zimmerman, 1991, 1992).

Third, teacher education topics are not central to research within the field. Research is usually conducted by higher education faculty members, graduate students, and independent scholars (Zimmerman, 1997b); although, practitioners in schools have been encouraged to participate in research studies (Galbraith, 1988; NAEA, 1996; Zimmerman, 1996). Yet many faculty members who work in research institutions show little interest in teacher education issues (Hutchens, 1997). Pankratz (1989) made the case that research topics are usually chosen by individual scholars and are based on their own interests and concerns, as well as on their own beliefs about art and art education. As Wilson (1994) remarked, researchers ideally relate their interests, values, and assumptions about life and human purpose to their research activities.

In a demographic survey of 332 art education educators in higher education institutions, Burton (1998) found that faculty and doctoral students principally pursue research in theoretical and conceptual areas, whereas master's-level graduate students most often focus on curricular and instructional topics related to the practicalities of teaching and teacher education. Anderson et al. (1998) surveyed 124 visual art education graduate programs in the United States and Canada to ascertain their location, scope, and nature. Their findings show that teacher education is also central to graduate study at the master's level, whereas in the leading doctoral programs, research is conducted on a variety of art education issues and concerns. Unfortunately, research at the master's level is rarely published in journals (Carroll & Kay, 1998); thus, much of this academic work remains unknown unless it is submitted to the *Dissertation Abstracts* database.

Galbraith (2001) found that many faculty members and other instructors responsible for preparing teachers, especially those in the smaller, more teaching-oriented institutions, tend not to conduct research or publish their work in established journals or texts. The form of "scholarship" and/or creative work that they pursue usually centers on teacher preparation, course design, and giving presentations and workshops.

A review of NAEA Annual Convention programs over the last 6 years found that a large number of presentations focus on teacher education issues (a few of which reflect demographic reports). However, a literature review could not ascertain how many of these presentations have been subsequently published. Burton and Boyer's (1998) listing of demographic studies in the status report of the NAEA Research Task Force on Demographics is extremely helpful as an indication of the types of demographic research conducted recently in art education. However, only three of the studies listed reflect demographic teacher education data (see Jeffers, 1994; Kautz, 1996; Spradling, 1995), and all of the studies are reported as presentations at NAEA annual conventions. Unfortunately, a search of the literature could not ascertain that these studies were subsequently published in refereed journals. As we suggest later, examining the types of scholarship and academic work undertaken by graduate students (especially at the master's level) and by faculty whose primary responsibilities involve the preparation of teachers may be helpful in providing a more succinct demographic profile of art teacher education (Galbraith, 2001).

Finally, the various national educational demographic databases, such as those developed by the Educational Testing Service and the National Center for Educational Statistics, rarely include data about teaching preparation in the arts in their research and reports (Hatfield, 2000, personal communication; Zimmerman, 1997b). They most often focus on the teaching areas of math, science, social studies, and language arts. Thus, if the arts are included, they are under the umbrella of other subject areas, or have been related to how students fare in the arts within schools (Eisner, 1999; Perskey, Sandene, & Askew, 1998), rather than on teacher education trends and practices. Nonetheless, these national reports provide essential demographic information that is helpful and should not be dismissed out of hand. National trends and statistics have great relevance to our field and to the future of teaching art (Day, 1997).

Developing a Positive Demographic Picture: Themes and Questions

Despite the lack of baseline data, developing a demographic picture (albeit broad) is a positive endeavor for art education. There is much to learn from examining existing demographic studies as well as from combing through other art education data looking for demographic insights, clues, and patterns (Zimmerman, 1997a). Arguably, there is also much to be learned from describing where "demographic gaps" exist and suggesting possibilities for future study. It should be noted that demographic research is a part of the larger research commitment made by the NAEA Research Commission. Also a recent survey of secondary art teachers (NAEA, 2001) spearheaded by Michael Day demonstrates the potential for further demographic research within the field.

As suggested earlier, this demographic inquiry focuses on three major themes: teacher education programs, preservice and inservice teachers, and teacher educators. Under the three thematic headings, we developed a series of questions that underscore our study. Some of the questions are as follows:

- Teacher Education Programs: In what kinds of institutions are these programs located and what are they like in terms of size and demographics? How many art teachers do these programs prepare on an annual basis? What are art teachers taught within these programs? What kinds of degrees and certification coursework do they offer? What do these degrees and options look like in terms of curricula, pedagogy, state and national standards, and graduation requirements? What types of student teaching and field placements exist in these programs? How do teacher education programs articulate within and across institutions, states, and nationwide?
- Preservice and Practicing Teachers: Who are these teachers? What demographic information about them is available? What is the role of art teacher education for preservice art teachers? What demographic information is available on elementary majors who take art education courses? What roles do school practitioners undertake in preservice art

education? What opportunities are there for inservice teacher education and professional development?

- Teacher Educators: Who prepares art teachers? Where do they teach? What are their backgrounds and qualifications? What and how do they teach? What are their responsibilities in terms of teaching, research and/or creative work, and professional service?

The questions listed here are not inclusive, and due to the complexity and interrelationship of art teacher education characteristics, natural overlaps and similarities of concepts are threaded throughout the themes. In the next part of this paper, we explore the three themes listed previously and address questions posed within them. We then examine other demographic issues and trends that serve to broaden our picture more extensively. Michael Parsons (2001) succinctly wrote the following about art education at the beginning of the 21st century:

> Along with the rest of schooling in the United States, it [art education] is about to undergo important and perhaps unprecedented demographic shifts. Large numbers of older teachers are ready to retire. New patterns of hiring and of teacher preparation are appearing. Student numbers are due to swell. Yet it remains that we do not know much about ourselves as art educators. Who are we? What are our goals? What do we believe about art, our students, our society? Are we happy in our institutional life? (p. 99)

Therefore, we examine art education data alongside and within the context of today's changing times and recent national reports that advocate change in the preparation and continuing education of teachers. Hopefully, we will learn more about ourselves as art teacher educators from the portraits painted of teacher education programs, preservice and practicing teachers, and teacher educators.

TEACHER EDUCATION PROGRAMS

There are an estimated 1,200 programs across the United States, which are responsible for preparing teachers of all subjects, each with their own individual approaches and traditions (Doyle, 1990). One quarter of these institutions are private institutions (Wenglinsky, 2000). Murray (1996) argued that there has been little change in the actual structure or content of teacher education programs during the 1980s and 1990s. Moreover, in many states, schools or departments of education do not need to be accredited; therefore, as Darling-Hammond (2000) cautioned, only about 500 of all of the teacher education programs in the United States meet common professional standards such as those advocated by NCATE.

An early descriptive study of teacher education programs within the United States was developed for the U.S. Office of Education (Howey et al., 1977). Since 1987 and each subsequent year, the Research About Teacher Education (RATE) project, supported by the American Association of Colleges for Teacher Education, has provided yearly detailed information on various aspects of teacher education (Ducharme & Ducharme, 1996). This project, for example, supplies data on student and faculty demographics, teacher salaries, and the nature of secondary methods courses (Richardson, 1996).

It is difficult determine the exact number of programs that prepare art teachers (Zimmerman, 1997b). There is a broad spectrum of degree and certification options available at the undergraduate, postbaccalaureate, and graduate levels for art specialists, and some programs only offer art education methods courses for elementary classroom majors. Hutchens (1997) has estimated that there are over 500 programs that prepare art teachers. Galbraith (1997) found that over 600 postsecondary institutions offer some form of art teacher preparation coursework for art specialists and elementary classroom generalists. Of these, 150 institutions offer certification coursework at the postbaccalaureate and graduate levels (Galbraith, 1997).

The institutions and their respective art teacher education programs vary considerably according to size, economics (private or state supported), orientations to research and teaching (Research I, land-grant, doctoral granting, undergraduate, etc.), and affiliation (professional art school, liberal arts, religious) (see, for example, Galbraith, 1997; Thompson & Hardiman, 1991; Zimmerman, 1997b). Some institutions, regardless of size and student enrollments, are described as universities, and others are known as colleges. These institutions are located within a diversity of settings, ranging from large metropolitan centers to more sparsely populated and rural areas across the United States. They also vary in terms of the undergraduate degrees and postbaccalaureate certification options offered, as well as in terms of opportunities for teacher education course work at master's and doctoral levels.

Institutional Demographics: Size, Location, and Enrollments

Acquiring knowledge about the institutions in which art education programs reside is vital if a demographic profile of art teacher education is to develop. Institutional size, location, enrollments, resources, commitment to art education, as well as their general characteristics (e.g., university, college, research, land-grant, church affiliation, liberal arts, 4-year school, doctoral granting, professional art school, etc.), are necessary data to collect. Moreover, the number of teachers who are actually prepared and the number of art education faculty are also key demographic indicators of program size.

Zimmerman (1997b), in her survey of teacher education programs in Indiana, identifies 18 institutions that offer art education coursework. She established that nine (50%) institutions had total student enrollments ranging from 900 to 3,000, five (28%) with 3,000 to 13,000, and four (22%) with 20,000 to 36,000. Galbraith (2001) in a study of 128 institutions (representing 43 states) uses slightly different criteria to classify institutional size and status. She found that art education coursework is offered in colleges and universities that run the gamut from small private liberal arts colleges with 600 to 1,500 students (e.g., Coker College, South Carolina; Dana College, Nebraska; Viterbo College, Wisconsin) to small state institutions with 1,500 to 3,500 students (e.g., Adams State College, Colorado; Black Hills State University, South Dakota; Castleton State College, Vermont; New Mexico Highlands University) to slightly larger institutions with 4,000 to 6,000 students (e.g., Alabama A & M University; Emporia State University, Kansas; University of the Pacific, California); midsize state and private institutions with 8,000 to16,000 students (e.g., Louisiana Tech University; Youngstown State University, Ohio, University of Minnesota-Duluth); larger universities with 18,000 to 26,000 students (e.g., Boise State University, Idaho; Ohio University; Southwest Texas State University; University of Kansas); and large research institutions with 35,000 to 52,000 students (e.g., The Ohio State University; Pennsylvania State University; University of Wisconsin). Whatever criteria were used to determine institutional size as well as geographical locations, these aforementioned data already suggest that programmatic differences will exist.

Art education programs can be found in every state within the United States, although many are concentrated in the Midwest, upper Midwest, East, and Southeast. For example, the state department of Ohio lists 36 institutions that offer teacher education programs (out of 56 teacher education programs statewide) for art teachers. Indiana, often known as "The Crossroads of America" (Zimmerman, 1997b, p. 38), has 18 art preparation programs. However, in Wyoming, there is only 1 higher education institution responsible for preparing art teachers (University of Wyoming in Laramie) (Galbraith, 2001). Programs can also be found in urban, suburban, and rural areas. To return to Zimmerman's (1997b) survey of Indiana institutions, eight institutions (18%) are located in urban areas (with populations over 500,000); six (33%), in suburban areas (with populations from 50,000 to 500,000); and eight (44%), in small towns (with populations under 50,000). Zimmerman also concluded that the larger institutions (56%) are generally state supported, whereas the smaller institutions (44%) are generally church supported.

Zimmerman (1997b) reported further that the majority of art education programs have an affiliation with colleges or schools of art. Thompson and Hardiman (1991) surveyed 350 institutions that granted undergraduate and graduate degrees in art education within the United States. The results of their study, based on 170 completed questionnaires (46.6%) with 121 from public state-supported colleges and 49 from private colleges and universities, found that 75% of art preparation programs that exist in doctoral-granting institutions are housed in colleges, schools, and departments of art. In institutions that did not offer a doctoral degree, 65% programs were affiliated with schools of art. The other programs in the study were affiliated with schools of education (6%), and others (19%) were affiliated with schools of both art and education. Zimmerman (1997b) noted in her Indiana survey that 16 of the 18 programs are affiliated with schools of art. Galbraith (2001) found a similar pattern in her study of 129 art education programs, in that 108 (73%) programs resided in schools or departments of art. Art teacher education programs exist in professional art schools; however, few studies have examined demographic data on these programs (see, for example, Caroll, Jones, & Sandell, 1995, for an overview of the program at the Maryland Institute, College of Art).

Few data have been acquired on the actual numbers of prospective teachers who are prepared within teacher education programs (Day, 1997). No large-scale systematic and longitudinal studies have examined graduation rates from the various individual art teacher education programs within North America. Also, no information exists on the number of art teachers prepared each year (Hatfield, November 2001, personal communication). However, individual state departments of education may have records relating to how many art teachers are certified. For example, correspondence with the Ohio State Department of Education confirmed that 189 multicertification art teaching certificates were awarded during the 1999 to 2000 academic year (Nichelson, 2001, personal communication).

Galbraith (1997, 2001) examined graduation rates from selected art education programs, but the numbers she acquired are estimates only, because they were derived from reports supplied by faculty rather than from actual figures supplied by educational institutions and/or state licensing and certification agencies. For example, a faculty member at Lawrence University, Wisconsin, a small private liberal arts college with a total enrollment of 1,100 students, reported that the college graduates 2 to 3 art education students per academic year. In another example, a faculty member at Stephen F. Austin University, Texas, a smaller university with a total enrollment of 12,000 students, reported that the program graduates 3 to 5 art teachers a year. And in a final example, a faculty member at Purdue University, Indiana, a large university with a total enrollment of 35,000 students, reported that the program graduates 15 to 20 art teachers a year.

Similarly, there are few data on the actual number of faculty who teach in art education programs. Anderson, Eisner, and McRorie (1998) indirectly address faculty issues in their study of graduate programs in the United States and Canada. They found that over 37% of respondents were sole full-time faculty art educators in their individual programs, and that 33 graduate programs were coordinated by either part-time or adjunct faculty members. It is not clear from these data if these faculty respondents mentioned are also responsible for teacher preparation. However, there is possible overlap, in that 81 programs surveyed offer K-12 certification coursework within their master's-level courses.

Degrees and Coursework

A number of degree and certification options exist for becoming an art teacher. Teachers can be prepared within traditional undergraduate programs that offer various undergraduate degrees (e.g., Bachelor of Arts in art education, Bachelor of Fine Arts in art education, Bachelor of Science in education, Bachelor of Science in art education). Some programs offer more than one bachelor's degree option at the undergraduate level (Galbraith, 1997). There are also certification options at the postbaccalaureate (postbaccalaureate certification) and graduate levels (e.g., Master of Arts in education, Master of Arts in art education, Master of Arts in teaching). In some cases, there are graduate-level programs that add an additional year (sometimes 2 years) to the traditional undergraduate 4-year degree, such as the fifth-year teacher education programs and professional development schools advocated by the Holmes Group of educational deans (Holmes Group, 1986). Some states (e.g., Arkansas and California) require teacher candidates to have a bachelor's degree before they enter a teacher preparation program. Many states offer certification from kindergarten to 12th grade; however, some make distinctions between elementary- and secondary-grade-level certification.

There is no one single degree or mandated set of courses that all prospective teachers are asked to take within the United States. Yet, the broader components of art teacher education programs are similar across the country (Davis, 1990; Galbraith, 1997; Sevigny, 1987). These components usually consist of credit hours in the following: art content (e.g., studio, art history requirements, and in some programs, aesthetics and/or art criticism), the theoretical foundations of art education (e.g., history and philosophy of art education, curriculum theory, instructional strategies), and supervised field experiences (e.g., student teaching and other types of clinical internships in elementary, middle, or high schools). Moreover, most programs require a semester grade point average of 2.5 or above for admission into teacher education programs (Galbraith, 1997).

Many programs also require preservice teachers to take coursework in professional education subject matter (e.g., educational psychology, child development, the history of American schooling), which is usually taught in schools, departments, or colleges of education (Davis, 1990). Undergraduate art education majors are usually required to take liberal arts and general education courses as part of their bachelor degrees. In many states in the United States, prospective teachers now are required to pass external examinations in art subject matter and professional education prior to or shortly after they begin teaching.

Curriculum and Coursework

Researchers have looked at the course content of teacher preparation programs over the years (Arnold, 1976; Davis, 1990; Eads, 1980; Galbraith, 1997; Hobbs, 1993; Sevigny, 1987; Willis-Fisher, 1991, 1993; Zimmerman, 1994b, 1997b). The average undergraduate art education degree program is composed of 120 to 130 semester credit hr (Galbraith, 1997), and these numbers have remained constant over the years (Arnold, 1976; Sevigny, 1987).

Changes took place in course offerings during the late 1980s and 1990s in relationship to discipline-based art education and the trend toward comprehensive art education (Day, 1997; Sevigny, 1987). Most preservice teachers are now expected to take some coursework (even if it is not taught in a separate class) in aesthetics and art criticism, as well as traditional emphases of studio art and art history (Day, 1997; Galbraith, 1997; Willis-Fisher, 1993). However, studio art is still the most prevalent component in the programs for education of art teachers (Davis, 1990; Galbraith, 1997; Hutchens, 1997; Willis-Fisher, 1991). Willis-Fisher (1991) surveyed a representative sample of state-approved undergraduate art education programs. Using data acquired from her questionnaire research, she found that preservice teachers take an average of 36 semester hr in studio coursework compared to an average of 9 semester hr in art history. Earlier, Sevigny (1987) surveyed 30 undergraduate programs in art education in order to ascertain if they were addressing course content required of discipline-based art education. After this baseline survey, he analyzed 14 programs in order to see if they had modified their programs in relation to discipline-based art education. His findings, as well as those of others (Rogers & Brogdon, 1990), suggested that studio courses are also the mainstay of the preservice experience. Studio offerings run the gamut from foundational courses to courses in more specialist areas, such as painting, ceramics, printmaking, and digital imagery.

The availability of courses is limited within smaller institutions (e.g., because of limited numbers of faculty, faculty expertise), and it is usually the larger programs (e.g., in terms of faculty and course offerings) that provide separate classes on aesthetics, art criticism, and other more specialized art education courses, such as those that examine multicultural issues and technology.

A review of the literature on curricular and course content suggested that the student teaching experience usually takes place during the final semester or term of a preservice teacher's program (Galbraith, 1997). Preservice teachers are assigned an elementary or secondary supervisory (or cooperating or mentor) teacher and spend the good part of a semester (or term) in the supervisory teacher's classroom. Faculty members, instructors, or graduate students from the preservice teachers' preparation programs then make regular supervisory visits to the student teaching classroom (Kowalchuk, 1999). There are exceptions to this state of affairs. For example, some teacher education programs are involved with professional development schools (e.g., The Ohio State University), and so opportunities for field and internship experiences are expanded (see, for example, Haynes & Schiller, 1994; Short, 1995). In many colleges and universities, student teaching experiences are conducted in liaison with schools or with departments of professional education.

There are few data that provide information on the impact of the NAEA's *Standards for Teacher Preparation* (NAEA, 1979, 1999) on teacher education curricular content. Murchison (1989) found that the Louisiana teacher preparation programs showed inconsistencies in their art requirements when compared to the 1979 NAEA *Standards*. In a study of the certification programs in Alabama's 14 colleges and universities, Rogers (1987) found that only two programs were close to compliance with the NAEA recommendations for art teacher education (NAEA, 1979). There are currently no data that examine whether art teacher education programs have adopted the current *Standards for Art Teacher Preparation* (NAEA, 1999). Galbraith (1997) also found that most faculty members in teacher education programs within or across states communicate little with one another, if at all. There are no data that indicate how statewide or nationwide programs articulate with one another.

There are also no large-scale demographic studies on the pedagogical practices employed and modeled within art teacher education programs, although there are reports on curricular activities and initiatives of individual art teacher education programs (Carroll, Sandell, & Jones, 1995; Roland, 1995; Thurber, 1989), as well as practices of individual faculty art educators (Grauer & Sandell, 2000; Myers & Grauer, 1994; Zimmerman, 1994c). Likewise, there are no demographic studies that examine the range of alternative art education approaches (e.g., feminist, social theory, critical pedagogy) within teacher preparation programs and the impact these approaches have made or are making on teacher preparation practices. Similarly, there is little demographic information on how preservice teachers are being taught to meet needs of diverse student populations, in terms of race, gender, disabilities, and sexuality (see, for example, Guay, 1993; Knight, 2000; Lampela, 1995, 2001).

The Canadian Context

In Canada, there are 48 universities and colleges that provide teacher education programs (Canadian Education Association, 2002). Of these, the 5 largest universities graduate over 1,000 new teachers each year. The majority of teacher education programs offer art education coursework. However, as is the case in the United States, teacher education is a diverse and complex field that has idiosyncrasies both within and across provinces (Irwin, Chalmers, Grauer, Kindler, & MacGregor, 1996). Depending on the province, it is possible to be certified as an art educator by graduating from programs in art schools, universities, and colleges, or from specific teacher education programs within colleges or universities. However, unlike the United States, the vast majority of art education programs in Canada are in universities, and the grade point average required for entry into these programs is the equivalent to that of the other university professional programs.

In Canada, it is possible to be certified as a generalist teacher for K-12 or as an art specialist in either secondary or elementary schools. Some provinces, like British Columbia, for example, certify the art specialist to teach all subjects in K-12, and this certification is accepted in all jurisdictions in Canada and in most countries around the world. However, in British Columbia, elementary generalist teachers are only required to take art education courses in one of the province's six teacher education programs, although art is a mandatory subject at the elementary level.

Like the United States, art education programs in Canada are typically housed in faculties of fine arts and/or faculties of education. Some are 3- or 4-year concurrent programs that grant a Bachelor of Education degree at the completion of course work and the student teaching practicum. Increasingly, fifth-year and postgraduate programs are becoming alternate routes for teacher certification. Future teachers entering these postgraduate degree programs must hold a Bachelor of Fine Arts or a Bachelor of Arts degree before admission. When they complete the program, they receive a second degree as well as certification. All the larger universities offer graduate degrees in art education, with the two largest graduate programs at the University of British Columbia in Vancouver and Concordia University in Montreal.

PRESERVICE AND PRACTICING TEACHERS

Preservice Teachers

Approximately 500,000 preservice teachers (Doyle, 1990) are enrolled each year in the 1,200 institutions that prepare teachers in general elementary teaching to secondary core subjects such as art, music, and mathematics within the United States. The number of preservice art teachers enrolled in art teacher education programs remains unknown (Hatfield, 2001, personal correspondence). Any existing data have been tabulated from individual faculty members who have reported data on their various programs (Galbraith, 2001).

It is unclear as to whether art education preservice teachers fit into the various national trends. Researchers have argued that studies of preservice teachers of all subject matter areas within the United States show uniformity in their demographic characteristics (Goodlad, 1990; Wenglingsky, 2000). Preservice teachers, in general, are mostly women (80%), and are less than 25 years old (87%). However, a good percentage of preservice students can be classified as nontraditional students in terms of both their age and when they chose to enter a degree or certification program (Wenglingsky, 2000).

Thompson and Hardiman (1991) found in their survey of art education programs that women art education students outnumber men by a ratio of 3:1 at all degree levels. However, their study did not focus entirely on students seeking certification; thus, some of the figures may not be accurate. However, Zimmerman's (1997b) analysis of the demographics of art teacher education concluded that 98% of art education students are White, and 68% are women.

Data on students entering visual arts departments suggest that teacher education candidates who enter university or college to pursue an individual subject discipline have relatively higher Scholastic Aptitude Test scores than those who do not pursue a specific college major (Wenglingsky, 2000). Additionally, there has been a steady increase in the number of visual and performing arts degrees conferred between 1987 and 1998. In the 1997 to 1998 academic year, over 50,000 degrees were conferred (National Center for Educational Statistics, 2000). There are no specific data available, however, on how art teacher education candidates fare as they move through their teacher education programs in terms of their coursework and, perhaps importantly, in terms of whether they actually become certified as teachers. Darling-Hammond (National Commission on Teaching and America's Future, 1996) described, using national data, how of the 600 students who entered a large 4-year teacher education program early in their college years, only 180 completed the program and only about 72 accepted teaching positions. Of these, only about 30 or 40 remained in the profession several years later. Thus, the overall attrition rate from the beginning of a traditional undergraduate teacher education through about the third year in teaching is 75%. Although graduate teacher education programs are more successful at finding jobs for their graduates and in keeping them in the teaching profession, these programs are still the exception to the rule.

Other studies on preservice teachers comprise small-scale or case study research. A small cluster of case studies is beginning to map out a demographic picture regarding preservice teachers' beliefs about art and teaching. Kowalchuk (1999), for instance, examined the beliefs of 37 preservice student teachers in a large teacher education program in the United States. She found that the preservice teachers were challenged not only by their discomfort with the technical aspects of teaching art especially in terms of classroom management and the use of pedagogical strategies but also by their lack of knowledge of art subject matter. In another example, Grauer (1998) examined the beliefs of preservice art specialists and elementary generalists in a year-long Canadian postbaccalaureate certification program. She concluded that preservice teachers' beliefs about what art education comprises is a much stronger indicator of their willingness to learn about art education than of their actual knowledge about art subject matter itself. Other studies have examined preservice teachers' beliefs and experiences through the use of journals, case studies, and personal stories and metaphors (see, for example, Grauer & Sandell, 2000; Roland, 1995; Zimmerman, 1994c).

This aforementioned research alerts art teacher educators and researchers to the ways in which subject matter content, instructional methods, and classroom management are shared preservice teacher beliefs, concerns, and experiences within and across art teacher education programs. Thus, demographic knowledge related to this population is valuable information when planning programs of study in teacher education (Myers & Grauer, 1994).

Preservice Elementary Classroom Generalists

There are no demographic data that examine the demographic characteristics of preservice elementary classroom teachers (Galbraith, 1991; Zimmerman, 1994a). Yet, teaching this population of preservice teachers is an essential component in the workloads of many faculty members and graduate teaching assistants (Galbraith, 2001; Jeffers, 1993). Jeffers (1993) surveyed members of the NAEA Higher Education Division in order to ascertain who taught elementary methods, but this study was related to the content and teaching of the methods courses. There is a small group of case studies that has examined elementary generalists' beliefs and concerns about art subject matter and teaching art (see, for example, Galbraith, 1991; Smith-Shank; 1992).

Practicing Teachers

It is estimated that there are 50,000 practicing art teachers within the United States (Hatfield, 2001 personal communication), with an estimated total of 35,000 at the secondary level (NAEA, 2001; National Center for Education Statistics, [NCES], 1998). Of these 35,000 art teachers, 90% are White, and 71% are female (NAEA 2001). Teachers of color represent 10% of art teachers. The percentage of art teachers who are women is above the national average within the United States, in that women teachers represent two thirds of the general K-12 teaching force (National Commission on Teaching and America's Future, 1996). However, the percentage of art teachers of color is below that of the national average in which teachers of color represent 13% of the general K-12 teaching force (National Commission on Teaching and America's Future, 1996).

The literature is sparse on specifically documenting how practitioners participate in art teacher education activities. As we began this chapter, we established that practitioners might be involved in art teacher education in a number of ways. For example, practitioners may be involved in the actual education of teachers, or they may be involved in their own teacher education, or they may be involved as research participants in related teaching and teacher education studies.

School practitioners are by necessity involved in the preservice education. They serve as cooperating or supervisory or mentor teachers when preservice teachers undertake student teaching or work in intern or field experience settings. There is, however, little demographic evidence about the role that art practitioners play in these clinical experiences. A review of the literature suggested that student teaching is a primary component of teacher education (Galbraith, 1997; Sevigny, 1987), yet it has rarely been documented within art education; although some teacher educators are trying both to make changes as to how student teaching has been traditionally conducted and to develop a better understanding of preservice teachers' concerns during the experience (Galbraith, 1997; Zimmerman, 1994c, 2000). No published demographic data exist on why practitioners serve as cooperating teachers or as mentors for student teachers; or on their backgrounds in relation to their qualifications, their time in the classroom, and their approaches to art. Some practitioners also serve as instructors (possibly as adjunct faculty) for their local teacher education programs. Galbraith (2001) found that some school practitioners taught methods courses for their local teacher education programs. However, this topic has never been fully studied.

Practitioners are also involved in their own education. They may be furthering their education with additional university or college coursework (e.g., toward a graduate degree of some kind) or they may be taking advantage of various professional development activities (which are considered teacher education activities) that school districts and other educational organizations offer. In some cases, additional professional coursework is mandatory as teachers seek to renew their licenses, request salary increases and promotions, and pursue other career goals.

It is clear from some studies (Burton, 1998; NAEA, 2001) that art teachers are pursuing or have pursued master's degrees or other forms of graduate-level course work. The NAEA survey of secondary art teachers reported that 52% of the respondents held master's degrees (NAEA, 2002). In their survey of 124 graduate programs in the United States and Canada, Anderson, Eisner, and McRorie (1998) reported that K-12 certification continued to be "the bread and butter" (p. 11) of graduate study at the master's level. A K-12 option for master's-level students was available in 81 programs, and 14 programs reported that they had certification options for art specialists. Nine programs also allowed certification coursework in their doctoral programs. In another study, Brewer (1999b) surveyed the educational background, educational needs, and scheduling preferences of 141 practicing art teachers in Florida. According to his survey, 67% of the art teachers did not have master's degrees; however, 55% were interested in pursuing one.

There is no large-scale data bank that has kept track of the types of professional development and teacher education courses available for teachers. Brewer (1999b) found in his survey of Florida teachers that most were more interested in taking studio courses, rather than courses in art education, aesthetics, criticism, or art history. However, the few research studies on inservice activities with teachers suggest that some practitioners have taken advantage of a wide spectrum of teacher education opportunities and offerings. For example, the Artistically Talented Program at Indiana University has provided art teachers with ways in which to develop their leadership skills in both their professional and their personal lives (Zimmerman, 1997c). From the mid-1980s to the 1990s, practitioners have benefited from inservice programs associated with the Getty Institute for Education in the Arts (formerly known as the Getty Center for Education in the Arts). The Getty's grants for its regional institutes in California, Florida, Minnesota, Nebraska, Ohio, Tennessee, and Texas totaled more than $24 million for arts-based research over 15 years (Duke, 1999). Wilson's (1997) report, *The Quiet Evolution: Changing the Face of Arts Education*, highlights how the regional Getty institutes brought about new developments in discipline-based art education and changes in art education practices as practitioners collaborated with administrators, consultants, and researchers.

Another professional development opportunity for art teachers is certification with the National Board for Professional Teaching Standards (1994; Goodwin, 1997). Day (1997) reported that during the 1994 to 1995 academic year, 44 teachers (of these, 84% were women) became national board-certified art teachers for early adolescence through young adulthood. As of the 1999 to 2000 academic school year, the number increased to 305. These teachers represent 11 states. As Day (1997) argued, these standards identify highly accomplished teachers, and the implications for preservice and inservice art teacher preparation are many. As yet there are no demographic data on these implications.

Third, practitioners have served as research participants in various ways, such as responding to surveys, allowing researchers in their classrooms, collaborating with researchers, or by conducting research themselves. In a national survey of instruction in secondary visual art education, Burton (2001) identified the instructional strategies that secondary teachers prefer to use. He found that teachers relied primarily on studio-oriented instructional strategies (direct instruction, demonstration, one-on-one conversations) rather than on strategies that encouraged self-inquiry and group work. Lampela (2001) surveyed elementary and secondary art teachers within the United States about their knowledge of and attitudes about including lesbian and gay artists in their curricula. She concluded that art teachers want to learn more about the lives and works of gay and lesbian artists, and that curricular materials and resources also are needed to help art teachers discuss the subject of sexual identity. In their nationwide survey, Mims and Lankford (1995) examined ways in which art is taught in elementary schools in the United States. One of the study's findings demonstrated that many teachers perceived themselves to be undervalued in the school curriculum. Considered together, results from these three demographic surveys alert us to the need for inservice (and preservice) teacher education and professional development coursework that address pedagogical practices; curricular resources about gays, lesbians, and other underserved groups; and the differences between how elementary and secondary art teachers are perceived in both art education and the teaching profession in general.

Additionally, the NAEA (2001) survey of art teachers in secondary schools within the United States found that the most performed professional activity by art teachers was planning art exhibits and events. The findings also indicated that about 60% of art teachers do not attend state art education association meetings, and 79% do not attend NAEA meetings.

A growing body of research is also emerging, as practitioners allow themselves to be observed and researched (see, for example, Anderson, 2000; Bullock & Galbraith, 1992; Galbraith, 1996; Hafeli, 1999; Stokrocki, 1988; Wolfe, 1997; Zimmerman, 1991, 1992), and not only provides the field (especially preservice art educators) with examples of the art educational practices of teachers but also provides practitioners (as research participants) with opportunities for professional and reflective growth as they work with researchers.

TEACHER EDUCATORS

There are few demographic studies of colleges- and university-level teacher educators—the teachers of teachers—within art education. Faculty work has rarely been examined and analyzed in terms of both art education (Galbraith, 1995, 2001; Hutchens, 1997) and general education literature (Ducharme & Ducharme, 1996; Lanier & Little, 1986).

It is difficult to assess, however, how many art education faculty members are directly responsible for preparing teachers, partly because few faculty members identify themselves as "art teacher educators" (Galbraith, 2001) and partly because specific data that relate to teacher preparation must be teased out of more general research on higher education and faculty issues within art education (see, for example, the research of Anderson et al. 1998; Thompson & Hardiman, 1991). Thus, it cannot be assumed that all postsecondary art education faculty teach preservice or inservice and professional development courses, although teacher education in the form of K-12 certification is the mainstay of many graduate-level programs and coursework (Anderson et al., 1998). Moreover, it should not be forgotten that teacher education, in its broadest designation, is the responsibility of not only all art educators (whatever their teaching interests and research specialization) but also other faculty campuswide (Howey & Zimpher, 1989).

Faculty members teach at various levels (e.g., instructor, assistant, associate, and full professor) within colleges and institutions. Some faculty members are tenured or are on tenure-track lines, whereas others are adjunct or have part-time status. Some instructors are also graduate teaching assistants who are working on degrees at the master's and doctoral levels. Thompson and Hardiman (1991) in their survey on art education programs found that 49% of the respondents were full professors, 28% were associate professors, and 23% were assistant professors. There were more women in the associate- and the assistant-level ranks, with more men in the full-professor ranks. Galbraith (2001), in her study of faculty working lives, also found that females are employed more in the associate and assistant professor ranks than at the full professor level. She also found that most of the part-time and adjunct faculty members are women, and in some cases, full-time secondary school teachers run art education programs on a part-time basis.

Galbraith's (2001) study involved surveying 500 faculty members who worked at a variety of institutions (e.g., research, teaching, liberal arts, religious, professional art school, private, public, large, small). The return rate of surveys was 33%, and of this percentage, 19 questionnaires were unusable because art education was no longer taught at that institution. Thus, she examined 148 faculty questionnaires representing 129 institutions and 43 U.S. states. Galbraith found that faculty members hold varying academic qualifications. Only 66% of the respondents held doctorate degrees in art education or in a related field such as curriculum and instruction or secondary education. Of the 34% respondents who did not hold doctorates, 7% taught art education without any graduate degree, whatsoever. The remaining respondents taught with master's level degrees, with 16% of the respondents holding a Master of Fine Arts degree.

The respondents who held doctorates (e.g., PhD or EdD) earned them from 34 different educational institutions, ranging from well-known art education programs such as The Ohio State University (16 respondents) and Pennsylvania State University (six respondents) to lesser known institutions such as Nova University (one respondent) and United States International University (one respondent). In their study, Thompson and Hardiman (1991) reported that 53% of faculty held doctorates. Thus, given these collective findings, a doctoral degree is not a requirement for teaching in many art teacher preparation programs, and in some cases, preservice teachers are taught by persons who do not hold any graduate degrees.

Faculty teaching loads are diverse in terms of numbers and types of courses taught. In some colleges or universities where teaching is valued more highly than research is (these tend to be smaller and less research-oriented institutions), loads of three to four courses per academic semester are typical, with some faculty teaching as many as four to five courses each semester (Galbraith, 2001). In the larger research and doctoral-granting institutions, the amount of faculty time assigned to teaching differs, although these teaching responsibilities are considered heavy by many faculty, given the research, institutional, and national service expectations (Thompson & Hardiman, 1991; Zimmerman, 1997b).

Most art education faculty members teach art education courses of some kind. However, not all faculty members teach courses directly related to teacher education (e.g., courses that involve teaching preservice teachers). Some faculty members teach studio coursework, as well as art history, art appreciation, and other art-related courses (and in some cases, professional education coursework). A large number of faculty are responsible for supervising student teaching and other field-based and clinical experiences. Galbraith (2001) reported that 61% of the respondents in her study taught elementary and secondary art education methods courses, and of this percentage, 34% were responsible for teaching methods coursework for elementary generalists.

There is little information available on the research and scholarly activities of faculty members. Many of the faculty members who prepare teachers (especially those faculty who work in more teaching-oriented institutions) tend not to pursue research on teacher education matters (Galbraith & Grauer, 1998; Hutchens, 1997). Their intellectual work primarily involves course design, professional and institutional service commitments, and local and state presentations or workshops; although some faculty members create and exhibit artwork (Galbraith, 2001).

However, interest in faculty perspectives on art teacher education is an important component of art teacher education. In a recent publication, renowned art education scholars have described "in their own words" the development of doctoral study within selected institutions (see Hutchens, 2001). These stories, along with other reflections on the role of art education in faculty lives (Eisner, 1998), are exciting to see and provide some understanding of teacher preparation philosophies and practices within higher education.

OTHER DEMOGRAPHIC RESEARCH AND ISSUES

There is a myriad of other demographic issues that need to be considered as we examine the state of the field of art teacher education today. For example, there are issues regarding alternative and certification and licensure measures for art teachers, the demands of recent education reform movements, and the effects of the teacher shortages at both K-12 and faculty levels.

Certification and Licensure

DiBlasio (1997) completed a comprehensive research on state requirements for art teacher certification and licensure in 1995. As she noted, changes have probably taken place since this time, given the wide disparity of teacher certification policies. Additionally, the teacher shortage at the beginning of the 21st century has brought about additional changes and modifications. Certification is given when candidates have met all of the coursework requirements and so forth required by their teacher education programs. Licensure is issued by each individual state when a teacher candidate has met all of the competency requirements for teaching (e.g., certification requirements, state teacher exams, probationary periods of teaching). However, as Sabol notes in his chapter in this volume, the terms *certification* and *licensure* are used interchangeably.

Schools of education usually recommend their preservice candidates for licensure (Darling-Hammond, 2000); thus, at some level, standards for certification vary in that some programs are not as good as others, given the education they offer in terms of coursework, faculty competencies, and adherence to various professional standards. In more than 40 states, alternative routes exist for teacher education beyond the traditional undergraduate teacher preparation program (Darling-Hammond, 2000). Some of these programs are sequential and planned postbaccalaureate options, whereas other options exist for emergency hiring. In some states (Arizona is an example), 2-year colleges now are able to offer teacher education courses and certify teachers; thus, some teachers hired on emergency certificates are seeking preparation programs that allow them to certify as quickly as possible.

Only 11 states (Alabama, California, Massachusetts, Minnesota, New Hampshire, Ohio, Oklahoma, Oregon, South Dakota, Texas, and West Virginia) license or certify teachers based on state standards specific to arts education (The Council of State Chief School Officers, 2001). At the time of this writing, two other states (Connecticut and Indiana) are developing licensure requirements based on their individual state arts standards.

Darling-Hammond (National Commission on Teaching and America's Future, 1996) pointed out that nearly one fourth (23%) of all secondary teachers do not have a college minor in their main teaching field, and this is especially true for more than 30% of mathematics teachers. However, the percentage in art and music is higher and more encouraging, in that 77.9% of K-12 teachers have a state license in their main field of art or music. The NAEA survey of secondary teachers (NAEA, 2001) concluded that the majority of teachers (93%) held bachelor's degrees in education and art, although the remaining percentage (7%) held degrees in other subject matter disciplines, including, English, language arts, dance, and music. Among teachers, nationwide, who teach a second subject, 36% are unlicensed in the field and 50% lack a minor (National Commission on Teaching and America's Future, 1996).

Standards and Quality

Recent reform movements in teacher education in the United States (see, for example, Holmes Group, 1986; National Commission on Teaching and America's Future, 1996) have argued not only for the development of new approaches and standards within teacher education programs but also for the incorporation of standards that exemplify what potential teachers should know. Various U.S. states are developing standards for examining and licensing teachers.

The push for teacher education standards is not solely the province of national reform movements or only a part of recent educational endeavors. The NAEA has had in place a set of voluntary teacher education standards for over 20 years (Day, 1997; NAEA, 1979). These standards have allowed teacher educators to work from a set of common assumptions about what qualities art teacher education might comprise. The standards were revised and rewritten during the late 1990s by an ad hoc committee of the NAEA. The new set of *Standards for Art Teacher Preparation* was subsequently published in 1999. These standards again reflect the NAEA's commitment to quality teacher education, and propose standards for teacher education candidates, teacher education programs, and teacher education faculty. The art standards also define the knowledge and skills that all beginning arts educators should possess in the visual arts for use in state teacher licensing and certification systems. Moreover, the revised standards are aligned with the *National Visual Arts Standards* (1994) and the *Early Adolescence through Young Adulthood/Art: Standards for National Board Certification* (National Board for Professional Teaching Standards, 1994). The teacher preparation standards also augment the NCATE and NASAD Standards. Copies of the teacher preparation standards were distributed nationwide to various campus and school administrators, deans, department heads, and officials.

Teacher Education as a Campuswide Endeavor

In a document entitled *A Move Forward: An Affirmation of Continuing Commitment to Arts Education* (2001), the Consortium of National Arts Education Associations, the International Council of Fine Arts Deans, and the Council of Arts Accrediting Associations challenge all campus leaders to become involved in teacher education. Members of the consortium not only endorse standards for K-12 arts teacher education but also argue that teacher preparation is an all-faculty and all-campus responsibility. There are unfortunately no data on how art teacher preparation is viewed on college campuses, and particularly in the schools or colleges in which art education programs are housed (e.g., visual art, fine arts, education, etc.). There are "stories," though, of art educators' experiences with studio faculty members and the historical divisions (and isolation) that have been created between studio and art education units. The pedagogical and curricular influences of studio, art history, and education faculty members on prospective art teachers remain unexamined.

In addition, as Lanier and Little (1986) noted, faculty members involved in teacher preparation are accorded less status in the hierarchy of college or university campus life than are their colleagues in arts and sciences, humanities, and other professional schools. However, most preservice teachers are taught not only by art education faculty but also by faculty in the arts and sciences, and in professional education; yet there are no demographic data on how these faculty members either instruct their classes, or serve as models (both positively and negatively) for potential teachers.

Teacher Quantity and Quality

A key issue within teacher education at the beginning of the 21st century is a consideration of how many teachers should be prepared (given the anticipated teacher shortage) and of the quality of these teachers (Wenglingsky, 2000). There are no demographic data that inform the field as to whether the anticipated teacher shortage in the early 21st century will seriously affect art education. Art education has always been hindered by the fact that not all school districts and/or states are willing to hire art teachers, especially when they are restricted by tight budgets.

Thompson and Hardiman (1990) predicted that there would be a number of retirements in terms of higher education faculty at the end of the 1990s. A cursory look at the job applications for art education postsecondary positions seems to indicate that faculty are indeed retiring and/or new positions are being filled and created. However, demographic research has not been conducted on this topic. Also, recent world events (e.g., September 11, 2001, and the ups and downs of the stock markets internationally) may have some long-term economic affects on university and college faculty and K-12 art teacher retirement and pension plans. Additionally, at the time of this writing, some states with the United States are reconsidering state funding for education and other resources, and some state-supported institutions are subject to hiring freezes.

A FEW REFLECTIONS

Demographic issues and concerns related to programs, teachers, and teacher educators are closely interwoven. One cannot understand the complexities of preparing teachers without addressing the nature of the teacher education programs in which they learn to teach. In turn, these programs are reflective of the working conditions of faculty art teacher educators, as well as of their backgrounds, understandings, and approaches to and beliefs about teaching art education.

There is a need to look more carefully at the various programs that prepare art teachers and help shape their development. It would be valuable to find some means that would allow for development of baseline data about teacher education programs. This task is enormous in scope, and as Day (1997) argues, some programs are more successful than others; yet it is important to differentiate between them. There is also the need to examine more thoroughly what is taught within these programs. Cochran-Smith (2000) reminds us that teacher educators have a responsibility to make sure that preservice teachers not only know their subject matter but also develop some understanding of the knowledge base of teaching and learning. This line of thinking aligns with the need to examine and describe not only the kinds of curricular and pedagogical approaches that are being taught within teacher preparation but also how future and current teachers (and teacher educators) can be informed about and introduced to alternative instructional and pedagogical practices and diverse art curricular resources. Murray (1996) referred to teacher education as the sharing of a collective body of knowledge about teaching. With this in mind, it is important that we begin to know more about the intellectual work and activities undertaken by the many faculty members who are responsible for preparing teachers.

CONCLUSIONS

As highlighted in this chapter, there is limited research on preservice programs, preservice and practicing teachers, and teacher educators. The demographic picture of art teacher education is incomplete. Associated with this partial research portrayal are growing societal and economic demands for change within teacher education. The challenge for art teacher education is to keep abreast of these developments and, at the same time, to keep core understandings related to art content and pedagogy central to the task of preparing teachers. Nonetheless, the potential for demographic research is exciting. It can only serve to enhance the ways in which art teachers are prepared and thus contribute to the evolving knowledge base within the field at large.

REFERENCES

Anderson, T. (2000). *Real lives: Art teachers and the cultures of school.* Portsmouth, NH: Heinemann.

Anderson, T., Eisner, E., & McRorie, S. (1998). A survey of graduate study in art education. *Studies in Art Education, 40*(1), 8–25.

Arnold, R. (1976). The state of teacher education: An analysis of selected art education art teacher preparation programs in the United States. *Art Education, 29*(2), 27–29.

Bresler, L. (1994). Imitative, complementary, and expansive: Three roles for visual arts curricula. *Studies in Art Education, 35*(2), 90–104.

Brewer, T. (1999a). Forty years of *Studies in Art Education*: 1979–1989. *Visual Arts Research, 25*(1), 14–18.

Brewer, T. M. (1999b). Art teacher profile and preference. *Studies in Art Education, 41*(1), 61–70.

Bullock, A., & Galbraith, L. (1992). Images of art teaching: Comparing the beliefs and practices of two secondary art teachers. *Studies in Art Education, 33*(2), 86–97.

Burton, D. (1991). *A survey of research interests among art education researchers.* Seminar for Research in Art Education: National Art Education Association.

Burton, D. (1996). Briefing paper on demographic research. In E. Zimmerman (Ed.), *Briefing papers: Creating a visual arts research agenda toward the twenty-first century.* Reston, VA: National Art Education Association.

Burton, D. (1998). Survey of current research in art education. *Studies in Art Education, 39*(2), 183–186.

Burton, D. (2001). How do we teach? Results of a national survey of instruction in secondary art education. *Studies in Art Education, 42*(2), 131–145.

Burton, D., & Boyer, G. (1998). Status report: The NAEA research task force on demographics. In E. Zimmerman (Ed.), *The NAEA research task force status reports* (pp. 3–8). Reston, VA: National Art Education Association.

Canadian Education Association. (2002). *The 2002 CEA handbook.* Toronto, Ontario: Canadian Education Association.

Carroll, K., & Kay, S. (1998). Status report: The NAEA task force on instruction. In E. Zimmerman (Ed.), *NAEA research task force status reports* (pp. 13–17). Reston, VA: National Art Education Association.

Carroll, K., Sandell, R., & Jones, H. (1995). The professional art school: A notable site for the preparation of art teachers. In L. Galbraith (Ed.), *Preservice art education: Issues and practice* (pp. 162–172). Reston, VA: National Art Education Association.

Chalmers, F. G. (1999). *Studies in Art Education*: The first 10 of 40 years. *Visual Arts Research, 25*(49), 2.

Chapman, L. (1982). *Instant art, instant culture: The unspoken policy for American schools.* New York: Teachers College Press.

Clark, A. (2001). The recent landscape of teacher education: Critical points and possible conjectures. *Teaching and Teacher Education. 17*(2), 599–611.

Clark, G., & Zimmerman, E. (1997). *Project ARTS: Programs for ethnically diverse, economically disadvantaged, high ability, visual arts students in rural communities: Identification, curriculum, evaluation* (ED 419765).

Clark, G., & Zimmerman, E. (2000). Greater understanding of the local community: A community-based art education program for rural schools. *Art Education, 53*(2), 33–39.

Cochran-Smith, M. (2001). Reforming teacher education: Competing agendas. *Journal of Teacher Education, 52*(4), 263–265.

Cochran-Smith, M. (2000). Teacher education at the turn of the century. *Journal of Teacher Education, 51*(3), 163–165.

Colbert, C., & Taunton, M. (2001). Classroom research in the visual arts. In V. Richardson (Ed.), *Handbook of research on teaching* (4th ed., pp. 520–526). Washington, DC: American Educational Research Association.

Colwell, R., & Richardson, C. (Eds.). (2002). *The New Handbook of Research of Music Teaching and Learning.* New York: Oxford University Press.

Consortium of National Arts Education Associations. (1994). *National standards for arts education: What every young American should know and be able to do in the arts.* Reston, VA: Music Educators National Conference.

Consortium of National Arts Education Associations; International Council of Fine Arts Deans; Council of Arts Accrediting Associations. (2001). *To move forward: An affirmation of continuing commitment to arts education.* Reston, VA: National Art Education Association.

Council of Chief State School Officers. (2001). *Gaining the arts advantage: More lessons from school districts that value arts education.* Washington, DC: Council of Chief State School Officers.

Darling-Hammond, L. (2000). How teacher education matters. *Journal of Teacher Education, 51*(3), 166–173.

Darling-Hammond, L., & Cobb, V. (1996). The changing context of teacher education. In F. Murray (Ed.), *The teacher educator's handbook: Building a knowledge base for the preparation of teachers* (pp. 14–62). San Francisco: Jossey-Bass.

Davis, J. D. (1990). Teacher education in the visual arts. In R. Houston (Ed.), *Handbook of research on teacher education* (pp. 746–757). New York: Macmillan.

Day, M. (Ed.). (1997). *Preparing teachers of art.* Reston, VA: National Art Education Association.

Degge, R. M. (1987). A descriptive study of community art teachers with implications for teacher preparation and cultural policy. *Studies in Art Education, 28*(3), 164–175.

DiBlasio, M. K. (1997). Certification and licensure requirements for art education: Comparison of state systems. In M. D. Day (Ed.), *Preparing teachers of art* (pp. 73–100). Reston, VA: National Art Education Association.

Doyle, W. (1990). Themes in teacher education. In W. R. Houston (Ed.), *Handbook of research on teacher education* (pp. 3–24). New York: Macmillan.

Ducharme, E. (1993). *The lives of teacher educators.* New York: Teachers College Press.

Ducharme, E., & Ducharme, M. K. (1996). Development of the teacher education professoriate. In F. Murray (Ed.), *The teacher educator's handbook: Building a knowledge base for the preparation of teachers* (pp. 691–715). San Francisco: Jossey-Bass.

Duke, L. L. (1999). Looking back, looking forward. *Arts Education Policy Review, 101*(1), 3–7.

Eads, H. (1980). *Art teacher education programs in the United States.* Unpublished doctoral dissertation, Illinois State University, Normal, IN.

Eisner, E. W. (1999). The national assessment in the visual arts. *Arts Education Policy Review, 100*(6), 16–20.

Ellingson, S. P. (1991). A comparison of two approaches to preparing preservice teachers to manage classrooms: Generic versus discipline-specific. *Studies in Art Education, 33*(1), 7–20.

Elliott, E. W. (1998). *The kind of schools we need: Personal essays.* Portsmouth, NH: Heinemann.

Galbraith, L. (1988). Research-oriented teachers: Implications for art teaching. *Art Education, 41*(5), 50–53.

Galbraith, L. (1990). Examining issues from general teacher education: Implications for preservice art education methods courses. *Visual Arts Research, 16*(2), 51–58.

Galbraith, L. (1991). Analyzing an art methods course: Implications for preparing primary student teachers. *Journal of Art and Design Education, 10*(3), 329–342.

Galbraith, L. (1995). The preservice art education classroom: A look through the window. In L. Galbraith (Ed.), *Preservice art education: Issues and practice* (pp. 1–30). Reston, VA: The National Art Education Association.

Galbraith, L. (1997). What are art teachers taught?: An analysis of curriculum components for art teacher preparation programs. In M. D. Day (Ed.), *Preparing teachers of art* (pp. 45–72). Reston, VA: National Art Education Association.

Galbraith, L. (2001). Teachers of teachers: Faculty working lives and art teacher education in the United States. *Studies in Art Education, 42*(2), 163–181.

Galbraith, L. (2002). Research in visual arts education: Implications for music. In Richard Colwell & Carol Richardson (Eds.), *The New Handbook of Research of Music Teaching and Learning* (pp. 962–974). New York: Oxford University Press.

Galbraith, L., & Grauer, K. (1998). Status report: The NAEA task force on teacher education. In E. Zimmerman (Ed.), *NAEA research task force status reports* (pp. 35–38). Reston, VA: National Art Education Association.

Getty Center for Education in the Arts. (1988). *The preservice challenge: Discipline-based art education and recent reports on higher education.* Los Angeles, CA: Getty Center for Education in the Arts.

Goodlad, J. (1990). *Teachers for our nation's schools.* San Francisco: Jossey-Bass.

Goodwin, M. A. (1997). The National Board for Professional Teaching Standards: Implications for Art Teacher Preparation. In M. D. Day (Ed.), *Preparing art teachers* (pp. 101–116). Reston, VA: National Art Education Association.

Grauer, K. (1998). Beliefs of preservice teachers toward art education.*Studies in Art Education, 39*(4), 350–370.

Grauer, K., & Sandell, R. (2000). *The visual journal and teacher development.* Paper presented at the annual Convention of the National Art Education Association, Los Angeles.

Guay, D. (1993). Cross-site analysis of teaching practices: Visual art education with students experiencing disabilities. *Studies in Art Education, 34*(4), 222–232.

Hafeli, M. (2000). Negotiating "fit" in student art work: Classroom conversations. *Studies in Art Education, 41*(2), 130–139.

Hamblen, K. (1989). Research in art education as a form of educational consumer protection. *Studies in Art Education, 24*(3), 169–176.

Hatfield, T. (2001, November). Personal communication.

Haynes, J. M., & Schiller, M. (1994). Collaborating with cooperating teachers in preservice art education. *Studies in Art Education, 35*(4), 218–227.

Hobbs, J. (1993). In defense of a theory of art education. *Studies in Art Education, 34*(4), 102–103.

Holmes Group. (1986). *Tomorrow's teachers: A report of the Holmes Group.* East Lansing, MI: Holmes Group.

Howey, K. R. et al. (1977). *Preservice teacher education.* Washington, DC: U.S. Office of Education (ED 146 210).

Howey, K., & Zimpher, N. (1994). *Informing faculty development for teacher educators.* Norwood, NJ: Ablex.

Howey K., & Zimpher, N. (1989). *Profiles of teacher education.* New York: State University of New York Press.

Hutchens, J. (1997). Accomplishing change in the university: Strategies for improving art teacher preparation. In M. D. Day (Ed.), *Preparing teachers of art* (pp. 139–154). Reston, VA: National Art Education Association.

Hutchens, J. (2001). *In their own words: The development of doctoral study in art education.* Reston, VA: National Art Education Association.

Irwin, R. L., Chalmers, F. G., Grauer, K., Kindler, A. M., & MacGregor, R. N. (1996). Art education policy in Canada. *Arts Education Policy Review, 97*(6), 15–22.

Jeffers, C. S. (1993). A survey of instructors of art methods classes for preservice elementary teachers. *Studies in Art Education, 30*(3), 142–156.

Jeffers, C. S. (1994). *A survey of Kansas art teachers' professional needs and interests.* Paper presented at the annual convention of the National Art Education Association, Baltimore, MD.

Jones, B. J., & McPhee, J. K. (1986). Research on teaching arts and aesthetics. In M. C. Wittrock (Ed.), *Handbook of Research on Teaching* (3rd ed., pp. 906–916). New York: Macmillan.

Kautz, P. (1996). *Preservice art educators' reasons for teaching: Career aspirations and demographics.* Paper presented at the annual Convention of the National Art Education Association, San Francisco.

Knight, W. B. (2000). *Preparing preservice teachers to work with diverse student populations: Implications for visual art teacher education.* Unpublished doctoral dissertation, Ohio State University, Columbus.

Kowalchuk, E. (1999). Perceptions of practice: What art student teachers say they learn and need to know. *Studies in Art Education, 41*(1), 71–90.

Lampela, L. (1995). A challenge for art education: Including lesbians and gays. *Studies in Art Education, 36*(4), 242–248.

Lampela, L. (2001). Lesbian and gay artists in the curriculum: A survey of art teachers' knowledge and attitudes. *Studies in Art Education, 42*(1), 146–162.

Lanier, J., & Little, J. (1996). Research on teacher education. In M. C. Wittrock (Ed.), *Handbook of research on teaching* (3rd ed., pp. 527–569). New York: Macmillan.

MacGregor, R. N. (1994). Assessment in the arts: A cross-Canada study (ED382560). Canada: British Columbia.

MacGregor, R. N. (1998). Two sides of an orange: The conduct of research. *Studies in Art Education, 39*(3), 271–280.

Mims, S., & Lankford, L. (1995). Time, money, and the new art education: A nationwide investigation. *Studies in Art Education, 36*(2), 84–95.

Murchison, E. M. (1989). *Visual arts education: A study of current practices in Louisiana.* Unpublished doctoral dissertation, Louisiana State University and Agricultural College, Baton Rouge.

Murray, F. B. (1996). Beyond natural teaching: The case for professional education. In F. B. Murray (Ed.), *The teacher educator's handbook: Building a knowledge base for the preparation of teachers* (pp. 3–13). San Francisco: Jossey-Bass.

Myers, S., & Grauer, K. (1994). *A comparison of beliefs and preconceptions of preservice teachers.* Paper presented at the annual meeting of the American Educational Research Association, New Orleans.

National Art Education Association. (1979). *Standards for art teacher preparation programs.* Reston, VA: National Art Education Association.

National Art Education Association. (1994a). *Art education: Creating a visual arts research agenda towards the 21st century.* Reston: VA: National Art Education Association.

National Art Education Association. (1994b). *The national visual arts standards.* Reston, VA: National Art Education Association.

National Art Education Association. (1996). *Briefing papers: Creating a visual arts agenda toward the twenty-first century.* Reston, VA: National Art Education Association.

National Art Education Association. (1998). *NAEA research task force status reports.* Reston, VA: National Art Education Association.

National Art Education Association. (1999). *Standards for art teacher preparation programs.* Reston, VA: National Art Education Association.

National Art Education Association. (2001). *Art teacher in secondary schools: A national survey.* Reston, VA: National Art Education Association.

National Board for Professional Teaching Standards. (1994). *Early adolescence through young adulthood/art: Standards for national board certification.* Washington, DC: National Board for Professional Teaching Standards.

National Center for Educational Statistics. (1998). *Digest of educational statistics.* Washington, DC: National Center for Educational Statistics.

National Center for Educational Statistics. (2000). *Digest of educational statistics.* Washington, DC: National Center for Educational Statistics.

National Commission on Teaching and America's Future. (1996). *What matters most: Teaching for America's future.* New York: National Commission on Teaching and America's Future.

National Council for Accreditation of Teacher Education. (2000–2001). *Teacher education: A guide to NCATE-accredited colleges and universities.* Washington, DC: National Council for Accreditation of Teacher Education.

Pankratz, D. B. (1989). Arts education research: Issues, constraints, and opportunities. In D. B. Pankratz & K. Mulcahy (Eds.), *The challenge to reform in arts education: What role can research play?* (pp. 1–28). New York: American Council for the Arts.

Parsons, M. J. (2001). Change again. *Studies in Art Education, 42*(2), 99–100.

Persky, H. R., Sandene, B. A., & Askew, J. M. (1998). *The NAEP 1997 arts report card: Eighth-grade findings from the National Assessment of Educational Progress.* U.S. Department of Education. Office of Educational Research and Improvement: National Center for Educational Statistics.

Richardson, V. (1996). The case for formal research and practical inquiry in teacher education. In F. B. Murray (Ed.), *The teacher educator's handbook: Building a knowledge base for the preparation of teachers* (pp. 715–739). San Francisco: Jossey-Bass.

Rogers, E. T. (1987). *A comparison of the course requirements in art teacher certification programs in the colleges and universities of Alabama.* Unpublished doctoral dissertation, Auburn University, AL.

Rogers, E. T., & Brogdon, R. (1990). A survey of NAEA curriculum standards in art teacher preparation programs. *Studies in Art Education, 31*(3), 168–173.

Roland, C. (1995). The use of journals to promote reflective thinking in prospective art teachers. In L. Galbraith (Ed.), *Preservice art education: Issues and practice* (pp. 119–134). Reston, VA: National Art Education Association.

Sevigny, M. J. (1987). Discipline-based art education and teacher education. *The Journal of Aesthetic Education, 21*(2), 95–128.

Short, G. (1995). Understanding domain knowledge for teaching: Higher-order thinking generated through the study of art criticism. *Studies in Art Education, 36*(3), 154–169.

Smith-Shank, D. (1992). *Art attitudes, beliefs, and stories of preservice elementary teachers.* Unpublished doctoral dissertation, Indiana University, Bloomington.

Spradling, K. (1995). *What methods teachers say they want and need in preservice courses.* Paper presented at the annual convention of the National Art Education Association, Houston, TX.

Stokrocki, M. (1988). Teaching preadolescents during a nine-week sequence: The negotiator approach. *Studies in Art Education, 1*(30) 39–46.

Thompson, C. M., & Hardiman, G. (1991). The status of art education programs in higher education. *Visual Arts Research, 17*(2), 72–80.

Thurber, F. E. (1989). *Linking the disciplines in art education: A study of a pilot course in discipline-based art education methods for preservice classroom teachers.* Unpublished doctoral dissertation, University of Nebraska-Lincoln, Lincoln, Nebraska.

Wenglingsky, H. (2000). *Teaching the teachers: Different setting, different result.* Princeton, NJ: Policy Information Center, Educational Testing Service.

Willis-Fisher, L. (1991). *A survey of the inclusion of aesthetics, art criticism, art history, and art production in art teacher preparation programs.* Unpublished doctoral dissertation, Illinois State University Press, Normal.

Willis-Fisher, L. (1993, Winter). Aesthetics, art criticism, art history, and art production in art teacher preparation programs. *NAEA Advisory.* Reston, VA: National Art Education Association.

Wilson, B. (1994). Reflections on the relationship among art, life, and research. *Studies in Art Education, 35*(4), 197–208.

Wilson, B. (1997). *The quiet evolution: Changing the face of arts education.* Los Angeles, CA: Getty Education Institute for the Arts.

Wilson, S., Floden, R., & Fernini-Mundy, J. (2001). *Teacher preparation research: Current knowledge, gaps, and recommendations.* Seattle, WA: Center for the Study of Teaching and Policy.

Wittrock, M. C. (Ed.). (1986). *Handbook of Research on Teaching* (3rd ed.). New York: Macmillan.

Wolfe, P. (1997). A really good art teacher would be like you, Mrs. C.: A qualitative study of a teacher and her artistically gifted middle school students. *Studies in Art Education, 3*(3), 232–245.

Zimmerman, E. (1991). Rembrandt to Rembrandt: A case study of a memorable painting teacher of artistically talented 13 to 16 year-old students. *Roeper Review, 13*(2), 76–81.

Zimmerman, E. (1992). A comparative study of two painting teachers of talented adolescents. *Studies in Art Education, 33*(3), 174–185.

Zimmerman, E. (1994a). *Art education: Creating a visual arts research agenda toward the 21st century.* Reston, VA: National Art Education Association.

Zimmerman, E. (1994b). Current research and practice about preservice art specialist teacher education. *Studies in Art Education, 35*(2), 79–89.

Zimmerman, E. (1994c). Concerns of pre-service art teachers and those who prepare them to teach. *Art Education, 1*(5), 59–67.

Zimmerman, E. (Ed.). (1996). *Briefing papers: Creating a visual arts research agenda toward the 21st century.* Reston, VA: National Art Education Association.

Zimmerman, E. (1997a). Whence come we? Wither go we? Demographic analysis of art teacher education programs in the United States. In M. D. Day (Ed.), *Preparing teachers of art* (pp. 27–44). Reston, VA: National Art Education Association.

Zimmerman, E. (1997b). Foreword. In S. D. La Pierre, & E. Zimmerman, E. (Eds). *Research methods and methodologies for art education* (pp. v–ix). Reston: VA: National Art Education Association.

Zimmerman, E. (1997c). I don't want to sit in the corner cutting out valentines: Leadership roles for teachers of talented art students. *Gifted Child Quarterly, 41*(1), 33–41.

Zimmerman, E. (Ed.). (1998). *NAEA research task force status reports.* Reston, VA: National Art Education Association.

20

Contexts for Teaching Art

Mary Stokrocki
Arizona State University

Contextual considerations that include the physical environment, sociocultural factors, and economic and political challenges are salient factors to consider with respect to teaching art. The form, content, meaning, and value of art teaching are determined by the context in which they are used. They range from the local to the global and are full of complexities and contradictions. Complexity in this case concerns the difficulty of conditions, and contradictions refer to those conditions that may not be solvable.

WHAT IS THE HISTORY OF CONTEXTUAL STUDIES IN ART EDUCATION?

In the first briefing papers of the National Art Education Association Task Force on Contextual Research, Congdon (1996) referred to research about teaching and learning contexts as "knowledge and insights into environments, cultures, and histories [that] provide important information throughout the development and implementation of art educational programming" (p. 51). She provided some background history of contextual research in art education and suggested questions and content areas of study, related to its history, values, culture, environment, instructional settings, collaborations, and policy. Stuhr and Ballengee Morris (1998) later added achievements of the Contextual Research Task Force that included symposiums, conferences, model programs, a list of contextual-based issues, action-oriented workshops, a task force newsletter, and anthologies of invisible histories (Bolin, Blandy, & Congdon, 2000) and histories of community-based art education (Congdon, Blandy, & Bolin, 2001). This chapter continues documentation of the history of contextual research and its implications for the field of art education.

WHY DID I SELECT THESE STUDIES?

This chapter focuses on instructional contexts and reveals their complexities and, at times, their contradictions. I searched the literature, from 1985 to 2002, for the word "contexts" and found 12 studies related to contexts for teaching art. Sources were the NAEA *Art Education Index, Studies in Art Education Index*, the *Journal of Multicultural and Cross-cultural Research in Art Education*, ERIC, NAEA publications, and several recent InSEA publications. Contextual studies also will be included in other chapters in this *Handbook*, such as curriculum research and historical research. Other useful terms searched were case studies, "hyper" (media or text), multicultural, and teaching art. Several art educators also offered suggestions of which studies to include. Some studies offer early attempts (Jones, 1977; Wilson, 1977), exemplify breakthrough areas of contextual research (Bullock & Galbraith, 1992; Garber & Stankiewicz, 2000), and present related issues about the area of context (Ballengee Morris, 1997). Other examples are well known to me (Clark & Zimmerman, 2000; Day, Eisner, Stake, Wilson, & Wilson, 1984); still others are marginal in that they deal with extreme cases such as jails (Congdon, 1984; Dennis, Hanes, Stuhr, Walton, & Wightman, 1997).

Lack of space, practical interests on instruction and student learning, and a focus on qualitative research limited this selection to approximately 50 studies. I borrowed categories of school, community, and multicultural contexts from Lieberman (1992); added the category of electronic contexts, and changed the term *multicultural* to *intercultural* to reflect changes in thinking "beyond multicultural perspectives" (Boughton & Mason, 1999). The categories that I use in this chapter are as follows:

- **School contexts:** These include school culture, schools as tribes, inservice programs, and effective and ineffective teaching.
- **Community contexts:** These include community-centered education, folk art sites, diverse population adaptations (lifelong learning and gender issues), and museum-enrichment programs.
- **Intercultural contexts:** These include multicultural clarifications, indigenous cultural understandings, cross-cultural comparisons, international summer schools, intercultural education, and globalization of popular culture.
- **Electronic contexts:** These include electronic environments such as videodiscs and hypertext, interactive Web sites, teleconferencing, and distance education courses. Selections occasionally may overlap.

WHAT IS A CONTEXT?

A *context* is a complex of factors, conditions, and contradictory elements that support or limit a historically and culturally related framework that is constantly changing. Some art educators have conceived of context as a sociocultural phenomenon (Anderson, 1995; Jones, 1988). Other art educators consider contexts as multi-interpretive because of differences in particular group values (Neperud, 1995). Contextual studies demand field study and an interpretive type of research that positions a local context, such as a class, a school, a community center, or an institution, within larger embedded contexts within a given culture (Graue & Walsh, 1998). For study in contextual research, a case can be a person, a class, an institution, a culture, or a hyper-mediated environment. Such studies can focus on individual sites or multiple cross sites. Because contextual research is multimodal, researchers have a wide selection of methods from which to choose. Methods range from qualitative examples such as case study, ethnography, and cross-site analysis to quantitative techniques of surveys, interviews, and computer data analysis.

WHAT CONTEXTUAL CONTRADICTIONS HAVE BEEN REPORTED IN ART EDUCATION?

Contradictions involving *school contexts* entail impersonal versus intimate settings (Guilfoil, 1990), structural and extrastructural learning (Wilson, 1977), and ethics that reflect and/or challenge the community (Stokrocki, 1986). Other conflicts include student-centered (Hafeli, 2000) versus discipline-centered instruction (Wilson, 1984b), popular culture versus fine art interests (Donnelly, 1990), dissonance (Bullock & Galbraith, 1992) or harmony, such as creativity concepts and ideals (Irwin & Reynolds, 1994), with inclusion or separation of students experiencing disabilities (Guay, 1993). Contradictions in *community contexts* include museum instructional differences between museum and art educators (Vallance, 1999), between leisure and lifelong learning (Lackey, 1999), and between ethnic and homogeneous art offerings (Young, 1985). *Intercultural contexts* deal with contrasts of assimilation or adaptation of indigenous people (Stuhr, 1986) and localization and globalization (Irwin, Rogers, & Wan, 1998). *Electronic contexts* favor student-centered versus teacher-centered instruction (Galbraith, 1996), interactive versus passive learning (Julian, 1997), multidirectional rather than linear thinking (Taylor, 2000), and a conversational learning style rather than a talking-heads television format (Garber & Stankiewicz, 2000).

WHAT ARE DOMINANT WORDS OR THEMES IN CONTEXTUAL RESEARCH?

One frequent term is the prefix "inter," noted at least 30 times in my review of research related to contexts in art education. Related themes are interests, interactive, interdisciplinary, intergenerational, international, and intercultural. The first theme of *interests* emerged with such studies as catering to preadolescents' popular culture interests (Stokrocki, 1997), determining family interests (Schrubbers, 1996), and sharing similar interests among people in diverse sites (Mason & Richter, 1999). Another theme is development of *interactive* sites, such as interactive exhibits found in museum-enrichment programs (Wilson, 2001), intense peer teaching and student interactions (Wolfe, 1997), cross-community communication (Clark & Zimmerman, 2000), cross-cultural interactions (Smith-Shank, 1997), and an interactive teleconference course (Garber & Stankiewicz, 2000). A third evolving theme is *interdisciplinary* or interrelated factors, such as ecology (Birt, Krug, & Sheridan, 1997; Julian, 1997), puppet plays and art and reading programs (Stokrocki, 1986), and the arts and integrated interdisciplinary curricula (Stuhr, in press). Four studies dealt with *intergenerational* contexts (e.g., Clark & Zimmerman, 2000; La Porte, 2000), and four studies involved the *Internet* (e.g., Julian, 1997; Rogers & Erickson, 1997). Finally, there are studies of *international* concern, such as promoting understanding of international perspectives (Irwin, Rogers, & Farrell, 1999) and studies of *intercultural* approaches concerning education (Davenport, 2000a, 2000b), citizenship (Hernandez, 2000), and exchanges of artwork and ideas (Stokrocki, 1989).

Variation of the word "critical" appears at least 10 times as an effort to expose hidden sociocultural differences among moral, political, and ecological concerns. Various usages of critical theory research related to contexts for teaching in art education revealed different styles of cultural representation (Mason, 1988), indigenous peoples' reactions to space (Sikes, 1992), and marginalized group learning (Dennis et al., 1997). Other occurrences of the term "critical" include complex ideas on identity and values (Stuhr, 1991), cultural patterns that are being replaced by economic values (Stokrocki, 1995), and ideas of economic and political power (Irwin, Rogers, & Wan, 1998). Critical examination of community centers further entailed ideological review of differences in the meaning of art, education, leisure, and work in school and in recreation centers (Lackey, 1994, 1997).

BIG SCHOOLS OR SMALL SCHOOLS?

At no time was the problem of school size noted by art educators in their research findings. Teachers complain of tight classroom spaces and high enrollments, yet schools tend to be problematic because of administration surveillance policies (Wilson, 1977), lack of articulation (Wilson, 1984b), working conditions (Sacca, 1996), environmental conditions (Asher, 2000), or spatial design (Guilfoil, 1990; Susi, 1990). Small schools are not always superior to large schools due to lack of subject choices, low funding, and social discrimination due to some students' family backgrounds. Large concentrations of disadvantaged students can become problematic because school administrators may neglect some of their needs. Thus, moderate-sized schools, schools within schools, or specialty areas are promising alternative environments (Lee, 2000). An arts complex or a community art wing can be an effective specialty area. Environments are complex entities. It takes an active collaboration of teachers and students to effect change. The emergence of art tribes, times when students separate themselves into their own communities, also can accelerate change (Wilson, 1977). Governance of public education is complex because of its many internal and external conditions and influences (Hodges Persell, 2000).

HOW DO CONTEXTUAL STUDIES CONTRIBUTE TO CONCEPTUAL PROGRESS?

Because some contextual studies may evolve from doctoral dissertations, they initially may have a narrow conceptual focus, such as behavioral considerations and space relations. More seasoned researchers can add breadth by comparing three or more contexts (Irwin et al., 1998). When researchers investigate multiple sites, their research scope can be broadened further. When researchers from several countries can address contextual issues, then their research can become global (Boughton & Mason, 1999).

There is a wealth of multicultural opinions in art education, but transnational research is lacking due to limited funding and vision; "more" sites, therefore, do not imply better research. Contextual concepts may seem sophisticated because they deal with multiple ideas; however, contextual studies need depth through consideration of multiple dimensions, including philosophical ideas.

SCHOOL CONTEXTS

School Culture

A school culture tends to be a complex phenomenon affected by students and teachers, curriculum content, and internal and external political and social forces. Champlin (1997) referred to school and culture as "the shared characteristics and features of the environmental conditions, physical space, human relationships and interactions, and pedagogical milieu within the instructional setting of the institution called the school" (p. 117). Over the last 100 years, rapid sociocultural changes have affected school cultures. These include "changes from an industry-oriented society and international dominance, demographic shifts, increase in the older population, a work force composed of immigrants, and negative assessment results of U.S. students' scores in sciences, critical, and problem-solving skills " (Darling-Hammond, cited in Lieberman, 1992, p. 112). McFee and Degge (1980) recognized the complexities of teaching and stated, "As our environment and our resources decrease and our numbers increase, we may need to understand our own needs, those of other individuals, and all groups to make our lives together workable" (p. 270). In their Perception Delineation Theory, they spoke of embedded contexts beginning with the readiness of the individual student, the psychocultural classroom environment, and the larger visual–physical learning environment. They believed that teachers who are aware of such complexities would be open to future contextual changes. Eisner (1998) explained, "Teaching always occurs in highly contextual situations; there is not now nor will there ever be a replacement for the teacher who understands which course of action and which decision is most appropriate in this particular circumstance at this particular time" (p. 209).

Environmental Conditions

Environmental factors and changes can affect teaching in many ways. Based on research observing classroom environments, Susi (1990) discovered the effects of environmental stress (bad lights and air, acoustics, white noise, intercom announcements, clutter, room temperature, and cleanliness) on effective teaching. He explained how environmental changes, such as seat location (eye contact and distance from speaker), space arrangements (clustered, circular, or theater style), and aesthetic quality (comfortable, pleasing, and flexible) can impact student behavior. Susi concluded that teachers could manipulate such variables to support student learning and that good environmental contexts result from informed decisions about social interaction patterns.

The culture of a school also has an invisible personality affected by environmental conditions bound by sociocultural characteristics (Birnbaum, 1988). Using participant observation techniques, Guilfoil (1990) observed the daily life in a rural Eskimo village for 3 months. She focused on behaviors and the built environment in a one-room school. By using behavioral mapping, she coded student location and movements on a floor plan, and through behavioral sketches, she described and determined social distances done at regular intervals between students and staff. Additional research and art teaching experiences involved informal interviews, essays, photography, and cognitive mapping—students' diagrams of what is important. Guilfoil interviewed elementary students for their ideas on school layout and noted their preference for close proximity and the constant issue of inappropriate settings—impersonal areas. She concluded that students learned valuable inquiry and spatial skills as they collaborated with her to discover the "intimate nature" of this rural school culture that included the importance of teachers and friends, close positioning, and small group spaces.

In another study involving action research, Asher (2000) explored her own teaching in an alternative high school in the Bronx, New York, with at-risk students from African American, Hispanic, Caribbean, and South East Indian backgrounds. She described the environment as a "landscape of hopelessness," a place of despair and decay. She offered a course called "Bronx as Art," which afforded students opportunities to view their environment in new ways and develop positive images of self and surroundings. Opportunities included sketching and photography in the school vicinity, collage, and silk painting. Besides teaching about past and contemporary artists who were influenced by their urban spaces, Asher invited a community artist who made paintings of his local neighborhood to share his work and experiences. She also encouraged memory writing, in which her students described and shared stories about where they lived, and engaged them in process writing, which is critical to thinking about their problems with unfamiliar materials and skills. The findings of Asher's study include successful activities such as making high-quality artworks, sharing of life experiences, developing trust among students, recognizing relationships in form and environment, creating new views of a familiar world, and developing a sense of beauty amidst the squalor.

Working Conditions

School culture also consists of a combination of working conditions that affect a school setting. Sacca (1996) reported a case study in a secluded logging camp in Vancouver Island in 1928. A lonely female art teacher wrote about her feelings of estrangement from her community and committed suicide. Some school board members unfairly criticized her teaching and ideas, which challenged their sociocultural values. The outraged community dismissed the school board and the Minister of Education and designated a welfare officer to investigate living and social conditions in rural districts. Sacca suggested that such conditions are similar to those academic curriculum controls and tight surveillance of teaching conditions under which women continue to work. She argued for additional action research undertaken by art teacher scholars who can readily pinpoint problems. Sacca concluded that socially conscious research modifications could help serve young teachers by addressing issues that affect teaching conditions, embrace contributions of women, develop new forms of collaborative research, and offer alternative means of publication.

Findings from studies of school culture, environmental conditions, and working conditions suggest that researchers and teachers can determine and change the nature of a school culture (from that of despair to that of hope), adjust environmental conditions, and affect positively negative working conditions.

Schools as Tribes

Schools also can be characterized as tribes with distinctive lore, symbols, and rites of passage (Deal & Peterson, 1999). Schools publicly proclaim their missions and mascots and arrange sports and academic rites. These rites include periods of separation, transition, and integration (Van Gennup, 1961). Schools separate academic disciplines into different subjects, such as art tribes, which further divide into art classes and student art groups. During the transition phase, students undergo trials and learn the sacred lore. Finally schools integrate students back into society at graduation.

Educational tribes can be public or private, dependent or independent. Art programs tend to be independent tribes in a school culture. The tribal character of an art program in which social interaction and knowledge tend to be loosely structured is as important as the intellectual character, where interaction and knowledge are highly structured.

Art teachers may allow and even instigate tribal behaviors and learning. Using ethnographic methods, Wilson (1977) described structural restraints of an extremely intense high school environment in New York where she taught. She noted conflicts between administrators and students who were angry and bored. In her drawing class, she focused on the emersion of "extrastructural learning," which is a form of relaxed attention. More specifically, she noticed the emergence of such playful and creative art forms as drawing games, making witty statements (puns on artists' names and class banter), role-playing (the jocks, greasers, heads, punks, and intellectuals), arranging rituals (class parties, portfolio arrangements, and art exhibitions), and developing an in-depth sense of community. She concluded that community cannot be forced but evolves around teachers who facilitate an atmosphere for learning and at the same time tolerate a degree of rule breaking.

Using similar methods, I (Stokrocki, 1997) also explored how an art teacher at the middle school level structured his teaching and captured his Southwest preadolescents' interests through focusing on rites of passage. He separated students into tribes, in which they named and designed related tattoos (a popular culture fad). He taught them the sacred lore, for example, about mask-making and death in different cultures. He furthered their camaraderie by assuming the role of jester and through videotaping that allowed for play and acting out of masked characters. He finally recommended that teachers use exaggerated stories and cultural events, such as the Day of the Dead, to capture student attention and ease their transition into the study of art history. Such teaching experiences appealed to his students' existential interests and may deepen their and other students' understandings of the social nature of art.

From studies focusing on schools or art classes as tribes, a few researchers concluded that schools and teachers publicly broadcast "structured" objectives, policies, and curriculum, but operate effectively at other levels as well. These other levels included extrastructural teaching or relaxed attention that allows for "antistructural" group identity and concerns metaphysical values that appeal to students' curiosity about life and death concerns.

Urban, Suburban, and Rural Inservice Contexts

Some tribes are dependent, and others are independent. A large corporation or university tribe may or may not highly influence school district policies by their philosophical methods and ideas through inservice connections. In order to determine what factors engender support of strong art programs in a school district and evidence of teaching art history, art criticism, and art production, the Getty Center for Education in the Arts funded cross-site case study analyses to discern similarities and differences in themes discovered in urban, suburban, and rural contexts. Focus was on a curriculum venture that was known as discipline-based art education (DBAE) and included content in areas of studio art, art history, art criticism, and aesthetics. The case study method began with a review of program materials including art curricula, declaration of philosophy, and such special components as school–museum collaborations. The next phase involved observation of instruction in schools and interviews with administrators, teachers, parents, students, and community members.

In Ohio, for example, the suburban Whitehall Schools had a long kinship connection to Ohio State University and with the State Supervisor of Art. Teachers were initially attracted to the DBAE curriculum package and their lessons were heavily studio based. For art history and criticism, they first relied on prepackaged slides, filmstrips, and *Art and Man* readings and activities. Unique experiences were planning and designing a (theoretical) museum and gaining cultural understanding through an archeological dig. It was suggested that the success of the DBAE curriculum was not only due to the content of the curriculum but also to the dynamic teachers, nurturing relationships, and local group support (Wilson, 1984a). The major problem, however, was the lack of teachers' ability to translate theory into practice into the DBAE content areas.

In contrast to dependent school districts in the Getty study were independent and decentralized school districts, such as Brooklyn District 15 in New York. In spite of this district's strong connections to museum and community resources and the initial enthusiasm and commitment of its administrators, it lacked a unified curricula and connections to university theorists (Wilson, 1984b). Research also revealed other contextual problems such as endless contests and competitions, student discipline concerns, low funding for special subjects, math and reading emphasis, and lack of superintendent support (Wilson, 1984b).

In addition to the Getty study, Gunter (2000) reported the impact of discipline-based art education on Southern rural middle school students. Students reflected problems of art education in the rural South, as they were unable to articulate an understanding of the components of the DBAE framework and felt disconnected from art in their everyday lives. The poorly implemented art curriculum at the middle school level had little relevance to the Southern rural females. Lack of experiences with art, especially with artists of color, women artists, and original works of art, contributed to an uncertainty about what art is and what artists do. In spite of dynamic leadership at the state level, lack of local coordinators, inadequate financial support, a misunderstanding of (DBAE) theory, and no input in curriculum planning, conditions led to younger teachers' apathy and burnout and division among veteran teachers. Recommendations included increased funding for art programs, use of coordinators for DBAE facilitation, a network for recruitment and retention of rural art educators, and the use of arts integration with a culturally diverse curriculum to provide relevance for students.

Researchers can conclude from studies of these inservice art programs that carefully planned and well-integrated curricula were helpful, but a nurturing theorist–practitioner relationship and local group support were equally significant. A major problem included lack of teachers' abilities to translate theory into practice. In addition, a program that is top-down with over-arching ideals may not fit every site, especially if articulation between levels and curriculum is fragmented or if the program does not consider the regional arts and conditions and differences among urban, suburban, and rural settings as sites for art teaching.

School Contexts Reflect and Challenge Community Ethics in Midwestern Settings

Using participant observation strategies, I (Stokrocki, 1986) noted environmental conditions that affected an elementary school teacher in a Midwest suburban community. These conditions included a tight schedule, limited space, students' expectations to make things and to celebrate holidays, and a teacher's interests in accelerating her own growth through color xerography. I discovered that this elementary art teacher could offer more opportunities to students when she stretched her limited 30-minute class with after-school art programs, interdisciplinary arrangements (puppet plays and art and reading programs), and university affiliations. Successful art teaching reflected the hard-work ethic of this working-class community.

Zimmerman (1992) compared two painting teachers of talented adolescents in a summer program at Indiana University. Their structured teaching practices included demonstrations, lectures, and individual and group critiques. She found that the instructor who shared secrets of the trade, told jokes, gave imitations of popular heroes, and related stories that dealt with moral or political problems was the one who realized his goals for art teaching. She advised those who teach talented students to be mindful of their students' needs to understand the contexts in which they create art, to examine their reasons for art making, and to discuss issues in the world of art. In addition, the context of summer programs seemed conducive to learning, because students were free from regular school obligations and probably accomplished more in a relaxed atmosphere than they did in their art classes during the school year. The academic university program challenged students from various parts of suburban and rural Indiana to learn about the nature of art in depth.

In a study of middle school students, many of whom were talented, Wolfe (1997) similarly focused on one art teacher in a Midwestern university community with rich artistic influences. By using constant comparative analysis and interrater reliability, she discovered the importance of good substantive teaching that consisted of a flood of images, student reflection in journals and sketchbooks, intense peer teaching and student interactions, and solid technical instruction. Assessment consisted of formal critique, exhibition, and in-process appraisal. She postulated that teachers should offer a plethora of organized artistic experiences and multimedia motivations while encouraging students to interact and react to what they were learning in art.

Using ethnographic methods that included daily observation and informal interviews, James (1997) postulated that instruction and creativity might emerge unpredictably from a class as an ecosystem of interacting people and materials. In other words, a class is a system of structure and nonstructure based on amplification of deviations. Through play and the utilization of the unexpected, one professor modeled deviating practices in a beginning metal sculpture class at a large university in the Midwest. He offered multiple ways of knowing (perceiving, analyzing, interpreting, and self-evaluating) so that students could deal with the hard–soft nature of the sculpture material and the physical diversions of bending, twisting, and wrestling with metal. An atmosphere of mutual engagement emerged as students worked alone and with others. The students' work evolved from mundane-found object sculpture to sturdy sculptural figures. In this context, the instructor primarily regarded sculpture as an expressive and formal aesthetic object. James concluded that teachers must understand the systematic complexity of their class context, namely, the creative and artistic processes. This class was based on an ethic of creativity that included divergence and uncertainty that was quite different from the conservative nature of their community.

In the previously cited contexts, teachers challenge their students. Outcomes regarding contexts pertain to excellent conditions outside the regular school environment that include university affiliations; high regard for art in the community; abundant program funding; and programs that are extrastructural, offer creative diversions, and encourage learning from peers.

Negotiation of Learning in Inner-City, Suburban, and Rural Settings

Contextual teaching and learning is all about "the individual creation of meaning and socio-cultural understanding through the development and recognition of different perspectives" (Hafeli, 2000). This meaning comes about through negotiation with students' viewpoints, school policies, and community interests.

Using participant observation techniques, I (Stokrocki, 1990) documented an African American teacher who was committed to developing both students' appreciation of their art heritages and confidence in artmaking and their recognition of art and avocational careers in inner city Cleveland. She presented an academic portrait lesson using artworks by famous African Americans and invited a Black cowboy artist to speak to her art class. She concluded that teachers of minority students must demonstrate how art is related to the students' lives, their heritages, their interests, and their future aspirations.

Using qualitative analysis and data collection, Bullock and Galbraith (1992) focused on the concept of "dissonance" found in two teachers' backgrounds, middle school policies, students' cultural heritages, and lack of art backgrounds in Tucson, Arizona. There was dissonance between internal sources, such as teachers' personal beliefs about art and teaching and their backgrounds, and external sources, such as students' cultural heritages, school curricula, and local policies. One teacher valued teaching more in-depth art experiences through a discipline-based approach as opposed to through the school's limited exploratory art curriculum. The other teacher who was Hispanic desired to advance her Hispanic students' skills and interests beyond "K-Mart aesthetics" and to teach them to appreciate their own Mexican heritage. To relieve some of this dissonance, researchers uncovered the teacher's use of popular cultural hooks, such as Madonna's preference for artworks by Frida Kahlo, to motivate young adolescents in this context. They concluded that teachers could easily modify their preferred teaching beliefs and practices to be more inclusive in their individual classroom contexts.

When teaching in an unemployed suburban context in Ireland, Donnelly (1990) serendipitously discovered popular culture references that motivated her large class of resentful adolescent girls. Whereas academic art history approaches of questioning and lecture failed, casual mention of the artist who cut off his ear (Van Gogh) piqued students' interests in existential concerns, caused emotional reactions, and inspired further student–initiated inquiry. Students showed further curiosity about Van Gogh's and other antiheroes' art philosophies, attitudes, and values that matched their own sense of rebellion. Students imitated Van Gogh's painting style through multimedia responses and empathetically initiated play.

By using participant observation and "stimulated recall," a sociological method of eliciting comments about photographs and video sequences, Hafeli (2000) analyzed class dynamics in a suburban middle school in New York State. She concentrated on middle school students' expressive self-portraits and on their paintings of people relating or not relating to each other. The assignment was to include as many people as possible in their paintings. She uncovered students' acts of resistance and negotiation, such as one student's bid to paint a ballgame from an aerial view, a more abstract approach to the painting. Such examples revealed a student-centered teaching approach and adaptive experiences that allowed students to form their own art education worldviews. These studies question the imposition of external standards regarding instruction and the need to modify practice to meet the needs, from a specific context, of the situation and of the students.

Using ethnomethodogy techniques that included intense observations, interviewing, audio- and videotapes and photography, Guay (2000) discovered the importance of personal stories to culturally diverse eighth graders in a working-class setting in Ohio. The observed teacher empowered students to make "outrageous" subject matter and thematic choices, showed them tricks with tools or textural materials, extended the project throughout the semester, and shared art examples as they related to each student's work. Results question the relevance of imposed standards, time constraints of teacher-designed assignments, and narrow objectives for all students.

Using a postmodern ethnography framework, Ballengee Morris (1997) explored cultural, political, and social issues in art education in collaboration with people in a rural context. She used interviews, observations, readings, and professional development with teachers. She presented a case study about the use of social reconstruction pedagogy through constructed stories that illuminate and address issues of power, voice, conflict, class, gender, and race. The goal was to help local people appreciate folk arts in an Appalachian mountain community of which she is a member. As participant observer, project coordinator, and co-artist, she focused on one rural elementary school in a West Virginia strip-mining town. Morris used peer coaching by modeling critical analysis to develop cultural pride, values, and a sense of place, voice, and identity in an elementary school. Students explored the sociocultural theme of John Henry, a local folk hero who was relevant to their culture. Activities included a visit to a coal mine, a student-scripted play, dancing body self-portraits and a flatfoot dance, a student-composed group song, and a culminating festival. Results included students' growing identity with their cultural selves through stories and an increase of self-understanding.

Clark and Zimmerman (2000) reported on their efforts to promote community interaction of teachers, parents, and community members in arts programs in rural areas that included populations with similar backgrounds. Project ARTS (Arts for Rural Teachers and Students) was a 3-year research and development program that included seven rural elementary schools in the United States. These rural areas included two different community schools in Indiana (Appalachian, English, and Scottish), two schools in New Mexico (Hispanic and Pueblo Indian), and three schools in coastal South Carolina (African American, Gullah heritage). The project aimed at having rural schools and communities determine their own objectives, curriculum, and activities based on the theme of celebrating their local communities. Parent and community member involvement was crucial, in that they helped develop and implement identification, curriculum, and assessment procedures. Some parents were local artists, who spoke to school children about their artwork. Students interviewed elders about local architecture, collected stories from local people, and illustrated and videotaped the stories. Authentic assessment procedures included (a) portfolios of unfinished work, peer critiques, self-evaluations, contracts, student journals; (b) teachers' observation comments; (c) videos of discussions with students about their artwork; (d) examination of students' artworks based on special assignments, final art displays, and group presentations that testified to art learnings. Students from rural pueblo and Indiana schools were surprised to discover they had similar interests, including basketball, and their art experiences and their awareness and appreciation of local community arts increased. Cross-community communications resulted in key findings that included sharing of interests in three sites, involvement of parents and community members for continuation of programs, locally designed evaluation forms and parent surveys, and continued incorporation of artistic heritages in local communities.

Findings involving inner-city and suburban settings, namely, at the middle school level, pointed to dissonance as a dominant condition in teaching students in diverse settings. These studies provided some reason to believe that a student-centered approach, negotiated learning, popular cultural hooks, and folk heroes were ingredients for successful art teaching. Key findings in rural sites also included sharing interests among sites, involvement of parents and community members for continuation of programs, locally designed evaluation forms, and continued incorporation in art curricula of artistic traditional and folk heritages in local communities. Effective teaching and programs appeared to be related to successful university connections and relaxed school environments. These studies also question imposition of external standards about art curricula offerings and assessments.

Inclusion and People Experiencing Disabilities

Inclusion is the education of students experiencing a so-called "disability" within a regular classroom as opposed to within a separate classroom. Blandy (1989) fought against a medical model of disability that assumed that disabled people needed to be cured and segregated into separate institutions away from normal contexts. Art teachers who used this model prepared "special" activities for disabled students, and learning became highly passive. He argued for an inclusive ecological approach, in which people and learning are interconnected, and for more "normal" or active utilization of their abilities and viewpoints. He referred to his case study at The Ohio State University Logan Elm Press and Papermill in which he worked with four youth apprentices in an arts-of-the book laboratory (Blandy, 1983). The so-called moderately mentally challenged apprenticed youths learned about book art skills, produced their own printed books, and shared their viewpoints. Blandy concluded that the book arts' context empowered these participants to develop autobiographical statements based on their life experiences as seen in their valued material culture and institutional ceremonies. Blandy (1994) further argued for inclusive education, a process in which art teachers create learning environments that are flexible, dynamic, and adaptable, to meet the needs of all participants in normal school settings. He also believed that universities should provide educational opportunities to facilitate involvement of preservice art teachers with groups who experience various challenges.

Using cross-site analysis, Guay (1993), for example, reported adaptive teaching practices of eight art teachers in included and segregated art programs in Ohio schools. She discovered a balance of expressive and responsive activities, use of task analysis and partial participation and incorporation of a variety of adaptive tools. Partial participation (the modification of instruction to individualize learning) and task analysis (the process of reducing techniques into simpler steps) were used effectively. She recommended that teachers focus on student similarities and include students in comprehensive art programs, instead of specially designed activities.

Research with people experiencing disabilities testifies to successes such as inclusion in regular art programs, promotion of pride and autonomy and social contact, and development of successful art works in a comprehensive art program. The role of the researcher as participant tends to become more demanding at times, especially research with people who have physical challenges, because the situation may demand that the researcher become a temporary teacher's aide or social advocate for the rights of the so-called disabled.

COMMUNITY CONTEXTS

Community-based contexts stress site-specific competencies and out-of-school knowledge, rather than in-school learning. They include ethnic community centers; intergenerational programs; museum outreach programs; and partnerships to develop ecological settings, recreation centers, senior adult centers, and correctional institutions.

Museum Outreach Programs

During the changing times of the 1970s, museums began to adjust their focus from enlightenment of a few to demand for knowledge raised by the general public and schools at all levels. Newsom and Silvers (1978) presented a comprehensive overview of museum contexts, such as outdoor museums (Massachusetts's Sturbridge Village), partnerships with schools (Cincinnati's Taft Museum), and mobile units (Ringling Art Caravan in Florida). Successful programs found in science museums and in children's museums, such as Teenage Explainers at the San Francisco Exploratorium, further challenged art museums to build concept-based exhibitions and participatory learning and outreach programs in rural areas (Berry & Mayer, 1989). Museum art programs now range from those for preschoolers and parents at the Cleveland Museum of Art to docent training and mobile arts programs for senior citizens at the Rochester, New York, Memorial Art Gallery.

From an international comparison of teaching methods used in museums, Jones (1977) found that personnel in American and European museums who participated both in her survey and in personal interviews favored school-visitation programs. Whereas in the United States museums educate volunteers to teach, Jones discovered that the European museums prepared paid teams of educational staff to accompany children and teachers on museum tours. In their field research, Ott and Jones (1984) later documented international museums and found remarkable exhibitions of children's art, such as those in the Muzeum Tornuniu in Torun, Poland, and those in the Museum of the Blind in Berlin. Art programs in many community contexts seem to be thriving, while the survival of art programs in schools is sometimes more challenging.

Folk Art as a Context for Art Teaching

Blandy and Congdon (1988) argued that teachers need to include traditional arts from their students' community in order for students to learn about their local folk backgrounds. Notable was their descriptive research on a controversial exhibit called "Boats, Bait, and Fishing Paraphernalia: A Local Folk Aesthetic" in Bowling Green, Ohio. They invited local experts from the fishing community to curate an exhibit and demonstrate such art processes as model boat constructing, fly tying, net making, rod wrapping, and taxidermy. Paraphernalia included fishing poles, photographs, lures, boats, clothes, and keepsakes (postcards). Also included were fish stories, movies, and food. Findings included controversial discussions, involving aesthetics, validation of local art forms, and national press attention. Because they do not represent static art heritages, these ethnic and folk sites also tended to incorporate new materials and ideas (Congdon & Blandy, 1999).

With interest in qualitative research in museum contexts, art educators also began to evaluate art programs in museum contexts. Through focus group meetings with staff members,

researchers uncovered hidden meanings and cultural problems embedded in museum education programs. In his institutional review of the Heard Museum (Phoenix, Arizona) which
involved Native people from diverse backgrounds, Sikes (1992), for example, discovered that
the museum's mission-style structure, especially its barred windows, resembled a prison to
these local Native people.

Research in museums abroad also revealed mistakes, successes, and differences in multicultural education contexts, content, and audience participation. In her effort to develop Turkish
immigrant families' interests in different museums in Berlin, for instance, Schrubbers (1996)
found that the splendor of the Charlottenburg Castle setting overwhelmed Turkish families,
especially when they discovered that the first Turkish migrants were servants in the castle. For
these Turkish families, however, the Berlin Museum's scale was more familiar and accessible.
Using qualitative observation, she discovered that group discussions of toys and discussions of
everyday life themes inspired reminiscences and were more successful than discussions about
fine arts. She concluded that tours for immigrant families needed to be better planned and
implemented. Dobbs (1996), who reviewed the research report, suggested that museum guides
tried to develop visitor motivation through personal and family interests, but needed more
information about dealing with cultural traits of diverse people. Due to language difficulties,
researchers needed to employ follow-up questionnaires to study the impact of museum visits
on participants.

Vallance (1999) clarified differences between the role of museum educator and that of
art educator in promoting multicultural awareness. For instance, while the museum educator
focuses mostly on objects, the art educator focuses mainly on students. To illustrate her point,
she conducted successful ethnographic case studies at the Saint Louis Art Museum. The first
study consisted of gallery talks that offered, as a kind of remedial education, a sample of
culturally different artifacts to a wide range of novice visitors. Another study involved thematic
cross-cultural tours that broadened the knowledge of multicultural issues for teachers with
some background in art, but not their students' understanding of multicultural art. A third
study entailed participatory programs, such as a middle school cultural crossroads program
that allowed small groups of racially mixed students during three gallery visits to discuss the
art on exhibit and to reinterpret it verbally and visually. As a result of this research, Vallance
challenged museums to determine what audiences actually learn in a multicultural sense and
what art teaching strategies might be most appropriate in museum contexts.

Deconstruction of museum power and place has been expanded with interactive approaches,
such as Fred Wilson's controversial installation "Mining the Museum." In this collaboration
with the Maryland Historical Society in Baltimore, Wilson (2001), an African American artist,
rearranged its collection with provocative titles that questioned the Eurocentric classification
of its collections. Such endeavors empower community members to reinterpret artworks and
artifacts through their own and others' cultural lenses.

Whereas some art museums tend to overwhelm people, others are more family oriented
and offer diverse art education programs. Some museums adjust their policies with input
from indigenous peoples and immigrant families. Still other museum programs may empower
disenfranchised and displaced people to communicate their spiritual and economic concerns
and help other peoples to understand changing ethnic heritages. Art teachers therefore need to
utilize such local museum programs as well and embrace similar practices such as family and
even immigrant community involvement in their art classes.

Ethnic Art Community Centers

Some communities developed art centers in an effort to enrich students' knowledge of their
ethnic heritage. Young (1985), for instance, described a community art program designed to

supplement the art education of African American students. Students learned about African American art history using prints from the local African American community as inspiration. They later learned about printing processes and made their own art prints. Young argued for the need for such programs to help teach students about their heritages at a time when there was a shortage of African American teachers who were knowledgeable about African American art.

Using such ethnographic techniques as interviews, videos, journals, observations, and photographs, La Porte (2000) documented how 10 high school students and 4 homebound senior citizens interacted during a 6-month intergenerational art program at a community center in Harlem, New York. La Porte asked young and old participants to describe an artwork, for example, Hayden's *Midsummer Night in Harlem,* and then encouraged students to direct questions to the older people so they could reminisce about their own experiences and relate stories of the context of life in Harlem in the 1940s. She concluded that the program dispelled ageism stereotypes; connected those who do not usually communicate; and encouraged art criticism discussions, oral history interviews, art history learning, and group collage making.

Art programs in ethnic community centers can impart knowledge, develop art skills, and build pride in one's heritage with the use of local art resources and volunteers. Students interviewing elderly adults and making art with them may stimulate pride in the arts of one's heritage and in the art created in other diverse contexts. Teachers, however, need to understand the history and sociopolitical position of such ethnic contexts that "provide a foundation for confronting the disproportionate degree of economic, social and educational problems some minority communities face" (Young, 1999, p. 29). Thus, these ethnic art centers have the potential to become active contexts for cultural change within a community and, hopefully, among communities.

Community partnerships are growing in response to community problems, such as ecological awareness in local environments. Pickering Elementary School in Ohio, for example, aimed to assist the school community in discovering the natural beauty within their own neighborhood (Birt et al., 1997). Students visited Pickering Ponds, a nearby wetland preserve, studied its ecology and wildlife, and later made their own clay tiles of the wildlife that was assembled into a mural and installed at the entrance of the preserve. With the help of teachers and university students from Ohio State University, an art teacher consequently transformed a poorly drained playing field near the school into a local wetland preserve. To create a supportive environment for local turtles, birds, and insects, participants added such ecological features as rocks, plants, dead branches, and even a raptor roost. According to Krug (Birt et al., 1997), "Art, culture, and nature can be investigated using cyclical inquiry processes that draw from direct experiences, observation and reflection, critical thinking, and collaborative action" (p. 9). These researchers concluded that schools should encourage interdisciplinary art teaching that seeks to investigate and solve real-life problems in community members' own backyards.

Art in the Backyard

People who need to escape everyday problems may find solace in a backyard garden. Kakas (2001) described, for instance, Hartman's historical rock garden that she stumbled upon during a road trip. This elaborate folk art site that was made during the Depression consisted of approximately 50 buildings and hundreds of cement figures strategically placed among flowerbeds. Kakas concluded that art teachers could teach folk art as a kind of healing. Folk artists may be untrained in art, yet are hardworking and dedicated people. They may employ artmaking processes that include collaborative appropriations of preexisting objects and images in one's neighborhood. Art teachers who are involved in community-based art education can effectively utilize neighborhood sites for learning about the contextual values and beliefs of local people (Congdon et al., 2001).

Recreation Centers

Nearly every community center in America has developed some kind of recreational art program. As art learning resources, these centers have been underexplored and denigrated as mere entertainment facilities. Lackey (1999), however, investigated the plight of recreation centers, "wrapped and trapped in fun" (p. 36). Based on qualitative methods, she earlier examined two Canadian community centers in Vancouver using analysis of documents, staff and parent interviews, and field notes. She discovered prevailing notions of pleasure, freedom, and commodity that are subject to socioeconomic pressures. She later examined contradictions inherent in leisure and lifelong learning and discussed work, play, free expression, and free choice as notions that are related to social restraints. Lackey noted tensions between educators and community facilitators that included low status and territoriality. She considered negotiation of notions of school art and lifelong learning as a way of allowing schools and communities to coexist and endure together. Lackey's reality-based example of a community art program seems to contradict the concept of genuine community that "builds on respect and recognition of multiple voices and perspectives" (Clark, 1999, p. 2).

Community Centers for Senior Adults

As both participant and observer, Barret (1998) reported results of her art program for African American elders in a senior center in Athens, Georgia. She discovered issues such as elders tiring easily or having health problems that may cause absences. From earlier surveys, she determined reluctant participation due to anxieties about lack of drawing ability and art's usefulness in older people's lives. She later found that the program's success was due to flexible art media, such as clay, thematic lessons, incorporation of individual life experiences (family, friends, and church), and multicultural concerns (art of West Africa); and elicited stories behind the artworks, which were used for motivation. She concluded that these community sites demanded much dedicated teaching as well as researchers who are dedicated to understanding art in community contexts.

Marginalized Settings

Finally, some contexts are so marginal that they challenge art educational goals. Congdon (1984) reported personal experiences, a kind of action research, teaching an all-women's art program in a Milwaukee county jail setting. She described women as minorities, unemployed, undereducated, drug users, and having a state of mind characterized as "in crisis." The environment where art teaching took place was small: Space was tight and the institutional climate was tense and restrictive. Congdon's goals were to develop pride and a sense of identity. The results were gift giving, sharing and discussing of values, and developing open communication between the teacher and the students and among the students themselves. The women decided to make clothes, embellishing them with embroidery and fabric jewelry, which resulted in garments that displayed their personal identities. Congdon concluded that the inclusion of inmates' interests, ideas, and concerns was paramount to successful teaching in such a restrictive context.

Dennis, Hanes, Stuhr, Walton, and Wightman (1997) developed a case study of an art program, initiated by residents, which was operated at a state correctional facility in the Midwest. They described the findings of their research which took place in a prison setting where they observed and interviewed residents, all of whom were men, and their administrators, all of whom were women. Using critical analysis, they concluded that the residents regarded the art room as a fraternal refuge, and their ideas about fine art views reflected preferences for realistic drawing and painting. Art produced by the residents for personal and social reasons was to be given as gifts. A power struggle between the residents and the administrators occurred over control of the art program. The atmosphere was relaxed and art instruction was informal and individualized to meet each resident's needs. Unfortunately the art program was later canceled. Researchers concluded the probable reason for program dismissal was the residents' hostile views toward the administrators.

Community partnerships appear to be growing in response to the need to investigate and solve real-life community problems, such as ecological issues. Several factors combined to influence successful art programs including promoting student pride and autonomy, enabling social contact between different social groups and age groups, and encouraging successful art making. Partnerships also provided some valuable learning tools such as understandings about oral history and local art resources. Some folk examples can be found in community members' backyards. The negotiation of notions of school art and lifelong learning as found in recreation centers is one way of allowing school and community art teaching to coexist and endure. Research in correctional institutions, however, revealed contradictions between freedom and constraints in these artmaking settings. Restrictive contexts may demand more liberating materials and relaxed control.

CONFUSION OVER MULTICULTURAL, GLOBAL, AND INTERCULTURAL CONTEXTS

In a search for cultural understanding, some art educators changed their research foci in response to local and world pressures. With growing interest in cross-cultural research, Eisner (1984) clarified the movement as "efforts made by the investigator to compare and contrast ideas or practices in more than one culture" (p. 28). After World War II, global education emerged to promote international understanding and ensure peaceful coexistence. Later, it widened its global stance to address issues of limited planetary resources and economic competition in the global marketplace. The goal was to promote responsible international citizens, encourage appreciation of cultural diversity, and advance understanding of the complexities of international systems (Sutton, 1998). Global education research differs from cross-cultural research in its focus of looking outside one's borders at people in other societies (Davenport, 2000a).

Multiculturalism

In the 1960s, during the civil rights movement in the United States, multiculturalism became a heated issue in art education. The term *multiculturalism* was a curriculum reform movement concerned with equal opportunity and human rights (Mason, 1988). Curriculum reform can only be successful with knowledge of diverse cultures or contexts. McFee (1995) felt that teachers needed to understand their students' diverse culture differences, notably their perception systems, roles, and aesthetic preferences, group or self-motivation, and propensity for cultural change. She consistently argued that "art and architecture be understood through diverse cultural aesthetics, cultural images, design, and ranges of creativity, [that] can help humanize people" (p. 7). Thus, a number of art education researchers focused on understanding their students from diverse backgrounds and reported conflicts over teaching practices.

Mason (1988), for example, used participant observation research methods such as note taking and interviewing to report her curriculum trials and experiences while teaching two small groups of multicultural students in Leicester, England. She motivated Hindu students to create an animated film and Muslim students to write and illustrate a story. She wanted children to depict their daily surroundings, hopes, anxieties, and fears and to provide an insider's view of ethnic minority children's lives today. Instead of the children depicting their so-called "real" settings, they portrayed family memories of life in India that were more fantasy based. Muslim children communicated the importance of Islamic religion in their life, by showing the daily task of praying. Children added script, which is an essential ingredient in the Koran, to their artwork. Novel, at that time, was the use of animated stories by the children to communicate their new bicultural lives. Cultural conflict arose over the English or Western style of mimetic representation and the children's Middle Eastern or Asian mythic and abstract styles of representation. The term *cultural pluralism* has evolved over time with demographic changes and disagreements over selection of content and ethnic identity in art education. Multicultural education ideologies, however, often are at odds with those of indigenous peoples who seek to preserve their own educational approaches that are more holistic than Western art education teaching strategies and curriculum content (Irwin, Rogers, & Farrell, 1999).

Indigenous Cultural Differences

Indigenous people are those who inhabited each continent before the arrival of Caucasian settlers. The encroachment of White people into indigenous areas caused and continued to cause a history of conflict over land, values, and teaching in places all over the world. In the United States in the mid-1980s, Stuhr (1986) examined classroom environments in several Wisconsin schools and found conflicts between Caucasian and Native American values and beliefs. Differences in social and educational beliefs included Native American sharing and close peer grouping versus Caucasian focus on individual achievement. Teaching methods such as Native American informal teaching and gentle banter opposed Caucasian instruction based on singular commands. Only one Bureau of Indian Affairs school considered the aesthetic heritage of Native American students in its curriculum. Stuhr recommended that teacher training include more courses and information on Native American value systems and art forms. Using participant observation, photographs, document review, and interviews, she further examined the complex traditional arts system of the Wisconsin Native American. This system included pipe carving related to the Peace Pipe Ceremony (honoring the coexistence of earth, plant, animal, and people) and derivative arts that modify form and use acculturated materials (such as beading that has its roots in stories of nature). She also examined their contemporary art forms that incorporate 20th-century art forms and materials of Euro-American influence. Wisconsin Native Americans tend to assimilate recycled materials and references to nature and adapt their tribal influences in order to make statements about their "Indianness." Thus, the idea of environment is related to a social process of preserving and adapting to cultural change and should be included in art teaching strategies when teaching this group of students.

Study about indigenous schooling practices also occurred in Arizona Navajo populations. Using microethnographic methods of participant observation, informal interview, photography, and data analysis, I (Stokrocki, 1995) studied schooling in rural Chinle, Arizona, and discovered that Navajo students are dualistically enculturated in American Indian education. Schooling included accommodating contextual differences of seasonal time, slow pacing habits, a need for free time, and a relaxed atmosphere. Insights from my research in several Navajo sites revealed the necessity of highly patterned art skills, basic schema, and arrangements for the more traditional Navajo students. Conflict exists among Navajo traditional, semitraditional, and nontraditional views on art education. Critical are the traditional cultural patterns that are being replaced by economic values that emphasize manual skills and trade exchanges in the context of a larger state economy. I concluded that successful art education for the Navajo seemed to be a blend of traditional and contemporary art forms and teaching methods.

From a phenomenological perspective in which a people's world and experiences are studied, Irwin and Reynolds (1994) also found similar notions of Amer-Indian instruction and aesthetics in Ojibwa (Canadian) experiences. They noted that instruction consisted of patience, repetition, and tools of listening, watching, and absorbing everything, which suggested a pervasive cultural experience. Through formal and informal interviews of 20 Ojibwa people, they focused on the socially constructed experience of creativity and concluded that creativity is a "negotiation of feeling and lived experience culminating in a synthesis of meaning" (p. 34). They summarized conditions for creativity: resource availability, sufficient times, cooperative rather than competition work, personal rather than external evaluation, need for psychological safety and freedom, and process valued over product.

Over the span of 2 to 4 years, Irwin et al. (1998) used ethnography to study the context of colonial destruction and reconstruction of indigenous cultures in Australia, Canada, and Taiwan. They discovered how contemporary artists reclaimed, reconciled, and reconstructed their local cultural roots through their art forms. Through oral history interviews and videos, researchers discovered how the artists developed new individual and community identities as they transformed conflicts in their lives. The authors further examined such global conflicts as economic and political power and how they might inform art teaching in their three different settings.

Such study of indigenous contexts may provide teachers guidance as they work with indigenous students who range from the traditional and semitraditional to nontraditional types. Teachers should be sensitive to traditional indigenous students' preferences for more informal instruction, close peer work, patterned models, and conditions for creativity. Indigenous peoples struggle with notions of creativity as individual freedom versus collective responsibility and the infringement of popular culture on their youth as well. They seem to prefer not to change their traditional ways, but to work toward changing how other cultures view them (Irwin et al., 1999).

Cross-Cultural Contexts

In contrast to interests in safeguarding art traditions is the desire to compare and contrast these traditions. Eisner (1984) found some problems in conducting cross-cultural research, such as conceptualization (shared frames of reference), implementation (grade and instructional equivalency), interpretation (contextual cues), and practical concerns (funding and publication). Using a phenomenological stance, Mason (1994) overcame such challenges and examined curriculum and instructional practices in Japan where education is quite formal and compared Japanese art education to British art education. She discovered, for example, that Japanese teachers had no incentive to display artworks and that process was more important than products. They worked long hours; curriculum was standardized; art was mandatory; and Japanese educators seemed uninterested in multiculturalism. What persisted was dedication to teaching traditional folk arts and everyday aesthetics and a commitment to moral education involving required trips to Japanese historical places. In contrast, British education tended to be more informal, emphasized the display of finished products, had less standardized curricula and incorporated multicultural strategies and aesthetic interests for use with immigrant students from former colonies. Such contextual examination, as in Mason's study, is the most significant part of cross-cultural understanding (Anderson, 1995).

Interest in examining craft education problems resulted in a comparison of information on courses, teacher attitudes, and curricula reform in both England and Japan (Mason, Najse, & Naoe, 1998). Using surveys, they discovered that both contexts had national curricula that included crafts under the rubric of Art, and they prioritized expression and technique; however, instruction in the crafts differed in both countries. In Britain, students learned from specially trained teachers and professional artifacts, whereas in Japan, secondary students learned to make crafts predominantly from standardized textbooks. Researchers discussed unique cultural factors and contributions to character education in each context. The Japanese, for example, based their values on the apprenticeship model that focuses on discipline, technique, and moral and spiritual concerns that are associated with traditional craft skills. Mason further questioned whose identity and values and what national heritage should pluralist societies transmit. To improve the low status and identity of craft programs, they argued for the addition of crafts as part of national British and Japanese examinations.

By observing women at home and using interviews, Mason and Richter (1999) also compared aesthetic values and interests of housewives from different ethnic backgrounds. Richter conducted research in Santa Maria, Brazil, and Mason examined examples in England. They noticed the dominance of working with conventional textile arts and realized that persistent values involved homemaking, caring, giving small gifts, and joyfully working in groups. The researchers concluded that strong moral and family cultures and art making are necessary to support a healthy society. Furthermore, they also felt that the (masculine) cultural trend toward self-fulfillment through expressive individualism in all walks of life was not compatible with many women's concerns in both contexts.

There seems to be a correlation among healthy societies, conventional arts, and moral education that includes the values of caring and cooperative art making. These concerns have great relevance for art teaching in a variety of cross-cultural contexts.

International Summer Schools

International education is a trend that emphasizes international understanding, exchange, and cooperation between two or more nations. Study of short- and long-term international art programs can promote similarities and differences of cultural understandings. An international summer school in Croatia, for instance, brought professors from three countries together to teach. By using a semiotic approach that involved an inquiry of meaning of a place in relation to signs within cultures, Smith-Shank (1997) reported how the ancient city of Stari-Grad off the coast of Croatia became a highly interactive classroom for learning. Just as this ancient city of Stari-Grad was a meeting place for past Greek, Roman, and Muslim peoples, it served as a neutral zone for exchange of world views between Chicago and Croatian students, who mapped places that were meaningful to their cultures. Students also shared their different ideas on schooling, art, architecture, and even war. Such international schools are forums of art teaching exchanges that may broaden understanding of people, places, signs, and meanings.

Intercultural Education

Intercultural contexts are those that cross physical or conceptual borders to link similarities and/or expose differences in peoples' cultural thinking. The idea of interculturalism developed in Europe and "provides students with cultural tools to explore their former and present cultures, personally recreate them, and know about, interact with, and appreciate others and their customs" (Ligtvoet, 1987). Through participant observation, I (Stokrocki, 1989) studied one intercultural educator of multicultural students in Rotterdam and described his instructional practices and unique curriculum in developing a passport as an art project. Components included a symbolic portrait identification (Who am I?), a composite of place (Where am I from?), and a country destination to visit (Where am I going?). Results included students sharing cultural differences, opening art history windows to the world, contrasting old and new cultural contexts, appropriating images for communication, and self-evaluating their own work. I concluded that success of intercultural teaching was due to his encouragement of students teaching each other about their cultural heritages, his individual work with students, and a supportive context of teachers and superintendent who worked as a team.

In Spain, Hernandez (2000) rebelled against the concept of homogenous society as a static entity composed of adjacent ethnic groups without links. He proposed the idea of education based on active *intercultural citizenship* that is based on a democratic nurturance of people's critical faculties to examine their life conditions in relation to those of others. He suggested ethnographic research as a way of examining such contexts.

Davenport (2000a) further suggested that the term *interculturalism*, which includes global, community-based aspects, enlightened by cross-cultural and anthropological views, replace the term *multiculturalism*. She further advocated the idea that interculturalism, which blends multicultural, community-based and global education, regards every student's culture as deserving study and stresses cross-cultural interactions or communication across distances. She presented her own intercultural research in action, which was a collaborative electronic exchange between first and fifth graders in Indiana and fourth graders in Japan (Davenport, 2000b). In one lesson, for example, elementary-age students exchanged stories and drawings about the adventures of a stuffed animal. She concluded that teachers could use the Internet to bridge great distances.

Globalization of Popular Culture

With the rapid exchange of global images that permeate daily life, it becomes necessary to examine their messages and influences. In the 1980s, Nadaner (1985) argued that students use social criticism to explore controversial subjects including sex and violence in the media. Duncum (1999) later proposed that art education should adopt a wider framework for aesthetic education to embrace study of everyday cultural and commercial sites. Examples he offered included theme parks, tourist spots, television, and the Internet. In so doing, students can critique their visual culture, namely, their gender, racial, and xenophobic values. Freedman (2000) suggested that contexts in practice include contexts of production (cultural purposes, conditions, and artists' personal histories), contexts of appreciation (institutional settings and meanings and functions of artworks), and structural properties of meaning (formal and technical qualities). An example of the practical teaching of popular culture via the Internet (Taylor, 2000) follows in the next section.

ELECTRONIC CONTEXTS

Electronic contexts for art education research include videodiscs, teleconferencing, hypermedia, and interactive Web sites and distance education courses, to name a few. Galbraith (1996) was one of the first art educators to explore, for research purposes, the use of hypermedia through the videodisc. A *videodisc* is a place to store data consisting of text, still images, or motion pictures. She transferred her case studies of elementary and middle school art teachers onto videodisc and presented them in multimedia hypertext. Hypermedia is a system of creating, retrieving, and linking data through different pathways that may be "linear, hierarchical, associative and multidirectional" (Keifer-Boyd, 1997, p. 29). These technologies enhanced pedagogical and contextual knowledge for her preservice art teachers. Fascinating were excerpts of teacher wisdom such as "reading a class is like scanning a painting—you do a great deal of detective work" (p. 97). Galbraith (1996) also offered videodiscs as valuable tracking devices of noticeable and hidden concepts and issues that can be used effectively for future art education research.

Taylor (2000) studied the effects of using hypertext at the high school level. She encouraged her art class to interpret Madonna's music video, *Bedtime Story*, with hypertext. Hypertext transfer protocol (http) is the main programming language that incorporates rules for transferring information on the Internet. Students generated a plethora of information related to Madonna's video, but lacked the means to interpret it. Taylor offered the hypertext computer program *Storyspace* as a way to compile data, rewrite ideas, share insights, and make connections that present an alternative to teacher-centered instruction. She also challenged students to find historic influences in contemporary art and culture on the Internet. Upon reflection, Taylor discovered critical questions for discussion with students involving racism, sexism, social group privilege, and appropriation. She concluded successful teaching included liberatory education—an approach that stimulates thought and feeling to challenge the social, political, and economic forces of their lives—combined with computer technology—a context and process for the exploration of ideas.

Julian (1997) explained that her hypermediated Web site, "A World Community of Old Trees," began with a postmodern research objective of decentering knowledge and examining potential of the World Wide Web as a communication and exchange site for ecological art education. Solitary tree paintings on canvas, strangled by static convention and stretcher bars, became an electronic, collaboratively authored, educational art piece. Through this hypermedia environment, she speculated that people of all ages produced their own content (tree paintings), created their own navigational pathways, forged a field of relationships, and left behind the linear character of the old print technology. She advocated an interactive Web site as an art teaching opportunity that can offer a unique, dynamic ecosystem composed of interrelated units of hardware and humanity and provide an opportunity for research, worldmaking, and creative thinking of the highest order. Distance education is the delivery of instruction of geographically separated people via electronic means. Little research is available, however, on results of using distance education for art teaching and art learning purposes. Most published work is descriptive technical information on electronic media and its issues (Gregory, 1997). Some advantages are cost efficiency, quick access to students from a wide variety of age levels and international locations, accommodation of large enrollments with a number of part-time tutors who have smaller student loads, and empowering of students as co-learners.

Garber and Stankiewicz (2000) reported their collaborative experiment in interactive distance education. They co-taught a course, "History and Philosophy in Art Education," through interactive television (Picturetel), e-mail, telephone, and face-to-face dialog. Early in the course, students who were all women expressed dislike of telephone interaction. They thought e-mail communication was more responsive for individual feedback. Students noted that they performed better as part of a learning community where professors become peer learners. Garber and Stankiewicz (2000) concluded that their students valued the "conversational learning style" (p. 37) rather than a talking-heads television format as a context for learning about art education.

In addition, a one credit, pass/fail, thematically based graduate course is available as part of Erickson's (1996) "Worlds of Art," a program on the Getty ArtsEdNet Web site. Rogers and Erickson (1997) revealed that the success of this curriculum resource Web site might be due to one person as the conceptual director, profuse corporate support, and layers of navigation. Since the first simple Web site and listserv-based efforts, which the Getty Education Institute funded, Erickson developed a much more sophisticated online course, again with major support from Getty. In collaboration with a computer expert and programmers at Arizona State University's Hispanic Research Center, she designed an online course, called "Art Appreciation and Human Development," consisting of both undergraduate and graduate versions. In addition, Erickson and Villeneuve (2001) have begun to analyze undergraduates' and graduate students' participation in online threaded discussion in an effort to gain insight into the design of developmentally appropriate online instruction. Using different tools, these electronic examples demonstrate that students and teachers can effectively communicate electronically and that collaborative teaching provides an important avenue for cross-site conversation.

In conclusion, models of teaching are changing from single-site or person instruction to collaborative and multicontextual operations with new electronic technology experiments. Such contexts seem to liberate teachers and students to become peer learners, to enable all parties to make conceptual connections, and to reflect on outcomes and make future plans for collaboration. However, electronic experiments involve factors often not reported, such as technical, logistical, access, and monetary problems. Teachers and researchers can examine information and research in depth and from different viewpoints in such interactive contexts.

FUTURE IMPLICATIONS

A wide range of contextual studies that deal with school, community, intercultural, and electronic sites already exist. Findings reveal that contexts are complex and involve contradictory factors that may not easily be resolved. Research is not only about reporting best practices and technocratic solutions but also about raising questions.

What Complex Issue Dominated This Review of Contextual Research in Art Education?

To understand a context primarily involves the *politics of identity*: not only how a person views him/herself but also how people regard themselves. Preadolescents, for example, explore possible identities through hero worship and tribal formations. School culture prepares students for societal rites and responsibilities in an academic society, but a culture consists of plural societies. The problem becomes compounded with the challenge of whose identity and values to transmit. Understanding further demands an examination of the historical effects of political struggles involving various subgroups' social and economic exploitation (jagodzinski, 1999). More specifically, indigenous people's rights, especially their essential relationship with the land and ownership of their sacred symbols, need to be addressed, not exploited. Although people may desire to preserve their traditional art forms and values, they also incorporate new art forms and materials (Congdon & Blandy, 1999). When studying a traditional context, teachers must also present its contemporary arts in relation to its living conditions with all its contradictory baggage. It is more important for art teachers to discuss such complexities and contradictions with students than to make imitative artworks. Teachers also should teach about the healthy benefits of societies that stress conventional arts and moral education and include the values of caring and cooperative art making.

Similar to Neperud's (1995) findings, several contextual research studies seem to question imposition of standards regarding curricula offerings with so many conflicting conditions and factors. More studies are needed on how art teachers survive in diverse contexts, adjust programs to meet the needs of different populations, examine their indigenous and community art forms with students, and challenge global pressures.

Does Contextual Research Represent Multiple Views?

Some studies present only one researcher's experience; other studies add participants' opinions. Still other studies incorporate multiple authors. Then, too, some studies encourage participants, such as indigenous peoples, to speak for themselves. At times, results from contextual investigation reveal differences of opinion that may not be resolved and need to coexist side by side. The future demands *negotiation of contextual findings* as a method of conflict resolution and as a result of the "push and shove" of democratic ways. Negotiation does not come without some degree of pain and heated argument. What is needed is research conducted in the same context but analyzed from a different perspective.

Does Contextual Research Reflect Realistic Concerns?

Contextual research for a real world (Anderson, 2000; Fehr, Fehr, & Keifer-Boyd, 2000) begins with thorough preparation—knowledge of school, community, culture, and intercultural contexts; careful analysis of data and relationships; and discussion of hidden issues and suggestions for improvement (Ulbricht, 2000). Researchers and teachers together need to investigate and solve real-life community problems in their own backyards. In order to democratize the study of art, teachers should investigate different art occupations in a community as sites for art teaching and broaden the definition of art, not just of the fine arts (Congdon, 1988). Schools and community centers should build linkages, for example, creative after-school art programs for latchkey kids that employ teachers who have art education backgrounds.

With school violence on the rise, the notion of "schools as tribes" warrants further investigation. Chambers (1978) earlier encouraged anthropological study of students' out-of-school tribal arts, such as comics and graffiti. Duncum (1999) believed that teachers could develop rich ethnographies of everyday aesthetic contexts to investigate popular arts more critically with students. An entire issue of *Visual Arts Research*, guest edited by Duncum (2003) dealt with contemporary tribal contexts, such as television, surfing, and shopping malls for further critical investigation.

What Are Methodological Concerns?

Researchers characterized their methodology as interpretive at least 8 times and more specifically their employment of interviews on approximately 15 occasions out of a total of approximately 51 reported studies. Contextual methods demand *role-reversals*, in which researchers become learners whenever they step into new situations. Researchers are teachers too. Following Lackey's (1994) advice, researchers should regard themselves as cultural workers for the betterment of equal access to art knowledge. They also need to be both ethical and self-critical (Bresler, 1996).

Are Contextual Findings Useful?

Translations of research findings are paramount if researchers expect to convince teachers to use contextual findings and the public to pay attention to contextual research results. Contextual studies and controversial problems can be presented on a Web site on which teachers and other researchers are invited to duplicate a lesson, research their own contexts, respond with alternate solutions, and critique results (e.g., Stokrocki, 1999). Translations of contextual research about teaching can take the form of NAEA *advisories* (e.g., Boughton et al., 2002), ERIC/ART reports (e.g., Zimmerman, 1990), and *translations* of theory into practice (e.g., Sandell & Speirs, 1999).

Researchers need to convert their research tools into teaching devices, such as interviews, and model critical analysis, by questioning hidden social issues such as power, voice, conflict, class, gender, and race. Teachers also need to model how to critique important issues in their own context with their own students (Freedman, 1997). More art-based methods of presenting contextual research findings can further readability. Researchers frequently used the word "stories" as a way of gathering data and reporting research. Examples include old wives' tales (Smith-Shank & Schwiebert, 2000), stories of everyday teachers (Anderson, 2000), and narrative books (Stuhr, in press).

How Should Researchers Deal With Future Uncertainties?

Contextual research necessitates the building of networks that empower art teachers, community people, and university educators to conduct research together to ensure equal access to knowledge about the best teaching practices discovered in a variety of contexts. A blending of qualitative and quantitative methods seems ideal. The quest for rigor (Sullivan, 1996) takes time, so researchers also need to follow their hunches, speculate on possible alternatives, and help each other attain success through thoughtful reflection. Researchers must not omit the human experiences of serendipity, caring, joy, love, adventure, and suspension of disbelief as characterized in artistic experience. Tough-mindedness also demands tender-heartedness in order to prevent research from being inhumane in regards to contextual issues. These conditions demand courage in order for researchers to proceed in spite of criticisms and challenges, so that the art education community is continually informed about effective art teaching practices in diverse educational contexts.

REFERENCES

Anderson, T. (1995). Toward a cross-cultural approach to art criticism. *Studies in Art Education, 36*(4), 198–209.

Anderson, T. (2000). *Real lives: Art teachers and the culture of school*. Portsmouth, NH: Heinemann.

Asher, R. (2000). The Bronx as art: Exploring the urban environment. *Art Education, 53*(4), 33–38.

Ballengee Morris, C. (1997). A mountain cultural curriculum: Telling our story. *Journal of Social Theory in Art Education, 17*, 98–116.

Barret, D. (1998). Organizing and developing visual arts programs in a senior center setting. In D. Fitzner & M. Rugh (Eds.), *Crossroads: The challenge of lifelong learning* (pp. 114–126). Reston, VA: National Art Education Association.

Berry, N., & Mayer, S. (Eds.). (1989). *Museum, education, history, theory, and practice*. Reston, VA: National Art Education Association.

Birnbaum, R. (1988). *How colleges work: The cybernetics of academic organization and leadership*. San Francisco, CA: Jossey-Bass.

Birt, D., Krug, D., & Sheridan, M. (1997). Earthly matters: Learning occurs when you hear the grass sing. *Art Education, 50*(6), 6–13.

Blandy, D. (1983). Printing poetry in Blissymbols: An arts-of-the book apprenticeship for four so-called moderately mentally retarded persons (Doctoral dissertation, The Ohio State University, 1983). *Dissertation Abstracts International, 44*, 2657A.

Blandy, D. (1989). As I see it: Ecological and normalizing approaches to disabled students and art education. *Art Education, 42*(3), 7–11.

Blandy, D. (1994). Assuming responsibility: Disability rights and the preparation of art educators. *Studies in Art Education, 35*(3), 179–187.

Blandy, D., & Congdon, K. (1988). Community-based aesthetics as exhibition catalyst and a foundation for community involvement in art education. *Studies in Art Education, 29*(4), 29–30.

Bolin, P., Blandy, D., & Congdon, K. (Eds.). (2000). *Remembering others: Making invisible histories of art education visible*. Reston, VA: National Art Education Association.

Boughton, D., & Mason, R. (Eds.). (1999). *Beyond multicultural art education: International perspectives* (pp. 49–64). New York: Waxmann.

Boughton, D., Freedman, K., Hausman, J., Hicks, L., Madeja, S., Metcalf, S., Rayala, M., Smith-Shank, D., Stankiewicz, M., Stuhr, P., Tavin, K., & Vallance, E. (2002). Art education and visual culture. *Advisory*. Reston, VA: NAEA.

Bresler, L. (1996). Ethical issues in the conduct of communication of ethnographic classroom research. *Studies in Art Education, 37*(3), 133–144.

Bullock, A., & Galbraith, L. (1992). Images of art teaching: Comparing the beliefs and practices of two secondary art teachers. *Studies in Art Education, 33*(2), 86–97.

Chambers, G. (1978). The art of contemporary 'tribes': Using the methods of cultural anthropology to study the out-of-school art of our students. In J. Condous, J. Howlett, & J. Skull (Eds.), *Arts in cultural diversity* (pp. 128–132). Papers presented at the 23rd World Congress of InSEA. Sydney, New York: Holt, Rinehart & Winston.

Champlin, K. (1997). Effects of school culture on art teaching practices: Implications for teacher preparation. In M. Day (Ed.), *Preparing teachers of art*. Reston, VA: National Art Education Association.

Clark, R. (1999). Where community happens. In R. Irwin & A. Kindler (Eds.), *Beyond the school: Community and institutional partnerships in art education* (pp. 5–13). Reston, VA: National Art Education Association.

Clark, G., & Zimmerman, E. (2000). Greater understanding of the local community: A community-based art education program for rural schools. *Art Education, 53*(2), 33–39.

Congdon, K. (1984). Art education in a jail setting: A personal perspective. *Art Education, 37*(1), 10–11.

Congdon, K. (1988). Occupational art and occupational influences on aesthetic preferences: A democratic perspective. In D. Blandy & K. Congdon (Eds.), *Art in a democracy* (pp. 110–123). New York: Teachers College Press.

Congdon, K. (1996). Contexts. In E. Zimmerman (Ed.), *Briefing papers: Creating a visual arts research agenda toward the 21st century* (pp. 51–58). Reston, VA: National Art Education Association.

Congdon, K., & Blandy, D. (1999). Working with communities and folk traditions: Socially ecological and culturally democratic practice in art education. In D. Boughton & R. Mason (Eds.), *Beyond multicultural art education: International perspectives* (pp. 65–83). New York: Waxmann.

Congdon, K., Blandy, D., & Bolin, P. (Eds.). (2001). *Histories of community-based art education*. Reston, VA: National Art Education Association.

Davenport, M. (2000a). Culture and education: Polishing the lenses. *Studies in Art Education, 41*(4), 361–375.

Davenport, M. (2000b). Using the Internet to bridge great distances: Japan & USA. Paper presented at the United States Society for Education through Art—Crossing Borders Conference. Arizona State University, Tempe.

Day, M., Eisner, E., Stake, R., Wilson, B., & Wilson, M. (Eds.). (1984). *Art history, art criticism, and art production: An examination of art education in selected school districts, Volume II: Case studies of seven selected sites*. Prepared for the Getty Center for Education in the Arts. Santa Monica, CA: Rand Corporation.

Deal, T., & Peterson, K. (1999). *Shaping school culture: The heart of leadership*. San Francisco: Jossey-Bass.

Dennis, D., Hanes, J., Stuhr, P., Walton, G., & Wightman, W. (1997). Resident initiated and operated prison art program: A group field study. *Journal of Multicultural and Cross-cultural Research in Art Education, 15*, 63–76.

Dobbs, S. (1996). Evaluation of museum art education programs. In D. Boughton, E. Eisner, & J. Ligtvoet (Eds.), *Evaluating and assessing the visual arts in education: International perspectives* (pp. 276–286). New York: Teachers College Press.

Donnelly, N. (1990). Stumbling on aesthetic experience: A factual account of the accidental discovery of aesthetic education in an Irish context. *Studies in Art Education, 1*(3), 149–157.

Duncum, P. (1999). A case for an art education of everyday aesthetic experiences. *Studies in Art Education, 40*(4), 295–311.

Eisner, E. (1984). Cross-cultural research in arts education: Problems, issues, and prospects. In R. Ott & A. Hurwitz (Eds.), *Art education: An international perspective* (pp. 39–51). University Park, PA: The Pennsylvania State University.

Eisner, E. (1998). *The kind of schools we need*. Portsmouth, NH: Heinemann.

Erickson, M. (1998). Worlds of art. The Getty Center for Education for the Arts, CA. Available online at http://www.getty.edu/artsednet/resources/Worlds/index.html

Erickson, M., & Villeneuve, P. (2001, Feburary 23–24). *The development of art knowledge and values*. Paper presented at The Arizona Symposium on Learning in the Arts called "Turning myth into reality," Tucson, AZ.

Fehr, D., Fehr, K., & Keifer-Boyd, K. (Eds.). (2000). *Real-world readings in art education: Things your professors never told you*. New York: Farmer.

Freedman, K. (1997). Critiquing the media: Art knowledge inside and outside of school. *Art Education, 50*(4), 46–51.

Freedman, K. (2000). Context as part of visual culture. *Journal of Multicultural and Cross-cultural Research in Art Education, 18*, 41–44.

Galbraith, L. (1996). Videodisc and hypermedia case studies in preservice art education. *Studies in Art Education, 37*(2), 92–100.

Garber, E., & Stankiewicz, M. (2000). An experiment in interactive distance education: Feminist perspectives. *The Journal of Gender Issues in Art and Education, 1*, 113–126.

Graue, M., & Walsh, D. (1998). *Studying children in context: Theories, methods, and ethics*. Thousand Oaks: Sage.

Gregory, D. (Ed.). (1997). *New technologies in art education: Implications for theory, research, and practice*. Reston, VA: National Art Education Association.

Guay, D. (1993). Cross-site analysis of teaching practices: Visual art education with students experiencing disabilities. *Studies in Art Education, 34*(4), 222–232.

Guay, D. (2000). Values, beliefs, behaviors, and artmaking in the middle grades: A teaching story. *Visual Arts Research, 26*(1), 38–52.

Guilfoil, J. (1990). An Eskimo village school: Implications for other settings and art education. In B. Young (Ed.), *Art, culture and ethnicity* (pp. 169–179). Reston, VA: National Art Education Association.

Gunter, S. (2000). *The history of DBAE in South Carolina and its impact on southern rural middle school students.* Unpublished doctoral dissertation, University of South Carolina.

Hafeli, M. (2000). Negotiating "fit" in student work: Classroom conversations. *Studies in Art Education, 41*(2), 130–145.

Hernandez, F. (2000). From multiculturalism to a new notion of citizenship. *Journal of Multicultural and Cross-cultural Research in Art Education, 17,* 32–34.

Hodges Persell, C. (2000). Values, control, and outcomes in public and private schools. In M. Hallinan (Ed.), *Handbook of the sociology of education* (pp. 387–407). New York: Kluwer.

Irwin, R., & Reynolds, J. (1994). Ojibwa perceptions of creativity. *Journal of Multicultural and Cross-cultural Research in Art Education, 12,* 34–49.

Irwin, R., Rogers, T., & Farrell, R. (1999). Multiculturalism denies the realities of Aboriginal art and culture. In D. Boughton & R. Mason (Eds.), *Beyond multicultural art education: International perspectives* (pp. 49–64). New York: Waxmann.

Irwin, R., Rogers, T., & Wan, Y. (1998). Reclamation, reconciliation, and reconstruction: Art practices of contemporary Aboriginal artists from Canada, Australia, and Taiwan. *Journal of Multicultural and Cross-cultural Research in Art Education, 16,* 61–72.

Jagodzinski, J. (1999). Thinking through/difference/ in art education contexts: Working the third space and beyond. In D. Boughton & R. Mason (Eds.), *Beyond multicultural art education: International perspectives* (pp. 303–329). European Studies in Education. New York: Waxmann.

James, P. (1997). Learning artistic creativity: A case study. *Studies in Art Education, 39*(1), 74–88.

Jones, B. (1988). Art education in context. *Journal of Multicultural and Cross-cultural Research in Art Education, 6*(1), 38–54.

Jones, L. (1977). Volunteer-guides and classroom teachers in school-visitation programs in European and North American art museums. *Studies in Art Education, 18*(3), 31–41.

Julian, J. (1997). Ecology art education on-line: A world community of old trees (Unpublished doctoral dissertation, New York University, 1997). Available online at http://www.nyu.edu/projects/julian

Kakas, K. (2001). Hartman's historical rock garden: Learning about art in someone's backyard. In K. Congdon, D. Blandy, & P. Bolin (Eds.), *Histories of community-based art education* (pp. 54–68). Reston, VA: National Art Education Association.

Keifer-Boyd, K. (1997). Interfacing hypermedia and the Internet with critical inquiry, In D. Gregory (Ed.), *New technologies in art education* (pp. 23–31). Reston, VA: NAEA.

Lackey, L. (1994). Art, education, work, and leisure: Tangles in the lifelong learning network. *The Journal of Social Theory in Art Education, 14,* 148–169.

Lackey, L. (1997). *Pedagogies of leisure: Considering community recreation centres as contexts for art education and art experience.* Unpublished doctoral dissertation, University of British Columbia, Vancouver.

Lackey, L. (1999). Art education wrapped and trapped in fun: The hope and plight of recreation centre art instructors. In R. Irwin & A. Kindler (Eds.), *Beyond the school: Community and institutional partnerships in art education* (pp. 36–45). Reston, VA: National Art Education Association.

La Porte, A. (2000). Oral history as intergenerational dialogue in art education. *Art Education, 53*(4), 40–44.

Lee, V. (2000). School size and the organization of secondary schools. In M. Hallinan (Ed.), *Handbook of the sociology of education* (pp. 327–344). New York: Kluwer.

Lieberman, A. (1992). *The changing contexts of teaching: Ninety-first yearbook of the national society for the study of education. Part I.* Chicago: University of Chicago.

Ligtvoet, J. (1987). *Arts education in a multicultural society.* Report of the International Association for Intercultural Education to the Council of Europe, Strasbourg, France. New York: Methuen.

Mason, R. (1988). *Art education and multiculturalism.* London and New York: Croom Helm.

Mason, R. (1994). Artistic achievement in Japanese junior high schools. *Art Education, 47*(1), 8–20.

Mason, R., Najse, N., & Naoe, T. (1998). Craft education at the crossroads in Britain and Japan. *Journal of Multicultural and Cross-cultural Research in Art Education, 16,* 7–25.

Mason, R., & Richter, I. (1999, September 20–22). Celebrating artful experience in the home: Case studies from Brazil. Paper presented at the InSEA 30th World Congress, Brisbane, Australia.

McFee, J. (1995). Change and the cultural dimensions of art education. In R. Neperud (Ed.), *Content, context, and community in art education: Beyond post-modernism.* New York: Teachers College Press.

McFee J., & Degge, R. (1980). *Art, culture, and environment: A catalyst for teaching.* Dubuque, IA: Kendall Hunt.

Nadaner, D. (1985). The art teacher as cultural mediator. *Journal of Multicultural and Cross-cultural Research in Art Education, 3,* 51–55.

Neperud, R. (1995). *Content, context, and community in art education: Beyond post-modernism.* New York: Teachers College Press.

Newsom, B., & Silvers, A. (Eds.). (1978). *The art museum as educator.* Berkeley, CA: University of California Press.

Ott, R., & Jones, L. (1984). International museums and art education. In R. Ott & A. Hurwitz (Eds.), *Art education: An international perspective.* University Park, PA: The Pennsylvania State University.

Rogers, P., & Erickson, M. (1997). *Layers of navigation: Hypermedia design for an ill-structured domain.* Paper presented at the 1997 National Convention of the Association for Educational Communications and Technology, St. Louis, MO.

Sacca, E. (1996). Women's full participation in art teaching and research: A proposal. In G. Collins, & R. Sandell (Eds.), *Gender issues in art education: Content, contexts, and strategies* (pp. 53–59). Reston, VA: National Art Education Association.

Sandell, R., & Speirs, P. (1999). Feminist concerns and gender issues in art education. *Translations.* Reston, VA: NAEA.

Schrubbers, C. (1996). Turkish families visiting Berlin museums. In D. Boughton, E. Eisner, & J. Ligtvoet (Eds.), *Evaluating and assessing the visual arts in education: International perspectives* (pp. 267–275). New York: Teachers College Press.

Sikes, M. (1992). Interpreting the Heard Museum as a metaphoric structure: A critical and ethnographic study. *Dissertation Abstracts International, 53*(3), 694-A.

Smith-Shank, D. (1997) Collaboration, exploration, and art education: The international summer school for art education. *Collaborative Inquiry in a Postmodern Era: A Cat's Cradle, 3*(1), 1–15.

Smith-Shank, D., & Schwiebert, V. (2000). Old wives tales: Questions to understand visual memories. *Studies in Art Education, 41*(2), 178–190.

Stokrocki, M. (1986). A portrait of an effective elementary art teacher. *Studies in Art Education, 27*(2), 81–93.

Stokrocki, M. (1989). Teaching art to multicultural students in Rotterdam: The art teacher as intercultural educator. *Journal of Multicultural and Cross-cultural Research in Art Education, 7*(1), 82–97.

Stokrocki, M. (1990). A portrait of a Black art teacher of preadolescents in the inner city. In B. Young (Ed.), *Art, culture and ethnicity* (pp. 201–218). Reston, VA: The National Art Education Association.

Stokrocki, M. (1995). Patterning of Navajo art skills, basic schema, and arrangements. *The Journal of Multicultural and Cross-cultural Research in Art Education, 13,* 67–76.

Stokrocki, M. (1997). Rites of passage for middle school students. *Art Education, 50*(3), 48–55.

Stokrocki, M. (1999). Qualitative research: Participant observation, teaching Southwest culture through art. Available online at http://www.public.asu.edu/~ifmls/POFolder/mainpage.html

Stuhr, P. (1986). *A field study which analyzes ethnic values and aesthetic education: As observed in Wisconsin Indian community schools.* Paper presented at the meeting of the American Educational Research Association.

Stuhr, P. (1991). Wisconsin Native American perspectives on environment and art. *The Journal of Multicultural and Cross-cultural Research in Art Education, 9,* 81–90.

Stuhr, P., & Ballengee Morris, C. (1998). Status report: The NAEA research task force on context. In E. Zimmerman (Ed.), *The NAEA Research Task Force, Status Reports* (pp. 18–24). Reston, VA: National Art Education Association.

Stuhr, P. (Ed.). (in press). *Teach: The arts and integrated interdisciplinary curriculum.* New York: Teachers College Press.

Sullivan, G. (1996). Critical interpretive inquiry: A qualitative study of five contemporary artists' ways of seeing, *Studies in Art Education, 37*(4), 210–225.

Susi, F. (1990). The art classroom as a behavior setting. In B. Little (Ed.), *Secondary art education: An anthology of issues* (pp. 93–105). Reston, VA: National Art Education Association.

Susi, F. (1999). The physical environment of art classrooms: A context for expression and response. In J. Guilford, & A. Sandler (Eds.), *Built environmental education in art education* (pp. 126–135). Reston, VA: National Art Education Association.

Sutton, M. (1998). *The uneven incorporation of global education into the social studies curriculum.* Unpublished research paper. Indiana University, Bloomington, IN.

Taylor, P. (2000). Madonna and hypertext: Liberatory learning in art education. *Studies in Art Education, 41*(4), 376–389.

Ulbricht, J. (2000). Preparing pre-service art teachers for uncertainty. *Texas Trends in Art Education,* 8–11.

Vallance, E. (1999). The multicultural world of art museums: Visible and programmatic choices for art education. In D. Boughton & R. Mason (Eds.), *Beyond multicultural art education: International perspectives* (pp. 33–48). New York: Waxmann.

Van Gennup, A. (1961). *The rites of passage.* Chicago: University of Chicago.

Wilson, M. (1977). Passage through communitas: An interpretive analysis of enculturation (Doctoral dissertation, Pennsylvania State University, 1977). *Dissertation Abstracts International, 38*(5), 2496-A. (University Microfilm #77-23, 291).

Wilson, M. (1984a). Theory into practice: The Whitehall story. In M. Day, E. Eisner, R. Stake, B. Wilson, & M. Wilson (Eds.), *Art history, art criticism, and art production: An examination of art education in selected school districts,*

Volume II: Case studies of seven selected sites (pp. 1-1–1-28). Prepared for the Getty Center for Education in the Arts. Santa Monica, CA: Rand Corporation.

Wilson, M. (1984b). Another view from the bridge: School art programs in Brooklyn District 15. In M. Day, E. Eisner, R. Stake, B. Wilson, & M. Wilson (Eds.), *Art history, art criticism, and art production: An examination of art education in selected school districts, Volume II: Case studies of seven selected sites* (pp. 5-1–5-49). Prepared for the Getty Center for Education in the Arts. Santa Monica, CA: Rand Corporation.

Wilson, F. (2001). Conversation with New York artist Fred Wilson. Presentation at the National Art Education Association Conference, New York City, March 17.

Wolfe P. (1997). A really good art teacher would be like you, Mrs. C: A qualitative study of a teacher and her artistically gifted middle school students. *Studies in Art Education, 38*(4), 232–245.

Young, B. (1985). Visual arts and black children. *Art Education, 37*, 36–38.

Young, B. (1999). An African American perspective on multicultural art education. In D. Boughton & R. Mason (Eds.), *Beyond multicultural art education: International perspectives* (pp. 21–32). New York: Waxmann.

Zimmerman, E. (1990). Teaching art from a global perspective. *ERIC/Art*. Eric Digest EDO-S0-90-10.

Zimmerman, E. (1992). A comparative study of two painting teachers of talented adolescents. *Studies in Art Education, 33*(3), 174–185.

21

Interaction of Teachers
and Curriculum

Mary Erickson
Arizona State University

The ultimate value of an art curriculum manifests itself for students when they experience the results of a teacher's complex engagement with that curriculum. This analysis examines the interaction between teaching and curriculum from three perspectives: (a) the wide range of competing and overlapping art curriculum theories that could guide teachers' curriculum decisions; (b) available research that could help teachers make judgments about the effectiveness of art curricula or particular curriculum components, or strategies; and (c) many factors that affect an individual teachers' decisions about selecting, developing, or adapting an art curriculum and then implementing it.

No handbook analysis can do justice to all the ideas and issues associated with the interaction of teaching and art curriculum. This analysis draws from art education books, journals, research reports, and conference proceedings, and focuses primarily on theory and research published from 1985 to 2001 in *Art Education, Studies in Art Education, Visual Arts Research*, and *The Journal of Multicultural and Cross-Cultural Research in Art Education*. These four journals are dedicated to art education, are refereed, and the last three are predominantly research oriented.

CURRICULUM THEORY

What Are Prominent Art Curriculum Theories With Which Teachers Can Interact?

The Historical Currents in Art Education section of the *Handbook* overviews 19th- and 20th-century curriculum rationales, many of which continue to influence teachers' curriculum decision making in the 21st century. Scholars have analyzed many art education curriculum theories and proposed general groupings. Wolf (1996) described the history of arts curriculum in the United States as moving through four phases (common curriculum; psychological contributions; development: symbols and rules; and apprentice). Efland, Freedman, and Stuhr (1996) outlined seven paradigm shifts in art education curriculum: academic, elements of design, creative self-expression, art in daily living, art as a discipline, and postmodern.

In a *Handbook* such as this, the full range of art curriculum visions set forth in the literature of art education in recent years can only be summarized, not analyzed in detail. Many diverse and overlapping theories emerge from humanities (Broudy, 1985; Levi & Smith, 1991; Smith, 1995): developmental (Erickson, 1995b; Housen, 1999) and cognitive (Dorn, 1999; Efland, 1995; Gardner, 1989; Gitomer, Scott, & Price, 1992; Magee & Price, 1992) foundations. Art educators also argue for inclusion of particular content within the larger art curriculum. Nadamer (1998) argued for continued importance of painting; Marschalek (1989, 1995), for design education and environmental design; and Lampela (1996), for gay and lesbian content, just to name a few. The literature of art education is replete with examples of curriculum reports that address particular concerns and outline approaches such as art created by artists from minority backgrounds within a nation's art curriculum (Wolcott & Macaskill, 1997), folk traditions (Congdon, Delgado-Trunk, & López, 1999), inquiry (Delacruz, 1997; Erickson, 2001), multiple artworlds (Erickson & Young, 2002), gender content (Collins & Sandell, 1996), and a socially defined studio curriculum (Anderson, 1985). Since the 1980s, ethnic and cultural issues have been a major focus of art curriculum theory and advocacy (Billings, 1995; Chalmers, 1996; Katter, 1987; Sahasrabudhe, 1992; Stuhr, 1994; Stuhr, Petrovich-Mwaniki, & Wasson, 1992; Young, 1990).

Discipline-Based Art Education Curriculum

During the 1980s and 1990s, advocacy and curriculum-reform efforts by the Getty Center for Education in the Arts (later the Getty Institute for Education in the Arts) focused a great deal of attention on an approach to art education called discipline-based art education (DBAE). A discipline-based approach can be seen as having evolved from an earlier apprentice, or at least role-model, approach (DiBlasio, 1985). An earlier version of DBAE, sometimes called discipline-centered art education, grew from Bruner's model of the spiral curriculum, which represents to young people the leading discipline ideas from the adult world in developmentally appropriate ways (Efland, 1995). Though DBAE students are not apprenticing to artists, art historians, art critics, and aestheticians, a DBAE curriculum draws its curriculum content from professional practice in the four disciplines of art making, art history, art criticism, and aesthetics.

The basic curriculum tenets of the Getty-advocated DBAE approach appear in several Getty publications and/or commissioned reports (Clark, 1991; Clark, Day, & Greer, 1987; Dobbs, 1998; Wilson, 1997). The most extensive presentation of the Getty position appears as a special issue (Vol. 21, No. 2) of the *Journal of Aesthetic Education* in 1987 (also published in book form, Smith, 1987). Within the last 2 decades many articles and at least two book series (Addiss & Erickson, 1993; Brown, & Korzenik, 1993; Cromer, 1990; Fitzpatrick, 1992; Lankford, 1992; Parsons & Blocker, 1993; Wolff & Geahigan, 1997; Zurmuehlen, 1990) have presented arguments and guidelines for building and implementing curricula that draw content from art making, art history, art criticsm, and aesthetics.

Art education is a field rich with proposals for curriculum reform, but generally poor in sustained, critical dialog. A marked exception is the mass of literature advocating, analyzing, extending, and criticizing DBAE (Burton, Lederman, & London, 1988; Calvert, 1988; Clark, 1997; Collins & Sandell, 1988; DiBlasio, 1987, 1997; Fleming, 1988; Greer, 1984, 1997; Hamblen, 1988, 1997; Johnson, 1988; Jones, 1988; Lovano-Kerr, 1990; Manley-Delacruz, 1990; Smith & Pusch, 1990; Villeneuve, 1997; Wilson & Rubin, 1997). Smith (2000) assembled an extensive anthology of readings in DBAE, which should prove useful in continuing the dialog. Stankiewicz (2000) reflected on the future of the art disciplines in art curriculum and proposed that "the future of art education depends on recognizing that knowledge and processes of inquiry are socially constructed, situated in sociopolitical contexts, and subject to change in response to intellectual climate" (p. 30). Time will reveal the extent to which DBAE will have lasting impact on teachers' interactions with art curriculum.

Two Recent Curriculum Challenges

Efland (1995) described the current postmodern era as a time when "pluralistic notions of the nature of art abound" and proposes that the postmodern curriculum challenge confronted by teachers of art is "to prepare ourselves and our students to approach the world of art in all its complexity" (p. 152). He argued for replacing the earlier curricular models with a more complex and flexible model. He envisioned a curriculum that "will serve the whole human person as an economic, social, cultural, and spiritual being" (Efland, 1996, p. 55). Recently, postmodern concerns (Clark, 1996, 1998; Efland et al., 1996; Hutchens & Suggs, 1997; Milbrandt, 1998) have drawn increased attention from curriculum theorists, for example, social action (Gude, 2000; Klein, 1992/3), community-based (Keifer-Boyd, 2000), lifeworld (Räsänen, 1997), everyday aesthetic experience (Duncum, 1999), intercultural art education (Davenport, 2000), and so forth. Global art education initiatives are discussed in the chapter Context's for Teaching Art of the Teacher and Teacher Education section of this *Handbook*.

A second challenge addressed by some contemporary art curriculum theorists is development of art curricula designed to enhance learning across the curriculum (Amdur, 1993; Bickley-Green, 1995: Efland, 2000; Hellwege, 1993; Kindler, 1987; Krug, 2000; Parsons, 1998). The fact that one of only six national visual arts standards addresses relationships among the arts is evidence of substantial and long-standing interest in integrated arts curriculum content. Interest has increased significantly in recent years in the direction of relationships between art learning and learning in other subject areas. Transfer theory has emerged as a vehicle for analyzing whether, and how, learning in art might transfer to other domains of achievement. Brown (2001) analyzed how different interpretations of evidence of transfer derive from assumed beliefs about the inherent or instrumental value of arts education. Erickson (2002a) proposed structuring an art curriculum in ways that use explicit teaching for transfer to promote cross-cultural understanding and higher order thinking. Koroscik (1996) described the crucial role that transfer plays in understanding artworks in the age of information.

How Do Teachers Make Curriculum Choices?

Different curriculum theories lead to quite different answers to key questions, such as: Why should art be taught? What should be the key/essential/central content of an art curriculum? How should instruction be designed/organized? How should an art curriculum function within the larger curriculum of the school? Research on the effectiveness of various curricula and curriculum components is one basis upon which teachers of art could inform their curriculum choices. Curriculum research is reviewed in the next section of this analysis. In addition, a great many other factors that also contribute to individual teacher choice are discussed. The third section of this analysis focuses on some of those other factors.

CURRICULUM RESEARCH

What Does Research Reveal About the Effectiveness of Art Curriculum?

Research in many fields of education has a bearing on research on art curricula. The Forms of Assessment in Art Education section of this *Handbook* offers guidance on the development of reliable and valid instruments and procedures for measuring and describing the effectiveness of the art curriculum. This analysis of curriculum research has two foci: (a) research into effects on student art learning of entire art curricula or of particular curriculum components and also on effects of various instructional strategies on student art learning, and (b) research into the effects of art curricula on learning beyond art.

Few large-scale studies are available that report on the effectiveness of entire curricula. Wilson (1997), an evaluator of the Getty's large-scale curriculum reform effort, reports on effects for teachers and schools, but not on the effects of DBAE curriculum on student learning. Tomhave (1999) compared the effectiveness of the Advanced Placement (AP) and International Baccalaureate (IB) Programs to determine whether studio performance by high school students was diminished when more comprehensive content replaced some studio time within the curriculum. He analyzed the IB program and concluded that it aligns closely with the tenets of DBAE. AP Studio Art teachers were randomly selected to implement the IB program. Other AP Studio Art teachers taught the usual AP program. Educational Testing Service AP adjudicators assessed portfolios produced by students in both programs. There was "no significant difference in the quality or quantity between the experimental group [IB/DBAE] and the control group [AP]" (Tomhave, p. 126). As teachers consider how to allocate time to art making and to art understanding within their art curricula, Tomhave's findings might lead them to rethink the assumption that more time devoted to art-making activities is the only way to improve artwork produced by students.

Effects of Art-Making Instruction

Several researchers have investigated the effectiveness of particular curriculum units on students' drawing performances. Brewer (1998) compared thematic and observational drawings made by third- and seventh-grade students in schools that provide formal art instruction with drawings by third- and seventh-grade students in schools that do not provide formal art instruction. He did not find significant differences. Because he did not identify the curriculum used in the formal art instruction in his study, even if he had found a statistically significant positive correlation between drawing ability and formal art instruction, curriculum implications would be unclear. Dowell (1990) was quite explicit about the type of art instruction offered in a program and its effects, which he attempted to measure. He compared drawings made by 9- through 12-year-old students after having received drawing instruction accompanied by practice with live models, practice with photographs, or practice with master drawings. He found no significant differences among the drawings made by students who practiced drawing in these three different ways. Such studies suggest that curriculum planners should examine assumptions they may have about effective drawing instruction. In an experimental study, Richards (1988) examined the effectiveness of drawing interventions that involved contour drawing, continuous-line drawing, and other strategies, on the drawing abilities of adolescents in both Jamaica and the United States. He found that the still-life drawing performance of students from both cultures improved significantly, but found no significant improvement in ability to apply drawing experiences to human-figure drawing for students from either culture.

Brewer has been involved in studies that compare the effectiveness of different strategies of ceramics instruction. In a study that compared the effectiveness of child-centered instruction to that of a discipline-based ceramics instruction, he found no significant difference between the "self concept, attitude toward art, knowledge of art, or ceramic products" (Brewer, 1991, p. 204) of students who received these two different types of instruction. His study calls into question assumptions that some curriculum planners may have about child-centered and discipline-based approaches. In another study, Brewer and Colbert (1992) examined the effects of three strategies of ceramics instruction on seventh-grade students' knowledge of ceramics vocabulary and production and on the quality of students' ceramic productions. Students in the studio/technical group observed demonstrations of studio techniques and worked with those techniques in clay. Students in the historical/cultural group received a lecture illustrated with ceramic vessel forms and did not work with clay. The teacher asked students in the questioning/discussion group about their own studio experiences and knowledge of ceramics. In their posttests, students in the first two groups scored significantly higher than did students in the third group. Teachers planning art activities may conclude from Brewer and Colbert's study (and also from Tomhave's IB/AP study 1999) that a balance of art-making and other art activities (in this case historical/cultural activities) is a sound curriculum choice.

Effects on Art Understanding

Short (1998) studied the effectiveness of a high school studio curriculum on improvements in their art understandings and appreciation not on improvements in the students' art making. She found that "studio experiences alone do not enhance students' ability to understand or appreciate well-known historical artworks" (Short, p. 46). She concluded that "to facilitate transfer of art understanding from one context to another, curricula on the high school level should include the critical activities of talking and writing about works of art" (Short, p. 62).

A number of researchers have attempted to determine the effects on the ability of students to understand about artworks through the curricula designed specifically to achieve that end. Johnston, Roybal, and Parsons (1988) studied the effects of instruction, "aimed at stimulating growth in both recognition and understanding of styles" (p. 61), on 6- to 8-year-olds and on 10- to 12-year-olds. They found that children of both ages increased their ability to recognize styles, but that neither group increased their ability to understand the expressiveness of style. In a small follow-up study, the majority of undergraduate students showed an ability to understand the expressiveness of style without instruction from the researchers. They concluded that curriculum planning should distinguish between style recognition and style understanding and that elementary children may not be developmentally prepared to understand the expressiveness of style.

Kakas (1995) observed young children experiencing developmental delays who participated in biweekly art criticism lessons. Her qualitative analysis of audiotapes, field notes, and discussions with the children's teacher led her to conclude that, over a period of a year, these 6- and 7-year-old students' art criticism skills improved in ways such as the abilities to label art forms; identify colors, shapes, and types of line; notice more in artworks; explain emotions in artworks; compare artworks; and understand the concept of portrait.

Erickson conducted several studies involving art history curriculum. She assessed students' abilities to interpret an artwork by referring to the historical artist (as distinct from references to art making in general), to historical viewers (viewers of the time when the artwork was made), and to the historical culture (culture in which the artwork was made). In a study of a year-long, roughly chronological, thematically organized curriculum, she found sixth-grade students scored significantly higher in their ability to refer to historical artists, to historical viewers, and to historical cultures than did second-grade students. She (Erickson, 1995a) also found that both groups referred more often to historical artists, next most often to historical viewers, and least often to historical cultures in their attempts to interpret artworks contextually. In another study, Erickson (1998) examined the effects of art history instruction on fourth- and eighth-grade students' attempts to interpret artworks contextually. She found that both groups of students improved in their use of references to the historical artist, but that only the eighth graders increased their use of references to historical viewers or historical culture. She suggests that planners of elementary art history curricula might consider students' prior knowledge of art-making processes as an avenue through which to introduce historical contexts to young learners. In addition, a middle-school-level art curriculum might effectively include an introduction of historical viewers and cultures as avenues to broader art historical understanding. Chanda and Basinger (2000) conducted an ethnographic study of third-grade children's abilities to construct culturally relevant understandings of artworks made by Kuba artists in what is now the Democratic Republic of the Congo. Their findings provide some reason to believe that students as young as third grade may be able to interpret artworks culturally if engaged in a curriculum that uses a constructivist inquiry approach.

Erickson (2002b) also studied the effectiveness of a curriculum unit built around the concept of artworlds on elementary and middle school students' understanding of their own artworlds. Activities in the unit presented the concept of artworld as a subculture that is centered on art. Instruction focused students' attention on people, places, activities, and ideas that are important in several different artworlds in North America (specifically in Mexican, Chicana/o, and African American artworlds). Teachers drew parallels to the students' own art experience as a basis for introducing these multicultural artworlds. She found a significant improvement in both elementary school students' and middle school students' understanding of all four artworld characteristics (artworld people, artworld places, artworld activities, and artworld ideas) measured on the pretest and postest. Such studies may provide some guidance to teachers as they plan developmentally appropriate art curricula that present artworks within their specific cultural and artworld contexts.

Stone (1997) compared the effectiveness of two different art museum tours, on elementary majors' learning both focusing on the same learning objectives. One tour took the form of a lecture; and the other, a format of a lecture/discussion. Stone reports that both tours were equally effective and that neither had strong long-term effects on the retention of information. Cason (1998) studied the effect of interactive multimedia on undergraduates' art history understandings. She found that students who studied art history with interactive multimedia "accessed more dimensions, demonstrated more lower-order understandings, and had significantly more higher order understandings... than students who supplemented their studies with slides" (Cason, p. 346). The Cason study may be of particular interest to teachers who are considering including new media in their art curriculum.

Others have attempted to measure the effects of circumstances surrounding the viewing of artworks on undergraduates' understanding. Seifert (1995) reported that the concurrent viewing of several artworks may affect students' responses to particular artworks. Koroscik, Short, Stravropoulus, and Fortin (1992) described the effects on undergraduates of viewing and writing about a reproduction of an artwork presented to them in three different contexts: (a) the artwork shown together with three other artworks by the same artist; (b) the artwork shown together with artworks by other artists displaying the same theme; and (c) the artwork shown in conjunction with a poem, a lithograph, and a videotaped dance, all of which were influenced by that artwork. The researchers also measured the effect of two verbal cues on students' writing: (a) initial prompts to look for common characteristics and (b) later, specification of the common characteristic (same artist, same, theme, or influence in other arts). They reported that contexts for viewing the artwork did, indeed, prompt students to view the artwork in different ways, and that the different contexts were most effective "when they were accompanied by explicit cues about the artworks' shared characteristics" (Koroscik et al., p. 163). These studies suggest that many factors, including developmental appropriateness of content, instructional strategies, and viewing contexts combine to influence what students' can learn as the result of curricula designed to increase art understandings.

Effectiveness Beyond the Art Curriculum

As noted previously in the Curriculum Theory section, learning across the curriculum is an area of considerable recent attention. A number of researchers have carried out studies attempting to determine the extent to which learning in art transfers to other areas of achievement. Caldwell and Moore (1991) compared the effectiveness of drawing and discussion as planning activities on second- and third-grade students' narrative writing. All students received instruction in such aspects of narrative writing as characterization, plot, and setting. The drawing group participated in follow-up drawing activities focused on those aspects of narrative writing. The control group participated in discussion of general language art content, such as oral language, listening, reading, and writing skills. Caldwell and Moore reported that the drawing group scored higher on a narrative rating scale than did the control group and that the difference between the two groups was statistically significant. Among the factors they cited to explain the effect of drawing on narrative writing are completeness of rehearsal, dual-code information processing, and increased student motivation.

Edens and Potter (2001) studied the effectiveness of drawing on fifth- and sixth-grade students' conceptual understandings in science. All students read a narrative text that explained the law of conservation of energy using roller coasters as examples. One group wrote what they learned; the text of the second group was illustrated and students copied the pictorial representation; the third group's narrative made their own pictorial representation. Students who had generated their own pictorial representations scored significantly higher on a posttest of conceptual understanding than did the students who wrote about what they learned. The scores of students who copied an illustration were not significantly higher than the scores of students who wrote in a science log. Edens and Potter also measured the effect of accuracy of drawing on posttest scores in science and found that students who created accurate drawings outperformed students who did not represent the concepts accurately. Edens and Potter (2001) concluded that "pictorial representation provides a viable way for students to learn scientific concepts" (p. 227). When teachers of art share the responsibility for learning in subjects outside their area of expertise, studies such as these may guide their collaborative planning with other teachers.

Other researchers have investigated how art instruction affects a wide range of non-art and sometimes art outcomes. Luftig (2000) studied the effects of an arts-infusion curriculum on creative thinking, academic achievement, affective functioning, and arts appreciation. The elementary arts-infusion program he studied was one that involved visual art, and also music, dance, and drama. "Classroom and arts teachers, arts specialists, artists employed for a residency, and the SPECTRA+ [infusion program] coordinator" (Luftig, 2000, p. 210) jointly planned activities in two schools. Luftig found significantly higher creative-thinking scores for students involved in the arts than for students in control groups. In one school, he found no difference in improvement in reading between arts-infusion students and control-group students. However, in the other school, arts-infusion students scored significantly higher than did control group students in reading. He found no significant difference in total and academic self esteem measures between arts-infusion and control-group students. "However, in the areas of social and parental self esteem decided advantages were found in the direction of the SPECTRA+ students" (Luftig, 2000, p. 224). There were no differences among student groups on locus-of-control scores. Arts-infusion students scored higher on arts appreciation and enjoyment than did students in control groups. Teachers concerned with curriculum may find Luftig's results useful in arguing to increase arts activities in schools. However because he does not describe the type of arts instruction in his study, only the amount (an hour a week in art, music, dance, and drama/theater), his research does not provide insights to guide teachers in making particular choices in selecting, developing, or implementing a visual arts curriculum.

Other researchers have attempted to measure the effects of unspecified types of arts instruction. Burton, Horowitz, and Adeles (2000) selected 12 elementary and secondary schools in four states in order to include as much diversity in types of arts education programs as possible. They did not attempt to affect the teaching and learning processes; rather they attempted to study relationships between, on the one hand, high-arts-involvement and low-arts-involvement students, and on the other hand, several variables such as creativity, self-concept, and personal traits as perceived by teachers. They found that high-arts-involved students scored higher for creativity. They found that teachers scored high-arts-involved students higher in "expression, risk-taking, and creativity-imagination dimensions, and lower in the cooperative learning dimensions" (Burton et al., p. 241). In addition, they reported "significant but weak correlations between academic self-concept scores and the arts teaching variables, and generally weak and not significant associations between non-academic self-concept and arts teaching variables" (Burton et al., p. 242). The researchers investigated learning in these 12 schools both quantitatively and qualitatively. They concluded that "transfer is probably only one of a complex of relationships interweaving arts learning with other domains" (Burton, Horowitz, & Adeles, 2000, p. 253). Catterall, Chapleau, and Iwanaga (2000) also looked for correlations between arts involvement and success in school. Theirs was a large, multiyear study of secondary students. They found significant associations between higher arts involvement (especially with music and drama) and academic successes. Because Burton et al.'s and Catterall et al.'s studies identified correlations between the various student outcomes and the amount of arts involvement, not correlations between those outcomes and any particular types of art instruction, direct implications for art curriculum development are unclear.

Haanstra (2000) analyzed effects of special, after-school arts programs in the Netherlands on the school achievement of 10- and 11-year-olds. Though the math scores of students in the arts program improved, the scores of students in the control group improved significantly more. Haanstra found no obvious effects of participation in after-school arts programs on students' social and emotional development. He concluded that transfer from arts activity to school success is not automatic and that "teachers of extended school activities should more explicitly teach for transfer of general cognitive skills in different contexts" (Haanstra, p. 26). At the same time he acknowledged that arts programs with more obvious relationships to core subjects may be less attractive to students. Teachers may wish to refer to such studies to bolster support for arts activities in general; but they will not find guidance in selecting, planning, or implementing an art curriculum.

Winner and Cooper (2000) conducted a meta-analysis of studies claiming associations between arts education and academic achievement. Where correlations are found, they caution that even though studying arts may have been the cause, other explanations are also possible. They argue that "for transfer to occur, teachers must teach explicitly for transfer" (Winner & Cooper, p. 63) and that teaching directly for transfer was not found to be the case in any of the studies they analyzed. Eisner (1998), Catteral (1998), and Perkins (2001) are among scholars who have reached different conclusions about the meaning of recent studies claiming learning in the arts transfers to academic achievement. In1998, Eisner found "no good evidence that transfer occurs [between art education and academic achievement] if what we count as evidence is no more than anecdotal reports that are often designed for purposes of advocacy" (Eisner, p. 10). Catteral was more optimistic. He "suspects that a panel composed of math, science, history, foreign language and elementary teachers would judge unanimously that ... dispositional outcomes of arts education would tend to boost academic achievement to some degree" (Catterall, 1998, p. 10) and concluded that new studies are needed. Perkins proposed that largely negative findings in a meta-analysis of arts education research "tell us not that the game is essentially over but that ... the game is not very well played yet" (Perkins, p. 124). He proposed that "thoughtful interventions ... offer reasonable prospects of transfer from visual arts to other academic areas" and argued that "learning in the arts needs to be designed with some finesse for effective indirect instruction, which generally it is not" (Perkins, p. 124).

When teachers go to research they may do so in search of persuasive evidence to help justify the existence of any sort of art activities or more specifically for insights to guide their selection, adaptation, development, or implementation of art curricula. The next section of this analysis is a review of some of the complex factors that are likely to influence how teachers, to the extent that they are aware of art curriculum research, might interpret findings and use conclusions in their own curriculum decision making.

TEACHER INTERACTION

What Influences Teacher Interaction With the Art Curriculum?

How teaching interacts with curriculum depends to a great extent on the teacher who is doing the interacting. Characteristics of persons choosing careers as art teachers are important factors. The National Art Education Association's recently commissioned national survey (Educational Research Service, 2001) provides some basic information about secondary art teachers. Of the 1,520 teachers who responded to the survey, 70.8 were women, 61% were over 45 years old, and 90.2% were White (1.6% African American/Black; 1.8% Hispanic/Latino; 0.9% Asian; 0.4% Native American, 1.0 biracial/multiracial; and 1.5% other). In addition, the survey revealed that the highest academic degree of 45% of secondary art teachers was a bachelor's degree, and 55% of secondary art teachers had received a master's degree.

Burton (1997) conducted a national survey of K-12 art teachers. He reported percentages of art teachers who claimed the following were major components in their art curricula: studio production (86.51), art history/art appreciation (79.76), art criticism (46.42), aesthetics (52.38), art exhibitions (61.90), computer technology (26.59), and interdisciplinary or multicultural concerns (59.52) (Burton, 1997). Although most art teachers follow a written curriculum, many do not. In a national survey, the Educational Research Service (2001) found that 75% of responding secondary art teachers reported that they had a written curriculum. In another national survey of secondary art teachers, Burton (2000) reported that "half of the respondents 'infrequently' and 'rarely or never' write detailed lesson plans."

Influences on art teachers' interactions with curriculum are wide-ranging. They include, among other factors, national, regional, state, and local traditions; preservice experiences; beliefs and practices of inservice teachers; practical realities; roles of governmental, professional, private, and other organizations; and processes involved in curriculum development and implementation.

Art Education Traditions

In various nations, teachers of art confront different challenges. Freedman and Hernandez (1998) collected a series of "international case studies of art education that illustrate the translation of cultural knowledge as part of a process of curriculum conceptualization, development, and implementation" (p. 3). In these case studies, art education in Japan, Australia, Canada, Spain, United States (New York), Sweden, Brazil, Morocco, Great Britain, Hungary, and Chile is reported. Within the United States, art teaching traditions differ considerably. In Eastern states there is a stronger tradition of elementary art teaching by certified art teachers. In Western states a great deal of the responsibility for elementary art teaching falls on general classroom teachers. In addition to traditional arts magnet schools, recently some states, such as Arizona, are chartering hundreds of schools, including schools centered on the arts.

Marché (1997) examined the effects of state mandates, preservice education, and local district administration on art program changes in one school district over a period of 68 years and found that "district administration decisions had the most visible and consistent effect on art programming" (Marché, 1997, p. 35). Marché (2000) cautioned that one must consider that factors influencing educational change are "situated within temporal, social, and geographic contexts" (p. 35). Congdon, Stewart, and White (2002) argued that "community influences persist and typically go unrecognized in curriculum decision-making" (p. 109). They reported on a process they used with inservice art teachers to provide "a means to intentionally reconsider the social and cultural dimensions of our lives that we bring into classrooms" (Congdon et al., p. 117). Clark and Zimmerman (2000) studied the positive effects of community-based art education programs in four culturally different rural communities in the United States. Studies such as these indicate that researchers have become increasingly aware of the role played by culture and community on the curriculum decision making of art teachers.

Preservice Experience

Preservice art teachers begin to interact with curriculum as it is introduced to them in their teacher education programs. The chapter on teacher education in the Teaching and Teacher Education section of this *Handbook* introduces the variety of programs that prepare students to become certified art teachers. Zimmerman (1994) reviewed research on preservice art education and reported results of her own small-scale survey of university art educators and examined research in three areas: knowing about subject matter content, how subject matter is put into practice, and the impact of outside influences. She found "a paucity of research about preservice art specialist education" and proposed "a carefully constructed research agenda" (Zimmerman, p. 79).

Short (1995) postulated that "art teachers frequently have autonomy in areas of curriculum planning and implementation in their schools" (p. 158). She found that preservice art teachers in her study, exhibited "over-simplifying tendencies characteristic of reductive bias" (Short, p. 161). Of seven dimensions of art (formal, descriptive, interpretive, historical, cultural, aesthetic, and critical), she found teachers whose art understandings ranged from just one dimension to six dimensions. In addition, Short found that the depth of art understanding of preservice art teachers correlated with their lesson-planning abilities. Students whose responses included two to six dimensions, when provided with additional information, were able to incorporate this content into their lessons. However, students who included only one dimension could not incorporate new dimensions into their lessons, but instead replaced one dimension with another. Short concluded that "despite their advanced learning status and visual art specialization, the majority of pre-service teachers demonstrated overly simplistic thinking, shallow understandings, and superficial domain knowledge. Their instructional decision-making, as reflected in lesson plans, exhibited similar characteristics" (Short, p. 167). When art teachers build their curricula on their own knowledge and understandings, and do not depend on published curricula, the depth of that art knowledge and understanding is particularly important.

Grauer (1998) argued that beliefs about art and art education are especially important factors influencing what and how teachers of art teach. She claimed that "unlike other subjects that are often driven by covering content in prescribed textbooks and by attempting to cover the content of government exams, decisions about the content and evaluation of art are very much in the hands of the classroom teacher" (Grauer, p. 362). In her study she examined the extent to which preservice teachers of art (both generalists and art specialists) changed their beliefs about art education within their teacher-preparation program. Grauer maintained that "there is a prevailing assumption that preservice teachers' prior beliefs are fixed and immutable" (1998, p. 266). Contrary to this assumption, she found that students' beliefs evolved in the direction of their art education courses and practical experiences. In her study, this evolution was away from a child-centered approach and toward a subject-centered approach.

A great deal of responsibility for implementing art curriculum in some school districts falls to elementary classroom teachers. Kowalchuk and Stone (2000) studied preservice elementary teachers' and inservice elementary teachers' attitudes toward art education. They found that both preservice and inservice elementary teachers' "attitudes about art and how it should be taught were often contradictory" (Kowalchuck & Stone, p. 29). Consistent with Grauer (1998), they found some evidence that preservice teachers moderated their values after participating in just one teacher-preparation course. To the extent that art curricula continue largely to be determined by art teachers, preservice education of art teachers becomes crucial. The art knowledge and beliefs about art and art education developed in preservice programs are the foundations upon which at least beginning teachers build their art curricula.

Beliefs and Practices of Inservice Teachers

Teachers of art, whether educated as certified art teachers or as general classroom teachers, whether certified to teach or serving as artists-in-the-schools, bring their own beliefs to their interactions with curricula and respond in various ways to professional development education. McSorley (1996) examined primary classroom teachers' conceptions of art criticism and found them wanting. She also found that the teachers' "choice of artworks was often guided by social studies" (McSorley, p. 169). She found no concern for multiculturalism or gender equity, nor any "philosophical or theoretical base from which art criticism is being taught" (McSorley, p. 167). The teachers in McSorley's study indicated no conception of art criticism as helping students create and derive meaning from visual art, but only a concern for fostering art appreciation. Anglin (1993) investigated the art curricula of 40 middle schools and reported that "participating teachers viewed art curriculum in three ways: what was written in the curriculum documents, what they taught, and what students learned" (Anglin, p. 61). These middle school teachers "emphasized media and production... and shared their frustration about including history, criticism, and aesthetics" (p. 63).

Bresler's (1994) ethnographic study of art curriculum in three elementary schools focused on the "curriculum as a dynamic entity by different individuals involved in the process" (Bresler, p. 91). She described a rote, teacher-centered orientation "more often than not [practiced] by classroom teachers with limited art background" (Bresler, p. 94). Classroom teachers and also special education teachers with little art background also practiced an open-ended, student-centered approach in which they invited students to create freely with little instruction, sometimes drawing ideas for art making from academic activities or holiday celebrations. Bresler found a third, higher order cognitive orientation "typically taught by teachers with professional art backgrounds, often artists-in-the-schools, sometimes classroom teachers who were practicing artists" (Bresler, p. 98). Teachers using this orientation transmitted "art-related knowledge and techniques as well as conceptual evaluation and feedback" (Bresler, p. 97). Although she made no observations of curriculum as practiced by professionally trained art teachers, Bresler's findings suggest significant differences of interactions of teachers and curricula related to whether those teachers had professional art backgrounds.

In some schools, parts of the art curriculum are delivered not by art teachers or classroom teachers but by artists. Zimmerman (1992) studied how two artists (who as faculty were experienced in teaching painting at the university level) adapted to the challenge of teaching talented adolescents between the ages of 13 and 16. She concluded that "preparation of professional artists before they enter a secondary level classroom is of paramount importance" (Zimmerman, p. 184). She proposed that such preparation include becoming aware of the particular needs and understandings of talented adolescents and experiences in organizing art classes for precollege students.

Bullock and Galbraith's (1992) case study of two secondary art teachers with quite different backgrounds, beliefs, and teaching practices revealed that dissonance was generated for both as they attempted "to confront recent paradigmatic shifts within art education curricula" (p. 96). Dissonance developed between, on the one hand, the teachers' backgrounds and experiences and, on the other hand, "school policy, ongoing external teaching debates, opinions about art education curricula, students' cultural heritages, and the lack of students' art background and readiness" (Bullock & Galbraith, p. 94).

Armstrong (1993) reported on the success of her effort to train six inservice elementary and secondary art teachers to incorporate an inquiry method into their studio art teaching. She concluded that "most teachers can change a teaching approach and students can respond to a new teaching method for a particular lesson very quickly" (Armstrong, p. 220). As teachers gain experience and success with various instructional strategies, their interest in reflecting on and improving their own art curricula may increase. The number of factors that art teachers and classroom teachers are responsible for and balance in their interactions with art curricula are indeed many and varied.

Practical Realities

Practical realities of art teaching also impact teachers' curriculum choices. The Contexts chapter of the Teacher and Teacher Education section of this handbook introduces a wide range of contexts in which art teachers function. May (1989) described details of an art teacher's workplace. She argues that curriculum reform is not likely to be effective "if it does not address the low status, morale, and recognition of teachers in general and the fringe status of art teachers in particular" (May, 1989, p. 146).

Mims and Lankford (1995) reported that time and money are two practical restrictions that can impinge greatly on elementary art teachers' curricula choices. They sent questionnaires to a sample of elementary art teachers and reported results of 332 returned questionnaires. They found that in a year teachers had an average of 29 contact hr per class. According to the Educational Research Service (2001) time restrictions are not as serious a constraint for secondary art teachers. They report that the median secondary art class is 55 min long, and that "about 75% of the [responding secondary] art teachers felt that their instructional time with students was adequate" (Educational Research Service, p. v).

In addition Mims and Lankford (1995) reported that the annual per student elementary art budget ranges from 20 cents to $20 with an average of $3.33 per student per year. In a national survey of art teachers, Burton (1997) found that high school teachers reported having more responsibility for the art budget than did elementary art teachers. Jeffers' (1996) survey of Kansas art teachers revealed that "beginning, mid-career, and veteran art teachers . . . have said quite clearly and unanimously that a lack of funding for low status of art programs, which in turn, threatened the viability of these programs, are major issues confronting them" (p. 111).

Jeffers and Fong (2000) investigated the impact of budgetary issues in Southern California schools and focused their attention on schools where art is taught by general classroom teachers. They compared the impact of funding in a poorer and a wealthier school district and found that "when support drops below [a] critical level, a downward spiral is likely to develop, such that teachers, even those who are very experienced and well-trained, begin to shut down and thus, shut off students' media usage" (p. 38). They argued that curriculum development should not ignore the "dynamic and complex relationship among media usage, funding support, and perceived performance" (Jeffers & Fong, p. 39).

Of course, in addition to time and money, many other day-to-day realities can affect teachers' interactions with curricula. Burton (1997) provided basic information about such practical realities that included assignment to a specialized art room; average classes taught per day; frequency of meeting times with students; block scheduling; class time; and resources.

Organizations and Institutions

The Policy Perspectives Impacting the Teaching of Art section of this *Handbook* outlines positions taken by professional organizations, government, private foundations, and commercial interests, that filter into teachers' thinking as they interact with art curriculum. Many organizations and institutions outside individual schools seek to affect art teachers and their curricula. Mims and Lankford (1995) reported that districtwide curriculum guides were not particularly influential on elementary art teachers' art programs.

State and national development and implementation of visual art curriculum standards and achievement tests are among the more recent ways that government has interacted with art teachers and their curricula. Since the publication of the National Visual Arts Standards in 1994, many art teachers have used those standards in curriculum planning. The Educational Research Service (2001, p. 17) reported that 86% of secondary art teachers agree that their curricula align with the national standards. Sobol (1998) analyzed state visual arts achievement tests and found inconsistency between the test items and the predominant content of most art programs. Thirty-seven percent of items tested vocabulary or concepts knowledge; 31%, art criticism; 5%, art history; 3%, aesthetics; and only 6% addressed production knowledge and skills. The number of production-related items was very disproportionate to the amount of curriculum content devoted to production.

Private foundations have also sought to influence art education programs. Freedman (1989) provided an historical perspective in her analysis of the complexity of missions of a Depression era philanthropic art education program: the Owatonna Project in Minnesota supported by the Carnegie Foundation. Wilson (1997) evaluated the impact of the J. Paul Getty Trusts' Regional Institute Project. He reported that after 7 years and the creation of an entirely new role for the art specialist, "the challenge of developing a comprehensive DBAE curriculum with a sequence of art-based instructional units [still] looms large" (Wilson, p. 20). He found that middleschool and junior high school art specialists were "more eager to accept the ideas of a comprehensive approach to art education" (Wilson, p. 21) than were high school art teachers. Yet, he concluded also that at the secondary level "much work remains . . . to build comprehensive DBAE curriculum" (Wilson, p. 20).

Wilson (1997) described differences in approaches taken by elementary classroom teachers and specialist art teachers within the context of a major curriculum reform program and argued for joint curriculum planning by elementary school classroom teachers and art specialists. He reported that after years of participation in the reform project, in the 235 schools he evaluated, "fully articulated exemplary units of instruction developed by classroom teachers and art specialists who take their cues from the themes, topics, and content of works of art are still somewhat rare" (Wilson, p. 151). Three years later, after the Getty Regional Institutes Program was completed, Eisner (2000), a long-time advisor to the Getty Education Institute, identified the absence of curriculum materials to be one of the problems with Getty's attempt to assume a leadership role in art education. He concluded that the approach advocated by Getty (discipline-based art education) "is an extremely demanding approach . . . for any teacher, even one well-trained in art. It is especially daunting for elementary school teachers, who often have little or no background in art" (Eisner, p. 131).

Many art museums have made efforts to become integrated into school art curricula. Stone's (1993) survey found that "secondary art specialists see the art museum as important for supplementing classroom instruction in studio art and in art history" (pp. 52–53). She recommended that preservice education be changed to help art teachers better integrate art museums into their programs.

Housen and Duke (1998) outlined a 3-year curriculum-development project initiated at New York's Museum of Modern Art, which used research findings from each preceding year to guide the evolution of a visual literacy curriculum into a visual thinking strategies (VTS) curriculum. Middle school and high school teachers and their students participated in the first-year study. The researchers found that "many teachers were . . . at the same stages as their students and a stage or more away from museum staff and experts" (Housen & Duke, p. 94) and that teachers with poor comprehension of information transmitted that information to their students in a distorted way. The basic aim of the revised second-year VTS curriculum "was to create teaching strategies that might help a teacher who is at the same aesthetic stage as his/her students to provide interesting and stage-appropriate challenges to those students" (Housen & Duke, p. 95). Also in the second year, one group of teachers received more education and took more responsibility for teaching with museum educators serving as mentors. Housen and Duke reported that the participants' learning of the art content was not strong, but that students, especially students in the group taught by mentored classroom teachers, showed significant growth in aesthetic stages of development, that is, in the ability to operate at more advanced aesthetic development stages. In preparation for the third year, the researchers provided "a structured way of introducing students to art which was simpler for teachers, and which used their skills and strengths" (Housen & Duke, p. 97). Housen and Duke report that "the revised curriculum changed the program's emphasis from helping participants become visually literate, analytical, and informed viewers to aiding their aesthetic developmental growth" (Housen & Duke, p. 98).

Commercial businesses have also had a role to play in influencing how art teachers interact with curriculum. Katter's (1985) historical analysis of hands-on instructional resources documented the evolving production of commercial materials for art teaching through the 20th century. The Educational Research Service (2001) reported that only 30.8% of secondary art teachers use textbooks or curriculum packages. Chapman (1985) outlined the process she used to develop an elementary art textbook series. She proposes that, because teachers are among those who produce most state, district, and local curriculum, her "analysis of such guides was viewed as a form of consultation with art educators [including teachers of art]" (Chapman, p. 207). Chapman developed and revised a detailed outline, which she sent along with a questionnaire to 410 individuals, including both art teachers and classroom teachers. In addition to promoting instructional materials and curriculum packages, and lobbying for textbook adoption, another major way that private business can influence art teachers' interaction with curricula is through their promotions of school art supplies, an issue not yet surfacing in art education research.

Curriculum Development and Implementation

As noted previously, teachers of art carry a great deal of responsibility not only for the implementation of curriculum but also for its development. In many instances, practicing art teachers collaborate with other educators as they develop, adapt, or select curricula. Dunn (1995) offered a structure that teachers of art might use to develop their own art curricula. Clover (2002) described how a group of art teachers adapted an online curriculum unit for implementation in several schools at both elementary- and secondary-grade levels. Irwin (1992) described the role of an art supervisor in the curriculum-development process. She concluded that "supervisors in many cases act in dialectical relationship between teachers and administrators and, as such, fulfill a unique interface role within a school district" (Irwin, p. 118).

Bergman and Fiering (1997) analyzed the evolution of a long-term curriculum-research collaboration among art teachers, an art supervisor, and a university researcher. They reported on the benefits derived from the struggle to reach common goals, which led the team "to shift from a totally researcher-driven model towards a co-investigational one" (Bergman & Fiering, p. 55) in which teachers and researcher negotiated goals, instruction, and procedures for assessing learning. Goldsmith-Conley and Bales (1994) reported on joint curriculum development by an art specialist and classroom teacher. Erickson and Stein (1993) outlined a 5-year team effort that involved 10 art teachers, a social studies teacher, and 3 university professors.

Art educators have attempted to describe the interaction of teachers and curricula through metaphor and key ideas. Ettinger and Hoffman (1990) used the metaphor of quilt making.

Erickson and Stein (1993) compared the process to baseball and dubbed it the curriculum negotiation game. MacGregor (1988) characterized it as reconceptualization. Sullivan (1989) described it as inevitably uncertain. The interaction of teachers and curriculum is elusive, complex, and continuously evolving.

RECOMMENDATIONS

Teachers of art who are interested in scholarly writing about art curriculum will find a tremendous range of curriculum visions from which to draw inspiration and help them develop their own visions. They will also discover that they can find sustained critical dialog regarding at least two of those visions: DBAE and correlations between arts education, or sometimes just arts involvement, and learning beyond the arts. Teachers of art also will benefit from collaborations between curriculum theorists and empirical researchers that result in evidence of effective implementation of particular theoretical curriculum proposals. They also can conduct their own action research investigations that have potential for developing new curriculum projects that can aid students' art learning.

Whatever art curriculum teachers ultimately implement in their classrooms, they must be attentive to how that curriculum is perceived by students, parents, school colleagues, and other policymakers and stakeholders. Unlike math teachers, science teachers, social studies teachers, and language arts teachers, teachers of art are often challenged to justify their curriculum to colleagues, stakeholders, and policymakers who themselves may lack any formal art instruction. When teachers learn of research results through sometimes oversimplified translations or within a politically charged context, critical reflection as a basis for their curriculum decision-making becomes increasingly difficult. Research designed to produce useful findings for art (or arts) education advocacy may not, at the same time, yield the kind of focused findings that can guide teachers in making specific curriculum decisions. Teachers who implement any of a variety of art curricula based on studies of undifferentiated art programs that "promise" particular outcomes may find that the desired outcomes are not forthcoming. The more researchers are able to specify the particular content, approach, or strategies of art curricula that they find to be effective, the better prepared teachers will be to make well-informed curriculum choices and decisions.

If teachers look to research to shed light on their selection, development, adaptation, or implementation of an art curriculum, they will find some evidence of the effectiveness of some curricula, curriculum components, and instructional strategies. However, research reports may be difficult for teachers to read and interpret. A study conducted in one context may have little or no generalizability or applicability in another. To help teachers understand the relevance of particular research findings to their own school situations, researchers should take special care to identify their basic assumptions about implementation. For example, did teachers implementing the curriculum have substantial or minimal art knowledge and skills? Was the study designed to produce evidence that will be useful to inservice teachers or to university art educators who have the responsibility of preparing new art teachers? Was the study carried out with minimal or optimal classroom time and instructional supply budget? Was the curriculum implemented in the lower grades, where most states mandate art instruction for all students, or in the higher grades, where the viability to a substantial portion of the art program may depend on its popularity with students who are free to elect, or more often not elect, to enroll in art classes?

Two general directions for future research emerge from this analysis of interaction between teaching and curriculum: One area focuses on effective curriculum; the other, on teachers. Researchers might design studies that manipulate key variables in order to develop and confirm various curriculum theories. Sequencing of art-making and art-viewing activities and also the use of verbal and visual cues to affect transfer are among variables researchers might manipulate to help determine the effectiveness of art curriculum on student learning. Compared with teachers of other subjects, many teachers of art have a great deal of autonomy in their art curriculum choices, especially in schools without visual arts supervisors and any standardized state art achievement tests. Researchers might design studies to describe the consequences of this situation as persons responsible for art teaching vary. That is, how do art curricula vary when art teachers, classroom teachers, artists in schools, art museum educators, volunteer parents, and others share all or part of the responsibility for a school's art curriculum?

How can researchers plan studies that teachers can understand and use? How can teachers free themselves from the many factors (personal, community, political, economic, and other) that impinge on their decision making, long enough to reflect on assumptions that may, consciously or unconsciously, override their curriculum decision making? Long-term collaborations among teachers, researchers, and others may be one way to listen, learn, and plan studies that can make a difference for teachers faced with the responsibility of selecting, adapting, developing, and implementing art curricula in their schools.

REFERENCES

Addiss, S., & Erickson, M. (1993). *Art history and education.* Urbana & Chicago: University of Illinois Press.

Amdur, D. (1993). Arts and cultural context: A curriculum integrating discipline-based art education with other humanities subjects art the secondary level. *Art Education, 46*(3),12–19.

Anderson, T. (1985). Toward a socially defined studio curriculum. *Art Education, 38*(5), 15–18.

Anglin, J. M. (1993). Three views of middle school art curriculum. *Studies in Art Education, 35*(1), 55–64.

Armstrong, C. (1993). Effects of training in an art production questioning method on teacher questioning and student responses. *Studies in Art Education, 34*(4), 209–221.

Bergman, L. M., & Fiering, N. C. (1997). Bridging the gap between the university researcher and the classroom teachers. *Art Education, 50*(5), 51–56.

Bickley-Green, C. A. (1995). Math and art curriculum integration: A post-modern foundation. *Studies in Art Education, 37*(1), 6–18.

Billings, M. M. (1995). Issues vs themes: Two approaches to a multicultural art curriculum. *Art Education, 48*(1), 21–24.

Bresler, L. (1994). Imitative, complementary, and expansive: Three roles of visual arts curricula. *Studies in Art Education, 35*(2), 90–104.

Brewer, T. M. (1991). An examination of two approaches to ceramics instruction in elementary education. *Studies in Art Education, 32*(4), 196–206.

Brewer, T. M. (1998). The relationship of art instruction, grade-level, and gender on third- and seventh-grade student drawing. *Studies in Art Education, 39*(2), 132–146.

Brewer, T. M., & Colbert, C. B. (1992). The effects of contrasting instructional strategies on seventh-grade students' ceramic vessels. *Studies in Art Education, 34*(1), 18–27.

Broudy, H. S. (1985). Curriculum validity in art education. *Studies in Art Education, 26*(4), 212–215.

Brown, N. (2001). The meaning of transfer in the practices of arts education. *Studies in Art Education, 43*(1), 83–102.

Brown, M., & Korzenik, D. (1993). *Art making and education.* Urbana & Chicago: University of Illinois Press.

Bullock, A. L., & Galbraith, L. (1992). Images of art teaching: Comparing the beliefs and practices of two secondary art teachers. *Studies in Art Education, 33*(2), 86–97.

Burton, D. (1997). *A survey of assessment and evaluation among U.S. K-12 teachers of art.* Richmond, VA: Art Education Department, Virginia Commonwealth University.

Burton, D. (2000). *1999 survey of secondary art education instruction in U.S. schools.* Richmond, VA: VCU Arts, Virginia Commonwealth University.

Burton, J. M., Horowitz, R., & Abeles, H. (2000). Learning in and through the arts: The question of transfer. *Studies in Art Education, 41*(3), 228–257.

Burton, J., Lederman, A., & London, P. (Eds.). (1988). Beyond DBAE: The case for multiple visions of art education. North Dartmouth, MA: University Council on Art Education.

Caldwell, H., & Moore, B. H. (1991). The art of writing: Drawing as preparation for narrative writing in the primary grades. *Studies in Art Education, 32*(4), 207–219.

Calvert, A. E. (1988). Native art history and DBAE: An analysis of key concepts. *Journal of Multicultural and Cross-Cultural Research in Art Education, 6*(1), 112–122.

Cason, N. F. (1998). Interactive multimedia: An alternative for studying works of art. *Studies in Art Education, 39*(4), 336–349.

Catterall, J. S. (1998). Does experience in the arts boost academic achievement? A response to Eisner. *Art Education, 5*(4), 6–8.

Catterall, J. S., Chapleau, R., & Iwanaga, J. (2000). *Champions of change. Involvement of the arts & human development.* Washington, DC: Council of Chief State School Officers.

Chalmers, F. G. (1996). *Celebrating pluralism: Art, education and cultural diversity.* Los Angeles: J. Paul Getty Trust.

Chanda, J., & Basinger, A. M. (2000). Understanding the cultural meaning of selected African ndop statues: The use of art history constructivist inquiry methods. *Studies in Art Education, 42*(1), 67–82.

Chapman, L. H. (1985). Curriculum development as process and product. *Studies in Art Education, 26*(4), 206–211.

Clark, G.A. (1991). *Examining discipline-based art education as a curriculum construct.* Bloomington, IN: ERIC: ART and Adjunct Clearinghouse for Art Education.

Clark, R. (1996). *Art education: Issues in postmodern pedagogy.* Reston, VA: National Art Education Association.

Clark, G. (1997). Critics, criticism, and the evolution of discipline-based art education. *Visual Arts Research, 23*(2), 12–18.

Clark, R. (1998). Doors and mirrors in art education: Constructing the postmodern classroom. *Art Education, 51*(6), 6–11.

Clark, G., Day, M., & Greer, W. D. (1987). Discipline-based art education: Becoming students of art. In R. A. Smith (Ed.), *Discipline-based art education: Origins, meaning, and development.* (pp. 129–196). Urbana and Chicago: University of Illinois.

Clark, G., & Zimmerman, E. (2000). Greater understanding of the local community: A community-based art education program for rural schools. *Art Education, 53*(2) 33–39.

Clover, F. (2002). How can artworld-centered online curriculum be used? In M. Erickson & B. Young (Eds.), *Multicultural artworlds: Enduring, evolving, and overlapping traditions* (pp. 27–31). Reston, VA: National Art Education Association.

Collins, G., & Sandell, R. (1988). Informing the promise of DBAE: Remember the women, children, and other folk. *Journal of Multicultural and Cross-Cultural Research in Art Education, 6*(1), 55–63.

Collins, G., & Sandell, R. (Eds.), (1996). *Gender issues in art education: Content, contexts, and strategies.* Reston, VA: National Art Education Association.

Congdon, K. G., Delgado-Trunk, C., & López, M. (1999). Teaching about the *Ofrenda* and experiences on the border. *Studies in Art Education, 40*(4), 312–329.

Congdon, K. G., Stewart, M., & White, J. H. (2002). Mapping identity for curriculum work. In Y. Gaudelius & P. Speirs (Eds.), *Contemporary issues in art education* (pp. 108–129). Upper Saddle River, NJ: Prentice Hall.

Cromer, J. (1990). *History, theory and practice of art criticism in art education.* Reston, VA: National Art Education Association.

Davenport, M. (2000). Cultural art education: Polishing the lenses. *Studies in Art Education, 41*(4), 361–375.

Delacruz, E. M. (1997). *Design for inquiry: Instructional theory, research and practice in art education.* Reston, VA: National Art Education Association.

DiBlasio, M. K. (1985). Continuing the translation: Further delineation of the DBAE format. *Studies in Art Education, 26*(4), 197–205.

DiBlasio, M. K. (1987). Reflections on the theory of discipline-based art education. *Studies in Art Education, 28*(4), 221–226.

DiBlasio, M. K. (1997). Twelve years and counting: Tracking a comprehensive effort at instructional and programmatic reform through DBAE. *Visual Arts Research, 23*(2), 34–42.

Dobbs, S. M. (1998). *Learning in and through art: A guide to discipline-based art education.* Los Angeles: Getty Education Institute for the Arts.

Dorn, C. M. (1999). *Mind in art: Cognitive foundations in art education.* Mahwah, NJ: Lawrence Erlbaum Associates.

Dowell, M. L. (1990). Effects of visual referents upon representational drawing of the human figure. *Studies in Art Education, 31*(2), 78–85.

Duncum. P. (1999). A case for an art education of everyday aesthetic experiences. *Studies in Art Education, 40*(4), 295–311.

Dunn, P. C. (1995). Curriculum: Creating curriculum in art. Reston, VA: National Art Education Association.

Edens, K. M., & Potter, E. F. (2001). Promoting conceptual understanding through pictorial representation. *Studies in Art Education, 42*(3), 214–233.

Educational Research Service. (2001). *Art teachers in secondary schools: A national survey.* Reston, VA: National Art Education Association.

Efland, A. D. (1995). The spiral and the lattice: Changes in cognitive learning theory with implications for art education. *Studies in Art Education, 36*(3), 134–153.

Efland, A. D. (1996). The threefold curriculum and the art. *Art Education, 49*(5), 49–56.

Efland, A. D. (2000). The city as metaphor for integrated learning in the arts. *Studies in Art Education, 41*(3), 276–295.

Efland, A. Freedman, K., & Stuhr, P. (1996). *Postmodern art education: An approach to curriculum.* Reston, VA: National Art Education Association.

Eisner, E. (1998). Does experience in the arts boost academic achievement? *Art Education, 51*(1), 7–15.

Eisner, E. (2000). A heroic effort to make a practical difference in art education. In E. Winner, & L. Hetland (Eds.), *Beyond the soundbite: Arts education and academic outcomes* (pp. 229–131). Los Angeles: J. Paul Getty Trust.

Erickson, M. (1995a). Second and sixth grade students' art historical interpretation abilities: A one-year study. *Studies in Art Education, 37*(1), 19–28.

Erickson, M. (1995b). A sequence of developing art historical understandings: Merging teaching, service, research, and curriculum development. *Art Education, 48*(6), 23–24, 33–37.

Erickson, M. (1997). Transfer within and beyond DBAE: A cognitive exploration of research issues. *Journal of Visual Arts Research, 23*(2), 43–51.

Erickson, M. (1998). Effects of art history instruction on fourth and eighth grade students' abilities to interpret artworks contextually. *Studies in Art Education, 39*(4), 309–320.

Erickson, M. (2001). Images of me: Why broad themes? Why focus on inquiry? Why use the Internet. *Art Education, 54*(1), 33–40.

Erickson, M. (2002a). Teaching about artworlds: A collaborative research project. In M. Erickson & B. Young (Eds.), *Multicultural artworlds: Enduring, evolving, and overlapping traditions* (pp. 33–39). Reston, VA: National Art Education Association.

Erickson, M. (2002b). *Stories of art.* Tucson, AZ: CRIZMAC.

Erickson, M., & Stein, S. (1993). The curriculum negotiation game. *Art Education, 46*(4), 14–20.

Erickson, M., & Young, B. (Eds.), (2002). *Multicultural artworlds: Enduring, evolving, and overlapping traditions.* Reston, VA: National Art Education Association.

Ettinger, L., & Hoffman, E. (1990). Quilt making in art education: Toward a participatory curriculum metaphor. *Art Education, 43*(4), 40–47.

Fitzpatrick, V. L. (1992). *Art history: A contextual inquiry course.* Reston, VA: National Art Education Association.

Fleming, P. S. (1988). Pluralism and DBAE: Towards a model for global multi-cultural art education. *Journal of Multicultural and Cross-Cultural Research in Art Education, 6*(1), 64–74.

Freedman, K. (1989). The philanthropic vision: The Owatonna art education project as an example of "private" interests in public schooling. *Studies in Art Education, 31*(1), 15–26.

Freedman, K., & Hernandez, F. (Eds.). (1998). *Curriculum, culture, and art education: Comparative perspectives.* Albany, NY: State University Press of New York.

Gardner, H. (1989). Zero-based arts education: An introduction to ARTS PROPEL. *Studies in Art Education, 30*(2), 71–83.

Gitomer, D., Scott, G., & Price, K. (1992). Portfolio culture in arts education. *Art Education, 45*(1), 7–12.

Goldsmith-Conley, E., & Bales, S. (1994). Development of a sophisticated early childhood art program: Collaboration and discovery. *Visual Arts Research, 20*, 78–91.

Grauer, K. (1998). Beliefs of preservice teachers toward art education. *Studies in Art Education, 39*(4), 350–370.

Greer, D. W. (1984). Discipline-based art education: Approaching art as a subject of study. *Studies in Art Education, 25*(4), 212–218.

Greer, D. W. (1997). DBAE and art education reform. *Visual Arts Research, 23*(2), 25–33.

Gude, O. (2000). Investigating the culture of curriculum. In E. D. Fehr, K. Fehr, & K. Keifer-Boyd (Eds.). *Real-world readings in art education* (pp. 75–81). New York: Falmer Press.

Haanstra, F. (2000). Dutch studies of the effects of arts education programs on school success. *Studies in Art Education, 42*(1), 20–35.

Hamblen, K. A. (1988). Cultural literacy through multiple DBAE repertoires. *Journal of Multicultural and Cross-Cultural Research in Art Education, 6*(1), 88–98.

Hamblen, K. A. (1997). Second generation DBAE. *Visual Arts Research 23*(2), 98–106.

Hellwege, P. (1993). Instructional resources: Aesthetic dialogue: Art and interdisciplinary curriculum. *Art Education, 46*(5), 25–28, 41–44.

Housen, A. (1999). *Visual Thinking Strategies.* Retrieved April 25, 2001, from http://www.vue.org/documents/vtsIntro. html, accessed

Housen, A., & Duke, L. (1998). Responding to Alper: Representing the MoMA studies on visual literacy and aesthetic development. *Visual Arts Research, 24*(1), 93–102.

Hutchens, J., & Suggs, M. (1997). *Art education: Content and practice in a postmodern era.* Reston, VA: National Art Education Association.

Irwin, R. L. (1992). A profile of an arts supervisor: A political image. *Studies in Art Education, 33*(2), 110–121.

Jeffers, C. S. (1996). Professional development in art education today: A survey of Kansas art teachers. *Studies in Art Education, 37*(2), 101–114.

Jeffers, C. S., & Fong, N. I. (2000). Funding issues & teacher expertise in elementary art teaching: A dynamic relationship. *Art Education, 53*(5), 33–39.

Johnson, N. R. (1988). DBAE in cultural relationships. *Journal of Multicultural and Cross-Cultural Research in Art Education, 6*(1), 15–25.

Johnston, M., Roybal, C., & Parsons, M. J. (1988). Teaching the concept of style to elementary school art students: A developmental investigation. *Visual Arts Research, 14*(2), 57–67.

Jones, B. J. (1988). Art education in context. *Journal of Multicultural and Cross-Cultural Research in Art Education, 6*(1), 38–54.

Kakas, K. (1995). Art criticism with young children experiencing developmental delays. In C. M. Thompson (Ed). *The visual arts and early childhood learning* (pp. 73–79). Reston, VA: National Art Education Association.

Katter, E. (1985). Hands-on instructional resources for the teaching of art: A historical perspective. In B. Wilson & H. Hoffa (Eds.), *History of art education: Proceedings of the Penn State Conference* (pp. 295–414). Reston, VA: National Art Education Association.

Katter, E. (1987). Within culture: The place for art in America's schools. *Journal of Multicultural and Cross-Cultural Research in Art Education, 5*(1), 73–82.

Keifer-Boyd, K. (2000). By the people: A community-based art curriculum. In D. E. Fehr, K. Fehr, & K. Keifer-Boyd, K. (Eds.), *Real-world readings in art education.* (pp. 155–165). New York: Falmer Press.

Kindler, A. (1987). A review of rationales for integrated arts programs. *Studies in Art Education, 29*(1), 52–60.

Klein, S. (1992–1993). Social action and art education: A curriculum for change. *Journal of Multicultural and Cross-Cultural Research in Art Education, 10/11,* 111–125.

Koroscik, J. S. (1996). Who ever said studying art world be easy? The growing cognitive demands of understanding works of art in the information age. *Studies in Art Education, 38*(1), 4–20.

Koroscik, J. S., Short, G., Stravropoulus, C., & Fortin, S. (1992). Frameworks for understanding art: The function of comparative art contexts and verbal cues. *Studies in Art Education, 33*(3), 154–164.

Kowalchuck, E. A., & Stone, D. L. (2000). Art education for elementary teachers: What really happens? *Visual Arts Research, 26*(2), 29–39.

Krug. D. H. (2000). Curriculum integration positions and practices in art education. *Studies in Art Education, 41*(3), 258–275.

Lampela, L. (1996). Concerns of gay and lesbian caucuses within art, education, and art education. *Art Education, 49*(4), 24–34.

Lankford, E. L. (1992). *Aesthetics: Issues and inquiry.* Reston, VA: National Art Education Association.

Levi, A. W., & Smith, R. A. (1991). *Art education: A critical necessity.* Urbana and Chicago: University of Illinois Press.

Lovano-Kerr, J. (1990). Cultural pluralism and DBAE: An issue (Fall,1988) revisited. *Journal of Multicultural and Cross-Cultural Research in Art Education, 11*(1), 61–71.

Luftig, R. L. (2000). An investigation of an arts infusion program on creative thinking, academic achievement, affective functioning, and arts appreciation of children at three grade levels. *Studies in Art Education, 4*(3), 208–227.

MacGregor, R. N. (1988). Curriculum reform. In *Proceedings of Issues in Discipline-Based Art Education: Strengthening the stance, extending horizons* (pp. 41–45). Los Angeles: Getty Center for Education in the Arts.

Magee, L. J., & Price, K. R. (1992). Propel: Visual arts in Pittsburgh. *School Arts, 91*(8), 43–45.

Manley-Delacruz, E. (1990). Revisiting curriculum conceptions: A thematic perspective. *Visual Arts Research, 16*(2), 10–25.

Marché, T. (1997). Examination of factors affecting change in a Pennsylvania school district's art program from 1924 to 1992. *Studies in Art Education, 39*(1), 24–36.

Marché, T. (2000). Toward a community model of art education history. *Studies in Art Education, 42*(1), 51–66.

Marschalek, D. (1989). A new approach to curriculum development in environmental design. *Art Education, 42*(4), 8–17.

Marschalek, D. G. (1995). A guide to curriculum development in design education. *Art Education, 48*(1), 14–20.

May, W. T. (1989). Teachers, teaching, and the workplace: Omissions in curriculum reform. *Studies in Art Education, 30*(3), 142–155.

McSorley, J. (1996). Primary school teachers' conceptions of teaching art criticism. *Studies in Art Education, 37*(3), 160–169.

Milbrandt, M. K. (1998). Postmodernism in art education: Content for life. *Art Education, 51*(6), 47–53.

Mims, S. K., & Lankford, E. L. (1995). Time, money, and the new art education: A nationwide investigation. *Studies in Art Education, 36*(2), 84–95.

Nadaner, D. (1998). Painting in an era of critical theory. *Studies in Art Education, 39*(2), 168–182.

Educational Research Service. (2001). *Art teachers in secondary schools: A national survey*. Reston, VA: National Art Education Association.

Parsons, M. J. (1998). Integrated curriculum and our paradigm in the arts. *Studies in Art Education, 39*(2), 103–116.

Parsons, M. J., & Blocker, H. G. (1993). *Aesthetics and education*. Urbana & Chicago: University of Illinois Press.

Perkins, D. (2001). Embracing babel: The prospects of instrumental uses of the arts for education. In E. Winner & L. Hetland, L. (Eds.), *Beyond the soundbite: Arts education and academic outcomes* (pp. 117–124). Los Angeles: J. Paul Getty Trust.

Räsänen, M. (1997). *Building bridges: Experiential art understanding, a work of art as a means of understanding and constructing self*. Helsinki, Finland: The University of Art and Design.

Richards, A. G. (1988). Perceptual training in drawing among students from two countries. *Studies in Art Education, 29*(2), 302–308.

Sahasrabudhe, P. (1992). Multicultural art education: A proposal for curriculum content, structure, and attitudinal understandings. *Art Education, 45*(3), 41–47.

Seifert, L. S. (1995). Concurrent viewing may alter verbal reports about artwork. *Visual Arts Research, 21*(2), 19–25.

Short, G. (1995). Understanding domain knowledge for teaching: Higher-order thinking in pre-service art teachers specialists. *Studies in Art Education, 39*(3), 154–169.

Short, G. (1998). The high school studio curriculum and art understanding: An examination. *Studies in Art Education, 40*(1), 46–65.

Smith, R. A. (Ed.). (1987). *Discipline-based art education: Origins, meaning, and development*. Urbana & Chicago: University of Illinois Press.

Smith, R. A. (1995). *Excellence II: The continuing quest in art education*. Reston, VA: National Art Education Association.

Smith, R. A. (Ed.). (2000). *Readings in discipline-based art education*. Urbana & Chicago: University of Illinois Press.

Smith, P., & Pusch, J. (1990). A cautionary tale: The stalling of DBAE. *Visual Arts Research, 16*(2), 43–50.

Sobol, R. F. (1998). What are we testing?: Content analysis of state visual arts achievement tests. *Visual Arts Research, 24*(1), 1–12.

Stankiewicz, M. A. (2000). Disciplines and the future of art education. *Studies in Art Education, 41*(4), 301–313.

Stone, D. L. (1993). The secondary art specialist and the art museum. *Studies in Art Education, 35*(1), 45–54.

Stone, D. L. (1997). A comparative study of two art museum tours and their impact on adult learning. *Visual Arts Research, 23*(2), 142–150.

Stuhr, P. L. (1994). Multicultural art education and social reconstruction. *Studies in Art Education, 35*(3), 171–178.

Stuhr, P. L., Petrovich-Mwaniki, L., & Wasson, R. (1992) Curriculum guidelines for the multicultural art classroom. *Art Education, 45*(1), 16–24.

Sullivan, G. (1989). Curriculum in art education: The uncertainty principle. *Studies in Art Education, 30*(4), 225–236.

Tomhave, R. (1999). Portfolio assessment in the visual arts: A comparison of advanced secondary art education strategies. *Dissertation Abstracts International, 60-06A*. (UMI No. AAI9935008)

Villeneuve, P. (1997). Paradigm to practice: Negotiating the first five years. *Visual Arts Research, 23*(2), 107–113.

Wilson, B. (1997). *The quiet evolution: Changing the face of arts education*. Los Angeles: Getty Center for Education in the Arts.

Wilson, B., & Rubin, B. (1997). DBAE and educational change. *Visual Arts Research, 23*(2), 89–97.

Winner. E., & Cooper, M. (2000). Mute those claims: No evidence (yet) for a causal link between arts study and academic achievement. *Journal of Aesthetic Education, 34* (3–4), 11–75.

Wolcott, A., & Macaskill, J. (1997). New Zealand: Integration of traditional Maori art and art education curriculum. *Journal of Multicultural and Cross-Cultural Research in Art Education, 15*, 24–32.

Wolf, D. P. (1996). Becoming knowledge: The evolution of art education. In P. W. Jackson (Ed.), *Handbook of research on curriculum* (pp. 945–963). New York: Macmillan.

Wolff, T. F., & Geahigan, G. (1997). *Art criticism and education*: Urbana & Chicago: University of Illinois Press.

Young, B. (1990). *Art, culture, and ethnicity*. Reston, VA: National Art Education Association.

Zimmerman, E. (1992). A comparative study of two painting teachers of talented adolescents. *Studies in Art Education, 33*(3), 174–185.

Zimmerman, E. (1994). Current research and practice about pre-service visual art specialist teacher education. *Studies in Art Education, 35*(2), 78–89.

Zurmuehlen, M. (1990). *Studio art: Praxis, symbol, presence*. National standards for arts education. Reston, VA: Music Educators National Conference.

22

Teacher Education as a Field of Study in Art Education: A Comprehensive Overview of Methodology and Methods Used in Research About Art Teacher Education

Frances Thurber
University of Nebraska at Omaha

Methodologies for research should be chosen that suit the questions that are asked and not the reverse. To establish a research agenda for the 21st century, content questions of direct concern to the role of art in education should be identified, then investigated through appropriate research methodologies.

—Zimmerman, 1994b, p. 10

The matching of an important problem to research questions and then to methodology constitutes one of the major issues to be encountered and resolved in the development of a coherent research agenda in teacher education.

—Yarger & Smith, 1990, p. 30

INTRODUCTION

Research should be conducted not merely to describe but to ground theory and inform practice. General educational research regarding teacher education contains major gaps in the content of existing studies and in recommendations for what should be studied about teacher education in the future (Yarger & Smith, 1990). Research in art education regarding teacher preparation has followed this national trend. Over the past 2 decades, this notion has been increasingly supported by several noted art education researchers (Davis, 1990; Day, 1997; Eisner, 1979, 1993a; Galbraith, 1995; Stokrocki, 1995a; Sullivan, 1996; Zimmerman, 1994a).

In this chapter significant research about preservice and inservice art teacher education will be discussed from the point of view of selected research methodologies rather than from a content or contextual focus. These issues are inextricably related, however, so no discussion can occur about art education research methodology without links to content of the research and to research contexts. Although minimally addressed in this study, chapters by Burton; Erickson; Galbraith and Grauer; Sabol; and Stokrocki, in this section on art teacher education of the *Handbook of Research and Policy in Art Education*, provide in-depth discussions of relevant issues, practices, perceptions, and contexts in which art teacher education research occurs.

The parameters for this chapter include an overview of selected studies from *Studies in Art Education* prior to 1991 that extended our knowledge of methodologies used in research about the education of teachers who teach art, as well as a more detailed review of methodologies used for significant research about teacher preparation and education published in that journal over the last decade. A review of methods used in studies about teacher education published 5 years prior to 2001 in *Visual Arts Research* also is provided. Central to this effort is research devoted to the preparation of K-12 art specialists at a preservice level and continued professional development of art educators at graduate or inservice levels. The chapter attempts to acknowledge methods used in those research efforts and further attempts to highlight emerging collaborative efforts at action research, where appropriate, conducted by university researchers and K-12 art education professionals. Review of the last decade of research conducted by art education doctoral candidates regarding teacher education adds to this body of knowledge. An overview of methods of research used for presentations about teacher preparation at National Art Education Association (NAEA) annual conferences in selected years in the last decade also provides insight into the shifts and trends of research methodology appearing in research forums about art teacher education.

SOME ASSUMPTIONS AND LIMITATIONS

It is beyond the scope of this chapter to rate or rank each study for methodological rigor or quality of methodological fit relative to its research questions or hypotheses. The cited studies' publication in the art education research literature served as basic acknowledgment of their contributions to the field. A critical assessment of this body of literature from the perspective of methodology could be a starting point for further and more in-depth research on methodology in research about art teacher education. In some reviewed studies, descriptions of methodology were sketchy or lacking altogether in either the abstracts or in the actual text of presentations, forums, or research papers.

This list of cited studies and their subsequent methodologies are by no means comprehensive. An informal review of the journals *Arts Education Policy Review, Journal of Aesthetic Education*, and *Art Education* revealed a number of studies written about methodology or art teacher education. Several of those are mentioned in this chapter when relevant to a particular discussion. An in-depth content analysis of method also was not conducted for research published in special-interest journals or in journals outside the venue of art education. This omission was considered in the interest of the length of this chapter. A systematic content analysis of methodological content within these documents is recommended for continued research.

Such publications recommended for continued research, but not part of this chapter, include research journals from NAEA affiliates, divisions, and partners, such as Women's Caucus (*Journal of Gender Issues in Art and Education*), Social Theory Caucus (*Journal of Social Theory in Art Education*), Seminar for Research in Art Education (*Annual Abstracts*), United States Society for Education through Art (formerly *Journal of Multicultural and Cross-Cultural Research in Art Education* now *Journal of Cultural Research in Art Education*), and Canadian Society for Education through Art (*CSEA Journal* and *Canadian Review of Art Education*). Other journals, including *Journal of Art and Design Education* (published in Great Britain), *Australian Art Education Journal*, and *Arts and Learning Research*, a special-interest-group (SIG) journal publication of the American Educational Research Association (AERA), are further possibilities for analysis of trends in methodology. Journals that do not directly focus on art education but sporadically emphasize art teacher education such as *Harvard Educational Review, Educational Leadership, Educational Horizons, Phi Delta Kappan*, and *Change* are also not included in this chapter. Another potential future research endeavor from data in this chapter would be a meta-analysis of each study's methodology focusing on which methods were selected by researchers across similar subject matter content and research contexts.

OVERVIEW OF METHODOLOGICAL TRENDS IN EDUCATIONAL RESEARCH

A significant shift in thinking about approaches to research, subsequently its methods, occurred in general education and in art education as well over the last quarter of a century (MacGregor, 1998). Researchers found that quantitative methodology based on a scientific inquiry model, and once the only respected methodological standard for educational studies, did not always offer an effective means of studying important questions arising in naturalistic settings (Ary, Jacobs, & Razavieh, 2002; Eisner, 1991; Ettinger, 1987; Galbraith, 1995; Pring, 2000). According to Eisner and Peshkin (1990), "the judgment that qualitative research is either beyond the pale or substandard no longer generally holds with overwhelming force. Not only is the contemporary interaction between quantitative and qualitative researchers less lopsided, it is increasingly less an encounter and more an interface" (p. 3).

Researchers apply quantitative research methods in controlled settings to test theory, to answer questions about relationships among variables, to analyze cause and effect, or to determine the current status of a situation or problem through a variety of statistical analyses of numerical data. Quantitative studies can be predictive and experimental in their approach or descriptive and observational (Koroscik & Kowalchuk, 1997). Because quantitative studies are deductive in nature, research design is determined prior to the study and standardized testing procedures are often applied to large populations. Quantitative research is based on philosophical views that emerged in the 19th century and include the positivistic notion that both scientific and social worlds are bound by recognizable and consistent principles. Within that context, hypotheses can be systematically tested as well as replicated by other researchers, and results can be applied to larger settings. Quantitative approaches to methodology include descriptive and causal-comparative designs, correlational research, and experimental designs. Meta-analysis is the most useful means of synthesizing statistical results from a number of studies focused on the same research problem. It often is used as a method for drawing conclusions across a variety of statistics and measures. It is important to realize that numerical data and statistical analysis are not exclusive to quantitative research design (Gall, Borg, & Gall, 1996; LaPierre, 1997).

Qualitative research methods, on the other hand, address questions directed toward a deeper understanding of social phenomena, providing thick (rich, detailed) descriptions of settings and participants in a specific context (Eisner, 1991). A qualitative study is inductive, in that it often generates theory rather than tests an existing theory. Qualitative methods emerge from a phenomenological approach, in which each social setting is unique. It is the researcher's task to richly describe human behaviors within that setting: behaviors determined by beliefs, perceptions, and attitudes of individuals existing in that context. Because variables unfold as a result of the research process, these studies do not begin with a hypothesis and are usually conducted with small populations (Ary, Jacobs, & Razavieh, 2002). Eisner (1991) attributed six features to qualitative research design: The studies are focused in naturalistic settings, use the researcher as the instrument, are interpretive in their quest to find meaning, use expressive language to communicate—allowing for voice to emerge—and pay attention to detail and subtleties within a particular context. They also are insightful, believable, and serve a purpose of finding meaning. Qualitative categories for methods often described in introductory research texts include ethnography, case study research, content analysis, participant observation, narrative, and historical research (Ary et al., 2002; Gall et al., 1996).

Choice of methods drawn from these two approaches is no simple matter. Prinz (2000), reflecting on the work of John Dewey (1934), cautions researchers to not get caught up in a "false dualism" (p. 33) by regarding quantitative and qualitative methodology as dichotomous ends. Eisner (1993b), referring to acceptance in the last 2 decades of qualitative research methodology (including the introduction of visual, narrative, and poetic forms of research) into the greater educational research community, reflected:

> If there are different ways to understand the world, and if there are different forms that make such understanding possible, then it would seem to follow that any comprehensive effort to understand the processes and outcomes of schooling would profit from a pluralistic rather than a monolithic approach to research. How can such pluralism be advanced? What would it mean for the way we go about our work? (p. 8)

A decade ago, Yarger and Smith (1990) designed a research framework for general study of teacher education that included three overarching themes or foci: antecedent conditions, process, and outcomes. They suggested that studies linking these foci, rather than treating them as distinct items, strengthen results of a research study. Within this framework, they described methodological domains that have been used as a means of conducting research in the previously mentioned arenas. Those methodological approaches are narrative research, case study research, survey research, correlational research, and causal/experimental research. La Pierre and Diket (1995) corroborated this framework by describing categories for art education research methodology as historical, descriptive, ethnographic, correlational, causal/comparative, and experimental.

According to Yarger and Smith (1990), narrative studies are basic to teacher education research. They are descriptive, inform readers with rich detail, and are often qualitative. However, they have a history of being not highly respected due to their lack of validity or reliability in the research field. Case studies are more organized in their structure than narratives and are usually written to shed light on a specific context. Although they are the most frequent form of research using qualitative methods in teacher education, case studies can function as only descriptive studies or they are capable of generating hypotheses.

Survey research poses questions rather than hypotheses, and results are most often reported in quantitative terminology. Information from survey research can lead to possibly significant hypotheses if a researcher builds that capability onto a research design. Correlational studies create relationships between two or more significant variables, and research results are also most frequently reported in quantitative form. Causal/experimental research, although the most respected and sophisticated in its initiation, is rarely effective in field settings; so its use has been limited in teacher education research—particularly in the last decade.

I (Thurber) thought it surprising that inquiry frameworks for philosophical and theoretical research were not routinely mentioned along with others previously mentioned in overviews of methodology in educational research and introductory research texts; however, description of methodology in philosophical inquiry occurs later in this chapter.

Summary of Conceptual Frameworks for Research in Art Teacher Education

It is, in fact, the nature of research questions that should determine whether the research design would be quantitative or qualitative in design (Wilson, 1997a; Zimmerman, 1997a). In studies about art teacher preparation, researchers have asked:

- What *was*? (uses historical research framework as methodology)
- What *is observable*? (uses descriptive research such as demographic surveys, longitudinal or cross-sectional studies, opinion surveys, ethnographic studies, qualitative

analyses including case studies, action research with participant/observer, content or trend analyses)

- What *will occur under controlled conditions*? (uses experimental and quasi-experimental studies such as single group, control group designs, or baseline studies)
- What *is possible or proposed*? (uses paradigm research or theoretical inquiry such as application of critical theory or feminist perspectives to research methodology or design)
- What *is meaningful, beautiful, good, true, or real*? (philosophical, theoretical, conceptual, evaluative, or prescriptive research such as posing a theory, policy statements, needs assessments, formative evaluations, program evaluations, curriculum evaluations)

I note that the last area of inquiry is somewhat problematic for contemporary researchers who determine that research settings and findings are highly contextual and socially constructed and that fixed constructs of goodness, truth, et cetera, may be readily and rightly challenged in today's research forums.

Figure 22.1 reproduces and expands Zimmerman's conceptual model (1997a) that described a spectrum of research methodologies appropriate for art education research. In order to ground discussion of emerging research methodologies used in research about art teacher education in this chapter, some additions have been made. Segmented lines and italicized text in the figure represent additional contemporary methodologies that researchers of art teacher education also are selecting as those methods continue to become increasingly acceptable choices in the evolving research landscape of general education. Thus, a variety of methodological choices are available to art education researchers within a broad quantitative–qualitative framework. La Pierre (1997), in fact, suggested that research methodology is actually a continuum and methods can be used in various combinations rather than in discreet designs.

A HISTORICAL CONTEXT FOR METHODOLOGY IN ART TEACHER EDUCATION

In the mid 1980s when a heightened concern for educational reform or renewal emerged in professional dialog and in general education research literature, a shift in the nature and methods of educational research also occurred. Chapman (1982) categorized research methodology into historical, philosophical, or observational (empirical) genres and addressed the difference between basic and applied research. Selected themes evolved beyond the issue of quality control or technical assessments of model practice and teacher performance. These themes included the purposes of teacher education, content and pedagogy of teacher education programs, characterization of successful teachers, and alternative means for teacher certification. An emerging emphasis on the importance of teacher knowledge and empowerment also caused a significant shift in the operant themes of national educational research (Doyle, 1990). Methodology for these studies underwent a shift as well, moving from an emphasis and occurrence of psychometric or quantitative research to a greater appreciation and occurrence of socioanthropological or qualitative approaches (Eisner, 1993a; Zeichner, 1978, 1999).

Art educational research in teacher education appears to have followed a similar evolving trend. A major factor in the last 2 decades affecting content, context, and methodology of research about art teacher education was the advent of a discipline-based approach toward teaching art; referred to as DBAE, and often labeled in recent literature as CAE (comprehensive art education). CAE's conception of visual art, shifting from a rather singular, but entrenched view of art only as art making, also embraced content and modes of inquiry from art history, art criticism, and aesthetics or philosophies of art. Sevigny (1987, 1988) pointed out that preservice teacher training became poised for significant change with the onset of a discipline-based approach to art education at all schooling levels (pre-K to postgraduate). An emphasis

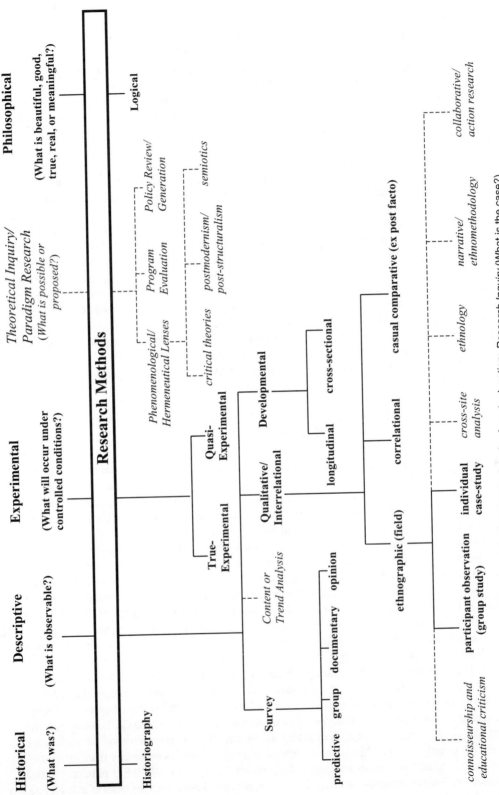

FIG. 22.1. Research methodologies for art education: *Research Inquiry* (What is the case?).

on and support for content-centered curriculum frameworks developed, particularly in the 1980s and onward. The nature of research questions—thus methodology—shifted as well, beginning with questions about the direction of preservice art education (Bolin, 1988). In 1986, ten national sites were selected by the Getty Center for Education in the Arts to explore possibilities for systemic change in existing preservice programs, including my campus (Thurber, 1990). Issues from this brief national preservice initiative were refined by 1988 and the Getty Center's attention began to be directed toward inservice education of teachers of art (Day, Gillespie, Rosenberg, Sowell, & Thurber, 1997; Wilson, 1997b).

According to Davis (1990), three ongoing concerns existed at that time in art education research regarding art teacher education. They included a content knowledge base, a professional knowledge base, and conceptions of quality teacher education in the visual arts. In his review of existing research, he concluded that that a limited number of studies attempted to explore content knowledge relative to art teacher education at preservice and inservice levels—particularly in the areas of studio art and art criticism (for example, Day, 1986). Research literature since the 1970s regarding art content had shifted to include content from aesthetics and disciplines of art history as well as art criticism. In the area of a professional knowledge base for teacher preparation in the visual arts, Davis indicated that this arena until 1990 was also limited in scope. It included studies relating to teacher values, attitudes, and perceptions; the nature of creativity and art education practice; teaching strategies; modes of inquiry; and pedagogical curriculum content. Regarding conceptions of quality teacher education in the visual arts, Davis suggested four major classifications: relationships and responsibilities among art educators, artists, and professional educators in preparation of both art specialists and art generalists; the level of entry for art teacher preparation; validation of general preparation of educators; and the role of teacher preparation in bridging the gap between theory and practice. The aforementioned issues are contested and continue to be debated in the 21st century.

In an effort to tighten the gaps in art education research, including research on preservice and inservice teacher education, the NAEA took the initiative in 1994 to establish an agenda and funding support for ongoing art education research, including research issues about teacher preparation (Zimmerman, 1994b, 1996, 1998). Research task forces were established to oversee major agendas for research. The task force on teacher education was one of eight task forces created by the 1994 NAEA research agenda.

Prior to that time, the NAEA annual conference hosted sporadic sessions on methodological approaches to art education research, but the new agenda provided impetus to involve many more educators in the research process. In 1994, in collaboration with the new research agenda, the Seminar for Research in Art Education (SRAE), an affiliate group of NAEA, held a preconference at the NAEA conference in Baltimore at which several active researchers held sessions specifically focused on the use of contemporary methods in art education research. Topics relating to methodology included sessions on historical research, authentic performance assessment, qualitative and feminist forms of research methods, artistic research method, and action research.

The SRAE, with the exception of a few years in the late 1980s, has published yearly monographs of research abstracts presented at NAEA conferences (Smith, 1992). In 1995 the abstracts also became available as ERIC documents (Connors, 1997). For example, in a review of the 1997 monograph, content in 11 of 72 research sessions dealt directly with issues or questions relative to preservice or inservice art teacher education. In the 11 sessions concerning preservice teachers and teaching, methodological approaches included historical research/autobiography (2), survey research (3), collaborative field-based research (2), as well as action research (4).

To date, just one former volume of *Studies in Art Education* (White, 1977) categorized research articles by methodology as well as by content. Those 20 studies were categorized as follows: 6 studies were identified to be descriptive/experimental; 1 study was historical; 2 studies were considered philosophical research; and 11 were placed in the category of tests and measures. (I found that volume's categorization to be very accessible, and helpful, and I recommend that a yearly breakdown by methodological category be reinstated and published in future years.) Research articles from *Studies in Art Education* recently have been classified by methodology in an online database on the Web site of the NAEA (National Art Education Association, 2002). In cross-checking my categorization of methodology for selected studies from the last decade, I found that very few method classifications of the studies yielded a discrepancy in opinion. Categorizations of methodology and methods in this database included "theoretical inquiry, philosophical inquiry, curriculum policy, and historical inquiry. The database used research design terms "descriptive, correlational, and experimental" to define research design for each of the studies found in the volumes. The following categorizations also were used: "exposition, survey, case study, interview, ethnography, action research, meta-analysis, and reviews/commentaries."

In the field of art education, researchers have challenged their colleagues to define and continue to refine methodological approaches in studies and texts they have written or edited. Eisner's text, *The Enlightened Eye: Qualitative Inquiry and the Enhancement of Educational Practice* (1991) gives researchers a virtual site map for using approaches of educational connoisseurship and educational criticism described later in this chapter. Eisner discussed methodologies for research that draw on the researcher's abilities to conduct research in artful ways, just as other researchers might conduct their research in a skilled scientific or mathematical manner. For thoughtful methodological approaches to educational criticism and program or process evaluation, researchers Boughton, Eisner, and Ligtvoet's text *Evaluating and Assessing the Visual Arts in Education* (1996) is valuable reading. Stokrocki's innovative monograph *New Waves of Research in Art Education* (1995b) and LaPierre and Zimmerman's, (1997) text *Research Methods and Methodologies for Art Education* provide comprehensive overviews of methodological frameworks discussed in this chapter that have been relevant to art education research. The texts discuss methodologies for research involving testing and authentic assessment; generation of theoretical or metaphorical research frameworks or paradigms regarding art education; and several other qualitative research approaches including phenomenology, ethnography, visual sociology, and case study methodologies. Readers of these texts will encounter a discussion of various aspects of descriptive versus predictive methodology and a comprehensive review of historical methodology. Action research as methodology and feminist approaches to research design also are issues explored in these texts.

Several books and other studies about art teacher education have helped inform art education researchers how to investigate, record, analyze, and interpret data about art teacher education as well as how to report results. Yakel's book (1992), *The Future: Challenge of Change*, offers contemporary discourse on emerging issues in art teacher education and other areas of concern in the field of art education. The texts *Preservice Art Education: Issues and Practice* (Galbraith, 1995), *Preparing Teachers of Art* (Day, 1997), and *Real Lives: Art Teachers and the Cultures of School* (Anderson, 2000) offer several examples of contemporary methods used in research on art teacher education. Anderson's book, for example, allows us to look deeply into the lives of six art teachers through his field observations and their own narratives. It was his intent that readers gain a deeper theoretical understanding of teaching through patterns of meanings that emerged in their stories.

Several notable articles from the last decade published in the journal *Art Education* are exemplars of applied research regarding research methodologies and the content of art teacher education: Szekely (1990) on the construct of teaching as performance; Parks (1992) on the artistic model as a framework for teaching; Eisner (1993a) on a shifting paradigm for arts education research; Smith-Shank (1993) on narrative methods used in preservice elementary education; Ryder (1994) on linking college classrooms to the community; Zimmerman (1994a) on case studies of students reflecting concerns of preservice teachers; Keifer-Boyd (1996) on postmodern thinking and preservice art education; Bergman and Feiring (1997) on a model for collaborative team research; Ament (1998) on feminist approaches to art education; Geahigan (1998) on classroom applications of critical inquiry; Henry (1999a) on reflective practice for art student teachers; Leshnoff (1999) on applied research in elementary art classrooms; Yokley (1999) on critical pedagogy; and ending with an exposition on cultural competencies of art educators (Andrus, 2001). Andrus defines cultural competency as a critical component of art teacher education in which art teachers have examined their own biases and understandings about cultural diversity and made a commitment to pursue ongoing multicultural education for themselves as well as for their students.

I wish to note that the journal *Educational Researcher*, published by the American Educational Research Association, consistently contains excellent research about methodology for research about teacher education. Examples include Cochran-Smith and Lytle's studies, conducted 10 years apart (1990, 1999), on issues that divide research on teaching and teacher education. I commend them for providing philosophical and historical overviews of key issues in research on teacher education and then revisiting them a decade later; reconceptualizing and rethinking these issues in a contemporary context. Art education researchers could follow such a model with extant literature on art teacher preparation. Another exemplar is Zeichner's article (1999) on methodology for a new scholarship in teacher education research. The previously mentioned studies, and others of their caliber, should encourage art educators to begin to look outside literature directed only at art education for innovative methodological advances in research. Postmodern, poststructuralist, and semiotic approaches to research are beginning to surface in mainstream educational research literature about teacher education, but not in an accelerated way (Grauer, 1999; Jeffers, 2000b; Smith-Shank, 1995).

CREATING A FRAMEWORK FOR CLASSIFYING SELECTED RESEARCH BY ITS METHODOLOGY

In raising the question about which research design frameworks would best suit a comprehensive overview of research methodology for studies about art teacher education, many choices became apparent as evidenced in this discussion (Figure 22.1). This array of choices indicates a broad variance of perception for classification of art educational research methods by various research theorists.

In an analysis of recent and contemporary research methodology for studies about art teacher education, I found little evidence of empirical experimental research, although researchers still use empirical research employing descriptive methodology often. For example, over the last 2 decades, several comprehensive demographic studies about preservice teacher preparation and inservice education programs for teachers of art have surfaced (for example, Brewer, 1999a; Burton, 2001; Davis, 1990; Galbraith, 1997b; Jeffers, 1993a; Lampela, 2001; Newby & Carli, 1987; Rogers & Brogdon, 1990; Zimmerman, 1994a, 1994c, 1997b).

Beyond demographic and other descriptive statistical methodology in recent research literature about art teacher education, conceptual frameworks often emerged using the following research methods: phenomenological research, particularly regarding teacher attitudes and beliefs; hermeneutics; constructivist or naturalistic analyses such as ethnographies or case studies; connoisseurship; content or trend analysis; critical theory; feminist approaches to research; historical research; paradigm research; philosophical/theoretical research; action research; and collaborative research among theorists or with art teacher practitioners. A brief description of these various approaches is necessary to set the groundwork for classification by method-ology of current research centered on the preparation and continuing education of teachers of art.

The most helpful conceptual framework that I found for situating the "overarching pur-poses" (p. 191) of contemporary qualitative research methodology with choices of method was the recent work of Donmoyer (2001), wherein he matched (a) "truth-seeking purposes" with methods situated in grounded theory; (b) purposes of thick description to anthropolog-ical and ethnographic methods; (c) purposes of measuring change among entities (people, groups, organizations) over time with quasi-historical methods; (d) purposes of personal inter-pretation with educational connoisseurship; and (e) purposes of social change with feminist, collaborative, postmodern and action research methods.

SOME CONTEMPORARY METHODOLOGIES BRIEFLY DEFINED

Phenomenology

Phenomenological research is an approach, often used to gather and interpret data about teacher attitudes and beliefs wherein the researcher is let in on an individual's own understandings and realities. Phenomenology focuses on the philosophical notion of consciousness and how that affects our capacity for understanding factual knowledge. It also supports the role of individual perceptions and recollections in the creation of meaning (Greene, 1995; Grumet, 1992; Jeffers, 1991, 1992; Walker, 1996). Reflection on the nature of mental acts, therefore, has for its subject matter the phenomena of consciousness. Prejudices should be set aside so researchers may be free to examine issues they select to study.

Hermeneutics

The term *hermeneutics* is best explained as an art and science of interpretation. It is a philosoph-ical stance that provides a series of questions about interpretation basic to a particular mode of inquiry. Its original use focused on interpretation applied to sacred writings; however, it is still extant in the 20th century and is applied to notions of reality and interpretation of meaning (Gall et al., 1996; Hamblen, 1989). According to Carreiro (2002), two opposing hermeneuti-cal methods exist. He suggested that one method views interpretation from a scientific basis when it is used in historical and human sciences, whereas the other is based on the work of the philosopher Heidegger (1996), who described what is being understood historically as an interchange between an interpreter and a text. Maitland-Gholson and Ettinger (1994) also examined hermeneutic methodology and its application to research in art education based on their earlier research about text analysis as a methodology (Ettinger & Maitland-Gholson, 1990). A brief discussion of their conceptual framework regarding text analysis appears later in this chapter.

Constructivist or Naturalistic Analyses

A constructivist methodological approach ensures that the researcher not only views his or her own perceptions as constructed phenomena but also regards future readers' views and perceptions as their own constructed realities (Schwandt, 1994). According to Stake (1995b) "the researcher needs to decide what effort to make to understand what potential readers already know, how they construct the world, and how new data and new interpretations can facilitate that construction. It calls for new interpretations of interpretation" (p. 4). Based on the work of Nelson Goodman (1978), Stake was convinced that constructivist methodology, in its validation of interpretation by the researcher, seeks to unearth undiscovered realities in a dynamic relationship.

Ethnography, Ethnology, and Ethnomethodology

Ethnography is a form of qualitative and constructivist research methodologies. Bresler (1994, 1996) described ethnographic research as an in-depth means of discovering shared values, knowledge, and practices of one culture or a specific group of people. Occurring in naturalistic settings, data can be interpreted through political, artistic, cultural, and psychological as well as sociological or anthropological lenses (Eisner, 1991). Ethnography is a way to study a human culture's uniqueness, universality, and emerging patterns from within those features of that culture (Gall et al., 1996).

Ethnology, frequently found in anthropological studies, is most often used as a method to study similarities and differences between or among various cultures. The purpose of ethnological research is to develop theories of culture as a result of a comparative analysis of data from two or more naturalistic settings (Chalmers, 1981).

Ethnomethodology, another constructivist methodology that is often used in sociology, espouses the notion that reality is developed or interactive rather than fixed or merely experienced and that socially constructed realities are a result of social practices by members of a culture. In an ethnomethodological approach, the researcher carefully attends to data unfolding as a person's story is told. This research attempts to study ways that individuals attempt to make sense of their everyday social lives, particularly in the tasks of communicating and decision making (Gall et al., 1996).

Narrative and Visual Sociology

Stokrocki (1998), in her explanation of *ethnographic storytelling* as a form of narrative method, stated that this "research is a kind of unraveling of meanings that warp around each other and conceal their identity.... Researchers re-weave meanings back together again into some whole. The historical story is the warp and the cultural meanings are the weft" (p. 66). Zurmuehlen (1991) also conducted much of her research using narratives as methodology for research about experiential aspects of art teacher education (Ulbricht, 1998).

Stokrocki (1995b) also defined *visual sociology* as an arts-based research method such as the use of photography as research instrument for analysis, elicitation of accurate information from those subjects photographed, and artful interpretation of data with an ultimate goal of moving beyond discreet findings to a rich sense of the character or essence of the observed context. Green (2000) further explored ethical issues arising in uses of imagery in art education settings.

Case Studies

Case studies are in-depth analyses of individuals, groups, or settings. These studies use several data-retrieval and analysis techniques to gather and triangulate significant data including interview, video, participant observation, and artifact collection (Doyle, 1991; Galbraith, 1991; Stake, 1995a; Stokrocki, 1997). Case study research is becoming a prevalent methodology in art education research on teacher education in the form of single-case, multiple-case, and cross-site analyses. Interest in this method was apparent in reviewing studies from the last decade, particularly when research questions addressed model teaching, exemplary art teacher education, or teacher attitudes and preferences.

Connoisseurship and Educational Criticism

Both connoisseurship and educational criticism are approaches to research in which the researcher is able to apply theory through his or her perception of subtleties within complex social settings or interactions. The aspect of connoisseurship allows a researcher to be very aware of nuances within an educational program, and the aspect of educational criticism provides a means for a researcher to describe and evaluate the appreciated entity (Bresler, 1994; Gall et al., 1996).

Eisner (1991) indicated that researchers using connoisseurship as a methodological approach are "aware that we have antecedent knowledge that informs our abilities to conduct the research" and that researchers have an obligation "to critically examine assumptions and values into which they have been socialized." Gaining expertise for conducting research in this mode of inquiry comes with repeated experiences "in description, interpretation, and appraisal of educational situations," and researchers must have an ability to "appreciate various uses of different forms of representation" (p. 239).

Educational criticism is important as a complementary methodology to connoisseurship in that it draws on an inquiry model from art criticism (analysis, interpretation, evaluation, and thematics). It can be complex, is able to expand in several directions, and is effectively employed in evaluation research. Evaluation research differs from assessment research in that it is normative rather than descriptive. Evaluation research methodology is put into place when a researcher wishes to assess quality of programs, serve as a gatekeeper for that quality rating, find out the level of quality existing within a program, ascertain the level of performance that students have attained relative to the goals of the program, identify trends in student performance (strengths and weaknesses) for that program, and most importantly, illuminate teachers' perceptions about their own teaching performances as integral to a program (Boughton et al., 1996).

Critical Theory: Critical Social Theory

In the formulation of critical theory, many contemporary research theorists in education and art education (Blandy & Congdon, 1987; Emme, 1995; Freedman, 1994; Hicks, 1994; Kincheloe & McLaren, 2000; Nadaner, 1984; Stokrocki, 1997; Stuhr, 1994) ascertained that research and research contexts must be critiqued. The individual perceptions, beliefs, and values of both researcher and research subjects need to be recognized within collaborative efforts at interpretation and evaluation. Further, critical theory is based on a set of principles that attempt to identify and critique relationships of power and resulting areas of oppression in social settings. According to Carreiro (2002),

> This methodology grapples with the social, political, cultural, economic, ethnic, and gender factors which shape the structures that are taken as "real" and immutable. The researcher and the researched are assumed to be interactively linked, with the values of the investigator influencing the inquiry. In critical theory the distinction between ontology and epistemology seen in positivism and post positivism gives way to a view that what can be known is intertwined with the interaction between a particular researcher and the particular group under study. (p. 2)

In actions beyond critique, critical social theory provides grounding for critical pedagogy, which is an opportunity for those identified as oppressed to experience possible emancipation from oppression and empowerment through their collaboration with researchers and teachers in the formation of knowledge (Giroux, 1988; Yokley, 1999). I have observed that action research efforts based on critical social theory are becoming increasingly more frequent in published art education literature. Although a thorough discussion of this trend is beyond the space limits of this chapter, the *Journal of Social Theory in Art Education*, an NAEA publication, is a worthwhile source of investigation for studies based on critical social theory.

Critical Theory: Feminist Approaches to Research

Defined at its most concrete level, feminist research is conducted by women, directed toward women and women's issues as subject matter in its content and research questions, and is often targeted for a female audience (Blaikie, 1992). It in its zeal to be part of the changing landscape of notions of culture, moving from canons that are fixed and immutable to cannons that are live and agents of social change, feminist research methodology perhaps initiated some intellectual waves of consideration regarding ontological and epistemological issues in research (Collins, 1977; Garber, 1992; Irwin, 1997a; Oleson, 1994; Sandell, 1997; Zimmerman, 1990). Feminist methodology encompasses new and valid interpretations and perhaps has allowed researchers to solidly confront sexism in content and to challenge male-centered educational contexts in the field of art education (Ament, 1998). Feminist research, although often conducted collaboratively (for example, Sandell, Collins, & Sherman, 1985; Thurber & Zimmerman, 1996), is not typically recognized by specific methods used within its approach. Rather, selected methods remain somewhat unique to questions posed as they do in other research methods just discussed (Collins & Sandell, 1995, 1997). Sandell (1979, 1997) applied theoretical constructs from feminist research to arrive at an understanding of the nature of feminist pedagogy and its ramifications in teacher education and art education classrooms.

Historical Research

Historical research about art teacher education serves to inform theorists and practitioners of art education about chronologies, key persons, events or issues, what they meant in their own time, and what they might mean today (Korzenik, 1985; Smith, 1995). Stankiewicz (1997) proposed that two processes operate in historical research: compilation of facts and shaping of findings into credible patterns of interpretation. Four styles of investigation usually are operant in historical research methodology. They include (a) a *realistic* approach, whereby the researcher seeks accurate facts as the focus of investigation; (b) a *formal* stance, through which an investigator is concerned with an order or structure that he or she can construct from analysis of past events; (c) an *expressive* mode, where the investigator is interested in making a critical interpretive statement about selected events from the past; and (d) a *pragmatic* interpretation, which is concerned with the past in order to confront issues and problems of the present (Erickson, 1985). Strategies for this methodology are drawn from historical or art historical strategies for data gathering and interpretation. Histories may be oral, written, or visual. As in all historical research endeavors, external criticism focuses on authenticity and originality of documents and artifacts when possible and internal criticism focuses on credibility of or believability of the source.

Paradigm Research

According to Carroll (1995), paradigms are "constellations of beliefs, values, laws and practices that govern practice and theory" and they tend to separate the larger community into discreet rather than connected social contexts. The methodology of paradigm analysis is important because art educators do not often have an awareness of influences, values, and circumstances that influence their own behaviors. She further stated: "More than a method of examining the status quo of a professional community, paradigmatic research is concerned about the structure of revolution and change" (p. 41). A research paradigm directs an investigator's approach to studying essential properties and structures of being and meaning. This method requires research skills similar to those of content analysis, but the difference is that the researcher wants to know why certain educational communities understand reality in the ways that they do. Carroll affirmed that this methodology provides an occasion for rich dialog across separate communities of discourse.

Philosophical/Theoretical Research

Conceptual, theoretical, or philosophical research (Jansen, 1995; May, 1992) is a way to organize and make sense out of complex connections from a variety of sources in any given context. Geahigan (1992) suggested that this form of research is a means whereby researchers not only critique educational discourse but also generate new learning or constructs about knowledge. He encouraged art educators to become more grounded in philosophical knowledge and processes about teaching and other aspects of education. Lankford (1992) argued that philosophical stances aim to justify our reasons for being, clarify our ideas, synthesize those ideas, make recommendations, and raise key questions. He defined theory as a "synthesis of ideas and research whose purpose is to provide a thorough account of some subject or phenomenon" (p. 198). Wilson (1994, 1997a) called for a more coherent effort in conducting research within the art education community. He suggested that research has potential to have a greater impact than currently experienced by being an agent for creation and evolution of theory in visual arts education. Theory, therefore, can be generated or proven. In recent years, it appears that generation of theory rather than refutation of theory has become more prevalent in research methodology related to art teacher education.

Content Analysis

Content analysis focuses on research directed at any recorded documentation within a specified context that is deemed to be authentic and valid. Such documentation includes texts, videos, diaries, stories, and other artifacts. After collection, data are analyzed and interpreted. The intent is to identify trends, emergent themes, possible conceptual frameworks, or theories as a result of analysis. Ettinger and Maitland-Gholson (1990) offered a framework for deconstructing text or textual objects from several dimensions. They ascertained that analysis of text was a valuable means of interpreting complex data. Their conceptual framework included a continuum of five orientations to text that determined meaning of the text(s) being defined. Five orientations included literal, classic content, semantic, structural, and hermeneutic approaches. Across these orientations, the role of the researcher shifts from expert, to objective describer, to model maker of internal contextual connections, to revealer of ideological generative codes, and finally, to rebuilder and receiver of meaning. Deconstructed into eight dimensions across each of the five orientations, the framework draws on the fields of psychology, sociology, education, philosophy, linguistics, anthropology, and literary criticism. The eight dimensions address such issues regarding text such as underlying assumptions, functions of text, roles of researchers, and historical origins.

Action Research and Other Collaborative Research

Action research presents practitioners as well as research scholars with opportunities to explore ways to become active critics of the shape and direction of their own learning as well as to improve practice for the education of others (Bresler, 1994; Irwin, 1997b). Research methodology is most often naturalistic, in which collected data, in the forms of interviews, participant observation field notes, video recording, photography, content analysis of reflective journals, and other artifacts, are analyzed and interpreted for emergent themes and issues that could initiate change or improvement within the research context. According to May (1993a, 1993b), these emergent issues are more significant than technical problem solving. In a recent review of research in art classrooms conducted since the 1960s, Colbert and Taunton (2001) found that much remains to be done in attempts at research within three areas of content: social contexts of art classrooms, portraits of effective teachers and competent learners, and planned instructional interventions. They, and other researchers (Hanes & Schiller, 1994; Irwin, 2000; Pankratz, 1989), encouraged collaborative methods of conducting action research as opposed to further idiosyncratic initiatives in art classroom contexts.

DISCUSSION OF THE METHOD FOR CATEGORIZING SELECTED STUDIES ACCORDING TO THEIR METHOD OF INVESTIGATION

After reading several research classifications or analyses of methodology in research texts, I decided to highlight the most frequently appearing categories as they emerged in a literature search of art education research. Those recurrences ultimately formed the basis for categorization of methodology and reporting research in this chapter. Thus, a review of the extant research literature informed the decision of which classifications to include.

My investigation of many worthwhile studies was greatly enhanced by looking at significant theme categories for research in art teacher education. Major themes now emerging in research on art teacher education call for appropriate research designs or methods. In the NAEA Research Agenda (Zimmerman, 1994b), research parameters are described for art teacher education as follows. I selected a few exemplary studies relative to their methodology for purposes of illustration of each thematic content area:

- Purposes, policies, and structure of teacher education programs (Duncum, 2001)
- Issues concerning preservice preparation of art teachers (Brewer, 1999a; Grauer, 1998; Short, 1993, 1995)
- Issues concerning inservice professional development of art teachers (Eisner, 1995a; Jeffers, 1994; Duncum, 1999)
- Alternative certification standards (Henry, 1999b)
- Lab and clinical experiences (Bullock & Galbraith, 1992)
- Post-baccalaureate certification and education (Anderson, Eisner, & McRorie, 1998)
- Diversity, special populations, and teacher education programs (Guay, 1993, 1994)
- Art teacher preparation for alternative settings—community centers, museums, or other public spaces (Stone, 1993)

Several research questions about art teacher preparation have appeared in research about art teacher education in the last 2 decades. These recurring questions can guide current researchers in their selection of content and appropriate methods for research (for example, Bolin, 1988; Chapman, 1982; Davis, 1990; Day, 1997; Doyle, 1990; Eisner, 1995a; Galbraith, 1996a, 1996b; Goodlad, 1990c; Henry, 1999b; Kowalchuk, 1999; May, 1993b; Zimmerman, 1994b, 1996). These broad questions include:

1. What do art teachers teach? (content: the disciplines of art, interdisciplinary content and art)
2. How do art teachers teach? (method: practices in art education including technology, learning and development, curriculum, and evaluation)

3. Why do art teachers teach? What do art teachers believe? (philosophy and perception)
4. Who do art teachers teach? (contexts and populations for teaching)
5. How well do teachers teach? (evaluation of a variety of factors; for example, effectiveness of teacher education programs or teacher leadership profiles)
6. Where did art teachers learn to teach? In traditional or nontraditional programs? How well prepared were they? (preservice practices and policies)
7. What should happen to keep them prepared? (inservice practices and policies including use of technologies, issues of diversity, integration of the arts into core curriculum—all challenges in art teacher education)
8. What are barriers to the preparation of teachers of art? (effects of culture and community on art teacher preparation)
9. What historical trends have occurred in art teacher preparation? (standards and licensing, use of portfolio, etc.)
10. What can art teachers teach the field about art teacher preparation? (reflective practice, teacher stories as research)
11. How, what, and why have art teachers conducted (or not conducted) certain types of research? What new types of research would enhance art teacher education? (teachers as researchers)
12. What are future directions for the preparation of teachers of art?

REPORTING, ANALYSIS, AND INTERPRETATION OF DATA

What are the findings? What do these findings suggest? What implications emerge for art teacher preparation and professional development as a result of research highlighted in this overview? These questions surfaced as this author was constructing the content framework of this chapter regarding methodology.

One professional arena in which many art educators participate, but do not make a written or published research contribution to the field, is the annual NAEA convention. Some written information regarding details about presentations is available, but detailed descriptions of proposed research, in whatever form they take, are not the norm. Based on self-reported descriptions of methodology used to create presentations and categorized by group or caucus affiliation, some interesting trends surfaced in a comparison of conferences held in 1992, 1997 (75th anniversary of NAEA), and 2001. A sample of three conferences was chosen to compare recurring issues and methods in the past decade. In 1992, 534 sessions were held with 92 sessions (17% of them) focusing on some aspect of art teacher education. In 1997, 622 sessions included 88 teacher education sessions or 14% of the total. The 2001 conference held 748 sessions with 19% (142) of them focusing on teacher preparation and professional development. Across the 3 years reported, only 9 sessions were devoted to expositions of methodology, with 6 of those occurring in 1997. No sessions were apparent that focused on experimental research design. The highest frequency of methodology reported was in the area of program or process description followed by sessions devoted to policy discussion or model development.

Nearly two dozen affiliate and partner groups coexist in NAEA. Within those groups, 3 affiliate groups reported the highest frequency of sessions, among other groups, on preservice or inservice art education. They were *Higher Education*, followed by *Research*, then *Elementary Education*. This ranking was consistent, and not surprising, across the 3 years reviewed. In 2001, a "Teacher Preparation Series" was featured as part of the conference agenda, with 22 sessions devoted to teacher education under that specific categorization. However, 16 of those were offered on the final morning of the conference. Also in 2001, nine student–member sessions regarding preservice art teacher preparation were held—up from 1 presentation in

1997 and 2 sessions in 1992. I regard that as a positive sign for the future of developing new research scholars in the field.

Categories of methodology that surfaced in this analysis are listed across the top row of Table 22.1. All presentations were considered with the exception of meal functions and business meetings. Issues forums and program descriptions had the potential to stimulate healthy interchanges at these conferences. It is possible, with some direction or mentoring, that these informal encounters could develop into written and permanent research contributions to the field, much as is done at AERA annual conferences (via *Educational Researcher, Arts in Learning Journal*, and online summaries of annual conference proceedings and abstracts).

In a review of 4 decades of *Studies in Art Education*, reports from Brewer (1999b), Chalmers (1999), Chapman (1999), and Collins (1999) indicated an apparent shift in published research methodology in the field of art education. Chalmers reflected that during the first decade of the publication (1959–1969), "one type of research seemed to count more than others and perhaps more than it does today" (p. 3). He referred to the scientific paradigm and empirical research so common in that decade and prior to paradigm shifts in research methodology. According to Chapman (p. 8), of the 245 entries for the decade 1979 to 1989, twenty-five articles were editorials, but more than half the remaining ones were empirical studies (with three-fourths of those being descriptive and one-fourth experimental). Within that total of empirical studies, 38 were about teachers and teaching and one half of those were experimental. One third of the total entries constituted philosophical inquiry, and nine historical studies and two commentaries were found. New perspectives about methods began to appear in this collection, for example, with feminist views (Collins, 1977; Sandell, 1979) and sociological/anthropological approaches to research (Chalmers, 1978). Chapman suggested that another important shift occurred—that in this decade, some research "foreshadowed concern about the voice of the researcher, how it shapes and expresses values beyond the research itself" (p. 11).

Brewer discussed the impact of discipline-based art education on teaching and its research content and methods. In his overview of seminal research regarding methods during the decade, Brewer selected three studies to highlight emerging methodology. He noted Beittel (1979), who challenged researchers to reconcile truth, language, and method in art education research, recognizing that art and its contexts is not value free and can have primal meaning in people's lives. Brewer highlighted Chalmers (1981) for his anthropological stance about research. He suggested a method modeled after ethnographers who study art and artifacts in a given culture in order to understand and appreciate the culture and its art. The third study stressed the importance of empirical evidence, involving testing and systematic evaluation (Hoepfner, 1984).

In Collins's overview of the decade 1989 to 1998, she indicated that of the 156 articles published during that time in *Studies*, 67 were theoretical, 56 were empirical, 16 were historical in methodological approach, and 17 were reviews of literature. She reflected:

> Perhaps a bit light on the empirical side, but from my point of view not too terribly so. Perhaps though there has been some talk of late about our research moving away from methodologies associated with the physical sciences to those associated with the social sciences and literary criticism, the empirical studies published during this period appear to be pretty evenly divided between those that are primarily quantitative and those that are primarily quantitative. If one sometimes gets the feeling that social concerns are beginning to outweigh subject matter concerns, if you're counting, articles published during this time period strike a pretty fair balance between those related to DBAE subject matter concerns and those that emphasize what might be called social critical perspective. (pp. 19–20)

She indicated that in her review of content for the studies previously cited, preservice and inservice art education for teachers proved to be the least prevalent topic of concern.

TABLE 22.1

Summary of Presentations on Teacher Preparation/Education at NAEA Reported by Method and Top Three Group Affiliations for Years 1992, 1997, and 2001

Year	NAEA Affiliation	Total	Program/ Project Description	Content Analysis	Historical/ Auto-biography	Process Description	Action Research	Quantitative Studies	Theoretical/ Philosophical/ Model Development/ Policy	Issues Forum	Interviews/ Narratives/ Case Study	Demographic Surveys	Methodology
1992	Higher education	29	5			6	1		8	5	3	1	
	Other	40							8				
	Research	13	4			1			1	1	2	1	1
	Elementary	10			1	3			7		2	1	1
1997	Higher education	32	13	1		5	2				2		
	Other	33			2				3	2	5	2	4
	Research	18	2			1					1	2	1
	Elementary	5		1									1
2001	Teacher preparation series	22	6			3	3		2	3	3		
	Higher education	27	7		1	7	1		9	1	1		
	Other	66											
	Research	16	3	1	3	6	3		4	1	2	1	1
	Elementary	11	3							2			

In the years prior to 1992, several studies appearing in *Studies in Art Education* contributed to the knowledge base about useful methodology for researchers in the area of teacher preparation. Chalmers (1981) explored the concept of art education as ethnology, and Rush and Kratochwill (1981) defined strategies for examining human behavior in classroom settings using descriptive research. Degge (1982) further examined patterns of inquiry used by classroom teachers. Part of Volume 26 of *Studies in Art Education* was devoted to historical research as a valid methodology, wherein Korzenik (1985) offered insights about quality historical research for preservice art education. Ettinger (1987), citing a tremendous increase in ethnographic research over the previous 20-year period (1966–1986), reinforced shifting trends in art education research by creating a taxonomy that defined styles of on-site descriptive research found in 31 existing studies. Text analysis and hermeneutics in art education research was also presented by Ettinger and Maitland-Gholson (1990) as previously discussed in the chapter.

Table 22.2 represents a classification by author and methodology of research about art teacher education in the journal *Studies in Art Education* published from 1992 to 2001. Note that out of concern for the length of this chapter, full citations for Table 22.2 (and Table 22.3) are not included in the reference section. The categories for classification in Table 22.2 surfaced as a result of reviewing each study for its approach and research design and creating an aggregate of those classifications. In terms of numbers of studies conducted, demographic studies—mostly surveys—are followed by conceptual/theoretical research in frequency of publication. Case study research, as well as other qualitative methods, is maintaining a steady presence in the journal. Very little historical or quantitative methodology was apparent across the decade's volumes.

Applying a similar categorization process to *Visual Arts Research*, one does not see a flurry of research activity devoted to art teacher preparation or inservice education in this publication, nor is there any emerging pattern of methodology used across six recent volumes (1996–2001). Perhaps if any claim can be made, historical research maintained a healthy presence relative to other methodologies during the target years.

In what research methodologies are new PhD's trained? This author would encourage continued tracking and dissemination of working papers presented yearly at NAEA conferences by graduate students from around the globe (Thunder-McGuire, 1997). One might assume that new researchers would continue to use methods in which they had developed some comfort in their graduate school or doctoral experience. However, it is hoped that their proposed research questions and content, as well as their knowledge of a wide variety of research protocols, will serve as primary determiners of methodology. Ideally, if content is informed by current issues in the disciplines of art and art education practice, recent graduates in art education should be familiar with an array of methodological approaches as they begin their work. In a recent survey of the most prestigious doctoral programs in art education, Anderson, Eisner, and McRorie (1998) reported that some responding institutions were unable to accurately describe methodological approaches required in their graduates' course of study. An interesting follow up to the previously mentioned findings about methodology in art teacher research would be a comparative study targeting national and international universities comparing what methods dominate the research that is being conducted. Another interesting and potential meta-analysis would be to design a study comparing data presented in this chapter and similar data from the descriptive research of research trends described a decade ago by Thompson and Hardiman (1991).

What current trends in methodology are research faculty and their doctoral or master's candidates using in research about art teacher education? Does mentoring occur between faculty and their students as evidenced in similar or parallel methodological choices in their individual research? For example, in Anderson et al.'s (1998) aforementioned study, Penn State University was ranked as one of the three most prestigious graduate institutions for art teacher education in the United States. Their online information site (Penn State University, 2002) profiles the research interests of their faculty as well as those of nine current doctoral candidates. Doctoral

TABLE 22.2

Classification of Methods Found in Studies on Art Teacher Preparation/Education From the Journal *Studies in Art Education*

	Vol. 33 1991–1992	Vol. 34 1992–1993	Vol. 35 1993–1994	Vol. 36 1994–1995	Vol. 37 1995–1996	Vol. 38 1996–1997	Vol. 39 1997–1998	Vol. 40 1998–1999	Vol. 41 1999–2000	Vol. 42 2000–2001
Quantitative: Experimental Research Designs	33(1), 7–20 Ellingson, S. P. [PS]									
Quantitative: Descriptive Research Demographic Surveys Unless otherwise noted		34(4), 233–243 Jeffers, C. S. [PS]	35(4), 228–236 Lampela, L. [NA] 35(3), 157–170 Freedman, K. [IS][a] 35(1), 45–54 Stone, D. L. [IS] 35(2), 79–89 Zimmerman, E. [PS]	36(1), 44–56 Guay, D. M. [IS] 36(2), 84–95 Mims, S. K. & Lankford, E. L. [IS]	37(2), 101–114 Jeffers, C. S. [IS] 37(4), 226–244 Makin, L.; White, M. & Owen, M. [IS]	38(1) 34–49 Williams, B. L. [IS]	39(4), 350–370 Grauer, K. [IS][a] 39(2), 183–186 Burton, D. [PS]	40(1), 8–5 Anderson, T.; Eisner, E., & McRorie, S. [PS/IS] 40(2), 162–179 Beck, R. J.; Martinez, M. E., & Lires, V. [PS]	41(1), 61–70 Brewer, T. M. [IS]	42(2), 131–145 Burton, D. [IS] 42(2), 146–162 Lampela, L. [IS][a] 42(2), 163–181 Galbraith, L. [IS]
Casual Comparative or Correlational Research Design	33(1), 21–35 Kakas, K. M. [IS]	34(4), 209–221 Armstrong, C. [IS] (ID by author, 'pre-experimental')					39(1), 57–73 Jeffers, C. S. [PS/IS]			
Philosophical/ Theoretical/ Conceptual/Model Development or Paradigm Research/Policy Studies	33(4), 226–243 May, W. [NA][a] 33(4), 210–225 Garber, E. [NA][a] 33(4), 195–200 Lankford, L. [NA][a]	34(2), 114–126 May, W. [PS/IS]	35(3), 179–187 Blandy, D. [PS][a] 35(4), 197–208 Wilson, B. [NA] 35(3), 135–148 May, W. T. [NA] 35(3), 149–156 Hicks, L. E. [NA] 35(3), 171–178 Stuhr, P. [NA][a]	36(1), 18–27 Maitland-Gholson, J., & Ettinger, L. [NA][a]	37(4), 245–252 Templeton, D. [NA][a] Bresler		39(2), 187 Zimmerman, E. [PS] 39(3), 271–280 MacGregor, R. N. [NA] 39(3), 270 Brewer, T. [NA] 39 (4), 293–308 Geahigan, G. [IS]	40(3), 279–283 Pariser, D. [NA][a] 40(4), 377–380 Congdon, K. G. [PS][a] 40(1), 26–27 Stankiewicz, M. [NA]	41(3), 197–201 Brewer, T. M. [PS, IS] 41(4), 87–91 LaPierre, S. [NA]	

	33	34	35	36	37	38	39	40	41	42
Historical Research (includes biography and autobiography)					37(3), 170–183 Smith, P. [IS]		39(1), 24–36 Marché, T. [IS]	40(2), 114–127 Smith, P. [NA]		42(1), 51–66 Marché, T. [NA] 42(4), 318–332 Eldridge, L. [NA]
Evaluation Studies (includes program or process analyses)										
Critical Analysis/Connoisseurship										
Text or Trend Analysis		34(3), 189–191 Stokrocki, M. [NA] (Book Review)	35(2), 121–123 Gray, J. [NA] (Book Review)					Pariser[a] (Book Review) Condon[a] (Book Review)	LaPierre[a] (Book Review)	
Case Study Research Qualitative single or Multiple-Site Studies.	33(2), 86–97 Bullock, A. L., & Galbraith, L. [IS] 33(3), 174–185 Zimmerman, E. [IS]	34(4), 222–232 Guay, D. M. [IS]	35(4), 218–227 Hanes, J. M., & Schiller, M. [PS/IS][a]	36(3), 154–169 Short, G. [PS]	37(2), 80–91 Walker, S. [PS/IS][a] 37(2), 92–100 Galbraith, L. [PS/IS]		39(1), 37–56 Anderson, R. [IS] 39(4), 321–335 White, B. [PS][a] Grauer		41(2), 130–145 Hafeli, M. [IS]	
Other Qualitative Traditions (includes ethnography, cross-site analysis, narratives, analysis, phenomenology, hermeneutics, semiotics, etc.				36(3), 170–188 Stout, C. [PS]	37(3), 160–169 McSorley. J. [IS] (phenom-onography)	38(4), 232–245 Wolfe, P. [IS]			41(1), 71–90 Kowalchuk, E. A., [PS] 41(2), 100–113 Morris, C. B.; Mirin, K.; & Rizzi, C. [IS]	

(Continued)

TABLE 22.2
(Continued)

	Vol. 33 1991–92	Vol. 34 1992–93	Vol. 35 1993–94	Vol. 36 1994–95	Vol. 37 1995–96	Vol. 38 1996–97	Vol. 39 1997–98	Vol. 40 1998–99	Vol. 41 1999–00	Vol. 42 2000–01
Action Research (includes teachers as researchers; collaborative research)			Hanes & Schiller[a]		Galbraith[a]				41(2), 146–163 James, P. [PS]	Lampela, L.[a]
Contemporary Research Method Lenses: Feminist, Gay/Lesbian/ Bisexual/ Transgendered, Post Modern, Critical/Social Reconstruction Theory, etc.	Garber[a]		May[a] Hicks[a] Blandy[a] Freedman[a] Stuhr[a]	36(2), 69–83 Collins, G. C. [NA]						
Significant Research about Methodology		May[a]		Maitland-Gholson & Ettinger	37(3), 133–144 Bresler, L. [NA]					

[a]Indicates a study already placed in one category above. Code: PS, = preservice focus; IS, = inservice focus; NA, = not specifically assigned.

TABLE 22.3

Classification of Methods Found in *Visual Arts Research* Studies on Preservice and Inservice Art Teacher Preparation/Education (1994–2000)

	Vol. 20 1994	Vol. 21 1995	Vol. 22 1996	Vol. 23 1997	Vol. 24 1998	Vol. 25 1999	Vol. 26 2000
(1) Experimental Research Designs Quantitative							26(2), 29–39 Kowalchuk, E. A., & Stone, D.
(2) Descriptive Research Designs Quantitative (demographic surveys unless otherwise noted)		21(1), 76–81 Stone, D. L.	22(1), 62–78 Alper, M. V.	23(2), 63–70 Schwartz, K. A.			
(3) Philosphical/Theoretical/ Conceptual/Model Development/Paradigm Research/Policy Studies				23(2), 52–62 Day, G., Gillespie M., Rosenberg, M., Sowell, J., Thurber, F.	24(2), 27–32 Deviston-Trochta, G. H.		
(4) Historical Research (includes biography and autobiography)				23(2), 124–134 Crespin, L., & Hartung, E.	24(2), 56–60 Ulbright, J.	25(1), 2–6 Chalmers, G. 25(1), 7–13 Chapman, L. 25(1), 14–18 Brewer, T. M. 25(1), 19–26 Collins, G. C.	
(5) Evaluation Studies (includes program or process analyses)/ Critical Analysis/ Connoisseurship				Day et al.[a]			

(*Continued*)

TABLE 22.3
(Continued)

	Vol. 20 1994	Vol. 21 1995	Vol. 22 1996	Vol. 23 1997	Vol. 24 1998	Vol. 25 1999	Vol. 26 2000
(6) Text or Trend Analysis						Chalmers[a] Chapman[a] Brewer[a] Collins[a]	
(7) Case Study Research Single-Multiple-Site Studies				23(1), 1–30 Graham, J.			26(2), 40–50 Wilson, T., & Clark, G. 26(1), 38–52 Guay, D. M.
(8) Other Qualitative Traditions (includes ethnography, ethnomethodology, cross-site analysis, narrative research, phenomenology, hermeneutics, semiotics)		21(1), 51–62 Stokrocki, M., & White, I. 21(2), 66–74 Hawke, D.			24(2), 61–66 Stokrocki, M.	25(1), 69–85 Kowalchuk, E. 25(2), 69–78 Stinson, S.	
(9) Action Research includes teachers as researchers and collaborative research)	20(1), 1–19 Bresler, L.						
(10) Contemporary Research Method Lenses: Feminist, G/L/B/T, Postmodern, Critical Social Theory, etc.							
(11) Significant Research About Methodolgy	Bresler[a]						26(2), 80–87 Anderson, T.

[a]Indicates placement in primary category but serves in another well.

TABLE 22.4
Frequency of Dissertations About Art Teacher Education Within Art Education Dissertations
as Reported in *Visual Arts Research*, Volumes 20–26

Year	1994	1995	1996	1997	1998	1999	2000	Total
Total Reported Teacher Education	78	64	106	80	121	27	75	551
as Focus	8	13	19	10	19	2	16	87
Percent of Teacher Education Dissertations	10.2%	20.3%	17.9%	12.5%	15.7%	7.4%	21.3%	Mean 14.5%

students' research included use of the following methodologies: development of conceptual frameworks; theoretical discourse grounded in contemporary critical theory, aesthetics, or cultural geography; case study; dramatic performance as research process; historical investigation; and ethnographic study.

During the period from 1994 to 2000, five hundred fifty-one art education dissertations were reported in the United States, and 87 of those focused on art teacher preparation or education. In Table 22.4, the frequency of dissertations about art teacher education is described from the pool of art education dissertations reported during 1994 to 2000. The mean for the frequency of those studies about teacher education occurring across those years was 14.5%.

In gathering data, I discovered that some abstracts were complete and clear in describing methodology applied to the study, whereas others were vague or unclear about reporting their design. However, Table 22.4 and Table 22.5 are offered to signify general trends in methodology

TABLE 22.5
Methodology for Dissertations About Art Teacher Education as Reported in *Visual Arts Research*,
Volumes 20–26

Year	Ethnographic Studies/ Narratives/ Teacher Perceptions etc.	Case Studies	Experimental/ Empirical Studies	Descriptive: Demographic Survey	Historical/ Biographical/ Autobiographical	Theoretical/ Philosophical/ Model Development	Process/ Program Evaluations	Total
1994	6	2						8
1995	6	3		1	1		2	13
1996	5	4		3	3	2	2	19
1997	4				1	4	1	10
1998	8	5		1	2	2	1	19
1999	1	1						2
2000	7	4				2	3	16
Total	37	19	0	5	7	10	9	87

relative to teacher education as research content. As a result of the overview, it became apparent that qualitative methods including case study research were most preferred. No evidence of experimental methodology was encountered. Some studies contained mixed designs but fell primarily into one major category.

PROFILES OF RESEARCHERS WHO USE CONTEMPORARY RESEARCH METHODOLOGY TO FOCUS ON IMPROVEMENT OF ART TEACHER PREPARATION THEORY AND PRACTICE

In considering possible future research initiatives, I reviewed research from several notable contemporary education researchers who not only eloquently address research questions regarding education for all teachers but also successfully model contemporary research methods as their conceptual studies unfold. Theoretical and philosophical contributions to an evolving research paradigm, reflective of the seminal work in art education research of John Dewey (1934) and Ken Beittel (1973, 1979), are found in the work of Eliot Eisner (1979, 1993a, 1993b, 1995a), John Goodlad (1990a, 1990b, 1991), and Maxine Greene (1986, 1993, 1995). Beyond the previously cited research, these scholars have contributed an extensive array of seminal research to the fields of art and education.

Several exemplary researchers of teacher education in art are currently informing the knowledge base about contemporary methodology (as well as conducting studies within those methodologies). The following roster is by no means fully comprehensive because several other notable art education scholars are conducting significant research in closely allied areas of content as well. Also, those mentioned herein continue to use other methodological approaches than those mentioned later, and the citations that follow represent only a small selection from their completed work.

Those scholars whose publication record and other evidence of scholarly leadership indicate an understanding of contemporary methodology and a repeated exploration of issues regarding preservice and/or inservice teacher education—and often in publications outside the field of art education as well as inside—include: Thomas Brewer (1999a, 1999b) and David Burton (1998, 2001), for descriptive approaches; Georgia Collins (1977, 1999) and Renee Sandell (1979; Collins & Sandell, 1995), for feminist approaches to methodology; Lynn Galbraith (1991, 1995), for case study methodology and other qualitative methods; Wanda May (1993a, 1993b), for action research and collaborative approaches; Mary Ann Stankiewicz (1997), for historical methods in research; Mary Stokrocki (1995a, 1995b, 1997) and Carol Jeffers (1993b, 1994, 2000), for constructivist and phenomenological approaches to research including narratives; and Sharon LaPierre (LaPierre & Diket, 1995; LaPierre, 1997), Brent Wilson (1994, 1997a, 1997b), and Enid Zimmerman (1994b, 1996, 1997b), for explication of appropriate theoretical research frameworks about art teacher education and issues of performance assessment for teachers. F. Graeme Chalmers (1978, 1981), Kit Grauer (1998, 1999, 2000), Rita Irwin (1997a, 1997b), and Ron MacGregor (MacGregor & Hawke, 1982; MacGregor, 1998), Canadian art education researchers, have informed art education's research field about ethnographic and also innovative arts-based research in their studies about art teacher education. They continue to work collaboratively with several postsecondary colleagues and K-12 teacher researchers (both in the United States and in the United Kingdom) and are models for other researchers who wish to approach research via research team methodology in the future (Irwin, Rogers, & Wan, 1999).

Since the inception of NAEA Foundation research awards, several of the previously cited researchers have benefited from the funding initiative. One recent research award was given to Galbraith and Grauer for a proposed study on preservice art generalists who teach art. No research grants for teacher education were awarded in the round of proposals that took place in 2001.

CONCLUSIONS AND RECOMMENDATIONS

Based on this discussion of research—frequency, value of the research (idiosyncratic or long term), rigor, and the relation of research to praxis, I make the following recommendations. Art educators in general and art education researchers in particular need to:

1. Pay more attention to emerging or shifting trends in methodology found in general educational research about teacher preparation and inservice education (McKean, 2001). Institutions that are responsible for teacher preparation in art education need to do a better job of encouraging their students, both undergraduate and graduate, to become familiar with literature in sociology, anthropology, psychology, other arts, and philosophy. Studies whose research base included research from these areas were thicker and richer in framing the studies. Institutions teaching research methods also should include in their content such contemporary approaches to research as critical theory, queer theory, feminist methodology, semiotics, and so forth.

2. Expand and connect research, drawing on certain methods used successfully by prior art education researchers. There needs to be more connection and preparation with past endeavors rather than idiosyncratic attempts at studies that are not based on the history of research in art education.

3. Increase collaboration among researchers in conducting research. In the review of research studies in this chapter, most were written by single authors or by a pair of researchers, with some notable exceptions.

4. Increase interaction among researchers from university settings and pre-K-12 institutions to produce findings to inform teacher education theory and practice (Manley-Delacruz, 1997; May, 1994).

5. Develop methodology for research on the merging of content from visual art education with content issues from the other arts, interdisciplinary content, multicultural and cross-cultural issues (La Pierre, Stokrocki, & Zimmerman, 2000), and moral dimensions of teaching as they integrate with content for art teacher preparation programs (Goodlad, 1994).

6. Promote action research created by art teachers in K-12 classrooms. This is not a new phenomenon. Many researchers (Degge, 1982; Irwin, 1997b; May, 1993) have encouraged their colleagues and students to participate in action research in the art education field. Their views are supported by Seidel (2001), in a recent report from an AERA symposium on research in arts education, and by Greene (1995). According to Greene, such research may "be a provoking of dialogues within the classroom space" (p. 26).

7. Explore uses of digital media and Internet technology to further communication and collaboration between and among researchers and practitioners interested in the art education of teachers (Keifer-Boyd, 1996). For example, in a recent review of available online resources about research in art teacher education, I encountered a theoretically based study by Duncum (2001) on the relationship between global culture and the practice of art education in classrooms. His research, revealed through his choices about contemporary methodology, is

hopefully just the beginning of a new wave of accessible research and opportunity for disseminating significant global research about art teacher education.

8. Make a concerted effort to publish research about art teacher education in journals related to education but outside the field of art education. Other researchers may offer insights to the work of art education if they had easier access to such specialized literature (e.g., Jeffers, 2000a; Thurber, 1997; Zimmerman, 1991).

FUTURE DIRECTIONS

1. In a recent AERA research symposium, a group of well-known researchers debated the merits and challenges of using fiction as a methodological framework for conducting innovative and artful research (Hussey et al., 2001). This discussion, and others like it, is opening up new visions for the nature of acceptable research methodology. Although a thorough discussion of arts-based research is outside the limits of this chapter, active involvement by art education researchers in active research groups such as AERA's Arts in Learning special interest group will be an asset to the future development of cutting-edge methods for art education.

2. As paradigms in education continue to shift, researchers and art teachers will need to collaborate more and to communicate more often to others the results of their collaborations. The NAEA Teacher Education Task Force has developed an interactive Web site (Krug, 2002) that includes a discussion board, an opportunity to publish research findings online, and access to others' research about art teacher preparation. Brought about by technological advances and a continuing commitment from exemplary art education researchers in the area of teacher preparation, such efforts at communication and dissemination should be applauded and supported by art educators. Established by Lynn Galbraith and subsequently managed by Kit Grauer, then Don Krug, the task force currently has 129 members who are primarily postsecondary art educators. There is significant room for expansion of this online opportunity in the areas of collaborative and action research. Galbraith and Grauer (1998) expressed concern that it was difficult to engage teachers in collaborative research because it was more time consuming and not rewarded by university bureaucracies in the tenure and promotion mill. I was struck by the relatively few research studies regarding teacher education in art authored by more than one, or sometimes two, researcher.

3. The *Standards for Art Teacher Preparation* (Henry, 1999b) offer excellent criteria for assessing (a) programs for art teacher education, (b) effectiveness of faculty in such programs, and (c) professional development of teacher candidates in art education. This comprehensive list of guidelines addresses the role of research in teacher preparation; however, further criteria may need to be added and monitored if research—and teacher knowledge of research methodology—is to become a more cohesive element in art teacher education.

The second standard for programs supports the notion of reflective practice and values teacher candidates' abilities for self-assessment as a part of their continuing growth. As an important extension, program standards could specifically "foster an appreciation for, encourage participation in, and provide access to appropriate research opportunities," so even undergraduate students could be introduced to research methodology at an earlier time in their professional development. In the section on faculty standards, postsecondary educators are challenged to stay current with research literature and to collaborate with colleagues in research endeavors.

Another standard regarding research that might be added would be to expect faculty to "provide opportunities for teacher candidates—undergraduate as well as graduate—to gain knowledge and an appreciation of research methodology" as an integral part of teacher preparation. Fortunately, in the third area (professional development of teacher candidates), Standards XII, XVII, and XIX specifically describe how teacher candidates should value research and its impact on classroom practice and should participate in action research in their classrooms. It is, however, the responsibility of faculty to initiate a focus on research in their art education preparation programs at all levels.

4. In recent reports (Arts Education Partnership, 1997; *Arts Education Research Agenda for the Future*, 1994), one of the highest priorities for future research, along with student learning, was for research identifying best practice in arts instruction and the most effective methods for ongoing professional development of teachers of art (Koroscik, 1994). Day (1997) and Wilson (1997a) suggested that there is little research theory—relative to praxis—that is useful, current, or reliable about teacher education. These key areas will provide research questions for future and needed research and concurrent methodologies.

Wilson offered the following themes for continued research: (a) types of teachers and the way they go about teaching—who they are—what motivates them—their gender/class and how this may affect teaching; (b) art teachers' interests and abilities in the disciplines of art; (c) teachers' conceptions of students and surrounding cultural contexts; (d) teachers' formal and informal philosophies of art education and actual or implicit goals they set for their students; (e) teachers' classroom behaviors, practices, instructional patterns; and (f) how art-teachers-to-be are prepared internationally, rites of passage into professionalization, professional development issues. These themes, and the research questions they will generate, will also determine future trends in methodological approaches to the education of teachers of art.

5. According to Hutchens (1997), many universities do not actually value collaborative or site-based research efforts on the part of their faculty. He stated:

> It has been demonstrated that faculty who are highly active in scholarly research tend to be more effective teachers than faculty who practice scholarly abstinence. . . . But many legislators, members of state university governing boards, students and in-service teachers have come to believe that most faculty research lacks any educational utility, is unrelated to and detracts from teaching, and is only a vehicle to enhance faculty and university affluence. (p. 145)

He further noted, along with Pankratz (1989), that even though research can be highly valued as a pursuit, it is often conducted by individuals pursuing their own scholarly interests, which is unfortunate when collaborative methods and applied action research can actually enhance both teaching and learning.

6. One final evolving issue that I find intriguing is increased acceptance of new forms of methodology for educational research, for example, the notion of artistry as a valid research framework. As evidenced in recent professional dialog at AERA, and at the urging of such educational visionaries as Eisner and Greene, researchers are beginning to be more open to as yet unexplored methodological paradigms. To this end, at an opening session of AERA in 1994, Eisner (1995b) stated:

> I think the question regarding what counts as research is a question of critical importance. I believe the answer turns on our conception of understanding. As I see it, the primary tactical aim of research is to advance understanding. The [art] works I have cited help us to understand because their creators have understood and had the skills and imagination to transform their understanding into forms that help us to notice what we have learned not to see. They provide us an image fresh to behold and in so doing provide a complement to the colorless abstraction of theory with renderings that are palpable. The consciousness and insight they provide make understanding possible. (p. 2)

Let us move forward—or within—as committed art education theorists and practitioners, to seek the knowledge we need for educating ourselves to receive and create research that will inform the practice of the next generation of educators who teach art. Let us all envision asking more questions about such intriguing ideas as semiotics, visual culture, and other poststructural issues, not as colorless theory but with the consciousness of our most colorful creative minds. Yet, at the same time we need to honor our past and make our research endeavors relevant to present concerns and future possibilities.

REFERENCES

Ament, E. (1998). Using feminist perspectives in art education. *Art Education, 51*(5), 56–61.

Anderson, T. (2000). *Real lives: Art teachers and the cultures of school.* Portsmouth, NH: Heineman.

Anderson, T., Eisner, E., & McRorie, S. (1998). A survey of graduate study in art education. *Studies in Art Education, 40*(1), 8–25.

Andrus, L. (2001). The culturally competent art educator. *Art Education, 54*(4), 14–19.

Arts Education Partnership. (1997). *Priorities for arts education research.* Washington, DC: Arts Education Partnership [Online]. Available at www.aep-arts.org

Arts Education Research Agenda for the Future. (1994). Washington, DC: U.S. Department of education (ERIC Document Reproduction Service No. ED 367587)

Ary, D., Jacobs, L. C., Razavieh, A. (2002). *Introduction to research in education* (6th ed.). Belmont, CA: Wadsworth/Thompson Learning.

Beittel, K. R. (1973). *Alternatives for art education research.* Dubuque, IA: William C. Brown.

Beittel, K. R. (1979). Unity of truth, language, and method in art education. *Studies in Art Education, 21*(1), 50–56.

Bergman. L. M., & Feiring, N. C. (1997). Bridging the gap between university researcher and the classroom teacher. *Art Education, 50*(5), 51–56.

Blaikie, F. (1992). Thoughts concerning a feminist emphasis in art education. *Art Education, 45*(2), 49–52.

Blandy, D., & Congdon, K. G. (Eds.). (1987). *Art in a democracy.* New York: Teachers College Press.

Bolin, F. S. (1988). The interrelationship between preservice and inservice education for art teachers and specialists. In *The preservice challenge: Discipline-based art education and recent reports on higher education* (pp. 201–212). Seminar proceedings, Snowbird, Utah. August 8–15, 1987. Los Angeles: Getty Center for Education in the Arts.

Boughton, D., Eisner, E. W., & Ligtvoet, J. (Eds.). (1996). *Evaluating and assessing the visual arts in education: International perspectives.* New York: Teachers College Press.

Bresler, L. (1994). Zooming in on the qualitative paradigm in art education: Educational criticism, ethnography, and action research. *Visual Arts Research, 20*(1), 1–19.

Bresler, L. (1996). Ethical issues in the conduct and communication of ethnographic classroom research. *Studies in Art Education, 37*(3), 133–144.

Brewer, T. M. (1999a). Art teacher profile and preference. *Studies in Art Education, 41*(1), 61–70.

Brewer, T. M. (1999b). Forty years of *Studies in Art Education:* 1979–1989. *Visual Arts Research, 25*(1), 14–18.

Bullock, A. L., & Galbraith, L. (1992). Images of art teaching: Comparing the beliefs and practices of two secondary art teachers. *Studies in Art Education, 33*(2), 86–97.

Burton, D. (1998). Survey of current research in art education. *Studies in Art Education, 39*(2), 183–186.

Burton, D. (2001). How do we teach? Results of a national survey of instruction in secondary art education. *Studies in Art Education, 42*(2), 131–145.

Carreiro, K. (2002). Add one part professor, another part phenomenology. Mix well into an educational plan of philosophical possibility and promise [Online]. Available at http://members.aol.com/joph00/carriero.htm

Carroll, K. L. (1995). Paradigm analysis, unsolved problems, and the call for intercommunity dialogue. In M. Stokrocki (Ed.), *New waves of research in art education* (pp. 41–47). Seminar for Research in Art Education. (ERIC Document Reproduction Service No. ED395871)

Carroll, K. L. (1997). Researching paradigms in art education. In S. D. LaPierre & E. Zimmerman (Eds.), *Research methods and methodology for art education* (pp. 171–192). Reston, VA: National Art Education Association.

Chalmers, F. G. (1978). Teaching and studying art history: Some anthropological and sociological considerations. *Studies in Art Education, 20*(1), 18–25.

Chalmers, F. G. (1981). Art education as ethnology. *Studies in Art Education, 23*(3), 6–14.

Chalmers, F. G. (1999). The first 10 of 40 years of *Studies in Art Education. Visual Arts Research, 25*(1), 2–6.

Chapman, L. H. (1982). *Instant art, instant culture: The unspoken policy for American schools.* New York: Teachers College Press.

Chapman, L. H. (1999). *Studies in Art Education*: Decade two. *Visual Arts Research, 25*(1), 7–13.

Cochran-Smith, M., & Lytle, S. L. (1990). Research on teaching and teacher research: The issues that divide. *Educational Researcher, 19*(2), 2–11.

Cochran-Smith, M., & Lytle, S. L. (1999). The teacher research movement: A decade later. *Educational Researcher, 28*(7), 15–25.

Colbert, C., & Taunton, M. (2001). Classroom research in the visual arts. In V. Richardson (Ed.), *Handbook of research on teaching* (4th ed., pp. 520–526). Washington, DC: American Educational Research Association.

Collins, G. C. (1977). Considering an androgynous model for art education. *Studies in Art Education, 18*(2), 54–62.

Collins, G. C. (1999). *Studies in Art Education*: 1989–1998. *Visual Arts Research, 25*(1), 19–26.

Collins, G., & Sandell, R. (Eds.). (1995). *Gender issues in art education: Content, context, and strategies.* Reston, VA: National Art Education Association.

Collins, G., & Sandell, R. (1997). Feminist research: Themes, issues, and applications in art education. In S. D. LaPierre & E. Zimmerman (Eds.), *Research methods and methodology for art education* (pp. 193–222). Reston, VA: National Art Education Association.

Connors, K. E. (Ed.). (1997). *Abstracts of research presentations.* Seminar for Research in Art Education presentations at the National Art Education Association Conference, New Orleans, LA, March 19–23.

Davis, D. J. (1977). Research trends in art and art education, 1883–1972. In S. S. Madeja (Ed.), *Arts and aesthetics: An agenda for the future* (pp. 109–147). St. Louis: Central Midwestern Regional Educational Laboratory.

Davis, D. J. (1990). Teacher education for the visual arts. In W. R. Houston, M. Haberman, & J. Sikula (Eds.), *Handbook of research on teacher education* (pp. 746–757). New York: MacMillan.

Day, M. D. (1986). Artist-teacher: A problematic model for art education. *Journal of Aesthetic Education, 20*(4), 38–42.

Day, G., Gillespie, M., Rosenberg, M., Sowell, J., & Thurber. F. (1997). A view from the field: Discipline-based art education for inservice teachers. *Visual Arts Research, 23*(2), 52–62.

Day, M. (Ed.). (1997). *Preparing teachers of art.* Reston, VA: National Art Education Association.

Degge, R. M. (1982). The classroom art teacher as inquirer. *Studies in Art Education, 24*(1), 25–32.

Donmoyer, R. (2001). Paradigm talk reconsidered. In V. Richardson (Ed.), *Handbook of research on teaching* (pp. 174–197). Washington, DC: American Educational Research Association.

Dewey, J. (1934). *Art as experience.* New York: Minton & Balch.

Doyle, W. (1990). Themes in teacher education research. In W. R. Houston, M. Haberman, & J. Sikula (Eds.), *Handbook of research on teacher education* (pp. 3–24). New York: MacMillan.

Doyle, W. (1991). Case methods in the education of teachers. *Teacher Education Quarterly, 17*(1), 7–15.

Duncum, P. (1999). What elementary generalist teachers need to know to teach art well. *Art Education, 52*(6), 33–37.

Duncum, P. (2001). Theoretical foundations for an art education of global culture and principles for classroom practice. *International Journal of Education and the Arts, 2*(3) [Online]. Available at http://ijea.asu.edu/v2n3

Eisner, E. W. (1979). Recent developments in educational research affecting art education. *Art Education, 32*(4), 12–15.

Eisner, E. (1991). *The enlightened eye: Qualitative inquiry and the enhancement of educational practice.* New York: MacMillan.

Eisner, E. W. (1993a). The emergence of new paradigms for educational research. *Art Education, 46*(6), 50–55.

Eisner, E. W. (1993b). Forms of understanding and the future of educational research. *Educational Researcher, 22*(7), 5–11.

Eisner, E. W. (1995a). Preparing teachers for schools of the 21st century. *Peabody Journal of Education, 70*(3), 99–111.

Eisner, E. W. (1995b). What artistically crafted research can help us understand about schools. *Educational Theory, 45*(1), 1–6 [Online]. Available at http://www.ed.uiuc.edu/EPS/Educational-Theory/Contents/45_1_Eisner.asp

Eisner, E. W., & Peshkin. (Eds.). (1990). *Qualitative inquiry in education: The continuing debate.* New York: Teachers College Press.

Emme, M. J. (1995). An editor's note: Critical theory, art and education. *Journal of Social Theory in Art Education, 14* [Online]. Available at www.art.ttu.edu/cstae/journal/journal.html

Erickson, M. (1985). Styles of historical investigation. *Studies in Art Education, 26*(2), 121–124.

Ettinger, L. F. (1987). Styles of on-site descriptive research: A taxonomy for art educators. *Studies in Art Education, 28*(2), 79–95.

Ettinger, L. F., & Maitland-Gholson, J. (1990). Text analysis as a guide for research in art education. *Studies in Art Education, 31*(2), 86–98.

Freedman, K. (1994). Interpreting gender and visual culture in art classrooms. *Studies in Art Education, 35*(3), 157–170.

Galbraith, L. (1991). *Crossing cultural boundaries: Case studies, reflective inquiry, and a common language in the preservice classroom.* Paper presented at the United States Society for Education in Art conference, September 12, Columbus, OH.

Galbraith, L. (Ed.). (1995). *The preservice classroom: Issues and practice.* Reston, VA: National Art Education Association.

Galbraith, L. (1996a). NAEA research task force briefing paper on teacher education research. In E. Zimmerman (Ed.), *Briefing papers: Creating a visual arts research agenda toward the 21st century* (pp. 78–85). NAEA Commission on Research in Art Education. Reston, VA: National Art Education Association.

Galbraith, L. (1996b). Teacher education in the fine arts. In F. B. Murray (Ed.), *The teacher educator's handbook: Building a knowledge base for the preparation of teachers* (pp. 179–193). San Francisco: Jossey-Bass.

Galbraith, L. (1997). What are art teachers taught? An analysis of curriculum components for art teacher preparation programs. In M. D. Day (Ed.), *Preparing teachers of art* (pp. 45–72). Reston, VA: National Art Education Association.

Galbraith, L., & Grauer, K. (1998). Status report: NAEA research task force on teacher education. In E. Zimmerman (Ed.), *The NAEA research task force: Status reports* (pp. 35–38). Reston, VA: National Art Education Association.

Gall, M. D., Borg, W. R., & Gall, J. P. (1996). *Educational research: An introduction.* White Plains, NY: Longman.

Garber, E. (1992). Feminism, aesthetics, and art education. *Studies in Art Education, 33*(4), 210–225.

Geahigan, G. (1992). Educating future teachers of art: The role of educational philosophy. In N. C. Yakel (Ed.), *The future: Challenge of change* (pp. 15–32). Reston, VA: National Art Education Association.

Geahigan, G. (1998). Critical inquiry: Understanding the concept and applying it in the classroom. *Art Education, 51*(5), 10–16.

Giroux, H. (1988). *Teachers as intellectuals: Toward a critical pedagogy of learning.* Granby, MA: Bergin & Harvey.

Goodlad, J. I. (Ed.). (1990a). *Places where teachers are taught.* San Francisco: Jossey-Bass.

Goodlad, J. I. (1990b). *Teachers for our nation's schools.* San Francisco: Jossey-Bass.

Goodlad, J. I. (1990c). Studying the education of educators: From conception to findings. *Phi Delta Kappan, 71*(9), 698–701.

Goodlad, J. I. (1991). Why we need a complete redesign of teacher education. *Educational Leadership, 49*(3), 4–6, 8–10.

Goodlad, J. I. (1994). *Educational renewal: Better teachers, better schools.* San Francisco: Jossey-Bass.

Goodman, N. (1978). *Ways of worldmaking.* Indianapolis, IN: Hackett.

Grauer, K. (1998). Beliefs of preservice teachers toward art education. *Studies in Art Education, 39*(4), 350–370.

Grauer, K. (1999). The visual journal as a semiotic contrivance for preservice art education. *Arts and Learning Research, 15*(1), 73–82.

Grauer, K. (2000). The art of teaching art teachers. *Australian Art Education Journal, 22*(2), 19–24.

Greene, M. (1986). In search of a critical pedagogy. *Harvard Educational Review, 56*(4), 427–441.

Greene, M. (1993). Reflection on Post Modernism and education. *Educational Policy, 7*(2), 106–111.

Greene, M. (1995). *Releasing the imagination: Essays on education, the arts, and social change.* San Francisco: Jossey-Bass.

Green, G. L. (2000). Imagery as ethical inquiry. *Art Education, 53*(6), 19–24.

Grumet, M. R. (1992). Existential and phenomenological foundations of autobiographical method. In W. Pinar & W. Reynolds (Eds.), *Understanding curriculum as phenomenological and deconstructed text* (pp. 28–43). New York: Teachers College Press.

Guay, D. M. P. (1993). Cross-site analysis of teaching practices: Visual art education with students experiencing disabilities. *Studies in Art Education, 34*(4), 222–232.

Guay, D. M. (1994). Students with disabilities in the art classroom: How prepared are we? *Studies in Art Education, 36*(1), 44–56.

Hamblen, K. A. (1989). Research in art education as a form of educational consumer protection. *Studies in Art Education, 31*(1), 37–45.

Hanes, J. M., & Schiller, M. (1994). Collaborating with cooperating teachers in preservice art education. *Studies in Art Education, 35*(4), 218–227.

Heidegger, M. (1996). *Being and time.* Albany, NY: SUNY Press.

Henry, C. (1999a). The role of reflection in student teachers' perception of their professional development. *Art Education, 52*(2), 14–20.

Henry, C. (Ed.). (1999b). *Standards for art teacher preparation.* Reston, VA: National Art Education Association.

Hicks, L. E. (1994). Social reconstruction and community. *Studies in Art Education, 35*(3), 149–156.

Hoepfner, R. (1984). Measuring student achievement in art. *Studies in Art Education, 25*(4), 251–258.

Hussey, C., Dunlop, R., Barone, T., Kilbourne, B., Neilsen, L., Eisner, E. et al. (2001). *The educated imagination: Fiction and knowledge.* Arts-based research symposium held at AERA, Seattle, WA, March 14.

Hutchens, J. (1997). Accomplishing change at the university: Strategies for improving art teacher preparation. In M. Day (Ed.), *Preparing teachers of art* (pp. 139–154). Los Angeles: J. Paul Getty Trust.

Irwin, R. L. (1997a). Pedagogy for a gender sensitive art practice. In R. L. Irwin & K. Grauer (Eds.), *Readings in Canadian art teacher education* (pp. 247–252). Boucherville, Quebec: Canadian Society for Education through Art.

Irwin, R. L. (1997b). Collaborative action research: A journey of six women artist-pedagogues. *Collaborative Inquiry in a Postmodern Era: A Cat's Cradle, 2*(2), 21–40.

Irwin, R. L., Rogers, T., & Wan, Y. Y. (1999). Making connections through cultural memory, cultural performance and cultural translation. *Studies in Art Education, 40*(3), 198–212.

Jansen, C. R. (1995). Philosophical research: Scenarios of art appreciation. In M. Stokrocki (Ed.), *New waves of research in art education.* Seminar for Research in Art Education. (ERIC Document Reproduction Service No. ED395871)

Jeffers, C. (1991). *Through the keyhole: Phenomenological glimpses of life in the preservice class, art for elementary teachers.* Unpublished doctoral dissertation, University of Maryland, College Park.

Jeffers, C. (1992). Research as art and art as research: A living relationship. *Art Education, 46*(5), 12–17.

Jeffers, C. S. (1993a). A survey of instructors of art methods classes for preservice elementary teachers. *Studies in Art Education, 34*(4), 233–243.

Jeffers, C. S. (1993b). Teacher education: A context for art education. *Journal of Aesthetic Education, 27*(3), 85–94.

Jeffers, C. S. (1994). Questioning the role of art in education: Paradoxical views of preservice teachers. *Journal of Aesthetic Education, 28*(4), 89–97.

Jeffers, C. (2000a). Between school and community: Situating service learning in university art galleries. *Michigan Journal of Community Service Learning, 7,* 109–116.

Jeffers, C. (2000b). Drawing on semiotics: Inscribing a place between formalism and contextualism. *Art Education, 53*(6), 40–45.

Keifer-Boyd, K. T. (1996). Interfacing hypermedia and the internet with critical inquiry in the arts: Preservice training. *Art Education, 49*(6), 33–41.

Kincheloe, J. L., & McLaren, P. L. (2000). Rethinking critical theory and qualitative research. In N. Denzin & Y. Lincoln (Eds.), *Handbook of qualitative research.* Newbury Park, CA: Sage.

Koroscik, J. S. (1994). Blurring the line between teaching and research: Some future challenges for arts education policymakers. *Arts Education Policy Review, 96*(1), 2–10.

Koroscik, J. S., & Kowalchuk, E. A. (1997). Reading and interpreting research journals. In S. D. LaPierre & E. Zimmerman (Eds.), *Research methods and methodology for art education* (pp. 75–102). Reston, VA: National Art Education Association.

Korzenik, D. (1985). Doing historical research. *Studies in Art Education, 26*(2), 125–128.

Kowalchuk, E. A. (1999). Perceptions of practice: What art student teachers say they learn and need to know. *Studies in Art Education, 41*(1), 71–90.

Krug, D. (2002). NAEA Task Force on Teacher Education. The Ohio State University [Online]. Available at www.accad.ohio-state.edu/~krug/teacher/NAEA/communication.html

Lampela, L. (2001). Lesbian and gay artists in the curriculum: A survey of art teachers' knowledge and attitudes. *Studies in Art Education, 42*(2), 146–162.

Lankford, E. L. (1992). Philosophy of art education: Focusing our vision. *Studies in Art Education, 33*(4), 195–200.

LaPierre, S. D. (1997). Introduction. In S. D. LaPierre & E. Zimmerman (Eds.), *Research methods and methodology for art education* (pp. xi–xvi). Reston, VA: National Art Education Association.

La Pierre, S. D., & Diket, R. M. (1995). Research methods and practices for the classroom art teacher. Presentation at NAEA, Houston. (ERIC Document Reproduction Service No. ED388532)

LaPierre, S. D., & Zimmerman E. (Eds.) (1997). *Research methods and methodology for art education.* Reston, VA: National Art Education Association.

La Pierre, S. D., Stokrocki, M., & Zimmerman, E. (Eds.). (2000). Research methods and methodologies for multicultural and cross-cultural issues in art education. (ERIC Document Reproduction Service No. ED438 224)

Leshnoff, S. K. (1999). What is going on in elementary classrooms? *Art Education, 52*(6), 6–12.

MacGregor, R. (1998). Commentary: Two sides of an orange: The conduct of research. *Studies in Art Education, 39*(3), 271–280.

MacGregor, R., & Hawke, D. (1982). Ethnographic research method and its application to an art setting. *Visual Arts Research, 16*(2), 36–46.

Maitland-Gholson, J., & Ettinger, L. F. (1994). Interpretive decision making in research. *Studies in Art Education, 36*(1), 18–27.

Manley-Delacruz, E. (1997). *Design for inquiry: Instructional theory, research and practice in art education.* Reston, VA: National Art Education Association.

May, W. T. (1992). Philosopher as researcher and/or begging the question(s). *Studies in Art Education, 33*(4), 226–243.

May, W. T. (1993a). 'Teachers-as-researchers' or action research: What is it, and what good is it for art education? *Studies in Art Education, 34*(2), 114–126.

May, W. T. (1993b). A summary of findings in art and music research traditions and implications for teacher education. (ERIC Document Reproduction Service No. ED360247)

May, W. T. (1994). The tie that binds: Reconstructing ourselves in institutional contexts. *Studies in Art Education, 35*(3), 135–148.

McKean, B. (2001). Concerns and considerations for teacher development in the arts. *Arts Education Policy Review, 102*(4), 27–32.

Nadaner, D. (1984). Critique and intervention: Implications of social theory for art education. *Studies in Art Education, 26*(1), 20–26.

National Art Education Association. (2002). [Online]. Available at http://www.naea-reston.org

Newby, M. P., & Carli, N. M. (1987). *Directions of art education in higher education: A survey of art teacher preparation programs in the United States, Canada, and Puerto Rico.* Reston, VA: National Art Education Association.

Oleson, V. (1994). Feminisms and models of qualitative research. In N. Denzin & Y. Lincoln (Eds.), *Handbook of Qualitative Research.* Newbury Park, CA: Sage.

Pankratz, D. (1989). Arts education research: Issues, constraints, and opportunities. In D. B. Pankratz & K. Mulcahy (Eds.), *The challenge to reform arts education: What role can research play?* (pp. 1–28). New York: American Council for the Arts.

Parks, M. E. (1992). The art of pedagogy: Artistic behavior as a model for teaching. *Art Education, 45*(5), 51–57.

Penn State University. (2002). [Online]. Available at psu.edu

Pring, R. (2000). *Philosophy of educational research.* New York: Continuum.

Rogers, E. T., & Brogdon, R. E. (1990). A survey of the NAEA curriculum standards in art teacher preparation programs. *Studies in Art Education, 31*(3), 168–173.

Rush, J. C., & Kratochwill, C. R. (1981). Time-series strategies for studying behavior change: Implications for research in visual arts education. *Studies in Art Education, 22*(2), 57–67.

Ryder, W. (1994). Linking the college classroom to the community. *Art Education, 47*(3), 23–24, 43–44.

Sandell, R. (1979). Feminist art education: An analysis of the women's art movement as an educational force. *Studies in Art Education, 20*(2), 18–28.

Sandell, R. (1997). The liberating relevance of feminist pedagogy. *Studies in Art Education, 32*(3), 178–187.

Sandell, R., Collins, G., & Sherman, A. (1985). Sex-equity in visual arts education. In S. Klein (Ed.), *Handbook for achieving sex equity through education* (pp. 298–318). Baltimore: John Hopkins University Press.

Schwandt, T. (1994). Constructivist, interpretist approaches to human inquiry. In N. Denzin & Y. Lincoln (Eds.), *Handbook of qualitative research.* Newbury Park, CA: Sage.

Seidel, K. (2001). Many issues, few answers—The role of research in K-12 arts education. *Arts Education Policy Review, 103*(2), 19–22.

Sevigny, M. J. (1987). Discipline-based art education and teacher education. *Journal of Aesthetic Education, 21*(2), 95–126.

Sevigny, M. J. (1988). Significance of recent national reports for preservice discipline-based art education. In *The preservice challenge: Discipline-based art education and recent reports on higher education* (pp. 134–152). Seminar proceedings, Snowbird, Utah (August 8–15, 1987). Los Angeles: Getty Center for Education in the Arts.

Short, G. (1993). Pre-service teachers' understanding of visual arts: The reductive bias. *Arts Education Policy Review, 94*(5), 11–15.

Short, G. (1995). Understanding domain knowledge for teaching: Higher-order thinking in pre-service art teacher specialists. *Studies in Art Education, 36*(3), 154–169.

Smith, P. (Ed.). (1992). *Abstracts of research presentations.* Seminar for Research in Art Education presentations at the National Art Education Association Conference, Phoenix, AZ.

Smith, P. (1995). Art education historical methodology: An insider's guide to doing and using. In M. Stokrocki (Ed.), *New waves of research in art education* (pp. 103–110). Seminar for Research in Art Education. (ERIC Document Reproduction Service No. ED395871)

Smith-Shank, D. L. (1993). Beyond this point there be dragons: Preservice elementary teachers' stories of art and education. *Art Education, 46*(5), 45–51. (Authors Note: This entire issue of *Art Education* is devoted to a special theme of preservice and inservice education containing eight other articles and studies using various methods from naturalistic inquiry about teacher education in art.)

Smith-Shank, D. L. (1995). Semiotic pedagogy and art education. *Studies in Art Education, 36*(4), 233–241.

Stake, R. E. (1995a). The art of case study research. Thousand Oaks, CA: Sage.

Stake, R. (1995b). Rene Magritte, constructivism, and the researcher as interpreter. *Educational Theory, 45*(1), 1–5. [Online]. Available at http://www.ed.uiuc.edu/EPS/Educational-Theory/Contents/45_1_Stake.asp

Stankiewicz, M. A. (1997). Historical research methods in art education. In S. D. LaPierre & E. Zimmerman (Eds.), *Research methods and methodology for art education* (pp. 57–73). Reston, VA: National Art Education Association.

Stokrocki, M. (1995a). A decade of qualitative research in art education: Methodological expansions and pedagogical explorations. *Visual Arts Research, 17*(1), 42–51.

Stokrocki, M. (Ed.). (1995b). *New waves of research in art education*. Seminar for Research in Art Education. (ERIC Document Reproduction Service No. ED395871)

Stokrocki, M. (1997). Qualitative forms of research methods. In S. D. LaPierre & E. Zimmerman (Eds.), *Research methods and methodology for art education* (pp. 33–55). Reston, VA: National Art Education Association.

Stokrocki, M. (1998). Looking for lost treasure: A narrative explanation of the meanings of a Turkish *kilim*. *Visual Arts Research, 24*(2), 61–66.

Stone, D. L. (1993). The secondary art specialist and the art museum. *Studies in Art Education, 35*(1), 45–54.

Stuhr, P. L. (1994). Multicultural art education and social reconstruction. *Studies in Art Education, 35*(3), 171–178.

Sullivan, G. (1996). Beyond the quantitative and qualitative divide: Research in art education as border skirmish. *Australian Art Education, 19*(3), 13–22. (ERIC Document Reproduction Service No. ED549820)

Szekely, G. (1990). The teaching of art as performance. *Art Education, 43*(3), 6–17.

Thompson, C. M., & Hardiman, G. (1991). The status of art education programs in higher education. *Visual Arts Research, 17*(2), 72–80.

Thunder-McGuire, S. (1997). *Working papers in art education, 14,* 1996–1997. Graduate student papers and presentations at the National Art Education Conference. (ERIC Reproduction Service Document ED424176)

Thurber, F. E. (1990). Linking the disciplines in art education: A study of a pilot course in discipline-based art education methods for preservice classroom teachers. (Doctoral dissertation, University of Nebraska, 1989). *Dissertation Abstracts International, 51*(2), 388A.

Thurber, F. (1997). Art education in rural settings. *The Rural Educator, 18*(2), 30–34.

Thurber, F., & Zimmerman, E. (1996). Empower not in power: Gender and leadership roles in art teacher education. In G. Collins & R. Sandell (Eds.), *Gender issues in art education* (pp. 144–153). Reston, VA: National Art Education Association.

Ulbricht, J. (1998). Reflecting on Marilyn Zurmuehlen's research interests. *Visual Arts Reesearch. 24*(2), 56–60.

Walker, S. R. (1996). Thinking strategies for interpreting artworks. *Studies in Art Education, 37*(2), 80–91.

White D. W. (1977). A registry of studies in art education: Volume 17, 1975–1976. *Studies in Art Education, 18*(3), 65–70.

Wilson, B. (1994). Studies in Art Education invited lecture: Reflections on the relationships among art, life, and research. *Studies in Art Education, 35*(4), 197–208.

Wilson, B. (1997a). The second search: Metaphor, dimensions of meaning, and research topics in art education. In S. D. LaPierre & E. Zimmerman (Eds.), *Research methods and methodology for art education* (pp. 1–32). Reston, VA: National Art Education Association.

Wilson, B. (1997b). *The quiet evolution: Changing the face of arts education.* Los Angeles: Getty Center for Education in the Arts.

Yakel, N. C. (Ed.). (1992). *The future: Challenge of change.* Reston, VA: National Art Education Association.

Yarger, S. J., & Smith, P. L. (1990). Issues in research on teacher education. In W. R. Houston, M. Haberman, & J. Sikula (Eds.), *Handbook of research on teacher education* (pp. 25–41). New York: MacMillan.

Yokley, S. H. (1999). Critical pedagogy in art education. *Art Education, 50*(5), 19–24.

Zeichner, K. (1978). *The student teaching experience: A methodological critique of research.* (ERIC Document Reproduction Service No. ED166145)

Zeichner, K. (1999). The new scholarship in teacher education. *Educational Researcher, 28,*(9), 4–15.

Zimmerman, E. (1990). Issues related to teaching art from a feminist point of view. *Visual Arts Research, 16*(2), 1–9.

Zimmerman, E. (1991). Rembrandt to Rembrandt: A case study of a memorable painting teacher of artistically talented 13 to 16 year-old students. *Roeper Review, 13*(2), 76–81.

Zimmerman, E. (1994a). Concerns of pre-service art teachers and those who prepare them to teach. *Art Education, 47*(5), 59–67.

Zimmerman, E. (1994b). *Creating a visual arts research agenda toward the 21st century: A final report.* Reston, VA: National Art Education Association.

Zimmerman, E. (1994c). Current research and practice about preservice art specialist teacher education. *Studies in Art Education, 35*(2), 79–89.

Zimmerman, E. (Ed.). (1996). Briefing papers. *Creating a visual arts research agenda toward the 21st century.* Reston, VA: National Art Education Association.

Zimmerman, E. (1997a). Forward. In S. D. LaPierre & E. Zimmerman (Eds.), *Research methods and methodology for art education* (pp. v–ix). Reston, VA: National Art Education Association.

Zimmerman, E. (1997b). Whence come we? What are we? Whither go we? Demographic analysis of art teacher preparation programs in the United States. In M. Day (Ed.), *Preparing teachers of art* (pp. 27–44). Los Angeles: J. Paul Getty Trust.

Zimmerman, E. (Ed.). (1998). Status reports. *The NAEA research task force.* Reston, VA: National Art Education Association.

Zurmuehlen, M. (1991). Stories that fill the center. *Art Education, 44*(6), 6–11.

23

An Overview of Art Teacher Recruitment, Certification, and Retention

F. Robert Sabol
Purdue University

INTRODUCTION

Calls for Educational Reform

Education in the United States has undergone phenomenal changes in the past 2 decades. Accepted educational paradigms were challenged by internal and external forces. Political, economic, cultural, technological, and social concerns drove these changes. Waves of educational reform were launched by the publications of *A Nation at Risk* (National Commission on Excellence in Education, 1983), *Beyond Creating: The Place for Art in America's Schools* (Getty Center for Education in the Arts, 1985), *A Nation Prepared: Teachers for the 21st Century* (Carnegie Corporation Task Force on Teaching as a Profession, 1986), *Tomorrow's Teachers* (Holmes Group, 1986), *Toward Civilization* (National Endowment for the Arts, 1988), *What Teachers Should Know and Be Able to Do* (National Board for Professional Teaching Standards, 1989), *America 2000: An Education Strategy* (U.S. Department of Education, 1991), and *Goals 2000: Educate America Act* (U.S. Department of Education, 1994).

Three Waves of Educational Reform

These and other publications focused national attention on public education. Ultimately, they led to examination of the nature and quality of education in the United States. Collectively, they contributed to three waves of reform that changed general education and art education. The first wave was predicated on the need for accepted content standards in each discipline. Curriculum content in most disciplines was a morass with minimal agreement among educators and stakeholders about content, knowledge, skills, and processes. The standards movement focused on identification of a common core of learning compatible with content of a discipline and best practices in a field.

Agreement was minimal among art educators about the fundamental structure and content for what should be taught in visual arts education programs. Visual arts education content lacked uniformity and largely reflected individual art educators' preferences. Numerous additional factors contributed to these differences including local funding, resources, facilities, staffing, enrollments, and the like. The Consortium of National Arts Education Associations developed national voluntary fine arts education standards (Day, 1997). In 1994 (Music Educators National Conference), and visual arts education content standards were published. The emergence of discipline-based art education in the mid-1980s and the publication of national fine arts standards acted as catalysts for restructuring state frameworks and proficiency guides and local visual arts curriculum guides. Peeno (1995) reported exemplary state and local adaptations of the national visual arts standards.

Calls for educational accountability and increasing concern about improving the quality of education in schools launched the second wave of educational reform. Stakeholders demanded proof that national and state standards were being met and to what degree. As a result, many state departments of education developed and implemented state-level assessments of learning in visual arts education (Council of Chief State School Officers, 1985, 1998; Olson, 2001; Peeno, 1997; Peterson, 1991; Sabol, 1990; Shuler & Connealy, 1998). Relationships were identified between content on these assessments and state and national visual arts content standards (Sabol, 1994, 1998a). After arts education was added to the national education goals (U.S. Department of Education, 1994), and Congress stated that "the arts are forms of understanding and knowing that are fundamentally important to education" (H. R. 6, 1994, p. 2), the fine arts were included in the National Assessment of Educational Progress (NAEP). In 1969, Congress established the NAEP for the purpose of surveying and monitoring changes in educational accomplishments of U.S. students. Previously, visual arts achievement was assessed on the 1974 and 1978 NAEP. Findings from the 1997 NAEP report in visual arts (Persky, Sandene, & Askew, 1998) and secondary analysis of its data (Burton, 2001; Diket, 2001; Sabol, 2001) focused attention on assessment of achievement in visual arts education. Established research agendas for visual arts education (Goals 2000 Arts Education Partnership, 1997; Goodwin, 2001; National Art Education Association 1994, 1995, 1996; The National Endowment for the Arts, 1994) included continued study of assessment and its impact on visual arts education.

The standards movement and intense attention on educational assessment provided impetus for the third wave of educational reform—teacher licensure and certification. Assessment results raised questions about why students were not meeting content standards. The business community demanded better prepared and better educated employees (Getty Education Institute for the Arts, 1996, 1997; U.S. Department of Education, 1991, 1994). Governing bodies raised concerns about threats to the welfare of society caused by inferior education (National Commission on Excellence in Education, 1983; U.S. Department of Education, 1991, 1994). A range of contributing factors were identified. The pivotal roles of teachers came under close scrutiny. Stakeholders rightly perceived that the quality of instruction students received crucially influenced their learning. Calls were made for rigorous teacher licensure standards and assessment of teachers (Council of Chief State School Officers, 1999; National Art Education Association, 1991; National Endowment for the Arts, 1988). Bodies responsible for teacher certification used energy from this wave to initiate reforms of state certification policies and procedures. Models for teacher preparation and certification standards were designed and published (Council of Chief State School Officers, 1992; National Art Education Association, 1999a). Peeno (1997) studied certification of art teachers and found variation among states' structures and requirements. Standards, assessment, and certification reforms raised a myriad of issues for teacher preparation programs, recruitment, and retention of teachers that remain today.

A Painting of the Current Landscape

Waves of educational reform occur in a landscape colored by larger forces that act to shape them. These forces combine to act as a backdrop against which recruitment, certification, and retention of teachers reforms can be examined. They bear directly on the field of visual arts education, though grounded in the larger picture of general education. For this reason, significant amounts of the remainder of this discussion will include references to and illustrations of themes and issues from the field of general education. Interpretations for visual arts education will be included when possible. Because visual arts education is a fundamental component in the broad definition of general education, it should be kept in mind that trends and developments in general education directly apply to visual arts education as much as to any other discipline.

Public school enrollment is projected to set new records every year until 2005 (Snyder & Hoffman, 2001). The National Center for Education Statistics (Nathanson, 2001) projected increased enrollment in public elementary and secondary schools from 43.2 million students in 1999 to 44.4 million students by 2006. Reports of increasing enrollments suggested a need for increasing numbers of teachers in the coming years (Gerald & Hussar, 2000; Henke & Zahn, 2001). Without more teachers, student to teacher ratios may increase dramatically (Hussar, 2001). An estimated 3.3 million elementary and secondary school teachers engaged in classroom instruction in the fall of 2000, with 2.0 million at elementary levels and 1.3 million at secondary levels (Snyder & Hoffman, 2001). The pool of available teachers is rapidly decreasing as the post-World War II baby-boom generation approaches retirement. Proportions of teachers who retire each year are expected to rise (Goodnough, 2000; Henke & Zahn, 2001). Hussar (2001) predicted that approximately 759,000 teachers will retire from 1998 through 1999 to 2008 through 2009. The National Center for Educational Statistics (Hussar, 2001) reported an annual demand for 150,000 new teachers. The projections for the number of newly hired teachers needed by the 2008 to the 2009 range are from 1.7 million to 2.7 million (Hussar, 2001). "Newly hired teachers" includes not only first-time teachers but also returning teachers and people who were formerly teaching in private schools (Hussar, 2001). Some of these newly hired teachers will be needed to replace those leaving the profession, and others will be needed as enrollments continue to increase. Inexperienced teachers are replacing retiring teachers from the baby-boom generation. The attrition rate for these teachers is higher than that for teachers in midcareer (Archer, 1999; Baker & Smith, 1997; Grissmer, & Kirby, 1997; Henke & Zahn, 2001).

This picture raises numerous disturbing questions yet to be answered. Challenges on the horizon may be viewed with foreboding or they may be embraced with optimism. Without question the future of education will be greatly influenced by directions taken in the recruitment, certification, and retention of teachers.

Arts education professional associations, state departments of education, colleges and universities, and arts schools should undertake efforts to attract capable students to arts teacher preparation programs, including minorities. (National Endowment for the Arts, 1988, p. 26)

People commit to the teaching profession for numerous and varied reasons. Teachers cited a "sense of calling," contributing to society, doing work they love, and having time with family as the most common reasons they entered the teaching profession (Wadsworth, 2001). Haselkorn and Harris (2001) suggested that the American public has high regard for contributions teachers make to society. Despite perceptions about problems with education, Americans ranked teaching as a profession that provides the most benefits to society, ahead of doctors, nurses, business persons, and public officials.

If teachers were guaranteed a salary of $60,000 a year, more than 8 in 10 Americans (82%) say they would recommend teaching as a career of choice to a member of their family. Indeed, 6 in 10 Americans (61%) would consider a teaching career themselves at these salary levels. (Haselkorn & Harris, 2001, p. 21)

Recruitment of students is influenced by an array of factors working in combination to draw students to preservice education programs and the profession or to block their participation in them. Discussion of a sampling of these will provide a foundation for understanding a number of issues related to recruitment of individuals to the field of art education.

In the fall of 2000, there were 3,252,000 public and private elementary through secondary teachers in the United States (Snyder & Hoffman, 2001). They taught 52,989,000 public school and private school prekindergarten through grade 12 students (Snyder & Hoffman, 2001). In 1993 to 1994 there were 144,119 art and music teachers in public schools and 26,381 in private schools (Whitener, Gruber, Lynch, Tingos, Perona, & Fondelier, 1997). Carey, Sikes, Foy, and Carpenter (1995) reported that 85% of public elementary schools offered visual arts education. In those programs, visual arts instruction was provided by specialists (43%), specialists and classroom teachers (29%), and by classroom teachers (28%). If numbers of students continue to grow, the need for trained teachers will increase and recruiting students for preservice programs will take on additional urgency. Researchers predicted teacher shortages for the past 2 decades (Darling-Hammond, 1984; Henke, Choy, Chen, Geis, & Alt, 1997; Olson & Hendrie, 1998). Ominous signals suggest that difficulties in hiring teachers are increasing. Often teacher shortages occur in selected fields rather than across fields (Bradley, 1999). Complicating matters further, particular states and localities are finding it harder than others to staff classrooms (Carey et al., 1995; Henke et al., 1997; Hussar, 2001; Whitener et al., 1997), and the number of teachers retiring continues to grow annually (Goodnough, 2000). In the fall of nineteen ninety-eight, 14,549,000 students were enrolled in institutions of higher education up from 12,097,00 in 1980 (Snyder & Hoffman, 2001). In nineteen ninety-seven to nineteen ninety-eight, 105,968 bachelor's degrees, 114,691 master's degrees, and 6,729 doctoral degrees were awarded in education (Snyder & Hoffman, 2001). During this same period, 1,545 bachelor's degrees, 668 master's degrees, and 25 doctoral degrees were awarded in art education (Snyder & Hoffman, 2001). The increasing need for teachers places an increased burden on colleges and universities to recruit students for preservice preparation programs.

Broughman and Rollefson (2000) studied career patterns of newly hired teachers. They grouped newly hired teachers from 1993 to 1994 (the latest year for which data are available) into four clusters including newly prepared teachers, delayed entrants, transfers, and reentrants. Newly prepared teachers were defined as those first-time teachers who attended college or had earned their highest degree in the previous year. Delayed entrants were considered as employed in fields outside education or in jobs related to education, such as teacher aids. Transfers were defined as teachers who were teaching in another school in the other sector (public or private), in another state, or within the same state and sector but in another school system. Reentrants were defined as individuals who had taken a break from teaching and were employed in nonteaching professions or were caring for family members. Of the newly hired public school teachers in 1993 to 1994, twenty-nine percent were newly prepared, 17% were delayed entrants, 31% were transfers, and 23% were reentrants. Broughman and Rollefson (2000) reported that within these groups the percentage of minorities hired in 1993 to 1994 increased slightly from 1987 to 1988. Across groups newly hired teachers were virtually the same in terms of degrees earned; however, 45% of delayed entrants were determined to be in need of alternative teacher training programs. Differences in the average age of newly hired teachers ranged from 27.6 years for newly prepared teachers to 31.9 years and 39.7 years for delayed entrants and reentrants, respectively.

Reforms of the 1980s and 1990s included focus on preservice teacher education programs. Among K-12 teachers working in 1994, nearly all reported that their jobs were related to their undergraduate field of study (97% among full-time teachers), whereas graduates who worked in other professions were less likely to report that their jobs related to their professions (62% or less in various professions) (Henke & Zahn, 2001). This high relationship between preservice education programs and employment illustrates that to a significant degree the quality of preservice programs contributes to recruitment of students.

Although the form and content of preservice teacher education programs experienced unprecedented change, teacher education programs have become more rigorous. The nature of these reforms has implications for recruitment of students for preservice education programs. The National Art Education Association published *Standards for Art Teacher Preparation* in 1999. This publication included standards for (a) art teacher preparation programs, including content for college and university art education programs; (b) higher education art education faculty in which competencies were delineated for faculty who have responsibility to prepare art teacher candidates; and (c) standards for art teacher candidates including detailed delineation of skills art teacher candidates should possess. These standards were written to be compatible with higher education accreditation standards from the National Association of Schools of Art and Design (NASAD) and the National Council for the Accreditation of Teacher Education (NCATE). Similar to NASAD and NCATE standards, *Standards for Art Teacher Preparation* (National Art Education Association, 1999a) consisted of guidelines for art teacher preparation. Art teacher candidate standards focused on understanding of the content of art, knowledge of students, curriculum development, instruction, assessment, and professional development. Separate standards were included for art education programs in higher education. These standards recommended that art education programs provide art teacher candidates with knowledge of content of the visual arts and knowledge of theory and practice of art education. Standards, such as these, have the power to improve preservice art education programs. In turn, these improvements can positively influence recruitment of students for preservice education programs by providing better quality training of future art educators.

Hutchens (1997) suggested strategies for improving preservice preparation programs to make them more attractive to students. He reported that few universities include teacher education in their mission statements. To make teacher education more attractive, he suggested that university policymakers must commit to teacher education and its reform. Those in higher education should communicate with university administration about the significant changes in theory and practice in teacher preparation that discipline-based and other forms of comprehensive art education can bring. Second, the research–teaching nexus in art education must be improved by stronger emphasis on needs of prospective teachers and through use of collaborative research teams, rather than remain on the idiosyncratic specialization and curiosity of faculty. Third, the disciplinary and conceptual entrenchment of faculty must be overcome. Reform initiatives have created a need for a closer community of educators. Adversarial perspectives among faculty can impede program development and leave faculty isolated in their own departments. Finally, development of a stronger constituency for art education must be built in state departments of education, university governing boards, and in business and private sectors. Alliances with members of these groups hold significant importance for influencing their decision making. Taylor (1992) identified four conditions needed to implement changes in preservice programs making them more attractive to students. The first of these conditions is a collective will to risk change. Preservation of outmoded programming and thinking prevents restructuring of preservice programs to meet demands of the changing field. A sense of collegiality in which cooperation and collaboration preserve individual identities is the second condition. Collegiality personalizes changes and provides assurances of support from colleagues. Third, administrative support is pivotal in implementing change. Continuous and vigilant efforts must be made to educate administration and cultivate productive relationships that favor art education preservice education programs. Finally, energy is required to work on several different fronts at the same time to rethink pedagogical issues, learn the inner politics of the institution, achieve interdependence within the working team, and develop necessary communication networks both within and across an institution and community.

Preservice education program reformers should design programs that are attractive to students while encompassing national teacher preparation standards (Council of Chief State School Officers, 1992; National Art Education Association, 1999a; National Board for Professional Teaching Standards, 1996, 2000), state certification and licensure standards, discipline content knowledge and skills, and technology. There is a great potential to enhance the attractiveness of individual programs and contribute to recruitment of students for them by using strategies—such as those recommended by Hutchens—and meeting conditions—such as those identified by Taylor—to build teacher preparation programs that are more responsive to the needs of future teachers.

The public has demanded that new teachers be more knowledgeable and skilled. State teacher licensing boards, administrators in higher education, and other decision makers reasoned that more demanding admission standards would draw more highly able students into preservice education programs. Consequently, the bar was raised for admission into preservice education programs at many colleges and universities. It remains to be seen whether raising admission requirements will encourage more highly able students to enter preservice education programs. Higher admission standards including increased grade point averages, SAT scores, and use of standardized tests such as the PRAXIS tests, the National Teacher Examination (NTE), or state proficiency tests have become commonplace. Tests such as these are routinely used for admission to teacher education programs (Feistritzer, 1999a). They also are used as gatekeeping devices for advancement through programs or at the completion of programs to measure knowledge and skills (Feistritzer, 1999a). In addition, they are used by state departments of education to assess qualifications of certification and licensure candidates. The public strongly supported passing a teacher competency test as a means of measuring capabilities of teachers (Haselkorn & Harris, 2001). Although assessments of these sorts may be seen as restrictive or exclusive, in fact, they act as mechanisms for measuring portions of the competencies and skills of those wanting to become teachers. A commonly held belief by those who advocate testing is that use of assessments positively affects recruitment both by attaching a quality of professionalism to teaching not previously achieved and by attracting more highly skilled and knowledgeable people to the profession. By contrast, increased emphasis on assessment may in fact be detrimental to recruitment efforts by eliminating people with potential to become accomplished teachers before and after they enter a field.

Recruiting students for preservice education programs is further complicated by the realization that teaching salaries are not commensurate with demands of the profession. Students are aware that teachers' salaries are not comparable with salaries of many of those who graduate in other areas of study. The average salary for public school teachers in 1998 to 1999 was $40,582 (Snyder & Hoffman, 2001). The median annual income in 1998 for year-round full-time college graduates with bachelor's degrees was $51,405 for men and $36,559 for women; median annual income for graduates with master's degrees was $62, 244 for men and $45,283 for women (Snyder & Hoffman, 2001). Figures like these combined with the booming economy of the late 1990s made teaching even less attractive. Archer (2000) reported the average salary for nonteachers with master's degrees increased by $17,505 from 1994 to 1998, after adjusting for inflation. The average salary for teachers with master's degrees rose by less than $200. Olson (2000) reported that 39% of teachers were working a second job to make ends meet. Gerald and Hussar (2000) projected an increase of only 6.9% in the average teachers' salary from 1998 through 1999 to 2009 through 2010. Low salaries, coupled with an understanding that opportunities for salary growth are limited and gender biased, pose particular barriers for recruitment of students.

During the past 2 decades, recruitment of students for preservice education programs has been of increasing concern and in all likelihood will continue to be a focus of attention for the foreseeable future. Smith (1995) raised a particularly unsettling question with important implications for recruitment of preservice education students. He concluded that as preservice education programs become more lengthy and include more rigorous standards, and while at the same time state departments of education set more rigorous certification and licensure standards combined with eroding school conditions and low salaries for teachers, potential art teachers may very well ask, "Is the cost of schooling worth it?" The demands of preservice education programs combined with harsh realities of the teaching profession have made the field of education less appealing than in decades past. In the end, the quality of teacher education may not be measured by the ideal of providing better preservice training to students but by students' answers to the question posed by Smith.

Some Issues Related to Recruitment for Preservice Education Programs

The field of education is concerned with a number of recruitment issues. Many of these issues have implications for the recruitment of teachers to the field of art education. In presenting these issues two caveats must be considered. First, issues selected represent a limited portion of those that could have been presented. This sampling of issues is not intended to be exhaustive. Second, details of implementation and specific procedures for operationalizing solutions to questions or problems they raise would be cumbersome and are beyond the specific province of this discussion.

States and school districts should become aggressive in their recruiting efforts. Recruiting teachers is complicated by the reality that teachers gravitate to schools with larger proportions of higher achieving students, nonminority students, and more affluent students (Archer, 2000). Wendy Kopp, the founder of Teach for America stated:

> We don't have a setup where our school districts believe and understand that it's up to them to develop an effective, aggressive recruitment strategy. In any other sector, this would be just bizarre. Corporations, law firms, whatever, spend so much on recruiting and developing effective people because they all know that people are everything. (Archer, 2000, p. 34)

The field of art education needs to develop recruitment strategies, as do all other fields of education. Archer (2000) recommended such strategies include marketing programs and media campaigns complete with public service announcements and advertisements similar to those in the business sector. He recommended training programs for personnel officers to make them more effective recruiters and designing hiring practices that provide free access to employment information and quick responses to employment queries. He reported that 27 states recruit teachers by providing job announcements on Web sites and that 9 states provide job applications online. Melville and Hall (2001) and Simmons (2001) recommended development of cadet teaching programs in high schools for recruitment purposes. Such programs provide opportunities for high school students to teach while helping them determine if teaching is a career they want to pursue. Approaching recruitment as a critical task for improving education may furnish much needed motivation for implementing these strategies.

Recruitment of minorities into the teaching profession is another concern art educators should address. Teachers from minorities represent 9% of U.S. public school teachers, and this number is expected to decrease to 5% in coming years (Feistritzer, 1998, 1999b; Jorgenson, 2001). The student body in public and private schools and in colleges and universities has become increasingly heterogeneous over the past quarter century. Pratt (2000) reported that minority enrollments have increased from 17% of all undergraduate students in the fall of 1976 to 26% in the fall of 1995. Feistritzer (1999a) specified that 8 out of 10 teacher candidates were White, 10% were Black, 6% were Hispanic, 3% were Asian or Pacific Islander, and 2% were American Indian. Newly hired public school teachers included slightly increasing numbers of minority teachers. In 1987 to 1988 minorities constituted 10% of newly hired teachers, whereas in 1993 to 1994 hiring of minorities increased to 16% (Broughman & Rollefson, 2000). Students from minority backgrounds constitute 40% of the total student body in the United States (Jorgenson, 2001). Recruiting minority students is compounded by the failure of the K-12 system to produce enough minority graduates (Archer, 2000). Minority groups are less likely to succeed in school and are equally less inclined to pursue teaching as a career according to Jorgenson (2001). Sabol (1998b, 1999) studied the ethnicity of urban and rural art educators in the Western Region of the National Art Education Association. Both studies revealed a predominance of Caucasian teachers in the field including 91% in urban settings and 97% in rural settings. African American art teachers were more common in urban settings (4%) than they were in rural settings (1%). Hispanic or Latino art teachers also were more common in urban settings (3%) than they were in rural settings (0.2%). American Indian and Asian art educators represented equal percentages in both urban and rural settings (1% each). In every category, nearly duplicate findings were produced in a study of secondary art educators conducted by the National Art Education Association (2000). Ethnic patterns, such as these, are generally comparable to ethnic distributions of teachers in public schools (Snyder & Hoffman, 2001). Findings from these studies suggest that teachers the field of art education are not ethnically diverse. Art education policymakers should aggressively develop recruitment strategies to improve ethnic diversity of the field. Various strategies for accomplishing this task were recommended by Jorgenson (2001). They included prioritizing the recruitment of ethnic educators, considering nontraditional sources of recruitment, expediting the application of ethnic applications, understanding how ethnically diverse employees perceive a school district, and creating a support network for educators of color. Policymakers and administrators should evaluate the merits of these strategies and implement those most appropriate for their school districts.

Olson (1998) contended that American schools are in the midst of an educational crisis of monumental proportions. Many school problems are influenced by site-specific factors (Williams & Newcombe, 1994; Williams & Woods, 1997). National attention has focused on problems in rural and urban schools. In the field of art education, Blandy and Congdon (1987) suggested that rural schools reflect traits, folkways, and learning styles that are different from other educational settings. Jones and Southern (1992) and Manifold (2000) studied the influences of rural values and beliefs on education and art education in rural schools. Clark and Zimmerman (2000) identified local rural history, cultures, traditions, and interests in rural art education curricula. Clark and Zimmerman (2000) and Sabol (1999) identified social problems and school-related factors that influenced art education in rural schools. Similar studies have identified factors and influences on education in urban schools. Ayers (1994), Meier (1997), Williams and Newcombe (1994), and Williams and Woods (1997) identified combinations of urban students' cultures, motivations, competencies, and opportunities. Sabol (1998b) identified social problems and school-related factors that influence art education in urban schools. Although the rural and urban school contexts are unique, they share common problems and deal with similar issues (Dorn, 1997; Olson, 1998, 1999; Shen, 1997a).

Teacher shortages are a common problem in rural and urban school districts (Feistritzer, 1999a; Haselkorn & Fideler, 1999; Olson & Hendrie, 1998; Olson & Jerald, 1998; Sabol, 1998b, 1999, in press; Tell, 2001; U.S. Department of Education 1991). New education graduates do not want to teach in urban or rural areas (Darling-Hammond, 2001; Feistritzer, 1999b). New teachers are less inclined to teach in urban schools where minorities comprise 43% of students and where 35% of students live in poverty (Olson & Jerald, 1998). They are less interested in teaching in rural and urban schools that on average are older than schools in towns and in the urban fringe (Pratt, 2000). Olson and Jerald (1998), Darling-Hammond (2001), and Ingersoll (2001) reported that newly hired teachers in urban schools are more likely than those in rural and suburban districts to have no teaching licenses or emergency or temporary ones. They stated that roughly 60% of urban new hires had emergency teaching licenses. Rural schools are plagued with the problem of hiring teachers who do not have a degree in the discipline they teach (Scherer, 2001). These are disturbing facts. The need for trained and licensed teachers in rural and urban schools is likely to keep pace with increasing enrollments and retirements. Because the field of art education mirrors general education in numerous ways, it is likely that recruitment problems for rural and urban schools are occurring in art education as well. However, research must be conducted in the field to explore these issues. Currently, such research has not been conducted.

The number of men in the teaching force is another ongoing recruitment issue. Education is predominantly a women's profession (Snyder & Hoffman, 2001). The percentage of men in the teaching force has steadily declined from a high of 34% in 1971 to 26% in 1996 (Pratt, Pfile, Conner, & Livingston, 2000; Snyder & Hoffman, 2001). In the field of art education men represent a slightly lower percentage of the teaching force and constituted only 17% of art educators at all teaching levels in both rural and urban schools (Sabol, 1998b, 1999). Of those teaching at the secondary level, 29% were men (National Art Education Association, 2000). Recruitment of men into the teaching profession is made problematic by low salaries, poor working conditions, lack of job satisfaction, limited opportunities for advancement, low job status, lack of interest for involvement with students, and student discipline problems (Darling-Hammond, 2001; Finn & Madigan, 2001; Whitener et al., 1997). Although conditions are even more challenging for women art teachers, they often bring supplementary income to their families and are not primarily responsible for providing family incomes. The NAEA and state art education associations must work with legislatures, the business sector, colleges and universities, local school districts, and other stakeholders to address these problems and to create policies and programs that will attract increasing numbers of men to the profession.

Increased use of teacher tests has contributed to recruitment problems for the profession. Increasingly, states, colleges, and universities are requiring teacher candidates to pass teacher competency tests for certification (Nagel & Peterson, 2001). Most teacher tests are technically sound and provide important information about content-related knowledge (Blair, 2001). Tests designed to measure teaching competency have been criticized for not measuring the range of knowledge and skills teachers need or to adequately predict classroom success (Blair, 2001; Nagel & Peterson, 2001; National Research Council of the National Academies, 2000, 2001; Scherer, 2001). Concerns about using a single teacher test to evaluate teacher competency were raised by Scherer (2001). Teacher tests, as in all assessments of learning, should be part of assessment programs that include multiple measures to determine teacher candidate competency (Nagel & Peterson, 2001; Scherer, 2001; Zimmerman, 1997). Blair (2001) reported that states are required by Congress to rank institutions by passing rates of teacher candidates on state teacher tests and, based on requirements of Title II of the Higher Education Act, authorized in 1998. According to this act, the federal government could limit funding to state and teacher preparation programs based on students' performances on state teacher tests. As a result some students may be highly successful in college, but if they do not pass the tests, they cannot enter the teaching profession. No one wants incompetent teachers in any classroom; however, teacher-testing programs have contributed to discouraging some from pursuing teaching as a career (Scherer, 2001). Studies of passing rates of art education teacher candidates on teacher competency tests have not been conducted. Such studies have great potential to contribute to understanding the impact this issue has had on recruitment of students to the field of art education.

An additional issue related to testing has contributed to recruiting problems. The current emphasis on adhering to standards and testing in the classroom has driven people out of the profession (Scherer, 2001). Teachers feel an increasing lack of control in planning curriculum and other aspects of their teaching because of pressures caused by national, state, and local testing programs. Testing programs have acted to determine what and how teachers teach. This takes away significant characteristics that define for teachers what it means to be a professional and acts to complicate recruitment of students by discouraging some who may want to become teachers. Sabol (1998b, 1999) reported that emphasis on state testing in the visual arts and in other disciplines was an increasing concern for art teachers in rural and urban schools. Teachers in both studies suggested that testing programs were distracting, time consuming, lacked sufficient scope to measure the full range of visual arts learning, and served to direct curriculum content. Stakeholders who demand accountability for learning in public schools should be made aware of the negative impact testing has had on students and teachers. Full understanding of the drawbacks of testing programs and their influences on learning may enable stakeholders to reevaluate demands for testing programs and tests' form and content.

Numerous and complex factors contribute to recruitment of teachers for the field. Researchers must actively engage in research that will provide information needed by policymakers and stakeholders to respond to recruitment needs in visual arts education.

TEACHER CERTIFICATION

About 2.8 million public school teachers are working in the United States (Olson, 2000). All states require teachers to possess licenses to teach in public schools. Ninety-three percent or 2,604,000 teachers are certified, whereas 7% or 196,000 teachers hold provisional, probationary, temporary, or emergency or waiver licenses (Pratt, 2000). Some states place the subject and grade level on a teacher license or certificate, whereas others award teachers generic licenses or certificates but allow or require them to attach "endorsements" related to specific grade levels or subjects. Teacher credentialing has no common set of terms. Some states require teacher candidates to obtain a "license," whereas others use the term "certificate" or " credential" (U.S. Department of Education, 1995). DiBlasio (1997) defined *certification* as completing the requirements (course requirements, competencies, internships, etc.) set by teacher education programs within institutions of higher learning. She defined *licensure* as recognition by the state as confirmation that all requirements have been met for competence in teaching. She goes on to say that the distinction between these terms becomes blurred when state professional standards boards or state boards of education defer to the judgment of teacher-training programs in granting licenses in a particular state. Review of the literature in the field revealed that these terms are used interchangeably, and for purposes of this discussion, the terms *certification* and *licensure* will be used as such.

The public depends on state Departments of Education to create, implement, enforce, and monitor certification of teachers in public schools. As a result certification systems are idiosyncratic with each state having its own criteria and procedures. Numerous calls for higher standards for teacher certification have been voiced over the past 2 decades (National Board for Professional Teaching Standards, 1996, 2000; National Commission for Excellence in Education, 1983; National Endowment for the Arts, 1988; U.S. Department of Education, 1991, 1994). Public concern about teacher quality has led a growing number of state Departments of Education to restructure certification policies, standards, requirements, and procedures. Sweeping certification reforms in states like Connecticut and Indiana (Indiana Professional Standards Board, 1997) served as models for certification restructuring in other states. In addition to revising art teacher standards, Connecticut, Indiana, and 11 other states license teachers based on state art standards (Council of Chief State School Officers, 2000; Hatfield, & Peeno, 2001; Indiana Professional Standards Board, 1997). Collaborations between states and professional organizations to restructure teacher licensing is ongoing.

> The National Commission on Teaching and America's future is working with a dozen states to improve teacher preparation, licensure, and assessment, by raising standards, encouraging more professional preparation, and providing more support for novices. (Olson, 2000, p. 18)

Reformation of teacher certification systems is currently being done in 35 states working with INTASC; 47 states have policies defining requirements for continuing professional development of teachers in order for teachers to be licensed by the state; and legislatures in 14 states have created autonomous Professional Standards Boards with jurisdiction to govern teacher training and licensing programs in their states (National Art Education Association, 1999b). Some states have developed career ladders with changing certification requirements at various points in the span of teachers' careers (Wall, 1997). These programs may award certificates at the completion of preservice preparation, after an induction period, and repeatedly during continuing professional development. Some states created licensure systems that award certificates for instructional levels or for developmental levels. Teacher testing is one of the most widely embraced school improvement initiatives of the past 15 years and it has become a lightning rod for controversy. In 1988, the National Endowment for the Arts recommended testing of teacher qualifications as a condition of teacher certification with inclusion of art content and pedagogy related to art teaching.

> State certifying agencies should develop tests to evaluate teacher preparation and teacher preparation programs. Such tests should assess the general (liberal arts) preparation of teachers, their knowledge of art in the context of history and culture, their ability to analyze art, their performance and skill competencies, their knowledge of issues in arts education, and their skill in lesson planning and pedagogy. (p. 26)

Haselkorn and Harris (2001) suggested that 70% of the American public felt it was very important for teachers to pass a teacher competency test. Many states require teacher candidates to pass tests of basic skills before they may be certified (Snyder & Hoffman, 2001). Tests such as PRAXIS I, a basic skills test, and PRAXIS II, tests of subject matter and tests of general and subject-specific knowledge designed by Education Testing Service, are widely used. PRAXIS III, a test of on-the-job skills is being piloted at this time (Bradley, 2000). Currently, 39 states require teacher candidates to pass a test of basic skills; but of those, 36 allow candidates to begin teaching without having passed the exam (Haselkorn & Harris, 2001; Jerald & Boser, 2000; Olson, 2000). Twenty-six states require candidates to pass pedagogical knowledge tests (Blair, 2001). Prospective high school teachers in 29 states are required to pass tests in the subjects they plan to teach to earn a beginning teaching license (Haselkorn & Harris, 2001; Jerald & Boser, 2000; Olson, 2000). Determining cutoff or passing scores is an issue of concern in most states. Low cutoff scores have been chosen in several states with high demands for teachers. In some states teachers can earn passing scores by correctly answering less than half of test questions correctly (Bradley, 2000). Most teacher tests include multiple choice items, but, depending on the subject, from 5 to 15 states also include essays or other performance measures (Jerald & Boser, 2000). High school teachers who fail to pass certification tests generally require annual renewal of permission to continue teaching; however, 11 states allow teachers hired on that basis to remain in the classroom indefinitely (Jerald & Boser, 2000).

Most people approve the concept of teacher certification reform, but there is disagreement about the effects that raising standards and making certification requirements more rigorous have on improving the quality of teaching or on improving student achievement. Making certification more demanding in a time of reported teacher shortages, increasing enrollments, and accelerating teacher retirement rates are viewed as unwise by some. Many current certification procedures have been viewed with skepticism by others. Still others question whether certification requirements can effectively identify high-quality teaching or predict classroom success (Blair, 2001).

"The paucity of solid evidence pointing to the effectiveness of teacher licensure is striking: There is little connection between licensing requirements and high-quality teaching," the Thomas B. Fordham Foundation concludes in a 1999 report, *The Quest for Better Teachers: Grading the States.* (Olson, 2000, p. 18)

Additional criticism focused on the adequacy of teacher candidate testing programs. (Blair, 2001; Nagel & Peterson, 2001; National Research Council of the National Academies, 2000, 2001; Scherer, 2001). Critics suggested that tests should match the grade level at which the teacher will teach; thus, specialized knowledge and skills needed for successful teaching at a specific level could be examined (Nagel & Peterson, 2001). Tests should be designed to measure a broad range of content knowledge and other pedagogical knowledge (Scherer, 2001). Use of authentic measures is advocated by some who recommend teaching portfolios with videotaped samples of instruction, journals, measures of student learning, visits by independent assessors, written peer and principal assessments, reflective essays, and other authentic assessments (Nagel & Peterson, 2001; Zimmerman, 1997).

Holding teachers accountable for student learning and improving quality of teaching in classrooms fueled education reforms of the 1980s that led to national certification of teachers. The structures and processes of state teacher certification programs were scrutinized. Wide variation among these programs was found (DiBlasio, 1997). Inconsistencies in practices and incomprehensible policies painted a portrait of confusion and contradiction for teacher certification in the field. Recognition that unified standards for teacher preparation, teacher certification, and teaching were needed by the teaching profession led to reflective examination of the nature of teaching. Questions about the fundamental essence of teaching and qualities accomplished teachers possessed were raised. Discussions about what highly effective teachers know and do were at the core of these examinations. Reformation of teacher certification culminated in creation of the National Board for Professional Teaching Standards (NBPTS) in 1987 (to be discussed in detail later).

State teacher certification bodies have created an array of policies and regulations. Certification programs in each state are idiosyncratic and represent unique approaches to credentialing teachers within the state. Some programs have been characterized as ranging from inventive to obsessive-compulsive (DiBlasio, 1997). With current demands for restructuring these programs, many states are at various stages of designing or implementing systematic changes in their programs. The state of flux that characterizes these programs has contributed to confusion and uncertainty about requirements and policies regulating certification.

In 1997, DiBlasio studied certification and licensure of visual arts teachers in the United States. The study consisted of a survey of state teacher licensing bodies and tabulation of licensing requirements. Detailed reports of requirements for general certification, art-related certification, professional education, and testing were produced. The report of art-related requirements for certification included descriptions of required numbers of semester hours; courses and course work; detailed requirements for certification; competency-based requirements; and listings of studio, art history, art criticism, art theory, or aesthetics requirements. The report of professional education requirements included art education methods requirements, general foundations requirements, and clinical experience requirements. The report of testing requirements was divided between general professional testing requirements and content-specific requirements. This landmark study provided a cogent foundation for comprehending the complexities and idiosyncrasies of certifying visual arts teachers in the United States at the end of the 1990s. Due to the rapid pace of change, maintaining accurate up-to-the-minute information about certification is challenging to say the least. This study, however, provided a foundation for identifying current trends and the nature of change in certification of visual arts teachers.

The NAEA conducted a complementary study of teacher certification in visual arts, music, theater, and dance in 1997. The study also included review of the status of state visual arts standards revisions, arts assessment, and arts requirements for high school graduation. The report of arts teacher certification, compiled in September of 1996, included listings of instructional level certificates for the visual arts. For example, some states certify visual arts teachers only for elementary or secondary instruction, whereas others issue K-9, 7-12, or K-12 certificates. In addition, the report included lists of visual arts instruction alternatives, such as states granting permission for elementary classroom teachers to teach art and music and alternative certification in visual arts instruction. Finally, the report detailed pending proposals for changes in certification of art teachers that included proposed policies, procedures, and requirements under consideration at the time of the study. This study provided a status report from which comparisons of state licensure structures could be made. Additional ongoing studies designed to track licensure changes and to identify current visual arts licensure status in the states are needed. Findings from these studies and postings of current certification information should be made easily accessible to the field of art education through electronic and printed means.

In 2000, the National Art Education Association published findings from a study of secondary visual arts educators in the United States. The study involved 1,520 secondary art teachers from 878 schools. A total of 672 (44%) secondary visual arts teachers from 520 (59%) schools responded to a questionnaire designed to elicit information about art education in secondary schools. The report, *National Survey: Secondary Art Education* focused on demographics, schools, curriculum, instruction, professional development, and teacher evaluation. The study revealed that 85% of respondents held standard teaching certificates in art education. The remaining 15% held elementary, history, supervisor, principal, or administrator certificates. Probationary and provisional certificates in art education were held by less than 4% of the respondents. Further information about certification structures, procedures, or requirements was not available. Similar studies of middle school and elementary school art educators are necessary along with longitudinal studies of art teacher certification.

In 1986 the Carnegie Corporation Task Force on Teaching as a Profession published *A Nation Prepared: Teachers of the 21st Century.* This report recommended creation of a National Board for Professional Teaching Standards (NBPTS). The NBPTS was founded in 1987. It is a nonprofit, nonpartisan organization governed by a 63-member board of directors, the majority of whom are teachers. The missions of the NBPTS include (a) establishing high standards for what accomplished teachers should know and be able to do, (b) developing a voluntary national system to assess and certify teachers who meet these standards, and (c) advancing related education reforms for the purpose of improving student learning (National Board for Professional Teaching Standards, 2000). All NBPTS standards are grounded philosophically in the policy statement *What Teachers Should Know and Be Able to Do* (National Board for Professional Teaching Standards, 1989). This statement identified five core propositions about accomplished teachers: (1) Teachers are committed to students and their learning; (2) teachers know the subjects they teach and how to teach those subjects to students; (3) teachers are responsible for managing and monitoring student learning; (4) teachers think systematically about their practice and learn from experience; and (5) teachers are members of learning communities (National Board for Professional Teaching Standards, 1989). The NBPTS has developed standards for nearly 30 fields. The NBPTS certification standards *Early Adolescence through Young Adulthood/Art* were published in 1996. The *Early Childhood and Middle Childhood/Art* standards were published in 2000. A unique aspect of National Board standards is that they were developed by practitioners from the field. The NBPTS represents an effort by the teaching profession to define its own high standards and to create a credential recognizing practitioners who meet those standards (Goodwin, 1997). The visual arts standards identified skills and understanding that teachers need in order to be effective facilitators of learning. These skills and understandings are related to student learning and understanding art. Goodwin (1997) wrote:

> The National Board promotes the role of the teacher as one who takes responsibility for providing an appropriate environment that encourages and supports student learning. The National Board also promotes an approach to teaching that transcends the classroom and extends to informing outside influences. The National Board encourages teachers to contribute to education reform beyond the classroom. (p. 112)

Harman (2001) reported that the National Board certified 10,000 teachers in the past 14 years and expects to certify 100,000 by 2006. Certificates are awarded by the developmental level of the students and the subject or subjects being taught. Developmental levels include early childhood, ages 3 to 8; middle childhood, ages 7 to 12; early adolescence, ages 11 to 15; and adolescence and young adulthood, ages 14 to 18+. Certification candidates must submit an application fee, currently $2,300, and a portfolio of required artifacts providing evidence that each standard has been met. Finally, candidates must complete assessment center exercises that match the certification standards, subject area, and developmental level for each certificate. In its effort to promote National Board certification of art teachers, the National Art Education Association published *NBPTS Board Certification for Art Teachers* (1998). This summary of National Board certification provided a foundation for understanding the background, procedures, and requirements for certification of art teachers. Since its publication, revision and restructuring of certification procedures and requirements have taken place and are likely to continue on a routine basis.

Teachers have received encouragement to achieve National Board certification in 40 states. Incentives such as fee reimbursement and salary supplements are currently available and vary from state to state. Some states offer a one-time bonus to National Board-certified teachers. Others have created National Board certified teacher pay categories and still others have added as much as 15% annual salary increases for the 10-year life of the certificate (Podgursky, 2001). Goodwin (1997) identified additional incentives for achieving National Board certification. He suggested that National Board certification provides much needed recognition for accomplished teachers in the field of art education. He cited National Board certification as a meaningful professional development opportunity that causes art teachers to closely examine what they do as teachers and to evaluate their knowledge and skills as visual arts teachers. Goodwin intimated that National Board certification standards and assessments could be used as models for restructuring teacher preparation programs, thereby producing visual arts teachers of higher quality. Finally, Goodwin predicted that National Board certification would positively impact state certification and standards by suggesting how they could be made broader and more rigorous. Additional incentives were identified in a case study of National Board certified teachers by Bohen (2001). The study suggested that the process of National Board certification positively influenced candidates teaching processes. Certified teachers reported greater professional confidence, improved analysis of instruction, clearer focus on student outcomes, greater commitment to professional growth, and increased prestige. Bohen also reported that

National Board-certified teachers claimed the certification process was the most intense and rewarding professional development opportunity they had experienced.

Since its inception, National Board certification has been the target of criticism. Podgursky (2001) detailed a number of points of contention about National Board certification. He suggested that the National Board certification process should be self-sustaining. Beginning in the early 1990s, the board began receiving federal funds. In recent years, Congress has appropriated roughly $20 million annually to this private, not-for-profit teacher organization. He raises the questions of why public tax dollars should be spent to support a private enterprise and why the $2,300 application fee does not enable the NBPTS to be self-sustaining. Criticism is leveled at evaluation of written work candidates must submit. Candidates are not penalized for grammatical or syntax errors in any of their written work, and artifacts are evaluated by part-time teacher evaluators who may not have requisite skills themselves. Podgursky cited training programs for certification evaluators in other professions, such as those in law and medicine, that provide rigorous and extensive training to evaluators of certification materials. He suggested that training of evaluators in those professions does not favorably compare with minimal training received by National Board evaluators. The certification process does not include input from parents, school supervisors, or principals; people, who Podgursky suggested, may be better able to evaluate candidates than National Board evaluators. He suggested that there is no evidence the costly and time-consuming process of National Board certification is any better at identifying superior teachers than assessments by supervisors, principals, and parents. Because the process depends on candidates independently creating and documenting their teaching, Podgursky contended that opportunities for cheating are inherent in the process. He suggested that parents, supervisors, or principals should be included in the collection and documentation process. Podgursky perceived a potential threat to authority of local school administrators in the National Board certification process. Podgursky was equally concerned about the long-range impact of National Board certification on the field and on graduate education programs in colleges and universities. He suggested that as the number of National Board teachers grows, National Board standards and processes will act to dictate state certification standards and procedures as states attempt to fall in line with the surge toward National Board certification. Graduate teacher education programs will be forced to restructure to be compatible with National Board guidelines in order to draw top-quality students. Complications of restructuring graduate programs may act to undermine the goals of graduate programs and diminish the appeal of these programs. Implicit in these concerns are questions of who controls the National Board and to whom is the National Board accountable? Since its inception in 1987, the National Board has received nearly $100 million in federal support; yet, no rigorous study has been undertaken to determine whether students of National Board-certified teachers actually learn more or perform better on state achievement tests or other standardized measures than students of noncertified teachers. Podgursky concluded that National Board certification tells us candidates know *how* to be good teachers; but whether they do it on a consistent ongoing basis is questionable. Further criticism was leveled at National Board certification when Podgursky suggested that National Board certification fosters elitism and contributes to divisiveness in the profession. The cost of certification may contribute to preventing some accomplished teachers from pursuing certification. Podgursky contended that a significant amount of teacher interest in National Board certification is based solely on salary rewards, and he questions further whether state funds should be used to reward teachers who achieve certification. Finally, he suggested that National Board certification can have double-edged impact on hiring and retention practices. Some school districts may actively seek National Board-certified teachers for various reasons while excluding applicants who are not certified. By contrast, in a time of diminishing funds for education, National Board-certified teachers may find themselves being excluded from teaching openings or removed from teaching positions because of higher salary paid to National Board-certified teachers in many states. The NBPTS launched an ambitious program to create national standards for teachers in various disciplines. National Board certification of teachers continues to be embraced by a growing number of leaders in the federal government, state legislatures, state Departments of Education, local school boards, and business. The long-term impact of National Board certification on the teaching profession remains to be seen. At this point in time, it has provided a model for state Departments of Education in restructuring licensing and assessment of teachers.

Some Issues Related to Certification of Visual Arts Teachers

A number of certification issues in the field of general education hold relevance for the field of art education. Discussion of a limited number of these will follow. In-depth examination of the selected and related issues is beyond the scope of this report. Implementation of solutions to problems and answers to associated questions may be under the direct auspices and legal control of state teacher-certification bodies. However, visual arts educators should monitor teacher certification and contribute to the dialog that shapes change in art teacher certification and the issues discussed here.

If predictions of teacher shortages become reality, making teaching more attractive as a profession will involve a number of significant certification changes. In the eyes of some, teaching is viewed as a profession with little appeal. Hussar contended that the supply of qualified teachers can be increased or decreased by changing certification requirements. "The certification requirements could be adjusted to favor more new or old college graduates for teaching positions" (Hussar, 2001, p. 12). Haselkorn and Harris (2001) reported that Americans strongly favored (88%) elimination of the practice of hiring unqualified teachers and also favored (76%) strengthening state requirements for becoming a teacher. Although intentions of advocates suggesting more rigorous standards for certification of teachers can potentially improve the quality of teaching and student achievement, harsh realities of supply and demand for teachers needed to fill classroom vacancies may dictate action and policies needed to meet these demands. Hussar (2001) predicted that 2 million newly hired public school teachers and 500,000 newly hired private school teachers will be needed between 1998 and 2008. He suggested that continuation rates of teachers, which are directly related to teacher projections, can be influenced by education policymakers and economic factors. To illustrate the point, Hussar stated that school districts can increase continuation rates among teachers by enacting incentives, such as increases in salary and benefits, which may encourage teachers to retain their positions rather than to retire, or they can enact policies to recruit people older than new college graduates into the teaching profession. Also, an economic downturn might make teaching positions more attractive because of their perceived stability. Job security associated with teaching holds power to draw numbers of people to the profession in times of economic uncertainty.

Teacher shortages in economically deprived settings and in rural and urban schools have caused school districts to hire teachers who may not meet state certification standards. Jerald and Boser (2000) studied state licensing requirements and identified "loopholes for bypassing minimum requirements." With the exception of New Jersey, each state provides a range of exceptions that permit teachers to enter the classroom without meeting full licensure requirements; these include waiving basic skills tests, subject-area tests, or subject-area courses requirements. Teachers permitted such exceptions are granted various credentials from emergency licenses and limited standard licenses to probationary certificates and hardship or out-of-field assignment licenses. These credentials remain valid for periods from 1 year to unlimited periods of time.

Art education is being provided at the elementary level by classroom teachers who may not be required to meet state art teaching standards (Brewer, 1999; Carey et al., 1995; Council of Chief State School Officers, 2000; Hatfield & Peeno, 2001; National Association of State School Boards of Education, 2000; National Endowment for the Arts, 1988). In elementary art education classrooms, over half (57%) of instruction is provided by specialists and classroom teachers (29%) or solely by classroom teachers (28%) (Carey et al., 1995). It is doubtful that all of these teachers possess adequate training in art education, because only 15 states certify teachers based on art standards (Council of Chief State School Officers, 2000; Hatfield & Peeno, 2001). Contributing to lower certification requirements for art education is the finding that only five states require statewide student assessment in art (Council of Chief State School Officers, 2000). Lack of these assessments frees school districts from being held accountable for maintaining quality art education programs or from providing visual arts education taught by certified visual arts specialists. All of these factors combine to lessen the need for school districts to seek, hire, and retain certified teachers for their art education programs.

Current teacher shortages and predicted shortages of 2 million teachers (Hussar, 2001) over the next decade have fueled calls for alternative certification programs for teachers in all disciplines. Findings from a national study of public attitudes toward teaching, educational opportunity, and school reform conducted by Haselkorn and Harris (2001) revealed that the American public strongly favors (83%) attracting more people currently working in other careers into teacher preparation. Development of alternative certification procedures for teachers has been recommended over the past 2 decades (National Commission on Excellence in Education, 1983; National Endowment for the Arts, 1988; U.S. Department of Education, 1991, 1994). In 1988, the National Endowment for the Arts called for states to:

> develop and implement flexible procedures that provide for special testing and certification of experienced practicing artists and arts professionals who can demonstrate a comprehensive background in the arts and substantial knowledge of the issues and methodologies of K-12 arts instruction. (p. 26)

Feistritzer (1998) defined "alternative teacher certification" as,

> every avenue to becoming licensed to teach from emergency certification to very sophisticated and well-designed programs that address the professional preparation needs of the growing population of individuals who already have a baccalaureate degree and considerable life experience who want to become teachers. (p. 2)

In coming to grips with the teacher supply issue, states have allowed teachers to become certified through specially designed programs and procedures that differ from those traditionally used (Feistritzer & Chester, 1991). People are now entering the teaching profession after careers in other fields. Today, alternative certification programs are available in 43 states (Berry, 2001; Broughman & Rollefson, 2000; Finn & Madigan, 2001; Haselkorn & Harris, 2001; Olson, 2000). In 1998 to 1999, alternative teaching credentials were issued to 24,000 teachers in the 28 states that keep these data, and during the past decade over 80,000 alternative licenses were issued (Berry, 2001). Evidence is emerging that minority candidates are attracted to alternative certification programs (Kwiatkowski, 1999).

A variety of alternative preparation and certification programs exist and contradictory and conflicting claims have been reported about them. Berry (2001) reported that two thirds of the 1,354 colleges and universities that prepare teachers have at least one teaching program for midcareer professionals. Finn and Madigan (2001) suggested that alternative certification programs commonly require a candidate to possess a bachelor's degree, pass a competency test and background check, and complete a compressed training program that includes hands-on experience. Graduates from many of these programs receive support from a supervisor or mentor teacher. Berry (2001) stated that typically preparation programs at these institutions last from 9 to 15 months. He suggested alternative preparation programs cannot be viewed as equal to traditional programs in terms of content, duration, rigor, and support for learning how to teach. To illustrate his point, he reported that "shortcut" programs typically include 4 weeks of training in classroom management, simplified instruction on developing lesson plans, and an introduction to the complex world of teaching. By contrast, Berry reports the existence of numerous high-quality programs and provided a listing of characteristics of these programs. They include strong academic and pedagogical course work, intensive field experience, requirements that candidates meet all state standards for subject matter and teaching knowledge for a standard teaching certificate; and guarantee that new teachers meet all state quality standards, including passing the same assessments given for traditional certification.

Candidates entering alternative certification programs often lack (a) a wide range of knowledge and skills necessary for effective teaching; (b) understanding of subject matter in ways that allow them to organize it and make it accessible to students; (c) understanding how students think and behave; and (d) recognizing student differences that may arise from culture, language, family background, and prior schooling (Berry, 2001). In a national study of 14,000 alternatively certified teachers, Shen (1997b) suggested that alternatively certified teachers had lower levels of educational accomplishment and higher out-of-field teaching assignments. By contrast, Berry (2001) reported that alternatively certified teachers have grade point averages that meet or surpass national averages of traditionally certified teachers. In fairness, it should be kept in mind that due to the higher numbers of teachers who have entered teaching through the traditional means, the grade point average of those teachers may be negatively skewed. Outcomes of studies have indicated that teachers from alternative certification programs have more difficulties with curriculum development, teaching methods, classroom management, and student motivation than traditionally prepared teachers (Berry, 2001; Darling-Hammond, 2001; Feiman-Nemser & Parker, 1990; Grossman, 1989). Contrary to these reports, Goldhaber and Brewer (1999) suggested that students of alternatively certified teachers produced results on assessments of learning that were comparable to those of teachers with conventional licenses.

More conflicting evidence is found in reports of studies of alternatively certified teachers and retention rates. Feistritzer (2000), Finn and Madigan (2001), and Klagholz (2000) suggested that teachers prepared through alternative routes have lower attrition rates than do conventionally certified teachers. However, they did not report specific retention percentages or rates for this group with which comparisons to conventionally certified teachers can be made. Darling-Hammond (2001) reported that nearly 30% of traditionally licensed new teachers and about 10% of teachers prepared in extended 5-year programs, which include a full year of student teaching, leave the field within 5 years with even higher rates in districts with disadvantaged student populations. Berry (2001) and Darling-Hammond (2001) reported that 60% of individuals who enter teaching through alternative certification programs leave the profession by the third year.

Alternative certification programs are an established part of the education landscape in the United States. Clearly, they provide a means of access to teaching that appeals to a particular group of individuals with interest in contributing to the education of students in American schools. For the foreseeable future, alternative certification programs are likely to continue providing teachers to meet increasing demands. Calls for federal and state assistance and support of these programs abound (Feistritzer, 1999b, 2000). Issues and controversies raised by alternative certification must continue to be examined and addressed by those in general education and art education. Despite a wide variation in alternative strategies, educators and policymakers should insist that all teachers meet the same high standards no matter how they enter the profession. The U.S. Department of Education (1995) identified encouraging signs that suggested reforms in education in the early 1990s were beginning to take hold. Teacher quality has been improved through reforms in certification policy, requirements, standards, and assessments. Pratt (2000) reported that 92% of teachers had regular or standard state certificates or advanced professional certificates, and the numbers of teachers with these certificates generally increased with years of teaching experience. Continued tracking of the results of these reforms is needed to determine their long-range effects.

RETENTION OF TEACHERS

Mark Twain once said, "Sometimes keepin' a good thing is harder than gettin' it." This witticism has significance for understanding issues and questions related to maintaining a viable teaching force. Startling figures continue to surface about the rates at which teachers leave the field. Archer (1999) and Grissmer and Kirby (1997) suggested that as baby-boomer teachers retire they will be replaced with younger teachers whose attrition rates are higher than those in midcareer. Haselkorn and Fideler (1999) reported that 20% of new teachers leave the classroom within 3 years and nearly 10% leave in the first year alone. Darling-Hammond (2001) stated that nearly 30% of new teachers leave within 5 years with even higher rates in disadvantaged districts. Olson (2000) found that over 50% of new teachers quit teaching after 5 years. Over the period from 1988 through 1989 to 1994 through 1995, the percentage of public school teachers leaving the field rose from 5.6 to 6.6% of all teachers in the United States (Snyder & Hoffman, 2001). Olson and Jerald (1998) reported that 58% of urban schools have at least one teacher leave before the end of the school year compared with 27% of nonurban schools. Among teachers who left during that period, the percentage of men rose by .5%, whereas the percentage of women who left rose by nearly 1.5 percentage points (Snyder & Hoffman, 2001). Also during that period, the percentage of teachers with minority backgrounds leaving public schools rose nearly 2.5 percentage points (Snyder & Hoffman, 2001). In the field of art education during the period from 1988 through 1989 to 1994 through 1995, the percentage of public school art teachers who left the field rose sharply from 4.2% to 7%; in private schools that rate dropped dramatically from 17.7% to 10.9% (Whitener et al., 1997). Olson (2000) reported that teachers who score in the top quartile on college entrance examinations were nearly twice as likely to leave the teaching profession as those from other quartiles. Teachers up to the age of 50 in private schools were more likely to leave teaching than those in public schools (Hussar, 2001; Rittenhouse, 1999).

Studies raising alarms about teachers leaving the field seem to suggest that the profession is in turmoil with an unstable population. Nothing is further from the truth. Henke and Zahn (2001) studied retention rates in various professions and found that among those who were employed as full-time K-12 teachers in 1994, eighty-two-percent were still teaching in 1997. Furthermore, none of the other occupations studied for this time period, including law enforcement (73%), engineers (71%), scientists (71%), business support (66%), financial services (66%), legal professionals (57%), computer and technical (53%), sales and service (45%), blue collar (39%), and clerical occupations (25%), proved more stable than teaching. Those least likely to leave the teaching profession were graduates of 5-year preservice programs (Darling-Hammond, 2001). Studies of teachers in this group have found that they are more satisfied with their preparation, they are more highly rated by their colleagues and principals, and are as effective with students as more experienced teachers (Andrew, 1990; Andrew & Schwab, 1995; Baker, 1993; Darling-Hammond, 2001).

Teachers left teaching for a range of reasons. Stress, working conditions, class size, low salaries, low prestige and lack of recognition, teacher burnout, discipline problems, governance of schools by legislatures and the courts, poor student motivation, lack of mentorship programs, difficult assignments, poor opportunity for professional development, and inadequate administrative support were the most common reasons teachers left the teaching profession or failed to consider teaching as a career option (Archer, 1999; Baker & Smith, 1997; Henke & Zahn, 2001; Goodlad, 1987; Hussar, 2001; Olson, 2000; Whitener et al., 1997). The two main reasons former teachers left teaching in 1994 through 1995 were retirement (27.4%) and pregnancy or child rearing (14.3%) (Rittenhouse, 1999; Whitener et al., 1997). New occupations of former teachers in 1994 to 1995 were self-employment or with private companies, businesses, individuals, or federal, state, or local government (Whitener et al., 1997).

Some Issues Related to Retention of Teachers

Retention of a quality teaching force poses a wealth of issues and questions for stakeholders to consider and address. The following is a sampling of some of them. Discussion of the selected issues is not intended to be exhaustive. As in previous sections of this discussion, the selected issues are approached from the standpoint of general education. However, the generic nature of these issues has direct implications for visual arts education. Specific themes related to these issues having special implications for art education will be discussed when appropriate. An essential point to keep in mind is that for each of these issues local school districts and state or national agencies can promote policies that affect retention and continuation rates for all teachers. Closer examination of opportunities, resources, and levels of support needed to do so is essential in making an impact on the retention of all teachers including art teachers.

Working conditions were cited among common reasons teachers left the field (Baker & Smith, 1997; Darling-Hammond, 2001; Henke & Zahn, 2001; Scherer, 2001; Whitener et al., 1997). Working conditions may include an array of factors. Class size, discipline problems, age of school buildings, lack of equipment and supplies, difficult assignments given to inexperienced teachers, and other contributing factors may make teaching conditions intolerable. Often these factors are related to funding limitations or the absence of policies designed to address them. The everyday stresses of teaching contribute to magnifying these factors to make them an irritant to teaching and learning. Improving working conditions requires continuous collaboration among teachers, administration, business and community leaders, parents, state education agencies, and professional associations. Students and teachers should be included in identifying factors that contribute to poor working conditions and provided with opportunities to suggest solutions for improving them. Policies should be enacted by decision makers that account for maintaining and improving favorable working conditions in all schools.

Low salaries was the second most common reason teachers left teaching (Archer, 2000; Darling-Hammond, 2001; Haselkorn & Harris, 2001; Jorgenson, 2001; Whitener et al., 1997). The tension between wanting to provide high-quality education for all students and providing funding for salaries to draw well-prepared and skilled teachers has long been an issue in education. Because public schools are supported with tax dollars, the public is hesitant to approve increases in taxes to provide funds for increasing salary needs of teachers. Studies of comparisons of salaries of teachers with those of equal educational qualifications in other fields reveal startling discrepancies. Average salaries of teachers compared with those in other professions dramatically illustrate the inequities of income. Salaries of teachers at the middle and senior levels of their careers should be increased. These individuals represent the knowledge and experience bases of the profession. Unfortunately, these groups are most affected by lowered incremental salary increases and salary compression (Archer, 2000). In other professions, people at these stages are sought after and rewarded. It is a common adage that "No one goes into teaching for the money"; however, training and demands of teaching coupled with the importance sound education has in all walks of life in our society still has not convinced the public to provide compensation commensurate with that importance. Clearly, increasing salaries of all teachers provides significant incentives that can affect teacher retention rates.

Entering the teaching profession is a daunting task no matter how rigorous teacher preparation programs may be. Naiveté, idealism, misconceptions, lack of information about policies and procedural requirements, curriculum development, assessments, classroom management, and a host of other factors converge on new teachers. Newly hired teachers frequently left teaching because of the absence of teacher induction programs despite reports that 50% of first-year public school teachers participate in some type of induction program and 60% of new teachers in urban schools participate in them (Haselkorn & Fideler, 1999). New teachers who left teaching felt isolated and bewildered by the lack of a means to support them during their "novice" period in the profession. Studies recommended that development and expansion of teacher induction programs hold particular potential for improving teacher retention rates (Darling-Hammond, 2001; Haselkorn & Fideler, 1999; Haselkorn & Harris, 2001; Henke & Zahn, 2001; Jerald & Boser, 2000; Olson, 2000; Olson & Hendrie, 1998; Whitener et al., 1997). Olson (2000) reported that 28 states currently have teacher induction programs. These programs consist of mentorship strategies, inservice training, administrative support, or support groups of other newly hired teachers. Providing induction programs designed with the needs of teachers in various subject areas in mind, such as those in art education, holds particular power to help teachers acclimate themselves to the demands of the profession while providing support and guidance in adjusting to them.

The teaching profession is in a constant state of flux. Teachers at all levels of experience need ongoing professional development to keep abreast of changes. New technology, laws, teaching materials, instructional methods, and other developments influence teaching in ways teachers must understand and learn. Lack of support for meaningful professional development opportunities have contributed to attrition rates of teachers (Darling-Hammond, 2001; Whitener et al., 1997). Repeated calls for professional development of teachers have been made (Goodwin, 2001; Haselkorn & Harris, 2001; Longley, 1999; Nathanson, 2001; National Endowment for the Arts, 1988; Pratt, 2000; U.S. Department of Education, 1995; Whitener et al., 1997). Art teachers reported that less than half (44%) of urban school districts (Sabol, 1998b) and slightly over half (52%) of rural school districts (Sabol, 1999) provided professional development activities. The three most common forms of support for urban art teachers were professional leave days and substitute teachers (63% each) and conference registration fees (47%) (Sabol, 1998b). Rural art teachers reported substitute teachers (78%), professional leave days (75%), and conference registration fees (68%) as most common professional development support (Sabol, 1999). Art teachers complained that professional development opportunities related to their needs were scarce and mandatory attendance at professional development activities unrelated to their needs was widespread (Sabol, 1998b, 1999). Teachers need to invest in themselves through their ongoing professional development. Participation in such activities has great potential to contribute to improving their knowledge and skills as professionals and their students will reap the dividends. Decision makers and policymakers need to understand the long-term importance of professional development to teachers and students alike. They need to make decisions, create policies, and use resources that foster the professional development of all teachers. Such policies and decisions can positively influence retention rates of teachers by creating more knowledgeable and skilled teachers who are better able to deal with changing demands of the field.

A significant factor in successful teaching is support from administration. School administrators control power that affects both teaching and learning. Lack of administrative support contributes to the deterioration of both. Former teachers reported lack of administrative support as a contributing factor in their decisions to leave teaching (Darling-Hammond, 2001; Haselkorn & Fideler, 1999; Haselkorn & Harris, 2001; Henke & Zahn, 2001; Olson, 2000; Olson & Hendrie, 1998; Whitener et al., 1997). Teachers depend upon administrators to provide guidance and assistance in meeting the goals of their programs. Creating positive relationships with faculty is a goal administrators and supervisors should strive to achieve. Sabol (in press) suggested critical factors for supervisors and administrators to consider in providing positive administrative support for art educators. Among them were involving teachers in administrative decision making; holding teachers accountable; setting high standards for teachers and maintaining them; working to provide increased funding for art programs; providing manageable schedules; improving student teacher ratios; being supportive of art education; supporting demonstrations of students' art achievement; and cultivating open dialog with teachers through active listening, constructive criticism, and positive involvement with the visual arts program. Administrative support for teachers is the product of long-term commitment and mutual respect for art and teachers.

Teaching provides its own set of incentives. However, retention of teachers may be improved by a group of incentives that would make teaching more appealing to those entering the profession and to those who have been in it for extended periods of time. Various researchers have concluded that offering teachers opportunities that are widely available in other professions requiring comparable education and training, such as signing bonuses; forgiving education loans; providing tax credits to teachers; awarding merit bonuses; raising salaries; improving fringe benefits; providing scholarships for professional development, advanced training, and degrees; and making housing allowances for mortgages or rent and moving expenses, would significantly raise retention rates (Archer, 2000; Darling-Hammond, 2001; Haselkorn & Harris, 2001; Henke & Zahn, 2001; Whitener et al., 1997). Members of other professions routinely change jobs in pursuit of improvements in any of these. Job applicants conscientiously investigate these factors in selecting jobs. Teachers are beginning to see opportunities of these kinds as becoming more commonplace. Olson (2000) found that 27 states currently have loan forgiveness programs, but only 10 states aim their programs at candidates willing to teach in hard-to-staff schools or regions. Isolated reports of other incentives designed to lure teachers to the profession or to retain them are beginning to become more widespread. Unfortunately, these incentives are financial in nature and most school districts cannot offer such enticements. If predictions of teacher shortages materialize, incentives such as these may become requirements for maintaining a high-quality teaching force rather than luxuries provided to a few.

Retention of teachers will continue to be a thorny issue in education. Unforeseen factors may give rise to new issues that will shape the teaching profession in the future. Teachers will need to become more circumspect about evaluating the rewards of teaching and the practical needs of living in a complex society of the 21st century in order to make judgments about the merits of teaching as a profession. In the future, the merits of teaching may increasingly depend on responses to some of the issues suggested here.

FUTURE DIRECTIONS FOR RECRUITMENT, CERTIFICATION, AND RETENTION OF TEACHERS

The previous discussion provided a brief summary of an increasing array of developments and issues for the recruitment, certification, and retention of teachers. It is uncertain if or how any of these issues can be resolved. However, it is reasonable to speculate about some possibilities they suggest. The following discussion will include a forecast based on conjecture about the future of some of them.

Some General Future Directions for Recruitment, Certification, and Recruitment of Teachers

The future of recruitment, certification, and retention of teachers will be affected by three dominant forces. The first is the continued emphasis on the standards movement. Standards needed for recruitment, certification, and retention of teachers will continue to be developed and revised to reflect future needs of the profession. The public will continue to require evidence that teachers are meeting these standards and they will demand that such standards continue to become more rigorous. An ongoing problem will be creation of means of holding teachers accountable to these standards while allowing others who fail to meet the standards to continue to teach due to possible teacher shortages.

A second force that will affect recruitment, certification, and retention of teachers will be assessment. There is great possibility that public dissatisfaction with schools and student achievement will grow and assessment will gain in power as an accountability measure. Assessment of teachers will become more comprehensive and more frequent. Teachers will be required not only to pass various assessments of their competence at all stages of their careers, but also to provide evidence of continued improvement in their students' achievements. In the future, employment of teachers may hinge on assessment results more than on any other single factor.

Technology is the third factor that will influence recruitment, certification, and retention of teachers. There are strong indications that local school districts and states will depend on technology to hire, certify, and retain teachers. Web sites that include job listings, applications, and interactive interviews will become commonplace. Certification of teachers also will be done with the aid of technology. State and national credentialing bodies will establish electronic methods for certification. Teachers will apply for teaching credentials and renew them through technological means. Teacher candidates will rely on technology by creating Web sites with their credentials, portfolios, and digital interactive examples of their classroom performances as teachers. Personnel directors and administrators will access teacher candidates and teachers through use of technology and evaluate their competencies. Further, use of technology in teaching will continue to expand. Teachers will use technology to expand their capabilities as teachers and their knowledge of subject matter content and pedagogy. Technology will become essential to recruitment and retention of teachers by creating professional development opportunities through distance learning.

Prognostications about the future may provide an agenda for possible action. Occasionally, predictions about the future become realities. Often they fail to materialize. If nothing else, they provide food for thought and contemplation. They encourage reflection and evaluation of the present while enticing the thoughtful to consider possibilities for the future. What the future of visual arts education holds is uncertain, but actions taken today can influence outcomes in the future.

RECOMMENDATIONS FOR FUTURE RESEARCH

Research will play a critical role in the future of recruitment, certification, and retention of teachers. Fundamental questions that bear directly on issues in these areas must be answered. Questions posed in this discussion were couched against the backdrop of general education. Each question and issue that is pertinent to general education must be explored and investigated in the field of art education. Unfortunately, relatively little research pertaining to recruitment, certification, and retention of art teachers has been done in visual arts education. Researchers from all levels of experience should consider investigations in these areas. The need exists for longitudinal, empirical, qualitative, philosophical, historical, ethnographic, case study, and other types of research. Findings from such research contribute to understanding and development of the field.

The previously discussed overview of some of the literature and studies of recruitment, certification, and retention of teachers raises a number of research questions for the field. These questions provide suggestions for an agenda for art education researchers that should foster awareness, clarify and describe situations, extend current knowledge, and contribute to translating research into practice.

The content areas of recruitment, certification, and retention of teachers are presented as an agenda for research. Examples of some general questions researchers may pursue in each of these areas are included.

In the area of recruitment of teachers, researchers may consider investigating the following questions:

Who is entering the field of visual arts education?
Why are people entering visual arts education?
What factors influence decisions to enter visual arts education?
What characteristics, knowledge, and skills do successful visual arts teachers possess?
At what instructional level(s) are teacher shortages likely to occur in visual arts education and when?
What are current enrollments in visual arts education preservice programs?
Will there be enough new art teachers produced by these programs to meet projected needs for the next decade and beyond?
What recruitment strategies have been successful in general education and other professions, and how can they be implemented in visual arts education?
What art teacher hiring practices currently exist?
What art teacher recruitment policies currently exist?
What art teacher recruitment policies will be needed in the future?

In the area of certification of teachers, researchers may consider the following questions:

What has been the historic development of visual arts teacher certification?
How has the nature of certification of visual arts teachers changed or remained the same over time?
What current certification requirements exist (standards, tests, portfolios, etc.)?
What alternative certification programs exist for art teachers?
What is the quality of alternative certification programs?
Do alternative certification programs produce quality art teachers for the field?
What impact has National Board certification of art teachers had on the field?
What numbers of art teachers have been certified by the National Board?
After receiving National Board certification, what affect has certification had on the teaching of those art teachers?
How have roles of National Board-certified art teachers changed after certification?
What incentives have been provided for National Board-certified art teachers?
Are these incentives equal to those provided to teachers in other subject areas?
What art teacher certification policies currently exist?
What art teacher certification policies will be needed in the future?

In the area of retention of art teachers, researchers may consider the following questions:

What factors contribute to art teachers' decisions to leave the field?
What factors encourage art teachers to remain in teaching?
At what rate do art teachers prepared through alternative certification programs leave the field?
How does this rate compare to retention of art teachers prepared through traditional means?
How do art teacher retention rates compare to those of teachers from other disciplines?
What are projected retirement rates for art teachers in the next decade and beyond?
What reduction in staff policies currently exist and how do they affect art teachers?
What art teacher retention policies currently exist?
What reduction in staff and retention of art teacher policies are needed?

Each question in this list of possible research questions may be investigated from local, state, and national perspectives. Most of the questions should be studied through a variety of research methods and methodologies. The meaning of findings from research related to any of these questions, as well as from their relationships to the recruitment, certification, and retention research contexts, can be interpreted. Baseline research in each of the content areas is needed to inform policymakers, direct preservice preparation of art teachers, and assist decision makers concerned with making judgments related to the field of art education.

CONCLUSION

Art teachers, like nearly everyone else, occasionally make judgments about the relative merits of entering or continuing in their chosen profession. Teaching art possesses a unique assortment of incentives. The intrinsic rewards for teaching are palpable to teachers. The desire to help students learn, pride in contributing to the education of fellow human beings, joy of watching students learn, love of teaching, and, for some, the satisfaction of answering a "call" are reasons enough to enter and continue teaching. But, the realities of the world in which art teachers live force some to make more weighty judgments about what they have chosen to do. Often they are driven to enter or leave teaching for practical reasons. These reasons may be related to character, financial, family, personal, or other concerns.

Demands for art teachers, as in those for all subject areas, will increase in the future. Recruitment of students for visual arts preservice preparation programs will increase proportionately, as will recruitment of art teachers. Restructuring efforts for certification of visual arts teachers will continue and, out of necessity to meet increasing demands for art teachers in the future, will become more broad in their design permitting a wider array of avenues through which individuals can enter the teaching profession. The need to retain art teachers will become critically important and new incentives will need to be creatively pursued.

Research focused at investigating recruitment, certification, and retention of visual arts teachers can inform the field about how visual arts teachers perceive themselves and understand their roles in the education of all students. Answers to research questions can help all art educators better understand and address issues of importance to the field. Findings from research can provide information and guidance in making decisions and in taking actions that will affect the field. Creating a research base for art education has great potential to provide a foundation upon which art education can be built and from which it can be judged in the future.

REFERENCES

Andrew, M. (1990). The differences between graduates of four–year and five-year teacher preparation programs. *Journal of Teacher Education, 41*, 45–51.

Andrew, M., & Schwab, R. L. (1995). Has reform of teacher preparation influenced teacher performance? *Action in Teacher Education, 17*, 43–53.

Archer, J. (1999). New teachers abandon field at high rate. *Education Week, 18*(27), 20–21.

Archer, J. (2000, January 13). Competition is fierce for minority teachers. *Quality Counts 2000, 19*(18), 32–34.

Ayers, W. (1994). City schools can be saved. *Educational Leadership, 51*(8), 60–63.

Baker, T. (1993). A survey of four-year and five-year program graduates and their principals. *Southeastern Regional Association of Teacher Educators, 2*(2), 28–33.

Baker, D. P., & Smith, T. (1997). Trend 2: Teacher turnover and teacher quality: Refocusing the issue. *Teacher College Record, 99*, 29–35.

Berry, B. (2001). No shortcuts to preparing good teachers. *Educational Leadership, 58*(8), 32–36.

Blair, J. (2001, April 4). Teacher tests criticized as single gauge. *Education Week*, A1, A19.

Blandy, D., & Congdon, K. G. (Eds.). (1987). *Art in a democracy.* New York: Teachers College Press.

Bohen, D. B. (2001). Strengthening teaching through national certification. *Educational Leadership, 58*(8), 50–53.

Bradley, A. (1999). States uneven teacher supply complicates staffing of schools. *Education Week, 18*(26), 10–11.

Bradley, A. (2000, January 13). The gatekeeping challenge. *Quality Counts 2000, 19*(18), 20–26.

Brewer, T. M. (1999). Art teacher profile and preference. *Studies in Art Education, 41*(1), 61–70.

Broughman, S. P., & Rollefson, M. R. (2000). *Teacher supply in the United States: Sources of newly hired teachers in public and private schools, 1987–88 to 1993–94.* (National Center for Education Statistics, NCES 2000-309). Washington, DC: U.S. Department of Education.

Burton, D. (2001). A quartile analysis of the 1997 NAEP visual arts report card. *Studies in Art Education, 43*(1), 35–44.

Carey, N., Sikes, M., Foy, R., & Carpenter, J. (1995). *Art education in public elementary and secondary schools.* (National Center for Education Statistics, NCES 95-082). Washington, DC: U.S. Department of Education.

Carnegie Corporation Task Force on Teaching as a Profession. (1986). A nation prepared: Teachers for the twenty-first century. Washington, DC: Carnegie Forum on Education and the Economy.

Clark, G., & Zimmerman, E. (2000). Greater understanding of the local community: A community-based art education program for rural schools. *Art Education, 53*(2), 33–39.

Council of Chief State School Officers. (1985). *Arts education in the states: A survey of state education policies.* (Department of Education). Washington, DC: U.S. Government Printing Office.

Council of Chief State School Officers. (1992). *Model standards for beginning teacher licensing and development: A resource for state dialogue.* Washington, DC: Council for Chief State School Officers.

Council of Chief State School Officers. (1998). *Key state education policies on k-12 education.* Washington, DC: Council for Chief State School Officers.

Council of Chief State School Officers. (1999). *Strengthening professional practice-state actions in five key areas: Recruitment, preparation, induction, professional growth, and career paths.* Washington, DC: Council of Chief State School Officers.

Council of Chief State School Officers. (2000). *Key state education policies on K-12 education: Results from the 2000 policies and practices survey of state departments of education.* Washington, DC: Council of Chief State School Officers.

Darling-Hammond, L. (1984). *Beyond the commission reports: The coming crisis in teaching.* Santa Monica, CA: RAND Corporation.

Darling-Hammond, L. (2001). The challenge of staffing our schools. *Educational Leadership, 58*(8), 12–17.

Day, M. (1997). Preparing teachers of art for 2000 and beyond. In M. Day (Ed.), *Preparing teachers of art* (pp. 3–25). Reston, VA: National Art Education Association.

DiBlasio, M. K. (1997). Certification and licensure requirements for art education: Comparison of state systems. In M. Day (Ed.), *Preparing teachers of art* (pp. 73–100). Reston, VA: National Art Education Association.

Diket, R. M. (2001). A factor analytic model of eighth-grade learning: Secondary analysis of NAEP arts data. *Studies in Art Education, 43*(1), 5–17.

Dorn, B. (1997). Youth violence: False fears and hard truths. *Educational Leadership, 55*(2), 45–48.

Feiman-Nemser, S., & Parker, M. B. (1990). *Making subject matter part of the conversation or helping beginning teachers learn to teach.* East Lansing, MI: National Center for Research on Teacher Education.

Feistritzer, C. E. (1998). *Alternative certification: An overview.* Washington, DC: National Center for Education Information.

Feistritzer, C. E. (1999a). *The making of a teacher: A report on teacher preparation in the U.S.* Washington, DC: National Center for Education Information.

Feistritzer, C. E. (1999b). *Teacher quality and alternative certification.* Washington, DC: National Center for Education Information.

Feistritzer, C. E. (2000). *Alternative routes to teaching escalate in just the last two years.* Washington, DC: National Center for Education Information.

Feistritzer, E., & Chester, D. (1991). *Alternative certification: A state-by-state analysis.* Washington, DC: National Center for Education Information.

Finn, C. E., & Madigan, K. (2001). Removing the barriers for teacher candidates. *Educational Leadership, 58*(8), 29–31.

Gerald, D. E., & Hussar, W. J. (2000). *Projections of education statistics to 2010.* U.S. Department of Education, National Center for Educational Statistics. Washington, DC: U.S. Government Printing Office.

Getty Center for Education in the Arts. (1985). *Beyond creating: The place for art in America's schools.* Los Angeles, CA: Getty Center for Education in the Arts.

Getty Education Institute for the Arts. (1996). *Educating for the workplace through the arts.* Los Angeles, CA: Getty Education Institute for the Arts.

Getty Education Institute for the Arts. (1997). *Arts education for life and work.* Los Angeles, CA: Getty Education Institute for the Arts.

Goals 2000 Arts Education Partnership. (1997). *Priorities for arts education.* Washington, DC: Council of Chief State School Officers.

Goldhaber, D. D., & Brewer, D. J. (1999). Teacher licensing and student achievement. In M. Kanstoroom & C. E. Finn Jr. (Eds.), *Better teachers, better schools* (pp. 83–102). Washington, DC: Thomas B. Fordham Foundation.

Goodlad, J. (1987). A place called school. In R. A. Smith (1987) *Excellence in art education: Ideas and initiatives* (pp. 86–89). Reston, VA: National Art Education Association.

Goodnough, A. (2000, January 21). Union says poll of teachers predicts wave of retirements. *The New York Times.*

Goodwin, M. (1997). The national board for professional teaching standards: Implications for art teacher preparation. In M. Day (Ed.), *Preparing teachers of art* (pp. 101–116). Reston, VA: National Art Education Association.

Goodwin, M. (2001). *Visual arts education: Setting an agenda for improving student learning.* Reston, VA: National Art Education Association.

Grissmer, D., & Kirby, S. N. (1997). Teacher turnover and teacher quality. *Teachers College Record, 99,* 45–56.

Grossman, P. (1989). Learning to teach without teacher education. *Teachers College Record, 91*(2), 191–208.

Harman, A. E. (2001). A wider role for the national board. *Educational Leadership, 58*(8), 54–55.

Haselkorn, D., & Fideler, E. F. (1999). *Learning the ropes: Urban teacher induction programs in the United States.* Belmont, MA: Recruiting New Teachers.

Haselkorn, D., & Harris, L. (2001). The essential profession: American education at the crossroads. Belmont, MA: Recruiting New Teachers.

Hatfield, T. A., & Peeno, L. N. (2001). *A report on state policy formation.* Reston, VA: National Art Education Association.

Henke, R. R., Choy, S. P., Chen, X., Geis, S., & Alt, M. N. (1997). *America's teachers: Profile of a profession, 1993–94* (National Center for Education Statistics, NCES 97-460). Washington, DC: U.S. Department of Education.

Henke, R. R., & Zahn, L. (2001). *Attrition of new teachers among recent graduates: Comparing occupational stability among 1992–93 graduates who taught and those who worked in other occupations* (National Center for Educational Statistics, NCES 2001-189.) Washington, DC: U.S. Department of Education.

Holmes Group. (1986). *Tomorrow's teachers: A report of the Holmes Group.* East Lansing, MI: Holmes Group.

Hussar, W. J. (2001). *Predicting the needs for newly hired teachers in the United States to 2008-09* (National Center for Educational Statistics). Washington, DC: U.S. Department of Education.

Hutchens, J. (1997). Accomplishing change in the university: Strategies for improving art teacher preparation. In M. Day (Ed.), *Preparing teachers of art* (pp. 139–154). Reston, VA: National Art Education Association.

Improving America's Schools Act of 1994, H.R. 6, 103d Cong. 2d Session. (1994).

Indiana Professional Standards Board. (1997). *Standards for teachers of fine arts.* Indianapolis, IN: Indiana Professional Standards Board.

Ingersoll, R. M. (2001). The realities of out-of-field teaching. *Educational Leadership, 58*(8), 42–45.

Jerald, C. D., & Boser, U. (2000, January 13). Setting policies for new teachers: States set sights on policies to ensure a qualified teaching force, but they're not there yet. *Quality Counts 2000, 19*(18), 44–61.

Jones, E. D., & Southern, T. (1992). Programming, grouping, and acceleration in rural school districts: A survey of attitudes and practices. *Gifted Child Quarterly, 36*(2), 112–117.

Jorgenson, O. (2001). Supporting a diverse teacher corps. *Educational Leadership, 58*(8), 64–67.

Klagholz, L. (2000, January). *Growing better teachers in the Garden State: New Jersey's "alternative route" to teacher certification.* Washington, DC: Thomas B. Fordham Foundation.

Kwiatkowski, M. (1999). Debating alternative teacher certification: A trial by achievement. In M. Kanstoroom and C. E. Finn, Jr. (Eds.), *Better teachers, better schools* (pp. 215–238). Washington, DC: Thomas B. Fordham Foundation.

Longley, L. (Ed.). (1999). *Gaining the arts advantage: Lessons from school districts that value arts education.* Washington, DC: President's Committee on the Arts and the Humanities and Arts Education Partnership.

Manifold, M. (2000). Valuing a rural aesthetic. *Art Education, 53*(4), 18–24.

Meier, D. R. (1997). *Learning in small moments: Life in an urban classroom.* New York: Teachers College Press.

Melville, S., & Hall, S. (2001). Growing our own teachers. *Classroom Leadership, 4*(48), 1–3.

Music Educators National Conference. (1994). *National standards for arts education: What every young American should know and be able to do in the arts.* Reston, VA: Music Educators National Conference.

Nagel, G., & Peterson, P. (2001). Why competency tests miss the mark. *Educational Leadership, 58*(8), 46–48.

Nathanson, J. H. (2001). *The condition of education 2000 in brief* (National Center for Educational Statistics, NCES 2001-045). Washington, DC: U.S. Department of Education.

National Art Education Association. (1991). National arts education accord. Reston, VA: National Art Education Association.

National Art Education Association. (1994). *Art education: Creating a visual arts research agenda toward the 21st century.* Reston, VA: National Art Education Association.

National Art Education Association. (1995). *A vision for art education reform.* Reston, VA: National Art Education Association.

National Art Education Association. (1996). *Implementing a visual arts education research program: Charting a journey toward the 21st century.* Reston, VA: National Art Education Association.

National Art Education Association. (1997). *Status of the states: Arts education reports.* Reston, VA: National Art Education Association.

National Art Education Association. (1998). *NBPTS Board certification for art teachers.* Reston, VA: National Art Education Association.

National Art Education Association. (1999a). *Standards for art teacher preparation.* Reston, VA: National Art Education Association.

National Art Education Association. (1999b, August 6). Art teacher preparation: Did you know? *NAEA Policy Watch.* Reston, VA: National Art Education Association.

National Art Education Association. (2000). *National survey: Secondary art education.* Reston, VA: National Art Education Association.

National Association of State Boards of Education. (2000, August). Arts education. *Policy Update, 8*(13), 1–2.

National Board for Professional Teaching Standards. (1989). *What teachers should know and be able to do.* Southfield, MI: National Board for Professional Teaching Standards.

National Board for Professional Teaching Standards. (1996). *Early adolescence through young adulthood/art.* Arlington, VA: National Board for Professional Teaching Standards.

National Board for Professional Teaching Standards. (2000). *Early childhood and middle childhood/art standards.* Arlington, VA: National Board for Professional Teaching Standards.

National Commission on Excellence in Education. (1983). *A nation at risk.* Washington, DC: U.S. Government Printing Office.

National Endowment for the Arts. (1988). *Toward civilization.* Washington, DC: National Endowment for the Arts.

National Endowment for the Arts. (1994). *Arts education research agenda for the future.* Washington, DC: National Endowment for the Arts.

National Research Council of the National Academies. (2000). Tests and teaching quality: Interim report. Washington, DC: U.S. Department of Education.

National Research Council of the National Academies. (2001). Testing teaching candidates: The role of licensure tests in improving teacher quality. Washington, DC: U.S. Department of Education.

Olson, L. (Ed.). (1998, January 8). Quality counts: The urban challenge. *Education Week, 17*(17), 6–270.

Olson, L. (Ed.). (1999, January 11). Quality Counts 1999: Rewarding results, punishing failure. *Education Week, 18*(17), 8–20.

Olson, L. (Ed.). (2000, January 13). Quality Counts 2000. *Education Week, 19*(18), 12–18.

Olson, L. (Ed.). (2001, January 11). Quality Counts 2001: A better balance: Standards, tests, and the tools to succeed. *Education Week, 20*(17), 12–22.

Olson, L., & Hendrie, C. (1998). Pathways to progress. In L. Olson (Ed.), Quality counts 98: The urban challenge. *Education Week, 17*(17), 32–46.

Olson, L., & Jerald, C. D. (1998). Barriers to success. Quality Counts 98: The urban challenge. *Education Week, 17*(17), 9–22.

Peeno, L. N. (Ed.). (1995). *Adaptations of the national visual arts standards: National, state, and district examples.* Reston, VA: National Art Education Association.

Peeno, L. N. (1997). *Status of the arts in the states.* Reston, VA: National Art Education Association.

Persky, H. R., Sandene, B. A., & Askew, J. M. (1998). *The NAEP 1997 arts report card: Eighth grade findings from the National Assessment of Educational Progress* (Office of Educational Research and improvement, NCES 1999-486). Washington, DC: US Department of Education.

Peterson, J. (1991). *States assessment survey*. Paper commissioned by the California Department of Education.

Podgursky, M. (2001, April 11). Should states subsidize national certification? *Education Week, 20*(30), 38–40.

Pratt, R. (Ed.). (2000). *The condition of education 2000*. (National Center for Education Statistics, NCES 2000-062). Washington, DC: U.S. Department of Education.

Pratt, R., Pfile, R., Conner, S., & Livingston, A. (Eds.). (2000). *The condition of education 1999* (Office of Educational Research and Improvement, NCES 1999-022). Washington, DC: U.S. Department of Education.

Rittenhouse, G. (Ed.). (1999). *The condition of education 1998*. (National Center for Education Statistics, NCES 98-013). Washington, DC: U.S. Department of Education.

Sabol, F. R. (1990). Toward development of a visual arts diagnostic achievement test: Issues and concerns. In M. Zurmuehlen (Ed.), *Working papers in art education, 1989-90* (pp. 78–85). Iowa City, IA: The School of Art and Art History of the University of Iowa.

Sabol, F. R. (1994). A critical examination of state visual arts achievement tests from state departments of education in the United States. *Dissertation Abstracts International, 9518525, 56*, 2A. (UMI No. 5602A)

Sabol, F. R. (1998a). What are we testing? Content analysis of state visual arts achievement tests. *Visual Arts Research, 24*(1), 1–12.

Sabol, F. R. (1998b). *Needs assessment and identification of urban art teachers in the Western region of the National Art Education Association*. Reston, VA: National Art Education Foundation.

Sabol, F. R. (1999). *Needs assessment and identification of rural art teachers in the Western region of the National Art Education Association*. Reston, VA: National Art Education Foundation.

Sabol, F. R. (2001). Regional findings from a secondary analysis of the 1997 NAEP art assessment based on responses to creating and responding exercises. *Studies in Art Education, 43*(1), 18–34.

Sabol, F. R. (in press). Supervision and administration of art education programs in rural and urban schools: Issues and answers. In V. Bodenhamer & B. Rushlow (Eds.), *The evolving roles of supervisors and administrators as leaders of change: Perspectives for the new millennium*. Reston, VA: National Art Education Association.

Scherer, M. (2001). Improving the quality of the teaching force: A conversation with David C. Berliner. *Educational Leadership, 58*(8), 6–10.

Shen, J. (1997a). The evolution of violence in schools. *Educational Leadership, 55*(2), 14–18.

Shen, J. (1997b). Has alternative licensure materialized it promise? A comparison between traditionally and alternatively certified teachers in public schools. *Educational Evaluation and Policy Analysis, 19*, 76–83.

Shuler, S. C., & Connealy, S. (1998). The evolution of state arts assessment: From Sisyphus to stone soup. *Arts Education Policy Review, 100*(1), 12–19.

Simmons, A. (2001). Teens to teachers: High school students fulfill their desire to teach. *Classroom Leadership, 4*(8), 7–8.

Smith, P. (1995). A brief history of preservice education for art teachers in the United States. In L. Galbraith (Ed.), *Preservice art education: Issues and practice* (pp. 147–159). Reston, VA: National Art Education Association.

Snyder, T. D., & Hoffman, C. M. (2001). *Digest of education statistics 2000* (NCES 2001-034). Washington, DC: U.S. Department of Education. National Center for Education Statistics.

Taylor, M. M. (1992). Teacher education of arts educators: Stepping into the future. In N. C. Yakel (Ed.), *The future: Challenge of change* (pp. 159–169). Reston, VA: National Art Education Association.

Tell, C. (2001). Making room for alternative routes. *Educational Leadership, 58*(8), 38–41.

U. S. Department of Education. (1991). *America 2000: An education strategy*. Washington, DC: U.S. Government Printing Office.

U. S. Department of Education. (1994). *Goals 2000: Education America act*. Washington, DC: U.S. Government Printing Office.

U. S. Department of Education. (1995). *Progress of education in the United States of America: 1990 through 1994*. Washington, DC: U.S. Department of Education. National Center for Educational Statistics, *Digest of Education Statistics*.

Wadsworth, D. (2001). Why new teachers choose to teach. *Educational Leadership, 58*(8), 24–28.

Wall, F. E. (1997). External standing committee moves to assessment. *IPSB Bulletin Board, 2*(1), 1–7.

Whitener, K. J., Gruber, K. J., Lynch, H., Tingos, K., Perona, M., & Fondelier, H. (1997). *Characteristics of stayers, movers, and leavers: Results from the teacher follow-up survey: 1994–95*. (Office of Educational Research and Improvement, NCES 97-450). Washington, DC: U.S. Department of Education.

Williams, B., & Newcombe, E. (1994). Building on the strengths of urban learners. *Educational Leadership, 51*(8), 75–78.

Williams, B., & Woods, M. (1997). Building on urban learners' experiences. *Educational Leadership, 54*(7), 29–33.

Zimmerman, E. (1997). Authentic assessment research in art education. In S. D. LaPierre & E. Zimmerman (Eds.), *Research methods and methodologies for art education* (pp. 149–169). Reston, VA: National Art Education Association.

24

The Practice of Teaching in K–12 Schools: Devices and Desires

Judith M. Burton
Teachers College Columbia University

INTRODUCTION

For many years it has been my practice to ask the graduate art education students I teach what influenced their decisions to become artists or embark on a teaching career. Almost without exception, responses have focused on the words or actions of past teachers; comments—often idiosyncratic and delivered in passing—have "stuck" with a force that might well have astonished their originators. Even if not precipitating a future direction or career, most of us look back on the practices of favorite teachers with benign nostalgia. Indeed, whenever we think about education, we inevitably think in terms of the practice of teachers as the single defining quality that marks our school experiences. Yet, and perhaps surprisingly, the practice of teaching is the least researched and possibly the most polemicized arena of art education. This chapter, thus, will be concerned with the practice of teaching: the instructional work teachers do, the lives they lead in art classrooms, and what we expect of them.

A LITTLE HISTORY

Those of us who have made the journey from pupil to teacher know how complex is the context in which teachers operate and of which they are a part. The 20th century has witnessed a radical and far-reaching evolution in our conceptions of schools, schooling, and what teachers are expected to know and be able to do (Efland, 1990; Eisner, 1998; Greene, 1994). Beliefs about the nature and worth of artistic knowledge and practice, how children should be taught, and the use of evaluation and assessment in instruction are certainly different today than they were even 20 years ago. Since the advent of Sputnik 1, American schools have been subject to a stream of reform efforts that have almost equally inspired and inhibited change (Cuban, 1990; Eisner, 1983, 1998; Gardner, 1991; Greene, 1994).

We know, for instance, at least theoretically, that the practice of teaching does not consist of a generic set of pedagogical skills; it is a complex performance involving interweaving dimensions (Berliner, 1986; Bullock & Galbraith, 1992; Giroux, 1988; Jackson, 1990; Schon, 1984). We no longer look for the one best method, for even a brief scan through the literature reveals art classroom practices of some variety (Carroll, 1996; Tyak, 1974). Within the working lives of art teachers we find that concerns and practices of older and younger teachers are different, as these are honed by experience and informed by different perceptions of past and present (Galbraith, 1995; Kowalchuk, 1999). Similarly, demands confronting practitioners at the elementary and secondary levels are shaped by distinctive developmental needs, learning styles, and changing patterns of experiences outside school that youngsters bring to their learning (Burton, 2000; Eisner, 1998; Gardner, 1990). The practical insights, wisdom, confidence, and self-esteem of teachers are sharply delineated along gender lines as are the classroom experiences of the boys and girls they teach (Brewer, 1998; Collins & Sandell, 1996; Tuman, 1999).

In an effort to confront diversity and difference in the art classroom, and be responsive to public demand for high standards and accountability, conceptions of subject matter and how children learn subject matter have also changed radically. Other aspects of art teachers' practices have taken on increasing importance in recent years as they have learned to work alongside professional practitioners in their classrooms and extended their attention to matters of collaboration both inside and outside their schools (Galbraith, 1995; Remer, 1996; Wilson, 1997). Such extensions have become more numerous, complex, and significant and thought to improve the quality of art teacher practice by grounding it within the socio cultural realities of particular school contexts. Given the variety of conditions that surround the working lives of teachers, it is, perhaps, not so surprising that there is little across-the-board agreement on what constitutes "best" practice (Fuller, 1999; Luftig, 2000; Smith, 1987; Wilson, 1997).

FUTURE IMPERFECT

The growing pressures of a postmodern society have, to a great extent, precipitated a collapse of moral, aesthetic, intellectual, and pedagogical certainties. As the work of teachers has come under public scrutiny and as teachers have taken on new mandates and problems, the norms of practice can no longer be defined in the context of permanence, singularity, and isolation. Like contemporary reform itself, the practice of teaching takes on coherence only if seen in the context of possibility and shifting relationships between parts and wholes. Meaningful and realistic analysis of the practice of teaching, thus, requires us to do more than balance out the advantages and disadvantages of particular ways of doing things, or isolating aspects of the work highlighted by research findings. Contemporary practice exists in a climate of change and challenge, which plays out within what Eisner and others have called the "ecology of the classroom" (Brofenbrenner, 1979; Bruner, 1996; Eisner, 1998). Yet, what do we know about the instructional practices of art teachers as they respond to the challenges of the modern world and the expectations of the contemporary classroom? For instance, how do art teachers conform to reform mandates, the imposition of standards, and what makes them dig in their heels and resist? For when all is said and done, if teaching remains central to the definition of what school and learning is all about, then research should have things to tell us about these issues.

DEVICES AND DESIRES

It is generally assumed that educational research will prove its legitimacy by offering new perceptions and stimulating improvements in teaching and learning. It is hoped that research findings will offer a more powerful knowledge base for practice including knowledge of subject matter, classroom management, pupil learning needs, and the pedagogy that teachers bring to bear on their everyday work. The assumption is that better art teachers help give substance to a school curriculum and, in consequence, make better schools. However, research on classroom practice has been somewhat of a stepchild in the field of inquiry in art education (Carroll, 1996; Carroll & Kay, 1998). What research there is has been inconsistent, methodologically diverse, and offers less than a consistent picture of the field. Findings appear to indicate that teachers adopt a variety of pedagogical strategies responsive to specific contexts and assumptions about subject matter, and there is little consensus on the benchmarks of what constitutes good practice (Berliner, 1986; Carroll, 1996; Carroll & Kay, 1998; Eisner, 1983).

Even more dispiriting, perhaps, is that art teacher practice appears to be somewhat impervious to the kinds of changes researchers and reformists suggest. Recent reforms in schools and the articulation of national standards appear to have had a small effect on classroom practice, including the arts (Chapman 1982; Cuban, 1990; Darling-Hammond, 1997; Eisner, 1998; Sarason, 1990). Research findings, while generally promoted in the art education journals, rarely appear to permeate the classroom, even though research articles are usually buttressed with suggestions and implications for practice and policy. Several reasons are suggested for the disjunction between the claims of reformers and researchers and the practices of art teachers. For instance, much research is "top down" and carried out by investigators who have not spent a great deal of time in art classrooms; thus, they often ask questions and represent findings in terms that do not fit easily within the complex demands of art teachers' everyday lives. Moreover, it is often the case that the questions and approaches of research are derived from theory rather than focused on practical questions of direct relevance to classrooms. Given that experienced teachers have worked to a level of security in their practice and assume the prerogative of their own personal ways of doing things, they often have little inclination to invest in the uncertainties of the new and different, however compellingly presented. Furthermore, until very recently, it was unusual for teachers themselves to be engaged in research on practice. Thus, the kinds of daunting questions that resonate most deeply with instructional practices have rarely been asked.

Recent experience tells us that although the desire to improve practice has been ever optimistic, at least among researchers and reformists, the devices by which practice might be improved have been somewhat elusive. With this in mind, this chapter presents trends in research on practices that will be examined for the insights they give us on the complexities and difficulties of art classroom life. Three major research trends focused on practices will be reported and their potential uses and limitations will be explored. Besides the general claims and constraints presented by each type of research, their implications will be further explored in light of what they tell us about how conceptions of subject matter, learners, and pedagogy shape the reality of art classroom events. It is important to note at this point that these three trends are not neatly compartmentalized, in that each is clearly and sharply delineated and singular in its concerns. There is much overlap here, because arguments and research findings appear and reappear within different interpretive frameworks. Thus, for the purpose of negotiating a minefield of complexity, the categories as delineated in the following sections simply highlight different aspects of this complex whole in order to help comprehension. In order to capture the various "voices" of the field in some fullness, a select group of projects has been chosen to stand as paradigmatic. Although limiting the range of the field, the virtue of depth in this instance is more advantageous than the kind of coverage the familiar listing of projects achieves.

TRENDS IN RESEARCH ON TEACHING

Research studies on the practice of art teaching may be categorized and, even, polemicized by their various purposes: by philosophical, psychological, or sociological orientation; by various conceptions of subject matter; by pedagogical practices; and by research methodology itself.

Because the purpose of this chapter is not to promote one purpose or methodology over any another, three rather broad categories of research on practice will be explored; I will call these the *speculative-theoretical,* the *inferential-empirical,* and the *descriptive-case study.*

It seems reasonable, as an opening gambit, to begin with the most broadly based research tradition of the field. Framed by particular viewpoints linking art, learning, and instruction, the work of Chapman, Gardener, Csikszentmihali, Eisner, the National Board for Professional Teaching Standards, and that of the more recent groups of theorists who form the growing fields of visual culture and critical pedagogy, offers a wide-lens view of what counts in instruction in the field. Each researcher and groups of researchers interweave a complex set of dimensions buttressing their assumptions and claims from experiences within their own teaching, scholar, research, practitioner lives. From within these speculative-theoretical frameworks, researchers and reformists offer both a trenchant critique of the problems besetting art classroom practice and provide compelling suggestions for change.

THE SPECULATIVE-THEORETICAL POSITION

Enlightened Citizenship

In her ground-breaking book, *Instant Art Instant Culture* (1982), Chapman argues for art education as critical to enlightened citizenship in a democratic society. Her critique of contemporary practice draws upon on an extensive review of national surveys carried out between 1977 and 1978, which cumulatively revealed youngsters graduating from schools with little or no instruction in art, and what study they had undertaken was largely confined to studio practice. Set against this picture, she argues for continuous in-school art education provision K–12, with art as core for all pupils and a curriculum that affirms creativity, imagination, and reflective thinking about art. For Chapman, the romantic view of the child as natural artist, adept at "doing" rather than at "thinking" about art has been a root cause of less than rigorous instruction. Thus, she argues for a practice that goes beyond studio experiences and which integrates the study of fine and popular arts of the cultures of Eastern and Western worlds. Learning gained from the study of others, Chapman envisions, both challenges the mind and offers important and useful knowledge to youngsters as their lives stretch beyond schools.

To accompany this more rigorous and comprehensive art education, Chapman foresees teachers who are broadly knowledgeable in the visual arts and more fully insightful about their role as guides to learning. Here she emphasizes art classroom instruction that is, "efficient, powerful, and representative of opportunities and issues in art" (p. 152). As central to instruction, teachers must recognize the experiences that pupils draw upon outside schools and be able to expand upon these experiences linking them to broad views of cultural practices. For Chapman, instruction in visual arts must respect the integrity of the discipline and be a primary responsibility of the school and the art teacher:

> Authentic reform does not lie in the direction proposed by various advocates who favor more emphasis on making art as the essence and end of arts education, or incidental instruction to be offered by artists and community agencies, or more use of the arts as tools for improving learning in other subjects, or more condensed and abbreviated instruction in the guise of "related art" or "interdisciplinary" arts courses. It is precisely this catch-as-catch can orientation which has taught school administrators that the arts are not worthy of inclusion in the curriculum on a par with the sciences and humanities. (p. 25)

Education for Understanding

Echoing many of the concerns of Chapman, about the practices and provisions of art education, in his book *The Unschooled Mind,* Gardner (1991) takes up the theme of what he terms "education for understanding." Referenced to education in general, including the arts, Gardner looks to research findings that point to the inability of students to master the learning that schools expect of them. In both the arts and sciences youngsters learn skills by rote, which they then cannot apply to new and different contexts. This inflexibility in thought, Gardner argues, derives from instruction that is not rooted in the intuitive or "unschooled" learning that youngsters bring with them to school and which underpins more traditional and disciplinary expertise. Neither is it rooted in instructional practices informed by concepts, knowledge, and skills derived from deep understanding of the various disciplines of schooling. In short, although the mind of the unschooled learner is often naive, and stereotypical, it nonetheless needs to be regularly and repeatedly recognized as a critical grounding for richer and deeper knowledge. Gardner also points to school curricula which prize coverage over depth of instruction and fragmentation over wholeness.

Developing and interweaving his central themes, Gardner argues that teaching for understanding in the arts involves creating and responding to symbols through which critical cognitive, reflective, and perceptual capacities are acquired. Youngsters need to work in-depth and over sustained periods of time, focusing on central problems within the discipline, problems derived from deep insight of the capacities exhibited and operations carried out by masters of a domain. Like Chapman, he argues for instruction related to the reality of youngsters lived experiences such that they are enabled to take multiple perspectives on concepts, issues, and ideas and link their growing insights to specialists in the field. Parting company from Chapman, somewhat, he privileges the role of practice as the central specialization of the discipline. He points to the work of Arts PROPEL as exemplifying an educational approach designed to enhance understanding, one that:

> … involves the mastery of the productive practices in a domain or discipline, coupled with the capacity to adopt different stances towards the work, among them the stance of audience member, critic, performer, and maker. The "understander" in the arts is one who can comfortably move among these various stances. (p. 239)

The ability to take multiple perspectives, which Gardner envisions as the hallmark of the flexible, adaptive mind and as critical to understanding, needs to be supported by an instruction that offers many and different opportunities for reflective examination. Good instruction, he suggests, should incorporate self assessment, assessment by peers, teachers, and outside experts, and should also include ongoing and extensive portfolio work.

Creativity: A Fundamental Human Capacity

One of the traditional and enduring leitmotifs of art education is that it promotes creativity which is an essential source of meaning in our lives. In his book *Creativity: Flow and the Psychology of Discovery and Invention* (1996) Csikszentmihalyi summarizes 30 years of research on the lives of creative people from the arts and sciences. To say that a child or adolescent is creative, he argues, is much too simplistic; nor, he suggests, is creativity a commodity that can be taught explicitly. Creativity arises from a synergy, an interaction, produced by deep knowledge of a symbolic domain, personal gifts, dispositions, and insights, and the recognition that is accorded by experts in the field who acknowledge and validate creative efforts. He argues that creativity is a fundamental capacity without which human culture would not have emerged and without which it will not survive.

Among the traits that are important to cultivate through instruction, and which define creative action, are what he calls opposed tendencies of curiosity and perseverance. In the best circumstances, interest and curiosity emerge early in development stimulated by childhood experiences, a supportive emotional environment, exposure to many different opportunities to explore and discover within the symbolic domain, and high expectations.

> So the first step toward a more creative life is the cultivation of curiosity and interest, that is in the allocation of attention to things for their own sake. On this score, children tend to have the advantage over adults; their curiosity is like a constant beam that highlights and invests with interest anything within range ... With age most of us lose the sense of wonder, the feeling of awe in confronting the majesty and variety of the world. Yes, without awe life becomes routine. Creative individuals are childlike in that their curiosity remains fresh even at ninety years of age; they delight in the strange and the unknown. And because there is no end to the unknown, their delight also is endless. (p. 346)

Creativity, a sense of wonder and awe, blossom in an environment that encourages both solitude and gregariousness and in which certain gender role flexibility is permissible. Echoing many of the themes of Gardner, he affirms that children need to be able to work alone, dig deep into a knowledge domain, and reflect on and incubate ideas. Similarly, they need also the challenges of different viewpoints offered through interactions with others. Although youngsters need in-depth knowledge within a domain, they also need opportunities to stand outside and explore ideas from the perspectives and skills of other domains. Opportunities to overflow the limits of a given domain, Csikszentmihalyi argues, is one of the most important instructional benefits that schooling has to offer. Conditions that foster creativity include appropriate in-depth training, high expectations, provision of resources, recognition by mentors, hope along with opportunities to exercise and display creativity, and rewards from experts in the field. Above all, creativity blossoms within what Csikszentmihalyi calls the "flow" experience, when the maker is enabled to dig deep, get lost, and, ultimately, find wonder and intrinsic enjoyment in an activity itself.

Personal and Shared Meaning

In his book *The Kinds of Schools We Need* (1998), Eisner interweaves a two-pronged view of the field: one directed to the need to redefine much of what passes for art education practice, and the other directed toward the kind of research needed to enlighten practice. Drawing upon earlier writing, he argues that artistic learning contributes to an expanded conception of literacy in that it both develops the ability to construct personal meaning and makes sense out of forms of representation created by others. Along with Gardner, Chapman, and Csikszentmihalyi, he envisions an art education directed toward the fundamental need for students to acquire competencies in the domain through exercising cognitive, affective, and sensory capacities. He sees expectations for arts learning frustrated by a limited view of activities of the mind, a fragmented curriculum, instruction unrelated to the realities of children's lives, and ignorance of the challenges of contemporary culture.

Eisner envisions many of the travails of contemporary instruction as offering potential challenges to research. However, along with other writers, he points to the small influence of research on art instructional practices and student learning outcomes. Along with Jackson (1990), he argues that life in classrooms is much too complex to be viewed from any single perspective and that research should be tied more closely to what he terms the "ecology of the classroom". Art education has for too long applied typical social science research paradigms to its problems, accepting results that offer only partial or limited views of practice. Such singularity and fragmentation of findings are ultimately unable to "take account of the unique particulars with which the practitioner must deal", thus, these findings are rendered redundant (p. 5). Here, he argues that research on practice should not only take a more ecological view of life in classrooms but also must take a broader view of knowledge, a more cultural view of mind, and a multiple view of intelligence.

For Eisner, practical implications for teaching impinge on art teachers' abilities to acknowledge the cognitive character of artistic learning; engage pupils in multiple forms of representation involving integrated learning; and use a variety of evaluation methods calibrated to specifics of art learning and not borrowed from other more quantitatively based disciplines. Beyond classroom practice, Eisner argues for "a finer and wider net through which the processes and outcomes of educational practice can be understood and appraised" (p. 108). He finds hope in what he calls naturalistic inquiry, illuminative evaluation, responsive evaluation, and his own educational connoisseurship. He quotes Gage (1978):

> Scientific method can contribute relationships between variables taken two at a time and even, in the form of interactions, three or perhaps four or more at time. Beyond say four, the usefulness of what science can give the teacher begins to weaken, because teachers cannot apply, at least not without help and not on the run, the more complex interactions. At this point, the teacher as an artist must step in and make clinical or artistic judgements about the best way to teach. In short, the scientific base for the art of teaching will consist of two-variable relationships and lower-order instruction. The higher-order interactions between four and more variables must be handled by the teacher as artist. (p. 197)

What Teachers Should Know and Be Able to Do

The desire to specify purposes and practices in education has been a dominant strand of American education for almost an entire century. Much criticized in the art educational literature for prescriptiveness, uniformity, superficiality, and mediocrity, the Standards movement has, nonetheless, made a vast sweep across the nation's school systems. Thus, in a different voice, but nonetheless-critical to the conversation about highly accomplished practice in the art classroom, is the booklet *What Teachers Should Know and Be Able To Do* produced in 1988 by the National Board for Professional Teaching Standards (NBPTS). This document sets forth five standards exemplifying accomplished practice, which remain still as a cornerstone for the expectations of teacher practice in the arts and in all other subject disciplines. As they stand, however, and although presented as "standards" these exhortations to good practice might, perhaps, be more properly read as a set of "criteria" or "guidelines" open to a good deal of individual and contextual interpretation. Indeed, the writers of the document recognized that any enumeration of expectations actually conceals the complexities, uncertainties, and dilemmas inherent in the work teachers do. But, read simply as criteria or guidelines to good practice, what is surprising is the degree to which the writers of the SE Standards highlight many of the deeper concerns of the speculative theorists. For example, the writers suggest that:

• Teachers should be committed to students and their learning as exemplified in practices that demonstrate equitable treatment of learners and recognition of diversity along with a broad array of insights into development and culture.
• Teachers should know the subjects they teach and how to teach those subjects to students. Accomplished teachers are expected to have a rich understanding of their disciplinary knowledge, how it relates to other disciplines, and how it is applied to real-world settings. They are, as a consequence, able to develop the critical and analytical capacities of their pupils, create multiple paths to learning, and enable pupils to pose and solve problems.

- Teachers should be responsible for managing and monitoring student learning. They are expected to employ a variety of instructional techniques, maintain a disciplined learning environment, set norms for social interaction, and be able to assess the progress of individuals as well as that of whole classes.
- Teachers should think systematically about their practice and learn from experience. They are expected to model those virtues and capacities they seek to inspire in their students. This calls for a range of capacities such as curiosity, tolerance, respect for diversity, and appreciation of cultural difference. In addition, teachers are expected to be able to draw on knowledge of development, subject matter, instruction, and understanding of their students to make principled judgments about sound practice.
- Teachers should be members of learning communities. Here, the Board stresses professional collaboration on instruction, curriculum development, allocation of resources, and an ability to work with parents.

The NBPTS writers did not intimate whether or not resources would be available to schools in order ensure parity in the accomplishments of the Standards; nor did they indicate the kinds of flexibilities of interpretation and applicability they had in mind, or how teachers were to be educated to fulfill the mission of the standards. However, in seeking to encourage new levels of professionalism in practice, the writers acknowledged both the tensions between current realities and emerging ideals and the need to carve out multiple paths to meet new certification standards.

Critical Pedagogy in a Visual Culture

A growing disenchantment with traditional trappings of art education over the past 20 or so years has produced a litany of criticism focused on instruction (Efland, 1995; Eisner, 1998; Neprud, 1995). Writers have noted the limitations of teacher-centered instruction, the preservation of the Western cannon as a model for style and subject matter, use of prescriptive rules for criticism and analysis, exclusion of diverse ways of knowing and experiencing, and fragmentation of the curriculum. In short, art educators have been seen to be out of step with the fast-paced, visual technological world beyond schools, a world that defines the realities of their pupils' lives. Outside art education, writers such as Bakhtin (1981), Bachelard (1964), Ellsworth (1997), Giroux (1981, 1988), and Greene (1978) have given intellectual sustenance to a growing cadre of adherents within. Two interrelated streams of concern form the substance of their proposals. The first has sought to widen the conception of art to include all instances and artifacts of visual cultures (Duncan, 2001; Freedman, 2000); the second focuses on the nature of encounters with visual cultures and makes recommendations for pedagogy and instruction (Betts, Fisher, & Hicks, 1995; Clark, 1998; Desai, 2000; Efland, 1995; Geahigan, 1998, 2000; Smith-Shank, 1999). The two streams are interactive, each informing the other in terms of theoretical position and practical application.

Adherents of both streams point out that most of us live in an envelope of visual culture including advertisements, graffiti, movies, fine arts, and the myriad productions of digital technology. We indeed live in a visual world designed not so much for creature comfort but to maintain a healthy economy and support systems of power. More than this, perhaps, the visual has become central to the creation, and dissemination of knowledge and to the construction of meaning. Visual artifacts are constitutive of beliefs and values that are historically and politically determined and socially situated and which should not be studied in isolation. Critical pedagogy promotes examination of such beliefs and allows for questioning of interest groups such as government, church, and other vehicles of institutional control. Engagement with instances of visual culture involves opening up vantage points and inviting questions that go beyond traditional norms. Here, the points of view and experiences of traditionally under represented voices from diverse cultures, sexual orientations, and physical capabilities become part of the larger conversation about how the world can be known.

Having layered the potential playing field, upon which no instance of visual culture is privileged in its own right, school based instruction opens up visual inquiry to multiple vantage points and a process of interrogation. In a similar vein, school and classroom hierarchies, once deconstructed, become open to authentic collaboration and collegiality. In order to explore the widest range of possibilities in learning, critical pedagogy offers non-rule-bound, participatory instruction, engaging the co-construction of knowledge among pupils and their teachers through careful listening and open dialog. This way of approaching both personal creative acts and engagement with the works of others calls for a considerable depth of study and sifting through alternative explanations and perspectives. It also involves critical and reflective capacities honed to the many ways in which identity, knowledge, value, and subjectivity are formed as a consequence of living in given political, economic, and aesthetic environments. The role of the teacher, in this instance, is that of a highly knowledgeable member of a community of learners.

Commentary

Taken as an ensemble, the works cited so far represent multiple vantage points on art education practice held by some of the leading writers in the field. Written at different points in recent times, and from different perspectives, the only consistency they hint at is inconsistency. There are some underlying threads, however, that interweave the various viewpoints. All agree, or intimate, that much needs to be improved in the world of art education practice. They see definitions of subject matter to be either too narrowly drawn around practice or too fragmented and broadly inclusive; they see an ignorance of the realities of pupils' lives both in and outside the classroom and in pedagogical practices that are impervious to change. They argue for the following: instruction that is flexible and that engages multidimensional knowledge of subject matter; insight into multiple ways of learning, difference, and diversity; the acknowledgment of the realities of youngster's lives and the demands of their cultures; ability to employ a variety of instructional and assessment techniques; and a willingness to transcend disciplinary boundaries and work collaboratively with others. Although opening our eyes to new possibilities for practice, such theories and speculations also come with limitations in that they have boundaries that exclude almost as much as they include. Left unstated by all writers are the specific practices that inform their critiques and those which they would offer for improvement. Just what are the topics so central to the discipline? What are the dimensions of overlap and connectedness to other disciplines? What is the relationship between "subject matter" and "developmental needs?" If we are to replace the fragmented curriculum, what form should an alternative take? Moreover, while there is much talk about "ecology" and "interaction" the precise mechanisms by which the various dimensions of instruction might be energized to produce a more articulate and better informed practice are left largely unstated.

THE EMPIRICAL-INFERENTIAL POSITION

What do teachers do when they teach? This seemingly simple question, as we have seen already, masks a complex of contradictory answers. Moving closer into the art classroom, responses come from a variety of sources: from surveys and demographic data of instructional practices and their outcomes, from empirical studies of specific features of arts learning, from research into the transfer of arts learning to other subjects, and from descriptions of specific programs that seek to promote certain types of instructional strategies. All such research-based efforts give rise to important inferences about practice even when, as we will see, they do not address specifically the instructional backgrounds of their subjects. Together, the data from these kinds of studies take us closer into actualities of art teachers' work.

The kind of research included here employs a social science paradigm and has mostly, but not exclusively, relied on scientific or quantitative methods. Often carried out by university art education faculties, these surveys and studies tend to focus on factor analysis of single, or several variables, chosen as pivotal to instruction. The populations of young people under study are depicted usually as representative of the population at large; thus, findings are amenable to generalization. Such studies are revealing and often claim correlations among variables or, more cautiously, hint at the presence of significant relationships among variables. Within this type of research, investigators tend to stand outside and distance themselves from the phenomena under study in order to minimize the contamination of personal subjectivity.

Surveys

Since 1969, The National Center for Educational Statistics has been engaged in continuous assessment of student achievement. Assessment of visual arts in American schools began with the 1977 National Assessment of Progress in Education (NAPE) and was taken up again 2 decades later in 1997. By far the most extensive survey of youngsters' accomplishments in the arts to have been carried out for 20 years, NAPE examined the artistic abilities of a nationally representative random sample of almost 3,000 eighth graders. Exactly one half of the sample reported that they had taken, or were taking, art in school during the current year. The tasks that youngsters were asked to undertake included those designed to assess knowledge and skills in creating and responding to selected artworks. In the creating block, youngsters were asked to make a self-portrait, a collage, a design, and a three-dimensional piece, after viewing selected works of master artists. A factor analysis of items included in the exercises revealed that there was no significant difference in the accomplishments of youngsters who were currently studying art and those who were not. Although the writers of the final report suggested that instruction had a negligible effect on the overall outcomes, nonetheless pupils with higher response scales were more likely to have studied art. On the creating segment of the test, only 6% of pupils received scores that the judges thought to be effective or adequate. Eighty-three percent of the work produced in the creating segment was scored as uneven or minimally adequate. Eleven percent of the pupils, thus, created work that was found to be unacceptable. Overall, a total of 94% of pupils failed to demonstrate even moderate creative abilities, although almost 50% of them reported being enrolled in art classes (Persky, Sandene, & Askew, 1998).

Similar results were evident in the responding segment, which focused on skills of analysis, description, and interpretation. For instance, only 29% of students could describe three ways in which Raphael created a sense of near and far in a Madonna and Child painting, and only 14% of youngsters could explain how Beardon created contrast between interior and exterior space in a collage. In addition, only 4% of students could write an acceptable essay linking explicit aesthetic features of artworks to interpretive meaning. The NAEP data revealed that experience in writing, accompanied by opportunities to work in three-dimensional media, positively impacted responding scores (Persky, Sandene, & Askew, 1998).

Other results from the NAPE survey indicated that portfolio activity, opportunities to exhibit art work, and out of school art activity were positively related to performance scores; that there was some measure of overlap in the creating and responding scores; and that museum visits, opportunities to talk to peers, and specialist art facilities impacted positively all results. In a secondary analysis of the original NAPE findings, Sabol (2001) found considerable regional variation in both creating and responding scores and also suggested that the data revealed combinations of variables such as portfolio activity, extracurricular art activity, and museum visiting which contributed either positively or negatively to the scores (Persky, Sandene & Askew, 1998).

There has been much criticism of the NAPE and other such standardized tests (Burton, 2001; Eisner, 1998; Greene, 1994; Sabol, 2001; Siegesmund, Dikert, & McCulloch, 2001). Concern has focused on the limited population studied, appropriateness of items to curriculum goals, narrowness and fragmentation of the scoring rubrics, and emphasis on following rules. Interestingly, the instructional implications of the NAPE results are highlighted in another survey focused explicitly on the art classroom practices of secondary teachers. Burton (2001a) investigated the quality and quantity of instruction in secondary public and private schools. He surveyed 177 teachers on their favorite teaching and classroom motivational strategies. In general, the survey showed that teachers focused on studio practice and favored working one on one with pupils, teaching mostly through step-by-step demonstration, showing examples, and lecturing. Most teachers favored working with a variety of media, developing technical skills, and learning how to apply the elements of art. In closing their lessons, and in their evaluation practices, teachers tended to be highly subjective, offering praise and showing pleasure in accomplishments based on direct observation of work, attitude, and general performance. According to their own reports, the teachers gave less focus to discussion, open ended questioning, reflection on practice, collaboration, field trips, learning about art history and criticism, and using technology. In contrast to suggestions made by other respondents to the NAEP data, learning and assessment derived through the use of art exhibitions and portfolio work were not priorities for the teachers included in Burton's survey.

Much of Burton's survey data confirm an earlier study that looked at instructional practices in Canadian high schools (Gray & Macgregor, 1991). This study also found a strong tendency toward studio instruction, step-by-step teaching, with a focus on elements, technical details, one-to-one advising, monitoring, and critiquing. In another study on teacher profile and preference, carried out 10 years later, Brewer (1999) found that out of 141 art teachers he surveyed, 67% had no master's degree. Asked if they would like to engage in further study, there was strong interest in taking studio courses and only moderate to low interest in taking courses in art education, art history, and criticism.

Formal Instruction

Because studio-based instruction appears to dominate the field of art education, what kinds of instruction are engaged in and to what ends? A wide range of research has spotlighted studio practice, mostly focusing on problems and possibilities inherent in handling various media. Investigators have examined capacities in drawing (Brewer, 1998; Burton, 1983; Hafeli, 2000; Tuman, 1999; Smith & the Drawing Study Group, 1998; Willatts, 1992), in painting (Amorino, 1999; Louis, 2000; Stokrocki, 1990), in ceramics (Brewer & Colbert, 1992; Graziano, 1999), and in working collaboratively with museums and artists (Anderson, 1997; Bresler, DeStefano, Feldman, & Garg 2000; Moore, 2002; Remer, 1996; Williams, 1996). Although investigators have also examined an array of studio topics, such as representation of space, memory and observation drawing, manipulation of elements, inclusion of features, and the impact of gender on style, comparatively little research has focused on the direct effects of instruction on studio abilities.

For instance, in a study carried out in 1999, Brewer examined the thematic and observational drawings made by 167 third graders and seventh graders, equally divided among those who had and had not received art instruction. In an echo of the NAEP findings, the presence or absence of art instruction was not clearly etched in the results. However, where art instruction impacted most strongly was in relation to gender and grade level. There was a diminishing trend in drawing achievement among the girls in the study on both drawing tasks. Brewer notes the startling fact that in one of the research settings it was necessary to explain to a group of third graders that an observation drawing meant to "look, see and draw."

The results of this study capture a general data trend that not only points to differential abilities between boys and girls in drawing tests but also suggests a general decline in drawing abilties with age. This reflects the oft-quoted U turn in artistic abilities, whereby most youngsters' capacities for drawing decline at the end of elementary school, leaving those with special gifts and talents to follow a stream of ongoing development (Gardner & Winner, 1982). When seen in the context of prevailing instructional practices, however, such results appear to echo teaching that focuses on technical skills, manipulation of formal elements, and a model of art embedded in the style of Western realism. Put simply, this model outcome is thought to require more of youngsters than the natural talents of childhood are able to sustain. Moreover, looked at from the perspective of an instruction based in another set of assumptions about development, artistry, and style, the outcomes can be perceived quite differently (Burton, 1998). For example, if adolescent drawings are examined for the questions and curiosities they pose, and the graphic possibilities they explore, this offers a very different picture of intentions and skills than do drawings calibrated to the canons of a post-Renaissance Western model. Studies by Amorino (1999), Burton (2000), Hafeli (2000), and Salander (2001) suggest that during the adolescence years a split emerges between youngsters' ideas about subject matter and their ideas about materials causing a temporary imbalance and tension. However, these researchers argue that this dislocation is a necessary and normative feature of ongoing artistic development and should not be interpreted as artistic decline. Similarly, the oft-noted decline in girls' studio abilities might also be attributed to instruction focused on the manipulation of fragmented elements and technical skills directed toward Western styles of realism. As compared with boys of the same age, girls whose thinking is perhaps more relational, holistic, and whose subjectivity informs conceptual insights, may find such instruction inhospitable to their personal needs and goals (Tuman, 1999).

The notion that research data can be alternatively represented, and changed assumptions about learning in art can cast outcomes and accomplishments in a new and richer light, is reflected in another study by Siegesmund, Dikert, and McCulloch (2001). These researchers re-administered the collage-creating and responding block used in the NAPE 1997 survey, but they re-designed the assessment in relation to the instructional goals of art teachers of the pupils to be tested. They developed the scoring rubrics of responding (addressing the problem posed), attending (shaping and identifying emotional responses to visual relationships), exploring (identify perceptual details), and relating (construct meaning). They also thought to give youngsters smaller paper to work on and more time to complete their work. In an interesting yet telling sidelight, the authors mention that the rubrics for the study developed by the teachers did not regularly appear on the curriculum frameworks for the art instruction they were expected to follow which placed heavy emphasis on skill acquisition and mastery of content. In other words, they noted a gap between the formal curriculum documents and the learning objectives that framed teachers' individual instruction. In brief, the data from this study, like the NAEP test, indicated only modest artistic achievement; however, they did offer a richer picture of the several capacities involved in creating and responding whether scores were high or more modest. In this study, exploring, attending, and relating emerged as dimensions of an ability to recognize and manipulate combinations of visual relationships in the construction of meaning in art.

Transfer Practices

Yet another perspective on instructional practice originates from studies that have examined evidence for transfer from art learning to other subject disciplines (Caterall, 1998; Erikson,

1997; Fisk, 1999; Perkins, 1989). Although the issue of transfer is, at best, problematic both as a research question and as a desirable outcome of arts instruction, results from such studies nonetheless offer important insights for teachers. If teachers think they are teaching for transfer, there is some evidence to suggest that they focus their teaching rather differently than if they believe they are teaching uniquely for artistic improvement. The outcome of teaching for transfer is usually measured in terms of its impact on other subject disciplines. Here, evidence for instruction resulting in higher order thinking, affective insight, increased perception, and enhanced creativity is usually sought. Teachers who teach for artistic outcomes alone, however, tend to focus more on manipulation of elements, techniques, and abilities to be discerning in judgments about artistic form and its quality and meaning.

In a complex investigation designed to estimate the impact of an arts infusion program on creative thinking, academic achievement, locus of control, and arts appreciation, Luftig (2000) studied 615 youngsters in grades 2, 4, and 5. Youngsters in a control group were engaged with the activities of Project SPECTRA, which offered experiences in making art, observing art and creative processes, critiquing art, learning art in historical and cultural contexts, learning about artistic materials, and integrating the arts into other subject disciplines such as science, math, and reading. Luftig's data suggested that creative thinking and originality, as measured by the Torrence Test of Creativity, were facilitated by involvement in the arts, as was resistance to premature closure among second-grade and fifth-grade grade pupils. There were moderate effects of arts learning reported on reading scores and, intriguingly, boys from the control group performed significantly better on mathematical tasks than did girls.

In perhaps the most complex study to date, Burton, Horowitz, and Abeles (2000) sought to determine whether cognitive skills such as higher order thinking had an effect on learning and thinking in general as well as on other subject disciplines. They speculated at the outset of their study that certain capacities, or ways of thinking, might be situated within the arts whereas others may have more general, across-discipline salience. They began their study by compiling a taxonomy of potential instructional outcomes in the arts derived from a careful but wide-ranging review of the art education literature. Included in this listing were focused perception and inquiry, reflective questioning, construction and layering of relationships, organization and appraisal of meaning, insight into alternative perceptions, imagining new possibilities, and multisensory learning. They administered a battery of tests, including the Torrence Test of Creativity, to 2,400 pupils from grades 4, 5, 7, and 8, from 12 schools. They also collected observational data and narratives and examples relating to the impact of arts learning from non-arts-subject-matter teachers.

In essence, the data from this study offered a picture of thinking in the arts, wherein a set of cognitive competencies including elaboration, creative thinking, fluency, originality, focused perception, and imagination grouped to form constellations in pedagogical contexts that demanded an ability to take multiple perspectives, layer relationships, and construct and express meanings in unified forms of representation. Not surprisingly, perhaps, the most positive scores in the data were associated with youngsters who had received art instruction for considerable periods of their schooling. Intriguingly, the study also revealed that the lowest test scores were associated with art curricula that were formalized and centralized. In general, the study did not offer clear evidence of transfer, or point to specific effects of transfer on other disciplines, although the data did suggest that the same constellation of competencies emerged in other subject disciplines when they called for the juggling of divergent perspective and layering of relationships. The writers of the report speculated that the relationship between learning in the arts and learning in other subject disciplines is interactive and involves ways of thinking that have general salience across the curriculum.

Common sense continues to tell the expert practitioner that engagement in the arts has an impact on youngster's motivation for school: how they develop and manipulate imagery; how they perceive and think about their worlds; how they access personal and shared meaning; how they work with others; and how they think in ways not encouraged in other subjects. Overall, the arts make possible the organization of sensory responses as these are marshaled in service of cognitive and expressive outcomes. There is very little good evidence that teaching art for instrumental outcomes that benefit other disciplines has any positive or lasting effect and may, in the long run, redound against the kind of rich and unique instruction needed to promote outcomes special to the discipline itself (Winner & Hetland, 2001).

Thematic Projects

In addition to surveys and studies of instructional practices calibrated to teaching given styles or concepts of art, the past 20 or so years have seen the emergence of a number of instructional programs linked to specific philosophical, curricular positions and practices and conceptions of artistry and arts learning. Looked at carefully, some of these programs such as the Chicago Arts Partnership in Education (CAPE) and Reading Instruction Through the Arts (RITA) are designed to impact learning in other disciplines; whereas other programs such as the Central Midwestern Regional Education Laboratory (CEMERAL), Discipline Based Art Education (DBAE), the Lincoln Center Institute (LCI), and Arts PROPEL are designed to overcome curricular fragmentation and enhance integration within the discipline.

Taking its credo from the work of Barkan (1955, 1962), Chapman (1982), Smith (1987), and Eisner (n.d.), and from the results of various empirical studies and surveys, DBAE, like its forerunner CEMERAL, was a response to growing sentiment in the field that studio practice was demonstrably a limiting focus for arts learning, particularly at the secondary level. The push for a more academic base for art education during the early 1980s, following the dismal results of the 1977 NAPE, was associated with needs to broaden instruction to include experiences in art history, art criticism, and aesthetics, which were seen to enlarge the scope of human awareness and be valuable not only to those students gifted in the practice of art but also essential to those who would be future audience members. There was, thus, a rejection of the centrality of "child art" and of the practices that promoted creativity and self-expression in favor of basing instruction on representative ideas drawn from the disciplines of art: art history, art criticism, aesthetics, and art production (Day, Eisner, Stake, Wilson, & Wilson, 1984). In order to create DBAE classrooms, both specialists and classroom teachers were offered inservice training in instruction in all four modes of the discipline. The practice of DBAE grew rapidly at all levels of schooling and became popular, because it served to support the more academic claims of art education at a time when the push for excellence in all forms of schooling was strong. In its initial form, DBAE required instruction in all four "disciplines." However, as it evolved, a less formal and fragmented set of practices emerged in which there was more interaction and integration among instruction across the four disciplines.

Not surprisingly, in a profession strongly committed to the centrality of instruction in studio practice, DBAE was regarded as a dissipation of the discipline. Many arts educators claimed that their instructional practices already engaged historical, critical, and aesthetic concerns, but were more holistically interwoven as they arose as natural concerns of practice. Other critics saw DBAE as promoting an essentially passive and conservative instructional response and an art education based in the Western cannon, offering little room for individual creativity and expression on the part of both teacher and pupil. Yet others saw the fragmentation of art education into four disciplines as an unwarranted watering down of instruction to meet the conveniences of the academic timetable (Burton, Lederman, & London, 1988; Clark, 1998, Collins & Sandell, 1988). Although not unmindful of some of the problems associated with instruction in DBAE classrooms, particularly in the hands of inexperienced teachers, thoughtful proponents such as Chalmers (1981), Hamblen (1987), McFee (1988), and Smith (1987) note that DBAE not only offers critical avenues to learning but also can be extended to encompass multicultural and global concerns in art education.

Arts PROPEL, like DBAE, constituted an effort to go beyond the exclusivity of practice and offer pupils formal and conceptual knowledge about the arts (Gardner, 1990). The project, as it developed in some of Pittsburgh's public middle schools and high schools, sought to create rich learning environments where students could "easily and naturally oscillate among different forms of artistic knowing" (p. 44). Originally designed to assess the growth of artistic intelligence, it became clear that students needed opportunities to work intensively with materials and ideas, if such assessments were to be well founded. Instruction included a focus on production or the making of works of art; perception including the discrimination of important features; and reflection on the meaning imbedded in artistic works, both those made by students themselves and those made by others; these three components were considered central to all arts education. As a means of melding the instructional components, PROPEL offered domain projects, or explorations of concepts and practices deemed central to a variety of art forms; the process portfolios, or collections of ideas, initial drafts, works in progress; written responses to and critiques of work of others. The process portfolio also constituted a forum for conversation and the assessments of benchmarks in learning. The fundamental belief of PROPEL is that historical, critical, and aesthetic considerations should arise as a natural response in pupils' own artistic work. Although PROPEL underscores the work of many excellent art teachers, Gardner nonetheless throws down a gauntlet for all teachers to rethink instruction along more rigorous and demanding lines:

> This approach seeks to build on what we know about the different streams of learning. . . . there is much evidence that on their own students do not connect material learned one way—say, as a craft skill—with that learned in a notational system or in a formal body of knowledge. There is every reason to expect that the same dissonance will occur in the arts. By explicitly fusing these activities together as much as possible, we hope to reconfigure artistic learning into a model of how forms of knowledge ought to be synthesized across the curriculum. (p. 45)

Arts PROPEL has not been subjected to the kinds of critical reviews directed toward DBAE. Perhaps because PROPEL has never attained the wide sweep across the nation achieved by DBAE, its measure and depth have not been extensively tested in a range of different settings. Like DBAE, however, the success of Arts PROPEL has relied on teachers being able to deliver the appropriate instructional content in ways that nurture and support pupil learning. Arts PROPEL with its focus on idea development, and the synthesis of broad-based knowledge in art practice can, perhaps, be seen to lean more heavily toward the specialist-artistic needs of secondary pupils. DBAE, on the other hand, with its clear focus within the art disciplines, and its stress on sequenced instruction, can be seen to appeal more generally to practitioners of K–12 education.

Commentary

There is widespread agreement among art educators on the importance of specifying levels of achievement and content standards if only to meet the demands of concerned schools and policymakers. The strength of studies and surveys that offer empirical evidence, or clear and demonstrable outcomes in arts learning, have intuitive appeal in a time of escalating demands for accountability. Although helpful, however, one needs to exercise caution over making causal links from research findings to instruction, however appealing. Most studies leave out of their introductory materials, detailed information about instructional practices, goals and objectives that underpin their findings; they also omit discussion of the kinds of developmental abilities and experiences that contextualize their subjects lives. In most cases, however, these omissions do not prevent writers of studies from offering implications for practice or drawing conclusions about artistic development at the conclusion of their papers. Classrooms are complex places, and even many well-conducted experiments have little of what Eisner calls ecological validity. When claims of generalizability accompany outcomes, they have intuitive appeal as models for practice; yet, read in isolation from their instructional context, they may be seen as arbitrary to the values, interests, and aspirations of diverse groups of learners and practitioners.

What we can learn from such studies and surveys, however, is the degree to which they reveal practices that are a long way from the aspirations of the more speculative theorists in the field. The NAEP results together with other formal empirical studies lend credence to the small effects of art instruction on children's lives. They suggest fragmentation within conceptions of subject matter and also within art classroom practice. Whether this is actually an artifact of the norm-referenced methodology used in many surveys and studies, or looking in the wrong places, or is an actual reflection of much instructional practice, must wait for further research. Clearly, research methodology borrowed from other traditions such as the social sciences may well parse out the very practices and outcomes that hold centrality in the discipline. Studies that have looked for transfer have begun to grapple with what it means to do this kind of research in complex art classroom settings. Similarly, thematic projects offer insights into fundamental purposes and rationales against which practices can be viewed.

THE DESCRIPTIVE CASE STUDY POSITION

An even closer look at life in art classrooms comes from the relatively few studies that have sought to capture the messy, often unpredictable and idiosyncratic practices of individual teachers. These studies have attempted to look non judgmentally at classroom practices and, unlike more quantative studies, have not tied their observations to outcome measures (May, 1993). Like other research activities, this more "grounded" route to knowledge and insight is not new, and we have in our literature some telling accounts of teachers' lives and practices, some constructed by participant observers (Amorino, 1999; Anderson; 2000; Beittel, Matill, Burgart, Hincaid & Steward, 1961; Degee, 1975; Duckworth, 1996, 2001; Duckworth & the Experienced Teachers Group, 1997; Jackson, 1990; McFee, 1968, Swann, 1986), and some by teachers themselves (Marshall, 1970; Richardson, 1946; Robertson, 1963). The insights afforded by such narrative accounts of classroom practices, composed from the perceptions and experiences of the various players, are vivid, truthful and, sometimes, uncomfortable especially when things go astray. Those who undertake such classroom-based, case study inquiry, are often self-identified practitioners interested in describing practice with the clear purpose of increasing understanding, rather than producing generalizations about practices and outcomes. These researchers adopt a close-up view of classroom life by attempting to capture language, gesture, movement, and verbal exchanges, as teachers interweave insights about pupils, subject matter, pedagogy, and engage in the negotiations and counter- negotiations that, of necessity, take place in teaching and learning encounters.

Getting Closer

In 1996, the National Art Education Association Commission on Research invited a series of briefing papers on critical issues in the field. In response to the briefing papers, the Commission established 8 task force groups and charged them to carry out research within their interests. The Task Force on Student Learning (TFoSL), comprised 20 professional practitioners from schools and colleges on the east coast of the United States, chaired by Judith M. Burton of Teachers College Columbia University. The TFoSL chose to examine student learning in the context of classroom practice. Taking cues from Bruner (1986, 1996), Coles, (1989), Jackson (1990), and Witherell and Noddings (1991) about looking at classrooms holistically and about the critical insights to be gained from narrative accounts, the TFoSL collected data by way of classroom videos, observational notes, formal interviews, and from more freewheeling conversations with teachers and pupils. In order to understand more clearly why teachers engaged in particular kinds of practices, they were invited to view a video of their classroom activities and reflect on the underpinnings of their thoughts and actions. A range of art activities was included in the study from elementary painting to middle school ceramics and drawing to museum visits. The research took place in schools and museums within the home sites of individual researchers. The populations studied included both public school and private school and special-needs pupils.

In general, the research group's early discussions were fairly freewheeling and ran to 5 or 6 hours with breaks. Videos were stopped and back-tracked, members made written descriptions and kept notes on the conversation as attention moved from the video presentation to the discussion and dissection of what had been seen. Initially, group members focused their attention on teacher pupil interactions attempting to identify how teachers were "reading" pupils' art-works and responding to their classroom behavior. The researchers also noted how the teachers used their insights as a basis for reviewing or re-directing instruction. As the research proceeded, it became clear that there were three salient themes emerging from the data. Looked at closely, these themes took the form of characteristic input variables that involved contextual setting, teacher responses, and pupil responses, each of which conditioned classroom interactions. Moreover, although the group found that characteristics appeared to nestle one within the other, each was distinguished by an array of output indicators that captured more directly how the teachers thought about content, learning, and pupil development.

The first characteristic to command attention was that of the contextual setting established by the art teachers' orientations to one or other or a combination of views about art education. In turn this orientation appeared to shape the manner in which pupils were invited to enter the learning process. The practices identified by the study group included activities such as focus on materials and making, focus on art concepts and making, focus on looking at artworks, focus on art techniques, focus on the experiential life of pupils, and focus on modeling or demonstrating ideas for pupils to exemplify.

As the research team looked closer, they found that some teachers adopted different motivating or motivational strategies from lesson to lesson, often combining strategies in one lesson, whereas others adopted a consistent strategy across all their teaching. However, the strategy or strategies chosen to invite pupils into the lesson then appeared to determine clusters of indicators such as classroom interactions and language use between teachers and pupils and among pupils; student engagement in reflection, attitudes toward enquiry, and willingness to move into the unexplored and unknown. For example, the team found that:

> ... in practice, a teacher might invite a class to begin considering work in a particular material, moving their attention gradually towards consideration of specific artistic conventions, and encouraging a willingness to move into the unknown. (Burton, 2002)

The second characteristic identified by the TFoSL involved the responses of the teacher, and these nestled within the framework of the contextual setting established at the outset of the lesson. Thus, moving into their chosen instructional strategy, teachers played out the drama of learning through the responses they made to youngsters as they worked. The indicators here were grouped under the following headings: encouraging exploration, posing reflective questions, promoting inquiry, inviting imagination, repeating pupil statements as confirming, eliciting ideas, making meaning out of complexity, giving directions, listing things, telling about process and expected outcomes, and negotiating conflicting perceptions and desires. For example, the team observed that:

> ... *the verbal responses of the teacher who began her lesson by inviting pupils to work with a particular material and who moved them toward exploration of the unknown, circles around her class promoting inquiry, reflection, and making sense out of complexit.* (Burton, 2002)

The third characteristic to emerge from the study involved initiating actions of pupils themselves. This initiating behavior involved both verbal and physical actions such as signaling the need for help or advice, interacting with each other on behalf of learning needs, and adopting various strategies to accomplish their ends. The amount of pupil interaction during the lesson and type of discourse used in this interaction appeared to be shaped by the way the teacher modeled such activities throughout the lesson. For example, if the teacher used the phrase "tell me about your work" as part of her repertoire of responses, pupils were likely to pick this up and apply it when making inquiries about the work of a peer. In addition, the TFoSL noted especially that the younger children in the study engaged in parallel discourse whereas, as they got older, youngsters' conversations were increasingly interactive, mingling art and social talk. Often young children would tell stories or dialog at length with each other over work considerations, or would work on each others' paintings or clay pieces as helping strategies. Younger children engaged in more direct and physically active initiating behaviors while older youngsters initiated an array of different types of verbal invitations and requests or, in contrast, displayed avoiding behaviors. For example:

> ... *in the lesson referred to above in which pupils were exploring new ideas about materials and artistic conventions a great deal of the classroom discourse among pupils revolved around looking at each other's works, sharing ideas and discussing possibilities.* (Burton, 2002)

This kind of close analysis of classroom practice helps identify critical dimensions and features of practice and suggests some ways in which they cluster as teachers carry out their art instruction. Other researchers are now taking even closer looks at the clustering effects of teacher actions and responses, examining topics such as the nature of exemplary practice (Alexander, 1980; Anderson, 2000; Carpet, 1986; Stokrocki, 1986; Zimmerman, 1991, 1992), discourse analysis (Krug & Cohen-Evron, 2000; Smith-Shank, 1999), the impact of different ways of thinking about subject matter (Amorino, 1999; Hubbard, 2001), students critiquing one another's work (Barratt, 1996), and students making judgments about their work (Hafeli, 2000; Wolf, 1988).

Two examples of close-up, rich, descriptive case study research reveal much that is important about art classroom practice. For example, Hafeli (2000) points out that pupils form their own personal perceptions on the work they do, and these can differ significantly from those of their teachers. In a study carried out in 1998, Hafeli sought to uncover the different avenues of approach adopted by pupils and their teachers as they attempted to make a fit between judgments about artworks. Taking a close-up view of the instructional practices of two middle school teachers she found that acts of resistance and negotiation characterized pupils' responses. Although sometimes pupils acquiesced to suggestions by their teachers, often situations arose in which pupils perceived contradictions between the teacher's expectations and their abilities to achieve them, which resulted in a clash of aesthetic preferences. Similarly, Siegesmund (1999) sought to capture the complexity of pedagogical practice in a classroom where cognitive curriculum was employed and cognitive outcomes were desired, both pursued through a concern with aesthetic knowing. Through a close examination of one pupil teacher interaction around a drawing newly transferred to a canvas, Siegesmund notes the strategies by which the teacher assists the youngster to think through his task. The teacher helps the young man to stand back, to take a more distanced view in order to break through his preconceptions; he also models and gives permission for the youngster to exercise a range of sensory responses. More importantly, perhaps, he honors the youngster's own responses even when they conflict with his own and, in so doing, he makes a connection with the young man through a shared concern for the work.

Commentary

These more "close up" views into classrooms represent yet other vantage points on the practices of teaching. Here, we encounter the teacher as the mediating variable in classroom life and in pupil learning. Taken as a whole, these studies show how art teachers assume responsibility for making sense out of an incredible array of information, combining and juggling thoughts about pupils and their diverse needs, fluctuating attitudes, and varied purposes. We encounter teachers making judgments and remaking them in the context of the fast pace of art-classroom life and different perceptions about artistic accomplishments. Outcome variables, of the kind encountered in the more quantitative studies, here assume a kind of partial relevance as they take their place in a larger and more complex pattern of actions.

Notwithstanding the pitfalls of this kind of research—not least of which are those dealing with vast amounts of data in different forms, calibrating research schedules to classroom timetables, and the inevitable interjection of subjectivity—it still get us closer to the nub of instruction. Seen as an outgrowth of classroom practice itself, such research studies can play a critical role in teachers' professional growth. Opportunities to reflect on their own practices may be, in fact, more congenial to teachers as an impetus to professional development than the imposition of standards or exhortations of reformist art supervisors. Making transparent how teachers translate their knowledge of subject matter into forms of practice that do or do not support youngsters' learning might be the subject of future conversations about conceptions of subject matter itself. Whether such studies are made by participant observers, or are action based and teacher led, they nonetheless promise much to our insights about, and possible improvement of, practice.

Looking Forward

Most of us would like to believe that research is useful to those engaged in the practice of art education. As Eisner (1998) points out, though, change in practice emanating from new views of subject matter, learner, and instruction more often precedes rather than follows the findings of research. It may well be that lists and litanies of strategies for excellence in instruction have little to say to experienced practitioners and may be problematic when imposed upon the inexperienced. As Schon (1984) points out, the experienced teacher develops elaborate schemas of instruction and insights into classroom events, and this occurs as knowledge about teaching is constructed and reconstructed, as ideas once held as true are reconsidered and reformed over time. Teachers develop repertoires of theories, practices, knowledge and values that influence how situations are defined, what is noted, and what kinds of questions are important to ask and what decisions are critical to make. The bulk, and best kind of teacher learning, comes from the everyday decisions teachers are forced to make in the real contexts of their teaching lives.

What we perhaps learn from studies that reflect on the practices of art teachers is that there are many vantage points and little consensus. Few studies have been replicated, and almost none of them are longitudinal, so that we have brief but vivid glimpses into art classroom lives but little consistent and dependable data. There remains considerable dispute about the subject matter teachers are expected to teach; whether subject matter is derived from studio practice or from the constituative disciplines; whether it is confined to the traditions of fine art or extended to embrace a more all-encompassing visual culture; whether it derives from the formal study of elements or from the life experiences of young people; or whether it is an intermingling of all vantage points, and, if so, what are the interconnecting threads? Very few studies that look at practice, either explicitly or implicitly, begin by staking out the developmental abilities and needs of the youngsters who are their subjects; nor do they set their subjects in the context of the classroom or their out-of-school lives. Instruction, thus, emerges as a set of activities involving the arts that are applied to young people, rather than engaging them at their own level and on their own terms. Notwithstanding contemporary calls for dialog, discourse, and constructivist learning, pupils still appear to be instructed on a one-to-one basis, through lectures and demonstration. Despite a premium given to creativity and imagination, youngsters are still expected to accomplish predetermined or standardized ends often modeled by the teacher or outside arts agencies. In spite of the call for diversity and respect for difference, there appears to be little tolerance for the truly divergent and different in the art classrooms of most American schools.

Although it is important that we research art-classrooms as complex ecological settings and envision teachers standing at the confluence of multiple dimensions of thoughts, insights, actions, and outcomes, it is nonetheless important to take a closer look at some of the fundamental dimensions from which practice is fashioned and put in place, and the supports that are needed to ensure professional excellence.

REFERENCES

Alexander, R. (1980). "Mr. Jewel as a model": An educational criticism of a high school art teacher. *Studies in Art Education, 2*(3), 20–23.

Amorino, J. (1999). *The reawakening of artistic expression in adolescence through the sensory emotional system: A study with a group of males.* Unpublished doctoral dissertation, Columbia University, Teachers College, New York.

Anderson, R. (2000). Real lives: Art teachers and the cultures of school. Portsmouth, NH: Heinemann.

Anderson, R. (1997). A case study of the artist as teacher through the video work of Martha Davis. *Studies in Art Education, 39*(1), 37–56.

Bachelard, G. (1964). *The poetics of space* (M. Jolas, Trans.). New York: Orian Press.

Bakhtin, M. (1981). *The dialogic imagination.* Austin, TX: University of Texas Press.

Barkan, M. (1955). *A foundation for art education.* New York: Ronald Press.

Barkan, M. (1962). Transition in art education: Changing conceptions of curriculum and theory. *Art Education, 15*(7), 12–18.

Barratt, T. (1996). *Criticizing photography: An introduction to understanding images.* (2nd. ed.). Mountain View, CA: Mayfield Publishing Co.

Beittel, K., & Mattill, E., with Burgart, H., Hincaid, C., & Steward, R. (1961). The effect of a "depth' vs. a "breadth' method of art instruction at the ninth grade level. *Studies in Art Education, 3*(1), 75–87.

Berliner, D. C. (1986). In pursuit of the expert pedagogue. *Educational Researcher, 15*(7), 5–13.

Bresler, L., DeStefano, L., Feldman, R. & Garg, S. (2000). Artists-in-residence public schools: Issues in curriculum integration impact. *Visual Arts Research, 26*(1), 13–29.

Betts, J. D., Fisher, P. & Hicks, S. J. (1995). Arts Integration: Semiotic transmediation in the classroom. *Visual Arts Research, 12*(1), 51–71.

Brewer, T. (1991). An examination of two approaches to ceramics instruction in elementary education. *Studies in Art Education, 32*(4) 196–206.

Brewer, T. (1998). The relationship of art instruction, grade level, and gender on third and seventh grade student drawings. *Studies in Art Education, 39*(2), 132–136.

Brewer, T. (1999). Art teacher profiles and preferences. *Studies in Art Education, 41*(1) 61–70.

Brewer, T. & Colbert, C. (1992). The effect of contrasting instructional strategies on seventh grade student ceramic vessels. *Studies in Art Education, 34*(1), 18–27.

Brofenbrenner, U. (1979). *The ecology of human development: Experiments by nature and design.* Cambridge, MA: Harvard University Press.

Bruner, J. (1986). *Actual minds, possible worlds.* Cambridge, MA: Harvard University Press.

Bruner, J. (1996). *The culture of education.* Cambridge, MA: Harvard University Press.

Bullock, A. & Galbraith, L. (1992). Images of art teaching: Comparing the benefits and practices of two secondary art teachers. *Studies in Art Education, 33*(2) 86–97.

Burton, D. (2001a). How do we teach? Results of a national survey of instruction in secondary education. *Studies in Art Education, 42*(2), 131–145.

Burton, D. (2001b). A quartile analysis of the 1997 NAEP Visual Arts Report Card. *Studies in Art Education, 43*(1), 35–44.

Burton, J. (1983). Transformations: Plots and casts of the interior dramas of adolescents. In A. Hurwitz (Ed.), *Drawing for the schools.* Baltimore, MD: Maryland Institute College of Art.

Burton, J. (1998). *A guide to teaching and learning in the visual arts: A handbook for teaching.* Unpublished manuscript. Columbia University, Teachers College, New York.

Burton, J. (2000). The configuration of meaning: Learner centered art education revisited. *Studies in Art Education, 41*(4), 330–345.

Burton, J. (Ed.). (2002). *(en)Lightening moments: Pausing to listen. A critical dimension of classroom practice.* (Under review various publishers.)

Burton, J., Lederman, A., & London, P. (Eds.). (1988). *Beyond DBAE: The case for multiple visions of art education.* New York: University Council for Art Education.

Burton, J., Horowitz, R., & Abeles, H. (2000). Learning in and through the Arts: The question of transfer. *Studies in Art Education, 41*(3), 228–257.

Carpet, M. (1986). *An exploratory study of teaching visual arts grades one through eight: A phenomenological account of teacher cues, assumptions, intuitions, and dialog during a studio experience, and their implications for future research.* Unpublished doctoral dissertation, University of California, Los Angeles.

Chalmers, G. (1981). Art education as ethnography. *Studies in Art Education, 22*(3), 6–14.

Chapman, L. (1982). *Instant art instant culture.* New York: Teachers College Press.

Caroll, K. L., & Kay, S. (1998). Instruction. In E. Zimmerman (Ed.), *The NAEA Research Task Force 1998 status reports* (pp. 13–17). Reston, VA: National Art Education Association.

Caroll, K. L. (1996). Instruction. In E. Zimmerman (Ed.), *The NAEA Commission on research in art education, briefing papers: Creating a visual arts research agenda towards the 21st. century* (pp. 41–50). Reston, VA: National Art Education Association.

Caterall, J. (1998). Do experiences in the visual arts boost achievement? *Art Education, 51*(4), 6–8.

Clark, R. (1998). Doors and mirrors in art education: Constructing the postmodernist classroom. *Art Education, 51*(6), 6–11.

Coles, R. (1989). *The call of stories: Teaching and the moral imagination.* Boston: Houghton Mifflin.

Collins, G., & Sandell, R. (1988). Informing the promise of DBAE: Remembering the women, children and other folk. *Journal of Multicultural and Cross Cultural Research in Art Education, 6*(1), 55–63.

Collins, G., & Sandell, R. (1996). *Gender issues in art education: Content, contexts, and strategies.* Reston, VA: National Art Education Association.

Csikszentmihalyi, M. (1996). *Creativity: Flow and the psychology of discovery and invention.* New York: Harper.

Cuban, L. (1990). Reforming again, and again, and again. *Educational Researcher, 19*(1), 3–13.

Darling Hammond, L. (1997). *The right to learn: A blueprint for creating schools that work.* San Fransisco: Jossey-Bass.

Day, M., Eisner, E., Stake, R., Wilson, B. & Wilson, M. (1984). *Art history, criticism and art production: Case study of seven selected sites* (Vol. 2). Santa Monica, CA: Rand.

Degee, R. (1975). *A case study and theoretical analysis of the teaching practices in one junior high art class.* Unpublished doctoral dissertation, University of Oregon, Eugene.

Desai, D. (2000). Imagining difference: The politics of representation in multicultural education. *Studies in Art Education, 41*(2), 114–129.

Dikert, R. (2000). A factor analytic model of eighth-grade art learning: Secondary analysis of NAEP arts data. *Studies in Art Education, 43*(1), 5–17.

Duckworth, E. (1996). *The having of wonderful ideas.* New York: Teachers College Press.

Duckworth, E. (2001). *"Tell me more": Listening to learners explain.* New York: Teachers College Press.

Duckworth, E. & the Experienced Teachers Group, (1997). *Teacher to teacher: Learning from each other.* New York: Teachers College Press.

Duncan, P. (2001). Visual culture: Development, definition and directions for art education. *Studies in Art Education, 42*(2), 101–112.

Efland, A. (1995). Change in the conception of art teaching. In R. Neprud (Ed.), *Context, content and community in art education: Beyond post modernism.* (pp. 25–40). New York: Teachers College Press.

Efland, A. (1990). *A history of art education.* New York: Teachers College Press.

Ellsworth, E. (1997). *Teaching positions: Difference, pedagogy and the power of address.* New York: Teachers College Press.

Eisner, E. (n.d.). The role of discipline-based art education in American schools. Los Angeles, CA: Getty Center for Education in the Arts.

Eisner, E. (1983). Can educational research inform educational practice? *Phi Delta Kappan, 65,* 447–452.

Eisner, E. (1985). *The educational imagination.* New York: MacMillan.

Eisner, E. (1998). *The kind of schools we need: Personal essays.* New York: Heinemann.

Erikson, M. (1997). Transfer within and beyond DBAE: A cognitive exploration of research issues. *Visual Arts Research, 23*(2), 43–51.

Fisk, E. (Ed.). (1999). *Champions of change: The impact of the arts on learning.* Washington, DC: Arts Education Partnership and The Presidents Committee on the Arts and Humanities.

Freedman, K. (2000). Social perspectives on art education in the USA: Teaching visual culture in a democracy. *Studies in Art Education, 41*(4), 314–329.

Fuller, M. (1999). On effecting change in art curriculum. *Arts Education Policy Review, 100,* 17–18.

Gage, N. (1978). *The scientific basis of the art of teaching.* New York: Teachers College Press.

Galbraith, L. (Ed.). (1995). *Preservice art education: Issues and practice.* Reston, VA: NAEA.

Gardner, H. (1990). *Art education and human development.* Los Angeles, CA: Getty Centre for Education in the Arts.

Gardner, H. (1991). *The unschooled mind: How children think and schools should teach.* New York: Basic Books.

Gardner, H., & Winner, E. (1982). First intimations of artistry. In S. Strauss (Ed.), *U-shaped behavioral growth.* New York: Academic Press.

Geahigan, G. (2000). Models of critical discourse and classroom instruction: A critical examination. *Studies in Art Education, 41*(2), 6–21.

Geahigan, G. (1998). Critical inquiry: Understanding the concept of art and applying it in the classroom. *Art Education, 51*(5), 10–16.

Giroux, H. (1981). *Ideology, culture and the process of schooling.* Phildelphia, PA: Temple University Press.

Giroux, H. (1988). *Schooling and the struggle for public life.* Minneapolis, MN: University of Minnesota Press.

Gray, J., & MacGregor, R. (1991). A cross Canada study of high school art teachers. *Canadian Journal of Art Education, 16*(1), 47–57.

Graziano, J. (1999). *Narratives and clay: The storied forms of early adolescence 10-14.* Unpublished doctoral dissertation, Teachers College Columbia University, New York.

Greene, M. (1978). *Landscapes of learning.* New York: Teachers College Press.

Greene, M. (1994). The arts and national standards. *The Educational Forum, 58,* 391–400.

Hafeli, M. (2000) Negotiating "fit" in student art work: Classroom conversations. *Studies in Art Education, 41*(2), 130–145.

Hamblen, K. (1987). An examination of discipline based art education issues. *Studies in Art Education, 28*(2), 68–78.

Hauge, C. (1994). *Evaluation of two teaching methods used to teach art to children.* Unpublished doctoral dissertation, Syracuse University, New York.

Hubbard, O. (2001). *The effect of format and context in the aesthetic experience of adolescents.* Unpublished paper, Teachers College Columbia University, New York.

Jackson, P. (1990). *Life in classrooms.* New York: Teachers College Press.

Kowalchuk, E. (1999). Perceptions of practice: What art student teachers say they learn and need to know. *Studies in Art Education, 41*(1), 71–80.

Krug, D., & Cohen-Evron, N. (2000). Curriculum integration positions and practices in art education. *Studies in Art Education, 41*(3), 258–275.

Leinhardt, G. (1922). What research in learning tells us about teaching. *Educational Leadership, 49,* 20–24.

Louis, L. (2000). *What children have in mind: A study of early graphic representation in paint.* Unpublished doctoral dissertation, Teachers College Columbia University, New York.

Luftig, R. (2000). An investigation of an arts infusion program on creative thinking, academic achievement, active functioning and art appreciation of children in three grades levels. *Studies in Art Education, 41*(3), 208–227.

MacGregor, R. (1997). The evolution of DBAE. *Visual Arts Research, 23*(2), 1–3.

Marshall, S. (1970). *An experiment in education.* London: Cambridge University Press.

May, W. (1993). Teachers-as-researchers, or action research: What is it and what good is it for art education? *Studies in Art Education, 34*(2), 114–126.

McFee, J. (1968). *Creative problem solving abilities in art of academically superior adolescents.* Washington, DC: National Art Education Association.

McFee, J. (1988). Art and society in issues in DBAE: Strengthening the stance, extending the horizon. *Seminar Proceedings Cincinnati 1977* (pp. 104–112). Santa Monica, CA: Getty Center for Education in the Arts.

Moore, J. (2002). Student learning in a museum setting. In J. Burton (Ed.), *(en) Lightening moments: Pausing to listen. A critical dimension of classroom practice.* (Under Review various publishers.)

National Board for Professional Teaching Standards (1989). *What teachers should know and be able to do.* Washington, DC.

Neprud, R. (1995). Transitions in art education: A search for meaning. In R. Neprud (Ed.), *Context, content and community in art education. Beyond post modernism.* New York: Teachers College Press.

Perkins, D. (1987). The arts as occasions of intelligence. *Educational Researcher, 45*(4), 36–43.

Perkins, D. (1989). *Smart schools: From training memory to educating minds.* New York: Free Press.

Persky, H. R., Sandene, B. A., & Askew, J. M. (1998). *The NAEP 1997 arts report card: Eighht grade findings from the National Assessment of Educational Progress* (NCREST 1999-486). United States Department of Education, Office of Educational Research and improvement: National Center for Educational Statistics.

Remer, J. (1996). *Beyond enlightenment.* New York: ACA Books.

Richardson, M. (1946). *Art and the child.* London: University of London Press.

Robertson, S. (1963). *Rosegarden and labyrinth.* London: Routledge & Kegan Paul.

Sabol, F. R. (2001). Regional findings from a secondary analysis of the 1997 NAEP Arts Assessment. *Studies in Art Education, 43*(1), 18–34.

Salander, B. (2001). *Adolescents' reflections on the mirror's role in identity and sense of self as outcomes of responding to paintings with mirror images.* Unpublished doctoral dissertation, Teachers College Columbia University, New York.

Sarason, S. (1990). *The predictable failure of educational reform.* San Fransisco: Jossey-Bass.

Schon, D. (1984). *The reflective practitioner: How professionals think in action.* New York: Basic Books.

Siegesmund, R. (1999). Reasoned perception: Aesthetic knowing in pedagogy and learning. *Arts and Learning Research, 15*(1) 35–51.

Siegesmund, R., Dikert, R., & McCulloch, S. (2001). Revisioning NAEP: Amending a performance assessment for middle school art students. *Studies in Art Education, 43*(1), 45–56.

Smith, N., & the Drawing Study Group. (1998). *Observational drawing with children.* New York: Teachers College Press.

Smith, R. A. (1987). *Excellence in art education: Ideas and initiatives.* New York: Wiley.

Smith-Shank, D. (1999). The signs of time in an art work. *Visual Arts Research, 15*(1), 151–154.

Stockrocki, M. (1986). A portrait of an effective art teacher. *Studies in Art Education, 27*(2), 82–93.

Stokrocki, M. (1988). Teaching art to students of minority cultures. *Journal of Mulicultural and Cross-cultural research in Art Education, 6*(1), 99–111.

Stokrocki, M. (1990). A cross-site analysis: Problems in teaching arts to preadolescents. *Studies in Art Education, 31*(2), 106–117.

Swann, A. (1986). *A naturalistic study of the art making process in preschool settings.* Unpublished doctoral dissertation, Indiana University, Bloomington.

Tuman, D. (1999). Gender style as form and content: An examination of gender stereotypes in the subject preferences of children's drawings. *Studies in Art Education, 41*(1), 40–60.

Tyak, D. (1974). *The one best system.* Cambridge, MA: Harvard University Press.

Willats, J. (1992). *What is the matter with Mary Jane's drawing?* In D. Thistlewood & E. Court (Eds.), Drawing Research and Development. Harlow, Essex: Longman.

Williams, B. L. (1996). Examination of art museum practices since 1984. *Studies in Art Education, 38*(1), 34–39.

Wilson, B. (1997). *The quiet evolution: Changing the face of art education.* Los Angeles, CA: Getty Education Institute for the Arts.

Winner, E., & Hetland, L. (2001). The arts in education: Evaluating the evidence for a causal link. *Journal of Aesthetic Education, 34*(3-4), 3–10.

Witherell, C., & Noddings, N. (1991). *Stories lives tell: Narrative and dialogue in education.* New York: Teachers College Press.

Wolf, D. (1988). Artistic learning: What and where is it? *The Journal of Aesthetic Education, 22*(1), 143–155.

Zimmerman, E. (1991). Rembrandt to Rembrandt: A case study of a memorable painting teacher of artistically talented 13-16 year old students. *Gifted Child Quarterly, 13*(2), 76–81.

Zimmerman, E. (1992). A comparative study of two painting teachers of talented students. *Studies in Art Education, 33*(3), 174–185.

V

Forms of Assessment
in Art Education

25

Assessment and Visual Arts Education

Elisabeth Soep
Youth Radio & University of California, Berkeley

The relationship between art and assessment is best characterized as awkward, if not overtly hostile. Arts educators tend to bemoan the impact of mandatory evaluations on imaginative practice. To make matters worse, accountability systems and testing conventions are often imported from academic subjects—domains of learning that may more easily "break down" into component questions with clear right answers, which students can conscientiously bubble in on multiple-choice tests. Visual arts projects can be messy, whether they involve hands-on production tasks or responses to work by established artists. It is difficult, and some might argue damaging, to evaluate student performance on these kinds of tasks according to predetermined standards. Matters get even more complicated when judgments about the quality of student work go beyond individual encounters between teachers and their students, when educators are answerable to state-sponsored mandates or external reviews.

This view, which pits art against assessment like two opponents in a boxing ring, is often justified. Nevertheless, much can be learned when we force ourselves to recognize what the work of visual art and the work of assessment have in common. Perhaps the two are not as oppositional as they initially appear.

1. Artworks and assessment works visualize the ineffable. Both visual artists and assessors are often in the business of rendering tangible something that defies easy articulation. Now, one could argue that plenty of tests merely require students to report bits of information— correct dates, names, and solutions, for example. But underlying individual test items is usually a drive to understand something much more elusive, like student learning, or what a young person knows and is able to do. Likewise, artists are not always interested in conveying some profound, ground-breaking message. Yet artworks function in a larger sense as objects that capture and convey complex meanings (even when they call into question the very possibility of "meaning" as an attribute of art). Both assessors and artists operate in worlds where tensions of translation are inevitable, in the always imperfect action of turning thoughts into things. In this section of the *Handbook*, Persky in particular explores these tensions, in her analysis of efforts by national assessors not to overburden visual arts tasks with verbal directions—a problem of translation across symbol systems. Despite or perhaps by virtue of these kinds of tensions, artworks and assessment works partially articulate some truth, or some lie, that would otherwise have remained invisible, had no effort taken place to make the ineffable concrete.

2. Artworks and assessment works tell stories. One way to look at individual art objects, collections of related works, or trajectories whereby whole traditions have emerged, dominated, and then fallen out of favor is to ask what stories these artifacts tell. The same is true for assessment. This point surfaces especially in one essay in this section by Myford and Sims-Gunzenhauser, where the authors describe the evolution of two national visual arts evaluation programs as a "story of contrasts" that reveals how educational priorities and assumptions have changed from the 1970s to the present. Art objects and histories, like assessment contents, structures, and rationales, expose who we are, as individuals and societies, at any given moment in time. Even the most antinarrative artwork and even the most statistics-driven evaluation have important stories to tell.

3. Artworks and assessment works provoke controversy. Related to point number 2 is this third connection: that art and assessment can tell us things about ourselves that we do not want to know. This observation seems obvious enough with respect to artworks. Societies have long tried to silence artists who expose painful realities or defy mainstream sensibilities, just as we depend on artists to advance avant-garde ideas and sensibilities. This same quality of provocation can be attributed to assessment, on at least two levels. First, there are the public outcries and "moral panics" that follow any large-scale report of student failure on standardized tests; often poor outcomes give rise to heated debates, new policy and curriculum interventions, and, predictably, ever more energetic testing efforts. Second, the difficult and provocative nature of assessment operates on a deeper level as well—when tests are exposed to be biased, or inhibiting to curricular innovation, or abused when applied to malevolent purposes. Artworks, and assessment works, can do harm *or* make good; both can yield uncomfortable moments of recognition when we are forced to contemplate our failings as artists and viewers, as test takers and test makers, and as participants in institutions that shape both realms of practice.

4. Artworks and assessment works simultaneously reflect *and* create the people who encounter these cultural products. The Brechtian idea that artworks are not merely mirrors held up to a society but hammers that shape it holds true as well for assessments. Artworks and assessment works are *technologies*, influenced by new materials and sources of knowledgeability, and also generative of these innovations through experimentation—for example, when affordable editing software became available to the grassroots video community, or with the advent of digital portfolios as a facet of visual arts assessment. The tools we have at our disposal not only serve or measure but also help shape what we make and know. Artworks and assessment works are also *ideologies* based in specific worldviews about the kinds of efforts worth undertaking and recognizing, as well as those deserving of little notice or loud resistance. It is possible to call an assessment tradition, like an arts tradition, "modernist," as Boughton does in his chapter for this section, with respect to standards-based multiple-choice testing. And there is growing interest today in what "postmodern" assessment might look like in contemporary classrooms (Fehr, Fehr, & Keifer-Boyd, 2000). Artists and assessors belong to, sustain, and ultimately unsettle specific movements and schools of thought and action. Just as "tests have invented all of us" (Hanson, 2000), so too do artworks transform those who make, consume, and critique visual culture.

5. Artworks and assessment works are social practices. Despite the persistent myth of the artist as a lone genius working under sequestered conditions, most artists and arts educators will attest from experience that artworlds are social fields, populated by peers, critics, mentors, models, and institutions including museums, popular culture industries, and schools. Even private moments of inspiration operate within minds and bodies shaped by histories of interaction with others. This same point about the social character of arts experience can be applied to assessment. Although it may seem intuitive to locate assessment projects squarely in the realm of scientific practice, even statistical methods and empirical findings develop out of social processes, which define quality and merit within a given realm of performance (Broadfoot, 2000). In this section of the *Handbook*, I make this sociocultural approach explicit, through my review of research on self- and peer assessment in visual arts education—processes that can range from formal and high-stakes "peer reviews" to informal and fleeting moments when a child comments on her classmate's drawing. Viewing artworks and assessment works as social practices draws attention to the complex orchestration of ideas, values, and institutional sanctions that support certain traditions within both fields. This approach also points to the possibility of intervening within these fields, by reminding us that these two realms of social practice are always in a process of reinvention.

Identifying these five features that artworks and assessment works have in common should in no way diminish the tensions that arise when arts educators are called on to evaluate their own pedagogical practices and their students' efforts and products. These conflicts are very real, and very significant, as the arts find themselves excluded from the vast majority of state-evaluation programs in the United States, even as arts educators are constantly expected to justify their place in the curriculum. This position is both a blessing and a curse. The arts are protected, to some extent, from the incursion of rigid standards and high-stakes pressures, but they are also overlooked in resource allocation and public recognition, thereby potentially reifying a marginalized place for the arts among school subjects.

The first author in this section, Doug Boughton, begins his chapter by exposing this odd position for the visual arts—a field that is rarely required for college acceptance, included in only seven states' mandatory testing policies, and yet caught up in a climate that demands accountability and public scrutiny for all subject areas that really matter in education. Boughton describes what he sees as a promising model for large-scale arts assessment administered in over 60 countries around the world—the International Baccalaureate (IB) program. In the IB program, trained external examiners assess portfolios documenting students' research and studio practices using predetermined holistic categories. Boughton argues that the portfolio is a far more appropriate measure of arts learning than paper-and-pencil tests, which "dismember" artistic performance and thereby stand to do more harm than good. The chapter holds relevance beyond the IB program in particular, as Boughton provides an overview of portfolio assessment in the arts, identifying the features associated with learning portfolios as distinct from professional portfolios. To function as an assessment tool within visual arts education, the portfolio should be more than a "repository" for homework assignments; Boughton says students should be the ones creating portfolio archives, including works in progress, sketches, and their own critical self-reflections. Two additional dimensions of the IB program also have broad relevance to debates in visual arts education: (1) A process called grade *moderation*, whereby multiple judges assess student work, promoting a climate of debate and a community of deliberation; and (2) an approach for developing assessment *benchmarks* based on exemplar student work embodying certain qualities, and not based on models put forth to be copied. Overall, Boughton makes a case for portfolio assessment in the arts without downplaying the tensions likely to arise when external measures are introduced within a U.S. arts educational climate that tends to privilege informal teacher judgments of student work.

The two subsequent chapters in this section of the *Handbook* also address large-scale arts assessments. Hilary Persky reports on the 1997 National Assessment of Educational Progress (NAEP) visual arts assessment. She sees NAEP as a model for capturing individual meaning-making and artistic thinking, assuming that the arts are integral to education "for all" and not only for the few who self-select or happen to attend schools with strong arts programs. Unlike the IB program, NAEP is a one-day, "drop-down," timed assessment for which students have no specific preparation. The visual arts section is just one of several academic and arts domains included in NAEP, which is administered to representative random samples of students across the United States, including those with absolutely no arts training. Needless to say, these conditions create unique challenges for designing a valid, reliable, and feasible evaluation constrained significantly by concerns about time limits, task sophistication, and labor and material costs. NAEP only works if the evaluators can get in and out of schools in a matter of hours, having never before met the students and knowing nothing about the specific contexts of the classrooms, schools, or communities where they are administering the test. It is a daunting undertaking indeed, says Persky, to devise tasks that allow students to create two- and three-dimensional objects, as well as to respond to the work of established artists, using various materials, all in the space of a few hours. Student work generated for NAEP is shipped off to external, trained judges for scoring, adding yet another significant challenge. Persky's chapter presents a case where assessors aim to recognize varied, imaginative, and experimental student responses despite fixed scoring criteria and strict format constraints. An additional contribution of the chapter is Persky's inclusion of several actual examples of student work—written and visual—produced in response to NAEP tasks, offering readers the artifacts themselves to consider alongside the scores these pieces actually earned, revealing the strengths and weaknesses of one of the most ambitious national visual arts assessments this country knows.

Persky's chapter provides a nice lead-in to the next one by Carol Myford and Alice Sims-Gunzenhauser, which chronicles the *evolution* of both NAEP and another national arts assessment, the Advanced Placement (AP) studio art program, over 3 decades. With respect to NAEP, the authors essentially compare the 1997 program with prior administrations of the assessment in 1975 and 1978. The 1970s favored breadth of coverage and behavioral objectives, whereas the 1997 version emphasized depth of knowledge and skill, range in tasks, and specific process and content standards. The most recent administration of the NAEP also showed increased sophistication in test design and scoring technologies and had a much larger evident impact on the research community. The AP assessment, unlike NAEP, has been given continuously since 1972, based on cumulative student portfolios rather than drop-down timed testing events. Over the years, the structure for the AP has shifted, but the evaluation of student portfolios has consistently depended on highly trained "readers," themselves high school- and college-level art teachers, who collaboratively review submissions based on holistic measures. Beyond analyzing the specific cases included in this chapter, Myford and Sims-Gunzenhauser address the more general tensions surrounding any assessment effort that extends over a significant period. The assessment needs to evolve and transform with the times. However, changes to the assessment can prevent comparison across groups of students who have taken different versions of the test (or experienced different approaches to the portfolio, or tackled different kinds of tasks). Herein lies the profound assessment challenge of balancing benefits for student learning and updated practice with social science principles that dictate valid, reliable, and significant comparisons among young people learning in diverse contexts. Myford and Sims-Gunzenhauser, in their discussion of the AP exam for studio art, also provide a glimpse into the kinds of deliberations that take place when panels of readers jointly assess work submitted within student portfolios.

In the final chapter of this section, I focus on the process of joint assessment among peers, as well as on individual self-assessment, by students themselves. The chapter begins with a discussion of relevant theories pertaining to self- and peer assessment in the visual arts, proposing a sociocultural view of the mind and outlining the notion of "artworlds" that assign value to specific arts practices while rendering others less visible or desirable. Organizing the chapter roughly along a developmental trajectory, I cast a wide net, reviewing research drawn from anthropology, cultural studies, education, and psychology that sheds light on how young artists formulate judgments of their own projects and those of their peers. As a complement to the other essays, which center on standardized national assessment programs, this chapter tends to zero in on small-scale, moment-to-moment assessment encounters among learners, and between students and teachers, which may or may not take place within formal evaluation events or accountability programs. This view of assessment as an unfolding process takes readers inside classrooms as well as to less recognized arts learning environments beyond school walls, expanding what counts as arts education in an era of increasingly pervasive and complex visual cultures.

Overall, the chapters contained in this section do not shrink from acknowledging the difficulties inherent in assessing visual arts learning. Perhaps one conclusion readers might draw is that there is, in fact, much to moan about when educators are asked to evaluate what their students know and are able to do in the arts. An alternative message to glean from these authors is a view of the unique challenges faced by arts educators not as burdens, but as opportunities. Every field of learning—including the arts and math and science and English—features relatively measurable skills as well as sophisticated performances that defy easy classification, especially when students make efforts that are truly experimental and unexpected. When assessments capture this full range of student abilities (as Myford and Sims-Gunzenhauser argue in their chapter), the dreaded act of "teaching to the test" actually results in "students working with commitment and passion at visual issues that stretch their knowledge, strengthen their conceptual abilities, and, of course, help them develop the framework of technical skills that are necessary to realize their ideas." Arts educators have no choice but to aim for these ambitions, simply because of the nature of our field. That surely makes the work harder, but it also puts the arts in a position of leadership with respect to innovative education, and assessment, across disciplines.

REFERENCES

Fehr, D., Fehr, K., & Keifer-Boyd, K. (2000). *Real-world readings in art education: Things your professors never told you.* London: Routledge-Falmer Press.

Broadfoot, P. (2000). Preface. In *Assessment: Social practice and social product.* In Ann Filer, (Ed.), London: Routledge-Falmer Press, ix–xii.

Hanson, F. A. (2000). How tests create what they are intended to measure. In A. Filer, (Ed.), (pp. 67–82). *Assessment: Social practice and social product.* London: Routledge-Falmer Press.

26

Assessing Art Learning in Changing Contexts: High-Stakes Accountability, International Standards and Changing Conceptions of Artistic Development

Doug Boughton
Northern Illinois University

INTRODUCTION

Underpinning art education since the 1940s has been the assumption that student autonomy is not only important but also central to their art making. It has been often argued that student experience in school art programs develops the capacity for independent thought and the ability to express ideas in visual form. Such individual expression has long been valued in American schools. Recent educational reforms have placed significant emphasis on testing as a way to improve standards in school subjects across the board in the United States. An unfortunate byproduct for the arts from these reforms has been the homogenization of student outcomes expressed as standards that are frequently measured with inappropriate assessment instruments. High-stakes tests, employed by state assessment authorities, provide the model for inappropriate assessment. These tests imply homogenous outcomes reflecting a single set of agreed standards is appropriate for the arts. The casualties in these reforms have been the most valued of all tenets of art education: the freedom of students to pursue independent learning pathways and the autonomy of their expression.

This state of affairs is more than an assessment problem; it is a complex curriculum issue. The intimacy of the relationship between assessment and curriculum is the focus of the discussion in this chapter. Here I will focus on three main themes that address the relationship between curriculum and assessment. The first is the importance of supporting student autonomy in their development of artistry; the second is to represent the ways in which the international community does this, with specific reference to the International Baccalaureate Organization; and the third is to provide a view of the potential use of technology in assessment to support a postmodern conception of artistic development that enables multiple pathways for students.

HIGH STAKES ACCOUNTABILITY AND STUDENTS' AUTONOMY
AS ARTISTS

Until recently the issue of student assessment in art education received scant attention in the United States. Between 1959 and 1974, for example, only 5% (14) of the articles published in *Studies in Art Education* dealt in any way with evaluation issues and these were concerned mainly with program evaluation rather than student assessment. However, current accountability pressures in the United States have caused arts educators to pay increased attention to the difficult business of assessing learning in the arts. High-stakes assessment in particular has heightened schools' awareness of the need to assess student learning in all subjects with an unprecedented intensity.

The arts, although currently subject to high-stakes assessment in only a few states have nevertheless been caught up in the backwash of the assessment momentum created by individual state accountability efforts. Arts teachers in the United States do not have the same history as their European counterparts in large-scale arts assessments, and are not as well equipped to deal with demands to demonstrate publicly the quality of their students' achievements through regularized assessments of their subjects. American teachers are much more accustomed to making individual classroom judgments about their students' learning that are not challenged by external reviewers or compared to the judgments made by other teachers in other schools. A large-scale survey of art teachers conducted by Burton found that the majority of art teachers conduct assessment by informal means, "such as observation of students (87.3%), viewing artwork (75%), critiques or evaluations upon completion of projects (62.7%), or conversations (50%)" (Burton, 1998, p. 1). This professional autonomy has long been treasured in the American context so that recent demands for public testing of students in the arts has lifted the curtain on what was previously a private stage for art teachers.

Overseas teachers of the arts are more familiar with public scrutiny. European and Australian countries, in contrast to the United States, admit students to university based on state or national public examinations of senior school subjects (including art), rather than on administering standardized university admission exams. Rigorous summative assessment procedures at the senior school level in art education have a lengthy tradition in Europe, the United Kingdom, Australia, New Zealand, and parts of Asia. Portfolios in various forms play a significant role in these assessments. This is the case, not only for art making but also for art history and design.

Unlike much of the rest of the developed world, high school grades, or aggregate high school scores, do not provide the sole or even the major gateway to universities in the United States. In only three states, Arizona, Kentucky, and Minnesota, do all universities require study of the arts for admission. In nine other states some universities require the arts for university admission. In other words the study of the arts in high school is not required for admission to university in three quarters of the nations' schools (2002–2003 State Arts Education Policy Database). Students in the United States gain admission largely on the basis of their ACT or SAT Scores. Admission to art schools on the other hand is largely based on portfolios for entry to foundations programs.

Public scrutiny of U.S. education has brought a search for more defensible art assessment procedures. For some insights into some alternative ways of conceiving large-scale assessments I will later look outside the United States to examine the portfolio assessment practices employed by the International Baccalaureate (IB) program at the senior school art level. The procedures employed in this large-scale assessment program, which is taught in over 60 countries, can inform both high stakes testing programs and individual classroom assessment practice.

The impetus for increased attention to assessment and teacher accountability has been growing steadily since the mid-1970s (Davis, 1993). In 1994, the Consortium of National Arts Education Associations published the *National Standards for Arts Education* as a major contribution toward the effort to improve arts teaching in the United States. It was assumed that these statements about the basic content of the field would provide a baseline reference for teachers across the nation and that assessment practices based on agreed outcome statements would improve the art learning of students. This claim was identical to that being made in other academic fields such as science, mathematics, and social studies … despite fundamental differences between the arts and other academic disciplines, and the ways in which excellence is judged in those disciplines. In the same year, the Goals 2000: Educate America Act emphasized the standards to be applied to curricular content, student performance, and opportunity to learn. In the 8 years since that publication, interest in assessment has accelerated in response to heightened accountability measures.

The development of national standards was regarded by many as an historic achievement in the United States (Armstrong, 1996). The majority of the United States has subsequently adopted a version of the national art standards that have formed the basis for state school curriculums and assessment practices. Of greater significance nationally has been the development of standardized high stakes testing designed as an accountability measure to determine which schools have been able to measure up and which have not. The basis for reference in the development of test items is the national standards or the state adaptations of them. Art, however, is rarely included in the basket of subjects used in these high-stakes tests. Only seven states require the arts to be tested statewide (2002–2003 State Arts Education Policy Database).

The majority of those seven states employ paper-and-pencil multiple-choice test formats. Some are combined with other options such as open-ended written responses and portfolios. Arts assessments are also commonly combined with other subjects within the humanities.[1] The effect of testing the standards through the use of multiple-choice tests is to atomize artistic knowledge to the point where assessment information gathered is virtually meaningless. Consider the following questions selected from the1996 Illinois state art test (Illinois State Board of Education, 1996). Students were required to answer 13 art questions in total. No assessment of art performance is undertaken in Illinois.

Q14. Which word best describes the theme for this sculpture?
   A. Unity
   B. Chaos
   C. Reality
   D. Tragedy
Q15. What is a style of writing that is also considered an art form?
   A. Graphic art
   B. Narrative art
   C. Iconography
   D. Calligraphy
Q19. Which art process uses a woodblock?
   A. Printmaking
   B. Painting
   C. Photography
   D. Weaving
Q22. Which painting has a horizon line below eye level?
   A. 1
   B. 2
   C. 3
   D. 4

---

[1] Information about art assessment in these states was gathered from state education Web sites and follow-up phone calls (October–November, 2002).

Q23. Which painting has a horizon line above eye level?
  A. 1
  B. 2
  C. 3
  D. 4

The national standards for arts education, between kindergarten and 12th grade contain 57 standards for the visual arts. Assessment information, if collected in relation to each one of these standards, provides detail about individual parts that have little intrinsic value. Examination of holistic acts of artistic achievement is complicated because the parts are interrelated and many standards are addressed simultaneously. Artistic performance is organic and cannot be dismembered without serious injury.

It is encouraging to see that the 1997 National Assessment of Educational Progress (NAEP) employed a wider range of assessment techniques than is common in state high-stakes tests. Students were asked to create, analyze, and interpret works of art (U.S. Department of Education, 1999). Although the NAEP assessment did not collect data over time portfolio style, the response to given tasks required students to produce artworks with relatively open-ended outcomes in addition to answering some multiple-choice questions about artworks.

Performance measures, such as portfolio or other "authentic" assessment techniques, however, are rare in statewide assessments of art, most likely due to the high cost of their implementation and the likely perception of policymakers that the arts are not worth the investment because their subjectivity compared to mathematics or science would make assessment unreliable. The result is that art is not tested in 43 states, which diminishes perception of its importance in the curriculum, and in the 7 states in which it is tested paper-and-pencil multiple-choice assessment formats are predominant. These kinds of assessments are not widely supported in the arts education assessment literature.

Thus, the current high-stakes assessment practice in the United States has created a parlous and no win scenario for art education. Art is not seen to be valued sufficiently by administrators in 43 states to warrant inclusion in their high-stakes assessment programs, and in the remaining 7 states testing is carried out using means that are largely inappropriate. In a national educational context in which the results of high-stakes assessments can affect the real estate values in school neighborhoods, the salaries of school administrators, and the professional futures of school faculties, art teachers increasingly feel the need to demonstrate student learning through systematic assessment that is ill suited to measuring the quality of holistic performances.

Portfolios as an Alternative to Paper-and-Pencil Tests

Questions about the appropriateness of testing as a means to determine artistic understanding have been raised by others (Gardner, 1996; Sullivan, 1993; Zimmerman, 1994) primarily because of the homogenizing effects of the testing process. Standardized testing using a series of discrete and unrelated items requires students to perform in ways that do not typify the kinds of behaviors that even young artists would use to display their knowledge in the broader social context; and in that sense, testing is an "inauthentic" way to determine whether someone possess specific kinds of cultural and practical knowledge in the arts. Other shortcomings of multiple-choice tests have been widely reported in the literature. They often require only lower order thinking skills; they fail to assess all the important and desirable educational outcomes; they can encourage teaching to the test; they can be used and interpreted improperly (Cizek, 1993).

Authentic assessment strategies, on the other hand, engage students in long-term tasks and meaningful projects that are challenging, complex, and reflect real-life situations (Gardner, 1996; Wolfe, 1988; Zimmerman, 1994). Assessment in the arts should not be conceived as information retrieval (Sullivan, 1993) but as a means to chart students' intellectual pathways. Insight into students' thinking and understanding is not always provided by end products. The Arts PROPEL project conducted in Pittsburg public schools (Gardner, 1989, 1996; Wolfe, 1988) was a long-term research effort that explored, among other things, alternative (authentic) assessment strategies based on portfolios, written reflective material, and dialog (Blaikie, 1994).

The Goals 2000 Educate America Act (1994) emphasized the intention of the U.S. education reform movement that advocated a preference for performance-based assessment as the most appropriate means to assess students' proficiency (Castiglione, 1996). The testing industry in the early 1990s invested considerable energy into retooling its instruments to meet the demand (Cizek, 1993). By 1996, at least 40 states were either exploring alternative testing procedures or were in the process of changing the process of student and professional performance (Castiglione, 1996). However, since the mid-1990s, the early enthusiasm for performance testing has declined significantly. For example, the California state testing program in the early 1990s supported locally developed exams that contained a high percentage of performance tasks. In 2002, the state's accountability index makes exclusive use of SAT9, a standardized, commercially produced, paper-and-pencil test.

Curiously, the idea of portfolio assessment, which is historically rooted in the visual arts, has, at the same time, been embraced as a viable solution to the shortcomings of paper-and-pencil testing in other subject areas and is largely ignored both by the state high-stakes assessment programs and by the teachers of the arts in the United States. Burton (1998) found that only 17.1% of teachers use portfolio review as a primary method of assessment.

Authentic Assessment and Portfolio Evidence

Portfolio evidence is one of the most important elements of alternative (authentic) assessment (Gitomer, Grosh, & Price, 1992). Both practice and research indicate that students may usefully collect within their portfolios work in progress; completed works; sketches and notes about ideas related to the work; assessments and commentaries by the student, teacher, and peers; essays about the work; photographs and other records of source materials. Portfolios have been employed widely and successfully for assessment in the visual arts by the Advanced Placement, International Baccalaureate, and Arts PROPEL programs (Blaikie, 1994), the Dutch National Assessment System (Schönau, 1996), the British GCSE art assessment (MacGregor, 1990), and Australian and New Zealand Year 12 state and national assessments (MacGregor, 1990, 1991).

CHANGING CONCEPTIONS ABOUT THE CONTENT OF THE FIELD

In the visual arts, the business of conducting large-scale assessments remains a vexed issue. The modernist philosophy underpinning the approach to assessment by standards assumes that artistic activity and its products can be deconstructed into discrete components, each of which can be assessed individually. The relationship between the components is not addressed by the standards. Assessment becomes a mechanistic gathering of bits of information that, taken one by one, contain no inherent value. In addition the organic nature of the arts is ignored; the relationship among history, culture, context, and production becomes disconnected; and complexity, which characterizes performance in the arts, is lost. In the end it is not the important and complex outcomes that are assessed but those individual pieces that are easy to measure.

In the modernist framework of standards-based assessment, life is oversimplified for teachers in comparison to the tangle of issues raised by changing conceptions of the field of art. The demands by politicians and school systems managers for art teachers to neatly characterize the nature and content of the field in terms of performance standards has occurred at a moment in the history of art and education which is characterized by vigorous challenges to established modernist orthodoxies. Specifically new approaches to art education, broadly categorized under the term *visual culture* question long-standing assumptions about both the nature of art and the content and practice of art education.

The visual culture approach is sufficiently well established in the literature to indicate the emergence of a significant challenge to established modernist art education orthodoxies (Efland, Freedman, & Stuhr, 1996; MacGregor, 1992b). Special issues of *Studies in Art Education* and *Art Education* in 2003 highlight this debate. Based on postmodern philosophy, visual culture approaches have proposed curriculum ideas that carry significant implications for assessment. Important among these are: (a) The meaning of visual images is as important as its form; (b) art reflects social issues such as equity, identity, and community, (c) the value of artworks is attributed by the viewer; (d) artworks are valued for the associative power of their symbols and social relevance in specific contexts; (e) art is best understood through sociocultural forms of analysis; (f) no distinction is made between fine and popular art forms with regard to their educational value; (g) contemporary art is relevant to students, (h) recycled imagery is appropriate in the context of postmodern art making; and (i) students are encouraged to take responsibility for their learning under the guidance of a teacher who initiates experiences in the full range of visual culture—including, among other things, comic books, video documentaries, film, computer games, and installations (Boughton et al., 2002).

Differences in views held by those who favor a modernist approach and by others holding postmodern perspectives continue to raise questions for educators about central pedagogical and assessment issues like the virtue of originality in image making (Freedman, 1994b; MacGregor, 1992a), the relationship of art and context (Chalmers, 1985; Blandy & Hoffman, 1993), the relative merits of popular art and fine arts (Duncum, 1996), the influence of new technologies on expression (Freedman & Relan, 1992), the relative value of Eurocentric forms of expression for students of diverse cultural backgrounds (Anderson, 1995; Garber, 1995; Stuhr, 1994), and gender issues in art and education (Freedman, 1994a; Sandell, 1991). Despite vigorous defense of traditional aesthetic values (Eisner, 2001; Feldman, 1992; Smith, 1992), the dust raised by the battle between the proponents of old and new ideologies has challenged the universality of traditional formalist criteria, such as the central role of the elements and principles of design, making it more difficult for teacher/evaluators in the United States to determine the parameters for assessing the quality of their students' artistic products.

The conceptions of content of the field in a visual culture approach to art education not only have changed, but also the understanding of the ways in which students progress through it have also changed, further complicating the assessment task for teachers. Traditional views of artistic growth presume the student enters the art program "from a naïve, uninformed state and exits from the program in a sophisticated state as a result of teacher interventions and educational activities..." (Clark & Zimmerman, 1978).

New approaches to art education assume students already possess sophisticated knowledge of the visual arts defined more broadly as visual culture. Students' capacities to understand the visual arts should not be underestimated, given the complexity of the computer games, feature-length films, and television commercials they experience every day. In most important ways, these forms of popular visual culture are as complex as fine art. As a result of their rich visual experiences, outside of school students today are making connections on their own among the diverse forms of visual culture they encounter daily and constructing a range of new knowledge through and about the visual arts.

The curriculum in this context is a creative process and a conceptual space in which students develop their ideas with the aid of teachers who act as critical partners. Curriculum is a form of mediation between and among students, teachers, and a wide range of texts and images from inside and outside of school. Assessment of student learning must reject homogeneity of outcomes and embrace the notion of individual student pathways. The IB program exemplifies this approach to curriculum, and its assessment provides the right environment for it to work. High-stakes assessment models in the United States do the exact opposite.

ASSESSMENT IN THE INTERNATIONAL CONTEXT

To this point I have argued that the current climate of accountability in the United States has raised the specter of public scrutiny of student learning in the visual arts, and that many arts teachers do not have a history that prepares them to respond to this demand well. I have argued also that despite the development of national and state-based standards for the teaching of art, current state testing formats are largely inappropriate to assess arts learning; and further, the field is undergoing a transition that points to a need for a more reflexive, holistic approach to both the construction of curriculum and the conduct of assessment. An implication from the aforementioned is that the relationship between curriculum and assessment needs to be reconsidered in the United States.

Looking more globally at the issues of assessment, the IB program is one that well reflects the challenge of achieving universal excellence variously expressed in multiple personal and cultural contexts. The IB is a system of international education taught in more than half the countries in the world. As described in documents accessed through the information page of the IB Web site, the centerpiece of the program is its flexibility in responding to local interests but at the same time providing access for students to what is shared and what is different in human experience.

> . . . developing citizens of the world-culture, language and learning to live together. building, and reinforcing students' sense of identity and cultural awareness fostering students' recognition and development of universal human values. (International Baccalaureate Organization [IBO], 2003a, p. 7)

Probably the most fundamental difference between the IB approach to assessment and the prevailing culture of assessment in the United States is summed up in the following:

> . . . in all such deliberations the primary consideration is always a recognition of the effect that any assessment structure has on classroom teaching. It is essential that assessment structures support good classroom practice. This is considered of greater educational importance than pure reliability of measurement. (International Baccalaureate Organization, 2003b, p. 15)

It is hard to imagine a greater possible difference in assessment cultures. Brent Wilson (1996), after spending 3 months in the Netherlands, England, Scotland, and Wales studying those countries national assessments, arrived at the conclusion that the United States could benefit by taking note of assessment practices in Europe and in England. He found that the public examinations in those countries "created high-level national expectations, and at the same time encouraged teachers to review the effectiveness of their own instructional practices, to collaborate with their colleagues to improve the general quality of art education, and to openly discuss issues relating to student performance" (p. 1).

To be fair, it is important to note that centralized assessment practices in the IB, Europe, Britain, and Australasia experience some important problems related to examiner training, the establishment of benchmarks, moderation systems, and the sheer volume of assessment materials handled. On balance, however, the portfolio-based moderated assessment systems used internationally are far more supportive of good classroom practice.

The IB program is one that uses both studio and research portfolios as a central assessment tools. A feature of the assessment is that few criteria are employed, and holistic judgments are employed to assess studio art learning.

THE INTERNATIONAL BACCALAUREATE PROGRAM

The IB program has a long tradition of public art portfolio examination in more that 60 countries, including the United States, where more than half the total world candidature is located. In the course of its history, the IB has developed examination procedures in art (and all other diploma subjects) that are accepted by universities in more than 110 countries (IBO, 2001). In the United States, 123 three universities accepted the IB diploma subjects for entry in 2001 including high status institutions such as Harvard and Stanford (International Baccalaureate North America, 2001). The International Baccalaureate Organization, IBO, was founded in 1968 as a nonprofit educational foundation based in Geneva, Switzerland. It has its origins as early as 1924, at which time international schools in Europe attempted to establish a common curriculum and university entry credentials. Thus, it had to develop a truly international program that would resonate in very different educational systems around the world. Critical thinking and exposure to a variety of points of view are believed to encourage not only intellectual and artistic, understanding but also *intercultural* understanding by IB students. The IB diploma is taken by students in the last 2 years of school before university studies, and the curriculum leads to what is now called a "baccalaureate," administered in 109 countries[2] and recognized by universities everywhere. Development of the diploma program was made possible by grants from UNESCO, the Twentieth Century Fund, the Ford Foundation, and other groups (International Baccalaureate Organization, 2002b).

The IB Curriculum

The diploma curriculum model is traditionally displayed in the shape of a hexagon with six academic areas surrounding a core. At the core of the program are three distinct components, a subject called "Theory of Knowledge," an extended essay, and a creativity/action/service component. The core components complement a traditional liberal arts curriculum in which the humanities and sciences are studied concurrently. The core subjects provide a critical role in linking the other content areas together, so that the arts become an integral part of education and not a repository of specialized bits of information. Knowledge in the arts is promoted as a way of knowing to which all humans should have access.

The diploma candidates are required to select at least one subject from each of the six subject groups. These are (a) Language A1, (b) Second Language, (c) Individuals and Societies, (d) Experimental Sciences, (e) Mathematics and Computer Sciences, and (f) the Arts. At least three and not more than four subjects are taken at a higher level (HL); and the others, at standard level (SL). A HL subject requires 240 teaching hours, whereas SL subjects are taught in 150 hours. This enables students to arrange their work to explore some subjects in depth and others more broadly over a 2-year period. Flexibility in choosing subject configurations allows the students to pursue areas of personal interest and to meet special requirements for university entrance (International Baccalaureate North America, 2001). The core subject,

---

[2] Art is offered in over 60 countries as an option within the IB diploma.

theory of knowledge, is one that informs all other subjects within the program and plays a vital role in developing critical perspectives required throughout the entire diploma.

The Visual Arts Program

Visual Arts is one of three options available within the arts subject grouping of the diploma. The others are Music and Theater Arts. Central to this program is the requirement for students to develop a critical perspective of visual arts within a variety of cultures and to pursue an independent pathway of learning through research and artistic practice. Each of the higher level and standard-level programs require students to complete two components: (a) studio work and (b) a research workbook. At the higher level, the studio component comprises a 70% of the total grade with 10% of that total grade being allocated to the determination of overall growth. The research workbook is allocated the remaining 30% of the total grade with 10% of that proportion allocated to a determination of the degree of integration between the research workbook and the studio work. The same weighting is applied to the Standard Level A program. The Standard Level B program reverses the proportions with 70% weighting allocated to the research workbook and 30% to studio exploration.

A distinctive feature of the entire IB program is the expectation that students take responsibility for defining their own learning pathways. Independence of research is a central expectation for both research and studio components. Imagination is integral to the studio components of both the HL and Standard Level A programs. Little is specified in terms of subject content, so that maximum flexibility is available to students to explore the visual arts in the context of various world regions and across different genres of art, which include a nonhierarchical examination of fine arts, popular arts, tribal arts, and design arts. The program takes pains to avoid the imposition of Western cultural hegemony on students who may be studying the subject in any of 60 or more countries. Two of the fundamental requirements are that students demonstrate knowledge of more than one cultural context, and that their studio work and research workbooks be closely related in terms of the investigations undertaken.

The role of the teacher in this context is to provide impetus for students, teach them how to conduct personal research, undertake analysis of context, engage in critical writing; provide resources, and work as a learning associate with the student as they progress through the program. The relationship of assessment strategies with the curriculum is one that is unique and serves as a useful model for comparison with existing practices in the United States.

Assessment in the IB Program

The learning pathway of students is, to large extent, defined by the assessment criteria used to evaluate both the research workbook and studio components. In this way the relationship between assessment and curriculum is intimate, yet the curriculum does not specify the content of study in advance. The content of programs is individual and negotiated between teacher and individual students. This is not to say instruction does not occur. Programs take shape in the context of student interest and instruction defined by the scope of the teachers' expertise and judgment about what is appropriate to the interest and abilities of students. Various imaginative approaches to instruction are taken in different schools. For example, Atlantic United World College in Cardiff, Wales, has used instructional salary flexibly to employ a permanent art teacher and temporary artists in residence on a term by term basis to most effectively service the specialized interests of students.

The International Baccalaureate Organization Visual Arts syllabus does not have units or modules from which the teacher constructs a course of study, but instead it provides a framework which allows teachers to choose a content and activities appropriate to their own and their students' interests and experience. When constructing the course of study the teacher is expected to bear in mind the visual arts assessment criteria and the specific requirements for the assessment tasks explained in this guide. (International Baccalaureate Organization, 2000, p. 7)

Choice of media and techniques are also negotiated.

Work in the studio may combine several techniques and any medium may be used. Artistic understanding and expression may be taught through various techniques from painting to puppetry, calligraphy to computer graphics, and sculpture to conceptual art. Students may demonstrate mastery in various ways, provided their course of study includes an introduction to arts concepts and techniques.

... Priority should not necessarily be given to drawing and painting. Design, for example, maybe as worthwhile an experience as observational drawing. A student may achieve a high degree of sensitivity and skill in, for example, photography, photography, ceramics, or the use of electronic media, without being able to draw or paint well. (International Baccalaureate Organization, 2000, p. 9)

The IB program is regularly reviewed by a committee constituted by the Curriculum Office in Cardiff. The most recent curriculum review of the visual arts conducted in 1997 to 1998, and chaired by this writer, redefined both the assessment criteria and the manner in which judgments are made about student learning to reflect a postmodern construction of the discipline and to remove Western cultural bias from the assessment criteria. In the previous assessment plan, weighted criteria were employed to assess studio work. *Imaginative and Creative Thinking and Expression* was weighted at 35%, *Persistence in Research* at 20%; *Technical Skill* at 15%, *Understanding the Characteristics and Function of the Chosen Media* at 10%, *Understanding the Fundamentals of Design* at 10%, and *Ability to Evaluate Own Growth and Development* at 10%. An analytical scoring system was used requiring separate marks to be assigned by examiners against each criterion and the previously cited weightings were then applied to arrive at the final studio grade. Such a process was viewed by the review committee to be inappropriate because it applied an inflexible modernistic construction of art to the assessment of culturally varied student work and promoted homogeneity of outcomes based on Western fine art traditions. Application of a single conception of excellence was contrary to the expressed philosophy of the IB program so the analytical scoring system was replaced by a holistic assessment of student work. In this model, criteria are used for reference, but examiners are free to pay attention to the work in the way that is most appropriate to its genre.

The specifics of these changes are discussed in the following section.

Assessment of the Studio Component

Students at the Higher Level and Standard Level A are required to exhibit a portfolio of their work containing both finished artworks and working pieces demonstrating the process of their visual research. An external examiner visits the school to interview each candidate for 30 to 35 minutes about their work. The examiner allocates a single holistic grade after the interview and following consideration of the work in relation to the following five criteria:

- *Imaginative Expression.* At the highest level of achievement, the candidate's explorations are creative and imaginative. Ideas and forms are consistently and intelligently presented in an adventurous manner, resulting in surprising and unusual images, which challenge existing conventions. Unusual combinations of forms, techniques, and media and/or combinations of form and content are frequently evident.

- *Purposeful Exploration.* At the highest level of achievement, there is evidence that the candidate's explorations of ideas are clearly and strongly integrated with his or her life and cultural context. The candidate includes both analysis and synthesis in the investigations, resulting in a powerful and significant body of work.
- *Meaning and Function.* At the highest level of achievement, the studio work exhibits a synthesis of conceptual content, formal knowledge, and technical skill. It has strong personal, sociocultural, or aesthetic meaning. The relationship between form, function, and meaning is very clear and appropriate.
- *Formal Qualities.* At the highest level of achievement, the studio work consistently shows strong evidence of a thoughtful and inventive use of elements and principles of design. This has resulted in the production of strongly unified works. A comprehensive ability to solve formal and technical problems is clearly evident as demonstrated by rigorous investigation of aspects of form in the body of work.
- *Technical and Media Skills.* At the highest level of achievement, the studio work shows an outstanding technical confidence and demonstrates a highly appropriate use of media in relation to the intended expressive purposes of the work (International Baccalaureate Organization, 2000).

Assessment of the Research Workbook Component

At the Higher Level and Standard Level A, this component is assessed by the teacher in relation to the following four equally weighted criteria using a six-level rubric for each.

- Independent research
- Critical research
- Contextual research
- Visual research

Moderation of Grades

What is moderation? It is a judgment process undertaken by teachers within the community of peers to ensure that the equivalent work done by students in different classrooms and different schools is rated equally. The grades issued by both external examiners and teachers are not the final grade. Moderation is a system of multiple judgments made by different examiners about the students' work. The intention of moderation is to reduce variations of interpretation among different examiners and serves to promote a climate of debate and discussion about the quality of student work. This debate is essential in assessment context where students are required to push the limits of their own understanding, to take risks, exercise imagination, and interpret the visual world critically. The best students frequently produce work that will perplex examiners, and this is the way it should be if art is properly taught in a postmodern context. A second, and sometimes third look, at student work is often necessary to determine its qualities and to serve students fairly.

This process is particularly important to the international Baccalaureate program given the wide geographic distribution of students who participate in the program. Different examiners are employed to visit schools in over 60 countries in which art is taught as part of the IB Diploma. Subsequent to the examiner visits to schools, photographic and photocopy samples of candidates' work is sent to a central location in Cardiff, Wales, where a team of experienced and trained moderators, under the direction of a chief examiner, compare the visiting examiners' and teachers' judgments against agreed benchmarks of performance. Benchmarks of the best work are drawn from the international student community and posted year by year on the IB virtual gallery accrossable via the internet. These works are available for access by teachers, students, and examiners. Benchmarks illustrating the range of achievement at specific levels from highest to lowest are sampled from student work and made available to examiners only.

The benefit of this process, in addition to ensuring more reliable judgments for students, is that examiners and teachers receive feedback about their judgments, thus developing a community of agreement about standards. The IB is not the only program to employ moderation procedures. Moderation is used on national scale in the United Kingdom (Steers, 1988), the Netherlands (Schönau, 1996), Australia (Boughton, 1994), and by the AP program in the United States (Askin, 1985).

Benchmarking

Central to the moderation process is the practice of benchmarking. In simple terms, benchmarks are samples of student work selected by moderators to exemplify specific levels of achievement. The work samples clearly indicate the limits of performance within each level. If, for example, five levels of performance are specified by performance descriptors, five collections of studio work are selected to define the limits of each level. Written performance descriptors alone tend to be limited in their ability to represent the qualities of visual art. Therefore the benchmarks take the form of actual examples of student work.

Benchmarking is an idea that has been much practiced in U.S. businesses (Codling, 1998) and is now finding favor in higher education (Alsete, 1996; Barak & Kniker, 2002; Tucker, 1996). However, in the United Kingdom and Europe, benchmarking has been practiced for many years in art assessments as well as in other fields. There are many approaches to the selection of benchmark work (Boughton, 1997). It is possible to select benchmarks each year from the cohort of candidates who are to be assessed. It is also possible to choose work from past years to represent benchmark standards. A combination of both past and present work may also be chosen. Irrespective of these choices, the idea is to choose multiple samples of work that represent the lower bound, the center, and the upper levels specified in the system. The visual arts are dynamic and unpredictable, thus, the intention is *not* to choose examples that must be matched by student candidates' work. Rather it is to choose samples of work that represent qualities rather than specific models of performance. In other words, an excellent painting of a scene depicting poverty in Indonesia is not intended to provide an image for students to copy in order to receive high grades. The painting is intended to exemplify an imaginative representation of a political statement, superior understanding of media, expressive use of form that is supportive of the content of the work. Students who attempt to make copies of benchmarks are penalized in their assessment.

The IB program provides benchmark of student work to examiners, selected from previous students' work. Teachers and students are provided with examples of high-level work chosen from previous years' examinations on the IB Web site (http://online.ibo.org/gallery/).

WHAT CAN BE LEARNED ABOUT ASSESSMENT FROM THE IB PROGRAM?

The foregoing description of the IB program provides a useful reference for analysis of trends in the assessment of student work in the visual arts. Research pertaining to art education assessment is scant, with far greater attention paid to the more attractive issues of curriculum content. As a result, assessment practice of student work in visual arts often draws important ideas from practice rather than from research. The IB program provides a unique model that incorporates best practice based on literature.

Important Defining Characteristics of the Portfolio

Although much has been written about the portfolio, it is an instrument that is frequently misused or misunderstood. The commonly understood characteristic of a portfolio is that it is *a collection of work accumulated over time.* There are, however, some other common features of traditional portfolios that, if overlooked, reduce the potency of the portfolio as an assessment tool. The first of these is that the content of the portfolio process is *embedded* in the ongoing program of instruction but *open ended* in the sense that students are encouraged to develop classroom experiences into independent explorations of ideas (Stecher & Herman, 1997).

This central intention here is that portfolio entries should be derived from regular instructional events and are not be the result of "on-demand" tasks. The student should be free to interpret the ideas encountered both inside and outside class and to develop independence in their exploration of art ideas. This characteristic, if present, enables students to take risks and move beyond classroom exercises.

Taking responsibility for learning and developing the capacity to work independently are important indicators of good art learning, and this is a central characteristic of the IB program. Not only does the portfolio serve as an assessment tool, it also plays a vital role in the meaningful elaboration of curriculum intentions. In short, the portfolio becomes integrated with curriculum in very important ways and is not simply a repository for all class assignments set throughout the year.

Burton's (1998) study found that 52% of all visual arts teachers surveyed in the United States assessed their students at the completion of each studio project or written assignment. The portfolio that contains only this collection of assigned work and lacks open-ended content is one where the teacher defines both the content and the outcome of each project. Such practice will ultimately proscribe the form and content of the portfolio. At the end of the term, semester, or year, students in the classes of these teachers will typically present portfolios that look very much the same as one another with products that meet the common project criteria demanded by the teacher. These kinds of portfolios do not reflect the student's capacity to work independently, nor do they reveal the degree to which students are willing to take risks in order to extrapolate from, and interpret, the ideas presented in class. By definition, the only thing these portfolios can do is showcase the teacher's capacity to invent tasks for student response and to direct their outcomes.

A second feature of good portfolios identified in the literature is that they contain *student-selected entries* (Castiglione, 1996; Stecher & Herman 1997). Although the idea of educational portfolios are prominent in the professional artworld the educational application of portfolios is different (Castiglione, 1996). The artist portfolio is usually a display of a person's public professional persona and does not usually contain works indicative of process, doubts, or failed explorations. The purpose of education portfolios is to promote students' knowledge of their own progress and to support their ability to demonstrate independence in researching and evolving projects of their own. Thus, works in progress, sketches, and reworked pieces are important as portfolio entries because they provide insight into student growth and the pattern of decisions students have made in relation to their evolving work.

Without student choice, there is no indication of the student's capacity to make informed decisions about his or her own ideas and progress. Often it is possible to discover as much about a student by what they choose to include as it is from the quality of the work itself. Clearly, the degree to which this is possible is determined to some extent by the age and sophistication of the students involved. Less is expected of younger students, whereas more fully resolved work can be anticipated from senior students. Nevertheless, some choice is possible at all levels of schooling. The IB assessment criteria, Purposeful Exploration (Studio), and Independence of Research (Research Workbook) have evolved from the understanding that portfolios effectively reveal these qualities in ways that other assessment instruments cannot.

A third feature of good portfolios is the importance of *student critical self-reflection*, which may appear in journals or portfolios in written, or taped form (Wolfe, 1988). In addition to the IB program teacher/examiner interviews have also been used in other programs, such Arts PROPEL (Blaikie, 1994). Ross, Radnor, Mitchell; and Bierton (1993) found that, during reflective discussions with students, teachers tend not to listen carefully to students; that they seem to drive their own agendas through teacher talk; that students understand more about their own feeling states and sensibilities than adults comprehend; and that dialog, properly conducted, can reveal valuable insights into the process of art making, particularly students' understanding of the quality of the work, the manner of its production, the reasons for choices, influences on the work, difficulties encountered, new ideas to explore, and so on. Here is an example from an IB student's candidate statement submitted as part of the exhibition of studio work:

> I found that seeing various artist's works has influenced me also. An example of this is Leon Kossoff's work: after seeing it, I immediately felt like painting in thick, bold brushstrokes. (International Baccalaureate student, May 1996)

This is another example from an IB student:

> Drawing human figures is one of my strengths. I used to copy human figures from comics. But then I found out that I needed to learn how to draw real human figures, so I started studying realistic human drawings and I learned a lot from these master drawings, especially Michelangelo, who is one of my favorite artists and has been my greatest inspiration. (International Baccalaureate student, May 2001)

Choosing Criteria for Assessment

The virtue of thoughtful and process focused portfolios resides in its capacity to collect assessment information over time. As was discussed earlier, not all portfolios are created equal. Without carefully considered judgment, the portfolio remains simply a repository of data. For portfolios to be effective, the relationship of assessment criteria to program intentions must be carefully articulated. In the case of the IB, assessment criteria are integral to the program, effectively defining expected outcomes of learning, and drawing upon the strengths of the portfolio strategy to reveal student learning. Choice of criteria can bear a strong relationship to the issue of validity in assessment. Examination of the literature indicates that there is a close relationship between IB criteria and those used by visual arts teachers in other programs internationally.

MacGregor's (1992a) examination of assessment practices in Britain, Holland, Australia, and New Zealand, showed that the broad criteria used by teachers vary little from country to country. Most teachers employ some variation of three categories of criteria: (a) relative ability to develop and interpret a theme, (b) level of technical expertise, and (c) relative ability to achieve sensitive personal expression through the use of a variety of techniques and processes. The particular strength of the portfolio strategy reflected in the IB program is the manner in which students' pursuit of ideas and themes can be tracked through both research workbook and studio work.

Making Judgments: Holistic Versus Analytic

One of the most difficult stages of the assessment process is making value judgments about student learning and student products. Considerable debate exists in the field about who should make these judgments and how. The IB program's reliance on external examiners and the use of moderation have succeeded in attracting widespread confidence in the reliability of judgments, and there is much to be said in support of the value of moderated assessments which are used throughout Europe, the United Kingdom, and Australasia (Boughton, 1996b; Blaikie, 1994; Wilson, 1996). Castiglione (1996) argues in support of the notion that faculty judgments in art instruction "are necessarily expected to involve commonly accepted standards, to transfer across individuals, and to generalize across judges—in short, to be independent of any criteria unique to the assessor."

In a comparison of the AP, IB, and Arts PROPEL projects, this is exactly what Blaikie (1994) found. All three programs depended on skilled judges with knowledge of the visual arts, using a set of established criteria to arrive at judgments of student work.

Schönau (1996) reported work done by the Dutch Institute for Educational Measurement (CITO) to examine the Dutch Central Practical Examination (CPE) in terms of the potential for achievement of common standards against national prescriptive criteria. In the first year of the exam, student work (1981) was judged by the student's teacher and a panel of five judges. In 1982 the jury was reduced to three, and from 1983 the work was judged by the students' own teacher and a specialist colleague from another school. The analysis of scores showed an acceptable level of judge difference between the scores allocated irrespective of the number of outside judges. However, Schönau also found that global judgments tended to produce higher judge agreement than analytical judgments using criterion analysis.

In 2001, the IB program moved from analytical criterion assessment of studio work to holistic judgments. The studio assessment prior to 2001 comprised six weighted criteria valuing imagination at more than twice the weighting given to technical skill. The problem confronted by curriculum developers was that the system of weighted criteria predetermined a western modernist construction of art that was universally applied across all cultures. Such a unilateral application of criteria was not responsive to cultural context or artistic genre. The move to holistic assessment enabled a far more reflective assessment strategy that took into account the complexity and variation of artistic expression without loss of reliability in the judgment process.[3] Different artwork demands different attention; thus, the use of a single holistic judgment enables judges to pay attention to the specific qualities of individual works. Application of standardized weighted criteria to all genres of work does not permit such flexibility.

What Are the Benefits of the Portfolio?

The greatest single benefit of the traditional portfolio is the flexibility it provides to the program for students to explore, take risks, reflect on their progress, and to exercise fully the skills required to perform in the complex ways demanded by the visual arts. A concomitant benefit is the insight it provides teachers and examiners to understand the students' development over time (Grace & Shores et al., 1994; Stecher & Herman, 1997). If students have the freedom to make choices about the content they include in their portfolios, and are also encouraged to explore ideas independently, outside the limitations of classroom exercises, then a clear picture of their intellectual footsteps is represented in the contents. I have seen this illustrated vividly in the portfolio exhibitions offered by IB students at their final examinations following 2 years of independent studio exploration.

A second benefit offered by the portfolio is the capacity that it can take multiple forms, each with the capacity to support distinctive ways of working (Grace & Shores et al., 1994). For

---

[3] An extensive research project was undertaken in 1998 to 1999 by this author in partnership with Kerry Freedman and the International Baccalaureate examinations office to compare the differences in reliability between analytical and holistic studio assessment methods. No statistical difference was found between the two methods using experienced examiners from different world regions.

instance, the *working portfolio* is an archive of works in progress that provides opportunity for teachers and students to reflect together on work done in the past and to revisit ideas and avenues that may have been forgotten or overlooked. The creation of an *exhibition portfolio*, on the other hand, requires students to select best work for exhibition or examination. In the context of an IB examination, students present their best work as an exhibition and provide the remainder to serve as *backup records* for reference, or to provide a point of discussion with the examiner or teacher.

A third benefit offered by portfolios is the motivation it provides to the student. The capacity to review work and see improvement can be a great stimulus for student learning. The reflective component of portfolios, if well used, can promote greater involvement by students with their work and also helps the teacher understand what is going on with student learning. Even math teachers have noted the benefits of portfolios. One algebra teacher reported that she came to use more varied kinds of instruction (e.g., more problem solving and more long-term situational problems) because she used portfolios in her algebra class so that her students ended up having a variety of items to choose from in creating their portfolio. This algebra teacher also noted that portfolios gave insight into students' maturity, self-esteem, writing ability, and their ability to evaluate their own and other students' work (Knight, 1992, cited in Lester, Lamdin, & Preston, 1997). Two other researchers, Lamdin and Walker (1994), found that students often became much more reflective about their own mathematical performance when they assumed responsibility for preparing a portfolio of their work.

DIGITAL PORTFOLIOS AND THE FUTURE

Given the frequent benefits of portfolio assessment evident in the IB program, it is important to raise the question of the potential of digital portfolio assessment. Faculty and students at Northern Illinois University have engaged for some years in examining this question at elementary, middle school, high school, college, and in-service levels. Stanley Madeja, working for the past 2 years with Charles Dorn, Robert Sabol, and others, has investigated the development of authentic assessment tools in the visual arts as part of a research grant funded by the National Endowment for the Arts (Dorn, Madeja, & Sabol, 2001).

This project involved the development of authentic assessment strategies with groups of art teachers in Florida, Indiana, and Illinois. Ten secondary teachers and one elementary teacher became interested in the application of digital portfolios for their own classrooms (Fitzsimmons, 2003). Two of these teachers, NIU graduate students, have played leadership roles in spearheading the trial of digital portfolios in state schools.

In their work with teachers using digital portfolios, NIU researchers found many benefits that are identified in the literature by people who have examined the same questions in other settings.

Efficiency: The most frequently mentioned benefits of electronic portfolios is the efficient handling and retrieving of information and images related to student work. First, electronic portfolios, like traditional portfolios, show a clear picture of growth over time (Wiedemer, 1998). But the work in traditional portfolios is far more difficult to organize in any desired sequence and takes far longer for the teacher to thumb through in order to analyze the collection. Pieces are more likely to get lost or distributed to other geographic locations. Electronic portfolios, on the other hand, offer the opportunity for work to be viewed in thumbnails all at once, and/or to be quickly organized into chronological or thematic order. In short, the benefit here is efficiency and safety of organization and data storage.

Second, parent–teacher conferences are easy with small, convenient, and accessible documentation (Guhlin, 1999). NIU graduate students/teachers reported that conversation with parents become much easier when electronic files or when hard-copy printouts of student portfolios are on the table. Reference is quick, and teachers have found that it is very easy to explain why a student is not getting good grades by comparing their work to benchmark exemplars produced by other students. This can also be done with traditional portfolios, but electronic versions are simply easier to handle. Again the payoff is efficiency.

Third, accessibility to records is enhanced. Fornander (1999) reported the benefits of electronic portfolios particularly accessibility, portability, utility for examination, and the capacity to widely distribute files. Information can be shared easily among colleagues, making dialog about images possible in a more efficient way.

Fourth, storage is easier. Work does not have to be kept in schools. Completed projects can be taken over immediately and not left to wait for grading. This is a particular benefit for three-dimensional work (Tuttle, 1997). In addition, far greater volumes of work can be stored on disk than could possibly be stored in the art room (Oros, Morgenegg, & Finger, 1998).

Motivation

Computers are effective motivational tools. Teachers and researchers alike reported on the enthusiasm demonstrated by students when working in electronic environments. Kerper (2000), an NIU researcher/observer in an electronic portfolio project classroom, reported high levels of enthusiasm demonstrated by elementary students even when working with inadequate technology. Electronic portfolios also seem to encourage ownership, pride, and an increased level of self-esteem, a factor noted by other researchers (Davis, 1999).

Curriculum Benefits

Because the craft of constructing an electronic portfolio becomes so much a part of the curriculum, NIU researchers have noted some additional curriculum effects. One teacher said that the portfolio process put more pressure on her to clarify her explanations and assessment standards. In short, she found it enforced a kind of discipline that was not necessary under traditional art teaching conditions (Fitzsimmons, 2003). Digital portfolios have the potential to stimulate students to further develop their art pieces made with traditional media. Once students have scanned their work, the possibility exists to enhance it, or even redevelop it in digital form.

Communication Benefits

Because the original artwork goes home after it is done, rather than remaining at school, parents are more aware of what is happening in school. Students are more likely to remember the concepts they have learned and not forget with the passage of time (Kerper, 2000).

Another communication benefit of digital portfolios is that students' work is able to travel with them throughout their career (Fornander, 1999). This has particular application at the college and university level.

Ancillary Benefit

Both students and teachers in schools have noted that electronic portfolios teach computing skills as ancillary benefit. Because the acquisition of computer skills are regarded as a good thing, the collateral learning in the area of digital technology that takes place is valued.

Assessment Gains

Having listed the Previous benefits, it would be easy to forget the major question: Can digital portfolios actually assist teachers to make better judgments about the quality of student learning? The direct assessment benefits identified both in the literature and by our Illinois teachers were the following:

Student Self-Assessment

Learners are able to see the big picture of their own progress more easily. Because of the ready access to their own record of progress, students seem to become more aware of both the quantity and the quality of their own work, particularly at the senior secondary level.

Teachers' Oversight of Curriculum

Program accountability becomes more evident. Teachers are able to keep a more comprehensive record of student work and overall progress of student groups. Comparison with program goals is easier, making diagnostic assessment easier as well.

Benchmarking

Electronic portfolios are useful for benchmarking (Guhlin, 1999; Niguidula, 1998) and are also very useful for the development of exit standards (Fornander, 1999). Traditional portfolios also serve this function, but the digital form has far greater utility.

CONCLUSION

It is clear that the current assessment climate in United States is not a healthy one for the arts. I have argued that the resilience of standardized tests and reliance on multiple-choice formats for determining the products of art instruction at the state level serve only to perpetuate an atomistic approach to the gathering of disconnected shards of information, which serves a limited purpose. Such testing has more to do with political posturing than it does with serving the interests of students.

In the classroom, teachers who are pressured to demonstrate the outcomes of their programs are not well prepared, nor well served, by the model of state assessment practices. Attempts to demonstrate that students have met national or state goals result in the gathering of disconnected pieces of information that are easy to collect but are not necessarily reflective of holistic engagement in art making and substantive understanding of the complexity of the arts.

The models of practice employed by the IB program and by other European and Australasian national assessment systems provide some insights into more productive ways to judge student learning. These approaches preserve the essential qualities of artistic performance at high levels and take into account the dynamic nature of the discipline of the visual arts across different cultural contexts. The fundamental instrument used to facilitate these assessment strategies is the portfolio. The portfolio on its own, however, is not the complete solution. There are important conditions that proscribe appropriate use of the portfolio that must be observed in order to achieve the good assessment outcomes.

Concomitant with the portfolio as an instrument are other essential elements of assessment that include benchmarking, moderation processes, and the institutionalizing of debate about the qualities of student art making among the community of peers involved in the education process. Admittedly, these are expensive practices to implement on the state level. However, there is no reason why, given the will, adaptations cannot be developed at the local level to achieve improvement in the benefits of assessment for both students and teachers. Some instances of attempts to do this have already been noted (Dorn, 2002).

The advance of technology has provided yet another possibility for the future. The potential of digital portfolios provides an expanded view of the ways in which assessment information may be gathered and managed. Ultimately the decision to deal with the issue of assessment is one that must be taken in the context of curriculum improvement. The unique quality of the IB program lies, not so much in the way in which the portfolio is used for assessment but in the intimate relationship between assessment practices and the curriculum itself.

If the United States wants to develop a more effective and appropriate approach to assessment of the visual arts in education, such as that found in the IB and European settings, there is a long way to go. However, current assessment practices draw on the unfortunate testing traditions of the past in United States that do not serve the current condition well in the arts. A perspective directed outwards rather than inwards may well serve us better to develop a more productive way forward.

REFERENCES

2002–2003 State Arts Education policy database: Arts Education Partnership. Council of Chief State School Officers, One Massachusetts Ave., NM, Suite 700, Washington, DC 2001-1431. www.aep-arts.org/policysearch

Alsete, J. (1996). *Benchmarking in higher education: Adapting best practices to improve quality.* Washington, DC: The George Washington University.

Anderson, T. (1995). Toward a cross-cultural approach to art criticism. *Studies in Art Education, 36*(4), 198–209.

Armstrong, C. (1996). A choice: Comfortable ambiguity or clearly translated standards. *Studies in Art Education, 37*(4), 253–256.

Askin, W. (1985). *Evaluating the Advanced Placement Portfolio in Studio Art.* Princeton, NJ: Advanced Placement and the College Board.

Barak, R., & Kniker, C. (2002). Using benchmarking to inform practice in higher education. Benchmarking by State Higher Education Boards: New Directions for Higher Education. *18* (Summer).

Blaikie, F. (1994). Values inherent in qualitative assessment of secondary studio art in North America: Advanced Placement, Arts PROPEL, and International Baccalaureate. *Studies in Art Education, 35*(4), 237–248.

Blandy, D., & Hoffman, E. (1993). Toward an art education of place. *Studies in Art Education, 35*(1), 22–33.

Boughton, D. (1994). *Evaluation and assessment of visual arts education.* Geelong: Deakin University Press.

Boughton, D. (1995). Six myths of National Arts Curriculum reform. *Journal of Art and Design Education, 14*(2), 139–152.

Boughton, D. (1996a). Assessing learning effects in the visual arts: What criteria should be used? *Art and fact: Learning effects of arts education.* Utrecht: Netherlands Institute for Arts Education.

Boughton, D. (1996b). Evaluating and assessing art education: Issues and prospects. In D. Boughton, E. W. Eisner, & J. Ligtvoet (Eds.), *Evaluating and assessing the visual arts in education: International perspectives* (pp. 293–309). New York: Teachers College Press.

Boughton, D. (1997) Reconsidering issues of assessment and achievement standards in art education. *Studies in Art Education, 38*(4), 199–213.

Boughton, D., Freedman, K., Hausman, J., Hicks, L., Madeja, S., Metcalfe, S., Rayala, M., Smith-Shank, D., Stankiewicz, M., Stuhr, P., Tavin, K., & Vallance, E. (2002). Art education and visual culture. *Advisory NAEA.* Reston, VA: National Art Education Association.

Burton, D. (1998). *A survey of assessment and evaluation among U.S. K-12 teachers of art.* Meeting of the NAEA Task Force on Demographic Research. NAEA convention, Chicago, April 2.

Castiglione, L. (1996). Portfolio assessment in art and education. *Education Policy Review, 97*(2), 2–9.

Chalmers, F. G. (1985). Art as a social study: Theory into practice. *Bulletin of the Caucus on Social Theory and Art Education, 5,* 40–50.

Cizek, G. (1993). Alternative assessments: Yes, but why? *Educational Horizon.* (Fall), 36–40.

Clark, G., & Zimmerman, E. (1978). A walk in the right direction: A model for visual arts education. *Studies in Art Education, 2*(19), 34–49.

Codling, S. (1998). *Benchmarking.* Brookfield, Vermont: Gower.

Consortium of National Arts Education Associations. (1994). *National Standards for Arts Education: What every young American should know and be able to do in arts education.* Reston, VA: Music Educators National Conference.

Davis, D. (1993). Art education in the 1990's: Meeting the challenges of accountability. *Studies in Art Education, 34*(2), 82–90.

Davis, H. (1999). *Portfolios, a guide for students and teachers* (sound recording series). Alexandria, VA: Association for Supervision and Curriculum Development.

Dorn, C. (2002). The teacher as stakeholder in student art assessment and program evaluation. *Art Education, 55*(4), 40–45.

Dorn, C., Madeja, S., & Sabol, R. (2001). *Evaluating expressive learning: Final report.* A project supported by the National Endowment for the Arts.

Duncum, P. (1996). From Seurat to snapshots: What the visual arts could contribute to education. *Australian Art Education, 19*(2), 36–45.

Efland, A., Freedman, K., & Stuhr, P. (1995). *Postmodern art education: An approach to curriculum.* Reston, VA: National Art Education Association.

Eisner, E. (2001). Should we create new aims for art education? *Art Education 54*(5), 6–10.

Feldman, E. B. (1992). Formalism and its discontents. *Studies in Art Education, 33*(2), 122–126.

Fitzsimmons, D. (2003). Visual arts teachers' perceptions on incorporation of electronic portfolios. Unpublished doctoral dissertation. DeKalb, IL: Northern Illinois University.

Fornander, M. (1999) *Digital portfolios. A district, school, and intermediate teachers' presentation on how to get started.* (Report). Boise State University, Idaho.

Freedman, K. (1994a). Interpreting gender and visual culture in art classrooms. *Studies in Art Education. 35*(3), 157–170.

Freedman, K. (1994b). Guest editorial: About this issue: A social reconstruction of art education. *Studies in Art Education, 35*(3), 131–134.

Freedman, K., & Relan, A. (1992). Computer graphics, artistic production, and social processes. *Studies in Art Education, 33*(2), 98–109.

Garber, E. (1995). A study in the borderlands. *Studies in Art Education, 36*(4), 218–232.

Gardner, H. (1989). Zero-based arts education: An introduction to Arts PROPEL. *Studies in Art Education, 30*(2), 71–83.

Gardner, H. (1996). The assessment of student learning in the arts. In D. Boughton, E. W. Eisner, & J. Ligtvoet (Eds.), *Evaluating and assessing the visual arts in education: International perspectives* (pp. 131–155). New York: Teachers College Press.

Gitomer, D., Grosh, S., & Price, K. (1992). Portfolio culture in arts education. *Art Education, 45*(1), 7–15.

Grace, C., & Shores, E. et al. (1994). *The portfolio and its use: Developmentally appropriate assessment of young children* (3rd ed.), Little Rock, AR: Southern Early Childhood Association.

Guhlin, M. (1999). *Electronic Portfolios.* Available at http://www.edsupport.cc/mguhlin/writings/portfolios.html

Illinois State Board of Education. (1996). *Illinois fine arts assessment series.* Springfield, IL.

International Baccalaureate North America. (2001). *University guide to the IB diploma program.* New York: International Baccalaureate North America.

International Baccalaureate Organization. (2000). *Diploma program visual arts guide: For first examination 2002.* Geneva, Switzerland: The International Baccalaureate Organization.

International Baccalaureate Organization. (2003a). *A basis for practice: The Diploma program.* http://www.ibo.org/ibo/index.cfm? contentid=000226E2-A4D7-1DE4-E1280C12645FD37&method=display&language=EN

International Baccalaureate Organization. (2003b). *A continuum of international education.* http://www.ibo.org/ibo/index.cfm? contentid=0000BAF7-A74F-1DE4-8E1280C12645FD37&method=display&language=EN

Kerper, A. (2000). *Digital portfolios implemented in the elementary program.* Unpublished paper. Northern Illinois University: Art Education Division.

Knight, P. (1992). How I use portfolios in mathematics. *Educational Leadership, 49*(8), 71–72.

Lamdin, D., & Walker, V. (1994). Planning for classroom portfolio assessment. *Arithmetic Teacher, 41*, 318–324.

Lester, F., Lamdin, D., & Preston, R. (1997). A new vision of the nature and purposes of assessment in the mathematics classroom. In Gary D. Phye (Ed.), *Handbook of classroom assessment* (pp. 287–319). London: Academic Press Limited.

MacGregor, R. N. (1990). Reflections on art assessment practices. *Journal of Art and Design Education.*

MacGregor, R. N. (1991). *Art assessment in South Australia, Victoria, and New Zealand: Comparisons and contrasts.* Unpublished paper submitted to the Ministry for Education, British Columbia. University of British Columbia: Vancouver.

MacGregor, R. N. (1992a). A short guide to alternative assessment practices. *Art Education, 45*(6), 34–38.

MacGregor, R. N. (September, 1992b). Post-modernism, art educators, and art education. *ERIC Digest ED348238.* Bloomington, IN: ERIC Clearinghouse.

NAEP 1997 arts report card: Eighth grade findings from the National Assessmant of Educational Progress, U.S. Department of Education (1999). Office of Education Research and Improvement. NCES 1999–486.

Niguidula, D. (1998). A richer picture of student work. In D. Allen, (Ed), *Assessing student learning: From grading to understanding* (pp. 183–198). New York: Teachers College Press.

Oros, L., Morgenegg, J., Finger, A. (1998). *Creating Digital Portfolios. Media & Methods, 34,* 15 (Jan/Feb).

Ross, M., Radnor, H., Mitchell, S., & Bierton, C. (1993). *Assessing achievement in the arts.* Buckingham, UK: Open University Press.

Sandell, R. (1991). The liberating relevance of feminist pedagogy. *Studies in Art Education, 32*(3), 178–187.

Schönau, D. (1996). Nationwide assessment of studio work in the visual arts: Actual practice and research in the Netherlands. In D. Boughton, E. W. Eisner, & J. Ligtvoet (Eds.), *Evaluating and assessing the visual arts in education: international perspectives* (pp. 156–175). New York: Teachers College Press.

Smith, R. A. (1992). Building a sense of art in today's world. *Studies in Art Education, 33*(2), 71–85.

Stecher, B., & Herman, J. (1997). Using portfolios for large scale assessment. In Gary D. Phye (Ed.), *Handbook of classroom assessment* (pp. 491–516). London: Academic Press Limited.

Steers, J. (1988). Art and design in the national curriculum. *Journal of Art and Design Education, 7*(3), 303–323.

Stuhr, P. (1994). Multicultural Art Education and Social Reconstruction. *Studies in Art Education, 35*(3), 171–178.

Sullivan, G. (1993). Art-based art education: Learning that is meaningful, authentic, critical and pluralist. *Studies in Art Education, 35*(1), 5–21.

Tucker, S. (1996). *Benchmarking: a Guide for Educators.* Thousand Oaks, California: Corwin Press Inc.

Tuttle, H. (1997). *The multimedia report: Electronic portfolios tell a personal story.* http://www.infotoday.com/MMSchools/jan97mms/portfol.html

Wiedemer, T. (1998). Digital Portfolios: Capturing and demonstrating skills and levels of performance. *Phi Delta Kappan, 79*(8), pp. 586–589.

Wilson, B. (1996). Arts standards and fragmentation: A strategy for holistic assessment. *Arts Education Policy Review. 98,* pp. 2–9.

Wolfe, D. (1988). Opening up assessment. *Educational Leadership, 45*(1), 24–29.

Zimmerman, E. (1994). How should students' progress and achievements in art be assessed? A case for assessment that is responsive to diverse students' needs. *Visual Arts Research, 20*(1), 29–35.

27

The NAEP Arts Assessment: Pushing the Boundaries of Large-Scale Performance Assessment

Hilary Persky
Educational Testing Service

INTRODUCTION

In 1997, the national assessment of students' visual arts knowledge and skills provoked both excitement and trepidation among many arts educators and educational policymakers. These sentiments were expressed throughout the process of assessment development, administration, and scoring by members of the National Assessment of Educational Progress (NAEP) visual arts development committee, many of whom had been part of the creation of the arts voluntary national standards and the NAEP arts education framework. Excitement and pride at the prospect of a national arts assessment combined with valid concerns about how fairly a standardized assessment could elicit and measure art making. As stated in the *1997 Arts Education Framework* that served as a blueprint for the NAEP arts assessment, "many arts educators worry that an assessment of the arts will artificially quantify the aspects of the arts that seem unquantifiable—inspiration, imagination, and creativity" National Assessment Governing Board [NAGB], (1994). (Audiences also frequently expressed this concern when my colleagues and I spoke to various state arts assessment organizations about the national assessment initiative.)

In spite of these concerns, the 1997 NAEP arts assessment was highly productive. A determination on the part of its creators both to push and to respect the limits intrinsic to national large-scale assessment made for an arts assessment that meaningfully informed the general public about the state of arts education in the schools. Further, many state arts assessment initiatives, including those in Maine, California, New Jersey, New York, and Maryland, have drawn and continue to draw on the national arts assessment model for item development, administration, and scoring. All five states requested presentations and workshops about the NAEP arts assessment, and information about how NAEP arts items were created and utilized was very positively received. Visual arts tasks that combine responding to works of art with creating tasks have been adapted from the national assessment model for use New Jersey, Maryland, and New York, that the author is aware of.

More broadly, the 1997 visual arts assessment provides a solid model for capturing the individual, expressive nature of making meaning, in ways that simulate good classroom practice, *and* still yield comparable, meaningful results from students with a wide range of exposures to arts education. Still, some would argue that NAEP was only partially successful in meeting these challenges (Beatty, 1999; Eisner, 1997). In presenting several strategies that designers and advisors adopted for the NAEP arts, this chapter will reflect on how far the 1997 effort took the arts assessment field. The final section of this chapter argues that although success at a national level is intrinsically limited, NAEP can offer informative and useful models for new approaches to large-scale arts assessment.

BACKGROUND TO THE NAEP 1997 ARTS ASSESSMENT

Since 1969, the National Assessment of Educational Progress (NAEP), also known as "the Nation's Report Card," has been the only nationally representative and continuing assessment of what America's students know and can do in various subject areas, including reading, mathematics, science, the arts, writing, U.S. history, civics, and geography. Under the current structure, the Commissioner of Education Statistics, who heads the National Center for Education Statistics (NCES) in the U.S. Department of Education, is responsible by law for carrying out NAEP projects. The National Assessment Governing Board, appointed by the Secretary of Education, but independent of the department, governs the program. NAEP does not provide scores for individual students or schools. Instead, the test offers results regarding subject-matter achievement, instructional experiences, and school environment for selected national populations of students (e.g., fourth-graders) and subgroups of those populations (e.g., female students, Hispanic students).

The NAEP 1997 arts assessment was the result of a multi-year process, described briefly in this volume (Myford & Sims-Gunzenhauser, 2002). Myford and Sims-Gunzenhauser discuss the collaboration among arts educators, artists, policymakers, and members of the public in the creation of the voluntary *National Standards for Arts Education* and The *1997 NAEP Arts Education Assessment Framework*. This collaboration resulted in two documents that share a set of ideas, although the standards describe what ought to be taught in the arts, and the framework describes what and how to assess. Both documents assume that an arts education is not just for the talented or the privileged, but is instead an integral part of education. As stated in the framework:

> Throughout their lives, [children] will draw from artistic experience and knowledge as a means of understanding what happens both inside and outside their own skin, just as they use mathematical, scientific, historical, and other frameworks for understanding. The expectation is not that they will become talented artists. What is expected is that they will have experienced enough of the discipline, the challenge, the joy of creating in different art forms to intimately understand the human significance of dance, music, theatre, and the visual arts. (NAGB, 1994, p. 1)

The notion that an arts education is not meant primarily to create talented artists should not be taken to mean that arts knowledge and skills are simple and easily attainable. Like other disciplines, dance, music, theater, and visual arts can be extremely challenging, and any assessment of arts knowledge and skills ought to elicit high levels of performance, not just minimum competency. Further, the standards and framework express the following principle: If a sequential and rigorous arts education is a crucial part of the curriculum, and such an education must emphasize creating, performing, studying and analyzing works of art, then any arts assessment ought to include chances for students to analyze, critique, and formulate value judgments about works of art, as well as to create and perform works of art.

Given these ambitions for a rigorous arts assessment, the tension between the depth and continuity of what can happen in an arts classroom and what can be managed in a large-scale arts assessment is a central concern of the arts assessment framework. In a classroom setting, teachers can evaluate students' arts knowledge and skills on the basis of prolonged observation. Students can ask questions and discuss artworks, their ideas, and artistic choices with peers and teachers; explore and experiment with different strategies for creating; and work on their projects over time. This is not the case in a drop-in timed assessment, for which students have had no specific preparation and that must be completed within a short period on a single day.

The task for those who created the NAEP visual arts assessment was therefore to encourage students to reflect about works of art, communicate ideas and feelings about works of art, and to take imaginative risks to solve artistic problems. At the same time, the assessment needed to be practical to administer and to yield responses that could be compared and scored on a large scale. This last was especially difficult because the students who were assessed had many different arts backgrounds. Teaching approaches to the arts vary widely. Further, because the arts are often not part of standard school curricula, some students had no arts background, whereas others had quite substantial arts experience, gained either in or outside of school. (The challenges of making assessment tasks accessible to a very wide range of students and of locating student samples that can meaningfully perform on an arts assessment are challenges that are somewhat peculiar to NAEP, as NAEP is mandated to assess representative national samples of students.)

To ensure that assessment tasks were as valid and reliable as possible, a team of arts experts was assembled to work alongside measurement specialists at Educational Testing Service (ETS). (ETS currently holds the NAEP development, analysis, and reporting contract.) This committee was composed of arts classroom teachers, arts curriculum experts, artists, and arts policymakers, many of whom had worked on the voluntary standards and the NAEP arts framework creation. Committee members brought their expertise to creating an arts performance assessment that would be as "authentic" and as valid as possible. This meant that all assessment tasks were created, reviewed, discussed, and refined by arts education experts who sought to adhere as closely as possible to the visions of the arts standards and framework; the goal was to develop exercises and scoring criteria that would measure important arts knowledge and skills in grade-appropriate ways. This included selecting and approving sets of exemplar students' works to be used to train raters to score assessment results. Some of the challenges confronted by ETS staff and the committee and the pros and cons of the strategies adopted to meet those challenges are explored in the following section.

Issues and Strategies Used in Assessment Development and Administration

This section will explore how visual arts tasks were developed and organized to accommodate administration concerns while being responsive to the arts framework. NAEP item development must always take place with an eye toward what will actually happen in schools. The most valid assessment task will fail if it cannot be administered, either because the task materials and space requirements are too complex or because the task itself is too complex to be understood and completed by students within a limited time frame. NAEP is a voluntary national assessment and must compete with many state-level assessments and standard curricula for student's time. Securing school participation in NAEP is often dependent on getting in and out of schools rapidly and as efficiently as possible; NAEP administrations thus cannot consume too much of school time or place undue burdens on schools for space or complex movements of students from one space to another.

To address the problem of balancing assessment depth with the time and space that could reasonably be asked for from schools, NAEP created separate assessments for the four arts subjects. This meant that any individual student participating in the assessment was assessed in only one arts subject, that is, dance, music, theater, *or* visual arts. Assessing each student on an individual basis in each subject area would have been prohibitively expensive and would have created massive time burdens on schools. Individual students usually spent an *average* of 90 minutes engaged in tasks for one arts subject, allowing a relatively in-depth assessment of the students' abilities in that subject. Separate assessments for each arts area were a natural first step to gain assessment depth (although it did preclude another framework goal of exploring relationships among the arts areas).

The arts framework also sought assessment authenticity. In visual arts, for example, students were to be offered a range of media and engage in a range of art-making processes including design. Further, arts processes were to be understood as inseparable: "The NAEP framework and the National Standards have framed a vision of arts education that integrates the aesthetic, social cultural, and historical contexts of the arts with the knowledge and skills necessary to participate in the arts. Skills will not be considered as separable . . ." (NAGB, 1994, p. 3). "The assessment will consist largely of multiple, related, exercise organized around an activity" (NAGB, 1994, p. 4). And finally, "Exercises should include a mix and a balance of creating exercises and responding exercises that engage a wide variety of knowledge and skills in studio production, art criticism, art history, and aesthetics" (NAGB, 1994, p. 7).

As will become evident from the following discussion, combining these processes, knowledge, and skills to give students enough time to create and respond meaningfully posed school burden challenges both in terms of time and space. Typically, students taking the NAEP in any subject area respond to two "blocks" (sets) of questions to be completed within a set time period (usually 50 minutes). Students complete anywhere from 15 to 24 assessment exercises, a combination of enough multiple choice and open-ended items to allow NAEP scaling and analysis. To enable efficient administration while being responsive to the framework, ETS staff and visual arts committee members decided to combine responding items requiring written responses to artworks with two-dimensional creating tasks, and then developed entirely separate tasks for three-dimensional creating. Both kinds of tasks were embedded in "focused" blocks concerned with a particular problem, issue, or genre. The logic and success of this design for the NAEP visual arts are discussed in the following section.

Challenges Associated With Administering Two- and Three-Dimensional Visual Arts Tasks

In developing assessment items for visual arts, pretesting revealed that a single block designed to measure students' responding abilities alone took anywhere from 40 to 50 minutes to complete, given the time students needed for absorbing visual stimuli and answering thoughtful questions in writing. If students then had to be given time for creating activities, the time for assessing any one student could easily extend to well over 2 hours. Two hours of assessment time would be compounded by time for setup, materials distribution, the gathering of materials, and cleanup, thus increasing assessment time for a set of visual arts tasks to a half-day or more.

Administering three-dimensional creating tasks posed a set of additional and unique challenges. Although two-dimensional works could be collected and shipped for eventual scoring, three-dimensional artworks needed to be photographed. It would have been impossible, given the realities of time, equipment, staff, and thousands of fragile artworks, to carefully wrap each three-dimensional work to ship it for scoring. Hence, administrators were taught during administrator training how to photograph each student's three-dimensional work from several different angles for scoring. Although this was surprisingly successful, it was certainly limiting;

it is always preferable to be able to look at three-dimensional works from every angle. There was some discussion of having experts score on site. However, organizing experts to be on site at the right time, given a nationwide assessment in which it is better not to use teachers of students at any given school to score, was problematic. NAEP prefers to train groups of expert, independent raters to agree on complex scoring criteria to demonstrate the validity of student responses.

Even apart from the photographing of student artworks, the complications involved in handing out and accounting for the complex materials necessary for three-dimensional tasks and the space required by students to create effectively with such materials made the tasks both very expensive and time consuming to administer. Two-dimensional tasks were difficult enough to administer; administrators had to be taught how to account for and distribute carefully packaged arts materials. Each kind of media and tool had to be separately bagged or bagged in sets, enabling administrators to easily check that a given school had received the correct shipment, and that each student received the appropriate number of and kind of media and tool. As an example, shown in the following is the materials list for a collage task that combines responding and creating activities. The list demonstrates the challenges of assessment administration caused by the justifiable efforts of assessment developers to make tasks as valid and as authentic as possible by supplying suitable ranges of materials for student creating. Students, after observing a Romare Bearden collage and answering questions about it, created their own collages, and each student required the following materials:

- Test booklet
- Pencil kit (one 2B pencil, one pink pearl eraser, one handheld sharpener)
- One portfolio containing:
    Glue stick
    Black ball-point pen
    12 in. × 18 in. 80 lb. drawing paper
    4 in. × 5 in. postcard of Bearden collage
    Set of 12 Cray-pas
    Set of 8 fine-tip watercolor markers
- Paper set containing:
    Two sheets 6 in. × 6 in. French marble
    One sheet 6 in. × 6 in. Okawara
    One sheet 6 in. × 6 in. dark green-backed foil
    One sheet 6 in. × 6 in. black Unryu paper
    Two sheets 6 in. × 6 in. corrugated cardboard
    Three sheets 12 in. × 15 in. tissue paper
    Two sheets 12 in. × 18 in. construction paper
- Poster of Bearden collage to be placed in room for distant view
- 8.5 in. × 11 in. print of Bearden collage
- 7 in. safety scissors

Once handed out, such materials had to be collected, along with student artworks, at the conclusion of each assessment session. Lengthy scripts were prepared to make distribution and collection standardizable and feasible, and of course administrators needed to ensure that students were able to follow directions and work individually. Three-dimensional tasks that included clay tools for working with plasticene (the chosen material so schools did not have to supply water and deal with the cleanup associated with clay), various other media such as wire and cardboard, and pencil kits for sketches were that much more difficult to prepare for and clean up, after which student responses had to be recorded by photography. Further, in some schools that had no special art room available, or even in schools that did, students did not always have the optimal space for creating.

It would have been simplest to duck the challenges posed by three-dimensional performance tasks. As Claudette Morton states in her article, *A National Arts Test*, "... [E]veryone was aware that because this assessment was so performance oriented, it was already the most expensive NAEP assessment that had ever been conducted" (Morton, 1999). Morton, a theater educator and member of the standards, framework, and assessment development committees, goes on to discuss how finally there was not enough money to assess all four arts areas at all three grades NAEP traditionally assesses. But to give up on in-depth three-dimensional creating would have meant giving up on an opportunity to explore a central component of art making, in the first large-scale, national assessment that could supply meaningful information about students' three-dimensional abilities.

The Strategy: Separating Responding and Two-Dimensional Creating From Three-Dimensional Creating

To respond to the framework's goals of combining assessment authenticity and depth, while attempting to mitigate administration and school burden, ETS staff and the arts development committee decided that only two-dimensional creating tasks could be combined with more than a few responding exercises. Students would complete paper-and-pencil exercises by describing, analyzing, critiquing, and interpreting works of visual arts, and then create a two-dimensional work of art linked to the responding exercises. Three-dimensional tasks that presented the additional administrative burdens discussed previously were administered separately with only a few written exercises meant to get students thinking. Even with this approach, not all students were able to take each kind of task during administration due to time constraints. Rather, some students did responding and two-dimensional creating only, and some a responding block and a three-dimensional creating task only. This arrangement had analysis implications.[1] Still, administration took as much as 2 hours or more. It fell to Westat, the company that holds the NAEP contract for assessment administration, to work with schools to secure ample time frames, promising that the quality and engaging nature of the arts assessment would compensate for the time involved. Although this often proved to be the case, the burden of administering the assessment was considerable.

Challenges Associated With Eliciting In-Depth Responses From Students

As stated earlier, a classroom is obviously a very different setting from a drop-down assessment, for which students have had no direct preparation and during which they cannot discuss options or choices with classmates or teachers. Within the constraints of the NAEP arts blocks, the arts committee and ETS staff worked hard to prepare students for meaningful responding and creating. The arts framework states: "Because art and design activities carried out in the classroom

---

[1] Creating results were not summarized on a standard NAEP scale, as were responding results. To scale assessment results, there must be a sufficient number of students taking a given group of exercises, and a sufficient number of exercises to be scaled of a given type. This was not the case for the creating visual arts tasks, given administrative constraints. Because they consumed far more assessment time than did written exercises, there were fewer exercises to group together into a scale. Given the complex administrative procedures associated with these tasks, each student took only one such task. This prohibited the use of the kind of scaling methodology used to summarize responding results. Instead of a scale, creating and performing results were presented in terms of an average percentage of the maximum possible score.

rely heavily on discussion with teachers, the assessment itself must encourage students in the absence of teachers" (NAGB, 1994, p. 27). Tasks were carefully structured to compensate—at least to a degree for the absence of classroom preparation and the fact that students' questions about content cannot be answered during the assessment. This compensation was important for another reason. As stated previously, NAEP assessments are usually administered to random national samples of students. This means that in the case of subjects like the arts, which may not be part of a school's regular curricula, students often have received little or no exposure to the subject. NAEP was confronted with the challenge of making assessment exercises accessible to students with little arts background yet meaningful to students with in-school exposure to the arts capable of high-level work. Short of teaching, inappropriate in an assessment, tasks were structured to create maximum context for thoughtful responding and creating.

Creating context was accomplished in several ways. All blocks, responding with two-dimensional creating or just three-dimensional creating, were organized around a single theme or problem and/or focused students on one or two stimuli. (Students were always offered high-quality reproductions as stimuli to encourage thoughtful looking. It would have been preferable to use video to display three-dimensional works, but in NAEP there were competing budgets for the theater and dance assessments, which required enormous video investments.) Building tasks around unified themes, issues, or genres gave students an opportunity to focus their attention, rather than skipping from artwork to artwork or theme to theme. This may have helped to mitigate the drop-down assessment effect and lack of time that contrasts so greatly with the kind of focused over time work that can be done in classrooms. In the two-dimensional tasks mixed with responding items, the responding items were intended to prepare students for two-dimensional creating. All tasks featured introductions to let students know what they would be doing, to supply information about the theme or artworks students would be observing, and to encourage careful work. As a rule, tasks began with simpler exercises to increase student comfort and exercises were "scaffolded" so students could address one part of a problem at a time.

Part of a responding/two-dimensional creating task for grade 8 is shown in the following section, and in its entirety at the conclusion of this chapter. In this task, or "block," students were asked to respond to a Romare Bearden collage and then to create collages of their own. The block is designed to help students build understanding as they move through the exercises to encourage students to take the time to look carefully and repeatedly at the artwork, to encourage thoughtful responses to stimulus artworks, and to prepare them for creating work. Note the sequence of the items shown in the following. (Nancy Pistone, member of the standards, framework, and arts development committees, created the task.)

Romare Bearden Collage Task (Responding and Two-Dimensional Creating)

Take time to look at the print you have been given and the poster hung on the wall. This is a work of art by Romare Bearden called *Pittsburgh Memories*. Bearden is one of America's outstanding 20th-century artists. Although he was born in North Carolina, Bearden spent time living in Harlem and in Pittsburgh. His memories of life in these places influenced his art. *Pittsburgh Memories* (1984) is an example of Bearden's style of the 1970s and 1980s.

You will have 17 minutes to answer some questions about *Pittsburgh Memories*. You will then do a collage of your own. The questions are designed to give you an opportunity to show how well you examine and respond to this work by looking at and thinking about what you see. You should, therefore, spend time studying the work.

Consider carefully the following questions about Romare Bearden's work, *Pittsburgh Memories*. Look thoughtfully at the work (your print and the poster); then write your answers as directed.

1. After you have taken some time to look at *Pittsburgh Memories*, think about your first impressions of the work. Write some words or short phrases that describe three of your first impressions. (Do NOT just state whether you think the work is good or bad, or that it is a collage.

   A _____

   B _____

   C _____

2. Take out a postcard, glue stick, and black felt-tip pen from your packet. Now paste your postcard in the space below. Look closely at the image. What features do you think Bearden wants you to notice in this work? Use your black felt-tip pen to draw arrows from the margin to at least <u>three</u> features you think Bearden wants you to notice. Label the features you have identified with brief but thoughtful descriptions, as shown in the example below.

3. Some art critics call this work a "visual narrative." A "narrative" is an orderly account of events or a story.

   Look again at the work. What do you think is the story Bearden tells in his memory of Pittsburgh? Put into words what you think the story is about. Talk about specific things you see in the work that help you see the story.

4. Identify something in the work that is unusual or unexpected. What is it and <u>how</u> <u>does</u> <u>it</u> <u>contribute</u> <u>to</u> <u>the</u> <u>work</u> <u>as</u> <u>a</u> <u>whole</u>? Be thoughtful and specific.

Questions 5–7 are designed to help you study some of the visual characteristics of *Pittsburgh Memories*. Choose the best answer for each question.

5. Key: B
   This work by Bearden is best described as a study of
   A a still life
   B an urban landscape
   C a factory interior
   D a human figure

6. Key: B
   Which of the following is emphasized in the work?
   A The use of shading to make the subject look realistic
   B A grid-like arrangement using horizontal and vertical rectangles
   C A composition that uses traditional approaches to perspective
   D The use of a single color scheme with varying values

7. Key: D
   Which of the following most clearly identifies the style of this work?
   A Impressionism
   B Photographic realism
   C Surrealism
   D Semiabstract representation

8. Look again at the Bearden work. How does Bearden show us the contrast between the interior and the exterior areas of the building? Be specific.

Note that the task shown above begins with an introduction to situate students and encourage them to spend time looking at the work (of which two views, close and distant) are supplied. The items then move the student from an initial response, a warm-up as it were, to noting parts of the work that capture attention. The task is designed to match the way a viewer might first respond to an artwork, feeling its overall impact, while the eye takes in various parts that jump out at the viewer. The questions increase in difficulty, asking students to try and articulate the overall "story" of the work after they have noted details, and then asking them to consider the work's technical aspects, after they have had the opportunity to explore its affective elements. Finally, students are asked to attend to a specific device (contrast between interior and exterior space) that will have significance for the collage-making task that immediately follows. The items in the block, both the nature of the responding items and their relationship to the creating task, represent one of the finer efforts to assess what Gardner and Grunbaum (1986) call "artistic thinking." Asking students to look carefully at artworks to explore their meanings and their forms of expression, both for preexisting works of art and those created by students in the assessment, sits at the center of the NAEP visual arts framework goals.

The importance of this goal raised concerns among members of the arts committee that students with high levels of arts knowledge and skills are not always skilled writers. Would they be able to express their responses to artworks in writing? There was discussion about other means of assessing students' responding skills, for example, by asking students questions orally and audiotaping their answers. Apart from the fact that it is not clear that students who cannot write do better at verbalizing their thoughts, the time constraints and administrative burdens already discussed made this an unrealistic choice. Previous experience in NAEP has shown that interviewing and audiotaping students involve enormous investments of resources in equipment and staff. Further, all students would have to be assessed individually, as opposed to in classroom-sized groups. To interview individual students, and then give them suitable amounts of time to create artworks, would have demanded even more substantial administration periods than those already required by complex creating tasks. When scoring student responses, every effort was made to avoid penalizing students because they could not write well; instead, the emphasis was always on knowledge and understanding of arts content.

In spite of the challenging nature of the assessment for students and such issues as writing burden, the visual arts responding/two-dimensional creating blocks did demonstrably engage students and elicit exciting work, in the judgment of arts committee members and audiences who have attended presentations about NAEP arts. This means that NAEP did experience some success at capturing high levels of student responding and creating skills. Further, even if other students did not respond or create in skillful ways, Westat administrators repeatedly observed that students were deeply engaged in assessment tasks and teachers observing assessments taking place were quite thrilled. This in itself is important information for those interested in further arts assessment initiatives. Here are some examples of very good student work; there are two written responses and two examples of student collages, in the first case with a self-evaluation. All responses shown received the highest scores (Persky, Sandene, & Askew, 1998, pp. 102–103).

Sample Student Response Receiving a Score of Acceptable

Identify something in the work that is unusual or unexpected. What is it and how does it contribute to the work as a whole? Be thoughtful and specific.

The big train is unusual because right next to it is an apartment building and it looks like it's going to run right into it. But the train adds more movement.

Identify something in the work that is unusual or unexpected. What is it and how does it contribute to the work as a whole? Be thoughtful and specific.

The bright mixed colors in only one area of the picture. It shows that he is happy when he goes home. It shows his emotions change as he goes from place to place.

Look carefully at your collage.

Describe in detail the ways that you show a memory of the place you chose and explain what your collage is about. Use evidence from your work to support your answer.

In my collage, I put it as a snowstorm. There are bright green trees on the snow, & there are black & white storm clouds. I also put a cave. In the cave I have 2 people by a fire, & behind them, are 2 windows.

Blank for Self-Evaluation. Either this student ran out of time because of the effort put into the collage, or simply skipped the last question in the block. Twenty-one percent of students left this question blank, suggesting the challenge in planning assessment time for a creative, hand-on activity.

(For further samples of student works, please see the NCES/NAEP site, http://nces.ed.gov/nationsreportcard/arts/)

Some Possible Problems Associated With the NAEP Visual Arts Block Design

Although the focused blocks such as the collage task did enable relatively in-depth assessment, it limited assessment breadth in terms of both artworks and issues. It also may have inhibited performances of students not engaged by a particular problem, theme, or artwork. Some assessment designers would argue that it is preferable to mix greater numbers of stimuli and questions to enable different students more access points to assessment exercises.

Members of the development committee also worried that the organization of "respond first and then create" was too limiting. In suggesting the movement of students from creating to responding and back, the framework was seeking to allow students to bring knowledge and skills together in as flexible a way as possible. It would have been preferable to have had more creative task arrangements involving combinations of responding, two- and three-dimensional creating. Almost all creating tasks, three-dimensional included, were followed by responding items asking students to evaluate their artworks; but students often had little time to complete these questions, because test administrators were told never to interrupt students creating work to compel them to move on to the concluding questions. In any event, student responses to such questions tended to be thin, perhaps because such reflection is difficult when art making has been so rapid and constrained.

On the other hand, there was concern that the absence from three-dimensional creating of leading in-depth responding exercises may have limited students' abilities to think through problems before undertaking such tasks. This could have been the case in spite of the context and guidance supplied by introductions and visual stimuli, and the fact that students made sketches prior to realizing three-dimensional artworks. Ultimately, any drop-down assessment in the arts (or perhaps any skills-based area) faces similar constraints as did the NAEP; creating works of art demands intellectual, emotional, and physical efforts that can be extremely difficult to generate on demand, and it is not possible to address every style. Given administrative constraints, the choice seemed to be between a set of responding exercises before a two-dimensional creating task, OR a lengthy introduction with at most two or three responding items before a three-dimensional creating task.

Shown in the following section is an example of such an introduction and two sketching exercises for a three-dimensional task, both intended to prepare students for creating:

In this task you will make a sculpture out of clay and wire. A sculpture is a work of art that is three-dimensional. Three-dimensional art is not flat so you can look at it from different sides.

Sculptures can be about many different things. The sculpture you will make today will explore the characteristics of kitchen utensils. You may have some of these utensils in your kitchen at home.

To help you think about sculptures, look at the artwork on page 3 of your booklet. [OLDENBURG] This sculpture explores the characteristics of a pair of scissors. Even though scissors are made of hard metal, the artist who made the sculpture used cloth and plastic to show scissors as soft and droopy.

Artists who make works like this sculpture are interested in exploring how we see and experience objects in the world around us. Their artworks are in part about how everyday objects, like a pair of scissors, can be seen as a kind of art.

Notice how this sculpture is surprising because it makes an everyday object into an unusual and unexpected shape. Look at how the artist has chosen to repeat shapes and to make certain shapes large and small. Think about how the artist may have wanted to make an artwork that would change the way people see and think about the everyday world around them.

1. Take out the page of photographs from your packet and unfold it. Look carefully at the photographs of the kitchen utensils. Look at the characteristics of each utensil. Notice different shapes, details, and the hard materials the utensils are made of.

Your goal is to use your imagination to plan and make a sculpture out of clay and wire that will explore characteristics of the kitchen utensils, like the sculpture you just looked at explored a pair of scissors. First, you will sketch shapes and details of the kitchen utensils that interest you, then you will sketch an idea for a sculpture that combines the shapes and details you noticed, and then you will create your sculpture.

To help you begin to plan your sculpture, imagine that the kitchen utensils you see in the photograph are melting and becoming soft and bendable, so that you can make a sculpture by

- Pulling them apart
- Changing their shapes
- Combining them in different ways

A. Think about which kitchen utensils you would pull apart to use in your clay and wire sculpture. Which shapes and details of different utensils would you combine to make a sculpture?

B. Now, right on the photographs, circle six of the shapes and details you would combine to make an imaginative sculpture.

C. In the space on page 5, draw a sketch of each of the six shapes and details you have chosen. In your sketch, use your imagination to change the shapes, sizes, and other characteristics of the six parts by showing how they would look if they were soft and bendable.

You will have 7 minutes to draw your sketch. If you finish before time is called, you may begin work on exercise 2 on page 6. Please start.

2. Now use the sketch you just made to make a second sketch that combines the different shapes and details of the kitchen utensils you chose into an idea for a sculpture. Make your sketch of what you want your sculpture to look like in the space below.

Remember that you will make your sculpture out of clay and wire. Use your sketch to plan how you will use the clay and wire to show how shapes and details of the utensils have become soft and bendable, and to make an imaginative, standing (three-dimensional) sculpture that explores the characteristics of the utensils.

You will have 6 minutes to do your sketch.

The task shown here is meticulously designed to introduce students to a contemporary art form and approach, and to engage them in thoughtful creating. It reflects many, many iterations, and yet it is till vulnerable to criticism on at least two counts: that of creating reading burden and tasks that consist of following directions. NAEP has been accused of both, in addition to the concerns about demanding too much student writing mentioned previously. One of the great challenges in the arts assessment was finding a balance among telling students exactly what was expected of them on assessment tasks, creating context for student activities, and not requiring students to read too much. The arts committee was especially concerned about this issue given that some students who are able in the arts may not be as able at reading. Measurement experts worked closely with the arts committee to find ways of diminishing reading burden where possible. For example, every attempt was made to use simple language; complex scripts for visual arts creating tasks (as in the kitchen sculpture task) were presented to students on audiotape with which they could read along; and arts terms students might not know were defined in exercise directions, unless students' knowledge of a particular term was being assessed (for example, *sculpture* and *three-dimensional* in the kitchen sculpture task). Nevertheless, although further analysis would need to be done with NAEP data to prove the point, directions and introductions to arts tasks were at times lengthy and may indeed have been prejudicial for some students with strong creating abilities. Reading burden is of course not a problem in arts assessment alone. But it is especially frustrating in an assessment where other skills are so valuable.

Sketch 1
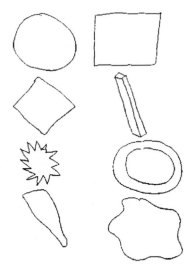

Sketch 2

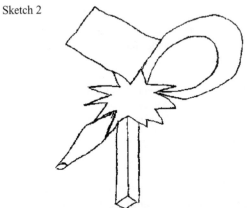

Photograph
of
sculpture

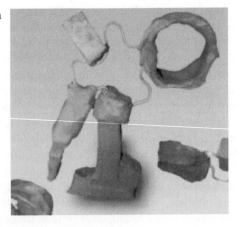

The other question is whether student imagination and creativity are limited by tasks that include too many directions and break out too many steps. The task script shown previously tells students what to notice and takes them through a fairly analytic process of choosing shapes and forms, taking them apart, and then putting them back together. As the following example shows, some students were able to create skilled and interesting work in responce to such direction (Persky et al., 1998, U.S. Department of Education, CD-ROM version). (For more examples of student kitchen sculptures, see the CD-ROM version of the 1997 NAEP Arts Report Card.)

Here is another example of task directions, this time for the collage-creating task that follows the responding items presented earlier:

Take time to look again at your print of *Pittsburgh Memories*. The collage you see visually expresses a memory of Bearden's own past, as well as his deep appreciation for aspects of everyday life. (A collage is a work of art in which different pieces of different kinds of materials are assembled and fastened onto a flat surface.)

Study the Bearden work, and think about how the collage shows the artist's memory of what life in Pittsburgh was like. Notice how Bearden combines and organizes objects and places in unusual and unexpected ways to express what it is like to remember. Look for the ways in which interesting contrasts between inside and outside areas and the use of details and colors communicate a memory.

Now think of a memory of a place where you once lived, where you live now, a friend's house, or another place important to you in your community. What kinds of pictures do you see in your mind when you remember what it was like to be there?

Being as creative as you can, create a memory collage of the place you choose. In your collage, communicate what you remember about what it was like both inside of this place and outside in the neighborhood.

To make your collage:

- Take out all of the materials from your packet. You may use your scissors and/or tear materials you choose for your collage.
- Assemble on your sheet of white drawing paper pieces of any of the materials provided to show both the inside of the place you choose and what it was like outside.
- Once you have pasted down these areas, you can add details with markers and oil pastels.

In both tasks, the directions are intended to clearly present a problem to be solved, and to help students thoughtfully create. Each problem is meant to be complex enough to engage students at a high level, and their detailed presentations are intended to reach students less schooled in art making. But the very attempt to increase student comfort and create clear task parameters that would yield scorable responses may have created directions too lengthy or detailed for some students to absorb, or too inhibiting for other students very concerned with following directions. Again, further study would be needed to prove or disprove the point. At the time, arts committee members and ETS staff chose very detailed, explicit directions not only for the reasons described above but also for the purpose of successful scoring.

BALANCING BEING OPEN AND CLOSED: ISSUES AND STRATEGIES USED IN ASSESSMENT DEVELOPMENT AND SCORING

It seems obvious that an arts assessment ought to elicit students' expressive abilities. The visual arts assessment tasks were all the creations of committed arts educators who greatly value student experimentation and expression. But assessment tasks also needed to yield scorable, comparable responses. NAEP scoring is accomplished by gathering all student responses for tasks in one central location, and assigning experts, in this case arts educators, to train small groups of qualified raters (those with suitable arts backgrounds and/or NAEP scoring experience) to assign scores to student responses. Scores are assigned to written and production work using scoring guides that feature multiple levels, or points, to accommodate a wide range of skill levels and range of responses. To train raters, experts choose sets of exemplars to demonstrate various levels of scoring criteria. As mentioned earlier, the arts committee vetted sets of exemplars to ensure that scoring matched the framework's specifications for expected levels of skill; NAEP is not a norm-referenced assessment. Given the goal of determining whether students were demonstrating specific kinds of knowledge and skills, it was crucial that tasks express clear expectations and that scoring criteria match these expectations. There was thus a constant tension between the goals of telling students what was expected of them in creating tasks, so their responses could be meaningfully scored, and leaving enough space for students to demonstrate their expressive abilities. Scoring guides for written responses were far less complex.

Why Create Constrained, Directed Creating Tasks?

Although this book is concerned with visual arts, an example from the dance assessment is instructive. In a dance assessment task (note that dance was ultimately not assessed in 1997 due to sampling constraints), students were asked to create and perform a dance built around the theme of metamorphosis: changing from one form to another. Students were told they needed to incorporate two different shapes, levels, and movement types into their dances. The task specified the amounts of time allowed for creating and practicing the dance. Within this structure, students were free to work with their partners in any way they chose; create dances of any genre or style as long as they incorporated the criteria; and experiment with any idea of metamorphosis that engaged them.

Giving students a theme to focus on and clear specifications for their dances gave them a useful structure within which their imaginations could play, a starting point, and helped them to respond to the task. It also ensured that student dances, even if they represented different dance styles, would be clear and comparable enough to score fairly. Finally, carefully timing different stages of activities, as was also done in the kitchen sculpture task shown previously, kept students focused and engaged, and ensured that all students in the sample would have the same opportunities for creating and performing.

The priority placed on being absolutely clear and constraining in directions did generate argument among arts assessment committee members and ETS staff. Would it have been better in various cases to open up tasks to enable student demonstration of skills? For example, was it necessary that the kitchen sculpture sketching directions be so constraining as regards modes of experimentation? The conclusion at the time was that it was important to direct students and to get them working, rather than have them spend a large amount of time wrestling with what to create. And it would have been far more difficult to compare student responses for scoring purposes had students been given too many choices of theme or subject. Certainly some degree of choice was allowed. For example, students were always given two or three drawing tools and told they could use their tools in any way they chose. And, when asked to create three-dimensional works of visual art, students were not *required* to base their final works on their sketches. However, as a general rule, choice was limited and directions were analytic to ensure a close match between task directions and scoring criteria.

NAEP 1997 Scoring Choices for Creating Tasks

Matching task expectations and scoring criteria is a basic assessment strategy, really rule, and not news to anyone. But even with quite constrained tasks, the visual arts assessment scoring guides went through many evolutions. The rule of matching task requirements and scoring criteria is far easier to apply in an assessment where measuring more widely accepted canons of specific knowledge and agreed-upon aspects of skill are in question, as in science or math. The creation of the 1997 assessment was an occasion when all the participants were learning as they developed and scored items for a large-scale arts performance assessment.

There were two initial approaches to scoring. In one, two guides were created for a given artwork to separately address technical and expressive qualities of student artworks. The other model meticulously broke out criteria into small units based on every aspect of a problem a students was asked to solve. As an example of the latter approach, here is the three-dimensional creating task for kitchen sculpture, followed by a set of criteria for scoring. Remember that students have been asked to create two sketches prior to creating their sculptures, both of which have encouraged them to focus on showing parts of kitchen utensils as soft and bendable and combining those shapes into a plan for a sculpture.

3. Now use the clay and wire you have been given in your packet to make your sculpture. Use the sketch you have just drawn to help you, but remember that your sculpture does not have to look exactly like your sketch.

- First work with some of your clay and/or wire to make the main shape of your sculpture.
- Then use more of your clay and wire to add other shapes and details to your sculpture.
- Experiment by pulling pieces of clay away from the main shape of clay and adding pieces of clay and wire to the main shape of clay.
- Use the tools you have been given to make textures, lines, and shapes.
- As you work, think about how your sculpture will look from different sides.

Scoring Criteria
You will have 30 minutes to create your sculpture and to answer a question about your work. The supervisor will help you keep track of the time.

Instructions: Rate each of the following items by circling the appropriate number. The numbers represent the following values:

1   Unsuccessful (did not do it)
2   Somewhat successful (partially did it)
3   Success (did it)
4   Very successful (did it very well)

How successful was the student in making a sculpture that meets each of the following criteria?

3.a 1 2 3 4   Student's solution recognizes the properties of clay in transforming the characteristics of the objects. This is demonstrated by the student's use of clay to show how the kitchen utensils have become soft and bendable.

3.b 1 2 3 4   Student's solution recognizes the properties of wire in transforming the characteristics of the objects. This is demonstrated by the use of wire to show how the kitchen utensils have become soft and bendable.

NOTE: Wire can be used to show detail, and/or as an armature.

3.c 1 2 3 4   Student integrated the materials in ways appropriate to the form.

Instructions: Rate each of the following items by circling the appropriate number. The numbers represent the following values:

1   Unsuccessful (did not do it)
2   Somewhat successful (sort of did it)
3   Successful (did it)

How successful was the student in making a sculpture that meets each of the following criteria?

3.d 1 2 3   Student incorporated shapes and details of the kitchen utensils into the sculpture. (Look for more than one object, shape, and detail.)

3.e   Student used the clay tools to make textures, shapes, and lines.

1 = Minimal evidence of tool use.
2 = Some evidence of tool use.
3 = Sufficient/adequate evidence of tool use.

3.f   Student's sculpture shows a variety of view points or sides and is freestanding, NOT a relief sculpture.

1 = completely flat work: limited detail, one object.
2 = transitional work: some detail/elaboration, more than one object.
3 = freestanding work: fairly detailed/elaborated, several objects, includes wire.

The criteria shown here do match what students have been asked to do, but after field-testing they were felt to be too constraining. Members of the arts development committee asked one another whether we were really scoring a sculpture, a piece of artwork. Arguably, the criteria reflect the analytic directions, but even so, it was decided at the time to append an additional guide that would more holistically address the set of criteria for the sculpture:

Holistic Guide

The student used imagination to create an inventive, freestanding sculpture of an everyday object that is soft, bendable, or distorted. Look for evidence of ability to explore the object in the photograph to inventively combine and organize shapes, colors, details and textures into an imaginative interpretation. The materials will be used in a creative way that enables the student to effectively capture the critical relationship between the materials and the idea the student is attempting to express.

1—UNSUCCESSFUL See visual examples.

2—SOMEWHAT SUCCESSFUL See visual examples.

3—SUCCESSFUL See visual examples.

4—VERY SUCCESSFUL See visual examples.

Although there is some overlap between the two kinds of criteria, the goal of the second kind of guide is clearly different. It both explicitly mentions creativity and combines sculptural attributes instead of breaking them out by material used, in this case clay (in fact plasticene) and wire. Certainly the guide was easier to use than the set of more detailed criteria, and some people experienced it as a better fit with the task. But whether it was felt to be a better fit because of its references to creativity, or in fact because it attends to the fact that students were asked to explore materials to create an integrated piece, not as an end in itself, is up for discussion.

In my view, a somewhat more successful combining of criteria to evaluate solution of the problems and technical and expressive qualities is shown in the scoring guide for the collage task. This guide evolved from two guides: the one dealing with technical skill; and the other, with expressive skills. After field testing, it was felt that student responses combined technical and expressive aspects in way that were too complex and varied to allow those qualities to be separated without overlap, that is, scoring the same thing twice. Just as the NAEP writing assessment has evolved from analytic scoring that separately evaluates grammar and development of ideas to primary trait guides that focus on a combination of prompt-related and writing skill criteria and, finally, to focused holistic guides that ask raters to evaluate the whole piece and treat the prompt purely as a springboard for writing, so many NAEP arts assessment guides ended up collapsing technical and expressive aspects into more holistic guides that score technical and expressive qualities across a number of levels, together. The arts guides did not abandon the specifics of the prompt as wholly as do the writing guides; the art "problem" students are asked to solve offers desirable parameters that enable comparisons across student responses, as demonstrated in the scoring guide for the collage task shown next.

1—UNACCEPTABLE No use of collage techniques, or very limited or ineffective use, and/or does not show inside or outside of place remembered. Objects are nonrecognizable.

2—MINIMAL The ability to use collage technique to express a memory about a place is barely evidenced in the work. Shows inside OR outside of place remembered, or shows both in a weak manner.

- Representations are of a single object or limited scheme and are simplistic and without detail.
- There is minimal exploration and variation of materials to depict objects, areas, ideas.
- A large degree of ambiguity exists because objects are incomplete; parts missing; objects float ambiguously on page.

3—UNEVEN The ability to use collage technique to express a memory about a place is evidenced in parts of the work. Shows inside OR outside of place remembered, or shows both in an uneven and unrelated manner.

- Choice and use of material show occasional awareness of pattern, texture, transparency, contrast, color, and the relationships of these qualities to depicted objects.
- Only parts of the work show exploration and variation of materials to depict objects, areas, or ideas.
- Lacks compositional unity.
- Fragments of the work evoke mood or feeling about place.

4—ADEQUATE The ability to use collage technique to express a memory about a place is evidenced throughout most of the work. Shows BOTH inside and outside of place remembered, and at least one is convincing and complex; though the two may not be well integrated, or both sides are evenly and well done (but not necessarily complex) and well integrated.

- Choice and use of material show some awareness of pattern, texture, transparency, contrast, color, and the relationships of these qualities to depicted objects.
- Forms and objects are generally shown with distinguishable features.
- Reasonably unified composition: Objects are shown in some relation to one another and to whole page.
- Work is moderately expressive.

5—EFFECTIVE The ability to use collage technique is evidenced throughout the whole work. Clearly shows BOTH inside and outside of place remembered, and the two are well integrated.

- Choice and use of material show good awareness of pattern, texture, transparency, color, and the relationships of these qualities to depicted objects.
- Material is placed in a careful, deliberate way to represent ideas.
- Forms and objects are shown with clearly distinguishable features.
- Unified composition: Objects are shown in clear relation to one another and to whole page.
- Work is very expressive.

The implied analogy made here between expressivity in art and development in writing is far from exact. Some might argue that a more apt analogy is between the creative quality in creative writing and the expressive quality in art. But it is very important to note that the language of making meaning versus that of being creative as an end in itself is closest to the arts framework. That document is most concerned with how well students can make meaning with what is available to them is a task; a concern with creativity is present in references to showing inventiveness in solutions and experimenting to seek goodness of fit with intended meaning. Creativity is seen as being embedded in experimentation and solutions that aptly express ideas, just as it is, with a very different medium; in writing. Just as the NAEP writing guides address precision in language, the ability to match word to meaning, the framework discusses using media and techniques to convey an intended meaning, and the collage guide evaluates matching collage material to idea. The distinction between successfully making meaning and being creative as an end in itself is an important distinction and fits best with a model of art education as being meaningful for many, versus a romantic model of the marginal and uniquely inspired artist.

Interestingly, it may have taken the framework writers some time to come to terms with the scoring implications of their own document, and the initial weddedness to expressivity as a separate, somehow elusive category may have been a stage in that evolution. There was much discussion about how to reward the students who seemed to demonstrate expressive skills without technical skills, but the framework does not seem to be designed to reward them. (Whether a future reworking of the framework might change this is another question.) Perhaps in this regard what is most successful about the collage guide is not its folding in of language about expressivity with technical skills, but instead its clear articulation of how well technical skills are brought to bear on making meaning. In this sense, the collage guide is very close to the NAEP holistic writing guides.

Possible Future Directions for Task Design and Scoring

A possible future approach would be to model large-scale arts assessment scoring guides even more closely on the NAEP writing assessment guides. In NAEP, students are creating what must be seen as artworks analogous to the drafty writing they create for the writing assessment. And it is precisely the fact that NAEP is an assessment meant to provide general results based on random sampling that makes it a good candidate for this holistic approach to task scoring. For example, just as writing scoring guides are organized in terms of how well students choose words, develop and organize ideas, and competently use technical skills to communicate ideas, so arts scoring criteria would reflect art educators' agreed-upon ideas about what students at various levels of knowledge and skill ought to be able to demonstrate regardless of a specific task's qualities. The collage guide shown previously is not too far from this, in that it takes for granted that students will apply what they may have learned about composition and use of media to create a meaningful work, just as, with only brief directions urging them to pay attention to clarity and development, students are expected to use what they know about writing in responding to NAEP writing prompts. If the collage guide were to more completely match the proposed model, it would not speak less in terms of the collage media per se and of the goal of depicting both inside and outside of a remembered place. Instead it would focus on the use of media, in general, to create an effect, in terms of integration, clarity, and so forth.

In fact, one very good quality of the NAEP writing assessment is the room for varied student responses that may address the prompt in the most glancing fashion, or that may mix "modes," for example, narrative and informative writing. The category of "off task" is quite rare, specifically because the writing prompts are intended to get student writing, not as ends in themselves. Instead, a specific set of writing skills is in question: word choice, development, organization, and control over conventions of grammar. In these circumstances, a student who fails to depict inside AND outside, for example, might still receive a high score, because he or she has demonstrated the ability to use arts skills to make meaning, even if that meaning is more tenuously related to the specifics of the problem students were asked to solve. (It should be noted though that students who write very "creative" narrative pieces, for example, undistinguished by technical competence, do generally receive low scores. What can be assessed and captured in a large-scale national assessment can never fulfill the promise of a small-scale, individualized, portfolio assessment, both in writing *and* in the arts. This is salient to the struggles mentioned previously about how to credit students who showed creative promise but seemed to lack the skill to bring that promise to fruition.)

One might even speculate as to whether arts-creating tasks could be simpler affairs, with fewer directions and steps. Such an approach would be one way to acknowledge the profoundly "draft" quality of the student artworks produced in timed assessment circumstances. Just as writing prompts, with as few words as possible, try to stimulate students to write, so arts prompts could ask students to use available tools and media to create a specific kind of two- or three-dimensional artwork, without complex directions guiding students through each step. Doing so would be less important because a wider range of student responses would be acceptable, given the more generic scoring criteria. Student responses could be standardized not in terms, for example, of whether every student attempts to depict both the inside and the outside of a place, but whether every student demonstrates suitable levels of skill in depicting anything related to the collage task. Further, as with writing planning, sketching for three-dimensional artwork would be optional, or if required, students would be told that it would not be scored, to encourage experimentation. Finally, just as the writing assessment offers students a short pamphlet on how to plan, revise, and edit their writing, so the NAEP arts assessment (or any large-scale arts assessment) could supply students with a brief pamphlet reminding them of ways to reflect on their work and its goals. This approach may enable greater student experimentation, more fluid combinations of responding and creating tasks, and simpler scoring.

Again, the analogy between arts and writing is far from perfect; it breaks down most when one considers the range of media and tools available to express art, versus writing, suggesting that art-making skills are firmly embedded in particular kinds of creating. This approach to arts task creation and scoring assumes that notions of what constitutes "good art," or art skill, can be as agreed upon as those of "good writing."[2] Last, assessment developers would still be confronted with how to make creating tasks accessible to a wide range of students, and it is this need that accounted for much of the complexity and lengthy directions in the NAEP arts tasks.

But the assumption that underlies this suggestion, that there are categories of skills that can be evaluated across tasks and students, is precisely what the arts framework itself assumes in its plan for scaling student creating abilities across tasks, along with student responding abilities.

---

[2]Given the struggle to come to terms with appropriate skills to be assessed in writing, it seems reasonable to assume that a given generation of arts educators can reach similar consensus.

The framework assumes that the ability to bring knowledge and skills to bear upon make meaning and responding to meaning using varied media (including writing) *is* an ability that can be generalized from many varied tasks. Further, in the experiment carried out by Siegesmund, Diket, and McCulloch (2001), student work was scored on a range of traits regardless of whether the student precisely followed directions, suggesting that there are skills or capacities of interest to arts educators that can be scored across tasks that vary greatly in nature. (Whether the framework's expression of such skills can be enriched with reference to the sorts of skills explored by the teachers in Siegesmund's research is an open question. Perhaps it is these skills that NAEP committee members were trying to capture in guides about how expressive a student work is, and the next generation of the arts framework can more fully articulate this goal.)

One way to accommodate skills that run across tasks yet attend to varied kinds of arts processes might be to create two creating scales, one for two-dimensional creating and one three-dimensional creating, and retain the 1997 NAEP model in which responding was treated separately. This might enable a more sensitive portrait of arts knowledge and skills; the peculiarity of tools and media in the arts is such that it is challenging to assess student skill without profoundly relating that skill to its expression with particular media and tools. Or, perhaps the scales are more properly divided by categories that capture the sensory, unique quality of art, as described by Siegesmund et al. (2001).

CONCLUSION

The previous discussion seeks to articulate several tensions in the creation and scoring of the NAEP arts assessment: making tasks feasible for administration yet authentic in the terms presented in the NAEP arts framework; encouraging thoughtful student responding and creating work without burdening students with too many directions and constraints; enabling students from a wide range of arts backgrounds to perform on the assessment, again without undue reading burden or constraints; and enabling student responses to be scorable without making tasks too limiting.

Clearly, certain compromises had to be made to successfully administer an arts performance assessment of a random national sample of students. Responding items to assess students skills at analyzing and articulating how artworks convey meaning required students to respond in writing, because interviewing individual students was not a possibility. Such items, designed also to move students thoughtfully toward creating activities, could not be used to precede three-dimensional creating tasks, because of the complexities inherent in the administration of such tasks. To compensate for lack of context created by the absence of responding items and to engage students of varying levels of exposure to arts education, directions and introductions to three-dimensional tasks were rather lengthy and complex. And, both two- and three-dimensional creating tasks limited, to some degree, student choice of problem, approach to solution, and media to ensure that students could complete assessment work in a limited time frame and to make tasks standardizable so student responses could be scored.

Concerns about the compromises made to create the NAEP arts assessment can be responded to in several ways. One way is to discuss the reasons behind the choices made, as this chapter does. The dilemmas of administrative and school burdens, limited budget, and reaching students of widely varying skill levels are not limited to NAEP, and are likely to be confronted by anyone seeking to assess large numbers of students in a drop-down assessment, even at the state or local level. Another response is to note that the assessment did yield results that many many people in the field of arts education have learned from. Although researchers and educators such as Siegesmund et al. (2001) are critical of some of the approaches NAEP took, they are nevertheless using the NAEP model as a starting point for future assessment design in the arts. Also, students enthusiastically wrote about and created artworks for the NAEP, and assessment results showed a range of skills from the most elementary grasp to the most sophisticated abilities. And, positive correlations were noted in the 1997 arts report card among various in (and out of school) arts activities and performances on both responding and creating tasks. (Persky et al., 1998, pp. 104–115). These correlations were sustained and further explored by secondary research, for example, that performed by Read M. Diket (2000). Finally, one can make suggestions for the future that may mitigate some of the problems of the assessment, such as more holistic scoring guides and associated simpler tasks.

Still, it is clear from the remarks above that success at assessing arts at a national level is intrinsically limited. The challenges posed by a large-scale administration are real. Further, it is inevitable, even appropriate, that an assessment of such large proportions, aimed at a random national sample of students, will offer a quite general measure of students' arts knowledge and skills. Again, in this respect, the NAEP writing assessment is similar; who would argue that the assessment offers the same picture of student skill as a portfolio assessment of students' works over several months, or the observations of a classroom teacher? But that general measure may be a fine snapshot of the state of arts education at a given time. State and local assessments may lose in budget what they gain in time and flexibility of administration. By demonstrating what *can* be achieved on a national level, the NAEP plays an extraordinarily important role in defining the outer limits of what is possible in large-scale arts assessment. The suggestions about holistic approaches to tasks and scoring offered earlier may make this role even more possible in the future.

TASK APPENDIX

Romare Bearden Collage Task (Responding and Two-Dimensional Creating)

Take time to look at the print you have been given and at the poster hung on the wall. This is a work of art by Romare Bearden called *Pittsburgh Memories*. Bearden is one of America's outstanding 20th-century artists. Although he was born in North Carolina, Bearden spent time living in Harlem and in Pittsburgh. His memories of life in these places influenced his art. *Pittsburgh Memories* (1984) is an example of Bearden's style of the 1970s and 1980s.

You will have 17 minutes to answer some questions about *Pittsburgh Memories*. You will then do a collage of your own. The questions are designed to give you an opportunity to show how well you examine and respond to this work by looking at and thinking about what you see. You should, therefore, spend time studying the work.

Consider carefully the following questions about Romare Bearden's work, *Pittsburgh Memories*. Look thoughtfully at the work (your print and the poster), then write your answers as directed.

1. After you have taken some time to look at *Pittsburgh Memories*, think about your first impressions of the work. Write some words or short phrases that describe three of your first impressions. (Do NOT just state whether you think the work is good or bad, or that it is a collage.)

   A _____

   B _____

   C _____

2. Take out a postcard, glue stick, and black felt-tip pen from your packet. Now paste your postcard in the space below. Look closely at the image. What features do you think Bearden wants you to notice in this work? Use your black felt-tip pen to draw arrows from the margin to at least <u>three</u> features you think Bearden wants you to notice. Label the features you have identified with brief but thoughtful descriptions, as shown in the example below.

3. Some art critics call this work a "visual narrative." A "narrative" is an orderly account of events or a story.

   Look again at the work. What do you think is the story Bearden tells in his memory of Pittsburgh? Put into words what you think the story is about. Talk about specific things you see in the work that help you see the story.

4. Identify something in the work that is unusual or unexpected. What is it and <u>how</u> <u>does</u> <u>it</u> <u>contribute</u> <u>to</u> <u>the</u> <u>work</u> <u>as</u> <u>a</u> <u>whole</u>? Be thoughtful and specific.

Questions 5–7 are designed to help you study some of the visual characteristics of *Pittsburgh Memories*. Choose the best answer for each question.

5. Key: B
   This work by Bearden is best described as a study of
   A a still life
   B an urban landscape
   C a factory interior
   D a human figure

6. Key: B
   Which of the following is emphasized in the work?
   A The use of shading to make the subject look realistic
   B A grid-like arrangement using horizontal and vertical rectangles
   C A composition that uses traditional approaches to perspective
   D The use of a single color scheme with varying values

7. Key: D
   Which of the following most clearly identifies the style of this work?
   A Impressionism
   B Photographic realism
   C Surrealism
   D Semiabstract representation

8. Look again at the Bearden work. How does Bearden show us the contrast between the interior and the exterior areas of the building? Be specific.

9. Take time to look again at your print of *Pittsburgh Memories*. The collage you see visually expresses a memory of Bearden's own past, as well as his deep appreciation for aspects of everyday life. (A collage is a work of art in which different pieces of different kinds of materials are assembled and fastened onto a flat surface.)

   Study the Bearden work, and think about how the collage shows the artist's memory of what life in Pittsburgh was like. Notice how Bearden combines and organizes objects and places in unusual and unexpected ways to express what it is like to remember. Look for the ways in which interesting contrasts between inside and outside areas and the use of details and colors communicate a memory.

   Now think of a memory of a place where you once lived, where you live now, a friend's house, or another place important to you in your community. What kinds of pictures do you see in your mind when you remember what it was like to be there?

   Being as creative as you can, create a memory collage of the place you choose. In your collage, communicate what you remember about what it was like both inside of this place and outside in the neighborhood.

To make your collage:

- Take out all of the materials from your packet. You may use your scissors and/or tear materials you choose for your collage.
- Assemble on your sheet of white drawing paper pieces of any of the materials provided to show both the inside of the place you choose and what it was like outside.
- Once you have pasted down these areas, you can add details with markers and oil pastels.

After you have completed your memory collage, you will answer a question about your collage. You will have 43 minutes to do your collage and to answer the question.

10. Look carefully at your collage.

Describe in detail the ways that you show a memory of the place you chose, and explain what your collage is about. Use evidence from your work to support your answer.

Kitchen Sculpture Task (Three-Dimensional)

In this task you will make a sculpture out of clay and wire. A sculpture is a work of art that is three-dimensional. Three-dimensional art is not flat, so you can look at it from different sides.

Sculptures can be about many different things. The sculpture you will make today will explore the characteristics of kitchen utensils. You may have some of these utensils in your kitchen at home.

To help you think about sculptures, look at the artwork on page 3 of your booklet. This sculpture explores the characteristics of a pair of scissors. Even though scissors are made of hard metal, the artist who made the sculpture used cloth and plastic to show scissors as soft and droopy.

Artists who make works like this sculpture are interested in exploring how we see and experience objects in the world around us. Their artworks are in part about how everyday objects, like a pair of scissors, can be seen as a kind of art.

Notice how this sculpture is surprising because it makes an everyday object into an unusual and unexpected shape. Look at how the artist has chosen to repeat shapes and to make certain shapes large and small. Think about how the artist may have wanted to make an artwork that would change the way people see and think about the everyday world around them.

1. Take out the page of photographs from your packet and unfold it. Look carefully at the photographs of the kitchen utensils. Look at the characteristics of each utensil. Notice different shapes, details, and the hard materials the utensils are made of.

Your goal is to use your imagination to plan and make a sculpture out of clay and wire that will explore characteristics of the kitchen utensils, like the sculpture you just looked at explored a pair of scissors. First, you will sketch shapes and details of the kitchen utensils that interest you, then you will sketch an idea for a sculpture that combines the shapes and details you noticed, and then you will create your sculpture.

To help you begin to plan your sculpture, imagine that the kitchen utensils you see in the photograph are melting and becoming soft and bendable, so that you can make a sculpture by

- Pulling them apart
- Changing their shapes
- Combining them in different ways

A Think about which kitchen utensils you would pull apart to use in your clay and wire sculpture. Which shapes and details of different utensils would you combine to make a sculpture?

B Now, right on the photographs, circle six of the shapes and details you would combine to make an imaginative sculpture.

C In the space on page 5, draw a sketch of each of the six shapes and details you have chosen. In your sketch, use your imagination to change the <u>shapes</u>, <u>sizes</u>, and <u>other</u> characteristics of the six parts by showing how they would look if they were soft and bendable.

You will have 7 minutes to draw your sketch. If you finish before time is called, you may begin work on exercise 2 on page 6. Please start.

Scoring Criteria

1—UNACCEPTABLE Characteristics in the sketch are not made to appear bendable, soft, or distorted. Or, student only shows one changed characteristic.

2—PARTIAL Characteristics in the sketch are made to appear bendable, soft, or distorted in minimal ways; little experimentation is in evidence. Or, student only shows two changed characteristics.

3—ESSENTIAL Characteristics in the sketch are made to appear bendable, soft, or distorted; some elaboration of details and experimentation is in evidence. Or, student only shows three or four changed characteristics.

4—EXTENDED Five or six characteristics in the sketch are made to appear bendable, soft, or distorted. There is strong evidence of elaboration and experimentation with shapes and details.

NOTE: Whereas simply eliminating a portion of a tool is change, showing distortion of that tool is experimentation. Experimentation of size, shape, and line can be understood as distortion of the following kinds:

- Elongation
- Integration
- Simplification
- Elaboration
- Abbreviation
- Stylization
- Juxtaposition
- Transformation/metamorphosis

2. Now use the sketch you just made to make a second sketch that combines the different shapes and details of the kitchen utensils you chose into an idea for a sculpture. Make your sketch of what you want your sculpture to look like in the space below.

Remember that you will make your sculpture out of clay and wire. Use your sketch to plan how you will use the clay and wire to show how shapes and details of the utensils have become soft and bendable, and to make an imaginative, standing (three-dimensional) sculpture that explores the characteristics of the utensils.

You will have 6 minutes to do your sketch.

Scoring Criteria

1—UNACCEPTABLE Sketch shows objects as they are. There is no evidence of variation and experimentation. No elaboration of details.

2—INSUFFICIENT Objects show limited evidence of variation and experimentation. Characteristics are made to appear bendable, soft, or distorted in minimal ways. Little or no elaboration of details. Images are ambiguous.

3—UNEVEN Objects show uneven or inconsistent evidence of variation and experimentation and are combined in predictable ways. Characteristics show evidence of appearing bendable, soft, or distorted. Minimal elaboration of details.

4—ADEQUATE Objects show sufficient evidence of variation and experimentation and are combined in fairly inventive ways. Characteristics show clear evidence of appearing bendable, soft, or distorted. There is clear evidence of elaboration of details.

5—ELABORATED Objects show considerable evidence of variation and experimentation and are combined inventively. Characteristics show strong evidence of appearing bendable, soft, or distorted. Details are well elaborated.

NOTE: Variation and experimentation of size, shape, and line can be understood as distortion of the following kinds:

- Elongation
- Integration
- Simplification
- Elaboration
- Abbreviation
- Stylization
- Juxtaposition
- Attenuation
- Transformation/metamorphosis
- QUANTITY of variation is less important than interesting contrasts and juxtapositions. Avoid a prejudice toward complexity.
- Whisks, unless the drawing is exceptional, are scored 1.

3. Now use the clay and wire you have been given in your packet to make your sculpture. Use the sketch you have just drawn to help you, but remember that your sculpture does not have to look exactly like your sketch.

First work with some of your clay and/or wire to make the main shape of your sculpture.

Then use more of your clay and wire to add other shapes and details to your sculpture.

Experiment by pulling pieces of clay away from the main shape of clay and adding pieces of clay and wire to the main shape of clay.

Use the tools you have been given to make textures, lines, and shapes.

As you work, think about how your sculpture will look from different sides.

You will have 30 minutes to create your sculpture and to answer a question about your work. The supervisor will help you keep track of the time.

Scoring Criteria
Instructions: Rate each of the following items by circling the appropriate number. The numbers represent the following values:

1   Unsuccessful (did not do it)
2   Somewhat successful (partially did it)
3   Success (did it)
4   Very successful (did it very well)

How successful was the student in making a sculpture that meets each of the following criteria?

3.a 1 2 3 4   Student's solution recognizes the properties of clay in transforming the characteristics of the objects. This is demonstrated by the student's use of clay to show how the kitchen utensils have become soft and bendable.

3.b 1 2 3 4   Student's solution recognizes the properties of wire in transforming the characteristics of the objects. This is demonstrated by the use of wire to show how the kitchen utensils have become soft and bendable.

NOTE: Wire can be used to show detail and/or as an armature.

3.c 1 2 3 4   Student integrated the materials in ways appropriate to the form.

Instructions: Rate each of the following items by circling the appropriate number. The numbers represent the following values:

1   Unsuccessful (did not do it)
2   Somewhat successful (sort of did it)
3   Successful (did it)

How successful was the student in making a sculpture that meets each of the following criteria?

3.f 1 2 3   Student incorporated shapes and details of the kitchen utensils into the sculpture. (Look for more than one object, shape, and detail.)

3.g Student used the clay tools to make textures, shapes, and lines.

1 = Minimal evidence of tool use.
2 = Some evidence of tool use.
3 = Sufficient/adequate evidence of tool use.

3.h Student's sculpture shows a variety of viewpoints or sides and is free-standing, NOT a relief sculpture.

1 = Completely flat work: limited detail, one object.
2 = Transitional work: some detail/elaboration, more than one object.
3 = Free-standing work: fairly detailed/elaborated, several objects, includes wire.

HOLISTIC GUIDE: The student used imagination to create an inventive, free-standing sculpture of an everyday object that is soft, bendable, or distorted. Look for evidence of ability to explore the object in the photograph to inventively combine and organize shapes, colors, details, and textures into an imaginative interpretation. The materials will be used in a creative way that enables the student to effectively capture the critical relationship between the materials and the idea the student is attempting to express.

1—UNSUCCESSFUL See visual examples.

2—SOMEWHAT SUCCESSFUL See visual examples.

3—SUCCESSFUL See visual examples.

4—VERY SUCCESSFUL See visual examples.

Look carefully at the sculpture you have made, and imagine that your sculpture is going to be part of an art exhibit at your school.

What would you want people looking at your sculpture to notice and think about? Be specific.

Explain why.

REFERENCES

Beattie, D. K. (1999, May). *An assessment or a demonstration: An analysis of the 1997 NAEP assessment of the visual arts*. Paper presented at the IAEA conference, Bled, Slovenia.

Diket, R. M. (2001). A factor analytic model of eighth-grade art learning: Secondary analysis of the NAEP report card in the visual arts. *Studies in Art Education, 41*(3), 202–207.

Eisner, E. W. (1999). The national assessment in the visual arts. *Arts Education Policy Review, 100*(6), 16–20.

Gardner, H., & Grunbaum, J. (1986). *The assessment of artistic thinking: Comments on the National Assessment of Educational Progress in the arts*. (ERIC Document Reproduction Service No. ED297677)

Morton, C. (Summer, 1999). A national arts test: An overview of the NAEP report. *Teaching Theatre, 10*(3), pp. 3–6.

Myford, C. M., & Sims-Gunzenhauser, A. (2004). *The evolution of large-scale arts assessment programs in the visual arts*. In E. Eisner, & M. Day (Eds.), *Handbook of Research and Policy in Art Education*. Mahwah, NJ: Lawrence Erlbaum Associates.

National Assessment Governing Board. (1994). *1997 Arts education assessment framework*. Washington, DC.

Persky, H. R., Sandene, B. A., & Askew, J. M. (1998). *The NAEP 1997 arts report card: Eighth-grade findings from the national assessment of educational progress*. U.S. Department of Education, Office of Educational Research and Improvement: National Center for Education Statistics.

Siegesmund, R., Diket, R., & McCulloch, S. (2001). *Re-visioning NAEP: Amending a performance assessment for middle school arts students*. Paper presented at the American Education research Association (AERA) in Seattle.

28

The Evolution of Large-Scale Assessment Programs in the Visual Arts

Carol M. Myford
University of Illinois at Chicago

Alice Sims-Gunzenhauser
Educational Testing Service

When designing a large-scale assessment, it is important to view the assessment as a dynamic, evolving system—not as a static system that is going to look the same in 20 years as it did when it was first implemented. The construct that is being measured may not change, but our knowledge of how best to carry out the measurement of that construct may. Those who design an assessment and those who use the assessment results should expect that the assessment will change over time and that modifications will be made. An assessment system needs to have the capacity to respond to sound research and evaluation studies that inform assessment practice. Advances in technology and in psychometrics, as well as advances in our practical knowledge of how to carry out the critical tasks of assessment design, administration, scoring, and reporting, should necessarily lead to improvements in the assessment over time.

As with many things in life, implementing change has its up side and its down side. When changes are made in an assessment with the aim of improving it, establishing score comparability for different forms of the assessment can become a thorny challenge. Suppose that students take an assessment, and then substantial changes are made in the assessment specifications the following year. A different blueprint is used to construct a new form of the assessment. Can we assume that students' scores on the two forms will be comparable? Will the inferences we make about a student's performance (and the decisions we might make about the student based on those inferences) be the same, regardless of which form of the assessment the student took? Are the alternate forms of the assessment truly interchangeable? Just how much change can we make in an assessment before lack of comparability of forms becomes an issue?

The *Standards for Educational and Psychological Testing*, a joint publication of the American Educational Research Association, the American Psychological Association, and the National Council on Measurement in Education (1999), provide a set of criteria for evaluating assessments, assessment practices, and the effects of assessment use. Several standards speak to the issue of establishing the comparability of assessments that evolve over time, acknowledging the difficulties encountered when the assessments "measure different constructs, ... differ materially in reliability, time limits, or other conditions of administration, or ... are designed to different specifications" (pp. 51–52).[1] Clearly, balancing the need for maintaining the comparability of assessment forms with the need to change an assessment to improve its measurement capabilities can be a tense struggle.

In this paper, we focus on two large-scale art assessments that have evolved over time and have borne witness to that struggle: the National Assessment of Educational Progress (NAEP) visual arts assessment and the Advanced Placement (AP) Studio Art portfolio assessment. Both have been in existence for over 25 years and have undergone significant changes while, at the same time, maintaining their integrity as psychometrically sound assessment programs. As we shall see, the two programs present an intriguing story of contrasts. They have different goals, and the assessment information they provide is used for very different purposes. Each has weathered its own set of "growing pains" over the years, and both have wrestled with concerns over the necessity of maintaining score comparability across different forms of the assessment.

In the next section of the paper, we describe what each assessment looks like, explain how each assessment has evolved since its inception, and discuss research and evaluation studies that have made use of these assessments. We then compare and contrast how each of the assessments has dealt with the issue of comparability. Finally, we close the paper with a discussion of the implications of these large-scale assessments for future assessments.

THE NATIONAL ASSESSMENT OF EDUCATIONAL PROGRESS VISUAL ARTS ASSESSMENTS

What Does the Assessment Presently Look Like?

The National Assessment of Educational Progress (NAEP) is an ongoing assessment of what America's students know and can do in a number of different subject areas. Assessments have been carried out since 1969 to provide information about students' knowledge and skills at ages 9, 13, and 17 (and in more recent years, for students in grades 4, 8, and 12). Policymakers, educators, and the general public use the assessment information to gauge the condition and progress of education at the state and national level. NAEP reports levels of student achievement and student- and school-reported background variables that are associated with those levels of achievement. For individual students, the NAEP assessment is a low-stakes assessment, because no individual scores are given. The major function of the assessment is to provide valid and reliable information about the knowledge, skills, and abilities of the nation's students—not to report on the performance of individual students, schools, or districts.

Design of the Assessment. The design of the NAEP 1997 visual arts assessment was guided by an arts education assessment framework that laid out the general parameters of the assessment, and by an assessment and exercise specifications document that provided the detailed information needed for devising the assessment instruments (National Assessment Governing Board, 1994a, 1994b). Additionally, at the time that the assessment framework was being developed, the Consortium of National Arts Education Associations (1994) was beginning its work to define national standards for education in the arts, specifying what

---

[1] Several standards are included that address the issue of establishing score comparability for alternate forms of an assessment (Standards 4.10 and 13.8). Other standards address comparability concerns that arise when the administration of an assessment has been modified to provide accommodations for individuals with disabilities (Standards 10.1, 10.4, 10.5, 10.7, and 10.11) or to provide linguistic modifications in an assessment adapted in a secondary language (Standards 9.5, 9.6, 9.7, and 9.9)

students should know and be able to do in dance, music, theater, and visual arts. The leadership of the two projects worked collaboratively toward establishing a common vision of the goals of arts education. The members of the visual arts group of the NAEP Planning Committee took the national achievement standards in the visual arts that had been developed by the Consortium project, identified those that were appropriate for a large-scale assessment, and then adapted those achievement standards so that they could be included in the content outlines that would be used to guide the development of the NAEP art assessment.

Structure of the Assessment.   The NAEP 1997 visual arts assessment consisted of a series of seven "blocks," or sets of multiple related exercises that were administered separately, each block to be completed within a particular time frame. A block included one or more stimuli and sets of multiple-choice exercises, short or extended constructed-response exercises, and/or creating exercises. The assessment was composed of three Creating blocks and four Responding blocks. All students who participated in the visual arts assessment took either one Responding block and one Creating block, or two Responding blocks.[2] (The NAEP assessments employ a matrix sampling approach to test design, which does not require that all students take the exact same form of the assessment. Rather, exercises are spiraled across forms so that more of the content domain can be covered in a single assessment.)

Administration of the Assessment.   The visual arts assessment was administered to a nationally representative random sample of public and nonpublic students in grade 8 ($N = 2,999$ students from 128 schools).[3] As part of the assessment, students and school administrators completed questionnaires to provide demographic and background information that would be used when reporting assessment results.

How Has the Assessment Evolved Since Its Inception? What Are the Major Changes It Has Undergone?

The 1997 assessment was the third NAEP assessment in the visual arts to be carried out. Earlier assessments were conducted in 1975 and in 1978. As the assessment has evolved over the years, there have been significant changes in its design, administration, scoring, and reporting.

Differences in Design.   The overarching design frameworks that have guided the development of the assessments have radically changed over the years. The assessment frameworks used in the 1970s defined the content domain of visual arts education in terms of a series of behavioral objectives (as was also the case in other disciplines that NAEP assessed during that time period). By contrast, in the more recent framework, the visual arts assessment was defined in terms of a design matrix that delineated the processes and content of arts education and a series of detailed content outlines that were based on that matrix.

Wilson (1970, 1971) explained the process of laying out the content domain for the 1975 NAEP visual arts assessment. A set of 5 fairly broad objectives that art educators agreed reflected major outcomes of art education were devised, and a set of specific behaviors supporting each of the broad objectives were prepared. There were 153 major and subobjectives that together defined the content domain for the assessment (Wilson, 1975) and provided the

---

[2]Even though some students took two Responding blocks in the visual arts assessment, all but one of the Responding blocks included some Creating exercises.

[3]The visual arts assessment was originally designed to be administered at grades 4, 8, and 12. However, due to budgetary constraints, the assessment could only be administered to one grade level.

TABLE 28.1
The "Produce Works of Art" Portion of the Content Outline for the 1974 NAEP
Visual Arts Assessment

III. Produce Works of Art

A. **Produce original and imaginative works of art.**

All Ages

1. Produce an imaginative work of art, such as an animal or other object that looks like no other object has looked before.
2. Given various forms or objects, invent new forms.

B. **Express visual ideas fluently.**

All Ages

1. Be fluent in generating ideas for works of art.
2. Be fluent in producing visual ideas.
3. Be fluent in the use of media.
4. Be fluent in composing visually.

C. **Produce works of art with a particular composition, subject matter, expressive character, or expressive content.**

Age 9

1. Produce a work of art that fulfills the intrinsic demands of a space or shape.
2. Produce a work of art containing specified subject matter.
3. Produce a work of art with a particular mood, feeling, or expressive character.

Age 13 (in addition to Age 9)

1. Produce a work of art with a particular mood, feeling, or expressive character.
   a. Produce a work that fits the mood of a poem or piece of music.
   b. Produce a work that shows a mood such as calmness, excitement, gaiety, or sadness.
   c. Produce a work (landscape, city, or town) that has a particular feeling such as coolness, loneliness, warmness, wetness, or spookiness.
2. Produce a work of art with meaning based on the use of established symbols.
3. Produce a work of art with meaning based on the use of new symbols.
4. Design a poster that advertises an event, product, etc.
5. Produce a work that has a particular type of order or variety.
6. Modify the form of an object to improve its aesthetic quality or functional character.

Age 17, A (In addition to Age 13)

Produce a work of art that has a particular composition such as vertical, horizontal, diagonal, concentric, symmetrical, and asymmetrical; that uses deep or shallow space; or that has an open or closed composition.

D. **Produce works of art that contain various visual conceptions.**

Age 9

1. Demonstrate the ability to represent spatial conceptions (one person standing in front of another, something close and something far, a street and a building, etc.).
2. Demonstrate the ability to represent accurately (depict the essential attitude and position of a model and indicate such things as clothing patterns).
3. Produce an accurate reportage drawing.
4. Produce works in which the subject matter aspects indicate expressions and emotions (running, walking, falling, laughing, crying, anger, fright, happiness, etc.).

Ages 13, 17, A (in addition to Age 9)

Demonstrate the ability to represent an object from different viewpoints and under different light conditions.

E. **Demonstrate knowledge and application of media, tools, techniques, and forming processes.**

Age 9 (None)

Ages 13, 17, A

1. Perform processes such as coiling a pot, cutting and printing a linoleum block, mixing specific colors, etc.
2. Select the appropriate tools to accomplish certain tasks such as printmaking, clay modeling, etc.

Note: This portion of the content outline was extracted from the full set of objectives found in chapter 3 of the 1971 National Assessment of Educational Progress publication, *Art Objectives*, edited by Eleanor L. Norris and Barbara Goodwin.

basis for exercise development. The 5 major objectives for the 1975 visual arts assessment were: (1) perceive and respond to aspects of art, (2) value art as an important realm of human experience,[4] (3) produce works of art, (4) know about art, and (5) make and justify judgments about the aesthetic merit and quality of works of art. Table 28.1 shows the content outline that was developed for the third major objective, "produce works of art" for the 1975 NAEP visual arts assessments for ages 9, 13, and 17.

The process used to delineate the content domain for the 1978 NAEP visual arts assessment was very similar (National Assessment of Educational Progress, 1981b). A sample of arts educators reviewed the objectives that had been prepared for the 1975 assessment to determine their appropriateness for the 1978 assessment. None of the objectives were changed, but changes were made in the recommended amount of assessment time to be allotted to certain objectives.

The assessment framework developed for the 1997 NAEP art assessment depicted visual arts education in terms of a design matrix of processes and content. Along the vertical axis of the matrix are two central processes that exemplary teaching in the visual arts seeks to foster: (1) *creating* works of art, defined as "expressing ideas and feelings in the form of an original work of art"; and (2) *responding* to existing works of art, defined as "observing, describing, analyzing, and evaluating works of art" (Persky, Sandene, & Askew, 1998, p. i). Along the horizontal axis of the matrix are two components of learning (*knowledge* and *skills*) that comprise the content of visual arts. Students studying in the visual arts work toward attaining "knowledge and understanding about the arts, including the personal, social, cultural, and historical contexts for works"; as well as "perceptual, technical, expressive, and intellectual/reflective skills" (National Assessment Governing Board, 1994a, p. 8). The matrix is shown in Figure 28.1.

The purpose of the 1997 assessment, then, was to measure students' knowledge and skills in creating and responding to works of art. The NAEP Visual Arts Planning Committee developed a series of content outlines to guide the design of exercises for the assessment, using the design matrix as the scaffolding for preparing their outlines. Table 28.2 shows the grade 8 visual arts content outline for the "creating" portion of the content domain.

A comparison of Tables 28.1 and 28.2 makes readily evident key differences in the two approaches to defining the production portion of the visual arts content domain. Clearly, the two committees charged with designing these assessments had differing conceptions of how this particular portion of the content domain should be defined. Although there is some obvious overlap in the two content outlines, there are important aspects unique to each. Similar conceptual differences are also evident when one compares the 1975 and 1997 content outlines that lay out the "responding" portion of the visual arts content domain. (For the interested reader, the assessment framework can be downloaded at the following Web site: http://www.nagb.org/pubs/artsed.pdf.)

The Nature of Innovation in Assessment Design Changes Over Time. All three NAEP arts assessments could be characterized as breaking ground for their time, pushing the envelope of assessment methodology in new directions, because there were few models for large-scale arts assessment upon which to draw when the NAEP assessments were developed. The arts assessments administered in the 1970s were certainly on the cutting edge of assessment design:

---

[4] A unique aspect of the assessments conducted in the 1970s was their inclusion of a number of exercises (i.e., about 20% of the assessment) to evaluate students' attitudes toward art to cover this second art objective. Some critics of these assessments (Gardner & Grunbaum, 1986) have voiced concern about allocating valuable assessment time to ask questions about students' attitudes toward art. The 1997 visual arts assessment did not tap attitudes, only knowledge and skills. Attitudes were not considered to be part of the content domain to be assessed.

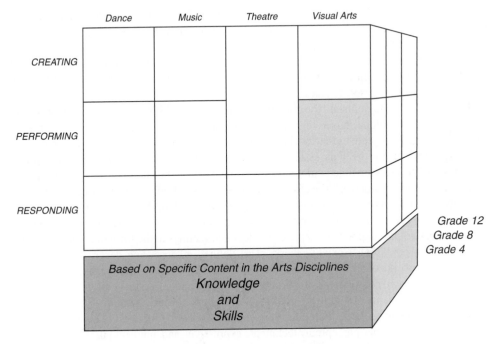

FIG. 28.1.   The framework matrix.

The item writers of both the art and music assessments were told to be innovative in developing test procedures and to ignore constraints of cost, time, administration, and scoring. Most important, they were not asked to restrict tasks to those that could be tested in multiple-choice formats scorable by machine. Although many innovative testing procedures were developed, most were set aside before the art and music assessments were undertaken because they were considered too difficult to administer and too expensive and time-consuming to analyze. Nonetheless, the National Assessment did result in an examination that went beyond a machine-scored format. (National Endowment for the Arts, 1988, p. 93)

Although all three assessments have included a blend of multiple-choice, constructed-response, and production exercises, the relative numbers of each exercise type (and amount of assessment time allocated to each) have changed over time. The authors of the *Design and Drawing Skills* report from the first NAEP art assessment (National Assessment of Educational Progress, 1978d) acknowledged an important design challenge faced by those who want to include art production exercises in large-scale assessments: obtaining adequate content coverage. Assessment time is quite limited, and the content domain of possible art production exercises is large. Given that such exercises are time consuming to administer and score, does it make sense to include any in large-scale assessments? The assessment developers struggled with this dilemma:

In developing the art objectives, National Assessment was aware of the fact that resources would not permit a comprehensive survey of student abilities to produce art. Nevertheless, NAEP considered it important to acknowledge as full a range of production goals as possible in the objectives. Hopefully, some of the goals that have not been measured will be measured in future assessments. Their exclusion from the first assessment does not suggest that they cannot be assessed. (p. 4)

The design strategies adopted for the 1975 and 1978 assessments placed a premium on assessing breadth of coverage within the content domain. To help accomplish that goal, the

TABLE 28.2
The "Creating" Portion of the Grade 8 Visual Arts Content Outline for the 1997 NAEP
Visual Arts Assessment

Visual Arts, Grade 8

I. Creating

A. Generate subjects, themes, problems, and ideas for works of art and design in ways that reflect knowledge and understanding of values (personal, social, cultural, historical), aesthetics, and context.

1. Speculate and discriminate among various ideas, making the most appropriate choices for specific artistic or design purposes.
2. Interpret and speculate on the ways that others have used subject matter, symbols, and ideas in visual, spatial, or temporal expressions, and how these are used to produce meaning or function that is appropriate in their own works.
3. Analyze the characteristics of art and design works of various eras and cultures to discover possible expressions or solutions to problems.
4. Speculate on how factors of time and place (such as climate, resources, ideas, and technology) influence the visual, spatial, or temporal characteristics that give meaning or function to a work of art or design.

B. Invent and use ways of generating visual, spatial, and temporal concepts in planning works of art and design.

1. Demonstrate the development of ideas across time.
2. Analyze and consider form, media, techniques, and process, and analyze what makes them effective or ineffective in communicating specific ideas.
3. Demonstrate knowledge of how sensory qualities, expressive features, and the functions of the visual arts evoke intended responses and uses for works of art and design.
4. Speculate about the effects of visual structures (elements and principles of design) and reflect on their influence on students' ideas.
5. Evaluate and discriminate among various ideas, making the most effective choices for specific artistic purposes or design uses.

C. Select and use form, media, techniques, and processes to achieve goodness of fit with the intended meaning or function of works of art and design.

1. Experiment, select, and employ form, media, techniques, and processes and analyze what makes them effective or ineffective in communicating ideas.
2. Utilize knowledge of characteristics of materials and visual, spatial, and temporal structures to solve specific visual arts and design problems.
3. Interpret the way that others have used form, media, techniques, and processes and speculate how these produce meaning or function.

D. Experiment with ideas (sketches, models, etc.) before final execution as a method of evaluation.

1. Evaluate, discriminate, and articulate differences among various ideas and forms, making the most effective choices for specific artistic purposes or design uses.
2. Simulate and articulate new insights and changes in direction that result from representation or simulation of ideas.
3. Employ organizational structures and analyze what makes them effective or ineffective in the communication of ideas.

E. Create a product that reflects ongoing thoughts, actions, and new directions.

1. Use media, techniques, and processes and analyze what makes them effective or ineffective in communicating ideas.
2. Integrate visual, spatial, and temporal concepts with content to communicate intended meaning in their art works.
3. Use subjects, themes, and symbols that demonstrate knowledge of contexts, values, and aesthetics that communicate intended meaning in art works.
4. Evaluate ideas and artwork throughout the creating process, making the most effective choices for specific artistic purposes or design uses.

(Continued)

TABLE 28.2
(Continued)

Visual Arts, Grade 8

F. **Reflect upon and evaluate their own works of art and design (i.e., students judge the relationship between process and product; the redefinition of current ideas or problems; and the definition of new ideas, problems, and personal directions).**
  1. Evaluate final compositions for use of compositional and expressive features.
  2. Demonstrate knowledge of the various purposes and reasons for works of visual art and design based on people's experiences (cultural backgrounds, human needs, etc.).
  3. Propose how works in the visual arts and design affect the way people perceive their experiences.
  4. Compare and evaluate the characteristics of works in two or more art forms that share similar subject matter, historical period, or cultural context.
  5. Describe new insights that have emerged from process and products of art and design that are meaningful to daily life.

Note: This portion of the grade 8 visual arts content outline was extracted from the full content outline found in the 1994 National Assessment Governing Board's publication, *1997 Arts Education Assessment Framework.*

assessments made relatively heavy use of multiple-choice items (i.e., at least half the exercises in each assessment were multiple choice), but the assessments still managed to include at least some production exercises. (The 1975 art assessment incorporated eight design and drawing exercises to evaluate students' production skills and abilities, whereas the 1978 assessment included four production exercises.)[5]

By contrast, in the 1997 assessment, the assessment and exercise specifications called for less emphasis on breadth of coverage and more emphasis on tapping depth of knowledge and skills within the domain (National Assessment Governing Board, 1994b). Consequently, many fewer multiple-choice items were used, and many more constructed-response exercises and production exercises were included (i.e., 12 multiple-choice items, 24 constructed-response exercises, and 10 Creating exercises). In the 1997 assessment, students spent 70% of their time working on Creating exercises and the remaining 30% engaged in Responding exercises (Persky et al., 1998).

Unlike the developers of the earlier NAEP arts assessments, the developers of the 1997 assessment created exercise "blocks." All the exercises included in a block made use of the same stimulus material and were organized around a single theme, issue, or problem. The exercises were designed to assess both creating and responding processes, integrating the two processes within the same block. (In this volume, chap. 27, Persky describes how exercise blocks were developed, administered, and scored. She provides an illustrative example of an exercise block from the visual arts assessment and presents its design rationale.) The adoption of this "exercise block" design strategy greatly facilitated the probing of the depth of students' knowledge and skills within the content domain.

The 1997 visual arts assessment also extended the range of art production tasks beyond those included in the 1974 and 1978 assessments, resulting in a widening of the definition of the visual arts. The production tasks employed in the 1974 and 1978 assessments were

---

[5]As Gardner and Grunbaum (1986) noted in their critique of these two assessments, about three fourths of the items required written responses.

limited to those appropriate for the assessment of design and drawing skills (i.e., draw a design for a piece of jewelry, a series of sketches representing ideas for a work of art, four people seated at a table from a particular perspective, three people on a playground, a person running; design a bedroom wall, a package for a specified product). By contrast, the 1997 assessment included an assortment of both two- and three-dimensional production tasks (i.e., create a self-portrait, a collage, a design for a package to carry a fish on a bicycle, a design for a package to hold a sound, a chipboard and plasticine monument, a plasticine and wire kitchen sculpture, a plasticine sculpture showing the metamorphosis of a man to a fish). In effect, the 1997 assessment became a national testing ground for learning how to design, administer, score, and report on a much wider variety of production tasks than had previously been attempted in any other large-scale visual arts assessment.

Differences in Administration.   In both the 1975 and 1978 art assessments, national stratified random samples of 9-, 13- and 17-year olds in and out of school took part in the 1975 assessment ($N = 27,500$ for 1975, and $N = 32,000$ for 1978). For the 1975 assessment, each student spent about 130 min in assessment-related activities, completing on average about 110 exercises. The 1978 assessment was a combined assessment that included art, writing, and music. Each student participating in the assessment responded to exercises in two of the subject areas. The assessment time allocated to art was significantly reduced in the 1978 assessment; each student spent about 45 min responding to art exercises and another 45 min responding to exercises in the other subject area. A much smaller nationally representative random sample of students that included only grade 8 students participated in the 1997 art assessment ($N = 2,999$). Because the 1997 assessment incorporated many more open-ended exercises than the previous NAEP art assessments, it was more time consuming and expensive to administer. Parallel assessments in music and theater that contained many open-ended exercises were also administered as part of this assessment. Therefore, it became imperative that smaller samples for each of the arts disciplines be used (and that students be assessed at only one grade level) in order for the assessment to be administratively feasible and stay within budget.[6]

Differences in Scoring.   In all three NAEP art assessments, the preparation of scoring guides to evaluate students' responses to the open-ended exercises has been a daunting enterprise. In the early 1970s, few guidelines for writing open-ended exercises and devising scoring guides were available. In short, the technology of designing and conducting large-scale performance assessment in the arts was in its infancy. Though arts educators had developed methods for informally evaluating students' works of art, a process for designing scoring guides that could be reliably applied by multiple judges in a cost-effective manner in a large-scale assessment context had not yet been developed. As Wilson (1975) noted, several of the scoring guides that were used in the 1975 assessment to score students art works were nearly 200 pages in length, reflecting the inherent complexity of the judgment task. Training scorers to use the scoring guides reliably was a time-consuming and costly task. Keeping track of all the relevant details in the scoring guides required much skill and concentration on the part of the scorer. The scoring became a major challenge for the assessment. Due to budget cutbacks, only half of the

---

[6]Jo Ann Pottorff, a member of the National Assessment Governing Board, served as spokesperson for NAGB when the results from the 1997 NAEP Arts Assessment Report Card were released. In her remarks, she noted that the NAEP arts assessment was an expensive effort, costing about $10 million dollars over a five-year period to develop, administer, score, and report. That figure did not include the development of the assessment framework and the assessment and exercise specifications. Those costs ($1.2 million) were borne by the National Endowment for the Arts and the Getty Center for Education in the Arts.

exercises requiring human scoring that had been administered were actually scored (National Assessment of Educational Progress, 1978d). Furthermore, only four of the eight production exercises that had been administered were scored and reported. (The unscored exercises were held back to be re-administered in the 1978 assessment.)

The 1978 assessment was designed to include many fewer open-ended exercises than the 1975 assessment, resulting in fewer responses to be scored. (The only open-ended exercises included in 1978 were ones that had been previously administered as part of the 1975 assessment.) Scoring guides used to evaluate examinees' responses to the six open-ended exercises administered in 1978 ranged from 15 pages in length for the two short constructed-response exercises that required written responses, to over 100 pages for each for the four production exercises that involved the evaluation of students' original works of art (National Assessment of Educational Progress, 1981b). High scoring costs again plagued the assessment, and students' responses to the six open-ended exercises could not be scored until 1980 when additional funding became available.

In the following 20 years, NAEP assessment staff gained considerable knowledge and experience in constructing and scoring complex performance assessments in disciplines outside the arts. NAEP assessment frameworks for these disciplines increasingly began to call for the inclusion of more open-ended exercises and fewer multiple-choice items in the assessments. Consequently, the development of a technology for designing, administering, and scoring large-scale performance assessments became a high priority for NAEP (and for statewide assessments as well). During this time period, NAEP assessment staff developed approaches to devising scoring guides that could be implemented in a cost-effective manner without sacrificing reliability or validity. The 1997 NAEP arts assessment directly benefited from these technological advances. (In this volume, chap. 27, see Persky for examples of scoring guides that were employed in the 1997 visual arts assessment.) Though there were many more open-ended exercises included in the 1997 art assessment than in the earlier art assessments, many fewer students took part in the 1997 assessment. Consequently, the scoring task was somewhat more manageable, because there were considerably fewer responses to score than in the previous two art assessments.

Differences in Reporting.   The initial reporting plan for the 1975 assessment called for the results to be reported by the five major objectives. However, just prior to the administration of the assessment, funding for the assessment was reduced, and the assessment plan had to be rather drastically scaled back. As a result, some of the major objectives had an insufficient number of exercises as measures of those objectives to justify reporting results by objectives (National Assessment of Educational Progress, 1978b). The remaining exercises comprising the assessment were categorized into three topics (i.e., knowledge about art, attitudes toward art, design and drawing skills). For both the 1975 and 1978 assessments, summary results were reported by topic rather than by major objective.

A unique aspect of the report on the 1978 assessment was the inclusion of value judgments that appeared alongside selected results. Several art consultants who had been hired by the National Assessment reviewed the findings of the assessment and provided commentary, interpreting various results for the art education community and discussing the implications of the findings for the field. For example, the report includes the following commentary by Brent Wilson regarding students' performance on drawing tasks included in the assessment:

> Wilson also felt that the drawing skills results were too low. "Elementary school curriculum guides often contain drawing units relating to the depiction of actions and expressions," he said. "But the assessment results for the 'draw an angry person' exercise show that students don't put much

action into their figures and that they do not draw expressively. These are not trivial things. One of the primary reasons young people draw is to produce visual symbolic models of themselves and their worlds so that they can anticipate and test future results. If children can't move the characters they create into action, if they can't show emotions, or if they can't draw expressively, then they are deprived of an extremely important way of developing and comprehending reality." (National Assessment of Educational Progress, 1981a, p. 15)

The National Assessment of Educational Progress published the results from the first visual arts assessment in five reports: *Design and Drawing Skills, Knowledge About Art, Attitudes Toward Art, Art Technical Report: Exercise Volume,* and *Art Technical Report: Summary Volume.* Results from the second visual arts assessment were published in three reports: *Art and Young Americans, 1974–79: Results From the Second National Art Assessment; The Second Assessment of Art, 1978–79, Released Exercise Set;* and *Procedural Handbook: 1978–79 Art Assessment.*

True to form, the 1997 NAEP arts assessment pushed the envelope of assessment reporting, just as it had pushed the envelope of assessment design, administration, and scoring. In the past, NAEP had produced report cards describing the results of the assessments conducted in the various disciplines. These reports were intended to be used to inform the decision making of policymakers, educators, and the general public.

When plans were being made for the 1997 arts assessment, a new approach was envisioned for reporting results and disseminating information about the assessment. Unlike previous NAEP arts assessments, that new approach was to involve heavy use of the internet as a dissemination tool. A NAEP arts assessment Web site was created (http://nces.ed.gov/nationsreportcard/arts/), and many of the assessment documents were posted there to make it easy for persons to access and download information about the design, administration, scoring, and reporting of the assessment.

The 1997 arts assessment report card had quite a different look and feel than did previous NAEP assessment reports in the arts (and in other disciplines, as well). For the first time, NAEP produced a full color report card (Persky et al., 1998) and an accompanying CD-ROM (National Center for Education Statistics, 1998b) to be used in conjunction with the report card. The CD-ROM included sample questions and student responses from the various exercise blocks, as well as some of the actual sights and sounds captured in the assessment. (The report card can be downloaded at the NAEP arts assessment Web site. The Web site also contains information for ordering a copy of the CD-ROM.) Additionally, the National Center for Education Statistics (1998a) published a full color brief report, "Arts Education: Highlights of the NAEP 1997 Arts Assessment Report Card," that provided a thumbnail sketch of the arts assessment and presented selected sample results in a brochure format intended to be accessible to a wide lay audience. (This document can also be downloaded from the Web site.) A series of short *Focus on NAEP* publications were prepared to provide brief nontechnical descriptions of the design of the arts assessment (Vanneman & Goodwin, 1998; Vanneman, Morton, & Allen, 1998; Vanneman, Shuler, & Sandene, 1998; White & Vanneman, 1998a, 1998b; White et al., 1998). Finally, a series of short *NAEP Facts* publications were prepared to present selected findings from the arts assessment (White & Vanneman, 1998a, 1998b, 1998c). (These reports can all be downloaded from the following Web site: http://nces.ed.gov/pubsearch/getpubcats.asp?sid=031#020.)

The approach taken to reporting results of the 1997 NAEP visual arts assessment was also quite revolutionary compared to the approach used in the 1970s. In 1997, results were presented in terms of the two key processes identified in the design matrix, Creating and Responding, rather than in terms of "topics" (as has been done in the 1970s). The results for Creating and Responding in the visual arts were presented separately. The report card included overall

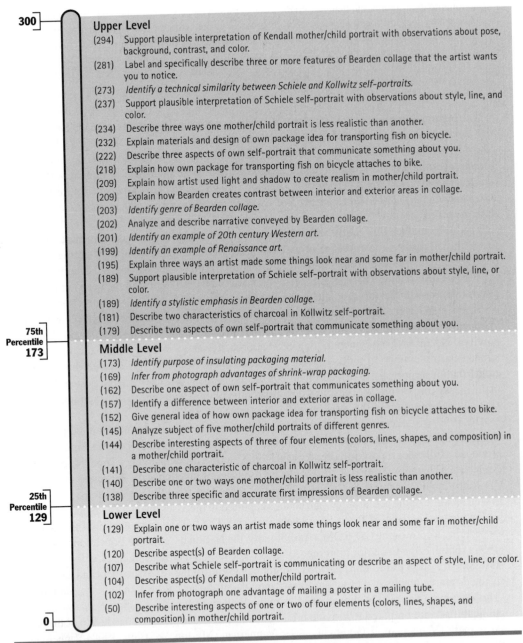

300

Upper Level

(294)   Support plausible interpretation of Kendall mother/child portrait with observations about pose, background, contrast, and color.

(281)   Label and specifically describe three or more features of Bearden collage that the artist wants you to notice.

(273)   *Identify a technical similarity between Schiele and Kollwitz self-portraits.*

(237)   Support plausible interpretation of Schiele self-portrait with observations about style, line, and color.

(234)   Describe three ways one mother/child portrait is less realistic than another.

(232)   Explain materials and design of own package idea for transporting fish on bicycle.

(222)   Describe three aspects of own self-portrait that communicate something about you.

(218)   Explain how own package for transporting fish on bicycle attaches to bike.

(209)   Explain how artist used light and shadow to create realism in mother/child portrait.

(209)   Explain how Bearden creates contrast between interior and exterior areas in collage.

(203)   *Identify genre of Bearden collage.*

(202)   Analyze and describe narrative conveyed by Bearden collage.

(201)   *Identify an example of 20th century Western art.*

(199)   *Identify an example of Renaissance art.*

(195)   Explain three ways an artist made some things look near and some far in mother/child portrait.

(189)   Support plausible interpretation of Schiele self-portrait with observations about style, line, or color.

(189)   *Identify a stylistic emphasis in Bearden collage.*

(181)   Describe two characteristics of charcoal in Kollwitz self-portrait.

(179)   Describe two aspects of own self-portrait that communicate something about you.

75th
Percentile
173

Middle Level

(173)   *Identify purpose of insulating packaging material.*

(169)   *Infer from photograph advantages of shrink-wrap packaging.*

(162)   Describe one aspect of own self-portrait that communicates something about you.

(157)   Identify a difference between interior and exterior areas in collage.

(152)   Give general idea of how own package idea for transporting fish on bicycle attaches to bike.

(145)   Analyze subject of five mother/child portraits of different genres.

(144)   Describe interesting aspects of three of four elements (colors, lines, shapes, and composition) in a mother/child portrait.

(141)   Describe one characteristic of charcoal in Kollwitz self-portrait.

(140)   Describe one or two ways one mother/child portrait is less realistic than another.

(138)   Describe three specific and accurate first impressions of Bearden collage.

25th
Percentile
129

Lower Level

(129)   Explain one or two ways an artist made some things look near and some far in mother/child portrait.

(120)   Describe aspect(s) of Bearden collage.

(107)   Describe what Schiele self-portrait is communicating or describe an aspect of style, line, or color.

(104)   Describe aspect(s) of Kendall mother/child portrait.

(102)   Infer from photograph one advantage of mailing a poster in a mailing tube.

(50)   Describe interesting aspects of one or two of four elements (colors, lines, shapes, and composition) in mother/child portrait.

0

NOTE: Italic type indicates a multiple-choice question. Regular type indicates a constructed-response question.
SOURCE: National Center for Education Statistics, National Assessment of Educational Progress (NAEP), 1997 Arts Assessment.

NAEP 1997 Arts Report Card

FIG. 28.2.   Map of selected questions on the NAEP visual arts responding scale: Grade 8.

summaries of Creating and Responding results and displayed the relationship of those results to student- and school-reported variables. Reporting results by artistic process was not in and of itself particularly revolutionary, however.

What was revolutionary was NAEP's exploration of the use of item response theory (IRT) to scale data from an art assessment. (Scaling methods had been routinely used in NAEP assessments in other disciplines for some time, but not in the arts assessments.) The 1997 visual arts assessment included a sufficient number of Responding exercises to make it possible to scale that portion of the assessment.[7] The Responding results were displayed on a 0 to 300 scale.

The "item map" that is produced when scaling is implemented is particularly useful as a means of visually representing what it means for students to be more (or less) proficient in terms of their performance on a set of exercises. The item map for the NAEP visual arts assessment orders the Responding exercises along a continuum, from those that were easier for students to perform well on (at the bottom of the map) to those that were harder for students to perform well on (at the top of the map). Figure 28.2 displays the item map. By reviewing the item map, one can readily identify the types of exercises that students at any given level along the scale had a high probability of having completed successfully, as well as those that they had a lower probability of having completed successfully.

Such reporting has potentially important instructional implications, because an art educator can review the item map and gain an understanding of how the Responding portion of the visual arts content domain is organized—In short, the art educator can see what it means to "get better" at Responding. If art educators would like to design instruction to help students become more proficient in responding to visual arts stimuli, the item map helps them determine what types of exercises to focus on in the initial phases of instruction (i.e., are the easiest for students to master). As students become more adept at responding, the item map helps art educators identify the types of exercises that could then be introduced that would likely be more challenging for students (i.e., those further up the scale that are more "difficult"). With this information in hand, art educators are in a far better position to be able to plan instruction that will foster deep learning of this critical aspect of the content domain. The inclusion of item maps in the NAEP Arts Assessment Report Card represents an important evolutionary step, because it moves us beyond our reliance on basic descriptive statistics for reporting results.

Have There Been Research/Evaluation Studies of This Assessment and Reports of Its Findings?

Following the publication of the reports from the two NAEP arts assessments administered in the 1970s, surprisingly only a few publications appeared that discussed the assessments. Chapman (1982), Wilson (1986), and Ward (1982) presented selected findings from the assessments and drew implications from those results for art education, whereas Gardner and Grunbaum (1986) critiqued the assessments and offered recommendations for future NAEP arts assessments. Several other publications included brief discussions of the assessments, their findings, and their implications for art teachers and administrators (National Endowment for the Arts, 1988; Wolf & Wolf, 1984; Zimmerman, 1984). However, despite all the time and effort spent in reporting on the assessments, the impact on the field was negligible. As Wilson (1986) lamented:

---

[7]Because the Creating exercises were much more involved and time consuming for students to complete, there were many few Creating exercises included in the assessment. Each student participating in the visual arts assessment took only one Creating exercise. Consequently, there were too few Creating exercises (and too few students taking a set of Creating exercises) for those exercises to be scaled. Rather, Creating results are reported in terms of average percent of the maximum possible score.

There has been virtually no response to the Assessment findings. In fact, within the field of art education, the results of the Art Assessment have been treated with indifference. The findings from the Art Assessment are unknown to most art teachers and supervisors. The findings have seldom been discussed in the art educational literature. (p. 7)

The first two NAEP arts assessments spawned few published research studies. One exception is Knight (1979), who analyzed data from the 1974 NAEP art assessment, looking for patterns in male–female performance on the assessment. She compared mean differences in performance between males and females on the NAEP art assessment to mean differences in performance between males and females on NAEP assessments in other content areas (i.e., music, literature, science, citizenship, social studies, and math). She found that patterns of male–female performance in art were different from those in the other content areas.

Following the release of the *1997 NAEP Arts Education Report Card*, several articles about the arts assessment appeared in a symposium issue of the electronic journal *Arts Education Policy Review*. The contributing authors (Eisner, 1999; Lehman, 1999; Stankiewicz, 1999) provided reactions to the assessment, commented on its strengths and weaknesses from their individual perspectives, and discussed implications of the assessment results for arts education. Creating and responding were appropriate domains for the visual arts assessment, Eisner noted; but the assessment report included little information about how the content of the items was chosen or how the performance expectations were determined. He pointed to the lack of information provided about the validity of the assessment, questioned whether the motivational tools used to engage students in the creating tasks were sufficient and whether the assessment may have depended too heavily on students' writing ability. Lehman applauded the "extraordinarily rich and diverse mix of artworks" that were included as stimuli and the important methodological contributions the assessment made "through its creative approaches to designing tasks and scoring rubrics for the assessment of skills in performing and creating" (p. 2). However, he questioned whether the framework specifications regarding the allocation of time to the different artistic processes were truly met and pointed to the lack of information on performance included in the Arts Report Card. Further, Lehman voiced concern over the small sample sizes and the consequent limitations that sampling imposed on the assessment's overall utility. Stankiewicz appreciated the comprehensiveness of the assessment framework and noted that the assessment provided art educators with "complex models of knowing and doing, and specific examples of performance assessments" (p. 4) that could be useful for designing state and local arts assessments. She too voiced concern about the use of small samples of only grade 8 students, which was not the intention of those who prepared the assessment framework. All three authors lamented the inability to directly compare students' results from the most recent assessment to the assessments conducted in the 1970s.

Beattie (1999) critiqued the 1997 NAEP visual arts assessment, examining the degree of correspondence between 15 specifications included in the assessment exercise and specifications document and the actual assessment that was designed from those specifications. She found that in a number of cases the specifications were only partially met (or, in some cases, not met at all).

Several researchers obtained a grant from the National Center for Education Statistics (NCES) to conduct secondary analyses of data from the 1997 NAEP visual arts assessment (Diket, Burton, McCollister, & Sabol, 2000; Diket, Sabol, & Burton, 2002). Diket (2001) sought to identify sets of variables that were related to variation in performance on the NAEP visual arts assessment. She conducted confirmatory factor analyses to evaluate a hypothesized structural model composed of sets of demographic variables, resources variables, and opportunity-to-learn variables. Sabol (2001) used multiple regression analysis to investigate the relationships between student and school variable sets and student performance on the NAEP visual arts assessment. The study's purpose was to determine whether there were variables that were associated with differences in regional performance on the Creating and Responding exercises. Burton (2001) employed quartile analysis to examine the performance of those students scoring in the highest and lowest quartiles on the NAEP visual arts assessment. His goal was to pinpoint variables that seemed to contribute most to differences in the performance of these two groups.

In all three NAEP arts assessments, the scoring of complex responses to constructed-response exercises has proven to be a challenge. The 1997 NAEP visual arts assessment has stimulated interest in research on scoring guides. Researchers have investigated varied approaches to evaluating student performance on Creating exercises included as part of the NAEP visual arts assessment. During the NAEP visual arts field test, raters experimented with descriptive graphic rating scales for evaluating students' performance on four of the production exercise blocks (Myford, 2002). Descriptive graphic rating scales are continuous score scales with two defined endpoints. A line connects these points, and descriptive phrases identify different points along the continuum. When a rater uses the scale, the rater makes a slash along the line to indicate where along the continuum the work lies. Descriptive graphic rating scales can incorporate different design features (i.e., presence or absence of a defined midpoint, presence or absence of hatchmarks along the line that connects the endpoints). Myford varied the design features of the descriptive graphic rating scales to learn about how raters used those features and to determine which features, if any, affected reliability. Siegesmund, Diket and McCulloch (2001) worked with middle school teachers to adapt the Collage exercise block for use as a classroom assessment tool. In the NAEP assessment, students' responses to the exercises included in this block were evaluated using a series of holistic scoring guides. The teachers worked with a consultant to devise a series of five analytic scoring guides to use instead. Their goal was to develop a scoring process that would enable them to derive information from the scoring of students' responses that would be more instructionally relevant than the limited information available from holistic scores.

THE ADVANCED PLACEMENT STUDIO ART PORTFOLIO ASSESSMENT

What Does the Assessment Presently Look Like?

The Advanced Placement Studio Art courses are three of the 34 subjects offered by the Advanced Placement (AP) program of the College Board. Like all AP subjects, the overriding mission is to document achievement in its field by high school students. Each AP course is intended to serve as an analog for the corresponding first-year or introductory college course. The annual assessments measure the degree to which students have met that challenge. In all subjects except studio art, students take exams that combine multiple-choice questions with substantial essay sections. The essays are scored by teachers of the relevant discipline in centralized, carefully monitored scoring sessions. AP grades in all subjects are reported on a scale of 1 to 5.[8] The AP Studio Art program is unique: It is not a written test, but rather a portfolio assessment. As radical as this may seem in the context of standardized testing, it is obviously not so in the world of art or art education; rather, its design makes it an unusually valid or "authentic" assessment. Students submit portfolios each May; the corresponding body of work is usually the product of at least a year's effort.

---

[8]The AP program provides the following description of the grades to both students and colleges: 5—Extremely Well Qualified, 4—Well Qualified, 3—Qualified, 2—Possibly Qualified, 1—No Recommendation. Some colleges will grant credit or advanced placement to students having grades of 3 or higher. Other colleges require grades as high as 4 or, in some cases, 5.

Currently, students interested in AP Studio Art may choose among three portfolios: Drawing, 2-D Design, and 3-D Design. Each consists of three sections, which are consistent across the portfolios. Section I, Quality, asks the students to submit five works that they feel best represent their accomplishment. In the cases of Drawing and 2-D Design, actual work is submitted; its only stipulation is that it must fit into the 18 in. × 24 in. portfolio that is sent to the schools for the exam. Students in 3-D Design do not submit any actual work; instead, they send slides (two views) of each of their five strongest works. Section II, Concentration, asks the students to submit 12 slides that document the investigation of a visual idea or problem of particular interest to the student, as well as a short written commentary. For Section III, Breadth, 12 slides in Drawing and 2-D Design, or 16 slides for 3-D Design (two views of each of eight works) are submitted to demonstrate a wide range of experiences germane to the particular portfolio.

Portfolios are most commonly submitted by high school seniors, although many juniors and even some sophomores also participate. The work in the portfolio, in many cases, has been developed over a longer period of time than 1 school year. Although many students are enrolled in classes specified as AP Studio Art classes, others work alongside somewhat less advanced or less motivated peers, and still others prepare portfolios outside of their high schools. Work may come from out-of-school as well as from in-school experiences. Thus, students are free to pursue this work in art from a wide range of vantage points; a small number, for example, prepare portfolios by working out informal mentor/apprentice arrangements with artists who are not teachers in the students' high schools.

The requirements for each section are intentionally broad and flexible; each portfolio should ideally serve as an equivalent to the college-level course that it parallels, but few, if any, assumptions are made about how a particular teacher in a particular school with a particular group of students will best achieve that goal. It is perhaps worth noting that the program strives to avoid the uneasy sense that teachers may be "teaching to the test" in the sense of providing students with what approaches canned assignments that seem to produce high scores. Although it is impossible to eliminate that as a possibility, "teaching to the test" in this case should result in students working with commitment and passion at visual issues that stretch their knowledge, strengthen their conceptual abilities, and, of course, help them to develop the framework of technical skills that are necessary to realize their ideas. At its best, the open-ended nature of the assessment serves these goals effectively.

Each year the College Board makes available a document called the *Advanced Placement Program Course Description: Studio Art*. In this document, the requirements for the portfolio are delineated. All of the requirements for the portfolios are determined by the AP Studio Art Development Committee, a group of college-level and AP teachers who meet regularly and who are also involved in the annual evaluation of the portfolios. The Committee does not believe that a single AP Studio Art course can or should exist but rather encourages art educators to exercise their creativity in designing courses that will enable students to produce portfolios meeting the stated guidelines. As Askin (1985) noted, the AP Studio Art course "does not consist of a fixed body of ideas, but is affected by ongoing reevaluations of both current and past art" (p. 7). Likewise, there is no one approved course outline and/or method of teaching. Teachers have a great deal of flexibility to create AP courses in studio art that will prepare their students for the portfolio assessment.

The College Board also publishes a full-color poster each year that students and teachers receive. The poster features exemplary artworks from portfolios submitted to the AP Studio Art program in the previous year and provides a condensed version of the portfolio requirements. The three sections of the portfolio are defined, and guidelines are included for submitting works appropriate for each section.

The evaluation of the portfolios is inextricable from the curricular requirements. Because of AP's history as a premier program rooted in holistic scoring, the Studio Art program was able to draw on the knowledge base of sample-picking, standard-setting (training evaluators), and evaluation procedures in general. In general AP terminology, those who evaluate the portfolios are known as Readers; they work under the Chief Reader and his or her assistants, Exam Leaders and Table Leaders, during the evaluation process, known as the Reading. Everyone who scores portfolios in any capacity is either an AP Studio Art teacher with at least 3 years of experience or a college faculty member who teaches comparable first-year classes. Each section of the portfolios is scored using a 6-point scale. Section I (Quality; usually actual work) is scored by three Readers working independently of one another; Sections II (Concentration) and III (Breadth) are each scored by two Readers.

Before the Reading actually begins, the Chief Reader, Exam Leaders, and Table Leaders spend at least 3 days choosing samples of each section of each portfolio to use as training samples for the Readers. Typically, these will include very clear samples (i.e., a solid example of each score point) to start off the training for each. As the training progresses, the sample sets become more complex; they may include borderline examples, bodies of work in which the achievement demonstrated varies widely (e.g., for a Quality section, two strong pieces, two middle-level pieces, and another that is weak), an array of work from several students that varies in achievement but is all unusually strong, another array focusing specifically on photography and digital art, and so on. Working in small groups, the Readers "grade" the samples and then engage in intensive discussions with their peers and the leaders. Not until the Chief Reader is convinced that all Readers understand and can apply the scoring guides does any actual scoring take place.

Once the Reading starts, quality control procedures are an inherent part of the process. If there is a discrepancy of 3 or more points between two scores given to the same section, the portfolio section is immediately pulled and forwarded to a team of Table Leaders for resolution. In the event that an individual Reader—or the whole group—appears to be drifting away from the standards, the individual may be engaged in conversation about samples; or in more unusual cases, the Chief Reader may stop the reading for supplemental training. With these procedures and the relatively large number of independent judgments, the score reliability of each portfolio as a whole is typically about .90. The current scoring guides for the portfolios can be found on the AP Web site, AP Central, at http://apcentral. collegeboard.com/repository/sg_studio_art_02_11395.pdf. Additional information on standard-setting and the portfolio evaluation process in AP Studio Art can be found in Askin (1985), Mitchell and Stempel (1991), Myford and Mislevy (1995), and Ott (1994).

Relative success on an AP exam is intended to carry with it the reward of placement out of the corresponding course, or credit towards a major, or simply toward graduation. Thus, the exams do not really fit the idea of "high-stakes" testing. On the other hand, despite the College Board's repeated statements that AP is not an admissions testing program, de facto policies at many institutions of higher education—particularly the most competitive ones—have informally made participation in and successful completion of AP courses highly desirable. Actual policies about how the AP grades are used vary tremendously across colleges and universities.

How Has the Assessment Evolved Since Its Inception?
What Are the Major Changes It Has Undergone?

In contrast to the NAEP visual arts assessment, AP Studio Art has a continuous history, with many modifications taking place over the last 30 years. When it began in 1972, AP Studio Art consisted of a single portfolio. Beginning with the 1979 to 1980 school year, at the behest of the Development Committee, the studio art portfolio was split into two exams, the General portfolio and the more focused Drawing portfolio. The General portfolio, which remained closer to the original design, was seen as being more tightly related to the way art is typically taught in most high schools; it was very open with respect to media, and it required a modest amount of three-dimensional work (which was persistently the section with the lowest average scores). The Drawing portfolio was conceived as more closely analogous to a basic college drawing course. Despite expectations that it would grow rapidly in volume, the Drawing portfolio remained at roughly one third of total submissions from 1980 through 2001. The two-portfolio format provided the basic outline of the AP Studio Art program throughout this period.

Sources of Change.   Over the course of the last 22 years, revisions ranging from slight to major have been made in the portfolios. The impetus for such changes may include a combination of factors such as:

- Data from statistical analyses of the portfolio scores that are produced annually
- Data from special studies conducted irregularly, such as college comparability studies
- Annual reports from the Chief Reader, which incorporate the group wisdom of all those who have evaluated the portfolios
- Pedagogical expertise of the members of the AP Studio Art Development Committee.

The role of research in AP Studio Art has largely taken the guise of these ongoing program analyses, supplemented by occasional special studies. From the beginning, ETS statisticians have produced annual analyses that track, among other statistics, the reliability of the evaluation of each section as well as of each portfolio as a whole, the correlations among the various sections, frequency distributions of scores, mean scores for every section of every portfolio, and historical distributions of the final AP grades. The analyses are produced annually, typically before meetings of the AP Studio Art Development Committee, which always reviews them. The Committee also has input into any special studies and, of course, reviews the results, which in many cases influence their subsequent decisions. This group, like all such AP committees, consists of college and university faculty members who teach the equivalent first-year courses, and experienced AP teachers. The Chief Reader, whose annual report is another mainstay of the program, attends and participates in the meetings, as do relevant ETS staff. It is the Development Committee, with the participation of the Chief Reader, which sets—and revises—the specifications for the portfolios.

Example 1: Statistical Information and Professional Expertise Intersect to Illuminate a Structural Problem.   In 1983, the Breadth section (then known as Section C) of the General portfolio consisted of several subparts that had existed since the inception of AP Studio Art. C1 (sometimes referred to as CI) consisted of 12 slides of drawings and was rated on a 9-point scale; C2 (similarly referred to by some as CII) had six different specifications, each of which was graded on a scale of 0 to 2. Each Reader summed his or her six individual scores for the parts of C2. Reliability and correlations of scores were calculated on the basis of each Reader's total score for C2, which logically ranged from 0 to 12. The six specified areas of C2 were defined as Technique, Color, Design, Spatial, Content, and Three-Dimensional. Students were required to submit at least one work in which each category was demonstrated, with a total of 14 slides among the six areas. The May 1980 *Advanced Placement Course Description: Art* (pp. 9–11) described them, in part, as follows:

Technique: a work in which the main thrust is a sensitive and personal use of specific materials and techniques.

Color: a work in which color is the major component and which clearly demonstrates the principle of visual operation of the color methodology used.

Design:	a work in which classic design components (elements and principles) are the major concept being presented.
Spatial:	a work emphasizing one or more approaches to creating the illusion of space or working with aspects of three-dimensional space.
Content:	a work in which the major consideration is his or her subjective or intuitive reaction to a specific subject or set of circumstances such as a reinterpretation of nature, an observed situation, or a personal experience.
Three-dimensional:	a work utilizing the partial and/or full potential of three dimensions through traditional, found or created, materials

Students received a poster that detailed the portfolio requirements and provided instructions for preparing their portfolios for evaluation. The instructions included on the portfolio reminded students that, "Although it is possible that a single work might have qualities that make it eligible for more than one of the categories, you may NOT submit the same work in more than one category of Part II."

In his report on the 1980 Reading, the Chief Reader, William A. Lewis (1980), commented on difficulties encountered in scoring Section CII of the portfolio:

> Section CII of the General Art portfolio is more complex [than CI], in the past it has been the source of difficulty for students and readers alike, and in the current reading still presents some unsatisfactory aspects. CII consists of six characteristics of art, all common to many forms of work, and generally regarded as important fundamental elements. These six categories are scored on a 00 to 02 scale, indicating the quality is not present by a 00 score, it is present in minimal, perhaps chance, fashion, or it is demonstrated deliberately, with intelligence and some distinction. (p. 3)

Lewis (1980) went on to summarize the idea behind each of the six categories and registered some of his concerns with those categories:

> For example, the terms Design and Color should elicit responses stating common principles learned in class. Too seldom was there evidence of such instruction. The term 3-Dimensional describes specific 3D objects which the slides should show, such as sculpture. This category was sometimes represented by slides of paintings, flat designs, other items of a 2-dimensional nature.... The term Content... continues to be ill understood by many students. When the idea of concept is understood, the works are frequently glorious to behold, presenting thought or concept far in excess of what a young person is usually deemed capable. (p. 4)

Perhaps not surprisingly, Lewis's concerns were reflected in statistical analysis of the portfolio evaluation. An internal ETS memo (Hecht & Bleistein, personal communication, February 8, 1980) reported that, "For the past two years, Section C-2 of the Studio Art examination has had a lower rating reliability than the other three sections of the evaluation" (p. 1). The memo then delineated the results of a study undertaken "to investigate possible explanations for the apparently lower rating reliability" (p. 1). In addition to noting a small percentage of addition errors by the readers, the study examined the rating reliability of each category, as well as the percentage of zero scores assigned by both readers for each category.

The discussion noted initially that the Three-dimensional category had the highest reliability of the categories; but it pointed out that 11% of the candidates in the study received two scores of zero in this category, and that "There is a near-perfect positive relationship, for the six criteria, between the reliability of the rating and the number of zero scores assigned" (p. 3). Almost certainly, many of the students who received zero scores for the Three-dimensional category were among those who Lewis pointed out misunderstood the category and actually submitted two-dimensional work. In the cases of Technique and Design, probably the most accessible to teachers and students and the most certain in their demonstration, the opposite case applied: Almost no students received zero scores, so that the rating scale was again compressed to two effective points, 01 and 02.

At the time of the 1980 study, the Development Committee met less frequently than once a year; because decisions involving the specifications for the portfolios reside with that group, consideration of the study and consequent action were relatively slow. In his report of the following year, Lewis (1981) noted that, "Though the Course Description has been rewritten for clarity's sake [an interim measure to try to improve the situation] and description of representative examples included, there remains more evidence of misunderstanding of the section than any other" (p. 3). In the fall of 1983, the Development Committee for AP Studio Art was convened. The results of the Hecht and Bleistein study were presented. Walter Askin, the Chief Reader who had succeeded Lewis, had continued to press the Readers' related concerns. In his report, Askin (1983) made the following points:

> ... sections CI and CII of the general portfolio should be combined for a more accurate and efficient evaluation. A mode has been provided for discussion combining eight slides of drawings (half figure studies and half spatial drawing), four color studies (excluding atmospheric and monochromatic color schemes), four design slides emphasizing compositional or formal organization (pure design, brochures, poster, calligraphy, album cover, etc.), and four slides of sculpture or three dimensional works describing two aspects of two works.... This will eliminate the more problematic and less apt areas of "technique" and "content." It will also, hopefully, make possible the use of [a] four point grading scale for each segment. (p. 1)

In fact, the Development Committee adopted this proposal almost exactly as presented, and went further to adopt a 4-point scale, not only for this section but for all sections of both portfolios. The one exception to the proposal was the Committee's decision not to make any stipulations as to the nature of the eight drawings, beyond saying that they must show breadth of experience. Reactions to the change were uniformly positive from all constituents—teachers and students had a clearer outline to follow, readers were therefore able to rate the work more confidently, and statisticians documented the result: reading reliability that was, finally, in keeping with the reliabilities for the other sections of both portfolios. This arrangement stood for several years; at about the same time that readers were beginning to chafe at the difficulty of distinguishing between Color and Design, the 1992 analysis revealed an estimated true-score correlation of .97 between the ratings for those two categories—high enough to suggest strongly that the two were not measuring distinct areas of accomplishment. Because the Development Committee was by then meeting annually, the decision to create a combined set of eight slides called "Color/Design" was made and implemented quickly. That structure, which allowed students to submit the eight slides that they felt best reflected their accomplishments in the combined area, remained in place through June 2001, after which the General portfolio was retired.

In 1996, a change was made to a 6-point rating scale, primarily as an effort to distribute scores more effectively. Other changes were more pedagogical than psychometric, for example, increasing the size of the standard portfolio (and the work it could contain) from 16 in. × 20 in. to 18 in. × 24 in., and the gradually increased inclusion of photography and digital art into more sections of the General portfolio over time.

Example 2: The Program Evolves for a Better Fit With the Field.   In 1998, in accordance with AP policy, a curriculum survey of colleges, universities, and art schools was conducted (Sims-Gunzenhauser, 1999, unpublished). Typically, surveys of this sort focus almost exclusively on questions about the content of the higher education course that the AP course is intended to parallel—for example, an art history survey might ask what percentage of the course is focused on the art of various time periods and/or parts of the world. For AP Studio Art, the needs were more complicated. Anecdotal evidence for years had suggested that students with the highest scores on the AP Studio Art exam were less likely than their colleagues in other subject areas to be granted credit or advanced placement by the colleges they attended. The Development Committee decided that the survey should step back a level and inquire not only into the content of particular courses but also, more generally, into the composition of first-year or foundation programs at the responding schools. In addition, the survey included questions that essentially focused on the respondent institutions' values with respect to what first-year students should be learning and on the kinds of work in a portfolio that would be most likely to be granted credit or advanced placement. In other words, the survey was conceived as a way of determining the best fit between the AP program and the institutions that the AP candidates might well attend.

The survey was mailed to the 300 colleges, universities, and art schools to which the greatest number of AP Studio Art candidates had sent their AP grades. Faculty members from 81 institutions responded. Table 28.3 summarizes the responses to the question about the content and organization of the first-year or foundation program.

The evidence from this set of schools, as is obvious, demonstrated a preponderance of programs that include drawing, two-dimensional design, and three-dimensional design. When the data were sorted to separate out art schools, the proportion reporting this constellation of courses was similar. Indeed, the data from this question provided a clear answer to the question of what the overall structure of the AP Studio Art offerings should be. With the support of the College Board, the decision was made early in 1999 to retire the General portfolio and introduce two new portfolios: 2-D Design and 3-D Design. These two, along with a slightly restructured Drawing portfolio, became active in the 2001 to 2002 school year. (The delay was considered critical in order for schools and teachers to have sufficient time to prepare new courses or to reorganize their existing courses.)

In order to make slightly finer decisions regarding the content of the new portfolios, the Development Committee referred to the results of a survey question that asked how likely the institutions would be to grant credit or placement for portfolios that were focused on any of a variety of art media. In practice, it has actually been unusual for a student's portfolio

TABLE 28.3
Which of the Following Best Describes the Organization and Content of Your Institution's Foundation Program?

	One-Year Program	Two-Year Program
A sequence of two-dimensional and three-dimensional design	9	1
A sequence composed of drawing, two-dimensional design, and three-dimensional design	32	21
A sequence that includes four-dimensional design as well as drawing and two- and three-dimensional design	2	3
A sequence that is organized around conceptual themes rather than more traditional courses	2	0
A sequence that is differentiated according to students' interests	0	1
A single, comprehensive course	3	
Other	13	7

to consist of work in a single medium; even the Drawing portfolio has always been open with respect to media, and most students tended to include work in a range of media, if only because the Breadth section made this a requirement for the General portfolio and a strong suggestion for the Drawing portfolio. On the other hand, students whose primary interest was in three-dimensional art forms, photography, or digital art were considerably more constrained than their colleagues. In the case of students primarily interested in three-dimensional art, the requirement to submit only flat work for Quality obviously limited their ability to present the strongest case for their achievement; in addition, eight drawings were required in the Breadth Section. Photographers and digital artists were able to submit prints of their work for Quality and slides for the Concentration, but were required to submit nontechnological drawings, as well as some sculpture, in the Breadth section.

Responses to the survey question about media showed that the level of acceptance ranged from a high of 91% positive for drawing to 48% for digital art, to the low of 38% responding positively to the possibility of a portfolio in film, video, or animation. On the basis of these results, the Development Committee decided to remove the restrictions on photography and digital art. Within the bounds of the 2-D Design portfolio, students may submit as much of the portfolio as they like—up to and including an entire portfolio—in photography or digital art. Obviously, the institution of the 3-D Design portfolio (for which Quality is evaluated through slides) accommodates the students working in that area. In all of these cases, indeed for any student who chooses to work in a single medium, there is still the need to demonstrate breadth of experience in that section of the portfolio. The same set of survey data, though, also constitute the rationale for eliminating film and video from inclusion in any of the AP portfolios, although stills from a film or videotape may be submitted for 2-D Design.

Though the information presented in Table 28.3 confirmed the course outlines for the portfolios, the Development Committee was also interested in knowing whether and to what extent the pedagogical thrust of the portfolios and the primary values inherent in the evaluation process were shared by the responding institutions. Still another survey question focused on the underlying values of the responding institutions. Over the years, the Development Committee and Chief Reader had spent a great deal of time and thought teasing out what they considered important in student art work; the simplest example would be the tension between the group's desire to reward students who took risks successfully and the much easier task of discerning (and rewarding) a high level of technical skill in a student's work. In concert with this effort, the scoring guides for the portfolios had evolved to address more overtly the aspects of a body of work that underlay judgments about its level of accomplishment and to articulate those aspects at each score point without becoming restrictive. Thus, another purpose of the curriculum survey was to try to see whether and to what extent these broader values were shared by the responding institutions. Table 28.4 summarizes the results from a survey question focused on these issues.

In this case, the results were the cause of some satisfaction. Had the results been primarily negative for the various categories listed, they would have given rise to a reexamination of the basic conceptual underpinnings of the program. In fact, the first two items in the left-hand column of the table, "broad experience" and "in-depth exploration," describe, respectively, Section III, Breadth, and Section II, Concentration, of the portfolios. The bottom three items identify the three basic strands that are woven throughout all of the scoring guides for the portfolios, as well as the program publications for teachers and students. Thus, these survey data suggest that both the overall direction of the portfolio specifications and the portfolio evaluation place the portfolios squarely in the accepted constructs of the domain, to the extent that those constructs are represented by the responding institutions. The program is optimistic about the scope and design of these changes; in June 2002, approximately 19,000 students submitted portfolios for assessment, an increase of nearly 25% from 2001.

TABLE 28.4
If You Were Considering What Kinds of Student Work Would Persuade You to Grant Credit or
Advanced Placement to a Student, How Important Would It Be to You to See Evidence of:

	Very	Moderately	(% Positive)	Neutral	Unimportant	Detrimental	Total
Broad experience	28 (39%)	23 (45%)	(84%)	13 (18%)	4 (6%)	3 (4%)	71
In-depth exploration	25 (35%)	30 (42%)	(77%)	8 (11%)	2 (3%)	6 (8%)	71
Concept/ideation	45 (63%)	19 (27%)	(90%)	7 (10%)	0	0	71
Originality/ creative exp	42 (59%)	24 (34%)	(93%)	4 (6%)	1 (1%)	0	71
Technical skill/ craftsmanship	43 (61%)	23 (32%)	(93%)	5 (7%)	0	0	71

What Are the Challenges That This Assessment Faces?

By definition, the AP Studio Art portfolios involve relatively unstructured tasks. Within the very general constraints of its three major divisions—Quality, Concentration, and Breadth—the program's philosophy is to allow teachers and students to work toward fulfillment of the requirements through the curriculum and teaching strategies that suit them best. Thus, there are literally an infinite number of ways of "solving" each section. A natural outcome of this fundamental stance is that the scoring guides for each section are holistic and quite general. Rather than trying to define in a restrictive or constrictive way what one should find in each section (barring the most basic guidelines, such as "12 slides"), the guides outline a variety of traits of work that one might find at each score level. For example, some students' work will be more technically competent and less interesting in terms of ideation, whereas other students may demonstrate relatively strong conceptual skills or be highly expressive but less accomplished in terms of skill in manipulating the medium. Similarly, not all of the works submitted for a single section will always demonstrate the same level of accomplishment. The scoring guides cover these situations. Great effort over many years has gone into making the scoring guides value free with respect to media, style, and content (e.g., middle-level, tightly rendered drawings should receive the same scores as highly expressive drawings that demonstrate an equivalent level of achievement). Reader training has evolved over time to focus carefully on these issues. To the extent that it is possible to discern such variables from artwork, care is also taken to keep the scoring value free with respect to the gender of the students, their ethnicity, or any other similar variables. In addition, special efforts have been made in recent years to augment reader training with respect to photography and digital art. These remain areas of concern, and efforts in these directions are ongoing.

Scoring guides are viewed as evolving documents and are reviewed each year. The introduction of the two new design portfolios logically necessitated the development of new scoring guides for 2-D Design and 3-D Design. These were initially rooted in the old guides for Color/Design and Sculpture/Three-Dimensional Design within Section III of the old General portfolio. They have, however, been worked through systematically and with considerably more depth. As the new portfolios become more familiar, it is likely that the guides will be revised further. Similarly, experience from the portfolio Reading will inform efforts to communicate more effectively with teachers about the nature of the two design portfolios and expectations for student work.

As with all AP subjects, the student's own teacher is not part of the assessment process. Many AP teachers serve as Readers, but if during the portfolio Reading, they see work by a student whom they know or whose work they recognize, they are required to ask another Reader or a Table Leader to evaluate that work. Not allowing the classroom teacher to participate in the evaluation (or contriving a systematic method of collecting input from classroom teachers) means that information regarding the context in which the work was produced is largely absent. Beyond what they may read in the student's written commentary on the Concentration, Readers do not know anything about the student—whether she or he has overcome unusual obstacles, or been a leader in the class, or any of a host of other factors that can affect performance. Because Readers are not only human, but are all teachers, probably every one of them has often wished for the chance to talk with students about their portfolios. On the other hand, one can argue that the body of work should stand on its own, because its qualities are the basis for the judgments that colleges and universities have to make about whether or not to grant credit or placement. There is also the inevitable argument that this form of evaluation is particularly objective in the sense that all students' work is evaluated on the basis of the same carefully worked-out scoring guides.

To date, only the single AP grade is reported for Studio Art. The high score reliability of the portfolios relies on pooling all of the judgments on all of the sections. It is the sense of the College Board and Educational Testing Service that only scores with high reliability should be reported. Each section by itself would not meet that statistical challenge. In the interest of supporting both student learning and teaching, it is hoped that this dilemma can be at least partially resolved in the future.

Have There Been Research/Evaluation Studies of This Assessment and Reports of Its Findings?

Several recent investigations have compared AP Studio Art to other approaches to teaching studio art. In Tomhave's (1999) study, students in two visual arts classrooms prepared portfolios that were then evaluated by AP-trained examiners. Students in one classroom were taught using the International Baccalaureate Art/Design curriculum, whereas students in the other classroom were taught using the AP Studio Art curriculum. Portfolio scores for the two classrooms were compared. Tomhave found no significant differences between the groups in the scores they received on their portfolios. The researcher also examined the relationship between the portfolio scores and the end-of-year course grades the students' teachers gave and reported that the correlation between the two was .01.

Willis (1999) conducted a qualitative study to compare and contrast the assessment procedures employed in the AP Studio Art program and in the International Baccalaureate Art/Design program. Through surveys and interviews, Willis studied the training of the teachers and the examiners who conduct the assessments, and the examiners' interpretations of various descriptors included in the scoring guides. He also compared the moderation processes employed in the two programs and the procedures used to handle discrepancies when examiners' scores of the same portfolio disagreed.

Blaikie (1994) investigated the assessment processes employed in three visual arts programs: Arts PROPEL, the International Baccalaureate Art/Design program, and the AP Studio Art program. Using content analysis, she reviewed curriculum materials prepared by each program and literature describing each program in order to identify a set of assessment criteria that she then employed to compare their assessment processes. Through her analysis, she identified common themes that crossed programs, as well as themes that were unique to individual programs.

Other researchers have conducted case studies of the AP Studio Art program. As part of his case study of the Virginia Beach art program, Wilson (1984, 1986) observed AP Studio Art classes in Kempsville High School and conducted interviews with the teacher and students to learn about the role that AP played within the Virginia Beach program. The Virginia Beach site was one of seven sites chosen for study by a team of investigators because it provided a well-rounded arts education program that included instruction in art history, art criticism, and art production.

Mitchell and Stempel (1991) prepared six case studies of performance assessments for the U.S. Office of Technology Assessment to illustrate what performance assessment is capable of accomplishing and to demonstrate its potential for assisting in educational reform efforts. One of their case studies focused on the AP Studio Art program as an example of a large-scale national portfolio assessment. To prepare their case study, they observed the 1990 portfolio reading, reviewed various program documents, and interviewed key program personnel as well as AP teachers, students, and college professors who teach introductory art courses.

Myford and Mislevy (1995) used two complementary approaches—quantitative and qualitative—to gather, analyze, and interpret information about critical aspects of the AP Studio Art assessment process. Their study provided an illustration of the use of the two approaches in tandem for the quality control monitoring of large-scale assessment systems. For the naturalistic portion of their study, they analyzed rating data from the 1992 AP Studio Art portfolio Reading using a many-faceted Rasch measurement model. They then engaged raters in discussions about hard-to-rate portfolios to discover why certain portfolios were more difficult to rate than others. Through their interviews, they gained an understanding of the cognitive processes underlying the unusual or discrepant patterns that the statistical analyses picked up in the ratings of these portfolios.

CONCLUSION

As is evident from this discussion, the NAEP visual arts assessment and the AP Studio Art assessment have evolved in very different ways since their inception. That evolution has created some concerns regarding the comparability of the scores provided by each of the two assessments over time.

In the case of the NAEP visual arts assessment, over 20 years had elapsed between the two most recent assessments. In that time, the field of visual arts education had changed rather dramatically, as Stankiewicz (1999) explained:

> More is expected of art education today. As part of the political construct arts education, the visual arts are expected to prepare students for work, to focus efforts for interdisciplinary learning, to provide challenging subject matter drawn from four foundational disciplines, and more. Expectations for student performance and learning are more complex as well. Memorizing art vocabulary, drawing figures in motion, designing a room of one's own, and other exercises that tend to call forth specific behaviors have given way to more complex, global ability areas [e.g., see Erickson et al., 1999]. We look for the ability to synthesize knowledge and skills, the integration of making and response. Those are positive advances. The NAEP arts framework was designed to encompass the complex nature of creating, performing/interpreting, and responding in the arts, to address specific content—knowledge and skills—in the arts disciplines. (p. 3)

As we have seen, the design framework used to construct the 1997 assessment differed radically from the frameworks used in 1975 and in 1978. Consequently, the assessment and exercise specifications arising out of those frameworks were also very different. Indeed, a close comparison of the content outlines driving those assessments might lead one to conclude that the construct of learning in the visual arts had been defined in very different ways. A convincing case could be made to argue that the constructs themselves may not have been comparable. As noted in the 1999 *Standards for Educational and Psychological Testing,* tests that measure different constructs or are built from different sets of specifications should not be considered comparable.

Several authors (Eisner, 1999; Lehman, 1999; Stankiewicz, 1999) have lamented the inability to directly compare students' results from the most recent assessment to the assessments conducted in the 1970s. As Lehman (1999) explains,

> Throughout its history, NAEP has emphasized the importance of identifying trends in student achievement and has compared the results of each assessment with those of previous assessments in that discipline. Indeed, measuring progress is so fundamental to NAEP that it is reflected in its name. Nevertheless, although there have been two previous NAEP assessments in music and two in visual arts, no information whatever has been provided concerning how student achievement in 1997 compares with that of previous years. That omission represents another huge lost opportunity. (p. 5)

NAEP has been able to maintain the comparability of assessments in other disciplines by implementing the statistical process of equating test scores from one assessment to the next. In theory, equating should be able to provide accurate score conversions for any set of students that are drawn from the population for which a given test has been developed and should then allow for comparisons to be drawn between student performances over time. Additionally, the same score conversion should be applicable irrespective of score interpretation or intended use. However, in the case of the NAEP arts assessment, equating was not feasible, nor would it have been a psychometrically acceptable practice in which to engage, given the warnings provided in the 1999 *Standards for Educational and Psychological Testing:*

> It is not possible to construct conversions with these ideal properties between scores on tests that measure different constructs; that differ materially in difficulty, reliability, time limits, or other conditions of administration; or that are designed to different specifications. (pp. 51–52)

It is important to note that comparisons *were* drawn between students' performances on selected exercises from the 1975 and 1978 assessments and reported (National Assessment of Educational Progress, 1981a). A set of common exercises were administered in both those assessments to allow for direct comparisons to be made. Great care was taken to ensure that the conditions of administration were comparable across the two assessments and that similar time limits were observed. For the six common open-ended tasks, the same scoring guides were employed to score students' responses in both assessments, and one set of raters scored all those responses (National Assessment of Educational Progress, 1981b). Having all those factors in place made it psychometrically feasible to draw justifiable comparisons and to identify trends in performance. However, none of these factors were in place for the 1997 assessment. There were no common exercises from earlier NAEP visual arts assessments, the conditions for assessment administration were very different from the conditions in effect in the 1970s, and different time limits were imposed. All these factors mitigated against being able to compare results from past NAEP visual arts assessments to results from the 1997 assessment.

In the case of the AP Studio Art portfolios, change over the last 30 years has, for the most part, been incremental. To maintain comparability of student scores from one year to the next, the AP Studio Art program relied in the beginning on the consistency of the group of people who served as Readers, and their passing on of accrued wisdom about levels of accomplishment. As the group of Readers has grown (there were 82 Readers in 2003), more formal and more specific scoring guides have been developed. The year 1996 can be seen as a watershed; it was then that section-specific rubrics were instituted. These have been refined with input primarily from the Chief Reader and Table Leaders but also, to some extent, from all of the Readers. Because there are no "questions" that change each year, the scoring guides work well as enduring, though, mutable, documents. Throughout the Reading, quality control procedures such as reviewing every instance of widely divergent scores given to the same body of work keep the group as a whole, or individual Readers, from drifting away from the standards.

In addition, the membership of the Reading group is relatively constant by design. Ideally, about 15% of Readers in any year are serving in that capacity for the first time. Not everyone who evaluates portfolios necessarily returns; the group as a whole, though, represents a strong and broad pool of expertise. Readers may serve a 6-year term, after which they retire if they do not move on to become Table Leaders. A critical aspect of the standard-setting discussions that serve as training is that all Readers, from the most to the least experienced, take part in them. Those with experience have obvious breadth of knowledge and familiarity with the assessment process to contribute; but those who are new often bring new viewpoints, or even new challenges, to the discussions. It is in part working through these divergences that keeps the program vital.

The final AP grades that are reported to candidates are determined through what is known as "grade-setting." All of the raw scores for each student are converted by a computer program into a single number, the composite raw score, which ranges from 0 to 72 points. In an intensive meeting with statisticians and program staff from both Educational Testing Service and the College Board, the Chief Reader decides what the lowest composite score will be for each AP grade on the 1 to 5 scale that is used for reporting. He or she is aided by historical data; at least as important, though, are detailed tables that show the average score on each section of the portfolio for students at each composite score point. Thus, the Chief Reader is able to make clear connections between actual judgments made by the Readers and the final AP grades.

Implications of These Large-Scale Assessments for Future Assessments.   At a time when accountability in education is again becoming a high-profile national issue, these two large-scale art assessments bear consideration. Their differences are obvious: NAEP relies on group data and reports no individual scores; nor does it have a direct impact on the future course of students' education. It required no particular curriculum in visual arts, but rather measured what students had learned from existing curricula. AP Studio Art, though its curricular requirements are broad and flexible, does demand support for some form of advanced study in art. It not only allows but also encourages an individual approach to curriculum and, therefore, individually distinctive results. Those results are then assessed for each student and do have some impact on the student's future work in the field.

Nonetheless, an overwhelming link between the two is, of course, the subject matter that they share. It is perhaps not coincidental that these two ground-breaking assessments exist in a field of endeavor that is frequently devalued by schools and is seen by the public as nonessential or less rigorous than the other core subjects. It is true that art is "different": To demonstrate mastery by definition means to demonstrate independent thinking and a willingness to move away from proven solutions. So, too, the two assessments profiled here have moved away from the traditional models that we have come to know as large-scale assessment. One might ask whether it is because of the perceived lesser importance of the arts that they have been allowed to do so. But one may also ask whether the traditional academic subjects might not benefit from this work. Imagine, for example, a large-scale history, chemistry, or Spanish assessment that included a requirement for students to define, pursue, and document an individual interest. Or, at a more basic level, common acceptance of classroom-based English composition assessment for which scoring guides actually acknowledged the writer's creativity as well as command of syntax and organization.

Were this to become an educational goal, a raft of difficulties would immediately arise: If work is accomplished outside of class, how can evaluators know that it is the work of the individual who turns it in? If creativity is to be assessed, what value does it hold relative to the mechanics of language? Will two or more evaluators ever be able to agree? The answers to these and other thorny questions are not simple. Designing assessment of this sort, whether for a national program or a district-based experiment, is arduous and intellectually demanding. NAEP and AP stand as evidence that it can be done, and done well. Perhaps expanded efforts of this sort are worth undertaking: If "teaching to the test" comes to mean "teaching students to work rigorously in a discipline, to think independently, and to tap their potential," then assessment will truly serve education.

ACKNOWLEDGMENTS

We would like to acknowledge the helpful comments and suggestions from Hilary Persky, Steve Lazer, Rick Morgan, and Dennie Palmer Wolf in the preparation of this paper. The material contained herein is based on work supported by the Educational Testing Service and the University of Illinois at Chicago. Any opinions, findings, conclusions, and recommendations expressed are those of the authors and do not necessarily reflect the views of the Educational Testing Service, the College Board, the University of Illinois at Chicago, the National Center for Education Statistics, or the National Assessment Governing Board.

REFERENCES

Askin, W. (1983). [Chief reader's report: Studio art]. Unpublished report.

Askin, W. (1985). *Evaluating the Advanced Placement portfolio in studio art.* New York: College Entrance Examination Board.

Beattie, D. K. (1999, May). *An assessment or a demonstration: An analysis of the 1997 NAEP assessment of the visual arts.* Paper presented at the IAEA conference, Bled, Slovenia.

Blaikie, F. (1994). Values inherent in qualitative assessment of secondary studio art in North America: Advanced Placement, Arts PROPEL, and International Baccalaureate. *Studies in Art Education, 35*(4), 237–248.

Burton, D. A. (2001). A quartile analysis of the 1997 NAEP visual arts report card. *Studies in Art Education, 43*(1), 35–447.

Chapman, L. H. (1982). *Instant art instant culture: The unspoken policy for American schools.* New York: Teachers College Press, Columbia University.

The College Board. (1980). *Advanced Placement course description: Art.* New York: College Entrance Examination Board.

College Entrance Examination Board. (2002). *Advanced Placement program course description: Studio art.* New York: College Entrance Examination Board.

Consortium of National Arts Education Associations. (1994). *National standards for arts education: What every young American should know and be able to do in the arts.* Reston, VA: Music Educators National Conference.

Diket, R. M. (2001). A factor analytic model of eighth-grade art learning: Secondary analysis of NAEP arts data. *Studies in Art Education, 43*(1), 5–17.

Diket, R. M., Burton, D., McCollister, S., & Sabol, F. R. (2000). Taking another look: Secondary analysis of the NAEP report card in the visual arts. *Studies in Art Education, 41*(3), 202–207.

Diket, R. M., Sabol, F. R., & Burton D. (2002). *Implications of the 1997 NAEP visual arts data for policies concerning artistic development in America's schools and communities.* Hattiesburg, MI: William Carey College.

Eisner, E. W. (1999). The national assessment in the visual arts. *Arts Education Policy Review, 100*(6), 16–20.

Erickson, M., Katter, E., Lankford, E. L., Roucher, N., & Stewart, M. (1999). *Scope and sequence: A guide for learning and teaching in art.* Available at ArtsEdNet, http://www.artsednet.getty.edu/ArtsEdNet/Resource/Scope.

Gardner, H., & Grunbaum, J. (1986). *The assessment of artistic thinking: Comments on the National Assessment of Educational Progress in the arts*. (ERIC Document Reproduction Service No. ED279677)

Joint Committee on Standards for Educational and Psychological Testing of the American Educational Research Association, American Psychological Association, and the National Council on Measurement in Education. (1999). *Standards for educational and psychological testing*. Washington, DC: American Educational Research Association.

Knight, S. S. (1979). *Sex differences in artistic achievement: A national study* (Report No. 06-A-51). Denver, CO: National Assessment of Educational Progress, Education Commission of the States. (ERIC Document Reproduction Service No. ED193314)

Lehman, P. R. (1999). Introduction to the symposium on the NAEP 1997 arts report card. *Arts Education Policy Review, 100*(6), 12–19.

Lewis, W. (1980). [Chief reader's report: Studio art]. Unpublished report.

Lewis, W. (1981). [Chief reader's report: Studio art]. Unpublished report.

Mitchell, R., & Stempel, A. (1991). *Six case-studies of performance assessment*. (ERIC Document Reproduction Service No. ED340777)

Morgan, R., Biddle, M., & Sims-Gunzenhauser, A. (1995, May). *The 1994 Advanced Placement college comparability study in studio art: Drawing*. Unpublished statistical report.

Myford, C. M. (2002). Investigating design features of descriptive graphic rating scales. *Applied Measurement in Education, 15*(2), 187–215.

Myford, C. M., & Mislevy, R. J. (1995). *Monitoring and improving a portfolio assessment system* (RR-94-05). Princeton, NJ: Educational Testing Service, Center for Performance Assessment.

National Assessment of Educational Progress. (1978a). *Art technical report: Exercise volume* (Art Report No. 06-A-20). Washington, DC: U.S. Department of Health, Education, and Welfare, National Center for Education Statistics.

National Assessment of Educational Progress. (1978b). *Art technical report: Summary volume. Selected results from the first national assessment of art* (Art Report No. 06-A-21). Washington, DC: U.S. Department of Health, Education, and Welfare, National Center for Education Statistics.

National Assessment of Educational Progress. (1978c). *Attitudes toward art: Selected results from the first national assessment of art* (Art Report No. 06-A-03). Washington, DC: U.S. Department of Health, Education, and Welfare, National Center for Education Statistics.

National Assessment of Educational Progress. (1978d). *Design and drawing skills: Selected results from the first national assessment of art* (Art Report No. 06-A-01). Washington, DC: U.S. Department of Health, Education, and Welfare, National Center for Education Statistics.

National Assessment of Educational Progress. (1978e). *Knowledge about art: Selected results from the first national assessment of art* (Art Report No. 06-A-02). Washington, DC: U.S. Department of Health, Education, and Welfare, National Center for Education Statistics.

National Assessment of Educational Progress. (1981a). *Art and young Americans, 1974–1979: Results from the second national art assessment* (Art Report No. 10-A-01). Denver, CO: National Assessment of Educational Progress, Education Commission of the States.

National Assessment of Educational Progress. (1981b). *Procedural handbook: 1978–79 art assessment* (Art Report No. 10-A-40). Denver, CO: National Assessment of Educational Progress, Education Commission of the States.

National Assessment of Educational Progress. (1981c). *The second assessment of art, 1978–79, released exercise set* (Art Report No. 10-A-25). Denver, CO: National Assessment of Educational Progress, Education Commission of the States.

National Assessment Governing Board. (1994a). *1997 Arts education assessment framework*. Washington, DC: Author.

National Assessment Governing Board. (1994b). *Arts education assessment and exercise specifications*. Washington, DC: Author.

National Center for Education Statistics. (1998a). *Arts education: Highlights of the NAEP 1997 arts assessment report card (Report No. NCES 98-455R)*. Washington, DC: Author. Available at: http://nces.ed.gov/nationsreportcard/arts/

National Center for Education Statistics. (1998b). *The NAEP 1997 arts report card: Eighth-grade findings from the National Assessment of Educational Progress* (CD-ROM). Washington, DC: Author.

National Endowment for the Arts. (1988). *Toward civilization: A report on arts education*. Washington, DC: Author.

Norris, E. L, & Goodwin, B. (Eds.). (1971). *Art objectives*. Denver, CO: National Assessment of Educational Progress, Education Commission of the States.

Ott, M. E. (1995). *Evaluating the Advanced Placement portfolio in studio art*. New York: The Advanced Placement Program, The College Board.

Persky, H. R. (in press). The NAEP arts assessment: Pushing the boundaries of large-scale performance assessment. In E. W. Eisner & M. Day (Eds.), *Handbook of research and policy in art education*. Hillsdale, NJ: Lawrence Erlbaum Associates.

Persky, H. R., Sandene, B. A., & Askew, J. M. (1998). *The NAEP 1997 arts report card: Eighth-grade findings from the National Assessment of Educational Progress* (Report No. NCES 1999-486). Washington, DC: National Center for Education Statistics, U.S. Department of Education. (ERIC Document Reproduction Service No. ED423213). Available at: http://nces.ed.gov/nationsreportcard/arts/

Persky, H. R., Sandene, B. A., & Askew, J. M. (1999). The NAEP 1997 arts report card: Eighth-grade findings from the National Assessment of Educational Progress. *Education Statistics Quarterly, 1*(1), 29–32. Retrieved January 17, 2002, from http://nces.ed.gov/naep/

Sabol, F. R. (2001). Regional findings from a secondary analysis of the 1997 NAEP art assessment based on responses to creating and responding exercises. *Studies in Art Education, 43*(1), 18–34.

Siegesmund, R., Diket, R., & McCulloch, S. (2001). Re-visioning NAEP: Amending a performance assessment for middle school art students. *Studies in Art Education, 43*(1), 45–56.

Sims-Gunzenhauser, A. (1999). [Results of the 1998 Advanced Placement studio art curriculum survey]. Unpublished raw data.

Stankiewicz, M. A. (1999). Spinning the arts NAEP. *Arts Education Policy Review, 101*(1), 29–32.

Tomhave, R. (1999). Portfolio assessment in the visual arts: A comparison of advanced secondary art education strategies (Advanced Placement, International Baccalaureate, Secondary Education). (Doctoral dissertation, University of Minnesota, 1999). *Dissertation Abstracts International, 60*, 1870A.

Vanneman, A., & Goodwin, M. (1998). NAEP and the visual arts: Framework, field test, and assessment. *Focus on NAEP, 3*(4). (ERIC Document Reproduction Service No. ED421452). Retrieved January 17, 2002, from http://nces.ed.gov/naep/

Vanneman, A., Morton, C., & Allen, L. B. (1998). NAEP and theatre: Framework, field test, and assessment. *Focus on NAEP, 3*(3). (ERIC Document Reproduction Service No. 447144). Retrieved January 17, 2002, from http://nces.ed.gov/naep/

Vanneman, A., Shuler, S., & Sandene, B. (1998). NAEP and music: Framework, field test, and assessment. *Focus on NAEP, 3*(2). (ERIC Document Reproduction Service No. ED421451). Retrieved January 17, 2002, from http://nces.ed.gov/naep/

Ward, B. J. (1982). A look at students' art achievements: Results from the National Assessment of Educational Progress. *Visual Arts Research, 8*(16), 12–18.

White, S., & Vanneman, A. (1998a). NAEP and dance: Framework and field tests. *Focus on NAEP, 3*(1). (ERIC Document Reproduction Service No. 422311). Retrieved January 17, 2002, from http://nces.ed.gov/naep/

White, S., & Vanneman, A. (1998b). The NAEP 1997 Arts education assessment: An overview. *Focus on NAEP, 2*(4). (ERIC Document Reproduction Service No. 421453). Retrieved January 17, 2002, from http://nces.ed.gov/naep/

White, S., & Vanneman, A. (1999a). Frequency of arts instruction for students. *NAEP Facts, 4*(3). (ERIC Document Reproduction Service No. ED436478). Retrieved January 17, 2002, from http://nces.ed.gov/naep/

White, S., & Vanneman, A. (1999b). Student musical activities and achievement in music: NAEP 1997 arts assessment. *NAEP Facts, 4*(1). (ERIC Document Reproduction Service No. ED436475). Retrieved January 17, 2002, from http://nces.ed.gov/naep/

White, S., & Vanneman, A. (1999c). Student subgroup achievement on the NAEP 1997 arts assessment. *NAEP Facts, 4*(2). (ERIC Document Reproduction Service No. ED436477). Retrieved January 17, 2002, from http://nces.ed.gov/naep/

White, S., Vanneman, A., Shuler, S., Sandene, B., Morton, C., Allen, L. B., & Goodwin, M. (1998). Focus on NAEP, 1998. *Focus on NAEP, 2*(4), *3*(1–4). (ERIC Document Reproduction Service No. ED447144). Retrieved January 17, 2002, from http://nces.ed.gov/naep/

Willis, S. (1999). A descriptive analysis of assessment procedures used in the Advanced Placement Studio Art program and the International Baccalaureate Art & Design programme (Doctoral dissertation, Florida State University, 1999). *Dissertation Abstracts International, 60*, 3591A.

Wilson, B. (1970). The status of national assessment in art. *Art Education, 23*(9), 2–6.

Wilson, B. (1971). A procedure for developing art objectives. In E. L. Norris & B. Goodwin (Eds.), *Art Objectives* (pp. 4–8). Denver, CO: National Assessment of Educational Progress, Education Commission of the States.

Wilson, B. (1975). National assessment and the future of arts education. *Peabody Journal of Education, 42*(3), 213–216.

Wilson, B. (1984). Tight structure, discipline, and quality: Art education in Virginia Beach. In *Art history, art criticism, and art production. An examination of art education in selected school districts. Volume II: Case studies of seven selected sites* (pp. 326–372). Santa Monica, CA: Rand Corp. (ERIC Document Reproduction Service No. ED257743)

Wilson, B. (1986). Testing and the process of change. *Design for Arts in Education, 88*(1), 6–11.

Wolf, T., & Wolf, D. P. (1984). How should we measure arts achievement? *Design for Arts in Education, 85*(3), 35–40.

Zimmerman, E. (1984). What art teachers are not teaching, art students are not learning. *Art Education, 37*(4), 12–15.

29

Visualizing Judgment: Self-Assessment and Peer Assessment in Arts Education

Elisabeth Soep
Youth Radio & University of California, Berkeley

A crayon-wielding toddler draws a wide oval, adds some energetic marks, and then proudly pronounces, "Mommy!" to the babysitter supervising her play. A 9-year-old examines the heavily muscled comic book character drawn on his classmate's binder: "That's tight," he says, "Wish I could draw like that." Members of a middle school art class gather with their instructor to critique the week's assignment, considering 1 by 1 the 15 self-portraits tacked on the wall. A senior voted "best artist" in her high school class makes selections from a year's worth of drawings and paintings for her AP portfolio. During a feedback session at a community-based youth media project, one participant challenges his peer's stereotypical description of a lead character as they prepare to create storyboards for a collaborative video. Five young people who have never met in real life communicate through e-mail and digital message boards to design an online fantasy role-play game, hoping their product will someday compete on the global market. Graffiti artists travel in small groups through their neighborhood at night, creating, admiring, ridiculing, and obscuring images on cement walls.

These snapshots of visual culture highlight the variety of ways that self- and peer assessments shape art objects, individual minds, and social worlds. In the field of education, researchers and policymakers tend to focus on teacher evaluation as a primary force that influences young people's short-term choices and lifelong trajectories within visual arts learning. Although that emphasis is unquestionably worthwhile, self and peers also play an important role in determining arts education experiences and destinies.

This chapter draws from numerous fields and orientations—from anthropological theory to critical pedagogy to cognitive developmental psychology—to explore self- and peer assessments in visual arts education. Out of this range in perspectives, a kind of conceptual framework crystallizes, perhaps to a greater extent than one would normally expect from a standard research review. Emphasis here centers on a sociocultural view of human and artistic development. Artmaking is a social practice (Pearson, 2001), whether an individual is working privately in a sequestered studio or collaboratively in a public art space. *Self-assessment* is a process of perceiving, interpreting, judging, and transforming one's own projects. Even silent and solitary moments of self-assessment are social, to the extent that the artist's choices are informed by and help shape histories of personal interaction and cultural tradition. *Peer assessment* is a process of seeing and responding to the current state of someone else's work, in some cases, offering clear value judgments ("this part is great...here it falls apart"); and in other cases, describing or otherwise interacting with the work in a way that is less obviously evaluative, and perhaps not even verbalized (e.g., by copying a peer with an admired style).

There are several viable alternatives to this sociocultural view. A psychoanalytic approach, for example, might focus on the dreams, fantasies, and pathologies of artists more than on their material social practices and entanglements. An emphasis on gifted and talented young artists (Bireley & Genshaft, 1991: Csikszentmihalyi, Rathunde, Whalen, & Wong, 2000) would identify the traits, processes, and environments associated with those with exceptional arts potential in contrast to others who are less remarkable. A review of artists' memoirs and biographies for evidence of self- and peer assessments might probe contemporary artists' personal correspondence or published statements (Cahan & Kocur, 1996; Stiles & Selz, 1996). Clinical perspectives would reveal the potential for art making to improve self-esteem and organize group therapy-based interventions (Carolan, 2001). All of these approaches bear considerable merit and to varying degrees inform the review offered here. But adopting primarily a sociocultural orientation makes sense for three reasons. (1) The expansiveness of this approach makes it possible to include a rich array of perspectives on art work and art worlds. (2) This focus represents a dominant interest within current arts education literature. (3) Given this interest, the sociocultural framework merits serious and critical consideration if it is to provide a generative basis for future research.

THREE TENSIONS

Before turning to specific theory and research, it is useful first to foreground some tensions that resonate through the work reviewed here. The first pertains to the pairing of self- and peer assessments as twin topics. Taken together, these processes suggest that producing visual art means knowing how to look critically at one's own practices and knowing when to turn to others as resources for critical response. Turning inward and reaching outward can be deeply interdependent, as personal assessments of a developing piece of work build on what the artist learns by hearing from others. The reverse is also true. Peer assessments are primarily meaningful to the extent that emerging artists can integrate classmates' judgments into their ongoing practices.

But there is also something of a contradiction built into this dual emphasis on the self and peers as sources of assessment. A focus on self conforms to the tradition in arts education research and practice that prioritizes individual development and self-expression. The child or adolescent generates and refines his or her own projects, with guidance and instruction from teachers, based on personal vision and meaning. Peer assessment, by contrast, invokes an educational ideology that privileges the social dimensions of learning and making. This second process forefronts the idea that every work of art emerges through joint participation in communities of practice. Some of the most interesting work reviewed in these pages maps out the territory where these two emphases overlap, when the individual student emerges as an artist whose mind "extends beyond the skin" (Wertsch, 1991).

A second tension surfaces with respect to the function of assessment according to arts education literature. There is a strong tradition for researchers to explore how young people learn to make specific judgments about particular works, and eventually to develop more generalizable (but never universal) standards and strategies for assessing their own work and that of their peers. This focus inflects self- and peer assessments with positive connotations, framing these processes as integral to continued interest and productivity within the arts. But there is a grimmer side. The research also suggests that many young people, at some point in middle childhood, assess themselves out of art making entirely. These students decide they are no good at drawing and abandon the activity altogether. In this latter sense, self-assessment may *alienate* young people from the arts, rather than empower them to continue to create. This tension highlights the importance of identifying just what modes of self- and peer assessment foster, rather than discourage, ongoing involvement in arts learning and making.

The third tension revolves around a familiar question in the field of education: What counts as assessment? Included among the studies reviewed here are those that may not be sorted in a library database as pertaining directly to "evaluation" as it is typically defined. The boundary that distinguishes description, interpretation, even free-flowing classroom conversation from assessment is difficult to pin down. To limit the scope of the chapter only to those studies that specifically consider formal evaluation conventions in visual arts education would overlook highly relevant inquiries into communication, interaction, and mental operations that have much to teach us about how young people develop judgment in and through the arts.

THEORIES OF MIND AND MAKING

This chapter may be a bit unusual in its foregrounding of theory alongside empirical research. I have chosen to organize the chapter in this way based on the contention that *what* we know about self- and peer assessment in the visual arts depends on *how* we know these things, and on *which* principles shape the inquiries researchers undertake. All research draws from and builds theory, whether the author spells out guiding concepts or implies them through the selection of methods and modes of analysis. Some of the theoretical luminaries considered in this section—people like Soviet psychologist Vygotsky and French critical anthropologist Bourdieu—would probably not identify as scholars of visual arts education. Yet their data, methods, and arguments derive from studies of people producing, interacting with, learning through and assigning value to visual texts. And their ideas have clear and often explicit ties to arts education research. The inclusion of these theorists situates their work within our field, where I would argue it rightfully belongs.

This theoretical discussion sets the stage for what follows—a review of contemporary studies relevant to self- and peer assessment, primarily those appearing in refereed journals and volumes, organized roughly (but not absolutely) along developmental lines. The review is, by necessity, selective and partial; my aim has been to include a body of work that is both representative and provocative. The chapter closes with a reflexive turn, where I consider evidence of recent efforts among arts education scholars to assess our own selves and peers, through influential critiques, debates, and meta-analyses with important implications for future research.

Sociocultural Minds

A major theoretical resource behind the sociocultural conception of mind is Soviet psychologist Vygotsky. His most significant contribution to studies of self- and peer assessments in visual arts education is the argument that thinking develops not inside the head but through engagement with other people, tools, practical activities, and "situations" (Vygotsky, 1978, 1986). In Vygotsky's view, "higher mental functioning in the individual derives from social life" (Wertsch, 1991, p. 19). Language is a key resource in this development, as words constitute one symbol system that mediates thinking, conceptualization, and problem solving. A thought "may be compared to a cloud shedding a shower of words," says Vygotsky (1986, p. 251), meaning language both produces thinking (just as moisture creates clouds) and develops out of thinking (just as rain flows from clouds). When applied to arts education, this view implies that even the youngest children depend on others to learn about visual conventions, categories, and vocabularies; and to master tools and materials. Three concepts pertaining to this socially mediated view of learning are especially relevant and influential in visual arts education literature: (a) egocentric speech, (b) the zone of proximal development, and (c) the idea that cognitive development occurs through participation in communities of practice.

Egocentric Speech. Anyone who has worked with or raised young children knows that toddlers often burst out in spontaneous speech, apparently talking for and to themselves. Vygotsky (1986) found that children tend to talk out loud to themselves especially when they hit a disruption in the flow of activity. A crayon may snap in half from pressing too hard on paper, for example, or a child has to figure out how to make the most of a misplaced or accidental mark, or to narrate a new approach that is not yet automatized. Vygotsky called the language children use under these conditions "egocentric speech," a concept he developed in part by observing what and when children spoke as they drew. Vygotsky described egocentric speech as a critical cognitive achievement that expresses "the process of becoming aware" (p. 30) heralding the onset of purposeful behavior. Without egocentric speech, said Vygotsky, children would never obtain inner speech—the capacity to reason through internal dialog. Egocentric speech is an intervening stage that allows children to transfer social or collaborative ways of knowing into intramental operations. Hence, when young children spontaneously assess their own drawings out loud, their words are not just charming outbursts. Rather, this language is a way for them to assign meaning and value to images while developing a private and interior source of judgment.

Zone of Proximal Development. The second sociocultural notion with relevance to visual arts education is what Vygotsky (1978, 1986, p. 187) called the zone of proximal development (ZPD): "the discrepancy between a child's actual mental age and the level he reaches in solving problems with assistance." A child drawing his mom, for example, might add new features, like ears and eyelashes, when prompted to do so by an older sibling. It is problematic, then, for researchers to look only at children's finished art works and reach conclusions about what they are capable of conveying graphically at a given stage of development. Such an approach ignores the potential influence of social environment and, specifically, that of peer assessment. Feedback can expand a child's evident performance within a certain range of cognitive and mechanical capacity. The existence of ZPD demonstrates that development in visual arts learning does not follow an inexorable pathway through identifiable stages corresponding neatly to a person's age. Rather, the logics and instincts young people exercise in visual arts activities are malleable, to some extent, based on the support or discouragement they receive from others in their environment.

Communities of Practice. Although Vygotsky himself is not known for this phrase, contemporary theorists (Lave & Wenger, 1991; Rogoff, 1994) have adapted his broader sociocultural theory to propose a conception of learning that is highly social and situated. Knowledgeability in this view is not a product one acquires through transmission but a mode of participating, with increasing sophistication, in communities of practice. Knowing how to judge one's own activities and respond to those of one's peers is necessary for achieving full participation in communities of visual arts practice. This notion of situated learning through joint activity, when applied to arts education, lends itself to analyses of collaborative creative undertakings—neighborhood murals, community garden projects, youth film festivals—as well as the study of social contexts for assessment shaping individual arts practices.

Artworld Geographies

Communities of practice are not neutral spaces. They are social worlds governed in part by assessment systems directed toward the self and others. Among adult working artists, assessment is the mechanism that determines which practitioners gain recognition and which get overlooked. More and more researchers interested in self- and peer assessment in visual arts education are considering these practices in light of the institutions, ideologies, and habitats that shape the criteria by which young artists and their works are judged. Three theoretical concepts are especially useful: (1) The notion of field derived from systems theory, (2) the concept of art worlds developed by Becker, and (3) Bourdieu's idea of cultural capital.

Fields of Creativity. Systems theorists define creativity as "any act, idea, or product that changes an existing domain, or that transforms an existing domain into a new one" (Csikszentmihalyi, 1996, p. 28; see also Feldan, Csikszentmihalyi, & Gardner, 1994). Complex factors, including standards of social evaluation, determine how creative works acquire value. Judging performance within a given domain depends on understanding how a field operates and on how participants in that field assign value to individuals, ideas, and objects (Csikszentmihalyi). A field is comprised of gatekeepers for a given domain—those who govern systems of inclusion and exclusion. Clearly young people in arts classrooms are not transforming domains with every family portrait or macaroni necklace or graffiti art piece or Web site interface they create. Nevertheless their assessment practices play a critical role in shaping and shifting domains. In their conception of fields, systems theorists tend to focus on evaluators with obvious power—for example, teachers and critics. Arts education researchers expand this view by accounting for how individual students themselves can serve as gatekeepers of inclusion and exclusion through formal and tacit standards for self- and peer assessments.

Art Worlds. In his sociological study of networks for art making, distribution, and interpretation, Becker (1982) focuses on interactions, institutions, and power relations. Complex artworld mechanisms sort out artists from nonartists, as well as good artists from bad artists. An individual art object is not the product of a single maker, according to Becker. It is an outcome of all the people and conventions that bring that work into existence and recognition (as well as critics of that work and those who aim to block resources from its maker). Self-assessment by arts learners derives at least in part from judgments channeled through peers and institutions. Young people's practices are shaped by the art worlds that contain their efforts—whether they participate in underground zine or comic book popular culture, excel in competitive Advanced Placement or International Baccalaureate classes, or manifest their artistry by producing camcorder tributes to screen legends like Jackie Chan and Francis Ford Coppolla. Becker's sociology tends to focus on networks of professionals. But arts education researchers have used this notion of artworlds to illuminate the networks of people and practices, standards, and values that come alive within visual arts learning environments. Self-reflection and peer review shape young people's pathways, propelling some toward recognition and exhibition and leaving others as casualties of unexamined assessment systems.

Cultural Capital. Pierre Bourdieu expands this interest in artworlds by framing aesthetic "taste" as a process that organizes whole societies (1984, 1991, 1993). Bourdieu argues that discourses of direct or disguised celebration transform a given work of art into an "object of belief" (1993, p. 35). Student artwork acquires value through the beliefs attached to it: estimations of worth; interpretations of meaning; associations with other objects, artists, and traditions; and so on. School classrooms are fertile grounds for the growth of these beliefs. A capacity to create objects that draw positive appraisal by peers and teachers is more than an aesthetic achievement. This ability can serve as a kind of "cultural capital," using Bourdieu's terminology, meaning bodies of knowledge, skills, and techniques that carry influence and authority within a given field of practice. Especially in the arts, cultural capital can pass for an innate gift. Nowhere is this belief more widespread than among peers, who often single out individual classmates as "great artists" without recognizing the systematic training—whether in homes or neighborhoods where art is valued, or in schools that educate children in the arts from an early age—that prepares some children for achievement. Arts education researchers use these ideas to frame assessment as a site of negotiation where identities and dispositions are formed, meanings are legitimated, and consequential choices are made. This view suggests that a fully realized education in the arts includes students in thoughtful discussions about not only the quality of their own images and those of their peers but also the criteria that shape categories of artistic performance and judgments of aesthetic quality. This kind of arts education includes young people as active participants in the complex workings of artworlds.

RESEARCH ON ARTWORK, ARTWORD, AND ARTWORLD AS SITES OF ASSESSMENT

This theoretical sketch suggests that art making is a mindful and mediated experience. Habits of mind, and experiments with the materials, tools, and techniques that mediate arts production, are shaped by participation in complex artworlds. Those artworlds are never value free, and as a result assessment of self and peer emerges as an especially important force that influences how minds and social contexts develop through visual arts activities. Arts education researchers have informed, responded to, and in some cases challenged this set of "big ideas" through careful study of young people actually making art under experimental conditions, as well as in their homes, classrooms, and public community spaces. Language is one, but not the only, data source that reveals self- and peer assessments at work. There is a tendency in the broader arts education research to dichotomize visual and verbal modes of expression, as if the two were hostile to one another, or even mutually exclusive. Although self- and peer assessments are not always verbalized, highly productive relationships exist between language and learning (Arnheim, 1998; Heath, 2001; Stibbs, 1998; Wolf, 2000; see also Eisner, 1992; and Richmond, 1998, for cautions), and words provide a key site of inquiry for arts education researchers interested in assessment as a dimension of production. "[W]e have limited access to culture without language," says Parsons (1998, p. 111) "and without language artworks have very limited connections with culture... to distinguish sharply between thinking visually and thinking linguistically is also to keep apart art and culture."

Youngest Children: The Onset of Self- and Peer Assessments

Freedman (1997) argues that it was once commonplace for scholars of drawing development to assume a linear trajectory through natural stages of graphic activity. Although yielding important findings, this "stage-by-age" approach fell out of favor in the 1960s and 1970s, says Freedman, eventually giving way to the realization that drawing was not a process of individual growth following a universal path. New models were necessary to account for the influence of context and history, the impact of collaborative art-making activities, and the extent to which arts fields are themselves cultural constructions.

These models recognize the role of self- and peer assessments even among the youngest children. Wolf and Davis Perry (1988, p. 21) demonstrate that children as young as 18 to 30 months monitor their own developing marks by "reading" meaning into them: "one loopy profile overlapping another can be called 'a pelican kissing a seal,' 'two pajamas,' or 'noodles in soup.'" This process, sometimes called "romancing" (Adijapha, Levin, & Solomon, 1998), provides evidence that young children assess, interpret, and translate their own drawings very early in life. By age 3, children have the capacity to match their form of graphic representation to dimensions of the task as a culturally defined endeavor, demonstrating responsiveness not only to their own personal meanings but also to larger social determinants (Wolf & Davis Perry). Similarly, Kindler and Darras's semiotic approach (1997) reveals that even before age 2, children begin to respond to feedback they receive about the relative value of different kinds of marks and shapes, and the significance of interaction dramatically increases among 2- and 3-year-olds, who "mimic each other's iconic gestures and sounds" (p. 28). This same focus on sociocommunicative context surfaces as well in Vinter's (1999) study of slightly older children (6- 10-year-olds) engaged in drawing tasks. However, although the youngest children in her study demonstrate some effect of meaning on how they draw, generally the older children are more likely to modify the graphic syntax of their images based on semantics introduced by experimental conditions.

Berk (1992) as well as Ramirez (1992) also report the use of drawing tasks to analyze the emergence of self-assessment and self-regulation among preschoolers, in this case using egocentric speech. These researchers identify the conditions under which egocentric speech promotes problem solving in visually oriented tasks. A "receptive social partner"—for example, an adult or more expert peer—enhances both the volume and the utility of egocentric speech, enabling young children to accomplish tasks that lie just beyond their independent capacity— in other words, within their zone of proximal development (Berk, 1992). Boyatzis (2000) analyzes drawings produced by his own stepdaughter, Janine, using Vygotsky's (1978, 1986) notion of ZPD to argue that the young child's art making from the earliest age takes place not in a social vacuum but through relationships with those around her, whose prompts encourage Janine to elaborate and interpret her imagery as it evolves, in effect integrating meaning and making.

Studies of Naturally Occurring Interaction. Although laboratory conditions and prompted interactions are one way to study the onset of self- and peer assessment in visual arts development, naturally occurring interactions lend further insight. Attention to real-life settings reveals how the artworlds educators and researchers create around children affect pedagogy and assessment. Using this term *artworld* explicitly, Pufall (1997, p. 176) argues that "early markmaking is neither private nor culturally unstructured." Children can judge whether their creations are socially valued and whether they are valued for making them. This process of valuing transpires through conventions like hanging finger paintings on refrigerators and seeing a classmate copy one's image. Wilson and Wilson remarked back in 1981 that in everyday life young children tend to draw together—not in isolation. As a result they imitate, model, and borrow what they see in peers' imagery through replication and reinterpretation. Debates about the educational implications of peer influence, as well as that of other kinds of models that can impinge on young children's "pure" instincts, were significant enough in the late 1980s to warrant a review article published by Duncum (1989) in *Studies in Art Education.* The review alludes to widespread agreement that an art education program comprised entirely of copying is not advisable; however, "sharing" imagery and technique among peers can be worthwhile.

In their study of preschool drawing practices, Thompson and Bales (1991) characterize drawing as "a performance unfolding in time, in which speech and gesture, word and image, are intertwined" (p. 43). Even when children work alone, they draw on social practices; even when they talk to themselves, they mimic social speech. These authors find that children's talk about their own images does not depend on instigation or facilitation by a teacher. By age 4, youngsters reflect on and monitor their own drawings, as well as raise questions about and evaluate images produced by peers. Their egocentric speech is "self-regulatory, marking those points in an activity when a child confronts a problem which requires thoughtful resolution" (p. 46). By age 7, egocentric speech can operate as a kind of spontaneous self-assessment process, one that eventually transforms into inner dialog. Key in this analysis is Thompson and Bales's observation that children's egocentric comments set off dialog, and "when children withdrew for more sustained consultation with themselves, their retreats were strategic and purposeful... [C]hildren spoke to themselves in order to plan or revise works in progress" (p. 53).

Thompson and Bales find that children can assess one another's drawings in harsh terms—the kinds of categorical evaluations one child relayed to the researchers by saying, "Michael doesn't like my dinosaurs" (p. 47). But critical comments often invigorate subsequent drawing activity among preschoolers in this study, as if in defiance of their peers' value judgments. Through peer feedback, children identify which aspects of their work draw admiration and which meet with criticism. This process moves them toward an ability to "modify their draw-ings to allow the graphic medium to carry their meaning, unassisted, to anonymous viewers" (pp. 47–48). In this sense, the spontaneous peer assessment that arises when young children converse about their artwork is preparation for eventually producing images that stand on their own and require no verbal explanation.

In a more recent study, Thompson (2000) once again looks into peer dialogs among young children, noting instances where children spontaneously develop mentor/tutor relation-ships within drawing tasks. Conversations are a dominant force during drawing time among preschoolers and kindergarteners. Ideas and images are freely circulated, admired, criticized, and copied. Solitary moments are uncommon, contends Thompson, in the lives of young chil-dren. Using Vygotsky's notion of ZPD, she argues that even preschoolers learn to judge and advance their own efforts and those of their peers through mediation by adults or more experi-enced children. The development of artistry is both personal and social—dependent not only on the intentions of the child but also on the extent to which those intentions are "mirrored or deflected in the response that one's work evokes in others" (p. 67).

Overall, contemporary efforts to understand the onset of both self-assessment and peer-assessment habits of very young children in the visual arts adumbrate multiple, uneven courses of artistic development, indicating the formation of aesthetic judgment at various points and within specific situations in the life of a child (Duncum, 2000). Self- and peer assessments help determine how, and whether, children develop into makers and interpreters of art.

Older Children: Assessment as Enhancement or Exit Strategy

The social dimensions of arts learning become further complicated as researchers locate older children's activities within specific environments and cultural contexts. Their vulnerability to peer opinion points to a risk in visual arts education. As children increasingly tune in to the sensibilities of their peers, ideals that dominate peer groups may actually discourage brave departures from conventional approaches to drawing, making children who "visualize otherwise" feel ashamed of their efforts and eventually abandon art making or modify their techniques to win admiration from classmates (Davis, 1997a).

Effects of Assessment Conditions.   In a study of the impact of evaluative comments on artistic performance and motivation, Gerhart (1986) investigates precisely what assessment conditions inspire or discourage further engagement with art projects. An impetus for the study is the hypothesis that children's motivation to continue drawing tends to diminish in late elementary school because young learners begin to question their abilities.

The author arranges four assessment conditions. In the case of *teacher evaluation*, Gerhart tells students the results of their drawing are important and will be graded. The *peer comparison* condition asks children to consider their own drawings in relation to other fourth-grade work, and to imagine how other fourth graders would evaluate their images. Researchers tell children in the *self-evaluation* group to assess their own work, based on whatever standards they deem appropriate. Finally, the *control group* receives no explanation. All children in the study are asked after they complete the assigned art task whether they want to come back to do more drawing and whether they would spend free time on similar tasks.

Gerhart's findings suggest that the different assessment conditions do not affect the quality of the children's drawings, but they do influence how children respond to the final questions. Self-evaluators express the highest degree of interest in continuing to participate in the drawing activities, whereas it appears that the teacher and peer evaluation conditions suppress participants' desire to continue with similar tasks. This finding conforms with an influential, though not uncontested, theory derived from creativity studies by Amabile (1989), who claims: "People will be most creative when they feel motivated primarily by the interest, enjoyment, challenge, and satisfaction of the work itself... and not by external pressures" (p. 54). Key to continued involvement with creative tasks, according to this view, is "the feeling that you are working on something for your *own* reasons and not someone else's" (p. 55).

In her analysis of how "children talk, write, dance, draw, and sing their understanding of the world," Gallas (1994) notes the diagnostic value of self-assessment. She focuses on how children communicate with her (the teacher), with one another, and with themselves as they participate in arts-infused projects with cross-disciplinary relevance—for example, a unit on the life cycle of an insect. One of Gallas's students began drawing an oversized insect that was supposed to be rendered to scale, and then she stopped, saying: "'Oops, that's way too big,' and she grabbed an eraser once again. After drawing a line that was much smaller, she continued, 'Aren't I smart? 'Cause I was thinking of him in the buttercups, so I had to make him smaller, or someone would come along and be terrified'" (p. 141). Observing this self-narrated artistic experience (a kind of egocentric speech), Gallas witnesses the student's conceptualization process, seeing that the girl had misunderstood some basic information but could correct herself and think through problems. When teachers attend to their students' spontaneous self-assessments, they gain access to thought processes that might otherwise remain hidden.

The same is true when an educator eavesdrops on peer conversations. When Adam, another of Gallas's students, grew frustrated with drawing and appeared ready to give up, Gallas encouraged him not to stop. Another student chimed in: "You don't have to make it perfect today. Just draw it, then do more tomorrow" (p. 135). In this encounter, the boundary between peer assessment and peer mentoring blurs, as students with varying degrees of comfort and proficiency in the arts are resources not only for evaluation but also for small moments of instruction. This kind of observation points to the tension produced by making sharp divisions among self-, peer, and teacher assessment.

Gallas's study reveals that students have their own ways of evaluating their works that can be distinct from the teacher's perspective—an observation Hafeli (2000) echoes in her analysis of art room conversations. Building on her own field work and prior scholarship (Swann, 1986; see also Taunton, 1984, 1986), Hafeli notes that the anticipation of teacher evaluation can shape even private conversations among peers: Because students are frequently asked what their images mean, "children tended to make up 'wild tales' based on adult questions and peer competition, in an effort to have their achievements acknowledged" (p. 131). Hafeli focuses on two middle school art classrooms, finding that student–teacher conversations tend to center on the assignment, subject matter, skill, and aesthetic codes. Resistance and negotiation also manifest themselves in interactions between students and teachers, as the teacher's suggestions can conflict with the students' sense of what they are capable of or what they want to convey in the artwork under review.

The content and style of teacher evaluations have significant impact on the standards students use to assess themselves and one another. Hafeli (2000) calls for further research to uncover the specific strategies teachers can use to promote and reward independent judgment and autonomy among students. She also makes the important point that the field needs new ways to integrate students' judgment capacities not only into how they individually are evaluated in a given class but also how large-scale assessment policies operate in the arts. When the latter derive from abstract public policy priorities, they can fall out of step with the concrete assessment practices that unfold within moment-to-moment classroom interactions.

Kakas (1991) considers student–teacher and student–student conversation in arts class-rooms in her analysis of fifth-graders' drawing lessons. Kakas is specifically interested in the potential benefit of peer conversation for performance and interest in the arts. Concur-ring with Hafeli (2000), Kakas contends that teachers' expectations and evaluations clearly affect peer interaction and help determine which standards of quality students exercise. An-alyzing peer interaction among 54 fifth-graders in nine classrooms, Kakas systematically in-troduces three conditions of student–teacher interaction: minimal feedback, questioning feed-back, and directive feedback. Her main interest is the impact of these three conditions on peer communication. Conversations among students cover a wide territory: The fifth-graders comment on subject matter and task difficulty, evaluate themselves (usually negatively) and others (usually positively), offer advice, express frustration, raise questions, and inquire about procedure.

Feedback conditions affect the frequency and nature of evaluative comments. Students in the directive feedback mode rely less on each other for advice and evaluation, apparently because they receive that kind of attention from the teacher/researcher. Peer interaction in this group tends to center on "nonteaching talk" about their pictures, procedures, and materials. Far more self-assessment takes place when the drawing task called for realistic representations. Students who appear more "insecure" about drawing are more likely to seek approval, consult other people's drawings more frequently, exhibit greater degrees of frustration, and self-evaluate. "Confident" children are more likely to mimic their teachers' modes of communicating—for example, offering support and advice and helping to manage classroom interaction.

Kakas's (1991) findings are instructive—and complex, when considered in light of other related research. When students evaluate themselves, they often deprecate their work. The fifth-graders in Kakas's classrooms who are least comfortable with drawing are the most likely to evaluate their own efforts verbally—and negatively. Peer evaluation is more likely to be positive, but it appears that primarily the more adept students in the class offer these kinds of appraisals, mixed with more explicit offers of instruction and guidance.

Contested Assessments and Developmental Trajectories.   The stakes associated with self- and peer assessments among older children come into extreme focus, given the finding within arts education literature that many young people reach a point where they lose faith and interest in visual art making entirely. In her influential study of the U-shaped curve in drawing development, Davis (1997a) argues that although five-year-olds gleefully produce images that resemble the work of professional artists in terms of expressive charac-teristics, this early prolific facility does not last. When youngsters in the United States enter middle childhood, they find themselves in classrooms that tend to privilege verbal language over visual modes of representation. Older children become increasingly perceptive about what drawing can do, at the same moment that visual arts opportunities often take a back seat to instruction in writing and math. With little reinforcement for drawing in contexts increasingly dominated by academics, and in light of the children's own frustration with a mismatch be-tween their capacities for perceiving and making, Davis finds that many older children and adolescents abandon art making altogether. In other words, the social environment conveys that drawing matters little, and children themselves often regard their own efforts as falling short of increasingly sophisticated expectations.

Although analysts of the U-shaped curve do not centrally focus on self- and peer assessments, their studies highlight the important role these procedures play in drawing development at middle childhood. Davis (1997a, 1997b, 1997c) argues that peer culture becomes increasingly influential for older children and adolescents, precisely at the time when popular-culture references gain favor over the more freely "expressive" images produced by younger children in her study. Self-assessment also holds sway here, as negative appraisals appear to factor in children's movement away from drawing as they struggle to achieve desired results.

Although pivotal in raising these matters, Davis's study also contributes a foundation for subsequent analysis of whether the U-shaped curve in graphic symbolization is a "universal" cognitive developmental pattern or a culturally mediated phenomenon (Davis 1997b, 1997c; Pariser & Berg 1997a, 1997b). The judges responsible for evaluating drawings in Davis's study used criteria derived from Western aesthetics to determine relative levels of expressivity (see, e.g., Goodman, 1976). Pariser and Berg set out to replicate Davis's study with drawings by a group of Chinese-Canadian children scored by U.S. and Chinese-Canadian judges. The Chinese-Canadian judges in Pariser's study, implementing both Davis's scoring protocol and another devised by Pariser, did not confirm the U-shaped configuration and assigned higher scores to the drawings by older children, compared to those by the youngest subjects. Once again, assessment surfaces as a process that is neither neutral nor natural. Evaluations—whether by adult judges, as is the case in these studies, or by classroom teachers, or peers, or young artists themselves—are influenced by subjective priorities, training, and culturally grounded artworld ideologies.

In a recent study of drawing development that takes up this question of the U-shaped curve, Kindler (2000) builds on Davis's original methodological protocol by adding a new dimension. To investigate systematically the judgment process itself, Kindler introduces several distinct panels of judges; some composed of adult artists and art educators and others made up of older children (ages 8 and 11) and teens. These various panels assessed over 600 drawings by Taiwanese children. Kindler finds that youth judges tend to be more critical in their appraisals than are the adults, perhaps due to different sets of standards in operation within the groups. That many of the adults are art teachers with an orientation toward positive affirmation of children's efforts may also play a role. The child and adolescent judges award their highest ratings to drawings they deem beautiful or lovely. They reject monotony, messiness, and nonsense imagery, regardless of expressive quality. The most robust difference between youth and adult judges comes down to priorities: Children in this study care about content, whereas the adults at this time and place focus on expressivity. This analysis holds significant implications for developmental theory and arts education policy: "If students' aesthetic criteria, artistic aspirations, and standards of satisfactory performance are at odds with those of their teachers, the grounds for effective educational interventions become seriously compromised" (Kindler, 2000, p. 27). (Further data on this point are contained in studies including those by Cunningham [1997], Kim [1998], and Kindler and Darras [1998], which identify qualities children from diverse cultural contexts admire in drawings, pointing to features such as beauty, expressiveness, color, neatness, evident effort, representational accuracy, and balance).

In his study of Japanese children's art-making practices, Wilson (1997) lends further insight into these matters. He compares children's drawings produced in the style of an enormously popular comic book called Manga with the imagery of formal arts training in Japan (see also Toku, 2001). In the U.S.-based literature, researchers have also noted the strong influence of comic book and commercial imagery on the artwork of older children, often characterizing these drawings as "crass forms that young people teach one another" (Wilson, 1997, p. 159).

Wilson unsettles the notion that "high art models" are superior to more readily accessible materials such as comic books and cartoons. He argues that Manga-inspired image making allows Japanese children to produce "their own little graphic worlds"—another artworld of sorts—through which they can experiment with significant life themes. Participation in peer culture then has the potential to channel back into new conceptions of self in society, as depicted and shaped through graphic configuration.

Overall, research reviewed in this section reveals a significant tension in the literature on self- and peer assessment in visual arts education. On the one hand, studies regard peer evaluation as a potential problem—a source of pressure that may rob the art-making experience of its intrinsic pleasure and sap children's imaginations. On the other hand, peer assessment can function as a source of learning for students, who perceive their own efforts in new ways by seeing them through others' eyes. Artworlds increasingly influenced by peer culture make their mark on the graphic productions of older children. Judging those images becomes increasingly complex, due to the various ways that scholars have linked child art to "high art" and popular culture models in diverse cultural locations. Literature on self- and peer assessments among adolescents further reveals the influence of artworlds and cultural fields, as adolescents experience and produce visual culture within school classrooms and inside arts-based communities of practice beyond school walls.

Youth: Social Participation, Community, and Critique

In 1976, Efland published a highly influential essay called "The School Art Style" in *Studies in Art Education*. In that essay he analyzes the school as an artworld that shapes student artwork in strong but sometimes subtle ways. School functions and philosophies—a humanistic orientation and the use of art as a kind of therapy, for example—register in the art style teachers and students value (see also Siegesmund, 2002). The work should be "relatively free of cognitive strain," liberated from external influence, and perceptually inviting (Efland, 1976, p. 42). Schools have changed in significant ways since Efland first described the school art style, but his larger point that educational institutions shape youth art production continues to resonate through arts education literature.

A key question in that literature centers on how young people learn, reproduce, and, in some cases critique institutionalized artworld values through their own practices of self- and peer assessments. Cotner (2001) approaches this question by focusing on "classroom art talk." Just as Efland identifies a particular style that marked the images students produced inside classrooms in the abstract expressionist-oriented 1970s, Cotner notes patterns in the modes of communication adolescents in art class use today. Like Efland (1976, 1995) Cotner finds that school conventions and priorities—assignments, grades, evaluation systems—shape what students come to value in their own work and that of their peers.

A Call for Self-Assessment.   Researchers and practitioners are currently reexamining school evaluation systems in the arts and beyond to create more meaningful opportunities for students to participate in self- and peer assessments. This orientation is not new. In 1985, Szekeley pointed out that teacher evaluation alone says nothing about how students value their own images or the experience of making them. The ability to self-assess, he argues, is key for goal setting and continued improvement: "Students therefore need to be taught a slower pace of seeing," with time to pause, reflect, and transform unfolding work (Szekeley, 1985, p. 39). As students carry increasing responsibility for "active seeing" and reevaluation of their own efforts and those of peers and established artists, teachers move into the role of audience for student reflections—a thoughtful questioner who facilitates young people's involvement in self-assessment.

With Szekeley (1985) as an early example, contemporary researchers intensify this interest in understanding and facilitating practices that foster self- and peer assessments. Hicks, Hicks, Powell, and Simonton (1996) call for a shift in arts education's evaluation "landscape" away from an emphasis on numbers, comparisons, and competition and toward an emphasis on personal assessment processes and outcomes: "Self-evaluation skills are a key to the future for everyone. This means that each of us must internalize evaluation options and be able to manipulate criteria appropriate for different settings" (Hicks et al. 1996, p. 55). When students are expected to generate, and not just respond to, assessment questions, these authors find improvement in student work, self-confidence, and overall skills with evaluation tasks. Like Hicks and colleagues, Anderson and Milbrandt (1998) advocate for new assessment strategies in "authentic" art instruction, with "self-reflection" playing an especially important role. This emphasis amounts to a shift toward shared responsibility for student learning, where young people are expected to discover the "real-life" relevance of specific arts tasks and skills and construct meaning from those connections. Anderson and Milbrandt (1998) emphasize that personal reflectiveness depends on high levels of social support and substantive conversation, once again pointing to the deep interdependence of self- and peer assessments, which they say together motivate and transform arts learning environments (see also Fowler, 2001).

Specific practices that invite self- and peer assessments include portfolios, exhibitions of understanding, journals, research workbooks, and reflective dialog, all of which factor prominently, to varying degrees and in different combinations, in contemporary visual arts curriculum and policy approaches including Discipline-Based Arts Education, National Standards, ARTS PROPEL, Advanced Placement, and International Baccalaureate programs (Anderson, 1990; Arnstein, 1990; Blaikie, 1994; Chalmers, 1989; Eisner, 1987, 1990; Gardner, 1989; National Standards for Arts Education, 1994; Ross, Radnor, Mitchell, & Bierton, 1993; Schultz, 2002; Studies in Arts Education, 1998; Winner, 1991). One curriculum practice that is especially steeped in processes of self- and peer assessmentss is critique.

Self- and Peer Critiques.   Critique in arts education takes its most prominent position in college and university art departments (cf, Barrett, 1988, 1997; Bulka, 1996; Cline, 1994; James, 1996; Laing, 1976; Lerman, 1993; Rogers, 1996; Roth, 1999), where students periodically display work and spend several hours discussing the strengths and weaknesses of each piece. Together with instructors, students describe what they see in the images displayed, offer advice, suggest new techniques, and notice connections with works by well-known artists (Soep, 1996, in press).

Although few theoretically grounded and empirically based studies of critique exist (Bulka, 1996), the practice has attracted attention from practitioners and scholars interested in the proper place for self- and peer assessment in arts education. Literature on critique highlights sessions that center on a completed piece or body of work, primarily within college or university art departments and dependent on skills and habits of the instructor. In her study of college critiques, Rogers (1996, p. 124) finds that discussions driven by aspiration (what a person wants within a given set of circumstances) promote more "integrative solutions" than does talk entrenched in position (what ideology a person claims). Art objects function as "interactants" in discussion, argues Rogers, as the works themselves help structure conversation. Tensions related to the status of the object as interactant emerge in an essay by Roth (1999). The contentiousness of a critique he describes intensifies, and the utility diminishes, when discussion veers away from the work itself; participants search for answers from the artist, entertaining theoretical debates with tenuous connection to paintings under discussion.

In her analysis of learning and teaching in a college-level sculpture studio, James (1996) takes a sociocultural approach. She characterizes critique as the final phase of instruction—coming after a foundational phase, where the instructor introduces basic techniques, and a studio phase, where students experiment heavily with materials. The critique phase should, according to James, create a safe environment through "spontaneity, empathy, and equality" (1996, p. 153), and the teacher should conclude the discussion by instilling key concepts using student work as examples. When this kind of positive educational environment fails to materialize, critique can give rise to an experience of painful self-exposure, argues Wernik (1985) in his study of the psychological aspects of critique in an art and design academy—as if the artist is "being hung naked on the wall and ridiculed" (p. 194). Wernik says critique should operate as a thoughtful dialog rather than as a judgmental verdict, and he is wary of sessions that lead students to negative self-evaluations or to create asymmetries within the group. Drawing on early work by Gibb (1961), Wernik identifies the characteristics that generate a supportive climate for critique. Along with spontaneity, empathy, and equality (the same features noted by James), Wernik also calls for a focus on description, a problem orientation, and a commitment to "provisionalism" in commentary offered in critique. Overall, research on college-level critiques demonstrates a marked duality: Critique can motivate learners on the one hand, fortifying their efforts, and intimidate on the other hand, with potentially counterproductive effects.

Few researchers have published refereed studies of critique in K-12 arts classrooms. Barrett (1994, 1997, 2000) is perhaps the most notable exception (see also Blythe, Allen, & Schieffelin Powell, 1999; Cotton, 1981; Ende-Saxe, 1990; House 2001). Artwork produced by peers constitutes a starting place for teaching students to think critically about art and its place in the world, says Barrett (1994, 1997, 2000)—a habit of mind that has the potential to translate into the strategies students develop to analyze adult exhibited art. Critique among young artists should not be judgmental, negative, prescriptive, oblique, lacking in approval, or directed exclusively by the instructor (1997, pp. 2–3). The process should have a purpose, invite participation, include positive and negative judgments supported by reasons, emphasize interpretation over evaluation, and privilege the viewer as the most important participant. Facilitators of critique should be prepared, says Barrett, to ask and elicit good questions, and to address fundamental issues pertaining to intent, content, subject matter, form, relationship of media to materials, sources of artistic influence, and social issues. In essence, Barrett (1994) views critique as a mode of argumentation and evidence-based persuasion. When students assess their own work and that of their peers, their interpretations reflect personal and communal ideologies. Barrett (2000) sees the model of mentoring as a useful way to approach critique facilitation, with the instructor playing the role of an "elder" who is affirming, loving and nurturing through a "reciprocal" relationship with learners marked by shared responsibility.

Whereas Barrett's work suggests that critique can play a role in classroom settings, this process occupies an especially important place in youth-based environments for art making beyond school walls. Relatively little research is available that considers the impact of nonschool conditions on how peers communicate and collaboratively produce in the arts. A 10-year national study of community-based youth organizations directed by Heath and McLaughlin (1994a, 1994b; Heath, 2001; Heath & Ball, 1993; Heath with Soep & Roach, 1998; Heath & Soep, 1998) is one exception (see also Davis, Soep, Maira, Putnoi, & Remba [1993] and Lawrence-Lightfoot & Davis [1998]). Heath and McLaughlin's research initially centered on the organizational features and cognitive and linguistic processes associated with educational experiences youth deem worthy of their discretionary time. Investigators later focused especially on arts-based activities—after-school mural-making projects, teen theater troupes, drum corps, and the like. In young people's eyes, some of the most robust features that distinguish the effective community-based arts sites are directly linked to self- and peer assessments.

Activities in these settings involve high levels of risk. Youth are expected to reveal personal stories, invest in projects with unpredictable outcomes, and collaborate with diverse groups of peers. These conditions make assessment of self and peer an ongoing, necessary process—the only way young people can move forward with the work and continually monitor its quality (Soep, 2002). There are no grades or tests—only collaboratively negotiated standards and anticipated audience or viewer reactions. As a result, young people use episodes of assessment not only to voice their own opinions but also to imagine how outside evaluators will respond to the work. An ongoing process of peer critique surfaces in these settings. The conditions of *risk*, *responsibility* for consequences, and continually shifting *rules* that characterize these sites promote an environment where self- and peer assessments are not assigned by an instructor, who ultimately serves as final arbiter. Rather, dimensions of the arts projects they undertake drive young people to turn to one another for advice, inspiration, and critique as they subject their work to internal group evaluation and prepare their work for release to outside audiences (Heath & Soep, 1998). Dimensions including mutual accountability, forced interdisciplinarity, and negotiated standards create conditions where critiques of self and peer provide a foundation for learning and making (Soep, 2003).

Communities of Critical Arts Practice.   Studies of nonschool settings for arts education illuminate how various communities of practice shape learning and assessment conventions. Contemporary researchers—especially those focused on adolescents—increasingly explore the ideologies and interactions that characterize community-based arts experiences (Campbell, 2001; Fleetwood, forthcoming; Keifer-Boyd, 2000; Paley, 1995; Trend, 1997) as well as the potential for the notion of "communities of practice" to transform arts learning inside classrooms (Fehr et al., 2000; Holloway & Krensky, 2001; Lowe, 2001; Neperud, 1995; Yokley, 1999). Many of these studies describe visual arts projects tied to local conditions and social justice concerns and organized through new media technologies and collaborative practice. The arts in this sense are a means to "act upon" communities (Marche, 1998) and act within communities through joint undertakings that matter for participants and for real audiences whose opinions count. The orientation of these visions for visual arts education range from critical pedagogy-inspired conceptions of the arts as engines of social change (see prior citations) to models derived from the design world that forefront the role of audience and joint problem solving (Davis, 1999) to paradigms based in visual culture as a site of critical understanding and empowerment (Duncum, 2002; Freedman, 2000), as well as to a system of "rhetoric" for everyday life (Cintron, 1997). These arts learning scenarios, diverse as they are, share the function of recasting the role of self- and peer assessment. Young people working in critical communities of arts practice hold themselves to standards that derive not solely from a personal expressive instinct, nor from an externally prescribed set of outcomes, but from a complex combination of these factors negotiated through ongoing reflection on one's own place in the world and the kind of work worth doing. As Sullivan (1993) argues in his call for a "meaningful, authentic, critical, and pluralist" arts education, when students plan projects, share responsibility for creative choices, and reflect critically on questions of meaning and cultural authority, self and peer emerge as key sites for assessment. At stake in such environments is not only the artwork as object, but the personal and collective meanings that object sustains.

CONCLUSION: VISUALIZED WORLDS

Although contemporary researchers call for meaningful, socially engaged, critically motivated orientations to the arts, they also continue to wrestle with an enduring debate in the field of arts education—whether participation in the arts boosts academic achievement (Darby & Caterall, 1994, 1998; Eisner, 1998; Hetland & Winner, 2001). A commitment to socially engaged arts experiences by no means precludes positive academic outcomes, as the former can promote cognitive skills and habits often linked to academic performance (Heath & Roach, 1999)—including capacities for self regulation (Jones & Davenport, 1996); creativity, fluency, originality, and elaboration (Burton, Horowitz, & Abeles, 1999); metacognition (Sullivan, 1993); thinking "within" a medium (Eisner, 2001) and integrated learning (Darby & Catterall, 1994). One might in fact argue that a capacity to assess the self and peers is among the most important determinants of achievement in more institutionally privileged domains like math, science, and English, as well as in the arts.

However, recent research calls into question the suggestion that these capacities necessarily migrate from one field of practice to another (Hetland & Winner, 2001). And very often researchers do not focus so much on these capacities anyway, because documented improvement on *test scores* in math and English, or elevated *grades* in academic courses, are the data that draw the most attention in academic, policymaking, and public debates. The pull toward these outcomes takes us two steps away from arts education. First, we translate the original arts experience in terms of academic implications. Second, we translate academic learning into a language of quantified measurement. The scenario can start to feel like a game of telephone, where the final message bears little in common with the original meaning.

That is not to say the arts should be fetishized within a sacred domain unto themselves, divorced from other related fields of practice, including academic pursuits and popular culture experience. Quite the contrary. A view of the arts as social practice reveals just how interconnected art making is with learning how to see the self, others, objects, and contexts in new ways. Several clear empirical questions surface out of this review of research on self- and peer assessments. What conditions promote self- and peer assessments as necessary activities rather than as empty exercises, and as edifying experiences rather than as encounters that ultimately turn young people away from art making? How can researchers better account for nonverbalized assessment? Although we have a sense of how young people communicate feedback to peers, more research is needed to understand how assessment recipients actually interpret, selectively heed, and in some cases totally reject the specific comments and implicit ideologies they gather from classmates and artworld institutions.

There are also more profound tensions evident in this body of literature. There are debates over what fields merit inclusion inside arts classrooms—not only "fine arts" models but also those operating within popular culture, underground artworlds, and digital environments. It is likely that young people would bring to these expanded fields new forms of authority and new systems of interpretation that would significantly shape the conventions of self- and peer assessments. A second key tension pertains to the relationship between large-scale assessment policies and moment-to-moment assessment-laced interactions young people and teachers experience on a daily basis. If the field primarily prioritizes external evaluation procedures distant from the kinds of things young people actually care and talk about in practice, not only do qualities of the art-making experience recede, but also potentially meaningful modes of self- and peer assessments are suppressed under the weight of institutionally sanctioned accountability demands.

These are the kinds of tensions that might shape new research questions within the field of visual arts education. But perhaps the most promising indicator of where the field is headed appears in the sense that more and more researchers are subjecting *themselves* to brave encounters with self- and peer assessment (Gee, 2001). Investigators are increasingly reflexive about how they use art world categories and assumptions about learning and child development. Meta-analyses and ongoing debates are opportunities for researchers to challenge one another and face hard truths about their own practices as analysts of arts experience. In this sense, arts education research is exactly like arts learning experience: deeply personal and absolutely social, at the same time.

REFERENCES

Adi-Japhe, E., Levin, I., & Solomon, S. (1998). Emergence of representation in drawing: The relation between kinematics and referential aspects. *Cognitive Development, 13*(1), 25–51.

Amabile, T. (1989). *Growing up creative*. New York: Crown.

Anderson, T. (1990). Attaining critical appreciation through art. *Studies in Art Education, 31*(3), 132–140.

Anderson, T., & Milbrandt, M. (1998). Authentic instruction in art: Why and how to dump the school art style. *Visual Arts Research, 24*(1), 13–20.

Arnheim, R. (1998). Why words are needed. *Journal of Aesthetic Education, 32*(2), 21–25.

Arnstein, D. (1990). Art, aesthetics, and the pitfalls of discipline-based art education. *Educational Theory, 40*(4), 415–422.

Atkinson, D. (1999). A critical reading of the national curriculum for art in light of contemporary theories of subjectivity. *Journal of Art and Design Education, 18*(1), 107–113.

Barrett, T. (1988). A comparison of the goals of studio professors conducting critiques and art education goals for teaching criticism. *Studies in Art Education, 30*(1), 22–27.

Barrett, T. (1994). Principles for interpreting art. *Art Education, 47*(5), 8–13.

Barrett, T. (1997). *Talking about Student Art. Art Education Practice Series*. Worcester, MA: Davis Publications.

Barrett, T. (2000). Studio critiques of student art: As they are, as they could be with mentoring. *Theory Into Practice, 39*(1), 29–35.

Baum, S., Owen, S., & Oreck, B. (1997). Transferring individual self-regulation processes from arts to academics. *Art Education Policy Review, 98*(4), 32–39.

Becker, H. (1982). *Art worlds*. Berkeley: University of California Press.

Berk, L. (1992). Children's private speech: An overview of theory and the status of research. In R. Diaz & L. Berk (Eds.), (pp. 17–53). Private speech: From social interaction to self-regulation. Hillsdale, NJ: Lawrence Erlbaum, Associates.

Bireley, M., & Genshaft, J. (1991). *Understanding the gifted adolescent: Educational, developmental, and multicultural issues*. New York: Teachers College Press.

Blaikie, F. (1994). Values inherent in qualitative assessment of secondary studio art in North America: Advanced placement, Arts PROPEL, and International Baccalaureate. *Studies in Arts Education, 35*(4), 237–48.

Blythe, T., Allen, D., & Schieffelin Powell, B. (1999). *Looking together at student work*. New York: Teachers College Record.

Bourdieu, P. (1984). *Distinction: A social critique of the judgment of taste*. Cambridge: Harvard University Press.

Bourdieu, P. (1991). *Language and symbolic power*. Cambridge: Harvard University Press.

Bourdieu, P. (1993). *The field of cultural production*. New York: Columbia University Press.

Boyatzis, C. (2000). The artistic evolution of mommy: A longitudinal case study of symbolic and social processes. *New Directions for Child and Adolescent Development, 90*, 5–29.

Bulka, J. (1996). You call that art? A critique of the critique. *The New Art Examiner, 23*(6), 22–25.

Burton, J., Horowitz, R., & Abeles, H. (1999). Learning in & through the arts: Curriculum implications. In E. Fiske (Ed.), *Champions of change: The arts & learning* (pp. 35–46). Washington, DC: Arts Education Partnership.

Cahan, S., & Kocur, Z. (1996). *Contemporary art and multicultural education*. New York: The New Museum of Contemporary Art.

Campbell, S. (2001). Shouts in the dark: Community arts organizations for students in rural schools with "urban" problems. *Education and Urban Society, 33*(4), 445–456.

Carolan, R. (2001). Models and paradigms of art therapy research. *Art Therapy, 18*(4), 190–220.

Catterall, J. (1998). Involvement in the Arts and Success in Secondary School. Washington DC. *Americans for the Arts, Monograph, 1*(9).

Chalmers, G. (1989). The international baccalaureate (I.B.) art/design program. *School Arts, 88*(9), 34–36.

Cintron, R. (1997). *Angels' town: Chero ways, Gang life, and rhetorics of the everyday*. Boston: Beacon Press.

Cline, B. (1994). *Critiquing student photographs in the college classroom*. Unpublished doctoral dissertation. Ohio University College of Education.

Cotner, T. (2001). Why study classroom art talk? *Art Education, 54*(1), 12–17.

Cotton, C. (1981). Critique: A middle school evaluation system. *School Arts, 80*(5), 46–47.

Cunningham, A. (1997). Criteria and processes used by seven-year-old children in appraising art work of their peers. *Visual Arts Research, 23*(1), 41–48.

Csikszentmihalyi, M. (1996). *Creativity: Flow and the psychology of discovery and invention*. New York: Harper Collins.

Csikszentmihalyi, M., Rathunde, K., Whalen, S., & Wong, M. (2000). *Talented teenagers: The roots of success and failure*. Cambridge: Cambridge University Press.

Darby, J., & Catterall, J. (1994). The fourth R: The arts and learning. *Teachers College Record, 96*(2), 299–328.

Davis, J. (1997a). Drawing's demise: U-shaped development in graphic symbolization. *Studies in Art Education, 38*(3), 132–57.

Davis, J. (1997b). Does the U in the U-Curve also stand for universal? Some reflections on Pariser's provisional doubts. *Studies in Art Education, 38*(3), 179–85.

Davis, J. (1997c). The what and the whether of the U: Cultural implications of understanding development in graphic symbolization. *Human Development, 40*, 145–154.

Davis, M. (1999). Design knowledge: Broadening the content domain of art education. *Arts Education Policy Review, 101*(2), 27–32.

Davis, J., & Gardner, H. (1992). The cognitive revolution in human understanding: Its consequences for the understanding and education of the child as artist. In R. Smith (Ed.), *The Arts, Education, and Aesthetic Knowing, Part II. National Society for the Study of Education Yearbook.* Chicago: University of Chicago Press.

Davis, J., & Gardner, H. (1993). The arts and early childhood education: A cognitive approach to the young child as artist. In B. Spodek (Ed.), *The Handbook of Research on the Education of Young Children.* New York: MacMillan.

Davis, J., Soep, E., Maira, S., Putnoi, D., & Remba, N. (1993). *Safe havens: Community arts centers that focus on education in economically disadvantaged neighborhoods.* Cambridge, MA: Harvard Project Zero.

Diaz, R., & Berk, L. (1992). *Private speech: From social interaction to self regulation.* Hillsdale, NJ: Lawrence Erlbaum Associates.

DiPardo, A., & Freedman, S. (1988). Peer response groups in the writing classroom: theoretical foundations and new directions. *Review of Educational Research, 58*(2), 119–147.

Duncum, P. (1989). To copy or not to copy: A review. *Studies in Art Education, 29*(4), 203–210.

Duncum, P. (2000). A multiple pathways/multiple endpoints model of graphic development. *Visual Arts Research, 25*(2), 38–47.

Duncum, P. (2002). Clarifying visual culture art education. *Art Education, 55*(3), 6–11.

Efland, A. (1976). The school art style: A functional analysis. *Studies in Art Education, 7*(2), 36–44.

Efland, A. (1995). The spiral and the lattice: Changes in cognitive learning theory with implications for art education. *Studies in Art Education, 36*(3), 134–153.

Eisner, E. (1987). *What is discipline-based arts education? The role of discipline-based arts education in American schools* (pp. 14–35). Los Angeles: Getty Center for Education in the Arts.

Eisner, E. (1990). Discipline-based arts education: Conceptions and misconceptions. *Educational Theory, 40*(4), 423–430.

Eisner, E. (1992). The misunderstood role of the arts in human development. *Phi Delta Kappan, 73*(8), 595–595.

Eisner, E. (1997). Cognition and representation: A way to pursue the American dream? *Phi Delta Kappan, 78*(5), 348–53.

Eisner, E. (1998). Does experience in the arts boost academic achievement? *Art Education, 51*(1), 7–15.

Eisner, E. (2001). Should we create new aims for art education? *Art Education, 54*(5), 6–10.

Ende-Saxe, S. (1990). The elementary antique. *School Arts, 90*(3), 22–23.

Fehr, D., Fehr, K., & Keifer-Boyd, K. (2000). *Real world readings in art education: Things your professors never told you.* New York: Falmer Press.

Feldman, D., Czikszentmihalyi, M., & Gardner, H. (1994). *Changing the world: A framework for the study of creativity.* Westport, CT: Praeger.

Fleetwood, N. (in press). Authenticating practices: Producing realness in youth videos. In S. Maira & E. Soep (Eds.), *Youthscapes: Popular cultures, national ideologies, global markets.* Philadelphia: University of Pennsylvania Press.

Fowler, J. (2001). If the shoe fits, make it into art. *Art Education, 54*(5), 18–23.

Freedman, K. (1997). Artistic development and curriculum: Sociocultural learning considerations. In A. Kindler (Ed.), *Child Development in Art,* 95–106. Reston, VA: National Art Education Association.

Freedman, K. (2000). Social perspectives on Art Education in the US: Teaching visual culture in a democracy. *Studies in Art Education, 41*(4), 314–329.

Freeman, N. H. (1997). Identifying resources from which children advance into pictorial innovation. *Journal of Aesthetic Education, 31*(4), 23–34.

Gallas, K. (1994). *The languages of learning: How children talk, write, dance, draw, and sing their understanding of the world.* New York: Teachers College Press.

Gee, C. (2001). The perils and parables of research on research. *Arts Education Policy Review, 102*(5), 31–38.

Gerhart, G. (1986). Effects of evaluative statements on artistic performance and motivation. *Studies in Art Education, 27*(2), 61–72.

Gibb, J. R. (1961). Defensive communication. *Journal of Communication, 11*(3), 141–148.

Goodman, N. (1976). *Languages of art.* Indianapolis: Hackett Publishing Company.

Gutierrez, K. (1992). A comparison of instructional contexts in writing process classrooms with Latino children. *Education and Urban Society, 24*, 244–262.

Hafeli, M. (2000). Negotiating "fit" in student art work: Classroom conversations. *Studies in Art Education, 41*(2), 130–145.

Hartung, E. S. (1995). The many faces of critique. *School Arts, 95*(2), 36–37.

Heath, S. B. (2001). Three's not a crowd: plans, roles, and focus in the arts. *Educational Researcher, 30*(7), 10–17.

Heath, S. B., & McLaughlin, M. (1994a). Learning for anything everyday. *Journal of Curriculum Studies, 26*(5), 549–567.

Heath, S. B., & McLaughlin, M. (1994b). The best of both worlds: Connecting schools and community youth organizations for all-day, all-year learning. *Educational Administration Quarterly, 30*(3), 278–300.

Heath, S. B., & Roach, A. (1999). Imaginative actuality: Learning in the arts during the non-school hours. In E. Fiske (Ed.), *Champions of change: The arts & learning* (pp. 35–46). Washington, DC: Arts Education Partnership

Heath, S. B., & Smyth, L. (1999). *ArtShow: Youth and community development, a resource guide.* Washington DC: Partners for Livable Communities.

Heath, S. B., & Soep, E. (1998). Youth development and the arts in the nonschool hours. *Grantmakers for the Arts, 9*(1), 9–16.

Heath, S. B., Soep, E., & Roach, A. (1998). Living the arts through language learning: A report on community-based organizations. *Americans for the Arts, 2*(7), 1–20.

Hetland, L., & Winner, E. (2001). The arts and academic achievement: What the evidence shows. *Art Education Policy Review, 102*(5), 3–6.

Hicks, J., Hicks, M., Powell, J., & Simonton, L. (1996). Evaluation: Need for a new landscape. *Art Education, 49*(3), 51–57.

Holloway, D., & Krensky, B. (2001). Introduction: The arts, urban education and social change. *Education and Urban Society, 33*(4), 354–365.

House, N. (2001). Critiques in the K-12 Classroom. *NAEA Advisory*, Spring.

James, P. (1996). The construction of learning and teaching in a sculpture studio class. *Studies in Arts Education, 37*(3), 145–159.

Jones, J., & Davenport, M. (1996). Self-regulation in Japanese and American art education. *Art Education, 49*(1), 60–65.

Kakas, K. (1991). Classroom communication during fifth grade students' drawing lessons: Student-student and student-teacher conversations. *Studies in Arts Education, 33*(1), 21–35.

Keifer-Boyd, K. (2000). By the people: A community-based art curriculum. In D. Fehr, K. Fehr, & K. Keifer-Boyd (Eds.), (pp. 155–166). Realworld readings in art education: Things your professor never told you. New York Falmer Press.

Kim, N. (1998). Age and test stimuli effects on children's preference for compositional balance. *Visual Arts Research, 24*(1), 48–64.

Kindler, A. (2000). From the U-curve to dragons: Culture and understanding of artistic development. *Visual Arts Research, 26*(2), 15–28.

Kindler, A., & Darras, B. (1997). Map of artistic development. In A Kindler (Ed.), *Child Development in Art* (pp. 17–44). Reston, VA: NAEA.

Kindler, A., & Darras, B. (1998). Culture and development of pictorial repertoires. *Studies in Art Education, 39*(2), 147–167.

Laing, R. (1976). *An application of the world hypothesis inquiry method to describe the quality of he verbal art critique.* Unpublished doctoral dissertation.

Lensmire, T. (1998). Rewriting student voice. *Journal of Curriculum Studies, 30*(3), 251–291.

Lerman, L. (1993). Toward a process of critical response. *High Performance, 16*, 46–47.

Love, J., & Wenger, E. (1991). Situated learning: Legitimate peripheral participation. Cambridge: Cambridge University Press.

Lowe, S. (2001). The art of community transformation. *Education and Urban Society, 33*(4), 457–471.

Marche, T. (1998). Looking outward, looking in: Community art education. *Art Education, 51*(3), 6–13.

Matthews, J. (1994). Deep structures in children's art: Development and culture. *Visual Arts Research, 20*(2), 29–50.

Montuori, A., & Purser, R. (1999). *Social Creativity* (Vol. 1). Cresskill, NJ: Hampton Press.

National standards for Arts Education. (1994). *What every young American should know and be able to do in the Arts.* Reston, VA: Music Educators National Conference.

Neperud, R. N. (1995). *Context, content and community in art education: Beyond Postmodernism.* New York: Teachers College Press.

Paley, N. (1995). *Finding art's place: Experiments in contemporary education and culture.* New York: Routledge.

Pariser, D., & Berg, A. (1997a). The mind of the beholder: Some provisional doubts about the U-shaped aesthetic development thesis. *Studies in Art Education, 38*(3), 158–178.

Pariser, D., & Berg, A. (1997b). Beholder beware: A reply to Jessica Davis. *Studies in Art Education, 38*(3), 186–192.

Parsons, M. (1998). Integrated curriculum and our paradigm of cognition in the arts. *Studies in Art Education, 39*(2), 103–116.

Pearson, P. (2001). Towards a theory of children's drawing as social practice. *Studies in Art Education, 42*(4), 348–365.

Pufall, P. (1997). Framing a developmental psychology of art. *Human Development, 40*, 169–180.

Ramirez, J. (1992). The functional differentiation of social and private speech: A dialogic approach. In R. Diaz, & L. Berk (Eds.), *Private speech: From social interaction to self-regulation* (pp. 199–214). Hillsdale, NJ: Lawrence Erlbaum Associates.

Richmond, S. (1998). In praise of practice: A defense of art making in education. *Journal of Aesthetic Education, 32*(2), 11–20.

Rogers, J. (1996). *The concept of framing and its role in teacher-student negotiations during desk critiques in the architectural design studio.* Unpublished doctoral dissertation.

Rogoff, B. (1994). Developing understanding of the ides of communities of learners. *Mind, Culture, and Activity, 1*(4), 209–229.

Ross, M., Radnor, H., Mitchell, S., & Bierton, C. (1993). *Assessing achievement in the arts.* Buckingham: Open University Press.

Roth, R. (1999). The crit. *Art Journal, 58*(1), 32–35.

Schultz, R. (2002). Apples, oranges, and assessment. *Arts Education Policy Review, 103*(3), 11–16.

Siegesmund, R. (2002). Bringing accountability to elementary art. *Kappa Delta Pi, 39*(1), 24–28.

Soep, E. (1996). An art in itself: Youth development through critique. *New Designs for Youth Development, 12*(4), 42–46.

Soep, E. (2002). Abnormal educational vision: Art in the city beyond school. *Kappa Delta Pi Record, 39*(1), 12–16.

Soep, E. (2003). Learning about research from youth media artists. *Penn GSE Perspectives on Urban Education, 1*(3).

Soep, E. (In Press). The making of hard core masculinities: Teenage boys playing house. In S. Maira & E. Soep (Eds.), *Youthscapes: Popular cultures, National ideologies, global markets.* Philadelphia: University of Pennsylvania Press.

Soep, E., & Cotner, T. (1999). Speaking the mind and minding the speech: Novices interpret art. *Studies in Art Education, 40*(4), 350–372.

Sperling, M. (1996). Revisiting the writing-speaking connection: Challenges for research on writing and writing instruction. *Review of Educational Research, 66*(1), 53–86.

Stibbs, A. (1998). Language in art and art in language. *Journal of Art Design Education, 17*(2), 201–209.

Sullivan, G. (1993). Art-based art education: Learning that is meaningful, authentic, critical, and pluralist. *Studies in Art Education, 35*(1), 5–21.

Swann, A. (1986). Child/adult interaction during art activities in a preschool setting: An achievement seeking response. *Arts and Learning Research, 4*(6), 73–79.

Szekeley, G. (1985). Teaching students to understand their artwork. *Art Education, 38*(5), 38–43.

Taunton, M. (1984). Reflective dialogue in the art classroom: Focusing on art process. *Art Education, 37*(1), 15–16.

Taunton, M. (1986). The conveyance of aesthetic values during art activities in grades one through three. *Arts and Learning Research, 4*(1), 56–63.

Taunton, M. (1987). Communication patterns during structured and unstructured art activities in an elementary classroom. *Arts and Learning Research, 5*(1), 62–74.

Thompson, C. (2000). Drawing together: Peer influences in preschool-kindergarten art classes. *Visual Arts Research, 25*(2), 61–68.

Thompson, C., & Bales, S. (1991). Michael doesn't like my dinosaurs": Conversations in a preschool art class. *Studies in Art Education, 33*(1), 43–55.

Toku, M. (2001). What is Manga? The influence of pop culture on adolescent art. *Art Education, 54*(2), 11–17.

Trend, D. (1997). The fine art of teaching. In H. Giroux & P. Shannon (Eds.), *Education and cultural studies: Toward a performative practice* (pp. 249–258). New York: Routledge.

Tudge, J., & Winterhoff, P. (1993). Vygotsky, Piaget, and Bandura: Perspectives on the relations between the social world and cognitive development. *Human Development, 36*, 61–81.

Vinter, A. (1999). How meaning modifies drawing behavior in children. *Child Development, 70*(1), 33–49.

Vygotsky, L. (1978). *Mind and society: The development of higher psychological processes.* Cambridge: Harvard University Press.

Vygotsky, L. (1986). *Thought and language.* Cambridge: MIT Press.

Wernik, U. (1985). Psychological aspects of criticism in an academy of art and design. *Journal of Creative Behavior, 19*(3), 194–201.

Wertsch, J. (1991). *Voices of the mind: A sociocultural approach to mediated action.* Cambridge: Harvard University Press.

Wilson, B. (1996). Arts standards and fragmentation: A strategy for holistic assessment. *Art Education Policy Review, 98*(2), 2–9.

Wilson, B. (1997). Types of child art and alternative developmental accounts: Interpreting the interpreters. *Human Development, 40*, 155–168.

Wilson, B., & Wilson, M. (1981). The case of the disappearing two-eyed profile or how little children influence the drawing of little children. *Review of Research in Visual Arts Education, 15*, 1–18.

Winner, E. (1991). *Arts propel: An introductory handbook.* Princeton: Educational Testing Service and the President and Fellows of Harvard University.

Wolf, D. (1997). Reimagining development: Possibilities from the study of children's art. *Human Development, 40*, 189–194.

Wolf, D. (2000). Why the arts matter in education or just what do children learn when they create an opera? In E. Fiske (Ed.), *Champions of change: The impact of the arts on learning.* Washington, DC: The Arts Education Partnership and The President's Committee on the Arts and the Humanities.

Wolf, D., & Davis Perry, M. (1988). From endpoints to repertoires: Some new conclusions about drawing development. *Journal of Aesthetic Education, 22*(1), 17–34.

Wood, J. (1999). Reconsidering critical response: Student judgments of purpose, interpretation, and relationships in visual culture. *Studies in Art Education, 40*(2), 128–142.

Yokley, S. H. (1999). Embracing a critical pedagogy in art education. *Art Education, 52*(5), 18–24.

Zimmerman, B. (1998). Acquisition of self-regulatory skill: From theory and research to academic practice. In R. Bernhardt, C. Hedley, G. Cattaro, & V. Svolopoulos (Eds). *Curriculum leadership: Rethinking schools for the 21st Century.* Cresskill, NJ: Hampton Press.

VI

Emerging Visions of the Field

30

Emerging Visions of Art Education

Arthur D. Efland
The Ohio State University

INTRODUCTORY ESSAY

This section of the *Handbook* explores the role that educational visions play in charting the future of art education. "What are educational visions, and "why do they arise periodically throughout history? Why do specific visions achieve dominance within educational theory, and what is their role in shaping practice in art education? What kind of research and policy issues are brought into play when new visions seize the professional imagination? Is the conceptual articulation of a vision a form of research, a declaration of educational policy; or are they forms of advocacy?

In *A History of Art Education* (Efland, 1990), I identified a series of trends or streams of influence coursing through the past 2 centuries, each having their origins in opposing conceptions of the individual, the nature of knowledge, the role of the visual arts in social and cultural life, and in rival educational purposes. The visions that dominated the last 100 or so years were responses to the challenges of modernity, which ushered in unprecedented changes in the forms of work, in economic and social organization, and especially in new forms of art. Each critiqued the practices in art education of its day, offered remedies, and promoted reform. They weathered periods of conflict before gaining acceptance and changing established practices.

Each chapter in this section offers a series of potential visions for the future of art education. Each expressly or by implication offers its critique of current practice. Definitions of "current practice" vary from writer to writer. For some, current practice might be an art education grounded in traditional studio practice, whereas for others it may be discipline–based art education (DBAE) prominent in the 1980s. Others see their position as a refinement or elaboration of the discipline–based position, whereas others abandon it in pursuit of differing directions. To understand the nature of educational visions, I compare it with the term *paradigm*.

Visions, Paradigms, and Models

The Paradigm

Change in the history of science has been likened to a sequence of revolutions called "paradigm shifts" by the noted historian of science, Thomas Kuhn. (Kuhn, 1970; p. viii see also Efland, Freedman, & Stuhr, 1996).[1] Heretofore, progress in science was pictured as an uphill march toward enlightenment. Each advance in knowledge eliminated the falsehoods that obscured human understanding. Kuhn challenged this representation of science history by characterizing the path to enlightenment as a sequence of conceptual conflicts or "revolutions," where established views of nature were overturned by more comprehensive ones. Paradigms in Kuhn's view were: "universally recognized scientific achievements that for a time provide model problems and solutions to a community of practicioners" (p. viii). These serve as bases for the activities of the scientific community. Newton's view of the universe was the basic paradigm for physics for over 2 centuries. Einstein's relativity theory eventually supplanted it. Kuhn described periods called "normal science" as times when the prevailing paradigm seems to work, in the sense that its relevant phenomena appear to be covered by the explanations it provides. But, often, anomalous findings appear that do not readily fit into existing explanatory schemes causing the scientific community to seek more adequate explanations eventuating in a shift away from the existing paradigm to form a new one.

A paradigm is a conceptual system of ideas shared by a community of practicioners, but it is a social construction as well. In fact one might say that allegiance to a particular paradigm is what creates a community of practicioners, and that by implication, the lack of a paradigm makes the formulation of coherent policies and practices difficult or impossible. In the arts, Arthur Danto claimed that what creates an artworld is the theory of art its members share. Moreover, paradigms are not permanent or absolute.

The art historian Suzi Gablik (1991) extends the notion of a paradigm to cover cultures or societies in saying that:

> A paradigm is very powerful in the life of society since it influences the way we think, how problems are solved, what goals we pursue and what we value. The socially dominant paradigm is seldom, if ever, stated explicitly, but it unconsciously defines reality for most people, whose view of the world does not normally transcend the limits imposed by this cultural conditioning. (1991, pp. 2–3)

An educational paradigm covers the ways we think about the realities of schooling including students, teachers, curricula, and educational settings. It identifies goals to pursue and values to guide the selection and organization of content and activities. Before proceeding, it should be clear that the educational visions described in this section are *not paradigms*!

Distinguishing Visions From Paradigms

A vision is not a paradigm. *It is a candidate for a paradigm!* What makes a vision paradigmatic is its degree of acceptance within the professional community of art teachers, textbook writers, planners of curricula, students, and the public at large. The process of achieving paradigmatic status entails a discursive process through which a community like the artworld, the scientific

---

[1] See Chapter Three entitled Visions of Progress in Art Education in Efland Freedman and Stuhr, 1996.

community, or the community of art educators achieves a relative degree of consensus.[2] The educational visions put forth here are tentative or speculative proposals. *If and only if they achieve a degree of acceptance in the marketplace of ideas will the vision become paradigmatic.*

A vision might also be deemed a theoretical possibility, one that conceptualizes what shall be taught, to whom, with what results, and for what purposes? Paul Hirst's (1963) distinction between theory in the scientific sense and theory as a term used by educational practicioners helps to distinguish the two.

> In the case of the empirical sciences, a theory is a body of statements that have been subjected to tests which express our understanding of the physical world. Such tested theories are the objects, the end products of scientific investigation; they are the conclusions of the pursuit of knowledge. Where, however, a practical activity like education is concerned, the place of theory is totally different. It is not the end product of the pursuit, but rather is constructed to determine and guide the activity. (pp. 51–64)

Models of Teaching and Curriculum

Along with visions that may lead to paradigms, there are entities called *models*. Joyce and Weil (1980) offer a variety of educational models to identify alternative approaches to teaching, whereas Eisner identified several conflicting conceptions of curriculum (Eisner, 1971). Models are analytic devices used by students of curriculum to map the organization of ideas within a given educational setting. Here one studies their coherence, their consistency, and their perceived social relevance. To exemplify, if one believes that art is creative self-expression, then lessons that have the student copy pictures would make little sense. The practice can be said to be incommensurate with the theory. However, if one believes that art is an imitation of nature, then learning by copying to make imitations might be warranted. The idea of *art as an imitation of nature* and the view that learning occurs *by imitation* are compatible. In this example, one finds compatibility between a particular philosophy of art and the behaviorist view in psychology, which explains the acquisition of new behaviors by imitating the behavior of influential persons such as parents and teachers. Compatibility is no guarantee that the connection is based on a true connection. Ideas may be compatible yet wrong.

The Role of Visions

Educational visions play a role in shaping the educational imagination. One such vision arose in the work of Jean Jacques Rousseau's novel *Emile*. Rousseau described the emergence of the child's mind through its encounters with nature as a self-evident source of truth and goodness, free of social corruption. Rousseau ascribed all forms of evil to social influences; thus, his prescription of social reform was to educate children in the lessons of nature as a sufficient source of the good and the true. Social reform would begin by abandoning the traditional agencies of education involving church and state. In the years following Rousseau, educators like Pestalozzi and Froebel were inspired to base their instructional practices on nature rather than on books. The vision came from Rousseau, whereas the practice came from the latter. Progressive educators like Parker and Dewey also drew strength from Rousseau, and, in effect, his influence on educational practice lasted for more than 200 years. A great vision does more than advocate change; it inspires it! Rousseau's vision had become paradigmatic.

---

[2] A working consensus implies that each is willing to accept the same foundational assumptions as a basis for their practice yet may take issue with particular aspects of the paradigm. Consensus does not imply absolute agreement.

The Past 100 Years

In the early 1900s the teaching of art was still synonymous with the teaching of drawing. Unlike drawing as taught in the 19th century, with its emphasis on geometry, drawing as a form of nature study became more prominent. Then, a bold new emphasis took hold based on *elements and principles of design*. Design had become a universal means to organize instruction both to produce works of art and to study their form. During the 1920s another shift occurred favoring *creative self-expression*. The new movement arose to free the imagination of students enabling them to express ideas and feelings by creative methods rather than by imitation. Then, as the Great Depression and World War II affected society, the emphasis shifted once again, from individual expression to the use of *art in daily living*—to art in the life of the community, the home, and workplace. Finally, curriculum initiatives inspired by the challenges of the Cold War gave rise to the teaching *of art as a discipline.* Instruction was based on the inquiries of artists, art critics, art historians, and philosophers of art. Before introducing the chapters, each with an emerging vision, I offer brief reviews of these past developments to illustrate the character of the previous visions that made an impact on practice in art education.

Elements and Principles of Design

Arthur Wesley Dow (1913) is generally credited with having introduced the teaching of art through such elements as line and color organized by specific principles of composition. He called it a "Synthetic method of teaching art approach[ed] through the teaching of Design instead of through Drawing."[3] Dow spent 5 years studying in French art schools only to find that the academic theory of art, which was the basis for the professional training of artists, had left him quite unsatisfied. His own account is quite informative:

> In a search for something more vital I began a comparative study of the art of all nations and epochs. While pursuing an investigation of Oriental painting and design at the Boston Museum of Fine Arts, I met the late Professor Ernest Fenollosa. He was then in charge of the Japanese collections, a considerable portion of which had been gathered by him in Japan.... He at once gave me his cordial support in my quest, for he also felt the inadequacy of modern art teaching. He vigorously advocated a radically different idea, based as in music upon synthetic principles. (pp. 4–5)

Dow's pedagogy arose in an era when social Darwinism was an influential doctrine. Educators were urged to eliminate subjects that lacked social efficiency, with this defined by its survival potential. In the world of the tough–minded businessman, the artist had become a marginal figure. Then, it made sense to move art teaching toward such quasi–scientific doctrines as formalism. The art curriculum with the best chances of acceptance and survival was one that could demonstrate a structure organized in a scientific way. Art, like chemistry, was shown to have its elements and principles. Like the laws of science they were assumed to have universal applicability. The extraordinary complexity of the visual arts was reducible to a set of universal, teachable rules.

Creative Self-Expression

Advocacy for an educational vision based on creative self-expression can be seen in Harold Rugg and Ann Shumaker's manifesto, *The Child-Centered School* (1928). They contrasted

---

[3]The statement appears on the dust cover of the 17th edition.

schools whose aim was social efficiency with those fostering creative growth. In their opinion organizing the school around models of industrial efficiency had lost credibility.

> The aim of conventional education was social efficiency. Growth was seen as increasing power to conform, to acquiesce to a schooled discipline; maturity was viewed from the standpoint of successful compliance with social demands .... In the new school, however, it is the creative spirit from within that is encouraged rather than conformity to a pattern imposed from without. (p. 3)

A number of gifted art teachers, including Franz Cizek in Vienna, Marion Richardson in England, and Victor D'Amico and Viktor Lowenfeld in the United States established pedagogies based on the premise that child art is inherently valuable in and of itself. A second premise was the idea that this is a vulnerable art, easily corrupted by inimical social forces. The child had to be protected from hostile influences poised and ready to crush his or her tender sensibilities. Children were encouraged to create their own art rather than imitate others.

But why had the change from the highly structured approaches of the early 1900s given way to self-expression in art? What led to progressive education? One reason may well have been the increasing popularity of Freudian ideas among artists and intellectuals that called into question the mechanisms of repression and neurosis as its consequence. Another may have been the rise of a large and well-educated urban, middle class responding to the rising pressures of urbanization and social conformity. Many questioned the standardized practices of public schooling as being inconsistent with democratic ideals.

Art in Daily Living

The economic optimism of the 1920s ended dramatically with the crash of the stock market in 1929 and the Great Depression that ensued. These events also brought about a transformation in art education theory and practice. Emphasis shifted from the study of timeless masterpieces to the application of art knowledge in the life of the common man. This is seen in the forward of Leon Winslow's (1939) text on art education:

> Activities that have become divorced from community life and purposes are perhaps suitable or even indispensable for a school purporting to give a timeless culture for its own sake, but they are unsuitable for a school as a living community .... Art as a cult, as an esoteric experience for privileged devotees, may be an art that is needed in a school of the first type. Art as a service to men living a common life, art as a means of attaining community goals, is certainly needed in the modern school.

Similarly, Melvin Haggerty (1935) took pains to distinguish art in the American mainstream from the art of these sophisticated elites:

> Art as the province of the sophisticated few lies outside the pattern of our thinking here. Art as a cult may be a hindrance rather than an aid to art as a way of life, and it clearly seems to be so in many cases. The teachers of art must be those of the broad and crowded avenues of life, the home, the factory, and the marketplace. It is this conception that must be clarified and dramatized in concrete ways if art is to take its place in the schools as a major and vital instrument of cultural education. (p. 41)

Art textbooks began to appear that were organized around such themes as art in the community or art in the home. These include books like *Art Today* (Faulkner, Ziegfeld, & Hill, 1942) and *Exploring Art* (Kainz & Riley, 1949)

The Discipline Orientation

In October 1957, as the cold war deepened, the Soviet Union launched its first artificial satellite, which resulted in a wave of criticism directed at the status of schooling in the United States. Science and mathematics had to be strengthened if the nation was to sustain its technological edge. Considering the ensuing psychological climate, it is easy to see how subjects like art and music might well have been dispensed with. However, several art educators felt that if art education was to survive, it would have to be approached as a "demanding and disciplined field" (Barkan, 1962). In an address before the Western Arts Association, Manuel Barkan reviewed the history of self-expression as a movement, arguing that it was an idea whose time was at an end. He began by recalling the revolution that resulted in self-expression:

> ... in my opinion the dynamic impetus and creative emergence of truly new conceptions of the teaching of art occurred primarily between nineteen twenty-five and nineteen thirty-five. That was the decade of sharp conflict, debate, and controversy, when old established conceptions about the nature of art met their demise, along with the academic teaching procedures which accompanied them. That was the decade when living, dynamic, and progressive thoughts in education and in the teaching of art began their full ascendancy. Those ten years were in fact the period in which truly new educational ideas were born. They were the years when the creative ideological visions were invented.[4]

Barkan (1966) presented his vision for art education and argued that artistic inquiry is structured and that the curriculum should be based on the kinds of questions artists deal with in their work. Art education conceived as a humanistic discipline would have as its principle task to lead students to ask similar questions. Moreover, in Barkan's view, the artist should be accompanied by the art critic and art historian as scholars deeply involved in the interpretation of the human meaning questions raised by artists. Each offered modes of inquiry because the particular ways that they conceived and acted on such questions would be identical with the ways art educators should have students study art.

A chapter on discipline-based art education (DBAE) by Stephen Dobbs follows this introduction. Though DBAE was a vision that can trace its beginnings to the curriculum reform movements spurred by the Cold War tensions of the late 1950s and 1960s, the vision continues to change and evolve. In summarizing its history, Brent Wilson recognizes the differentiation of its practices by referring to DBAE as the "quiet evolution" (Wilson, 1997). A number of the educational visions presented in this section can be identified as modifications or outgrowths of DBAE. However, in all fairness, some authors regard their particular conception of the curriculum to be an outright repudiation of this particular tradition.

Table 30.1 summarizes the major characteristics of the dominant visions of 20th-century art education.

These visions inevitably spurred conflict with some being the result of simple inertia, a reluctance to change how things were done; but conflict was also driven by deeply felt divisions of opinion regarding the nature of art, the purposes of education, developmental issues, different beliefs about learning, and the like. Table 30.2 summarizes the issues in contention with each other.

---

[4]The extracts quoted from Barkan appeared in the draft of Barkan's address that was given before the Western Arts Association Conference in Cincinnati, Ohio, in 1962. They did not appear in the version published in *Art Education*.

TABLE 30.1
Four Dominant Visions of 20th-Century Art Education

Movement	Nature of Art	Content and Methods	Value of Art
Academic Art 17th–19th Centuries	Mimetic aesthetics: Art imitates nature.	Copying from artists or copying from nature as in life drawing.	Values are found in the accuracy of representations.
Elements of Design: Early 20th Century	Formalist aesthetics: Art is formal order.	Teach elements and principles through a sequence of exercises.	Values are found in the excellence of formal organization and in the resulting aesthetic experience.
Creative Self-Expression: Early to Mid-20th Century	Art is an expression of the individual artist.	Free the child's imagination. Eliminate rules. Don't impose adult ideas or standards.	Values are found in the originality of personal expression.
Art in Daily Living 1930–1960	Art is an instrument for enhancing the individual's surroundings.	Apply knowledge of art and design to the home or community.	Values are found in the intelligent solutions to problems in daily life.
Art as a Discipline 1960–1990	Art is an open concept, a problem for artistic, and scholarly inquiry.	Base activities upon modes of inquiry used by artists, critics and art historians.	Values are found in the increased understanding of art.

THE STUDY OF VISIONS AS A MODE OF CURRICULUM INQUIRY

To be an educational vision within art education, three additional features need to be present that I call *continuity*, *revision*, and *depth-and-breadth*. These are explained in the following passages where I attempt to identify these attributes as they will appear in the chapters comprising this section of the Handbook:

Continuity

A proposed vision must show connections with aspects of past practices. If the new vision lacks continuity with art education's past, it becomes a separate, unrelated narrative, not readily seen as part of the story of the field. For example, Parsons points to the attempts at integrated curricula in the history of the Progressive Education Movement. He reiterates certain aspects or approaches followed in the 1920s and 1930s, yet he also identifies differences between current initiatives and past practice. Similarly, Freedman and Stuhr see visual culture as a further elaboration of art education's concern with popular culture. Earlier involvements were adversarial in character as past art educators strove to cultivate a taste for canonical masterpieces in order to wean students from the crass allurements of popular culture. Similarly, my chapter on imaginative cognition invites comparison with the creative self-expression that appeared in progressive schools of the late 1920s and 1930s. It differs from past efforts in drawing strength from recent advances in the cognitive sciences, and pursues a different

TABLE 30.2

Summations of Key Ideas in 20th-Century Art Education

20th Century Visions	Critique of Status Quo	Proposed Reform	Issues in Conflict	Claims for Progress
Elements and Principles of Design	Voiced dissatisfaction with academic art teaching because it traditionally emphasized the human form, the most difficult subject.	Teach elements and principles synthetically starting with simple lines, shapes, and colors.	When first introduced it opposed drawing as the basis for art education.	Approaching the arts through universal elements and principles enabled students to discover beauty in all cultures and periods.
Creative Self–Expression	Critiqued the growing emphasis on social conformity and loss of individuality in education.	Free the imagination. Eliminate rules. Don't impose adult ideas or standards on children.	One of the first major culture wars that divided educators into traditional vs. progressive enclaves.	Freeing the expression of the child through the arts was warranted by claims to promote psychological health.
Art in Daily Living	Critiqued the imposition of elitist taste on the masses of people. Favored art and design to improve daily living.	Focus on problems in everyday life rather than on remote art masterpieces.	Opposed the excessive emphasis on the self and lack of a social focus.	Art is integrated into the daily life of the individual.
Art as a Discipline	Critiqued the lack of disciplinary rigor and lack of structure in the teaching of the visual arts.	Focus the curriculum on the human meaning questions dealt with in the arts.	Opposed excessive emphasis on studio activities and superficial activities like holiday art.	Promotes the appreciation of works of art as well that of as artists, critics, and art historians for their contributions to civilization.

purpose for art education, namely, to argue for the enhancement of cognitive ability through art experience.

Revision

Though the new vision must demonstrate continuity with past traditions, it also must critique and possibly repudiate these traditions by offering changes in purposes and practices. Otherwise it merely continues to retain the same footing that supported past efforts. It must revise the historical narrative so that it can look forward to a different future. If it is unable to do this, the historical narrative merely continues or reaches its end. Furthermore, the critique has to propose the pursuit of alternate objectives, teaching methods or content. For example, though Freedman and Stuhr demonstrate the continuity of their vision with art education's troubled connection with popular culture, they repudiate aspects of past practice, advancing new objectives and content. In a similar vein Dobbs' chapter on DBAE repudiates creative self-expression as a practice though DBAE continues to retain a studio component as one of the four sub-disciplines.

Depth and Breadth

The proposals offering visual culture and integrated curricula as alternative visions would promote change along a broad front, each with a potentiality to alter objectives of instruction, teaching methods, activities, not to mention the subject matter covered. But a vision might go into depth in a single area of knowledge. Barrett's chapter is a personally reflective account of his journey from academic art criticism sometimes called "school-art-criticism" to criticism based on practices of critics operating in the real world of art. Though Barrett maintains allegiance to the discipline-based conception of art education (continuity), he questioned the lock-step procedures of academic art criticism and procedures like "aesthetic scanning" as ones offering false representations of what critics do in their efforts to develop adequate interpretations of artworks. His essay describes more than a shift in method; it documents research as conducted by a reflective practicioner, in this case himself. Through trial and error with critical methods used with students in various age groups, he shaped his personal vision of practice including the change over time in his own views of what art criticism entails as a practice and the ways it might be taught.

Similarly, Graeme Sullivan revisits the tradition of studio practice. Like Barrett, his is a personally reflective account of his experience in the dual role of educational researcher and artist. He reestablishes a connection with the tradition of art production that remains the dominant practice in art education classes. But his vision is built on the analogy between educational research as a scientific enterprise and the activity of artists as they investigate their experience and attempt to embody it in the various media of their particular art form. Here, studio practice becomes more than expression; it also becomes a thoughtful mode of inquiry and understanding.

As I end this introductory essay I realize that I have left certain questions unanswered. First, what kind of educational inquiry is the thought process that results in an educational vision? What kind of educational inquiry is it? Is it a form of educational research in the traditional (largely empirical) sense; and if so, what is the nature and object of such inquiries? Second, is the comparative examination of particular visions a fitting topic for educational investigation? Are such inquiries forms of curriculum inquiry? Is it policy study? These are questions I leave to readers to answer for themselves. In the final analysis, the reader has the final say in whether the visions offered herein are tenable ones for the future.

REFERENCES

Barkan, M. (1962). Transition in art education: Changing conceptions of curriculum and theory. *Art education, 15*(7), 12–18.

Barkan, M. (1966). Curriculum problems in art Education. In E. Mattil (Ed.), *A seminar in art education for research and curriculum development.* (pp. 240–255) (U.S. Office of Education Cooperative Research Project No. V-002). University Park: Pennsylvania State University.

Dow, A. W. (1913). *Composition*. New York: Doubleday Doran.

Efland, A. (1990). *A history of art education: Intellectual and social currents in teaching the visual arts.* New York: Teachers College Press.

Efland, A., Freedman, K., & Stuhr, P., (1996). *Postmodern art education: An approach to curriculum.* Reston VA: National Art Education Association.

Eisner, E. (1971). *Confronting curriculum reform.* Boston: Little Brown.

Gablik, S. (1991). *The reenchantment of art.* New York: Thames & Hudson.

Faulkner, R., Ziegfeld, E., & Hill, G. (1942). *Art today.* New York: Holt Rinehart & Winston.

Haggerty, M. (1935). *Art a way of life*. Minneapolis: University of Minnesota Press.

Hirst, P. (1963). Philosophy and educational theory. *British Journal of Educational Studies, 12*, pp. 51–64.

Joyce, B., & Weil, M. (1980). *Models of teaching*. Englewood Cliffs, NJ: Prentice–Hall.

Kainz, L. C., & Riley, O. (1949). *Exploring art*. New York: Harcourt Brace.

Kuhn, T. (1962). *The structure of scientific revolutions*. (2nd ed., 1970). Chicago: University of Chicago Press.

Rousseau, J. J. *Emile*. (Several editions available).

Rugg, H., & Shumaker, A. (1928). *The child-centered school*. New York: World Book Co.

Wilson, B. (1997). The quiet evolution: Changing the face of arts education. Los Angeles: Getty Institute for the Arts.

Winslow, L. (1939). *The integrated school art program*. New York: McGraw-Hill.

31

Discipline-Based Art Education

Stephen Mark Dobbs
Bernard Osher Foundation and Taube Foundation

THE EDUCATIONAL VISION OF DBAE

Definition of Discipline-Based Art Education

Discipline-based art education (DBAE) is a comprehensive approach to teaching and learning in the visual arts, developed primarily for K-12 schooling but also useful in art museums and adult education. It features systematic and sequential learning experiences in four distinctive domains of art to help students create, understand, and appreciate art, artists, artistic processes, and the roles of art in cultures and societies. DBAE draws its content primarily from these basic art disciplines, each of which enables students to have broad and rich experiences with works of art:

1. By creating works of art, through the skillful application of both experience and ideas, with tools and techniques in various media (*art making*).
2. By describing, interpreting, evaluating, and theorizing about works of art for the purposes of increasing understanding and appreciation of works of art and clarifying the functions of art in society (*art criticism*).
3. By inquiring into the historical, social, and cultural contexts of art objects by focusing upon aspects of time, place, tradition, functions, and styles to better understand the human condition (*art history*).
4. By raising and examining questions about the nature, meaning, and value of art, which lead to insights as to what distinguishes art from other kinds of phenomena, the issues that such differences give rise to, and the development of criteria for judging and evaluating works of art (*aesthetics*).

Rationale for Art in the Curriculum

DBAE regards art as an indispensable component of a quality general education. Thus, art shares with other subject matters the basic school missions, among others, of building minds,

701

of creating problem solvers, and of transmitting cultural heritage. Art contributes to all of these general goals of education and to others as well. In fact, art has historically sought to justify its place in the curriculum by its contributions to such student needs as language development or personality and social development. But whereas the general educational goals are important, they only furnish an instrumental or contextualist rationale, not one based on what only art can indispensably provide.

There is justification for art as well in its indigenous and unique contributions, unrelated to its service to nonart goals. Art is a distinctive form of human experience, and the study of it in schools ought to focus on what other subject fields do not. For example, shaping form to possess aesthetic character, and understanding types of aesthetic experience (in DBAE's case that of visual images), is not a goal of any other subject in the school curriculum. Idiosyncratic frames of reference such as the aesthetic are ways of knowing which are not addressed in the typical school program. DBAE teaches the specialness of art. It does so to introduce and sustain forms of experience which can enhance the lives of students who encounter and experience it.

The Interdisciplinary Approach

As a comprehensive approach the scope of DBAE is as broad as that of the four key domains of art experience. It assumes that works of art are multidimensional, and that to apprehend and understand them successfully involves a broad exposure and extensive examination that generally exceeds what has been traditionally provided by educational programs. The four foundational disciplines of art making, art criticism, art history, and aesthetics embrace the knowledge base; characteristic tools of inquiry; and specialized vocabulary for perceiving, understanding, and making works of art. Each of the disciplines is a lens through which one might experience art from different perspectives.

But DBAE is more than learning about four art disciplines. It is a partnership among those domains designed to work together in an integrated fashion so as to maximize learning opportunities. Thus, DBAE is a form of interdisciplinary study, with the disciplines each contributing to the awakening and development of student awareness of art and its capacity to influence our lives. This partnership among the art disciplines naturally leads to a more holistic experience of art than when the curriculum is based on a single discipline, such as art making. In that circumstance, which reflects a paradigm that long held sway in art education, the student became a maker of objects without the benefit of tutorial by the great traditions of artistry and history which have created cultural artifacts of great power and meaning. Each of the disciplines offers a valuable and informative individual or "field-centric" perspective. However, in DBAE their effectiveness comes from their coordination and unity.

Policy Implications

DBAE defines the character of the art classroom experience by treating art as a substantive, complex subject matter, one with a large knowledge base, a wide assortment of inquiry skills, and rich traditions. This has policy implications for teaching and learning, as DBAE's claim to instructional time is based on its essential character and status as a valuable subject matter. DBAE, thus, has consequences, among other things, for teacher training, curriculum development, instructional resources, research, and evaluation. Accordingly, each effort to establish DBAE necessarily addresses a wide range of issues.

For example, a school district that chooses to adopt DBAE must create a support system for the classroom teacher for which there is almost no precedent in the history of art education. No other approach or paradigm has ever required as much of schools as does DBAE, whether it be professional development activities for the teaching staff, allotment of instructional time and budget, or the ongoing interest and "buy-in" of administrators. The requisite changes in attitude needed to develop such a supportive professional infrastructure and policies must be patiently but steadily cultivated and reinforced. Administrative advocacy from the school board down to the individual principal is required to make DBAE adoption and implementation meaningful, successful, and enduring.

HISTORICAL ORIGINS AND PRECURSORS OF DBAE

Jerome Bruner's "Process of Education"

The discipline-centered conception of art flowed initially from the influence of educator Jerome Bruner, whose "structure of the disciplines" was a seed concept for DBAE in the 1960s. He endorsed studying the structure of a field rather than just facts about it. This in turn could be learned by studying the practitioners who are the source of knowledge about a field. To know and understand, say, architecture, one would consult architects and determine what, why, and how they do what they do. The process of education is about assimilating the knowledge, skills, and traditions of the master craftsmen who in effect define the field. Such an inquiry would reveal the "structure" of the discipline, including its basic organization and principles, challenging issues, characteristic tools, and technical vocabulary. These ideas entered art education principally through the influence of Manuel Barkan of Ohio State, who featured them at the 1965 Penn State Seminar in Art Education where a variety of new ideas and reforms were discussed.

The implications for art are clear: The studio artist, the art critic, the art historian, and the aesthetician are the paradigm practitioners of the four art disciplines. They demonstrate how their respective disciplines shape and influence their work, and how the discipline provides a field or arena of artistic inquiry and experience. But studying only a single discipline or even several of them is insufficient to provide a comprehensive picture. Thus, Bruner's model is one in which the integrated character of DBAE is anticipated by several decades.

Seminar for Research in Art Education

Also in the1960s a special interest group formed within the National Art Education Association. These art educators came from diverse fields, including in addition to the foundational disciplines of art other disciplines with related interests, such as philosophy; psychology and cognitive science; anthropology; and cultural studies, linguistics, sociology, and information science. A common interest in building an academic research agenda for art education led to the creation of the seminar and publication of *Studies in Art Education* early in the decade. Later journals like the *Journal of Aesthetic Education*, *Visual Arts Research*, *Arts Education Policy Review*, and *Journal of Multicultural and Cross-Cultural Research in Art Education* would also contribute to a growing milieu of research and systematic study in art education in the final third of the 20th century. This would help feed practice and stimulate interest in art education in more complex and ambitious curricula and teaching strategies.

The investment of professionals in art education in empirical and other types of research was not a brand new development in art education, which had featured studies of children's drawings, visual perception, and other inquiries of early psychologists going back to the 19th century. Pioneer educational researchers had sought to demonstrate the utility of research for determining questions of curriculum and instruction. By and large, most art teachers were indifferent to such investigations which generally took place in the universities, distant from school classrooms.

The emergence a little more than a generation ago of heightened research interests and the attraction to the field of people with related interests to those of art educators was the first time that experimental research was widely incorporated in the professional priorities and training programs of the field. Professors and doctoral students began to pursue serious, academic quality research focused on learning in art and the enhancement of pedagogy. Crossing boundaries by drawing on different disciplines became commonplace, another anticipation of DBAE.

This turn to empirical research (philosophical and historical research has been addressed as well) had strong consequences for shaping the field. In addition to leading to conferences and publications, it helped ground the field in substantive inquiry about art education, offering an alternative to those who preferred the appeal to "creativity," "the mystique of art," and attractive romantic but unproven conceptions of the child as artist. Research to standards furnished a basis for increasing the credibility of art education as a subject matter that merited a place in the curriculum.

Kettering Project at Stanford

One of the significant precursors to the concept of disciplines in DBAE was a curriculum project in elementary art, sponsored by the Kettering Foundation and developed at Stanford University from 1967 under the leadership of Elliot Eisner. The Kettering project sought to demonstrate that even younger children could apprehend concepts in different domains of art, and that their own art work could benefit from guided inquiry and experience in production, criticism, and historical curricular activities.

Kettering assumed that in most situations the classroom teacher in elementary grades is not an art specialist and has no more than a minimum of professional training in teaching art. Therefore the art education was as much about the teacher as the student. Kettering provided extensive instructional support for the teacher, including a "Kettering Box" filled with materials designed to facilitate learning in the productive, critical, and historical domains of art. In these classrooms children learned about art as well as produced it. Kettering anticipated the use of the art disciplines and included activities with a family resemblance to those that would take place in DBAE classrooms 20 years later.

Providing training and support for the teacher, including a written curriculum and an assortment of instructional resources, was also a feature of Kettering that would become important for organizing tenets of discipline-based art education. Finally, Kettering placed a premium on evaluation of the learning experience to ascertain what impacts it made on children's knowledge and on the understanding of art. Here too the value placed on assessment linked Kettering to DBAE.

R&D Activity in Government Labs

Still another historical piece that led to the development of DBAE was the establishment in the 1960s, as a result of a massive Elementary and Secondary Education Act passed by Congress, of a network of research laboratories which became the headquarters for many government-sponsored research and demonstration projects, including some in art. Thus, federal dollars helped support a burgeoning research ethos throughout the subject areas of schooling, including art.

At their peak, the federal R&D laboratories and centers numbered more than a dozen and over the years spent hundreds of millions of dollars inquiring into virtually every facet of American education. Most of the labs, established at or affiliated with research universities, took on specialized interests. Two of these with interests in art were CEMREL, the Central Midwestern Regional Laboratory; and CAREL, the Central Atlantic Regional Educational Laboratory.

CEMREL eventually developed a series of curriculum packages and materials ("kits") in various art forms, including visual art, music, theater, and dance. These were multidimensional in character, offering information and ideas, learning activities, instructional resources, and procedures for assessment. CAREL's principal product was the creation of a catalog or dictionary of statements about the various art forms, expressed in terms of the information students ought to learn about art. These were intended to establish a knowledge base for students in experiencing each of the respective art forms.

The R&D laboratories which focused on the arts were important because they not only supported research and tried to address the arts in a comprehensive fashion that was unprecedented in the field but also represented the claim of American education on the federal government to invest in the arts as a significant subject matter for schools. By virtue of such support, art education began growing in credibility during the decades prior to the emergence of DBAE. Progressive developments included the adoption by the National Art Education Association of a broad and ambitious set of general aims for art education (which closely prefigure the multidisciplinary approach) and the creation of the National Endowment for the Arts with its support of art education in schools through the "Artists in Schools" programs.

DBAE & IDEOLOGICAL CHOICE IN ART EDUCATION

DBAE Versus Creativity/Self-Expression Paradigm

Discipline-based art education is based on a paradigm different from that which had dominated the field of art education for more than 50 years. The "creativity/self-expression" paradigm took root in the early 20th century based on the work of Franz Cizek and other European and American educators who endorsed art for its value as relief from the rigors of the academic curriculum, its presumed capacity for nurturing the expressive life of children, and the opportunities offered in art for "making" and creative work. These goals were absent elsewhere in the curriculum, so it fell to art. But these goals of recreation and play and self-enrichment were not necessarily valued by schools, as shown by the marginal role of art in most school programs.

By midcentury, the leadership of the psychologist Viktor Lowenfeld focused art educators almost exclusively on "creative and mental growth." Art was a tool for socialization and personality development. Creativity and self-expression theory cherished the untutored and naive emanations of child art, which many art specialists believed would be contaminated by even talking about student work. Art's capacity to provide unique contacts with and learning about the works of art of mature artists was subordinated to art's capacity to reinforce the goals of child development. Few efforts were made to utilize the vast heritage of world art for such learning tasks as understanding its role in human history; nor were questions of aesthetic content or import raised with children lest art be "intellectualized." A bias against reading or talking about art (basically against anything that seemed "academic" or made art resemble other subjects) caused defenders of the paradigm to retreat to soft stances regarding the mystique of art and its essentially nonacademic character.

Subject Field-Centered Versus Student-Centered Rationale

Discipline-based art education basically challenged the creativity/self-expression paradigm by putting the work of art, rather than the student, at the center of the art lesson. Student self-discovery as the chief goal of art is replaced in DBAE with the acquisition of competence in art as a field of study and engagement. The DBAE-educated young person is able to view and talk about works of art, how they are made, and what they mean. He or she can analyze the contents of an image and situate it in an historical and/or cultural context. The DBAE student can handle questions of value and purpose in works of art. None of these subject-centered abilities are priorities for the creativity/self-expression paradigm.

However, it would be a mistake to entirely diminish the importance of works of art created by students themselves in a DBAE setting. The conception, design, and execution of student works of art are the goals of the art-making or art production discipline. But rather than view those works as being primarily of service to students' personal and social development, DBAE considers such works as having been shaped and influenced in positive fashion by the exposure and input of the other disciplines.

General Classroom Teachers Versus Art Specialists

Perhaps the most controversial feature of DBAE programs is its appeal and utility to the general classroom teacher who has had little or no professional preparation in art. Yet in thousands of classrooms across America, such teachers in the elementary grades are expected to teach art, despite their lack of training. Some classrooms may enjoy a periodic and limited visit by an art specialist, but in many places even those are lacking. Budget priorities have eviscerated the art specialist profession in some states, such as California.

Art specialists who teach in elementary schools have described their apprehension about training classroom teachers to teach art. Art specialists in junior and senior high schools have sometimes also opposed DBAE because they feared that training classroom teachers was a step backwards, and that more art specialists should be retained to do that job in grade schools. DBAE recognizes the special professional contributions of art specialists who have so much to offer to students at all levels. But the reality is that in thousands of elementary classrooms throughout the country the students will have little or no art instruction at all unless their classroom teachers are trained and motivated to teach it. At the same time, DBAE offers even the art specialists the opportunity to broaden their approach to art with their students in secondary schools, many of which are wedded to the creativity/self-expression paradigm.

Pluralism in Art Education

Art education is a field in which individual differences count, reflecting the values of idiosyncrasy and boundary breaking in fashioning, knowing about, understanding, and appreciating works of art. DBAE offers a flexible approach that acknowledges the differences among students, teachers, administrators, school districts, facilities, community resources, budgets, and curricular opportunities. In fact, during the development of DBAE in the 1980s and 1990s, a number of training institutions and theoreticians in art education traveled their own paths, guided by the general axioms of DBAE (foundational art disciplines, written sequential curriculum, engagement with works of art, etc.) but leaving many decisions to choice based on local circumstance, energy, and intention.

This pluralism is entirely consistent with discipline-based art education, which acts as an umbrella or central locus for related explorations which take art seriously as a subject matter, and which build a knowledge base in students that will help equip them for their own experience. DBAE is not a specific curriculum, but rather an approach to pluralism in art.

DISTINCTIVE FEATURES AND CHARACTERISTICS OF DBAE

Balanced Content From Four Foundational Art Disciplines

Discipline-based art education draws its substance, its content, from the four foundational art disciplines of artmaking, art criticism, art history, and aesthetics. Knowledge, skills, and tools from other disciplines also furnish potential resources for DBAE, which embrace concepts from anthropology, cognitive science, linguistics, philosophy, cultural studies, and other disciplines. The proportions of instructional time and attention allocated to the individual art disciplines may vary with the nature and scope of the individual lesson and local circumstance, such as the training and interests of the teacher, or availability of resources such as art reproductions or an art museum in the community. There is no formula that dictates the extent or proportion of the input from individual disciplines, only that the lesson be "balanced" to reflect the multiple interests involved, that alternative perspectives be available, and that a variety of resources might be utilized.

Systematic and Sequential Written Curriculum

One of the ways in which DBAE considers art to be like other academic subject matters is in the requirement for a written, sequential curriculum. This helps ensure that students move along grade-level and age-appropriate learning tracks in which lessons are reinforced but not repeated, and which incrementally build the knowledge, skills, and understandings that are the overall goals of the process. The written curriculum for a DBAE lesson will feature certain characteristics, including a clear statement of the learning idea or behavior on which the lesson is focused, a rationale that describes the significance of what is to be learned, basic questions that might be asked about it, and alternative learning activities to fulfill the lesson.

A written curriculum will also specify instructional materials required (such as art images or media), provide readings or references to additional background information (such as about an artist, an era, a style, etc.), and delineate an assessment procedure or mechanism that helps teachers and students ascertain what has been learned. Other features of a written curriculum might include tapes and questions for discussion, compact disks, games, posters, and so forth.

Developmentally Suitable and Age-Appropriate Activities

Although DBAE does not hold the personal and social development of the child to be the principal purpose of the art lesson, as it is for many followers of the creativity/self-expression paradigm, DBAE does recognize the importance of devising developmentally suitable and age-appropriate activities for students in the elementary grades. This issue has arisen in part because some critics fear that the hands-on emphasis of the traditional studio art approach will be displaced by an emphasis in DBAE on verbal analysis of works of art, an "intellectualizing" or "academicizing" of the learning experience in art which replaces doing and making with talking about it.

In fact, there may be at least initial limitations that may flow from teachers' and students' general unfamiliarity with using words (instead of paint or clay) to express one's ideas and feelings about visual images, especially when technical vocabulary is utilized. Part of the agenda in DBAE is to build student competence to express and share one's perceptions, and to become informed from listening to those of other people about the capacities of art works for eliciting a variety of divergent reactions.

A second impediment for some is DBAE's embrace of aesthetics, the discipline which of the four foundational art disciplines is likely to be the most unfamiliar to adults and children alike. To include aesthetics or philosophy of art in the basic art education regime is considered by some to be "inappropriate," but tweed-jacketed British philosophers are not the only ones interested in questions about the value and meaning of art. In fact, even young children can address basic aesthetic questions when these are couched in developmentally suitable and age-appropriate language. Why are some works of art "pretty" and others are "ugly"? Why do some works of art make us happy and others make us sad? Can you make a beautiful picture of something that isn't beautiful?

Engagement With Works of Art

A critical feature of discipline-based art education is engagement with works of art by mature artists. Although students' own works of art are valued by DBAE as significant personal statements, it is the works of accomplished adult artists that best reflect the lessons about art that are taught in DBAE. An enormous inventory of works of art suitable for reproduction exists in various formats (book illustrations, posters, slides, videos, compact disks, etc.). Improvements in color printing technology and access to Internet resources make it easier than ever for instructors to acquire the images they need to teach and talk about art.

An additional advantage of drawing on established works of art is that they provide examples of the range of art across different world civilizations and cultures. One consequence of "globalization" is the immediacy of cultural diversity, which is expressed most vividly in the American melting pot. Cultural diversity in art is routinely embraced by DBAE. A salutary development during the 1990s was the decision by commercial publishers to publish and make available art reproductions and other media of non-Western art. Of course, every effort needs to be made by the teacher of DBAE to give students opportunities to view original works of art. These are available in museums and galleries, and in the community (architecture, sculpture in public places, etc.). It is always preferable to view original works of art; but in their absence, the high-quality art reproductions now available are generally adequate for classroom use.

THE ROLE OF THE GETTY EDUCATION INSTITUTE

Getty's Interest in DBAE

Discipline-based art education enjoyed a singular champion and catalyst for almost 20 years, the Getty Center for Education in the Arts (later renamed the Getty Education Institute), a program of the J. Paul Getty Trust of Los Angeles. No organization in the history of American philanthropy ever attempted a more ambitious program of support for art education in the public schools than did "The Getty." The Trust, originally established to administer the Graeco-Roman Getty Museum in Malibu, California, diversified in the early 1980s into related areas, including art education. Under the leadership of President Harold Williams and Program Director Leilani Lattin Duke, the Getty Center became the leading exponent of the DBAE approach and its major funder in universities where it was developed and in school districts where it was implemented throughout the United States.

The Getty Center in its early days canvassed the thinkers and doers in the field and gathered a long list of ideas for potential philanthropic investment. The Getty leadership decided to address the low status and uneven quality of art education in the public schools. A search for the type of program that Getty might undertake focused on the comprehensive approach that would be subsequently named (in 1984) "discipline-based art education." Support for such an approach existed in the antecedents of Jerome Bruner, the Kettering Project at Stanford, and the R&D efforts in the regional laboratories.

It also followed as an outcome of a national report commissioned by Getty from the RAND Corporation. They evaluated seven school districts around the United States that featured exemplary programs in art. Successful projects were found, unsurprisingly, to exhibit such characteristics as strong administrative support, opportunities for professional development, and links with the community. These and other progressive factors were echoed in the Getty Center's inaugural publication, *Beyond Creating: The Place for Art in America's Schools* (1985). This became the clarion call for DBAE and for change in art education.

Private Philanthropy in Partnership With Public Schools

Getty's approach to disseminating DBAE was ambitious and deliberate. Its activities spanned the arenas of advocacy, theory development, professional training, curriculum studies, model programs, and assessment. Between the early 1980s and the late 1990s, the Center sponsored workshops, seminars, and major national conferences; developed major summer in-service training programs in a half-dozen states; and sponsored preservice pilot programs in more than a dozen universities where teachers are trained.

The Getty Center also commissioned dozens of scholarly papers and monographs; supported development of new instructional resources, such as the Multicultural Art Print Series; ran a fellowship program for doctoral students; and formed alliances and networks with more than three dozen national "cooperating organizations," such as the Parent Teachers Association, National School Boards Association, and the National Endowment for the Arts. They supported curriculum research and development of model lessons; launched a broad program of publications and created art education's first national Web site; ran retreats for school administrators such as principals, superintendents, and school board members; and, explored the school-to-career options for students interested in art. The central theme of all of these activities was discipline-based art education.

Facilitating Change in Art Education

The Getty Trust's intervention in the field of art education was unprecedented in American education and American philanthropy, but the magnitude of the challenge to improve the status and quality of the field required no less. Art education has been generally far behind its subject matter cohorts in the curriculum when it comes to public understanding, administrative support, financial resources, and instructional time.

Due to Getty's continuing promotion of the issues, many reforms were achieved, including the upgrading of art as a high school graduation requirement in many states, the bolstering of a number of university preservice programs, and the public expression of support for art by major figures including the Secretary of Education, chair of the National Endowment for the Arts, and other community leaders. Getty was open about its motives for its involvement in art education: It was even rather logical for the Getty Trust, which operated one of America's best known and richest museums, to help ensure that museum audiences of the future would be better prepared to understand and enjoy what was available for visitors. Improving art education in schools might have a positive impact on the citizenry, whose children could become informed and appreciative museum goers.

But Getty did more than bankroll the effort: It provided leadership, energy, forums, programs, and enterprise. In one sense, DBAE was itself a huge research experiment, looking at what it was feasible for one private organization to accomplish. Harold Williams and Lani Duke's strategy was to create alliances and networks so that Getty, which obviously could not do it all alone, would have plenty of assistance and support from its partners. Furthermore, Getty set out directly to facilitate major change, not to just study the problem, create task forces, and issue reports. Like the J. Paul Getty Trust itself, which as an operating foundation staffs and runs its own programs, the Getty Center for Education in the Arts played a pro-active, front-line position on the team.

Of course, it did cost large sums to pay for summer institutes, conferences, publications, and a host of other initiatives. The financial commitment was obviously millions of dollars a year. But whatever the outcomes of its efforts, even critics could agree that the Getty Center never wavered in its support of DBAE (which itself was evolving over the entire duration). Throughout its existence the Center sought to shift the field toward the more rationalistic, academically oriented DBAE, and away from the creative/self-expression approach, which many felt was responsible for art education's low estate in schools. The Getty Center sought to build commitment to a successor paradigm that would galvanize the field and help shape the profession of art teachers over coming decades.

Sponsoring Theory and Practice

The Getty Center understood that DBAE needed to be built on a solid foundation of theory and practice, so it invested in both. On the theory side, the Getty Center commissioned a major monograph about the theoretical premises and underpinnings of DBAE and invited 100 art educators to meet and critique it. Monographs were also written by major educational figures, such as Gestalt psychologist Rudolf Arnheim, philosopher Harry Broudy, cognitive scientist Howard Gardner, and Stanford professor Elliot Eisner.

On the practical side, Getty invested in far more than professorial scholarship. Major commitments to professional training were made in the Los Angeles Institute for Educators on the Visual Arts (1983–1989), six Regional Institutes; and a plethora of smaller projects in school districts, colleges and universities, state departments of education, national organizations, art museums, and community organizations.

Special task forces or working groups were also established to focus on advocacy for art, on curriculum ideas, on multicultural diversity in instructional materials, and on assessment. Model and demonstration programs were funded. Art educators attending regional and national conferences heard a multitude of reports from the field about both the practical and the theoretical work taking place under the auspices of the Getty Center.

Building the Art Education Infrastructure

The Getty Center worked with the people and organizations who held the authority, power, and opportunity to change the direction of the field. The National Art Education Association, art education's national professional guild, became a major partner of the Getty, co-sponsoring projects and providing a visible venue for tracking and reporting on DBAE's progress. A significant portion of the program at each of the annual conferences of the NAEA was devoted to discipline-based art education, which had aroused the consciousness of the field.

Perhaps the most astute initiative of the Getty was to attempt to create an infrastructure for DBAE within the many schools and school districts to which Getty had access by virtue of the Regional Institutes or other Getty-sponsored programs. That infrastructure included a "lighthouse person" or team within each school whose responsibility was to provide leadership, model commitment, and work for the steady implementation of a permanent DBAE program. In one place, that might be a teacher; in another, a supervisor; in still another, a principal. Even superintendents and school board members were cultivated by the Center to contribute their interest and energy to the team establishing the DBAE paradigm, which usually began with putting an in-service training program in place. Getty cultivated administrators, school board members, and community policymakers and other influential figures (i.e., museum directors, art critics, artists) to participate.

IMPLEMENTATION OF DBAE

Professional Training

Successful learning may be predicated on successful teaching. A priority for discipline-based art education from its inception was its focus on professional development. Preservice preparation in the training institutions, the colleges and universities where school teachers obtain their degrees and teaching credentials, closely mirrors the values and belief systems of the deans and senior professors who run such institutions. Some senior figures in art education, heavily invested in the creativity/self-expression paradigm after decades of professional work in the field, might be less open to the idea of a paradigm shift than would a younger faculty member who attended college in the 1970s or 1980s when integrated and interdisciplinary studies cut a wide swath across the nation's campuses.

Inservice programs received the greater share of the Getty Center's attention because of the obvious need to work with teachers who were already on faculties and teaching art in the classroom. Literally thousands of workshops were held during the Getty era, primarily in schools, to address the needs of staff for training in art. DBAE had to first be taught to and understood by the teachers who would be charged with its exercise, and only then might it be conveyed to students. This was a formidable research project, to determine what training strategies might work best when teachers were working with a subject area in which they generally had little training and were usually unfamiliar with domains like aesthetics and art criticism.

Of course, the Getty constantly worried about the fate of the inservice professional development programs which were established and facilitated by the foundation's grants and contracts. Who would take up the cause if Getty were to withdraw from the scene? At a time when the *Nation at Risk* report (1983) revealed a crisis in American schools, what was the long-term viability of the Getty interventions? No one could say.

Curriculum and Instructional Materials

No single program ever received the imprimatur of being "The DBAE Curriculum." Rather, diversity of pedagogical tactics, instructional resources, choice of art images, and opportunities for connecting to the general curriculum was encouraged. Adherence to well-known basic principles (i.e., balanced content from the four art disciplines, engagement with works of art, integration where feasible with nonart subject matter, rigorous assessment, etc.) created a family resemblance among a number of different DBAE-styled programs across the country.

An important threshold was reached in the mid-1980s when the commercial publishers that supplied textbooks and curriculum "kits" to art specialists noticed the growing interest in DBAE. They came up with their own DBAE-like curricula packages, which were advertised in art education publications and featured at the national conferences. It became clear that the vendors were listening to the buzz about DBAE and to their customers who were asking for multidisciplinary, comprehensive materials. Vendors offered their written curriculum in handsomely designed binders with supporting videos, compact disks, and other media.

Soon there were abundant new choices for DBAE users, including reproductions of works of art, new historical information about familiar masterpieces, thematic presentations uniting works in common support of a central social or cultural concept, and gender and culturally sensitive materials. The advent of the Internet would bring even more art resources to the teacher's doorstep.

Administrative and Political Support

Ultimately the success of DBAE implementation relied on the sympathetic interest and support of the administrators: principals, district art curriculum supervisors, superintendents, school board members, state directors of education, and even higher government functionaries (such as members of Congress who support the National Endowment for the Arts, which since the 1960s gave grants for art education initiatives). Efforts to involve administrators in DBAE were intense in the recent decades of the 20th century, perhaps more so than at any time in the history of art education. A steady flow of information about new DBAE art programs was paired with special retreats to focus on the indispensable contributions of administrative support to successful DBAE teams.

Principals, superintendents, and school board members were courted and involved. Some became the leading voices for art education in their respective district or region. State directors of art also were convened by Getty and encouraged to work together on such issues as state frameworks, curriculum guidelines, graduation requirements, assessment protocols, and teacher certification standards.

Community Relationships

Discipline-based art education connects with and draws upon the community in several ways. First, it identifies the local sources where students might view original works of art: museums, art galleries, art in public spaces. Second, it includes people resources, such as practitioners of the four foundational art disciplines (i.e., the artist who has been commissioned by the local arts council to create a work for a public place, or the art critic who writes for the local newspaper). One of the singular experiences for students in DBAE is to have the opportunity to be visited by or to go to the workplace of an artist, critic, historian, or philosopher (aesthetician). Third, DBAE reaches out to parents of the students to inform them and help them better understand what is at stake and what is being accomplished in their children's art lesson, something most parents have paid little attention to beyond affixing youthful art work to the refrigerator.

DBAE AND EDUCATION REFORM

The Basic Education Movement

Discipline-based art education was a reform movement itself when it appeared on the art education scene in the early 1980s. It proposed overturning or replacing the old paradigm of creativity/self-expression with a new approach that would be academically respectable and actually teach children about works of art in a stimulating and effective manner. In a sense, the DBAE movement in art education resembled the "back to basics" movement, as it was promoted by organizations like the Council for Basic Education (a Getty "cooperating organization"), which valued a return to educational fundamentals.

These were the courses that instilled in students the basic skills they would need to make their way in the society, including verbal and number skills. For example, art education was perceived to sharpen perception, which in turn enabled students to make fine-grained distinctions that nurtured linguistic abilities. DBAE would also equip students with the basic skills they needed to function as intelligent observers, consumers, and makers of art.

Basic education focused on "core" subjects; favored discarding what it considered curricular effluvia, such as topical offerings, which were filling up the high school curriculum (i.e., "family life" and "consumer education"); and, strongly emphasized good reading and writing skills. DBAE itself also pursued a traditional approach, offering a comprehensive education in basic art. This resemblance in objectives helped gain a seat at the table of school improvement for art educators.

State Frameworks

The Constitution reserves to the States the responsibility and authority to provide for public education. Although there exists a federal Office of Education, it does not set specific standards or requirements for schools in all of the states. Decisions as to what subjects students study, how much of the subject is taught, and other pedagogical and curricular questions are made by the individual states, which determine graduation requirements for high schools and other curriculum-controlling issues. Although local school boards ultimately govern and adopt basic requirements for district schools, the state departments of education play a substantial role in educational decision making at both the curricular and the budgetary levels. Course requirements are set forth in the state frameworks, documents that list goals and describe the learning program intended to fulfill them, including courses, student competences and behaviors, and other variables. These are sometimes complemented by a separate document furnishing specific curriculum guidelines.

DBAE advocates worked hard, state by state, to make their voices heard on the framework committees, which periodically review and revise such documents. In the absence of a curriculum-controlling central educational authority, such as exists in such other countries as Japan, frameworks come as close to being a set of normative requirements as anything promulgated. In most states, the creativity/self-expression approach had been enshrined in state frameworks since the 1950s or even earlier, but toward the end of the century the old paradigm was being supplanted by variants of discipline-based art education.

A major achievement of DBAE has been to alter perceptions at the state level as to what constitutes an adequate art education. Policy changes usually follow an extended period of debate and discussion, and in many states the replacement of a mainly studio-oriented curriculum in art with a broader approach did not occur overnight. However, by the late 1990s the majority of the states featured new or recently revised frameworks that elucidated the principles of a comprehensive education in art for K-12 schools. The adoption of such frameworks gave important credibility to the efforts of DBAE advocates statewide. For example, the *California Framework for the Visual Arts* (1972, revised 1990) describes four cornerstones of a quality art education: artistic perception, creative expression, historical and cultural context, and aesthetic valuing. Although the nomenclature varies, the basic curricular structure of the four foundational disciplines is adopted. Similar goals and organizing concepts are to be found in the documents of Ohio, Pennsylvania, and other states.

National Standards

DBAE's efforts to improve the status and quality of art education also benefited from the interest in and trend towards developing national standards for subject matters and for teacher certification. The *National Standards for Art Education: What Every Young American Should Know and Be Able to Do in the Arts* (1994) sets up voluntary standards for educators, policymakers, and the general public. This effort to develop a common point of departure for improving arts education in America's schools shows the significant influence of DBAE in the formulation of reasonable expectations of K-12 students educated in art. Similar progress in developing national standards occurred in teacher certification, for which the National Board for Professional Teacher Standards (NBPTS) issued guidelines (1995).

Accountability Within Art Education

The determination of general progress in the field on a national scale falls to the National Assessment of Educational Progress (NAEP), a government-sponsored program that rotates its attention to subject matters. Every few years it assesses students' knowledge and understanding in art. It is of course difficult to describe with confidence a connection between student performance on a national examination and the adoption of a particular approach to the teaching of art. Discipline-based art education would have to be much more widely implemented in thousands of additional school districts for there to be any likelihood of its impacts showing up short term on the National Assessment.

Complicating the picture is the fact that assessment has not always been a priority for art educators. Under the creative/self-expression paradigm, objective or standardized instruments were disregarded because their application was deemed inconsistent with the personal and expressive outcomes presumably produced by the curriculum. To evaluate performance in the art classroom was conceived to be a violation of the integrity and individuated character of student art.

Discipline-based art education holds to the practical standard of an assessment that provides useful feedback to teacher and student alike. There is simply no other way to ascertain whether the DBAE approach is achieving its objectives than to take a searching, neutral look at how, if at all, student performance is affected in the DBAE classroom. Failing to find out leaves DBAE's most avid proponents grasping for explanations of performance, whether salutary or not. So DBAE commands assessment efforts, although few art educators have specific training or competence in application of the highly specialized tools and procedures of qualitative and quantitative assessment. One might examine such factors as student interest in art, ability to apply critical concepts, acquisition of social and cultural understandings, the use of technical vocabulary, explorations in various media, and awareness of the philosophical issues raised by art.

RESEARCH IN AND THROUGH DBAE

Cognitive Science as a Resource for DBAE

Research in art education began in the late 19th and early 20th century when psychologists examined children's drawings for clues to their personality and expressive/affective character. The influence of Freud and Jung reinforced the notion that children's art might be a door or mirror to their inner lives. Educators like Walter Sargent at Chicago and Earl Barnes at Stanford conceived of art as a language, and found that perceptions of the forms of that language constitute an important type of literacy (which was later named "visual literacy"). By the middle of the 20th century, influential psychologist/educators included Rudolf Arnheim, whose studies of perception resulted in his conviction that art is a form of "visual thinking," and Viktor Lowenfeld, who taught that art stimulated "creative and mental growth" and development.

By the 1980s, Howard Gardner was exploring the concept of visual intelligence, and how artists manifest this specific form of intellectual functioning, in his books such as *Frames of Mind: The Theory of Multiple Intelligences* (1983). At Harvard Project Zero, cognitive scientists like David Perkins explored the relationship between artistic creativity and intellectual development. Art education drew strength and credibility from the links established by cognitive studies between visual imagery and the formation of ideas and concepts. This was important because it tied art education's fortunes to the major purposes of schooling. If art education helped students become more efficient problem solvers, perhaps that might help justify an expanded role in the curriculum. Actually, art educators such as Kenneth Lansing and Brent and Marjorie Wilson had demonstrated in their research since the 1960s the links among artistic perception, language, and critical understanding.

The linkages between art and mind have been explored throughout the recent history of research in art education. Such research demonstrates the contributions that art education can make to general education, a goal of discipline-based art education. Furthermore, the embrace of such cognitively related functions as talking and reading about art, as part of the study of art, reinforces the notion that art can share with other subject matters the responsibility for helping students in concept formation and problem solving.

Models of Professional Training

Because professional development plays such a key role in the DBAE approach, research related to both preservice and inservice training programs became an important source of validation and verification for advocates. The central role of teacher preparation also occupied many of the stakeholders, including school districts, educational policymakers, teacher training institutions, art education professional organizations, and funders.

By far the most extensive and searching examination of DBAE professional development programs was the 7-year effort (1983–1989) sponsored by the Getty Center for Education in the Arts relating to the Los Angeles Institute for Educators on the Visual Arts, and the Regional Institutes in the states of California, Florida, Minnesota, Nebraska, Ohio, Tennessee, and Texas. Each of these was a major initiative to experiment with varying models of DBAE and their concomitant specifications for teacher training.

Probably no other initiative of the Getty Center had more direct consequence in classrooms than its R&D in professional development. These programs reached thousands of students and teachers in the seven states where core projects existed, and in many others as well. Substantial resources were devoted to ongoing and rigorous assessment of these programs to ascertain what worked and what did not. Under Brent Wilson's leadership, a wealth of solid research data resulted from years of careful study and documentation. *The Quiet Evolution: Changing the Face of Art Education* (Wilson, 1997) is the evaluative report of a large research experiment in discipline-based art education. The report also charts the progress of the Regional Institutes in transforming the teaching of art in American schools. DBAE's links to the larger picture of school change and the reform process are elucidated. One of the major findings in Wilson's report is that the arts can move from the margins of the curriculum to the center and may even facilitate school renewal.

Focus on the Art Disciplines

During the most influential period of DBAE's tenure (early 1980s through the late 1990s) many related areas of concern attracted research interest, including the aforementioned cognitive studies and professional development. Another source of rich ideas for DBAE in classrooms was mined through philosophical, historical, curricular, and empirical research in the four foundational art disciplines. Much of this research resulted from the ongoing development of the respective disciplines, each of which was undergoing its own spirited professional dialog. For example, the College Art Association was ridden with controversies over feminism and other special interests in art history even while DBAE advocates worked to establish the theory and practice of art history (with or without a feminist orientation) in schools. Because content for DBAE was drawn from those disciplines in a certain flux, the journals that reported research and the conferences that debated the issues at hand became more significant than ever before for art educators.

Again the Getty Center was responsible for creating multiple linkages between art educators and theorists and practitioners in the four art disciplines. Artists, art critics, art historians, and aestheticians were invited to conferences where they described the changes occurring within their respective domains the research such process might lead to. In various publications, the Getty, National Art Education Association, state departments of education, and other national organizations gave visibility and value to the professional work of the discipline specialists, including their research interests. The artist, perhaps the only one of the four whose inquiries do not regularly result in writing and publication, is perceived in DBAE as conducting "qualitative research" by exploring possibilities and resolving problems in media.

Moving From Theory to Practice

Classroom teachers and art specialists are less likely than professors and teacher trainers to read research journals or attend research seminars. But well-trained teachers ought to possess the most current ideological resources to assist in their advocacy and pursuit of DBAE. Professional inservice development programs should provide instructors with a steady stream of selected studies which translate theory to practice. As a practical matter many teachers learn their craft on the job. It is important to retain their interest in professional improvement, and the research literature is one principal way to remain current. At the same time, policies affecting art education might take root in the faculty lunchroom as much as they might issue from research findings or the decisions of school boards.

Furthermore, different functions fall to different roles in the field. Theorists, usually professors and writers in the colleges and universities, formulate theory and disseminate their ideas at professional meetings and through publications. Practitioners, usually working in classrooms in schools, carry out their teaching assignments informed or not about the latest theories and research findings. The lack of control groups makes it difficult to compare experimental treatments (i.e., a DBAE curriculum) across classrooms.

THE LEGACY OF DBAE

Facilitating Interdisciplinary Studies

The nature of DBAE, drawing content from four art disciplines, makes it by definition "interdisciplinary," and a model for interdisciplinary studies. The approach provides an example of unity and convergence in a subject field, and among different but related subject areas in school curricula beset by fragmentation. By emphasizing the relationships among the four art disciplines, as well as their connections to knowledge from other domains, an opportunity is created to integrate and consolidate a student's education around comprehensive ideas, broad themes, and holistic practices. DBAE is largely about discovering and exploring those connections. The art disciplines do not exist in completely independent fashion, but actually relate to one another at many levels. Thus, a student encountering a work of art might address it through the view or perspective of any one of, or even all of, the disciplinary lens furnished by DBAE.

At one point the Getty Center and the College Board co-sponsored a national integration project with the title *The Roles of the Arts in Unifying the High School Curriculum* (1995). The project envisioned art playing a central role in an integrated approach to secondary learning. Following DBAE's lead, art might be productively studied in connection with language and literature, history, social and cultural studies, and even science. Some might call DBAE a "humanities approach" to education.

Adoption by Other Art Forms and Subject Fields

The model of the four art disciplines might be plausibly applied to other art areas as well. Although DBAE was initially developed for teaching and learning in the visual arts, there is no impediment to its application in other art forms. In fact, since its inception, discipline-based art education has attracted the interest of performing arts educators, especially music educators, and of the Music Educators National Conference, which was headed for a time by a former head of the National Art Education Association.

Some music educators, such as Bennet Reimer, have taken the lead in discussing DBAE (with "A" = arts) as a conceptual framework. Music educators are often partial to the importance of music history, and to a lesser extent criticism, as components of a comprehensive music education. DBAE as an organizing construct for the performing arts has also been the subject of speculation and discussion in theater and dance education. Members of the American Association for Theater Education also have shown interest, attending DBAE conferences and writing for publications. Perhaps most significant, funders other than Getty have invested in establishing the Southeast Center for Education in the Arts at the University of Tennessee in Chattanooga and the South Carolina Center for Dance Education.

The relevance of DBAE to other subject areas beyond the arts has not yet attracted much research or advocacy enthusiasm. This may be because curricular areas tend to experience their respective internal reformations idiosyncratically. Perhaps practitioners of other disciplines or school subject areas are reluctant to borrow a model from art because they are unaware of the connections that bind art to the larger purposes of school life, nor are they familiar with art's unique contributions to student learning.

Impacts of Electronic Technologies

Like every part of the curriculum, the rapid emergence of the computer and electronic communications over the last 2 decades has profoundly affected schooling. The first manifestation of this in art education occurred in the 1970s and 1980s, when computer graphics programs began to be established in art and design (sometimes art education) departments in American universities. For example, The Ohio State University was one of the pioneers in art education, developing programs for graphic artists which offered previously unimaginable capacities for practically instant graphic design. These students would help create a computer culture in art education, one which is consonant with the DBAE platform which endorses a far-ranging search for interesting and appropriate images and ideas. Using every technological advantage available to expand and enhance students' art experience is good DBAE practice.

Students of all ages now have immediate access to extraordinary resources. Ideas and data flow in unending profusion from the Internet. The ability to explore art is unprecedented, from downloading images of works of art in museums all over the world to encyclopedic entries on artists, art styles, and issues in both historical and contemporary art. Simply finding the time to review such abundant resources (much less connect them to one's situation) is a logistical challenge for teacher and student alike.

The National Art Education Association and the Getty Center were the first to utilize the Internet for national art education Web sites. Getty's *ArtsEdNet.com* carried basic program and project information intended to disseminate good ideas, such as curricular practices evolving out of the Regional Institutes. Resources posted to the site included reproductions of works of art, information about artists and art movements, suggestions for classroom topics and treatments, updates on pending federal and state legislation affecting art education, texts of important speeches delivered at professional conferences, and other items.

The likelihood is that Internet improvements will continue to increase access for learning in art. The development of recent wireless technologies will enable students to fold a laptop computer into their backpacks and with such devices gain entree at their convenience to museums and galleries, artist's studios, public art sites, scholarship, and other art-related information from around the world.

The Future of DBAE in Schools

Discipline-based art education set out to transform the face of American art education, and its report card after more than 20 years reveals achievement as well as disappointment. Notwithstanding the substantial professional talent, material resources, and energy expended in the movement to establish and implement DBAE, it must be admitted that the process of change has proved to be more complicated and problematic than anyone imagined.

DBAE advocates are justified in the satisfaction they can take in having created a more substantive, academically respectable approach to K-12 art education. This has included some significant accomplishments, including advocacy strategies, theory development, professional training programs, curriculum units, instructional materials, and tools for evaluation. Such positive developments as the adoption of standards for teacher performance in art instruction are also significant advances which benefit DBAE. But these and most other commitments are only voluntary. Survival beyond being a trend, and perpetuation as a permanent legacy in schools, will depend on how successful DBAE advocates are in altering perceptions about teaching and learning art. The change process is incremental over time, and reform of schools as well as the subject matters taught within them is probably a multi-generational task. A key requirement for programs that become part of the school's cultural bedrock and core curriculum is identifying those "lighthouse" people and their successors, so that the comprehensive approach to art (and other subjects) endures.

A large disappointment for DBAE practitioners has been the abrupt withdrawal from the field of art education by the Getty Education Institute, the primary patron and promoter of discipline-based art education since the term was coined in 1984. When Harold Williams stepped down in 1998 as president of the Getty Trust, the program became vulnerable and was shortly thereafter eliminated by his successor. This occurred despite the widespread evidence that Getty's program had indeed made a difference in one way or the other in the lives of thousands of students and teachers in hundreds of schools around the country.

A plethora of firsthand accounts by teachers who were associated with DBAE programs at different levels testified to the impact it had on many teachers' lives and careers. In addition, DBAE was responsible for a myriad of ways in which the field of art education was galvanized and supported over the approach's almost 20-year run. However, the movement could not overcome the disappearance of its champion, and the Getty's surprising (and unexplained) abandonment of its own progeny remains a mystery.

Meanwhile, although the central fiscal source for so many DBAE-related projects and activities has disappeared, the professional commitment to DBAE lives on in many places: in the concept of a substantive, academically rigorous, and multifaceted comprehensive art education, a goal which continues to be worthwhile and has many adherents; in textbooks and scholarly materials which advocates of the comprehensive approach continue to produce; and, in the posture and perspective of the teachers, art supervisors, professors, researchers, and sympathetic administrators who joined in the great effort to transform the face of art education and who remain committed to its development, with or without a major private philanthropic patron.

At its base DBAE owes allegiance to a humanistic philosophy that holds that art has limitless power to sustain and enhance human life, and to reveal and enable us to better appreciate the human condition. These are reasons enough for the inclusion of discipline-based art education in school programs. The final chapter is far from written.

REFERENCES

Addis, S., & Erickson, M. (1993). *Art History and Education.* Urbana: University of Illinois Press. A volume in the series *Disciplines in Art Education: Contexts of Understanding.*

Admur, D. (1993). Arts in cultural context: A curriculum integrating discipline-based art education with other human-ities subjects at the secondary level. *Art Education, 46*(3), 12–19.

Anderson, J., & Wilson, B. (1996). Professional development and change communities. *Music Educators Journal, 83*(2), 38–42, 50.

Anderson, T. (1990). Attaining critical appreciation through art. *Studies in Art Education, 31*(3), 132–40.

Armstrong, C. (1994). *Designing assessment in art.* Reston, VA: National Art Education Association.

Arnheim, R. (1990). *Thoughts on art education.* Occasional paper 2. Los Angeles: Getty Center for Education in the Arts.

Asmus, E., Lee, K., Lindsey, A., Patchen, J., & Wheetley, K. (1997). DBAE: A conceptual framework for learning and teaching in the arts. *Visual Arts Research, 23*(2), 114–123.

Bakewell, E., Beeman, W., & Reese, C. (1988). In Marilyn Schmitt (General Ed.), *Object, image, inquiry: The art historian at work.* Santa Monica, CA: J. Paul Getty Trust.

Barrett, T. (1994). *Criticizing art: Understanding the contemporary.* Mountain View, CA: Mayfield.

Barrett, T. (1994). Critics on criticism. *Journal of Aesthetic Education, 28*(2), 71–82.

Baumgarner, C. (1993). *Artists in the classroom: An analysis of the Arts in Education Program of the National Endowment for the Arts.* Unpublished PhD dissertation, The Pennsylvania State University.

Boston, B. (1996). *Connections: The arts and the integration of the high school curriculum.* New York: College Board.

Boughton, D., Eisner, E., & Ligtvoet, J. (1996). *Evaluating and assessing the visual arts in education: International perspectives.* New York: Teachers College Press.

Boyer, B. (1989). DBAE and CLAE: Relevance for minority and multicultural students. *Journal of Social Theory in Art Education, 9,* 58–63.

Brickell, E., Jones, N., & Runyan, S. (1988). An art curriculum for all students. *Educational Leadership, 45*(4), 15–16.

Broudy, H. (1987). *The role of imagery in learning.* Occasional Paper 1. Los Angeles: Getty Center for Education in the Arts.

Broudy, H. (1994). *Enlightened cherishing: An essay on aesthetic education.* Urbana: University of Illinois Press. (First published 1972)

Brown, M., & Korzenik, D. (1993). *Art making and education.* Urbana: University of Illinois. A volume in the series *Disciplines in Art Education: Contexts of Understanding.*

Burton, J., Lederman, A., & London, P. (1988). *Beyond DBAE: The case for multiple visions of art education.* North Dartmouth: Art Education Department, Southeastern Massachusetts University.

California Framework for the Visual Arts, Sacramento: State Department of Education. (1972, revised 1990).

Chalmers, G. (1987). Beyond current conceptions of discipline-based art education. *Art Education 40*(5), 58–61.

Chalmers, G. (1996). *Celebrating pluralism: Art, education, and cultural diversity.* Occasional Paper 5. Los Angeles: Getty Education Institute for the Arts.

Chapman, L. (1982). *Instant art. Instant culture: The unspoken policy for American schools.* New York: Teachers College Press.

Clark, G., Day, M., & Greer, D. (1987). Discipline-based art education: Becoming students of art. *Journal of Aesthetic Education 21*(2), 129–193.

Clark, G. (1991). *Examining discipline-based art education as a curriculum construct.* ERIC: ART. Bloomington: Social Studies Development Center. Indiana University.

Clark, G. (1997). Critics, criticism, and the evolution of discipline-based art education. *Visual Arts Research, 23*(2), 12–18.

Collins, G., & Sandell, R. (1988). Informing the promise of DBAE: Remember the women, children, and other folk. *Journal of Multi-cultural and Cross-cultural Research in Art Education, 6*(1), 55–63.

Consortium of National Art Education Associations. (1994). *National standards for the Arts: What every young American should know and be able to do in the arts.* Reston, VA: Music Educators National Conference.

Cowan, M., & Clover, F. (1991). Enhancement of self-concept through discipline-based art education. *Art Education, 44*(2), 38–45.

Crawford, D. (1987). Aesthetics and discipline-based art education. *Journal of Aesthetic Education, 21*(2), 227–39.

Crespin, L., & Hartung, E. (1997). Metacognition as a necessary strategy for teaching training in DBAE: Facilitating theory into practice. *Visual Arts Research, 23*(2), 124–34.

Cromer, J. (1990). *History, theory, and practice of art criticism in art education.* Reston, VA: National Art Education Association.

Csikszentmihalyi, M., & Robinson, R. (1990). *The art of seeing: An interpretation of the aesthetic encounter.* Santa Monica, CA: Getty Center for Education in the Arts.

Day, M. (1985). Evaluating student achievement in discipline-based art programs. *Studies in Art Education, 26*(4), 232–242.

Day, M. (1987). Discipline-based art education in secondary classrooms. *Studies in Art Education, 28*(4), 234–242.

Day, M. (1989). The characteristics, benefits, and problems associated with implementing DBAE. *NASSP Bulletin, 73*(517), 43–52.

Day, M. (1997). Influences of discipline-based art education within the field of art education. *Visual Arts Research, 23*(2), 19–24.

Delacruz, E. (1988). *A conceptual framework for teaching aesthetics to elementary students.* Unpublished PhD dissertation, The Florida State University, Tallahassee.

Delacruz, E., & Dunn, P. (1995). The evolution of discipline-based education. *Journal of Aesthetic Education, 30*(3), 67–82.

DiBlasio, M. (1987). Reflections on the theory of discipline-based art education. *Studies in Art Education, 28*(4), 221–26.

DiBlasio, M. (1997). Twelve years and counting: Tracking a comprhensive effort at instructional & programmatic reform through DBAE. *Visual Arts Research, 23*(2), 34–42.

Dobbs, S. (1989). Discipline-based art education: Some questions and answers. *NASSP Bulletin, 73*(517), 7–13.

Dobbs, S. (1992). The Kettering Project: Memoir of a paradigm. In P. Amburgy et al. (Eds.), *The History of Art Education: Proceedings from the Second Penn State Conference, 1989* (pp. 186–190). Reston, VA: National Art Education Association.

Dobbs, S. (1998). *Learning in and through art: A guide to discipline-based art education.* Los Angeles: Getty Education Institute for the Arts.

Dobbs, S. (1988). *Perceptions of discipline-based art education and the Getty Center for Education in the Arts.* Santa Monica, CA: Getty Center for Education in the Arts. (ERIC Document Reproduction Service ED388599)

Dobbs, S. (Ed.). (1988). *Research readings for discipline-based art education: A journey beyond creating.* Reston, VA: National Art Education Association.

Duke, L. (1990). Mind building and arts education. *Design for Arts in Education, 91*(3), 42–45.

Duke, L. (1984). The Getty Center for Education in the Arts. *Phi Delta Kappan, 65*(9), 612–614.

Duke, L. (1986). The role of private institutions in art education. *Journal of Aesthetic Education, 20*(4), 48–49.

Duke, L. (1999). Looking back, looking forward. *Arts Education Policy Review, 101*(1), 3–7.

Dunn, P. (1995). Integrating the arts: Renaissance and reformation in art education. *Arts Education Policy Review, 96*(4), 32–37.

Dunn, P. (1996). More power: Integrated interactive technology and art education. *Art Education, 49*(6), 6–11.

Dunnahoo, D. (1992). *Content analysis of elementary art teacher preparation textbooks: A study of the status of discipline-based art education in art teacher preparation texts.* Unpublished PhD dissertation, University of Georgia, Athens.

Efland, A. (1990). Curricular fictions and the discipline orientation in art education. *Journal of Aesthetic Education, 24*(3), 67–81.

Eisner, E. (1988). Discipline-based art education and its critics. *Art Education, 41*(6), 7–13.

Eisner, E. (1990). Discipline-based art education: Conceptions and misconceptions. *Educational Theory, 40*(4), 423–430.

Eisner, E. (1988). The principal's role in art education. *Principal, 67*(3), 6–10.

Eisner, E. (1987). *The role of discipline-based art education in America's schools.* Los Angeles: Getty Center for Education in the Arts.

Eisner, E. (1988). Structure and magic in discipline-based art education. *Journal of Art & Design Education, 7*(2), 185–196.

Eisner, E. (1998). The Getty Education Institute for the Arts. *Studies in Art Education, 40*(1), 4–7.

Eisner, E., & Dobbs, S. (1986). *The uncertain profession: Observations on the state of museum education in twenty American museums.* Los Angeles: Getty Center for Education in the Arts.

Erickson, M. (1995). A sequence of developing art historical understandings: merging teaching, service, research, and curriculum development. *Art Education, 48*(6), 23–24, 33–37.

Erickson, M. (1997). Transfer within and beyond DBAE: A cognitive exploration of research issues, *Visual Arts Research, 23*(2), 43–51.

Ewens, T., (Ed.). (1986). *Discipline in art education: An interdisciplinary symposium.* Providence: Rhode Island School of Design.

Eyestone, J. (1990). A study of emergent language systems and their implications for discipline-based art education. *Visual Arts Research, 16*(1), 77–82.

Fehr, D, (1994). From theory to practice: Applying the historical context model of art criticism. *Art Education, 47*(5), 52–58.

Feldman, E. (1982). *The artist.* Englewood Cliffs, NJ: Prentice-Hall.

Feldman, E. (1993). *Practical art criticism.* Englewood Cliffs, NJ: Prentice-Hall.

Fitzpatrick, V. (1992). *Art history: A contextual inquiry course.* Reston, VA: National Art Education Association.

Fleming, P. (1988). Pluralism and DBAE: Towards a model for cultural art education. *Journal of Multi-cultural and Cross-cultural Research in Art Education, 6*(1), 66–74.

Garber, E. (1990). Implications of feminist art criticism for art education. *Studies in Art Education, 32*(1), 17–26.

Gardner, H. (1983). *Frames of mind: The theory of multiple intelligences.* New York: Basic Books.

Gardner, H. (1990). *Art education and human development.* Occasional Paper 3. Los Angeles: Getty Center for Education in the Arts.

Gardner, H., & Perkins, D. (Eds.). (1988). Art, mind, and education: Research from Project Zero. Urbana: University of Illinois Press. First published as a special issue of the *Journal of Aesthetic Education, 22*(1), (1988).

Gaughan, J. (1990). *One hundred years of art appreciation education: A cross comparison of the picture study movement with the discipline-based art education movement.* Unpublished PhD dissertation, University of Massachusetts, Boston.

Geahigan, G. (1996). Conceptualizing art criticism for effective practice. *Journal of Aesthetic Education, 30*(3), 23–42.

Gentile, J., & Murnyack, N. (1989). How shall students be graded in discipline-based art education? *Art Education, 42*(6), 33–41.

Getty Center for Education in the Arts. (1985). *Beyond creating: The place for art in America's schools.* Los Angeles: Getty Center for Education in the Arts.

Getty Center for Education in the Arts. (1988). *Discipline-based art education: What forms will it take?* Proceedings of the First National Invitational Conference, 1987. Santa Monica, CA: Getty Center for Education in the Arts.

Getty Center for Education in the Arts. (1988). *The preservice challenge: Discipline-based art education and recent reports on higher education.* Los Angeles: Getty Center for Education in the Arts.

Getty Center for Education in the Arts. (1990). *From snowbird I to snowbird II: Final report of the Getty Center's preservice education project.* Los Angeles: Getty Center for Education in the Arts.

Getty Center for Education in the Arts. (1990). *Inheriting the theory: New voices and multiple perspectives on DBAE.* Seminar Proceedings. Los Angeles: Getty Center for Education in the Arts.

Getty Center for Education in the Arts. (1991). *Future tense: Arts education technology.* Proceedings of the Third National Invitational Conference. Los Angeles: Getty Center for Education in the Arts.

Getty Center for Education in the Arts. (1993). *Discipline-based art education and cultural diversity.* Seminar Proceedings. Santa Monica, CA: Getty Center for Education in the Arts.

Getty Center for Education in the Arts. (1994). *Perspectives on education reform: Arts education as catalyst.* Proceedings of the Fourth National Invitational Conference, 1993. Santa Monica, CA: J. Paul Getty Trust.

Goldyne, J. (1988). The uniqueness and overlap among art production, art history, art criticism, and aesthetics: An artist's viewpoint. *The Preservice Challenge: Discipline-Based Art Education and Recent Reports in Higher Education.* Los Angeles: Getty Center for Education in the Arts.

Goodson, C., & Dulin, E. (1996). Integrating the four disciplines. *Music Educators Journal, 83*(2), 33–37.

Gray, S. (1992). *The effects of modified discipline-based art instruction on mainstreamed students' attitudes, achievement, and classroom performance in a public school system.* Unpublished PhD dissertation, Brigham Young University, Provo, UT.

Greer, D. (1984). Developments in discipline-based art education (DBAE): From art education towards arts education. *Studies in Art Education, 34*(2), 91–101.

Greer, D. (1984). Discipline-based art education: Approaching art as a subject of study. *Studies in Art Education, 25*(4), 212–218.

Greer, D. (1987). A structure of discipline concepts for DBAE. *Studies in Art Education, 28*(4), 227–233.

Greer, D., & Hoepfner, R. (1986). Achievement testing in the visual arts. *Design for Arts in Education, 88*(1), 43–47.

Gregory, D. (1989). Review of elementary and junior high school DBAE instructional resources. *Art Education, 42*(3), 14–21.

Hagaman, S. (1990). Feminist inquiry in art history, art criticism, and aesthetics: An overview for art education. *Studies in Art Education, 32*(1), 27–35.

Hamblen, K. (1987). An examination of discipline-based art education issues. *Studies in Art Education, 28*(2), 68–78.

Hamblen, K. (1990). An art education future in two world views. *Design for Arts in Education, 91*(3), 27–33.

Hamblen, K. (1993). Developmental models of artistic expression and aesthetic response: The reproduction of formal schooling and modernity. *Journal of Social Theory in Art Education, 13*, 37–56.

Hamblen, K. (1997). Second generation DBAE. *Visual Arts Research, 23*(2), 98–106.

Harris, W. (1996). *A qualitative study of elementary teachers implementing multicultural content with discipline-based art education*. Unpublished PhD dissertation, The Ohio State University, Marion, OH.

Hurwitz, A. (Ed.). (1986). *Aesthetics education: The missing dimension*. Baltimore: Institute College of Art.

Judson, B. (1987). Teaching aesthetics and art criticism to school children in an art museum. *Museum studies journal, 2*, 4.

Journal of Multi-cultural and Cross-cultural Research in Art Education (1988). *6*(1). Special Issue on DBAE.

Kaelin, E. (1989). *An aesthetics for art education*. New York: Teachers College Press.

Kern, E. (1987). Antecedents of discipline-based art education: State departments of education curriculum documents. *Journal of Aesthetic Education, 21*(2), 35–56.

Kindkler, A. (1992). Discipline-based art education in secondary schools. *Journal of Art and Design Education 11*(3), 345–355.

Kleinbauer, E. (1987). Art history in discipline-based art education. *Journal of Aesthetic Education, 21*(2), 205–215.

Korzenick, D. (1984). The studio artist. In E. Katter (Ed.), *Coming together again: Art history, art criticism, art studio, aesthetics*. Kutztown, PA: Kutztown University.

Lachapelle, R. (1997). Experiential learning and DBAE. *Visual Arts Research, 23*(2), 135–144.

Lanier, V. (1985). Discipline-based art education: Three issues. *Studies in Art Education, 26*(4), 253–256.

Lankford, L. (1992). *Aesthetics: Issues and inquiry*. Reston, VA: National Art Education Association.

Lankford, L. (1990). Principles and risk in teaching aesthetics. *Art Education, 43*(5), 50–56.

Levi, A., Smith, R. (1991). *Art education: A critical necessity*. Urbana: University of Illinois Press. (A volume in the series Disciplines in Art Education: Contexts of Understanding)

Lovano-Kerr, J. (1985). Implications of DBAE for university education of teachers. *Studies in Art Education, 26*(4), 216–223.

MacGregor, R. (1985). An outside view of discipline-based education. *Studies in Art Education, 26*(4), 216–223.

MacGregor, R. (1989). DBAE at the secondary level: Compounding primary gains. *NASSP Bulletin, 73*(517), 23–29.

MacGregor, R. (1997). The evolution of discipline-based art education. *Visual Arts Research, 23*(2), 1–3.

Mason, R., & Rawding, M. (1993). Aesthetics in DBAE: Its relevance to critical studies. *Journal of Art & Design Education, 12*(3), 357–370.

Matthews, M. (1994). *Mindful body, embodied mind*. Unpublished PhD dissertation, Stanford University.

Moody, W. (Ed.). (1993). *Artistic intelligences: Implications for education*. New York: Teachers College Press.

Moore, R. (Ed.). (1995). *Aesthetics for young people*. Reston, VA: National Art Education Association.

Myers, S. (1992). *A description and analysis of preconceptions about art and art education held by preservice elementary education students*. Unpublished PhD dissertation, The University of Arizona, Tucson.

Nation at Risk, (1983), Washington DC: Government Printing Office.

National Endowment for the Arts. (1988). *Toward Civilization: A Report on Arts Education*. Washington, DC: Government Printing Office.

National Standards for Art Education: What every young American should know and be able to do in the Arts, Washington, DC: Office of Education (1994).

Parsons, M. (1994). Can children do aesthetics? A developmental account. *Studies in Art Education 28*(3), 33–45.

Parsons, M. (1987). *How we understand art: A cognitive developmental account of aesthetic experience*. New York: Cambridge University Press.

Parsons, M., & Blocker. G. (1993). *Aesthetics and education*. Urbana: University of Illinois Press.

Patchen, J. (1996). Overview of discipline-based music education. *Music Educators Journal, 83*(2), 19–26.

Perkins, D. (1994). *The intelligent eye: Learning to think by looking at art*. Occasional Paper 4. Los Angeles: Getty Center for Education in the Arts.

Posey, E. (1988). Discipline-based arts education: Developing a dance curriculum. *Journal of Physical Education, Recreation, and Dance 59*(9), 61–63.

RAND Corporation. (1984). *Art history, art criticism, and art production: An examination of art education in selected school districts* (3 vols.). Santa Monica, CA: RAND Corporation.

Reimer, B. (1991). Would discipline-based music education make sense? *Music Educators Journal, 77*(9), 21–28.

Risatti, H. (1987). Art criticism in discipline-based art education. *Journal of Aesthetic Education, 21*(2), 217–225.

Rubin, B. (1989). Using the naturalistic evaluation process to assess the impact of DBAE. *NASSP Bulletin, 73*(517), 36–41.

Rubin, B., & Wilson, B. (1997). DBAE and educational change. *Visual Arts Research, 23*(2), 89–97.

Rush, J. (1986). Discipline-based art education: Pragmatic priorities for realistic research. *Journal of the Institute of Art Education* (Australia) *10*(1), 23–35.

Rush, J., Greer, D., & Feinstein, H. (1986). The Getty Institute: Putting educational theory into practice. *Journal of Aesthetic Education, 20*(1), 85–95.

Russel, R. (1986). The aesthetician as model in learning about art. *Studies in Art Education, 27*(4), 186–197.

Schwartz, K. (1987). *Educators' perceptions of an institutional supervision system for discipline-based art education.* Unpublished PhD dissertation, The University of Arizona.

Sevigny, M. (1987). Discipline-based art education and teacher education. *Journal of Aesthetic Education, 21*(2), 95–126.

Shipps, S. (1994). *Last impressions? Aesthetic theory and outcomes in 'Art 101.'* Unpublished PhD dissertation, Harvard University, Cambridge, MA.

Sibbald, M. (1989). *A humanistic approach to discipline-based music education.* Unpublished PhD dissertation, University of Illinois at Urbana-Champaign.

Silverman, R. (1988). The egalitarianism of discipline-based art education. *Art Education, 41*(2), 13–18.

Silverman, R. (1997). Testing the in-service hypothesis: The Getty's Los Angeles DBAE Institute. *Visual Arts Research, 23*(2), 4–11.

Simmons, S. (1990). Art history and art criticism: Changing voice(s) of authority. *Controversies in Art and Culture, 3*(1), 54–63.

Slavik, S. (1995). *An examination of the effects of selected disciplinary art teaching strategies on the cognitive development of selected sixth-grade students.* Unpublished PhD dissertation, The Florida State University, Tallahassee.

Smith, R. (1993). Art and its place in the curriculum. *School Administrator, 50*(5), 23–30.

Smith, R. (Ed.). (1989). *Discipline-based art education: Origins, meaning, development.* Urbana: University of Illinois Press. First published as a special issue of *Journal of Aesthetic Education, 21*(3) (1987).

Smith, R., & Simpson, A. (Eds.). (1991). *Aesthetics and arts education.* Urbana: University of Illinois Press. A volume in the series *Disciplines in Art Education: Contexts of Understanding.*

Soren, B. (1992). The museum as curricular site. *Journal of Aesthetic Education, 26*(3), 91–101.

Southeast Center for Education in the Arts. (1994). *Discipline-based music education: A conceptual framework for the teaching of music.* Chattanooga: Southeast Center for Education in the Arts.

Spitz, E. (1994). Aesthetics for young people: Some psychological reflections. *Journal of Aesthetic Education, 28*(3), 63–76.

Spratt, F. (1987). Art production in discipline-based art education. *Journal of Aesthetic Education, 21*(2), 204.

Stankiewicz, M. (2000). Discipline and the future of art education. *Studies in Art Education, 41*(4), 301–313.

Stinespring, J. (1992). Discipline-based art education and art criticism. *Journal of Aesthetic Education, 26*(3), 106–112.

Swanger, D. (1990). Discipline-based art education: Heat and light. *Educational Theory, 40*(4), 437–442.

Taunton, M. (1983). Questioning strategies to encourage young children to talk about art. *Art Education, 36*(4), 40–43.

Van de Pitte, M. (1994). Discipline-based art education and the new aesthetics. *Journal of Aesthetic Education, 28*(2), 1–14.

Villeneuve, P. (1993). *Contending art education paradigms and professionalization.* Unpublished PhD dissertation, The University of Arizona.

Villeneuve, P. (1997). Paradigm to practice: Negotiating the first five years. *Visual Arts Research, 23*(2), 107–113.

Walsh, D. (1992). *A discipline-based art education model for criticism and inquiry directed to non-western art.* Unpublished PhD dissertation, Texas Tech University, Lubbock.

Williams, B. (1997). Recent changes in museum education with regard to museum-school partnerships and DBAE. *Visual Arts Research, 23*(2), 83–88.

Williams, H. (1991). *The language of civilization: The vital role of the arts in education.* Washington, DC: President's Commission on the Arts and Humanities.

Williams, H. (1993). *Public policy and arts education.* Santa Monica, CA: J. Paul Getty Trust.

Wilson, B. (1996). Arts standards and fragmentation: A strategy for holistic assessment. *Arts Education Policy Review, 98*(2), 2–9.

Wilson, B. (1997). *The quiet evolution: Changing the Face of Arts Education.* Los Angeles: Getty Institute for the Arts.

Wolff, T., & Geahigan, G. (1997). *Art criticism and education.* Urbana: University of Illinois Press. A volume in the series *Disciplines in Art Education: Contexts of Understanding.*

Zurmuehlen, M. (1990). *Studio art: Praxis, symbol, presence.* Reston, VA: National Art Education Association.

INSTRUCTIONAL RESOURCES

Alexander, K. (1994). *Learning to look and create: The SPECTRA Program*. Menlo Park, CA: Dale Seymour. Text, slides, poster.

Alexander, K., & Day, M. (1991). *Discipline-based art education: A curriculum sampler*. Los Angeles: Getty Center for Education in the Arts.

Art Forum: Professional development audiotapes. (1996). Tucson: CRiZMAC Art & Cultural Educational Materials. D. Greer (Introduction to DBAE); M. Day (Art Production); Terry Barrett (Art Criticism); M. Stewart (Aesthetics); and E. Katter (Assessment).

Barrett, T. (Ed.). (1994). *Lessons for teaching art criticism*. ERIC: ART. Bloomington: Social Studies Development Center, Indiana University.

DiBlasio, M., & DiBlasio, R. (1987). *smART curriculum: Sequentially managed art curriculum, grades 1 to 6* (6 vols.). ARTWORLD Press: St. Paul.

Discover Art K-8 Program. Worcester, MA: Davis Publications. Curriculum programs: texts, prints, audiovisual materials.

Erickson, M. (Ed.). (1992). *Lessons about art in history and history in art*. ERIC:ART. Bloomington: Social Studies Development Center, Indiana University.

Greer, D. (1977–91). *SWRL elementary art program*. Bloomington: Phi Delta Kappa. Teachers guides and filmstrips.

Hobbs, J., & Salome, R. (1995). *The visual experience* (2nd ed.). Worcester, MA: Davis Publications. Texts, prints, and audiovisual materials.

Hubbard, G. (1986). *Art in action, 1–8*. San Diego: Coronado Publishing.

Hurwitz, A., & Day, M. (1995). *Children and their art: Methods for the elementary school* (6th ed.). Fort Worth: Harcourt Brace.

Katz, E., Lankford, L., & Plank, J. *Themes and Foundations of Art*. St. Paul: West Publishing. A high school text.

Mack, S. (1995). *Masterpack 4–6*. Tucson: CRiZMACK Art & Cultural Educational Materials. Text and videotape.

Mittler, G. (1994). *Art in focus* (3rd ed.). Westerville, OH: Glencoe. Ninth grade.

32

Investigating Art Criticism
in Education:
An Autobiographical Narrative

Terry Barrett
The Ohio State University

INTRODUCTION

When invited to write this chapter, I decided to construct a personal narrative of my life in art education to pass on lessons learned during 30-some years. In the telling I hope that I am neither inflating nor minimizing the work in which I have been engaged as an art educator interested in art criticism. When I began teaching, I viewed myself as an artist who had to teach, but I now view myself as an art educator and writer who wants to teach and write. Since 1990, most of my writing has been books. The editors' request of me to write a chapter for this anthology provides me occasion to take a reflective pause in the midst of two larger writing projects. The first is a book titled *Interpreting Art: Reflecting, Wondering, and Responding* (Barrett, 2003). It encourages college students to actively interpret the art that they see and study rather than passively receive interpretations from their professors and other scholars. The second project is a book for college art majors titled *Art: Form & Meaning.* I especially look forward to this project because the publisher is providing 300 reproductions, 200 in color—many more images than I have been able to use in other books—and my wife Susan, an art museum educator (Hazelroth & Moore, 1998; Hazelroth-Barrett & Moore, 2003) and Montessori teacher, is working on the book with me.

Interpreting Art and *Art: Form & Meaning* follow publication of a third edition of *Criticizing Photographs: An Introduction to Understanding Images* (Barrett, 2000a) originally published in 1990, and a second edition of *Criticizing Art: Understanding the Contemporary* (Barrett, 2000b) first published in 1994. They are books for college students that explain what professional critics do, how, and why, so that students can then engage with art more deeply, read criticism more intelligently, and write criticism more insightfully. *Talking about Student Art* (1997) is a book I wrote for art teachers, kindergarten through high school, to encourage teachers to engage their students in more and better talk and deeper thought about the art that they and their classmates make. I am 57, have been teaching at The Ohio State University for more than 30 years, and I am still eager to get up each morning and write and teach, and then come home and make art. What follows is an attempt to make public sense of my continuing involvement in art education especially through art criticism.

TEACHING HIGH SCHOOL

I graduated from college in December of 1967. A year prior to graduation, I had left a prayerful and usually silent monastic life of poverty, chastity, and obedience that I had been part of from age 13 to 22. My philosophical education, within monastic studies, was an incompatible mix of Plato, Aristotle, Augustine, Aquinas, and Existentialists, especially Sartre, Camus, Nietzsche, Dostoyevsky, Kierkegaard, and Beckett. The latter group, predominantly atheistic, was more convincing to me than the former, so that I eventually found myself in the uncomfortable position of being an agnostic humanist studying to become a monastic priest. Through Existentialism I came to believe that "existence precedes essence": That is, one can define oneself by choices and through actions rather than follow one's predetermined nature. I left the monastery and completed a degree in art and philosophy at Webster College in St. Louis. At that time Webster was a small, Catholic, predominantly female college with a progressive educational philosophy. At Webster I was persuaded by Sister Jacqueline Grennan, college president and an educational advisor to President Kennedy, not to look for a place to fit but to make a place.

As a child in the 1950s attending the Catholic grade school in Westmont, a small town outside of Chicago, I experienced minimal art education, if it can be called that. On occasional Friday afternoons between about 2:15 and 3:00 dismissal, had we been "good" and if nothing else was more pressing, Sister would place pages torn from coloring books on a counter below the chalkboard. We would line up, pick a page, receive one precious piece of coarse manila paper, and attempt to copy the coloring book picture onto the drawing paper with pencil and then color it in with crayons. With no instruction from Sister, this was at first very difficult and frustrating, but somehow I became good at it and frequently got to parade my colored drawing copying of rearing horses through other admiring classes of children. This constituted art education for me from about fourth grade through eight grade. My father brought my older sister and me to the Art Institute of Chicago to joyfully gaze at paintings. I supplemented my school drawing by saving allowances or birthday money and bought Walter T. Foster's (1938) learn-to-draw books, one at a time. Each purchase was exciting. Animals were my favorite subjects. From Foster's books I learned to successfully copy, step by step, his mountain lions and antelopes onto paper and call the pencil drawings mine. A kind and nurturing aunt and uncle applauded these and my school drawings. I was unable, however, to transfer any knowledge learned from Foster's step-by-step method to be able to draw any other animal, person, or thing without Foster's books. I still do not draw well representationally, despite successfully completing drawing courses in college.

In high school, a Catholic seminary, I was fortunate to participate in art classes taught by Margaret Dagenais, an artist who made liturgical art and who taught in Chicago at Loyola and De Paul universities. She did not "teach" us other than to provide materials, show some minimal techniques, and offer encouragement. Somehow I was successful, and made liturgical mosaics, unglazed terracotta ceramic saints and crucified figures, and Madonnas with Latin phrases painted onto cloth and hung as banners. The priest who brought the artist to us in the seminary, Fr. Gregory O'Brien, taught me a love of reading and writing in his English classes, and I am forever indebted to both him and Ms. Dagenais for my lifelong involvement in art and writing. Jann Gallagher (1994) included me in her dissertation as one in a series of biographical case studies of "lifelong writers" and what influenced them to be such. She won an award for her study. Similar studies on lifelong art lovers, I think, would be helpful in our field.

My college education in art was that of a studio major, with emphasis in graphic design and with active interests in photography, experimental film, and environmental design, along with courses in classical figure drawing and sculpture. Webster's art department was split between a faculty entrenched in classical drawing and sculpture and a faculty committed to aesthetic and social change through functional art. I saw benefits to and enjoyed both orientations. Photography was struggling in the artworld to be recognized as a legitimate art form. An itinerant photographer happened by the college and got three of us to clean up an abandoned darkroom, showed us the rudiments of photographic chemistry, and we taught ourselves, not so well, the magic of making black and white prints, enough so that my senior project was in photography.

When I graduated, America's involvement in Vietnam's civil war was escalating rapidly. I was strongly opposed to that war, but the day I graduated I was no longer automatically deferred from the draft by being a student. I still had some options, however: get drafted into the military and likely be thrown into Vietnam; avoid the draft by fleeing the country (some classmates chose Canada); feign being insane or gay (the draft boards considered them similarly); or teach school because my local draft board had enough young men in its pool that they were not drafting teachers. My advisor, Sister Gabriel Mary, who was also opposed to the war, generously found me a teaching vacancy in the Public Schools of the City of St. Louis. When I began teaching art at Sumner High School in January 1968, I did not know that I would be teaching art ever after.

Sumner, an inner-city school in the heart of the St. Louis ghetto, was the first African American high school west of the Mississippi, and for many years the only African American high school in segregated St. Louis. Some famous black people attended Sumner, including pop singer Tina Turner, operatic singer Grace Bumbry, and tennis star Arthur Ashe. Having grown up in white suburbs, I feared putting myself into a black school. Two African American friends at Webster who had graduated from Sumner furthered my anxieties by teasing me with funny but macabre and threatening stories about the school. However, I had more repulsion for and trepidation of shooting and being shot by the Vietnamese. Also, something in me wanted to face the challenge of teaching in that school, and I believed in the political cause of integration and the promise of social equality that Sumner was presumed to represent. The school's enrollment was about 2,000 students, all African American. There were about 100 teachers, all African American except three White teachers. The principal openly referred to the three of us as "hippies" and many of the students addressed us in the hall as "white muh-fuhs."

The Black Power movement was emerging. Race rioters burned neighborhoods in Detroit in 1967. The very evening of the day that Martin Luther King was assassinated, our school principal held a prescheduled PTA meeting but made no mention of the murder, although riots were raging in over 100 American cities as he spoke. King at that time was anathema to conservative black citizens who thought him too radical and likely a Communist. The FBI was surreptitiously spreading negative misinformation about King. When some politically progressive students in the high school founded a Black Power Club, the only faculty member willing to be their sponsor was the white woman on the faculty.

I was sympathetic to and sometimes active in the Civil Rights movement. I was aggressively opposed to the war and to the social inequities brought about by "Ma Bell" and American capitalism. I occasionally participated in protest marches against the war and worked on an "underground paper" that supported civil rights. In the summer of 1968, two of my college professors and I went to Mississippi to make photographs of the Deep South for educational materials. Whenever we went into black communities, we were bumper-to-bumper tailed by squad cars driven by white sheriffs or their deputies. At the time, I was reading books such as John Howard Griffin's *Black Like Me* (1961), Eldridge Cleaver's *Soul on Ice* (1968), and novels by James Baldwin (1953, 1963). I was also reading popular books critical of education such as *Up the Down Staircase* (Kaufman, 1964), *Teaching as a Subversive Activity* (Postman & Weingartner, 1969), and Jonathan Kozol's *Death at an Early Age: The Destruction of the Hearts and Minds of Negro Children in the Boston Public Schools* (1967). Regardless of my liberal social beliefs and readings, I was unprepared for an African American urban environment and had no formal preparation to teach art.

The students in my classes were friendly and I felt safe with the students who knew me, but the school was large and the psychological environment was violent and stressful to me. Discipline in the high school was primarily by the threat of violence. I was physically slight at the time, weighing 148 pounds, and being a nonviolent, war-avoiding person, I maintained discipline by keeping the students interested in what we were doing. I projected an external look of fearlessness (not at all true) and was respectful of the students. Confounded by my lack of violent displays or threats, some students fabricated the rumor that I possessed a black belt in karate. I did not attempt to dispel the rumor.

I believed that my primary responsibility was to provide a kind of art therapy for my students, helping them feel some success in life, and in this case, in making things. I taught one art history class, the last class of a long teaching day, when both the students and I were tired and ready to go home. I attempted to bring African art history into the course that was based on Western art history. The theory on the ghetto streets was that Blacks ought to be proud of their heritage and would be, especially if young Blacks were exposed to positive African influences such as African art. My students, however, wanted nothing to do with what were to them strange and embarrassing masks with large lips and wide noses or totems with pointy breasts or prominently erect penises. Neither, however, were they or I particularly interested in various forms of Greek columns and other topics I had been expected to learn. With tacit consent, we all sloughed off that art history class.

My other classes were studio based. Two of them were composed of TEs, that is, "terminal education students," who the school system had determined were *not educable*. They were to be maintained in school only until they had reached the age of 16 when they would be dismissed from public education. The art classes had names like Art I, Art II, but I taught the same material in each class, inventing new projects on a daily basis to meet what I assumed to be the students' short attention spans, and I did not know how to expand a lesson beyond 1 or 2 days, and storage of long-term projects was a constant challenge that I could not meet. In retrospect, my lessons were narrow in scope (making modern art) and random in sequence. I exhausted myself in curriculum invention: short studio projects that would have a high chance of resulting in things that looked like contemporary art and that would be personally gratifying to the students. Often they achieved things that looked like respectable modern art but things that were not satisfying to students: They could not understand why I valued what they had made. Had I known more crafts, I would have taught more crafts, teaching the students how to make things they could be genuinely proud to show.

Two books that were of help to me as an art teacher were *100 Ways to Have Fun With an Alligator & 100 Other Involving Art Projects* (Laliberté & Kehl, 1969) and Jean Mary Morman's (1967) *Art: Of Wonder and a World*. I still do not understand the title, but the book's attitude toward art and teaching was upbeat and inspiring. Sister Corita Kent's graphical *Damn Everything but the Circus* (1970) was also attitudinally inspiring.

Teaching was a me–them situation. I was clearly white: My students were not frequently exposed in person to white people. To me, they were clearly black: I had never been in a black person's home. I tried hard to bridge gaps, to find out about their lives, their views. They were surprisingly naïve about the lack of social necessities and niceties they had access to in the ghetto. To them, the world seemed mostly fine, or at least the way it was, which was all right with most of them. One of the young men, whom the administrators thought most likely to retire in prison, believed he could be president of the United States. He was tall and wore a long black coat and a gentleman's large hat and he could alternately be charming and intentionally menacing. One afternoon after school I invited him to my apartment to meet some of my college friends, but outside of his neighborhood he reverted to a little shy boy, almost autistic. Intellectually, I was conflicted between my belief that existence could precede essence and my awareness of the oppression of being born black in the United States of America.

The value of art for me at the time was attitudinal and instrumental. With an aesthetic attitude, an artistic way of looking at the world, both human-made and natural, one could transform the ordinary into the extraordinary, or recognize that the ordinary was not at all ordinary, but beautiful. Susan Sontag (1978) would later characterize some aspects of my view negatively as "aestheticizing" the brutality of social reality to make it acceptable and to relieve us of the burden of improving social conditions. Although I might be able to teach my students to aesthetically appreciate aspects of their daily lives, an aesthetic response would not alleviate their poverty or rectify the social imbalances of the city and society in which they were born and kept by skin color, class, negative societal expectations, and meager opportunities.

I brought other beliefs about art to my teaching: Art ought to be fun—*Damn Everything but the Circus*. These were the days of Pop Art. Art ought to be experimental and innovative and expansive: "Art is anything you can get away with" (McCluhan & Fiore, 1967). These were the days of Happenings (Kaprow, 1993), the days when art styles and movements in the New York galleries changed in a New York-minute. The Bauhaus was also an educational influence: Artists can and ought to improve society through art and design. Art and design are more similar than dissimilar and allied rather than competing. Art and design ought to be in the service of better designed communities and more socially equitable societies. Tom Wolfe would later satirize the consequences of some of the Bauhaus architectural beliefs and consequences in *From Bauhaus to Our House* (1981), but many of the Bauhaus's premises remain influential in my life and teaching today.

As both an aspiring artist and an art teacher, I was unconcerned with art critics and unaware of art criticism as a discipline. I browsed art, design, and craft magazines for personal visual inspiration to me as an artist, and as potential sources of curriculum—that is, art-making ideas, but I did not read the magazines for art ideas articulated in language. I was quickly forced to abandon my ambitions to make art during the school year. As a fellow teacher (mathematics) told me, the best way to prepare for teaching was to be asleep by eight o'clock in the evening. From college studio critiques, I learned that criticism is usually judgmental and negative, and I was committed to be a positive force in my school students' lives. From college critiques, I also knew that one should say *something* after students have finished a project. Therefore, I hung up my students' work and said nice things about it.

I taught 2 years at Sumner before I accepted an opportunity to work with teachers and students in a "media lab" housed in a high school in University City, a progressive, innovative, and racially integrated school system neighboring the city of St. Louis. The schools were supported in part by the John D. Rockefeller III Fund "to provide all the arts for every child" (Madeja, 1973). Nearby, Stanley Madeja was running CEMREL, the Central Midwestern Regional Educational Laboratory, where one of my friends from Webster College worked. She informed me about "aesthetic education" and making exciting and innovative "educational packages" to infuse school curriculum with arts-based learning. CEMREL was buzzing with consultants coming and going, people whose names at the time I did not recognize: Jack Davis, David Ecker, Elliot Eisner, Jerome Hausman, Guy Hubbard, Al Hurwtiz, and Mary Rouse.[1]

Two years later, in 1972, I was hired onto the faculty of Art Education at The Ohio State University by Ken Marantz to teach future art teachers about photography, sound,

---

[1]My colleague Candace Stout (2002) has written a book, *Flower Teachers*, about art teachers who began their profession around this time and their parallel experiences.

film—"newer media" with which they could enhance their teaching of art—in a laboratory that Manuel Barkan had founded a couple of years before his death. Barkan had hired Robert Strobridge from Webster College to establish the experimental space. I joined Tom Linehan, also from Webster, in "the media lab." Prior to coming to Ohio State, I had not heard of Barkan nor had I known that there was such a field as "art education." Barkan's notion that art education ought to include art history and art criticism in addition to art making made quick intuitive sense to me and was logically compelling. I wished that I had had an art education like the Ohio State students were receiving before I taught at Sumner.

When I visit inner-city schools today, I do not see much educational difference from 30 years ago when I taught in St. Louis. Students and their teachers still work in oppressive conditions and prevailing negativity. I think there is still a great need for as yet undiscovered ways to innovatively and engagingly teach African American youngsters about improving their lives with and through art. Were I to teach again now at a school like Sumner, I would want to have been born a person of color, and I would bring to the students artworks by contemporary American artists of color, especially those working with social concerns such as Anthony Barboza, Michael Ray Charles, Mel Chin, Renée Cox, Jimmie Durham, Guillermo Gómez-Peña, David Hammons, Edgar Heap of Birds, Amalia Mesa-Bains, Willie Middlebrook, Adrian Piper, Faith Ringold, Lorna Simpson, Clarissa Sligh, Kara Walker, Pat Ward Williams, Carrie Mae Weems, and Fred Wilson. We would have a curriculum centered on art that mattered to the students, and especially art about the students' lives as children of color in a racist society.

EARLY COLLEGE TEACHING

During the Uses of Newer Media classes I taught at Ohio State in the early 1970s, I would hang on the wall photographs made by the students and try to initiate a discussion about them. By now having learned of Edmund Feldman and his method of criticism (1970), I would ask students to first describe the photographs. In response, they would look at me as if I had asked a silly question. These were photographs we were looking at and what we were seeing seemed obvious to them, too obvious to bother describing them. They could be coaxed into some formal analysis, the second step of Feldman's method, because they were used to hearing about form in their painting and sculpture courses. They experientially knew that the photographs were in part mechanically produced, so *interpretation* seemed to be a matter of reading too much into a picture. They resisted looking for meaning beyond whatever reason the photographer gave for making the photograph. My critiques limped along, more often than not turning into a spontaneous and sometimes good and sometimes a not so particularly good class. I took these failures as impetus to investigate whether other photography instructors were having similar problems trying to engage their students in discussions about photographs. Sure enough, they were. The study resulted in my master's thesis (1974) and then some articles on the subject of teaching photography criticism (Barrett, 1977, 1978; Barrett & Linehan, 1977).

My early work in criticism was heavily influenced by Morris Weitz (1979), the aesthetician who applied Wittgenstein's ideas to aesthetics and who is best known for defining art as "an open concept." Arthur Efland advised me to look at Weitz's *Hamlet and the Philosophy of Literary Criticism* (1964) in which Weitz analytically studied the major writings of critics on Shakespeare's *Hamlet*. Weitz drew many notable conclusions: When critics criticized, they primarily described, interpreted, judged, and theorized. Any one of these activities can constitute criticism. Description alone can constitute criticism. Criticism need not entail judgment. When critics interpret, they answer many different kinds of questions. Description can yield true and false information, but the other procedures do not. One cannot truly define art but attempts at definitions are valuable because they identify what critics find meritorious in works of art.

Although not explicitly stated by Weitz, it also became clear that there was not an established method of criticizing art, but likely as many methods as there were critics. Weitz's work on criticism was liberating.

WRITING AND EDITING CRITICISM

Between 1971 and 1983, I exhibited photographs, as art, in galleries and museums, and published photographs as illustrations and covers for books and magazines. As a part-time graduate student studying photography, and a full-time faculty member teaching photographic media, I was frequently part of studio critiques. On occasions more rare, my work was mentioned in published critical reviews. To have had my own work the subject of criticism and to have it ignored by critics was a humbling experience. Consequently, I have empathy for artists whose work I might criticize.

For about 10 years beginning in 1983, at the urging of my colleague Robert Arnold, I edited a local newsprint journal of art criticism called *Columbus Art*. The paper came out every 2 months and covered exhibits and art events in the Central Ohio area. As editor I recruited critics; coached them; edited their reviews and feature stories; identified exhibitions that ought to be covered; chose content for covers; and oversaw layout and design, printing, and distribution. As editor of art criticism, I had an insider's view of some of the business of the artworld. Some shows were covered for political, personal, or economic reasons. I could not always obtain the writers I wanted. Some writers would promise a review of an important show, one by Deborah Butterfield, for example, and then never deliver it and the show would go unreviewed and the journal would look uninformed.

Many writers could not resist their urge to include some (unwittingly) condescending bits of advice for artists, to show that they were indeed being "critical." Some writers felt the need to be superior to the artists they were reviewing; others saw their role as subservient to the artist's work. Some writers relied too heavily on predigested fact and information sheets about the artist provided by the sponsoring gallery; others ignored these press packets altogether. Some critics paid studio visits or interviewed artists they were reviewing; others kept a distance. Some manuscripts required virtual rewrites; others required little or no editing.

I would like to see research done on the formal and informal policies of art journals and magazines that are published for regional, national, and international audiences. I would also like to see research that "shadows" professional critics when they observe shows, write, and read what they have written after it is published. Such projects would make art criticism more real and less ideal. For this reason, I like reading about critics and the artworld. Janet Malcolm (1986a, 1986b) provided two articles on art critics that were delightfully informative about some baser aspects of the critical profession. She reveals that Rosalind Krauss is "quick, sharp, cross, tense, bracingly derisive, fearlessly uncharitable—makes one's own 'niceness' somehow dreary and anachronistic" (Malcolm, 1986a, p. 49). Krauss herself is quoted saying that Max Kozloff, in editorial meetings of *Artforum*, "was very busy being superior" and that there was "quite an unpleasant quality emanating" from him (p. 49). Krauss says Thomas McEvilley is "a very stupid writer" who dreadfully "seems to be another Donald Kuspit" (Malcolm 1986a, p. 51). Malcolm quotes John Coplans, founder of *Artforum*, saying in contrast that McEvilley is "first rate, absolutely first rate" (p. 52). Eight days from the press run, Ingrid Sischy, then the editor of *Artforum*, was still waiting for articles from McEvilley and Rene Ricard. For 3 nights she went to Ricard's apartment to work with him on his promised piece, staying till two or three in the morning until she finally got it from him.

This kind of information, admittedly gossipy, provides me with the knowledge that criticism is difficult work for professional critics, psychologically as well as intellectually. Critics, too, are human. Peter Plagens, currently art critic for *Newsweek* magazine, admits to insecurities as a critic: "I wonder if I've *ever* had a real art idea" (Plagens, 1986, p. 119). Critics also can be vicious in their judgments of one another. Their condemnations strike fear in my heart that I must confront, overcome, or at least avoid when I sit down to write about art. There is some comfort that one critic finds another "very stupid," whereas another finds him "absolutely first rate." There is also comfort, and annoyance with the magazine, knowing that even one of its former editors finds much in *Artforum* "unreadable" (Sischy in Malcolm, 1986a, p. 52).

I wrote some criticism for *Columbus Art* and for *New Art Examiner, Dialogue*, and more scholarly journals such as *Camera Lucida* (Barrett, 1982). I was encouraged to write criticism, in part, by the biography of A. D. Coleman, a pioneering photography critic who started writing about photography while he was a drama critic and became interested in photographic images. He first wrote photography criticism for the *Village Voice* in 1968 and eventually defined his criticism as simply "the intersecting of images with words" (Coleman, 1979, p. 204). I adopted attitudes about criticism from other working critics. Jonas Mekas, a critic of independent (not Hollywood) films for the *Village Voice* in the 1970s and 80s, said that he only wrote about films he admired. Lucy Lippard (1988), the prolific art critic, wrote that she wanted to "forge simple words that even the children understand" (p. 184).

As one who sometimes writes criticism (e.g., Barrett, 1992a), I have experienced how daunting and intimidating the task can be. A critic writes for an anonymous public that likely includes the artist, other artists, and other critics, and undoubtedly some who know more about the art than the writer, and some who know too little to be informed by a review that is so limited in length. I am always appreciative of editors who allow me to refuse to write about a show: I often feel that I have too little to say about a show to accept an assignment. Sometimes I have to struggle to find enough words to fill a column, and other times I have to cut many more words than I want in order to fit a required word count. I choose to write about that which I think I have something to say but I still worry that I have insights of import about the exhibition or a work. I learned that writing criticism is putting into permanent print tentative thoughts about new work and new ideas, of the artist or of the critic. One hopes that readers are aware of the tentative nature of art criticism.

Whether writing criticism or research, I have always tried to write clearly. In *Artforum* Peter Schjeldahl (1994) admitted that he has "written obscurely when [he] could get away with it. It is very enjoyable, attended by a feeling of invulnerability." Then he added, "Writing clearly is immensely hard work that feels faintly insane, like painting the brightest possible target on my chest" (p. 69). I've tried to maintain the posture of being clear so that I could be shown to be wrong if I was. I resent authors who do otherwise, who hide behind language or who attempt to intimidate readers into accepting their positions or to let them go unchallenged. I agree with Karen-Edis Barzman (1994), a feminist art historian, who complains about writers who have "a dependence on so much erudition that the reader is disarmed and even daunted at the moment of reception, a moment in which asymmetrical power relations between writer and reader are at least implicitly affirmed" (p. 331).

Having written criticism has affected how I teach criticism. I first and foremost stress that critics engage in critical dialog *for an audience*, and one that is much larger than the artist who made the work. Art criticism in schools and universities too often is reduced to comments made to the artist who is present in the room, and students leave art classes wrongly believing that art criticism is for the artist who made the work rather than for the audience who reads the magazine or paper in which the criticism appears. I ask my student critics to determine an audience for their papers or I identify their audience as the university community whose readership is composed of art majors, an occasional art history professor, and undergraduates who may know little about art. I believe that good criticism will speak, somewhat, to all of these readers. I sometimes ask my students to write criticism for their grandmothers or grandfathers or for young nieces and nephews or for best friends who are not arts majors. When able, I give students a choice of works to write about rather than imposing a single work. I establish a word limit. I stress that professional critics are writers. If one is to be an art critic, one better enjoy writing and write well enough that a reader wants to read what is written.

WRITING BOOKS ABOUT CRITICISM

I earned tenure at the rank of instructor at Ohio State in 1978 based on articles, editing, good teaching, and exhibitions of my photographs. Sometime after receiving tenure, I put aside art making, continued writing and editing criticism, and pursued a doctorate. For my doctoral dissertation (Barrett, 1983), I theorized about how we derive meaning from photographs. It was a philosophical study. In it I identified three unique characteristics of photographs: selectivity, instantaneity, and credibility. I also saw that photographs could be categorized as descriptive, explanatory, interpretive, aesthetically evaluative, ethically evaluative, or theoretical. These categories are overlapping and are meant to be used heuristically by a viewer to discover how a photograph was meant to be used and how its meaning could be altered through contexts. I saw that meaning was highly dependent on three types of context that I identified as internal, external, and original.[2] I do not know if I discovered these distinguishing concepts about photographs or invented them. My research methodology was to draw on my experience as a photographer; my experience of writing about photographs as a critic, synthesizing and applying what other scholars and photographers have written about photography; and my own teaching of photography.

I was working on theoretical issues of photography in the 1970s and 1980s during a time when aestheticians were becoming aware that photography is an interesting phenomenon (e.g., Arnheim, 1974; Barthes, 1981; Cohen, 1988; Scruton, 1983; Sekula, 1975; Sontag, 1978; Walton, 1984). I wrote articles (1980, 1981) about some of the ideas I was pursuing before rewriting them for my dissertation. I also rewrote sections of the finished dissertation for articles for research journals (1986a, 1986b), and then I differently addressed these ideas for teachers who might want to teach about photography (1986c, 1986d, 1986e). Gill Clark and Enid Zimmerman encouraged me to reposition and rewrite ideas for different audiences. Writing as art educator for photography professors who taught studio courses felt like risky business; so did writing about photography for art educators in art education journals. For a long time I felt like an outsider to both groups.

I wrote my dissertation two pages at a time, every day, for about an academic year. I was going through a divorce at the time, and dissertation work was a pleasant relief from that emotional turmoil. The daily page limit is somewhat arbitrary, but the motivation is compelling for me. I do not know from whom I learned the strategy, but it is to write one or two or three pages a day, whatever limit you set for yourself. I have read that Stephen King writes six to 8 pages a day (1998). If you finish by nine in the morning you can quit and go to the beach. If it takes you till eleven at night, then you stick with if for that long. I write finished pages, double spaced with proper margins, and with accurate footnotes and references. In a week, I have 14 pages; in a month, 60 pages; and in about 9 months, a dissertation-length manuscript. I still use this strategy. Sometimes, when I am very busy with teaching and committees, I may have to set the goal to a paragraph a day. When I am really struggling to write something that I would rather avoid, then I switch to an hour a day until I can get over my resistance, and then go back to a page count per day. I also learned, from Hemingway, I think, to end a day's

---

[2]Mary Ann Stankiewicz (2002) has shown how these types of contexts can be used to teach fifth-grade students about the photographic work of Lorna Simpson and other artists.

session in the middle of a sentence so that I know just how to start the next day. When I do not keep this routine because I am traveling or for other reasons, I find that when I get back to writing, I anxiously waste time, chasing away demons before I can write again.

Before I write, I read and take copious and carefully transcribed quotations from what I am reading. I enter these single-spaced and accurately referenced. Sometimes I include parenthetical notes to myself about how I might use the quoted material. When writing *Interpreting Art: Reflecting, Wondering, and Responding*, for example, I relied on 68 pages of single-spaced quotations from scholars writing on interpretation of art and literature. Among aestheticians who write on topics of interpretation, I gathered dense quotations from Nelson Goodman (1976), Arthur Danto (1981), Israel Scheffler (1991), Richard Margolis (1995), Noël Carroll (1997), Robert Stecker (1995), and George Dickey (1997). Quotations from literary scholars and philosophers writing about interpreting literature include insights of Umberto Eco (1992), Jonathan Culler (1992), and Richard Rorty (1992). Critics such as Suzi Gablik (1970) and Griselda Pollock (1996) provided me with their thoughts on the work of specific artists, René Magritte and Edouard Manet, respectively. I used a short appreciative essay by David Carrier (2000) on the comics of Gary Larson and another by Michel Foucault (1983) on Magritte's painting *This Is Not a Pipe*. In preparation for *Art: Form & Meaning*, I compiled 100 pages of single-spaced notes. I feel confident that I have sufficient material when I stop finding surprises in what new material I am reading.

When I have finished gathering relevant material, I sort it into topics or chapters and start writing. I do not necessarily write from the first chapter to the last, nor from the first paragraph to the last. Sometimes I start with what is easiest for me to write; sometimes I start with what is most difficult. Sometimes I know what I am going to say before I say it; other times writing is a discovery process for me as much as a telling to another. I always try to leave time to put a finished piece away for a while, and come back to it and revise. I sometimes read what I have written out to catch clumsy phrasing, and I sometimes ask my wife Susan to read it aloud to me to hear where she stumbles and how it will sound to a reader new to the material.

I have learned to appreciate editors both professional and amateur. I revise a piece until I am happy with it and then find one or more readers to review what I have written.[3] Sometimes I choose readers who I predict will provide encouragement if I feel I need that: Sydney Walker (2000), an Ohio State colleague, responded positively and helpfully to early chapters of *Talking about Student Art*, specifically encouraging me to articulate and include in the book more of my own insights into my thinking process as I conducted the discussions with students which are the heart of that book. Sometimes I choose a reader who will give me a general critical reading: Michael Parsons, my chairperson at the time, read each manuscript chapter of *Criticizing Art: Understanding the Contemporary* (Barrett, 1994) as I wrote them. He would tell me what he found interesting and about what he would like to read more of. When I broach areas I am insecure about, I seek someone in that discipline to read what I have tentatively finished. Sometimes I want a general reader to respond to new material: My older sister Barrie Jean, an independent software trainer with an MA in English, responded to chapters of *Interpreting Art*, telling me what she found most interesting, what she needed more discussion of, and what she found tedious. Susan is my "ideal reader," genuinely eager to read new pages that I bring home daily or every other day, penciling comments in margins about what she finds exciting or what is troublesome to her because the idea is not yet fully realized in the writing.

A former editor of the *Village Voice* is said to have said that his job as editor was to keep writers from making asses of themselves in public. (When reading my *Criticizing Art* manuscript, Mike Parsons pointed out that I had Kant in the wrong century.) Editors also have

---

[3]This piece has been improved by suggestions from my wife Susan and my colleague Candace Stout. Stout (1995) is the author of *Critical Thinking and Writing in Art*.

a job of keeping the journals they publish from appearing foolish. Book editors want their books to sell and help their authors revise to better speak to their intended readers. Mayfield Publishing Company, now owned by McGraw-Hill, sent out prospectuses and sample materials to reviewers, professors who might use such a book in their teaching, and then later sent the finished manuscript to a different set of scholars and professors. The editor forwarded the reviews to me verbatim, summarized her reading of them, and then we negotiated what changes I would make. Waiting for such reviews considerably slows the process, but as an author I like knowing that my Mayfield and McGraw-Hill books have already gone through rigorous scrutiny from other scholars. Sometimes the reviewers the editors choose lack tact and kindness and offer this writer, at least, unnecessary obstacles to overcome—their sarcasm or meanness, for instance. (I want to be a kind critic.) I enjoy a good copy editor, one who makes wise suggestions as to how to improve my prose. Making revisions of a piece with copy editor's suggestions is to me like matting and framing a finished photograph, procedures I also enjoy. I have regretted the few times I have bypassed or shortchanged editorial processes because that material is not as good as it might have been.

During and after I completed my dissertation in 1983, I decided that I would no longer both make art for exhibition and write because I felt that I could not simultaneously do both to my satisfaction. It was also apparent that I could not write, teach, and devote as much time to art making as did my colleagues in the art department. I decided to keep writing: I was enjoying it and thought I was making more important contributions to the world with my words than with my images. Getting published motivated me more than having my photographs exhibited. While driving Jesse, my young son, back to his and his mother's home after Christmas holidays, we passed time by making New Year's resolutions. We were jointly resolving, and Jesse was transcribing. I made a resolution to get an article published in *The Journal of Aesthetic Education*, in my mind, the premier art education journal in the 1980s. Jesse needed to know how to spell *aesthetic* and wanted to know what it meant. When the article came out the following year (Barrett, 1985), I sent him the first copy.

I was proud to see my work in print and continue to be. At conferences or wherever it may happen, I am inspired to continue writing by an occasional spontaneous compliment from someone who has read a piece or whose students have benefited from one. Around 1997, I began making art again, for personal enjoyment, not for exhibition. I now find that I am professionally happiest when I am teaching well, have a writing in progress at school and a painting in the works at home. The hierarchy is important to me. I think I have been able over the years to gainfully integrate teaching, writing, and art making: Each feeds the other.

As I was writing my dissertation, I thought it had potential to become a published book. I did not simply revise and publish it for college students. I had intended to do that, but reviewers of the proposal reported that they liked the proposed book, would want it on their personal bookshelves, would list it as a recommended text on their syllabi, but would not require it. This was economically troubling to Mayfield who was in the textbook business, and intellectually puzzling, to me. From reading between the lines of the reviewers' comments, I inferred that the book was too much my theory, and that they would not use it as a common text if they could not feel more ownership of the material. I revised the contents considerably and then rewrote. Unlike what I did in the dissertation, I took up Weitz's (1979) distinctions of critical procedures—description, interpretation, judgment, and theory—as the organizing structure of the book. I eliminated my properties of photographs that I call "selectivity," "instantaneity," and "credibility." I kept my six categories and my three types of contexts but subsumed them under Weitz's general category of interpretation. The published book has chapters on criticism in general, how critics describe, what interpretation entails, interpretive categories for photographs, contexts from which to derive interpretive conclusions, how critics judge photographs, theories of photography, and a final chapter on how students can write and talk about photographs. The reviewers liked the changes; Mayfield published the book as *Criticizing Photographs: An Introduction to Understanding Images* (1990), and it is in its third edition with a fourth edition planned by McGraw-Hill.

The publication of *Criticizing Photographs* was serendipitous. I admired Barbara and John Upton's book *Photography* (1976) adapted from the luxurious multivolume set, *Life Library of Photography* (Time-Life, 1970). It is well written, in large format, with many lushly printed duo-tone black-and-white and color reproductions. I wanted *Criticizing Photographs* to be like it. I sent a prospectus and a sample chapter to Little Brown, who first published *Photography*, and another to an editor I had met at Harcourt Brace, who also produced lushly illustrated art books. The latter quickly said that such a book was "not in their plans," and I eventually received an uninformative form letter of refusal from Little Brown. There was a marginal note on my returned prospectus from Little Brown: "Does he realize the cost?" I had not realized the lack of a market for an expensive photography criticism textbook. Discouraged, I put the prospectus in my file drawer and returned to writing articles. One day, Jan Beatty, an acquisitions editor from Mayfield, was scouting campuses for publishing ideas and knocked on my door seeking general information about art education and what books I thought the field might need. During our conversation, I remembered my idea for *Criticizing Photographs* and told her about it and its two rejections. Jan asked to take the prospectus and sample chapter and send them out for review. Shortly after, I had a contract and about 2 years later—a year to write, a year in production—I had a published book and felt like an author.

Criticizing Art: Understanding the Contemporary (1994) followed. It presented new fears and challenges for me to face. Well aware of status divisions in academia and art, I had overcome my hesitancy to enter the photography world as an art educator, but now I was going to put my writing forward into the larger and "higher" world of art. Professors of art and art history would have to approve of the ideas of an art educator involved in photography and adopt the book, were it to be successful.

To write that book, methodologically I first polled about 50 friends and colleagues who knew current artists and critics and asked them which they thought should be included in *Criticizing Art*. I used several of the people they suggested and favorite artists and critics whom I already knew I wanted to include. I obtained a small grant from my college, hired an undergraduate art education student as a research assistant on hourly wages, gave her a list of artists and a list of critics, and sent her to the library to find and copy articles in current criticism journals and magazines. I sorted through the large stacks of material she brought me and read and took notes in the form of exact quotations.

In both *Criticizing Photographs* and especially in *Criticizing Art*, along with the scholarship of critics, aestheticians, historians, photographers, and artists, I wove in valuable insights of art educators who have influenced my thinking, including Manual Barkan (1955), Barkan, Laura Chapman, and Evan Kern (1970), Rogena Degge and June McFee (1980), David Ecker (1967), Arthur Efland (1983), Elliot Eisner (1972), George Geahigan (1983), Vincent Lanier (1982), and specifically cited considerations of art criticism articulated by art educators Tom Anderson (1988), Harry Broudy (1972), Kristen Congdon (1991), Arthur Efland (1990), Edmund Feldman (1973, 1987), Elizabeth Garber (1991, 1992), George Geahigan (1983), Sally Hagaman (1990), Karen Hamblen (1987), Sun-Young Lee (1988), Wanda May (1992), Michael Parsons (1987), Harold Pearse (1992), Ralph Smith (1973, 1992), and Brent Wilson (1997).

To organize what I read and what I knew, I continued using Weitz's categorical topics of description, interpretation, judgment, and theory. Although these clearly emerge from a modernist perspective, I find them and my use of them to be adaptable to postmodern concerns. These four topics constitute the basis of chapters in *Criticizing Art: Understanding the Contemporary* with an introductory chapter on art criticism in general and a final chapter on college students' writing and talking about art. In the second edition of *Criticizing Art*, I moved the

theory chapter from the end of the book to the beginning. I had first placed it toward the end because it contained the most difficult material and I did not want to lose readers early. However,
theory is so essential to criticism that I placed it early in the next edition, after satisfactorily
trying that new placement with students I taught.

The theory chapter was most difficult to write: It contrasts postmodernism and modernism,
and I struggled to make postmodernism clear for readers who are new to the ideas but sufficiently
sophisticated to satisfy graduate students and professors of art theory. The most enjoyable
chapter to write was the first, an overview of art criticism. In my work with art students of
all ages, teachers, and professors, I have heard strongly held assumptions about art critics and
criticism, many of which I think are mistaken and misguided. When introducing myself to
a group of fourth graders, for example, I asked, "What do art critics do?" The first answer I
received was, "They make fun of artists." Adults' assumptions are often similar. I have found
it difficult to convince learners that criticism is a positive activity rather than a negative one.
Many art professors are cynical about critics and criticism and they pass along their doubts
to their students, many of whom become art professors and art teachers. Art teachers often
think of art criticism as "advice" to artists to improve their artmaking. The premise of both
Criticizing Art and *Criticizing Photographs*, and that of my later book (Barrett, 1997), *Talking
about Student Art*, is that criticism in all schools would be better if it were closer in spirit and
practice to what professional critics do when they criticize art.

I believe that the introductory chapters on criticism and the later chapters on interpretation
are the most valuable in both *Criticizing Photographs* and *Criticizing Art*. Both books set forth
photography criticism and art criticism, in the words of photography and art critics, as *positive*
activities that are meant to engage audiences of readers that may or may not include the artist
about whose work the critic is writing. Criticism is generally not written for an artist. Art critics
generally love the work that they do and are much more often positive in their remarks than
they are negative, and spend considerably more print space describing and interpreting art,
rather than judging it. When they do judge art, their judgments are more often positive than
negative. I present criticism as an ongoing conversation among people interested in art. Most
critics believe their statement to be provisional and open to revision. Criticism is usually about
new art, not old art; when criticism is about old art, critics consider the old art as it affects us
now.

The interpretation chapters offer and explain *principles* for interpreting art. I have devised
or appropriated the following principles from literature on interpretation, and experiences
with interpreting art, as a tentative set of *guides* for making meaning about works of art and
other items of visual culture. I have eclectically compiled and fashioned these principles from
scholars of art (e.g., Danto, 1981; Dickey, 1997; Goodman, 1976), literature (e.g., Culler, 1992;
Eco, 1992; Hirsch, 1967), philosophy of knowing (e.g., Margolis, 1995; Rorty, 1992; Scheffler,
1991), art educators (Chapman, 1978; Feldman, 1970; Parsons, 1987), art critics (e.g., Hickey,
1997; Plagens, 1986; Raven, 1988), artists (e.g., Charles, 1998; Close, 1997; Fischl, 1990;
Skoglund, 1998), and from many personal experiences in interpreting art by myself as a critic
and especially with groups of many kinds in schools, museums, community centers, and at
dinner tables as a facilitator of art criticism (Barrett, 1991, 1992a, 1992b, 2002).

The principles constitute a set, but a loose set that can be expanded or contracted. I believe the
set to be noncontradictory. All the principles are asserted as reasonable, but not all reasonable
people concerned with matters of interpretation will agree with any one of them or all of
them as a set. All of the principles are open to revision, and none of them are meant to be
dogmatic. These principles are offered to help guide any interpreter of any artistic object or
event. They may well provide directions to any and all interpretive endeavors, and not just to
making meaning of artworks and artifacts of visual culture. Interpretation in realms other than
the artistic are beyond the chosen scope of my research. The principles are meant to provide

the security of some stability to the insecurity of the risky and exhilarating efforts of making meaning of artistic objects and events that seem to shift as we gaze at them and change as we reflect upon them.

If these principles are followed, interpreters can be confident that their interpretive efforts are in a right direction and of a right spirit. One may also use the principles as methodological ways to begin and continue constructing an interpretation of a painting, a dance, a poem, or a poster. Any single one of the principles will set one on one's way toward a meaningful encounter with a work of art. To apply all principles to every interpretive situation would likely be beneficial, but prohibitively exhausting except in cases of serious and thorough pursuit. In some interpretive discussions and for some works of art, it is likely that the interpreter will find some of the principles more pertinent than others in the set.

- Artworks are about something.
- SUBJECT MATTER + MEDIUM + FORM + CONTEXT = MEANING
- To interpret a work of art is to understand it in language.
- Feelings are guides to interpretation.
- The critical activities of describing, analyzing, interpreting, judging, and theorizing about works of art are interrelated and interdependent.
- Distinctions between form and content are dubious.
- Artworks attract multiple interpretations and it is not the goal of interpretation to arrive at single, grand, unified, composite interpretations.
- There is a range of interpretations any artwork will allow.
- Meanings of artworks are not limited to what their artists meant them to be about.
- Interpretations are not so much right, but are more or less reasonable, convincing, informative, and enlightening.
- Interpretations can be wrong.
- Interpretations imply a worldview.
- Good interpretations of art tell more about the artwork than they tell about the interpreter.
- The objects of interpretations are artworks, not artists.
- All works of art are in part about the world in which they emerged.
- All works of art are in part about other art.
- Good interpretations have coherence, correspondence, and inclusiveness.
- Interpreting art is an endeavor that is both individual and communal.
- Some interpretations are better than others.
- The admissibility of an interpretation is determined by a community of interpreters and the community is self-correcting.
- Good interpretations invite us to see for ourselves and continue on our own.

AN ART CRITIC IN EDUCATION

In 1986, Scott Noppe-Brandon, a former student of mine who was then working for the Ohio Arts Council and who is currently director of education at the Lincoln Center Institute in New York, encouraged me to become an "Art Critic in Education" and visit schools and engage children and teens in discussions about contemporary art. By courtesy of the Ohio Arts Council, the state of Ohio enjoys a robust artist-in-education program, sponsoring artists and writers in long-term residencies in schools throughout the state. The artists work from a studio model and Scott and the Council were interested in expanding their programs to include more reflection on and responses to studio products and practices. My first invitation was to join a contemporary dance workshop in a public elementary school to do interpretive work with students who had performed with the visiting company as well as with students who had seen the work but had not been active in making it.[4]

I responded to the invitation tentatively and contingent on meeting the dancers and seeing their work. I had hesitancies: I enjoyed modern dance as an audience member, but could I lead an informed critical discussion of it? Were the artists antagonistic or favorable toward critics and criticism? Would their dance works hold enough personal interest for me to want to discuss them? Would children be interested in talking about these dances? These are the questions I continue to ask about artifacts and educational opportunities when choosing artifacts and groups of learners. After attending a rehearsal and talking with the choreographer and dancers, my hesitancies quickly evaporated.

This first experience of Art Critic in Education was successful: The children talked intelligently, insightfully, and enthusiastically for 45 minutes about the dance works. I facilitated the children in orally recalling what they saw and felt, prompting them with video clips when their memories failed, and asked what some of the aspects of the dance meant to them and why. Our discussion was descriptive and interpretive, what Ralph Smith (1973) might call "exploratory aesthetic criticism." The professional dancers, too, were pleased with the children's verbal articulations and insights. Were the professional dancers not pleased with our interpretive endeavors and results, intellectual and political conflicts would have ensued and would have required resolution.

Buoyed by this experience with the elementary students, I accepted a second invitation to engage high school students in art criticism in a Catholic high school. This experience was key for my development as a critic in education, but it was a negative experience for me. A product of Catholic schooling myself, in preparing for my visit I had nostalgic memories and optimistic hopes for a warm and honest homecoming, of sorts, mediated through works of art that I imagined would be in the students' artroom. There was little art in the art room to discuss; the students were very reticent to say *anything* out loud; they seemed self-consciously aware of visitors who observed from the back of the room; and the 45-minute period seemed to me to drag interminably. I was humbled by my naive expectations and embarrassed by my poor performance, especially in the presence of the sponsors who had observed it.

I learned important lessons from that experience: Always have too many works of art to be able to talk about rather than too few. Realize that observers or participants new to the core group will affect the psychological atmosphere of the classroom. Know that when I am a visitor or part-time teacher, the personality of the class I am teaching will have already been largely shaped by the school or by the students' primary teachers. As a visitor, I will always inherit certain but unpredictable givens and must patiently accommodate. For example, the students may have never before talked in an organized way about works of art. Indeed, some classes have never talked publicly in an organized way about any topic. Students may not be knowledgeable about or comfortable with speaking in front of their peers and teachers and to a stranger. Many students do not know how to listen to one another in group discussions. Many students have not been taught to think for themselves or encouraged to honestly express their views. Many art students have been taught to believe that works of art "speak for themselves." Many students have been allowed to put one another down; thus, individuals are very reluctant to speak and expose themselves to subtle or obvious psychologically painful criticism from their peers or teachers.

After many sessions as a visiting critic, I have found that if my schedule is Art I or Art II, Ceramics II, and Photography I, for example, it will likely be a more challenging day for me than if my schedule is English, English II, Social Studies, and AP English. We teachers have generally taught art students not to talk about art, although we have generally taught them to verbally and orally engage with ideas in humanities and social studies classes.

---

[4]Stuart Pimsler Dance & Theater, Lima City Schools, Lima, Ohio, 1986.

"Learning readiness" *is* a key concept in art and other subjects: Some people are not ready for some works of art, nor should they be expected to be. Therefore, choosing which artworks to show to which audiences also quickly became crucial to my success or failure as a facilitator of discussions. I have had educational success with pre-K, K, and early elementary students talking about stuffed animals; boxes of breakfast cereals; photographs made by William Wegman; 20th-century paintings of animals by Picasso, Chagall, and Marc; and works that the children themselves have made. I have also learned not to underestimate students' abilities to handle challenging works of art. A group of girls and boys in a middle-school home economics class, for example, taught me that they could be very intelligently engaged with political and postmodern works of art made by Barbara Kruger. These same artworks can also be stimulating to older learners including adults. Fourth graders have insightfully discussed installations that they have built in their schools with visiting artists. Fourth graders have intelligently discussed Native American professional dance performances and written about the paintings of René Magritte (Barrett, 2002) and installations made by Sandy Skoglund. High school students have insightfully engaged with art made by Richard Avedon, Romare Bearden, Deborah Butterfield, Salvador Dali, Helen Frankenthaler, Jenny Holzer, Jacob Lawrence, Sean Scully, Cindy Sherman, Jerry Uelsmann, works that the students themselves have made, graphical tee-shirts, TV commercials, popular magazine ads and covers, and clips from Hollywood feature films.

I have had occasions to facilitate discussions about difficult art, some of which have been made controversial. Sharon Rab, a public school English teacher and sponsor of an after-school art club, The Muse, invited me to her high school to prepare students to see in person Robert Mapplethorpe's exhibition, "The Perfect Moment," when it was shown in nearby Cincinnati after it had been shut down by the sheriff and then reopened, but under litigation concerning Cincinnati's pornography laws. This visit resulted in an article that I co-authored with Sharon Rab (Barrett & Rab, 1990) in which we heavily quoted the students with whom we worked. I had a second occasion to work with high school students and Mapplethorpe's photographs in a Columbus public school.[5] Both cases demonstrate that teenagers in school, when given the opportunity, a psychologically safe environment, and facilitation, are able and willing to talk about subject matter that their teachers and parents might think too difficult to discuss.

Similarly, fourth- and fifth-graders in a public school in a rural area of Ohio[6] were able to insightfully write about photographs made by Sally Mann of her children, sometimes partially nude. These photographs (Mann, 1992) are controversial for some adults and are sometimes targeted by groups demanding that they be removed from bookstores. Mann's photographs were not controversial for the fourth- and fifth-graders who saw them, but the photographs did provoke the students to think and talk and write passionately about Mann's children and their mother, as well as all children and mothers and growing up (Barrett, 2000c).

Two full classes of fourth-graders and a core group of 12 fifth-graders selected from their regular classes talked and wrote about the Mann images. Twelve high school students went to and wrote about the Mapplethorpe exhibit. About 30 students in the Columbus high school talked about Mapplethorpe images in their art room. Only two of the parents of all these elementary and high school students objected to the material: One mother did not want her daughter seeing Mann's or any nude and partially dressed children, and one parent of a high school student asked that her daughter be excused from the discussion of Mapplethorpe photographs. Administrators in both schools supported the teachers, me, and the students working with photographs by Mapplethorpe and Mann. Although I recognize the difference between *intelligent selection* of artworks for the curriculum and *censorship*, I think that many art teachers

---

[5]Columbus Alternative High School, Lisa Vottero, sponsoring art teacher, Columbus, Ohio, May 1992.
[6]Forest Park Elementary School, Jann Gallagher, sponsoring teacher, Euclid, Ohio, March 1992.

unfortunately and unnecessarily self-censor their curricula. What is difficult for some adults may not be difficult for those whom they teach: "Difficult" is a relative term.[7]

There are many artists who make art that challenges aspects of American society. This art, in the hands of wise and sensitive teachers, could benefit students. Works made by African American artists such as Robert Colescott, Carrie Mae Weems, and Michael Ray Charles can serve here as examples. Each of these artists deals in confrontational ways with racism. Colescott employs sarcastic humor in many of his paintings, depicting historical white figures as if they were black, sometimes uses sexual narratives to make his points. (Brent Wilson once wisely remarked, "If you don't want to talk about blowjobs, don't show Colescott's *George Washington Carver Crossing the Delaware.*")[8] Carrie Mae Weems (1994) has made photographs with texts. *White Patty*, for example, is a photograph of an African American girl, about age 10, wearing boxing gloves, with a confident and threatening facial expression, with text in bold caps: "WHITE PATTY, / WHITE PATTY, / YOU DON'T SHINE, / MEET YOU AROUND THE CORNER, / AND BEAT YOUR BEHIND." I believe a skilled teacher could use this image and talk with young girls and boys about pain inflicted by racism and about conflict resolution in response to it.

Michael Ray Charles (1998) appropriates stereotypical representations of African Americans into his paintings, using Aunt Jemima, Sambos, minstrels, and pickaninnies in degrading postures and situations. I think these images are generally inappropriate for young children, but may be very salient for high schoolers, particularly for African American students in all-black classrooms and in racially mixed groups. Using such material, however, requires intellectual and emotional maturity on the part of the teacher and the students. The work that Charles makes is volatile: Many African American viewers find them objectionable and want neither to display them nor to talk about them.[9] Warning: Charles's paintings might be especially volatile subjects for high school students in racially mixed classrooms who do not know how to talk about controversial subjects. During the late 1960s and early 1970s, when I was working in high schools, I recall classroom fist fights among students erupting when well-meaning but socially and psychologically naive teachers showed historic films of Negroes being lynched in the American South.

With teachers and art museum docents I have used images by Weems, Charles, Andres Serrano, The Chapman Brothers, Joel-Peter Witkin, and by other artists whose content is justifiably challenging to many. I do not necessarily recommend that the teachers use such imagery with their students: I encourage teachers to decide what content they will use based on their knowledge of their students, school, and culture in which they teach. I do think it important that teachers become comfortable talking about uncomfortable images if they plan to use such images with their students. I also believe that art teachers have a professional responsibility to be aware of and articulate about art made during their lives and the lives of their students regardless of whether they teach about *all* of that art. As a profession, art education has, I think, irresponsibly removed itself from the fray of public controversy over some artworks made by Mapplethorpe, Andres Serrano, Chris Ofili, Renée Cox, and many others. If we want a citizenry that can deal with difficult art in a more sophisticated and

---

[7]When Susan Barrett and I were recently invited to work with docents on "difficult art" in an art museum, we prepared material with which we and the docents could talk about issues of sex, religion, and politics that works of art raise. Some artworks that entailed these issues were difficult for the docents; but more difficult for them, to our surprise, was abstract painting and sculpture.

[8]Brent Wilson, public discussion following a workshop that I led at Penn State University, February 24, 1995.

[9]When invited in 1997 to prepare tour guides for a Michael Ray Charles exhibition at the Austin Museum of Art in Texas, no African American docents attended the workshop; nor did any choose to tour the exhibition. See Juliet Bowles (1998) for a published account of controversy within African American communities surrounding images of Blacks by artists such as Charles, Colescott, and Kara Walker.

enlightened way than either censorship or blind acceptance, we need to educate the present and future citizenry. If we don't, who will? A sheriff in Cincinnati, a mayor of New York City, a senator from South Carolina.

STUDIO CRITIQUES AND ART CRITICISM

Studio critiques are a peculiar form of art criticism that have tremendous import in the teaching of art at all levels, but especially in colleges and graduate-degree programs of art. Studio critiques are a special form of criticism. Critiques are generally for artists whose art is being discussed in a school setting. They are often directed to the artist who made the work being discussed, and usually with the understanding that the critique is for the purpose of the artist improving his or her art making. Art criticism, however, is usually a written form of discourse about art published in magazines and newspapers for the benefit of an audience of many readers who are interested in art. Perhaps too simply put, art criticism is discourse about art meant to increase understanding and appreciation of art in those who participate in the discourse by reading and writing and talking: Studio critiques are a special form of art criticism usually directed at the artist to improve his or her art making (Barrett, 1988). Unfortunately, people who have participated in studio critiques when they took art studio courses often mistake critiques for art criticism.

When critiques are confused with art criticism, art criticism too quickly becomes judgmental, and frequently degenerates into giving advice to artists. Whereas art criticism can generally be understood as discourse around topics of description, interpretation, judgment, and art theory (aesthetics or philosophy of art), studio critiques frequently bypass much description, often ignore interpretation, and proceed quickly to judgment or even begin and end with judgment with no interpretive talk in between. When art is interpreted during studio critiques, the interpretation that ensues usually rests on the artist's intent (or the intent of the instructor who gave the art assignment). Intentionalism is a very limited but widely used and frequently flawed form of art criticism. When items of visual culture are included in the art curriculum, current models of studio critiques will be of little use to deciphering those items, their meanings, and values.

Since 1993, I have been collecting answers to open-ended questions about studio critiques from groups of individuals in colleges across the United States. I have hundreds of responses to different questionnaires from faculty and art students at 26 institutions including some in Canada and Australia. All respondents confirm that studio critiques have been influential in their lives, both in positive and especially in negative ways. Some of the results of these questionnaires have been published with suggestions for improving studio critiques by generally adapting positive notions of and by paying more attention to the implied meaning of works of art, regardless of the artist's intent in making the work (Barrett, 2000d).

Art teachers have been influenced by their own participation in studio critiques while they were in college, taking art courses. Many art teachers have had more art courses than they have had courses in art education. Art teachers' experiences about art criticism from studio professors are likely more influential than whatever they read by or heard of Edmund Feldman and other art educators who write about improving art criticism in art education. Moreover, many art professors have negative attitudes about art critics and consciously or subconsciously communicate these to their students.

A long-term goal of mine has been to merge professional art criticism and studio critiques in schools of all levels. *Talking about Student Art* (Barrett, 1997) is a book I wrote for art teachers. It attempts to insert into practice lessons learned from professional art critics and aestheticians with children as young as 4 years old, children in elementary and middle schools, teenagers in high schools, and with adults who make art occasionally. There are many educational advantages of bringing art education into closer alignment to some artworld professional practices: a most important advantage is that the art room becomes more like what the learners will experience in the artworld outside of school, and thus learners will be better prepared to interact intelligently with art outside of their classrooms. Another important advantage of using appropriate professional critical practices is that by doing so, children learn that their art, when made seriously, can be taken seriously and approached with serious questions, many of the same questions posed by professional critics about art made by professionally mature artists.

Talking about Student Art consists of about 30 case studies of discussions with students about the works of art that the students made. The book employs action research to find ways to improve the quality as well as quantity of students' thinking about their peers' and their own art by using critical strategies employed by critics and other art professionals. The book contains transcriptions of dialogs between the students and me as guest critic about art the students have already made as assigned to them and supervised by their art teachers. The discussions include reflections about the dialogs and the choices I made as discussion facilitator, what was good and not so good about my choices, and how the discussions could have been better.

Following are some key suggestions, strategies, and questions for students, derived from research for *Talking about Student Art*, that are based in part on real-world practices of art critics. Because critics write for specific audiences, I ask middle or high school students to write interpretively about an artwork so that a younger brother or sister—or a class of second- or third-graders—would understand the criticism. I ask the writers to read their writing to their intended audience to see how effectively it communicates.

A teacher could ask a student or a team of students to curate a show of student work. Explain to the students that a curator is a person who usually works for an art museum, and decides what to show, why to show it, and how. The student curators could consider these questions:

- Will you show the work of one student or many?
- If you hang a group show, which artists will be included and why?
- What pieces will you select and why?
- Will you display them chronologically or by some other organizing principle?
- Will you hang the work according to themes of subject matter, similarity of media, or some other organizing principle?
- How many works by each artist will you include?
- Will you hang all of one artist's work together, or disperse them among other artists' works?

These are two sets of questions meant to elicit *interpretive* discussions about works of art made by the students and other artists. The questions bring student artists and viewers to consider aspects of art larger than what the artist likely had in his or her mind when making the work. The following questions, if answered, will lead art teachers to consider carefully the assignments they make and the consequences of those assignments of which they may be unaware. The questions are also very appropriate for items of visual culture such as TV commercials, music videos, printed tee-shirts, and posters.

- What seems most important in this artwork? How do you know?
- What do you think the artwork is for or against?
- What political, religious, or racial views does the artwork seem to uphold?
- What would this artwork have you believe about the world?
- Does the artwork represent a male or a female point of view?

- What does this artwork indicate about the time in which it was made? Could it have been made at *any* time and place, or only at a *specific* time and place? What evidence do you have for your answers?
- What does the artwork assume about the viewer?
- Is the artwork directed at a certain age group, a certain class of people?
- Is this an optimistic or a pessimistic view of what is shown?
- Who might most like this artwork?
- Might some people be offended by the work?

The next set of questions for middle and high school students will likely move the discussion effortlessly and naturally from criticism into *aesthetics* (philosophizing about art and visual culture). Ask:

- Is there truth in fiction?
- Is there truth in art?
- What is factual and what is fictional about an artwork or artifact? This question is particularly appropriate for artworks that have realistically depicted subject matter, such as photographic work.

Artists who work in one medium think differently when they then work in another medium. A photographer, for instance, always has something in the viewfinder and thinks about what to include and exclude as the photographer moves the camera up, down, in, and out. The painter, however, starts with a blank canvas and adds to it. Photography, in this sense, is a subtractive medium. Painting is an additive medium. Ask learners to discuss *how they think* when they are using different media:

- What are the advantages and disadvantages of any particular medium?
- What are the limitations of any particular medium?
- What does any one particular medium allow an artist to do best?
- Are there "wrong" or improper uses of media?
- Teachers in the Bauhaus workshops wanted a medium to look like the medium it was. For example, they believed poured concrete for a building's wall should look like poured concrete. They would leave the newly poured concrete walls textured from their wooden forms, and natural gray instead of painting them. They considered cardboard to be beautiful, and would use it, undisguised, to make furniture and other items. Do you agree with these "honesty of materials" principles? Why or why not?

The next questions will engage students in both critical and aesthetic (philosophical) discussions of their art and *all* art. The questions are concerned with *the role of the artist's intent* in making a work of art when interpreting that work:

- Can we know an artist's intent? Ever? Always? Do some artists work intuitively, drawing on the subconscious, and even intentionally block specific intent?
- Is an artist's intent, when available, always relevant to the meaning of the artwork?
- Can an artist mean to express one thing, but then express more than that, or something different from that?
- Should the artist's stated intent be the final arbiter when determining the accuracy of an interpretation?
- As a teacher, what are your beliefs about artistic intent? Are you consistent or contradictory when you teach about artistic intention, art making, and art interpretation?

Studio critiques, at any age, quickly, easily, and unintentionally turn *negative*. Teachers can redirect unnecessarily negative discussions. When students are being overly and unproductively negative during a critique, teachers can point out that the students are being negative, and redirect questions to elicit more positive answers: "Tell me what's *good* about this artwork." "Tell me what the artist *has done*, not what you think the artist *should have done*." When discussing work that the teacher thinks is good but students do not, allow the students their preferences (what they *like*), but challenge them to think about why others might think it is a *good* work of art (what some people *value*). "Why do museum personnel regard this work of art to be good enough to be preserved, protected, and displayed?" Ask: "You don't have to like this artwork, but why do you think someone else might think that it is good? Can you think of reasons why someone might value this work of art?"

When purposely engaging learners in judgmental questions about works of art, teachers can elicit *positive* critical judgments by phrasing judgmental questions in ways such as these:

- How is this a good work of art?
- What is the most effective part or aspect of this work of art?
- How or why are the artist's choices good ones?
- How would you persuade others to appreciate this artwork as much as you do?
- How could you convince someone to appreciate a particular artwork that he or she thinks is not good?
- What artists throughout history might most appreciate this artwork?

Questions can also be addressed to expose the underlying values of works of art and items of visual culture:

- What are the social implications of what is depicted?
- Do you want to be part of a society that upholds the values implied in this artifact?

CONCLUDING REMARKS

As I reflect on what I have done in the past and what motivates me today, I am aware of being rooted in *art* and humanities in my formal education and professional life, more so than in the field of *education*. I have spent my university career in a college of the arts, not in a college of education, and daily pass by or through a gallery filled with ever-changing exhibitions of contemporary art, some of it still wet. I am daily grateful that I see such art on my way to my office rather than what I see on bulletin boards when walking through the halls of the college of education. Nonetheless, my research and practice is informed by education literature and practice, especially my own many and frequent experiences working with children and teenagers in schools. I think it would be informative for someone to research the beliefs and attitudes about art and education held by those educated within and working within colleges of education versus colleges of art. I think some significant differences would emerge, and these differences will likely have import for debating and implementing educational reform.

I am drawn to contemporary art and Western art more than to historical art and art of other cultures, although I continually seek to learn about and enjoy all art. When faced with art that is foreign to me, I am awestruck by the amount of knowledge and experience it takes to comprehend and appreciate such work. I recall informal comments by David Ecker, who wondered how anyone could assume to understand another culture or its artifacts without intimately knowing the language of the culture. I worry about shortchanging that artwork by well-intended but shallow introductions of it to students. It seems self-apparent to me that there is a distinct educational advantage in working with contemporary art that is made and displayed in one's own culture. It is of us and from us and therefore accessible. I think that it is common sense to start with art around us and then move to art that is further removed from us by time or geography or culture. Yet, many art teachers and museum docents fear contemporary art as foreign, strange, and difficult to teach about.

I approach the teaching of art with the sensibility of an artist, a critic, and an aesthetician, but I do not necessarily give any one of these sensibilities hierarchical status over the other, and I do not engage in all three simultaneously. I privilege one over the other depending on context, circumstance, and purpose. When painting, I have a need to consciously block the critic and aesthetician from my consciousness so as not to be so self-conscious of critical and philosophical issues as to become hampered and constricted while making art. When I teach art making, I want students to inhale an art spirit and think; and make art as mature artists might think, feel, and make. As an art teacher, I want reflective art making from students about feelings and ideas about which they genuinely care, followed by thoughtful and respectful reflections by their classmates on what they have made. I believe art making constitutes a unique way of being in the world. I believe art making is a uniquely valuable way of experiencing and knowing the world. I believe works of art give us new knowledge, and without works of art, the world would lack this knowledge and suffer for the lack.

When I look at art as a critic and when I engage students in critical looking and thinking, I emphasize *interpretation* of works of art:

- What do they mean?
- How do they mean?
- What do they mean to me?
- What do they mean to others? How do I know?
- How might these artworks change my life?
- How might they change others' lives? Are such changes morally desirable?

When criticizing art and engaging others in its criticism, I generally deemphasize judgment in favor of interpretation. Judgment without interpretation is irresponsive and irresponsible. Thorough interpretation often renders judgment unnecessary or transparently obvious. Interpretation ought to include *consequences of content* in artworks and items of visual culture, and such thinking entails judgment. Interpretation entails description, as needed, and formal analysis and how it affects meaning, but the distinction between form and content often held by art teachers and professors is dubious. Distinctions between aesthetics and ethics are artificial and merely academic.

Although I appreciate many types of art, I especially cherish art that is socially engaged. When I make art, however, it is usually abstract, and I intend it to be more than about itself and to be about living life optimistically. The "more" that my art is concerned with is spirituality of a humanistic sort. As a critic and aesthetician and especially as an art educator who teaches students in schools and future art teachers in college, I am resistant to Formalism, the 20th-century theory of art that insists that art is about itself and of itself and apart from all else in the world. I appreciate formalist art, and want to teach others to be able to appreciate it, as one type of art among many choices. Attention to form is essential to thoughtful attention to any artifact, but many art teachers confuse form and Formalism and the conflation of form and Formalism has seriously hampered the teaching of art in the last 50 years and continues to limit art instruction today.

As an art educator, my leanings are toward social reconstructionism and libratory pedagogy, which, I believe, can be furthered by art making and by critical and philosophical thinking about art and culture. I believe art education should actively embrace the critical study of popular culture in addition to the art we find in contemporary art galleries and historical art museums. I think visual culture and fine art culture are mutually informing, and that study of one can enlighten understanding of the other. If the study of either does not genuinely engage the learner with issues of life, however, neither is worth pursuing in the manner it is being pursued. These are the presumptions that motivate my work in art education through art criticism.

REFERENCES

Anderson, T. (1988). A structure for pedagogical art criticism. *Studies in Art Education, 30*(1), 28–38.

Arnheim, R. (1974). On the nature of photography. *Critical Inquiry, 1*(1), 149–161.

Baldwin, J. (1953). *Go tell it on a mountain.* New York: Dial Press.

Baldwin, J. (1963). *The fire next time.* New York: Dial Press.

Barkan, M. (1955). *A foundation for art education.* New York: Ronald Publications.

Barkan, M., Chapman, L., & Kern, E. (1970). *Guidelines: Curriculum development for aesthetic education.* St. Louis: CEMREL.

Barrett, T. (1974). *Toward critical discourse about photographs.* Unpublished master's thesis, The Ohio State University, Columbus.

Barrett, T. (1977). Educating for response: Criticism in the curriculum. *Exposure: The Journal of the Society for Photographic Education, 16*(4), 20–23.

Barrett, T. (1978). Reading as a method of photographic criticism. *Exposure: The Journal of the Society for Photographic Education, 15*(4), 3–5.

Barrett, T. (1980). A structure for appreciating photographs. *Exposure: The Journal of the Society for Photographic Education, 18*(3, 4), 50–54.

Barrett, T. (1981). Photographs in teaching: Epistemological confusions. *Philosophical Studies in Education Proceedings,* 114–121.

Barrett, T. (1982). The offset works of Les Krims: An interpretive critique. *Camera-Lucida: The Journal of Photographic Criticism, 5,* 49–57.

Barrett, T. (1983). *A conceptual framework for understanding photographs.* Unpublished doctoral dissertation. The Ohio State University, Columbus.

Barrett, T. (1985). Photographs and contexts. *Journal of Aesthetic Education, 19*(3), 51–64.

Barrett, T. (1986a). A theoretical construct for interpreting photographs. *Studies in Art Education, 27*(2), 52–60.

Barrett, T. (1986b). A conceptual framework for understanding photographs. *Visual Arts Research, 12*(1), 68–77.

Barrett, T. (1986c). Teaching about photography: Types of photographs. *Journal of Art Education, 39*(5), 41–44.

Barrett, T. (1986d). Teaching about photography: Photographs and contexts. *Journal of Art Education, 39*(4), 33–36.

Barrett, T. (1986e). Teaching about photography: Credibility, instantaneity, and selectivity. *Journal of Art Education, 39*(3), 12–15.

Barrett, T. (1988). A comparison of the goals of studio professors conducting critiques and art education goals for teaching criticism. *Studies in Art Education, 30*(1), 22–27.

Barrett, T. (1991). Criticizing art with others. In D. Blandy, & K. Congdon (Eds.), *Pluralistic approaches to art criticism* (pp. 66–72). Bowling Green, OH: Bowling Green State University Popular Press.

Barrett, T. (1992a). *American pluralism: Artists at The Ohio State University,* an exhibition catalogue for venues in Belgium, England, Scotland, Norway, Finland, Hungary and Germany. Columbus, OH: The Ohio State University.

Barrett, T. (1992b). Criticizing art with children. In A. Johnson (Ed.), *Art education: Elementary* (pp. 115–129). Reston, VA: NAEA.

Barrett, T. (1997). *Talking about student art.* Worcester, MA: Davis.

Barrett, T. (2000a). *Criticizing photographs: An introduction to understanding images* (3rd ed.). Mountain View, CA: Mayfield.

Barrett, T. (2000b). *Criticizing art: Understanding the contemporary* (2nd ed.). Mountain View, CA: Mayfield.

Barrett, T. (2000c). About art interpretation for art education. *Studies in Art Education, 42*(1), 5–19.

Barrett, T. (2000d). Studio critiques in college art courses as they are and as they could be with mentoring. *Theory into Practice, 39*(1), 29–35.

Barrett, T. (2002). Interpreting art: Building communal and individual understandings. In Y. Gaudelius & P. Speirs (Eds.), *Contemporary issues in art education for elementary majors* (pp. 291–300). Upper Saddle River, NJ: Prentice-Hall.

Barrett, T. (2003). *Interpreting art: Reflecting, wondering, and responding.* New York: McGraw-Hill.

Barrett, T., & Linehan, P. (1977). Photographic criticism in an educational context. *Afterimage, 5*(1, 2).

Barrett, T., & Rab, S. (1990). Twelve high school students, a teacher, a professor and Robert Mapplethorpe's photographs: Exploring cultural difference through controversial art. *Journal of Multicultural and Cross-Cultural Research in Art Education, 8*(1), 4–17.

Barthes, R. (1981). *Camera lucida: Reflections on photography*. New York: Hill & Wang.

Barzman, K-E. (1994). Beyond the canon: Feminists, postmodernism, and the history of art. *The Journal of Aesthetics and Art Criticism, 52*(3), 327–339.

Bowles, J. (1998). Extreme times call of extreme heroes. *International Review of African American Art, 14*(3), 3–7.

Broudy, H. (1972). *Enlightened cherishing*. Champaign-Urbana, University of Illinois Press.

Carrier, D. (2000). *The aesthetics of comics*. The Pennsylvania State University Press, 2000.

Carroll, N. (1997). The intentional fallacy: Defending myself. *The Journal of Aesthetics and Art Criticism, 55*(3), 305–308.

Chapman, L. (1978). *Approaches to art in education*. San Francisco: Harcourt Brace Jovanovich.

Charles, M. R. (1998). *Michael Ray Charles, new paintings*. New York: Tony Shafrazi Gallery.

Cleaver, E. (1968). *Soul on ice*. New York: McGraw-Hill.

Close, C. (1997). *The portraits speak*. New York: A.R.T. Press.

Cohen, T. (1988). What's special about photography? *The Monist,* April, 293–303.

Coleman, A. D. (1979). *Light readings: A photography critic's writings 1968–1978*. New York: Oxford University Press.

Congdon, K. (1991). Feminist approaches to art criticism. In D. Blandy & K. Congdon (Eds.), *Pluralistic approaches to art criticism* (pp. 15–23). Bowling Green, OH: Bowling Green State University Popular Press.

Culler, J. (1992). In defense of overinterpretation. In U. Eco, *Interpretation and overinterpretation* (pp. 109–124). New York: Cambridge University Press.

Danto, A. (1981). *Transfiguration of the commonplace*. New York: Farrar, Straus, Giroux.

Degge, R., & McFee, J. (1980). *Art, culture and environment*. Dubuque, IA: Kendall Hunt.

Dickey, G. (1997). *Introduction to aesthetics: An analytic approach*. New York: Oxford University Press.

Ecker, D. (1967). Justifying aesthetic judgments. *Art Education, 20*(5), 5–8.

Eco, U. (1992). *Interpretation and overinterpretation*. New York: Cambridge University Press.

Efland, A. (1983). School art and its social origins. *Studies in Art Education, 24,* 49–57.

Efland, A. (1990). *A history of art education: Intellectual and social currents in teaching the visual arts*. New York: Teachers College Press.

Eisner, E. (1972). *Educating artistic vision*. New York: MacMillan.

Feldman, E. (1970). *Becoming human through art: Aesthetic experience in the school*. Englewood Cliffs, NJ: Prentice-Hall.

Feldman, E. (1973). The teacher as model critic. *Journal of Aesthetic Education, 7*(1), 50–57.

Feldman, E. (1987). *Varieties of visual experience* (3rd ed.). Englewood Cliffs, NJ: Prentice-Hall.

Fischl, E. (1990). *Scenes and sequences: Recent monographs by Eric Fischl*. Hood Museum of Art, Dartmouth College, New York: Abrams.

Foster, W. T. (1938). *How to draw animals*. Hollywood, CA: Walter T. Foster.

Foucault, M. (1983). *This is not a pipe*. Berkeley: University of California Press.

Gablik, S. (1970). *Magritte*. New York: Thames & Hudson.

Gallagher, J. (1994). *Developing life-long writers*. Unpublished doctoral dissertation, Kent State University, Ohio.

Garber, E. (1992). Feminism, aesthetics, and art education. *Studies in Art Education, 33*(4), 210–225.

Geahigan, G. (1983). Art criticism: An analysis of the concept. *Visual Arts Research, 9*(1), 10–22.

Goodman, N. (1976). *Languages of art* (2nd ed.). Indianapolis, IN: Hackett.

Griffin, J. H. (1961). *Black like me*. Boston: Houghton Mifflin.

Hagaman, S. (1990). Education in philosophy and art in the United States: A feminist account. In *Das philosophische denken von kindern* (pp. 213–219). Sankt Augustin, Germany: Academia Verlag.

Hamblen, K. (1987). Beyond universalism in art criticism. In D. Blandy & K. Congdon (Eds.), *Pluralistic approaches to art criticism* (pp. 7–14). Bowling Green, OH: Bowling Green State University Popular Press.

Hazelroth, S., & Moore, J. (1998). The web of inclusion: Creating a structure of collaboration between schools and museums. *Journal of Art Education, 51*(2), 20–24.

Hazelroth-Barrett, S., & Moore, J. (2003). Postmodernism and art museum education: The case for a new paradigm. In L. Tickle, V. Sekules, & M. Zanthoudaki (Eds.), *Visual arts education in museums and galleries*. The Netherlands: Kluwer Academic Publishers.

Hickey, D. (1997). *Air guitar: Essays on art and democracy*. Los Angeles: Art Issues Press.

Hirsch, E. D. (1967). *Validity in interpretation*. New Haven, CT: Yale University Press.

Kaprow, A. (1993). *Essays on the blurring of art and life*. Berkeley: University of California Press.

Kaufman, B. (1964). *Up the down staircase*. Englewood Cliffs, NJ: Prentice-Hall.

Kent, C. (1970). *Damn everything but the circus*. New York: Holt, Rinehart & Winston.

King, S. (1998*). Bag of bones*. New York: Scribner.

Kozol, J. (1967). *Death at an early age: The destruction of the hearts and minds of negro children in the Boston public schools*. Boston: Houghton Mifflin.

Laliberté, N., & Kehl, R. (1969). *100 ways to have fun with an alligator & 100 other involving art projects*. Blauvelt, New York: Art Education.

Lanier, V. (1982). *The arts we see: A simplified introduction to the visual arts*. New York: Teachers College Press.

Lee, S-Y. (1988). *A metacritical examination of contemporary art critics' practices: Lawrence Alloway, Donald Kuspit and Robert Pincus-Witten for developing a unity for teaching art criticism*. Unpublished doctoral dissertation, The Ohio State University, Columbus.

Lippard, L. (1998). Some propaganda for propaganda. In H. Robinson (Ed.), *Visibly female: Feminism and art today*. New York: Universe.

Madeja, S. (1973). *All the arts for every child*. New York: The JDR 3rd Fund.

Malcolm, J. (1986a). A girl of the zeitgeist—I, *The New Yorker*, October 20.

Malcolm, J. (1986b). A girl of the zeitgeist—II, *The New Yorker*, October 27.

Mann, S. (1992). *Immediate family*. New York: Aperture.

Margolis, J. (1995). Plain talk about interpretation on a relativistic model. *Journal of Aesthetics and Art Criticism, 53*(1), 1–7.

May, W. (1992). Philosopher as researcher and/or begging the question(s). *Studies in Art Education, 33*(4), 226–243.

McLuhan, M., & Fiore, Q. (1967). *The medium is the massage*. New York: Bantam Books.

Morman, J. M. (1967). *Art, of wonder and a world*. Blauvelt, NY: Art Education.

Parsons, M. (1987). *How we understand art: A cognitive developmental account of aesthetic experience*. New York: Cambridge University Press.

Pearse, H. (1992). Beyond paradigms: Art education theory and practice in a post-paradigmatic world. *Studies in Art Education, 33*(4), 244–252.

Plagens, P. (1986). Peter and the pressure cooker. In P. Plagens (Ed.), *Moonlight blues: An artist's art criticism* (pp. 119–130). Ann Arbor, MI: UMI Press.

Plagens, P. (1986). *Moonlight blues: An artist's art criticism*. Ann Arbor, MI: UMI Press.

Pollock, G. (1996). The "View from Elsewhere": Extracts from a semipublic correspondence about the visibility of desire. In B. Collins (Ed.), *12 Views of Manet's Bar* (pp. 278–313). New Haven, CT: Princeton University Press.

Postman, N., & Weingartner, C. (1969). *Teaching as a subversive activity*. New York: Delacorte Press.

Raven, A. (1988). *Crossing over: Feminism and art of social concern*. Ann Arbor, MI: UMI Press.

Rorty, R. (1992). The pragmatist's progress. In U. Eco (Ed.), *Interpretation and overinterpretation* (pp. 89–108). New York: Cambridge University Press.

Scheffler, I. (1991). *In praise of the cognitive emotions and other essays in the philosophy of education*. New York: Routledge.

Schjeldahl, P. (1994). Critical reflections, *Artforum*. Summer.

Scruton, R. (1983). Why photography is not art. In Methuen (Ed.), *The aesthetic understanding*. New York: Routledge.

Sekula, A. (1975). On the invention of photographic meaning. *Artforum*, January, 15–25.

Skoglund, S. (1998). *Reality under siege: A retrospective*. New York: Abrams.

Smith, R. (1973). Teaching aesthetic criticism in the schools. *Journal of Aesthetic Education, 7*(1), 38–49.

Smith, R. (1992). Problems for a philosophy of art education, *Studies in Art Education, 33*(4), 253–266.

Sontag, S. (1978). *On photography*. New York: Farrar, Straus, & Giroux.

Stankiewicz, M. A. (2002). Three: Reading Lorna Simpson's art in context. In Y. Gaudelius & P. Speirs (Eds.), *Contemporary issues in art education* (pp. 384–394). Upper Saddle River, NJ: Prentice-Hall.

Stecker, R. (1995). Relativism about interpretation. *Journal of Aesthetics and Art Criticism, 53*(1), 14–20.

Stout, C. (1995). *Critical thinking and writing in art*. Minneapolis, MN: West.

Stout, C. (2002). *Flower teachers: Stories for a new generation*. Reston, VA: NAEA.

Time-Life Books. (1970). *Life library of photography*. New York: Time-Life.

Upton, B., & Upton, J. (1976). *Photography: Adapted from the life library of photography*. Boston: Little, Brown.

Walker, S. (2000). *Teaching meaning in artmaking*. Worcester, MA: Davis.

Walton, K. (1984). Transparent pictures. *Critical Inquiry*, December, 246–259.

Weems, C. M. (1994). *Carrie Mae Weems*. Washington, DC: The National Museum of Women in the Arts.

Weitz, M. (1964). *Hamlet and the philosophy of literary criticism*. Chicago: University of Chicago Press.

Weitz, M. (1979). The role of theory in aesthetics. In D. Goldblatt & L. Brown (Eds.), *Aesthetics: A reader in philosophy of the arts*. Upper Saddle River, NJ: Prentice Hall.

Wilson, B. (1997). *The quiet evolution: Changing the face of arts education*. Los Angeles: J. Paul Getty Trust.

Wolfe, T. (1981). *From Bauhaus to our house*. New York: Farrar Straus Giroux.

33

Art Education as Imaginative Cognition[1]

Arthur D. Efland
The Ohio State University

Imagination is more important than knowledge.
—Albert Einstein.

INTRODUCTION

Imagination is no stranger to art education. Like creative self-expression it was one of those labels used by Progressive educators of the 20th century to characterize their vision of school reform. Allowing the child's imagination to unfold in unforeseen ways was the goal, and the method consisted of freeing children from the constraints of the traditional school with its demand for social conformity, obedience to rules, and silence. With the removal of external coercion, imagination was thought to unfold spontaneously if parents and teachers would but allow it. The child by nature was imaginative, though this quality of mind could be thwarted by the designs of an insensitive pedagogy. Indeed, in the heyday of Progressivism the best teaching was the least teaching.

Harold Rugg and Ann Shumaker's *Child-Centered School* was based on the child–is–artist metaphor, and the struggle of artists to emancipate themselves from the strictures of academic convention was adopted to characterize progress. The "lid of restraint is being lifted from the child of the common man in order that he might come to his own best self-fulfillment" (Rugg & Shumaker, 1928, pp. 62–63). And the proof of success was not to be found in the parroting of facts read in books but in the child's production of original products including works of art. Teaching art was synonymous with freeing the imagination.

---

[1] This chapter is based on Chapter Six of my book *Art and Cognition* (Efland, 2002), which is based on the theoretical and empirical work by George Lakoff and Mark Robertson. I have reworked the original text to bring it into conformity with their more recent writing, especially their recent book, *Philosophy in the Flesh.* (Lakoff & Johnson, 1999). I first encountered the term *imaginative cognition* in Rudolf Steiner's book The Philosophy of Freedom.

From the 1920s through the 1950s, a number of gifted teachers of art based their pedagogy on their understanding of artistic imagination,[2] with particular emphasis on the originality of artistic accomplishments as the mark of authenticity. These include Franz Cizek in Vienna Austria; Marion Richardson in England; and Florence Cane, Victor D'Amico and Viktor Lowenfeld in the United States (Efland, 1990). Though insightful, their pedagogical activities were not grounded in an understanding of imagination as a cognitive endeavor (Efland, 2002, pp. 42–43).

Throughout most of the 20th century, educational practice was guided by behavioral psychology and had little use for imagination. Its program of research was largely limited to investigations of stimulus and response conditions, conditioning, habit formation, and the effects of reinforcement. Intelligence was characterized quantitatively by the IQ that was set at birth, whereas achievement was measured by the number of facts recalled in testing. Mind and imagination were outside the bounds of legitimate science. Cognition was narrowly conceived in terms of literacy and numeracy, and the arts by default were identified as noncognitive studies, relegated to the "affective domain," to educational romanticism. In limiting itself to S–R bonds as the unit of analysis, behavioral science never adequately explained how higher cognitive processes like abstract thinking could emerge from these simple units of behavior.[3] With the appearance of the cognitive sciences in the latter half of the 20th century, questions about the role of imagery in thinking rekindled interest in the imagination. "Work in a number of fields is converging toward a rhabilitation of imagination as a fundamental scientific topic..." (Fauconnier & Turner, 2002, p. 15).

Aside from its use as an honorific what does cognitive science have to say about imagination? Does it arise spontaneously when the proverbial lid of restraint has been lifted, or does it have to be cultivated in particular ways? Does the imagination have a role in helping individuals understand their world and communicate about it, or does it lead to day–dreaming and escape? And the key question: Can current conceptions of cognition offer art educators a basis for reshaping itself into a domain hospitable to the imagination and creativity? I begin by identifying several factors affecting the current understanding of cognition to identify where imagination fits into the story.

The Cognitive Revolutions

The Mind as a Computer

Six major developments had to transpire before cognitive explanations of learning could arise. The first was the cognitive revolution, itself, which got under way in the late 1950s which offered an alternative explanation of learning from the behaviorism that dominated research and practice throughout the first half of the last century. In its initial phases this revolution was centered on ideas about symbolic computation (Gardner, 1987). With its software and hardware divisions, the computer became a fitting metaphor for the mind. It investigated such topics as pattern recognition, problem solving, artificial intelligence, the operation of symbol systems in thinking and information processing, areas where the mind is most like a computer. George Lakoff and Mark Johnson (1999) refer to such developments as belonging to a first generation of cognitive science:

> The mind, from this "functionalist" perspective, was seen metaphorically as a kind of abstract computer program that could be run on any appropriate hardware. A consequence of the metaphor

---

[2]Many were practicing artists in their own right.

[3]Imagination was a topic of investigation throughout the 18th and 19th centuries, and appeared in the epistemologies of Hume and Kant.

was that the hardware... [the body] was seen as determining nothing at all about the nature of the program. (pp. 75–76)

Howard Gardner's multiple intelligence theory was one of the more fruitful outcomes of the symbol systems approach in that he conceived of the mind as an ability to devise multiple symbol systems. This expanded the conception of cognition by describing a variety of symbolic forms including music, numbers, and verbal competence. Each of the intelligences had its unique assemblage of symbols. But explanations of cognition, based on a symbol systems approach, were plagued by a dualism where the mind was characterized in terms of its formal operations unconstrained by the body. Thinking occurred in the brain and entailed the use of these symbol systems. As in computer languages, the symbols were meaningless in themselves, and thinking was defined as the manipulation of such symbols according to formal rules.

The Body in the Mind [4]

In the late 1970s, a second generation of cognitive theories offered alternatives to symbol systems approaches. Evidence began mounting demonstrating that abstract concepts and reason were far more dependent on bodily and sensory encounters than was initially thought to be the case. Lakoff and Johnson refer to this second generation as "the cognitive science of the embodied mind" (1999, p. 77). In particular their investigations in cognitive linguistics studied the construction of metaphors and categories in human thought and demonstrated the interconnectedness of body and mind.

Changes in Theories of Language

Additional revolutionary developments also occurred within cognitive linguistics itself. One is the change from the formalist perspective of Noam Chomksy, where language is thought by him to be an autonomous faculty of mind with its innate universal grammar and syntax independent of aspects external to the body. Supplanting this view is one where language is studied more broadly to provide a fuller description of how symbols and concepts get their meaning.

According to Andrew Ortony (1993), ordinary language was traditionally characterized as a literal affair, without figures of speech or ornamental embellishment. The language of science represented this use of communication in its purest form. Privileged by logical positivism, scientific explanation rested on the foundational assumption that reality could be represented objectively in symbolic form and that other uses of language such as figurative speech and metaphor either were essentially meaningless or had to be reduced to literal terms before understanding could take place. Literal language reigned supreme in education, and, to an extent, this is still the case. By the 1980s and 1990s, constructivist views of knowledge and representation called into question the basis for a rigid differentiation between the literal and the figurative uses of language. In short, the gulf between the objective language of the scientist and the figurative language of the poet was no longer as wide as it once was thought to be. It is now possible to see metaphor "as an essential characteristic of the creativity of language" rather than "as deviant and parasitic upon normal usage" (Ortony, 1993, p. 2).

Constructivist Views of Learning

Recent cognitive explanations of learning are characterized as constructivist views. Accordingly, individuals construct their understanding of reality guided by their knowledge-seeking

---

[4]The paragraph heading is from the title of Mark Johnson's book of the same name.

purposes. Emphasis is placed on human agency where meaning-making is guided by the dispositions and purposes of the learner. Constructivism also characterizes learning as a process where new knowledge is understood through its integration into one's base of prior knowledge. Hence, knowledge constantly undergoes reconstruction. This classical view of constructivism is largely derived from Piaget's late writings. Recent views of constructivism still retain the broad outlines of the Piagetian view but differ in one important aspect in recognizing the social context of learning. The progress individuals make in their learning is not undertaken in isolation. Individuals make use of the "cultural tools," and these include specific knowledge domains through which inquiries are addressed.

Domains of knowledge are cultural communities in their own right, each with distinctive practices. This emphasis on cultural practices does not necessarily deny the possibility of independent discovery learning perse, but recognizes that various fields of knowledge such as the sciences or the arts have their social dimension, and that teaching within these domains enculturates learners into the specific discourses of each field. For example, the tools of science include such conceptual tools as atoms, ions, and genes as well as particular metaphors that enable understanding of these entities to occur. For example, my understanding of the structure of the atom came about through its analogy with the solar system, though current views have abandoned this.

Similarly, works of art are understood through the metaphor of living organisms, as integrated wholes greater than the sum of its parts.

Metaphors as Mappings

In describing his contemporary theory of metaphor, Lakoff (1993) argues that metaphorical expressions are, in a sense, not matters of language but forms of thought based on underlying conceptualizations of reality. He describes metaphors as involving a mapping across conceptual domains, and these exist in many forms: in ordinary or everyday language, in the practice of creative writers and poets, in the image making of visual artists, and in the language of science. An example of the latter is provided by M. Mitchell Waldrop, who describes certain changes in current scientific thinking as shifting away from "the Newtonian metaphor of clockwork predictability... [toward] metaphors more closely akin to the growth of a plant..." (1992, p. 329).

Metaphor involves the way we conceptualize one mental domain in terms of another. The words of the poet or the images of the visual artist are surface indicators of these deeper conceptual metaphors through which we organize our understanding. To make this point, Lakoff (1993) illustrates the systematic character of the conceptual metaphor he calls "LOVE-IS-A-JOURNEY".[5] "The metaphor involves understanding one domain of experience, love in terms of a very different domain, namely journeys." It involves a mapping from a source domain, in this case, a knowledge of journeys, to a target domain, in this case, love (1993, pp. 206–207). He asks us to consider these expressions:

> Our relationship has hit a dead-end street.
> We may have to go our separate ways.
> We're spinning our wheels.
> Our relationship is off the track.
> The marriage is on the rocks.
> We may have to bail out of this relationship. (p. 206)

---

[5]Here I use Lakoff and Johnson's system of naming metaphors by using capital letters and hyphens. This system is used throughout this essay.

He explains:

> The metaphor is not just a matter of language but of thought and reason. The language is secondary. The mapping is primary, in that it sanctions the use of source domain language and inference patterns for target domain concepts... This view of metaphor is thoroughly at odds with the view that metaphors are linguistic expressions. If metaphors were merely linguistic expressions, we would expect different linguistic expressions to be different metaphors. Thus "we've hit a dead-end street" would constitute one metaphor. "We can't turn back now" would constitute another, entirely different metaphor... Yet we don't seem to have dozens of metaphors here. We have one metaphor in which love is conceptualized as a journey. And this unified way of *conceptualizing* love metaphorically is realized in many *linguistic* expressions." (p. 208)

And later he adds,

> The fact that the love-is-a-journey mapping is a fixed part of our conceptual system explains why new and imaginative uses of the mapping can be understood instantly, given the ontological correspondences and other knowledge about journeys. Take the song lyric, "we're driving in the fast lane on the freeway of love." The travelling knowledge called upon is this: when you drive in the fast lane, you go a long way in a short time and it can be exciting and dangerous. (p. 210)

Lakoff lists five false assumptions regarding the distinction between the literal and the figurative uses of language:

1. All everyday language is literal, and none is metaphorical.
2. All subject matter can be comprehended literally, without metaphor.
3. Only literal language can be contingently true or false.
4. All definitions in the lexicon of a language are literal not metaphorical.
5. The concepts used in the grammar of a language are all literal; none are metaphorical (Lakoff, 1993, p. 204).

Visual Metaphors

This concern for metaphor would certainly apply to the literary arts, but does it apply to the visual arts? Are there such things as visual metaphors whose meaning is conveyed directly by images rather than by words, and if so, how do they differ from verbal metaphors? Noel Carroll (2001) raised this question and answered by noting that images differ from words in being recognized "simply by looking" without having to be decoded (Carroll, 2001, p. 348). Images can be symbolic like the dove on the flag of the United Nations, though not all images are necessarily metaphoric. The family photographs taken on my last vacation are not visual metaphors.

However, a work like Man Ray's photomontage entitled *Violin d'Ingres* (1924)[6] qualifies as a visual metaphor. In the Man Ray, the bare back of a female nude model is shown reminiscent of the odalisques of Ingres from the early 19th century. However, he placed two black f-shaped holes such as those found in violins or cellos on the back of the model. This realization suggests something quite shocking: that this woman is no longer a person but an instrument, that is, something to be played with—perhaps an instrument of sexual desire! This interpretation is reinforced by the turban on the model's head which brings to mind Ingre's paintings of harem odalisques. The image plus the title gives rise to the metaphorical insight that Ingre's odalisques are violins, or conversely that violins are odalisques. Lakoff's view that conceptual metaphors are not matters of words but matters of thought lends credence to the idea that visual images are also forms of thought, and that thought is not restricted to the literary arts. They are cognitive.

---

[6]The Man Ray example was used by Carroll.

Again, the primary condition for the formation of the metaphor is the mapping of one domain onto another, in this case the odalisque as a violin.

Implications for Art Education

This traditional dichotomy between the literal and the figurative uses of language is akin to the gulf separating "cognitive" from "noncognitive" subjects in the school curriculum. This distinction is being repudiated by recent explanations of learning, especially the constructivist view, which holds that individuals construct their views of reality guided by their own knowledge-seeking purposes. As noted previously, emphasis is placed on human agency where meaning-making is guided as much by personal interest and effort as well as by the phenomenon singled out for educational attention. And the implications for general education are plain to see. Cognition involves more than the acquisition of knowledge found in books and lectures compiled and organized by scholars. It also involves the construction of meaning by the learner. If the purpose of education is to enhance the cognitive capabilities of individuals, it must offer experiences within domains calling for an array of abilities, and differing domains have differing structures requiring differing approaches in instruction.

What Makes Certain Domains Complex and Ill Structured?

The domains of the sciences exemplify what Rand Spiro and his colleagues have called "well-structured domains," because they are organized around laws and generalizations that cover numerous cases. In such domains, learning involves the task of retrieving appropriate generalizations or principles. However, many domains are "ill structured" including the arts. Learning in such domains often must proceed without the guidance of broad generalizations or principles. Instruction in law and medicine is also based on cases rather than on generalizations.

In ill-structured domains, learners are forced to organize their understanding by assembling knowledge from individual cases (Spiro, Vispoel, Schmitz, Samarpungavan, & Boerger, 1987, p. 2). By seeing multiple cases, the learner comes to understand the relative influence of various contexts in which each case is embedded. The learner must do more than take in knowledge; she must engage in a constructive process where experience with a large number of cases is assembled. A well-educated person is one who can function in both well–structured and ill–structured learning situations. Cognitive flexibility is the attribute of having an array of strategies, but it also includes the ability to select and match the appropriate strategy for knowledge acquisition for use in domains with differing structural properties.

There is an additional factor that adds complexity to the domain of the arts, namely, that artworks are themselves metaphoric structures—"cross-domain mappings" to use Lakoff's term. Such mappings exist wherever metaphor occurs, and metaphor occurs throughout what Lakoff and Johnson call "the cognitive unconscious" (1999, pp. 11–12). It is not exclusive to the arts, but the arts are domains where metaphoric forms of thought serve as principal objects of inquiry. The arts are places where the structure of metaphors and their meanings are actively explored, including such aesthetic attributes as freshness and evocative power. By contrast the conceptual metaphors that are built into our cognitive unconscious largely go unnoticed.

The current understanding of cognition is more complex than was heretofore thought. And cognitive ability, which traditionally has been limited to the acquisition of propositional or literal forms of thought, needs to be broadened to include conceptual activities that entail nonpropositional forms of thought including the arts. In what follows, I discuss the role that imagination plays both in propositional and in nonpropositional forms of thought.

IMAGINATION IN COGNITION

After offering definitions of imagination, I describe three kinds of research including anecdotal studies of mental imagery, empirical studies of mental images, and cognitive linguistic studies. It is mainly within the latter type of study that the nature of metaphor is revealed as a major function of the imaginative in cognition.

Defining Imagination

Imagination is the act or power of forming mental images of what is not actually present to the senses, or what has not actually been experienced. It is also the act or power of creating new ideas or images through the combination and reorganization of previous experiences. This latter power "is often regarded as the more seriously and deeply creative faculty which perceives the basic resemblances between things. . ." (*Websters New World Dictionary, College Edition,* 1964, p. 725). We have a tendency to dismiss or discount ideas if they exist "only in the imagination," as when we say that someone's imaginary notions or ideas lie "beyond belief." and we tend to be wary of individuals having "an overactive imagination." Yet, in many contexts, imagination and imaginative are used as honorifics, as when we discuss the creative talent of an artist or the achievements of scientists.

As used here, imagination refers to the cognitive processes that enable individuals to organize or reorganize images, to combine or recombine symbols as in the creation of metaphors, or narrative productions. The honorific associations of the term also imply that the products of imagination differ from everyday, ordinary thinking by being more innovative and less concerned with typical or conventional communication. The term *imaginative* can refer to innovation in formal arrangement, meaning, or both. It adds novelty to the cultural landscape, and terms like *imaginative* or *imaginary* also carry social designations about particular objects or events, rather than about a specific class of cognitive operations. It is not any one specific cognitive operation or faculty in the Kantian sense but the result of cognitive acts that enable individuals to construct meanings that are generally less dependent on conventional, rule-governed, or propositional forms of thinking and communication. The creation of a fresh metaphor in spoken or written expression would be one example, whereas the juxtaposition of images in a collage to generate a new image would be another (Efland, 2002, p. 134).

Imagination in Education

As long as poets, musicians, and visual artists employed devices that transcended those needed for daily communication in the individual's lifeworld, their elimination from schooling was seen as having minimal impact on the cultivation of the individual's cognitive abilities. Education in the arts was seen as an indulgence, fine for those having the leisure and the means to engage in its obscure enchantments, but not essential for the development of the learner's mental powers. The metaphors one encounters in daily speech are sufficient to produce and convey meaning; thus, one could argue that for everyday purposes, high levels of metaphoric competence rarely become necessary to create meanings and understandings. Indeed, quite the opposite is the case. Being plainspoken is itself a virtue. Such a view is shortsighted, because processes like metaphor, which operate by the mapping of one domain onto another, enable the mind to go beyond what is known, to reach what has yet to be learned. This happens in all domains, to be sure, and each domain of knowledge (each discipline if you will) has its rules and constraints, including the arts.

As used in the arts, metaphor creates a space in human cognition where individuals are free to rehearse new ideas of expression and form and to express personal visions, social issues, and moral ideals. This assumes a level of autonomy for the arts as with other domains, yet the arts do not exist for the sake of their own purity but for the freedom of the cultural life they enable. Works of art are also active agents in mediating the culture of which they are part (Wolff, 1995 p. 134). The work of art becomes an arena for the discursive production of meanings and values in society. Becoming conscious of the power of metaphor has the potential to extend the reach of human communication. The arts are not transcendental realms above and beyond daily experience, but a place where novel metaphors and images stand out in experience by their exceptionality and power. Indeed, *art* is the honorific we give to especially notable moments.[7]

Investigations of Imagery and Imagination

The paucity of psychological studies of imagination throughout the 20th century is not the result of oversight. It was widely discussed in literary and philosophical circles throughout the 18th and 19th centuries. Its neglect throughout most of the last century reflects the constraining influence of positivism, a legacy from which we have yet to shake ourselves free. With the rise of the cognitive science perspective, the cognitive character of imagery and imagination became a new candidate for psychological research, especially in work by Roger Shephard, Stephen Kosslyn, and others (Kosslyn, 1980; Shephard, 1978a; Shephard, 1978b). In raising the issue of how to explain the function of mental imagery in cognition, these psychologists also raised fundamental questions about the adequacy of computational models of mind which were generally restricted to the use of propositional symbol systems. In particular the models of mind advanced during the first generation of the cognitive revolution were unable to account for the role of mental imagery in cognitive functioning.

Anecdotal Studies of Mental Imagery

There have been three kinds of studies that have dealt with the topic of mental imagery: First, there have been compilations of anecdotal studies including self-reports of individuals whose significant scientific discoveries or artistic accomplishments were occasioned by strong acts of imaginative creativity. In particular, Shephard (1978a, 1978b) collected accounts of the imaginative activity of scientists. These provide dramatic portrayals of the role that mental imagery played in the thought processes that led these individuals to do their most important work or to make key discoveries. Shephard cited Albert Einstein, who reported that verbal processes did "not seem to play any role" in his processes of creative thought. In fact he maintained that his particular ability did not lie in mathematical calculation either, "but rather in *visualizing . . . effects, consequences and possibilities.*" He performed what he called his *gedanken* or thought experiment where he imagined himself traveling alongside a beam of light at speeds of 186,000 miles per second. What he mentally "saw" did not correspond to anything "that could be experienced perceptually as light nor to anything described by Maxwell's equations, which specified in mathematical terms the relationships between the various forms of electromagnetic energy. It was these visualizations that prompted him to formulate the special theory of relativity" (Shephard, 1978a, 1978b).

Empirical Studies of Mental Images

A second approach involved empirical studies, where the utilization of mental imagery was compared with ordinary perceptual activity (Shephard & Metzler, 1971), or was contrasted with information presented in verbal, linguistic form (Kosslyn, 1983). Results obtained by Shephard

---

[7]This opens the argument on behalf of aesthetic experience as the principal criterion marking the presence of a work of art. This paper does not address this issue.

and Metzler indicate that in many instances mental imagery is remarkably able to substitute for actual perception with subjects seemingly able to make the same judgments about mental objects as they do about real objects encountered in perception. Kosslyn and his colleagues have also devised a comprehensive theory of what they call a "quasi-pictorial form of mental representation called "imagery." According to Gardner, "this form of mental representation is as important for an understanding of cognition as is the more usually invoked propositional form" (Gardner, 1987, p. 327). Gardner suggested, "the fact that computers can—and usually do—transmit information in only one symbolic form is no reason to assume that human beings do the same" (1987, p. 129) Indeed, his theory of multiple intelligences aggressively denies that limitation.

Cognitive Linguistic Studies

I already introduced the third approach to the study of imagination in referring earlier to the work of George Lakoff and Mark Johnson (1980, 1999), who collaborated to study the cognitive foundations of such seemingly abstract mental activities as categorization and metaphor as observed through empirical studies of linguistic behavior. They maintain that there is a growing body of evidence for the existence of what they call "an image-schematic level of cognitive operations." Like the concept of schemata in Piaget's theory, these exist at a level of generality and abstraction that allows them to serve repeatedly as identifying patterns in a variety of experiences similarly structured in relevant ways, but they differ from Piagetian schemata in some important ways to be discussed later (Johnson, 1987, pp. 26–28).

The image schemata postulated by Lakoff and Johnson begin with images that arise directly from bodily experiences, acquired directly in perception. These provide the foundation for categorization, abstract reason, propositional and nonpropositional forms of thinking, metaphor, and narrative. In Lakoff and Johnson's recent writing, they introduce terms like "cognitive unconscious" and "conceptual metaphor" to refer to the larger and more inclusive structures of mind composed of these schemata. Image schemata should not be confused with the images we recall from prior perceptions like yesterday's sunset. Rather they are cognitive structures that are conceptualized from a variety of images. Johnson exemplifies with one he calls "compulsive force." He described a resemblance between a jet airplane being forced down the runway by the power of its engines, the geological forces acting on continental plates, and social pressures acting on his social conscience that obliged him to join the PTA. The meaning of compulsive force is embodied directly in the percepts acquired in experience and does not have to await additional actions put forth by the mind for comprehension.

Lakoff and Johnson's image schemata initially resemble schemata in the cognitive developmental theories of Piaget, in that both begin as structures based on images derived from bodily and perceptual experiences. Piaget calls this early stage of development "sensimotor operations." These schemata are abstract structures that summarize information from many different cases, but tied to these structures is the awareness of particular operations (actions to be undertaken by the mind) to understand what is given in perception. Piaget describes the development of these cognitive structures as becoming increasingly mentalistic, abstract, and less dependent on the senses. Their cognitive operations become less physical and more formal so that the development of schemata in his account is a narrative that details the development of human cognition as the progress we make toward disembodied mental life. Cognitive development thus proceeds through several stages marked by changes in these structures. In his "formal operations" stage, Piaget describes the mind's power to organize symbolic structures in logical and scientific propositions that describe, explain, and reliably predict events in nature. His main work consisted of tracking the evolution of these structures from the first actions undertaken by the infant, like the grasping of objects, to the formation of abstract, formal structures, comprised of numbers and letters which, though meaningless in themselves, are understood as representations of the actual world.

Piaget did *not* discuss the possibility that schemata might take the form of mental imagery resulting from perception. Indeed, he did not regard perception as a form of intelligence, but rather defined it in terms of the actions or operations the mind takes on its perceptions in order to understand them (Flavell, 1963, pp. 31–33). Piaget's account also does not explain how metaphor happens. He left unanswered the question of why human beings apparently seem to develop an ability to conceptualize one mental domain in terms of another. By contrast, Lakoff and Johnson's theory accounting for image schemata as nonpropositional structures of imagination does provide a basis for establishing such connections through such devices as metaphor.

THREE IMAGINATIVE PROCESSES

Image Schemata in Cognition

In what follows, three processes involving the imaginative in cognition are described. The first involves the development of image schemata and processes of metaphoric projection or elaboration as arising from such schemata. Image schemata derived from bodily and perceptual experiences are shown to form the foundation for abstract thinking.

The second offers a contemporary theory of categorization, which indicates that the power to develop category systems including their extensions also relies heavily on imaginative activity having its origins in bodily and perceptual experiences. The third describes cognition as resting on a vast system of conceptual metaphors essentially built up through cross-domain mappings. Each of these processes is heavily reliant on image schemata as bases for cognition. Moreover, each demonstrates that the abstract powers of the mind have their origins in bodily and perceptual experience and that the mind is not separate from the body.

As described by Lakoff and Johnson cognition begins with a preconceptual, bodily experience (Lakoff, 1987, p. 267). Johnson illustrates the concept of an image schema with one arising from the experience of *balance*. Initially, balance acquires meaning through experiences where we orient ourselves physically within our environment. We live in a gravitational field and resist the pull of gravity as we learn to maintain our equilibrium when learning to walk. He writes:

> It is crucially important that we see that balancing is an *activity that we learn with our bodies* and not by grasping a set of rules or concepts. First and foremost balancing is something we *do*. The baby stands, wobbles, and drops to the floor. It tries again, and again, until a new world opens up—the world of balanced erect posture. (Johnson, 1987, p. 74)

The image schema of balance is acquired by actions like learning to stand and walk, experiences which are learned in the course of development, often before there are words to name or describe them; hence, their nonpropositional character. Once established, they provide a basis for elaboration through metaphor. Thus, the attributes of balance get mapped onto to other entities, as in expressions like "a balanced personality." Balance is also applied to the equation in mathematics and to the balance of justice in the workings of the legal system. Johnson explains how such schemata give rise to metaphor.

> In the case of *balance*, for example, we saw how certain very abstract concepts, events, states, institutions, and principles (such as psychological states, arguments, moral rights, and mathematical operations) are metaphorically structured as entities or physical events. And it is by virtue of metaphorically imposed structure that we can understand and reason about the relevant abstract

entities. It is the projection of such structure that I am identifying as the creative function of metaphor, for it is one of the chief ways we can generate structure in our experience in a way we can comprehend. (Johnson, 1987, p. 98)

Metaphoric Projection and Elaboration

Lakoff and Johnson postulate that higher order, rational thinking can be accounted for through extensions of these image-schematic structures by *metaphoric projection.* To understand the nature of these structures and their actions, I summarize Lakoff's account.

A metaphor has three parts: a source domain, a target domain, and a mapping function that enables the attributes of one domain to be applied to another (1987, p. 276). To understand the logic behind the metaphor, we have to see how the mapping function ties these elements together. In many of Lakoff and Johnson's examples, the source domain is grounded in basic-level bodily experience as seen previously with balance.

Metaphors establish connections among objects and events that are seemingly unrelated, and they are encountered in all studies, the arts included. Metaphoric projection is thus a means through which abstract thought arises. This is important because it explains how abstract thinking in human cognition can emerge from bodily and sensory experience. Lakoff and Johnson's main claim is that image schemata, which come about from bodily actions and perceptions, can reach the mental, epistemic, or logical domains in cognition. What is typically referred to as higher order thinking, the larger understandings that are called abstract and disembodied reason, has its beginnings with the formation of image schemata in bodily experience.

It is here where Lakoff and Johnson differ from Piaget, in that for Piaget *actions* are *operations of the mind* that work on the perceptions it receives as opposed to *actions of the body* like learning to walk. Piaget's schemata are used to explain how the mind devises formal, propositional structures, whereas the image schemata of interest to Lakoff and Johnson, are *of the body.* However, in Johnson's epistemology, body and mind are undivided.[8] Piaget's understanding of the cognitive was a journey from experience at the sensory level toward formal abstraction. Piaget conceived of the mind's formal operations as being less dependent on, if not entirely separate from, the body.

By contrast, Lakoff and Johnson's intellectual journey reveals a basic level of bodily and perceptual experience as the foundation of cognition and the source of meaning. Like Piaget, they sought to provide an alternative to the Kantian view that higher order logical structures emerge "a priori as the universal essence of rationality" (Johnson, 1987, p. 99), to argue that such higher order cognitive structures emerge from our embodied, concrete experience.

The Kantian conception of imagination was problematic because it divided the mind into a physical or material side governed by strict deterministic natural laws, which included our bodily being, including sensations and feelings; whereas on the other side of the mind was the formal realm of the understanding. This gulf separated understanding from perceptual experience, the mind from the body, in a dualism traceable to the rationalism of Descartes, and which survives in Piaget's tendency to separate thinking from feeling and perception from understanding. However, the imagination as initially conceived by Kant had the potential to bridge this gap, as Johnson explains:

I would suggest that though Kant could never admit it, that his remarkable account of imagination actually undermines the rigid dichotomies that define his system, showing very powerfully that they are not absolute metaphysical and epistemological separations. Hence imagination is a pervasive

---

[8]Both Lakoff and Johnson reject what they term the myths of objectivism and subjectivism in favor a metaphysics they call experiential realism. See Chapter 11 in Lakoff's *Women, Fire and Dangerous Things.* See also Chapters 25 to 28 in Lakoff and Johnson's *Metaphors We Live By.*

structuring activity by means of which we achieve coherent, patterned, and unified representations. The conclusion ought to be, therefore, that imagination is absolutely essential to rationality, that is, to our rational capacity to find significant connections, to draw inferences, and to solve problems. Kant, of course, pulls back from this conclusion because it would undermine the dichotomies that underlie his system. (Johnson, 1987, p. 168)

Kant's problem disappears when we deny the alleged gap among understanding, imagination, and sensation. Johnson asks, "what if, following the consensus of contemporary analytic philosophy, we deny the strict separation of the formal realm from the material?" If we were to regard these as poles on a continuum, there would be no need to exclude imagination from the cognitive. Kant recognized a vast realm of shared meaning structure in imagination but could not bring himself to grant this dimension cognitive status.

Categories in Cognition

Classical Categories

Categories in the classical, formal sense are bound up with rules that define the conditions of membership or nonmembership of objects, events, or persons as the mind organizes and classifies things and actions into like groups. These rules form the basis for the logic used in the operation of propositional forms of thought, areas *not* commonly regarded as fertile ground for the development and cultivation of imagination. For example, romantic theories of imagination often characterized it as unconstrained thinking without rules.

Categorization also refers to how people group things in the world of everyday, common-sense experience. We learn about the natural world through our senses, through the multiple sensations of sights and sounds, warmth and coolness, roughness and smoothness, tastes and smells. We also learn within a social world through mediations with family members, peers, and the community at large. Our understanding emerges from these encounters. With experience, our world picture becomes increasingly diverse, and to control this vast enumeration of things, we organize it by categories, by samenesses and differences, friends and foes— even by likes and dislikes. It is the power to select—to include and exclude. We organize our world on the basis of common attributes. Categories are containers into which like things are grouped.

It is more efficient to learn about groups of things by their shared characteristics than by each in isolation. Categorization involves thinking about things in terms of commonalities, not about the uniqueness of individual cases. This action is mostly automatic and unconscious, giving rise to the view that objects and events in the world come in natural kinds, but categories also are cognitive achievements, not properties of the world as such. They emerge from the mind's effort to organize what is given in perception in its effort to secure meaning. Were it not for the capacity to categorize, we would soon become "slaves to the particular."[9]

Categories are also used to group things and people and serve as a basis for social behavior. Jokes about women drivers or mother-in-laws assume that members of these groups share common (in these cases pejorative) characteristics. Such categories and their affective loadings are built into everyday language; they can disseminate sexist or racist stereotypes. These are negative applications of categorization. On the constructive side, the common-sense classification of birds, flowers, and fish into groups of like things provides the basis for organizing knowledge used in everyday affairs and in the school curriculum.

---

[9]I attribute the expression to Jerome Bruner.

Limitations of Classical Categories

We tend to assume that the category groupings we form in our everyday affairs offer reliable representations of things as they are in the world, leading to a reliable view of reality, itself. Lakoff explains:

> From the time of Aristotle to the later Wittgenstein categories were thought to be well understood and unproblematic. They were assumed to be abstract containers with things either inside or outside the category. Things were assumed to be in the same category if, and only if, they had certain properties in common, and the properties they had in common were taken as defining the category. (Lakoff, 1987, p. 6)

Wittgenstein's Family Resemblance Categories

According to Lakoff (1987, p. 16), Ludwig Wittgenstein realized that people do not necessarily organize experience by classical modes of categorization; that often they tend to devise alternative systems to circumvent the constraints imposed by such categories. He exemplified this with the concept of *game*. There is no single collection of properties that all games share; thus, it is impossible to devise a definition that includes all things called games that simultaneously excludes nongames. What unites games as a category is what Wittgenstein called *family resemblance*. According to Lakoff, "... games like family members are similar to one another in a wide variety of ways. That, and not a single, well-defined collection of common properties is what makes them a category" (p. 16). Moreover, people in everyday life are not troubled by this lack of a definition. We have no difficulty recognizing the objects and events called games.

Art as a Category

Morris Weitz (1956) argued that *art* as a concept also functions as a family-resemblance category, in that the existing definitions of art are unable to cover all cases of art. Art also has extendable boundaries as new media and styles come into being and as new works are created.[10] When art was defined as formal order, the curriculum featured the study of formal principles stressing elements and principles of design, but when art was defined as the expression of the artist's feelings, pedagogies based on creative self-expression were prevalent. When Weitz suggested that these definitions were, at best, argued for recommendations to view art from a particular vantage point, art educators began recognizing the possibility of multiple perspectives in the curriculum. This change from a traditional, classical conception of categorization to a family-resemblance system began surfacing in proposals for eclectic curricula open to various ideas about what can be art.[11]

Prototype-Based Categories

In classical theory, a category shares a collection of common properties possessed by all of its members, where these attributes define the category. Consequently, no member of a set would have any special status (Lakoff, 1987, p. 40). Yet in the early 1970s, Eleanor Rosch began identifying certain effects she called *prototype effects* within categories like *color*, *birds*, or *chairs*. When people were asked to group colors that seem to belong together, they would

---

[10] Answers to the question, "What is art?" were traditionally thought to be *true definitions*, in the sense that they were advanced as covering all cases of art. Weitz argued that "What is art?" is the wrong question, that a more appropriate one would ask "what sort of concept is art?" or how is it being applied in a given context?

[11] For example, Laura Chapman's widely used text *Approaches to Art Education* adopted an eclectic stance. My "Conceptions of Teaching" paper traced a succession of orientations in art education that were prominent throughout the 20th century.

put all the reds together, all the blues, and so forth. But, if asked to select the best or most typical example of red or blue, most people could readily do that as well. These optimal color selections act like specific prototypes often based on family resemblance by which individuals mark their experiences of colors. Because prototypes suggest that some members of a group are more representative of the category than others, the idea of prototypes is at variance with classical theory where all cases should have the same standing as exemplars of the category.

Prototypes in Art

From the time of Weitz, philosophers of art have continued to struggle with the problem of defining art, especially as the category of what is admissible as art expands. Now it is quite common to include graphic communication, architecture, folk art, and the multiple forms of popular culture as well as many contemporary art forms such as installations. One can ask people to extend this list and most individuals can do this quite readily. Yet if we were to ask the same people to select from their list those forms they consider to be the most typical or most representative forms of art, they will very likely choose drawings, paintings, and sculpture rather than installations, political cartoons, or corporate logos.

Basic-Level Categories

Akin to prototype-based categories are what Roger Brown called "basic-level" categories (Brown, 1958, 1965, pp. 317–321). Like Rosch, he found that there are levels of membership within categories. To exemplify, when children learn about flowers as a category they may be involved in such actions as planting, picking, and smelling the blossoms. At the same time they learn that they are called flowers, mentally establishing them as a class of things. Later learning may add knowledge of more kinds of flowers, like roses, or the knowledge that flowering plants are members of a larger group called the plant kingdom. As a basic-level category, flowers occur in the midlevel of a larger system. The basic level is that which is learned first, and with increasing expertise, the category system extends outward to create subordinate and superordinate levels.

Subordinate and Superordinate Levels of Categorization

The basic-level categories that are learned first are attributed to physical bodily actions that are undertaken while the category is being established mentally (Lakoff, 1987, pp. 32–33; Lakoff & Johnson, 1999, p. 2). With additional learning, categories become more elaborate, thus forming a "superordinate level" made up of generic categories. Thus, the plant kingdom becomes an all-encompassing category that supersedes flowers. Categorization can also proceed downwards to form "subordinate" levels of categories, for example, the various varieties of roses. Categorization at the sub- and superlevels are less likely to be learned in conjunction with bodily actions, and for this reason these additional levels are what Brown called "achievements of the imagination." These imaginative extensions, though initially the result of bodily and perceptual experience are sense free (Lakoff, 1987, pp. 32–33).

When our thinking occurs at the basic level of categories, our mind frequently gives rise to mental images for them. This is because they were first learned through the perception of images or through actions of the body, like sitting in chairs, smelling flowers, or riding in cars. We can mentally visualize a flower or a car, but we cannot call up a mental image of the plant kingdom as a whole, or an image of a generalized vehicle distinct from any particular vehicle like a train or a bicycle. We can visualize other vehicles like trains, but no generic image comes to mind that represents the vehicular domain as a totality (Lakoff & Johnson, 1999, p. 27).

Art as a Basic-Level Category

Earlier I made the point that there is a kinship between basic-level categories and prototypes. Art as a concept also has many of the qualities of a basic–level category. Ask a child in the primary grades what art is and he or she will describe activities like drawing, painting, or clay modeling, that is, actions undertaken when the category is being established mentally. Later he or she will learn that the things he or she calls art stand within more encompassing categories such as the "fine arts" or "visual culture" that include folk art, graphic design, and the various aspects of the popular culture as well as traditional fine art. Should he or she major in art as a young professional, he or she will develop subordinate levels of the concept of art that might include such cultural practices as art criticism, or he or she might specialize in the study of Chinese Jade carving.[12]

The Cognitive Unconscious as a Conceptual System

Primary Metaphors

As we have seen, an imaginative element in cognition appeared in the elaboration of category systems described previously, and earlier, in the explanation of image schemata. In their later writing, Lakoff and Johnson deepen their characterization of metaphor by introducing the notion of levels into their discussion. They discuss "primary" metaphor using the analogy of atoms joining together to form the more complex structures of molecules, or in this case "complex" metaphors. Examples of primary metaphors include "KNOWING-IS-SEEING" as exemplified in expressions like "I see what you mean," or "PURPOSES-ARE-DESTINATIONS," where the expression "He'll ultimately be successful, but he is not there yet" serves as an illustration (Lakoff & Johnson, 1999, pp. 56–59). Primary metaphors are acquired automatically and unconsciously via the normal process of neural learning and we are generally unaware that we have them. They are part of the "cognitive unconscious" (pp. 11–12).

> We have a system of primary metaphors simply because we have the bodies and brains we have because we live in the world we live in, where intimacy does tend to correlate significantly with proximity, affection with warmth, and achieving purposes with reaching destinations. (Lakoff & Johnson, 1999, p. 59)

Complex Metaphors

Complex metaphors emerge from combinations of primary metaphors. The LOVE-IS-A-JOURNEY metaphor referred to earlier is an instance of a complex metaphor. Lakoff and Johnson also describe the complex metaphor they call "A-PURPOSEFUL-LIFE-IS-A-JOURNEY." Such a metaphor is comprised of the primary metaphors called PURPOSES-ARE-DESTINATIONS and ACTIONS-ARE-MOTIONS. This leads to a more complex mapping, where

A Purposeful Life Is A Journey.
A Person Living A Life Is A Traveler.
Life Goals Are Destinations.
A Life Plan Is An Itinerary.

---

[12]If my assertion is correct, the proposal to transform art into visual culture may be difficult to achieve since from a cognitive perspective, it exists as a concept at the superordinate level. If change is to take place in one's understanding of art as a form of visual culture it will need to address the understandings one has constructed at the basic level.

Unlike primary metaphors, complex metaphors are not directly grounded in bodily experiences. Rather, the grounding occurs within the primary metaphors that make up the complex metaphor. Thus, A-PURPOSEFUL-LIFE-IS-A-JOURNEY is grounded through its constituent primary metaphors, namely, PURPOSES-ARE-DESTINATIONS and ACTIONS-ARE-MOTIONS. Indeed, our most important abstract concepts such as life, love, and morality are conceptualized via multiple complex metaphors, and though they are abstract, they are not disembodied. In the examples cited, love and life are conceptualized metaphorically as journeys. However, they can be conceptualized in other ways as well. Using love as an illustration, Lakoff and Johnson point out that

> Love is conventionally conceptualized...in terms of...physical force, illness, magic, madness, union, closeness, nurturance, giving of oneself...and heat...Our most important abstract philosophical concepts, including time, causation, morality and the mind, are all conceptualized by multiple metaphors, sometimes as many as two dozen. (1999, p. 71)

In Marc Chagall's painting *The Birthday* (1915) one sees a couple literally swept off their feet by the feeling of love. Is love in this portrayal a physical force, or a kind of magic which permits suspension of the laws of nature? Is it a union of opposites? Because love is so central in human experience, it is bound to be conceptualized metaphorically in complex ways. Understanding the painting is a task of seeing how the various primary metaphors that seem to be involved here give rise to a meaning that is greater and more complex than that provided by such metaphors in isolation. "The cognitive reality is that our concepts have multiple metaphorical structurings" (p. 71). And these are meanings constructed by the imagination.

Implications

The work on cognition reviewed in these last sections described three arenas where imagination comes to light as an emergent phenomenon, where the abstract or sense-free aspects of thinking and understanding are accounted for as having their origins in bodily and perceptual imagery.

First, they appear in metaphoric projections from image schemata. Here we saw how schemata for *balance*, which are acquired through such physical actions as learning to walk, ultimately give rise to structures of imagination that can be applied in a number of abstract domains like mathematics, or to describe the system of checks and balances in the organization of government, or to the personality of individuals.

The second appeared in the elaboration of category systems, with the emergence of superordinate and subordinate hierarchies of concepts within categories. The creation of such cognitive extensions was also identified as an achievement of the imagination.

Third, we saw that undergirding conscious thought is a vast network of conceptual metaphors that enable us to make connections among the things of the world in our understanding. In their book *The Way We Think* (2002), Gilles Fauconnier and Mark Turner offer a similar characterization of the mind by their term "conceptual blending" to refer to the mental processes that bind together and integrate these elements into complex ideas. Like Lakoff and Johnson, they make a compelling argument for the role of imagination in our conceptual lives.

Implications for Education

Cognition is not purely literal. It has metaphorical and imaginative attributes as well. The subjects in the school curriculum utilize multiple forms of cognition including thinking as a propositional process and nonpropositional thinking involving images, metaphor, and imagination. Propositional thought is more likely to be evidenced in philosophy, physics, and mathematics than in the arts; whereas it is principally in the arts where one encounters the use of imagery, metaphor, and imagination. Yet conceptual metaphors do appear in the language of scientists, though they are likely to remain hidden as seen in the illustration that follows. Notice that in each of these statements, references to the physical attributes of buildings or processes of construction are mapped onto theories.

Is that the *foundation* for your theory?
You'll never *construct* a *strong* theory on those assumptions.
I haven't figured out what *form* our theory will take.
Here are some more facts to *shore up* your theory.
Evolutionary theory won't *stand* or *fall* on the *strength* of that argument.
So far we have only put together a *framework* of the theory.
He *buttressed* the theory with *solid* arguments. (Johnson, 1987, p. 104)

Each of these expressions is clear and unproblematic, underscoring the point that the THEORY-ARE-BUILDINGS metaphor is meaningful in the conventional communication forms of everyday life and within the scientific community. In fact, members of the scientific community would not likely recognize the metaphoric character of their speech. The discussion of Marc Chagall that follows demonstrates that metaphor plays quite a different role in the arts.

Chagall's Clocks

In several of Chagall's paintings done in the 1930s to 1940s, a recurrent image is the flying clock sometimes accompanied by images of other objects in flight. In one such work, *Time Is a River Without Banks* (1930–1939), the clock dominates the center of the composition, accompanied by a flying fish and a violin. In the lower right-hand corner one sees a pair of lovers. Another is entitled *Clock with Blue Wing* (1949). We know literally that clocks do not fly; nor do fish; nor do they have wings enabling them to do so. So a question for the viewer becomes, "What meaning do the flying clocks have in these works? Do these images refer to the folk metaphor that *time flies*? Does the pair of lovers have any special significance in a painting that seems to comment on the passage of time, perhaps the artist's remembered youth in Russia, or a former love affair. Is the clock emblematic of the beating of the human heart or the ticking away of life; or is it a reference to the heart as a symbol of love? Numerous critics also refer to Chagall's use of images of people in flight to represent the emotional ecstasy of the pair of lovers as referred to earlier in *The Birthday* (1915).

There is no way to be sure which of these interpretive conjectures is tenable. Each viewer will map the connections between things somewhat differently. Some will account for the flight of the clock using the primary metaphor TIME–IS–MOTION. Others might map time onto life with the ticking of the clock mapped onto the beating of the heart. For this reason, such works of art open what David Perkins calls a "reflective intelligence" (Perkins, 1994, p. 14). The clock has become an object for thought, for interpretation. The clock metaphor is active and can enliven the cognitive activity of the viewer; but the metaphor is complex, offering multiple meanings. It is active and enlivens cognitive activity. The point of these two illustrations is to show that metaphors are likely to work passively in scientific discussions, whereas in the arts they delve directly and deeply into what the work is about.

Toward a Theory of Imagination

Johnson suggested that "an adequate account of meaning and rationality (as well as that of understanding and communication) awaits a comprehensive theory of imagination. Such a theory would complement and influence our present theories of conceptualization, propositional content, and speech acts. In its broadest sense, it would provide a comprehensive account of structure in human experience and cognition (1987, p. 171). He then listed several features of what a cognitive account of imagination would entail, some of which are listed in the following sections.

Categorization

By categorization, he means not the classical view of categorization but a view that describes the way human beings actually "break up their experience into comprehensible kinds." Prototypical or basic-level categorization is preferred over one that seek sets of necessary and sufficient conditions. The power to elaborate and extend categories into superordinate and subordinate levels of classification is an achievement of the imagination (Johnson, 1987, p. 171).

Schemata

Johnson (1987) cites the need for a comprehensive theory of schemata, i.e., "general knowledge or event structures." We need to survey the basic kinds of schemata to see how they can be developed metaphorically, to investigate their complex interrelations, and to explore their connections with propositional structures" (p. 171).

Narrative Structure

When it comes to explaining how humans make sense of their world "there must be a central place for the notion of narrative unity. Not only are we born into complex and communal narratives, we also experience, understand, and order our lives as stories we are living out" (pp. 171–172).

Interpretations as Narratives

Although Johnson identifies the structure of narrative as one of the components in a comprehensive theory of imagination (1987, pp. 171–172), he does not elaborate how the capacity for narrative is related to other features of imagination such as metaphor. But narrative structure does share certain common features with metaphoric structure, in that they have a source point in human experience where they originate with some kind of problem or situation. Jerome Bruner uses the term "trouble" to identify the starting points in many narratives (Bruner, 1996). A typical narrative will open with a phrase like:

> "I was walking down the street, minding my own business when..." The action unfolds leading to a breach, a violation of legitimate expectancy. What follows is either a restitution of initial legitimacy or a revolutionary change of affairs with a new order of legitimacy. (Bruner, 1996, p. 94)

There is also a target point (some kind of resolution, outcome, or moral of the story); and finally there are pathways that map the intervening connections.

Narrative in Bruner's view is also a disciplined mode of thought for construing the present, past, and possible human conditions (Bruner, 1996, p. 100). Narratives do not provide explanations; rather, they lead to understanding, with understanding defined as "the outcome of organizing and contextualizing essentially contestable, incompletely verifiable propositions in a disciplined way (p. 90). The narrative mode of meaning-making tells us a story of what something is about. "Understanding, unlike explaining, is not preemptive. One way of construing the fall of Rome narratively does not rule out other interpretations." Some narratives about "'what happened'" are simply righter, not just because they are rooted in factuality, but because they are better contextualized, rhetorically more 'fair minded' and so on" (pp. 90–91).

Bruner also identified the broad implications of narrative in education, decrying the tendency in schooling to treat them as mere decoration rather than as a way, perhaps the best way, for individuals to construct meaning.

> It has been the convention of most schools to treat the arts of narrative—song, drama, fiction, theatre, whatever—as more "decoration" than necessity, something with which to grace leisure ... Despite that, we frame the accounts of our cultural origins and our most cherished beliefs in story form ... Our immediate experience, what happened yesterday or the day before, is framed in the same storied way. Even more striking , we represent our lives (to ourselves as well as to others) in the form of narrative. (p. 40)

> The importance of narrative for the cohesion of culture is as great very likely, as it is in structuring an individual life. . . . "trouble narratives" appear again in mythic literature and contemporary novels, better contained in that form than in reasoned and logically coherent propositions. It seems evident, then, that skill in narrative construction and narrative understanding is crucial to constructing our lives and a "place" for ourselves in the possible world we will encounter. (p. 40)

Relevance to Art Education

For most people the term *imagination* "connotes artistic creativity, fantasy, scientific discovery, invention and novelty"—having little or no correspondence to the everyday world of occurrences. Such beliefs are holdovers from 19th-century romanticism. Lakoff and Johnson were intent to explain how catgeorization, image schemata, metaphor, and narrative, as components of the imaginative in cognition, operate across the whole gamut of human cognition and thus are not limited to the arts.

But because they so thoroughly implicate imagination as the quintessential component of higher forms of cognition including abstract reason, it has unmistakable implications for the arts as well, as places where metaphoric leaps of imagination are prized for their power and aesthetic excellence. Moreover, it is in the arts, where the structures of imagination should become the principle object of study. Typically this happens when one creates works of art, yet imagination also comes into play in the interpretation of works of art. Deepening the wellspring of the imagination and the role it can play in the creation of personal meaning and in the transmission of culture becomes the point and purpose for having the arts in education.

Making a place for the arts means giving oneself over to neither the ornamental fringes of knowledge nor to the abandonment of the hard facts of reality. Indeed, quite the reverse is true. For example, before a metaphor can become active in the learner's mind—*as a metaphor!*—he or she must understand the underlying reality or context where the metaphorical nature of the image or expression is active.

Let me emphasize this point once more—that the arts are places where the constructions of the imagination can and should become the principle object of study, where it is necessary to understand that the visual image or verbal expression are not literal facts but embodiments of meanings to be taken in some other light. It is *only in the arts where the imagination is encountered and explored in full consciousness—where it becomes the object of inquiry.*

Having learners understand the imaginative as ornamental devices like metaphor, used mainly by artists and poets, is of secondary importance. I lean more toward activities where the learner comes to an understanding of the world referred to in works of art, and the role that the artist's imagination plays in constructing that world and giving it meaning. Moreover, an art education that fails to recognize the metaphoric character of meanings in the arts is without serious educational purpose.

Implications for General Education

Cognition entails more than meaning situated in propositional forms; it takes nonpropositional forms as well. Yet schooling for most students occurs within a curriculum where knowledge is experienced as a series of isolated, random facts. This compartmentalized curriculum reflects a long tradition in Western philosophy, which in large part is the consequence of a divided mind. On one side is cognition proper, the province of reason, conceptualization, logic, and formal propositional discourse. On the other hand is the bodily, perceptual, material, emotional, and imaginative side of our nature.

> The most significant consequence of this split is that all meaning, logical connection, conceptualization and reasoning are aligned with the mental or rational dimension, while perception, imagination and feeling are aligned with the bodily dimension. As a result both non-propositional and figuratively elaborated structures of experience are regarded as having no place in meaning and the drawing of rational inferences. (Johnson, 1987, p. xxv)

These polarities have reified themselves into structures of consciousness. If thinking is cognitive, then its contrary (feeling) is noncognitive. If cognition involves the use of verbal and mathematical symbols to construct rational or formal propositions, then perceptual imagery is taken to be nonpropositional and hence noncognitive. This tendency has relegated half of mental life to the lesser realm of affect.

Moreover, this structure of belief has become the structure of the curriculum. The sciences were placed in the cognitive domain, whereas the arts were dispatched to the domain of feelings and emotions. To be sure, the arts were highly praised as sources of wonderment, amusement, delight, embellishment, or beautification (icing on the cake); but rarely were they taken to be active sources of insight, knowledge, or understanding. Education should have as its ultimate purpose the maximization of the cognitive potential of individuals, and this includes the use of the imagination—in all subjects to be sure but certainly in the arts.

The arts are educationally important when they equip individuals with the relevant tools to interpret their lifeworlds. The tools or cognitive strategies that are entailed in this learning process include imagination as a schematizing function and its extensions by metaphoric projection. Metaphor, in particular, constructs linkages that enable us to understand and structure one domain of knowledge in terms of the knowledge in a different domain; thus, it establishes connections among seemingly unrelated things. The subjects that give play to these aspects of cognition should lie at the core of the curriculum where they can become bases for understanding.

We may have multiple forms of cognizing (propositional vs. nonpropositional), but in my view these do not stand in opposition to each other. Rather, both emerge from the same common source, the basic level of experience originating in bodily and perceptual encounters with the environment including culture. The reason why the hunches of the scientist or the imagination of the artist can be intuitive is that their foundation is built on an undivided world, the world that the physicist David Bohm calls "the implicate order," a world beyond dualisms that divide the body from the mind, thinking from feeling, or individuals from their social world. The building of lifeworlds requires access to such sources as represented and extended symbolically in thinking, feeling, and willed action. Such building is, in the final analysis, an "achievement of the imagination."

Teaching Art as Imaginative Cognition

Imagination is the act or power of forming mental images of what is not actually present to the senses, or what has not actually been experienced. It is also the power of creating new ideas or images through the combination and reorganization of images from previous experiences. Creative imagination through arbitrary combinations of images can be found in the notebooks of Leonardo DaVinci, who described his procedure for inventing fantastic creatures by combining the head of an animal such as a lion with the body of another, adding perhaps the wings of a bird. He also describes an exercise where he looks at cracks in the plaster of a wall, allowing the lines to suggest the shape of mountains and other details of landscapes. In both instances, Leonardo drew on imagery stored in memory. Fantastic animals can form the basis of an activity where students combine animal images cut from old magazines and newspapers to invent a new animal never seen before. To many experienced art teachers, such a lesson on fantastic animals is hardly a new idea. Other ideas invite the learner to suspend the everyday expectations that have become customary in our lives by asking "What if" types of questions. What if the sun will not rise tomorrow? What if there were time travel or teleportation?

Previously the point was made that imagination also consists of cognitive strategies that establish links among things enabling one's understanding to move from the known to the unknown. I referred to Lakoff and Johnson's term "cross–domain mapping" to characterize this process. The known is found in the learner's source domains, the sensory knowledge obtained early in life that is in one's cognitive unconscious. Teaching involves the kind of instructional prompts that bring the relevant schemata to consciousness because they are likely to be inert, or in a state of dormancy. The teacher must create the situation where such knowledge is called upon.

I will offer two examples: In the first, the teacher introduces the principle of balance as encountered in the teaching of design. It is common for teachers to refer to a composition as having symmetrical or asymmetrical balance or sometimes to the lack of balance in particular artworks. In pure design, with no reference to any particular expressive content, an activity might involve exercises where students manipulate compositional elements with differing visual weights. Two darkly colored rectangles on one side of a composition might offset a larger single rectangle, and so on. It is unlikely that such activities would activate balance as a source domain. Lessons in the abstract in all probability will not fully engage the learner.

In a second lesson, balance is used to characterize the moral attributes of different personalities. The expressive task is more complex because schemata learned many years earlier now have to be mapped onto the character of a given personality. The teacher might introduce a lesson with a discussion of different personalities, perhaps fictional characters like Batman and the Jester as prototypes of good and evil. Batman is portrayed as a morally *upright* hero with the *backbone* to *stand up* to evil. References to his moral stature are reinforced by his balanced, erect posture, not to mention his good looks. On the other hand, there is something sinister about his rival, the Jester, whose villainy demonstrates the opposing attributes. He is an *unbalanced, underhanded* character who has *fallen* from grace and who is disfigured.[13]

Think of how many times the references to posture and balance are brought into this discussion to characterize the differing identities of the hero and the villain? It is through such conversation that the teacher builds the scaffolding needed to help the student become conscious of the conceptual metaphors at work just below the threshold of consciousness. Once such connections are established, a vast bank of images is brought within reach that can be used to motivate studio activities or to open a critical conversation about a given portrait. Knowing that our concepts for moral goodness are physically correlated with upright posture may help

---

[13]It also occurs to me that in this example both the hero and the villain are disguised.

us understand how advertisers present political candidates either positively or negatively in television commercials.

Balance might extend to color as when we talk of a person being *green* with envy, *red* with anger, a cowardly *yellow*, or feeling *blue*. Also such formal qualities of line have their origins in bodily experiences like the physiognomy of smiles and frowns. Straight, clean–cut features are for heroes, whereas crooked snearing features personify dishonesty and evil. Some of these associations are the result of cultural conditioning such as the pairing of green with envy or yellow with cowardice. This is knowledge very likely embedded in the cognitive unconscious.

When I offered some of these ideas to a graduate class of art teachers, mainly at the elementary and middle school levels, I learned that many had taught lessons on self–portraits or heroes and that what I was suggesting as lessons with an imaginative twist actually seemed quite familiar. This leads to the question asked at the outset; namely, "what can current conceptions of cognition offer art educators as a basis for reshaping itself into a domain hospitable to the cultivation of imagination?

To quite an extent, the new understanding of what cognition entails lends credence to much that art teachers presently offer. The change that is required must be at the level of purpose, where the constructions of the imagination become principle objects of study. This kind of exploration must be done consciously and can begin with conversations in the language and imagery of the lifeworld, and that undergo discussion in daily speech.

It is also important to recognize that awakening the imaginative aspect of cognition does not happen in a vacuum but must be actively cultivated. Freeing the child from the rigid structures of traditional subjects was thought to be sufficient generations earlier. It now appears that it also involves the intentional preparation of curriculum plans and resources. The content of the curriculum becomes the strategies one uses to cultivate the imaginative. One sees it in the superodinate levels of categorization, in the mapping of one domain on another as in metaphor, and finally in the ability to engage in the complex networks of meaning we call our world.

REFERENCES

Brown, R. (1958). How shall a thing be called? *Psychological Review, 65,* 14–21.

Brown, R. (1965). *Social Psychology.* New York: Free Press.

Bruner, J. (1996). *The culture of education.* Cambridge MA: Harvard University Press.

Carroll N. (2001). *Beyond aesthetics: Philosophical essays.* New York: Cambridge University Press.

Efland, A. (1990). *A history of art education: Intellectual and social currents in teaching the visual arts.* New York: Teachers College Press.

Efland, A. (2002). *Art and cognition: Integrating the visual arts in the curriculum.* New York: Teachers College Press.

Fauconnier, G., & Turner, M. (2002). *The way we think: Conceptual blending and the mind's hidden complexities.* New York: Basic Books.

Flavell, J. H. (1963). *The developmental psychology of Jean Piaget.* Princeton NJ: Van Nostrand.

Gardner, H. (1987). *The mind's new science: A history of the cognitive revolution.* New York: Basic Books. (originally published in 1984)

Gruber, H. E., & Voneche, J. J. (1981). *The essential Piaget.* London: Routledge & Kegan Paul.

Johnson, M. (1987). *The body in the mind: The bodily basis of meaning, imagination and reason.* Chicago: University of Chicago Press.

Kant, I. (1997). *Critique of pure reason.* P. Guyer and A. Wood (Eds. & Trans.). New York: Cambridge University Press.

Kosslyn, S. (1980). *Image and mind.* Cambridge, MA: Harvard University Press.

Kosslyn, S. (1983). *Ghosts in the mind's machine: Creating and using images in the brain.* New York: Norton.

Lakoff, G. (1993). The contemporary theory of metaphor. In A. Ortony (Ed.). *Metaphor and thought (2nd ed.),* Cambridge, UK: Cambridge University Press.

Lakoff, G., & Johnson, M. (1980). *Metaphors we live by.* Chicago: University of Chicago Press.

Lakoff, G. (1987). *Women, fire and dangerous things: What categories reveal about the mind.* Chicago: University of Chicago Press.

Lakoff, G., & Johnson, M. (1999). *Philosophy in the flesh: The embodied mind and its challenge to Western thought.* New York: Basic Books.

Ortony, A. (1993). Metaphor, language and thought. In A. Ortony (Ed.), *Metaphor and thought (2nd ed.).* Cambridge, UK: Cambridge University Press.

Rugg, H., & Shumaker, A. (1928). *The child–centered school.* New York: World Book Co.

Shephard, R. N. (1978a). The mental image. *American Psychologist,* February, 125–137.

Shephard, R. N. (1978b). Externalization of mental images and the act of creation. In B. S. Randhawa & W. E. Coffman (Eds.), *Visual learning, thinking and communication.* New York: Academic Press.

Shephard, R. N., & Metzler, J. (1971). Mental rotation of three dimensional objects. *Science, 171,* 701–703.

Spiro, R. J., Vispoel, W. P., Schmitz, J. G., Samarpungavan, A., & Boerger, A. E. (1987). *Knowledge acquisition and application: Cognitive flexibility and transfer in complex content domains* (Tech. Rep. No. 409). University of Illinois at Urbana–Champaign. Center for the Study of Reading.

Waldrop, M. (1992). *Complexity: The emerging science at the edge of order and chaos.* New York: Simon & Schuster.

Wolff, J. (1995). Against sociological imperialism: The limits of sociology in the aesthetic sphere. In R. W. Neperud (Ed.), *Context, content, and community in art education.* New York: Teachers College Press.

Weitz, M. (1956). The role of theory in aesthetics. *Journal of Aesthetics and Art Criticism, 15,* 27–35.

34

Art and Integrated Curriculum

Michael Parsons
The Ohio State University

A RENEWED INTEREST IN INTEGRATED CURRICULUM

We are currently witnessing a renewed interest in integrated curriculum in both art education and in education in general. Integrated curriculum, not always with that name, has been a recurrent interest in American education since the late 19th century, though the circumstances in which it arises are each time different (Kliebard, 1995). One thread in what follows is that society has changed in such a way as to make integrated curriculum again a concern today. Simultaneously, I believe that the artworld and our general modes of communication have also changed in such a way as to make art potentially more central to the curriculum. In this chapter, I will review the literature on integrated curriculum in art education, seeking to articulate the vision that lies behind it. I hope the review suggests two things: for art educators, that an integrated approach might enhance the teaching of art; and for educators, in general, that art has a significant role to play in integrated curricula.

The reasons for the revival of interest are several. Most important may be the sense that our society and the kinds of problems we face are changing rapidly. Our problems are becoming more complex, have a faster turnover rate, and require more information from more different sources. This is true at work, at home, and in our social and political life. A socially relevant education would prepare students by focusing the curriculum on such problems. In addition, students need a more integrated personality, greater awareness of self, and more understanding and tolerance of others, goals with which our present system does poorly. For art educators, there is a third kind of reason, having to do with changes in the contemporary artworld and concern over the enormous growth of visual communications in our society.

The current interest has not yet produced a consensus on the theory or practice of integrated curriculum, much less an articulated and organized movement (Ulbricht, 1998). The literature in art education is scattered and the practices are undertheorized.[1] The result is that many different practices go by the name of integrated curriculum and there are many names for similar practices (The Consortium of National Arts Education Associations, 2002). There is considerable variation in the scope of intentions involved. At its least ambitious, the interest is in connecting together the various school subjects to make them more meaningful to students. At its most ambitious, the interest is in the promotion of democratic schooling, via student choice, self-reflection, and active inquiry; and of democratic society, via the investigation of social problems and their solutions. Alternative names include interdisciplinary, multidisciplinary or cross-disciplinary curriculum, the experience curriculum, activity-centered curriculum, and project method.

In the introduction to his recent book, one of the rare sustained current attempts to deal with curriculum integration in a theoretical way, James Beane complains that the conservativism of our times has reduced discussions of integrated curriculum to questions about how to connect the content of the different school subjects (Beane, 1997). He says:

> It is possible that someone might come to this book expecting to learn about the overlaps or connections among school subjects and how to create thematic units out of them. This would not be surprising, since the term *integrated curriculum* has too often been used to describe arrangements that amount to little more than rearranging existing lesson plans. (Beane, 1997, p. x)

Beane urges the importance of the connections with democratic schooling, the whole child, social problem solving, and learning through inquiry that were so prominent in the progressive era. Discussions of integrated curriculum, he complains, have tended to lose connection with these bigger issues and to become discussions of efficient curriculum structure. I do not believe this charge is always true of the literature in art education. Although this literature is not voluminous, the more interesting parts often connect curriculum with bigger issues. I hope this review will suggest that art educators who adopt an integrated approach are both responding to contemporary changes and also making connection with traditional concerns of the field from times prior to the current disciplinary movement.

It is necessary at the outset to make it clear that integrated curriculum is not primarily an issue of how to schedule the school day, not primarily about "the egg-box curriculum." It is about meaning and understanding. Integration occurs when students make sense for themselves of their varied learning and experiences, when they pull these together to make one view of their world and of their place in it. It takes place in their minds or not at all. Advocates of integrated curriculum are fundamentally concerned to make learning meaningful to students. They stress the importance of understanding as the primary goal of education and often contrast it with "lower level" goals such as learning facts and routine skills. This contrast is traditional in educational discussions, of course, and many educators who support the traditional curriculum also emphasize understanding. The difference is that a good traditional curriculum aims at an understanding of disciplines, whereas a good integrated curriculum aims at an understanding of the lifeworld (Habermas, 1981). Does the school curriculum help students connect academic learning with their personal experience? Does it deal with their real-life issues, that is, with issues that they are already aware of as important in their life? Are their emotions, attitudes, and values related to what they learn in school? Does their learning enable them to make sense

---

[1] I mean by this that there are more attempts by art teachers to integrate their curriculum in practice than there is public discussion of underlying goals and principles. This may be a hopeful situation, because it suggests that many teachers are seeking change in their practice. Of the books and articles that have been published, there are many more descriptive accounts than there are reflective ones. It is impossible to mention all of the descriptive material in this chapter, and I shall not try to do so.

of their place in the world? Are they helped to understand social problems and to be better citizens of our complex, diverse democracy? These are the kind of questions we should ask of an integrated curriculum.

It is worth emphasizing that an integrated curriculum is inherently concerned with ideas. It is necessarily a curriculum that encourages students to think about important ideas, to interpret them and relate them to themselves, their own time and context. It is above all a thoughtful curriculum, full of ideas rather than of activities (Burnaford, Aprill, & Weiss, 2001). This is because only with ideas can students integrate their world, combine its various aspects in one stable understanding. And the key claim is that the kinds of ideas that enable them to do this usually transcend the disciplines. They are more general and multifaceted than the ideas central to academic disciplines and, not coincidentally, they are the kinds of ideas often dealt with in art. On the other hand, they can be looked at from the perspective of several individual disciplines, and an integrated curriculum does not reject disciplinary perspectives. Rather it uses them when they are helpful and helps students to integrate them into a larger picture.

There is massive resistance, of course. Most efforts at school improvement tend to favor further emphasis on school subjects, especially on reading, writing, science, mathematics, and technology. They often stress teacher expertise in the disciplines and call for more rigor in their teaching. Some authors favor teaching for understanding within disciplines; others emphasize basic skills and the ubiquitous standardized achievement tests. In art education, there is a continuing tradition that promotes the autonomy and independence of art as a discipline or set of disciplines. In short, many educators want more, not less, emphasis on teaching separate school subjects.

ATTITUDES TOWARD DISCIPLINES

I have so far spoken of both "school subjects" and "academic disciplines." It is important to see that the relationship between the two is not a simple one. One might say that a "school subject" is an adaptation of an academic discipline in light of educational considerations, primarily students' learning abilities and social needs. This was Bruner's notion, for example, and it was much discussed by the progressives before him (Bruner, 1960; Dewey, 1990). But the desirable scope and character of this adaptation are complex questions and they lie at the heart of all curriculum issues, including the calls for an integrated curriculum. In spite of this, some of the current literature for and against integrated curriculum tends to speak of academic disciplines and school subjects as if they were identical.

The organization of the curriculum into school subjects has characterized American public schooling since it began. But as long ago as 1918 it was officially agreed that the disciplines are to be regarded as tools to be used for an understanding of life and the solution of life's problems (U.S. Bureau of Education, 1918). In other words, they are not to be taught primarily as ends in themselves, and the traditional organization is not self-justifying. Yet there is little agreement on what this means in practice. One disagreement is about sequence. Should knowledge of disciplinary content be considered prerequisite for problem solving or an outcome of it? Do students need to learn the tools first, before being able to use them, or should they address problems first and learn to use the tools as they need them?

The most common answer is that disciplines are very complex and difficult to master, and they require separate study before they can be used (e.g., Broudy, Smith, & Burnett, 1964). This follows a long-standing tendency among educators to break learning down into its constituent parts and to teach the simpler elements before the complex wholes. In this case, the disciplines are simpler and are to be taught before the problems. The notion is that this sequence of simple to complex, part to whole, is required by logic, and it is usually associated with claims of efficiency. It underlies traditional practice, except that too often the problems are not addressed at all.

The contrary view comes from the greater concern for meaning. Meaning lies in the whole, it is argued, and the parts should be learned after their place in the whole is grasped. Tools have meaning only when their usefulness is understood; indeed their meaning lies in what they can be used to do. This means that students should grapple with the problems first and learn to use the tools as they find them helpful. Dewey notably championed this view (Dewey, 1990). However, he regarded an understanding of the disciplinary character of knowledge as *one* of the desirable goals of education. This is in line with his general view that an important mechanism of learning is the transformation of means into ends. The disciplines represent, he said, "the possibilities of development inherent in the child's immediate crude experience" (Dewey, 1990, p. 190). This means that students should eventually come to understand the different kinds of knowledge, and their value, as a consequence of a long period of using them to solve problems that they care about. Disciplines, on this view, serve teachers as guides to clarify the direction that student learning should take. In other words, disciplines retain a significant educational role in an integrated curriculum, even though they do not constitute the primary educational goals. They are tools for problem solving and guides for teachers.

As I have already argued, the scheduling of school subjects in the school day is a relatively minor question and does not lie at the heart of issues about integrated curriculum. In actual practice, there are many ways to schedule the school day in an integrated curriculum. One can maintain the traditional pattern of school subjects with specialist teachers for the whole day or for part of the day, or one can abandon it. The key questions are the content and manner of the students' learning.

ART, CONTEMPORARY SOCIETY, AND INTEGRATED CURRICULUM

It is common to analyze curriculum discussions in terms of three kinds of issues (Kliebard, 1995). One is social, having to do with the needs and character of contemporary society, to which education must in some way respond. Another is psychological, having to do with the way students learn and organize their knowledge, their abilities, and their interests. And the third is epistemological, having to do with the nature of knowledge. This includes issues about disciplines, their nature, origins, functions, and so on. These categories are admittedly very general, but I will use them in my discussion.

I begin with a review of the arguments having to do with the character of society. The basic argument here is simple. Our society has become increasingly complex and is in constant change, and students should study these changes, and their attendant problems, to prepare them to participate well in society. A socially relevant democratic education, it is argued, must engage students in this way. This requires integrated studies, because the issues involved transcend disciplinary boundaries.

Versions of this argument appear in discussions of both work and public life. The discussion of work is not much found in the art education literature today (an exception is Boston, 1996) but I think it is influential with many teachers. It says that workers today will likely encounter complexities on the job, have to deal with ambiguity and change, evaluate their own performance, and in general solve problems that go beyond individual disciplines. They will also need to be able to work well with others, take multiple points of view, and be tolerant of diversity of all kinds. In art education the same points are more often made about social problems. Most of our social problems exceed the limits of single disciplines and require a matching range of capacities of citizens. Problems that are often cited include poverty, violence, environmental deterioration, the development of technology, gender differences. For example, the new national curriculum in Taiwan requires 20% of school time to be spent on integrated curriculum and specifies six topics for study: the environment, the community, identity, gender, human values, and home economics (Huang, 1999). In the art education literature, there is often a social reconstructionist tone that says that students should go beyond the study of social problems and do something that promotes their solution (Freedman & Stuhr, 2001). This educational activism is mirrored by the rise of social activism in the artworld. A number of contemporary artists intend their art not only to raise awareness of social problems but also to make the world better by modeling solutions (Gablik, 1991; Spaid, 2002).

A topic[2] commonly suggested for integrated study is the local community. Many school reformers favor this because it can bring school and community closer together. For instance, it encourages local people to come into the school and students to go out into the community. There are many ways one can study the community. Depending on teacher and student interests, one could study, for example, its garbage, ethnic diversity (Stuhr, 1994), food, government, entertainments, architecture, monuments. In one case, some teachers in a Cleveland elementary school chose to study local bridges (Wiseman, 1999). The children talked with a local engineer about the different structures and designs of bridges. They went to study particular bridges in the neighborhood. Because there are many bridges in Cleveland, the topic led to a study of traffic patterns, the history of transport and industry in Cleveland, and inquiry about the history of specific bridges. The students took photographs, made drawings, created model bridges, looked at paintings of bridges, and wrote essays and letters about bridges. Local history and the local built environment are in general rich topics for cultural, historical, social, and architectural inquiry in an integrated curriculum (Burnaford, Aprill, & Weiss, 2001; Guilfoil, 2000; Marche, 1998; Thurber, 1997).

Such topics have a long history in American education (Cremin, 1961). What is new today, because of changes in the contemporary artworld, is a greater possibility of making art central to their study. Contemporary art is frequently about the sort of topics just mentioned, including at least the first five of the six topics in the new Taiwanese curriculum. It is particularly easy to find artworks in and about local communities. There have always been murals, statues, and monuments; and since the creation of the National Endowment for the Arts, there has been an important expansion and development of public art (Lacy, 1995; Raven, 1993). The commissioning of artworks by communities has become a regular feature of the artworld. An artist commissioned to make a public work today is usually expected to research the local history, character, people, occupations, architecture, and to make a work that is about some aspect of the community that commissioned it. This happens at many levels. Prominent examples at the national level might be the Vietnam Wall and the current discussions of what is to be built on Ground Zero in New York City. These both offer opportunities for the study in school of significant historical events and national attitudes. There are many examples at the level of the local community, especially because today artworks are often required in new public buildings and renovations. An interesting case is the program of public art in the village of Dublin, Ohio, which for 12 years has biennially commissioned a public work to celebrate the identity of the village (Dublin Arts Council, 2002). The program has been very successful and has become a kind of model for other communities. In short, both the making and the study of public art in a community are also necessarily the study of aspects of the community.

This process of commission, research, and making can also be adapted in schools. Students can be "commissioned" to design artworks for a particular space and asked to think about some aspect of their community and to submit designs to a committee composed of either

---

[2]The use of the term *topic* is questioned by some authors. They may prefer *issues, themes, problems,* or *ideas.* I see little value in arguing such distinctions and hope to convey my meanings sufficiently through the use of examples.

local people or other students. This would require study both of the local community and of other public artworks. A further step would be actually to make and install the work.

There is often an activist aspect to this topic. Public art is often intended somehow to affect the community by drawing attention to some aspect of it. Increasingly it is used in efforts to improve deteriorating neighborhoods. The idea is to make artworks that celebrate or improve local features, histories, facilities, often in conjunction with other efforts at renovation. An example is the 8-year-old "Art in the Market" program to restore the old Findlay market in Cincinnati. This old, still substantial marketplace is in an impoverished neighborhood called *Over-the-Rhine*. The program seeks to help the neighborhood recognize and use its own resources. Teenagers from the area are encouraged in a school program to create artworks around the marketplace in response to their study of the market and the people using it (Russell & Russell, 2001). Another example is the creation of a playground for children in an inner-city neighborhood. In this case, local parents came together to renovate a small delapidated park for the safe use of their children and to enhance community identity. With the help of a small grant, they engaged local artists to create artworks in the park that the children can play with, each with an African American theme. For example, one is a steel sculpture of a baobob tree that the children can climb on or gather round. Another is an African story board that encourages children to tell stories about selected visual prompts. The Kwanzaa Playground in Columbus has been a great success (Chanda & Daniel, 2000; Daniel, 2001). Cases like this may seem ambitious for an individual school, but there are many smaller opportunities. There are always local histories, buildings, events, people to inquire into; and walls, vacant spaces, and walkways that could support an artwork. The educational opportunities in the study of communities are many.

Another well-developed topic that calls for art in an integrated curriculum is the natural environment. Again, there is plenty of precedent in the contemporary artworld. Many artists have taken the natural environment as their theme, including increasingly artists who attempt to improve the environment through their work (Spaid, 2002). Students can approach the natural environment through studies of particular aspects of it, such as a stream, the needs of local wildlife, the quality of the air, making a garden. In one well-documented case, elementary school students studied a local wetlands park, together with a visiting environmentalist and children's author. They examined the plants and animals, wrote and drew about them, followed the seasons, and created a large ceramic mural installed in the park. The next year, influenced by the artwork of Lynne Hull, they created their own wetlands on the school grounds, made habitats for particular species of wildlife, and studied the gradual development of the wetlands (Birt, Krug, & Sheridan, 1997). In another example, Taylor used the model of Mazeud's well-known river-cleaning work in service-learning activities in a teacher education program (Gablik, 1991; Taylor, 2002, pp. 119–122). The work of Don Krug provides many more illustrations of these possibilities (Krug, 1997). These examples all involve ideas from biology, chemistry, economics, history, math, and literature, and they use art as a central activity that enables students to make sense of them.

I have mentioned some developments in the contemporary artworld that lie behind these examples and enable art to be central to the integrated curriculum. But perhaps the most fundamental change in this respect is the huge increase in our use of visual images for communication of all kinds—in advertising, magazines, on the Internet, through videos, and so on. This is a very large change in our society, and it has been much commented on. Mitchell, for example, speaks of our time as having taken a "visual turn" that has profoundly changed its character (Mitchell, 1994). The development of visual communication has blurred the distinction between fine art and popular culture so far that it is often not clear which parts of it should be considered part of the contemporary artworld. Are advertisements art, for example? Perhaps only some of them? Are videos, comic strips, fashion designs art? There is no definitive answer, of course, and it is often proposed that therefore aspects of visual communication should be studied in art education (Duncum, 2001; Freedman, 2000). There are endless possibilities here. How is war portrayed, for example, on TV, in the movies, in the newspapers, in videogames? We know that the *image* of war is important psychologically, politically, perhaps even militarily. How are other cultures, or racial or national differences, represented? What are the popular images of children, teenagers, schooling? What kinds of people become celebrities on television? What kinds of images are presented of film stars, sports players, politicians, businessmen? How are cigarettes and alcohol advertised? There is an endless series of questions that would require a study of both visual images and of the realities that lie behind the images. Taylor, for example, gives an example where high school students studied a video of Madonna's and made conceptual webs of the many connections they saw between its details and their own lifeworld (Taylor, 2000). One advantage of such approaches is that they present art as part of students' life, something not to be found only in museums and galleries.

More radically, it is sometimes suggested that the whole of art education should become the study of visual culture. A separate chapter of this volume is devoted to this movement, so I will not dwell on it here, nor detail its bibliography. But clearly the study of visual culture, as a part or the whole of art education, is a natural ally of integrated curriculum. One can advocate an integrated curriculum without also advocating the study of visual culture, but the reverse is implausible. One cannot seriously study visual communications without also thinking about their content and function, about the representations made in them, and about the corresponding realities in one's own experience, without, in short, an integrated approach to the curriculum.

A topic often associated with the study of visual communications is gender. Many contemporary artists have made art about gender; Cindy Sherman and Barbara Kruger are well-known examples. But the images that most influence young people come from the popular media, especially commercial advertising and entertainment. Many people feel that this influence is unhealthy, especially for girls and young women, and that a number of personal and social problems flow from it (Shandler, 1999). Consequently, it is often suggested that we should study in art education the way girls and boys and men and women are represented in popular images, especially in advertising and movies (Freedman, 1994).

There is some negative reaction to these proposals on the grounds that art education might disappear. To discuss, for example, popular visual representations of gender would probably also require discussing the nature of advertising and fashion and perhaps that of our commercial and entertainment systems as a whole. The discussion could easily move to the power relations obtaining in those systems and the many connections with other aspects of social structure, such as poverty and inequality. At this point, one begins to hear objections that the art has been lost from art education; that art education has become something else. Art, it is said, first becomes visual imagery in general, and then visual imagery becomes politics. These objections will no doubt be discussed in the chapter on visual culture. My reason for mentioning them here is that the fear of losing what is important about art haunts all discussions of integrated curriculum. It arises particularly in connection with issues of visual culture, but it is more general than that. If we integrate the study of art with other subject matters, will we lose our focus on the nature of the images themselves? Will art become only the "handmaiden" of other concerns? I will return to this fear in a later section.

Many other topics deriving from the character of our society could be mentioned in this section. They conform with what was suggested earlier: They target important social problems; they are complex and transcend the limits of individual disciplines; they are ambiguous and need to be understood from several points of view. The connection of integrated curriculum with such topics is very strong in the art education literature, and it suggests that, although at the level of practice the field may be more conservative, Beane's charge of conservatism does not easily apply to the literature in our field.

Art, the Student, and the Integrated Curriculum

In general, art educators interested in integrated curriculum have done much less with psychological issues of learning than they have with the social ones just reviewed. This is perhaps surprising, because the integration of the whole child was a major theme of the expressive movement of earlier decades. Viktor Lowenfeld, emblematic of that movement, wrote memorably about the importance of "self-identification" in the early pages of *Creative and Mental Growth* (Lowenfeld & Brittain, 1982). He spoke of the need for children to be able to express their ideas and feelings, to learn through their bodily senses, and to relate what they learn in school with their own experience. The major goal of the movement Lowenfeld represented was the psychological integration of the child in lived context through the expression and interconnection of mental contents. After the "cognitive revolution" (Davis & Gardner, 1992), Lowenfeld's reputation suffered because he did not speak in cognitive terms, nor talk much about self-awareness, nor at all about the social construction of the mind. But his theme—the personal integration of students' thoughts, feelings, attitudes—remains fundamentally important. To see this, one has only to think of the many current school problems with drugs and alcohol, ethnic intolerance, obesity, depression, bulimia, and violence. Schooling today is stressful for many students and sometimes disorienting, moreso perhaps than it was in Lowenfeld's time. Personal wholeness has long been linked with art education (Burton, 2002) and is the fundamental goal of curriculum integration. It can be achieved only by students relating together their thoughts, feelings, and attitudes in a more comprehensive understanding. The goal is for students through their learning to construct a consistent picture of their world and their place in it, especially by making sense of their own experience and life-world. The reason for the study of social problems, reviewed earlier, can not be really (in my judgment) to solve the problems but to provide a meaningful context for this integrated understanding.

Integrated curriculum is usually associated with a constructivist psychology. The student is thought of as actively constructing the meanings of what is learned, inquiring into topics of interest, relating what is learned with what is already known. This view of the learner as an active meaning-maker is virtually required, because it is the students, not the teacher, who integrate what is learned in their own understanding. Constructivist views are frequently referenced in the art education literature, especially the visual culture literature. A related issue, often mentioned, is the relation of teachers and students (The Ohio State University TETAC Mentors, 2002). Constructivist psychology suggests that teachers and students become more like research collaborators than is usual, with the students helping to determine topics, research activities, constructive projects, and criteria for assessment.

The relative lack of attention in art education to the psychological aspects of integrated curriculum does not occur in education at large. Much of the general literature on integrated curriculum is concerned with student learning and personality. Clincy, for example, says:

> ... the world of the 21st century (calls) for a profoundly different, deeply democratic system of public schooling based on constant attention to the lives of individual children and to the familial and community worlds from which those children come. It is a system of schooling whose most important aim is the creation of decent, compassionate, human individuals who are, in Anita Teeter's words, "caring adults, builders of communities, sharers of learning, lovers of the printed word, citizens of the world, nurturers of nature." (Clincy, 1997, pp. 8–9)

There is also an important concern in education for developmentally appropriate practices, matching curriculum demands with the abilities and needs of students (Bredekamp & Copple, 1997; Charbonneau & Reider, 1995; Hart, Burts, & Charlesworth, 1997). This concern, too, is found much less often in the art education literature. Charlesworth, speaking of early childhood, makes clear the connection of developmentally appropriate practice with integrated curriculum. She says:

> The primary criteria of developmental appropriateness are age appropriateness, individual appropriateness and cultural appropriateness. DAP is defined as including integrated curriculum based on children's natural interests, allowing for construction of concepts through exploration of concrete materials, and adjusting to the diversity in our society. . . (Charlesworth, 1997, p. 51)

The discussion of developmental appropriateness and personal integration occurs in connection with all levels of schooling but is probably most vigorous in preschool and middle school. In preschool, there is emphasis on "the whole child," and the project method is very popular. The name "project method" was first coined by Kilpatrick and it covers a wide variety of practices (Kilpatrick, 1936). One well-known set of examples is provided by the schools of Reggio Emilia (Katz, 1998; Spaggiari, 1987). The project method encourages young children to investigate topics of their own choice, such as where shadows come from, how to organize a long-jump competition, or how to make an amusement park for birds.[3] It is a response to the ways young children explore the world and at the same time develop ways to express their thoughts "in a hundred languages." Many of these languages, of course, belong to the visual arts and are frequently central to the projects in this method (Rabitti, 1994; Ranklin, 1998)). Pitri discusses an American project that combined archeological inquiries with art (Pitri, 2002). Other examples of the role of art in developmentally appropriate early childhood programs have been discussed by Colbert and Taunton (Colbert, 1997; Colbert & Taunton, 1992).

In 1995, Brazee and Capelluti, arguing for integrated curriculum, said of the middle school curriculum:

> The middle level curriculum landscape has changed dramatically in the last five years. Beginning with the publication of James Beane's from *Rhetoric to Reality* in 1990, the curriculum conversation, as it has come to be called, has exploded. . . . Serious and reasoned consideration of what the middle school curriculum should be (and *how* it should be) is of utmost concern. (p. 15)

In the middle school literature, the dominant issue is identity (Middle Level Curriculum Project, 1993). Middle school students are increasingly aware of issues of self-presentation and social interaction, of the inwardness of feeling and the outwardness of appearance, of stereotyping and group membership, and of the differences among people. These developments are a central issue in middle schools and many believe that they call for an integrated curriculum (and we might add they also call for more work with art). *Self* and *identity* are the words we use for the integration of understanding into a coherent whole. Our identity, we can say, *is* the understanding we have of our self. Building that understanding is a continuous process, requiring middle school students to make sense of traditionally difficult antitheses, such as those between inner feeling and outward appearance, values and practice, among the different perspectives of people, between life in school and experience at home, and between mind and body. To relate these aspects of experience together in a satisfactory way is to construct a stable self and a meaningful identity.

Art has traditionally been associated with this construction. *Self* is a frequent topic in the art classroom. Art teachers commonly ask students to make works that represent some aspect of

---

[3]The examples come from the exhibition of children's work in Reggio Emila schools, *The one hundred languages of children*, that toured the United States in the summer of 2002.

their self. They call for works about family, vacations, hobbies, ideals. Sometimes assignments move into students' feelings, fears, dreams, and social relations. The more ambitious projects encourage students to think of self as having a number of elements, through the use of collections of images brought together in collages, boxes, notebooks, portfolios. Of course, such projects do not automatically promote an *integration* of self. Everything depends on the details of the project. One can always ask questions about actual cases. For example, do the assignments promote reflection or self-stereotyping? Do they touch on issues of real concern to students? Do they suggest hard questions or easy answers? Do they promote inquiry? Are students encouraged to acknowledge different elements of self?

A contemporary view would rather speak of identity than of self, stressing the social and cultural influences on individuals. Today we prefer to speak of students' construction of identity from the materials offered by their culture rather than of their discovery of self. Given this view, the topic of *self* readily moves into the study of the cultural environment. Popular culture in particular provides many of the elements that students use to construct their identity. Wagner-Ott, for example, discusses a case where students studied the characteristics of popular dolls and action figures, with an emphasis on gender differences (Wagner-Ott, 2002). A common suggestion is to study popular stereotypes of the various groups—gender, race, nationality, and so on—to which students may belong. These stereotypes too easily become accepted as aspects of self unless they are examined critically. When students analyze the stereotypes, they analyze parts of their own identity, becoming aware of influences they can accept or reject. As already suggested, this kind of examination is a major motif of the visual culture movement. So far, however, the chief interest of that movement has been the analysis of the visual culture rather than that of students' own response to it. It has shown a stronger interest in the social issues than in the psychological ones. These latter include, for example, the kinds and degrees of awareness of or critical attitude toward stereotypes that students have. How do they use the arts to integrate their understandings of complex issues? What images do they use to integrate their bodily, emotional, and social experience? How far do they consider the point of view of others in their interpretations? How and when do they understand the images of popular culture, especially their commercial intent? Questions like these, about the uses of imagery and the development of self-awareness, are important to integrated learning and they are continuous with the traditional concerns of art educators. In short, the psychological issues of integrated curriculum have been important in art education, though the current literature has not much dwelt on them.

It may be worthwhile asking why this is so. Perhaps we could say that, in the same way that the visual culture movement now tends to underplay psychological interests in favor of social and political ones, the disciplinary movement of the last 30 years has also underplayed them in favor of disciplinary interests. Most of the attention of the disciplinary movement was on the structures, methods, content, of the arts disciplines and their translation into the school curriculum. Its interest in learning was oriented mostly to studies of learning to think in disciplinary ways. There were the many studies of the recognition of artistic styles, for instance (Gardner, 1990), of learning to think in the arts as separate languages (Goodman, 1978), and of visual thinking as opposed to verbal thinking (Arnheim, 1969). Their common idea was a separatist one: that thinking proceeds differently in different disciplines (or in different media, languages, or sensory organs), an idea that is not hospitable to curriculum integration (Parsons, 1998). The most influential outcome of this kind of theory is probably the idea of "multiple intelligences" (Gardner, 1983). This theory has provided important political and ideological support for teaching the arts in schools, but it does not easily support their integration with other subjects.

The work of Arthur Efland is an exception in that it does address the psychological interests of learning in an integrated curriculum (Efland, 2002a). Efland describes art as an essentially "ill-structured" discipline in which there are many exceptions to general statements and procedures (Spiro, Coulson, Feltovich, & Anderson, 1988). It is an endeavor where ambiguity and intuition are as important as logic and where connections run in multiple directions. Efland argues that in consequence art is best taught through case studies. Major artworks can serve the cognitive function that significant landmarks and buildings do in cities (Efland, 2000). Landmarks orient people to the city, offer varied perspectives on its parts, and let people locate themselves. In the same way, artworks can be approached from many directions, can connect different areas of knowledge together, and let people know where they are. They can serve as organizers of an integrated understanding of complex situations.

Efland is influenced by current efforts in psychology to understand the mind as closely related to the body and its experience, in reaction to the cognitive science metaphor of the mind as a computer (Johnson, 1987; Varela, Thompson, & Rosch, 1991). A promising idea is that our important metaphors derive from bodily experience, as when we speak of an upright character, the grasp of meaning, or a burning passion (Lakoff & Johnson, 1980). We elaborate meanings by elaborating metaphors. They are the source of new meanings as we move in the world from situation to situation, trying to find continuities among them. It is in the arts that we are most encouraged to work with metaphors—both to create and to reflect on them.

Arguments About the Nature of Art

There has been an important change in attitudes toward disciplines, especially in art. This can be seen in the metaphors commonly used to describe them. When the "new" disciplinary curricula of the 1960s were introduced, the disciplines were understood as conceptual structures, in which certain unique ideas lay at the heart of a discipline and gave it its character and power (Bruner, 1960). These ideas were linked to one another in particular ways, forming a characteristic "structure"; for example, the ideas of electron, nucleus, and atom are linked and form the structure of atomic physics. Such a distinctive set of fundamental ideas was thought to be the defining characteristic of every discipline, and much effort went into identifying them, especially in the case of the less "well-structured" disciplines of the arts and humanities. In schools, the educational goal was to be an understanding of these conceptual structures and their component key ideas, as contrasted with low-level learning such as remembering particular facts and practicing specific skills. The focus on conceptual structure, it was argued, would ensure that the curriculum is meaningful to students. This metaphor of ideas and structures was influential on the discipline-based approach to teaching art, which usually focused on teaching ideas that are uniquely important in art.

Nowadays, another metaphor is more common. Disciplines are more often thought of as "fields" or "domains," as having boundaries in the way that kingdoms and other domains do, boundaries that are historically arrived at, are somewhat arbitrary and reveal the exercise of power. We are more aware that academic disciplines are the constructions of self-promoting and powerful elites that require varied acts of exclusion for their maintenance. And, in a further step, boundaries like this are likely to be impediments to knowledge, just as boundaries to real domains are obstacles to travel. Meaning, the metaphor suggests, is as likely to be found in crossing borders as in remaining in the center.

This shift of metaphors is due, no doubt, in part to the fact that the dreams about meaning of the "new" disciplinary curricula were overtaken by subsequent pressures toward social efficiency, including the behavioral objectives movement, the cognitive science movement, and the current emphasis on high-stakes achievement tests. But it also reflects postmodern doubts about disciplines. We now have a greater recognition of their historical character and an increased suspicion of their relations to power. The traditional art disciplines in particular are sometimes seen as elitist repositories of politically correct knowledge and as undemocratically excluding the works and judgments of common people, folk art, the art of some other traditions, and visual culture in general.

Perhaps most importantly for art educators, there is no agreement that its most important ideas are unique to art. We have had more than 30 years of an emphasis on the arts disciplines, but there is no agreement about the conceptual structures or the central ideas of any of them, including art making, art history, art criticism, or the philosophy of art. It is also doubtful that they have unique methods of working or research paradigms. We can no longer identify them in terms of a single identifying method or logic. The idea of *art* itself has become so loose that, given the flood of visual images in our society, it is impossible to sort the art images from the non-art ones.[4] The ideas sometimes called the *elements and principles of design* (such as line, shape, color, and balance, contrast, focus) may be unique to art but they are no longer thought to be the most important. The idea of the *aesthetic* is often suggested both as the most fundamental idea in art and as unique to it, providing the purpose of art education and giving it coherence (Eisner, 2001; Smith, 1995). Artworks have aesthetic qualities, it is said, and the purpose of art education is help students to grasp those qualities. If we do not attend to the aesthetic qualities of images, their study becomes something other than art education: cultural anthropology, perhaps, or media studies. The fear is that we will lose the aesthetic qualities of images and the art in art education.

In my opinion, a better response is to accept the account of the "ill-structured" character of art and its disciplines and to continue to use them nevertheless. Instead of looking for essential ideas, we can teach the disciplines through a study of cases, extracting from them characteristic and useful, but not essential, ideas and ways of proceeding (Barrett, 1994, 1996; Harris, 2001; Walker, 2001). In practice, artists, art critics, art historians, and others have many ways of making and arguing, and practitioners use whatever makes most sense of the situation. When we look at their practice, we can identify a number of ideas and ways of proceeding and we can teach others to use them. These are tools worth learning, though they are context dependent, hard to generalize, and subject to dispute; they are useful, though their use requires judgment and sensitivity to context. And they are often variously connected with real-world issues and so are hospitable to integrated approaches to curriculum. I believe that this response, which accepts the multiplicity of art forms, procedures, and qualities rather than looking for an essential common element, reflects the character of contemporary art.

One can make the same point via the notion of the "artworld." The artworld is a social institution, a recognizable and important part of our society, with particular practices, ideas, institutions, narratives, and histories (Efland, 2002b). It is both more comprehensive and more indeterminate than the different art disciplines but can be substituted for them as the focus of study in art education. The key point is then that the artworld is to be understood as much in social as in intellectual terms and to understand it requires more than a knowledge of the art disciplines.

---

[4]These kinds of doubts are often used to support the movement to expand the idea of art to include all of visual culture. It is the first argument, for example, in the recent summary of the case in an *Advisory* of the NAEA. This document is significant because it was written by a group of 12 prominent scholars in the field. The summary says, in part:

Conceptions of art are changing and expanding. The boundaries that inform our understanding of art institutions, forms, practices, and values, are in flux. Recent theoretical and philosophical shifts have emerged in and across various domains of knowledge....New self-conscious trans-disciplinary fields of study have emerged to challenge conceptual dichotomies, such as fine/popular arts. As a result of these changes, it has become necessary to expand the concept and practice of art education to the realm of visual culture. (NAEA, 2002, p. 1)

The *Advisory* adds a second argument, which I have already discussed in the context of the psychological interests of integrated curriculum: that the visual images that we meet in everyday life greatly influence our students' beliefs, feelings, and values.

I have already abundantly traded on an assumption about art that is related to these issues and is fundamental in thinking about art in an integrated curriculum. It is that artworks are always *about* something; they have meanings to understand, as well as qualities to grasp, and these meanings are central to their character as artworks. Especially they can be about social or personal issues, sometimes deep and abiding ones. This point would not always have been accepted in the Modernist period, but it has been reiterated in many ways since Arthur Danto argued it (Danto, 1981). The assumption enables us to say that, although artworks certainly have characteristic ideas, media, techniques, principles, and histories, what is most important about them are their meanings (Parsons, 2002). The thought leads directly to an integrated curriculum. If students are to study art, they must think about meanings. If they are to understand a work by someone else, they need to inquire into its topic; and conversely, if they are to study a topic, they can explore and express their thoughts by making works about it. Art in this light is already an integrated subject. It is a medium for the exploration and expression of views about topics, in which an understanding of a topic cannot easily be divorced from its expression. In this way, it is like language, though in other ways very different. Students can neither understand nor write a good essay about a topic they do not understand; nor can they understand or make an interesting artwork about it. In practice, students in school might study a topic and make both verbal and visual works about it (essays, videos, digital presentations, artworks). The use of a combination of media leads to further conceptual and experiential integration and is often more motivating.

In principle, then, students must think about two kinds of things when studying art. One is the substantive topic, which may involve social studies, science, or math; and the other has to do with ideas and techniques of expression, which is the traditional content of art class. When these two elements are taken seriously and coordinated into one enterprise, the curriculum is integrated. For example, if the topic for study is a local stretch of river, the substantive element consists of the biological (or chemical, economic, social, political) character of the river. The artistic element consists of finding ways to represent the river that convey the students' evolving understandings and attitudes toward it. This may of course require looking at other works about rivers by other artists and the practice of relevant techniques; but it also requires the study of some aspect of the river itself.

In the practice of integrated curriculum, there can be great differences in the balance between these two elements, the substantive and the artistic. In some cases the substantive element almost disappears. The art teacher may assume that students already know enough about the river and should concentrate on how to represent it. This tends to reduce art to matters of technique, sometimes to the techniques of capturing the appearances of things. This is not good integrated curriculum because the students are not inquiring into any substantial ideas, and it also may not be good art education.

In other cases, the art element almost disappears. This is often because the teachers have a number of expectations to meet and art is not prominent among them. It may also be that they have relatively little training in art, as is often true. Teachers are often encouraged to integrate art into their curriculum and they may wind up using artworks only as illustrations of nonart topics. For example, they may show paintings to illustrate historical events, or get students to make drawings to illustrate them. In such cases, there are no ideas or procedures deriving from the artworld, no discussion of the character of the images as images or attention to the subtleties of their possible meanings. The spread of such teaching practices is a major fear of opponents of integrated curriculum (Eisner, 1986). This fear is associated with another: that integrating the curriculum will be an excuse in elementary schools for not employing specialist art teachers. Whether these fears are realistic depends on circumstances, mostly on how educators, including art teachers, understand both art and integrated curriculum. They may also depend on budgets. It must be said that a good integrated curriculum is more, and not less, demanding of teachers than one oriented toward disciplines. Cremin reached this conclusion in his history of progressive education, suggesting that a reason for the persistence of the traditional organization is that it is easier for teachers to teach it and cheaper to prepare them to do it (Cremin, 1961). Advocacy of integrated curricula does not imply that teachers do not need to understand one or more disciplines. Quite the reverse. And it is always desirable to have art specialist teachers in schools, even in preschools, where students are clearly not expected to think about the disciplines. The Reggio Emilia preschools, for example, usually have an art specialist on their staff (Rabitti, 1994). This follows from the Deweyan thought suggested earlier: that in an integrated curriculum, a knowledge of disciplines serves as a guide to teachers about where the students' learning can go.

Other practices sometimes occur in the name of integration that give it a bad image among art educators. Especially there are projects in which teachers engage students in a variety of activities but engage them with no significant ideas. Wiggins and McTighe (1998, p.1), for example, cite a unit of activities about apples. Another example is the practice in elementary schools of choosing a geographical continent each year and devising activities related to it. Where these curricula are not guided by significant ideas it is unreasonable to call them integrated. Curricular activities can only be integrated by promoting thought about a common idea.

An Example of Integrated Curriculum

I will close this chapter by presenting an example with which I am personally acquainted. A number of faculty and students at The Ohio State University recently worked together on a 5-year grant[5] to help some local schools integrate their curriculum through a focus on the arts (The Ohio State University TETAC Mentors, 2002). The example comes from this work and was the result of the efforts of several groups of faculty, teachers, and students working together. At the same time, the reflections on it that follow are mine and may not be shared by all.

We adopted two ways of talking about ideas and their role in integrated curriculum: *Key ideas* and *essential questions* (Jacobs, 1989). Without these, we found curriculum projects tended to disintegrate into a set of parallel activities that had little more in common than the use of the same name. *Key ideas* can be thought of at two levels of generality. At the more general level, they are very similar to what I called topics previously; for example, community, environment, identity, violence, gender. A key idea is very general and names a kind of important contemporary problem. It does not belong to the artworld, though it is something that artists have made works about. It suggests many questions, is full of complexities, has many instantiations, and encourages different points of view. Teachers especially may find key ideas provocative. For instance, in one school a small group of teachers met to discuss the natural environment as a topic for their integrated curriculum. They spent an hour debating whether they should say, in their assignments to students, *the* environment, *our* environment, or *my* environment. The discussion reached no consensus but was full of new insights.

To make key ideas more easily understood and more manageable for inquiry, however, we found it useful to formulate them at a less general level. For example, community can be studied by investigating the local shopping mall, the garbage system, or the local bridges. These all reflect the community in some way and provide a suitable target for investigation. The environment topic can become the study of a wetland, a garden, or a stretch of road.

---

[5]The grant was part of the national Transforming Education Through the Arts Challenge and was funded jointly by the Getty Center for Arts in Education and the Annenberg Challenge (The National Arts Education Consortium, 2002).

Similarly, students can think about identity more easily by focusing on clothing styles, images of gender, or racial stereotypes. The point is that a key idea needs to be couched at a level that engages its audience. For students, one usually needs a more specific formulation to guide inquiry and to take advantage of local resources and interests. It may be generalized later but needs an initial more particular focus. Among other things, the desirability of beginning with local issues means that an integrated curriculum at the school level can be planned at a national level only in very general terms (Burns, 1995).

Essential questions turn the idea into questions that can be pursued by students. They are articulations of some of the ambiguities and depths of the idea, questions that resist easy answers, call for sustained inquiry, and lead on to further questions. For example, about the environment we might ask: How is the (local) environment changing? What causes the changes? Or: What is garbage? What does our garbage tell us about us? Can we imagine a community without garbage? Questions like these give direction to student thought, calling for both data collection and inquiry into further issues.

An example comes from a rural high school where a number of teachers worked together to integrate part of their curriculum. Here I need to say that the account that follows does not conform to the actual case closely. I have extended and idealized it somewhat for the sake of clarity. The reality of this curriculum of course encountered a number of difficulties, having mostly to do with time constraints, scheduling problems, and competing priorities. Nevertheless, it is clearly recognizable in this account.

One year, wanting particularly to raise value issues for the students, the group of teachers (about six of them, teaching a variety of different subjects) chose the key idea of *heroes*. In terms of the previous discussion, this is a particular case of *identity*, because of course to study one's heroes is also to study oneself. The teachers agreed to have their students pursue the following essential questions wherever possible throughout their first year of high school:

> *What are our heroes like?*
> *How are heroes represented in art, literature, and the popular media?*
> *Why do people have heroes?*
> *How do heroes reflect different societies?*
> *What do our heroes tell about us?*

The teachers kept returning in class to these questions at different times during the whole year and they met frequently to discuss progress and coordinate topics. During the year, the students engaged in many sorts of activities in their classes, as appropriate to the different school subjects. In art and language arts classes, they identified and discussed their own heroes; their choices initially were dominantly sports or entertainment stars and other figures from popular culture. They collected stories and images of them from popular media and other sources, wrote biographies, and made portraits of them. They also looked at representations of heroes in the history of art and literature. An extended example in literature was the figure of Odysseus from the Odyssey. In art they spent some time looking at Warhol and making Warholesque portraits of their heroes. This exercise led to extended discussions of the difference between celebrities and heroes, a distinction that was full of insight for many and that caused some to change their choice of hero. It led also to discussion of the ambiguities of Warhol's own attitudes toward celebrities: admiring, descriptive, or critical? They also spent time with Rauschenberg's collage portraits of the Kennedys, again making their own collage portraits of their heroes. This led to discussion about the relation of heroes to the time and culture that makes them heroes, a step toward the essential question: *What do our heroes tell about us?*

In history class, they studied American presidents and the ways they have been represented. In one case, they focused on the photographs and other representations of Franklin Delano

Roosevelt over the years, because it was during that year (1999) that a public artwork—the new statue in Washington, D.C.—revealed openly the presence of the wheelchair to which he was bound. They also did a survey of the heroes of the adults in their community and collected photographs of the local statues and memorials. This project connected local with national history and also gave them a sense of changes in local tastes and values. In social studies, they looked at heroes in different cultures around the world, which led to further discussions of the relations between societies and the people they choose as heroes. Throughout all of this, there was attention to the way in which heroes are represented in both language and visual imagery and how those representations guide attitudes.

In these activities as described, art stands beside the other school subjects as one of several disciplinary approaches to the essential questions, which themselves overflow disciplinary distinctions. The curriculum could very well have stopped with that design. In this example, however, art was also used in a further and somewhat more ambitious way: as a medium for an exercise in the comprehensive integration of the students' discoveries about their heroes.

For the end of the year, the students were asked to design an outdoor sculpture about their heroes. They were commissioned by the group of teachers to design a work that expressed their understandings and feelings about their heroes. The students were to work in small groups to create the designs, one of which was to be chosen for actual installation in a space at the rear of the school. The process was adapted from the commissioning process mentioned earlier in the discussion of contemporary community public art and in itself taught the students something about how the contemporary artworld works. First they were to design a work that expressed their understanding of and attitudes toward their heroes. The design was to be drawn on paper and discussed in an artists' statement. It was then to be presented formally to the rest of the students acting as a selection jury. The criteria for selection were announced beforehand. They were three: the degree to which the design reflected learning from the year's work; interest and expressiveness, including appropriateness to the particular hero(es); and issues of practicality, including the relation of the design to the space. There were questions and answers at the end of each presentation, and then the students voted to select the best five designs. This presentation and selection process required special scheduling for 3 consecutive school afternoons and the collaboration of the teachers of the various disciplines, including math and science.

Subsequently, the five successful teams were given time to improve their design and to make three-dimensional models or computer simulations. They also revised their presentations, having learned considerably from the first round of presentations. They were then asked to make their presentations again in the evening before a jury of local adults, including the principal, a local politician, and an artist, and in front of an audience of parents and students. At the end of the evening the jury chose one design for actual construction and implementation. Teachers and students, together with a local engineer, labored for several weeks in the evenings to install it. This has now resulted in the beginning of an "art park" at the rear of the school, where a new work, on a different topic, is to be added each year.

This process was a practical and highly motivating experience of art criticism and discussion, one that engaged many students and teachers and a number of other local adults. Most importantly, it offered the students a way to digest and express their thoughts on a complex topic they had studied for the whole year. They used visual media to integrate their understanding, trying to create a work that expressed the complexities and points of view they had reached. They could of course have written essays or narratives that tried to do the same thing but there are advantages to using visual media for this purpose. One is, simply, motivational. So much of school is already verbal that the challenge to work with visual media was energizing for many students. Another is the mixture of media, visual and verbal, which is inherently stimulating intellectually: They had to discuss what they were doing with each other, explain it to audiences, and to write an artists' statement. A third is the communication and publicity value, through the involvement of local adults and the permanent presence of the piece on the school grounds.

CONCLUSION

In this review, I have tried to articulate a vision that I think lies within the current interest in integrated curriculum in art education. It is a vision that harks back to the progressive era and at the same time responds to contemporary developments in the artworld and in society in general. It connects integrated curriculum with a focus on significant ideas, an interest in social problems, and a concern for students' struggle for a stable and healthy identity. It focuses on students' understanding of important topics and on their ability to connect school learning with their real daily world. With respect to the arts, it sees significantly greater opportunities for their role in the curriculum because of current changes in the artworld and in our modes of communication.

I have argued that integrated curriculum need not deny the value of the academic disciplines when they are understood as tools for problem solving. Indeed, an integrated curriculum calls for more highly trained teachers than does a disciplinary one. Both need an understanding of their discipline; the teacher in the integrated curriculum needs to know a discipline well in order to judge how it can be useful as a tool for the students. In addition the teacher in the integrated curriculum needs to understand the social developments and attendant problems that are to be studied and also have an understanding of the lifeworld and developmental needs of the students. A good teacher in an integrated curriculum must herself be able to integrate these three different kinds of things in her classroom. In addition, there must be a supportive school culture for integrated approaches to teaching (a topic I have not touched in this paper, though it is important). The vision is therefore a demanding one. It is a question whether we have a sufficiently supportive school culture or a sufficiently well-educated teaching force to carry it off in the majority of our public schools and whether, in a conservative time, we are willing to supply the resources required. We should not forget that the progressive education movement had many successes but ultimately foundered on these rocks.

At the same time, there are many benefits for teachers, as well as for students. Teaching an integrated curriculum in small groups can be an engaging and powerful form of professional development, as well as a source of insights into social and personal problems. There are many excellent teachers and schools at all levels where integrated curricula are practiced, where students work together to identify important problems and inquire into ideas for their solution, and where students can develop a consistent understanding of self and others in their world. In addition, in some of these schools, the arts are valued as modes for the exploration and integration of thought. I hope that the current wave of interest will swell their number.

REFERENCES

Arnheim, R. (1969). *Visual thinking.* Berkeley, CA: The University of California press.

Barrett, T. (1994). *Criticizing art: Understanding the contemporary* (2nd ed.). Mountain View, CA: Mayfield.

Barrett, T. (1996). *Criticizing photographs: An introduction to understanding images* (2nd ed.). Mountain View, CA: Mayfield.

Beane, J. (1997). *Curriculum integration: Designing the core of democratic education.* New York: Teachers College Press.

Beane, J. (1993). *The middle school curriculum: From rhetoric to reality* (2nd ed.). Columbus, OH: The National Middle School Association.

Birt, D., Krug, D., & Sheridan, M. (1997). Earthly matters: Learning occurs when you hear the grass singing. *Art Education, 50*(6), 6–13.

Boston, B. (1996). *Connections: The arts and the integration of the high school curriculum.* New York: The College Entrance Examination Board and the Getty Center for Education in the Arts.

Brazee, E., & Capelluti, J. (1995). *Dissolving boundaries: Toward an integrative curriculum.* Columbus, OH: The National Middle School Association.

Bredekamp, S., & Copple, C., (Eds.). (1997). *Developmentally appropriate practice in early childhood programs: Revised.* Washington, DC: National Association for the Education of Young Children.

Broudy, H., Smith, B., & Burnett, J. (1964). *Democracy and excellence in American secondary education: A study in curriculum theory.* Chicago: Rand, Mcnally.

Bruner, J. (1960). *The process of education.* Cambridge, MA: Harvard University Press.

Burnaford, G., Aprill, A., & Weiss, C. (2001). *Renaissance in the classroom: Arts integration and meaningful learning.* Mahwah, NJ: Lawrence Erlbaum Associates.

Burns, R. (1995). *Dissolving the boundaries: Planning for curriculum integration in middle and secondary schools.* Charleston, WV: Appalachia Educational Laboratory.

Burton, J. (2000). The configuration of meaning: Learner centered art education revisited. *Studies in Art Education, 41*(4), 330–345.

Chanda, J., & Daniel, V. (2000). Recognizing works of art: The essences of contextual understanding. *Art Education, 53*(2), 6–11.

Charbonneau, M., & Reider, B. (1995). *The integrated elementary classroom: A developmental model of education for the 21st century.* London: Allyn & Bacon.

Charlesworth, R. (1997). Mathematics and the developmentally appropriate integrated curriculum. C. Hart, D. Burts, & R. Charlesworth (Eds.), *Integrated curriculum and developmentally appropriate practice* (pp. 51–74). Albany, NY: SUNY Press.

Clincy, E. (1997). *Transforming public education: A new course for America's future.* New York: Teachers College Press.

Colbert, C. (1997). Visual arts in the developmentally appropriate integrated curriculum. In C. Hart, D. Burts, & R. Charlesworth (Eds.), *Integrated curriculum and developmentally appropriate practice.* Albany, NY: SUNY Press.

Colbert, C., & Taunton, M. (1992). *Developmentally appropriate practices for the visual arts education of young children.* Reston, VA: The National Art Education Association.

The Consortium of National Arts Education Associations. (2002). Authentic connections: Interdisciplinary work in the arts. Reston, VA: The National Art Education Association.

Cremin, L. (1961). *The transformation of the school: Progressivism in American education, 1876–1957.* New York: Knopf.

Daniel, V. (2001). Art education as a community act: Teaching and learning through the community. In *Proceedings of the International Symposium in Art Education* (pp. 49–71). National Taipei University, Taiwan.

Danto, A. (1981). *The transfiguration of the commonplace.* Cambridge, MA: Harvard University Press.

Davis, J., & Gardner, H. (1992). The cognitive revolution: Consequences for the understanding and education of the child as artist. In B. Reimer & R. Smith (Eds.), *The arts, education, and aesthetic knowing* (pp. 92–123). Chicago: University of Chicago Press.

Dewey, J. (1990). *The school and society; and the child and curriculum.* Chicago: The University of Chicago Press. (originally published in 1902)

Dickie, G. (1984). *The art circle: A theory of art.* New York: Haven Press.

Dublin Arts Council. (2002). *Dublin's museum without walls.* Dublin, OH: Dublin Arts Council.

Duncum, P. (2001). Visual culture: Development, definitions, and directions for art education. *Studies in Art Education, 42*(2), 101–112.

Efland, A. (2000). The city as metaphor for integrated learning through the arts. *Studies in Art Education, 41*(3), 276–295.

Efland, A. (2002a). *Art and cognition: Integrating the visual arts in the curriculum.* New York: Teachers College Press.

Efland, A. (2002b). *Emerging visions of art education.* NAEA conference, Miami Florida.

Eisner, E. (2001). Should we create new aims for art education? *Art Education, 54*(5), 6–10.

Eisner, E. (1986). *The role of discipline-based art education in America's schools.* Los Angeles, CA: Getty Center for Education in the Arts.

Freedman, K. (1994). Interpreting gender and visual culture in art classrooms. *Studies in Art Education, 35*(3), 156–168.

Freedman, K. (2000). Social perspectives on art education in the US: Teaching visual culture in a democracy. *Studies in Art Education, 41*(4), 314–327.

Freedman, K., & Stuhr, P. (2001). *Visual culture: Broadening the domain of art education*. Council for Policy Studies in Art Education meeting, unpublished.

Gablik, S. (1991). *The reenchantment of art*. New York: Thames and Hudson.

Gardner, H. (1990). *Art education and human development*. Los Angeles: J. Paul Getty Trust.

Gardner, H. (1983). *Frames of mind: The theory of multiple intelligences*. New York: Basic Books.

Goodman, N. (1978). *The languages of art* (2nd ed.). Indianapolis: Hackett.

Guilfoil, J. (2000). From the ground up: Art in American built environment education. *Art Education, 53*(4), 6–12.

Habermas, J. (1981). *The theory of communicative action*. Thomas McCarthy (Trans.). Boston: Beacon Press.

Harris, J. (2001). *The new art history: A critical introduction*. London: Routledge

Hart, C., Burts, D., & Charlesworth, R. (Eds.). (1997). *Integrated curriculum and developmentally appropriate practice*. Albany, NY: SUNY Press.

Huang, H. (1999). Educational reform in Taiwan. *International Journal of Educational Reform, 8*(2), 145–153.

Jacobs, H. (1989). *Interdisciplinary curriculum: Design and implementation*. Alexandria, VA: Association for Supervision and Curriculum Development.

Johnson, M. (1987). *The body in the mind*. Chicago: The University of Chicago Press.

Katz, L. (1998). What can we learn from Reggio Emilia? In C. Edwards, L. Gandini & G. Forman (Eds.), *The hundred languages of children: The Reggio Emilia approach* (pp. 27–45). Norwood, NJ: Ablex.

Kilpatrick, W. (1936). *Remaking the curriculum*. Chicago, Newson.

Kliebard, H. (1995). *The struggle for the American curriculum, 1893–1958* (2nd ed.). New York: Routledge.

Krug, D. (1997). *Art and ecology: Interdisciplinary approaches to the curriculum*. Santa Monica, CA: Getty Center for the Arts in Education. http://www.getty.edu/artsednet/resources/ecology/curriculum/inter.html

Krug, D., & Cohen-Evron, N. (2000). Curriculum integration: Positions and practices in art education. *Studies in Art Education, 41*(3), 258–275.

Lacy, S. (Ed.). (1995). *Mapping the terrain: New genre public art*. Seattle: Bay Press.

Lowenfeld, V., & Brittain, W. (1982). *Creative and mental growth* (8th ed.). New York: Macmillan. (1st ed. by Lowenfeld, V. in 1947)

Lakoff, G., & Johnson, M. (1980). *Metaphors we live by*. Chicago: University of Chicago Press.

Marche, T. (1998). Looking outward, looking in: Community in art education. *Art Education, 51*(3), 6–13.

Middle Level Curriculum Project. (1993). Middle level curriculum: In search of self and social meaning. In T. Dickinson (Ed.), *Readings in middle school curriculum: A continuing conversation*. Columbus, OH: The National Middle School Association.

Mitchell, W. (1994). *Picture theory*. Chicago: University of Chicago Press.

NAEA (2002). *Art education and visual culture*. NAEA advisory. Reston, VA: National Art Education Association.

The National Arts Education Consortium. (2002). *Final project report. Transforming education through the arts challenge*. Columbus, OH: The Department of Art Education, The Ohio Sate University.

The Ohio State University TETAC Mentors. (2002). Integrated curriculum: Possibilities for the arts. *Art Education, 55*(3), 12–22.

Parsons, M. (1998). Integrated curriculum and our paradigm of cognition in the arts. *Studies in Art Education, 39*(2).

Parsons, M. (2002). Aesthetic experience and the construction of meanings. *The Journal of Aesthetic Education, 36*(2), 24–37.

Pitri, E. (2002). Project learning: Exploration, discussion, and discovery. *Art Education, 55*(5), 18–24.

Rabitti, G. (1994). An integrated art approach in a preschool. In L. Katz & B. Cesarone (Eds.), *Reflections on the Reggio Emilia approach* (pp. 51–68). Urbana, Ill: ERIC Clearing House on Elementary Education.

Ranklin, B. (1998). Curriculum development in Reggio Emilia: A long-term curriculum about dinosaurs. In C. Edwards, L. Gandini & G. Forman (Eds.), *The hundred languages of children: The Reggio Emilia approach* (pp. 215–237). Norwood, NJ: Ablex.

Raven, A. (Ed.). (1993). *Art in the public interest*. New York: Da Capo Press.

Russell, F., & Russell, R (2001). *Art in the market: A program integrating service learning with asset-based community development in Cincinnati*. Paper presented at the 27th annual meeting of Social Theory, Politics and the Arts. St. Louis, MO.

Shandler, S. (1999). *Ophelia speaks: Adolescent girls write about their search for self*. New York: Harper Smith, R. (1995). *Excellence II: The continuing quest in art education*. Reston, VA: The National Art Education Association.

Smith, R. (1995). *The continuing quest in art education*. Reston, VA: The National Art Education Association.

Spaid, S. (2002). *Ecovention: Current art to transform ecologies*. Cincinnati: The Contemporary Art Center.

Spaggiari, S. (1987). *The hundred languages of children*. Reggio Emilia, Italy: Department of Education.

Spiro, R., Coulson, R., Feltovich, P., & Anderson, D. (1988). *Cognitive flexibility theory: Advanced knowledge acquisition is ill-structured domains*. (Tech. Rep. No. 441) University of Illinois at Urbana-Champaign, Center for the Study of Reading.

Stuhr, P. (1994). Social reconstructionist multicultural art curriculum design: Using the Powwow as an example. In R. Neperud (Ed.), *Context, content, and community in art education* (pp. 193–221). New York: Teachers College Press.

Taylor, P. (2002). Service learning as postmodern art and pedagogy. *Studies in Art Education, 43*(2), 124–140.

Taylor, P. (2000). Madonna and hypertext: Liberatory learning in art education. *Studies in Art Education, 41*(4), 376–389.

Thurber, F. (1997). A site to behold: Creating curricula about local urban environmental art. *Art Education, 50*(6).

Ulbricht, J. (1998). Interdisciplinary art education reconsidered. *Art Education, 51*(4), 13–17.

U.S. Bureau of Education. (1918). *Cardinal principles of secondary education: A report of the commission on the reorganization of secondary education* (U.S. Bureau of Education, Bulletin, 1918, no. 35). Washington, DC: Government Printing Office.

Varela, F., Thompson, E., & Rosch, E. (1991). *The embodied mind.* Cambridge, MA: MIT Press.

Wagner-Ott, A. (2002). Analysis of gender identity through doll and action figure politics in art education. *Studies in Art Education, 43*(3), 246–263.

Walker, S. (2001). *Teaching meaning in artmaking.* Worcester, MA: Davis.

Wiggins, G., & McTighe, J. (1998). *Understanding by design.* Alexandria, VA: Association for Supervision and Curriculum Development.

Wiseman, V. (1999). Unpublished paper, Cleveland City Schools.

35

Studio Art as Research Practice

Graeme Sullivan
Teachers College, Columbia University

STUDIO ART AS RESEARCH PRACTICE

Research in art education involves asking questions and seeking answers that allow us to better understand how to make art, study art, and teach art. In devising methods of inquiry, educators mostly seek to adapt practices from existing research traditions in the human sciences. For instance, in the early 1960s, art educators struggled to assess the theoretical robustness of the field (Arnstine, 1965; Ecker, 1965; Efland, 1964; Eisner, 1964; Kaufman, 1959). A central question asked was whether art was a discipline and whether it was possible to construct a theoretical framework from which explanatory structures of knowledge could be drawn. To do so meant to adopt the research protocols of science, as this was how knowledge about human thought and action was best believed to be revealed.

In later decades, the use of qualitative research methods in educational inquiry found strong support in art education (Bresler; 1994; Chalmers, 1981; Eisner, 1985; 1991; May, 1993; Stokrocki, 1997). Here the quest to ground the theoretical adequacy of art education gave credence to the teacher as a plausible source of knowledge and the praxis of the classroom and the community as a viable basis for theory. This grounded approach was seen to account more closely for the authenticity of art learning and teaching. As a result, as conceptions of art education changed so did the methods of inquiry. The reliance on expressive and psychological foundations of creating art broadened to embrace culturally grounded frameworks for interpreting art and this brought language-based experiences clearly into the picture (Parsons, 1992). Yet the continued need to confirm the theoretical status of art education remained wedded to the practices prescribed by dominant discourses in the social sciences (Sacca, 1989).

Despite the emergence of qualitative approaches to educational inquiry that achieve a more adequate "goodness of fit" for the kind of learning seen in the classroom and the studio, the need to construct theories that "explain" phenomena is still assumed to be the ultimate goal of research. I argue that "understanding" is as significant as explanation as a goal of research, and more so when outcomes are applied in educational contexts. If this is accepted, then making art and interpreting art become the basis for constructing theories of artistic knowing. This quest for understanding sees individual and social transformation as a worthy educational goal, and this is what art educators seek as they develop theories about learning and teaching art. Consequently, if art education is to establish a theoretically robust foundation, then the research approaches deployed should not only be informed by what the social sciences have to offer but also must be grounded in practices located within the domain of art. To continue to merely borrow research methods from other fields denies the intellectual maturity of art practice as a plausible basis for raising significant theoretical questions, and as a viable site for applying important educational ideas.

QUESTIONING THE RESEARCH TRADITION WITHIN ART EDUCATION

Despite the expansion of the methodological landscape, debates about educational inquiry continue. Although the postmodern critique of institutional practices revealed the problematic status of traditional boundaries–be they discipline divisions, arts areas, or cultural divides– many saw the need to reconcile the apparent incompatibility of the quantitative and qualitative paradigms (Jackson, 1990; LeCompte & Goetz, 1982; Smith & Heshusius, 1986). Eisner (1993) highlights this dilemma in his discussion of the tension between "what is individual and distinctive" and what is "patterned and regular." He asks:

> How do we avoid the verificationist's constipation of conceptual categories on the one hand and the radical relativist's free-for-all, anything goes, no-holds-barred nihilism on the other? Or are these really untenable alternatives that nobody really believes? Maybe so. (p. 8)

The emergence of qualitative methodologies as viable approaches to research in the human sciences has, of course, not been without its critics (Gross & Levitt, 1994). Cizek (1995) questions the "crunchy granola" character of qualitative methods that favors "thick texture" rather than scientific analysis. He asks:

> If one accepts the notion that all understanding is contextualized, if all experience is embedded in culture, and if all knowledge is a personalized construction, and so on, than can any interpretivist claims be rejected? If not we are not only poststructuralist, postconstructivist, and postmodernist, but probably postscientific as well. (p. 27)

In many cases the arguments about the relative merits of different research paradigms seem to offer theoretical barriers rather than guidelines to cross borders. There is, however, plenty of evidence to suggest that the reality of research practice readily blurs these distinctions. Amundsen, Serlin and Lehrer (1992) adopt a "postpositivist" perspective and suggest that unlike the positivists' past emphasis on observation and prediction, a realistic approach is to seek more global criteria such as simplicity and theoretical consistency. Salomon (1991) offers an approach to research that identifies discrete and interdependent elements within complex educational phenomena that subsequently require different modes of inquiry. Although based on different conceptions of knowledge such as the distinction between specific outcomes and multiple meanings, the "analytic" and "systematic" (p. 13) approaches serve to complement each other in data analysis. Salomon's nested approach seeks to capture the complexity of learning environments, whereby the precision of analysis helps to maintain focus, whereas systematic data management ensures that outcomes are authentic.

Although the conceptual and methodological frameworks that shape the research land-scape these days are clearly more flexible (Creswell, 2002; Tashakkori & Teddlie, 1998), it is necessary to review some underlying assumptions about research if a more comprehensive approach to studio art research is to be realized. For instance, to maintain the mythic mantle of the objective observer as being the only rational way of investigating phenomena denies the complex ways that humans encounter the world around them. Further, the way constructs such as causality, objectivity, falsifiability, and verification are reified within the research community continues to keep certain theoretical and methodological divisions in place.

Causality and Meaning

Within the scientific tradition it is readily accepted that things have causes, and although this notion may serve the natural sciences well, it is less convincing when applied to the human sciences. Identifying cause and effect has rich predictive power, but human nature remains tantalizingly obscure in revealing underlying causal structures or discrete patterns of behavior. For instance, when the decoding of the human genome was revealed to the world in February 2001, the result was unexpected. There was no neat underlying structure or causal network to be found. There was no coded map that fully explained the distribution of human attributes. It was apparent that the soupy pool of genes and protein was just as complicated as the unwieldy world of human encounters that confront us.

To assume that there are some psychobiological constructs that cause all human action is to place far too much faith in determinism. Social effects may be the result of multiple causes rather than a single cause, or be the product of human agency, for individuals have the capacity to choose how they might respond in social situations. There are obvious links in the way humans are shaped in part by their neural architecture and their interactions with socio cultural settings. But to focus on causes seems unnecessarily reductive when the more interesting questions center on the kind of decisions and choices people and cultures make that lead them to do the things they do. Even a committed educational researcher such as Jerome Bruner (1990) ceased to ask the causal question, "How do children learn?" and began to ask, "How are meanings made?" This took him out of the clinical setting and into the "real" world in order to understand the culture of education (Bruner, 1996). In a way, giving undue emphasis to the linear logic of causality is similar to assuming that an artwork is merely the consequence of artistic intention, when obviously there are an array of factors that influence the making and reading of visual images. To acknowledge the continual interplay between subjective and objective ways of knowing provides a plausible account of the interrelationships that shape human understanding.

Objectivity, Subjectivity, and Intersubjectivity

The tendency to try to reside on either side of the objective subjective divide is to adopt an overly simplistic stance. For instance, to resort to extreme relativism is to ignore the idea that there are aspects of an objective world "out there." Although we might view empirical reality through a personally constructed lens, there is no mistaking that we understand certain things better than before because of accumulated knowledge. Truth may well be provisional, but making use of what is currently known about certain phenomena is a very useful starting point. To neglect such information is to ignore the necessary distinction between knowledge and opinion.

A broader conception of objectivity is therefore required to deal adequately with complex realities. The positivist belief is only a partial account and needs to be supported by the inter-subjectivity that characterizes how individuals and cultures construct meaning. By intersub-jectivity, I refer to Michael Parson's definition that there exists a realm of "shared symbolically mediated meanings" (1995, p. 12) that facilitate individual and community understanding. In

true testing include both types.

methodological terms this means there is a need to consider the *observer* and the *observed* as legitimate sources of knowledge. It is instructive to remember that it was Einstein who helped us understand that when interpreting events some things will remain the same, and others will change according to the viewpoint taken. Similarly, Heisenberg affirmed this uncertain relationship between the observer and the observed, and this is readily understood by anyone who understands the "push and pull" of painting where intervention, action and reflection have different consequences when seen up close and from afar.

Falsifiability, Verification, and Self-Confirmation

Another powerful construct used to confirm the robustness of scientific inquiry is the notion of falsifiability. Eloquently argued by Karl Popper (Miller, 1985), the basic principle is that there is more merit in trying to expose something to failure rather than trying to confirm its probable truth. Being able to subject untenable propositions to rigorous testing is a way to uncover those that do not stand up to analysis, and those that can be confirmed that are the best theoretical fit. The steely eye of the science community and the methodological safety net of hypotheticodeductive reasoning serve as an additional basis for monitoring and correcting the accumulation of knowledge.

It would be wrong, however, to assume that there are no traditions or practices in the arts, whereby theories are not subject to empirical risk. As Efland (1995) notes, visual arts is an "ill structured domain" (p. 143) and does not have the self-correcting features of prescribed methods and replicability that characterizes the formalisms of the sciences. If, however, we subscribe to the view that empiricism involves verifying things through observation, then those involved in the arts routinely put theories and practices up for empirical review through a *self-confirming* critical process. This is precisely what happens when the arts are seen as systems of engagement that include artworks, artists, cultural commentators, and educators. These agencies become arenas for debate and intersubjective agreement through the use of the self-confirming processes of peer review and historical legacy.

The conventions of quantitative research provide a clear structure for generating questions grounded in accumulated knowledge. Although it is readily acknowledged that hypothetical constructs must be measurable and testable, they need not lack imagination. Yet the quest for verification and the demands of control and reductionism often leave little room for speculative maneuvers. Kirk and Miller (1986) note:

> When confirmatory research goes smoothly, everything comes out as expected. Received theory is supported by one more example of its usefulness, and requires no change. As in everyday social life, confirmation is exactly the absence of insight. (p. 15)

However, radical insights in science emanate as much from serendipitous events, happy accidents, or intuition as they do from following prescriptions (Feyerabend, 1991; Perkins, 2000; Weisberg, 1993). Situating inquiry that builds on previous research may be sound research practice, but scholarship is also about ideas. Obviously, in science as in art, knowing one's craft heightens the awareness of not only what is probable but also what is possible. But hypothesis testing is not the only way to go about systematic inquiry. Confirming or not confirming a null hypothesis only really allows the researcher to claim that certain effects or relationships are probably the result of chance or not. Levels of statistical significance are customarily used as a numerical indicator of the odds. Yet, if the principle of subjecting predictions to the risk of empirical rejection is adopted, then there are several strategies that can be followed in arts inquiry.

The criteria for assessing the viability of qualitative findings are not so much a matter of whether an outcome is statistically significant, but whether it is meaningful. Therefore for those researchers seeking insight and understanding, the emphasis on discovery requires one to maintain an especially vigilant pose in dealing with issues of validity and reliability (Kirk & Miller, 1986). This involves sound reasoning, systematic analysis, and sustained focusing, along with the process of subjecting emerging findings to continual empirical challenge as new observations inform existing interpretations. As Bruner (1996) notes, the purpose is to achieve understanding rather than explanation, and in the process we construct meanings.

> The object of interpretation is understanding, not explanation; its instrument is the analysis of text. Understanding is the outcome of organizing and contextualizing essentially contestable, incompletely verifiable propositions in a disciplined way... The requirement, rather, is verisimilitude or "truth likeness," and that is a compound of coherence and pragmatic utility, neither of which can be rigidly specified. (p. 90)

Isn't this what thoughtful art critics do? In helping describe how art critics might assist others who feel a need to understand and assess art according to whatever prescribed criterion is set Arthur Danto (2001) explains:

> I would be eager to point out the complexities of interpretation... and that the panelists should consider the art the way it is considered by a critic, from the perspective of what view is being visually advanced. Seen this way, it becomes a matter of finding plausible critical hypotheses and then seeing whether they could *not* [italics added] be true. (p. 33)

Probable and Plausible Conceptions of Reality

In many basic texts on educational research a foundation principle given for distinguishing qualitative and quantitative approaches is the difference in underlying conceptions of reality. Conceptions of social reality shape most of what we think, say, and do and are defined by assumptions about some of the most basic questions we ask when we inquire into human thought and action. When the question, "What is real?" is asked, answers will be framed by a range of ontological beliefs: A realist will claim a reality independent of individual interest or influence; a contextualist will claim reality is socially constructed and exists in many forms. In a similar way, concerns about how knowledge is acquired and communicated will raise epistemological distinctions about objective states and subjective experience. In another way, the manner by which individuals shape, or are shaped by their environment, reflects basic assumptions about human nature. These differing conceptions are most often seen as opposing perspectives positioned along various continua that highlight alternative ways the world is seen. Consequently, research outcomes are understood as instances of what is believed to be true.

In qualitative inquiry the criteria for assessing outcomes relies on their plausibility rather than their probability. Rather than explain phenomena in terms of differences in degree, the interest of qualitative researchers is to compare differences in kind. This rests on the premise that generalizing results from specific samples to the general population is not the only way to configure research outcomes. The plausibility of research findings grounded in observations of real-world actions, events, and artifacts relies on the agreement that outcomes can be interpreted as connections between the "specific and the specific." In other words, what is seen to be real in one observed setting can have a parallel relevance in a similar situation. Eisner (1991) calls these kinds of outcomes "prospective" and "retrospective," whereby "generalizations [made] through art provide a heuristic or canonical image with which to see more clearly" as "they give you something to look for or to reflect on" (1999, p. 20).

The Possibility of Transformative Research

Although criteria for quantitative results are based on the probable likelihood of occurrences, and findings from qualitative inquiries are assessed by the plausibility or relevance of outcomes, the possibility of insight remains an elusive criterion for judging the significance of research. If a measure of the utility of research is seen to be the capacity to create new knowledge that is individually and culturally transformative, then criteria need to move beyond probability and plausibility to *possibility*.

The possibility of gaining new understanding involves accessing, designing, and investigating issues of personal and public interest. Research of this kind is imaginative and logical and includes the exploration of one's tacit knowledge and the insight of others as both experience and reasoning come into play. Generally the goal of research is to describe, interpret, or explain phenomena; but if the desire is to see inquiry as having the capacity to change human understanding, then our sight needs to be set on a bigger picture. For instance, when Marvin Minsky and Seymour Papert were looking for images to conceptualize their ideas about artificial intelligence, they realized there was no single structure on which they could model their smart machine. Their "society-of-mind" theory made use of multiple structures and variable resources. Minsky noted that "you can't understand anything unless you understand it in several different ways, and the search for the single truth–the pure, best way to represent knowledge–is wrongheaded" (cited in Brockman, 1996, p. 163). According to Minsky and Papert, for new knowledge to have individual and cultural significance, it has to be able to be negotiated and represented in different forms within the framework of a continually changing world. Therefore, creating knowledge that is informative and transformative is necessary if the theories and practices of educational research are to have personal and public impact.

My argument that the goal of educational research in general, and art education research in particular, should be the production of transformative knowledge is grounded on two premises. The first is that there is a schism of thought whereby institutionalized traditions make it difficult for many to move beyond the safety of accepted practices. In the mid-20th century C. P. Snow's description of *The Two Cultures* (1959) highlighted this polite cultural clash between the humanities and the sciences as a dispute between the "intellectuals" and the "boffins." In a more recent publication edited by John Brockman titled *The Third Culture* (1996), he chronicles a series of conversations among a highly regarded list of scientists. Brockman describes them as "third-culture thinkers" (p. 18) who seem to be filling the gap identified by C. P. Snow 50 years ago. What is intriguing to me is that there is no set agenda, no accepted canon, and no standardized way these scientists think about things. Just as many artists move with insight and imagination within and beyond boundaries, many scientists do the same. So the unnecessary reification of research practices is more a consequence of institutionalized thinking. I would argue that history, convention, power, and position are the kind of cultural blinders that limit the capacity to see and act in different ways.

My second premise argues that to better understand how art education can contribute to human understanding, there is a need to ground art educational research within the theories and practices that surround art making. It is from this central site of investigation that other derivative practices such as critical and philosophical analysis, historical and cultural commentary, and educational praxis emerge. The notion that art is a warm, fuzzy, and essentially private experience now extends to acknowledge the cognitive capacities that inform artistic making and thinking (Efland, 2002; Goodman, 1976).

A RATIONALE FOR THEORIZING STUDIO ART PRACTICE
AS RESEARCH

The process of "theorizing" is a basic procedure of inquiry and hence a core element in research. We construct theories about how the world works all the time. Some of these are based on how we apply systems of knowledge to help solve problems and understand things. In these instances, our observations of some perplexing issue or event are reconciled or resolved as we draw on known theoretical knowledge to help explain what we see. In other situations, intuition, experience and tacit knowledge grounded in context-specific circumstances provide an empirical base for constructing new frameworks of understanding.

To accommodate the call for a broader notion of what the outcomes of research might be, three types of theorizing can be identified (Mithaug, 2000). First, *constructive theorizing* describes the conceptual and analytical process whereby theoretical explanations result from systematic reasoning based on the analysis of credible information. This kind of theorizing is most common within academic circles where established procedures are deployed to help direct reasoning and to apply criteria for assessing the credibility of evidence and the argument or proposition being advanced.

Critical theorizing is another approach that is based on the deconstructive practices used in postmodern discourse where theoretical structures seen to be problematic are critiqued. Underlying theoretical systems and received histories are challenged if they can be shown to maintain theories and practices that privilege particular positions, marginalize others, or deny multiple forms of discourse. The critical incursion is a process that acknowledges interpretive flexibility and is part of a system of thinking that renders texts of all sorts subject to reflexive analysis. Yet the process of critical theorizing is both a deconstructive and reconstructive process as the challenge to underlying theoretical systems and received discourse gives rise to new possibilities about how histories, ideas and practices can be re-imagined (Brown, 2003).

A third type of theorizing Mithaug (2000) identifies is *practitioner theorizing*, which I expand on in the remaining part of this chapter. Practitioner theorizing is a method commonly used in the field (the studio, classroom, community, Internet) where individuals and groups use a range of inductive and performative methods to find and solve problems, assess and enact change, and critique and create new practices. Practitioner theorizing, however, needs to be seen within broader systems of knowledge whereby the inventive insights associated with theories grounded in commonsense empiricism add to, and sometimes challenge, existing knowledge domains. "Folk" theories that we might absorb from authorities, influential sources, or homespun wisdom, therefore can prove to be insightful and novel. Yet they will remain naïve until located within a broader realm that is personally relevant and culturally valued.

The challenge of theorizing studio art practice requires the construction of a robust and defensible framework for considering the relationship between the theories and the practices that inform how art is made and how it can be studied and taught. There are several good reasons for constructing an analytical framework that describe the relationship between theory and practice.

- First, the identification of a range of theoretical issues and a breadth of constituent interests underscore the notion that art practice is a multidisciplinary endeavor that is firmly centered on art making.
- Second, such a framework can serve as a forum for considering debates in the field and ensuring that the boundaries that frame ongoing discussion are subject to continual review.
- Third, research studies that are undertaken can be located and critiqued within particular domains of theory and practice.

- Fourth, newer approaches to research such as the use of visual methods (Banks, 2001; Emmison & Smith, 2000; Pink, 2001; Rose, 2001) and computer-based qualitative data analysis (Fielding & Lee, 1998; Gahan & Hannibal, 1998; Tesch, 1990) can be assessed in terms of the domains of theory and practice in art education.
- Finally, a framework offers the possibility that art practice can be readily translated into other disciplinary forms of research discourse if the purpose demands it. In this way the research culture remains grounded in the theories and practices of art.

The need to be cautious about describing an analytical framework for theorizing art practice as a site for research is obvious. Any systematic structure has the potential to usher in a new orthodoxy as preferred interests and methods function to normalize practices. To this end it is essential that the goal of critical reflexivity is maintained and the boundaries shown in Figure 35.1 are seen as bridges rather than as barriers. I have high hopes that this dynamic stance could be readily maintained, and this should be the case as long as links to contemporary studio practices and critical cultural commentary remain central to any inquiry.

The structure described in Figure 35.1 connects the domains of practice and theory. The domain of practice describes the various constituents involved in the process of making art, studying art, and teaching art. The *artist* is the key figure in the creation of new knowledge that has the potential to change the way we see and think. Therefore the studio experience is a form of cognitive inquiry and is a site where research can be undertaken that is sufficiently robust to yield knowledge and understanding that is transformative, trustworthy, and socially and culturally relevant. The main research interest is to investigate how knowledge is created *in* the process of making art. Research in art therefore asks questions about the processes and products of artistic knowing. To do this the artist is both the researcher and the *object* of study. Many of the self-study protocols available can be deployed (Bullough & Pinnegar, 2001; Ellis & Flaherty, 1992; Reed-Danahay, 1997) if the desire is to formally investigate and subsequently communicate the outcomes of an inquiry to a wider constituency. Alternatively, the artist can be the *subject* of a case study.

	DOMAIN OF PRACTICE			
		Artist	Art Writer	Artwork	Visual Culture
DOMAIN OF THEORY	**Ends**	Research "IN" art Research Interest: Understanding "in" art by individual insight Characteristic: Individual–social constructed ideas	Research "ABOUT" art Research Interest: Understanding "about" art by interpretation Characteristic: Theoretical–institutional constructed views	Research "OF" art Research Interest: Understanding "of" art by knowledge Characteristic: Historical–cultural constructed forms and events	Research "THROUGH" art Research Interest: Understanding "through" art by contextualization Characteristic: Cultural–political constructed situations
	Means	Data Source: Self Method: Self-study Case study	Data Source: Others Method: Art criticism Art history	Data Source: Objects Method: Material culture study	Data Source: Contexts Method: Cultural study Educational study

FIG. 35.1. Theorizing art practice.

Art writers respond to the art they see and offer insights that take the art experience to new levels of engagement and understanding. As producers of new knowledge *about* art, critics, historians, and philosophers give insights into why and how art is made and interpreted, and ways it functions in society. The main research interest is to study the forms, methods, and meanings of art by making interpretations about art. To do this the art writer makes use of the many theoretical, conceptual, and methodological approaches available to study art (Adams, 1996; Carrier, 2003; Harris, 2001). These studies are shaped by the purpose of the inquiry, but like all areas of human engagement they are subject to individual, ideological, and institutional influences. Yet like any researcher, the task of the art writer is to produce work that is grounded in evidence that justifies the questions raised and supports the claims made.

The artwork carries its own status as a form of knowledge. Research *of* art subsequently communicates new insights into the ways that objects carry meaning about ideas, themes, and issues. As an object of study, an artwork is an individually and culturally constructed form that can be used to represent ideas and thus can be examined as a source of knowledge. Historical research provides an array of ways that images can carry meaning whether by means of description, representation, expression, or symbolization (Minor, 1994). More recent cultural discourse disrupts the relationship among the artwork, the artist, and the viewer and provides much more scope in the potential for meaning making that might result from an encounter with a work of art. This ensemble of influential factors allows the researcher to adopt many perspectives where the focus of study might be on the work of art itself, or other surrounding contexts that shape the way artworks take on cultural meaning. And the range of nondiscursive forms the art object assumes is continually expanding as artists craft new technological means into service.

Researchers, who study the way that art practice might function to assist us to better understand the contexts surrounding art so as to exercise control over the visual information we confront, will be interested in the communicative and political roles of art. Here the approach is to seek understanding by conducting research *through* art so as to determine the many functions and purposes to which art can be put. Using visual forms as agencies to advance various social, cultural, political, and educational ends has a long history, and the pervasive impact of visual culture warrants critical study. The analysis of artworks, artifacts and other mediated texts and the circumstances surrounding their production and presentation means that both the forms themselves and the viewing public are subjects of study. To move beyond the realm of critique and to a state of empowerment, there is a need for visual culture researchers to produce knowledge that can be acted on (Freedman, 2003). This educational role requires the use of a range of critical processes that are neither constrained by discipline boundaries nor restricted to particular textual forms. As a socially constructed process, "visuality" is a pervasive form of cultural knowledge and among other things warrants research responses that deploy a suitably critical image base.

The framework for theorizing art practice incorporates several of the dimensions of inquiry covered in the art education literature, especially debates about the importance of interpretation (Berger, 1980; Danto, 1986; Parsons, 1992), the study of artworks (Barrett, 2000; Lankford, 1992), and the advocacy for visual culture (Duncum & Bracy, 2001). What is not so apparent in the field is the study of the studio setting as a place of inquiry and as a site for sustained research that has the potential to yield significant knowledge. For some art educators the studio is a unique place for problem finding and problem solving, media exploration, and giving form to ideas of personal and social relevance (Beittel, 1979; Nadaner, 1998; Zurmuehlen, 1990). For others, it is the educational consequences of the studio experiences that offer tangible outcomes, and these tend to change in relation to different socio cultural circumstances and political interests (Brown & Korzenik, 1993). Understanding the studio art experience by doing case studies of artists that reveal insights into the creative mind as an individual and cultural construct is a common approach used to model artistic learning processes (Harris, 1990; Irwin & Miller, 1997; Krug, 1992/3; La Chapelle, 1991; Stuhr & Freedman, 1989; Taylor, 1989).

Another approach to exploring the studio experience is to identify connections between art-making processes and methods of inquiry that seek to confirm art practice as a form of research. Montgomery-Whicher (1997), for instance, draws parallels between the practice of drawing and the practices of phenomenological research.

> The abilities and attitudes necessary for phenomenological research, like those required for draw-ing, can be described in visual terms. Just as people learning to draw learn to temporarily set aside their usual conceptual knowledge of their subject matter in favor of vivid perceptual analysis, researchers must learn to see "with attentiveness and wonder," to see the everyday as worthy of attention, to see through surface appearances and worn-out clichés, to attend to what we ordinarily overlook, in short, to re-search. (p. 18)

Although this strategy helps highlight links among various studio-based learning processes with approaches found in certain research methodologies, a larger theoretical task remains. There is a necessity to construct theories of art practice that establish the legitimacy of the studio experience as a site that is capable of yielding plausible and trustworthy knowledge. In order to theorize about art practice in this way, one needs to consider the studio to be a place where philosophies and practices can be located and investigated, developed, and applied. The studio is also seen as a site of inquiry that is neither bounded by walls nor removed from the daily grind of everyday social activity. Further, studio art experiences are inclusive of the full range of ideas and images that inform individual, social, and cultural actions. Then there is a need to examine the kind of issues that arise at the institutional level and within the orbit of the artworld, as these can be quite diverse. These are some of the potential conditions that inform studio-based art practice and need to be seen as part of broader theoretical systems. Only when these kinds of issues are examined and the arguments are sufficiently robust to withstand scrutiny, may it be possible to explain the phenomena that we see in studios where individuals are transformed by the knowledge gained through art making.

Towards a Postdiscipline Research Practice

Can art practice be accepted as a form of research? That the studio practice of artists could share the imaginative scope, intellectual rigor, and systematic inquiry of the traditional sciences generate responses that range from acceptance, ambivalence to outright hostility. And these varied views come both from the broader academic community and from within the artworld. There is a general unease at the university level about how to accommodate artists' practice as research, and the need to identify and clarify problems of definition, equivalent practices and assessment issues.

The dilemma of how to integrate the arts within the academy is of course not new. The institutionalization of art practice has a long and illustrious history (Hubbard, 1963; Singerman, 1999). In each era, the formal training of the fine artist invariably has created a schism between those within the institution who see a need to uphold the canon and those from without who challenge it (Chadwick, 1990; Efland, 1990; Nochlin, 1988). Many advocates of the training of artists see the marketplace of the artworld as the arbiter that offers professional success, with institutions being mostly responsible for technical training. Those who seek academic status for the profession invariably have to respond to the challenge of setting creative practice on a more grounded disciplinary foundation. As such, the university setting exerts its own institutional power. The challenge is how to accommodate these demands yet also maintain a degree of integrity about what constitutes art as a field of study. It is in the area of research where these distinctions become the sharpest.

Two main strategies characterize the quest to confirm the academic status of studio-based research. The first involves assessing "equivalency" whereby the features of art practice are set on a scale that is comparable to levels of scholarship associated with the more traditional disciplines. Yet there is an inherent folly in assuming that practices from different fields can be validly compared if the criteria used are drawn from the discipline that holds the power. In the case of the sciences, the prevailing emphasis on marketplace research mostly assesses outcomes in terms of product yield and economic return. This utilitarian focus is an inadequate basis on which to assess the outcomes of art research. Perhaps, despite the acknowledgment that the arts and the sciences may share the same interest in the search for new ways of thinking about things, there can be parallel paths but no common road. Acceptance that a shared goal can be achieved by different means is a realization that is born as much from cultural maturity as it is from discipline interests.

The second institutional criterion used to assess the relative position of art practice in the academy is "benchmarking" or moderating. This is an evaluative process for identifying practices of merit based on the principle of peer assessment. The procedure involves the nomination of benchmarks that are grounded within local interpretations of what constitutes high-quality performance. Although this approach acknowledges diversity, it is labor intensive and requires considerable documentation to substantiate assessments and to offset perceived problems of lack of objectivity and comparability. Research in university settings is also characterized by its dissemination to a wide audience of professionals who are in a position to evaluate the outcomes against agreed on, if often unstated, performance indicators. In some cases the criteria applied will be external to the discipline, such as the amount of competitive research funding secured or other similar institutional measures.

Benchmarking, with its obvious similarity to the refereeing procedures used in the humanities and the sciences, comes close to the kind of peer-review process that is part of artworld practices. But what needs to be acknowledged is the existence of a multiplicity of artworlds (Young, 2001). Whether located within the domain of contemporary art, or within institutional settings, different artworld agencies will exercise somewhat different performance criteria. However, like all forms of public adjudication, the criteria for assessment centers on the interpretive decisions made and the congruence between the outcomes sought and the evidence presented.

Artists also make informed choices about the imaginative and intellectual approaches they use when they create and respond to art. The process of making insightful decisions when carrying out research *in* art is not predicated on the assumption that there is a prescribed body of knowledge one learns and then applies. Notwithstanding the repertoire of prior knowledge about relevant processes and products, at the outset there is little in the way of prevailing explanatory systems of knowledge within which new advances might be framed. Various theories of human processes, communal practices and cultural agencies obviously abound, and these serve as both a grounded set of conditions and an interpretive framework around which inquiry is referenced. This is as basic to creative inquiry as it is to scholarly research. However, making informed choices about creative ends and means involves selecting, adapting, and constructing ways of working and ways of seeing, and to do this one has to construct the tools of inquiry from an array of practices. When working from a base in contemporary art, the conceptions of the discipline are uncertain and the informing parameters are open-ended; yet the opportunity for inventive inquiry is at hand. In these circumstances the artist-researcher is seen to be participating in a "post-discipline" practice. Here there is little reliance on a prescribed content base; rather it is the deployment of a suitable methodological base that supports the questions being asked, which may take the researcher beyond content boundaries. In many cases, it is in universities where these opportunities may be best realized.

Studio-based programs at the university level that seek to move beyond the terminal exhibition as the principal form of documentation are required to meet the research criteria set by the parent institution for the completion of research degrees. This is most often seen to be the contribution of new knowledge to the field and is framed by reference to prevailing theories and practices. In the field of art education, this mostly means completing the academic requirements for doctoral study using established research protocols. In those institutions that confer higher degrees that incorporate a studio component the expectation is that a "thesis" topic might be investigated through studio-based inquiry. This is generally accompanied by an "exegesis," which is a critical interpretation that provides a context for the work undertaken. The thesis and exegesis are thus seen to constitute a body of research.

In completing projects within the academic setting the methods deployed by a studio-based researcher in "surrounding"[1] a research problem will be necessarily broad yet be personally relevant. There will also be public considerations if it is accepted that the creation and exhibition of art is an educational act that can have an impact on others. Even if the artist eschews public commentary or critical response, the artwork occupies a public space for others to encounter. As the artwork is subject to public discourse, it enters into a set of institutional relations and as such becomes part of an interpretive regime. Once the personal is made public, an exchange that involves others is underway. And if the artist-researcher, whether using self-study strategies or other research methods, gathers evidence that is grounded and defensible rather than merely confessional, then the outcomes open up educational discussion.

> Like other forms of research, self-study invites the reader into the research process by asking that interpretations be checked, that themes be critically scrutinized, and that the "so what" question be vigorously pressed. In self-studies, conclusions are hard won, elusive, are generally more tentative than not. The aim of self-study research is to provoke, challenge, and illuminate rather than confirm and settle. (Bullough & Pinnegar, 2001, p. 20)

Part of the legacy of conceptualizing studio art practice as research is the opportunity it gives to reconsider the inextricable relationship between theory and practice. Assembling a variety of new historical and critical traditions of fine arts alongside equally diverse studio practices means that the alliance between the artist and the art writer is seen as a collaboration that interrogates the artwork in a speculative quest to explore the unknown. For the artist, the artwork embodies the questions, ideas, feelings, impulses, and images; whereby for the critic, the word becomes the vehicle to advance new realms of investigative possibility. In this case, the coalition between the visual and the verbal is both critical and supportive.

ART AS TRANSCOGNITIVE PRACTICE AND TRANSFORMATIVE RESEARCH

Many theories and approaches have been applied to study the workings of the creative mind (Gardner, 1982; Gruber, 1981; West, 1997). Initially seen as a human capacity contained within the inventive headspace of the gifted but socially mute individual, recent conceptions of the mind see creativity as a social construct (Goodman, 1984; Weisberg, 1993). As such, the outcomes of creative thought and action are seen to be different when positioned relative to existing ideas. The outcome of these kinds of inquiries continues to influence art education and

---

[1] I am reminded of a radio interview with Gloria Steinem when she was asked how she "solved problems." After pausing a moment, she responded that one doesn't "solve problems," rather a more comprehensive approach is to "surround problems." This image nicely captures the approach used by artist-researchers.

our understanding of creative practices for imaginative thinking is at the heart of learning and teaching art. To better understand the cognitive coalition at the heart of the studio experience, there is a need to critique two long-term theoretical constructs, process and product, and assess them in relation to practices found in contemporary art. For it can be argued that what contemporary artists "do" provides access to foundational thinking in the field (Sullivan, 1993, 2002a).

At various times in the history of art education the prevailing belief has been that art learning should emphasize the *process* and at other times the *product* (Efland, 1990). One outcome of poststructuralist discussion was a critique of the merit of using binary opposites as conceptual organizers and the limits this tendency imposes on how the interdependency of structural relationships might be considered. Various dichotomies have been deconstructed such as objective-subjective, form and content, fact and fiction, cognition and affect, and female and male. A serious deficiency with the process-product dichotomy is apparent when the cognitive processes associated with artistic thinking are reviewed (Sullivan, 2000b).

A prominent position in art education is taken by the description of artistic thinking as primarily being the consequence of thought and action that is manifest in the creative product. Drawing as it does from analytical and Gestalt psychology as the defining paradigms, *thinking in a medium* is a useful description of this orientation. Research in the mid-20th century studied perceptual processes, as this seemed the most obvious way to approach what Arnheim (1969) labeled "visual thinking." Later approaches took more of a systems approach describing cognitive functioning as a form of symbolic processing (Gardner, 1973; Sullivan, 1986; Winner, 1982), and in some cases different cognitive functions were associated with different media (Carey & Gelman, 1991). The extrapolation of these ideas relative to the creative processes in adults (Gardner, 1993) further emphasized that artists think in a medium.

Artistic thinking is also seen as a cognitive process that is socially mediated (Berger, 1980). This view has its genesis in social constructionism (Vygotsky 1986; Wertsch, 1985), European interpretive theories (Habermas, 1984; Ricouer, 1981), and semiotics (Barthes, 1968; Hodge & Kress, 1988). Rather than focusing on behavioral outcomes to study cognition, one tries to make sense out of the intrinsic way language is used to construct stories and meanings through art talk, or discourse, that derives from encounters with art (Barrett, 2000; Carrier, 2003). In art education this cognitive orientation emphasizes the process and is best described as *thinking in a language* (Parsons, 1992). In this view, knowledge of cognition is built on the basis of the way linguistic signs function and understanding emerges as a process mediated by social and cultural conventions. Therefore thinking *in* art and thinking *about* art is language dependent and understanding about art is mediated by artworld conventions and the lifeworld context of the individual.

Art as Transcognitive Practice

The importance of context as an agent that informs our understanding is central to many recent arguments about cognitive development (Efland, 2002; Harris, 1998; Light & Butterworth, 1993; Sternberg & Wagner, 1994). Different contextual influences include human involvement as well as situational factors, physical features, and other environmental and cultural cues. Perkins (1992) for instance, describes "distributed cognition" as a process whereby thinking takes place within an interactive system that includes the self and others, and the artifacts we use. Situated cognition, on the other hand, is sometimes called sociocultural cognition whereby reality is a social construct and understanding emerges as a consequence of commonsense transactions in language and in other forms of communication (Efland, 2002; Rogoff & Lave, 1984). Inquiries into other factors such as discipline-specific influences and psychobiological constraints appear to be offering additional insights into the cognitive ensemble that informs artistic functioning (Changeux, 1994; Frith & Law, 1995).

Describing cognition as mental and physical activities that take place within a socio cultural context requires one to abandon the idea that art learning is best located in the process or the product. Viewing art practice as displaying cognitive processes that are distributed throughout the various media, language, situational, and cultural products offers the possibility of a more plausible account of artistic thinking. The belief that process and product inform each other does not mean that we reduce things to their common elements in the manner of viewing two overlapping circles, much like a Venn diagram. Rather, there is the expectation that both process and product represent complex systems of skill and understanding. Therefore when the processes and products of artistic experiences interact, the connections are strategic and purpose driven, rather than being all encompassing or reductive.

Inquiries into contexts that inform art practice generally focus on identifying artists' working processes (Csikzentmihalyi, 1990; Sullivan, 1996), or the products of artistic activity (Arnheim, 1986). These conform to the emphasis placed on either process or product described earlier. To examine a wider set of contextual factors that influence how artists think a study was undertaken with two artists who were invited to participate in a research project that culminated in an exhibition of their work in a commercial gallery (Sullivan, 1998). The aim of the project, titled Critical Influence, was to investigate approaches to contemporary visual arts practice so as to be able to better understand how artists' think, and act in response to the challenge of preparing work for an exhibition. Other artworld agents such as the exhibition setting, the gallery director, a critic, and the researcher also wearing a curatorial hat, were all considered to be active elements in the artistic endeavor. As well as producing artworks for exhibition, each artist also participated in a qualitative case study over several months leading up to the exhibition that mapped the influences on their art practice. Information was collected in the form of a series of interviews with each artist, along with studio observations recorded in written, photographic, and video formats. Interviews were also conducted with those involved in the exhibition process, including the gallery director and an art critic, whom both wrote catalog essays.

The outcomes of the Critical Influence project indicate that in mapping the cognitive character of artistic practice there is a need to reject the process-product dichotomy, as it does not adequately account for the range of activities observed. It was more appropriate to meld the psychological view that describes art learning as *thinking in a medium,* and the interpretive position that describes art knowing as *thinking in a language.* The resolution confirmed findings of an earlier study (Sullivan, 1996) that described the cognitive coalition observed as *thinking in a setting.* This cognitive ensemble involves an ongoing dialog between, within and around the artist, artwork, viewer, and context, where each has a role in co-constructing meaning. This process is ongoing in a constructivist way and strategic in nature as meaning is encompassed and negotiated. I describe this as *transcognition.*

> Transcognition is a process where the 'self' and 'others' are parallel and necessary agents of mind that inform each other through analysis and critique... The strategic interaction between the self and others occurs over time and involves iteration and negotiation as individual purpose is mediated by situational factors. During this time, concerns about process and product serve as a basis upon which practice is grounded. (Sullivan, 2002b, p. 9)

The outcomes of these studies of artists' practice confirm the distinctive transcognitive way artists think and create. Further, the studies reveal insights about how activities that take place in the studio constitute a form of research that is responsive, reflexive, and strategic and yields actions that construct new realities. In this case it is spurious to compare artistic inquiry to scientific inquiry, because even though the quest for human insight is similar, artists and scientists follow different paths. After all, scientists think about how progress leads to change, and artists think about how change leads to progress.

Art Practice as Transformative Research

During modernist times the prevailing construct was: "to *see* is to know." This was grounded in an empirical understanding based on direct experience and was mostly achieved by participation in the grand tradition of cultural tourism. During postmodern times we live in a constructed visual world where there is little distinction between the real and the virtual. If we understand the constructions that shape what we see, then "to *know* is to see" (Rose, 2001). Therefore there are different ways of seeing and knowing the world. The critical task is to determine the social impact of these different visions and the creative task is to create forms of representation that have the capacity to reveal, critique, and transform what we know. This quest for understanding can be achieved by conceiving of art practice as a form of transformative research that makes full use of the potential of visual images to help reveal insights and understandings about issues of human concern. But what is the status of the visual image as a data source in research?

A review of recent research methods texts highlights a growing disquiet with the lack of a critically reflexive attitude (Brown & Jones, 2001; Scheurich, 1997; Stronach & MacLure, 1997). Although those advancing a perspective grounded in critical theory have advocated an emancipatory role for research for a long time (Kemmis & McTaggart, 1988; McTaggart, 1997) many of those deploying *visual* methods of research are content to see these approaches as merely a way of expanding the range of data available for analysis (Ball & Smith, 1992; Banks, 2001). This renewed interest in how images might be used as data has a long history of debate, particularly in sociology and anthropology, regarding the status of still and moving images. For many, the use of photography and film is questioned, as these forms of data are too subjective and messy and resist systematic analysis. It is somewhat ironic that many researchers in disciplines that pioneered field-based research remain wedded to practices that see the image as a device for documentation and the interpretation of visual forms mostly as an exercise in content analysis (Prosser, 1998). For instance, the use of photography is still being presented as an illustrative travelog and this severely misinterprets what a photograph is.

> Photographs of people and things stand for evidence in a way that pure narrative cannot. In many cases, visual information of what the people and their world looks like provide harder and more immediate evidence than the written word; photographs can authenticate a research report in a way that words alone cannot. (Ball & Smith, 1992, p. 9)

It seems that the telling quip that "cameras don't take photographs, people do" is not fully understood.

What is missing from much of the visual research method literature is an acknowledgment that the interpretation of visual data is not so much about trying to describe visual content. Rather, the task of the researcher is to understand how those who make images–artists and other cultural communicators–and those who interpret images–critics and other cultural commentators–construct their meanings as they present them in visual form. Obviously the image-based researcher also creates and interprets visual data so a central consideration is to address the need to be critical in assessing how the researcher makes meanings.

> The idea that subjective experience can be translated into objective knowledge is itself problematic for reflexive ethnography. Therefore an "analysis" through which visual data becomes written

academic knowledge has little relevance. Instead, ethnographers need to articulate the experiences and contexts from which their field notes, video recordings, photographs and other materials were produced, their sociological or anthropological understanding of these ethnographic contexts, and their relevance to wider academic debates. (Pink, 2001, p. 97)

This critical imperative implies that the visual image is more than a product that can be isolated and contextualized. The image is also constitutive of cultural practices, individual process, and information systems that are located within spaces and places; is evidence of mediated processes; and is indicative of visual regimes that may be tangible or invisible (Emmison & Smith, 2000; Rose, 2001; Van Leeuwen & Jewitt, 2001).

The pattern seen in areas of visual anthropology and visual sociology reflects a move in life science research whereby the visual image is being seen as a form of data representation that has particular properties and possibilities. As such, it is no longer sufficient to accept the visual image as merely an alternative form of data that is assessed in relation to the dominant modes of representation. Visual images *cannot* be understood by comparing them to words or numbers. Rather, a different set of theoretical parameters is needed to fully understand the way images reveal insights and understandings. This principle is accepted by art historians and cultural theorists who understand the dynamic, interpretive relationships among the object, creator, and viewers; and related cultural, political, and institutional regimes that influence how knowledge is constructed and made problematic; and how meanings are made (Bal, 1996; Heywood & Sandywell, 1999; Hooper-Greenhill, 2000).

To understand the role of the artist as a creator of visual images, and the potential to conduct research "in" art using studio practice, there is a need to consider the changing function of the artist. The idea of the artist as social recluse or a cultural lamplighter of genius is an inadequate representation. Nor is it reasonable to accept the image of the artist-teacher as someone whose creative expertise is merely a model to emulate. The contemporary artist adopts many patterns of practice that dislodge discipline boundaries, media conventions, and political interests, yet still manages to operate within a realm of cultural discourse that is both reflexive and coercive at the same time. The image of the artist as creator, critic, theorist, teacher, activist, and archivist partly captures the range of art practice today.

The artist-researcher is a notion that is not inconceivable nowadays, as the kind of practices that constitute what can happen in the studio can readily be placed within the discourse of cultural and educational research. This is especially apparent if the trends evident in research continue to move beyond the quest for explanatory paradigms as the long dominant positivist practices reveal themselves unable to cope with the breadth and depth of human action. This is evident if the changing role of the visual image is considered. Originally conceived as an object or icon representative of a time or place, or as an informational record, the associated research method defined the visual image as an instrument of culture, and the research task was to determine how it was used in explaining the way the world worked. More recently, however, visual images are seen as textual forms of all sorts and as sites for ideas that are taken up by an interpretive community. The research method defines the visual image as an agent of change, and the research task is to reveal how it helps us understand the transformative power of knowledge.

Researching art practice can therefore be seen as a viable way to reveal the kind of knowledge that is unique to artistic understanding. The approach to inquiry runs parallel to the ideas and methods from the social sciences that promote the critical application of visual research methods. For instance, adventurous social science researchers are beginning to use the visual image not merely to record or illustrate social texts, but as a means to create and critique new knowledge by applying methods that highlight the contested nature of visual cultural practices (Rose, 2001). Others are not trying to make "truth" claims and instead are applying ethnographic methods as an imaginative and reflexive act that reveals new insights about others (Hine, 2000; Pink, 2001). Yet, although research practices in the visual arts are found in the studio, in galleries, in communities, on the street, in texts, or on the Internet, they have yet to find a rightful place within the academy. Therefore the question to be asked is whether it is possible to conceive of research projects in art that incorporate a range of ways of presenting, encountering, and analyzing information that is sufficiently robust to move beyond explanatory theory to produce new knowledge that is transformative? Is it possible to consider "the visual," not only as a descriptive or interpretive form but also as an agent of transformation in *constructing* new knowledge, not *finding* it? Seen from this perspective, the role of visual data in research can be used to move beyond the contribution to explanatory knowledge production, and to a more ambitious state of transformative knowledge construction.

CONCLUSION

As an area of individual, social and cultural inquiry, visual arts has, for the most part, remained outside the mainstream of community debate. Although no stranger to controversy due to the capacity to divide public opinion, as a serious social phenomenon, visual arts remains mostly sequestered within a limited cultural and political orbit. At worst, visual arts is seen as elitist, at best visual arts is misunderstood. Even when included in schools and institutions of higher education, visual arts programs and art education courses struggle for acceptance as important areas of the curriculum. Existing misconceptions about the intellectual status of learning in visual arts means that the scholarly, cultural and social significance of art is grossly under valued. To redress this I explored the theoretical basis of artistic practice and position this within the discourse of research.

The approach taken examines visual arts as a form of inquiry within the theories, practices and contexts used by artists. The critical and creative investigations that occur in studios, galleries, on the Internet, in community spaces, and other places where artists work, is presented as a form of research that is grounded in art practice. Rather than adopting methods of inquiry from the social sciences, the research practices advocated here subscribe to the view that while similar research goals can be set, they can be achieved by following different yet complementary paths. What is common is the attention given to rigor and systematic inquiry, but in a way that privileges the role imagination and intellect plays in constructing knowledge that is not only new but has the capacity to transform human understanding.

A central claim made in this chapter is that understanding is a viable goal of educational research and that explanatory theories of human learning need to be supplemented with transformative theories of individual and social action. It is further contended that these emancipatory theories can be found within the thoughts, ideas, and actions that result from making art. This posits the view that art practice can be claimed to be a legitimate form of research and that approaches to inquiry can be located within the studio experience. Therefore, studio art practice needs to be seen as a valuable site for raising theoretically profound questions and exploring them using robust visual methods that have the potential to yield critically grounded and individually transforming outcomes. Artistic practice therefore comprises a critical coalition that involves an ongoing dialog between, within and around the artist, artwork and context where each has a role to play in the creation of meaning. With these provisions in mind it appears highly likely that a new era of art education research is possible for those who see studio art as transcognitive practice and visual methods as a central means for conducting transformative research.

REFERENCES

Adams, L. S. (1996). *The methodologies of art: An introduction.* Boulder, CO: Westview Press.

Amundsen, R., Serlin, R. & Lehrer, R. (1992). On the threats that do not face educational research. *Educational Researcher, 21*(9), 19–23.

Arnheim, R. (1986). *New essays on the psychology of art.* Berkeley and Los Angeles, CA: University of California Press.

Arnheim, R. (1969). *Visual thinking.* Berkeley and Los Angeles, CA: University of California Press.

Arnstine, D. (1965). Needed research and the role of definitions in art. *Studies in Art Education, 7*(1), 2–17.

Bal, M. (1996). *Double exposure: The subject of cultural analysis.* New York: Routledge.

Ball, M. S., & Smith, G. W. H. (1992). *Analyzing visual data.* Newbury Park, CA: Sage.

Banks, M. (2001). *Visual methods in social research.* London: Sage.

Barrett, T. (2000). *Criticizing art: Understanding the contemporary* (2nd ed.). Mountain View CA: Mayfield.

Barthes, R. (1968). *The elements of semiology* (A. Lavers and C. Smith, Trans.). New York: Hill and Wang.

Beittel, K. R. (1979). Unity of truth, language, and method in art education. *Studies in Art Education, 21*(1), 50–56.

Berger, J. (1980). *About looking.* New York: Pantheon Books.

Bresler, L. (1994). Zooming in on the qualitative paradigm in art education: Educational criticism, ethnography, and action research. *Visual Arts Research, 20*(1), 1–19.

Brockman, J. (1996). *The third culture: Beyond the scientific revolution.* Touchstone: Simon & Schuster.

Brown, T., & Jones L. (2001). *Action research and postmodernism.* Buckingham: Open University Press.

Brown, M., & Korzenik, D. (1993). *Art making and education.* Urbana, IL: University of Illinois Press.

Brown, N. (2003). Art as a practice of research. *Proceedings of the 31st InSEA World Congress: InSEA Member Presentations Papers and Workshops CD-ROM.* New York: The Center for International Art Education, Inc., Teachers College Columbia University.

Bruner, J. (1990). *Acts of meaning.* Cambridge, MA: Harvard University Press.

Bruner, J. (1996). *The culture of education.* Cambridge, MA: Harvard University Press.

Bullough, R. V., Jr., & Pinnegar, S. (2001). Guidelines for quality in autobiographical forms of self-study. *Educational Researcher, 30*(3), 13–21.

Carey, S., & Gelman, R. (Eds.). (1991). *The epigenesis of mind: Essays in biology and cognition.* Hillsdale, NJ: Lawrence Erlbaum Associates.

Carrier, D. (2003). *Writing about visual art.* New York: Allworth Press.

Chalmers, F. G. (1981). Art education as ethnology. *Studies in Art Education, 22*(3), 6–14.

Chadwick, W. (1990). *Women, art, and society.* London: Thames and Hudson.

Changeux, J. (1994). Art and neuroscience. *Leonardo, 27*(3), 189–201.

Cizek, G. (1995). Crunchy granola and the hegemony of the narrative. *Educational Researcher, 24*(2), 26–28.

Creswell, J. W. (2002). *Research design: Qualitative, quantitative, and mixed methods approaches* (2nd Ed.). Thousand Oaks, CA: Sage.

Csikzentmihalyi, M. (1990). *Flow: The psychology of optimal experience.* New York: Harper & Row.

Danto, A. C. (1986). *The philosophical disenfranchisement of art.* New York: Columbia University Press.

Danto, A. C. (2001, May 28). In the bosom of Jesus. *The Nation,* 30–34.

Duncum, P., & Bracy, T. (Eds.). (2001). *On knowing: Art and visual culture.* Christchurch, NZ; Canterbury University Press.

Ecker, D. W. (1965). Editorial: On the possibility of theory in art. *Studies in Art Education, 6*(2), 1–6.

Efland, A. D. (1964). Theory and research in art education. *Studies in Art Education, 6*(1), 8–13.

Efland, A. D. (1990). *A history of art education. Intellectual and social currents in teaching the visual arts.* New York: Teachers College Press.

Efland, A. D. (1995). The spiral and the lattice: Changes in cognitive learning theory with implications for art education. *Studies in Art Education, 36*(3), 134–153.

Efland, A. D. (2002). *Art and cognition: Integrating the visual arts in the curriculum.* New York: Teachers College Press and Reston, VA: National Art Education Association.

Eisner, E. W. (1964). Toward a new era in art education. *Studies in Art Education, 6*(2), 54–62.

Eisner, E. W. (1985). *The art of educational evaluation: A personal view.* London: The Falmer Press.

Eisner, E. W. (1991). *The enlightened eye: Qualitative inquiry and the enhancement of educational practice.* New York: Macmillan Publishing Company.

Eisner, E. W. (1993). Forms of understanding and the future of educational research. *Educational Researcher, 22*(7), 5–11.

Eisner, E. W. (1999). Rejoinder: A response to Tom Knapp. *Educational Researcher, 28*(1), 19–20.

Ellis, C., & Flaherty, M. G. (Eds.). (1992). *Investigating subjectivity: Research on lived experience.* Newbury Park, CA: Sage.

Emmison, M., & Smith, P. (2000). *Researching the visual: Images, objects, contexts, and interactions in social and cultural inquiry.* London: Sage.

Feyerabend, P. (1991). *Three dialogues on knowledge.* Oxford, UK: Blackwell Publishers Ltd.

Fielding, N. G., & Lee, R. M. (1998). *Computer analysis and qualitative research.* London: Sage.

Freedman, K. (2003). *Teaching visual culture.* Reston, VA: National Art Education Association.

Frith, C., & Law, J. (1995). Cognitive and psychological processes underlying drawing skills. *Leonardo, 28*(3), 203–205.

Gahan, C., & Hannibal, M. (1998). Doing qualitative research using QSR NUD•IST. London: Sage.

Gardner H. (1973). *The arts and human development.* New York: Wiley.

Gardner, H. (1982). *Art, mind and brain: A cognitive approach to creativity.* New York: Basic Books.

Gardner, H. (1993). *Creating minds.* New York: Basic Books.

Goodman, N. (1976). *Languages of art.* Indianapolis, IN: Hackett.

Goodman, N. (1984). *Of mind and other matters.* Cambridge, MA: Harvard University Press.

Gross, P., & Levitt, N. (1994). *Higher superstition: The academic left and its quarrels with science.* Baltimore: Johns Hopkins University Press.

Gruber, H. (1981). *Darwin on man: A psychological study of scientific creativity.* Chicago: University of Chicago Press.

Habermas, J. (1984). *The theory of communicative action. Volume 1, Reason and the rationalization of society* (T. McCarthy, Trans.). Boston, MA: Beacon Press.

Harris, I. B. (1990). The creative process from the perspective of artists. *Arts and Learning Research, 8*(1), 163–188.

Harris, J. D. (1998). *The nurture assumption.* New York: Touchstone: Simon & Schuster.

Harris, J. H. (2001). *The new art history: A critical introduction.* London: Routledge.

Heywood, I., & Sandywell, B. (Eds.) (1999). *Interpreting visual culture: Explorations in the hermeneutics of the visual.* New York: Routledge.

Hine, C. (2001). *Virtual ethnography.* London: Sage.

Hodge, R., & Kress, G. (1988). *Social semiotics.* Ithaca, NY: Cornell University Press.

Hooper-Greenhill, E. (2000). *Museums and the interpretation of visual culture.* New York: Routledge.

Hubbard, G. (1963). The development of the visual arts in the curriculum of American colleges and universities. *Dissertation Abstracts International.* (University Microfilms No. 63-4607).

Irwin, R., & Miller, L. (1997). Oral history as community-based participatory research: Learning from First Nations women artists. *Journal of Multicultural and Cross-Cultural Research in Art Education, 15,* 10–22.

Jackson, P. (1990). The functions of educational research. *Educational Researcher, 19*(7), 3–9.

Kaufman, I. (1959). Some reflections on research in art education. *Studies in Art Education, 1*(1), 9–18.

Kemmis, S., & McTaggart, R. (Eds.). (1988). *The action research planner.* Victoria, Australia: Deakin University.

Kirk, J., & Miller, M. L. (1986). *Reliability and validity in qualitative research.* Newbury Park, CA: Sage Publications.

Krug, D. (1992/3). The expressive and cultural practices of a non-academically educated artist, Ellis Nelson, in the micro and macro environment. *Journal of Multicultural and Cross-Cultural Research in Art Education, 10/11,* 20–48.

LaChapelle, J. R. (1991). In the night studio: The professional artist as an educational role model. *Studies in Art Education, 32*(3), 160–170.

Lankford, E. L. (1992). *Aesthetics: Issues and inquiry.* Reston, VA: National Art Education Association.

LeCompte, M. D., & Goetz, J. P. (1982). Problems of reliability and validity in ethnographic research. *Review of Educational Research, 52,* 31–60.

Light, P., & Butterworth, G. (Eds.). (1993). *Context and Cognition: Ways of learning and knowing.* Hillsdale, NJ: Lawrence Erlbaum Associates.

May, W. T. (1993). "Teachers-as-researchers" or action research: What is it, and what good is it for art education? *Studies in Art Education, 34*(2), 114–126.

McTaggart, R. (Ed.). (1997). *Participatory action research: International contexts and consequences.* Albany, NY: State University of New York Press.

Miller, D. (Ed.). (1985). *Popper selections.* Princeton, NJ: Princeton University Press.

Minor, V. H. (1994). *Art history's history.* Englewood Cliffs, NJ: Prentice-Hall.

Mithaug, D. E. (2000). *Learning to theorize .* Newbury Park, CA: Sage.

Montgomery-Whicher, R. (1997). Drawing from life: The practice of art and research. *N.S.C.A.D. papers beyond form: Transformation through imagery and action.* Nova Scotia, Canada: Nova Scotia College of Art and Design.

Nadaner, D. (1998). Painting in the era of critical theory. *Studies in Art Education, 39*(2), 168–182.

Nochlin, L. (1988). *Women, art, and power and other essays.* New York: Harper & Row.

Parsons, M. (1992). Cognition as interpretation in art education. In B. Reimer & R. Smith (Eds.), *The arts, education, and aesthetic knowing.* Chicago: The National Society for the Study of Education.

Parsons, M. (1995). Art and culture, visual and verbal thinking: Where are the bridges? *Australian Art Education, 18*(1), 7–14.

Perkins, D. (1992). *Smart schools.* New York: Basic Books.

Perkins, D. (2000). *The Eureka effect: The art and logic of breakthrough thinking.* New York: Norton.

Pink. S. (2001). *Visual ethnography.* London: Sage.

Prosser, J. (1998). *Image-based research: A sourcebook for qualitative researchers.* London: Falmer Press.

Reed-Danahay, D. E. (Ed.). (1997). *Auto/Ethnography.* New York: Berg.

Ricœur, P. (1981). *Hermeneutics and the human sciences: Essays on language, action, and interpretation* (J. B. Thompson, Trans.). New York: Cambridge University Press.

Rogoff, B., & Lave, J. (Eds.). (1984). *Everyday cognition: Its development in social context.* Cambridge: Harvard University Press.

Rose, G. (2001). *Visual methodologies.* London: Sage.

Salomon, G. (1991). Transcending the qualitative-quantitative debate: The analytic and systematic approaches to educational research. *Educational Researcher, 20*(6), 10–18.

Sacca, E. (1989). Typologies in art education: How to live with them and how to live without them. *Visual Art Research, 15*(2), 58–70.

Scheurich J. L. (1997). *Research method in the postmodern.* London: Falmer Press.

Singerman, H. (1999). *Art subjects: Making artists in the American university.* Berkeley, CA: University of California Press.

Smith, J. K., & Heshusius, L. (1986). Closing down the conversation: The end of the quantitative-qualitative debate among educational inquirers. *Educational Researcher, 15*(1), 4–12.

Snow, C. P. (1959). *The two cultures.* Cambridge: Cambridge University Press.

Sternberg, R. J., & Wagner, R. K. (1994). *Mind in context: Interactionist perspectives on human intelligence.* New York: Cambridge University Press.

Stokrocki, M. (1997). Qualitative forms of research methods. In S. D. La Pierre & E. Zimmerman (Eds.), *Research methodologies for art education* (pp. 33–55). Reston, VA: National Art Education Association.

Stronach, I., & MacLure, M. (1997). *Educational research undone: The postmodern embrace.* Buckingham, UK: Open University Press.

Stuhr, P., & Freedman, K. (1989). A field study of two prominent and successful fine artists. *Arts and Learning Research, 7*(1), 38–51.

Sullivan, G. (1986). A covariance structure model of symbolic functioning: A study of children's cognitive style, drawing, clay modelling and storytelling. *Visual Arts Research, 12*(1), 11–32.

Sullivan, G. (1993). Art-based art education: Learning that is meaningful, authentic, critical and pluralist. *Studies in Art Education, 35*(1), 5–21.

Sullivan, G. (1996). Critical interpretive inquiry: A qualitative study of five contemporary artists' ways of seeing. *Studies in Art Education, 37*(4), 210–225.

Sullivan, G. (1998). *Critical influence: A visual arts research project with Jayne Dyer and Nikki McCarthy.* CD-ROM, College of Fine Arts, University of New South Wales.

Sullivan, G. (2002a). Ideas and teaching: Making meaning from contemporary art. In Y. Gaudelius & P. Speirs (Eds.), *Contemporary issues in art education* (pp. 23–38). Upper Saddle River, NJ: Prentice-Hall.

Sullivan, G. (2002b). Artistic thinking as transcognitive practice: A reconciliation of the process-product dichotomy. *Visual Arts Research, 22*(1), 2–17.

Tashakkori, A., & Teddlie, C. (1998). *Mixed methodology: Combining qualitative and quantitative approaches.* Thousand Oaks, CA: Sage.

Taylor, C. (1989). The work of art as hermeneutic process: An artist "takes on" Heidegger. *Visual Arts Research, 15*(2), 52–57.

Tesch, R. (1990). *Qualitative research: Analysis types and software tools.* Basingstoke, Hampshire: The Falmer Press.

Van Leeuwen, T., & Jewitt, C. (Eds.). (2001). *Handbook of visual analysis.* Thousand Oaks, CA: Sage.

Vygotsky, L. (1986). *Thought and language* (A. Kozulin Trans.). Cambridge, MA: The MIT Press.

Weisberg, R. W. (1993). *Creativity: Beyond the myth of genius.* New York: Freeman.

Wertsch, J. V. (1985). *Vygotsky and the social transformation of mind.* Cambridge, MA: Harvard University Press.

West, T. G. (1997). *In the mind's eye.* Amherst, NY: Prometheus Books.

Winner, E. (1982). *Invented worlds: The psychology of the arts.* Cambridge, MA: Harvard University Press.

Young, J. O. (2001). *Art and knowledge.* London: Routledge.

Zurmuehlen, M. (1990). *Studio art: Praxis, symbol, presence.* Reston, VA: National Art Education Association.

36

Curriculum Change for the 21st Century: Visual Culture in Art Education

Kerry Freedman
Northern Illinois University

Patricia Stuhr
The Ohio State University

CURRICULUM AND VISUAL CULTURE

National and international art educators have begun to move away from the emphasis on traditional fine arts disciplines toward a broader range of visual arts and cultural issues (Ballengee-Morris & Stuhr, 2001; Barbosa, 1991; Blandy, 1994; Congdon, 1991; Duncum, 1990; Freedman, 1994, 2000; Garber, 1995; Garoian, 1999; Hernández, 2000; Hicks, 1990; Jagodzinski, 1997; Neperud, 1995; Smith-Shank, 1996; Tavin, 2000). These contributors to the field have argued for a transformation of art education in response to changing conditions in the contemporary world where the visual arts, including popular arts and contemporary fine art, are an increasingly important part of the larger visual culture that surrounds and shapes our daily lives. In the process of this transformation, art educators are replacing older views of curriculum and instruction with an expanded vision of the place of visual arts in human experience.

The change in art education has historical roots. From the beginning of public school art education in the late 19th century, a range of design forms have been included in the field. For example, early art education focused on industrial drawing and handicrafts; children's interests became a topic of art education by the 1920s; art in daily life was a slogan of the 1930s; during World War II, visual propaganda was taught in school; and during the 1960s, crafts increased in popularity. In the following 2 decades, a few art educators addressed important issues in the uses of popular culture and mass-media technologies, contextualizing these in relation to students' lives (Chalmers, 1981; Grigsby, 1977; Lanier, 1969; 1974; McFee & Degge, 1977; Neperud, 1973; Wilson & Wilson, 1977; Wilson, Hurwitz, & Wilson, 1987).

Substantial differences exist between those roots of a generation or more ago and the contemporary movement. This is the case, in part, because the global virtual culture only suggested by theorists before the availability of interactive, personal computers in the early 1980s has now become a reality with its associated proliferation of images and designed objects. The current transformation of art education is more than just a broadening of curriculum content and changes in teaching strategies in response to the immediacy and mass distribution of imagery. It includes a new level of theorizing about art in education that is tied to emergent postmodern philosophies based on this growing environment of intercultural, intracultural, and transcultural visualizations.

The shift to visual culture not only refers to expanding the range of visual arts forms included in the curriculum but also to addressing issues of imagery and artifacts that do not center on form per se. This includes issues concerning the power of representation, the formation of cultural identities, functions of creative production, the meanings of visual narratives, critical reflection on technological pervasiveness, and the importance of interdisciplinary connections. The focus in recent decades on fine arts disciplines in U.S. art curriculum and standardized testing have resulted in the exclusion of such critical aspects of visual culture in art education. In fact, these aspects of the visual arts have been given more attention in "nonart" school subjects such as anthropology and sociology and feminist, cultural, and media studies (Collins, 1989; Mirzoeff, 1998; Scollon & Scollon, 1995; Sturken & Cartwright, 2001). If the intention of education is to prepare students for personal fulfillment and to constructively contribute to society, then art education must deal with newly emerging issues, problems, and possibilities that go beyond the constraints of learning offered by a discipline-based curriculum and standardized forms of assessment.

The purpose of this chapter is to discuss art education in terms of the broadening realm of visual culture and to theorize about curriculum change. The development of a conceptual framework for postmodern visual culture is vital to any contemporary teaching with a goal of critical reflection. Although scholars in art education and other fields have begun to develop theoretical underpinnings for understanding visual culture, the topic from an educational perspective remains severely undertheorized. As a result, much theoretical work needs to be done in order to promote appropriate interpretations and applications of visual culture in art education. In this chapter, we have drawn on scholarship from inside and outside of the field to lay a foundation for curriculum theory. In the following main section, we support the argument for broadening the domain of art education by presenting the visual arts in their contemporary, sociocultural context. After discussing this context of visual culture, we address shifts in recent theory and practice of art education in the second main section.

BROADENING THE DOMAIN OF ART EDUCATION

A global transformation of culture has occurred that is dependent on visual images and artifacts ranging from what we wear to what we watch. We live in an increasingly image-saturated world where television news may control a person's knowledge of current events, where students spend more time in front of a screen than in front of a teacher, and where newborn babies are shown videos to activate still-developing neurons. Visual culture is pervasive and it reflects, as well as influences, general cultural change. The pervasiveness of visual cultural forms and the freedom with which these forms cross various types of traditional borders can be seen in the use of fine art icons recycled in advertising, computer-generated characters in films, and the inclusion of rap videos in museum exhibitions. The visual arts are the major part of this larger visual culture that includes fine art, advertising, folk art, television and other performance arts, housing and apparel design, mall and amusement park design, and other forms of visual production and communication. Anyone who travels, watches rock videos, sits on a chair, enters a building, or surfs the Web experiences the visual arts. Visual culture is the totality of humanly designed images and artifacts that shape our existence.

The increasing number of visual culture objects and images shapes not only art education in the 21st century but also the intergraphical and intertextual connections between visual forms (Freedman, 2000, 2003). The conceptual and physical interactions of various images and artifacts, forms of representation, and their meanings are fundamental to the way in which the visual arts are interpreted and understood. Art now crosses many old borders of culture and form. For example, advertising photography, body fluids, and Star Wars paraphernalia are all exhibited in art museums. As a result, knowledge of what has traditionally been considered fine art objects and "good" taste can no longer be seen as the only visual cultural capital to serve elementary, secondary, or higher education students. Fine art is still of great value in education and an important part of historical and contemporary visual culture; however, the broader, creative, and critical exploration of visual culture, and its local, state, national, and global meanings is a more appropriate focus if we want students to understand the importance of visual culture.

In this section of the chapter, we discuss four conditions of the contemporary world that contextualize art education and lead to changes in the production and study of visual culture by students. First, important characteristics of personal and communal identities are discussed in terms of representations constructed in and through the range of visual culture. Second, increasing daily interactions with newer media, particularly visual technologies, are addressed as a major part of contemporary human experience. Third, the permeable quality of disciplinary boundaries and the significance of interdisciplinary knowledge to the complexity of visual culture are discussed. Fourth, the importance of critical processes of interpretation in understanding the complexity of visual culture is presented. Although, we have delineated these conditions into sections for this chapter, the contents of these sections actually blur and interact.

Social Issues and Cultural Identities

At one time, sociologists thought popular forms of visual culture merely reflected social life. Contemporary images and artifacts, however, are a major part of social life. Visual culture teaches people (even when we are not conscious of being educated) and, in the process, we recreate ourselves through our encounters with it. As we learn, we change, constructing and reconstructing ourselves. Global culture functions through visual culture (television, radio, newspapers, telephones, faxes, World Wide Web, etc.) to produce hegemonic, virtual realities, including our social consciousness and identities.

The influence of visual culture on identity occurs on personal and communal levels. Various aspects of personal identity are made up of many cultural bits. Culture is a collage of many cultural identities that are selected and translated on a continuing basis (Clifford, 1988). Far from being a unified whole, any particular identity is a combination of others, with its resulting contradictions and incongruities. These identities include age, gender, and/or sexuality, socioeconomic class, exceptionality (giftedness, differently abled, health), geographic location, language, ethnicity, race, religion, and political status.

All we can ever understand of a cultural group is based on individual, temporal experience as lived or expressed. Fragmented knowledge of identity is all that can exist, making it difficult to understand even our own cultures and social groups. However, the more that is learned about visual culture, the better we can grasp the concept of identity; and the more that is learned about the various members of a particular group, the more richly we can understand their visual culture (Stuhr, 1999). A recognition of our own sociocultural identities and biases makes it easier to understand the multifaceted identities of others. It also helps us to understand why and how students respond to visual culture as they do (Ballengee-Morris & Stuhr, 2001; Freedman & Wood, 1999).

Communal identity is constructed by social groups at the international, national, regional, state or province, county, and local community levels where institutions, laws, and policies interact and change. These communal levels are continually being constructed and reconstructed in accordance with sociopolitical positions. Communal identity is an important conceptual site where cultural beliefs and values are formed, sanctioned, and/or penalized as it mediates the uncertainty and conflict of daily life and change.

Global visual culture is created through commodification and distributed at an international level. The merchandise of global visual culture has expanded beyond products to ideology, spirituality, and aesthetics. This merchandizing can be a useful tool when coopted for positive educational purposes, such as for saving endangered species, protecting the environment, or promoting human rights; however, it can have negative effects as well when it colonizes, stereotypes, and disenfranchises. As a result of the expanding, global influence of visual culture in the formation of identity and lived experience, art education has a new global significance. Through lived experience with the increasing range, availability, and speed of visual forms, many art educators have come to understand that visual culture is in a continual state of becoming and should be taught as such.

Visual Technologies

A critical issue of visual culture is the place of visual forms produced through the use of computer and other advanced technologies. Computer technology is not only a medium but also a means that has enabled people to see things previously unimagined and to cross borders of form from the fine arts to the mass media to scientific visualization. Visual technologies allow people to create, copy, project, manipulate, erase, and duplicate images with an ease and speed that challenges distinctions of talent, technique, and the conceptual location of form. It could be argued that many of the issues that are seen as critical to postmodern visual culture have existed historically in other forms; however, the global technological presence of images and objects, the ease and speed with which they can be produced and reproduced, and the power of their pervasiveness demand serious attention in education.

Contemporary visual technologies have promoted the collapse of boundaries between education and entertainment. Advertisements, Web sites, and even the news, combine education and entertainment to promote the sale if products and/or ideas. Consumers are approached as audiences through the instantaneous transmission of sound and imagery to even the most remote areas. Goods and ideas are pitched under the guise of enjoyable and addicting entertainment. This edu-tainment has fictional qualities that have become an important part of daily reality and the sensual qualities of the imagery are as seductive as they are didactic. It is the wide distribution of this interaction of seduction, information, and representation that makes newer visual technologies so powerful.

Although experiences with visual technologies were once considered an escape into a fictional, virtual world, students using technology today are understood as engaging with complex, global communities at multiple cognitive levels. We now experience technology as reality and appropriate visual culture as life experience, turning it into attitudes, actions, and even consciousness (Rushkoff, 1994). While we are being shaped by technological visual culture, we shape it through our fashion, toy, music, and other preferences. Corporations and advertising agencies videotape students in teen culture focus groups, who act as informants on the next "hot" or "cool" thing, which are then developed into products. The products are subsequently advertised and sold inside, as well as outside, of school to their peers through global visual technologies. The process illustrates one of the parts visual technologies plays in the fusion of education and entertainment as well as in the collapse of boundaries between student culture and corporate interests.

Visual culture forms are merging. Rarely do contemporary artists specialize in painting on canvas or sculpting in marble; painters do performance art; actors do rock videos; video artists recycle film clips; filmmakers use computer graphics, which are adapted for toys and T-shirt advertising; and advertisers appropriate paintings. Today's visual arts have moved beyond painting and sculpture to include computer graphics, fashion design, architecture, environmental design, television, comics and cartoons, magazine advertisements, and so on.

Visual culture also overlaps with arts not usually categorized as visual, such as dance and theater. Performance artists of many types use computerized lighting and sound to create atmospheric and dramatic effects. The performing arts are part of visual culture. Even music has become more visual through the increased use of rock videos and complex technologically produced light shows during concerts. Through the use of technology, such as computer graphics and audio software, art objects have increasingly become recycled bits of other objects that are collaged, reconstructed, and reproduced.

In the process of changing the visual arts, advanced technologies have changed what it means to be educated in the arts. In the context of postindustrialized culture, the visual arts can no longer be seen as isolated from general culture, the products of a few alienated, individual artists working in a small fine art community of museums, collectors, and galleries. Museum or gallery exhibition contact with original fine art objects is now only one of many possible experiences with the visual arts. Newer technologies have enabled encounters with the visual arts to become embedded in all aspects of our daily lives.

Permeable Arenas of Knowledge

It is becoming more difficult to distinguish the fine arts from other aspects of visual culture because the qualitative differences among these forms have become less discrete. Visual culture is a mode of experience that connects people through many and varied mediators. The variety and complexity of the experience are dependent on the possibility of *a range of quality* related to form, none of which should be inherently excluded from the investigation, analysis, and critique enabled by art education. Even concepts and objects previously considered fairly stable are in flux. Truth has shifted from an epistemological to an ontological issue: That is, it becomes less about what we know than who we are. Time has lost its neat linearity, space appears to expand and contract, and boundaries of various sorts have become blurred. Perhaps most important, postmodern visual culture makes imperative a connectedness that undermines knowledge as traditionally taught in school. It involves interactions among people, cultures, forms of representation, and professional disciplines. As suggested earlier, this condition has been particularly promoted through the use of visual technologies.

In light of these contemporary conditions, it seems less important than it once was to focus determinations of either worthiness of study or quality of object in education on distinctions of taste or between "high" and "low" arts. Such distinctions may be important to understanding some aspects of artistic practice, such as private collecting, museum exhibition, and the use of fine art in advertising. These distinctions of visual form have long been based on socioeconomic differences and are therefore contrary to the democratic purposes of schooling. Although such distinctions might be understandable as boundaries of professional training in a period of increasing specialization, we now live in a time that includes important challenges to extreme specialization. Such challenges are made by even highly specialized professionals who realize that solving the most serious and important problems of the world demand interdisciplinary and cross-disciplinary knowledge.

The realm of the visual arts inherently overlaps with other disciplinary domains. Artists and other cultural producers draw on all types of knowledge and cognitive processes to create. Recent research on cognition, and even predictions by labor leaders, suggests that learning in the future will have more to do with developing a range of knowledge that involves disciplinary, interdisciplinary, and interpersonal relationships than with the boundaries of professional disciplines (Solso, 1997). Connecting content typically considered part of other school subjects in the curriculum helps students to understand the importance and power of the visual culture and their place in the world.

Processes of Understanding Complexity

As a part of the process of concept formation in education, the arts have often been dichoto-mously categorized, inhibiting understanding and reducing the complexity of visual culture. The process of learning new concepts does involve dichotomous distinctions. For example, children with pets may begin to learn that a cow is a cow by learning that is not a dog or a cat; they learn to discern one style of painting by learning its differences from other styles (Gardner, 1972). However, if attempts to understand visual culture are successful, the dichotomies of early concept formation are overcome, the complexity of concepts becomes increasingly ap-parent, categories blur, and hard and fast distinctions become less discrete. At this level of understanding, oppositions become dualisms ("two sides of the same coin"), multiple perspec-tives are valued, and oversimplifications (such as stereotypes) are replaced by more complex representations.

Contemporary visual culture is too complex to be represented in a dichotomous fashion. The complexities are illustrated by practices such as image recycling, the difficulties of defin-ing creativity as originality, and the effects of maintaining conceptual oppositions (including distinctions such as fine vs. popular arts and male vs. female capabilities). As discussed earlier, it is not easy to view cultures or their creations as totally separate because they interact on many levels and through many media. Fine artists borrow imagery from popular culture, men borrow from women, and artists in one country borrow from those in other countries. These intersections are revealed and supported in and through visual cultural forms.

An increasing body of contemporary theory and artistic practice represents the seductive infusion of meaning in aesthetics as the power of visual culture (e.g., Ewen, 1988; Shusterman, 1989). The integral relationship between deep meaning and surface qualities is one of the reasons that visual culture is so complex. It is not the surface qualities of form that make art worth teaching in academic institutions; rather, it is the profound and complex qualities, based on their social and cultural contexts and meanings, that are attached to forms. In part, postmodern visual culture producers of various types reflect and enable this refocusing of aesthetic theory. They often reject formalistic uses of the elements and principles of design in favor of symbolic uses that suggest multiple and extended social meanings.

Making meaning from complex visual cultural forms occurs through at least three overlap-ping methods: (a) *communication*, (b) *suggestion*, and (c) *appropriation* (Freedman, 2003). Communication involves a fairly direct line of thought between the maker and the viewer. The maker has a message that she or he intends for viewers to understand, and the message is conveyed in as direct a manner as possible to an intended and understood audience. Suggestion involves a process by which association is stimulated in viewers by a maker (whether intended or not), resulting in the extension of meaning beyond the work. Appropriation involves the creative interpretation by a viewer who encounters a visual culture form in which the maker has intentionally diffused meaning. In a sense, viewers complete any work of art by drawing on their prior knowledge and experiences as they construct meaning. However, contemporary visual culture is often complex because postmodern artists deliberately confound the construc-tion of meaning. These conditions illustrate the importance of teaching visual culture as a process of creative and critical inquiry.

NEW APPROACHES TO ART EDUCATION: VISUAL CULTURE INQUIRY

In part, visual culture inquiry challenges traditional forms of art education because it is sen-sitive to the social and cultural issues discussed in the previous section. The foundation of art education conceptualized as visual culture inquiry is a matter of teaching for life in and through the visual arts. It helps students to recognize and understand the ambiguities, conflicts, nuances, and ephemeral qualities of social experience, much of which is now configured through imagery and designed objects.

In part, freedom in contemporary democracies is reflected through the ways in which visual realities are constructed, cutting across traditional artistic and social boundaries. Students and teachers are becoming aware of the power of visual culture in the formation of attitudes, beliefs, and actions. In dynamic ways, visual culture shapes the ways we look at ourselves and perceive others, often portraying individuals and groups in ways contradictory to the democratic purposes of schooling. At the same time, education is one of the last public forums for a potentially free critique of the products of mass distributed visual technologies that make up the media and visual culture and for thoughtful student reflection on their own production and uses of visual culture. The critical necessity of teaching visual culture in this context is seen in the lack of serious debate even in the "free" media as it becomes increasingly focused on entertainment (e.g., Aronowitz, 1994; Morley, 1992).

Perhaps the people most influenced by visual culture are children and adolescents. Students incorporate the social codes, language, and values of visual culture into their lives (Freedman & Wood, 1999; Tavin, 2001). Visual culture influences students' knowledge, affects their identity construction, and shapes their aesthetic sensibilities.

In the following sections, we first argue the importance of moving from a school foundation of modernist aesthetic policy based on industrial training to a more meaningful and relevant art education. Second, we discuss problems of atomizing visual culture in curriculum. Third, we focus on teaching as a process of helping individuals and learning communities to make meaning through the fusion of creative and critical inquiry.

Reconceptualizing Modernist Aesthetic Policy: Art Education Responds to Industrial Training

An unstated aesthetic policy has developed through the educational application of an aesthetic canon that underlies all of what we do. As policy, the canon has calcified and reproduced itself, through century-long practices of schooling. Like any educational policy, this aesthetic policy implies a social contract that is revealed through the modernist, industrial curriculum and standardized tests taken by students and teachers. It is a historical artifact that was important in its time for the development of the visual arts in the United States and, in public school art education, has been based on industrial design at least since Walter Smith's work in the 1870s. Times have changed, however, and the contract is being renegotiated. The new perspective of art education responds to contemporary change in what students need to know in and through the arts.

The industrial training model of education carries with it regimented, mechanistic training and the reproduction of traditional forms of knowledge through group conformity. As a result, students working within this model often make art that looks very much alike. These assembly-line-looking products, such as color wheels, are produced by rote and repeated in multiple grade levels. The emphasis on this model has enabled the development of the school art style (Efland, 1976, 1983) and has cramped teacher and student freedom in the exploration of conceptual complexity in both making and viewing. Of course, some technical exercises are important to art education, but to emphasize this model of instruction confounds the importance of art.

Like other school subjects, art education adopted industrial training as its basic approach in the late 19th century. Today, the business community has changed from a focus on modern, industrial production techniques to postmodern market information and services, in which home loans and vacations can be bought on the Web, children learn about outer space through role-play computer games, and people access maps through satellite connections in their cars. As discussed earlier, the history of art education is replete with examples of the inclusion of popular culture images and objects. The current movement leaves behind the technical emphasis of industrial training that alienates producers from the larger meanings associated with their production. Instead it gives attention to the multiple connections between form and meaning.

The industrial model in art education is based on analytical aesthetics. This aesthetic perspective has been treated in curriculum as if it is objective: That is, analytical aesthetics is not generally taught as if it were a socially constructed and culturally located philosophical stance. In curriculum, the analytic emphasis is formalism. Formalism is a pseudoscientific conception of aesthetics that developed in the late 19th and early 20th century at a time when science was gaining currency in application to all areas of social life. Other conceptions of aesthetics exist but have largely been ignored as philosophical analysis in art education.

Even when the focus of instruction is not formal per se (that is, when formal qualities are understood as supports for ideas) the educational presentation of formal qualities is not always responsive to social and cultural issues. Consider the example of frontal views of authority figures, which is often included as part of the aesthetic canon students must learn. Not only is this concept relatively trivial in the big picture of the small amount of time we have to teach students, but also it is Eurocentric. In certain African cultures, authority has been represented traditionally in female relief form in which its femaleness (protruding breasts and buttocks) is intended to be viewed from the side. Another instance where the Western canon of pictorial frontal views of authority does not hold up is in the context of traditional Plains Native American shields and teepees where authority figures are represented as part of symbolic narratives. Their authority might be recognized by headgear, size, and so on. Even in European art, the authority of male figures has been symbolically shown by uniforms, weapons, and even by connection to a spouse as in a pair of profile portraits. These examples illustrate that the focus of curriculum must change if students are to develop an understanding of the complexity of thought concerning visual imagery and artifacts.

The traditional focus on historical, fine art exemplars has tended to suggest a single line of Western stylistic development. Formal and technical qualities have been represented in curriculum as the most important connection between art objects. Even the educational emphasis of content, such as the figure, landscape, or still life, has often become formal and technical when teachers assign students to "make a Van Gogh sunflower painting" with paper plates and dry markers. In the past, the rich conceptual connections among images, objects, and other forms of culture, which are often their reasons for being, have been missed or hidden in such endeavors. The complex, interdisciplinary reasons we value such artists' ideas are neglected. Under these conditions, visual culture objects are transformed through education, often losing important attached cultural meanings.

Curriculum as Process: Challenging Atomistic Content and Assessment

Recently, general curriculum theorists have been struggling with the project of reconceptualizing curriculum from postmodern perspectives (Giroux, 1992; Pinar, 1988; Pinar, Reynolds, Slattery, & Taubman, 1996). This project is a response to the many social and cultural changes that are now influencing students' lives. The project of developing appropriate educational responses to such change is increasingly important as societies and cultures leave the secure thinking of modernistic forms of education, where knowledge and inquiry methods are represented as stable and curriculum is intended to be reproductive. For example, postmodern curriculum theorists point out that curriculum is not a neutral enterprise; it is a matter of selection. As a result, curriculum contains and reflects the interests of individuals and social groups. Patrick Slattery (1995) has argued that curriculum expresses autobiography because it is created by human beings who leave parts of themselves in their teaching and writing. He has suggested that curriculum should focus on issues of the self, because that is where learning takes place, and he argues that educators can use the concept of autobiography to better understand educational conditions. A postmodern understanding of the personal and social processes of curriculum planning and enactment exemplifies the aesthetic character of education and the importance of considering individual learning in relation to social contexts.

The modernist problem of curriculum may be thought of as having allowed a veil to fall over such social issues, hiding or obscuring them. This veil has covered the complexity and connections of artistic relationships as modernist curriculum has sought to continually break down knowledge into minute bits of information. As the curriculum has become more focused on small objectives and traditional, fine art exemplars are used over and over again, art has been transformed from visual expressions of multiple and complex ideas to oversimplified uses of formal and technical qualities.

The postmodern problem of curriculum is to lift the veil and thus make art education more meaningful than mere sensory experience. This could be accomplished by challenging students with inquiry based on creative production and critical reflection involving deep interrogations of images, artifacts, and ideas that approach the complexity of visual culture as experienced. This often requires some school subject integration.

The major issue of curriculum integration now can no longer be whether to integrate, but rather what, when, and how to teach students most effectively through the construction of integrated knowledge. Schools are adopting integrated approaches to curriculum in an effort to teach students the conceptual connections they need to succeed in contemporary life. Art education should help students know the visual arts in their integrity and complexity, their conflicting ideas as well as their accepted objects, and their connections to social thought as well as their connections to other professional practices.

As discussed earlier, confining the visual arts to narrow learning objectives and assessment strategies based on traditional notions of excellence in fine art disciplines is highly problematic. The old constructs of knowledge about the visual arts have included at least one other set of boundaries that has resulted in difficulties for an art education. It involves the question: Where do the boundaries of art stop and other school subjects begin? Reproducing narrow constructs of knowledge should not be the purpose of contemporary art education. Not only is finding a perimeter for the open concept of art difficult, but also it may be an ineffective way to approach curriculum. From a contemporary educational standpoint, our goal is to make as many connections as possible because connections produce integrated learning.

In order to reconceptualize curriculum in this way, it is necessary to understand curriculum as a process rather than as a single text. The process of curriculum *is* its product. Curriculum is not a unified whole. It is a collage of bits of information based on knowledge (Freedman, 2000, 2003). It is flexible, at some times sequential and at other times highly interactive, making connections not only to the previous lesson but also to life experiences.

An integral relationship exists between assessment and curriculum. Both must be of quality in order to have a successful program. An authentic perspective of assessment and curriculum is to develop both through community discourse. Criteria for assessment must be developed through community debate, but not allowed to be trivialized through excessive fragmentation and overassessment (Boughton, 1994, 1997).

Art education is no different in the dissolution of its boundaries from other areas and disciplines. Postmodernism and advances in computer and media technologies have enabled boundary erosion that has prompted new ways of conceptualizimg subject areas and what constitutes important disciplinary knowledge. As a result, new methods for investigation and data collection are continually being invented and developed. The arts figure prominently in these new methodological configurations (Barone & Eisner, 1997; Gaines & Renow, 1999; Prosser, 1998; Rose, 2001).

Artistic Production: Making Meaning Through Creative and Critical Inquiry

In the past, the focus on formal and technical attributes of production has limited our conception of curriculum and has been constrained by at least four interconnecting, historical foundations. First, there has been a focus on realistic representation as a major criterion for quality in student art. Teachers often cite parent and administrative pressure for this focus. A focus on realism, without conceptual foundation, addresses only one form of artistic production and ignores the importance of abstract and symbolic representations of ideas that are vital to human experience. Creative and critical problem investigation and production based on various forms of abstraction, fantasy, science-fiction, and so on can only be promoted through open-ended, independent inquiry leading to connective forms of representation.

Second, in conflict with the focus on realism, but coexisting with it is an emphasis on expressionistic characteristics and maintaining childlike qualities in student art. This has resulted in products that have formal and technical qualities that look somewhat like young children's art regardless of the conceptual sophistication of the student. The painterly quality of child art is valued as evidence of individual self-expression (in part, based on fine art styles such as abstract expressionism) and is a foundation of the aesthetic of late modernism. However, these expressionistic qualities are not necessarily evidence of individuality because they have been socially constructed and have become a criterion for group assessment.

Third, as discussed earlier, the industrial training model has led to a focus on formal and technical qualities, but these are also easy to teach and assess. Curriculum content is often selected and configured to be efficiently handled in the institutionalized settings of classrooms. With the emphasis on standardized curriculum and testing, the reliance on simplistic, easily observed products or results and procedures is convenient. Although these practices often trivialize art and are generally irrelevant to students' lives, they are considered efficient and effective by administrative and governing bodies, and teachers have been encouraged to perpetuate these practices.

Fourth, art teachers are forced to compete for funds and advocate for programs through art exhibitions for parents and administrators who are not well educated in the arts. As a result, teachers are often placed in a position of defending their place in the school community based on the success of exhibitions, which depend on a student art aesthetic that demonstrates a high degree of formal and technical skill, but is not intellectually demanding. Rather than acknowledging that art involves a range of life issues, abilities, and concepts, art teachers have been pressured to think that their worth is based on students' technical production skills and knowledge of a few art historical facts.

The new conception of curriculum and student artistic inquiry opens up the possibility of moving away from these problems. A curriculum based on visual culture takes into consideration students' daily, postmodern experiences and their future lives. Most students will not be professional artists, but all students need to become responsible citizens of the world. In a democracy, an aim of education is to promote the development of responsible citizens who think critically, act constructively in an informed manner, and collaborate in the conscious formation of personal and communal identities. In order for art curriculum to fulfill this aim in the contemporary context, students' studio experience must be thought of as part of visual culture and as a vital way to come to understand the visual milieu in which they live. Student studio experience is essential to teaching and learning about visual culture because it (a) is a process of creative/critical inquiry, (b) helps students understand the complexities of visual culture, and (c) connects and empowers people.

Artistic Production Is a Process of Creative/Critical inquiry

Creative production and critical reflection are not separate in art; they are dualistic and mutually dependent. Creative production is inherently critical, and critical reflection is inherently creative. When we look at an image or artifact, we create it in the sense that we give it meaning. It is important to conceptualize these processes as being interconnected if art educators are going to teach in ways appropriate to understanding visual culture.

Many different types of studios (i.e., commercial arts, fine arts, computer graphics, video and film production) and studio practices exist. Studio practices include conceptualizing, viewing, analyzing, judging, designing, constructing, and marketing visual forms. An important part of studio practice is participation in the discourses of various communities (professional, student, ethnic, gender, environmental, etc.) to develop contexts through which connections can be made between production and social life. As discussed earlier, a critical aspect of teaching visual culture is making connections and crossing borders. This is accomplished through conceptually grounded processes of creative/critical inquiry that promote synthesis, extend knowledge, and enrich relationships. These are the powers of the arts and vital aspects of studio production. Conceptually grounded production processes cross over traditional boundaries of form, breaking down old borders of media-driven curriculum, and turning curriculum upside-down, so that the development of ideas are given attention first and the techniques and processes emerge as the expression of those ideas. In this way, technique and media are related to and enhance the making of meaning in creative/critical inquiry. Visual culture is an expression of ideas through the use of technical and formal processes, but these processes are not the main purpose of artistic production.

Creative/critical inquiry is not only for secondary level students; in fact, it should begin at the elementary level. Young students are already adopting postmodern visual culture as a framework for understanding reality outside of school. For instance, elementary students analyze, role-play, draw, and construct environments based on the Harry Potter books, films, and toys from interdisciplinary perspectives of casting, acting, designing, costume styling, narration, and mechanization.

Making Visual Culture Can Help Students Grasp Complexities of Culture

Traditionally, art has been represented in education as inherently good. The term *art* has carried with it assumptions of quality, value, and enrichment. However, the visual arts are not *inherently* good. The great power of the visual arts is their ability to have a variety of effects on our lives; but that power can make them manipulative, colonizing, and disenfranchising. The complexity of this power needs to be considered as part of educational experience. For example, advertising images are produced by artists and are thought of as good for the companies whose products they are intended to sell, but, they often represent stereotypes and cultural biases that damage viewers' self-concepts. Another example is the astronomical amount of money paid to sports stars and for historical fine art, which seems inconsistent with the ideals of moral responsibility. As a result of such complexities, investigations of issues of empowerment, representation, and social consciousness are becoming more important in art education.

Cultural Production Connects and Empowers People

Visual culture connects makers to viewers through communication, identity formation, and cultural mediation. Addressing aspects of visual communication, identity formation, and cultural mediation has become a vital issue in art education (e.g., Ballengee-Morris, & Striedieck, 1997; Freedman, 1994; Stuhr, 1995). Studio production can aid students to understand that visual culture involves personal and communal codes of symbols, images, environments, artifacts, and so on. Investigating the relationship between makers and viewers of visual culture can help them to identify and recognize ethnocentric perspectives at the national, regional, state, and local levels. This process is important because it creates possibilities for the critique of visual culture at all levels to achieve democratic educational goals intended to guide the preparation of reflective and responsible citizens, consequently leading to a more socially conscious and equitable society. From a visual culture perspective, production empowers makers and viewers by promoting critique through the process of making, encouraging analysis during viewing, and enabling makers and viewers to claim ownership of images and designed objects.

CONCLUSION

Art education based on teaching visual culture requires new curriculum and instructional roles, content, and strategies to shift the focus of the field from narrow, conventional approaches to open processes of creative and critical inquiry. A new language is necessary for art education that does not solely depend on fine arts discourse. Ideally, it should involve discourses on all the visual arts, such as media studies, design education, cultural critique, and visual anthropology. Art teachers should be educated to become involved citizens in the various communities in which they live and work. They should strive to enrich the communities to create pride in cultural heritage and address contemporary problems through artistic solutions. Art should be approached as an equally legitimate school subject and conceptually integrated with the rest of the school curriculum. All educators should teach the concepts and skills necessary to function effectively in a democratic society now and in the future.

New instructional strategies include teachers becoming role models of leadership in their professional community. To conceptualize art education as different from other school subjects inadvertently disengages it from the legitimate school curriculum. In the larger sense, art teachers focus on what other teachers consider important: the concepts and skills necessary to function effectively in a democratic society now and in the future. But, art teachers do this through visual culture, which is as profound in its effect as written texts.

Teacher education programs need to prepare teachers to act as facilitators of student creative and critical inquiry. As part of teaching visual culture, we must shift from a focus on didactic instruction to an education that promotes student responsibility. When students are allowed to investigate the range of visual culture with the guidance of a teacher, they can actively discover complex meanings, multiple connections, and enriched possibilities for creation and critique. Art classrooms should be conceptualized as multitasking arenas where images and objects cross over and are produced and discussed to lead students and teachers through the investigation of ideas, issues, opinions, and conflicts.

Through technological advancements, visual culture is becoming increasingly pervasive and affecting the lives of students and teachers worldwide. The professional field must respond to the challenge of this significant social change by educating new art teachers and retraining current art teachers to use technology to create students who are aware of the world they live in and to take an active responsible role in improving life for all.

ACKNOWLEDGMENT

The authors wish to thank Ron Neperud for his careful reading and thoughtful comments on this chapter.

REFERENCES

Aronowitz, S. (1994). Technology and the future of work. In G. Bender & T. Druckrey (Eds.), *Culture on the brink: Ideaologies of technology* (pp. 15–30). Seattle: Bay Press.

Ballengee-Morris, C. B., & Striedieck, I. M. (1997). A postmodern feminist perspective on visual art and visual culture in elementary teacher education. In D. R. Walling (Ed.), *Under Construction: The role of the art and visual culture and humanities in postmodern schooling* (pp. 193–215.) Indianapolis: Phi Delta Kappa.

Ballengee-Morris, C., & Stuhr, P. L. (2001). Multicultural art and visual cultural education in a changing world. *Art Education, 54*(4), 6–13.

Barbosa, A. M. (1991). Art education and environment. *Journal of Multicultural and Cross-Cultural Research in Art Education, 9*(1), 59–64.

Barone, T., & Eisner, E. (1997). Another example of arts-based research. *Complementary Methods for Research in Education.* Washington, DC: American Educational Research Association.

Blandy, D. (1994). Assuming responsibility: Disability rights and the preparation of art educators. *Studies in Art Education, 35*(3) 179–187.

Boughton, D. (1994). *Evaluation and assessment in visual arts education.* Geelong, VIC: Deakin University.

Boughton, D. (1997). Reconsidering issues of assessment and achievement standards in art education. *Studies in Art Education, 38*(4), 199–213.

Chalmers, F. G. (1981). Art education as ethnology. *Studies in Art Education, 22*(3), 6–14.

Clifford, J. (1988). *The predicament of culture: Twentieth-century ethnography, literature, and art.* Cambridge, MA: Harvard University Press.

Collins, J. (1989). *Uncommon cultures: Popular culture and post-modernism.* New York: Routledge.

Congdon, K. G. (1991). A folk art focus. *Journal of Multicultural and Cross-cultural Research in Art Education, 9,* 65–72.

Duncum, P. (1990). Clearing the decks for dominant culture: Some first principles for a contemporary art education. *Studies in Art Education: A Journal of Issues and Research, 31*(4), 207–215.

Efland, A. (1976). The school art style: A functional analysis. *Studies in Art Education, 17,* 37–44.

Efland, A. (1983). School art and its social origins. *Studies in Art Education, 24,* 49–57.

Ewen, S. (1988). *All consuming images: The politics of style in contemporary culture.* New York: Basic Books.

Freedman, K. (1994). Interpreting gender and visual culture in art classrooms. *Studies in Art Education, 35*(3), 157–170.

Freedman, K. (1995). Educational change within structures of history, culture, and discourse. In R. W. Neperud (Ed.), *Context, content, and community in art education.* New York: Teachers College Press.

Freedman, K. (2000). Social perspectives on art education in the U.S.: Teaching visual culture in a democracy. *Studies in Art Education, 41*(4), 314–329.

Freedman, K. (2003). *Teaching visual culture.* New York: Teachers College Press.

Freedman, K., & Wood, J. (1999). Student knowledge of visual culture: Images inside and outside of school. *Studies in Art Education, 2*(40), 128–142.

Garber, E. (1995). Teaching art in the context of culture: A study in the borderlands. *Studies in Art Education, 36*(4), 218–232.

Gardner, H. (1972). The development of sensitivity to figural and stylistic aspects of paintings. *British Journal of Psychology, 63,* 605–615.

Gaines, J. M., & Renow, M. (Eds.). (1999). *Collecting visible evidence.* Minneapolis, MN: University of Minnesota Press.

Garoian, C. (1999). *Performing pedagogy: Toward an art of politics.* Albany: SUNY Press.

Giroux, H. (1992). *Border crossings: Cultural workers and the politics of education.* New York, London: Routledge.

Grigsby, J. (1977). *Art & ethnics.* Dubuque, Iowa: Wm. C. Brown.

Hernandez, F. (2000). *Educatión y cultura visual.* Barcelona: Octacdro.

Hicks, L. (1990). A feminist analysis of empowerment and community in arts education. *Studies in Art Education, 32*(1), 36–46.

Jagodzinski, J. (1997). The nostalgia of art education: Reinscribing the master's narrative. *Studies in Art Education, 38*(2), 80–95.

Lanier, V. (1969). The teaching of art as social revolution. *Phi Delta Kappan, 50*(6), 314–319.

Lanier, V. (1974). A plague on all your houses. *NAEA Journal, 27*(3), 12–15.

McFee, J. K., & Degge, R. (1977). *Art, culture, and environment: A catalyst for teaching.* Belmont, CA: Wadsworth.

Mirzoeff, N. (Ed.). (1998). *Visual culture reader.* New York: Routledge.

Morley, D. (1992). *Television, audiences, and cultural studies.* London: Routledge.

Neperud, R. (1973). Art education: Towards an environmental aesthetic. *Art Education, 26*(3).

Neperud, R. (Ed.). (1995). *Context, content, and community in art education.* New York: Teacher College Press.

Parsons, M. (1998). Integrated curriculum and our paradigm of cognition in the arts. *Studies in Art Education, 39*(2), 103–116.

Pinar, W. F. (Ed.). (1988). *Contemporary curriculum discourses.* Scottsdale, AZ: Gorsuch Scarisbrick.

Pinar, W. F., Reynolds, W. M., Slattery, P., & Taubman, P. M. (1996). *Understanding curriculum.* New York: Peter Lang.

Prosser, J. (Ed.). (1998). *Image-based research: A sourcebook for qualitative researchers.* Bristol: Falmer.

Rose, G. (2001). *Visual methodologies.* London: Sage.

Rushkoff, D. (1994). *Media virus: Hidden agendas in popular culture.* Sydney: Random House.

Scollon, R., & Scollon, S. W. (1995). *Intercultural communication.* Cambridge, MA: Blackwell.

Shusterman, R. (1989). *Pragmatist aesthetics: Living beauty, rethinking art.* Oxford: Blackwell.

Slattery, P. (1995). Postmodernism as a challenge to dominant representations of curriculum. In J. Glanz & L. Behar-Horenstein (Eds.), *Paradigm debates in curriculum and supervision.* New York: Greenwood.

Smith-Shank, D. (1996). Microethnography of a Grateful Dead event: American subculture aesthetics. *Journal of Multicultural and Cross-cultural Research in Art Education, 14*, 80–91.

Solso, R. (1997). *Mind and brain sciences in the 21st century.* Cambridge, MA: MIT Press.

Stuhr, P. L. (1995). A social reconstructionist multicultural art curriculum design: Using the powwow as an example. In R. W. Neperud (Ed.), *Context, content, and community in art education: Beyond postmodernism.* New York: Teachers College Press.

Stuhr, P. L. (1999). Response to Brian Allison's article, "Colour, culture, language, and education." *Journal of Multicultural and Cross-cultural Research in Art Education. 18*(1), 14–15.

Sturken, M., & Cartwright, L. (2001). *Practices of looking: An introduction to visual culture.* Oxford, England: Oxford University Press.

Tavin, K. (2000). Just doing it: Towards a critical thinking of visual culture. In D. Wiel & H. K. Anderson (Eds.). *Perspectives in critical theory: Essays by teachers in theory and practice* (pp. 187–210). New York: Peter Lang.

Tavin, K. (2001). Teaching in and through visual culture. *Journal of Multicultural and Cross-Cultural Research in Art Education, 18*(1), 37–40.

Wilson, B., & Wilson, M. (1977). An iconoclastic view of the imagery sources of the drawing of young people. *Art Education, 30*(1), 5–11.

Wilson, B., Hurwitz, A., & Wilson, M. (1987). *Teaching drawing from art.* Worchester, MA: Davis.

Author Index

Note: Numbers in italics indicate pages with complete bibliographic information; n indicates footnote.

Subject Index

Note: n in a locator references a footnote.

A